A Reader on the Sanskrit Grammarians

Studies in Linguistics
edited by Samuel Jay Keyser

1. A Reader on the Sanskrit Grammarians
   J. F. Staal, editor

A Reader on the Sanskrit Grammarians

Edited by J. F. Staal

The MIT Press Cambridge, Massachusetts, and London, England

This book was designed by the MIT Press Design Department.
It was set in Monotype Gill Sans
and printed on Finch Textbook Offset
by Halliday Lithograph Corporation
and bound in Whitman POC Gold
by Halliday Lithograph Corporation
in the United States of America.

Library of Congress Cataloging in Publication Data

Staal, Johan Frederik comp.
A reader on the Sanskrit grammarians.

Bibliography: p.
1. Sanskrit philology—Collections. 2. Scholars, Sanskrit—Collections.
I. Title.
PK402.S8 491.2'08 77–122265
ISBN 0–262–19078–8 (hardcover)

अनन्तपारं किल शब्दशास्त्रं
स्वल्पं तथायुर्बहवश्च विघ्नाः ।
सारं ततो ग्राह्यमपास्य फल्गु
हंसैर्यथा क्षीरमिवाम्बुमध्यात् ॥

anantapāraṃ kila śabdaśāstraṃ
svalpaṃ tathāyur bahavaś ca vighnāḥ/
sāraṃ tato grāhyam apāsya phalgu
haṃsair yathā kṣīram ivāmbumadhyāt//

Boundless indeed is the science of language,
but life is short and obstacles are numerous.
Hence take what is good and leave what is worthless,
as geese take milk from the midst of water.

Early Accounts

1

2

The Foundations of Western Scholarship

The Romantic Period

47

4

The Golden Days

Plates

Preface

The study of the Sanskrit grammarians, and in particular of Pāṇini, has been regarded for almost a century as a hyperspecialist occupation. Only the specialists of *vyākaraṇa* ('grammar') among specialists of Sanskrit philology were considered capable of arriving at an understanding of the difficult texts of the Indian grammatical tradition. Pāṇini was accordingly treated even by linguists as an object of Indological investigation, not as a deceased colleague of great genius. This view has not always been predominant, however, and today, for reasons that will be sketched here, it is once again beginning to change. It is now generally recognized that Pāṇini, despite his exclusive preoccupation with Sanskrit, was the greatest linguist of antiquity, if not of all time, and deserves to be treated as such. Accordingly, linguists, dissatisfied with mere lip service, are beginning to turn to him and to the Sanskrit grammarians, just as logicians turn to Aristotle. But the difficulties awaiting them are still formidable. Pāṇini's insights about language are disguised in his metalinguistic analysis of Sanskrit in Sanskrit, which presupposes some familiarity with the complexities of the Sanskrit language. Also, the arguments and patterns of reasoning of Pāṇini, Patañjali, and many later grammarians are no less compact, precise, and profound than those of Aristotle. In addition, neither is Sanskrit as familiar as Greek, nor are notions in contemporary linguistics derived from Pāṇini in the way many notions in modern logic are derived from Aristotle.

The text of Pāṇini's grammar, the *Aṣṭādhyāyī*, is accessible in Boehtlingk's edition and translation of 1887, reprinted in 1964. There are at least two other translations, one by Renou of 1948–1954 and one by S. C. Vasu of 1891, reprinted in 1962. However, all of these are difficult to use without the help of a competent guide. In addition, there is not available at present an introduction to Pāṇini that is adequate and up-to-date. The two most important existing monographs are one by Goldstücker of 1861 (reprinted in India and in Germany during recent years) and one by Liebich of 1891 (one chapter from the latter is reproduced in the present volume). Many important articles do exist, but they have often been published in out-of-the-way places and they are difficult to find even in good libraries. Accordingly, it is difficult not only for linguists but also for Sanskritists to acquaint themselves adequately with Pāṇini and the Indian grammarians.

One of the aims of this book is to render the work of the Sanskrit grammarians more easily accessible. In the absence of a helpful introduction to the subject, there is no better way to achieve a first understanding than through studying some of the best articles that have appeared during the last one and a half centuries. However, the following selection may pave the way for, and in due course supplement, a new general introduction to the study of the Sanskrit grammarians, which is presently under preparation (Joshi, Kiparsky, and Staal).

The second aim of the book is to throw some light on an interesting line of development within Western linguistics itself. In doing so it may also dispel two widespread but erroneous notions. The first is that the Sanskrit grammarians have in the past been studied by philologists but neglected by linguists. The second, turning the previous supposition into a principle of research, is that the materials have first to be made available and interpreted by philologists before they can be evaluated by linguists. The circularity of such a principle is apparent. We shall see how, on the contrary, the results of philological research have often been colored by underlying linguistic views.

In India itself, the grammatical tradition, which is largely but not exclusively concerned with Pāṇini and his school, has been revived several times and continues to the present day. Its foremost living authorities are the traditional grammarians or paṇḍits of *vyākaraṇa*, whose knowledge is handed down almost entirely in Sanskrit. Such Indian scholars trained the Western Sanskritists who first devoted close attention to the Indian grammarians. Without their assistance the original sources would have remained unintelligible.

The history of the study of the Sanskrit grammarians from outside the tradition falls into several periods, to which the chapters of this volume correspond. The earliest information was provided by Buddhist pilgrims from China and Tibet, by Muslim travelers from the Near East, and by Christian missionaries from Europe. The foundations of Sanskrit studies in the West was laid by British scholars who worked in India, often as administrators and civil servants, and who were assisted by Indian paṇḍits. Colebrooke, foremost among them, provided detailed and accurate information on the Sanskrit grammarians. This was followed on the Continent and especially in Germany by a wave of enthusiasm for ancient Indian culture, resulting in linguistic evaluations of Pāṇini by A. W. von Schlegel and W. von Humboldt. For some time, discussions on the Sanskrit grammarians continued to be part and parcel of general linguistics. This development, combined with renewed contacts with the living grammatical tradition in India, led to a deeper understanding of the Sanskrit grammarians, culminating, less than a century ago, in the work of Bhandarkar and especially of Kielhorn. A relapse followed, with a nadir in Whitney, resulting in a general decrease of understanding and an accordingly low evaluation of the "native" grammarians. But the tradition founded by Kielhorn was not entirely destroyed, and it led eventually to the modern period of rather specialized philological work to which Western, Indian, and Japanese scholars contribute.

Contemporary scholarship within this philological perspective continues to produce valuable results that are new to Western scholars though often perfectly well known to Indian paṇḍits. All the same, there is a recent revival of interest in the Sanskrit grammarians which is partly linked with the extraordinary developments that have taken place during the last decade and a half in Western linguistics. This new and much wider interest is marked by the participation of linguists as well as Sanskritists and constitutes in this respect a kind of return. But now there are at least two totally new reasons for such a revival. First, the activities of the Indian grammarians are the closest parallel in history to contemporary linguistics. Second, it appears that only contemporary insights can pave the way for adequate interpretations of the work of the Sanskrit grammarians themselves. There are many parallels for such a state of affairs in other domains where progress has not been linear, for example, in the history of philosophy or logic. It is indeed not at all surprising that Pāṇini and his colleagues cannot be properly understood unless they are taken seriously for what they were, that is, linguists. This change of perspective has definite consequences, for it is an illusion to imagine that it is possible to do justice to the Sanskrit grammarians as linguists without considering the linguistic problems with which they themselves were coming to grips. It is at the same time clear, however, that this contemporary approach should not lead to what might be called retrospective interpretation. In particular, it remains important that the valuable insights and results of earlier generations of scholars be preserved. This book, then, sets out to perform part of a task that in the wake of new discoveries seems of some urgency.

The articles and fragments reproduced here are selected mainly in view of their analytic and linguistic relevance, excluding, on the one hand, purely historical and philological articles and, on the other hand, papers that deal with the interpretation of particular rules in Pāṇini's grammar without elucidating problems of general interest. These considerations have sometimes been overruled by the desire to provide selections from a variety of viewpoints. This work seeks to go beyond a mere collection of articles by providing a connected historical outline, especially with regard to the earlier periods. The introductory notes preceding the selections include information about related work, contain excerpts from other sources, and explain particular points of a more technical nature. They sometimes give additional references to later publications treating the same or similar topics or exhibiting a similar approach.

The selections included here are in English, German, and French. A few passages quoted in Latin and Greek have been provided with an English translation. For Chinese, Tibetan, and Arabic texts, use has been made of existing translations. For Sanskrit terms and passages, a translation has been generally supplied whenever it would be difficult to follow the argument otherwise. But Sanskrit expressions treated as elements of the object-language, and quoted on account of certain formal features, have not been translated. Similarly, *sūtras* and linguistic rules are often left untranslated when their function in the context is clear and when a mere translation would be intelligible only when in turn accompanied by a fuller analysis. Editor's translations and explications are generally placed within square brackets.

The transliteration from Sanskrit into Roman script has had many vicissitudes since the beginning of Western scholarship, and quotations in the articles here reproduced had to be modified accordingly. The original transliteration has been retained only where it was of some independent historical interest, as in the work of Pons and Colebrooke. Elsewhere the transliteration has been unified throughout. For more precise information in this respect, see the editor's Note on Sanskrit Transliteration.

Unlike most linguistic books, where illustrations are confined to such things as sound waves or the vocal chords, this volume has been illustrated with a variety of plates, emphasizing that "*homo foneticus indicus* was no mere cross-sectioned larynx sited under an empty cranium . . .; on the contrary, the whole man, belly, heart and head, produced voice" (J. E. B. Gray 1959, 520, with textual support from the *Mahābhāṣya* and the *Pāṇinīyaśikṣā*). It is perhaps risky to publish illustrations that may reinforce the trend to regard linguistics in India as an exotic growth, but the articles included provide enough material to correct such tendencies.

Other features of the book are more self-explanatory. The list of abbreviations reflects the idiosyncrasies of a variety of authors, some changing their method of referring to texts more than once even within a single article. It may be added here that abbreviations consisting of three numerals (in various forms, for example, II, 3.5 or 2.3.5) always refer to Pāṇini's *Aṣṭādhyāyī*, specifying *adhyāya*, *pāda*, and *sūtra*. The bibliography lists all publications referred to in the introductions and explanatory notes accompanying the selections. To have included the sources referred to in the selections themselves would have led to at least a fivefold increase.

The motto that introduces this book occurs in the *Pañcatantra* and in other collections and has here been quoted from Otto Boehtlingk's *Indische Sprüche*, St. Petersburg, 1870–1873 (reprint Osnabrück, 1966), vol. I, p. 45, no. 243.

Now there remains the pleasant task of thanking numerous persons and institutions for their help in preparing this book. I am first of all grateful to the authors who have permitted me to reprint their articles: Professors John Brough (Cambridge), Yutaka Ojihara (Kyoto), K. A. Subramania Iyer (Lucknow), and Paul Thieme (Tübingen). The authors of the majority of articles here reproduced are no longer living. But an attempt has been made to obtain permission in all cases for republication, even if the material has long been in the public domain. I am greatly indebted to the following persons, publishers, and institutions for their assistance and for their permission to reprint articles: *Acta Orientalia*; Akademie der Wissenschaften, Göttingen; The Asiatic Society of Bombay, Bombay; Bhandarkar Oriental Research Institute, Poona; Calcutta University Press, Calcutta; Clarendon Press, Oxford; Éditions E. de Boccard, Paris; H. Haessel Verlag, Frankfurt; Indian Research Institute, Calcutta; International Academy of Indian Culture, New Delhi; Japanese Association of Indian and Buddhist Studies, Tokyo; Johann Ambrosius Barth, Leipzig; The Johns Hopkins Press, Baltimore, Maryland; Johnson Reprint Corporation, New York; *Journal of the American Oriental Society*; Dr. S. M. Katre, M.A., Ph.D. (Lond.), Poona; Kuppuswami Sastri Research Institute, Madras; Lambert Schneider, Heidelberg; Longmans Green & Co. Ltd., Harlow; Österreichische Akademie der Wissenschaften, Vienna; Philological Society, Oxford; Routledge & Kegan Paul, London; S. Hirzel Verlag, Stuttgart; Société Asiatique, Paris; Walter de Gruyter & Co. Verlag, Berlin.

I owe special gratitude to the following scholars, who have helped me with their encouragement, criticism, and suggestions, or who have answered specific queries: Professors George Cardona (Philadelphia), Murray B. Emeneau (Berkeley), Jean Filliozat (Paris), Morris Halle (Cambridge, Mass.), J. C. Heesterman (Leiden), S. M. Katre (Poona), Paul Kiparsky (Cambridge, Mass.), B. A. van Nooten (Berkeley), Gerhard Oberhammer (Vienna), and John W. M. Verhaar (Djakarta). The Theology Department, University of San Francisco, helped me by providing information on Jean François Pons. I am particularly indebted to Professors Kiparsky and van Nooten, who read an earlier version of the entire manuscript and provided me with a wealth of ideas and suggestions. I am also very grateful to those who have assisted me in various ways in connection with the illustrations: the Director General of the Archaeological Survey of India (New Delhi), Mr. J. E. B. Gray (London), Dr. J. C. Harle (Oxford), Professor V. Raghavan (Madras), Dr. R. Ramachandran (Annamalainagar), Dr. S. T. Satyamurti (Madras), the late Mr. J. M. Somasundaram Pillai (Annamalainagar), and Mr. C. Srinivasan (Madras). I wish in particular to thank my secretary, Mrs. Barbara Sinclair, without whose acumen and care this book might not have seen the light of day.

In a book of this kind, replete with quotations, references, footnotes, technical terms, and diacritical marks, proofreading presents a formidable task. My gratitude goes to the University of California, which provided me with research assistance during the proofreading, and to Mr. Tai Shung Paik for his sharp eye and expert assistance at this stage and for preparing the indexes. I also thank the staff of The MIT Press for its assistance at all times.

J. F. S.

Berkeley, California

Notes on the Frontispiece: Patañjali

Patañjali the grammarian and author of the *Mahābhāṣya* is traditionally identified with Patañjali the philosopher and *yogī*, author of the *Yogasūtra*. Whether the two Patañjali's were really the same person has been a matter of much dispute. The date of the *Yogasūtra*, at any rate, is rather uncertain, and the name Patañjali is fairly uncommon. J. H. Woods, the American translator of the *Yogasūtra* and its main commentaries, compared the treatment of the concept of substance in the *Yogasūtra* and in the *Mahābhāṣya* and, as a result of this study, doubted the identity of their authors (Woods 1914, xiii–xvii). Surendranath Dasgupta, one of the leading experts on Indian philosophy in general and on the Yoga system in particular, controverted Woods's conclusions and argued that the two were identical (Dasgupta 1922, 230–238). Several other scholars have contributed to the controversy (for a survey see Eliade 1954, 363–364), which, however, remains unresolved.

This personage Patañjali, to whom the *Mahābhāṣya*, the *Yogasūtra*, and also sometimes a medical work are attributed, is represented traditionally as a snake from the waist down and sometimes with a large hood composed of five serpents above his head (cf. this volume, pp. 25, 38). There are numerous legends connected with this figure, particularly in South India, where Patañjali is regarded as one of the two sages to whom Śiva manifested himself as Śiva Naṭarāja, namely, in his cosmic dance (the other sage being the more mythical Vyāghrapāda, "tiger foot"). According to one legend Patañjali, who as a *yogī* did not wish to crush insects with his feet, obtained from Naṭarāja the favor of being partially changed into a serpent. Another legend relates how Patañjali fell (*pat*) into the hollow of the hand (*añjali*) of Pāṇini in the shape of a snake (Jouveau-Dubreuil 1937, 51–52). There is at least one shrine in South India especially connected with Patañjali, the Anantīśvara temple in Cidambaram (Somasundaram Pillai 1955, 146). The temple has recently been restored and the image of Patañjali installed there is of recent origin. There are images of Patañjali in many Śiva temples in the South, but rarely published or described (for Teṅkāśi, see Gopinatha Rao 1916, 255; for Śucīndram, see Pillay 1953, 386–387). The most important Naṭarāja temple in India is the large temple complex in Cidambaram, where the oldest and most interesting images of Patañjali are found.

The frontispiece pictures a stone image of the East *gopura* or temple gateway at Cidambaram (built around the middle of the thirteenth century during the Late Coḷa period), where Patañjali is represented on two large serpent coils, with fangs and with his hands in *añjali* pose with a beaded chaplet pressed between his palms (Harle 1963, 121; illustrated in Krishna Sastri 1916, 85). This illustration is by courtesy of the Archaeological Survey of India.

Note on Sanskrit Transliteration

The selections reproduced in this book come from a great variety of sources, adopting a bewildering variety of transliterations of Sanskrit. Moreover, in many of the originals, especially those published in India, Sanskrit terms and passages were printed in the Nāgarī script (this applies to the articles by Bhandarkar, Kielhorn, Boehtlingk, Bühler, Chatterji, and Subramania Iyer). The oldest transliterations into Roman script, that is, those by Pons and Colebrooke, are interesting as attempts not only at transliteration but also at phonological analysis; they have therefore been retained. Elsewhere the Nāgarī has been transliterated into Roman script, and all transliterations have been unified, adopting the system that is now in common use by Sanskritists all over the world. Sometimes the spelling used for a Sanskrit word has also had to be regularized. All this occasioned quite considerable changes in spelling, especially with regard to the older selections, where, for example, the retroflex fricative was written as *sh* instead of *ṣ*, the palatal fricative as *ç* instead of *ś*, *anusvāra* as *ṁ* instead of *ṃ*, and where the vowel *ṛ* and the diphthongs *ai* and *au* were written as *ṛi* and *āi* and *āu*, respectively. Lengthening signs over vowels used to be the circumflex ^ instead of the horizontal bar ¯. Some modern authors use the circumflex only over vowels when they result from sandhi; this practice has been retained in the one paper where it was adopted, that is, in Ojihara's paper. More idiosyncratic and confusing uses, such as, *j* for the liquid nowadays written *y*, had to be modified also. The lengthening signs used by Kielhorn over e and *o* have been dropped; though the marked vowels may be phonetically long (as reflected in the practice of South Indian manuscripts written, for example, in Grantha script), the distinction between short and long *e* and *o* is not phonemic in Sanskrit. Among the later papers only Brough's transliteration has been changed, involving the replacement of the curly hooks that some British linguists were in the habit of attaching to letters by the customary diacritics.

All Roman transliterations now in use go back to William Jones's "A Dissertation on the Orthography of Asiatick Words in Roman Letters" of 1786. As Sir M. Monier Monier-Williams told the Royal Asiatic Society in 1890: "as a result of a kind of natural selection or survival of the fittest, the practice of all Oriental scholars — so far as Āryan languages are concerned — is settling down into an acceptance of Sir William Jones' principles of transliteration" (quoted by G. H. Cannon in Sebeok 1966, I, 56).

The transliteration adopted is given in the following table.

The Sanskrit Alphabet

			glottal	velar	palatal	retroflex	dental	labial
Consonants								
stops	voiceless	unaspirated		*k* क	*c* च	*ṭ* ट	*t* त	*p* प
		aspirated		*kh* ख	*ch* छ	*ṭh* ठ	*th* थ	*ph* फ
	voiced	unaspirated		*g* ग	*j* ज	*ḍ* ड	*d* द	*b* ब
		aspirated		*gh* घ	*jh* झ	*ḍh* ढ	*dh* ध	*bh* भ
nasals				*ṅ* ङ	*ñ* ञ	*ṇ* ण	*n* न	*m* म
liquids					*y* य	*r* र	*l* ल	*v* व
fricatives	voiceless		*ḥ* ः		*ś* श	*ṣ* ष	*s* स	
	voiced		*h* ह					
Vowels								
		short	*a* अ		*i* इ	*ṛ* ऋ	*ḷ* ऌ	*u* उ
		long	*ā* आ		*ī* ई	*ṝ* ॠ		*ū* ऊ
					e ए			*o* ओ
					ai ऐ			*au* औ

Abbreviations

AĀ	Aitareyāraṇyaka
AB	Aitareyabrāhmaṇa
AiGr	(Wackernagel's) *Altindische Grammatik*
AKM	*Abhandlungen zur Kunde des Morgenlandes*
APr, AthPrāt, AVPr	Atharvaprātiśākhya
ĀpŚ(S)	Āpastambaśrauta(sūtra)
Āśv(GS)	Āśvalāyana(gṛhyasūtra)
Āśv(ŚS)	Āśvalāyana(śrautasūtra)
AV	Atharvaveda
B(ŚS), Bau(ŚS)	Baudhāyana(śrautasūtra)
BĀU	Bṛhadāraṇyakopaniṣad
Bau(GS)	Baudhāyana(gṛhyasūtra)
BB	*Bezzenberger's Beiträge zur Kunde der indogermanischen Sprachen*
Bh, Bhāṣ	Mahābhāṣya
Bhā(ŚS), Bhār(ŚS)	Bhāradvāja(śrautasūtra)
Bhāg	Bhāgavata
Bhām	Bhāmaha
Bhar	Bharata
Bhāṣāv	Bhāṣāvṛtti
Bhaṭṭ	Bhaṭṭoji Dīkṣita
BibInd	*Bibliotheca Indica*
BM	Bālamanoramā
Br	Brāhmaṇa
BR	Boehtlingk-Roth *Sanskrit-Wörterbuch*
Bṛhaddev	Bṛhaddevatā
BSS	Bombay Sanskrit Series
C(V)	Candra(vṛtti)
ChU	Chāndogyopaniṣad
Daśak	Daśakumāracarita
Dhanv	Dhanvin
Dhātuprad	Dhātupradīpa
DhSū	Dharmasūtra
Dra	Dravya(samuddeśa)
DŚS, DrāhŚ	Drāhyāyaṇaśrautasūtra
Durgh	Durghaṭavṛtti
Gaṇaratn	Gaṇaratnamahodadhi
GB	Gopathabrāhmaṇa
GGA	*Göttingische gelehrte Anzeigen*
GN	*Nachrichten von der Gesellschaft der Wissenschaften zu Göttingen*
GS	Gobhilagṛhyasūtra
H, Hem, Hemac	Hemacandra
Helā	Helārāja
Hir(ŚS)	Hiraṇyakeśi(śrautasūtra)

IA, IndAnt	*Indian Antiquary*
IHQ	*Indian Historical Quarterly*
IndCu	*Indian Culture*
Ind Sprüche	(Boehtlingk's) *Indische Sprüche*
ISt, IndStud	(Weber's) *Indische Studien*
J	Jainendra
J, Jaim	Jaimini, Jaiminīya
Jā	Jāti(samuddeśa)
JA, Jas	*Journal asiatique*
JAOS	*Journal of the American Oriental Society*
JB	Jaiminīyabrāhmaṇa
J.Dep.Letters	*Journal of the Department of Letters, University of Calcutta*
jñāp	jñāpaka
JRAS	*Journal of the Royal Asiatic Society*
JS	Jaimini's Mīmāṃsāsūtra
JUB	Jaiminīyopaniṣadbrāhmaṇa
K, Kāś	Kāśikāvṛtti
Kā	Kālasamuddeśa
Kai, Kaiy	Kaiyaṭa
kār	kārikā
Kāt, Kāty	Kātyāyana
Kauś	Kauśika
KāvMī	Kāvyamīmāṃsā
KB	Kauṣītakibrāhmaṇa
Kiel	Kielhorn
KP	Kāvyaprakāśa
Kri	Kriyā(samuddeśa)
KS	Kāṭhakasaṃhitā
Kṣīratar	Kṣīrataraṅgiṇī
KŚS, KātyS	Kātyāyanaśrautasūtra
Kt	Kātantra
Kuval	Kuvalayānanda
KZ	*Zeitschrift für vergleichende Sprachwissenschaft* (begründet von A. Kuhn)
LŚS, LāṭŚ	Lāṭyāyanaśrautasūtra
LŚŚ, Laghuś	Laghuśabdenduśekhara
M, Mbh, Mohā	Mahābhāṣya
Mī(Sū)	Mīmāṃsā(sūtra)
MS	Maitrāyaṇīsaṃhitā
MSL	*Mémoires de la Société Linguistique de Paris*
MŚ(S), MānŚ(S)	Mānavaśrauta(sūtra)
N	Nyāsa
Naiṣ	Naiṣadhīya
Nār	Nārada

Ng, Nāg, Nāgoj	Nāgojībhaṭṭa
NIA	*New Indian Antiquary*
NidSū	Nidānasūtra
Nigh	Nighaṇṭu
Nir	Nirukta
NM	Nyāyamañjarī
Nyāyaprak	Nyāyaprakāśa
Ny(Sū)	Nyāya(sūtra)
P, Pāṇ	Pāṇini
Padamañj	Padamañjarī
Pañcavidh	Pañcavidhasūtra
paribh	paribhāṣā
Paribh, ParibhInduś, ParibhŚ, PŚ	Paribhāṣenduśekhara
Pat, Patañj	Patañjali
PB	Pañcaviṃśabrāhmaṇa
PGS	Pāraskaragṛhyasūtra
Piṅg	Piṅgala
Pitṛme	Pitṛmedha
Pr	Pradīpa
Pr, Prāt	Prātiśākhya
PrakKaum	Prakriyākaumudī
Pratijñ	Pratijñāsūtra
praty	pratyāhāra
Pur	Purāṇa
Puṣp	Puṣpasūtra
Rktan	Ṛktantra
RPr, RkPrāt	Ṛkprātiśākhya
RV, RgV	Ṛgveda
s, sū	sūtra
Ś, Śaṅk	Śaṅkara
Ś(ŚS)	Śāṅkhāyana(śrautasūtra)
ŚA	Śāṅkhāyanāraṇyaka
SāhDarp	Sāhityadarpaṇa
Saṃ	Saṃbandha (samuddeśa)
SaṃhUB	Saṃhitopaniṣadbrāhmaṇa
Sāṃkhyakār	Sāṃkhyakārikā
Sarvānukram	Sarvānukramaṇī
ŚB	Śatapathabrāhmaṇa
ṢB, ṢVB	Ṣaḍviṃśabrāhmaṇa
SB(B), SB(Bayer)	*Sitzungsberichte* (*der bayerischen Akademie der Wissenschaften*)
SK, SiddhK, SiddhKaum	Siddhāntakaumudī
ŚK, Śabdakaust	Śabdakaustubha
SKĀ, SKĀbh, SarKĀbhar	Sarasvatīkaṇṭhābharaṇa
Skand	Skanda(svāmin)
Skt	Sanskrit
ŚṛṅgPrak	Śṛṅgāraprakāśa

ŚS	Śivasūtra
ŚS	Śrautasūtra
sv	svāmin
SV	Sāmaveda
TĀ, TaittĀr	Taittirīyāraṇyaka
TB	Taittirīyabrāhmaṇa
TPr	Taittirīyaprātiśākhya
TPS	*Transactions of the Philological Society*
Tribhāṣy	Tribhāṣyaratna
TS	Taittirīyasaṃhitā
TV	Tantravārttika
Ud	Uddyota
Up	Upaniṣad
v	vṛtti
V(Pr)	Vājasaneyi(prātiśākhya)
V(ŚS)	Vaitāna(śrautasūtra)
vā, vārtt	vārttika
Vaidikābhar	Vaidikābharaṇa
Vaidyan	Vaidyanātha
Vaiś(Sū)	Vaiśeṣika(sūtra)
Vām	Vāmana
Vāyup	Vāyupurāṇa
Ve(Sū)	Vedānta(sūtra)
Viṣṇudharmott	Viṣṇudharmottara(purāṇa)
VP, Vāk, Vākyapad	Vākyapadīya
VS	Vājasaneyisaṃhitā
W, Wack	Wackernagel
Wh	Whitney
WZKM	*Wiener Zeitschrift für die Kunde des Morgenlandes*
Yājñav	Yājñavalkya
Yājñik	Yājñikadeva
Yo(Sū)	Yoga(sūtra)
YV	Yajurveda
ZDMG	*Zeitschrift der deutschen morgenländischen Gesellschaft*

Table of the Sanskrit Grammarians

Vedic	Pāṇinīya	Kātantra	Cāndra	Jainendra, etc.
Padapāṭha: SV RV AV TS/VS } X–VIII B.C.				
Prātiśākhya: Ṛk Atharva (2) Taittirīya Vājasaneyi Sāma } VI–IV B.C.	(10) Pāṇini V B.C. Kātyāyana 300 B.C. Patañjali 150 B.C.			
Nirukta VI–IV B.C.		Śarvavarman I A.D.		
	Bhartṛhari V		Candra- gomin VI	Devanandin VI
	Kāśikā VII			
	Jinendra- buddhi VIII	Durgasiṃha VIII		ŚĀKAṬĀYANA IX
	Kaiyaṭa XI			
	Puruṣottama XII			HEMACANDRA XII
	Śaraṇadeva XII			JAUMARA XII–XIII
	Haradatta XIII			VOPADEVA XIII
	Rāmacandra XV			SĀRASVATA XIII?
	Nārāyaṇa- bhaṭṭa			SAUPADMA XIV
	Bhaṭṭojī- dīkṣita XVII			
	Nāgojībhaṭṭa XVIII			

A Reader on the Sanskrit Grammarians

I

Early Accounts

Plate I

Plate I reproduces a later sculpture from Cidambaram, representing, from left to right, the sages Jaimini (author of the *Mīmāṃsāsūtra*: see this volume, pages 286–297), Vyāghrapāda (with tiger paws, carrying an implement probably used for picking flowers and fruit) and Patañjali. I owe this illustration to the kindness of the late Mr. J. M. Somasundaram Pillai. See also p. xxi and Kulke 1970.

I

Hsüan Tsang (602-664)

Throughout the centuries the Sanskrit grammarians occupied a central place in the complex fabric of Indian civilization. Grammar (*vyākaraṇa*) was the science of sciences, to which scholars in other fields looked for inspiration and technical assistance. It is not surprising, therefore, that foreigners who came in close contact with Indian culture have left accounts of the grammatical tradition. In addition to the Western scholarly occupation with the Sanskrit grammarians, which itself constitutes an account of this kind, it is of some interest to look at other accounts.

Among foreign observers, the one exception in this respect was that of the classical Greeks. The Greeks had quite extensive information about India, and their narrations are invaluable for the study of classical Indian history. But as far as Indian civilization is concerned, they seem to have been mainly struck by the more spectacular aspects of Indian philosophies and religions. There does not appear to have been a single Greek account of the Sanskrit grammarians or, for that matter, of the Sanskrit language. All the Greeks seem to have known is that there were many languages in India and that people did not always understand each other: *ἔστι δὲ πολλὰ ἔθνεα Ἰνδῶν καὶ οὐκ ὁμόφωνα σφίσι* 'there are many nations among the Indians, and they don't speak the same language' (Herodotus, *Historiae* 3.98).

The situation is quite different with respect to Asian nations; the Chinese, the Tibetans, and Muslims from different Near Eastern countries have left detailed accounts of Indian civilization, not excluding references to the grammatical tradition. That their interest in India was on a more advanced level than that of the ancient Greeks is also apparent from the fact that some of these foreign scholars knew something of Indian languages, and, in particular, of Sanskrit.

The Chinese who left us such accounts had good reasons for being interested in India. They were pious Buddhists who traveled to India as pilgrims to see the country where the founder of their religion had lived and taught. One of the most celebrated of these was Hsüan Tsang, who left China for India on foot in A.D. 629 and stayed in India for many years. He described his experiences in a large work entitled *Records of the Western Countries* (*Si-yu-ki*). We have additional information about his experiences from his biographer, and pupil, Hwui Li. While many Chinese pilgrims were very superstitious, Hsüan Tsang was obviously a good scholar. He was not averse to reporting local legends, but he also provided detailed and reliable information.

The first book of the *Records* describes Central Asia up to the Northwest Indian frontier. The second book contains a description of the first Indian areas that Hsüan Tsang visited but starts with a long introduction that provides general information about India. This introduction contains about one paragraph about the language and a brief reference to grammar (Beal 1885, I, 77–78; Julien 1857, I, 71–73):

> The letters of their alphabet were arranged by the god Brahmā, and their forms have been handed down from the first till now. They are forty-seven in number, and are combined so as to form words according to the object, and according to circumstances (*of time or place*): there are other forms (*inflexions*) used. This alphabet has spread in different directions and formed diverse branches, according to circumstances; therefore there have been slight modifications in the sounds of the words (*spoken language*);

but in its great features there has been no change. Middle India preserves the original character of the language in its integrity. Here the pronunciation is soft and agreeable, and like the *language* of the Devas. The pronunciation of the words is clear and pure, and fit as a model for all men. The people of the frontiers have contracted several erroneous modes of pronunciation; for according to the licentious habits of the people, so also will be the corrupt nature of their language.

The most striking feature of this Chinese approach to Sanskrit remains a characteristic of all later Chinese studies. To the Chinese, the alphabet meant everything. They simply assumed that knowledge of the Sanskrit script was as important a feature of Sanskrit as knowledge of characters is of Chinese. Hence they had only a very vague notion of what was involved in knowing the Sanskrit language beyond knowing its alphabet.

After the introductory paragraph, previously quoted, Hsüan Tsang goes on to say that the young in India are instructed from the age of seven in five sciences (*vidyā*), of which "The first is called the elucidation of sounds (*śabdavidyā*). This treatise explains and illustrates the agreement (*concordance*) of words, and it provides an index for derivatives."

After this introduction Hsüan Tsang describes in his second chapter how he reached the area of Gāndhāra (on the upper Indus); after relating various further events, he describes how he reaches a town called So-lo-tu-lo (Beal 1885, I, 114–117; Julien 1867, I, 125–128). Part of his account agrees with the Indian tradition that the *pratyāhāra-sūtras* (*a*, *i*, *u*, etc.), which occur at the beginning of Pāṇini's grammar and form an integral part of it, were divinely inspired (they are, therefore, sometimes referred to as *Śivaśūtra*). Attempts have been made to utilize Hsüan Tsang's description to help date Pāṇini, but this seems impossible. All we are told in this passage is that some five hundred years after the death of the Buddha, Pāṇini was reborn. It might at most be argued that the original Pāṇini must have lived *after* the Buddha, for otherwise it would have been unreasonable to suppose that he had incurred an amount of demerit sufficient to be reborn by not embracing the teachings of the Buddha.

I have here reproduced Beal's translation (with minute changes) mainly because it is in English. But the text was first translated into French, by Stanislas Julien (Julien 1857–1858). Beal claims that his translation is independent of Julien's (Beal 1885, Introduction xxii). But Waley (1952, 11) says: "I found that almost everything European writers have said about him [that is, about Hsüan Tsang] is taken, directly or indirectly, from an incomplete and very imperfect translation of his biography by Stanislas Julien." This probably applies to the *Records* as well. These translations pose many problems to Sanskritists, for just as the Chinese must have been greatly puzzled by the structure, and in particular by the inflections of Sanskrit, Western Sinologists may have missed technical references to Sanskrit grammar. The expression in Beal's translation "there are other forms (*inflexions*) used" has no parallel in Julien. Similarly, Julien has merely "sens des mots" where Beal translates "agreement (*concordance*) of words." The Chinese equivalent for *śabdavidyā* (which also occurs in I Tsing: see page 12) might be an equivalent for *śabdānuśāsana*, which is a well-known Sanskrit expression for grammar.

A. Records of the Western Countries (Seventh Century)

Hsüan Tsang

To the north-west of U-to-kia-han-c'ha, 20 li or so, we come to the town of So-lo-tu-lo (Śalātura). This is the place where the Ṛṣi Pāṇini, who composed the *Ching-ming-lun* (*vyākaraṇa*), was born.

Referring to the most ancient times, letters were very numerous; but when, in the process of ages, the world was destroyed and remained as a void, the Devas of long life descended spiritually to guide the people. Such was the origin of the ancient letters and composition. From this time and after it the source (*of language*) spread and passed its (*former*) bounds. Brahmā Deva and Śakra (*Devendra*) established rules (*forms* or *examples*) according to the requirements. Ṛṣis [seers] belonging to different schools each drew up forms of letters. Men in their successive generations put into use what had been delivered to them; but nevertheless students without ability (*religious ability*) were unable to make use (*of these characters*). And now men's lives were reduced to the length of a hundred years, when the Ṛṣi Pāṇini was born; he was from his birth extensively informed about things (*men and things*). The times being dull and careless, he wished to reform the vague and false rules (*of writing and speaking*)—to fix the rules and correct improprieties. As he wandered about asking for right ways, he encountered Īśvara Deva, and recounted to him the plan of his undertaking. Īśvara Deva said, "Wonderful! I will assist you in this." The Ṛṣi, having received instruction, retired. He then laboured incessantly and put forth all his power of mind. He collected a multitude of words, and made a book on letters which contained a thousand *ślokas* ['verses']; each *śloka* was of thirty-two syllables. It contained everything known from the first till then, without exception, respecting letters and words. He then closed it and sent it to the king (*supreme ruler*), who exceedingly prized it, and issued an edict that throughout the kingdom it should be used and taught to others; and he added that whoever should learn it from beginning to end should receive as his reward a thousand pieces of gold. And so from that time masters have received it and handed it down in its completeness for the good of the world. Hence the Brāhmans of this town are well grounded in their literary work, and are of high renown for their talents, well informed as to things (*men and things*), and of a vigorous understanding (*memory*).

In the town of So-lo-tu-lo is a *stūpa*. This is the spot where an Arhat [elder] converted a disciple of Pāṇini. Tathāgata [that is, the Buddha] had left the world for some five hundred years, when there was a great Arhat who came to the country of Kaśmīr, and went about converting men. Coming to this place, he saw a Brahmacārin occupied in chastising a boy whom he was instructing in letters. Then the Arhat spake to the Brāhman thus: "Why do you cause pain to this child?" The Brāhman replied, "I am teaching him the *Shing-ming* (*Śabdavidyā*), but he makes no proper progress." The Arhat smiled significantly, on which the Brāhman said, "Shamans [that is, Buddhist monks] are of a pitiful and loving disposition, and well disposed to men and creatures generally; why did you smile, honoured sir? Pray let me know!"

The Arhat replied, "Light words are not becoming, and I fear to cause in you incredulous thoughts and unbelief. No doubt you have heard of the Ṛṣi Pāṇini, who compiled the *Śabdavidyā Śāstra*, which he has left for the instruction of the world." The Brāhman replied, "The children of this town, who are his disciples, revere his eminent qualities, and a statue erected to his memory still exists." The Arhat continued: "This little boy whom you are instructing was that very (*Pāṇini*) Ṛṣi. As he devoted his vigorous mind to investigate worldly literature, he only produced heretical treatises without any power of true reason in them. His spirit and his wisdom were dispersed, and he has run through the cycles of continued birth from then till now. Thanks to some remnant of true virtue, he has been now born as your attached child; but the literature of the world and these treatises on letters are only cause of useless efforts to him, and are as nothing compared to the holy teaching of Tathāgata, which, by its mysterious influences, procures both happiness and wisdom."

B. The Life of Hsüan Tsang (Seventh Century)

Hwui Li

Hwui Li, the biographer of Hsüan Tsang, relates in his *Life of Hsüan Tsang* how his teacher (whom he calls thoughout his work "the Master of the Law") learned Sanskrit grammar in the Nālanda monastery. He inserts a little treatise on this subject, "no doubt," says Waley (1952, 47), "to impress us with the difficulties that Tripitaka [that is, Hsüan Tsang] overcame in his study of Sanskrit writing and grammar." This treatise is reproduced here in full from Beal's translation (Beal 1911, 121–125), though the biography has also been translated by Julien (Julien 1853).

There is a recent English translation of Hwui Li's biography by Li Ying-hsi, published under the auspices of the San Shih Buddhist Institute by the Chinese Buddhist Association and printed in the People's Republic of China (Peking 1959); this passage occurs on pages 117–120. The references to Sanskrit have been regularized; for example, *bhavataḥ* has been inserted in the proper place, and the case endings are the correct ones. But *vyati*, considered an ending (like "underneath the nine inflections" in this context), remains still unexplained, and it is unclear whether the regularization is based upon new manuscript material (in the Foreword by Chao Pu-chu it is said that "the Ching Ling Buddhist Text Society at Nanking has completed the task of carving new printing blocks to replace the lost ones for the complete works translated or written by the Ven. Hsüan-tsang").

Pāṇini's grammar consists of just under 4000 *sūtras*, but the Chinese writers on India always seem to measure the size of writings in terms of *ślokas*. *Aṣṭa-dhātu* can refer neither to the *Dhātupāṭha* (which has ten chapters, corresponding to the ten verb classes), nor to Pāṇini's grammar itself, the *Aṣṭādhyāyī* (eight chapters), as it is distinguished from both by I Tsing (see page 13). But *Aṣṭadhātu* may be an elementary book, such as is referred to under that name in the *Durghaṭavṛtti* (Renou 1940, Introduction, 60). The terms *tiṅanta* and *subanta* for "what ends in *tiṅ*, i.e., verbal endings" (verbs) and "what ends in *sup*, i.e., nominal endings" (nouns) are undoubtedly Pāṇinian. The expressions *tiṅantapadam* ("a word ending in *tiṅ*") and *subantapadam* ("a word ending in *sup*") are generally used in this connection, but *vājya* could stand for *vākya* (in general meaning "sentence" but here perhaps "expression"). *Parasmai(pada)* and *Ātmane(pada)* are also Pāṇinian terms for the Active and Middle endings, respectively. The reference to *vyati* (or *ve*, *ya*, *ti*) is puzzling (the process here referred to is described differently in Pāṇini 3.4.78–80)*. The explanation of

* The ending of the first person singular Middle is (e.g., *bhave*); the element *-ya-* is attached to the root before the endings of the Passive (e.g., *kriyate*); the ending *-ti* occurs only in the Active.

the cases, with the exception of the Genitive, is reminiscent of Pāṇini's *kāraka* theory. However, Pāṇini did not consider the Vocative a separate case, but regarded it as a special use (*āmantrita*) of the Nominative. Last, it is apparent that there was considerable confusion with regard to the case endings. For some further discussion see van Gulik (1956, 14–18).

The Master of the Law whilst he stopped in the convent, heard the explanation of the Yoga-śāstra, three times: the Nyāyā-Anusāra-śāstra, once; the *Hin-hiang-tui-fă-ming*, once; the Hetu-vidyā-śāstra and the Śabdavidyā and the *tsah liang* śāstras, twice; the Prāṅyamūla śāstra-ṭīkā, and the Śata-śāstra, thrice. The Koṣa, Vibhāṣā, and the Ṣaṭpadābhidharma śāstras, he had already heard explained in the different parts of Kaśmir; but when he came to this convent he wished to study them again to satisfy some doubts he had: this done, he also devoted himself to the study of the Brāhman books and the work called Vyākaraṇa on Indian letters, whose origin is from the most remote date, and whose author is unknown.

At the beginning of each Kalpa, Brahma-rāja first declares it [the Vyākaraṇa], and then transmits it for Devas and men to use. Being thus declared by Brahma-rāja, therefore men call it *Fan*, or Brahmā, writing. The words of this book are very extensive, comprising a hundred myriad ślokas. It is the same as the old commentary calls the Vyākara(*ṇa*)-śāstra, but this pronunciation is not complete. If correct, it would be Vyākaraṇam, which is another name for 'a treatise relating to the record of the science of sounds.' It treats at large, in a mnemonic way, on all the laws of language and illustrates them, hence the name.

At the beginning of the Kalpa of perfection (*vaivarta kalpa*) Brahma-rāja first declared this book; it then comprised 100 myriad [thousand] of ślokas; afterwards, at the beginning of the *Vaivarta-siddha-Kalpa*, that is, the kalpa, or period, of establishment, Ti-shih (*Śakra-raja*) reduced them to ten myriad ślokas. After this a Brahman of the town Śalātura in Gandhāra of North India, whose name was Pāṇini Ṛṣi, reduced them to 8000 ślokas. This is the work at present used in India.

Lately a Brahman of South India, at the request of a king of South India, reduced them further to 2500 ślokas. This work is widely spread, and used throughout all the frontier provinces, but the well-read scholars of India do not follow it as their guide in practice.

This then is the fundamental treatise relating to sounds and letters of the Western world, their branch-divisions, distinctions and mutual connections.

Again, there is a Vyākaraṇam work (*mnemonic treatise*) of a short kind having 1000 ślokas; again, there is one of 300 ślokas on the roots (*bases*) of letters (*i.e. letter roots* or *bases*); again, there are (*treatises on the*) two separate kinds of letter-groupings, one named Maṇḍaka in 3000 ślokas, the other called Uṇādi in 2500 ślokas. These distinguish letter-groupings from letter-roots. Again, there is the treatise called Aṣṭa-dhātu (*Dhātuvṛtti?*) in 800 ślokas; in this work there is a brief conjunction of letter-bases and letter-groupings. These are all the Vyākaraṇa treatises.

In distinguishing active and passive expositions (*i.e.* in expounding the principles of grammar, relating to active and passive verbs), there are these two rules: the first, called Ti-yen-to-shing

(*Tiṅanta-vājyam*) having eighteen inflections; the second Su-man-to-shing (*Subanta-vājyam*), having twenty-four inflections; the Tiṅanta "sounds" are used in elegant compositions, but seldom in light literature. The twenty-four "sounds" are used in all kinds of composition alike. The eighteen inflections of the Tiṅanta "sounds" are of two characters: 1st, Parasmai, 2nd, Ātmane; each of these has nine inflections, and so together there are eighteen. With respect to the nine which come first: we know that in ordinary discourse *everything* has three ways of being viewed (*i.e. as one thing*, or *two things*, or *many things*); *every other person* has three ways of being considered (*i.e. as one other*, *two other*, or *many other*); and also "oneself" can be considered in three ways (*i.e.* as *I myself*, *two of us*, or *many of us*). Thus every single thing may be regarded in these three ways, as one, two of a class, or many; here, then, are three (three *persons* and three *numbers*, altogether *nine*). In both (*voices*) the root-word is the same, but the (*final*) sounds are different. So there are two sets of nine.

Now, taking the Parasmai sounds: we may speak of a thing as existing or not existing, in all cases. Supposing then we say a thing exists, there are three ways of putting (*naming*) this fact; we may say "it exists" (*bhavati*) or, "two things exist" (*bhavapa*)[1] or, "they exist" (*bhavanti*). And so, speaking of another, we may say "thou dost exist" (*bhavasi*), or, "you two exist" (*bhavapa*, for *bhavathaḥ*), or "you all exist" (*bhavatha*); and so again speaking of oneself we may say "I exist" (*bhavāmi*), or, "we two exist" (*bhavāvaḥ*), or, "we all exist" (*bhavāmaḥ*).

With regard to the nine case-endings of the Ātmane class, they simply take underneath the nine inflections just named the word "*vyati*," (or, the words *ve*, *ya*, *ti*); in other respects they are the same as the above.

Thus touching these things, we see how a skilful writer in this language is saved from ambiguity, and also how his meaning may be expressed in the most elegant manner.

With respect to the twenty-four inflections of the Subanta "sound (endings)," it is to be observed that every word has altogether eight inflections (*cases*), and that each of these cases or inflections is subject to three conditions as to number, viz., when one, or two, or many, are concerned. Hence arise the twenty-four (*sound-endings*). Then, again, in connection with these twenty-four inflections we have three other terms, viz., the masculine sound ending, the feminine, and the neuter. But regarding the eight inflections, the first exhibits the substance, or basis, of the thing conceived (*nominative*); the second exhibits the deed done (*objective*); the third, the means by which, and the doer (*instrumental*); the fourth, for whom the thing is done (*dative*); the fifth, what causes the thing (*ablative*); the sixth, whose is the thing (*genitive*); the seventh, that which determines (*localises*) the thing (*locative*); the eighth, the calling, or summoning, the thing (*vocative*). Now, for example, let us take the masculine ending, as in the word "man," and go through the eight cases named above.

The word "man" in Indian speech is *puruṣa*. The root-word has three inflexions, viz., *puruṣaḥ*, *puruṣau*, *puruṣās*. The thing done (*object*) has three, *puruṣam*, *puruṣau*, *puruṣān*; the instrument by which the thing is done by the doer has also three inflexions—*puruṣeṇa*, *puru(ṣā)bhyām*, *puruṣābhiḥ* or *puruṣaiḥ*; "for whom the

[1] For *Bhavataḥ*.

thing is done" [is rendered by] *puruṣāya, puruṣābhyām, puruṣeṣu*; "the cause from which the thing proceeds," [by] *puruṣāt, puruṣābhyām, puruṣeṣu*; "whose is the thing," [by] *puruṣasya, puruṣābhyām, puruṣāṇām*; "the place where," [by] *puruṣe, puruṣayos, puruṣāṇām*; "the calling case," [by] *hi puruṣa, hi puruṣau, hi puruṣāḥ*.
From these one or two examples, other cases may be understood; it would be difficult to make a full statement of particulars.

The Master of the Law thoroughly investigated the language (words and phrases), and by talking with those men on the subject of the "pure writing," he advanced excellently in his knowledge. Thus he penetrated, and examined completely, all the collection (of Buddhist books), and also studied the sacred books of the Brahmans during five years.

2

I Tsing (634-713)

Another Chinese scholar-pilgrim, I Tsing, left China in A.D. 671 by sea for India via Indonesia. He was then thirty-seven years old. Before he entered India proper, he stayed six months in Sumatra to learn Sanskrit. This would hardly be the place to learn that language nowadays, but in the seventh century, Eastern Sumatra was the center of the Śrīvijaya empire and, at the same time, a center for Buddhist, and therefore also Sanskrit, learning. After leaving Sumatra, I Tsing had many adventures on the way to India and in India, where he visited mainly the Ganges plain. He returned again via the sea route and Indonesia. Before reaching China in 695, he spent at least another four years in Sumatra. Here he wrote, probably during 691–692, his *Record of Buddhist Practices sent home from the Southern Sea*. This work, translated by Takakusu, gives a very detailed account of life in India and contains a long chapter (the thirty-fourth) on "The method of Learning in the West."

In the beginning of this chapter, I Tsing discusses Sanskrit and Buddhist philosophy. He stresses that the highest truth (*paramārtha-satya*) is beyond language, but admits that lower truth (*saṃvṛti-satya*) "may be explained by words and phrases." He then continues with a detailed account of the Sanskrit grammarians, which, despite its fascination with numbers and enumeration, is full of precious information (Takakusu 1896, 168–180, omitting most of the notes).

A fair amount of literature has been devoted to these compact pages: Max Müller (1883, 210–213, 281–366; also in Takakusu 1896, ix–xvi); F. Kielhorn (1883, 226); B. Liebich (1930, 266–270, 281–284). Many difficulties of interpretation remain, and the text ought to be studied anew.

The Method of Learning in the West (691-692)

I Tsing

The old translators have seldom told us the rules of the Sanskrit language. Those who lately introduced the Sūtras to our notice spoke only of the first seven cases. This is not because of ignorance (*of grammar*), but they have kept silence thinking it useless (*to teach the eighth*), (i.e., the vocative). I trust that now a thorough study of Sanskrit grammar may clear up many difficulties we encounter whilst engaged in translation. In this hope, I shall, in the following paragraphs, briefly explain some points as an introduction to grammar.

(Note by I-tsing): Even in the island of Pulo Condore (in the south) and in the country of Sūli (in the north), people praise the Sanskrit Sūtras, how much more then should people of the Divine Land (China), as well as the Celestial Store House (India), teach the real rules of the language! Thus the people of India said in praise (*of China*): "The wise Mañjuśrī is at present in Ping Chou, where the people are greatly blessed by his presence. We ought therefore to respect and admire that country, &c."

The whole of their account[1] is too long to be produced.

Grammatical science is called, in Sanskrit, Śabdavidyā, one of the five Vidyās; Śabda meaning 'voice,' and Vidyā 'science.' The name for the general secular literature in India is Vyākaraṇa, of which there are about five works, similar to the Five Classics of the Divine Land (China).

I. The Si-t'an-chang (Siddha-composition) for Beginners*

This is also called Siddhirastu, signifying 'Be there success' (in Sanskrit, the Chinese text has 'complete be good luck!') for so named is the first section of this small (book of) learning.

There are forty-nine letters (of the alphabet) which are combined with one another and arranged in eighteen sections; the total number of syllables is more than 10,000, or more than 300 ślokas. Generally speaking, each śloka contains four feet (pādas), each foot consisting of eight syllables; each śloka has therefore thirty-two syllables.

Again there are long and short ślokas; of these it is impossible here to give a minute account.

Children learn this book when they are six years old, and finish it in six months. This is said to have been originally taught by Maheśvara-deva (Śiva).

II. The Sūtra

The Sūtra is the foundation of all grammatical science. This name can be translated by 'short aphorism,' and signifies that important principles are expounded in an abridged form. It contains 1000 ślokas, and is the work of Pāṇini, a very learned scholar of old, who is said to have been inspired and assisted by Maheśvara-deva, and endowed with three eyes; this is generally believed by the Indians of today. Children begin to learn the Sūtra when they are eight years old, and can repeat it in eight months' time.

[1] I-tsing seems to be quoting these passages from a book.

[* Kielhorn (1883, 226), quoted by Takakusu, considers this an elementary *Siddhānta*, "which teaches the letters, their combinations, the organs with which they are pronounced, etc." The words *siddhir astu* 'let there be success' may occur at the beginning of almost any book.]

III. The Book on Dhātu*

This consists of 1000 ślokas, and treats particularly of grammatical roots. It is as useful as the above Sūtra.

IV. The Book on the Three Khilas**

Khila means 'waste land,' so called because this (part of grammar) may be likened to the way in which a farmer prepares his fields for corn. It may be called a book on the three pieces of waste land. (1) Aṣṭadhātu consists of 1000 ślokas; (2) Wen-ch'a (Maṇḍa or Muṇḍa) also consists of 1000 ślokas; (3) Uṇādi too consists of 1000 ślokas.

1. Aṣṭadhātu This treats of the seven cases (Sup) and ten Las, and eighteen finals (Tiṅ, 2 × 9 personal terminations).

α. The Seven Cases Every noun has seven cases, and every case has three numbers, i.e. singular (Ekavacana), dual (Dvivacana), and plural (Bahuvacana); so every noun has twenty-one forms altogether. Take the word "man," for instance. If one man is meant it is 'Puruṣaḥ', two men, 'Puruṣau', and three (or more) men, 'Puruṣāḥ'. These forms of a noun are also distinguished as heavy and light (probably 'accented and unaccented'), or as pronounced by the open and closed breathings (perhaps 'nouns with an open vowel or those with a closed vowel'). Besides the seven cases there is the eighth,—the vocative case (Āmantrita), which makes up the eight cases. As the first case has three numbers, so have the remaining ones, the forms of which, being too numerous to be mentioned, are omitted here. A *noun* is called Subanta, having (3 × 8) twenty-four (inflected) forms.

β. The Ten Las There are ten signs with L (*for the verbal tenses*); in conjugating (lit. expressing) a verb, the distinctions of the three times, i.e. past, present, and future, are expressed.

γ. The Eighteen Finals (Tiṅ). These are the forms of the first, second, and the third person (*of the three numbers of a verb*), showing the differences *of the worthy and unworthy, or this and that.*[2] Thus every verb (*in one tense*) has eighteen different forms which are called Tiṅanta.

2. Wen-ch'a (Maṇḍa or Muṇḍa) This treats of the formation of words by means of combining (a root and a suffix or suffixes). For instance, one of many names for "tree" in Sanskrit is *vṛkṣa*. Thus a name for a thing or a matter is formed by joining (the syllables) together, according to the rules of the Sūtra, which consist of more than twenty verses.

[* This is obviously the *Dhātupāṭha*.]

[** The word *khila* means 'appendix,' but what the *Aṣṭadhātu*, also mentioned by Hwui Li (Liebich 1930, 282: "eine Sammlung von Deklinations- und Konjugationsparadigmen") and the *Maṇḍa* or *Muṇḍa* are is unclear. Like *sup* and *tiṅ* (see page 7), *L* is a technical expression in Pāṇini's grammar. It is the initial sound of the technical names of the ten tenses and moods (i.e., *laṭ* 'present,' *liṭ* 'perfect,' *luṭ* 'periphrastic future,' *lṛṭ* 'future,' *leṭ* 'subjunctive,' *loṭ* 'imperative,' *laṅ* 'imperfect,' *liṅ* 'optative,' *luṅ* 'aorist,' and *lṛṅ* 'conditional'). For *Uṇādi* suffixes see page 62.]

[2] We should expect here 'Ātmanepada and Parasmaipada.' 'This and that' may be a vague way of expressing the grammatical terms 'Ātmane' and 'Parasmai,' for Chinese has no grammatical terms for these. Still, 'worthy and unworthy' is very strange.

3. The Uṇādi This is nearly the same as the above (Maṇḍ a), with the exception that what is fully explained in the one is only mentioned briefly in the other, and vice versa.

Boys begin to learn the book on the three Khilas (or 'three pieces of waste land') when they are ten years old, and understand them thoroughly after three years' diligent study.

V. The Vṛtti-sūtra (Kāśikāvṛtti)*

This is a commentary on the foregoing Sūtra (i.e. Pāṇini's Sūtra). There were many commentaries composed in former times, and this is the best of them.

It cites the text of the Sūtra, and explains minutely its manifold meaning, consisting altogether of 18,000 ślokas. It exposes the laws of the universe, and the regulations of gods and men. Boys of fifteen *begin to study this commentary*, and understand it after five years.

If men of China go to India for study, they have first of all to learn this (*grammatical*) work, then other subjects; if not, their labour will be thrown away. All these books should be learnt by heart. But this, as a rule, applies only to men of high talent, while for those of medium or little ability a different measure (method) must be taken according to their wishes. They should study hard day and night, without letting a moment pass for idle repose. They should be like the Father K'ung (i.e. Confucius), by whose hard study the leather binding of his Yi-king was three times worn away; or imitate Sui-Shih, who used to read a book a hundred times. The hairs of a bull are counted by thousands, but a unicorn has only one horn.[3] The labour or merit of learning the above works is equal to that of proceeding to (the grade of) the Master of Classics ('Ming-king').

This Vṛtti-sūtra is a work of the learned Jayāditya. He was a man of great ability; his literary power was very striking. He understood things which he had heard once, not requiring to be taught twice. He revered the Three Honourable Ones (i.e. Triratna), and constantly performed the meritorious actions. It is now nearly thirty years since his death (A.D. 661–662). After having studied this commentary, students begin to learn composition in prose and verse, and devote themselves to logic (Hetuvidyā) and metaphysic (Abhidharmakośa). In learning the Nyāya-dvāra-tāraka-śāstra, they rightly draw inferences (Anumāna); and by studying the Jātakamālā their powers of comprehension increase. Thus, instructed by their teachers and instructing others, they pass two or three years, generally in the Nālanda monastery in Central India, or in the country of Valabhī (Walā) in

[* The first part of the *Kāśikāvṛtti* commentary (though Belvalkar 1915, 35, doubts that this text is meant here by the term *vṛttisūtra*, the regular name being *sūtravṛtti*; but Liebich, 1930, 283, is not taken aback by this inversion) was written by Jayāditya; its second part, by Vāmana possibly after I Tsing had left India. The dates 661–662, which are undoubtedly too precise, are based upon this important passage alone. In a grammatical context a reference to "the Three Honourable Ones" is most readily interpreted as a reference to the *munitrayam* 'three sages' or 'three *ācāryas*' (see below page 86), viz., Pāṇini, Kātyāyana and Patañjali. Moreover, the Buddhist *triratna*—Buddha, law, and order—consists of at most one person.]

[3] That is to say, 'Few are clever.'

Western India. These two places are like Chin-ma, Shih-ch'ü, Lung-mên, and Ch'ue-li in China, and there eminent and accomplished men assemble in crowds, discuss possible and impossible doctrines, and after having been assured of the excellence of their opinions by wise men, become far famed for their wisdom. To try the sharpness of their wit (lit. 'sharp point of the sword'), they proceed to the king's court to lay down before it the sharp weapon (of their abilities); there they present their schemes and show their (*political*) talent, seeking to be appointed in the practical government. When they are present in the House of Debate, they raise their seat and seek to prove their wonderful cleverness.

When they are refuting heretic doctrines, all their opponents become tongue-tied and acknowledge themselves undone. Then the sound of their fame makes the five mountains (of India) vibrate, and their renown flows, as it were, over the four borders. They receive grants of land, and are advanced to a high rank; *their famous names are*, as a reward, *written* in white on their lofty gates. After this they can follow whatever occupation they like.

VI. The Cūrṇī*

Next, there is a commentary on the Vṛtti-sūtra entitled Cūrṇī, containing 24,000 ślokas.

It is a work of the learned Patañjali. This, again, cites the former Sūtras (Pāṇini), explaining the obscure points (lit. 'piercing the skin') and analysing the principles contained in it, and it illustrates the latter commentary (Vṛtti), clearing up many difficulties (lit. 'removing and breaking the hair and beard of corn').

Advanced scholars learn this in three years. The labour or merit is similar to that of learning the Ch'un-ch'iu and the Yi-king in China.

VII. The Bhartṛhari-śāstra**

Next, there is the Bhartṛhari-śāstra. This is the commentary on the foregoing Cūrṇī, and is the work of a great scholar Bhartṛhari. It contains 25,000 ślokas, and fully treats of the *principles* of human life, as well as of grammatical science, and also relates the reasons of the rise and decline of many families. The author was intimately acquainted with the doctrine of 'sole knowledge' (Vidyāmātra), and has skilfully discussed about the Hetu and Udāharaṇa (the cause and example of logic). This scholar was very famous throughout the five parts of India, and his excellences were known everywhere (lit. 'to the eight quarters'). He believed deeply in the Three Jewels (i.e. Ratnatraya), and diligently meditated on the 'twofold nothingness' (Śūnya).[4] Having desired *to embrace* the

[* As Max Müller (1883) and Kielhorn (1883) have pointed out, *Cūrṇi* is a name used for Patañjali's *Mahābhāṣya*.]

[** The date and religion of the celebrated philosopher-grammarian Bhartṛhari have been the subject of ample discussion. Despite I Tsing's testimony, Bhartṛhari is nowadays generally believed to have been a Hindu (see, for example, Biardeau 1964b) and is sometimes believed to have lived in the fifth century (because the Buddhist logician Diṅnāga appears to quote him: Frauwallner 1959; cf. Ruegg 1959, 57–60). Portions of what is extant of the commentary on the *Mahābhāṣya* mentioned here have been published only recently.]

[4] The 'twofold nothingness,' 'both Ātman and Dharma are but an empty show.'

excellent Law he became a homeless priest, but overcome by worldly desires he returned again to the laity. In the same manner he became seven times a priest, and seven times returned to the laity. Unless one believes well in the truth of cause and effect, one cannot act strenuously like him. He wrote the following verses, full of self-reproach:

Through the enticement of the world I returned to the laity.
Being free from secular pleasures again I wear the priestly cloak.
How do these two impulses
Play with me as if a child?

He was a contemporary of Dharmapāla. Once when a priest in the monastery, being harassed by worldly desires, he was disposed to return to the laity. He remained, however, firm, and asked a student to get a carriage outside the monastery. On being asked the cause, he replied: 'It is the place where one performs meritorious actions, and it is designed for the dwelling of those who keep the moral precepts (Śīla). Now passion already predominates within me, and I am incapable of adhering to the excellent Law. Such a man as myself should not intrude into an assembly of priests come here from every quarter.'

Then he returned to the position of a lay devotee (Upāsaka), and wearing a white garment continued to exalt and promote the true religion, being still in the monastery. It is forty years since his death (A.D. 651–652).

VIII. The Vākya-discourse

In addition there is the Vākya-discourse (Vākyapadīya). This contains 700 ślokas, and its commentary portion has 7000 (ślokas). This is also Bhartṛhari's work, a treatise on the Inference supported by *the authority* of the sacred teaching, and on Inductive arguments.

IX. The Pei-na*

Next there is Pei-na (probably Sanskrit 'Beda' or 'Veda'). It contains 3000 ślokas, and its commentary portion is in 14,000 (ślokas).

[* Bhartṛhari is not known to have written anything apart from the *Mahābhāṣya* commentary and the *Vākyapadīya*. Takakusu's reference to a *Beḍāvṛtti*, mentioned by Bühler and occurring in Bhandarkar's Catalogue of MSS in the Deccan College (Takakusu 1896, 225) is not particularly illuminating. Liebich (1930, 266–267) believes "Pei-na" to mean *Prakīrṇa*, the third part of the *Vākyapadīya*, which is very long and sometimes regarded as a separate work. This was in fact the viewpoint of Kielhorn, who had already drawn attention to the fact that South Indian manuscripts call this third part (which is linguistically the most interesting part) *Prakīrṇaka*, and that Helarāja called his commentary on this part *Prakīrṇa-prakāśa* (Kielhorn 1883, 227). Also Abhinavagupta (about A.D. 1000) wrote a work called *Prakīrṇa-kavivaraṇam*, now lost, which was probably a commentary on the third part of the *Vākyapadīya*. Recently, Aklujkar (1969), has shown that the title *Vākyapadīya* was in fact originally given to the first two books only. Another possibility is that the name of Puṇya (rāja), a commentator on Bhartṛhari's *Vākyapadīya*, is referred to by the Chinese "Pei-na." There are difficulties with either interpretation as long as it is not certain who the Dharmapāla that I Tsing referred to was (cf. Aklujkar 1969, 549, n. 8).]

The śloka portion was composed by Bhartṛhari, while the commentary portion is attributed to Dharmapāla, teacher of the Śāstra. This book fathoms the deep secrets of heaven and earth, and treats of the philosophy of man (lit. 'the essential beauty of the human principles'). A person who has studied so far as this (*book*), is said to have mastered grammatical science, and may be compared to one who has learnt the Nine Classics and all the other authors of China. All the above-mentioned books are studied by both priests and laymen; if not they cannot gain the fame of the well-informed (lit. 'much heard,' Bahuśruta, or 'Knowing much of the śruti').

3

Fa Tsang (643-712)

Though Hsüan Tsang and I Tsing are the most famous of the Chinese pilgrims who provided information on India, there were other Chinese scholars who referred to Sanskrit and, in such references, to the Sanskrit grammarians. Fa Tsang (643–712) was a Buddhist monk of Sogdian descent and a prolific author who lived in China. He was the main authority on the *Avataṃsaka sūtra*, a Buddhist *Mahāyāna* work that taught the sameness of everything and became very influential in China and Japan. In Fa Tsang's *Account of Exploring the Mysteries of the Avataṃsaka Sūtra*, a passage occurs which deals with Sanskrit grammar. Van Gulik, who stresses that the Chinese knowledge of Sanskrit was generally confined to the script, quotes this passage in order to prove that "it would have been quite possible to draw up a complete Chinese version of Pāṇini's rules accompanied by a commentary." The quotation proves no such thing, and it does not refer directly to the Sanskrit grammarians. In fact, its explanation of the cases is rather different from the one we are given by Pāṇini. But some of Fa Tsang's examples may be traced back to the grammatical tradition. The *Kāśikā*, for example, uses *paraśunā chinatti* 'he cuts with an axe' to illustrate the Instrumental (commenting on Pāṇini 1.4.42, 2.3.18). Fa Tsang's passage has been published and translated by van Gulik (1956, 19–20).

It is remarkable that both van Gulik and Fa Tsang talk about eightfold declension, and then proceed to discuss seven cases. As we have seen (on page 13), their practice accords with the Indian tradition.

Account of Exploring the Mysteries of the Avataṃsaka Sūtra (Seventh Century)

Fa Tsang

The cases refer to the (grammatical) rules of the Western countries. If one wants to examine and read the sacred and secular books one has to know the rules for the eightfold declension. If one does not understand these, one cannot know the meaning and arrangement of the text.

1. *puruṣaḥ*, the case of direct indication; for instance, in the sentence 'The man cuts down the tree', this case points directly to that man [nominative].
2. *puruṣam*, the case indicating that to which something happens. As in the sentence 'The tree that is cut' [accusative].
3. *puruṣeṇa*, the case indicating the instrument with which something is done, as in the sentence 'to cut a tree with an axe' [instrumental].
4. *puruṣāya*, the case indicating for whom something is done, as in 'to cut a tree for a man' [dative].
5. *puruṣāt*, the case indicating a causal relation, as in 'to build a house on behalf of a man' [ablative].
6. *puruṣasya*, the case indicating possession, as in 'the slave belongs to the master' [genitive].
7. *puruṣe*, the case indicating staying with, as in 'the guest stays with his host' [locative].

4

Abū Raiḥān al-Bīrūnī (973-1048)

The expansion of Islam and scholarly curiosity seem to be the two main factors that explain the large number of Arabic and Persian publications dealing with India. Foremost among these is the Arabic treatise of the Persian scholar Abū Raiḥān Muḥammad Ibn Aḥmad al-Bīrūnī (973–1048), referred to as "Indica" by its editor and translator, Edward Sachau. This detailed and scholarly work, the real title of which is *An Accurate Description of All Categories of Hindu Thought, Those Which Are Admissible as well as Those Which Must Be Rejected*, was written in 1030. Al-Bīrūnī, who was not only a Sanskrit scholar but also an astronomer, wrote a large number of works on Indian astronomy and mathematics. While writing his "Indica" he was also engaged, as he tells us, in translating Euclid's *Elements*, Ptolemy's *Almagest*, and writing a treatise of his own on the construction of the astrolabe into Sanskrit *ślokas*.

The "Indica" contains detailed descriptions of Hindu religion, philosophy, literature, and especially astronomy, al-Bīrūnī's specialty. In the beginning of his book al-Bīrūnī discusses the reasons why "the Hindus entirely differ from us in every respect." The foremost reason he cites is their language, which is "of an enormous range, both in words and inflections, something like the Arabic, calling one and the same thing by various names, both original and derived, and using one and the same word for a variety of subjects, which, in order to be properly understood, must be distinguished from each other by various qualifying epithets. For nobody could distinguish between the various meanings of a word unless he understands the context in which it occurs, and its relation to both the following and the preceding part of the sentence. The Hindus, like other people, boast of this enormous range of their language, whilst in reality it is a defect" (Sachau 1910, 17–18). This last topic is a theme to which al-Bīrūnī occasionally returns, for example, when discussing the variety of geographical names: "Of course, in all of this the Hindus are actuated by the desire to have as many names as possible, and to practice on them the rules and arts of their etymology, and they glory in the enormous copiousness of their language which they obtain by such means" (Sachau 1910, 299). Al-Bīrūnī's disapproval is related to the ensuing difficulty of learning "the whole of the language" (pages 228–229):

The Hindus and their like boast of this copiousness, whilst in reality it is one of the greatest faults of the language. For it is the task of language to give a name to everything in creation and to its effects, a name based on general consent, so that everybody, when hearing this name pronounced by another man, understands what he means. If therefore one and the same name or word means a variety of things, it betrays a defect of the language and compels the hearer to ask the speaker what he means by the word. And thus the word in question must be dropped in order to be replaced either by a similar one of a sufficiently clear meaning, or by an epithet describing what is really meant. If one and the same thing is called by many names, and this is not occasioned by the fact that every tribe or class of people uses a separate one of them, and if, in fact, one single name would be sufficient, all the other names save this one are to be classified as mere nonsense, as a means of keeping people in the dark, and throwing an air of mystery about the subject. And in any case this copiousness offers painful difficulties to those who want to learn the whole of the language, for it is entirely useless, and only results in a sheer waste of time.

Another reason for the differences between Muslims and Hindus is that "the [Hindus'] language is divided into a neglected vernacular one, only in use among the common people, and a classical one, only in use among the upper and educated classes, which is much cultivated, and subject to the rules of grammatical inflection and etymology, and to all the niceties of grammar and rhetoric" (page 18). Furthermore, the language is very difficult to pronounce ("we have sometimes written down a word from the mouth of Hindus, taking the greatest pains to fix its pronunciation, and afterwards when we repeated it to them, they had great difficulty in recognising it" (page 18); with characteristic self-confidence, al-Bīrūnī attributes this to his informants' carelessness). Lastly, the Hindus like to compose their works in meters in order to facilitate their being learned by heart. "Now it is well known that in all metrical compositions there is much misty and constrained phraseology merely intended to fill up the metre and serving as a kind of patchwork, and this necessitates a certain amount of verbosity. This is also one of the reasons why a word has sometimes one meaning and sometimes another" (page 19).

The thirteenth chapter of the "Indica" is devoted to "their [the Hindu] grammatical and metrical literature." Though not apparently an admirer of poetry, al-Bīrūnī was interested in Sanskrit meters and in the way the Hindus used arithmetic in their metrical system. Most of the chapter is devoted to this topic, but in the beginning he also provides some information on grammatical works and schools (Sachau 1887, 65; 1910, I, 135–136; II, 300–301).

A further description of the books listed in the text of this article is as follows:

1. An "Aindra" school of grammar has often been construed as a pre-Pāṇinian school of Sanskrit grammarians (last by A. C. Burnell 1875); but a grammarian Indra(gomin), probably much later than Pāṇini, is known only by name. The confusion may be partly due to traditions which connect the god Indra with the origin of grammar (cf. page 136 of this volume and Patañjali's Introduction to the *Mahābhāṣya*, quoted in Staal 1969, 501–502). The earliest of these traditions is of Vedic origin: *Taittirīya-saṃhitā* 6.4.7 "Speech indeed spoke formerly without manifestation (*avyākṛta*). The gods said to Indra: 'do manifest this speech for us'... Indra approaching it from the middle made it manifest (*avyākarot*). Therefore speech is manifest (*vyākṛta*)" (hence *vyākaraṇa* 'making manifest, analysis, grammar').
2. This is the most popular Buddhist grammar; Candra(gomin)'s date is uncertain (estimates range from the fifth to the seventh century A.D.).
3. The author of the grammar, not his *ḳabīla* 'tribe', is Śākaṭāyana; he was a Jain who probably lived in the ninth century.
4. The reading of the manuscript is *pānriti*, the result of an effort to render the retroflex feature of Sanskrit "*ṇ*" (Chatterji 1951, 90; cf. Sachau 1910, II, 300–301).
5. This is the oldest non-Pāṇinian grammar.
6. This work is not known to me.
7. Not known to me; this could not be a misspelling of *Durghaṭavṛtti*, since this work was written in the twelfth century.
8. Deciphered by Kielhorn (Sachau 1910, II, 301); cf. Belvalkar (1915, 91); Renou (1940, Introduction 59).

An Accurate Description of All Categories of Hindu Thought (1030)

Abū Raiḥān al-Bīrūnī

The two sciences of grammar and metrics are auxiliary to the other sciences. Of the two, the former, grammar, holds the first place in their [the Hindus'] estimate; [it is] called *vyākaraṇa*, i.e. the law of the correctness of their speech and etymological rules, by means of which they acquire an eloquent and classical style both in writing and reading. We Muslims cannot learn anything of it, since it is a branch coming from a root which is not within our grasp—I mean the language itself. That which I have been told as to titles of books on this science is the following:—

1. *Aindra*, attributed to Indra, the head of the angels.
2. *Cāndra*, composed by Candra, one of the red-robe-wearing sect, the followers of Buddha.
3. *Śākaṭa*, so called by the name of its author. His tribe, too, is called by a name derived from the same word, viz. *Śākaṭāyana*.
4. *Pāṇini*, so called from its author.
5. *Kātantra*, composed by Śarvavarman.
6. *Śaśidevavṛtti*, composed by Śaśideva.
7. *Durgavivṛtti*.
8. *Śiṣyahitāvṛtti*, composed by Ugrabhūti.

I have been told that the last-mentioned author was the teacher and instructor of Shāh Ānandapāla, the son of Jayapāla, who ruled in our time. After having composed the book he sent it to Kashmīr, but the people there did not adopt it, being in such things haughtily conservative. Now he complained of this to the Shāh, and the Shāh, in accordance with the duty of a pupil toward his master, promised him to make him attain his wish. So he gave orders to send 200,000 *dirham* and presents of a similar value to Kashmīr, to be distributed among those who studied the book of his master. The consequence was that they all rushed upon the book, and would not copy any other grammar but this one, showing themselves in the baseness of their avarice. The book became the fashion and highly prized.

Of the origin of grammar they give the following account:* One of their kings, called Samalvāhana, i.e., in the classical language Śātavāhana, was one day in a pond playing with his wives, when he said to one of them *Mā udakaṃ dehi*, i.e. do not sprinkle the water on me. The woman, however, understood it as if he had said *modakaṃ dehi*, i.e. bring sweetmeats. So she went away and brought him sweetmeats. And when the king disapproved of her doing so, she gave him an angry reply, and used coarse language towards him. Now he was deeply offended, and in consequence, as is their custom, he abstained from all food, and concealed himself in some corner until he was called upon by a sage, who consoled him, promising him that he would teach people grammar and the inflexions of the language. Thereupon the sage went off to Mahādeva, praying and fasting devoutly. Mahādeva appeared to him, and communicated to him some few rules, the like of which Abul'aswad Addu'alī has given for the Arabic language. The god also promised to assist him in the further development of this science. Then the sage returned to the king and taught it to him. This was the beginning of the science of grammar.

[* This account of the origin of grammar is a patriarchal version of the traditional legend of the origin of the Kātantra school, where it is the ignorant king Śātavāhana who, when requested by his queen *modakaṃ dehi*, offered her sweets (Belvalkar 1915, 82–83). Śātavāhana is the name of a dynasty of South Indian kings (approximately 50 B.C.–A.D. 250).]

5

Tāranātha (Born 1573)

The interests of the Tibetan Buddhist scholars were similar to those of the Chinese Buddhists, but they were closer to India, had easier access to a large number of sources, and had been familiar with Sanskrit for a longer period. They also seemed to have had a predilection for describing fantastic events. Among the earlier historians, Bu-ston (1290–1364) provides the most information, though much of it is in mythical form. According to Bu-ston, a great *śāstra* dealing with grammar was first composed in heaven by the god Sarvajñāna and was subsequently lost. Thereupon the god Indra composed the *Indravyākaraṇa*, which was studied and propagated by the divine perceptor, Bṛhaspati. It became known in India, but gradually lost popularity. Thereupon Pāṇini appeared (Schiefner 1869, 294).

The work of the Tibetan scholar Tāranātha (born 1573) on the history of Buddhism in India, which was completed in 1608, also incorporates numerous legends, but its aim appears to be more strictly historical. This book begins with a description of the age of the Buddha and the reign of the king of Magadha, Ajātaśatru, who killed and succeeded his father Bimbisāra about 490 B.C. About 413 B.C. king Nanda overthrew this earlier dynasty and established a new one, known as the Nanda dynasty. When relating events during the reign of king Nanda, Tāranātha speaks about Pāṇini and provides some information about grammars (from the German translation in Schiefner 1869, 53–54).

Tāranātha does not talk about these grammatical works in the manner of a person who is at all familiar with their contents. Kalāpa is another name for Kātantra (*kalāpa*, literally 'that which holds single parts together,' hence 'bundle,' in particular 'peacock's tail.'

A. Geschichte des Buddhismus in Indien (1608): I

Tāranātha

Ein Genosse des Königs Nanda war der Brahmane Pāṇini, welcher im Westen in Bhīrukavana geboren war. Als er einen Handliniendeuter gefragt hatte, ob er die Wortlehre innehaben werde oder nicht, und dieser es verneint hatte, machte er sich mit einem scharfen Scheermesser Handlinien, wandte sich an alle Meister der Sprachlehre auf der Erde, trieb dieselbe eifrigst und da er noch immer nicht befriedigt war, bannte er durch seine Ausdauer seinen Schutz-Gott herbei. Als dieser sein Antlitz zeigte und *a*, *i*, *u* aussprach, erlangte er alle Stücke der in der Dreiwelt befindlichen Laute. Die Heterodoxen [the Hindus] behaupten, dass es Īśvara gewesen, haben jedoch dafür keine eigenen Quellen, die Orthodoxen [the Buddhists] aber sagen, dass es Avalokiteśvara gewesen und haben als Quelle die Vorhersagung aus dem Mañjuśrīmūlatantra: "Der Brahmanensohn Pāṇini wird sicherlich mit der vollendeten Einsicht eines Śrāvaka [a Buddhist monk], meiner Vorhersagung gemäss, die Majestät des Herrn der Welt durch seinen Zauberspruch herbeibannen". Dieser Pāṇini verfasste das Pāṇinivyākaraṇa genannte grammatische Sūtra, welches 2000 Śloka's umfasst und zwar 1000 Śloka's der Wortbildung and 1000 Śloka's der Erläuterung. Dies ist gleichsam die Wurzel aller Grammatiken. Vor ihm gab es keine schriftlich abgefassten Śāstra's der Wortbildung und da kein System, welches die Sache unter Gesichtspunkte brachte, bestand, so wurden die einzelnen Sprachkundigen, wenn jene von zwei bis zwei Verbindungen anfangend einzelnes zusammenbrachten, für besonders gelehrt gehalten. Obwohl es in Tibet heisst, dass das Indravyākaraṇa älter sei, so wird unten gesagt werden, dass es, obwohl es vielleicht in der Götterregion früher da war, in Āryadeśa nicht früher erschien. Wenn auch die Paṇḍita's behaupten, dass das ins Tibetische übersetzte Candravyākaraṇa mit Pāṇini, das Kalāpavyākaraṇa mit dem Indravyākaraṇa übereinstimme, so sagt man doch allgemein, dass besonders das Pāṇinivyākaraṇa durch die ausgedehnte Ausführlichkeit der Bedeutungen und die systematische vollständige Einsicht etwas sehr Seltenes sei.

B. Geschichte des Buddhismus in Indien (1608): II

Tāranātha

In the fifteenth chapter of his "History," Tāranātha describes the events that took place at the time of the Buddhist philosopher (*ācārya* 'teacher') Nāgārjuna, a person around whom numerous legends were woven and who is said to have converted king Udayana to Buddhism. The *purohita* or domestic priest of king Udayana was friend of Nāgārjuna and a grammarian. His name, Vararuci, is in fact another name of Kātyāyana, the author of the *vārttikās* or rules of interpretation (see page 104 of this volume) on Pāṇini's grammar. Tāranātha then gives some information about Vararuci and the relationship between the Pāṇinian and the Buddhist systems of grammar (Schiefner 1869, 73–76).

The form *mamodakāsiñca* as used in this selection seems to be a corruption combining several words as they occur in the sentences describing this episode; for example, in the *Kathāsaritsāgara* (6.114-116), the queen first said, *modakair deva paritāḍaya mām*, 'don't hit me with water, my lord' and then explained it later by dissolving the *sandhi* between *mā* and *udakair*, as follows: *udakaiḥ siñca mā tvam mām*, 'don't (you) splash me with water.' But *modaka* is also a kind of sweetmeat. The linguistic part of the legend is reported more accurately by al-Bīrūnī (see page 22). The legends reported here probably reflect ancient rivalries between grammatical schools. *Ṣaṇmukhakumāra* 'the six-faced

youth' is a name of the god Kārttikeya, whose vehicle is a peacock (hence *kalāpa* 'peacock's tail'). *Varṇasamāmnāya*, 'enumeration of sounds,' refers to the *pratyāhārasūtra* or *Śivasūtra*. Patañjali, whom tradition identifies with the author of the *Yogasūtra* of that name, is represented in iconography as a sage who is a serpent below the waist (cf. frontispiece, Plate I).

Der Freund desselben Ācārya, der Ācārya und Brahmane Vararuci lebte als Purohita des Königs Udayana. Zu der Zeit kannte eine jüngere Gattin des Königs ein wenig die Grammatik, der König kannte sie aber nicht. Zur Zeit als sie im Lusthain im Wasser spielten und der König sie mit Wasser bespritzte, sagte sie zu ihm: mamodakāsiñca d.h. in tibetischer Sprache "Bespritze mich nicht mit Wasser." Der König aber verstand in Uebereinstimmung mit der Sprache des Südens einen in Sesamöl gekochten Erbsenkuchen und gab ihr einen solchen. Da dachte die Königin, dass es besser sei zu sterben als mit einem solchen ochsengleichen Könige zu leben und schickte sich an sich zu tödten, wurde aber vom Könige ergriffen, welcher sich ans Lernen der Sprache machte und von dem Brahmanen Vararuci fleissig lernte, allein da er nicht im Geringsten vorwärts kam, nahm er Unterricht vom Ācārya Saptavarman. Die Geschichte des Ācārya Vararuci ist folgende. Der der Buddha-Lehre eifrig ergebene Brahmane, welcher der sechs Werke beflissen war und zu der Zeit als der ehrwürdige Nāgārjuna Paṇḍita in Nālanda war, mit ihm bekannt wurde, stammte aus dem östlich von Magadha belegenen Lande Chagala. Als er 12 Jahre hindurch das ehrwürdige Avalokiteśvaramantra hergesagt hatte und ihm endlich ein Brandopfer mit Zurüstung von 400,000 in Gold gebracht hatte, erschien Avalokiteśvara offenbar und fragte, was er wolle. "Ich wünsche durch die acht grossen Siddhi's [magical attainments] das Wohl aller belebten Wesen zu bewirken, und dass du Mahākāla zu meinem Diener machest." Als ihm dies gewährt war, konnte er fortan jeden Zauber nach Wunsch vollziehen und durch die acht Siddhi's die Kügelchen u.s.w. erwies er tausendfach den belebten Wesen Nutzen; die 8000 Siddhi-Besitzer erkannten ihn als ihren Lehrer an, und alle Wissenschaften hatte er von selbst inne ohne sie gelernt zu haben. Als er sich darauf nach dem Süden begeben hatte, wohnte er im Lande des mit grossem Reichthum versehenen Königs Śāntivāhana und nachdem er dort durch die Mantra's und Tantra's den lebenden Wesen Nutzen schaffend gelebt hatte, erwies er, als er nach Vārāṇasī kam, wo zu der Zeit der König Bhīmaśukla herrschte, den lebenden Wesen noch grösseren Nutzen . . . Als er darauf nach dem Süden gekommen war und dort der König Udayana die Sprache lernen wollte, aber keinen Lehrer finden konnte, welcher Pāṇini's Buch vollständig kannte und als er erfahren, dass der Nāgarāja [king of snakes] Śeṣa den Pāṇini vollständig kenne, so rief der Brahmane Vararuci diesen durch die Kraft der Mantra's herbei und vermochte ihn eine ausführliche Erklärung des ganzen Sinnes von Pāṇini in 100,000 Śloka's zu geben, welche der Ācārya niederschrieb; beide waren aber durch einen Vorhang getrennt. Als 25,000 Śloka's vorüber waren, wünschte der Ācārya zu sehen, welcher Art sein Körper wäre, lüftete den Vorhang und erblickte eine grosse sich hinstreckende Schlange, welche voll Schande davon lief. Darauf schrieb der Ācārya selbst die Erklärung weiter, aber es sind dort nicht mehr als 12,000 Śloka's. Diese beiden Werke zusammen sind bekannt unter dem Namen der von dem Nāga gelehrten Grammatik. Es wird dort von der Sprache und anderen Wissenschaften vielfach gelehrt. Endlich soll ihn Mahākāla auf seine Schultern genommen und ihn auf den Gipfel des Sumeru nach Pārijātaka getragen haben. Da der König Udayana der von dem Ācārya Vararuci gemachten Erklärung nicht traute, befahl er dem Brahmanen Saptavarman den Ṣaṇmukhakumāra zu bannen. Als dieser herbeigebannt war, fragte er, was er wolle. "Gieb mir das Indravyākaraṇa." Als der Gott nur die Worte Siddhovarṇasamāmnāya ausgesprochen hatte, erfasste er die Bedeutung aller der Laute. Früher wurde in den in Tibet bekannten Geschichten erzählt, dass Ṣaṇmukhakumāra vom Kalāpa [see page 25] die vier ersten Capitel dictirt habe und Kalāpa als Zusammenfügung der Theile zu fassen sei, so wie in den Pfauenschweiffedern die verschiedenfarbigen Theile zusammengefügt werden. Allein es verhält sich nicht so; Kalāpa ist von Saptavarman selbst verfasst und die Bedeutung Zusammenfassung der Theile ist die, dass alle nöthigen Theile zusammengefasst sind. Ebenso wird der Name dieses Ācārya falsch als Īśvaravarman erklärt, wie sich die Form Sarvavarman fälschlich eingeschlichen hat; Saptavarman bedeutet aber: Siebenpanzer.

2

The Foundations of Western Scholarship

Plate II

A bronze image of Patañjali, which shows a beard and an enlarged rounded cranium that are the marks of sages in late South Indian iconography. This bronze of the fourteenth or fifteenth century is in a private collection.

6

Jean François Pons (1698–1752)

Among the first Western scholars to hear about linguistics in India was Filippo Sassetti (1540–1588). Sassetti was greatly impressed by the Indian discovery that different sounds are produced by the various movements of the mouth and the tongue. He himself extended this idea even further by attributing the large number of sounds in Indian languages to the widespread native custom of chewing betel leaves and areca nuts (Thieme 1957a, 267 note).

Several missionaries who worked in India came in closer contact with Sanskrit and wrote grammars of Sanskrit in Latin, for which they most probably made use of the Indian tradition. Around 1660, Henrich Roth, S.J., composed a grammar of Sanskrit, the manuscript of which was recently discovered in the National Central Library in Rome by A. Camps, O.F.M. In 1790 a grammar was brought out in Rome by Paulinus of St. Bartholomew, O.C.D. Little is known about these grammars, and they do not seem to have had any direct bearing on the origins of Indology.

Some specific information about the Indian grammarians was provided by another Jesuit who worked in India, Father Jean François Pons, S.J. (1698–1752). Pons, who was born in Rodez, France, left for India in 1726. He wrote a letter from Karikal, in Southeast India, on November 23, 1740 to Father du Halde, another Jesuit priest. This letter was soon published in *Lettres édifiantes et curieuses, écrites des Missions Étrangères, par quelques Missionaires de la Compagnie de JESUS, XXVI.* Recueil (Paris 1743). Pons refers to an abridgment of a grammar which he had earlier made and sent to Rome, but about which nothing was known until Filliozat discovered the manuscript in Paris in the Bibliothèque du Roi, where it had been studied by A. L. de Chézy, who occupied the first chair of Sanskrit (founded for him in 1814) at the Collège de France (Filliozat 1937; for Chézy see below page 50). Pons's manuscript was also studied by Anquetil-Duperron, the first translator of the Upaniṣads (from a seventeenth-century Persian version), which were in turn made famous by Schopenhauer.

The second part of Pons's letter (printed on pages 222–227 of the *Lettres édifiantes*) is reproduced here. Of particular interest is the stress laid on the "small number of primitive elements," themselves not used (i.e., themselves abstract) from which the Sanskrit grammarians are said to derive "the infinite variety of actual forms in use"; and also the implication that the rules of grammar are described explicitly, so that someone who "knows nothing but grammar" can apply them. The title here chosen from the table of contents of the *Lettres édifiantes* (page 453), i.e., "Richesse et énergie . . ." contains a prefiguration of Humboldt's *energeia* or *Thätigkeit*.

Anubhūtisvarūpācārya is the traditional founder of the Sārasvata school of grammar, a non-Pāṇinian school called after the goddess of speech, Sarasvatī. The Sārasvata grammar is indeed greatly abridged, but is probably not older than the thirteenth century A.D. The passage about king Jamour refers to the Jaumara school of grammar, another non-Pāṇinian school, founded in the thirteenth century by Kramadīśvara. The school derives its name from its most famous grammarian, Jumaranandin, who is referred to in the manuscripts as *mahārājādhirāja* 'sovereign king of great kings', and who was accordingly ridiculed by opponents as a member of the low weaver caste (Belvalkar 1915, 91–96, 108–109).

Richesse et énergie de la langue Samskret, et comment et par qui elle a été réduite en Grammaire (1740)

Jean François Pons

La Grammaire des Brahmanes peut être mise au rang des plus belles sciences; jamais l'Analyse & la Synthése ne furent plus heureusement employées, que dans leurs ouvrages grammaticaux de la langue *Samskret* ou *Samskroutan*. Il me paroît que cette langue si admirable par son harmonie, son abondance, & son énergie, étoit autrefois la langue vivante dans les pays habités par les premiers Brahmanes. Après bien des siécles elle s'est insensiblement corrompue dans l'usage commun, de sorte que le langage des Anciens *Richi* ou Pénitens dans les *Vedam* ou livres sacrés, est assez souvent inintelligible aux plus habiles, qui ne sçavent que le *Samskret* fixé par les grammaires.

Plusieurs siècles après l'âge de *Richi*, de grands Philosophes s'étudièrent à en conserver la connoissance, telle qu'on l'avoit de leur tems, qui étoit, à ce qu'il me semble, l'âge de l'ancienne poësie. *Anoubhout* fut le premier qui forma un corps de grammaire, c'est le *Sarasvat*, ouvrage digne de *Sarasvadi*, qui est, selon les Indiens, la Déesse de la parole, & la parole même. Quoique ce soit la plus abrégée des grammaires, le mérite de son antiquité l'a mise en grande vogue dans les écoles de l'Indoustan. *Pania* aidé du *Sarasvat* composa un ouvrage immense des régles du *Samskret*. Le Roi *Jamour* le fit abréger par *Kramadisvar*; & c'est cette Grammaire, dont j'ai fait l'abrégé, que j'envoyai, il y a deux ans, & qui vous aura sans doute été communiquée; *Kalap* en composa une plus propre aux sciences. Il y en a encore trois autres de différens Auteurs, la gloire de l'invention est principalement dûe à *Anoubhout*.

Il est étonnant que l'esprit humain ait pû atteindre à la perfection de l'art, qui éclatte dans ces Grammaires: les Auteurs y ont réduit par l'Analyse la plus riche langue du monde, à un petit nombre d'élémens primitifs, qu'on peut regarder comme le *caput mortuum* de la langue. Ces élémens ne sont par eux-mêmes d'aucun usage, ils ne signifient proprement rien, ils ont seulement rapport à une idée, par exemple *Kru* à l'idée d'action. Les élémens secondaires qui affectent le primitif, sont les terminaisons qui le fixent à être nom ou verbe, celles selon lesquelles il doit se décliner ou conjuguer un certain nombre de syllabes à placer entre l'élément primitif & les terminaisons, quelques propositions, &c. A l'approche des élémens secondaires le primitif change souvent de figure; *Kru*, par exemple, devient, selon ce qui lui est ajoûté, *Kar*, *Kār*, *Kri*, *Kir*, *Kīr &c*. La Synthése réunit & combine tous ces élémens & en forme une variété infinie de termes d'usage.

Ce sont les régles de cette union & de cette combinaison des élémens que la grammaire enseigne, de sorte qu'un simple écolier, qui ne sçauroit rien que la grammaire, peut en opérant, selon les régles, sur une racine ou élément primitif, en tirer plusieurs milliers de mots vraiment *Samskrets*. C'est cet art qui a donné le nom à la langue, car *Samskret* signifie synthétique ou composé.

Mais comme l'usage fait varier à l'infini la signification des termes, quoiqu'ils conservent toujours une certaine analogie à l'idée attachée à la racine, il a été nécessaire de déterminer le sens par des Dictionnaires. Ils en ont dix-huit, faits sur différentes méthodes. Celui qui est le plus en usage, composé par *Amarasimha*, est rangé à peu près selon la méthode qu'a suivi l'Auteur de l'*Indiculus Universalis*. Le Dictionnaire intitulé *Visvābhidhānam*, est rangé par ordre alphabétique, selon les lettres finales des mots.

Outre ces Dictionnaires généraux, chaque science a son introduction, où l'on apprend les termes propres qu'on chercheroit en vain par tout ailleurs. Cela a été nécessaire pour conserver aux Sciences un air de mystère, telement affecté aux Brahmanes, que non contens d'avoir des termes inconnus au vulgaire, ils ont enveloppé sous des termes mystérieux les choses les plus communes.

7

Henry Thomas Colebrooke (1765–1837)

It is uncertain how much Sanskrit any of the early missionaries actually knew. The distinction of being the first European who knew Sanskrit well goes to Sir Charles Wilkins (1749?–1836). Sir William Jones (1746–1794), who was on all accounts the founder of Sanskrit studies in the West, was rather pessimistic about the future of these studies. He wrote to Wilkins on April 24, 1784: "Happy should I be to follow you in the same track; but life is too short and my necessary business too long for me to think at my age of acquiring a new language" (Mukherjee 1968, 94). And on October 6, 1787: "You are the first European that ever understood Sanskrit, and will, possibly, be the last" (Windisch 1917, I, 23 note). But earlier in the same year, on July 22, 1787, Jones had written to George John Spencer (his former pupil and lifelong friend): "I have the delight of knowing that my studies go hand in hand with my duty, since I now read both Sanscrit and Arabick with so much ease that the native lawyers can never impose upon court in which I sit. I converse fluently in Arabick with Maulavis and in Sanscrit with Pundits and in Persian with nobles of the country" (Mukherjee 1968, 129). Others judged differently, as we learn from an anecdote related by G. H. Cannon (1958) from William Dick's letter to Sir Walter Scott of August 23, 1819: "Shortly after arriving in Calcutta, Jones found himself using his Persian. He was sitting beside a Persian scholar when several learned Indians came to pay their respects. He addressed them in his 'Persian,' which was so incomprehensible that they thought it was English" (in Sebeok 1966, I, 55).

Wilkins appears to have been the first to write a grammar of Sanskrit in English, for he informs us that the first printed sheet of his work was destroyed by fire in 1795 (Müller 1870², vi). The earliest grammars written by Englishmen were the result of studies with the help of Indian pandits and were based directly or indirectly on works in the Indian grammatical tradition—in particular, on two works in the Pāṇinian tradition, i.e., the *Kāśikā* by Jayāditya and Vāmana (A.D. seventh century) and the *Siddhāntakaumudī* of Bhaṭṭojidīkṣita (seventeenth century); and on one in the non-Pāṇinian tradition, i.e., the *Mugdhabodha* of Vopadeva (thirteenth century?). The first published and the best (*facile princeps*, as Max Müller was to call it) among these early grammars was written by Henry Thomas Colebrooke (1765–1837). It was published in 1805 but was never completed, because the printing of Sanskrit characters, manufactured in Calcutta, was so crude that the examples Colebrooke needed to illustrate his statements would have required an excessively large volume (A. W. von Schlegel, page 58 of this volume). Other early grammars were written by H. P. Foster (who delivered his manuscript to the Council of Fort William at Calcutta in 1804) and by W. Carey (published 1806). These four authors must have all been familiar to some extent with Indian methods of grammatical analysis, as their grammars, especially the one by Colebrooke, demonstrate.

The question of whether any of the early Sanskritists knew Pāṇini (Pons had referred to him as Pania) has been raised particularly with reference to Jones, who is known to have studied the *Siddhāntakaumudī*; Jones informs us in a letter of August 18, 1792 that he finished "the attentive reading of this grammar" (Emeneau 1955, 148). It has been doubted whether Jones knew Pāṇini (Master 1956, 186–187). But such discussions result from confusion. Both the *Kāśikā* and the *Siddhāntakaumudī* are commentaries on Pāṇini's *Aṣṭādhyāyī* and quote, explain, and illustrate the *sūtras* or rules of this grammar. One difference between the two commentaries is that the *Kāśikā* adheres to the order of rules as given by Pāṇini, whereas the *Siddhāntakaumudī* rearranges the rules in a different order. Whoever studies either of these commentaries is, therefore, faced with a study of Pāṇini's rules, and even a less attentive student than Jones could not fail to observe that there is a *sūtrakāra* 'maker of rules,' whose teachings the commentary seeks to explain. Of course, Sir William might not have known that Pāṇini had lived some two millenia before Bhaṭṭojīdīkṣita. But to say that he knew the *Siddhāntakaumudī* without knowing Pāṇini makes no sense. This conclusion is further corroborated by the fact that a statement of Colebrooke's implies that Jones knew Pāṇini. According to Colebrooke, Jones called the *sūtras* of Pāṇini, when studied without a commentary, "dark as the darkest oracle."

Colebrooke, one of the first and best Western Sanskritists, had scientific rather than literary interests. Though he laid the foundations for a variety of Sanskrit studies, he contributed especially to the study of Hindu mathematics, astronomy, law, and epigraphy. Similar to al-Bīrūnī in these respects, he also had no taste for poetry. His son and biographer wrote that "the false taste of Oriental poetry especially repelled him" ("But then, there is no evidence that he enjoyed English poetry either": Ingalls 1960, 193). He did, however, like al-Bīrūnī, write on Sanskrit meter and poetics. Ingalls is of the opinion that in all probability "he read and understood more Sanskrit texts than all the Europeans of his time put together" (loc. cit. 194). Colebrooke also turned to the study of the Indian grammarians, from which "he derived something of the same pleasure he derived from mathematics" (Ingalls loc. cit., 193). He was a practical scholar and saw to it that first things were done first. He was largely responsible for the publication of Pāṇini's grammar in 1809 in Calcutta (begun by Dharaṇīdhara and completed by Kāśinātha). This led in turn to Boehtlingk's editions of the *Aṣṭādhyāyī*.

Colebrooke also provided the first reliable and detailed information on the Indian grammarians, in an article "On the Sanskrit and Prácrit Languages," *Asiatic Researches* 7 (1803, 199–231), from which the first twenty pages, dealing with Sanskrit, are here included (omitting some of the footnotes).

There are remarkably few inaccuracies in this account, notwithstanding its wealth of detail. Mention may here be made only of the confusion around Bhartṛhari. The philosopher-grammarian by that name wrote a commentary on the *Mahābhāṣya* (see page 392 of this volume), but did not write the *kārikās* which occur in the text. He was also not the same as the poet, Bhartṛhari, author of the three *śatakas* (each theoretically of a hundred stanzas). Among the interesting remarks Colebrooke made, attention may be drawn to his characterization of the discovery of the linguistic zero. The characterization of the text, "the addition or the substitution of one or more elements," fits context-free rules perfectly well.

The chart reproduced at the beginning of this volume gives a survey of the Sanskrit grammarians, their schools (in capitals), and their approximate dates. A Vedic column has been added, since the earliest activity of linguistic analysis was setting up the *Padapāṭha* or 'word-for-word analysis' of each of the oldest Vedic texts. Pāṇini mentioned ten predecessors by name (cf. pages 104–106 of this volume).

On the Sanscrĭt and Prácrĭt Languages (1803)

Henry Thomas Colebrooke

In a treatise on rhetorick, compiled for the use of Manicya Chandra, *Rájá* of *Tirabhucti* or *Tirhút*, a brief enumeration of languages, used by Hindu poets, is quoted from two writers on the art of poetry. The following is a literal translation of both passages.

"Sanscrĭta, *Prácrĭta*, *Paiśáchí* and *Mágad'hí*, are in short the four paths of poetry. The Gods, &c. speak *Sanscrĭta*; benevolent genii, *Prácrĭta*; wicked demons, *Paiśáchí*; and men of low tribes and the rest, *Mágad'hí*. But sages deem *Sanscrĭta* the chief of these four languages. It is used three ways; in prose, in verse, and in a mixture of both."

"Language, again, the virtuous have declared to be fourfold, Sanscrĭta [or the polished dialect,] *Prácrĭta* [or the vulgar dialect], *Apabhranśa* [or jargon], and *Miśra* [or mixed]. *Sanscrĭta* is the speech of the celestials, framed in grammatical institutes; *Prácrĭta* is similar to it, but manifold as a provincial dialect, and otherwise; and those languages which are ungrammatical, are spoken in their respective districts."

The Paiśáchí seems to be gibberish, which dramatick poets make the demons speak, when they bring these fantastic beings on the stage. The mixture of languages, noticed in the second quotation, is that which is employed in dramas, as is expressly said by the same author in a subsequent verse. It is not then a compound language, but a mixt dialogue in which different persons of the drama employ different idioms. Both the passages above quoted are therefore easily reconciled. They in fact notice only three tongues. 1. *Sanscrĭt*, a polished dialect, the inflections of which, with all its numerous anomalies, are taught in grammatical institutes. This the dramatic poets put into the mouths of Gods and of Holy personages. 2. *Prácrĭt*, consisting of provincial dialects, which are less refined, and have a more imperfect grammar. In dramas it is spoken by women, benevolent genii, &c. 3. *Mágad'hí*, or *Apabhranśa*, a jargon destitute of regular grammar. It is used by the vulgar, and varies in different districts: the poets accordingly introduce into the dialogue of plays a provincial jargon spoken by the lowest persons of the drama[1].

The languages of India are all comprehended in these three classes. The first contains Sanscrĭt, a most polished tongue, which was gradually refined until it became fixed in the classic writings of many elegant poets, most of whom are supposed to have flourished in the century preceding the Christian æra. It is cultivated by learned Hindus throughout India, as the language of science and of literature, and as the repository of their law civil and religious. It evidently draws its origin (and some steps of its progress may even now be traced) from a primeval tongue which was gradually refined in various climates, and became Sanscrĭt in India;

[1] *Sanscrĭta* is the passive participle of a compound verb formed by prefixing the preposition *sam* to the crude verb *crĭ*, and by interposing the letter s when this compound is used in the sense of embellishment. Its literal meaning then is "adorned;" and when applied to a language, it signifies "polished." *Prácrĭta* is a similar derivative from the same crude verb, with *pra* prefixed: the most common acceptation of this word is "outcast, or man of the lowest class;" as applied to a language, it signifies "vulgar." *Apabhranśa* is derived from *bhraś* to fall down: it signifies a word, or dialect, which falls off from correct etymology. Grammarians use the *Sanscrĭta* as signifying "duly formed or regularly inflected;" and *Apabhranśa* for false grammar.

Pahlaví in Persia, and Greek on the shores of the Mediterranean. Like other very ancient languages, Sanscrĭt abounds in inflections, which are, however, more anomalous in this, than in the other languages here alluded to; and which are even more so in the obsolete dialect of the Védas, than in the polished speech of the classick poets. It has nearly shared the fate of all antient tongues, and is now become almost a dead language; but there seems no good reason for doubting that it was once universally spoken in India. Its name, and the reputed difficulty of its grammar, have led many persons to imagine that it has been refined by the concerted efforts of a few priests, who set themselves about inventing a new language; not like all other tongues, by the gradually improved practice of good writers and polite speakers. The exquisitely refined system by which the grammar of Sanscrĭt is taught, has been mistaken for the refinement of the language itself. The rules have been supposed to be anterior to the practice, but this supposition is gratuitous. In Sanscrĭt, as in every other known tongue, grammarians have not invented etymology, but have only contrived rules to teach what was already established by approved practice.

There is one peculiarity of Sanscrĭt compositions which may also have suggested the opinion that it could never be a spoken language. I allude to what might be termed the euphonical orthography of Sanscrĭt. It consists in extending to syntax the rules for the permutation of letters in etymology. Similar rules for avoiding incompatible sounds in compound terms exist in all languages; this is sometimes effected by a deviation from orthography in the pronunciation of words, sometimes by altering one or more letters to make the spelling correspond with the pronunciation. These rules have been more profoundly investigated by Hindu grammarians than by those of any other nation, and they have completed a system of orthography which may be justly termed euphonical. They require all compound terms to be reduced to this standard, and Sanscrĭt authors, it may be observed, delight in compounds of inordinate length; the whole sentence too, or even whole periods, may, at the pleasure of the author, be combined like the elements of a single word, and good writers generally do so. In common speech this could never have been practised. None but well known compounds would be used by any speaker who wished to be understood, and each word would be distinctly articulated independently of the terms which precede and follow it. Such indeed is the present practice of those who still speak the Sanscrĭt language; and they deliver themselves with such fluency as is sufficient to prove that Sanscrĭt may have been spoken in former times with as much facility as the contemporary dialects of the Greek language, or the more modern dialects of the Arabic tongue. I shall take occasion again to allude to this topick after explaining at large what are and by whom were composed, those grammatical institutes in which the Sanscrĭt language is framed, according to the author above quoted; or by which (for the meaning is ill conveyed by a literal translation) words are correctly formed and inflected.

Páńini, the father of Sanscrĭt grammar, lived in so remote an age, that he ranks among those ancient sages whose fabulous history occupies a conspicuous place in the Puráńas, or Indian theogonies. The name is a patronymick, indicating his descent from Pańin; but according to the Pauráńica legends, he was grandson of Dévala, an inspired legislator. Whatever may be the true history of Páńini, to him the Sútras, or succinct aphorisms of grammar, are attributed by universal consent. His system is grounded on a profound investigation of the analogies in both the regular and the anomalous inflections of the Sanscrĭt language. He has combined those analogies in a very artificial manner; and has thus compressed a most copious etymology into a very narrow compass. His precepts are indeed numerous[2], but they have been framed with the utmost conciseness; and this great brevity is the result of very ingenious methods which have been contrived for this end, and for the purpose of assisting the student's memory. In Páńini's system the mutual relation of all the parts marks that it must have been completed by its author; it certainly bears internal evidence of its having been accomplished by a single effort, and even the corrections, which are needed, cannot be interwoven with the text. It must not be hence inferred, that Páńini was unaided by the labours of earlier grammarians; in many of his precepts he cites the authority of his predecessors[3], sometimes for a deviation from a general rule, often for a grammatical canon which has universal cogency. He has even employed some technical terms without defining them, because, as his commentators remark, those terms were already introduced by earlier grammarians.[4] None of the more ancient works, however, seem to be now extant; being superseded by his, they have probably been disused for ages, and are now perhaps totally lost.[5]

A performance such as the Páńiníya grammar must inevitably contain many errors. The task of correcting its inaccuracies has been executed by Cátyáyana,[6] an inspired saint and law-giver, whose history, like that of all the Indian sages, is involved in the impenetrable darkness of mythology. His annotations, entitled *Várticas*, restrict those among the Páńiníya rules which are too vague, enlarge others which are too limited, and mark numerous exceptions which had escaped the notice of Páńini himself.

The amended rules of grammar have been formed into memorial verses by Bhartrĭ-hari, whose metrical aphorisms, entitled *Cáricá*, have almost equal authority with the precepts of Páńini, and emendations of Cátyáyana. If the popular traditions concerning Bhartrĭ-hari be well founded, he lived in the century preceding the Christian Æra[7]; for he is supposed to be the same with the brother of Vicramaditya, and the period when this prince reigned at Ujjayiní is determined by the date of the Samvat Æra.

The studied brevity of the Páńiníya Sútras renders them in the highest degree obscure. Even with the knowledge of the key to their interpretation, the student finds them ambiguous. In the application of them when understood, he discovers many seeming

[2] Not fewer than 3996.

[3] Sácalya, Gárgya, Cáśyapa, Gálava, Sácat'áyana, and others.

[4] In a few instances he quotes former grammars to refute them.

[5] Definitions of some technical terms, together with grammatical axioms, are also cited from those ancient works in the commentaries on Páńini. They are inserted in a compilation entitled Paribháshá, which will be subsequently noticed. The various ancient grammars of the Sanscrĭt tongue, as enumerated in a memorial verse, are eight in number, and ascribed to the following authors; viz. Indra, Chandra, C'aśa, Critsná, Písálí, Śácatáyana, Páńini, and Amera Jinéndra.

[6] This name likewise is a patronymick.

[7] A beautiful poem has been composed in his name, containing moral reflections, which the poet supposes him to make on the discovery of his wife's infidelity. It consists of either three or four Śatacas, or centuries of couplets.

contradictions; and, with every exertion of practised memory, he must experience the utmost difficulty in combining rules dispersed in apparent confusion through different portions of Páńini's eight lectures. A commentary was therefore indispensably requisite. Many were composed by ancient grammarians to elucidate the text of Páńini. A most copious one on the emendations of his rules was compiled in very ancient times by an uncertain author. This voluminous work, known by the title of *Mahábháshya*, or the great commentary, is ascribed to Patanjali, a fabulous personage, to whom mythology has assigned the shape of a serpent. In this commentary every rule is examined at great length. All possible interpretations are proposed: and the true sense and import of the rule are deduced through a tedious train of argument, in which all foreseen objections are considered and refuted; and the wrong interpretations of the text, with all the arguments which can be invented to support them, are obviated or exploded.

Voluminous as it is, the *Mahábháshya* has not exhausted the subject on which it treats. Its deficiencies have been supplied by the annotations of modern grammarians. The most celebrated among these scholiasts of the *Bháshya* is Caiyát'a, a learned Cashmirian. His annotations are almost equally copious with the commentary itself. Yet they too are loaded by numerous glosses; among which the old and new *Vivaranás* are most esteemed.

The difficulty of combining the dispersed rules of grammar, to inflect any one verb or noun through all its variations, renders further aid necessary. This seems to have been anciently afforded in vocabularies, one of which exhibited the verbs classed in the order implied by the system of Páńini, the other contained nouns arranged on a similar plan. Both probably cited the precepts which must be remembered in conjugating and declining each verb and noun. A catalogue of verbs, classed in regular order, but with few references to the rules of etymology, is extant, and is known by the title of *D'hátupát'a*. It may be considered as an appendix to the grammar of Páńini; and so may his own treatise on the pronunciation of vocal sounds, and the treatise of Yásca on obsolete words and acceptations peculiar to the Véda. A numerous class of derivative nouns, to which he has only alluded, have been reduced to rule under the head of Uńádi, or the termination *u*, &c.; and the precepts, respecting the gender of nouns, have been in like manner arranged in Sútras, which are formed on the same principles with Páńini's rules, and which are considered as almost equally ancient. Another supplement to his grammar is entitled *Gańapát'a*, and contains lists of words comprehended in various grammatical rules under the designation of some single word with the term "&c." annexed to it. These supplements are due to various authors. The subject of gender alone has been treated by more than one writer reputed to be inspired, namely by Cátyáyana, Góbhila, and others.

These subsidiary parts of the Páńiníya grammar do not require a laboured commentary; excepting only the catalogue of verbs, which does need annotation; and which is in truth a proper ground work for a complete review of all the rules of etymology, that are applicable to each verb.[8] The *Vrĭttinyása*, a very celebrated

[8] The number of verbal roots amounts to 1750 nearly; exclusive of many obsolete words omitted in the *D'hátupáta*, but noticed in the Sútras as the roots of certain derivatives. The crude verbs, however, are more numerous, because many roots, containing the same radical letters, are

work, is, I believe, a commentary of this sort.[9] It is mentioned by Maitréya Racshita, the author of the *D'hátu pradípa*, as the work chiefly consulted by him in compiling his brief annotations on the *D'hátupát'a*. A very voluminous commentary on the catalogue of verbs was compiled under the patronage of Sayańa, minister of a chieftain named Sangama, and is entitled *Mád'havíyá vrĭtti*. It thoroughly explains the signification and inflection of each verb; but at the same time enters largely into scholastick refinements on general grammar.

Such vast works as the *Máhábháshya* and its scholia, with the voluminous annotations on the catalogue of verbs, are not adapted for general instruction. A conciser commentary must have been always requisite. The best that is now extant is entitled the *Cáśicá vrĭtti*, or commentary composed at Varáńaśi. The anonymous author of it, in a short preface, explains his design: 'to gather the essence of a science dispersed in the early commentaries, in the *Bháshya*, in copious dictionaries of verbs and of nouns, and in other works.' He has well fulfilled the task which he undertook. His gloss explains in perspicuous language the meaning and application of each rule: he adds examples, and quotes, in their proper places, the necessary emendations from the *Várticas* and *Bháshya*. Though he never deviates into frivolous disquisitions, nor into tedious reasoning, but expounds the text as succinctly as could consist with perspicuity, his work is nevertheless voluminous; and yet, copious as it is, the commentaries on it, and the annotations on its commentaries, are still more voluminous. Amongst the most celebrated is the *Padamanjarí* of Haradatta Miśra; a grammarian whose authority is respected almost equally with that of the author, on whose text he comments. The annotators on this again are numerous; but it would be useless to insert a long list of their names, or of the titles of their works.

Excellent as the *Cáśicà vrĭtti* undoubtedly is, it partakes of the defects which have been imputed to Páńini's text. Following the same order, in which the original rules are arranged, it is well adapted to assist the student in acquiring a critical knowledge of the Sanscrĭt tongue. But for one who studies the rudiments of the language, a different arrangement is requisite, for the sake of bringing into one view the rules which must be remembered in the inflections of one word, and those which must be combined even for a single variation of a single term. Such a grammar has been compiled within a few centuries past by Rámachandra, an eminent grammarian. It is entitled *Pracríyacaumudí*. The rules are Páńini's, and the explanation of them is abridged from the ancient commentaries; but the arrangement is wholly different. It proceeds from the elements of writing to definitions; thence to orthography: it afterwards exhibits the inflections of nouns according to case, number, and gender; notices the indeclinables; and

variously conjugated in different senses: the whole number of crude verbs separately noticed in the catalogue exceeds three thousand. From each of these are deduced many compound verbs by prefixing one or more prepositions to the verbal root. Such compounds often deviate very widely in their signification, and some even in their inflections, from the radical verb. The derivative verbs again are numerous; such as causals, frequentatives, &c. Hence it may be readily perceived how copious this branch of grammar must be.

[9] I have not yet had an opportunity of inspecting either this or its gloss. It has been described to me as a commentary on the *Cásicá vrĭtti*.

proceeds to the uses of the cases: it subjoins the rules of opposition, by which compound terms are formed; the etymology of patronymicks and other derivatives from nouns; and the reduplication of particles, &c. In the second part, it treats of the conjugation of verbs arranged in ten classes: to these primitives succeed derivative verbs, formed from verbal roots, or from nouns. The rules concerning different voices follow: they are succeeded by precepts regarding the use of the tenses; and the work concludes with the etymology of verbal nouns, gerunds, supines, and participles. A supplement to it contains the anomalies of the dialect, in which the Véda is composed.

The outline of Páńini's arrangement is simple; but numerous exceptions and frequent disgressions have involved it in much seeming confusion. The two first lectures (the first section especially, which is in a manner the key of the whole grammar) contain definitions; in the three next are collected the affixes, by which verbs and nouns are inflected. Those which appertain to verbs, occupy the third lecture: the fourth and fifth contain such as are affixed to nouns. The remaining three lectures treat of the changes which roots and affixes undergo in special cases, or by general rules of orthography, and which are all effected by the addition or by the substitution of one or more elements.[10] The apparent simplicity of the design vanishes in the perplexity of the structure. The endless pursuit of exceptions and of limitations so disjoins the general precepts, that the reader cannot keep in view their intended connexion and mutual relation. He wanders in an intricate maze; and the clew of the labyrinth is continually slipping from his hands.

The order in which Rámachandra has delivered the rules of grammar is certainly preferable; but the sútras of Páńini thus detached from their context are wholly unintelligible. Without the commentator's exposition, they are indeed what Sir William Jones has somewhere termed them, dark as the darkest oracle. Even with the aid of a comment, they cannot be fully understood until they are perused with the proper context. Notwithstanding this defect, Bhát't'ójí Dícshita,[11] who revised the *Caumudí*, has for very substantial reasons adhered to the Páńiníya sútras. That able grammarian has made some useful changes in the arrangement of the *Pracríya*: he has amended the explanation of the rules, which was in many places incorrect or imperfect: he has remedied many omissions; has enlarged the examples; and has noticed the most important instances where the elder grammarians disagree, or where classical poets have deviated from the strict rules of grammar. This excellent work is entitled *Sidd' hánta Caumudí*. The author has very properly followed the example of Rámachandra, in excluding all rules that are peculiar to the obsolete dialect of the Véda, or which relate to accentuation; for this also belongs to the Véda alone. He has collected them in an appendix to the *Sidd'hánta Caumudí*; and has subjoined in a second appendix rules concerning the gender of nouns. The other supplements of Páńini's grammar are interwoven by this author with the body of his work.

The Hindus delight in scholastick disputation. Their grammarians indulge this propensity as much as their lawyers and their

[10] Even the expunging of a letter is considered as the substitution of a blank.

[11] Descendants of Bh'át't'ojí in the fifth or sixth degree are, I am told, now living at Benares. He must have flourished then between one and two centuries ago.

sophists.[12] Bhát't'ójí Dícshita has provided an ample store of controversy in an argumentative commentary on his own grammar. This work is entitled *Prant'a manóramá*. He also composed a very voluminous commentary on the eight lectures of Páńini, and gave it the title of *Śabda Caustubha*. The only portion of it I have yet seen reaches no farther than to the end of the first section of Páńini's first lecture. But this is so diffusive, that, if the whole have been executed on a similar plan, it must triple the ponderous volume of the *Mahábháshya* itself. I have reason, however, for doubting that it was ever completed.

The commentaries on the *Sidd'hánta Caumudí* and *Manóramá* are very numerous. The most celebrated shall be here briefly noticed. 1. The *Tatwa bod'hiní* expounds the *Sidd'hánta*: it is the work of Inyánéndra Saraswati, an ascetick, and the pupil of Vamanéndra Swámí. 2. The *Śabdendu śec'hara* is another commentary on Bhát't'ójí's grammar. It was composed by a successor, if not a descendant, of that grammarian. An abridgment of it, which is very generally studied, is the work of Nágéśa, son of Śiva Bhat't'a, and pupil of Hari Di'cshita. He was patronised, as appears from his preface, by the proprietor of *Srĭngavéra púra*.[13] Though called an abridgment, this *Laghu Śabdéndu* is a voluminous performance. 3. The *Laghu Śábdaratna* is a commentary on the *Manóramá* of Bhát't'ójí Dícshita, by the author's grandson, Harí Dícshita. This work is not improperly termed an abridgment, since it is short in comparison with most other commentaries on grammar. A larger performance on the same topicks, and with the same title of *Śábda ratna*, was composed by a professor of this school. 4. Bála sarmań Págońdiya, who is either fourth or fifth in succession from Bhát't'ójí, as professor of grammar at Benares, has written commentaries on the *Caustubha*, *Śábda ratna*, and *Śabdéndu śéc'hara*. His father, Baidyarat'ha Bhat't'a, largely annotated the *Paribháshéndu śéc'hara* of Nágójí Bhat't'a, which is an argumentative commentary on a collection of grammatical axioms and definitions cited by the glossarists of Páńini. This compilation, entitled *Paribháshá*, has also furnished the text for other controversial performances bearing similar titles.

While so many commentaries have been written on the *Sidd'hánta Caumudí*, the *Pracríya Caumudí* has not been neglected. The scholiasts of this too are numerous. The most known is Crĭshńa Pand'ita; and his work has been abridged by his pupil Jayanta, who has given the title of *Tatwa chandra* to a very excellent compendium.[14] On the other hand, Crĭshńa Pand'ita has had the fate common to all noted grammarians; since his work has employed a host of commentators, who have largely commented on it.

The *Caumudís*, independently even of their numerous commentaries, have been found too vast and intricate for young students. Abridgments of the *Sidd'hánta Caumudí* have been therefore attempted by several authors with unequal degrees of success. Of three such abridgments, one only seems to deserve present

[12] Many separate treatises on different branches of general grammar are very properly considered as appertaining to the science of logick.

[13] A town on the Ganjes, marked Singhore in Rennel's maps. It is situated above Illahabad.

[14] Finished by him, as appears from a postscript to the book, in the year 1687 of the Samvat era. Though he studied at Benares, he appears to have been born on the banks of the Tapati, a river marked Taptee in Rennel's map.

notice. It is the *Mad'hya Caumudí*, and is accompanied by a similar compendium of annotations, entitled *Mad'hya Mánoramá*. The name indicates, that it holds a middle place between the diffuse original, and the jejune abstracts called *Laghu Caumudí*, &c. It contains such of Páńíni's rules as are most universal, and adds to each a short but perspicuous exposition. It omits only the least common exceptions and limitations.

When *Sanscrĭt* was the language of Indian courts, and was cultivated not only by persons who devoted themselves to religion and literature, but also by princes, lawyers, soldiers, physicians, and scribes; in short, by the first three tribes, and by many classes included in the fourth; an easy and popular grammar must have been needed by persons who could not waste the best years of their lives in the study of words. Such grammars must always have been in use; those, however, which are now studied are not, I believe, of very ancient date. The most esteemed is the *Sáraswata*, together with its commentary named *Chandricá*. It seems to have been formed on one of the *Caumudís*, by translating Páńini's rules into language that is intelligible, independently of the gloss, and without the necessity of adverting to a different context.

Another popular grammar, which is in high repute in Bengal, is entitled *Mugd'habód'ha*, and is accompanied by a commentary. It is the work of Vópadéva, and proceeds upon a plan grounded on that of the *Caumudís*; but the author has not been content to translate the rules of Páńini, and to adopt his technical terms. He has on the contrary invented new terms, and contrived new abbreviations. The same author likewise composed a metrical catalogue of verbs alphabetically arranged. It is named *Cavicalpadruma*, and is intended as a substitute for the *D'hátupát'a*.

The chief inconvenience attending Vópadéva's innovation is, that commentaries and scholia, written to elucidate poems and works of science, must be often unintelligible to those who have studied only his grammar, and that writings of his scholars must be equally incomprehensible (wherever a grammatical subject is noticed) to the students of the *Páńiníya*. Accordingly the Pandits of Bengal are cut off in a manner from communication on grammatical topics with the learned of other provinces in India. Even etymological dictionaries, such as the commentaries on the metrical vocabularies, which I shall next proceed to mention, must be unintelligible to them.

It appears from the prefaces of many different grammatical treatises, that works, entitled *Dhátu* and *Náma páráyańa*, were formerly studied. They must have comprehended, as their title implies, "the whole of the verbs and nouns" appertaining to the language; and, since they are mentioned as very voluminous, they must probably have contained references to all the rules applicable to every single verb and noun. Haradatta's explanation of the title confirms this notion. But it does not appear that any work is now extant under this title. The *D'hátupát'a*, with its commentaries, supplies the place of the *D'hátupáráyańa*. A collection of dictionaries and vocabularies in like manner supplies the want of the *Náma páráyańa*. These then may be noticed in this place as a branch of grammar.

The best and most esteemed vocabulary is the *Amera cósha*. Even the bigotry of Sancar Ácharya spared this, when he proscribed the other works of Amera Sinha. Like most other Sanscrĭt dictionaries, it is arranged in verse to aid the memory. Synonymous words are collected into one or more verses and placed in fifteen different chapters, which treat of as many different subjects. The sixteenth contains a few homonymous terms, arranged alphabetically in the Indian manner by the final consonants. The seventeenth chapter is a pretty full catalogue of indeclinables, which European philologists would call adverbs, prepositions, conjunctions, and interjections; but which Sanscrĭt grammarians consider as indeclinable nouns. The last chapter of the *Ameracósh* is a treatise on the gender of nouns. Another vocabulary by the same author is often cited by his commentators under the title of *Ameramálá*.

Numerous commentaries have been written on the *Ameracósh*. The chief object of them is to explain the derivations of the nouns, and to supply the principal deficiencies of the text. Sanscrĭt etymologists scarcely acknowledge a single primitive amongst the nouns. When unable to trace an etymology which may be consistent with the acceptation of the word, they are content to derive it according to grammatical rules from some root to which the word has no affinity in sense. At other times they adopt fanciful etymologies from Puráńas or from Tantras. But in general the derivations are accurate and instructive. The best known among these commentaries of the *Amera cósha* is the *Padra chandricá*, compiled from sixteen older commentaries by Vrĭhaspati surnamed Mucut'a, or at full length Ráya Mucut'a Mańi. It appears from the incidental mention of the years then expired of astronomical eras, that Mucut'a made this compilation in the 4532d year of the *Caliyug*, which corresponds with A. D. 1430. Achyuta Jallací has abridged Mucut'a's commentary, but without acknowledgment, and has given the title of *Vyác'hyá pradípa* to his compendium. On the other hand, Bhánují-Dícshita has revised the same compilation, and has corrected the numerous errors of Mucut'a: who often derives words from roots that are unknown to the language; or according to rules which have no place in its grammar. Bhánují has greatly improved the plan of the work, by inserting from other authorities the various acceptations of words exhibited by Amera in one or two senses only. This excellent compilation is entitled *Vyách'ya sud'há*.

The *Amera cósha*, as has been already hinted, gives a very incomplete list of words that have various acceptations. This defect is well supplied by the *Médiní*, a dictionary so named from its author Médinicar. It contains words that bear many senses, arranged in alphabetical order by the final consonants; and a list of homonymous indeclinables is subjoined to it. A similar dictionary, compiled by Mahéśwara, and entitled *Viśwa pracáśa*, is much consulted, though it be very defective, as has been justly remarked by Médinicar. It contains, however, a very useful appendix on words spelt more than one way; and another on letters which are liable to be confounded, such as *v* and *b*; and another again on the gender of nouns. These subjects are not separately treated by Médinicar; but he has on the other hand specified the genders with great care in the body of the work. The exact age of the *Médiní* is not certainly known; but it is older than Mucut'a's compilation, since it is quoted by this author.

Amera's dictionary does not contain more than ten thousand different words. Yet the Sanscrĭt language is very copious. The insertion of derivatives, that do not at all deviate from their regular and obvious import, has been very properly deemed superfluous. Compound epithets, and other compound terms, in which the Sanscrĭt language is peculiarly rich, are likewise omitted; excepting such as are especially appropriated, by a limited acceptation, either as titles of Deities, or as names of plants, animals, &c. In fact compound terms are formed at pleasure, according to the rules of grammar; and must generally be interpreted in strict conformity with those rules. Technical terms too are mostly excluded from general dictionaries, and consigned to separate nomenclatures. The *Ameracósh* then is less defective than might be inferred from the small number of words explained in it. Still, however, it needs a supplement. The *Háravalí* may be used as such. It is a vocabulary of uncommon words, compiled by Purushóttama, the author of an etymological work, and also of a little collection of monograms, entitled *E'cácshara*. His *Háravalí* was compiled by him under the patronage of D'hrĭta Sinha. It is noticed by Médinicar, and seems to be likewise anterior to the *Viśwa*.

The remaining deficiencies of the *Ameracósh* are supplied by consulting other dictionaries and vocabularies; such as Heláynd'ha's, Váchespati's, the *Dharańicósha*, or some other. Sanscrĭt dictionaries are indeed very numerous. Purushóttama and Médinicar name the *Utpaliní*, *Sabdárnáva* and *Sansárávárta*, as works consulted by them. Purushóttama adds the names of Váchespati, Vyád'i and Vicramáditya; but it is not quite clear whether he mentions them as the authors and patrons of these, or of other dictionaries. Médinicar adds a fourth vocabulary called *Námamálá*, and with similar obscurity subjoins the celebrated names of Bháguri, Vararuchi, Sáśwata, Bópálita and Rantidéva. He then proceeds to enumerate the dictionaries of Amera, Śubhánga, Heláynd'ha, Góverd'hana, Rabhasa Pála, and the *Ratnacósha*; with the vocabularies of Rudra, Dhananjaya, and Gangád'hara; as also the *Dharańicósha*, *Háravalí*, *Vrĭhadamara*, *Tricáńd'asésha* and *Ratnamálá*. Many of these are cited by the commentators on Amera, and by the scholiasts on different poems. The following are also frequently cited; some as etymologists, the rest as lexicographers: Swámí, Durga, Sarvadhara Vámana, Chandra, and the authors of the *Vaijayntí Námanid'hána*, *Haima*, *Vrĭhat-nighanti*, &c. To this list might be added the *Anécárt'ha*, *dwani manjari Nánárt'ha*, and other vocabularies of homonymous terms; the *Dwiructi*, *Bhuriprayóga cósha*, and other lists of words spelt in more than one way; and the various *Nighantis* or nomenclatures, such as the *Dhanwantari-nighanta* and *Rájanighanta*, which contain lists of the materia medica; and the *Nighanti* of the *Véda*, which explains obsolete words and unusual acceptations.[15]

Before I proceed to mention other languages of India, it may be proper to mention, that the school of Benares now uses the *Siddhánta caumudí*, and other works of Bhattóji, as the same school formerly did the *Cáśicá vrĭtti*. The *Pracríya caumudí*, with its commentaries, maintains its ground among the learned of Mit'hilá or Tirhút. In both places, however, and indeed throughout India, the *Mahábháshya* continues to be the standard of Sanscrĭt grammar. It is therefore studied by all who are ambitious of acquiring

[15] The *Niructi*, as explained in Sir William Jones's treatise on the literature of the Hindus, belongs to the same class with the *Nighanti* of the *Véda*: and a small vocabulary under both these titles is commonly annexed to the *Rĭgvéda* to complete the set of *Upavédas*. There is however a much larger work entitled *Niructi*; and the commentators of it are often cited upon topics of general grammar.

a critical knowledge of the language. The *Haricáricá*, with its commentaries by Héláràja and Punjarája, was probably in use with a school that once flourished at Ujjayiní: but it does not seem to be now generally studied in any part of India.

3 The Romantic Period

8

August Wilhelm von Schlegel (1767–1845)

After the foundations for the study of the Sanskrit grammarians had been laid by the early English Sanskritists, the Germans took to its study with the enthusiasm worthy of the Romantic period. The British and especially Colebrooke had had firsthand experience of India. Their scholarship was sound and often related to practical problems. Some of their interests (e.g., in Hindu lawbooks) were due to the requirements of the East India Company. The first English Sanskritists were in fact not altogether dissimilar to some of the Muslim scholars who had visited India earlier. Islam had also in other respects paved the way for the British Raj.

The first German Sanskritists were free from such mundane preoccupations, but they were also much less well informed. During the Romantic period, many scholars were especially interested in Indian philosophies and religions. Though not quite so superstitious, they were like the Chinese and Tibetan Buddhists in this respect. The Germans at any rate blamed the British for neglecting the ancient culture of India. However, Colebrooke himself had done the groundwork in this area also in his *Essay on the Philosophy of the Hindus* (1823). He reacted with characteristic self-confidence to the charges from the continent in a letter to H. H. Wilson of December 24, 1827: "Careless and indifferent as our countrymen are, I think, nevertheless, that you and I may derive some complacent feelings from the reflection that, following the footsteps of Sir W. Jones, we have with so little aid of our collaborators, and so little encouragement, opened nearly every avenue, and left it to foreigners, who are taking up the clue we have furnished, to complete the outline of what we have sketched" (Windisch 1917, I, 36).

The manifesto of the Romantic tradition in Indian studies was Friedrich von Schlegel's *Über die Sprache und Weisheit der Inder* (1808). Though this book does not refer to the Indian grammarians, the author says in the *Preface* that he has "für die indische Sprache" made use of a manuscript written in Bengali characters. "Es enthält" (among other things) "eine kurze Grammatik des Sanskrit nach dem Mugdhobōdho des Vōpodevo" and "den Omorokōsha." Friedrich von Schlegel (1772–1829) had tried to study Sanskrit in Paris. He learned his grammar from Alexander Hamilton (1762–1824), an officer of the British navy and one of the early members of the Asiatic Society of Bengal, who was on parole as a prisoner of war during the Napoleonic wars in Paris, where he had come to collect Sanskrit manuscripts for an edition of the *Hitopadeśa* (Rocher 1968b; Schwab 1950, 74–75). There are conflicting early accounts of the activities of this remarkable Scotsman, now superseded by Rocher's monograph (1968b). In the present context, it is worth mentioning that Hamilton wrote a booklet entitled *Terms of Sanskrit Grammar* (1814).

On May 15, 1803, Friedrich von Schlegel wrote from Paris to his brother August Wilhelm that he had been doing very well:

Denn vieles, vieles hab' ich erlernt. Nicht nur im Persischen Fortschritte gemacht, sondern endlich ist auch das grosse Ziel erreicht, dass ich des Samskrit gewiss bin. Ich werde binnen vier Monaten die Sakontala in der Urschrift lesen können, wenn, ich gleich alsdann die Uebersetzung wohl auch noch brauchen werde. Ungeheure Anstrengung hat es erfordert, da eine grosse Complication und eine eigne Methode des Divinirens und der Mühe; da ich die Elemente ohne Elementar-Bücher erlernen musste. Zuletzt ist mir noch sehr zu Statten gekommen, dass ein Engländer Hamilton, der einzige in Europa ausser Wilkins der es weiss, und zwar sehr gründlich weiss, mir mit Rath wenigstens zu Hülfe kam. (Rocher 1968b, 45; Windisch 1917, I, 57–58).

It seems likely that Friedrich von Schlegel never managed to learn Sanskrit well.

Friedrich's older brother, August Wilhelm von Schlegel (1767–1845), came to Paris to study Sanskrit in 1815. At that time A. L. de Chézy had begun to give courses on Sanskrit at the Collège de France. Chézy, who had studied Sanskrit from the manuscript of Pons's grammar which was preserved in the Bibliothèque du Roi, does not appear to have been an exciting scholar or teacher (Windisch 1917, I, 73–74). A. W. von Schlegel was not satisfied with his courses and tried instead to learn Sanskrit from Franz Bopp, who himself had come to Paris to learn the language. But to learn Sanskrit in Paris during those days was an enterprise fraught with difficulties. Bopp had come in 1812, when no Indian languages were studied at all. Chézy's appointment did not do much to improve the situation. Bopp wrote in 1814 that neither he nor Chézy himself could understand a text that had not already been translated (Windisch 1917, I, 69). This was partly due to the lack of a good dictionary. The dictionary of H. H. Wilson did not appear until 1819 in Calcutta; it was difficult to get and extremely expensive (Windisch 1917, I, 69).

Much of the situation is reflected in an essay "Ueber den gegenwärtigen Zustand der Indischen Philologie," which August Wilhelm von Schlegel wrote in 1819 and which was first published in the *Jahrbuch der preussischen Rhein-Universität*, then in French translation in the *Bibliothèque universelle*, and again in the *Revue encyclopédique* (how much in demand such information must have been!), and finally in Schlegel's own periodical, *Indische Bibliothek* (1, 1820, 1–27). It contains an interesting evaluation of the Indian grammarians and a brief description of dictionaries, here quoted from the *Indische Bibliothek* (pages 10–13).

The observation that Pāṇini's rules and techniques may be compared to the formulas and methods of algebra, here made by Schlegel, is often found in later works (for example, Whitney, page 140 of this volume). Colebrooke had been even more specific, as we have seen, by drawing attention to techniques of addition and substitution (see page 40). It took more than a century before the formalization that these observations suggested was beginning to be attempted (cf., for example, Staal 1965a, 1965b).

A. Ueber den gegenwärtigen Zustand der indischen Philologie (1819)

August Wilhelm von Schlegel

Es sind nun auch bereits drey Original-Werke über die Indische Grammatik gedruckt: die Sprüche des Pāṇini nebst einer Auswahl von den Anmerkungen der Scholiasten, die Siddhānta-Kaumudī, und die kurze Sprachlehre des Vopadeva, unter dem Titel Mugdha-Bodha.[1] Diese gehören aber nicht zu den Hülfsmitteln für Anfänger, sondern zu dem ans Licht geförderten Vorrath von Erzeugnissen der Indischen Gelehrsamkeit. Denn so schwere Bücher können nur erfahrne Kenner des Sanskrit lesen, und auch solchen wird Inhalt und Einkleidung noch Schwierigkeit genug machen, besonders da sie mit keiner Uebersetzung oder Erklärung in einer bekannten Sprache ausgestattet sind. Indessen ist es sehr wichtig, sie zu haben: die grammatischen Arbeiten der Europäischen Philologen können in der Folge mit diesen authentischen Quellen verglichen, darnach geprüft, daraus berichtigt oder bestätigt werden. Die Methode der alten Indischen Sprachlehrer ist strenge wissenschaftlich, und sie legen es keineswegs darauf an, die Anfangsgründe zu erleichtern. Sie sprechen die allgemeinen Gesetze in Formeln aus, welche den algebraischen an Kürze gleichen, und mit ihnen den Vortheil gemein haben, dass, wenn man sie einmal begriffen hat, alle darunter befassten Fälle mit Sicherheit aufgelöst werden können. Was sich nicht unter eine Regel bringen lässt, wollen sie dem Gedächtnisse durch allerley mnemonische Kunstgriffe eingeprägt wissen. Sie haben auf Köpfe gerechnet, denen das spitzfindigste bald geläufig wird, und nach dem grossen und dauerhaften Ruhm ihrer Schriften zu urtheilen, haben sie sich nicht betrogen.

Das nächste Bedürfniss nach der Sprachlehre sind die Wörterbücher, und hierin sind wir noch längst nicht so gut berathen als in jenem Fache. Wir haben nichts als den Amara-Koṣa,[2] freylich in der vortrefflichen bearbeitung von Colebrooke. Allein der Amara-Koṣa ist kein alphabetisches, sondern ein metrisch abgefasstes Real-Wörterbuch, dessen Hauptzweck ist, das Geschlecht der Nenn- und Eigenschaftswörter zu bestimmen: diese werden nicht als zwey verschiedene Classen betrachtet, sondern die letzten nur als dreygeschlechtige bezeichnet. In den ersten beyden Büchern sind die Benennungen nach der Folge der Gegenstände geordnet; dann kommen im dritten Bande vermischte; vieldeutige Wörter, auch die der Biegung nicht empfänglichen. Die Zeitwörter sind ausgeschlossen. Der Herausgeber hat ein alphabetisches Register beygefügt, und die Stelle oder die Stellen, wo jedes Wort vorkommt, nach der Seiten- und Verszahl angegeben. Es ist also immer ein doppeltes, oft ein mehrfaches Nachschlagen nöthig; nicht selten sucht man vergeblich, denn bey vielen andern Verdiensten hat das Buch keineswegs das der Vollständigkeit. Indessen wird es immer zu Rathe gezogen werden müssen, wenn wir auch künftig ein alphabetisches Wörterbuch besitzen, weil es merkwürdige Aufschlüsse über die Eigenthümlichkeit und den Zusammenhang der Indischen Begriffe von der Geisterwelt, der Natur und dem menschlichen Leben giebt. Da die Ausgabe

[1] The Grammatical Sūtras or aphorisms of *Pāṇini* with selections from various Commentators. *Nagarī* Character. 2 Vol. 8. Calcutta, 1809. The Siddhānta-Kaumudī, a Grammar conformable to the system of Pāṇini by *Bhaṭṭojī Dīkṣita*. *Nagarī* Character, 1 Vol. 4to. Calcutta, 1812. The *Mugdha Bodha*, a Grammar by *Vopadeva*. Bengali Character, 1 Vol. 12, Serampore, 1807.

[2] *Koṣa* or Dictionary of the Sanscrit language, by *Amara Sinha*. With an English Interpretation and Annotations. By *H. T. Colebrooke*, Esq. Serampoor, 1808.

von Colebrooke schon sehr selten geworden ist, (ich besitze sie nur durch die Güte meines verehrten Freundes Sir James Mackintosh) so wäre sehr zu wünschen, dass in England ein neuer Abdruck veranstaltet werden möchte, der sich bey den Vortheilen der Europäischen Typographie leicht um vieles bequemer einrichten liesse. Auf den in Calcutta erschienenen Abdruck des Textes von Amara-Koṣa nebst drey andern ähnlichen Wörterbüchern[3] ohne alle Erläuterung, ist dasselbe anzuwenden, was ich oben von den Original-Sprachlehren sagte.

B. Réflexions sur l'étude des langues asiatiques (1832)

August Wilhelm von Schlegel

Though Franz Bopp (1791–1867) acted as August Wilhelm von Schlegel's Sanskrit teacher in Paris, he had himself never had proper training. Whatever the extent of his knowledge, there was no one in Germany at the time who knew more Sanskrit than he did. Yet, out of the translations from the Sanskrit that accompanied his book *Über das Conjugationssystem der Sanskritsprache in Vergleichung mit jenem der griechischen, lateinischen, persischen und germanischen Sprache* of 1816, only a fragment from the *Mahābhārata* had not been translated before, and this contained many elementary mistakes (Windisch 1917, I, 69). How his frustrated liaison with Sanskrit relates to his linguistic interest is not known. Bopp himself later considered all his work in Sanskrit subordinate to his general occupation with language. He wrote for example in 1829: "Mir ist von Allem, was Indien anbelangt, die Sprache das wichtigste, und nur in Zergliederung ihres Organismus, in Untersuchungen über ihr Verhältniss zu den verwandten Dialekten und ihre Bedeutung in der allgemeinen Sprachenwelt trete ich mit wahrer Lust und innigem Vertrauen als Schriftsteller auf" (Windisch 1917, I, 68).

Bopp's knowledge of the Sanskrit grammarians was very limited. Had it been otherwise, modern linguistics might look different. This accords at any rate with Schlegel's interesting opinion: "Herr Bopp hat allerdings grammatischen Sinn: wenn er nur die Indischen Grammatiker fleissiger studirt hätte, wenn er nicht immer Originalität anbringen wollte, wo sie nicht hingehört, so hätte er etwas recht gutes leisten mögen" (writing to Humboldt, June 23, 1829: Leitzmann 1908, 244). Bopp's limited knowledge in this area may account for his low evaluation of the "National-Grammatiken." Thus Delbrück: "Bopp hatte sie [viz., the Indian grammarians] wenig studiert, konnte auch in dem damaligen Studium der wissenschaftlichen Entwicklung wenig Nutzen aus ihnen ziehen, hätte dann aber freilich auch seine gelegentliche Polemik unterlassen sollen" (Leitzmann 1908, *Einleitung*, XVI). Boehtlingk had judged Bopp in harsher terms (which he later, in conversations with Delbrück, regretted) in the Preface to his edition of Vopadeva's *Mugdhabodha* of 1847: "Der zweite Grund (für den Entschluss, dies Buch herauszugeben) war der, dass Carey und Forster bei ihren Grammatiken Vopadevas Werk zugrunde gelegt haben, und Bopp, der weder bei seinen grammatikalischen noch bei seinen lexikalischen Werken andere als sekundäre Quellen benutzt, teilweise dem letzteren von den beiden eben genannten englischen Grammatikern folgt" (Delbrück quoted in Sebeok 1966, I, 264).

[3] The *Amara Koṣa*, *Medini Koṣa*, *Tricānda Śeṣa*, and *Hārāvalī*, four original Vocabularies, I Vol. 8, *Nagarī* character. Calcutta, 1807.

The avowed aim of Bopp's *Ausführliches Lehrgebäude der Sanskrita-Sprache* of 1827, written in Berlin and dedicated to Humboldt, is stated in the introduction: "Ich habe die Bearbeitung einer Grammatik der Sanskrit-Sprache in der Überzeugung unternommen, dass, nach dem was besonders von Wilkins und Forster in diesem Gebiete Verdienstliches geleistet worden, eine weitere Förderung des Gegenstandes nicht etwa von einer ausgedehnteren Benutzung der eingebornen Grammatiker ausgehen könne, sondern nur von einer unabhängigen Kritik der Sprache selbst"; with a footnote: "Wilkins und Forster hatten ihre Grammatiken nicht einmal auf Pāṇini, sondern auf jüngere einheimische Systeme basirt" (page v; quoted in Liebich 1891, 42). The materials for this grammar were in fact largely taken from the grammars of Forster and Wilkins, which Bopp held in high regard. He had to rely very heavily on these two, for his was, in fact, the first grammar not written by someone in close contact with native speakers. His judgment about Colebrooke and the Indian grammarians, on the other hand, is typical. He considered Colebrooke's grammar "ebenso lehrreich als Einleitung in das Studium der National-Grammatiken, als ungenügend und höchst dunkel als Lehrbuch der Sprache" (Windisch 1917, I, 54).

Bopp's grammar was the topic of a long critical review by Christian Lassen in the *Indische Bibliothek* (3, 1830; cf. also Verburg in Sebeok 1966, I, 229–231). Lassen commented as follows upon the words from Bopp's introduction quoted above: "Der Anfang dieser Stelle wird, ich zweifle kaum daran, bei vielen Anstoss erregen, und ich gestehe, dass, allgemein betrachtet, der darin enthaltene Grundsatz, sich mit abgeleiteten Quellen zu behelfen, und die ursprünglichen zu vernachlässigen, auf keinem Gebiete historischer Forschung gutgeheissen werden kann." This is a curious indictment of Western linguistics by Western philology on behalf of Indian linguistics. Lassen's own views on the usefulness of the Sanskrit grammarians are expressed as follows:

> Wir müssen also die Texte der Grammatiker kritisch prüfen, und, wo sie verdorben sind, herzustellen suchen; dann zum vollen Besitz ihres Verständnisses uns hindurch arbeiten; wir müssen dann die von ihnen vorgetragenen Lehren mit unbefangenem Blicke der Kritik unterwerfen, und bei diesem Geschäft mit desto grösserer Vorsicht zu Werke gehen, je mehr zu befürchten ist, dass das Gewicht dieser Lehren, welches uns in der That gross sein muss, uns nicht mit sich fortreisse, so dass wir einen eigenen freien und festen Standpunkt nicht behaupten; und nach allen diesen Studien haben wir noch immer dibselbe Verpflichtung, die Sprache selbst, wie sie im wirklichen Geerauch sich zeigt, zu Rathe zu ziehen, die Sprache des freien Lebens mit der der strengen Schule zu vergleichen [both quotations from Liebich 1891, 42–43].

Bopp was also criticized because he defended the view that the Indian grammarians had created many forms to serve as roots which were not known from Sanskrit texts, and which were therefore not "real" roots. This empiricist note was to have a great future. Bopp himself says in the Preface to his *Glossarium comparativum linguae sanscritae* (quoted from the third edition of 1867): "Multae sunt a grammaticis Indicis inter radices receptae sunt formae non verae sunt radices, sed verborum denominativorum themata, ut e.c. *kumār*, *kartr*, *mantr*, *stom*" ('Many forms which are included by the Indian grammarians amongst the roots are not real roots, but are the stems of verbs derived from nouns, as for example *kumār*,' etc.). Westergaard defended the opposite point of view and went even further in his *Radices linguae sanscritae* of 1841: "Quum autem multas radices neque ex nominibus inde derivatis cognoscamus, neque earum usum locis e libris classicis sumptis probare possimus, sunt qui contendant, tales radices omnino non in lingua exstitisse, sed a grammaticis nescio cur mere esse fictas. Mira tamen assertio, quum tam paululum literae Indicae notae sint" (quoted in Liebich 1891, 43: 'There are many roots which we do not know from nouns derived from them, and of which we cannot establish the use from classical passages and books. For this reason there are people who claim that such roots have never existed in the language at all, but have merely been invented—I wouldn't know why—by the grammarians. But such an assertion is astonishing, given the fact that so little is known of Indian literature').

Though A. W. von Schlegel had started to learn Sanskrit from Bopp, he was soon his equal (as for example his corrections of the latter's translations show: Windisch 1917, I, 76). Schlegel was on the whole inclined to agree with Lassen, and both scholars criticized Bopp for neglecting the Sanskrit grammarians, who in their view constituted the final court of appeal in matters pertaining to Sanskrit grammar. Bopp defended himself against Schlegel, saying that he did not regard further studies of the Indian grammarians as useless and that he had in fact recommended such work to some of his best students. But he excluded himself from such research, at least for the time being, while he continued to arrive at results in linguistics: "Ich selbst mag diese Arbeit nicht unternehmen, so lange wenigstens nicht, als mich ein selbständiges Forschen und das Streben die Sprache durch sich selbst zu begreifen und die Gesetze zu erkennen, nach denen sie sich entfaltet, zu neuen Resultaten führt" (letter to Schlegel of May 26, 1829: Windisch 1917, I, 77). Schlegel did not continue with this correspondence, for he noted (as he wrote to Bopp) that "vertrauliche Mittheilungen Bopp unwilkommen seien, sobald eine Divergenz der Meynungen hervortrete" (Windisch loc. cit.).

A few years later, A. W. von Schlegel published his *Réflexions sur l'étude des langues asiatiques* (1832). In the course of this book he discusses several Sanskrit grammars, lastly Bopp's, after which he holds forth on the Indian grammarians (with an excursus on the Vedas and their accents). The passage included here is quoted from the Bonn–Paris edition of 1832, pages 31–37.

The program outlined by Schlegel at the end of this passage still awaits completion, though much work toward its partial fulfillment has been done, for example, by Kielhorn, Thieme, and Renou. The monograph on the Sanskrit grammarians which is forthcoming (Joshi, Kiparsky, and Staal, in preparation) will be a further step toward its realization. The beginnings of a "catalogue" (as mentioned under item (2)) had in fact been provided by the *Terms of Sanskrit Grammar* (1814) of Alexander Hamilton, the teacher of August Wilhelm's brother Friedrich. Later Renou published his *Terminologie grammaticale du Sanskrit* (1942, 1957[2]). The formalization suggested under (3) has recently begun to receive some attention. Item (4) shows that Schlegel did not know the *gaṇapāṭha*. It may be noted that Schlegel's statement that the Vedas are in modern times recited in monotone is incorrect, both then and now.

M. *Bopp* s'est occupé avec prédilection de l'analyse comparative des langues: il a donné sur ce sujet plusieurs traités, dont l'un écrit en anglais,[1] remplis d'aperçus fins et ingénieux. Sa grammaire est exacte et méthodique; on ne saurait le blâmer d'avoir essayé de montrer comment les formes variées du sanscrit découlent de certains principes fondamentaux. Mais dans les recherches sur l'unité primitive des langues d'une même famille, lorsque nous essayons de nous faire une idée de leur formation graduelle, et de remonter à une époque de l'antiquité dont il n'existe point de monumens écrits, nous sommes sur un autre terrain que quand il s'agit des règles positives d'une langue fixée par l'usage depuis un temps immémorial. À mon avis, M. Bopp a un peu trop confondu les deux genres: il accorde trop de place à ses idées favorites et même à ses hypothèses. Les nombreuses innovations qu'il a introduites, ne seront probablement pas approuvées par ceux qui pensent que dans un langue anciennement cultivée et fixée, il faut respecter l'usage et les autorités classiques.

La partie la moins satisfaisante dans toutes ces grammaires c'est la syntaxe: MM. Colebrooke et Bopp ne sont pas arrivés jusque-là; et chez les autres le petit nombre de pages réservées à ce chapitre, peut à peine mériter ce nom. Cependant la syntaxe est d'une importance majeure dans l'interprétation et la critique des textes.

La grammaire, dans l'opinion des Brahmanes, occupe un rang très-élevé parmi les sciences humaines. Ils la mettent dans un rapport immédiat avec la théologie, à cause de son utilité pour bien comprendre leurs saintes écritures, et pour préserver de toute corruption ce dépôt sacré. Ils considèrent le sanscrit même comme une révélation. Sans quitter le point de vue profane d'une origine naturelle, on doit leur accorder qu'un organe aussi parfait de la pensée et de toutes les jouissances intellectuelles, est une noble prérogative. L'histoire nous fait voir, que chez plusieurs nations possédant des langues pareilles, l'heureux instinct qui avait présidé à leur formation, s'est perdu ensuite, et que les langues ont dégénéré. Les anciens sages de l'Inde ont pensé qu'il ne fallait pas abandonner le sanscrit aux caprices variables et à la négligence du vulgaire. Ils l'ont enseigné de bonne heure par les modèles et les préceptes, et ils ont réussi à le fixer sans en gêner le développement régulier moyennant la dérivation et la composition des mots. Ils ont approfondi la théorie de ces deux moyens d'enrichir leur langue, tandis que les grammairiens grecs ne se sont pas seulement doutés que cela fût possible. La grammaire a été si anciennement cultivée dans l'Inde que les fondateurs de cette science, *Pāṇini*, *Kātyāyana* et *Patañjali*, sont devenus des personnages mythologiques. Pāṇini passe pour le plus ancien; en y regardant de près, on voit pourtant qu'il a eu des prédécesseurs, puisqu'il cite dans ses aphorismes huit autres grammairiens. M. Colebrooke pense que les écrits de quelques-uns d'entr'eux, peut-être de tous, existent encore. Mais ceux que j'ai nommés sont les oracles du langage classique. "Si leurs opinions sur quelques points diffèrent, dit M. Colebrooke, on peut opter, mais s'ils sont d'accord, il faut se soumettre à leur autorité." Cependant on irait peut-être trop loin en disant que, dans aucun cas, il n'est permis de les contredire. Ils sont des témoins irrécusables sur des questions de fait; mais une partie de leur doctrine est spéculative: par exemple l'étymologie, dès qu'elle dépasse le cercle des

[1] *Annals of oriental litterature*, *London* 1824, P. I., *Analytical comparison of the Sanscrit, Greek, Latin, and Teutonic Languages, shewing the original identity of their grammatical structure*. By F. Bopp.

analogies grammaticales. Ils savaient parfaitement leur langue maternelle, mais ils n'en connaissaient pas d'autre; nous savons moins bien le sanscrit, mais nous pouvons le comparer avec d'autres langues, et rectifier par là nos vues générales.

Néanmoins M. Bopp, dans la préface de l'édition allemande de sa grammaire, congédie formellement les grammariens nationaux du sanscrit; il soutient qu'après ce qui en a été extrait déjà, ils ne peuvent plus rien nous apprendre. C'est une grande erreur, je n'hésite pas à le dire. Je pense au contraire que, pour marcher d'un pas assuré dans la critique des textes, il faut être suffisamment initié dans le système des principaux grammairiens indiens, pour savoir les consulter au besoin. M. Colebrooke l'a pensé de même: c'est d'après ses ordres que deux ouvrages importans, les *Aphorismes* de Pāṇini, avec un extrait des commentaires, et la *Siddhānta-Kaumudī*, ont été imprimés à Calcutta. Sans doute, la méthode de ces grammairiens diffère totalement de celle à laquelle nous sommes habitués; elle est fort abstruse. Mais en revanche ils se distinguent par une briéveté et une précision admirables, par l'esprit scientifique dans la recherche des principes, et par l'exactitude scrupuleuse qu'ils mettent à constater le fait de l'usage. Outre la terminologie ordinaire puisée dans la langue même, et appropriée seulement à un emploi spécial, Pāṇini et ses successeurs ont imaginé un autre système de termes techniques. Ce sont des mots fictifs, des signes abrégés, qu'on peut comparer à ceux de l'algèbre. Il faut en avoir la clé, sans quoi les Aphorismes de Pāṇini ressemblent à des énigmes plus obscures que les oracles de Bacis; de même qu'un écolier qui ne sait que les élémens de l'arithmétique, ne comprendra rien aux formules algébriques.

Quel que soit notre jugement sur cette méthode, nous ne pouvons pas vouloir l'ignorer. Les commentateurs indigènes sont nécessaires pour l'intelligence des livres difficiles, et les commentateurs, dans tout ce qui a rapport à la grammaire, se servent de ces termes techniques. On voudra bien arriver finalement à la lecture des *Vedas*, de ce monument mémorable de l'antiquité, source première de la doctrine brahmanique. Or les Vedas sont écrits dans un langage suranné, dont les licences qui se trouvent par-ci par-là chez les plus anciens poètes épiques, ne sont qu'un dernier reste. Pāṇini marque dans un grand détail la différence du style sacré et de l'usage profane. Outre que la connaissance en est nécessaire pour la critique et l'explication des Vedas, ces formes viellies sont intéressantes pour la théorie générale et la comparaison des langues. Quelques-unes sont de vraies déviations, des irrégularités que l'instinct grammatical a rejetées plus tard; d'autres fois la forme des mots et les inflexions anciennes sont plus rapprochées de celles qu'on trouve dans des langues affiliées, et concourent à prouver leur unité primitive.

Les règles de l'accentuation ont été laissées de côté par tous les grammairiens européens du sanscrit. Aujourd'hui dans les écoles des Brahmanes on pronounce les vers des anciens textes uniquement d'après la quantité des syllabes, avec une récitation monotone. Mais jadis le sanscrit a été accentué comme toutes les langues vivantes, et cette accentuation nécessairement a dû avoir de l'influence sur la formation de la langue. Pāṇini en donne les règles qui ne sont pas faciles à comprendre, parce que les accents ne se trouvent écrits nulle part.

Ces raisons, auxquelles je pourrais ajouter plusieurs autres, suffiront pour montrer combien l'étude des anciens grammairiens indigènes est importante. Mais elle est d'un abord très-difficile.

Les deux ouvrages que je viens de nommer, ne sont accompagnés d'aucun mot anglais depuis le titre jusqu'à l'errata; leur extérieur même est rébutant: c'est un labyrinthe où l'on perd son temps à chercher des éclaircissemens sur telle ou telle matière. Ainsi que tous les livres sanscrits imprimés à Calcutta d'après les ordres de M. Colebrooke, et exécutés parle libraire *Bābou-Rāma*, ce ne sont pas des éditions comme nous l'entendons, ce sont des manuscrits multipliés par l'impression.

Une introduction générale à l'étude des grammairiens originaux serait donc un ouvrage fort utile à entreprendre. Pour remplir son but elle devra contenir: (1) une analyse de leur méthode, éclaircie par des exemples; (2) un catalogue de tous les termes techniques avec leur définition, arrangé par ordre alphabétique; (3) la terminologie par signes abrégés et formules, expliquée dans le plus grand détail; (4) un répertoire de toutes les séries de mots sujets à une règle particulière, lesquelles sont désignées par le premier mot, placé arbitrairement à la tête en y ajoutant *et caetera*.

C. Controversy with H. H. Wilson

Horace Hayman Wilson (1784–1860), who was the author of the Sanskrit-English dictionary (1819) and who worked for many years in India with the assistance of pandits, wrote in 1830, in Calcutta, a *Memorandum* in which he attempted to show that he was the only deserving candidate for the newly established Boden chair of Sanskrit at Oxford. The Bishop of Calcutta forwarded this *Memorandum* (which stressed, among other things, the usefulness of the knowledge of Sanskrit for the Indian chaplaincy and the mission) to the Principal of Magdalen College, and Wilson was appointed in due course. The *Memorandum* formulated requirements for the incumbent of the new chair such as were satisfied by Wilson but not, for example, by continental scholars:

I should think it an indispensable requisite in the first Professor of the Sanscrit Language, that he had acquired his knowledge in India. It is true that considerable proficiency has been attained by some learned men on the Continent, but it is evident from their publications that their reading has been very limited, and that they are far from possessing any degree of conversancy with the great body of Sanscrit Literature. Their knowledge is, in fact, of the most elementary kind, and restricted to the grammar of the language. The publications of Bopp are chiefly of this description; and Schlegel has not ventured in translation beyond those works which have been previously translated by English Scholars. With the different departments of Hindu classical literature, with any one of them in a variety of details, and even with its grammar as studied in India, they are unfamiliar; and they must be very incompetent therefore to prepare a Student for this country, or even where general information only is sought, to convey comprehensive and correct notions of the classical writings of the Hindus, of their poetry, mythology, philosophy, and science. . . . If, however, instruction in the language alone be the object to be kept in view, the Lecturer will have to confine himself to the elements of the Sanscrit tongue, its grammar, syntax, and prosody: to explain these satisfactorily, however, he should be familiar not only with the grammars compiled by European scholars, as Wilkins, etc. but with the original grammars read by the Pundits, the Sūtras of Pāṇini, the Siddhānta Kaumudī, and Mugdhabodha; for although it is by no means advisable to teach the grammar after those systems, they alone furnish a clue to the intricacies of Sanscrit grammar, without which it is not easy to make a profitable use even of modern European compilations (quoted in Schlegel 1832, Appendix F, 201–202).

Though this *Memorandum* was first treated as a confidential document, the Bishop of Calcutta wrote to the Principal of Magdalen on May 31, 1831: "I could wish this valuable paper, which was drawn up at my request, to be circulated widely" (quoted in Schlegel 1832, 200). When this somehow reached Schlegel, who was in the habit of sending his offprints to Wilson, he went into a fit of rage and wrote Wilson a long letter, which he published as an appendix in his *Réflexions* in 1832. In this letter Schlegel points out numerous mistakes and inaccuracies in Wilson's own work, suggests that he had left much of the really hard work to the pandits working for him in Calcutta, complains about the high prices of Sanskrit books published in England and the curious restrictions on the sale of inexpensive Indian books outside England, etc. The letter ends with a warning: when Wilson returns to Europe, his activities will be reviewed critically. (Schlegel 1832, 167–168).

Toutefois, ne craignez rien de la part de nous autres vétérans. Nous devons imiter l'impassibilité de ces Brahmanes dont nous admirons les sages maximes. Nous nous rappelons que Viśvāmitra perdit tout le fruit de ses pénitences pour s'être laissé entraîner à un mouvement de colère, quoique la provocation fût assez forte. . . . Mais je ne vous réponds pas de nos jeunes Indianistes: ils sont aussi fongeux que zélés pour leur étude, et pourraient être tentés de venger leurs ancient maîtres. Si vous publiez quelque ouvrage, on sera à l'affût de vos méprises: et qui n'en commet pas? Si, au contraire, vous ne publiez rien, on dira qu'en partant de Calcutta, vous avez oublié d'embarquer votre savoir [an obvious reference to Wilson's pandit informants]. Croyez-moi, faites votre paix le plutôt et le mieux que vous pourrez; je vous offre mes bons offices comme médiateur.

(It is interesting to read, in this connection, what Weber wrote 20 years later: "It is certainly very discouraging to see that Professor Wilson during all the time since he got his one professorship in Oxford, has not succeeded in bringing up even one Sanskrit scholar who might claim to be regarded as one who has done at least some little service to our Sanskrit philology": from a letter of Weber to Salisbury of December 28, 1852 (quoted in Sebeok 1966, I, 405).

These exchanges show, if not a tinge of imperialism, at least how knowledge regarding Sanskrit that could almost exclusively be obtained in India, such as knowledge of the Sanskrit grammarians, was beginning to become controversial. Such feelings remained in existence for a long time. In 1899, for example, no less distinguished a scholar than Hermann Oldenberg called Sir William Jones "ein unermüdlich coquettirender Schönreder" (quoted in Sebeok 1966, I, 11). The Germans, in turn, were criticized not only by the English but also by the French. The skeptic Jacquemort wrote: "L'absurde de Bénarès et l'absurde de l'Allemagne n'ont-ils pas un air de famille?" (Schwab 1950, 238 note).

9

Wilhelm von Humboldt (1767–1835)

From 1818 to 1831 A. W. von Schlegel had an extensive correspondence with Wilhelm von Humboldt (1767–1835), in which Sanskrit studies figured prominently (edited by Leitzmann 1908; cf. Windisch 1917, I, 205–207). Humboldt defended Bopp against some of Schlegel's criticisms and asked Schlegel at the same time numerous questions about the Indian grammarians. Schlegel had unlimited admiration for them and encouraged Humboldt to study them: "Ich hege für sie [the Indian grammarians] eine gränzenlose Bewunderung, und wollte nur, ich verstände sie erst vollkommen. Ich zweifle nicht, es wird Ihnen einen grossen Genuss gewähren, in der Folge an die Originalwerke dieser wissenschaftlichen Köpfe selbst zu gehen, da Sie gewohnt sind, schwere Räthsel aufzulösen" (writing to Humboldt in 1821, Leitzmann 1908, 19). As this passage shows, Schlegel knew that his own information on this topic was rather scanty. A letter of 1822, too, makes it clear that he was not sure whether the Sanskrit grammarians had ever dealt with syntax—a question in which Humboldt had expressed interest: "Ew. Excellenz legen zuerst Hand an eine schwere wissenschaftliche Aufgabe: die Syntaxis des Sanskrit; denn die paar Blätter bei Carey und Wilkins, welche diese Überschrift führen, sind ja kaum der Rede werth. Sind die Indischen Grammatiker eben so karglaut? Haben sie ihren Scharfsinn so ganz an der Wortbildung erschöpft, dass ihnen für die Wortfügung gar nichts übrig blieb? Ich weiss es nicht . . ." (Leitzmann 1908, 86).

Humboldt was close to both Bopp and Schlegel and could not fail to get involved in their battles, and hence in an evaluation of the Indian grammarians. He preferred the Greek grammarians to the "Formelwesen" of the Indian grammatical tradition, as he stated in a letter to Schlegel of June 16, 1829, in which he passes judgment on Bopp after stressing that his own position is fully unprejudiced:

> Ich stehe ganz unpartheiisch zwischen Ihnen beiden. Ich kann mich, soviel Belehrung ich auch Ihnen beiden schuldig bin, einen Schüler von keinem von Ihnen nennen, Sie haben beide selbst meine Irrthümer und Unkenntnisse mit fast überhöflicher Schonung behandelt, meine langjährige Freundschaft mit Ew. Hochwohlgeboren, meine lebhafte Zuneigung und Theilnahme an Bopp stellt mich Ihnen beiden nahe, mir kann keine Eifersucht beiwohnen, da ich Sie beide in diesen Studien weit über mir erkenne. Mein Zeugniss kann mithin von keiner Seite der Partheilichkeit verdächtig seyn. . . . Ich gebe vollkommen zu, dass Bopp die Indischen Grammatiker nicht selbst studirt hat, und ob ich gleich, wie ich augenblicklich sagen werde, dies in ihm gerechtfertigt finde, so billige ich nicht, dass er oft zu sehr dies Studium überhaupt für nicht nothwendig erklärt. Ich thäte das schon nicht, weil gerade ein solches Urtheil mit vielem Studium verbunden seyn müsste, es ist aber auch gegen meine Ueberzeugung, wiewohl ich, was hier zu lang zu rechtfertigen wäre, keine so vortheilhafte Meinung von den eingeborenen Grammatikern und ihrem Formelwesen habe, als Ew. Hochwohlgeboren, und die guten Griechischen für weit vorzüglicher halte (Leitzmann 1908, 232–233).

Humboldt had great admiration for the Sanskrit language, which he seemed mainly to have studied from Wilkins' grammar ("ich habe mein Sanskrit ganz eigentlich zuerst ans ihm gelernt": writing to Schlegel, June 16, 1829), from Bopp's grammar, and from Bopp's and Schlegel's editions of texts. We do not know how much he knew (he called both Bopp and Schlegel "weit über mir" in the letter just quoted), but Bopp praised his rapid progress in a letter to the French Sanskritist Jean-Louis Burnouf (Windisch 1917, I, 83). Humboldt himself published several studies on Sanskrit, for example, on the so-called gerunds ending in *-tvā* and on the *Bhagavad-Gītā*. To Humboldt, Sanskrit was the zenith of the development of inflected languages. Only because of Sanskrit was a serious and fruitful study of language possible (Dove in Sebeok 1966, I, 98; Windisch 1917, I, 82–86). Humboldt was the first to recognize the extent of Sanskrit influence in Southeast Asia (in his *Über die Kawi-Sprache auf der Insel Java* of 1832).

The Indian grammarians are mentioned several times in Humboldt's most well known work, the Introduction to the *Kawi-Sprache*, published separately under the title *Über die Verschiedenheit des menschlichen Sprachbaues und ihren Einfluss auf die geistige Entwicklung des Menschengeschlechts* (1836). Recently Chomsky has drawn attention to Humboldt's emphasis in this work on the creative aspect of language use (Chomsky 1964, 17–21; 1966, especially 19–28). Humboldt in fact relates some of the views he expresses on this topic to the Sanskrit grammarians. His concept of language as *Erzeugnis* finds expression in the "Regeln der Redefügung" and in the rules of *Wortbildung* (Chomsky 1966, 19). With respect to the former, Humboldt could not refer to the Indian grammarians, for Schlegel had not enlightened him on this matter. With respect to the *Wortbildung* he says: "Man kann den *Wortvorrath* einer Sprache auf keine Weise als eine *fertig daliegende Masse* ansehen. Er ist, auch ohne ausschliesslich der beständigen Bildung neuer Wörter und Wortformen zu gedenken, so lange die Sprache im Munde des Volks lebt, ein fortgehendes *Erzeugniss* und Wiedererzeugniss des *wortbildenden Vermögens*, zuerst in dem Stamme, dem die Sprache ihre Form verdankt, dann in der kindischen Erlernung des Sprechens, und endlich im täglichen Gebrauche der Rede" (Humboldt 1836, 109–110). He then explains why this cannot be merely due to memory. Next he considers how it becomes possible for the vocabulary of a language to form a unity, on account of the *Erzeugung* of words (Humboldt 1836, 111–112).

A. Über die Verschiedenheit des menschlichen Sprachbaues (1836): I

Wilhelm von Humboldt

Die *Indischen Grammatiker* bauten ihr, gewiss zu künstliches, aber in seinem Ganzen von bewundrungswürdigem Scharfsinn zeugendes System auf die Voraussetzung, dass sich der ihnen vorliegende Wortschatz ihrer Sprache ganz durch sich selbst erklären lasse. Sie sahen dieselbe daher als eine ursprüngliche an, und schlossen auch alle Möglichkeit im Verlaufe der Zeit aufgenommener fremder Wörter aus. Beides war unstreitig falsch. Denn aller historischen, oder aus der Sprache selbst aufzufindenden Gründe nicht zu gedenken, ist es auf keine Weise wahrscheinlich, dass sich irgend eine wahrhaft ursprüngliche Sprache in ihrer *Urform* bis auf uns erhalten habe. Vielleicht hatten die Indischen Grammatiker bei ihrem Verfahren auch nur mehr den Zweck im Auge, die Sprache zur Bequemlichkeit der Erlernung in systematische Verbindung zu bringen, ohne sich gerade um die historische Richtigkeit dieser Verbindung zu kümmern. Es mochte aber auch den Indiern in diesem Punkte wie den meisten Nationen bei dem Aufblühen ihrer Geistesbildung ergehen. Der Mensch sucht immer die Verknüpfung, auch der äusseren Erscheinungen, zuerst im Gebiete der *Gedanken* auf; die *historische* Kunst ist immer die späteste, und die reine *Beobachtung*, noch weit mehr aber der *Versuch*, folgen erst in weiter Entfernung idealischen oder phantastischen Systemen nach. Zuerst versucht der Mensch die Natur von der Idee aus zu beherrschen. Dies zugestanden, zeugt aber jene Voraussetzung der Erklärlichkeit des Sanskrits durch sich allein von einem richtigen und tiefen Blick in die Natur der Sprache überhaupt. Denn eine wahrhaft ursprüngliche und von fremder Einmischung rein geschiedene müsste wirklich einen solchen thatsächlich nachzuweisenden Zusammenhang ihres gesammten Wortvorraths in sich bewahren. Es war überdies ein schon durch seine Kühnheit Achtung verdienendes Unternehmen, sich gerade mit dieser Beharrlichkeit in die Wortbildung, als den tiefsten und geheimnissvollsten Theil aller Sprachen, zu versenken.

B. Über die Verschiedenheit des menschlichen Sprachbaues (1836): II

Wilhelm von Humboldt

Thus, according to von Humboldt, the Indian grammarians unrealistically regarded the Sanskrit vocabulary as closed and not subject to change. But despite these limitations, they recognized the principles of word formation by which the entire vocabulary is knit together, and which constitute "the deepest and most mysterious portion of all languages."

In the following pages Humboldt specifies this thesis in greater detail. After referring to pronouns, prepositions, and interjections, he comes to roots. Thereupon, referring to Bopp, to Sanskrit, and to the Indian grammarians, he develops a theory which resembles Bopp's idea that there is a one-to-one correspondence between the smallest morphological and semantic elements of language (cf. Kiparsky 1970). He introduces the notion of postulated or underlying roots, which Bopp, as we have already seen, had repudiated as far as the Sanskrit grammarians were concerned. But according to Humboldt, such roots might be the object of linguistic analysis without being given in actual performance: "... die Wurzeln brauchen nicht der wahrhaften Sprache anzugehören.... Denn die wahre Sprache ist nur die in der Rede sich offenbarende, und die *Spracherfindung* lässt sich nicht auf demselben Wege abwärts schreitend denken, den die *Analyse* aufwärts verfolgt" (page 115).

These roots may be invisible in certain languages (in particular, in inflected languages) and they may have to be postulated. But Humboldt believed that they were quite real in the sense that they had originally existed and might still be found in other languages. This is most clearly expressed in a letter to Schlegel of 1829, in which he contrasts his views with those of Bopp and says that the Indian grammarians, when postulating roots, also isolated them by a kind of purification:

In etwas, das bei Bopp hier noch zum Grunde liegt, bin ich mit ihm verschiedener Meinung. Er betrachtet, wozu freilich auch Colebrooke Anlass giebt, die Wurzeln als grammatische Abstracta. Ich hingegen halte sie für uralte Grundwörter, die aber in der ganz flectirten Sprache, als solche, verschwinden. Höchstens möchte ich zugeben, dass die Grammatiker, welche sie (wenige Fälle ausgenommen) allerdings bloss als wissenschaftliche Hülfsmittel brauchten, sie von gewissen Nebenlauten befreiten oder sonst Lautveränderungen mit ihnen vornahmen, um sie zu durchaus lauteren Quellen aller aus ihnen entspringenden Formen zu machen. Ich suche daher immer nach dem Erscheinen dieser Wurzeln in nicht-Sanskritischen Asiatischen Sprachen, und habe wohl Einiges, aber nicht Vieles bisher gefunden (Leitzmann 1908, 238).

It is in this context that it becomes especially clear how Humboldt's ideas about the creative use of language as manifested in word formation, foreshadowed in fact by Pons' "élémens primitifs" (page 31 of this volume), were influenced by the Indian grammarians and by the long discussions about their "invented" roots between Bopp, Lassen, Schlegel, and others.

Humboldt believed that they were quite real in the sense that they had originally existed and might still be found in other languages. This is most clearly expressed in a letter to Schlegel of 1829, in which he contrasts his views with those of Bopp and says that the Indian grammarians, when postulating roots, also isolated them by a kind of purification:

> In etwas, das bei Bopp hier noch zum Grunde liegt, bin ich mit ihm verschiedener Meinung. Er betrachtet, wozu freilich auch Colebrooke Anlass giebt, die Wurzeln als grammatische Abstracta. Ich hingegen halte sie für uralte Grundwörter, die aber in der ganz flectirten Sprache, als solche, verschwinden. Höchstens möchte ich zugeben, dass die Grammatiker, welche sie (wenige Fälle ausgenommen) allerdings bloss als wissenschaftliche Hülfsmittel brauchten, sie von gewissen Nebenlauten befreiten oder sonst Lautveränderungen mit ihnen vornahmen, um sie zu durchaus lauteren Quellen aller aus ihnen entspringenden Formen zu machen. Ich suche daher immer nach dem Erscheinen dieser Wurzeln in nicht-Sanskritischen Asiatischen Sprachen, und habe wohl Einiges, aber nicht Vieles bisher gefunden (Leitzmann 1908, 238).

It is in this context that it becomes especially clear how Humboldt's ideas about the creative use of language as manifested in word formation, foreshadowed in fact by Pons' "élémens primitifs" (page 31 of this volume), were influenced by the Indian grammarians and by the long discussions about their "invented" roots between Bopp, Lassen, Schlegel, and others.

In his *Über die Verschiedenheit*, Humboldt then raises the question whether or not the roots thus arrived at are really the smallest elements and cannot be subject to further analysis. Claiming that this is not mere speculation, he arrives at a kind of language atoms, the *Wurzellaute*, and argues that these are always expressed by the verb, since it is there that they are combined with the greatest variety of additional forms. This leads him again to the Indian grammarians, and he treats at some length their distinction between two kinds of word-forming suffixes, namely *kṛt* suffixes and *uṇādi* suffixes. The facts as we now know them are as follows. Whereas *kṛt* suffixes are attached to roots to form derivatives in accordance with Pāṇini's rules, which specify their syntactic function and often their meaning, *uṇādi* suffixes are postulated to account for a series of words which are formed from roots in irregular ways. Such words are therefore not subject to the regular analysis provided by Pāṇini; they are characterized as *avyutpanna* 'unanalyzable'. Schlegel had said about these suffixes in a letter to Humboldt (1821) that they "sind allerdings der Theorie zu Liebe ersonnen" (Leitzmann 1908, 16), which is, therefore, not quite correct. Humboldt refers to them in connection with his theory of the *Wurzellaute* on pages 115–119 of the 1836 edition of *Über die Verschiedenheit des menschlichen Sprachbaues*, of which the beginning sentences have already been quoted.

The work of Pott to which Humboldt refers is *Etymologische Forschungen* (1833–1836). Pāṇini refers twice to *uṇādi* suffixes, so called because a list of them begins with *uṆ* 'the suffix *u*' (where *Ṇ* is a metalinguistic marker: Pāṇini 3.3.1 and 3.4.75). It is uncertain whether Pāṇini was in fact the author of such a list; the lists that are presently known are of much later date. One list was published in 1844 by O. Boehtlingk; another, by Th. Aufrecht, appeared in 1859 together with a *vṛtti* 'gloss' of Ujjvaladatta. For a recent study see Renou (1956b).

Chomsky's emphasis on the value of Humboldt's ideas has been timely but should not obscure the fact that some of Humboldt's formulations can lead rather easily, and have in fact led, to mystification. Contemporary Neo-Humboldtianism (with its admixture of Hegelianism) has a large share of this, and even the Sanskrit grammarians have not remained unaffected. The following is a recent example of a singularly ill-informed and muddled piece of interpretation in this tradition: "Und um diesem Zauber-Worte [*brahman*] seine ursprüngliche Zauber-Kraft zu erhalten, haben die alten Inder schon vor 3000 Jahren eine raffinierte Grammatik erfunden, die in Europa erst in den letzten 100 Jahren erreicht und überholt worden ist. In Griechenland aber ist das magisch-beschwörende Wort der Sprache zu dem wissenschaftlichen Begriff geworden, in dem diese ursprüngliche magisch-beschwörende Kraft, um mit Hegel zu sprechen, erst ihre Wirklichkeit und Wahrheit erreicht hat" (Lohmann 1960, 183–184).

Mit dem Namen der *Wurzeln* können nur solche Grundlaute belegt werden, welche sich unmittelbar, ohne Dazwischenkunft anderer, schon für sich bedeutsamer Laute, dem zu bezeichnenden Begriffe anschliessen. In diesem strengen Verstande des Worts, brauchen die Wurzeln nicht der wahrhaften Sprache anzugehören; und in Sprachen, deren Form die Umkleidung der Wurzeln mit Nebenlauten mit sich führt, kann dies sogar überhaupt kaum, oder doch nur unter bestimmten Bedingungen der Fall sein. Denn die wahre Sprache ist nur die in der Rede sich offenbarende, und die *Spracherfindung* lässt sich nicht auf demselben Wege abwärts schreitend denken, den die *Analyse* aufwärts verfolgt. Wenn in einer solchen Sprache eine Wurzel als Wort erscheint, wie im Sanskrit, *yudh*, Kampf, oder als Theil einer Zusammensetzung, wie in *dharmavid*, gerechtigkeitskundig, so sind dies Ausnahmen, die ganz und gar noch nicht zu der Voraussetzung eines Zustandes berechtigen, wo auch, gleichsam wie im Chinesischen, die unbekleideten Wurzeln sich mit der Rede verbanden. Es ist sogar viel wahrscheinlicher, dass, je mehr die Stammlaute dem Ohre und dem Bewusstsein der Sprechenden geläufig wirden, solche einzelnen Fälle ihrer nackten Anwendung dadurch eintraten. Indem aber durch die Zergliederung auf die Stammlaute zurückgegangen wird, fragt es sich, ob man überall bis zu dem wirklich *einfachen* gelangt ist? Im Sanskrit ist schon mit glücklichem Scharfsinn von Bopp, und in einer, schon oben erwähnten, wichtigen Arbeit, die gewiss zur Grundlage weiterer Forschungen dienen wird, von Pott gezeigt worden, dass mehrere angebliche Wurzeln zusammengesetzt oder durch Reduplication abgeleitet sind. Aber auch auf solche, die wirklich einfach scheinen, kann der Zweifel ausgedehnt werden. Ich meine hier besonders die, welche sich von dem Bau der einfachen oder doch den Vocal nur mit solchen Consonantenlauten, die sich bis zu schwieriger Trennung mit ihm verschmelzen, umkleidenden Sylben abweichen. Auch in ihnen können unkenntlich gewordene und phonetisch durch Zusammenziehung, Abwerfung von Vocalen, oder sonst veränderte Zusammensetzungen versteckt sein. Ich sage dies nicht, um leere Muthmassungen an die Stelle von Thatsachen zu setzen, wohl aber, um der historischen Forschung nicht willkührlich das weitere Vordringen in noch nicht gehörig durchschaute Sprachzustände zu verschliessen, und weil die uns hier beschäftigende Frage des Zusammenhanges der Spra-

selben von dieser bestimmten Art ist. Die *Uṇādi*-Suffixe begreifen, gerade im Gegentheil, nur Benennungen concreter Gegenstände, und in den durch sie gebildeten Wörtern ist der dunkelste Theil gerade das Suffix selbst, welches den allgemeineren, den Wurzellaut modificirenden Begriff enthalten sollte. Es ist nicht zu läugnen, dass ein grosser Theil dieser Bildungen erzwungen und offenbar ungeschichtlich ist. Man erkennt zu deutlich ihre absichtliche Entstehung aus dem Princip, alle Wörter der Sprache, ohne Ausnahme, auf die einmal angenommenen Wurzeln zurückzubringen. Unter diesen Benennungen concreter Gegenstände können einestheils fremde in die Sprache aufgenommene, andrentheils aber unkenntlich gewordene Zusammensetzungen liegen, wie es von den letzteren in der That erkennbare bereits unter den Uṇādi-Wörtern giebt. Es ist dies natürlich der dunkelste Theil aller Sprachen, und man hat daher mit Recht neuerlich vorgezogen, aus einem grossen Theile der Uṇādi-Wörter eine eigne Classe dunkler und ungewisser Herleitung zu bilden.

Das Wesen des Lautzusammenhanges beruht auf der kenntlichkeit der *Stammsylbe*, die von den Sprachen überhaupt nach dem Grade der Richtigkeit ihres Organismus mit mehr oder minder sorgfältiger Schonung behandelt wird. In denen eines sehr vollkommenen Baues schliessen sich aber an dem *Stammlaut*, als den den Begriff individualisirenden, *Nebenlaute*, als allgemeine, modificirende, an. Wie nun in der Aussprache der Wörter in der Regel jedes nur Einen Hauptaccent hat, und die unbetonten Sylben gegen die betonte sinken, . . . so nehmen auch, in den einfachen, abgeleiteten Wörtern, die Nebenlaute in richtig organisirten Sprachen einen kleineren, obgleich sehr bedeutsamen Raum ein. Sie sind gleichsam die scharfen und kurzen Merkzeichen für den Verstand, wohin er den Begriff der mehr und deutlicher sinnlich ausgeführten Stammsylbe zu setzen hat. Dies Gesetz sinnlicher Unterordnung, das auch mit den rhythmischen Baue der Wörter in Zusammenhange steht, scheint durch sehr rein organisirte Sprachen auch formell, ohne dass dazu die Veranlassung von den Wörtern selbst ausgeht, allgemein zu herrschen; und das Bestreben der Indischen Grammatiker, alle Wörter ihrer Sprache danach zu behandeln, zeugt wenigstens von richtiger Einsicht in den Geist ihrer Sprache. Da sich die Uṇādi-Suffixe bei den früheren Grammatikern nicht gefunden haben sollen, so scheint man aber hierauf erst später gekommen zu sein. In der That zeigt sich in den meisten Sanskritwörtern für concrete Gegenstände dieser Bau einer kurz abfallenden Endung neben einer vorherrschenden Stammsylbe, und dies lässt sich sehr füglich mit dem oben über die Möglichkeit unkenntlich gewordener Zusammensetzung Gesagten vereinen. Der gleiche Trieb hat, wie auf die Ableitung, so auch auf die Zusammensetzung gewirkt, und gegen den individueller oder sonst bestimmt bezeichnenden Theil den anderen im Begriff und im Laute nach und nach fallen lassen. Denn wenn wir in den Sprachen, ganz dicht neben einander, beinahe unglaublich scheinende Verwischungen und Entstellungen der Laute durch die Zeit, und wieder ein, Jahrhunderte hindurch zu verfolgendes, beharrliches Halten an ganz einzelnen und einfachen antreffen, so liegt dies wohl meistentheils an dem durch irgend einen Grund motivirten *Streben* oder *Aufgeben* des inneren Sprachsinnes. Die Zeit verlöscht nicht an sich, sondern nur in dem Maasse, als er vorher einen Laut absichtlich oder gleichgültig fallen lässt.

4 The Golden Days

Plate III

A page from a manuscript in the India Office, London, of Pāṇini's *Aṣṭādhyāyī*, reproduced by courtesy of Her Majesty's Secretary of State for Foreign and Commonwealth Affairs. The manuscript is modern (see No. 2451, Catalogue Eggeling 1887). The sūtras, of which groups of twenty are numbered, constitute 3.2.88–144. The text is the following:

bahulaṃ chaṃdasi//sukarmapāpamaṃtrapuṇyeṣu kṛñaḥ//some suñaḥ// agnau ceḥ//karmaṇy agnyākhyāyāṃ// karmaṇīnir vikriyaḥ//dṛśeḥ kvanip// rājani yudhikṛñaḥ//sahe ca//saptamyāṃ janer ḍaḥ//pañcamyām ajātau upasarge ca saṃjñāyāṃ//anau karmaṇi//5//anyeṣv api dṛśyate//niṣṭhā// suyajor ṅvanip//jīryater atṛn//chaṃdasi liṭ//liṭaḥ kānaj vā//kvasuś ca// bhāṣāyāṃ sadavasaśruvaḥ//upeyivānanāśvānanūcānaś ca//luṅ//anadyatane laṅ//abhijñāvacane lṛṭ//na yadi //vibhāṣā sākāṃkṣe//parokṣe liṭ// haśaśvator//laṅ ca praśne cāsannakāle //laṭ sme//aparokṣe ca//nanau pṛṣṭapratīvacane//6//nanvair vibhāṣa// puri luṅ cāsme//vartamāne laṭ//laṭaḥ śatṛśānacāv aprathamāsamānādhikaraṇe//saṃbodhane ca//lakṣaṇahetvoḥ kriyāyāḥ tau sat//pūṅyajoḥ śānan// tācchīlyavayovacanaśaktiṣu cānaś// iṅdhāryoḥ śatr akṛcchriṇi//dviṣo mitre//suño yajñasaṃyoge//arhaḥ praśaṃsāyāṃ//ā kves tacchīlataddharmatatsādhukāriṣu//tṛn//alaṃkṛññirākṛñprajanotpacotpatonmadarucyapatrapavṛtuvṛdhusahacaraḥ iṣṇuc// ṇeś chaṃdasi//bhuvaś ca//glājisthāś ca ksnuḥ//trasigṛdhidhṛṣikṣipeḥ knuḥ //7//śamityaṣṭābhyo ghinuṇ//saṃpṛcānurudhāṅyamāṅyasaparisṛsaṃsṛjaparidevisaṃjvaraparikṣipaparirataparivadaparidahaparimuhaduṣadviṣadruhaduhayujākrīḍavivicatyajarajabhajāticarāpacarāmuṣābhyāhanaś ca//vau kaṣalasakatthasrambhaḥ// ape ca laṣaḥ//pre . . .

The following is a translation of these rules. Most references through *anuvṛtti* to preceding sūtras have been supplied between parentheses. There is *anuvṛtti* of 3.2.84 *bhūte* "when the past is expressed" through 3.2.122, but this has been generally omitted in the following translations. Capital letters denote metalinguistic indicatory elements.

(3.2.88) In the Veda sometimes (the suffix *KVIP* is attached to *han* 'kill'). (3.2.89) (The suffix *KVIP* is attached) to *kṛÑ* 'do' when compounded with *su* 'well,' *karman* 'work,' *pāpa* 'evil,' *mantra* 'sacred formula,' and *puṇya* 'merit.' (3.2.90) (The suffix *KVIP* is attached) to *suÑ* 'press' when compounded with *soma* 'the soma (-stalk).' (3.2.91) (The suffix *KVIP* is attached) to *ci* 'construct' when compounded with *agni* 'fire altar.' (3.2.92) (The suffix *KVIP* is attached to *ci*) when compounded with a term designating a fire altar when an object is referred to [by the entire expression]. (3.2.93) The suffix *inI* is attached to *vikrī* 'sell' when an object is referred to. (3.2.94) The suffix *KvanIP* is attached to *dṛś* 'see' (when an object is referred to). (3.2.95) (The suffix *KvanIP* is attached) to *yudh* 'fight' and *kṛ* 'do' when combined with *rājā* 'king.' (3.2.96) (The suffix *KvanIP* is attached to *yudh* 'fight' and *kṛ* 'do') also with *saha* 'with.' (3.2.97) The suffix *Ḍa* is attached to *jan* 'be born' when a locative is expressed. (3.2.98) (The suffix *Ḍa* is attached to *jan*) when an ablative not denoting a class is expressed. (3.2.99) (The suffix *Ḍa* is attached to *jan*) also with a preposition when a name is expressed. (3.2.100) (The suffix *Ḍa* is attached to *jan*) with *anu* when combined with an object. *//5//* (3.2.101) (The suffix *Ḍa* is attached to *jan*) also in other cases. (3.2.102) *NIṢṬHĀ* [that is, the suffixes *ta* and *tavat*] is used (when the past is expressed). (3.2.103) The suffix *ṄvanIP* is used with *su* 'press' and *yaj* 'sacrifice.' (3.2.104) The suffix *atṚN* is used with *jṛ* 'grow old.' (3.2.105) The perfect is used in the Veda. (3.2.106) [However,] the suffix *KānaC* is used optionally in the place of the perfect endings (in the Veda). (3.2.107) The suffix *KvasU* is also used (optionally in the place of the perfect endings in the Veda). (3.2.108) In the vernacular (the suffix *KvasU* is also used optionally in the place of the perfect) after *sad* 'sit,' *vas* 'live,' and *śru* 'hear.' (3.2.109) *upeyivān* 'who has come near,' *anāśvan* 'who has not eaten' and *anūcānaḥ* 'who has studied' are also used (optionally in the place of the perfect). (3.2.110) The aorist is used (when the

अष्टा. वहुलंछंदसि सुकर्मपापमंत्रपुण्येषुकृञः सोमेसुञः अग्नौचेः कर्मण्यग्न्याख्यायां
८ कर्मणीनिविक्रियः दृशेःक्वनिप् राजनियुधिकृञः सहेच सप्तम्यांजनेर्डः पंचम्यामजा
तौउपसर्गेचसंज्ञायां अनौकर्मणि ५ अन्येष्वपिदृश्यते निष्ठा सुयजोर्ङ्वनिप् जीर्य
तेरतृन् छंदसिलिट् लिटःकानज्वा क्वसुश्च भाषायांसदवसश्रुवः उपेयिवाननाश्वा पिं
ननूचानश्च लुङ् अनद्यतनेलङ् अभिज्ञावचनेलृट् नयदि विभाषासाकांक्षे परो
क्षेलिट् हशश्वतोर्लङ्च प्रश्नेचासन्नकाले लट्स्मे अपरोक्षेच ननौपृष्टप्रतिवचने
६ नन्वोर्विभाषा पुरिलुङ्चास्मे वर्तमानेलट् लटःशतृशानचावप्रथमासमानाधि
करणे संबोधनेच लक्षणहेत्वोःक्रियायाः तौसत् पूङ्यजोःशानन् ताछील्यवयोव
चनशक्तिषुचानश् इङ्धार्योःशत्रकृच्छ्रिणि द्विषोमित्रे सुञोयज्ञसंयोगे अर्हःप्रशं
सायां आक्वेस्तछीलतद्धर्मतत्साधुकारिषु तृन् अलंकृञ्निराकृञ्प्रजनोत्पचोत्पतो
न्मदरुच्यपत्रपवृतुवृधुसहचरइष्णुच् णेश्छंदसि भुवश्च ग्लाजिस्थश्चग्स्नुः त्रसिगृ
धिधृषिक्षिपेःक्नुः ७ शमित्यष्टाभ्योघिनुण् संपृचानुरुधाङ्यमाङ्यसपरिसंसृजप
रिदेविसंज्वरपरिक्षिपपरिरटपरिवदपरिदहपरिमुहदुषद्विषद्रुहदुहयुजाक्रीडवि ८
विचत्यजरजभजातिचरापचरामुषाभ्याहनश्च वौकषलसकत्थस्रंभः अपेचलषः प्रे

past is expressed). (3.2.111) The imperfect is used (when the past is expressed) excluding the present day. (3.2.112) The future is used (when the past is expressed, excluding the present day) when a memory is voiced. (3.2.113) But not in combination with *yad* 'that.' (3.2.114) In construction with another sentence there is an option. (3.2.115) The perfect is used when the speaker was not present. (3.2.116) It is also used with the particles *ha* 'indeed' and *śaśvat* 'frequently.' (3.2.117) The imperfect is also used in a question about the recent past [the last two rules are divided differently in the printed editions]. (3.2.118) The present is used (when the past is expressed and the speaker was not present) with the particle *sma*. (3.2.119) Also when the speaker was present. (3.2.120) With the particle *nanu* in answer to a question. //6// (3.2.121) There is option with the particles *na* and *nu*. (3.2.122) The aorist may also be used with the particle *purā* when the particle *sma* is not present. (3.2.123) The present tense is used when what is presently happening is expressed. (3.2.124) The suffixes *ŚatṚ* and *ŚānaC* are used in the place of the present when coreferential with a noun not in the Nominative. (3.2.125) But (the suffixes *ŚatṚ* and *ŚānaC* are used in the place of the present when coreferential with a noun) [even when] (in the Nominative) in modes of address. (3.2.126) (The suffixes *ŚatṚ* and *ŚānaC* are used in the place of the present) when they characterize an action or express its cause. (3.2.127) These (suffixes are called) *SAT*. (3.2.128) The suffix *ŚānaN* is attached to *pū* 'purify' and *yaj* 'sacrifice.' (3.2.129) The suffix *CānaŚ* is attached to express a habit, one's age, or a capacity. (3.2.130) The suffix *ŚatṚ* is attached to *iṄ* 'go' and the causative of *dhṛ* 'hold' when no difficulty is involved. (3.2.131) (The suffix *ŚatṚ* is attached) to *dviṣ* 'hate' in the meaning of 'enemy.' (3.2.132) (The suffix *ŚatṚ* is attached) to *suÑ* 'press' when there is a connection with a sacrifice. (3.2.133) (The suffix *ŚatṚ* is attached) to *arh* 'deserve' when praise is expressed. (3.2.134) Up to 3.2.177, suffixes are attached to express habit, obligation, and ability. (3.2.135) The suffix *tṛN* is attached (to express these meanings). (3.2.136) The suffix *iṣṇuC* is attached to *kṛÑ* 'do,' preceded by *alam* and *nirā*, to *janA* 'be born,' by *pra*, to *pacA* 'ripen,' by *ud*, to *patA* 'fly,' by *ud*, to *madA* 'be mad,' by *ud*, to *rucI* 'shine', *trap* 'be ashamed,' by *apa*, to *vṛtU* 'turn,' *vṛdhU* 'grow,' *sahA* 'prevail,' *car* 'move' (3.2.137) In the Veda (the suffix *iṣṇuC* is attached) to causatives. (3.2.138) (The suffix *iṣṇuC* is attached) also to *bhū* 'be.' (3.2.139) The suffix *Ksnu* is attached to *glā* 'be exhausted,' *ji* 'conquer,' *sthā* 'stand,' as well (as to *bhū*). (3.2.140) The suffix *Knu* is attached to *trasI* 'tremble,' *gṛdhI* 'be greedy,' *dhṛṣI* 'dare,' *kṣipI* 'throw.' //7// (3.2.141) The suffix *GHinUṆ* is attached to the eight roots beginning with *śam* 'be calm.' (3.2.142) (The suffix *GHinUṆ* is attached) also to *pṛc* 'mix' preceded by *sam*, to *rudh* 'obstruct,' by *anu*, to *yam* 'hold,' by *āṄ*, to *yas* 'exert,' by *āṄ*, to *sṛ* 'run,' by *pari*, to *srjA* 'emit,' by *sam*, to *devI* 'lament,' by *pari*, to *jvarA* 'burn,' by *sam*, to *kṣipA* 'throw,' by *pari*, to *ratA* 'howl,' by *pari*, to *vadA* 'talk,' by *pari*, to *dahA* 'burn,' by *pari*, to *muhA* 'err' by *pari*, to *duṣA* 'make a mistake,' *dviṣA* 'hate,' *druhA* 'hurt,' *duhA* 'milk,' *yuj* 'join,' *krīḍA* 'play,' preceded by *ā*, to *vicA* 'separate,' by *vi*, to *tyajA* 'abandon,' *rajA* 'desire,' *bhajA* 'dispense,' *carA* 'move,' by *ati* and *apa*, to *muṣA* 'rob,' by *ā*, to *han* 'kill,' by *abhyā*. (3.2.143) (The suffix *GHinUṆ* is attached) to *kaṣ* 'hurt,' *lasA* 'sport,' *katthA* 'praise,' *srambh* 'believe,' preceded by *vi*. (3.2.144) (The suffix *GHinUṆ* is attached) to *laṣ* 'desire,' preceded by *apa* as well (as by *vi*).

Sūtra 3.2.123 has been made use of for dating Patañjali (cf. pages 79–81). Many sūtras in this fragment are discussed by Louis Renou in his article "La théorie des temps du verbe d'après les grammairiens sanskrits" (in the last section of this volume, pp. 500–525).

10

Ramkrishna Gopal Bhandarkar (1837–1925)

During the first half of the nineteenth century the foundations for the serious study of the Indian grammarians had been laid primarily by British Sanskritists, and some of the real importance of the subject had been recognized, mainly by German linguists. In the second half of the century this study began to flourish and yield results of lasting value. The most important contributions were due to Franz Kielhorn, a German scholar who spent part of his life in India. His contributions include the edition of Patañjali's *Mahābhāṣya*, the translation of Nāgojībhaṭṭa's *Paribhāṣenduśekhara*, a work of the eighteenth century, and many smaller studies. But there were also many other contributors, among whom O. Boehtlingk, T. Goldstücker, A. Weber, and, a little later, B. Liebich may be mentioned. A special place was occupied by Sir Ramkrishna Gopal Bhandarkar (1837–1925) who without being a pandit himself combined traditional scholarship and Western training (he regarded himself as an Indian scholar "of the new stamp"). His grammatical training was his main characteristic. "Bhandarkar's Physiologie ist die der indischen Grammatik," wrote Windisch (1921, 13). Bhandarkar became the best-known Indian Sanskritist of the nineteenth century. Kielhorn and Bhandarkar were colleagues at the Deccan College at Poona before Kielhorn was appointed at Göttingen. Many important papers by these two scholars, dealing with the Sanskrit grammarians, appeared in the *Indian Antiquary*, a periodical founded in 1872, published from Bombay, and first edited by James Burgess.

Before Bhandarkar and Kielhorn began to write, several important publications appeared, some of which should be mentioned. Boehtlingk published an edition of Pāṇini's *sūtras* in 1839, which depended largely on the *editio princeps* of Calcutta of 1809. It was not until 1887 that he brought out a much better edition, this time accompanied by a translation and extensive indexes (reprinted 1964). Boehtlingk also published the text of Vopadeva's *Mugdhabodha* (1847). In the meantime the Prātiśākhya literature, which deals mainly with Vedic phonology and phonetics (to be more exact, which provides for each Vedic text the rules to derive the *saṃhitā* from the *padapāṭha*), was beginning to become known. The first editor of the *Ṛkprātiśākhya* was the French Vedic philologist Adolphe Regnier; it appeared between 1856 and 1858 in the *Journal Asiatique*. Max Müller had begun an edition and translation of this text in 1856, but it was not published until 1869. Other Prātiśākhya texts were edited and translated by A. Weber (1858) and W. D. Whitney (1862, 1871). Another important early work, the *Nirukta*, dealing with Vedic etymology, was also beginning to be studied; the text was published in 1852 by Rudolph Roth.

In 1861 Theodor Goldstücker (1821–1872) published *Pāṇini: His Place in Sanskrit Literature*, a very remarkable monograph which evinces his quite extensive familiarity with the *Aṣṭādhyāyī* (recently reprinted twice: Varanasi 1965, Osnabrück 1966). Goldstücker had studied with A. W. von Schlegel and Lassen in Bonn, and with Eugène Burnouf (the famous son of Jean-Louis Burnouf, mentioned previously) in Paris. Wilson invited him to come to England to prepare a new edition of the Sanskrit dictionary. He was subsequently appointed as an honorary professor at the University College, London, in 1852. Goldstücker planned to bring out an edition of the *Mahābhāṣya*, and under his supervision two photolithographic reproductions of manuscripts of that text, one accompanied by Kaiyaṭa's commentary, were published (1874a and 1874b; see Plate IV; and see this volume, page 151, note 7).

Goldstücker's *Pāṇini*, an extraordinarily aggressive book, consists very largely of long refutations of the German Sanskritists, Roth, Boehtlingk (whom he always called the "editor" of Pāṇini's grammar), Weber, Max Müller, and others. This work did not in fact establish much. But it raised important problems and devoted much attention to the historical relationships among Pāṇini, Kātyāyana, Patañjali, the *Prātiśākhyas*, and the *Nirukta*. Goldstücker defended (as did Thieme more than half a century later) the priority of Pāṇini with regard to the Prātiśākhyas against the prevalent view of Roth, Müller, and Weber. He also attempted to settle Pāṇini's date and tried, with the help of an ingenious argument, to determine that Patañjali had written a certain portion of the *Mahābhāṣya* between 140 and 120 B.C.

Goldstücker's work attracted much criticism, and much of it was well deserved. Albrecht Weber devoted 176 pages of his periodical *Indische Studien* (5, 1862) to a critical review. He tried to show that almost all of Goldstücker's conclusions were untenable, or at least open to doubt. But Weber's own work was not free from defects, and the real shortcomings of Goldstücker became apparent only later.

Despite these activities, it was only with Kielhorn that a really new era of scholarship began. This was largely due to the fact that continental scholars such as Bühler and Kielhorn had now begun to deepen their knowledge of Sanskrit in India. Earlier, says Wackernagel, "eine Fahrt nach Indien oder gar längerer Aufenthalt daselbst kam gar nicht in Frage. — Nun aber begann eine ganz neue Periode. Nun wurden europäisches und indisches Können in Verbindung gebracht, nun der Forschung aller aus dem Boden Indiens eine Fülle neuer Schätze zugeführt" (Wackernagel 1908, 5).

Bhandarkar had written a review of Goldstücker's *Pāṇini*, which first appeared in a local newspaper, *Native Opinion*, on August 21 and 28, 1864. At Kielhorn's suggestion, it was reprinted in the *Indian Antiquary* (6, 1877, 108–113). It is a good specimen of Bhandarkar's style and scholarly qualities and deserves to be republished if only because of the recent reprints of Goldstücker's work. In addition, it is of particular interest because it deals with Pāṇini's treatment of names and his use of technical terms, both called *saṃjñā* or *sanjñā* in Sanskrit.

A. Review of Goldstücker's Pāṇini (1864, 1877)

Ramkrishna Gopal Bhandarkar

Dr. Goldstücker is undoubtedly one of the most learned, laborious, and accurate European Sanskrit scholars we have known, and the wide and, in many cases, precise knowledge he has shown of Indian grammatical literature is particularly striking to a Hindu, especially when we call to mind that he has not had the advantage of oral instruction, which is available only in India. Of course a minute knowledge of the complicated and subtle speculations of Indian grammarians can only be acquired after a hard study of at least five years, and from a Paṇḍit-teacher. But much of what they have written is barren and useless, and no European Sanskritist, or Indian scholar of the new stamp, would consider it worth his while to study it. The doctor's critical acumen, the skill with which he has brought together stray facts to illustrate and prove his points, and the success with which he has combated the opinions of several scholars, command our admiration, though we are rather inclined to think he has handled some of his German friends somewhat roughly. His book is, however, not without its weak points, and there are three or four places where it appears to us to be particularly so. It is not our intention at present to write an elaborate review of it, but we will notice one point which bears materially on his theory about Pāṇini, the Indian grammatical legislator.

At page 166, Dr. Goldstücker lays down the four following propositions:—

1. That his (Pāṇini's) Grammar does not treat of those *sanjñās* or conventional names which are known and settled otherwise.
2. That this term *sanjñā* must be understood in our rule to concern only such conventional names as have an etymology.
3. That it applies also to grammatical terms which admit of an etymology, but not to those which are merely grammatical symbols.
4. That such terms as *ṭi*, *ghu*, and *bha were known and settled before Pāṇini's Grammar*, but that nevertheless they are defined by Pāṇini, because they are not etymological terms.

These four statements contain, according to Dr. Goldstücker, the principles which guided Pāṇini in the composition of his work, and are deduced as conclusions from one of his *sūtras*, Patañjali's *Bhāṣya* on it, and Kaiyaṭa's gloss on the latter. Leaving these points for fuller examination at the end, let us in the first place consider if these principles are worthy of being made the basis of a stupendous grammatical superstructure, and bear an air of truthfulness about them, or if there is any external evidence to support them.

According to the first two statements, Pāṇini does not propose to teach *sanjñās*, and such *sanjñās* only as have an etymology. Does he, then, propose to teach *sanjñās* which are without etymology? The "only" would show that he does propose this. What, then, is meant by *sanjñās without etymology?* Are such *sanjñās* as *Pañcālāḥ*, *Varaṇāḥ*, *Aṅgāḥ*, which are given by the commentators as instances of this *sūtra* and the previous one to which it refers, and which, therefore are the *sanjñās* Pāṇini, according to them, does not propose to teach,—are these *sanjñās*, we ask, without etymology? If they are, according to Dr. Goldstücker, Pāṇini should teach them. If they are not, no instance can be given of a word existing in the language which is a *sanjñā* without etymology. If we bear in mind that two schools of etymology existed in India, viz. *vyutpatti pakṣa*, according to which all words have an etymology, and *avyutpatti pakṣa*, according to which some have, and some have not, and that Pāṇini belonged to the latter, as is asserted and believed by all śāstris, such words as *pañcālāḥ* and *aṅgāḥ* are *sanjñās* without etymology. And if this be joined with Dr. Goldstücker's statement it will follow that Pāṇini should teach them. But as a fact he does not, if we believe the commentators. Now with regard to the *vyutpatti pakṣa*, we see that the rule in question contradicts its doctrine, for according to that *pakṣa* all words, *sanjñās* included, have etymology, while the rule makes a distinction between words *with* and words *without* etymology. If we suppose, then, that Pāṇini belonged to this *pakṣa*, and at the same time that he observed the rule given by Dr. Goldstücker, we must either suppose him to have possessed an extremely illogical mind, or not to have proposed such a rule for his guidance. Upon either view of etymology, therefore, we maintain that the rule laid down in statements Nos. 1 and 2 could not have been followed by Pāṇini. We perfectly agree with statement No. 1 if it be separated from No. 2, and not interpreted according to the sense of the word *sanjñā* given in the latter.

In the next two statements, this rule is applied to grammatical *sanjñās*. Such as are settled are not to be defined, but an exception is to be made in favour of such as have no etymology, e.g. *ṭi*, *ghu*, *bha*, &c. We see no reason why Pāṇini should select for definition, out of settled *sanjñās*, such as have no etymology. For, both those with and those without etymology are settled, *i.e.* have a fixed meaning. The mere circumstance of some *sanjñās* having etymology, which may be considered as the reason why they are not to be defined, is immaterial, as the presence of etymology in the one case is nearly the same thing as its absence in the other. The etymology of a technical term is not sufficient to explain its sense, and in some cases it affords no clue to it whatever. How can the etymology of the terms *bahuvrīhi*, *pratyaya*, &c. enable one to understand their grammatical signification? In so far, then, as words with etymology are used in philosophical treatises in a sense different from the etymological, or from that they have in common language, they are in the same predicament as unmeaning words, such as *ṭi*, *ghu*, &c. We see, therefore, no reason why Pāṇini should have selected the latter for definition, and not the former.

Having laid down this theory about Pāṇini's technical terms, Dr. Goldstücker proceeds to test its accuracy with reference to several *sanjñās* which he knows were settled before Pāṇini's time, such as *pratyaya*, *prathamā*, *dvītīyā*, *tatpuruṣa*, &c., and finds that he has not defined them, as they have an etymology. He then mentions other *sanjñās*, such as *karmadhāraya*, *sanyoga*, *anunāsika*, *hrasva*, *dīrgha*, *udātta*, *anudātta*, &c., and since they are defined and possess etymology, he concludes that they must have been first used by Pāṇini himself. We cannot help thinking that there is here an instance of the fallacy of *reasoning in a circle*, or of the *anyonyāśraya* of Hindu logicians. In order that Dr. Goldstücker's theory may be true, it is necessary that these defined *sanjñās* possessing etymology should be inventions of Pāṇini, and they are inventions of Pāṇini because the theory is true. Or, in plainer terms, the theory is true because these defined *sanjñās* are Pāṇini's inventions, and they are Pāṇini's inventions because the theory is true. These defined *sanjñās* may have been settled *before* Pāṇini's time, in which case the doctor's theory would be false. And in fact we have reason to believe that such *sanjñās* as *hrasva*, *dīrgha*, *pluta*, *udātta*, *anudātta*, &c. were invented before Pāṇini. We are sorry we have not got any treatise on *Śikṣā* to refer to just now, but considering that the names for accents and for long and short vowels must have been very early invented by grammarians, as they are the most elementary distinctions, and likely to strike a lingual philosopher before many others, and bearing also in mind that if different terms for these had existed before Pāṇini, they would not have been altogether lost, and we should have known them, we are inclined to believe that the names in question were settled before his time. Dr. Goldstücker himself mentions one such word (*dvandva*), and is not inclined to disbelieve that there may be many more. But the supposition he makes, to save his theory, that Pāṇini used them in a sense somewhat different from that in which they were before used, has, in our opinion, no basis.

We have all along used the word *definition* in Dr. Goldstücker's sense. He seems to understand by the term *definition* such a definition as is commonly given in European books, viz. that which unfolds the connotation or comprehension of a term. But the principal object of a definition is to point out or distinguish certain things (*definitum*) from the rest, and this may be done in other ways than by unfolding the connotation. Unfolding the extension or denotation is often an easier process, and may in several cases be resorted to. Even European logicians call this latter a definition, no less than the former. Sanskrit writers do not confine themselves to the former, but frequently use the latter and several other kinds. For instance, in Viśvanātha Pañcānana's *Muktāvali* (p. 71 Asiatic Society's edition) the fallacy *anaikāntika* is defined as that which is any one of *Sādhāraṇa*, &c., *i.e. anaikāntika* is either *Sādhāraṇa*, *Asādhāraṇa*, or *Anupasanhārin*. The fallacy is thus defined by enumerating its several kinds. We need not stop here to quote other instances. Any one who takes the trouble will find many in any Sanskrit philosophical treatise. What we maintain, then, is that, so far as this view of definition is concerned (and we are convinced that that is the Hindu view), Pāṇini *has* defined the terms *pratyaya*, *tatpuruṣa*, *bahuvrīhi*, &c., which Dr. Goldstücker says he has not; but he has defined them by enumerating the several kinds or individuals contained under them. To Hindu writers such a definition is as good as the other, especially when the latter is difficult to give. We think Pāṇini in defining terms by enumeration was not guided by any such rule as the learned doctor lays down, but he simply consulted his own convenience. When he found it difficult to give a connotative definition, he gave a denotative one. How difficult would it have been to give a connotative definition of *bahuvrīhi*, for instance, containing as it does such compounds as *uttarapūrvā* [Northeast], *saputra* [accompanied by his son], *daṇḍādaṇḍi* [stick against stick], so different from such a one as *kamalanayana* [lotus-eyed].

We now proceed to examine the principal evidence upon which Dr. Goldstücker's theory is based. As we said before, he quotes a *sūtra* of Pāṇini, the *bhāṣya* on it, and Kaiyaṭa's gloss on the latter, and deduces his theory from these. When we read this portion of the book for the first time, we were surprised to find that the doctor had not understood one of the passages correctly. The *sūtra* referred to is *tad aśiṣyaṃ saṃjñāpramāṇatvāt*. Dr. Goldstücker's translation:— "Such matter will not be taught by me, for it falls under the category of conventional terms which are settled (and therefore do not require any rule of mine;" *literally*, "for it has the authority of a *sanjñā* or conventional term)."

This translation is generally correct. We would, however, translate it more closely, thus:—"About that no rule ought to be made, *or*, that should not be taught, for (the knowledge derived from) the meaning of conventional terms in common usage is an authority in itself." The word *saṃjñā* is explained by Patañjali as *saṃjñānam*, which again Kaiyaṭa interprets by *saṃpratyayaḥ, avagamaḥ, i.e.* knowledge obtained (from usage). In a note on that portion of the *Siddhānta Kaumudī* (Cowell's edition), where this *sūtra* is explained, we find the following:—*saṃjñānāṃ lokavyavahārāṇām evātra pramāṇatvam*, "*sanjñās*—that is, usages—are here an authority or evidence."

The *bhāṣya* on this *sūtra* is as follows:—*kiṃ yā etāḥ kṛtrimāṣ ṭighubhādisaṃjñās tatprāmāṇyād aśiṣyam | netyāha | saṃjñānaṃ saṃjñā |*. Dr. Goldstücker's translation:—"When Pāṇini speaks of conventional terms which he will not teach, because they are settled, does he mean, by this expression, such technical terms as *ṭi, ghu, bha*, and the like? No; for *sanjñā* is here the same as *sanjñāna*, understanding (*i.e.* a name which has a real meaning, that may be traced etymologically)."

We do not see whence he gets the first portion up to "settled." If by implication, we do not think it necessary to understand anything. There is nothing even in the *sūtra* which has the sense of the words "which he will not teach, because they are settled." For what Pāṇini says he will not teach is *that* something which he has alluded to in the last *sūtra* but one, and which we shall explain hereafter. We do not deny that this sense may be inferred from what Pāṇini actually says. We have, however, a particular objection to the expression "are settled" if it is to be made applicable to the terms *ṭi, ghu, bha* &c., and understood to mean "settled before Pāṇini's time." There is nothing in the original corresponding to the words enclosed in brackets in the above extract, nor is the sense deducible from any word occurring in the Sanskrit passage. There is, no doubt, the word *sanjñānam*, but we do not know upon what authority Dr. Goldstücker renders it by "a name which has a real meaning that may be traced etymologically." Kaiyaṭa explains it by *avagama, saṃpratyaya*, as noticed above, which means '*knowing, comprehending*,' as is evident from his use of the word *avagati* (differing from *avagama* only in the form and not in the sense of the termination) in the sentence which follows. It is this:—*tatra yathāpo dārāḥ sikatā varṣā ity ukte liṅgasaṃkhyāviśeṣāvagatir utpadyamānā pramāṇam evaṃ pañcālā varaṇāḥ ity ādāv api*:— "As when one pronounces the words *āpaḥ, dārāḥ, sikatāḥ, varṣāḥ*, the *avagati* (knowledge or comprehension) of a particular number and gender which is produced is authority, so is it in the case of *pañcālāḥ, varaṇāḥ*," &c. Our translation of the passage in question is as follows:—"Is it on account of the *authority* of (or evidence afforded by) such artificial *sanjñās* as *ṭi, ghu, bha*, &c. that *that* (the thing mentioned in a previous *sūtra* alluded to before) should not be taught." "No," says he (Gonardīya—Patañjali). "*Sanjñā* is *knowing, comprehending*." Upon the whole, Dr. Goldstücker's translation of these two passages is not very objectionable, but they do not afford any basis for his theory, except for that portion of it which is comprehended in the first statement. But the quotation from Kaiyaṭa is altogether misunderstood. It runs thus:—

kiṃ yā etā iti | pratyāsattinyāyāśrayeṇa praśnaḥ nety āheti | pratyāsatteḥ sāmarthyaṃ balavat | nahi ṭighubhādisaṃjñānāṃ pramāṇatvaṃ yuktavadbhāvaśāstrasyāśiṣyatve hetur upapadyate | saṃbandhābhāvāt | saṃjñānam iti | avagamaḥ saṃpratyaya ity arthaḥ |

And Dr. Goldstücker's translation of this is as follows:—

"The question of Patañjali is suggested by the rule of analogy. His answer is in the negative because the context itself has greater weight than (mere) analogy. Now, though such terms as *ṭi, ghu, bha*, and the like, are settled terms, this circumstance would not have been a sufficient reason in an *etymological* work (like that of Pāṇini) for leaving them untaught, for they have no etymology. 'Understanding' (as Patañjali paraphrases *sanjñā*), means mentally entering into, understanding the component parts of a word (or it means the words which admit of this mental process)."

In the first sentence of this, the word *analogy* is not, we think, a correct translation of *pratyāsatti*, though it will do. "Proximity" is the word that is equivalent to it, and it ought to have been used here, for a reason which we shall presently explain. But it is the third sentence that is the most objectionable of all. We have no hesitation in saying that the translation here is totally wrong, and it is upon this misapprehension of the sense of the original that the doctor's peculiar theory is based. We hope our readers will excuse us for the assurance with which we speak; for we feel that no native scholar acquainted with grammatical phraseology would ever think of translating or interpreting the passage thus. As Dr. Goldstücker translates it, he appears to connect the nouns *pramāṇatvam* and *aśiṣyatve* with the genitive *ṭighubhādisaṃjñānām* and renders the former by "being settled." But *aśiṣyatve* ought really to be taken with the genitive *yuktavadbhāvaśāstrasya*; and then the translation would be "for leaving *yuktavadbhāvaśāstra* untaught," instead of "for leaving them (i.e. *ṭi*, *ghu*, *bha* &c.) untaught," as the Doctor translates it. *Yuktavadbhāvaśāstra* is rendered "an etymological work," which, if one remembers what the *sūtra* is about, he will at once see is altogether wrong. The word can by no stretch of sense mean that. *Śāstra* means here '*a rule*,' as it frequently and primarily does, and not '*a work*.' Various instances may be quoted in support of this, the last *pāda* of the verse about Uṇādi, *etac chāstram uṇādiṣu*, being one. *Saṃbandhābhāvāt* is rendered as "having no etymology," for which, however, there is not the slightest authority. *Saṃbandha* never means *etymology*; it means *connection*. Besides, from the context it is clear that the sentence cannot have the sense Dr. Goldstücker attaches to it. For, the whole subject here discussed by these several writers is this:—The last but one *sūtra* of Pāṇini is *lupi yuktavadvyaktivacane*, which is thus explained in the *Siddhānta Kaumudī*:— *lupi sati prakṛtivalliṅgavacane staḥ* | *pañcālānāṃ nivāso janapadaḥ pañcālāḥ* | *kuravaḥ* | *aṅgāḥ* | &c., meaning that when an elision called *lup* takes place, the gender and number (of the noun) are like those of the base; *pañcālāḥ* &c. are instances. This requires some explanation. In virtue of the *sūtra tasya nivāsaḥ* 4,2,69, the termination *aṇ* should be added to the noun *pañcālāḥ* for instance, when we have to form a derivative signifying '*the place of residence or the country* of the Pañcālās,' a race of Kshatriyas (hence the above example from the *Kaumudī* is worded *pañcālānāṃ nivāso janapadaḥ*). Now, this termination is elided in virtue of the *sūtra janapade lup* 4, 2, 81. If the termination were not dropped, the word expressing 'the country of the Pañcālās' would be *pāñcālaḥ*. Then the question is, when it is dropped, what should be the gender and number of the noun signifying the *country*? Should it be masculine and singular, as the word *janapada country* is? If so, the derived word would be *pañcālaḥ*. But "No," says Pāṇini (in the *sūtra lupi yuktavat* &c.); "the gender and number should be like those of the original base," which is *pañcālāḥ*, and, consequently, masculine and plural. Hence the noun signifying the residence or country of the Pañcālās is *pañcālāḥ*. "Now," says Pāṇini (in the *sūtra tad aśiṣyaṃ saṃjñāpramāṇatvāt*), "what is the use of teaching by a rule the number and gender of these?" though he himself, in conformity with the practice of former writers, has done so. "They are to be learnt from usage, which has itself an authority, just as the gender and number of *āpaḥ* and *dārāḥ* are, and the authority of a grammarian is not required. For *pañcālāḥ*, *aṅgāḥ*, &c. in the plural are actually the names of certain countries, and, as such, ought to be used in the plural, in deference to the existing usage, and there is no necessity of a grammarian's teaching it." Upon this Patañjali raises the question, "Pāṇini speaks of the authority (of usage in matters) of names. Are they such names as *ṭi*, *ghu*, *bha* &c., which have an authority" (as used by Pāṇini, not necessarily by any other writer)? "No," says he. Kaiyaṭa explains why Patañjali put to himself such a question. "He was led," he says, "to it by the proximity of these artificial grammatical *sanjñās*, or that he wanted to determine which were the *sanjñās* meant by Pāṇini; because if he did not do so, a reader might, on reading the *sūtra* in question, be led to think first of them (the grammatical names) rather than of any other, on account of their proximity to or connection with the science he is studying. In order, therefore, to avoid all such confusion, he proposes the question, and answers it by saying 'No.'" Why not? "(*hi*) Because," says Kaiyaṭa, "(*ṭi-ghubhādisaṃjñānāṃ pramāṇatvam*) the authority of the grammatical *sanjñās ṭi*, *ghu*, *bha* &c. (*na hetur upapadyate*) is no reason (as the authority of *sanjñās* in common language such as *Pañcālāḥ*, *Aṅgāḥ*, &c. is) why *yuktavadbhāvaśāstram* (a *sūtra* or rule expounding that when a termination is elided by the use of the term *lup*, the gender and number are like those of the base) (*aśiṣyatve*) should not be taught." And why is it no reason? "(*saṃbandhābhāvāt*) Because there is no connection" (*i.e.* no connection between such *sanjñās* as *ṭi*, *ghu*, &c. and *yuktavadbhāva*). This is the whole sense of the three quotations. *Yuktavad*, *i.e.* like the base, is the word used by Pāṇini in the last but one *sūtra* (*lupi yuktavat*), &c.; and Kaiyaṭa first adds the word *bhāva* to it, when the whole means "the being like the base," and then the word *śāstram*, *a rule*, and thus the expression *yuktavadbhāvaśāstram* signifies *literally* "the rule about the being like the base," and not an *etymological work*, as Dr. Goldstücker understands.

It will thus be apparent that Dr. Goldstücker's theory is based upon a misapprehension of a passage in Kaiyaṭa; and, now that we have explained its true sense, and have also shown that the theory is not supported by any external evidence, it must, we think, be given up. The first of the doctor's four propositions if separated from the second we agree with, as we have already intimated. Dr. Goldstücker's opinion, that the *sanjñās ṭi*, *ghu*, and *bha* were known before Pāṇini's time, may be true, for aught we know, but it does not at all follow from anything in the passages commented on. He was, no doubt, led to it by the expression *ṭighubhādisaṃjñānāṃ pramāṇatvam*, which he renders by "such terms as *ṭi*, *ghu*, *bha*, are settled terms." We would translate it as *the authority of such sanjñās or terms as ṭi*, *ghu*, *bha*, &c., and this authority they derive from their having been used and defined by Pāṇini. The whole grammatical literature based on his work does not admit the authority of any other person except him, his continuator and critic Kātyāyana, and his *bhāṣyakāra*. And even if we take Dr. Goldstücker's translation, the expression "are settled terms" does not necessarily mean "settled" *before Pāṇini's* time, or by any other person than Pāṇini himself.

Dr. Goldstücker has also misunderstood the sense of the *sūtra pradhānapratyayārthavacanam arthasyānyapramāṇatvāt*, which is thus explained in the *Kaumudī*: *pratyayārthaḥ pradhānam ity evaṃ rūpaṃ vacanam apy aśiṣyam | kutaḥ | arthasya lokata eva siddheḥ* | *i.e.* "the saying that the sense of a termination is the principal sense of a word (and that that of the base is attributively joined to it) should not be taught. Why? Because the sense (of a word) is to be gathered from, or is established by, *usage*." We do not know whence Dr. Goldstücker brings in the idea of a compound and its "principal part" in his translation. We do not think it necessary to enter at greater length into the explanation of the *sūtra* in this place.

We must here close our remarks; our space does not admit of a more lengthened notice, at least for the present. We hope our observations will be calmly and patiently attended to by European Sanskritists.... In several cases, though not in all, native students of Sanskrit have a greater right to be listened to than Europeans. We are also desirous that these few remarks should not give pain to Dr. Goldstücker, who, especially by his articles on our religious difficulties published in the *Westminster Review*, has shown himself to be our decided friend, who sympathizes with our fallen condition, and is ready to help us by his friendly advice in our race towards a brighter future.

B. On the Date of Patañjali and the King in Whose Reign He Lived (1872)

Ramkrishna Gopal Bhandarkar

In "On the date of Patañjali and the King in Whose Reign He Lived" (1872), Bhandarkar turned to Patañjali's *Mahābhāṣya* and found further evidence to corroborate the date Goldstücker had proposed. The argument is of special interest because it illustrates how the Sanskrit grammarians' carefully recorded observations on the use of tenses could be used for the determination of historical data. This line of research was later developed by others (for example, Liebich 1930, *Einleitung zu Anhang* III, 265–289). The paper also refers to Pāṇini's *sūtra* 1.1.68, which introduces the distinction between "use" and "mention" and which was for that reason studied by Brough three quarters of a century afterward (see pages 402–414 of this volume). Bhandarkar's article was published in the *Indian Antiquary* (1, 1872, 299–302).

Patañjali's date has been dealt with again in a more recent study (Frauwallner 1960), in which a later date than the traditional second century B.C. is suggested; see also Staal (1967, 48–49). The pivotal sūtra 3.2.123 occurs on the manuscript page illustrated in Plate III.

In Patañjali's *Mahābhāṣya* or great commentary on Pāṇini, a rule (vārtika) laid down by Kātyāyana, is given, teaching that the Imperfect should be used to signify an action not witnessed by the speaker but capable of being witnessed by him and known to people in general. Of this rule Patañjali gives two instances: "The Yavana besieged (aruṇat) Sāketa" and "The Yavana besieged (aruṇat) the Mādhyamikas." The siege of Sāketa, therefore, must be considered to have been an event capable of being witnessed by the speaker, *i.e.* by Patañjali himself, in other words, some Yavana king must have besieged Sāketa in Patañjali's time. Sāketa is the usual name for Ayodhyā. Reasoning in this way, the late Prof. Goldstücker arrived at the conclusion that the Yavana here spoken of must have been Menandros, King of Baktria, who is said to have pushed his conquests in India to the river Yamunā Menandros, according to Prof. Lassen, became king about 144.

B.C. Patañjali therefore must have lived about that time.

But there is another passage in Patañjali not noticed by Prof. Goldstücker, in which the name of the king of Pāṭaliputra, during whose reign he flourished, is given, and which enables us to arrive at the date of the author of the Mahābhāṣya in another way and from other data. In his remarks on Pāṇ. III. 2–123, Patañjali quotes a *vārtika* of Kātyāyana, the meaning of which is "A rule should be made teaching the use of the present tense (*laṭ*) to denote an action or undertaking which has been begun but not finished." The examples given by Patañjali are:—"Here we study;" "Here we dwell;" "Here we perform (as priests) the sacrifices (instituted) by Puṣpamitra." Then Patañjali asks "How is it that Pāṇini's rule III. 2–123, (*vartamāne laṭ*), which teaches that the present tense should be used to denote present time, does not extend to these cases?" The answer is, "the time here involved is not present time." How not? This question is answered by Kaiyaṭa, whose gloss upon this runs as follows:—"The phrase 'here we study' means that study has begun but not ended. When the students being engaged in dining and doing such other things do not study they cannot then properly say 'we study' (according to Pāṇ. III. 2–123, *i.e.*, they cannot use the present tense, for it is not *study* that is then going on, and consequently the time is not present;) hence the rule by Kātyāyana."[1] The sense of the whole is, that when an action, such as that of studying or performing the great sacrifices, spreads over many days, the present tense should be used to denote it, if the action has begun but not ended, even though at the time of speaking the speaker may not be actually performing the action. "Here we sacrifice for Puṣpamitra," is Patañjali's example. Now this cannot be an imaginary instance, for such a one would not bring out the distinctive sense that Patañjali wishes to convey, namely, that the action has begun but not ended. This example then expresses a fact; *i.e.*, that at the time Patañjali wrote, there lived a person named Puṣpamitra and a great sacrifice was being performed for him and under his orders. If he employed priests to perform the great sacrifices for him he must have been a king; for in the olden days it was Indian kings that propitiated the gods and patronized the Brahmans in this way. The sacrifices were always expensive, and were treated rather as extraordinary festivals than ordinary religious performances. But in another part of the *Mahābhāṣya* we are actually told who this Puṣpamitra was. Pāṇini (in I. 1, 68) tells us that any grammatical change or operation that he may have in his work prescribed in the case of a certain word ought to be made applicable to that word alone and not to what it signifies, or to its synonyms. This, however, does not hold in the case of his own technical terms. Thus, for instance, to form derivatives in a certain sense from the word *agni* (fire) the termination *eya* should, he says, be applied to *agni*. The meaning of this rule should not be stretched

[1] Pāṇini *vartamāne laṭ* III. 2, 123, Kātyāyana *pravṛttasyāvirāme śiṣyā bhavanty avartamānatvāt* | Patañjali *pravṛttasyāvirāme śāsitavyā bhavanti* | *ihādhīmahe* | *iha vasāmaḥ* | *iha puṣpamitraṃ yājayāmaḥ* | *kiṃ punaḥ kāraṇaṃ na sidhyati* | *avartamānatvāt* | Kaiyaṭa *pravṛttasyeti* | *ihādhīmaha ity adhyayanaṃ pravṛttaṃ prārabdhaṃ na ca tad viratam* | *yadā ca bhojanādikāṃ kriyāṃ kurvanto nādhīyate tadā 'dhīmaha iti prayogo na prāpnotīti vacanam* | Patañjali then proceeds to say that the sense is conveyed by Pāṇ. III-2-123 and no new rule is required, but this has no bearing on the present question.

so as to make it applicable not only to *agni*, but to other words also, having the sense of *agni*. *Vahni* for instance also means fire but does not take that termination. But in the case of the technical terms of grammar, the change or operation should be effected in the case of the things (which of course are words) signified by that term. Thus, for instance, when he tells us to apply a certain termination to *ghu*, it is to be applied, not to *ghu* itself, but to the roots to which the name *ghu* is given by him. Now Patañjali, after a long discussion of this rule, in the course of which he shows that it is not wanted, though out of respect for the great Ācārya he does not distinctly say so, tells us that there are some sūtras in which the rules given are applicable,—1, sometimes to the synonyms of the words,—2, sometimes to the individuals comprised under the species denoted by the words,—3, sometimes to the words alone, and, sometimes to any two of these three. In these cases some indicatory letters ought, he says, to be attached to the words to show to which, or to which two, of the three categories the rule is to be applied. Then in such rules as II. 4, 23, which teaches that a Tatpuruṣa compound ending in the words *sabhā* (court or assembly) preceded by *rājan* (king) becomes neuter he tells us that *j* should be attached to *rājan* and others, to show that the rule is applicable only to the synonyms of *rājan* and others, and not to *rājan* or others themselves, or to the individuals comprised under the species denoted by *rājan* and others. And the instances he gives to show that it is not applicable to individual *rājās* or kings are *Puṣpamitra-sabhā* (the assembly or court of Puṣpamitra) and *Candragupta-sabhā*[2] (the assembly or court of Candragupta) in which we see that the compound is not neuter but feminine. We thus come to the conclusion that Puṣpamitra was the name of a king.

Now we know that the most powerful kingdom during a few centuries before Christ, the sovereigns of which extended their sway over a large portion of India, was that of Magadha, the capital of which was Pāṭaliputra. And Patañjali so often speaks of this city in his work[3] that we must infer that he had a great deal to do with Pāṭaliputra, and perhaps lived there for some time, and that on that account the city and things concerning it were uppermost in his thoughts. The Puṣpamitra then that he speaks of in the two cases here pointed out, must have been king of Pāṭaliputra in his time. And the fact of his being mentioned along with Candragupta in one of the two cases strengthens this inference. For Candragupta the Maurya was king of Magadha, and there was no other Candragupta till several centuries afterwards when the Gupta dynasty came into power.

Now looking into the Purāṇas we find that there was only one king of Magadha of the name of Puṣpamitra, the founder of the Śunga dynasty, which succeeded the Mauryas. He was the Commander-in-Chief of Bṛhadratha, the last Maurya king, and usurped the throne after having killed his master. The ten Mauryas are said to have ruled the kingdom for 137 years. The

[2] Patañjali *jitparyāyavacanasyaiva rājādyartham | jinnirdeśaḥ kartavyaḥ | tato vaktavyaṃ paryāyavacanasyaiva grahaṇaṃ bhavati | kiṃ prayojanam | rājādyartham | sabhā rājām anuṣya-pūrvām | inasabham īśvarasabham | tasyaiva na bhavati | rājasabhā tadviśeṣāṇāṃ ca na bhavati | puṣpamitrasabhā | candraguptasabhā |*

[3] See amongst others his comments on I-3-2, II-1-16, II-3-28, III-3-134, and 136 and V-3-57. In the second of these, one of the examples given is *anuśoṇaṃ pāṭaliputram.*

accession of Candragupta, the first of these ten, has been fixed about 315 B.C. Puṣpamitra, therefore, must have raised himself to the throne about 178 B.C. The Mātsya Purāṇa assigns him a reign of 36 years, *i.e.* from 178 B.C. to 142 B.C. It follows then that Patañjali wrote his comments on Pāṇ. III. 2, 123 some time between these limits. The limits assigned by Dr. Goldstücker, reasoning from the one example he considers, are 140 and 120 B.C. But there is apparently no reason why he should not take into account the earlier years of Menandros's reign. For, according to Prof. Lassen, Menandros must have become king about 144 B.C. The passage in the Mahābhāṣya, on which I base my conclusion, is not far from the one noticed by Dr. Goldstücker. The latter occurs in the comments on III. 2, 111, while the former in those on III.2, 123. We thus see that when this portion of the Bhāṣya was written, a Yavana king (who must have been Menandros) had laid siege to Sāketa or Ayodhyā, and Puṣpamitra was reigning at Pāṭaliputra; and if we adhere to Lassen's chronology these two things could have happened only between 144 B.C. and 142 B.C.; for there is, I think, no reason to distrust the chronology of the Purāṇas here, since the date arrived at from the statements contained in them coincide in a remarkable degree with that determined from the evidence of coins. And even supposing that Prof. Lassen's date is not quite accurate, it must be admitted that it cannot be very far wrong.

We thus see that Patañjali lived in the reign of Puṣpamitra, and that he probably wrote the third chapter of his Bhāṣya between 144 B.C. and 142 B.C. And this agrees with the conclusion drawn by Prof. Goldstücker from a statement in another part of the work that the author of the *Mahābhāṣya* flourished after the Maurya dynasty was extinct. Since all the passages then, and the different historical events they point to, lead us to about the same period, the date of Patañjali so derived must be regarded as trustworthy, and in the History of Sanskrit Literature it is of great importance.

C. Ācārya, the Friend of the Student, and the Relations between the Three Ācāryas (1876)

Ramkrishna Gopal Bhandarkar

The preceding paper of Bhandarkar's, along with another one dealing with the age of the *Mahābhārata*, led to a long discussion with Weber. These discussions of Bhandarkar with European scholars are interesting in more than one way. Quite apart from their scholarly content, they show quite clearly that Indian scholars were in a better position to contribute to Sanskrit scholarship in such fields as the Indian grammarians (and Indian scholarly (*śāstra*) literature in general) than European scholars had first thought they would be. Discussions of this sort led to interesting reactions on both sides. Bhandarkar expressed his own feelings about European scholarship only much later, when describing to the Bombay branch of the Royal Asiatic Society, his visit to the Vienna Oriental Congress of 1886 (printed in the *Bombay Journal* (17, 1889, 72–95) and reprinted in the *Collected Works* (I, 1933, 332–360)). His is an entertaining observation which throws much light on the general situation of Sanskrit studies in Europe at the time. After describing the main achievements of European scholars in the field of Sanskrit studies, Bhandarkar addressed his Bombay audience as follows (pages 348–351 of the reprinted version):

In this work of study and research the Germans, of all the nations of Europe, have been the foremost. Most of the great achievements I have briefly indicated above are due to their patient industry and critical acumen. We have had one great French scholar, and there are now two or three. Englishmen first of all discovered Sanskrit, as was of course to be expected from the fact of India's having fallen into their hands, and we have had first-class English scholars, such as Colebrooke and Wilson. But somehow Sanskrit and philological studies have not found a congenial soil in the British isles. While there are at present twenty-five German scholars at least who have been working in the different branches of Sanskrit literature and have published something, we have not more than five among Englishmen. England employs Germans in connection with her philological work. The best Sanskrit scholar in the country is a German, and the Professor of Sanskrit at Edinburgh and the Librarian of the India Office are Germans. There is a German in charge of Manuscripts in the British Museum and the Assistant Librarian at the Bodleian is a Hungarian. The Germans are the Brahmans of Europe, the French the Kṣatriyas, and the English the Vaiśyas; though, as was the case in India, the Brahmans of Europe have now taken to a military occupation. The great excellence of German scholarship consists in the spirit of criticism and comparison that is brought to bear on the facts that come under observation, and in the endeavour made to trace the gradual development of thought and language and to determine the chronological relations of events.

So much for the bright side of the picture. But it has also a dark side, to shut our eyes to which will do no good to the cause or to anybody. The proper and fruitful exercise of the critical and comparative, or what might be called the historical spirit, depends upon innate ability and a naturally sound judgment. These are not to be found everywhere, and often we meet with instances in which very comprehensive conclusions are based upon the most slender evidence. Though it is true that a native does not easily look at the language, thought, and institutions of his country from the critical standpoint, while the first impulse of an intelligent foreigner is to do so, still there are some disadvantages under which the foreigner must labour. He has no full and familiar knowledge of what he subjects to a critical examination. In the case of European Sanskrit scholars there is besides always a very strong disinclination to admit the high antiquity of any book, thought, or institution, and a tendency to trace Greek influence everywhere in our literature; while not seldom the major premise in the reasoning is that the Indians cannot have any good in them, since several times in the course of their history, they allowed themselves to be conquered by foreigners. Oftentimes the belief that the Brahmans are a crafty race prevents a full perception of the truth. Of course, scholars of ability and sound judgment shake off such tendencies and prejudices; and among these I may mention, since I do not wish to make invidious comparisons between living scholars, Dr. Muir of Edinburgh and Prof. Goldstücker.

But independently of such defects in the exercise of the critical faculty, there are very important branches of Sanskrit literature which are not understood in Germany and Europe. I had a conversation with Dr. Kielhorn on this subject the day after I reached Vienna. I said it appeared to me that works in the narrative of Purāṇic style and the dramatic plays were alone properly understood in Europe, while those written in the style of discourse or works on philosophy and exegesis were not. He replied that even several of the dramatic plays and works on Poetics were not understood. Mistakes are constantly made when a scholar endeavours to interpret and criticise a work or passages in a work belonging to any of the Śāstras, as we call them; and often the sense of passages containing idiomatic expressions in other works also is not perceived. A scholar reads such a work or interprets such expressions and passages with the aid of a grammar and a dictionary; but a clear understanding of them requires an amount of previous knowledge which cannot be derived from either. As to positive command over Sanskrit, I had an illustration in the shape of a card which was given to me by a Professor at the Congress on which two verses in the easiest of Sanskrit metres, the Anuṣṭubh, composed by him, are printed. In three of the four lines the metre is violated, and there is a bad compound in the second verse. If the study of Greek was not successfully carried on in Western Europe before the fall of Constantinople drove many learned Greeks into that part of the continent, it is of course not reasonable to expect that Sanskrit literature should be properly understood in Europe without instruction from the old Pandits of India. This defect was first of all clearly perceived by those German scholars who spent a good many years in India; and now it has been acknowledged by others also, though there are still some whose reliance on a grammar and a dictionary continues unbounded. And the Germans have already begun to remedy the defect. Dr. Garbe was sent more than a year ago to this country at the expense of the Prussian Government to study Indian philosophy. He lived at Benares for a year and read one or two works with some of the Pandits there, and has recently returned to his country. Dr. Kielhorn has undertaken to publish an edition of the Kāśikā, an old commentary on Pāṇini's Sūtras, containing copious notes and explanations of a nature to enable the European scholar to understand the intricacies of the style of grammatical exegesis....

A little later in his address, after briefly referring to the European wars, Bhandarkar related an incident that led him to another attitude regarding the Germans (page 354 of the reprint):

A German Sanskrit Professor once said to me that he liked social equality being given to the natives of India, but not political equality, and that he considered the Ilbert Bill to be mischievous. I told him that in Ceylon and the presidency towns the native magistrates did actually exercise the power of trying European offenders. He did not know that, he said, but still proceeded to defend his position, and, bringing his oriental learning to his aid, observed, "Oh, Buddhism has softened the Ceylonese, so that they might exercise that power; but the case is different in India." I listened quietly, thanking my country's stars that she had not fallen into the hands of Germans.

The controversy with Weber about the dates of Patañjali and of the *Mahābhārata* took place about one and a half decades before the Vienna congress which prompted the above excursus. Weber (*Indian Antiquary* 2, 1873, 57–59) complained that Bhandarkar did not know his (Weber's) review of Goldstücker's *Pāṇini* of 1862 in the *Indische Studien*, and maintained that the beginning of the first century A.D. was a more likely date for Patañjali. Bhandarkar, replying in *Indian Antiquary* (2, 1873, 59–61), maintained that his own conclusions were in no way affected by what Weber had written. It is true that Weber in his review had already referred to the passage containing the expression *Puṣyamitra-sabhā*

(Bhandarkar insisted on saying *Puṣpamitra*, claiming that the other spelling was due to a scribal error; but here he was wrong). But Bhandarkar shows that his argument depended on the expression *iha puṣpamitraṃ yājayāmaḥ* 'here we perform the sacrifices (instituted) by Puṣpamitra' (*Mahābhāṣya* on Pāṇini 3.2.123), which was referred to neither by Goldstücker nor by Weber.

Next, Bhandarkar discussed the passage *aruṇad yavano mādhyamikān* "the Yavana besieged the Mādhyamika,' from which Goldstücker and Weber had derived different conclusions with regard to Patañjali's date. "The truth is," said he in *Indian Antiquary* (2, 1873, 60)

> that the name 'Mādhyamika' has been misunderstood both by Dr. Goldstücker and Professor Weber; and hence, in giving Dr. Goldstücker's argument in my article, I omitted the portion based on that name. The expression *aruṇad Yavano Mādhyamikān* makes no sense, if we understand by the last word, the Buddhist school of that name. The root *rudh* means 'to besiege' or 'blockade;' and the besieging or blockading of a sect is something I cannot understand. Places are besieged or blockaded, but not sects. I am aware that Professor Weber translates this verb by a word which in English means 'to oppress;' but I am not aware that the root is ever used in that sense. By the word "Mādhyamika" is to be understood the people of a certain place, as Dr. Kern has pointed out in his preface to his edition of the Bṛhat Sanhitā, on the authority of the Sanhitā itself. We are thus saved the necessity of making a string of very improbable suppositions; and in this way, Professor Weber's argument, based as it is on the hypothesis that the Mādhyamikas alluded to by Patañjali were the Buddhist sect of that name, falls to the ground. The first of Dr. Goldstücker's passages (the word "Yavana" occurring in both of them), and the passage I have for the first time pointed out, taken together, determine the date of Patañjali to be about 144 B.C. And this agrees better with the other passages pointed out by Dr. Goldstücker. For if Patañjali lived in the reign of the founder of the Śunga dynasty, one can understand why the Mauryas and their founder should have been uppermost in his thoughts; but if he lived in 25 A.D., when the Andhra Bhritya dynasty was in power, one may well ask why he should have gone back for illustrating his rules to the Mauryas and Candragupta, and passed over the intermediate dynasties of the Śungas and the Kānvas.

Weber replied with characteristic promptitude (*Indian Antiquary* (2, 1873, 206–210)) that he was not convinced, since Bhandarkar's arguments (which he apparently did not understand) only showed that Patañjali did not live *before* Puṣpamitra and that they merely established that, during Patañjali's time, "the memory of this king was still cherished by the Brahmans." As to the Mādhyamikas, Bhandarkar's silence in his first article "far from implying that he did not coincide with the interpretation of it given by Goldstücker, would seem to show, on the contrary, that he acquiesced in it, not being yet aware of all the difficulties of the case" (page 207). Though he remained unconvinced, Weber continued, after a few more quibbles, to congratulate Bhandarkar in a friendlier spirit "as a most welcome fellow-labourer in our common studies," and he even condescended to commend his critical spirit and sagacity. In his final reply (*Indian Antiquary* (2, 1873, 238–240)), Bhandarkar complained politely about Weber's lack of good faith, and reiterated his position. If we were, in these days, to give an instance of a rule such as the present tense denotes actions that have begun but not ended, he asked, "should we give such a one as 'Johnson edits the *Rambler*', or 'Gibbon is writing the *History of the Decline and Fall*'? Would not, on the contrary, our instances be such as 'Drs. Boehtlingk and Roth are compiling a Dictionary of Sanskrit'? I think we should use such as this latter, for in the former the actions of editing and writing have long been over, and consequently they would be of no use to illustrate the rule, which specially requires they they should not be over."

At about the same time Weber published a long study about the *Mahābhāṣya* in his *Indische Studien* (13, 1873, 293–496), where many of these topics were treated again and equally unsatisfactorily (the discussion about Puṣpamitra occurs in almost identical terms on pages 309–313). Weber gave translations from the *Mahābhāṣya*, in which he distinguished the passages where Patañjali quoted Kātyāyana from passages by Patañjali himself. He arrived at the view that the *Mahābhāṣya* text in its present form was more the work of his pupils than of Patañjali himself. Boehtlingk took this up in two articles in the *Zeitschrift der deutschen morgenländischen Gesellschaft* (29, 1876, 183–190 and 483–490). In the first he gave a full translation of the commentary on Pāṇini (3.2.123), dealing with the present tense, and of a fragment from the Introduction to the *Mahābhāṣya*. He concluded from this that the *Mahābhāṣya* must be interpreted as a dialogue between Kātyāyana and Patañjali, which is quoted and commented on by a third person, who is the author. Therefore, the author must be different from Patañjali. "Wollten wir Patañjali für den Berichterstatter halten, dann müssten wir ihm eine Selbstverleugnung zumuthen, die uns geradezu in Staunen versetzen würde" (page 190).

In his second article Boehtlingk attempted to corroborate these conclusions further with the help of a translation of the commentary on 6.1.64, a rule which teaches the substitution (for metalinguistic reasons) of retroflex ṣ for the initial dental s of certain monosyllabic verbs. "Wie im ersten Artikel," said Boehtlingk, "erscheinen auch hier Kātyāyana und Patañjali als einander gegenüberstehende Klopffechter. Die Palme der Spitzfindigkeit und des Dünkels können wir getrost Patañjali zuerkennen" (page 483). Actually it is not impossible that Boehtlingk, in the interpretation of this rule, made use of an excellent and detailed exposition of Pāṇini's treatment of these verbs, provided by Max Müller in section 103 of his *Sanskrit Grammar* of 1866. This initial ṣ had puzzled scholars for a long time. It is discussed, for example, in a letter of Schlegel's addressed to Humboldt of 1822 (Leitzmann 1908, 106–107).

Western scholars complaining about overingenuity and obscurity in the Indian grammatical texts they have attempted to explain have often been proved wrong. Weber's and Boehtlingk's view regarding both the date and the structure of the *Mahābhāṣya* were incorrect. This became increasingly clear from the work of Bhandarkar and especially of Kielhorn. In 1874 Kielhorn published his translation of Nāgojībhaṭṭa's *Paribhāṣenduśekhara* (reprinted in 1960), an extremely difficult work and one of the major works of the later Pāṇinian tradition. He was at that time also preparing an edition of the *Mahābhāṣya*, which appeared in three volumes in 1880–1885 (second edition 1892–1909; third edition I: 1960, II: 1965). Ballantyne had earlier published a portion of this text in Mirzapore, 1856; and Rājarāmaśāstrī and Bālaśāstrī had published the text in Banaras, 1872. Goldstücker reproduced two manuscripts, as we have seen (1874a and 1874b; cf. Plate IV). Kielhorn (using these manuscripts, among others) not only produced a reliable edition, but specified also where Patañjali quoted Kātyāyana's *vārttikās*, thus structuring a text which was unintelligible otherwise (as Weber's and Boehtlingk's hypotheses had amply demonstrated).

In addition, Kielhorn wrote a series of important papers in which he dealt authoritatively with some of the problems brought up by Weber. Many of these papers appeared between 1876 and 1887 in the *Indian Antiquary*. In the first of these, "On the *Mahābhāṣya*" (*Indian Antiquary* 5, 1876, 241–251), Kielhorn established two important conclusions partly through refutations of the opposite views of Weber: (1) the *Mahābhāṣya* was written by Patañjali himself, and not by his pupils; (2) the text of the *Mahābhāṣya* had not been "several times newly arranged" (as Weber had argued from two passages from the *Rājataraṅgiṇī* and the *Vākyapadīya*), but the text given by the manuscripts was the same as it was about two thousand years earlier. The passages discussed by Weber (and earlier by Goldstücker and A. C. Burnell) established only that the text of the *Mahābhāṣya* was *recovered*, not *reestablished* or *reconstructed*, by Candra and others (i.e., about the sixth century A.D.). Weber replied, but his argument remained rather unconvincing (*Indian Antiquary* 6, 1877, 301–307).

In 1876 Kielhorn published a booklet that in due course became rather well known, *Kātyāyana and Patañjali* (recently reprinted twice: Varanasi 1963, Osnabrück 1965). Here he elucidated the exact relationship (which was later specified with complete precision in his *Mahābhāṣya* edition) between the two great Indian grammarians, and their relation to Pāṇini. In the same year Bhandarkar published an article, "Ācārya, the Friend of the Student, and the Relation between the Three Ācāryas," in the *Indian Antiquary* (5, 1876, 345–350) in which he arrived at a characterization of the three *ācāryas* ('teachers') Pāṇini, Kātyāyana, and Patañjali, which is in some respects even more accurate than Kielhorn's. Since Kielhorn's booklet is now readily available, Bhandarkar's conclusion at least deserves to be quoted here (page 350).

We thus see (1) that Kātyāyana explains and supports the *sūtras*, sometimes by raising questions about them and answering them, sometimes without resorting to this procedure; (2) that he amends them, and thus must be understood to criticize them, or find fault with them; and (3) that he supplements them. Patañjali (1) comments on the *vārtikas* in accordance with his own definition of *vyākhyāna*; (2) agrees with Kātyāyana; (3) refutes him; (4) recasts Pāṇini's *sūtras*; (5) affirms that they, or a word or words in them, are not wanted, even in cases when Kātyāyana justifies them or defends Pāṇini; (6) discusses and explains *sūtras* or words in them, notwithstanding that there is no *vārtika*; and (7) gives supplementary rules called *iṣṭis*, which, however, occur very rarely, very little being left for him to do in this respect, by his predecessors. It will thus appear that in writing the *vārtikas*, Kātyāyana *did* "mean to justify and to defend the rules of Pāṇini" also, and that a *vārtika is* often "a commentary which explains;" and that the *Mahābhāṣya* contains such varied matter, arguments of such length, so consistent, so well connected, and so subtle, that it by no means deserves the title of "a skilful compilation of the views of Pāṇini's critics and of their refutation by Patañjali," or of a "mere refutation of Kātyāyana," or of "a synopsis of arguments for and against the details of Pāṇini's system, or a controversial manual." The only tenable theory is that Kātyāyana's work is an edition of Pāṇini with notes, explanatory, critical, and supplementary; and that Patañjali's is a commentary on this edition, explaining in detail the notes of Kātyāyana, but discussing *at length* all points connected with the system of Pāṇini and with grammar generally, whether Kātyāyana notices them or not, in a manner favorable or otherwise to his author. The object of both was the same, viz. to teach grammar by following and explaining the system of Pāṇini, endeavouring to perfect it, even though this sometimes required a remodelling of his *sūtras* or their entire refutation, and to complete it by supplying the omissions and bringing up the knowledge of Sanskrit grammar conveyed therein to their own times.

D. Development of Language and of Sanskrit (1883)

First Wilson Lecture

Ramkrishna Gopal Bhandarkar

In an article in the *Journal of the Bombay Branch of the Royal Asiatic Society* (16, 1883–1885, 181–189), P. Peterson, a professor at the Bombay Elphinstone College for whom Bhandarkar had served as an assistant, had questioned the date of Patañjali for which Goldstücker and Bhandarkar had argued. Bhandarkar replied in the same journal (same volume, pages 199–222 and 343–345). Having been involved in various discussions, the time had come for Bhandarkar to give a more systematic exposition of his ideas. This was done in the Wilson Lectures delivered at the University of Bombay and published in the Bombay *Journal* (volumes 16 and 17). Of these lectures the most relevant in the present context are I, "Development of Language and of Sanskrit" (*Journal of the Bombay Branch of the Royal Asiatic Society* 16, 1883–1885, 245–274) and VII, "Relation between Sanskrit, Pâli, the Prâkṛits and the Modern Vernaculars" (in the same volume, pages 314–342).

Bhandarkar began the first lecture with some general facts about Sanskrit, the origins of linguistic studies in India, phonetics, and different language families, and then he proceeded to analyse a specimen of Vedic Sanskrit. He also gave a sketch of a general theory of the development of language, illustrated with Indian examples, reproducing the *communis opinio* of the historical linguistics of his day. Next he traced the development of Sanskrit from the Brāhmaṇa literature onward, in due course arriving at Patañjali, whose style he characterized and illustrated with a translation from the Introduction of the *Mahābhāṣya*, beginning with the same passage which Boehtlingk had translated in the *Zeitschrift der deutschen morgenländischen Gesellschaft* (29, 1876, 189–190) (see this volume page 85). He ended the lecture by specifying the types of Sanskrit presupposed by the grammatical analysis of Pāṇini, Kātyāyana, and Patañjali (pages 266–274). Of special interest is Bhandarkar's translation from Patañjali, where the latter discusses the need for rules describing forms that are not in use.

It was in the field of philosophy, dialectics, and exegesis, scriptural or grammatical, that this nominal style was greatly cultivated and developed. The earliest work of the kind we know of is Patañjali's Mahābhāṣya on Kātyāyana's Vārtikas or notes on Pāṇini's Sūtras. Nearly the whole of the philosophical literature of the Sanskrit is written more or less in the style of disputation. An Indian author does not lead his readers into the processes his own mind has gone through in arriving at the doctrines he lays down; in other words, he does not tell us how he has come by the opinions he holds, but lays down these doctrines and sets forth those opinions and conceives objections that may be raised and answers them. Or before actually stating the true doctrine or *siddhānta*, certain others, more or less opposed are stated, and reasons given in support of them (*pūrvapakṣa*) which are, of course, refuted. The Mahābhāṣya is written in this manner, but it differs in a good many respects from later works of the kind. Unlike the latter, it gives the very words that an opponent, speaking in his own person, may be expected to use. It therefore really consists of a series of dialogues, often smart, between one who maintains the *pūrvapakṣa*, and another who lays down the *siddhānta*. Hence, the language is plain and simple, and the sentences are short, and such as a man may naturally use in ordinary conversation or oral disputation. The nominal style, however, as I have ventured to call it, in contradistinction to that of the Brāhmaṇas and also of Yāska is observable; but it has of course not yet degenerated into the long compounds and algebraic expressions of modern times, and is perfectly natural. In this respect it keeps pace with the language of the Itihāsaṣ and Smṛtis. Vātsyāyana's Bhāṣya on Gotama's Nyāya Sūtra, and Śabarasvāmin's on that of Jaimini, as well as the Bhāṣyas on some of the sacrificial Sūtras, are written in the same sort of simple and lively style, though however they present a further stage in the downward progress. But gradually this manner of writing ceased to be used, and the philosophical style went on progressing until it has come to be what it is now. Śaṃkarācārya's Bhāṣya presents it in a middle stage. The sentences are much longer than those of the earlier writers, the construction is more involved, there is a freer use of attributive adjuncts, and the form is that of an essay or a lecture, instead of an oral disputation. But the great Ācārya's style is perspicuous throughout, fluent and charming, and not solidified or petrified, as that of later writers is. These latter hardly ever use a verb, and of the cases only a few are to be met within their works. The nominative and ablative singular prevail, and long compounds are constantly employed. All our ideas are thrown into the form of nouns, mostly abstract, and even the participles have become rare. This style is the style of formulas rather than of discourse. It has reached its climax in the works of recent *Naiyāyikas*, but it has been more or less used by modern writers in all the Śāstras. The movement which began with a less frequent use of verbal forms and the employment of attributive expressions has thus ended in making Sanskrit a language of abstract nouns and compound words.

I have used the word style in describing this movement, to show what important changes in the structure of a language may originate from what is in the beginning but a style or mode of speaking or writing. If everybody thought and spoke about all matters as the Naiyāyika does in his own subject our language would be just like his. It would almost have no verbs, no participles, and no cases except one or two. But it is not so. The movement could not be carried so far in other subjects. Hence the real classical Sanskrit is the Sanskrit of the Epics, the Purāṇas, the metrical law-books, the better or earlier specimens of Kāvyas or poems and dramatic plays, and of the early philosophical or exegetical works. And if we examine this literature we shall find that the greater use of attributive or nominal forms of expression gradually drove out a large portion of the Sanskrit verb, and gave a new character to the language, which may be thus described:— Very few verbal forms are used besides those of such tenses as the Present and Future; participles are frequently met with; the verbal forms of some roots, especially of those belonging to the less comprehensive classes, have gone out of use, and in their place we often have a noun expressive of the special action and a verb expressive of action generally; compound words are somewhat freely employed; and a good many of the Taddhita forms or nominal derivatives have disappeared, and in their stead we have periphrastic expressions. If the treatises of Pāṇini and others had perished, and we had to construct a grammar of the Sanskrit from the classical literature I have above indicated, our Verb and the Taddhita portion would be very meagre. Professor Benfey attributes the condition which the language thus assumed to the influence of the Prākṛts or the spoken vernaculars. But the process appears to me perfectly natural, and no such influence need be supposed. The change may in some respects be likened to that which rendered the Vedic subjunctive and other grammatical forms obsolete in the later stage of the language. The Prākṛts may have given some words to the Sanskrit, but that they should in this manner have influenced its grammatical structure is very unlikely. It is more natural to suppose that it was the Sanskrit from which the Prākṛts evidently sprang which gave to these latter their peculiar character. I shall endeavour to determine the exact relation between the Sanskrit and these dialects in the concluding lecture.

We have thus observed and determined the change that came over Sanskrit after the period that elapsed between the Brāhmaṇas and Yāska from an examination of the literature itself. But the fact is borne witness to by Kātyāyana, who observed it in his time and made it the subject of a few *vārtikas*. Patañjali discusses the points raised in the following manner. An objector or *Pūrvapakṣin* is introduced, who says:

Pūrv. *asty aprayuktaḥ* There exist (some) words which are not used; for instance, *ūṣa*, *tera*, *cakra*, *peca*. (These are forms of the second person plural of the Perfect.)

The *Siddhāntin*, or the principal teacher, who advocates the doctrine that is finally laid down asks:—

Sid. What if they are not used?

Pūrv. You determine the grammatical correctness of words from their being used. Those then that are not now used are not grammatically correct.

Sid. What you say is, in the first place, inconsistent, viz., that words exist which are not used. If they exist they cannot be not used; if not used, they cannot exist. To say that they exist and are not used is inconsistent. You yourself use them (utter them) and say (in the very breath) there are words which are not used. What other worthy like yourself would you have to use them in order that they might be considered correct? (lit. What other person like yourself is correct or is an authority in the use of words).

Pūrv. This is not inconsistent. I say they exist, since those who know the Śāstra teach their formation by (laying down) rules, and I say they are not used, because they are not used by people. Now with regard to [your remark] "What other worthy, &c." [when I say they are not used] I do not mean that they are not used by me.

Sid. What then?

Pūrv. Not used by people.

Sid. Verily, you also are one amongst the people.

Pūrv. Yes, I am *one*, but am not *the people*.

Sid. (Vārt. *asty aprayukta iti cen nārthe śabdaprayogāt*). If you object that they are not used, it will not do (the objection is not valid).

Pūrv. Why not?

Sid. Because words are used to designate things. The things do exist which these words are used to designate. (Therefore the words must be used by somebody. If the things exist, the words that denote them must exist).

Pūrv. (Vārt. *aprayogaḥ prayogānyatvāt*). (It does not follow.) Their non-use is what one can reasonably infer.

Sid. Why?

Pūrv. Because they (people) use other words to designate the things expressed by these words; for instance, *kva yūyam uṣitāḥ* ['where did you live?'] in the sense of **ūṣa*; *kva yūyaṃ tīrṇāḥ* ['where did you cross?'] in the sense of **tera*; *kva yūyaṃ kṛtavantaḥ* ['where did you act?'] in the sense of **cakra; kva yūyaṃ pakvantaḥ* ['where did you cook?'] in the sense of *peca*. (We here see that participles had come to be used for verbs of the Perfect Tense).

Sid. (Vārt. *aprayukte dīrghasattravat*). Even if these words are not used, they should be essentially taught by rules just as long sacrificial sessions are. It is in this way. Long sacrificial sessions are such as last for a hundred years and for a thousand years. In modern times none whatever holds them, but the writers on sacrifices teach them by rules, simply because [to learn] what has been handed down by tradition from the Ṛṣis is religiously meritorious. And moreover (Vārt. *sarve deśāntare*) all these words are used in other places.

Pūrv.—They are not found used.

Sid.—An endeavour should be made to find them. Wide indeed is the range over which words are used; the earth with its seven continents, the three worlds, the four Vedas with their aṅgas or dependent treatises and the mystic portions, in their various recensions, the one hundred branches of the Adhvaryu (Yajur-Veda), the Sāma-Veda with its thousand modes, the Bāhvṛcya with its twenty-one varieties, and the Ātharvaṇa Veda with nine, Vākovākya, the Epics, the Purāṇas, and Medicine. This is the extent over which words are used. Without searching this extent of the use of words, to say that words are not used is simple rashness. In this wide extent of the use of words, certain words appear restricted to certain senses in certain places. Thus, *śavati* is used in the sense of motion among the Kambojas; the Āryas use it in the derived form of *śava; hammati* is used among the Surāṣṭras, *raṃhati* among the eastern and central people, but the Āryas use only *gam; dāti* is used in the sense of 'cutting' among the easterners, *dātra* among the northerners. And those words which you think are not used are also seen used.

Pūrv.—Where?

Sid.—In the Veda. Thus, *saptāsye revatī revad ūṣa* ['on (the god) with seven mouths (i.e., Bṛhaspati) have you shone riches, o rich ones?': Ṛgveda 4.51.4] | **yad vo revatī revatyāṃ tam ūṣa* ['you

[* Three sentences quoted from the *Mahābhāṣya* have a better reading in Kielhorn's edition (I, 9): *kiṃ yūyaṃ tīrṇāḥ* 'what did you cross?,' *kiṃ yūyaṃ kṛtavantaḥ* 'what did you do?,' *kiṃ yūyaṃ pakvavantaḥ* 'what did you cook?' The second (unidentified) sentence attributed to the Veda also has a reading in Kielhorn's edition (I, 10) which is probably more correct: *yad vo revatī revatyaṃ tad ūṣa*.]

have shone on us what is full of riches, o rich ones'] | *yan me naraḥ śrutyaṃ brahma cakra* ['the glorious brahman which you, o heroes, have made me': Ṛgveda 1.165.11] | *yatrā naś cakrā jarasaṃ tanūnām* ['in which you have determined the age of our bodies': Ṛgveda 1.89.9].

We here see that the objector says that certain words or forms are not used by people, and therefore they should not be taught or learnt. The instances that he gives are forms of the perfect of some roots and he observes that the sense of these forms is expressed by using other words which are perfect participles of these roots. These statements are not denied by the Siddhāntin, but he does not allow that the forms should not be taught on that account. Though not used, they should be taught and learnt for the sake of the religious merit consequent thereon, just as the ceremonial of long sacrificial sessions, which are never held, is. Then the objector is told that though not used by people, the words may be current in some other country, continent, or world, or they must have been used somewhere in the vast literature of the language. As regards the particular instances, two of them are shown to be used in the Vedas.

It thus follows that in the time of Kātyāyana and Patañjali, such verbal forms had become obsolete, and participles were used in their place. But it must have been far otherwise in the time of Pāṇini. He gives minute rules for constructing the innumerable forms of the Sanskrit verb. Our grammarians proceeded upon a strictly scientific basis. Nothing is more clear from several observations scattered throughout the work of Patañjali, besides those contained in the above passage, than this, that the Indian Grammarians do not give us the inventions of their own brains as they are supposed by some scholars to do. The very perfection of their observation and analysis has rendered them liable to this reproach. But notwithstanding all that, there can be *no doubt whatever* that they scrupulously adhered to usage. If so, the verbal forms taught by Pāṇini must have been current in the language at some time. We do meet with them in the Brāhmaṇas, but our grammarian does not include these forms among the peculiarities he has given of the Vedic or Chandas and Brāhmaṇa dialect, and thus does not restrict them to those works. They must therefore be understood as having been in use in the Bhāṣā or current language, the grammar of which he teaches in his Sūtras. And the Bhāṣā that he means must be that which was current in his time. In Pāṇini's time, therefore, the fluent or verbal style of speech was in use, as I have observed before. But it may be argued that though he refers these forms to the Bhāṣā, the Bhāṣā he means may not be that which prevailed when he lived, but another current before his time and preserved in its literature, on which Pāṇini based his rules. It matters very little even if we make this supposition. The only effect is that the period when the non-Vedic Sanskrit was rich in verbal forms is placed before Pāṇini; but the fact itself that there was such a period is undeniable. The supposition, however, is unreasonable. For it is not at all likely that he should neglect the language prevalent in his time and teach that which was current before him, and speak of it as the Bhāṣā, which word literally signifies the "spoken language" or vernacular. And the occurrence in the Sūtras of words that became obsolete in later Sanskrit confirms this view. The following are such words:—*anvavasarga* 'allowing one his own way,' *niravasita* 'excommunicated,' *pratyavasāna* 'eating,' *abhividhi* 'including,' *svakaraṇa* 'marrying,' *utsañjana* 'throwing up,' *abhreṣa* 'equitableness.' You will have seen that the Vārtika of Kātyāyana which starts the discussion I have translated, and Patañjali's comment on it speak of words generally as having ceased to be used though the examples given consist of certain verbal forms only. It is, therefore to be understood that the observation is applicable to other forms and expressions also taught by Pāṇini which we do not meet with in the later literature. Among such may be noticed *upājekṛ* and *anvājekṛ* 'to strengthen,' *nivacanekṛ* 'to be silent,' *kaṇehan*, and *manohan* 'to fulfil one's longing,'[1] &c. *kaṇehan* occurs in Yāska also. Most of the verbal derivatives ending in the technical termination *ṇamul* must also be so considered, such as *brāhmaṇavedaṃ bhojayati* 'feeds every Brāhmaṇa that he finds,' *celaknopaṃ vṛṣṭaḥ* 'rained till the clothes were wet'; *svapoṣaṃ puṣṇāti* 'supports by his own means,' *ūrdhvaśoṣaṃ śuṣyati* 'withers standing,' &c. A good many Taddhita forms taught in Pāṇini's Sūtras must also, I think, be put in the same category.

And there is another circumstance which shows that Pāṇini's Sanskrit was more ancient than Kātyāyana's. Kātyāyana's Vārtikas on Pāṇini, which I have already spoken to you of, touch on various points concerning grammar and the system of Pāṇini. The purpose of a great many of them is the proper interpretation of the Sūtras, and there are some which supply the links that are wanting in the system, also a good many which teach forms not taught by Pāṇini, or give the correct forms, when by the strict application of Pāṇini's rules we arrive at such as are incorrect. Now, this strict application of Pāṇini's rules is often in the manner of a quibbling logician, and consequently it was probably never meant by Pāṇini himself. Again, it may also be allowed that some forms existing in the language may have escaped Pāṇini's notice. But even after making allowance for all these considerations, a good many forms taught by Kātyāyana are left which it is impossible to believe Pāṇini did not observe or know, if they existed in the language in his time. Though not infallible, Pāṇini was not an indifferent grammarian. He justly deserves the reputation he has all along enjoyed of being the preeminent teacher of grammar. He has noticed even stray facts about the language. If so, the only reasonable supposition is that these forms did not exist in the language at the period when he lived. For instance, according to Pāṇini's rules the vocative singular of neuter nouns ending in *an* such as *brahman* and *nāman* is *brahman* and *nāman*, but Kātyāyana in a Vārtika on VIII. 2, 8 tells us it is *brahman* or *brahma* and *nāman* or *nāma*. Pāṇini teaches that the forms of the dative, ablative, genitive, and locative singular of the feminine of *dvitīya* and *tṛtīya* are optionally like those of the corresponding pronouns, *i.e.* we have either *dvitīyāyai* or *dvitīyasyai*, *dvitīyāyāḥ* or *dvitīyasyāḥ* &c., but Kātyāyana in a Vārtika on I. 1, 36 extends this option to the masculine also, and according to him we have *dvitīyāyaḥ* or *dvitīyasmai*, *dvitīyāt* or *dvitīyasmāt* &c., while Pāṇini gives us only the first. Pāṇini's rule IV. 1, 49 allows of *mātulānī* only as the feminine of *mātula*, but Kātyāyana gives *mātulī* also; *upādhyāyānī* is not noticed by Pāṇini, while Kātyāyana lays down that as well as *upādhyāyī* in the sense of 'wife of the *upādhyāya*.' So also *āryā* and *kṣatriyā* are according to Pāṇini, 'a female Ārya' and 'a female Kṣatriya,' but Kātyāyana gives *āryāṇī* and *kṣatriyāṇī* as well as *āryā*

[1] Professor Goldstücker has used the argument based on the occurrence of obsolete words in the Sūtras and that set forth in the next paragraph, to prove the archaic character of the language as it existed in Pāṇini's time, and some of the instances quoted in the text are the same as his.

and *kṣatriyā*. A good many more instances of a similar nature may be given from other parts of Sanskrit Grammar. Are we then to suppose that the forms *brahma, nāma, karma* &c. of the vocative singular, *dvitīyasmai* of the dative of *dvitīya* &c., *mātulī, upādhyāyānī, āryāṇī, kṣatriyāṇī* and many more such, escaped the observation of such a grammarian as Pāṇini, or that he did not know them? Is the supposition that they did not exist in the language in his time not more reasonable? It therefore appears clear to me that the language in Pāṇini's time was in a different condition from that in which it was in Kātyāyana's. The chief differences, to point out which has been the object of this discussion, may be thus stated:—In Pāṇini's time a good many words and expressions were current which afterwards became obsolete; verbal forms were commonly used which ceased to be used in Kātyāyana's time, and some grammatical forms were developed in the time of the latter which did not exist in Pāṇini's.

Pāṇini's Sanskrit must, therefore, be identified with that which preceded the Epics, and he must be referred to the literary period between the Brāhmaṇas and Yāska. Hence it is that the Brāhmaṇas, as observed before, are the best existing representatives of the language of which Pāṇini writes the grammar. Kātyāyana, on the other hand, wrote when the language arrived at that stage which we have called classical. Thus then, we have been able to trace three distinct periods in the development of Sanskrit. First, we have the Vedic period, to which the Ṛgveda Saṃhitā, the Mantra portion of the Yajurveda, and the more antiquated part of the Atharva-Saṃhitā are to be referred. Then commences another period, at the threshold of which we find the Brāhmaṇas, which, so to say, look backwards to the preceding, that is, present the Vedic language in the last stage of its progress towards Pāṇini's Bhāṣā; and, later on, we have Yāska and Pāṇini. This may be called the period of Middle Sanskrit. And last of all, there is the classical period to which belong the Epics, the earliest specimens of Kāvyas and dramatic plays, the metrical Smṛtis, and the grammatical work of Kātyāyana. Pāṇini's work contains the grammar of Middle Sanskrit, while Kātyāyana's that of classical Sanskrit, though he gives his sanction to the archaic forms of the former on the principle, as he himself has stated, on which the authors of the sacrificial Sūtras teach the ritual of long sacrificial sessions, though they had ceased to be held in their time. Patañjali gives but few forms which differ from Kātyāyana's, and in no way do they indicate a different stage in the growth of the language; hence his work is to be referred to the same period. The form which the language assumed at this time became the standard for later writers to follow, and Kātyāyana and Patañjali are now the generally acknowledged authorities on all points concerning the correctness of Sanskrit speech.

E. Relations between Sanskrit, Pāli, the Prākṛts and the Modern Vernaculars (1883)

Seventh Wilson Lecture

Ramkrishna Gopal Bhandarkar

In his seventh and last Wilson Lecture, Bhandarkar addressed himself to the thesis of several European scholars, that the Prākṛts were not spoken languages but artificial adaptations. This led in turn to a discussion of the question whether Sanskrit itself was a spoken language. Bhandarkar dealt with this topic lucidly and authoritatively, with the aid of numerous references to the grammarians and quoting passages from the *Mahābhāṣya*, including a famous passage concerned with the native speakers of Sanskrit (pages 326–336 of the original).

There is positive evidence that Sanskrit was a spoken language. Yāska in the Nirukta frequently refers to the Vedic dialect and to another called Bhāṣā, the peculiarities of which mentioned by him are observable in classical Sanskrit. Pāṇini in his Grammar gives a good many rules which are exclusively applicable to the dialect of the Vedas, to which he refers by using the words *Chandas*, *Nigama*, *Mantra*, and *Brāhmaṇa*, and others which are applicable to the Bhāṣā alone, but by far the largest number of his sūtras have reference to both. Now since Bhāṣā, or the ordinary Sanskrit, is thus distinguished from the dialect of the Vedas, it must be the language in use at the time when these writers lived. "Bhāṣā," as used by them, is a proper name, but in later Sanskrit it acquired a generic signification and meant language generally. The root from which the word is derived signifies "to speak," wherefore the original sense of the word as a proper noun must have been the "speech" or "the spoken language." And because this was its signification it afterwards came to denote "explanation." When we ask for an explanation of something that is obscure and unintelligible, what we mean is that the sense should be expressed to us in the ordinary language of men, a language that we can understand. Thus such a sentence as *sthitaprajñasya kā bhāṣā* means "what is the Vernacular of *sthitaprajña*?" an expression similar to "what is the English of it?"

Pāṇini refers certain points expressly to popular usage. He says that the names of countries are conventional, and no grammatical analysis should be given of them, because it is fictitious. These should be used as we find them used. Similarly he says grammarians should not make rules to teach such things as these:—That the two words of a compound express the thing denoted by the principal word as qualified by the sense of the subordinate word; as for instance, *rājapuruṣa*, a compound of *rājan* "a king" and *puruṣa* "a man" does not denote "a king," but "a man," and not "man" *alone* but *as connected with a king*, *i.e.* a king's man or officer; and that the base and the termination express the sense of the termination as qualified by that of the base; as *aupagava* signifies not *upagu* but a child, and not a child *alone* but a child *as connected with upagu i.e.* Upagu's child. For the significations of words are to be learnt from usage.

In the introduction to the Mahābhāṣya Patañjali tells us that some persons in his or Kātyāyana's time considered the study of grammar to be unnecessary. For said they, "Vedic words or forms we know from the Veda, and those current in popular usage from that usage; grammar is useless." Now the grammar which is thus declared useless is the grammar both of the Vedic and classical Sanskrit; and the depreciators of the science profess to derive a knowledge of the first dialect from the Vedic books, and of the second not from other books but from popular usage. Hence Sanskrit must have been in the times of those two grammarians a spoken language.

Similarly in the passage from the same work which I placed before you in the first lecture, you will remember that the objector (or *pūrvapakṣin*) argues that since usage is the authority upon which the grammarians go, certain verbal forms which are no longer used by people ought not to be taught by the grammarians, and says that instead of those verbal forms participles are employed. The principal teacher (*Siddhāntin*) does not deny the facts but refers the objector to the vast literature of the language, where he may find them used, though obsolete at the time. It is evident from the whole passage, that Sanskrit was then a spoken language, though some of its verbal forms had fallen into desuetude. I have also shown that the language was considerably changed between the times of Pāṇini and Kātyāyana, and called the Sanskrit that prevailed when Pāṇini and Yāska flourished Middle Sanskrit, and that which was current in the time of Kātyāyana classical Sanskrit. Now these changes from the one form to the other could not have taken place if the language had been dead or petrified into a merely literary language.

I am at a loss to see why some scholars should find it so difficult to believe that Sanskrit was a vernacular. If its declensions and conjugations are considered too complicated for the language of everyday life, it must not be forgotten that such a fact did not prevent the ancient languages of Europe from becoming spoken languages. And this objection would do equally well against the Vedic dialect, which, or others like which, are regarded as the vernaculars of their times, and which are richer in inflexions than the later Sanskrit. Then it is held that the artificial regularity of Sanskrit makes it improbable that it should have been a vernacular. Where is this artificial regularity? On the contrary, it is the absence of regularity that renders its grammar so difficult and complicated. There is a freedom in the choice of words, expressions, and forms. In every department of its grammar there are innumerable optional forms; nouns and verbal roots are often declined and conjugated in several ways. One same root in a good many cases forms its special tenses in more ways than one, and in the nominal derivatives, the verbal derivatives, the formation of the feminine, and the uses of cases and tenses there is a freedom which some may consider a license. The only difference is that Sanskrit has had the most perfect grammarians in the world, who observed all the facts of their language and laid them down as unchangeable facts, and it is this which gives that language a stiffened appearance. Then the Saṃdhi or euphonic combinations of letters which are necessary in Sanskrit, are regarded as inconsistent with the character of a spoken language. It is however not denied that such combinations are observable in all languages, and particularly so in Latin and Greek; but it is urged that in Sanskrit there is a regularity or universality about them which is not found anywhere else. It should not however be forgotten that Saṃdhi in the same word and the same compound, and of a preposition with a root is alone necessary. Between different words it is optional, which means that it was on occasions neglected. Now Saṃdhi in the same word is necessary by a law of nature. The Sanskrit does not allow a hiatus; and this is a characteristic of most of the modern idioms also. Some languages, such as our Prākṛts and the old languages of Europe tolerate it. But the euphonic combination of consonants in the same word is necessary even in Latin; as in rex = reg-s, scriptus = scrib-tus, cinctum = cing-tum, lectum = leg-tum, tractum from traho, though the *h* like the Sanskrit *ha* stands for an original *gh*; *d* and *t* combine to form an s, as defendo, defensum; sedeo, sessum; claudo, clausum; &c. Prepositions are really parts of words, and hence by the same law they also must form one harmonious sound with the initial letter of the word to which they are attached; and modern vernaculars have got corruptions of the combined words which shows that they must have been used in those forms in the colloquial Sanskrit. Sk. *paryasta*, Pr. *pallaṭṭa*, M. *pālaṭ*; Sk. *pratyabhijñānā*, Pr. *paccahiāṇa*, H. *pahicān*; Sk. *atyartha*, Pr. *accaṭṭa*, M. *acāṭ*, &c.

Now as to compounds, this peculiarity of the Sanskrit has been carried to an extravagant extent by later writers, but Pāṇini allows only certain formations of this nature. These grew up as independent words in the language, and hence in the matter of Saṃdhi were treated like other words. In the spoken language the euphonic combinations we have been considering were not consciously made, but the words themselves acquired those forms by habitual use in the same manner as in other tongues. The grammarians however discovered and laid down these rules; and the practice of using them in books even in combining different words gained ground, though however many instances in which there is no such Saṃdhi are found in the Itihāsas and the Purāṇas. But if in colloquial speech such a combination was not possible, the grammarians do not enjoin that it should be made; and very probably it was not made.

And traces of many expressions which only a colloquial use of language can generate have been preserved, not so much in the literature as by the grammarians. Such is one expressive of an intensive or excessive action, composed of the Imperative second person form of a root repeated, followed by a verbal form of the same in any tense of the Indicative and in any person or number; as *khāda khādeti khādati*, lit. 'eat, eat, he eats,' *i.e.* eats much, *kuru kurv iti karoti* 'do, do, he does,' *i.e.* does much. This expression exists in Marāṭhī and is considered so colloquial that no Marāṭhī grammarian has noticed it, as *khā khā khāto*, *kar kar karato* in which as in Sanskrit *khā* and *kara* are the forms of the Imperative second person singular. A similar expression is used when several actions are attributed to the same agent; as *odanaṃ bhuṅkṣva saktūn piba dhānāḥ khādety evāyam abhyavaharati* 'eat rice, drink barley water, devour fried grain, in this way he fills his stomach'; which in Marāṭhī is *bhāt jev pej pī lāhyā khā asem poṭ bharato*. In this case the Indicative should signify a general action of which the Imperatives denote the species, and we may have here *karoti* 'does' instead of *abhyavaharati*. Similarly those innumerable expressions consisting of a form made up by adding *am*, technically *ṇamul*, to a root, preceded by a noun, and of a verbal form of the same root must be colloquial; as *hastagrāhaṃ gṛhṇāti* 'holds by the hand,' *jīvanāśaṃ naśyati* 'he perishes,' *udarapūram bhuṅkte* 'eats a stomachful,' *yathākāram aham bhokṣye tathākāraṃ bhokṣye kiṃ tavānena* 'I, will eat as I eat (as I like), what have you to do with it?' &c. Etymologically *hastagrāham*, *jīvanāśam* &c. are accusatives, and they may in these cases be called cognate accusatives, and the expressions somewhat resemble such ones in English, as "run a race," "walk a walk," "die a death," &c. The compounds *daṇḍādaṇḍi*, *keśākeśi* &c. meaning 'a scuffle in which there is a brandishing of sticks and seizing each other by the hair;' and a great many others made up of Imperative forms of verbs, or of a verb and its object which are used as nouns, are of a nature suited for the purposes of a light conversation; as *atra khādatamodatā vartate* "'eat and enjoy' is the rule here," *atrāśnītapibatā vartate* "'eat and drink' is the rule here," *uddharotsṛjā tasya dānaśauṇḍīr asya gṛhe* "'take out and give' is what takes place in the house of a bountiful man," *jahistamboyam* "he is one who constantly says, 'strike the sheafs of corn'"; *ehisvāgatā vartate* "'come, welcome to thee' is the practice" &c.

Sanskrit was not the only language spoken in the times of Kātyāyana and Patañjali. In the Mahābhāṣya there are several passages which contain allusions to a dialect arising from a corruption of Sanskrit. Thus in the comment on the Vārtika *Siddhe śabdārtha-saṃbandhe*, we are told with reference to the question whether words are created or exist of themselves, that Pāṇini's rules suppose that they are not created but exist of themselves; and so is the relation between them and the things they denote, *i.e.* their power of expression uncreated and self-existent; and according to another interpretation of the Vārtika, the things also which words denote are so. How is it known that all these are self-existent? Because in the affairs of the world or in ordinary life men think of certain things and use words to express them; they do not set about producing words before doing so. But this is not the case with those things that are created and not self-existent. If a man wishes to do something with an earthen pot, he goes to the house of a potter and says, "Make a pot for me, I have to do something by its means." Now if he has to use words, he does not in the same way go to the house of a grammarian and say, "Make words, I want to use them"; but immediately that he thinks of this thing and that he uses words (for expressing them). Well then, if words are to be taken from ordinary life (and are not made by grammarians) what is it that the Śāstra (grammar) does: "The Śāstra lays down a restriction by observing which a man may attain religious merit. It does what other Śāstras in ordinary life do. Thus while it is possible to satisfy hunger by eating anything whatever, it is enjoined that one shall not eat domesticated fowl or pig; and the object is that he may by regulating his conduct thus attain religious merit. In the same way this Śāstra (grammar) tells us that while it is possible to express one's meaning by using correct words or incorrect words, correct ones alone which it teaches should be used to secure the religious merit arising therefrom." After this follows the discussion translated in the first lecture; and then we have another of which the following is a portion.

Pūrv. Does religious merit arise from a knowledge of correct words or from their use.

Sid. What is the difference?

Pūrv. If you say religious merit arises from their knowledge, religious demerit also must arise. For he who knows what words are correct, also knows what words are incorrect. If merit results from the knowledge of those that are correct, demerit must result from the knowledge of those that are incorrect; or greater demerit must arise (from their knowledge), as the number of incorrect words is larger, and that of correct words smaller. For the corruptions of one correct word are manifold; as, for instance, the corruptions of the correct word *gauḥ*: are *gāvī*, *goṇī*, *gotā*, *gopotalikā* &c. And the Ṛṣi also indicates (in a passage which is quoted) that the restriction as to correct words concerns their use (and not knowledge).

Sid. Well, then, let it be that religious merit arises from their use (and not from knowledge).

Pūrv. If from their use, the whole world would obtain heavenly felicity.

Sid. And now why should you be jealous if the whole world obtain heavenly felicity?

Pūrv. No, certainly, I am not jealous. But what I mean is that it thus becomes useless to make any effort; such effort only as is fruitful should be made. If you get the fruit without any effort, the effort is useless. (The effort meant is that involved in the study of grammar, *i.e.* of correct words. People use some correct words at least without studying grammar, and if eternal felicity results from the *use* of such words they get it without making the effort of studying the subject).

Sid. Why, verily those who make the effort will largely use correct words, and will obtain a large amount of heavenly felicity.

Pūrv. That the fruit does not follow the effort is also an observed fact. For there are persons who though they have made the effort are seen to be incompetent (in the use of correct words), while others who have not, are competent; wherefore it is possible the fruit, *i.e.* heavenly felicity, may not follow.

Sid. Well then, religious merit arises not from knowledge alone, neither from use alone.

Pūrv. From what then?

Sid. Heavenly felicity arises from the use of correct words when it is accompanied by the knowledge that they are correct, derived from a study of the Śāstra.

And thus it goes on.

Now it is clear from all this that correct words, *i.e.*, Sanskrit, was spoken in those days by all, but that incorrect words had got mixed up with it, and the object of grammar was to teach how to avoid incorrect words or corruptions, though there were men who could speak correctly without knowing grammar. And this is the state in which more or less all languages are at all times; and even at the present day the purpose of grammar is considered to be to teach how to speak correctly. By the way, it will be seen how Sanskrit grammarians distinctly declare that they teach nothing that does not exist, they do not create words, but separate the correct ones from such as are incorrect. But what did Patañjali consider to be the standard of correct Sanskrit, who was it that spoke the language correctly, and in whose speech were corruptions observable? This is clear from another passage at the beginning of the third pāda of the first chapter of the Mahābhāsya. Patañjali interprets the sūtra *bhūvādayo dhātavaḥ*: (I, 3, 1.) in a manner to yield such a connotative definition of a dhātu or root as this, that a dhātu is that which denotes action or being. Then a question is raised, if this is the way to distinguish a root why should a list of roots be given; in other words, if we have got a connotative definition, a definition by enumeration is not wanted. In this case there is a difference of opinion between Kātyāyana and Patañjali.

Pūrv. If you have given a connotative definition now, enumeration should not be made, *i.e.* a list of roots should not be given.

Sid. It should be made.

Pūrv. What for?

Sid. The enumeration of (the verbal roots) *bhū* and others should be made for the purpose of excluding nouns (*prātipadika*) and the verbs that begin with *āṇapayati*. (*i.e.* If the roots are not actually enumerated, nouns also which express action or being may come under the connotative definition. In the same way it will extend to roots used in ordinary life, which are not Sanskrit, such as *āṇapayati* and others.)

Pūrv. What verbs are those which begin with *āṇapayati*?

Sid. *Āṇapayati*, *vaṭṭati* and *vaḍḍhati*. And enumeration should also be made in order that the *anubandhas* or indicatory letters and accents of roots may be made known; *i.e.*, that one may know what the accents and indicatory letters of roots are. It is not possible to know the accents or indicatory letters unless the roots are enumerated. (*Anubandhas* are certain letters attached to roots to denote some conjugational or other peculiarity belonging to them.)

Pūrv. Now those roots whose accents are capable of being inferred, *i.e.* are *udātta*, and which have no *anubandhas*, but still are inserted in the list, may be omitted from it. (*i.e.* When those roots which have the *anudātta* accent are enumerated, it may be inferred that the rest have the other or *udātta* accent.)

Sid. Even these should be enumerated in order that *āṇapayati* and others (*i.e.*, corrupt Sanskrit roots) may be excluded.

Hereupon Patañjali disagrees with Kātyāyana and says:—

Pat. No. *Āṇapayati* and others will be excluded, because the usage of the educated or Śiṣṭas is to be followed. This usage of the Śiṣṭas must be necessarily referred to in other cases even; for instance, in order to exclude the altered forms of those roots that are enumerated. For in ordinary life, they use *kasi* for *kṛṣi* and *disi* for *dṛśi*. (The sense is, that since in grammar we follow the usage of the Śiṣṭas or educated, these verbs *āṇapayati*, *vaṭṭati* and *vaḍḍhati*, and also *kasi* for *kṛṣi* and *disi* for *dṛśi* which are not used by them will necessarily be excluded from our connotative definition; hence for the purpose of excluding them enumeration is not wanted.)

Now *āṇapayati* is a corruption of the Sanskrit *ājñāpayati*, *vaṭṭati* of *vartate*, and *vaḍḍhati* of *vardhate*, *te* Ātm. being replaced by *ti* Parasm., and *kas* of *kṛṣ*, and *dis* of *dṛś*. These and such other corruptions were in use at the time, but Patañjali clearly lays down that they were not used by the Śiṣṭas or educated people, and therefore they belonged to the language of the vulgar. Now all these roots are found in the Pāli in these very forms, *āṇapayati* being, however, *āṇāpayati*; but the reading in the MSS. and the Benares lithographed edition which I have consulted is faulty. So also of the corruptions of the word *go* given by our author, we find *gāvī* in Professor Childers' Pāli Dictionary, and *goṇa* the masculine of *goṇī*.

Thus our grammarians recognise one language only, the Sanskrit, and these words and forms which are found in the Pāli they assign to the speech of the vulgar.

In another passage still we are told more definitely who the Śiṣṭas were that spoke the Sanskrit language correctly without studying Pāṇini's grammar, and whose usage was the standard of correctness. Pāṇini's Sūtra VI. 3, 109, lays down that such words as *pṛṣodara* ['with a spotted belly'] should be regarded as correct in the form in which they are upadiṣṭa, *i.e.*, used or uttered; the changes in them such as the elision, or augmentation of letters or the alteration of their forms do not obey any general rules laid down by him, but still the words exhibiting those changes should be taken as correct, just as they are used. Now the Pūrvapakṣin raises the question.

Pūrv. What is meant by *upadiṣṭa*?

Sid. Uttered (used).

Pūrv. How does it come to mean that?

Sid. The root 'diś' signifies 'uttering.' One utters (uses), letters, and says that they are thus upadiṣṭa.

Pūrv. By whom upadiṣṭa (uttered or used)?

Sid. By the Śiṣṭas.

Pūrv. Who are the Śiṣṭas?

Sid. The grammarians.

Pūrv. How so?

Sid. The character of a Śiṣṭa is conferred upon one by the knowledge of the science (Śāstra); and the grammarians know the science (of grammar).

Pūrv. If a man is made Śiṣṭa by the science, and the science depends upon a man's being Śiṣṭa, this is reasoning in a circle. An argument in a circle does not hold. (The circle is, one is Śiṣṭa, and consequently an authority in matters of language if he has studied grammar; and grammar itself depends on the usage of the Śiṣṭas).

Sid. Well, then, the character of a Śiṣṭa is conferred upon one by the country in which he lives and by his conduct. That sort of conduct must be associated with residence in Āryāvarta alone, (lit. that sort of conduct must be in Āryāvarta alone).

Pūrv. Which is Āryāvarta?

Sid. The country which is to the east of the Ādarśa, west of Kālakavana, south of the Himālaya, and north of the Pāriyātra. Those Brahmans in this country of the Āryas who do not store up riches (lit. who keep only so much grain as is contained in a jar), who are not greedy, who do good disinterestedly, and who without any effort are conversant with a certain branch of knowledge are the worshipful Śiṣṭas.

Pūrv. If, then, the Śiṣṭas are an authority as regards language, what function does the Aṣṭādhyāyī (Pāṇini's grammar) perform?

Sid. The purpose of the Aṣṭādhyāyī is to enable us to find out the Śiṣṭas.

Pūrv. How is it possible to find out the Śiṣṭas by means of the Aṣṭādhyāyī?

Sid. A student of the Aṣṭādhyāyī finds a man who has not studied the book using words just as they are taught in the Aṣṭādhyāyī. He then thinks, "Verily, this man possesses some good luck or innate nature by means of which, though he has not studied the Aṣṭādhyāyī, he uses words just as they are taught in that book. Verily he knows other words also" (not taught in the Aṣṭādhyāyī, such as *pṛṣodara*). Thus, the purpose of the Aṣṭādhyāyī is to enable one to find out who is a Śiṣṭa (in order that he may refer to him and learn such words as do not obey the rules laid down by Pāṇini, but still are correct).

Here then we have the clearest possible evidence that Sanskrit was the vernacular of holy or respectable Brahmans of Āryāvarta or Northern India, who could speak the language correctly without the study of grammar. The corrupt language mentioned by Patañjali which was composed of correct and incorrect words, that is, a dialect like the Pāli must, therefore, have been the vernacular of the other classes. And this is what you may say even with regard to the modern vernaculars. Who is it that speaks good or correct Marāṭhī? Of course, Brahmans of culture. The language of the other classes is not correct Marāṭhī. The word Śiṣṭa may be translated by "a man of education or culture;" and this education or culture has, since remote times, been almost confined to Brahmans. Thus the dialects of the inscriptions of Aśoka and the Pāli were the vernaculars of the non-Brahmanic classes; but a greater importance must evidently have been attached to them in the times of Aśoka than is now assigned to the Marāṭhī of the non-Brahmanic classes since they are used by him in the inscriptions. They are however not recognized as independent languages by our grammarians who treated them as we treat the Marāṭhī of the lower classes; but they were in use and bore the same relation to Sanskrit that low Marāṭhī does to high Marāṭhī, the English of the lower classes in England to the speech of the higher. And the English of the lower classes contains, as we have seen, a great many such grammatical forms as "I knowed," and "you says," along with others that are correct.

11

Franz Kielhorn (1840–1908)

Franz Kielhorn (1840–1908) studied Sanskrit mainly with A. F. Stenzler, who was influenced by Bopp. His first publication was an edition of Śāntanava's *Phiṭsūtra*, a treatise dealing with the accent. He then went to Oxford to work with Monier Monier-Williams (to whom Weber had recommended him) on the Sanskrit dictionary. Subsequently Kielhorn proceeded to Poona, this time with recommendations from Max Müller, to take up a professorship of Oriental Languages (that is, Sanskrit) at the Deccan College. He stayed in India for more than fifteen years and kept in close contact not only with Georg Bühler at the Elphinstone College at Bombay but also with numerous Indian scholars, including Bhandarkar. Bühler and Kielhorn initiated a new era in Western Sanskrit scholarship. Wackernagel says about Kielhorn's work in India: "Kielhorn war nun im Besitz einer Kenntnis der grammatischen Litteratur der Inder, wie sie vor ihm bloss Colebrooke in ähnlicher Tiefe besessen hat, nach ihm vielleicht niemand wieder besitzen wird" (Wackernagel 1908, 6).

One of the first articles written by Kielhorn on the subject of the Sanskrit grammarians, "Der Grammatiker Pāṇini" (1885), was a reaction to a paper by Pischel, who had defended the view that Pāṇini had lived in the sixth century A.D. at the earliest. The second part of Kielhorn's article deals with the text of Pāṇini's grammar as known to the authors of the *Kāśikā*. The material of this second half was published later in English in Kielhorn's "The text of Pāṇini's Sūtras, as given in the *Kāśikā-Vṛtti*, compared with the text known to Kātyāyana and Patañjali" of 1887. As this second article is also included in this volume, only the first part of "Der Grammatiker Pāṇini" will be reproduced here (*Nachrichten von der königlichen Gesellschaft der Wissenschaften und der Georg-Augusts-Universität zu Göttingen* 5, 1885, 185–190). Needless to say, Kielhorn's conclusions with regard to the chronology of the early grammarians are now universally accepted.

A. Der Grammatiker Pāṇini (1885)

Franz Kielhorn

Prof. Pischel hat in der Zeitschr. d. D. Morg. Ges. XXXIX S. 95—98 zwei Verse eines Dichters *Pāṇini* aus *Nami's* Rudraṭakāvyālaṃkāraṭippanaka mitgeteilt und wahrscheinlich zu machen gesucht daß der Dichter und der Grammatiker Pāṇini eine Person seien. Dieser Pāṇini würde in das 6te, frühestens 5te Jahrhundert nach Chr. zu setzen sein, und es würde dann keine so große Lücke zwischen der *Aṣṭādhyāyī* und der *Kāśikā* bestehen 'wie man jetzt annehmen muß, und wie es ganz unwahrscheinlich ist'.

Ich will versuchen mit wenigen Worten darzulegen was uns über das gegenseitige Verhältniß der erhaltenen grammatischen Werke der Inder von Pāṇini bis etwa zur Mitte des 7ten Jahrhunderts nach Chr. bekannt ist. Vorher jedoch bemerke ich daß Nami's Worte ebensowenig wie eine anonyme Strophe ein Beweis für die Identität des Dichters und des Grammatikers Pāṇini sein können und daß die von Nami citirten Stellen eher gegen als für solche Identität sprechen.

'Obgleich', so übersetze ich abweichend von Pischel, 'der Gebrauch falscher Formen schon indirect dadurch verboten ist daß vom Dichter umfassende gelehrte Bildung (und deshalb natürlich auch eine Kenntniß der Grammatik) verlangt worden ist, so tadelt der Verfasser doch noch ausdrücklich den Gebrauch solcher Formen um zu zeigen daß man besondere Aufmerksamkeit auf ihre Vermeidung verwenden müsse, weil er findet daß sogar große (und mit der Grammatik vertraute) Dichter (aus Unachtsamkeit) falsche Formen gebraucht haben'. Als Beweise für den Schluß des Satzes citirt Nami zwei Stellen Pāṇini's in denen *gṛhya* fälschlich für *gṛhītvā* und *paśyatī* fälschlich für *paśyantī* gebraucht worden sind. Ist es aber wahrscheinlich, daß der Grammatiker Pāṇini seine eigenen Regeln VII, 1, 37 *samāse 'nañpūrve ktvo lyap* und VII, 1, 81 *śapśyanor nityam* vergessen haben sollte?

Wichtiger ist die Frage nach dem Zeitalter dieses Pāṇini. Wenn ich hier zunächst meine eigene Ansicht aussprechen darf, so ist es die daß Pāṇini der vedischen Litteratur weit näher steht als der sogenannten classischen; daß er einer Zeit angehört in der das Sanskrit mehr war als eine Sprache der Gelehrten.

Ich gebe zu, daß das Bestreben die Zeit eines Grammatikers aus den von ihm gegebenen Beispielen bestimmen zu wollen, zu einem sichern Resultate deshalb nicht immer führen kann, weil wir nicht wissen ob solche Beispiele von ihm selbst gebildet oder seinen Vorgängern entnommen sind. Dieselben Beispiele finden sich in den Werken der jüngeren wie in denen der älteren Grammatiker. Wäre das Mahābhāṣya verloren gegangen, so würden wir aus den Beispielen der Kāśikā für den Gebrauch des Imperfectums (Kāś. III, 2, 111) und aus der Erwähnung des Puṣyamitra für das Alter dieses Werkes vielleicht dieselben Schlüsse ziehn die jetzt für das Mahābhāṣya gezogen werden trotz der Thatsache daß Patañjali ältere Werke ebenso benutzt hat wie es die Verfasser der Kāśikā gethan haben. Wenn aber Pāṇini z. B. in Uebereinstimmung mit dem vorherrschenden Gebrauche der ältern Sprache das Periphr. Perfectum nur mit dem Verbum kṛ bildet, während die Schriftsteller des 6ten Jahrhunderts kṛ, bhū und as ohne Unterschied gebrauchen; wenn seine Lehre über die Verwendung des Aorists durch die Praxis der Brāhmaṇas bestätigt wird, während die spätere Zeit das Verständniß für die Unterschiede der Tempora der Vergangenheit verloren hat; wenn seine Regeln für den Gebrauch der Casus in einem Brāhmaṇa bis in die geringfügigsten Details beobachtet werden, Abweichungen von denselben dagegen bei classischen Schriftstellern nicht selten sind, so fühlen wir daß wir auf festerem Boden stehn, und werden Pāṇini eher Jahrhunderte vor Chr. als zusammen mit *Kālidāsa*, *Bhāravi* u. a. etwa in das 5te oder 6te Jahrhundert nach Chr. setzen.

Wie aber verhält es sich dann mit der Lücke welche in diesem Falle zwischen Pāṇini und der Kāśikā bestehen würde und deren Vorhandensein Prof. Pischel als unwahrscheinlich bezeichnet hat? A priori ist es vollständig gleichgültig, ob wir die Kāśikā 200 oder 1200 Jahre nach Pāṇini verfaßt sein lassen, denn wir haben nicht den geringsten Grund anzunehmen daß sie einer der frühesten oder überhaupt einer der alten Commentare zu Pāṇini's Grammatik gewesen sei. Die uns bekannten Thatsachen erhärten vielmehr das Gegentheil. Von mehr als funfzig Regeln können wir beweisen daß sie in der Kāśikā anders lauten als sie Pāṇini gegeben hat. Nicht nur werden in jedem Kapitel die Lesarten und Erklärungen Anderer mit Kecit, Kaścit, Anye, Apare, Aparaḥ, Eke, Pāṭhāntara, Smṛtyantara, Śāstrāntara, Granthāntara u.s.w. eingeführt, sondern einer der Verfasser berichtet im Eingange seines Werkes ausdrücklich, er fasse kurz das Beste von dem zusammen was sich in den Commentaren (zu Pāṇini) und andern Werken zerstreut finde. Einige Namen der Verfasser solcher Commentare sind uns erhalten worden.

Außer älteren Commentaren haben die Compilatoren der Kāśikā auch das *Mahābhāṣya* benutzt. Das Mahābhāṣya ist von *Bhartṛhari* commentirt worden, und da wir durch M. Müller's für die Geschichte der Grammatik epochemachende Entdeckung wissen daß dieser Bhartṛhari vor den Verfassern der Kāśikā gelebt hat, so verdienen sein Verhältniß zum Mahābhāṣya und seine Mittheilungen über die Geschichte dieses Werkes unsere besondere Aufmerksamkeit. In der Vorrede zum 2ten Bande meiner Ausgabe habe ich gezeigt, daß Bhartṛhari oft verschiedene Lesarten des Textes des Mahābhāṣya mitgetheilt und daß er noch häufiger die abweichenden Erklärungen anderer Commentatoren erwähnt hat, deren Werke verloren gegangen sind. Würden wir schon hieraus schließen daß Patañjali und Bhartṛhari durch einen vielleicht nach Jahrhunderten zu bemessenden Zeitraum von einander getrennt sind, so wird diese Ansicht in vollem Maße bestätigt durch die bekannten Verse am Schlusse des 2ten Buches des Vākyapadīya. Dort nennt Bhartṛhari das Mahābhāṣya das Buch des *Ṛṣi*; er berichtet daß es eine Zeit gab in der das Werk nicht verstanden wurde, und fügt hinzu daß wir seine Wiedereinführung in den Kreis der grammatischen Studien dem *Ācārya Candra* und andern Gelehrten verdanken. Absichtlich übergehe ich die Nachricht nach der Candrācārya unter *Abhimanyu* von *Kaśmīr* gelebt haben soll, und ebensowenig will ich den Stil und den eigenthümlichen Sprachgebrauch des Mahābhāṣya als Argumente für das Alter dieses Werkes benutzen. Soviel denke ich erwiesen zu haben daß es im höchsten Grade gewagt sein würde auch nur Patañjali in eine so späte Zeit wie das 5te Jahrhundert nach Chr. setzen zu wollen. Und welcher Zeitraum liegt zwischen Patañjali und Pāṇini!

Das Mahābhāṣya ist zunächst ein Commentar zu *Kātyāyana's Vārttikas*, aber es ist ebensowenig der älteste Commentar zu jenem Werke wie Bhartṛhari's der älteste Commentar zum Mahābhāṣya oder die Kāśikā der älteste Commentar zur Aṣṭādhyāyī gewesen sind. Denn wir erfahren von Patañjali, daß Andre nicht nur eine ganze Anzahl von Vārttikas anders als er selbst erklärt (vgl. z. B. meine Ausgabe Vol. I, pag. 10, 64, 237, 247, 357, 366, 450, 465, 473 u. s. w.), sondern daß sie auch den Text gewisser Vārttikas anders abgetheilt (z. B. I, pag. 193, 422), oder überhaupt anders gelesen hatten (z. B. I, pag. 179, 314). Auch hatte es in der Zeit zwischen Kātyāyana und Patañjali Gelehrte gegeben welche die Lehren des Vārttikakāra zu vereinfachen, zu erweitern, oder ihnen durch die Hinzufügung näherer Bestimmungen eine exactere Fassung zu geben sich bemüht hatten (vgl. z. B. I, pag. 367; 230, 281, 443; II, pag. 103, 273, 304, 397; I, pag. 468, 489; II, pag. 136 u. s. w.). In dieselbe Periode fallen, um von vereinzelt genannten Persönlichkeiten nicht zu reden, zwei Schulen von Grammatikern, welche beide auf der von Kātyāyana eingeschlagenen Bahn weiter gegangen waren, und von denen die einen, die *Bhāradvājīyās*, in engerem Anschlusse an Kātyāyana hauptsächlich dessen Werk zu verbessern oder zu vervollständigen bestrebt gewesen waren (vgl. I, pag. 73, 136, 201; II, pag. 46, 70, 233; III, pag. 199, 230), während die andern, die *Saunāgās*, in mehr selbständiger Weise ihre kritischen Bemerkungen gegen Pāṇini selbst gerichtet hatten (vgl. I, pag. 416; II, pag. 105, 228, 238, 325; III, pag. 76, 159; vgl. auch Kāśikā zu P. VII, 2, 17). Was wird aus den Generationen von Gelehrten von denen wir aus dem Mahābhāṣya allein Kunde haben, wenn Pāṇini selbst frühestens im 5ten Jahrhundert nach Chr. gelebt haben soll?

Und dies ist nicht Alles. Die Tradition berichtet daß Patañjali sein eigenes Werk verfaßte als ein älteres grammatisches Werk, dessen Titel er uns selbst überliefert hat, unverständlich geworden war und daß seine Lehren auf die in jenem Werke enthaltenen Lehren basirt sind. Wie dem auch sei, soviel läßt sich aus dem Mahābhāṣya selbst ersehen daß Patañjali ein oder mehrere in Versen geschriebene Werke vor sich hatte, die nach der Zeit des Kātyāyana verfaßt waren und die Patañjali in so ausgedehntem Maße benutzt hat daß manche Stellen seines Werkes kaum anders denn als Prosaversionen metrischer Originale bezeichnet werden können. Wenn nun die Verfasser jener von Patañjali benutzten Schriften Kātyāyana (II, pag. 121) den Vārttikakāra (II, pag. 176) den *Bhagavān Kātyaḥ* (II, pag. 97) 'den heiligen Kātya' nennen, gerade wie Bhartṛhari den Verfasser des Mahābhāṣya den *Ṛṣi* Patañjali gennant hat, so reden sie offenbar nicht von einem Zeitgenossen, sondern von einem Gelehrten der schon für sie—und wieviel mehr für Patañjali—ein Weiser der Vorzeit war.

Und was für das Verhältniß des Patañjali zu Kātyāyana gilt, gilt in gleichem Maße für das Verhältniß des Kātyāyana zu *Pāṇini*. Auch für ihn ist Pāṇini schon der *Bhagavān Pāṇiniḥ* (vergl. III, pag. 467), auch er hatte seine Vorgänger in der kritischen Behandlung der Aṣṭādhyāyī (vgl. z. B. I, pag. 211, 365; II, pag. 19, 133, 216; III, pag. 265, 377), auch er kannte ebenso wir Patañjali Commentare zu Pāṇini, denn seine Bemerkungen beziehn sich in vielen Fällen nicht sowohl auf den Text der Sūtras als auf die Erklärungen, von denen sie begleitet gewesen sind. Daß das Sanskṛt in der Zeit zwischen Pāṇini und Kātyāyana in grammatischer wie lexicalischer Hinsicht manchen Veränderungen unterworfen gewesen war, daß in derselben Zeit eine neue Litteratur entstanden war, daß während derselben Periode die Sanskṛtsprechenden Hindus weite Landstrecken Indiens in Besitz genommen hatten, ist von andern Gelehrten erwiesen worden, und ich glaube nicht daß die hierfür wie überhaupt für das Alter der Aṣṭādhyāyī vorgebrachten Beweise einfach durch die Identification eines Dichters und des Grammatikers Pāṇini zunichte gemacht werden können.

B. The Authorities on Grammar Quoted in the Mahābhāṣya (1887)

Franz Kielhorn

Kielhorn contributed a number of studies on the Indian grammarians to the 1886 and 1887 volumes of the *Indian Antiquary*. As many of them are full of textual references, only some will be reproduced here; others will be briefly described. Kielhorn's interest was not confined to the grammatical works of the Pāṇinian tradition. In "Indragomin and other grammarians" (*Indian Antiquary* 15, 1886, 181–183), for example, he showed that there was no school of Aindra grammarians prior to Pāṇini as had been argued by A. C. Burnell (in his Essay on "The Aindra School of Sanskrit Grammarians," 1875), by Peterson and others (including al-Bīrūnī, as we saw on pages 21–22). Kielhorn showed, however, that a grammar composed by Indra, whose full name was Indragomin, must have existed as it had been used by Hemacandra (in the twelfth century). After discussing some grammarians referred to by Hemacandra, Kielhorn arrived at the conclusion that Indragomin's grammar was probably related to the grammar of Candragomin (sixth century ? cf. page 158).

In "The *Cāndra-Vyākaraṇa* and the *Kāśikā-Vṛtti*" (*Indian Antiquary* 15, 1886, 183–185), Kielhorn turned to Candragomin's grammar and found that the authors of the *Kāśikā* commentary "diligently used that grammar, although they never actually mention it." In this paper he also contrasted some of Pāṇini's technical terms with those of Candra.

Kielhorn published seven "Notes on the *Mahābhāṣya*" in the *Indian Antiquary*, as follows:

1. *Ācāryadeśīya* (1886, 80–81)
2. Goṇikāputra and Gonardīya (1886, 81–84)
3. On some Doubtful *Vārttikas* (1886, 203–211)
4. Some Suggestions Regarding the Verses (*Kārikās*) in the *Mahābhāṣya* (1886, 228–233)
5. The Authorities on Grammar Quoted in the *Mahābhāṣya* (1887, 101–106)
6. The Text of Pāṇini's Sūtras, as Given in the *Kāśikā-Vṛtti*, Compared with the Text Known to Kātyāyana and Patañjali (1887, 178–184)
7. Some Devices of Indian Grammarians (1887, 244–252)

In the first, "*Ācāryadeśīya*," Kielhorn showed with the help of a selection of quotations from the grammatical commentaries that the *Mahābhāṣya* is written in the form of a dialogue, in which the principal interlocutors are the *Śiṣya*, the *Ācāryadeśīya*, and the *Ācārya*: "The *Śiṣya* brings forward his doubts and asks questions; the *Ācāryadeśīya* is ready to solve these doubts and reply to the questions raised, but . . . his answers are given hastily and without a full knowledge of all the difficulties of the matter under discussion; so that finally the *Ācārya* must step in to overrule him, and to explain the true state of the case" (80).

In the second, "Goṇikāputra and Gonardīya," Kielhorn argued that these two names are the names of grammarians quoted by Patañjali, and do not denote Patañjali himself. The latter view had been defended by other scholars and had led to the assumption that Patañjali was the son of Goṇikā and a native of Gonarda.

In the third, "On some Doubtful *Vārttikas*," Kielhorn, considering the principles for the reconstruction of the *vārttikas* of Kātyāyana from the *Mahābhāṣya* in which they are quoted, discusses a few cases where it is doubtful whether a passage occurring in the *Mahābhāṣya* should be regarded as a *vārttika*.

In the fourth, "Some Suggestions Regarding the Verses (*Kārikās*) in the *Mahābhāṣya*," Kielhorn showed that most of these

verses are not the work of Kātyāyana or Patañjali, but are borrowed from older versified grammatical works, composed after the *vārttikas*.

In the fifth article, "The Authorities on Grammar quoted in the *Mahābhāṣya*," Kielhorn collected passages or expressions in which older authorities, other than Pāṇini or Kātyāyana, were referred to by Patañjali. Though this article, like most of the others, is written mainly for students specifically of the *Mahābhāṣya*, it contains information of general interest and is reproduced here (*Indian Antiquary* 16, 1887, 101–106).

In the preceding note I have tried to show, that the *Kārikās*, which we meet with in the Mahābhāṣya, are taken from grammatical works composed after the *Vārttikas*, and that Patañjali has probably used the same works, even where he does not actually quote from them. In the present note I intend to collect those passages or expressions, in which Kātyāyana and Patañjali, or the authors of the verses preserved in the Mahābhāṣya, are distinctly quoting or referring to authorities on grammar, other than Pāṇini or Kātyāyana.

Pūrvasūtra

Grammars older than Pāṇini are referred to by the term Pūrvasūtra,[1] which is used by both Kātyāyana and Patañjali, as well as in the *Kārikās*, and which occurs six times in the Mahābhāṣya. According to Kātyāyana (Vol. II. p. 205), Pāṇini may have employed the word *upasarjana* in the rule IV. 1, 14, in the sense of *apradhāna*, in accordance with the usage of former grammars. According to Patañjali (Vol. I. p. 248), Pāṇini has similarly used *vṛddha* for *gotra* in I. 2, 65. In a *Kārikā* in Vol. I. p. 36, the term *akṣara* is said to have been employed in former grammars in the sense of *varṇa*, 'a letter.' In Vol. III. p. 104, Patañjali refutes a suggestion of Kātyāyana's by intimating, that the term *citaḥ* in P. VI. 1, 163, need not necessarily be the Genitive of *cit*, but may be taken to be the Nominative of *cita*, 'containing a suffix that has the Anubandha *c*,' the Nom. having been employed by Pāṇini in accordance with the practice of former grammars, in which that which undergoes an operation was put in the Nom., not in the Gen. case.[2] According to Patañjali (Vol. III. p. 455), the word *ahnaḥ* in P. VIII. 4, 7, may, by the same reasoning, be taken to be the Nom. of *ahna*, not the Gen. of *ahan*. Lastly, in Vol. III. p. 247 it is suggested that Pāṇini may have taken the term *auṅ* which he uses in VII. 1, 18, from an older grammar, a suggestion intended to show, why the operation, which in Pāṇini's work usually takes place before a termination with the Anubandha *ṅ* does not take place in the case of the terminations under discussion. This last passage has occasioned Patañjali's general remark, which has been made much of by the late Prof. Goldstücker,[3] that Anubandhas used in former grammars have no effect in the grammar of Pāṇini.

[1] Kaiyata on P. IV. 1, 14:—*pūrvasūtraśabdena pūrvācāryakṛtavyākaraṇam ucyate.*

[2] Kaiyaṭa on P. VI. 1, 163:—*pūrvavyākaraṇe prathamayā kāryī nirdiśyate*; and on P. VIII. 4, 7:—*pūrvācāryāḥ kāryabhājaḥ saṣṭhyā na niradikṣann ity arthaḥ.*

[3] See Goldstücker's *Pāṇini*, p. 181; Burnell's *On the Aindra School of Sanskṛt grammarians*, p. 40.

From all this we learn little about the works of Pāṇini's predecessors. That some of their technical terms differed from those used by Pāṇini, is probable enough, but Kātyāyana's and Patañjali's remarks regarding the particular terms mentioned are hardly of more value than the similar statements concerning *Pūrvācārya-saṃjñāḥ* or *Prācāṃ saṃjñāḥ* of later writers. It may also be true that some ancient grammarians, like some modern ones,[4] did use the Nom. in the way stated, and that they did employ other Anubandhas. I am quite aware too of the fact, that Pāṇini occasionally does use the Nom. case, where we should have expected the Gen.; and *ahnaḥ* in P. VIII. 4, 7, undoubtedly *is* the Nom. of *ahna*, just as *vanam* in VIII. 4, 4 is the Nom. of *vana*, and *vāhanam* in VIII. 4, 8 the Nom. of *vāhana*. At the same time Patañjali's explanations look too much as if they had been invented for the occasion. At any rate, to take the word *citaḥ* as a Nominative is impossible; and as regards the term *auṅ*, I cannot help thinking that Patañjali would have given his explanation in a more direct and positive manner, had he in this particular instance really been possessed of any authentic knowledge regarding the more ancient works, from which he supposes Pāṇini to have borrowed.

Āpiśali and Śākaṭāyana

Two only of the grammarians, who are mentioned by Pāṇini himself, are quoted in the Mahābhāṣya by name, Śākaṭāyana and Āpiśali.[5] But regarding the former all we are told (Vol. II. p. 138) is, that in his opinion all nouns are derived from verbs, a statement which has been copied from the *Nirukta*.[6] And of Āpiśali, only the single rule is referred to (Vol. II. p. 281), that *dhenu* takes the suffix *ka*, provided it be not compounded with the negative *a*. Thus much would appear to be certain, even from this solitary quotation, that both the author of the *Kārikā*, who alludes to Āpiśali's rule, and Patañjali, who more fully explains his remark, were really acquainted with the text of that grammarian's *Sūtra*.[7]

[4] e.g. the author of the *Kātantra*. Compare also in the *Kārikās* such constructions as *vālavāyo vidūram* (*scil. āpadyate*), Vol. II. p. 313.—The use of the cases in the technical structure of Pāṇini's rules requires a separate and full investigation. In this respect, Pāṇini is most uncertain. He undoubtedly employs the Ablative and Genitive cases in a promiscuous manner, and he often has the Nominative, where we should least have expected it. Nor are the commentators wrong, when they speak of *avibhaktika nirdeśa*. And from their point of view, I am quite ready to endorse the maxim *chandovat sūtrāṇi bhavanti*. [On this point, see Birwé 1966.]

[5] Śākaṭāyana is mentioned also in Vol. II. p. 120.—In Vārt. 3. on P. IV. 1, 14, Kātyāyana has *āpiśalam adhīte*. In Vol. I. p. 12, Patañjali gives the instances *pāṇinīyam āpiśalam kāśakṛtsnam*, and in Vol. III. p. 125 *āpiśala-pāṇinīyavyāḍīyagautamīyāḥ*

[6] The passage of the *Nirukta* referred to in the above (Roth's edition, p. 35) has not yet been satisfactorily explained; here I would only state that the term *saṃvijñāna* is used in the sense of *avyutpanna prātipadika* in the Mahābhāṣya, Vol. III. p. 436, l. 11, a meaning which is not given in our dictionaries. The grammar of the old Śākaṭāyana must have been lost in very early times, for, so far as I know, there is no reference to it in any grammatical work later than Pāṇini.

[7] Regarding Āpiśali see the preface of Vol. II. of my edition of the Mahābhāṣya, p. 20, note. On P. II. 3, 17, Kaiyaṭa reports, that Āpiśali's reading of that rule was *many akarmaṇy anādara upamāne vibhāṣāprāṇiṣu*. On P. V. 1, 21, he states, that for the word

Anye Vaiyākaraṇāḥ; Anya Ācāryāḥ

"Other Grammarians" are mentioned by Patañjali twice; "other Ācāryas" only once. In one of these passages (Vol. I. p. 87) the expression "other grammarians" may possibly denote Kātyāyana, whose Vārt. 1. on P. VI. 1, 144, teaches exactly what the *others* are stated to have taught. The two other passages are of some interest, because one of them (Vol. I. p. 48) contains the technical term *Saṃkrama*, 'a termination having the Anubandha, or *kṅ* which ordinarily prevent the substitution of Guṇa and Vṛddhi,' a term which has not yet been met with anywhere else; while the other (Vol. III. p. 177), instead of *antaraṅga*, has the word *pratyaṅga* which in this technical sense is found in a *Kārikā* on P. VI. 4, 110, and in the quotation from Gonardīya on P. 1. 1, 29.

I may add here that Patañjali undoubtedly is quoting a rule of other grammarians, although he does not actually say so, in the words *lakṣaṇaṃ hi bhavati yvor vṛddhiprasaṅga iyuvau bhavata iti* in Vol. I. p. 310, and that very probably one or two more rules of others are alluded to elsewhere in the Mahābhāṣya.[8]

Eke; in Vārttikas

In the *Vārttikas*, as they are printed in my edition, Kātyāyana seven times introduces other scholars by the word *eke*, 'Some,' which is always placed at the end of a *Vārttika*, and for which Patañjali generally supplies the verb *icchanti* 'they maintain.' According[9] to the Vārt. on P. I. 2, 38 (Vol. 1. p. 211) only *some* agree with Pāṇini, the practical result of which is, that Pāṇini's rule may be regarded as optional. In Vārt. 1 on P. II. 1, 1, Kātyāyana explains *sāmarthyam by pṛthag arthānām ekārthībhāvaḥ*; in Vārt. 4 (Vol. I. p. 365) he states, that *some* take it to be *parasparavyapekṣā*. In Vārt. 1 on P. III. 1, 8, he teaches, that the suffix *kyac* must not be added to a base ending in *m* nor to an indeclinable; in Vārt. 2 (Vol. II. p. 19) he adds, that, according to *some*, *kyac* is added to *go*, to a base ending in a simple vowel, and to bases ending in *n*. In Vārt. 2 on

aśate of Pāṇini's rule Āpiśala and Kāśakṛtsna read *agranthe*. Kāsakṛtsna is besides mentioned by Kaiyaṭa on P. II. 1, 51, where the rule *pratyayottarapadayoḥ* is ascribed to him. A rule of the Āpiśalāḥ is given in the Kāśikā on P. VII. 3, 95. And of the Āpiśalāḥ and Kāśakṛtsnāḥ it is reported by Helārāja, in his commentary on the *Prakīrṇaka*, that they had not given the rule *tadarham* (P. V. 1, 117. Bhartṛhari merely says *tadarham iti nārabdhaṃ sūtraṃ vyākaraṇāntare*).

[8] On the Vārt. 23 on P I. 4, 2 (Vol. I. p. 310) Kaiyaṭa has the remark—*prasaṅgena vyākaraṇāntare lakṣaṇaṃ vicārayitum āha yaṅādeśād*. On the Vārt. 3 on P. II. I, 36 (Vol. I. p. 388) Kaiyaṭa calls the statement *vikṛtiḥ prakṛtyā*, with which the *Vārttika* begins, a *Pūrvācārya-sūtra*. From the remark in Vol. I. p. 100, I. 18, it appears, that the grammarians whose views are given there, instead of *asya cvau* (P. VII. 4, 32), had read the rule *asya cvāv anavyayasya*. (The modern Śākaṭāyana has the rule *cvau cāsyānavyayasyeḥ*; see also *Gaṇaratnamahodadhi*, p. 28). And from Patañjali's remark *prātipadikasyāntaḥ* in Vol. II. p. 7 and Vol. III. p. 87, it would seem, that he knew some such rule as is given in the first *Phiṭsūtra*. The *Phiṭsūtra* IV. 6 *nyaṅsvarau svaritau* would seem actually to occur in Vol. I. p. 262, I. 12, but I have strong reasons to suspect, that in that passage the text given by the MSS. has been interpolated.—I purposely have omitted here all references to the Prātiśākhyas, or *Chandaḥśāstrāṇi*, as Patañjali calls them.

[9] In the following I am merely giving the general import of the *Vārttikas* referred to, not an accurate and full translation of them.

P. III. 2, 146, Kātyāyana says, that Pāṇini has taught the addition of *vuñ* to *nind*, etc., in order to show that the suffixes taught in P. III. 2, 134, 177 necessarily supersede the suffix *ṇvul* of P. III. 1, 133; in Vārt. 3 (Vol. II. p. 133) he adds, that, according to *some*, what is shown by P. III. 2, 146, is, that the suffixes mentioned necessarily supersede, not merely *ṇvul* but all suffixes taught in general rules. In Vārt. 1 on P. IV. 1, 39, Kātyāyana states that, contrary to Pāṇini's rule, *asita* and *palita* form *asitā* and *palitā*; in Vārt. 2 (Vol. II. p. 216) he adds, that, according to *some*, they form *asiknī* and *paliknī* in the Veda. In Vārt. 4 on P. VII. 1, 72 he teaches that, contrary to Pāṇini's rule, the Nom. Plur. Neut. of *bahūrj* is *bahūrji*; in Vārt. 5 (Vol. III. p. 265) he adds, that according to *some*, it is *bahūrñji*. Finally, in Vārt. 3 on P. VIII. 1, 51 (Vol. III. p. 377) he states, that *some* object to the interpretation of Pāṇini's rule by which the words *na cet kārakam sarvānyat* are taken to mean *na cet kartā sarvānyaḥ*.

To the above we must add three similar statements, which undoubtedly are *Vārttikas*, but which have disappeared from the MSS. because Patañjali's explanations of them happened to commence with identically the same words.[10] The first is *dyudrubhyāṃ nityārtham eke*, which should be inserted before 1, 4 of Vol. II. p. 396; the second, *upasamastārtham eke* which has to be added before the last line in Vol. III. p. 104; and the third, *samo vā lopam eke*, which has disappeared before 1. 8 of Vol. III. p. 425. By the Vārt. 3 on P. V. 2, 97, the repetition of *anyatarasyām* in P. V. 2, 109, merely indicates, that P. V. 2, 96 prescribes only the two suffixes *lac* and *matup*, in other words, the repetition of *anyatarasyām* is regarded as a *jñāpaka*; in the Vārt. *dyudrubhyāṃ nityārtham eke* Kātyāyana adds, that, according to *some*, the repetition of *anyatarasyām* is not a *jñāpaka*, but is necessary in order that the rule P. V. 2, 108 may not be taken to be an optional rule. In Vārt. 1 on P. VI. 1, 166, Kātyāyana shows that the term *jasaḥ* of Pāṇini's rule is superfluous; in the Vārt. *upasamastārtham eke*[11] he adds, that, according to *some*, *jasaḥ* is necessary because, without it, Pāṇini's rule would be applicable also in forms like *atitisrau*. Lastly, in the Vārt. *samo vā lopam eke* on P. VIII. 3, 5, Kātyāyana states that, according to *some*, the final of *sam* may be elided before *skṛ*, which is contrary to Pāṇini's and to Kātyāyana's own teaching.

From this, I fear, somewhat tedious exposition it is evident, that Kātyāyana was acquainted with the works of other scholars who, before him, had tried both to explain and to amend Pāṇini's grammar, and who had subjected the wording of the *Sūtras* to that critical examination, which is so striking a feature of Kātyāyana's own *Vārttikas*. Those who are familiar with the history of Indian grammar will probably be inclined to suspect, that Kātyāyana may have borrowed from his predecessors, even where he does not distinctly refer to them; certain it is, that he was not the first Vārttikakāra.

[10] None of the MSS. compared by me give these statements as separate *Vārttikas*, but the stops put after two of them in some MSS. and the absence of Saṃdhi between °*meke* and *icchanti* suggest, that the text of the *Vārttikas* has disappeared. The *Vārttika 'sarvamukhasthānam avarṇam eke' may* have disappeared before the words *sarvamukhasthānam avarṇam eka icchanti* in Vol. I. p. 61, l. 21; at any rate, Patañjali nowhere else uses the phrase *eka icchanti*, except when he is explaining a *Vārttika*.

[11] Nāgojībhaṭṭa considers this to be a remark of Patañjali's.

Vājapyāyana, Vyāḍi, and Pauṣkarasādi

Compared with this, Kātyāyana's references to individual scholars are of slight importance; and it may even be doubted if the three scholars named by him were really all grammarians. According to Vārt. 35 on P. I. 2, 64 (Vol. I. p. 242), Vājapyāyana maintained, that words mean a genus, while according to Vārt. 45 (Vol. I. p. 244) Vyāḍi held the opposite doctrine, that words mean individual things.[12] In Vārt. 3 on P. VIII. 4, 48 (Vol. III. p. 465) the rule, that a tenuis before a sibilant is changed to the corresponding aspirate (*vatsaḥ* to *vathsaḥ*), is ascribed to Pauṣkarasādi.[13]

Apara āha; Kēcid āhuḥ: Apara āha; or Apara āhuḥ

Patañjali most usually introduces the opinions of other grammarians by the phrase *apara āha* 'another says,' which occurs no less than 83 times in the Mahābhāṣya. From an examination of the statements so introduced it appears, not only that Patañjali knew of grammarians whose views in individual cases differed from those of Kātyāyana, or who had tried to add to, to simplify, or to render more exact, and generally to improve on, the *Vārttikas* of that scholar, but also, and to this I would draw particular attention, that there had been those who, *before* Patañjali, had *explained* the *Vārttikas*. Patañjali's quotations certainly prove, that others had interpreted or even read certain *Vārttikas* differently; and more than once he even places before us two different explanations, by others, of one and the same *Vārttika*. Besides, he introduces, by *apara āha*, opinions that are at variance with his own, also where he is not explaining Kātyāyana; and he employs the same phrase before a number of *Kārikās*.

I shall not weary the reader by fully discussing here every one of the many passages which have occasioned these remarks. A few simple examples will, I trust, sufficiently illustrate what I have said above. According to Kātyāyana (Vol. III. p. 321) the word *saṃvatsara* in P. VII. 3, 15 indicates merely, that P. VII. 3, 17 is not applicable, e.g., in the formation of *dvaisamika*, according to *another*, the same word indicates generally, that words denoting time are nowhere in Pāṇini's grammar included in the term *parimāṇa*, and that accordingly we must, e.g., by P. IV. 1, 22 form *dvivarṣā*, notwithstanding the fact that that rule contains an exception regarding words denoting a measure. On P. I. 3, 25, Kātyāyana has the remark (Vol. I. p. 281), *upoddevapūjāsaṃgatakaraṇayoḥ*; another has *upoddevapūjāsaṃgatakaraṇamitrakaraṇapathiṣu*. To the rule P. IV. 2, 7, Kātyāyana appends the note (Vol. II. p. 273) *kaler ḍhak*; *another* gives the general rule *sarvatrāgnikalibhyāṃ ḍhak*. In Vol. I. p. 367, Kātyāyana defines a sentence to be *ākhyātaṃ sāvyayakārakaviśeṣaṇam*) ['the verb together with indeclinables, *kāraka*-relations and their attributes']; *another*, simplifying that definition, merely says *ākhyātaṃ saviśeṣaṇam* ['the verb together with its attributes']. In Vol. I. p. 468 *another* permits the two constructions *śobhanā khalu pāṇineḥ* or *pāṇininā sūtrasya kṛtiḥ*, which is contrary to the teaching of both Pāṇini and Kātyāyana.

[12] For Patañjali's reference to the *Saṃgraha*, which is reported to have been composed by Vyāḍi, see below.

[13] Compare the *Atharva-prātiśākhya* II. 6; *Taittirīyaprāt.* XIV. 12; *Vājasaneyi-prāt.* IV. 119; and *Ṛk-prāt.* CDXXX. It may be noted that, contrary to his usual custom, Kātyāyana in his *Vārttika* puts the name *pauṣkarasādi* in the Gen., not in the Nom. case.

In Vol. I. p. 179, Patañjali's reading of two *Vārttikas* is *savarṇe'ngrahaṇam aparibhāṣyam ākṛtigrahaṇād ananyatvāc ca*; *another*, we learn, reads °*dananyatvam*. In Vol. I. p. 192, Patañjali explains the reading *jāgro'guṇavidhiḥ*. In Vol. I. p. 314 he shows, that *another* reads the Vārt. 6 without the particle *ca*; in Vol. I. p. 422, that *another* reads *dravyasya* instead of *adravasya*. In Vol. I. pp. 10, 20, 64, 237, 247, 357 and elsewhere, Patañjali gives us his own explanations of *Vārttikas* and also those of *another*. Regarding the Vārt. 2 on P. VI, 1, 3, he informs us (Vol. III. p. 8), that *some* supply for *tṛtīyasya* the word *ekācaḥ*, while *another* supplies *vyañjanasya*; and regarding the Vārt. 2 on P. VI. 4, 106 (Vol. III. p. 215), that *some* supply *chandograhaṇaṃ kartavyam*, and *others vāvacanaṃ kartavyam*. In a similar manner he records different explanations in Vol. I. p. 424 and Vol. II. pp. 92 and 171.

Again, in Vol. I. p. 390 Patañjali himself proposes to substitute *bhayabhītabhītibhībhiḥ* for the one word *bhayena* of P. II. 1, 37, and he tells us, that *another* would substitute *bhayanirgatajugupsubhiḥ*. In Vol. III. p. 30 he explains the word *apaspṛdhethām* in P. VI. 1, 36, to be a reduplicated form of the word *spardh*, and he adds, that *another* derives the same word from *apa-spardh*. In Vol. III. p. 244, he tells us, that either the rule P. VII. 1, 8 or the rule P. VII. 1, 10, is superfluous, and he adds, that according to *another* the word *bahulaṃ* of P. VII. 1, 8 *and* the rule P. VII. 1, 10, may be dispensed with. In the same manner he mentions opinions of others, that differ from his own, in Vol. I. pp. 172, 210, 290 and elsewhere; and he records the views of different scholars in Vol. I. p. 427, and Vol. II. pp. 19, 120, 151 and 254.

That Patañjali introduces some of the *Kārikās* by *apara āha*, I have already mentioned in a previous note.[14] I will only add here, that the authors of the *Kārikās* themselves allude to the opinions of other scholars, who are referred to by the words *Eke* or *Kecid*, in Vol. III. pp. 217 and 414.

The Bhāradvājīyāḥ, Saunāgāḥ, and Krōṣṭrīyāḥ

Of individual grammarians or schools of grammarians those most frequently referred to by Patañjali are the Bhāradvājīyas and the Saunāgas. The former are actually quoted ten times (Vol. I. pp. 73, 136, 201, 291; Vol. II. pp. 46, 55, 70, 233; and Vol. III. pp. 199 and 230), and the latter seven times (Vol. I. p. 416; Vol. II. pp. 105, 228, 238, 325; and Vol. III. pp. 76 and 159), but it does not seem at all improbable that some of the statements, which are introduced by the phrase *apara āha*, or which would appear to contain suggestions of Patañjali himself, may likewise really belong to either of those schools.[15] Both may be described as authors of *Vārttikas*, and both flourished after Kātyāyana. But, while to amend the *Vārttikas* of Kātyāyana appears to have been the main object of the Bhāradvājīyas, the Saunāgas, so far as we can judge, would seem to have criticized the text of Pāṇini's grammar more independently. This is indicated also by the manner in which both are quoted in the Mahābhāṣya. Whereas Patañjali usually places the dicta of the Bhāradvājīyas by the side of those of Kātyāyana, as it were, to point out the differences between the two, and to show how the

[14] *ante*, Vol. XV. p. 231, note 17.

[15] In Vol. II. p. 209, l. 8, it seems as if Patañjali himself were attempting to improve on a *Vārttika* of Kātyāyana's; from Vol. II. p. 105, l. 7 and p. 238, l. 10 we see that he is merely repeating a statement of the Saunāgas.

former have tried to improve on the latter,[16] he generally cites the Saunāgas in support of his own statements, and without any such distinct reference to Kātyāyana's *Vārttikas*.[17] Thus it happens, too, that in six out of seven cases the remarks of the Saunāgas are introduced by the phrase *evaṃ hi saunāgāḥ paṭhanti*, preceded by *iṣṭam evaitat saṃgṛhītam* or some similar expression, while the dicta of the Bhāradvājīyas are always introduced simply by *bhāradvājīyāḥ paṭhanti*. That of the *Vārttikas* of the Bhāradvājīyas which are cited in the Mahābhāṣya, one (in Vol. III. p. 199) is in verse, I have already had occasion to state in my remarks on the *Kārikās*.[18]

A third school of grammarians, the Kroṣṭrīyas, is mentioned in the Mahābhāṣya only once (Vol. I. p. 46). All we learn about them is, that they considered the two rules, P. I. 1, 3 and 52 to be quite independent of each other, and were of opinion, that in any case where both rules might happen to be simultaneously applicable, the former ought to supersede the latter, an opinion which is not shared by Patañjali.

Goṇikāputra, Gonardīya, *Kuṇaravāḍava*, Sauryabhagavat, and Vāḍava[19]

The passages in which Patañjali quotes Goṇikāputra (Vol. I. p. 336) and Gonardīya (Vol. I. pp. 78 and 91; Vol. II. p. 76; and Vol. III. p. 309), I have already discussed in my second note (*ante*, Vol. XV. p. 81); and I have there tried to show, that Gonardīya was a writer of grammatical *Kārikās*, who in all probability lived after Kātyāyana. About Goṇikāputra it is difficult to say anything. Later than Kātyāyana is also Kuṇaravāḍava, for the two statements ascribed to him by Patañjali (Vol. II. p. 100 and Vol. III. p. 317) are distinctly directed against Kātyāyana, whose *Vārttikas* they show to be superfluous. Whether this Kuṇaravāḍava is really the same as Vāḍava, who together with the *Sauryabhagavat* is mentioned by Patañjali in the difficult passage in Vol. III. p. 421, I have no means of deciding; nor do I know what scholar is meant to be denoted by the term *Sauryabhagavat*, 'the *Ācārya* of the town Saurya,' as Kaiyaṭa explains it.[20] Nāgojībhaṭṭa takes Vāḍava to be the author of the Vārt. 3 on P. VIII. 2, 106, a statement, the correctness of which I doubt.

The Saṃgraha of Dākṣāyaṇa

This work, on which Patañjali is reported to have based his own work, is cited in the Mahābhāṣya only once, in connection with the first *Vārttika* (Vol. I. p. 6). From that passage we learn, that

[16] On P. I, 1. 20, Kātyāyana has *ghusaṃjñāyāṃ prakṛtigrahaṇaṃ śidartham*, the *Bhāradvājīyas* read *ghusaṃjñāyāṃ prakṛtigrahaṇaṃ śidvikṛtārtham*; on P. III. I, 38, Kātyāyana has *viderāmkit* the *Bhāradvājīyas* add *nipātanād vāguṇatvam* etc.

[17] But the Saunāgas also more fully explain the meaning of a *Vārttika* of Kātyāyana in Vol. I. p. 416, and they improve on another *Vārttika* in the statement alluded to in note 15 above. A *Vārttika* of the Saunāgas, which has not been taken from the *Mahābhāṣya*, is given in the *Kāśikā* on P. VII. 2, 17. In commenting on that passage, Haradatta explains *saunāgāḥ* by *sunāgasyācāryasya śiṣyāḥ*.

[18] *ante*, Vol. XV. p. 230.

[19] I purposely have omitted in the above Vārṣyāyaṇi; the passage, in which his name occurs (Vol. I. p. 258), has been copied by Patañjali from the *Nirukta* (Roth's edition, p. 31).

[20] A town Śaurya is mentioned in Vol. I. p. 474.

the question, as to whether words are *nitya* or *kārya*, had been fully discussed in the *Saṃgraha*, and that the science of grammar had been shown to be necessary, whichever view might be taken regarding the nature of words. Elsewhere we are told that the *Saṃgraha* was composed by Vyāḍi; Patañjali himself incidentally calls the author of it Dākṣāyaṇa, in Vol. I. p. 468.

Considering the great bulk of the Mahābhāṣya, it is disappointing that we do not learn from it more regarding the history of Indian grammar, and particularly, that, what we are told in it of the predecessors of Pāṇini, is wellnigh valueless. But I trust, that my survey of the grammatical authorities referred to by Kātyāyana and Patañjali will at least make this much clear, that Kātyāyana cannot have been the first author of *Vārttikas*, and that between him and Patañjali there intervene a large number of writers, writers in prose and in verse, individual scholars and schools of grammarians, who all have tried to explain and to amend the works of both Pāṇini and Kātyāyana. To what extent Kātyāyana and Patañjali were indebted to those that went before them, we shall never know; judging from the analogy of the later grammatical literature of India we may, in my opinion, certainly assume, that, like Pāṇini himself, both have based their own works on, and have preserved in them all that was valuable in, the writings of their predecessors.

In conclusion, I would here draw attention to the fact, that instead of the regular terms of the *Pāṇinīya* and also in addition to them, occasionally, both in the *Vārttikas* and in the *Kārikās*, we meet with a number of other grammatical *termini technici*. Most of those terms had doubtless been in use already before Pāṇini, and they were generally adopted in several of the later grammars, in preference to the more artificial terms of Pāṇini. But a few are themselves highly artificial symbols, which may have been invented by grammarians later than Pāṇini, and which remind one of the terms used in the *Jainendra*, where indeed one of them actually occurs.

Thus, Kātyāyana occasionally employs the terms *svara* for Pāṇini's *ac* (Vol. I. pp. 59, 123, etc.), *vyañjana* for *hal* (Vol. I. pp. 26, 42, etc.), *samānākṣara* for *ak* (Vol. I. p. 24 and Vol. II. p. 19), *saṃdhyakṣara* for *ec* (Vol. I. pp. 22, 24, etc.); *sparśa* and *aghoṣa* (Vol. I. p. 355); *prathama*, *dvitīya*, *tṛtīya*, and *caturtha* for the first, second, third, and fourth consonants of the five *Vargas* (Vol. III. pp. 218, 465, and Vol. I. p. 154); *ayogavāha*, *jihvāmūlīya*, and *upadhmānīya* (Vol. I. p. 28 and Vol. III. p. 431). For *laṭ*, *luṭ*, *lṛṭ*, and *luṅ* he has *bhavantī*, *śvastanī*, *bhaviṣyantī* and *adyatanī* (Vol. I. p. 443; Vol. II. pp. 114, 123, 160; Vol. II. p. 143; Vol. I. p. 474; Vol. II. p. 114; Vol. III. p. 217). For the phrase *saṃjñāchandasoḥ* he uses the artificial term *taṇ* (Vol. I. p. 488; Vol. II. pp. 99 and 221); and, strange to say, for Pāṇini's *ṣaṣ*, which he himself has, e.g. in Vol. II. p. 199 and Vol. III. p. 107, he employs *ḍu* in Vol. I. p. 304.

In addition to some of these terms we find in the *Kārikās*, *parokṣā* for *liṭ* (Vol. I. p. 199), *kārita* to denote the Causal (Vol. II. p. 415), and *cekrīyita* and *carkarīta* to denote the two forms of the Intensive (Vol. II. p. 232 and Vol. III. p. 359). In the *Kārikās* we also meet with *la* for *lopa* (Vol. II. pp. 284, 378, and 425), and with *ghu*[21] (or perhaps *dyu*) for Pāṇini's *uttarapada* (Vol. III. pp. 229, 247, and 318).

[21] See *ante*, Vol. XV. p. 231, note 14.

C. The Text of Pāṇini's Sūtras, as Given in the Kāśikā-Vṛtti, Compared with the Text Known to Kātyāyana and Patañjali (1887)

Franz Kielhorn

In the sixth article of his series of notes on the *Mahābhāṣya*, Kielhorn turned to Pāṇini's text itself. This grammar was commented upon in the *Mahābhāṣya*, and again some eight centuries later in the *Kāśikā* (beginning of the seventh century; see p. 33 of this volume). It is therefore important to see whether the texts presupposed in these two commentaries are the same, and whether they are the same as the text that has been handed down to us. Kielhorn discusses this problem in a fundamental article, "The Text of Pāṇini's Sūtras, as given in the *Kāśikā-Vṛtti*, Compared with the Text Known to Kātyāyana and Patañjali," which is reproduced here (*Indian Antiquary* 16, 1887, 178–184). As was mentioned before, much of the material presented here had already appeared in the second half of the article "Der Grammatiker Pāṇini" of 1885, the first half of which has been included earlier in this volume.

Considering the almost unrivalled position which Pāṇini's *Aṣṭādhyāyī* holds in Indian literature, it may be interesting to inquire, what alterations, if any, the text of that work has undergone, and to collect those rules which can be shown to be additions to the original text, or the wording of which has in any way been altered, since the rules were first enunciated by Pāṇini. To contribute towards the solution of this question, I intend in the present note to show, so far as this may be possible, to what extent the text of the Sūtras which is given in the *Kāśikā-Vṛtti*, the oldest extant commentary, differs from the text that was known to Kātyāyana and Patañjali. In attempting to do this, I shall be mainly guided by the remarks that have been appended to certain Sūtras by Kaiyaṭa, Nāgojībhaṭṭa, and Haradatta, and I shall have only few occasions to go beyond, or to differ from, what has been already stated by those commentators.

But before entering upon the question with which I am more immediately concerned here, I cannot help drawing attention to the fact that the text of Pāṇini's rules has neither in the editions of the *Aṣṭādhyāyī* nor in that of the *Kāśikā-Vṛtti*—however valuable those editions may be otherwise—received that critical care and attention, which it undoubtedly deserves. For years I have been content to regard the printed text of the Sūtras, allowing for some misprints, as trustworthy beyond doubt. It is only lately that I have become somewhat suspicious, and having compared such MSS., as were within reach, I have come to the conclusion, that in the case of a considerable number of rules the printed text differs, more or less, from the text which is furnished by the best MSS., and that wrong readings have in succession crept from one edition into another. A few examples may show this:

P. III. 1, 109 all the printed texts have *etistuśāsvṛ*°. Here three old and valuable MSS. of the *Kāśikā*, and an old MS. of the *Aṣṭādhyāyī* which I owe to the kindness of Dr. Bhandarkar, have *etistuśāsuvṛ*°; the MSS. of the *Mahābhāṣya* GAaK, which here as elsewhere give only the beginning of the rule, have *etistuśāsu*°, and in the *Mahābhāṣya* Vol. II. p. 2, where the rule is quoted, the MSS. aK have °*śāsuvṛ*°. From this there can be no doubt, that the right reading is °*śāsuvṛ*° (not, as in P. VII. 4, 2, °*śāsu-ṛ*°).

P. III. 2, 21 all the printed texts have *divāvibhāniśā*°, and all accordingly have *niśākaraḥ* in the commentaries. In this case the MSS. of the *Mahābhāṣya* are of no value, because they only give the commencement of the rule *divāvibhā*°; nor is this rule quoted anywhere in the *Mahābhāṣya*. But all the three MSS. of the *Kāśikā* omit *niśā* from the rule and *niśākaraḥ* from the commentary, and the MS. of the *Aṣṭādhyāyī* has *niśā* added *secundā manu* in the margin. Accordingly there can in my opinion be no doubt, that Pāṇini has not taught the formation of the word *niśākara*. Judging from the quotations in Böhtlingk and Roth's Dictionary, *divākara*, which *is* taught by Pāṇini, is an old word, occurring twice in the Atharva-veda, but *niśākara* is *not*.

P. IV. 1, 62 all the printed texts have *sakhyaśiśvīti*°. This rule is neither treated of nor quoted in the *Mahābhāṣya*. The three MSS. of the *Kāśikā* and the MS. of the *Aṣṭādhyāyī* have *sakhyaśiśvī*, without *iti*[1], and so reads Candra.

P. IV. 3, 119 all the printed texts have °*pādapādañ*. This rule is neither treated of nor quoted in the *Mahābhāṣya*. The three MSS. of the *Kāśikā*, both in the rule and in the commentary, and the MS. of the *Aṣṭādhyāyī* have °*pātapādañ*, and Candra has the rule *nāmni vātapādañ*.

P. V. 4, 68 all the printed texts have *samāsāntāḥ*. The MSS. of the Mahābhāṣya GaK and originally A, as well as the three MSS. of the *Kāśikā*. both in the rule and in the commentary, and the MS. of the *Aṣṭādhyāyī* read *samāsāntaḥ* which singular form is supported by Mahābhāṣya, Vol. II. p. 438, lines 23 and 25, and p. 443, l. 15, and is no doubt correct.

Not taking into account rules such as these, to which I might add a fairly large number of other rules for which the MSS. furnish a better text than the one printed, the Sūtras of the *Kāśikā-Vṛtti*, which can be shown to differ from the Sūtras as known to either Kātyāyana or Patañjali, may be treated of under four heads. 1. Excepting as regards the observation of the rules of *Saṃdhi*, the wording of the text has remained unchanged, but several consecutive words, which originally were *one* rule, have been separated so as to form *two* or even *three* rules. The technical name for this proceeding is *Yoga-vibhāga*, 'the splitting-up of a rule (into two or more rules).' 2. One or more words have been added to the original text of a rule. 3. The wording of rules has been altered otherwise than by the addition of one or more words. 4. Whole rules have been added to the original text of the *Aṣṭādhyāyī*. The particulars under each of these four heads are as follows:—

1. Yoga-vibhāga

P. I. 1, 17 *uñaḥ*[2] and 18 *ūṁ* originally formed the one rule *uña ūṁ*, and the splitting up of that rule into two was first suggested by

[1] I may perhaps draw attention here —as to a real gem of ingenious interpretation—to the manner, in which this word *iti* of the above rule has been explained by the author of the *Siddhāntakaumudī* (New Bombay Ed. No. 517). It is well known (although nothing is said about it in our Dictionaries), that at any rate in works of the Indian middle ages *iti* sometimes conveys the sense of *prakāra* or *ityādi* 'words like this,' 'this and similar words.' When Hemacandra in his *Śabdānuśāsana* says *pāṇigṛhītīti*, that term means, and is by Hemacandra himself explained to mean,—*pāṇigṛhītiprakārāḥ* 'words like *pāṇigṛhīti*,' '*pāṇigṛhīti* and similar words'; and when in his *Liṅgānuśāsana* he says *apatyam iti*, he himself tells us that he means *apatyādayaḥ*. This use being well known to Bhaṭṭojīdīkṣita, that scholar connects the word *iti* of the above rule of Pāṇini's with, and in construing the rule, wishes us to place it *after*, *bhāṣāyām*, and he then explains *bhāṣāyām iti* to mean *bhāṣādau*, i.e., *bhāṣāyāṃ chandasi ca*. Comment appears superfluous.

[2] This word, taken by itself, does not fit into Pāṇini's text, because it is in the Genitive case.

Kātyāyana (Vol. I. p. 72). Pāṇini's one rule would allow only *ūṁ iti* or (according to P. I. 1, 14) *u iti*, while from Kātyāyana's two rules we also obtain *viti*.

P. I. 4, 58 *prādayaḥ* and 59 *upasargāḥ kriyāyoge* originally formed the one rule *prādaya upasargāḥ kriyāyoge*, which has been split in two by Kātyāyana (Vol. I. p. 341). To quote an example given by Kaiyaṭa, Pāṇini's one rule would not allow us to account (by P. VI. 2, 2) for the accent of *prā'cārya*, because here *pra* would not be termed *Nipāta*. Kaiyaṭa, who knew the *Kāśikā*, has the remark—*yadā prāg eva prādaya iti yogo vibhajyate tadā prayojanakathanāya vārttikam| yadā tu prādaya upasargāḥ kriyāyoga ity eko yogaḥ paṭhyate tadā yogavibhāgaḥ kartavyatvena codyate.*

P. II. 1, 11 *vibhāṣā* and 12 *apaparibahirañcavaḥ pañcamyā* originally formed the one rule *vibhāṣāpaparibahirañcavaḥ pañcamyā*. The division of that rule into two has been suggested by Patañjali (Vol. I. p. 380), to make it quite clear that *vibhāṣā*, as an *Adhikāra*, is valid also in the following rules P. II. 1, 13, etc.; for, as Kaiyaṭa observes, *anyathehaivāsyopayoga āśaṅkyeta yogavibhāge tv adhikāro gamyate.*

P. IV. 3,117 *saṃjñāyām* and 118 *kulālādibhyo vuñ* originally formed the one rule *saṃjñāyāṃ kulālādibhyo vuñ*. The division of that rule has been suggested by Kātyāyana (Vol. II. p. 317), to enable us to account by the rule *saṃjñāyām* for the words *mākṣika*, *sāragha*, etc. (p. 316). Kaiyaṭa appends the note—*saṃjñāyāṃ kulālādibhyo vuñ iti sūtraṃ vibhaktam ity arthaḥ.*

P. V. 1, 57 *tad asya parimāṇam* and 58 *saṃkhyāyā saṃjñāsaṃghasūtrādhyayaneṣu* originally formed the one rule *tad asya parimāṇaṃ saṃkhyāyā saṃjñasaṃghasūtrādhyayaneṣu*, so quoted in Vol. II. p. 343, 1. 13. The division of that rule has not been actually proposed by either Kātyāyana or Patañjali, but it may justly be argued that Kātyāyana's Vārt. 6 in Vol. II. p. 353 would have been superfluous, if to him the words *tad asya parimāṇam* had been a separate rule; and Kaiyaṭa and Nāgojībhaṭṭa are therefore in my opinion quite right, when they say, the former *tad asya parimāṇam iti yogavibhāgaḥ kartavya ity uktaṃ bhavati*, and the latter (in the *Laghuśabdenduśekhara*) *uttareṇa yogavibhāgo'tra bhāṣye dhvanitaḥ*. I need hardly add, that the very general rule *tad asya parimāṇam* allows us to account for a number of words, which otherwise could not have been explained by Pāṇini's rules.

P. VI. 1, 32 *hvaḥ saṃprasāraṇam* and 33 *abhyastrasya ca* originally formed the one rule *hvaḥ saṃprasāraṇam abhyastrasya ca*. That rule has been split in two by Kātyāyana (Vol. III. p. 29), in order to account by *hvaḥ saṃprasāraṇaṃ* (*ṇau ca saṃścaṇoḥ*) for the forms *juhāvayiṣati* and *ajūhavat*.

P. VI. 1, 164 *taddhitasya* and 165 *kitaḥ* originally formed the one rule *taddhitasya kitaḥ*, so quoted in Vol. III. p. 116, 1, 13. The division of that rule has been suggested by Patañjali (Vol. II. p. 253, 1.22), who by *taddhitasya* (*citaḥ*) wishes to account for the accent of words like *Kauñjāyanā'ḥ*. But for this new rule such words, being formed with the suffix *cphañ* (P. IV. 1, 98), would be *ādyudātta* by P. VI. 1, 197, a rule which here would supersede the rule P. VI. 1, 163.

P. VII. 3, 117 *idudbhyām*, 118 *aut*, and 119 *ac ca gheḥ* originally formed the one rule *idudbhyām aud ac ca gheḥ*, so quoted in Vol. I. p. 116, 1. 9, and Vol. II. p. 404, 1. 15. Kātyāyana, after having in Vol. III. p. 342, 1. 10 divided that rule into the two rules *idudbhyām* and *aud ac ca gheḥ*, in 1. 14 proposes to divide the latter rule again into the two rules *aut* and *ac ca gheḥ*, but in 1. 22 he himself shows this second division to be unnecessary. (Compare also the *Kāśikā-Vṛtti* on P. VII. 3, 119). Pāṇini's one rule would only permit the locative cases *kṛtau*, *dhenau* etc., not *kṛtyām*, *dhenvām*, etc.

The above are, in my opinion, all rules, in the case of which *Yoga-vibhāga* can with certainty be proved to have taken place. It is true, that according to Nāgojībhaṭṭa the two rules P. VI. 2, 107 *udarāśveṣuṣu* and 108 *kṣepe* also, originally were one rule, apparently because *udarāśveṣuṣu kṣepe* has been so quoted in Vol. III. p. 121, 1. 14 and p. 133, 1. 17; but I should not now venture to conclude from the fact that two or more rules are quoted together, that they must necessarily have been regarded as only one rule, unless indeed such conclusion could be supported by other arguments. No less than eleven times we find in the *Mahābhāṣya* the quotation *ato dīrgho yañi supi ca* (P. VII. 3, 101 and 102), and yet P. VII. 3, 101 and 102 undoubtedly are two separate rules, of which the former has been quoted by itself four times, and the latter twice. Similarly P. VI. 2, 143 and 144 have been quoted together eight times, although they are separate rules; and the same might be said of other rules. Besides, the verse in Vol. III. p. 121, 1. 13 appears to me to prove that P. VI. 2, 108 *kṣepe*, even before the time of Patañjali, was regarded as a separate rule.

2. One or more words added to the original text of a rule

P. I. 3, 29 *samo gamyṛcchipracchisvaratyartiśruvidibhyaḥ* originally was only *samo gamyṛcchibhyām*. The verbs *vidipracchisvarati* and *artiśru* have been added from Kātyāyana's Vārttikas (Vol. I. p. 282). *Dṛś*, which also is given by Kātyāyana, is mentioned in the *kāśikā* only in the commentary, whereas Candra has made it part of the rule. Kaiyaṭa appends to the Vārttikas on P. I. 3, 29 the remark—*samo gamyṛcchibhyām ity etāvat sūtram iti vārttikam ārabdham.*

P. III. 1, 95 *kṛtyāḥ prāṅ ṅvulaḥ* originally was only *kṛtyāḥ*. The addition of the words *prāṅ ṅvulaḥ* has been suggested by Kātyāyana in his Vārt. 1 on Pāṇini's rule, but shown to be in reality superfluous in Vārt. 2 (Vol. II. p. 81). On the Vārt. 1 Kaiyaṭa has the note —*kṛtyā ity etāvat sūtram ity āha kṛtyasaṃjñāyām iti.*

P. III. 1, 118 *pratyapibhyāṃ graheś chandasi* originally was only *pratyapibhyām graheḥ*. The word *chandasi* has been added by Kātyāyana (Vol. II. p. 87).

P. III, 1, 126 *āsuyuvapirapilapitrapicamaś ca*. Here *lapi* has in my opinion been inserted from Kātyāyana's Vārt. 3 on P. III. 1, 124 (Vol. II. p. 88). *Dabhi*, which is mentioned in the same *Vārttika*, is in the *Kāśikā* given in the commentary on P. III. 1, 126.

P. III. 3, 122 *adhyāyanyāyodyāvasaṃhārādhārāvāyāś ca* originally did not contain the words *ādhāra* and *āvāya*, which have been inserted from Kātyāyana's Vārttika on the preceding rule (Vol. II. p. 155). The word *avahāra*, which is mentioned in the same Vārttika, is in the *Kāśikā* given in the commentary on P. III. 3, 122. In the *Mahābhāṣya*, Vol. II. p. 146, l. 20, where the rule has been quoted, the MSS. give it as read in the *Kāśikā*, excepting that the MS. K omits from it *ādhāra*. Kaiyaṭa on P. III. 3, 121 has the remark—*adhyāyasūtra ādhārāvāyaśabdau vārttike darśanād abhiyuktaiḥ prakṣiptau.*

P. IV. 1, 15, which in the *Kāśikā* ends °*kvarapkhyunām*, originally was ending °*kvarapaḥ*. The term *khyun* has been added from Kātyāyana's Vārt. 6 (Vol. II. p. 209), and it occurs also in a Vārttika of the Saunāgas (Vol. II. p. 105, l.8; p. 209, l.8; and p. 238, l. 11; quoted without *khyun* in the *Kāśikā* towards the end of the commentary on P. IV. 1, 15) as well as in the corresponding rule of Candra's grammar. The original ending of the rule may be seen from Patañjali's words *kañkvarapo yañaś ceti* on P. IV. 1, 16; and Kaiyaṭa has the note—*sūtre khyunaḥ pāṭho'nārṣaḥ*.

P. IV. 2, 2 *lākṣārocanāśakalakardamāṭṭak* originally did not contain the words *śakala* and *kardama*, which have been inserted from Kātyāyana's first Vārttika (Vol. II. p. 271) on the rule. Here again Kaiyaṭa has the note—*sakalakardamayoḥ sūtre pāṭho'nārṣaḥ*. (Incidentally I may add here that the statement *śakalakardamābhyām aṇapīṣyate* which occurs in the *Kāśikā* on P. IV. 2, 2, is based on Candra's rule *śakalakardamād vā*).

P. IV. 2, 21 *sāsmin paurṇamāsīti saṃjñāyām*. The word *saṃjñāyām* has been added in accordance with Kātyāyana's Vārttikas on the rule, but has been declared superfluous by Patañjali (Vol. II. p. 275). Kaiyaṭa appends the note—*saṃjñāgrahaṇaṃ sūtre'nārṣam iti vārttikam ārabdham*.

P. IV. 2, 43 *grāmajanabandhusahāyebhyas tal* originally did not contain the word *sahāya*, which has been taken from Patañjali's note on the rule (Vol. II. p. 279). *Gaja*, which also has been mentioned by Patañjali and which Candra has in the rule, is given in the *Kāśikā* on the commentary.

P. IV. 4, 17 *vibhāṣā vivadhavīvadhāt* originally was only *vibhāṣā vivadhāt*. *Vīvadha* has been added from Patañjali's note on the rule (Vol. II. p. 329), and is also given by Candra. Haradatta has the note—*vīvadhaśabdo vārttike darśanāt sūtre prakṣiptaḥ*.

P. V. 2, 101 *prajñāśraddhārcāvṛttibhyo ṇaḥ* originally did not contain the word *vṛtti*, which has been added from Patañjali's note 3 on the rule (Vol. II. p. 396) and has also been given by Candra. Here again Haradatta has the note—*sūtre vṛttiśabdo vārttike darśanāt prakṣiptaḥ*.

P. V. 4, 50 *abhūtatadbhāve kṛbhvastiyoge sampadyakartari cviḥ* originally did not contain the word *abhūtatadbhāve*, which has been added in accordance with Kātyāyana's first Vārttika on the rule (Vol. II. p. 436). Kaiyaṭa has the note—*abhūtatadbhāvagrahaṇaṃ vārttike dṛṣṭvānyaiḥ sūtre prakṣiptam*.

P. VI. 3, 6 *ātmanaś ca pūraṇe* originally was only *ātmanaś ca*, and the addition of *pūraṇe* is Kātyāyana's (Vol. III. p. 143). Such evidently is the opinion of Bhaṭṭojīdīkṣita (*Siddhānta-Kaumudī*, new Bombay Ed. No. 963), which I now accept as correct. Haradatta, misled by the fact that the Vārttika *ātmanaś ca pūraṇe* in the MSS. of the *Mahābhāṣya* has been put under P. VI. 3, 5, and by Patañjali's explanation *ātmanaś ca pūraṇa upasaṃkhyānaṃ kartavyam*, instead of *ātmanaś ca pūraṇa iti vaktavyam*, takes the whole *ātmanaś ca pūraṇe* to be an addition to Pāṇini's original text (*vārttikam evedaṃ sūtrarūpeṇa paṭhitam*); but the words *ātmanaś ca* are necessary for the following rule P. VI. 3, 7, and Nāgojībhaṭṭa (in the *Uddyota* and *Laghuśabdenduśekhara*) has not, in my opinion, been successful in proving that we can do without those words (*atrātmanaś ca pūraṇa iti viśiṣṭaṃ vārttikam ity atratyabhāṣyasvarasādāyāti vaiyākaraṇākhyāyām ity atra parasya ceti cena paraśabdapratidvandvitayātmaśabdasyaiva grahaṇaṃ tad ubhayaṃ caikasūtram ity āhuḥ*).

P. VI. 3, 40 *svāṅgāc ceto'mānini* originally was only *svāṅgāc cetaḥ*, and *amānini* has been added from Kātyāyana's Vārttika *svāṅgāc ceto'mānini* (Vol. III. p. 156; compare also Vol. II. p. 193, l. 2 and Vol. III. p. 157, l. 11). Kaiyaṭa has the note—*svāṅgāc ceta ity etāvat sūtram iti matvā vārttikārambhaḥ*.

P. VI. 3, 83 *prakṛtyāśisyagovatsahaleṣu* originally was only *prakṛtyāśiṣi*, to which *agovatsahaleṣu* has been added in accordance with the suggestions of Kātyāyana and Patañjali. For Kātyāyana has amended Pāṇini's original rule by adding to it *agavādiṣu*, and Patañjali in explaining the Vārttika has given the example *sagave savatsāya sahalāya* (Vol. III. p. 171). Kaiyaṭa has the note—*agovatsahaleṣv iti bhāṣyavārttikadarśanāt sūtre kenacit prakṣiptam.*

P. VI. 4, 100 *ghasibhasor hali ca.* Kātyāyana's Vārttika on the rule (Vol. III. p. 213) shows that the rule originally did not contain the particle *ca*, which has been added for the very purpose of making the rule, in accordance with Kātyāyana's suggestion, more widely applicable. In Vol. III. p. 213, l. 19 some MSS. of the *Mahābhāṣya* read the rule without, others with *ca*. Kaiyaṭa appends the note—*anyatrāpīti vacanād vārttikakāraś cakāraṃ na papāṭheti lakṣyate.*

P. VIII. 1, 67 *pūjanāt pūjitam anudāttaṃ kāṣṭhādibhyaḥ* originally did not contain the word *kāṣṭhādibhyaḥ*, which has been added in accordance with the suggestion of Kātyāyana (Vol. III. p. 379). Kaiyaṭa has the note—*kāṣṭhādibhya iti sūtre vārttikadarśanāt kaiścit prakṣiptam.*

P. VIII. 3, 118 *sadisvañjyoḥ* (such is the reading of the MSS. of the *Kāśikā*) *parasya liṭi* originally was only *sadeḥ parasya liṭi*. *Svañji* which is given also by Candra, has been added from Kātyāyana's Vārttika on the rule (Vol. III. p. 451).

P. VIII. 1. 73 *nāmantrite samānādhikaraṇe sāmānyavacanam* and 74 *vibhāṣitaṃ viśeṣavacane bahuvacanam* originally were 73 *nāmantrite samānādhikaraṇe* and 74 *sāmānyavacanaṃ vibhāṣitaṃ viśeṣavacane*. The new division of the two rules and the addition of *bahuvacanam* are suggested by Patañjali (Vol. III. pages 383 and 384), but at the same time Patañjali himself adds that the word *sāmānyavacanam* or, according to others, *viśeṣavacanam* may be omitted from the rules. Kaiyaṭa on 73 remarks—*nāmantrite samānādhikaraṇa iti sūtraṃ paṭhitaṃ tataḥ sāmānyavacanaṃ vibhāṣitaṃ viśeṣavacana iti dvitīyam*, and on 74—*bahuvacanagrahaṇam apāṇinīyam iti.*

Finally, it may appear doubtful, if the rule P. VIII. 2, 12 from the beginning did contain the word *kakṣīvat*, because the formation of that word has been specially taught in Vārt. 7 on P. VI. 1, 37 (Vol. III. p. 33). The opinions of native scholars are divided on this point, for, while Kaiyaṭa (on P. VI. 1, 37) rejects the Vārttika as superfluous (*āsandīvad aṣṭhīvad ity atra kakṣīvacchabdasya nipātanād vārttikam nārabdhavyam*), Nāgojībhaṭṭa reports that others consider the word *kakṣīvat* to be spurious in P. VIII. 2, 12 (*etad bhāṣyaprāmāṇyāt tatra*, i.e. in P. VIII. 2, 12, *kakṣīvacchabdapāṭho'nārṣa ity anye*).

3. The wording of rules altered otherwise than by the addition of one or more words

P. V. 3, 5 *etado'ś*. Patañjali's remarks on this rule (Vol. II. p. 403) show that the reading known to him was *etado'n*. Patañjali considered the *n* superfluous, and by doing so suggests the reading *etado'ś*. Kaiyaṭa has the note—*iha kecid aśaṃ paṭhanti kecid anam.*

P. VI. 1, 115 *prakṛtyāntaḥ pādam avyapare*. Kātyāyana's reading of this rule was *nāntaḥ pādam avyapare* (Vol. III. p. 86). But from Vol. III. p. 89, lines 7 and 18, p. 91, l. 8, and other passages in the *Mahābhāṣya* it appears, that the reading *prakṛtyā*, instead of *na*, was known already to Patañjali. In the *Kāśikā* we have the note—*kecid idaṃ sūtraṃ nāntaḥ pādam avyapara iti paṭhanti.*

P. VI. 1, 124 *indre ca nityam*, and 125 *plutapragṛhyā aci*. Patañjali's reading of these two rules was 124 *indre ca*, and 125 *plutapragṛhyā aci nityam* (Vol. III. p. 87, l. 24); but on p. 89, l. 18 he declares the word *nityam* to be altogether superfluous, and in Vol. 1. p. 66 and Vol. III. p. 53 he cites the rule 125 without *nityam*. Kaiyaṭa (on Vol. III. p. 87, l. 24) has the note—*indre ceti ye sūtraṃ paṭhanti plutapragṛhyā aci nityam iti tu dvitīyaṃ tanmatenaiṣa praśnaḥ*.

P. VI. 1, 137 *saṃparyupebhyaḥ karotau bhūṣaṇe*, and 138 *samavāye ca*. In the place of these two rules Patañjali has had only the one rule *saṃparibhyāṃ bhūṣaṇasamavāyayoḥ karotau*, which is so quoted in Vol. III. p. 216, l. 1, and the first word *saṃparibhyāṃ* of which has been explained by Patañjali in Vol. III. p. 93, l. 13. (Compare the similar explanation of *sudurbhyām* in P. VII. 1, 68, in Vol. III. p. 262, l. 21.)

P. VI. 1, 150 *viṣkiraḥ śakunir vikiro vā* originally was *viṣkiraḥ śakunau vā*, a wording of the rule which was not approved of by Kātyāyana (Vol. III. p. 95). In his opinion, *viṣkiraḥ śakunau vā* would mean, that 'after *vi*, *kṛ* takes the augment *suṭ*,—optionally, when one wishes to denote a bird,' whereas the real meaning of the rule is assumed to be that 'after *vi*, *kṛ* may take *suṭ* in case one wishes to denote a bird;' in other words, the bird may be called *vikira* or *viṣkira*, while in the case of any other meaning the only right form would be *vikira*. (Differently Goldstücker, *Pāṇini*, p. 125). Of the commentators, Kaiyaṭa has the note—*viṣkiraḥ śakunau veti sūtrapāṭham āśritya vārttikārambhaḥ*; Haradatta—*yathā tu bhāṣyaṃ tathā viṣkiraḥ śakunau vety etāvat sūtram* and Nāgojībhaṭṭa—*viṣkiraḥ śakunir vikiro vety anārṣaḥ pāṭha iti bhāvaḥ*.

P. VI. 4, 56 *lyapi laghupūrvāt* originally was *lyapi laghupūrvasya*. The substitution of the Ablative for the Genitive case has been suggested by Kātyāyana (Vol. III p. 204). In the *Mahābhāṣya* the rule has been quoted in its original form in Vol. III. p. 288, lines 4 and 11, and in its altered form p. 191, l. 12, and p. 212, lines 1 and 14. Kaiyaṭa has the remark—*kecid ācāryeṇa lyapi laghupūrvasyeti ṣaṣṭhy antamadhyāpitā anye tu laghupūrvād iti pañcamy antam*.

P. VII. 1, 25 *adḍḍatarādibhyaḥ pañcabhyaḥ* originally was *ad ḍatarādibhyaḥ pañcabhyaḥ*. The addition to *ad* of the Anubandha *ḍ* has been suggested by Kātyāyana (Vol. III. p. 250). Compare also Vol. I. p. 87, lines 17 and 18, and Vol. III. p. 48.

P. VII. 3, 75 *ṣṭhivuklamvācamāṃ* (such is the reading of the MSS. of the *Kāśikā*) *śiti* originally was *ṣṭhivuklamucamāṃ śiti*. The alteration of the wording of the rule has been suggested by Kātyāyana (Vol. III. p. 334). In Vol. III. p. 333, l. 15, where the rule is quoted, the best MSS. of the *Mahābhāṣya* give the altered form of it, which has been adopted also by Candra. Kaiyaṭa has the note—*ṣṭhivuklamucamāṃ śitīti sūtrapāṭhād āha . . . athavā sūtre tantram āṇ na tu yathopeyivān ity atropaśabdo 'tantram iti pradarśanāya vārttikārambhaḥ*.

P. VII. 3, 77 *iṣugamiyamāṃ chaḥ* originally was *iṣagamiyamāṃ chaḥ*, as may be inferred from Kātyāyama's Vārttika on the rule (Vol. III. p. 334)—*iṣu°* is the reading also of Candra. The *Kāśikā* has the remark—*ya iṣim uditaṃ nādhīyate te'cīty anuvartayanti*, and Kaiyaṭa appends the note—*iṣugamīti pātho'nārṣa ity āheṣeś chatvam ahalīti*.

P. VIII. 4, 28 *upasargād bahulam* originally was *upasargād anotparaḥ*, as may be seen from Patañjali's remarks on the rule. The reading *upasargād bahulam* has been suggested by Patañjali (Vol. III. p. 460).

4. Whole rules added to the original text of the Aṣṭādhyāyī

P. IV. 1, 166 *vṛddhasya ca pūjāyām* is really a Vārttika of Kātyāyana's on IV. 1, 163 and P. IV. 1, 167 *yūnaś ca kutsāyām* is based on the Vārttika *jīvaṃdvaśyaṃ ca kutsitam* on IV. 1, 162 (Vol. II. p. 265). As regards, however, the explanation of the two rules in the *Mahābhāṣya* and in the *Kāśikā*, there is the difference, that in the former they are considered obligatory, while in the latter, by supplying *vā* from IV. 1, 165, they are made optional. Owing to the employment of the Genitive cases *vṛddhasya* and *yūnaḥ*, neither rule fits into the text of Pāṇini's *Aṣṭādhyāyī*. On Kātyāyana's Vārttikas Kaiyaṭa has the remarks—*sūtreṣu tu kaiścid vṛddhasya ca pūjāyām iti vārttikadarśanāt prakṣiptam*, and *yūnaś ca kutsāyām iti sūtram anārṣam iti vacanam.*

P. IV. 2, 8 *kaler ḍhak* is really part of Kātyāyana's Vārttika on the preceding rule IV. 2, 7 (Vol. II. p. 273).

P. IV. 3, 132 *kaupiñjalahāstipadād aṇ* and 133 *ātharvaṇikasyekalopaś ca* are really two Vārttikas of Kātyāyana, which in the *Mahābhāṣya* are placed under P. IV. 3, 131 (Vol. II. p. 320). On 132 Kaiyaṭa has the note—*apāṇinīyaḥ sūtreṣu pāṭhaḥ*. Regarding 133 the opinions of the commentators differ; according to Kaiyaṭa the rule is an original Sūtra, but Haradatta rightly remarks—*pūrvaṃ ca sūtram idaṃ ca vārttike darśanāt sūtreṣu prakṣiptam*, and on the margin of the MS. a of the *Mahābhāṣya* we have the note—*idam api vārttike dṛṣṭvā sūtreṣu prakṣiptam.*

P. V. 1, 36 *dvitripūrvād aṇ ca* is really a Vārttika of Kātyāyana's on the preceding rule. (Vol. II. p. 350). By Candra the wording of that Vārttika has been altered to *dvitryāder aṇ ca*. Kaiyaṭa has the note—*dvitripūrvād aṅ cety sūtreṣv anārṣaḥ pāṭha iti vārttikārambhaḥ*.

P. VI. 1, 62 *aci śīrṣaḥ* is really a Vārttika of Kātyāyana's on the preceding rule (Vol. III. p. 41). Here too, Kaiyaṭa has the note—*vārttikam dṛṣṭvā kaiścit sūtreṣu prakṣiptam.*

P. VI. 1, 100 *nityam āmneḍite ḍāci* is really a Vārttika of Kātyāyana's on P. VI. 1, 99 (Vol. III. p. 77). Kaiyaṭa again has the note—*vārttikadarśanāt sūtre kaiścit prakṣiptam.*

P. VI. 1, 136 *aḍabhyāsavyavāye'pi* teaches the same as, and is clearly based on, Kātyāyana's Vārttikas 5 and 6, *aḍvyavāya upasamkhyānam* and *abhyāsavyavāye ca*, on P. VI. 1, 135 (Vol. III. p. 92). Kaiyaṭa has the note—*aḍabhyāsavyavāye'pīti sūtrasyāpāṭhe vārttikapravṛttiḥ*, and Nāgojībhaṭṭa adds—*anārṣaḥ sūtre pāṭhaḥ*.

Finally, P. VI. 1, 156 *kāraskaro vṛkṣaḥ* has been taken from Patañjali's notes on P. VI. 1, 157 (Vol. III. p. 96). Here the *Kāśikā* itself has the remark—*kecid idaṃ sūtraṃ nādhīyate pāraskaraprabhṛtiṣv eva kāraskaro vṛkṣa iti paṭhanti.*

The result of this inquiry then is as follows:—The text of the *Aṣṭādhyāyī*, which is given in the *Kāśikā-Vṛtti*, differs in the case of 58 rules (excluding here the somewhat doubtful case of P. VIII. 2, 12) from the text which was known to Kātyāyana or Patañjali. 10 of those 58 rules are altogether fresh additions to the original text (by which I mean here the text known to Kātyāyana or Patañjali). 17 rules were from the beginning part of the text, but in the original text those 17 rules did not form 17, but were only 8 separate rules. 19 rules, which also belong to the original text, have each had one or more words added to them. The wording of 10 original rules has been changed otherwise than by the addition of one or more words, and one rule has been altered in addition to being split up into two rules (P. VI. 1, 137 and 138). Altogether the text given in the *Kāśikā-Vṛtti* (and that of the *Aṣṭādhyāyī* in the editions) contains 20 more Sūtras than the original text.

The origin of the changes, which the text has undergone, can in most cases be traced in the Mahābhāṣya. Out of 8 cases of *Yogavibhāga*, 5 have been suggested by Kātyāyana and 2 by Patañjali. In the case of 19 rules, which have received additions, the words added have in 13 rules been taken from the Vārttikas, in 4 rules from Patañjali's notes, and in one rule jointly from Kātyāyana's and Patañjali's remarks; in the case of one rule the word added has not been actually taken from a Vārttika, but the addition has been made to comply with a suggestion of Kātyāyana's. In the case of 12 rules, which have been otherwise changed, the changes can in 5 rules be traced to Kātyāyana's and in one rule to Patañjali's suggestions. Of the 10 rules, which have been added to the original text, 7 are Vārttikas of Kātyāyana, 2 are based on Vārttikas, and one is a note of Patañjali's.

Have the rules of the *Aṣṭādhyāyī* since the time of the composition of the Mahābhāṣya undergone any changes besides those which have been indicated in the preceding, and in particular, is there any reason to suppose that other new rules have been added to the original text? After the careful study which I have given to the Mahābhāṣya and the literature connected with it, I feel no hesitation in answering this question in the negative. Besides the 1,713 rules, which are actually treated of by Kātyāyana and Patañjali, nearly 600 rules are fully and about 350 other rules partly quoted in the Mahābhāṣya. And as a large number of other rules is absolutely necessary for the proper understanding of those rules for which we have the direct testimony of Patañjali, and for the formation of words used by that scholar in the course of his arguments—I refer to the numerous quotations at the foot of the pages in my edition—we may rest satisfied that our text of the *Aṣṭādhyāyī*, or rather the text of the best MSS., does not in any material point differ from the text which was known to Patañjali.

D. Some Devices of Indian Grammarians (1887)

Franz Kielhorn

The seventh and last article of the series of "notes" on the *Mahābhāṣya* deals with "Some Devices of Indian Grammarians." The study of this topic, though fundamental to the study of the Sanskrit grammarians, was resumed only half a century later (for example, in Boudon 1938, below pages 358–391, and Renou 1940, Introduction, ch. III "Les procédés d'interprétation chez les grammairiens sanskrits"). In Pāṇini's grammar there are certain metarules or *paribhāṣās*, which state how the *sūtras* of the grammar have to be used and interpreted. Later commentators added other similar rules, but also introduced numerous other devices. These are the subject of Kielhorn's article (*Indian Antiquary* 16, 1887, 244–252).

In the present note I intend to enumerate, and to illustrate by a few simple examples, some of the devices—other than regular Paribhāṣās—which the commentators on Pāṇini are in the habit of resorting to in the course of their discussions. The general aim of these devices is, to secure the right interpretation and proper application of Pāṇini's rules; to refute objections that might be raised to them; to extend the sphere of the rules of the *Aṣṭādhyāyī*, so as to make them apply where at first sight they would seem to be inapplicable, and to render additional rules unnecessary; and sometimes also to shorten or simplify those rules. In the Vārttikas of Kātyāyana their number is comparatively small; it is greatly increasing already in the work of Patañjali; and, to a certain extent, one may perhaps venture to say that, the later an author, the greater is the number and the more artificial the nature of the devices with which he operates.

In accordance with the plan of these notes, I shall confine my remarks generally to the works of Kātyāyana and Patañjali; but I shall try to indicate by one or two examples, how the practice of those older writers has been more fully developed in the *Kāśikā-Vṛtti*.

1. Jñāpaka[1]; *ācāryapravṛttir jñāpayati*; *jñāpayaty ācāryaḥ*.—In addition to what he teaches directly, Pāṇini teaches many things indirectly. Regarding the interpretation of P. I. 1, 45 *ig yaṇaḥ saṃprasāraṇam*, there arises the question,—Is *Samprasāraṇa* a name for the vowels *i*, *u*, etc., substituted for *y*, *v*, etc., or is it equivalent to the phrase '*i*, *u*, etc. take the place of *y*, *v*, etc.'? Pāṇini indirectly teaches (*jñāpayati*), that *Samprasāraṇa* has both meanings; for, when in VI. 3, 139 he says that *Samprasāraṇa* is lengthened, he shows that *Samprasāraṇa* denotes the vowels *i*, *u*, etc., substituted for *y*, *v*, etc., because only vowels can be lengthened; and, when in VI. 1, 13 he rules that *Samprasāraṇa* shall be substituted for a certain suffix, he shows that the word *saṃprasāraṇam* must also be equivalent to *the phrase ig yaṇaḥ* '*i*, *u*, etc., take the place of *y*, *v*, etc.' (Vol. I. p. 111). On P. III. 2, 16, it may be doubtful whether we should supply only *adhikaraṇe* from the preceding rule, or also *karmaṇi* from P. III. 2, 1; in other words, whether a word like *kurucara*, which is formed by the rule, means only *kuruṣu carati*, or means also *kurūṃś carati*. Our doubt is solved by Pāṇini himself; by giving in III. 2, 17 a special rule for *bhikṣāṃ carati*, Pāṇini clearly intimates that in III. 2, 16 we are not to supply *karmaṇi*. Accordingly, *kurucara* can only mean *kuruṣu carati*, not *kurūṃś carati* (Vol. II. p. 101).

The idea, which underlies the notion of *jñāpaka*, is a perfectly sound one. We must, in the first instance, allow Pāṇini himself to explain his own work. But as Pāṇini does not speak out openly, there is the danger lest we should make him suggest more than he really meant to say. And this danger is greatly increased when the *Aṣṭādhyāyī* is regarded as an absolutely perfect work,[2] in which every seemingly irregular or unaccountable proceeding must have been intentionally resorted to for the purpose of indirectly instructing the student. In IV. 2, 42, Pāṇini teaches that the suffix *yan* is added to certain bases enumerated in the rule. Patañjali here raises the question: 'Why this new suffix? Why is not the suffix *yañ*, which in every respect would serve the same purpose as *yan*, valid from IV. 2, 40?' And his answer is, that Pāṇini has purposely employed a new suffix, in order to suggest that this new suffix shall be added to *other* bases besides those actually enumerated. Here it will be sufficient to point out that Patañjali, in the application of the principle of indirect teaching, is going far beyond Kātyāyana. Kātyāyana, instead of regarding the superfluous *yan* in P. IV. 2, 42

[1] Kātyāyana resorts to this device 44 times, Patañjali far more frequently. And since Patañjali has two Ācāryas to deal with, Pāṇini and Kātyāyana, he is enabled to refer us also to the indirect teaching of Kātyāyana, and he has actually done so six times. As regards Pāṇini, it may be added that there are *jñāpakas* in his *Gaṇapāṭha* and *Dhātupāṭha*, as well as in his *Aṣṭādhyāyī*.

[2] *na hi kiṃcid asmin paśyāmi śāstre yad anarthakaṃ syāt* ['I don't see anything in this work which is meaningless'] Vol. III. p. 54.

as a *jñāpaka*, makes a separate new rule for the word which in his opinion should have been distinctly mentioned by Pāṇini (Vol. II. p. 279).

That *jñāpakas* are often and rightly made use of in the Mahābhāṣya to establish the validity for Pāṇini's grammar of certain general maxims of Paribhāṣās, I have had frequent occasions to show in my edition of the *Paribhāṣenduśekhara*. Here, too, maxims may be deduced from some peculiar wording of the Sūtras, which possibly have never presented themselves to Pāṇini himself; and occasionally (as in Vol. I. p. 486, Vol. II. p. 64, and elsewhere) the commentators themselves differ both as regards the validity of a particular maxim and the *jñāpaka* by means of which such maxim is sought to be established. It *is* strange, that Pāṇini should have employed the same Anubandha *ṇ* in the first and in the sixth of the so-called Śivasūtras, because by doing so he has made it difficult for us to decide whether the Pratyāhāras *aṇ* and *iṇ* are formed with the first or with the second *ṇ*. But did Pāṇini really adopt this stratagem in order to suggest, that in every doubtful case of this kind we should have recourse to the (traditional) *interpretation* of his rules (Vol. I. p. 35),—a maxim to which Patañjali draws our attention no less than a dozen times in the course of his discussions?

On P. V. 1, 115 Kātyāyana gives the special rule, placed in the Mahābhāṣya under V. 1, 118, that the suffix *vat* is added also to *strī* and *puṃs*, to form *strīvat* and *puṃvat*. Kātyāyana considers such a rule necessary, because without it the suffixes *nañ* and *snañ* taught for *strī* and *puṃs* in P. IV. 1, 87, would supersede the suffix *vat* of P. V. 1, 115. According to Patañjali, on the other hand, Pāṇini himself shows that the suffixes taught in IV. 1, 87 do not supersede the suffix *vat*, inasmuch as he uses the word *puṃvat* in his rule VI. 3, 34. And when we object, that even so there would be no reason why we should form also *strīvat*, we are told that our objection is futile, because (yogāpekṣaṃ jñāpakam) 'the *jñāpaka* (*puṃvat* in VI. 3, 34) has reference to the *whole* rule (IV. 1, 87),' *i.e.* Pāṇini, by employing *puṃvat*, indirectly teaches that the whole rule IV. 1, 87 is superseded by V. 1, 115. This example of a *yogāpekṣa jñāpaka*[3] naturally leads me on to—

2. Nipātana.[4]—By incidentally employing a word or any form whatever, Pāṇini shows that that word or that form is correct;[5] and if such a word or form should happen to be contrary to any rule of his, that rule must, in this particular instance, be understood to be superseded. The incidental employment of a word or form is thus like a special rule superseding a general rule. In *sarvanāman* the initial (dental) *n* of *nāman* should by P. VIII. 4, 3 be changed to the (lingual) *ṇ*; but that change does not take place, because Pāṇini in I. 1, 27 puts down *sarvanāmāni* with a (dental) *n* (Vol. I. p. 86). On P. III. 3, 90 Kātyāyana demands a special rule, to teach that the root *prach* before the suffix *naṅ*, is not by P. VI. 1, 16 changed to

[3] Patañjali in Vol. I. p. 83; Vol. II. pp. 81, 238, 347, 365. Compare also *aviśeṣeṇa jñāpakam* in Vol. II. p. 110. The expression *yogāpekṣaṃ jñāpakam* has been curiously misunderstood in the late Prof. Goldstücker's *Pāṇini*, p. 116.

[4] Kātyāyana in Vol. I. pp. 52, 86, 478; Vol. II. p. 406; Vol. III. pp. 103, 105, 123, 194, 255; (compare also 455). Patañjali twice as often. In Vol. III. p. 224 Patañjali refers us by the phrase *nipātanād etat siddham* to a Vārttika of Kātyāyana's.

[5] Compare Vol. II. p. 413 *deśyāḥ sūtranibandhāḥ kriyante i.e. deṣṭavyāḥ sādhutvena pratipādyā ete sūtre nibadhyante prasaṅgena sādhutvapratipādanārtham.*

pṛch; in other words, that *prach* + *naṅ* = *praśna*, not *pṛśna*. According to Patañjali, no such special rule is needed, because Pāṇini employs the word *praśna* in III. 2, 117. (Vol. II. p. 151). On P. I. 1, 47 Kātyāyana makes a special rule to account for *bharūjā* and *marīci*. Patañjali considers such a rule superfluous, because Pāṇini has the two words in his Gaṇas (Vol. I. p. 115).

3. Anabhidhāna.[6]—Grammar is not to invent new words or new meanings, but has to concern itself with existing words only, to show which are right words, and to explain their formation and usage. The grammarian need not take into account any *possible* wrong words which nobody would think of employing; he does his duty if he gives his rules in such a manner as to account for the right words, and to exclude wrong words which people actually do use. Reasoning like this would appear to have led to the device of *anabhidhāna*, which has been frequently resorted to by Kātyāyana and Patañjali, especially in those chapters of Pāṇini's grammar which treat of the addition of suffixes, sometimes to show that Pāṇini has said more than he need have said, and sometimes to defend him from the charge of having said too little. If nobody thinks of using a particular word, or of using a word in a particular sense, it may be said that such a word would mean nothing, or would not convey the requisite meaning, and it may therefore seem unnecessary to forbid its use or its employment in that particular sense. According to P. IV. 2, 1, a certain suffix is added to a word denoting a colour to signify 'coloured by (or with) that.' The suffix is said to be added 'to a word denoting a colour,' apparently to prevent its addition, e.g., to *devadatta*, in the expression *devadattena raktaṃ vastram* 'cloth coloured by Devadatta.' According to Kātyāyana, Pāṇini might have omitted the words 'to a word denoting a colour,' for the suffix taught by Pāṇini is added to denote the meaning 'coloured by (or with),' and that meaning would not be denoted by *daivadatta* in *daivadattaṃ vastram*. Everybody will understand this phrase to mean 'cloth belonging to Devadatta,' and nobody would employ *daivadattaṃ vastram* in the sense of 'cloth coloured by Devadatta'[7] (Vol. II. p. 271). In III. 2, 1, Pāṇini is not obliged to tell us that the suffix, which in accordance with his rule is added in *kumbhakāra*, must not be added to *dṛś*, to express the sense of *ādityaṃ paśyati*, because the word *ādityadarśa* would not convey the requisite meaning, or in other words, because nobody would think of using the word *ādityadarśa*.[8] (Vol. II. p. 94). On P. V. 2, 65

[6] Kātyāyana, in Vol. I. p. 424; Vol. II. pp. 12, 13, 94, 146, 234, 271, 325; Vol. III. p. 365; and in other passages, where *anabhidhāna* is referred to by the word *uktam* or the phrase *uktaṃ vā*. Patañjali in Vol. I. p. 177; Vol. II. pp. 25, 250, 274, 307, 308, 309, 319, 334, 341, 351, 358, 382 (twice), 387, 395, 398, 399. I may perhaps draw attention to the fact, that most of these references are to Vol. II. of the Mahābhāṣya, which, generally speaking, treats of Kṛt and Taddhita-suffixes.

[7] The device of *anabhidhāna* may appear so strange, that it is perhaps advisable to quote the following from Kaiyaṭa on P. IV. 2, 1: *raktādīnaṃ śabdānāṃ yo'rthaḥ sa eva yadi laukike prayoge pratyayenābhidhīyate tadā pratyayo bhavati nānyathā prayuktānāṃ śabdānām sādhyasādhuvivekāya śāstrārambhāt | devadattena raktaṃ vastram iti vākyāyo'rtho'vagamyate nāsau daivadattaṃ vastram ity ato'vagamyate svasvāmisaṃbandhasyaivātaḥ saṃpratyayāt |*

[8] See Kaiyaṭa on P. III. 2, 1—*anabhidhānād iti | nityānāṃ śabdānām idam anvākhyānamātram | na cādityaṃ paśyatītyādy arthapratipādanāyād ity adarśādayaḥ śabdā loke prayujyanta iti śāstreṇāpi sādhutvena nānuśiṣyanta ity arthaḥ |*

Kātyāyana would wish to alter the wording of Pāṇini's rule, so as to make it quite clear that the words *dhanaka* and *hiraṇyaka*, which, are formed by the rule, mean 'a desire for wealth' and 'a desire for gold,' and do not mean 'desirous of wealth' and 'desirous of gold.' According to Patañjali, Pāṇini's rule need not be altered; the suffix taught by Pāṇini cannot be added in the sense of 'desirous of,'—(*anabhidhānāt*), because *dhanaka* and *hiraṇyaka* would not convey that meaning (Vol. II. p. 387).

These instances will sufficiently prove, that the device of *anabhidhāna*, beyond acquainting us with the views of the commentators who happen to make use of it, is really of no value whatever. We know that a word cannot be used, or does not convey a particular meaning, and therefore we want no rule forbidding its use, or its employment in a particular sense. Why, we may well ask, do we study grammar at all, if we know beforehand what words cannot be used? It is right to add, that at any rate Kātyāyana, in general, has had recourse to *anabhidhāna* only as to an alternative proceeding, and that the weak point of the device has been clearly perceived by the Indian grammarians themselves. Haradatta, when commenting on P. III. 2, 1, says that *anabhidhāna* must be resorted to, only where the authorities tell us to do so, and that elsewhere we must simply follow the rules of grammar.[9]

4. Vivakṣā.[10]—Similar to *anabhidhānu*, and liable to the same objection, is the device of *vivakṣā*, which is a few times made use of in the Mahābhāṣya, and is more frequently employed in the *Kāśikā-Vṛtti*. *Vivakṣā* means 'the wish to say a thing'; and *vivakṣā* or *laukikī vivakṣā*, as understood here, is the desire of those who speak a language to convey certain meanings by certain words, the manner in which people employ the words of their language, the prevailing and generally understood usage of words (*prāyasya*, i.e. *lokasya*, *saṃpratyayaḥ*). According to Patañjali, Pāṇini refers us to this common usage by the word *iti*, which he occasionally employs in a rule. By that *iti* Pāṇini, according to Patañjali, indicates that such a rule of his must not be observed generally and under all circumstances, but has its application limited by general usage. The rule must be observed only so far as it may lead to the formation of such words as are used by people, or of words which are really used in the particular sense indicated by the rule. We may by P. V. 1, 16 say *prāsādīyaṃ dāru* ['palatial timber'], to convey the meaning *prāsādo'sya dāruṇah syāt* ['timber sufficient to build a palace'], but we cannot by the same rule form *prāsādīyo devadattaḥ* ['palatial Devadatta']: in the sense of *prāsādo devadattasya syāt* ['Devadatta sufficiently able to build a palace'], because people would not understand this meaning from *prāsādīyo devadattaḥ* (Vol. II. p. 343).

5. Yogavibhāga is the splitting up of a rule into two or more separate rules. This proceeding has been suggested about 25 times by Kātyāyana, and rather more than 70 times by Patañjali. Its general purport is, without altering the wording of the text of the *Aṣṭādhyāyī*, simply by a different division of that text, to obviate objections that might be brought against Pāṇini's rules, and to

[9] Haradatta on P. III. 2, 1,—*tac cānabhidhānaṃ yatrāptair uktaṃ tatraiva | anyatra tu yathālakṣaṇaṃ bhavaty eva | tathā ca paṭhati yathālakṣaṇaṃ bhavaty eva | tathā paṭhati yathālakṣaṇam aprayukta iti |*

[10] Kātyāyana in Vol. II. p. 282. Patañjali in Vol. II. pp. 275, 342, 393. See also *Kāśikā-Vṛtti* on P. II. 2, 27; IV. 2, 21, 55, 57, 58, 67; IV. 4, 125; V. 1, 16; V. 2, 45, 77, 94, 95, 107, 112, 115; V. 4, 10.

make those rules teach more than they would teach otherwise, or that Pāṇini has taught himself. Examples, both from the Vārttikas and from the Mahābhāṣya, have been already given in my last note.

I may add here that the commentators, without resorting to actual *yogavibhāga* and thus increasing the number of the Sūtras, occasionally meet objections by joining the first word or words of one rule on to a preceding rule, or by dividing the words of the text differently from what they themselves show to be the ordinary or generally accepted division of it. In Vol. I. p. 272 Kātyāyana suggests the possibility of dividing the text of the rule P. I. 2, 11 *svaritenādhikāraḥ*, usually divided into *svaritena* and *adhikāraḥ*, into the three words *svarite*, *na*, and *adhikāraḥ*. In Vol. I. p. 271 Patañjali proposes to join the word *svaritena* of the same rule on to the preceding rule, which would then read *yathāsaṃkhyam anudeśaḥ samānāṃ svaritena*, and to make P. I. 3, 11 consist of only the one word *adhikāraḥ*. In Vol. II. p. 228 Patañjali proposes to transfer the word *sarvatra* from the beginning of P. IV. 1, 18 to the end of the preceding rule IV. 1, 17. In Vol. II. p. 11 he meets an objection by dividing the words *dīrghaś cābhyāsasya* of P. III. 1, 6, usually divided into *dīrghaś ca* + *abhyāsasya*, into *dīrghaś ca* + *ābhyāsasya*. In Vol. III. p. 11 he divides *jakṣityādayaḥ* (= *jakṣiti* + *ādayaḥ*) of P. VI.1, 6 into *jakṣ* + *ity ādayaḥ*; in Vol. I. p. 152 °*vareyalopa*° of P. I. 1, 58 into °*vare* + *'yalopa*°, etc.

6. Ekayogaḥ kariṣyate.[11]—As a single rule may be split in two, so two rules may be joined together, so as to form one rule. The advantage sought to be derived from this device, which has been five times resorted to by Patañjali, may be seen from the following example. It may be argued that *guṇavṛddhī* in P. I. 1, 3 (*iko guṇavṛddhī*) is superfluous, because *vṛddhiḥ* and *guṇaḥ* will be valid from P. I. 1, 1 *vṛddhir ād aic* and P. I. 1, 2 *ad eṅ guṇaḥ*. The objection to this would be, that *vṛddhiḥ* of P. I. 1, 1 would be valid also in P. I. 1, 2, and that accordingly *a*, *e*, *o* would by P. I. 1, 2, be termed both *Guṇa* and *Vṛddhi*. But that objection is met by the suggestion, that P. I. 1, 1 and 2 should be made one rule, *Vṛddhir ād aij ad eṅ guṇaḥ*. In this single rule the term *vṛddhiḥ*, with which the rule opens, would not be valid in the concluding portion of the same rule, and from this rule both *vṛddhiḥ* and *guṇaḥ* could then be supplied in the following rule (Vol. I. p. 44).

7. Sambandham anuvartiṣyate; *sambandhānuvṛtti*; *sambandhavṛtti*.[12]—But the objection raised to the validity of the term *vṛddhiḥ* of P. I. 1, 1, in P. I. 1, 3, may be met also by another device, which Patañjali has resorted to more frequently. In P. I. 1, 2 the *whole* rule *vṛddhir ād aic* may be regarded as valid, and subsequently *guṇaḥ* and *vṛddhiḥ* may be regarded as valid in P. I. 1, 3. The case in fact would stand thus,—

P. I. 1, 1 *vṛddhir ād aic*.
P. I. 1, 2 *ad eṅ guṇaḥ*;—*vṛddhir ād aic* valid from the preceding.
P. I. 1, 3 *ikaḥ*;—*guṇaḥ* and *vṛddhiḥ* valid from the preceding.

8. Maṇḍūkagatayo 'dhikārāḥ;[13] *maṇḍūkapluti*.—And there is even a third way of meeting the same objection. There is no reason at all why *vṛddhiḥ* of P. I. 1, 1, should be valid in P. I. 1, 2. Like a frog, it may leap across P. I. 1, 2 and alight on P. I. 1, 3. This device has been resorted to by Patañjali seven times.

[11] Patañjali in Vol. I. pp. 44, 482; Vol. III. pp. 25, 162, 315.
[12] Patañjali in Vol. I. pp. 44, 190, 457, 482; Vol. II. pp. 127, 151, 267, 290, 372; Vol. III. pp. 25, 52, 8, 148, 238, 271, 410, 425, 431, 433.
[13] Patañjali in Vol. I. pp. 44, 457, 482; Vol. II. p. 372; Vol. III. pp. 25, 161, 314.

9. Iṣṭavācī paraśabdaḥ.[14]—In I. 4, 2 Pāṇini prescribes that of two conflicting rules the subsequent (*para*) rule, in the order of the *Aṣṭādhyāyī*, shall take effect in preference to the preceding rule. Now Kātyāyana on various occasions shows that Pāṇini's rule is not universally true, and he points out a number of *pūrva-vipratiṣedhas*, *i.e.* instances in which the preceding rule must take effect in preference to the subsequent rule. According to Patañjali, on the other hand, the special rules given by Kātyāyana are unnecessary, and the objections of that grammarian only show that he has not fully understood the word *para* in P. I. 4, 2. *Para*, amongst other things, also means 'desired' (*iṣṭa*), and what Pāṇini really teaches is, that of two conflicting rules it is the *desired* rule that should take effect, *i.e.* that rule, whatever be its position in the *Aṣṭādhyāyī*, the application of which will lead to correct words. Here again, then, we ought to possess a perfect knowledge of the language, if we would rightly apply the rules of Pāṇini's grammar.

10. Pratyāhāragrahaṇa.[15]—A term ending with an Anubandha, which at first sight would appear to denote a single suffix, root, etc., is occasionally by Patañjali explained to be a collective term denoting a series of suffixes, roots, etc. Thus *mātrac* in P. IV. 1, 15 is not, as might be supposed, the suffix *mātrac* taught in P. V. 2, 37, but is taken to be a *Pratyāhāra* or collective term, formed of *mātra* in P. V. 2, 37 and the Anubandha *c* of *ayac* in P. V. 2, 43, and denoting, accordingly, all suffixes from *mātrac* in the former up to and including *ayac* in the latter rule (Vol. I. pp. 106 and 138). The most interesting example occurs in Vol. I. p. 289, and again in Vol. II. p. 47. In the older works of Sanskrit literature the Periphrastic Perfect is formed only with *kṛ*; and this is exactly what Pāṇini teaches in III. 1, 40, where he says, that *kṛñ*, *i.e. kṛ* which has the Anubandha *ñ*, is employed in the Periphrastic Perfect. Patañjali, however, desirous of accounting by Pāṇini's rules for Perfects such as *ihām āsa*, *īhāṃ babhūva*, explains *kṛñ* in P. III. 1, 40 to be a Pratyāhāra, formed of *kṛ* in P. V. 4, 50 and the Anubandha *ñ* of *kṛñ* in P. V. 4, 58, and including therefore *bhū* and *as*, which in P. V. 4, 50 follow immediately upon *kṛ*.

11. Praśliṣṭanirdeśa.[16]—A long or even a short vowel often results from the coalition of two or more vowels. How this simple fact may be turned to account in grammatical discussions, may be seen from the following examples. In Vol. I. p. 501, Kātyāyana states that the single vowel *ā* (*ḍā*), which by P. II. 4, 85 is substituted in the Periphrastic Future for the ordinary personal terminations *ti* and *ta*, takes the place of the *whole* original terminations (and not merely, according to P. I. 1, 52, of their *final* letters), because *ā* may be regarded as a combination of the two vowels *ā* + *ā*; and that for this reason Pāṇini is justified in not attaching the Anubandha *ś* to the substitute *ḍā* (compare P. I. 1, 55). According to Patañjali, Pāṇini might similarly have omitted the Anubandha *ś* of the term *aś* in P. II. 4, 32 (Vol. I. p. 481), and of the same term *aś* in P. VII. 1, 27 (Vol. III. p. 251), because even (short) *a* may be regarded as a combination of *a* + *a*. According to Patañjali, again, *loka*° in P. II. 3, 69 may be regarded as the result of the combination of *la* + *u* +

[14] Patañjali in Vol. I. pp. 46, 194, 306, 404; Vol. II. pp. 237, 279, 337; Vol. III. pp. 18, 99, 134, 201, 238, 276.

[15] Patañjali in Vol. I. pp. 106, 138, 141, 289, 470, 488; Vol. II. pp. 47, 130, 203.

[16] Kātyāyana in Vol. I. p. 501. Patañjali in Vol. I. pp. 47, 88, 139, 140, 469, 481; Vol. II. pp. 46, 52, 184, 403; Vol. III. pp. 151, 212, 251, 273, 312. Compare *vikāranirdeśa*, Kātyāyana in Vol. I. p. 202.

uka°, and no additional rule is required to teach that words like *cikīrṣu*, which are formed with *u*, are not construed with the Genitive case (Vol. I. p. 469).

12. Ekaśeṣanirdeśa.[17]—Pāṇini, according to the commentators, also employs other terms once only, instead of repeating them. An instance is afforded by the same rule P. II. 4, 85, which has been mentioned under the last heading. In that rule Pāṇini teaches that *ḍāraurasaḥ*, *i.e.* as one would say, *ḍā*, *rau*, and *ras*, are substituted for the third personal terminations of the Periphrastic Future. Here it may be objected that, as there are six such terminations, three in the Parasmaipada and three in the Ātmanepada, and only three substitutes, the rule P. I. 3, 10, which determines the order in which substitutions take place, would not be applicable, and that Pāṇini therefore ought to have shown in some other way, how the substitution should take place. Such objection is met by the statement that *ḍāraurasaḥ* is an *ekaśeṣa-nirdeśa*, for *ḍāraurasaḥ* + *ḍāraurasaḥ*, i.e. *ḍā rau ras* + *ḍā rau ras*; and the number of substitutes having thus been shown to *be* six, the order of substitution is after all regulated by P. I. 3, 10 (Vol. I. p. 500). To P. I. 1, 27 *sarvādīni sarvanāmāni* Kātyāyana wishes to append the note that *sarva* etc., when used as proper names, are *not* termed *Sarvanāmāni*. Such a note, however, is by Patañjali regarded as superfluous, because *sarvādīni sarvanāmāni* may be taken to stand for *sarvādīni sarvādīni sarvanāmāni sarvanāmāni*. '*sarva* etc., are (termed) *Sarvanāmāni*; (and the) *sarva* etc., (here spoken of) are nouns denoting anybody' (not proper names). (Vol. I. p. 88).

13. Avibhaktiko nirdeśaḥ.[18]—Pāṇini on rare occasions does put down in his Sūtras certain terms without the case-terminations, which we should have expected him to attach to them.[19] But this will hardly be considered to justify the commentators in assuming an *avibhaktika nirdeśa*, 'the employment of a term without termination,' in instances like the following. The wording of P. VII. 3, 82 and 83 is *mider guṇaḥ jusi ca*, or, when the two rules are joined according to the rules of euphony, *mider guṇo jusi ca*. To meet certain objections, Patañjali in Vol. I. p. 47 takes the first rule to consist of the three words *mid eḥ guṇaḥ*, where the base *mid* would stand for the Genitive case *midaḥ* ('Guṇa is substituted for the *i* of *mid*'); and in Vol. III. p. 335 he further divides *guṇojusi ca* into *guṇa* + *ujusi ca*, where the base *guṇa* would stand for the Nominative case *guṇaḥ* ('Guṇa is also substituted before *jus*, when *jus* commences with *u*').

14. Luptanirdiṣṭa.[20]—Occasionally a consonant (usually *y* or *v*) is supposed to have been elided in the text of the Sūtras. Such consonant would of course have to be replaced, when explaining the text. On P. I. 3, 7, Kātyāyana demands a special rule, to teach that, contrary to Pāṇini's rule, the initial *c* of the suffixes *cuñcup* and *caṇap* is *not* an Anubandha. According to Patañjali, no such rule is required because the two suffixes really begin with the letter *y*, which has been elided in the text (Vol. I. p. 263).

[17] Kātyāyana in Vol. I. pp. 261, 350, 369; Vol. III. pp. 167, 467. Patañjali in Vol. I. pp. 88, 156, 212, 500.

[18] Patañjali in Vol. I. pp. 21, 25, 47; Vol. II. p. 46; Vol. III. pp. 242, 335, 414.

[19] Compare e.g. P. III. 3, 17 *sṛ*; III. 3, 30 *kṝ*; III. 3, 48 *vṛ*; VI. 1, 184 and VI. 4, 6 *nṛ*; VI. 3, 62 *eka*; VI. 4, 142 *ti*.

[20] Patañjali in Vol. I. pp. 49, 263 (twice); Vol. II. p. 52; Vol. III. pp. 43, 245, 257. The letters supposed to have been dropped are *y*, *v*, and once *n*.

15. Dvi-kārako nirdeśaḥ.[21]—More often Pāṇini is supposed to have employed a double consonant, where the actual text of the Sūtras has only a single consonant. On P. VIII. 3, 5, *samaḥ suṭi* Kātyāyana suggests that, before the augment *suṭ* (in *sam* + *skartā*), *s* (not *ru*) should be substituted for the final of *sam* (= *saṃskartā*). According to Patañjali, Kātyāyana's remark is superfluous, because the substitution of *s* has been taught in Pāṇini's own rule, the wording of which really is *samaḥ ssuṭi* (or *samasssuṭi*), *i.e.* '*s* is substituted for (the final of) *sam* before *suṭ*' (Vol. III. p. 425). Theoretically it is perfectly true that, by the rules of euphony, original *samaḥ ssuṭi* might have been changed to *samaḥ suṭi*, but how little importance can be attached to Patañjali's remark, may be seen from the fact that quite a different meaning has been assigned by him to the same rule *samaḥ ssuṭi* in Vol. III. p. 94.

16. Anvarthasaṃjñā.[22]—Technical terms are employed for the sake of economy or brevity. When, then, Pāṇini uses other than short technical terms, he does so to show that the application of those terms accords with their etymological meaning. On the rule I, 1, 23, in which Pāṇini teaches that *bahu*, *gaṇa*, etc. are termed *Saṃkhyā*, Kātyāyana would wish it to be distinctly stated that the ordinary numerals *eka*, *dvi*, etc. also are termed *Saṃkhyā*, because otherwise these numerals would not in Pāṇini's grammar be denoted by the term *Saṃkhyā*. But Kātyāyana's suggestion is rejected by Patañjali, on the ground that *Saṃkhyā* is an *anvartha-saṃjñā*. The term *Saṃkhyā* denotes the ordinary numerals *eka*, *dvi*, etc., because *saṃkhyā* is derived from *sam* + *khyā* 'to count together,' which is exactly what the ordinary numerals do (Vol. I. p. 81).

17. Tadvadatideśa.[23]—Or it may be said, that in the rule mentioned Pāṇini has used the word *saṃkhyā* in the sense of *saṃkhyavat*. Pāṇini does not say at all that *bahu*, *gaṇa*, etc., are *termed Saṃkhyā*; what he teaches is, that *bahu*, *gaṇa*, etc., are treated as *if they were* numerals[24] (Vol. I. p. 81).

18. Prakarṣagati.[25]—As in ordinary life, so here, sometimes the mere fact that Pāṇini employs a word is sufficient to show that particular stress is laid on such word; that the word has reference to things which under all circumstances, or in a high degree, or more than other things (*sādhīyaḥ*), are what the word means. When in I. 1, 56 Pāṇini uses the term *al-vidhi* 'an operation depending on *a letter*,' he means such operations as depend on letters as such, not operations which depend on suffixes that happen to be letters (Vol. I. p. 136). When in III. 1, 94 he speaks of *asarūpa* (*i.e.* not uniform) suffixes, he must mean suffixes which are *asarūpa*

[21] Patañjali in Vol. I. p. 139; Vol. III. pp. 94, 254, 425; (*dvisakārako nirdeśaḥ*);—Vol. I. p. 155; Vol. II. p. 68; Vol. III. pp. 37, 188, 208; (*dvila*°);—Vol. I. p. 170; (*dviśa*°);—Vol. II. p. 20; (*dvica*°);—Vol. III. pp. 48, 250; (*dviḍa*°);—Vol. III. pp. 108, 410; (*dvina*°); Vol. III. p. 257; (*dvima*°);—Vol. III. p. 351 (*divita*°, *trita*°). This is perhaps the right place for the remark that the wrong reading *kkṅiti ca* of the rule P. I. 1, 5 (*kṅiti ca*) owes its origin to Patañjali's suggestion in Vol. I. p. 269 and Vol. II. p. 132, *kakāre gakāraś cartvabhūto nirdiśyate*. Compare a similar expression in Vol. III. p. 110.

[22] Patañjali in Vol. I. pp. 81, 89, 96, 215, 324, 346, 378; Vol. II. pp. 3, 76. Compare *anvarthagrahaṇa* in Vol. I. pp. 88, 209, 227, 229, 237, 472; Vol. II. pp. 303, 416; Vol. III. pp. 98, 120, 415.

[23] Patañjali in Vol. I. pp. 81, 191, 469. *Vatinirdeśa* in Vol. III. p. 272.

[24] Accordingly, Hemacandra in his rule I. 1, 39 has *ḍatyatu saṃkhyāvat*.

[25] Patañjali in Vol. I. pp. 136, 261, 283 (twice), 329, 355, 370, 380; Vol. II. pp. 80, 334; Vol. III. pp. 164, 369, 430.

in the ordinary language as well as in the language of grammar, because in the latter *all* suffixes are *asarūpa* (Vol. II. p. 80). And when in I. 3, 3 he speaks of a *last* consonant, he must be understood to mean the final consonant of complete roots, suffixes, etc., and Kātyāyana need not have attempted to improve on Pāṇini's rule (Vol. I. p. 261).

19. Akāro matvarthīyaḥ; matublopaḥ.[26]—To meet objections of various kinds, a noun ending in the vowel *a* is occasionally regarded as a derivative noun formed with the possessive suffix *a*; or it is stated that the possessive suffix *matup*, which should have been added, has been dropped. A simple instance is furnished by the word *anudātta* in P. VI. 1, 158. As the meaning of that rule (*anudāttaṃ padam ekavarjam*) is, that 'with the exception of one vowel, a word contains only *anudātta* vowels,' one might have expected Pāṇini to say (not *anudāttaṃ padam*, but) *anudāttāḥ pade* or *anudāttāḥ padasya*. The actual wording of the rule is nevertheless correct, because *anudāttam* does not mean *anudātta*, but means 'containing *anudātta* vowels;' either the possessive suffix has been dropped, or the final *a* of *anudātta* is the possessive suffix *a*. (Vol. III. p. 97.)

20. Tādarthyāt tācchabdyam;[27] sāhacaryāt tācchabdyam;[28] tātsthyāt tācchabdyam.[29]—Things subservient to something else, or things which are in company with something else, or things which are in a particular place, may be called by the names of the things to which they are subservient, or in company with which they appear, or of the place where they are. It is thus that the term *samāsa* in P. I. 2, 43, denotes *the rules* which teach the formation of compounds (*samāsārthaṃ śāstram*; Kātyāyana, in Vol. I. p. 214); and that *tatpuruṣaḥ* in P. I. 2, 42 means the words forming a Tatpuruṣa-compound (Patañjali, against Kātyāyana in Vol. I. p. 214). Thus, too, the rule P. I. 1, 30 *tṛtīyāsamāse* is supposed to account for the fact that, e.g., in *māsena pūrvāya dehi* ['give earlier by a month'] the word *pūrva* does not follow the pronominal declension. (Vol. I. p. 92.) And, by a similar reasoning, suggestions of Kātyāyana have been rejected by Patañjali in Vol. II. p. 388 and p. 437.

As might have been expected, most of these devices which I have collected from the Mahābhāṣya, have been made use of also in the Kāśikā-Vṛtti. In addition to them, the compilers of that commentary have employed other devices among which the two following, with which I conclude this list, are perhaps those most commonly resorted to.

21. Vyavasthitavibhāṣā.[30]—When Pāṇini teaches that an operation takes place optionally, we naturally understand him to mean, that such operation may or may not take effect in every individual instance which may fall under the rule. This, too, is clearly the opinion of the earlier commentators, as may be seen from various critical remarks which they have appended to some of Pāṇini's

[26] Patañjali in Vol. I. pp. 156, 208; Vol. II. pp. 104, 179, 376, 377; Vol. III. pp. 30, 97, 104, 171.

[27] Kātyāyana in Vol. I. p. 214; Vol. II. p. 312. Patañjali in Vol. I. pp. 91, 92, 214, 225, 332, 452, (twice); Vol. II. pp. 283, 331, 338, 359; Vol. III. p. 32.

[28] Patañjali in Vol. I. pp. 180, 202; Vol. II. pp. 284, 309, 360, 388.

[29] Patañjali in Vol. II. p. 437. Compare also Vol. II. p. 218, 1. 15. *Kāśikā-Vṛtti* on P. III. 1, 144.

[30] See e.g. *Kāśikā-Vṛtti* on P. I. 2, 21; I. 3, 70; I. 4, 47; II. 3, 17; 60; III. 1, 11; 90; 143; III. 2, 124; III. 3, 14; III. 4, 85, 86; VI. 1, 27, 28, 51.—Compare also *Mahābhāṣya*, Vol. II. p. 165; III. p. 350.

optional rules. To obviate such remarks, and generally with a view to account by Pāṇini's own rules for the actual facts of the language as known to them, later grammarians have invented the device of *vyavasthita-vibhāṣā*. An optional rule need not be optional in every case, but may be taken to teach, either, that an operation in particular instances necessarily must take place, while in others it is not allowed to take place at all; or, that the operation is really optional in a limited number of instances only, while in other instances, as the case may be, it must necessarily take place or may not take place. In I. 2, 21 Pāṇini teaches that in certain forms roots with penultimate *u* optionally take Guṇa;—*dyut* thus forms *dyutita* or *dyotita*. According to Kātyāyana, Pāṇini's rule is too wide; it should have been limited to roots of the first class only. According to the *Kāśikā-Vṛtti*, the rule affords an instance of *vyavasthita-vibhāṣā*; the operation taught by it optionally takes place in roots of the first class; in the case of other roots it does not take place at all. By P. III. 1, 143 *grah* forms either *graha* or *grāha*; but, the rule being a *vyavasthita-vibhāṣā*, *grah* forms only *graha* in the sense of 'a planet,' and only *grāha* in the sense of a 'shark.' According to P. I. 4, 47 the verb *abhiniviś* governs the Accusative case; Jayāditya, in order to account by Pāṇini's rule for the Locative case which also is found occasionally with the same verb, makes the rule optional by supplying for it (by *maṇḍūkapluti*) *anyatarasyām* from P. I. 4, 44, and he then declares P. I. 4, 47 to be a *vyavasthita-vibhāṣā*. *Abhiniviś* in some phrases governs only the Accusative, in others only the Locative. The interpretation of Pāṇini's rules is again dependent on and regulated by the actual usage of the language.

22. Anuktasamuccayārthaś cakāraḥ.[31]—On P. I. 3, 93 *luṭi ca kḷpaḥ*, Patañjali shows that the *ca* of that rule is superfluous, because even without it the term *syasanoḥ* of the preceding rule would be valid in the rule under discussion; and he adds the general remark that in like manner all the particles *ca* of the *Aṣṭādhyāyī* may be dispensed with (Vol. I. p. 295). In other places meanings have been assigned by him to *ca*, which that particle does not convey ordinarily. Thus *ca* is taken in the sense of *eva* (*avadhāraṇārtha*) in Vol. I. pp. 381 (P. II. 1, 17); 392 (P. II. 1, 48), 406 (P. II. 1, 72); in the sense of *iti* in Vol. I. p. 415 (P. II. 2, 14). More strange even Patañjali's proceeding must appear to us, when we see him refute certain criticisms of Kātyāyana by means of the particle *ca* in P. II. 4, 9 and P. VI. 1, 90,—a proceeding which, I may add, has been imitated by Jayāditya on P. II. 3, 16 and P. III. 1, 2. But there is one meaning which Patañjali has never assigned to *ca*, and which in grammar has to my knowledge been assigned to it first by the authors of the *Kāśikā-Vṛtti*,—the meaning indicated in the above heading *anuktasamuccayārthaś cakāraḥ*. The word *ca* serves the purpose of adding to the words actually enumerated in a rule others that have not been mentioned; or, in other words, Pāṇini indicates by the particle *ca*, that his rule applies to other words besides those actually mentioned by him. On P. V. 1, 7 *khalayava-māṣatilavṛṣabrahmaṇaś ca*, Kātyāyana has the note that *ratha* takes the same suffix as the words enumerated (Vol. II. p. 339). According to the *Kāśikā-Vṛtti*, the particle *ca* at the end of the rule is by Pāṇini meant to show that the suffix taught by the rule is added to other words *besides* those actually enumerated, and the word which

[31] See, e.g. *Kāśikā-Vṛtti* on P. II. 4, 18; III. 1, 126; III. 2, 30, 138, 188; III. 3, 119, 122; IV. 1, 74, 96, 123; IV. 2, 82; IV. 4, 29; V. 1, 7; V. 4, 25, 145; VII. 1, 48; VII. 2, 16.

Pāṇini had in view in thus employing *ca* is said to have been *ratha*. On P. III. 2, 30 *nāḍīmuṣṭyoś ca*, Patañjali adds to the word given by Pāṇini *ghaṭī* and others (Vol. II. p. 102); in the *Kāśikā* we are told that these very words *ghaṭī* etc., are suggested by the particle *ca* of Pāṇini's own rule. In P. IV. 4, 29 Pāṇini has *parimukhaṃ ca*; the corresponding rule of Candra's grammar is *parer mukhapārśvāt*; according to the *Kāśikā*, the particle *ca* of Pāṇini's rule shows that the suffix taught by the rule is added to other words besides *parimukha*, and the word which Pāṇini had in his mind, when thus employing *ca*, is the very *paripārśva* which is actually given by Candra. According to the *Kāśikā*, the *ca* of P. V. 4, 145 shows that one also says *ahidat* or *ahidanta*, *mūṣikadat* or *mūṣikadanta* etc.; *ahi*, *mūṣika* etc., are the very words which the corresponding rule of Candra actually enumerates, in addition to the words *agra*, *anta* etc., which are enumerated by Pāṇini. Unluckily we do not possess yet a complete copy of Candra's grammar; but judging from what we do possess of it, I feel little hesitation in saying that, wherever the device of which I am speaking is resorted to in the *Kāśikā-Vṛtti*, the words which Pāṇini is supposed to suggest by the employment of the particle *ca*, have invariably been taken by the compilers of the *Kāśikā* from the Vārttikas, or from the Mahābhāṣya, or from the grammar of Candra. The compilers have invented nothing; not caring for, or having no notion of, the history of grammar, they have tried to show, how Pāṇini's own rules can be made to account for a number of words, for which Pāṇini's more immediate successors had given additional rules.[32]

[32] See a paper on *ca* and *iti* by Dr. Bühler in *Wiener Zeitschrift für die Kunde des Morgenlandes*, Vol. I. p. 13.

5

The Sceptics and Their Critics

Plate IV

A page from the text of Patañjali's commentary on Pāṇini's grammar, *Mahābhāṣya*, with Kaiyaṭa's sub-commentary, *Bhāṣyapradīpa*, as it was reproduced in 1874 by photolithography under the supervision of Goldstücker from an undated manuscript (Goldstücker 1874b). The ten lines in somewhat larger type in the middle of the page constitute the following discussion from the Introduction of the *Mahābhāṣya* — a discussion that starts with the question of whether in the teaching of grammar, grammatical forms, or ungrammatical forms, or both should be taught:

kiṃ punar atra jyāyaḥ laghutvāc chabdopadeśaḥ / laghīyāñ chabdopadeśaḥ garīyān apaśabdopadeśaḥ ekaikasya śabdasya bahavo'pabhraṃśāḥ / tad yathā / gaur ity asya śabdasya gāvīgoṇīgotāgopotalikādayo'pabhraṃśāḥ / iṣṭānvākhyānaṃ khalv api bhavati / athaitasmiñ chabdopadeśe sati kiṃ śabdānāṃ pratipattau pratipadapāṭhaḥ kartavyaḥ gaur aśva puruṣo hastī śakunir mṛgo brāhmaṇa ity evam ādayaḥ śabdāḥ paṭhitavyāḥ nety āha / anabhyupāya eṣa śabdānāṃ pratipattau pratipadapāṭhaḥ / evaṃ hi śrūyate / bṛhaspatir indrāya divyaṃ varṣasahasraṃ pratipadoktānāṃ śabdānāṃ śabdapārāyaṇaṃ provāca nāṃtaṃ jagāma / bṛhaspatiś ca pravaktā iṃdraś cādhyetā divyam varṣasahasram adhyayanakālaḥ na cāṃtaṃ jagāma kiṃ punar adyatve yaḥ sarvathā ciraṃ jīvati sa varṣaśataṃ jīvati caturbhiś ca prakārair vidyopayuktā bhavati // āgamakālena svādhyāyakālena pravacanakālena vyavahārakāleneti / tatra cāsyāgamakālenaivāyuḥ kṛtsnaṃ paryupayuktaṃ syāt tasmād anabhyupāyaḥ śabdānāṃ pratipattau pratipadapāṭhaḥ / kathaṃ tarhīme śabdāḥ pratipattavyāḥ / kiṃcit sāmānyaviśeṣaval lakṣaṇaṃ pravartyaṃ yenālpena yatnena mahato mahataḥ śabdaugān pratipadyeran / kiṃ punas tad utsargāpavādau kaścid utsargaḥ kartavyaḥ kaścid apavādaḥ kathaṃ jātīyakaḥ punar utsargaḥ kartavyaḥ kathaṃ jātīyako'pavādaḥ sāmānyenotsargaḥ kartavyaḥ tad yathā karmaṇy aṇ / tasya viśeṣeṇāpavādaḥ tad yathā ātonupasarge kaḥ

"Now which of these is better? The teaching of grammatical forms, because of simplicity. The teaching of grammatical forms is simpler; the teaching of ungrammatical forms is more complicated. (The reason is that) corresponding to each grammatical form there are many corrupt forms. For example, to the grammatical form *gauḥ* 'cow' correspond the corrupt forms *gāvī*, *goṇī*, *gotā*, *gopotalikā*, and so forth. Moreover, (in the teaching of grammatical forms) the enumeration of the desired forms arises also. Now if grammatical forms are taught, must this be done by the recitation of each particular word for the understanding of grammatical forms? Must, for example, the grammatical forms 'cow,' 'horse,' 'man.' 'elephant,' 'kite,' 'deer,' 'Brahman,' be recited? No, says the author [that is, Patañjali], the recitation of each particular word is not a means for the understanding of grammatical forms, for there is the following tradition. Bṛhaspati addressed Indra during a thousand divine years, going over the grammatical forms by speaking each particular word, and still he did not attain the end. With Bṛhaspati as the instructor, Indra as the student, and a thousand divine years as the period of study, the end could not be attained, so what of the present day when he who lives a whole lifetime lives at most a hundred years? Knowledge is used in four ways: at the time of acquisition, at the time of study and rehearsal, at the time of teaching, and at the time of practice and application. But since in the present case the period of acquisition occupies the entire life-span, the recitation of each particular word is not a means for the understanding of grammatical forms. But then how are grammatical forms acquired? Some work containing the general and the particular has to be composed, so that men will acquire vast collections of forms with minimal effort. Of what would this consist? General rules and exceptions. Some general rule and some exception has to be formulated. What kind of general rule and what kind of exception? A general rule has to be formulated in all generality, for example, *karmaṇy aṇ* [Pāṇini 3.2.1: "*aN* is attached to the root when there is an object"]. An exception to that should be formulated with full particulars, for example, *āto'nupasarge kaḥ* [Pāṇini 3.2.3: "after a root ending in *ā* not preceded by a preverb the affix is *Ka*"]."

The two lines at the top of the page continuing with the four lines at the bottom constitute Kaiyaṭa's subcommentary on this passage of the *Mahābhāṣya*. See also page 97 of this volume and Staal 1969, 501–502.

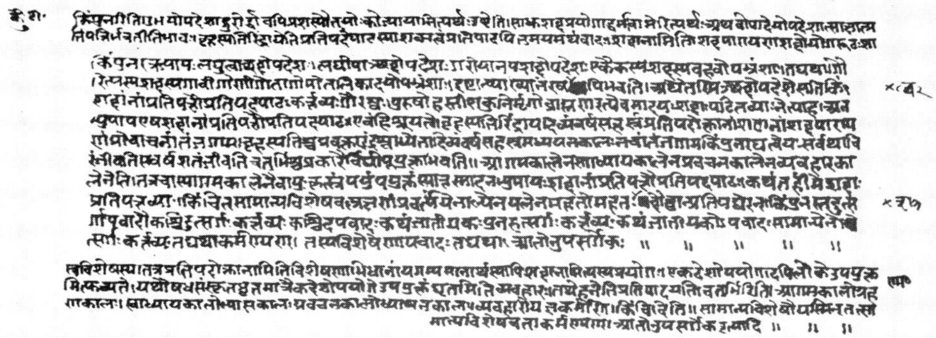

12

William Dwight Whitney (1827-1894)

From the very beginning of the study of the Indian grammarians there have been scholars who doubted that there ever was a language that conformed to the extremely numerous and complicated rules of Pāṇini and the other Sanskrit grammarians. This skepticism is not surprising for at least four reasons: (1) Sanskrit was regarded as a language which was no longer spoken; (2) literature in Sanskrit was only beginning to be known—text editions were relatively few, manuscripts were only beginning to be discovered, and access to them was rare; (3) people—especially philologists, but also linguists—tend to confound language with a body of literature; and (4) European scholars were not used to such painstaking detail in grammatical description as was displayed by grammatical rules in the Indian tradition. Such specificity and complexity was generally associated only with priestly cunning (there is, in fact, a close relationship between Indian ritualistic studies and the Sanskrit grammarians; see below pages 435–469). Even at present, there are people who are distrustful of a grammar when it looks complicated or contains very many rules.

Colebrooke had already referred to such skepticism and brushed it aside (see page 36 of this volume). Bopp during the Romantic period, however, was of the opinion that the Indian grammarians had set up forms to serve as roots, which were in fact merely postulated "underlying" forms, and not "real" (page 53). He was criticized, especially by Lassen (page 53), but also by philologists like Westergaard (who emphasized that too little was known of Sanskrit literature to warrant such a judgment), and, at least implicitly, by linguists like Humboldt (who regarded such postulated roots as real even if they did not come to the surface in a given language; see page 63). We have also seen that Bhandarkar in his lectures not only showed that Sanskrit was a spoken language, but also determined historically which stage of the language was in conformity with the grammatical rules given by specific grammarians—in particular, by Pāṇini, Kātyāyana, and Patañjali page 91). Kielhorn and Liebich contributed further to this kind of research.

Though the Sanskrit grammarians had not become widely known and their study remained a specialty even among Sanskritists, Western scholars had become familiar with at least some of their techniques. Apart from *guṇa* and *vṛddhi*, the distinction between roots and suffixes, and similar distinctions of a very fundamental nature, most Sanskrit scholars were acquainted with such specimens of the Sanskrit grammarians as were quoted by Max Müller in his excellent *Sanskrit Grammar for Beginners* of 1866 (which is much indebted to and collated throughout with Pāṇini's grammar). In the introduction to this grammar Müller gave the following example of the complexity of Pāṇini's grammar (quoted from the second edition of 1870, ix–x):

By this process [i.e., by collating the whole of the grammar with Pāṇini] which I have adopted, I believe that on many points a more settled and authoritative character has been imparted to the grammar of Sanskrit than it possessed before; but I do by no means pretend to have arrived on all points at a clear and definite view of the meaning of Pāṇini and his successors. The grammatical system of Hindu grammarians is so peculiar, that rules which we should group together, are scattered about in different parts of their manuals. We may have the general rule in the last, and the exceptions in the first book, and even then we are by no means certain that exceptions to these exceptions may not occur somewhere else. I shall give but one instance. There is a root *jāgṛ*, which forms its Aorist by adding *iṣam*, *īḥ*, *īt*. Here the simplest rule would be that final *ṛ* before *iṣam* becomes *r* (Pāṇ. VI. 1, 77). This, however, is prevented by another rule which requires that final *ṛ* should take Guṇa before *iṣam* (Pāṇ. VII. 3, 84). This would give us *ajāgariṣam*. But now comes another general rule (Pān. VII, 2, 1) which prescribes Vṛddhi of final vowels before *iṣam*, i.e. *ajāgāriṣam*. Against this change, however, a new rule is cited (Pāṇ. VII., 3, 85), and this secures for *jāgṛ* a special exception from Vṛddhi, and leaves its base again as *jāgar*. As soon as the base has been changed to *jāgar*, it falls under a new rule (Pāṇ. VII. 2, 3), and is forced to take Vṛddhi, until this rule is again nullified by Pān. VII. 2, 4, which does not allow Vṛddhi in an Aorist that takes intermediate *i*, like *ajāgariṣam*. There is an exception, however, to this rule also, for bases with short *a*, beginning and ending with a consonant, may optionally take Vṛddhi (Pāṇ. VII. 2, 7). This option is afterwards restricted, and roots with short *a*, beginning with a consonant and ending in *r*, like *jāgar*, have no option left, but are restricted afresh to Vṛddhi (Pāṇ. VII. 2, 2). However, even this is not yet the final result. Our base *jāgar* is after all not to take Vṛddhi, and hence a new special rule (Pāṇ. VII. 2, 5) settles the point by granting to *jāgṛ* a special exception from Vṛddhi, and thereby establishing its Guṇa. No wonder that these manifold changes and chances in the formation of the First Aorist of *jāgṛ* should have inspired a grammarian, who celebrates them in the following couplet:

guṇo vṛddhir guṇo vṛddhiḥ pratiṣedho vikalpanaṃ/
punar vṛddhir niṣedho'to yaṇ pūrvāḥ prāptayo nava//

'Guṇa, Vṛddhi, Guṇa, Vṛddhi, prohibition, option, again Vṛddhi and then exception, these with the change of *ṛ* into a semivowel in the first instance, are the nine results.'

Though much new information was becoming accessible, this was not always accompanied by an adequate understanding of the nature of the work of the Sanskrit grammarians. Actually, not only had the skeptical view not died, its extreme form was only beginning to be explicitly formulated—and passionately defended. In 1874, after being dormant for perhaps half a century, when Bopp had defended a much weaker and much more balanced version, the view was put forward by Theodor Benfrey in the Introduction to his Vedic grammar "dass uns von den Indern, diesen grössten Grammatikern der Welt, auf der einen Seite (in den Veden) die wunderbarste Sprache ohne eine sich auf sie stützende Grammatik hinterlassen worden sei, auf der andern dagegen die wunderbarste Grammatik ohne die Sprache, auf welche sie gestützt ist. Wir haben daher kein äusseres Hilfsmittel, wodurch wir die Richtigkeit dieser letzteren zu prüfen, ja auch nur zu controliren vermöchten" (quoted in Liebich 1891, 44). However, the main proponent of the view that there was a "grammarians' Sanskrit," which was "a thing of grammatical rule merely, having never had any real existence as a language" was William Dwight Whitney, the first important American Sanskritist.

William Dwight Whitney (1827–1894) studied Sanskrit first at Yale with Edward Elbridge Salisbury, who himself was interested mainly in Arabic but who had studied some Sanskrit with Bopp in Berlin and later with Lassen in Bonn. At an early date Whitney also made use of the second edition of Bopp's Sanskrit grammar, which his elder brother had brought with him from Europe in

1847. Later Whitney studied in Germany with Weber, Bopp, and Roth (cf. T. D. Seymour and C. R. Lanman in Sebeok 1966, I, 399–439). He became widely known also as a general linguist. As a Sanskritist his fame was mainly due to his work on the *Atharvaveda* and to his *Sanskrit Grammar*, which was first published in Leipzig in 1879 together with a German translation. This grammar was based upon very extensive textual materials, and there is nothing in it that cannot be substantiated by examples from the extant and available corpus of Sanskrit texts. It was in fact mainly praised because of this new, so-called "statistical" approach (see page 204) of this volume). As we shall see, Whitney held strong views with regard to the "reality" of roots given by the Sanskrit grammarians. He went even further in his grammar, in that he never set up an underlying root unless it was somewhere (phonetically) manifested in the language (for a fuller discussion of this and other characteristics of Whitney's grammar see McCawley 1967). Needless to say, Whitney's grammar did not rely on Pāṇini's grammar, which the Preface attacks for its "highly artful and difficult form of about four thousand algebraic-formula-like rules in the statement and arrangement of which brevity alone is had in view, at the cost of distinctness and unambiguousness" (xi).

Apart from the fact that Whitney appears to have had a low opinion of Indian scholarship in general (for example, see page 151, note 7), his misinterpretations of the Sanskrit grammarians may be traced back not only to the general skeptical trend, but also to his own linguistic convictions and philological activities. First, he was convinced that a linguistic description is nothing but an inventory of elements. Chomsky has quoted one of Whitney's statements as expressing most clearly perhaps this view of linguistics: "language in the concrete sense . . . is . . . the sum of words and phrases by which any man expresses his thought" (Whitney 1874, 372 in Chomsky 1964, 22). His Sanskrit grammar is a perfect illustration of this approach. Second, Whitney does not appear to have done any work himself on the Sanskrit grammarians, though he had worked widely in the Prātiśākhya literature and published and translated the *Atharvaveda-prātiśākhya* (in 1862) and the *Taittirīya-prātiśākhya* (in 1871). This does not, however, conflict with his general linguistic outlook; on the contrary, it confirms it, for there is a characteristic difference between the Prātiśākhya literature and the tradition of the Sanskrit grammarians. Each *prātiśākhya* specifies for a given branch of the Veda how the *saṃhitā* (or continuous text, in which the *sandhi* rules, etc. are applied) must be derived from the *padapāṭha* (or word-for-word analysis, in which the *sandhi* is dissolved). Each *prātiśākhya* is, therefore, by its very nature confined to the analysis of a specific corpus of utterances. The *prātiśākhya*s do not, in general, give linguistic rules, though it often happens that the rules which they provide for the derivation of the *saṃhitā* from the *padapāṭha* coincide with linguistic rules (cf. Staal 1967, ch. II; 1970a).

The approach of the Prātiśākhya literature was congenial to Whitney because it accorded with his general outlook in linguistics. He checked the completeness of the statements of the *prātiśākhya*s with the corpus which they purported to describe, and often found to his satisfaction complete agreement. For example, commenting on the passages of the *Taittirīya-prātiśākhya* which describes the conversion from dental *n* in the *padapāṭha* to retroflex *ṇ* in the *saṃhitā*, he noted: "I have not discovered in the Saṃhitā any case of a lingual nasal arising in the conversion of pada text into saṃhitā which is not duly provided for in this chapter" (Whitney 1871, 180). And similarly: "The Prātiśākhya's enumeration of the cases of occurrence of the lingual nasal is, so far as I have been able to determine, complete" (Whitney 1871, 281). But this does not mean that Whitney understood the linguistic position of the Sanskrit grammarians. Hence the inadequacy of such evaluations as the following, voiced by T. D. Seymour (in Sebeok, 1966, I, 416): "That he [i.e., Whitney] did not discredit and slight the old Hindu grammarians because of any lack of acquaintance with them is shown by his own work and publications in that field. He published not only the Atharva-Veda-Prātiśākhya (text, translation, and notes, in 1862), but also a similar edition of the Taittirīya-Prātiśākhya, with its commentary, the Tribhāṣyaratna, in 1871."

Whitney's influential views on the Sanskrit grammarians were expressed in an article in the *American Journal of Philology* (5, 1884, 279–297) which is here reproduced.

A. The Study of Hindu Grammar and the Study of Sanskrit (1884)

William Dwight Whitney

To the beginning study of Sanskrit it was an immense advantage that there existed a Hindu science of grammar, and of so high a character. To realize how great the advantage, one has only to compare the case of languages destitute of it—as for instance the Zend. It is a science of ancient date, and has even exercised a shaping influence on the language in which all or nearly all the classical literature has been produced. It was an outcome of the same general spirit which is seen in the so careful textual preservation and tradition of the ancient sacred literature of India; and there is doubtless a historical connection between the one and the other; though of just what nature is as yet unclear.

The character of the Hindu grammatical science was, as is usual in such cases, determined by the character of the language which was its subject. The Sanskrit is above all things an analyzable language, one admitting of the easy and distinct separation of ending from stem, and of derivative suffix from primitive word, back to the ultimate attainable elements, the so-called roots. Accordingly, in its perfected form (for all the preparatory stages are unknown to us), the Hindu grammar offers us an established body of roots, with rules for their conversion into stems and for the inflection of the latter, and also for the accompanying phonetic changes—this last involving and resting upon a phonetic science of extraordinary merit, which has called forth the highest admiration of modern scholars; nothing at all approaching it has been produced by any ancient people; it has served as the foundation in no small degree of our own phonetics: even as our science of grammar and of language has borrowed much from India. The treatment of syntax is markedly inferior—though, after all, hardly more than in a measure to correspond with the inferiority of the Sanskrit sentence in point of structure, as compared with the Latin and the Greek. Into any more detailed description it is not necessary to our present purpose to enter; and the matter is one pretty well understood by the students of Indo-European language. It is generally well known also that the Hindu science, after a however long history of elaboration, became fixed for all future time in the system of a single grammarian, named Pāṇini (believed, though on grounds far from convincing, to have lived two or three centuries before the Christian era). Pāṇini's work has been commented without end, corrected in minor points, condensed, re-cast in arrangement, but never rebelled against or superseded; and it is still the authoritative standard of good Sanskrit. Its form of presentation is of the strangest: a miracle of ingenuity, but of perverse and wasted ingenuity. The only object aimed at in it is brevity, at the sacrifice of everything else—of order, of clearness, of even intelligibility except by the aid of keys and commentaries and lists of words, which then are furnished in profusion. To determine a grammatical point out of it is something like constructing a passage of text out of an *index verborum*: if you are sure that you have gathered up every word that belongs in the passage, and have put them all in the right order, you have got the right reading; but only then. If you have mastered Pāṇini sufficiently to bring to bear upon the given point every rule that relates to it, and in due succession, you have settled the case; but that is no easy task. For example, it takes nine mutually limitative rules, from all parts of the text-book, to determine whether a certain aorist shall be *ajāgariṣam* or *ajāgāriṣam* (the case is reported in the preface to Müller's grammar): there is lacking only a tenth rule, to tell us that the whole word is a false and never-used formation. Since there is nothing to show how far the application of a rule reaches, there are provided treatises of laws of interpretation to be applied to them; but there is a residual rule underlying and determining the whole: that both the grammar and the laws of interpretation must be so construed as to yield good and acceptable forms, and not otherwise—and this implies (if that were needed) a condemnation of the whole mode of presentation of the system as a failure.

Theoretically, all that is prescribed and allowed by Pāṇini and his accepted commentators is Sanskrit, and nothing else is entitled to the name. The young pandit, then, is expected to master the system and to govern his Sanskrit speech and writing by it. This he does, with immense pains and labor, then naturally valuing the acquisition in part according to what it has cost him. The same course was followed by those European scholars who had to make themselves the pupils of Hindu teachers, in acquiring Sanskrit for the benefit of Europe; and (as was said above) they did so to their very great advantage. Equally as a matter of course, the same must still be done by any one who studies in India, who has to deal with the native scholars, win their confidence and respect and gain their aid; they must be met upon their own ground. But it is a question, and one of no slight practical importance, how far Western scholars in general are to be held to this method: whether Pāṇini is for us also the law of Sanskrit usage; whether we are to study the native Hindu grammar in order to learn Sanskrit.

There would be less reason for asking this question, if the native grammar were really the instrumentality by which the conserving tradition of the old language had been carried on. But that is a thing both in itself impossible and proved by the facts of the case to be untrue. No one ever mastered a list of roots with rules for their extension and inflection, and then went to work to construct texts upon that basis. Rather, the transmission of Sanskrit has been like the transmission of any highly cultivated language, only with difference of degree. The learner has his models which he imitates; he makes his speech after the example of that of his teacher, only under the constant government of grammatical rule, enforced by the requirement to justify out of the grammar any word or form as to which a question is raised. Thus the language has moved on by its own inertia, only falling, with further removal from its natural vernacular basis, more and more passively and mechanically into the hands of the grammarians. All this is like the propagation of literary English or German; only that here there is much more of a vernacular usage that shows itself able to override and modify the rules of grammar. It is yet more closely like the propagation of Latin; only that here the imitation of previous usage is frankly acknowledged as the guide, there being no iron system of grammar to assume to take its place. That such has really been the history of the later or classical Sanskrit is sufficiently shown by the facts. There is no absolute coincidence between it and the language which Pāṇini teaches. The former, indeed, includes little that the grammarians forbid; but, on the other hand, it lacks a great deal that they allow or prescribe. The difference between the two is so great that Benfey, a scholar deeply versed in the Hindu science, calls it a grammar without a corresponding language, as he calls the pre-classical dialects a language without a grammar.[1] If such a statement can be made

[1] Einleitung in die Grammatik der vedischen Sprache, 1874, pp. 3, 4.

with any reason, it would appear that there is to be assumed, as the subject of Hindu grammatical science, a peculiar dialect of Sanskrit, which we may call the grammarians' Sanskrit, different both from the pre-classical dialects and from the classical, and standing either between them or beside them in the general history of Indian language. And it becomes a matter of importance to us to ascertain what this grammarians' Sanskrit is, how it stands related to the other varieties of Sanskrit, and whether it is entitled to be the leading object of our Sanskrit study. Such questions must be settled by a comparison of the dialect referred to with the other dialects, and of them with one another. And it will be found, upon such comparison, that the earlier and later forms of the Vedic dialect, the dialects of the Brāhmaṇas and Sūtras, and the classical Sanskrit, stand in a filial relation, each to its predecessor, are nearly or quite successive forms of the same language; while the grammarians' Sanskrit, as distinguished from them, is a thing of grammatical rule merely, having never had any real existence as a language, and being on the whole unknown in practice to even the most modern pandits.

The main thing which makes of the grammarians' Sanskrit a special and peculiar language is its list of roots. Of these there are reported to us about two thousand, with no intimation of any difference in character among them, or warning that a part of them may and that another part may not be drawn upon for forms to be actually used; all stand upon the same plane. But more than half—actually more than half—of them never have been met with, and never will be met with, in the Sanskrit literature of any age. When this fact began to come to light, it was long fondly hoped, or believed, that the missing elements would yet turn up in some corner of the literature not hitherto ransacked; but all expectation of that has now been abandoned. One or another does appear from time to time; but what are they among so many? The last notable case was that of the root *stigh*, discovered in the Māitrāyaṇī-Saṃhitā, a text of the Brāhmaṇa period; but the new roots found in such texts are apt to turn out wanting in the lists of the grammarians. Beyond all question, a certain number of cases are to be allowed for, of real roots, proved such by the occurrence of their evident cognates in other related languages, and chancing not to appear in the known literature; but they can go only a very small way indeed toward accounting for the eleven hundred unauthenticated roots. Others may have been assumed as underlying certain derivatives or bodies of derivatives—within due limits, a perfectly legitimate proceeding; but the cases thus explainable do not prove to be numerous. There remain then the great mass, whose presence in the lists no ingenuity has yet proved sufficient to account for. And in no small part, they bear their falsity and artificiality on the surface, in their phonetic form and in the meanings ascribed to them; we can confidently say that the Sanskrit language, known to us through a long period of development, neither had nor could have any such roots. How the grammarians came to concoct their list, rejected in practice by themselves and their own pupils, is hitherto an unexplained mystery. No special student of the native grammar, to my knowledge, has attempted to cast any light upon it; and it was left for Dr. Edgren, no partisan of the grammarians, to group and set forth the facts for the first time, in the Journal of the American Oriental Society (Vol. XI, 1882—but the article printed in 1879—pp. 1–55), adding a list of the real roots, with brief particulars as to their occurrence.[2] It is quite clear, with reference to this fundamental and most important item, of what character the grammarians' Sanskrit is. The real Sanskrit of the latest period is, as concerns its roots, a true successor to that of the earliest period, and through the known intermediates; it has lost some of the roots of its predecessors, as each of these some belonging to its own predecessors or predecessor; it has, also like these, won a certain number not earlier found: both in such measure as was to be expected. As for the rest of the asserted roots of the grammar, to account for them is not a matter that concerns at all the Sanskrit language and its history; it only concerns the history of the Hindu science of grammar. That, too, has come to be pretty generally acknowledged.[3] Every one who knows anything of the history of Indo-European etymology knows how much mischief the grammarians' list of roots wrought in the hands of the earlier more incautious and credulous students of Sanskrit: how many false and worthless derivations were founded upon them. That sort of work, indeed, is not yet entirely a thing of the past; still, it has come to be well understood by most scholars that no alleged Sanskrit root can be accepted as real unless it is supported by such a use in the literary records of the language as authenticates it—for there are such things in the later language as artificial occurrences, forms made for once or twice from roots taken out of the grammarians' list, by a natural license, which one is only surprised not to see oftener availed of (there are hardly more than a dozen or two of such cases quotable): that they appear so seldom is the best evidence of the fact already pointed out above, that the grammar had, after all, only a superficial and negative influence upon the real tradition of the language.

It thus appears that a Hindu grammarian's statement as to the fundamental elements of his language is without authority until tested by the actual facts of the language, as represented by the Sanskrit literature. But the principle won here is likely to prove of universal application; for we have no reason to expect to find the grammarians absolutely trustworthy in other departments of their work, when they have failed so signally in one; there can be nothing in their system that will not require to be tested by the recorded facts of the language, in order to determine its true value. How this is, we will proceed to ascertain by examining a few examples.

In the older language, but not in the oldest (for it is wanting in the Veda), there is formed a periphrastic future tense active by compounding a *nomen agentis* with an auxiliary, the present tense of the verb *as* 'be': thus, *dātā 'smi* (literally *dator sum*) 'I will give,' etc. It is quite infrequent as compared with the other future, yet common enough to require to be regarded as a part of the general Sanskrit verb-system. To this active tense the grammarians give a corresponding middle, although the auxiliary in its independent use has no middle inflection; it is made with endings modified so

[2] I have myself now in press a much fuller account of the quotable roots of the language, with all their quotable tense-stems and primary derivatives—everything accompanied by a definition of the period of its known occurrence in the history of the language.

[3] Not, indeed, universally; one may find among the selected verbs that are conjugated in full at the end of F. M. Müller's Sanskrit Grammar, no very small number of those that are utterly unknown to Sanskrit usage, ancient or modern.

as to stand in the usual relation of middle endings to active, and further with conversion in 1st sing. of the radical *s* to *h*—a very anomalous substitution, of which there is not, I believe, another example in the language. Now what support has this middle tense in actual use? Only this: that in the Brāhmaṇas occur four sporadic instances of attempts to make by analogy middle forms for this tense (they are all reported in my Sanskrit Grammar, §947; further search has brought to light no additional examples): two of them are 1st sing., one having the form *se* for the auxiliary, the other *he*, as taught in the grammar; and in the whole later literature, epic and classical, I find record of the occurrence of only one further case, *darśayitāhe* (in Naiṣ. V 71.)![4] Here also, the classical dialect is the true continuator of the pre-classical; it is only in the grammarians' Sanskrit that every verb conjugated in the middle voice has also a middle periphrastic future.

There is another and much more important part of verbal inflection—namely, the whole aorist-system, in all its variety—as to which the statements of the grammarians are to be received with especial distrust, for the reason that in the classical language the aorist is a decadent formation. In the older dialects, down to the last Sūtra, and through the entire list of early and genuine Upaniṣads, the aorist has its own special office, that of designating the immediate past, and is always to be found where such designation is called for; later, even in the epos, it is only another preterit, equivalent in use to imperfect and perfect, and hence of no value, and subsisting only in occasional use, mainly as a survival from an earlier condition of the language. Thus, for example, of the first kind of aorist, the root-aorist, forms are made in pre-classical Sanskrit from about 120 roots; of these, 15 make forms in the later language also, mostly sporadically (only *gā*, *dā*, *dhā*, *pā*, *sthā*, *bhū* less infrequently); and 8 more in the later language only, all in an occurrence or two (all but one, in active precative forms, as to which see below). Again, of the fifth aorist-form, the *iṣ*-aorist (rather the most frequent of all), forms are made in the older language from 140 roots, and later from only 18 of these (and sporadically, except in the case of *grah*, *vad*, *vadh*, *vid*), with a dozen more in the later language exclusively, all sporadic except *śaṅk* (which is not a Vedic root). Once more, as regards the third or reduplicated aorist, the proportion is slightly different, because of the association of that aorist with the causative conjugation, and the frequency of the latter in use; here, against about 110 roots quotable from the earlier language, 16 of them also in the later, there are about 30 found in the later alone (nearly all of them only sporadically, and none with any frequency). And the case is not otherwise with the remaining forms. The facts being such, it is easily seen that general statements made by the grammarians as to the range of occurrence of each form, and as to the occurrence of one form in the active and a certain other one in the middle from a given root, must be of very doubtful authority; in fact, as re-

[4] Here, as elsewhere below, my authority for the later literature is chiefly the Petersburg Lexicon (the whole older literature I have examined for myself), and my statements are, of course, always open to modification by the results of further researches. But all the best and most genuine part of the literature has been carefully and thoroughly excerpted for the Lexicon; and for the Mahābhārata we have now the explicit statements of Holtzmann, in his Grammatisches aus dem Mahābhārata, Leipzig, 1884.

gards the latter point, they are the more suspicious as lacking any tolerable measure of support from the facts of the older language. But there are much greater weaknesses than these in the grammarians' treatment of the aorist.

Let us first turn our attention to the aorist optative, the so-called precative (or benedictive). This formation is by the native grammarians not recognized as belonging to the aorist at all—not even so far as to be put next the aorist in their general scheme of conjugation; they suffer the future-systems to intervene between the two. This is in them fairly excusable as concerns the precative active, since it is the optative of the root-aorist, and so has an aspect as if it might come independently from the root directly; nor, indeed, can we much blame them for overlooking the relation of their precative middle to the sibilant or sigmatic aorist, considering that they ignore tense-systems and modes; but that their European imitators, down to the very latest, should commit the same oversight is a different matter. The contrast, now, between the grammarians' dialect and the real Sanskrit is most marked as regards the middle forms. According to the grammar, the precative middle is to be made from every root, and even for its secondary conjugations, the causative etc. It has two alternative modes of formation, which we see to correspond to two of the forms of the sibilant aorist: the *s*-aorist, namely, and the *iṣ*-aorist. Of course, a complete inflection is allowed it. To justify all this, now, I am able to point to only a single occurrence of a middle precative in the whole later literature, including the epics: that is *rīriṣīṣṭa*, in the Bhāgavata-Purāṇa (III 9, 24), a text notable for its artificial imitation of ancient forms (the same word occurs also in the Ṛg-Veda); it is made, as will be noticed, from a reduplicated aorist stem, and so is unauthorized by grammatical rule. A single example in a whole literature, and that a false one! In the pre-classical literature also, middle precative forms are made hardly more than sporadically, or from less than 40 roots in all (so far as I have found); those belonging to the *s* and *iṣ* aorists are, indeed, among the most numerous (14 each), but those of the root-aorist do not fall short of them (also 14 roots), and there are examples from three of the other four aorists. Except a single 3d pl. (in *īrata*, instead of *īran*), only the three singular persons and the 1st pl. are quotable, and forms occur without as well as with the adscititious *s* between mode-sign and personal ending which is the special characteristic of a precative as distinguished from a simply optative form. Here, again, we have a formation sporadic in the early language and really extinct in the later, but erected by the grammarians into a regular part of every verb-system.

With the precative active the case is somewhat different. This also, indeed, is rare even to sporadicalness, being, so far as I know, made from only about 60 roots in the whole language—and of these, only half can show forms containing the true precative *s*. But it is not quite limited to the pre-classical dialects; it is made also later from 15 roots, 9 of which are additional to those which make a precative in the older language. Being in origin an optative of the root-aorist, it comes, as we may suppose, to seem to be a formation from the root directly, and so to be extended beyond the limits of the aorist; from a clear majority (about three-fifths) of all the roots that make it, it has no other aorist forms by its side. And this begins even in the earliest period (with half-a-dozen roots in the Veda, and toward a score besides in the Brāhmaṇa and Sūtra); although there the precative more usually makes a part of a general aorist-formation: for instance, and especially, from the root *bhū*, whose precative forms are oftener met with than those of all other roots together, and which is the only root from which more than two real precative persons are quotable. How rare it is even in the epos is shown by the fact that Holtzmann[5] is able to quote only six forms (and one of these doubtful, and another a false formation) from the whole Mahābhārata, one of them occurring twice; while the first book of the Rāmāyaṇa (about 4500 lines) has the single *bhūyāt*. Since it is not quite extinct in the classical period, the Hindu grammarians could not, perhaps, well help teaching its formation; and, considering the the general absence of perspective from their work, we should hardly expect them to explain that it was the rare survival of an anciently little-used formation; but we have here another striking example of the great discordance between the real Sanskrit and the grammarians' dialect, and of the insufficiency of the information respecting the former obtainable from the rules for the latter.

Again, the reduplicated or third form of aorist, though it has become attached to the causative secondary conjugation (by a process in the Veda not yet complete), as the regular aorist of that conjugation, is not made from the derivative causative stem, but comes from the root itself, not less directly than do the other aorist-formations—except in the few cases where the causative stem contains a *p* added to *ā*: thus, *atiṣṭhipat* from stem *sthāpaya*, root *sthā*. Perhaps misled by this exception, however, the grammarians teach the formation of the reduplicated aorist from the causative stem, through the intermediate process of converting the stem back to the root, by striking off its conjugation-sign and reducing its strengthened vowel to the simpler root-form. That is to say, we are to make, for example, *abūbhuvat* from the stem *bhāvaya*, by cutting off *aya* and reducing the remainder *bhāv* or *bhāu* to *bhū*, instead of making it from *bhū* directly! That is a curious etymological process; quite a side-piece to deriving *varīyas* and *variṣṭha* from *uru*, and the like, as the Hindu grammarians and their European copyists would likewise have us do. There is one point where the matter is brought to a crucial test: namely, in roots that end in *u* or *ū*; where, if the vowel on which the reduplication is formed is an *u*-vowel, the reduplication-vowel should be of the same character; but, in any other case, an *i*-vowel. Thus, in the example already taken, *bhāvaya* ought to make *abībhavat*, just as it makes *bibhāvayiṣati* in the case of a real derivation from the causative stem; and such forms as *abībhavat* are, in fact, in a great number of cases either prescribed or allowed by the grammarians; but I am not aware of their having been ever met with in use, earlier or later, with the single exception of *apiplavam*, occurring once in the Śatapatha-Brāhmaṇa (VI ii, 1, 8).

Again, the grammarians give a peculiar and problematic rule for an alternative formation of certain passive tenses (aorist and futures) from the special 3d sing. aor. pass.; they allow it in the case of all roots ending in vowels, and of *grah*, *dṛś*, *han*. Thus, for example, from the root *dā* are allowed *adāyiṣi*, *dāyiṣyate*, *dāyitā*, beside *adiṣi*, *dāsyate*, *dātā*. What all this means is quite obscure, since there is no usage, either early or late, to cast light upon it. The Ṛg-Veda has once (I 147, 5) *dhāyīs*, from root *dhā*; but this, being active, is rather a hindrance than a help. The Jaim. Brāhmaṇa has once (I 321) *ākhyāyiṣyante*; but this appears to be a form anal-

[5] In his work already cited, at p. 32.

ogous with *hvayiṣyate* etc., and so proves nothing. The Bhāg. Purāṇa has once (VIII 13, 36) *tāyitā*, which the Petersburg Lexicon refers to root *tan*; but if there is such a thing as the secondary root *tāy*, as claimed by the grammarians, it perhaps belongs rather there. And there remains, so far as I can discover, only *asthāyiṣi* (Daśak. [Wilson], p. 117, l.6) and *anāyiṣata* (Ind. Sprüche, 6187, from the Kuvalayānanda); and these are with great probability to be regarded as artificial forms, made because the grammar declares them correct. It seems not unlikely that some misapprehension or blunder lies at the foundation of these rules of the grammar; at any rate, the formation is only grammarians' Sanskrit, and not even pandits'; and it should never be obtruded upon the attention of beginners in the language.

Again, the secondary ending *dhvam* of 2d pl. mid. sometimes has to take the form *ḍhvam*. In accordance with the general euphonic usages of the language, this should be whenever in the present condition of Sanskrit there has been lost before the ending a lingual sibilant; thus: we have *aneḍhvam* from *aneṣ* + *dhvam*, and *apaviḍhvam* from *apaviṣ* + *dhvam*; we should further have in the precative *bhaviṣīḍhvam* from *bhaviṣī-ṣ-dhvam*, if the form ever occurred, as, unfortunately, it does not. And, so far as I know, there is not to be found, either in the earlier language or the later (and as to the former I can speak with authority), a single instance of *ḍhvam* in any other situation—the test-cases, however, being far from numerous. But the Hindu grammarians, if they are reported rightly by their European pupils (which in this instance is hard to believe), give rules as to the change of the ending upon this basis only for the *s*-aorist; for the *iṣ*-aorist and its optative (the precative), they make the choice between *ḍhvam* and *dhvam* to depend upon whether the *i* is or is not "preceded by a semivowel or *h*:" that is, *apaviṣ* + *dhvam* gives *apaviḍhvam*, but *ajaniṣ* + *dhvam* gives *ajanidhvam*, and so likewise we should have *janiṣīdhvam*. It would be curious to know what ground the grammarians imagined themselves to have for laying down such a rule as this, wherein there is a total absence of discoverable connection between cause and effect; and it happens that all the quotable examples—*ajaniḍhvam*, *artiḍhvam*, *aindhiḍhvam*, *vepiḍhvam*—are opposed to their rule, but accordant with reason. What is yet worse, however, is that the grammar extends the same conversion of *dh* to *ḍh*, under the same restrictions, to the primary ending *dhve* of the perfect likewise, with which it has nothing whatever to do—teaching us that, for instance, *cakṛ* and *tuṣṭu* + *dhve* make necessarily *cakṛḍhve* and *tuṣṭuḍhve*, and that *dadhr-i* + *dhve* makes either *dadhriḍhve* or *dadhridhve*, while *tutud-i* + *dhve* makes only *tutudidhve*! This appears to me the most striking case of downright unintelligent blundering on the part of the native grammarians that has come to notice; if there is any way of relieving them of the reproach of it, their partisans ought to cast about at once to find it.

A single further matter of prime importance may be here referred to, in illustration of the character of the Hindu grammarians as classifiers and presenters of the facts of their language. By reason of the extreme freedom and wonderful regularity of word-composition in Sanskrit, the grammarians were led to make a classification of compounds in a manner that brought true enlightenment to European scholars; and the classification has been largely adopted as a part of modern philological science, along even with its bizarre terminology. Nothing could be more accurate and happier than the distinction of dependent, descriptive, possessive, and copulative compounds; only their titles—'his man' (*tatpuruṣa*), 'act-sustaining' (? *karmadhāraya*), 'much-rice' (*bahuvrīhi*), and 'couple' (*dvandva*), respectively—can hardly claim to be worth preserving. But it is the characteristic of Hindu science generally not to be able to stop when it has done enough; and so the grammarians have given us, on the same plane of division with these four capital classes, two more, which they call *dvigu* ('two-cow') and *avyayībhāva* ('indeclinable-becoming'); and these have no *raison d'être*, but are collections of special cases belonging to some of the other classes, and so heterogeneous that their limits are hardly capable of definition: the *dvigu*-class are secondary adjective compounds, but sometimes, like other adjectives, used as nouns; and an *avyayībhāva* is always the adverbially-used accusative neuter of an adjective compound. It would be a real service on the part of some scholar, versed in the Hindu science, to draw out a full account of the so-called *dvigu*-class and its boundaries, and to show if possible how the grammarians were misled into establishing it. But it will probably be long before these two false classes cease to haunt the concluding chapters of Sanskrit grammars, or writers on language to talk of the six kinds of compounds in Sanskrit.[6]

Points in abundance, of major or minor consequence, it would be easy to bring up in addition, for criticism or for question. Thus, to take a trifle or two: according to the general analogies of the language, we ought to speak of the root *gṛh*, instead of *grah*; probably the Hindu science adopts the latter form because of some mechanical advantage on the side of brevity resulting from it, in the rules prescribing forms and derivatives: the instances are not few in which that can be shown to have been the preponderating consideration, leading to the sacrifice of things more important. One may conjecture that similar causes led to the setting up of a root *div* instead of *dīv*, 'play, gamble': that it may have been found easier to prescribe the prolongation of the *ī* than its irregular gunation in *devana* etc. This has unfortunately misled the authors of the Petersburg Lexicons into their strange and indefensible identification of the asserted root *div* 'play' with the so-called root *div* 'shine': the combination of meanings is forced and unnatural; and then especially the phonetic form of the two roots is absolutely distinct, the one showing only short *i* and *u* (as in *divam*, *dyubhis*), the other always and only long *ī* and *ū* (as in *dīvyati* -*dīvan*, and -*dyū*, *dyūta*); the one root is really *diu*, and the other *dīū* (it may be added that the Petersburg Lexicon, on similar evidence, inconsistently but correctly writes the roots *sīv* and *srīv*, instead of *siv* and *sriv*).

It would be easy to continue the work of illustration much further; but this must be enough to show how and how far we have to use and to trust the teachings of the Hindu grammarians. Or, if one prefers to employ the Benfeyan phrase, we see something of what this language is which has a grammar but not an existence, and in what relation it stands to the real Sanskrit language, begun

[6] Spiegel, for example (Altiranische Grammatik, p. 229), thinks it necessary to specify that *dvigu*-compounds do, to be sure, occur also in the Old Persian dialects, but that they in no respect form a special class; and a very recent Sanskrit grammar in Italian (Pulle, Turin, 1883) gives as the four primary classes of compounds the *dvandva*, *tatpuruṣa*, *bahuvrīhi*, and *avyayībhāva*—as if one were to say that the kingdoms in Nature are four: animal, vegetable, mineral, and cactuses.

in the Veda, and continued without a break down to our own times, all the rules of the grammar having been able only slightly to stiffen and unnaturalize it. Surely, what we desire to have to do with is the Sanskrit, and not the imaginary dialect that fits the definitions of Pāṇini. There is no escaping the conclusion that, if we would understand Sanskrit, we may not take the grammarians as authorities, but only as witnesses; not a single rule given or fact stated by them is to be accepted on their word, without being tested by the facts of the language as laid down in the less subjective and more trustworthy record of the literature. Of course, most of what the native grammar teaches is true and right; but, until after critical examination, no one can tell which part. Of course, also, there is more or less of genuine supplementary material in the grammarians' treatises—material especially lexical, but doubtless in some measure also grammatical—which needs to be worked in so as to complete our view of the language; but what this genuine material is, as distinguished from the artificial and false, is only to be determined by a thorough and cautious comparison of the entire sytem of the grammar with the whole recorded language. Such a comparison has not yet been made, and is hardly even making: in part, to be sure, because the time for it has been long in coming; but mainly because those who should be making it are busy at something else. The skilled students of the native grammar, as it seems to me, have been looking at their task from the wrong point of view, and laboring in the wrong direction. They have been trying to put the non-existent grammarians' dialect in the place of the genuine Sanskrit. They have thought it their duty to learn out of Pāṇini and his successors, and to set forth for the benefit of the world, what the Sanskrit really is, instead of studying and setting forth and explaining (and, where necessary, accounting for and excusing) Pāṇini's system itself. They have failed to realize that, instead of a divine revelation, they have in their hands a human work—a very able one, indeed, but also imperfect, like other human works, full of the prescription in place of description that characterizes all Hindu productions, and most perversely constructed; and that in studying it they are only studying a certain branch of Hindu science: one that is, indeed, of the highest interest, and has an important bearing on the history of the language, especially since the *dicta* of the grammarians have had a marked influence in shaping the latest form of Sanskrit—not always to its advantage. Hence the insignificant amount of real progress that the study of Hindu grammar has made in the hands of European scholars. Its career was well inaugurated, now nearly forty-five years ago (1839–40), by Böhtlingk's edition of Pāṇini's text, with extracts from the native commentaries, followed by an extremely stingy commentary by the editor; but it has not been succeeded by anything of importance,[7] until now that a critical edition of the Mahābhāṣya, by Kielhorn, is passing through the press, and is likely soon to be completed: a highly meritorious work, worthy of European learning, and

[7] For the photographic reproduction, in 1874, of a single manuscript of Patañjali's *Mahābhāṣya* or 'Great Comment' (on Pāṇini), with the glosses upon it, was but a costly piece of child's play; and the English government, as if to make the enterprise a complete *fiasco*, sent all the copies thus prepared to India, to be buried there in native keeping, instead of placing them in European libraries, within reach of Western scholars. [cf. Plate IV].

likely, if followed up in the right spirit, to begin a new era in its special branch of study. Considering the extreme difficulty of the system, and the amount of labor that is required before the student can win any available mastery of it, it is incumbent upon the representatives of the study to produce an edition of Pāṇini accompanied with a version, a digest of the leading comments on each rule, and an index that shall make it possible to find what the native authorities teach upon each given point: that is to say, to open the grammatical science to knowledge virtually at first hand without the lamentable waste of time thus far unavoidable—a waste, because both needless and not sufficiently rewarded by its results.

A curious kind of superstition appears to prevail among certain Sanskrit scholars; they cannot feel that they have the right to accept a fact of the languages unless they find it set down in Pāṇini's rules. It may well be asked, on the contrary, of what consequence it is, except for its bearing on the grammatical science itself, whether a given fact is or is not so set down. A fact in the pre-classical language is confessedly quite independent of Pāṇini; he may take account of it and he may not; and no one knows as yet what the ground is of the selection he makes for inclusion in his system. As for a fact in the classical language, it is altogether likely to fall within the reach of one of the great grammarian's rules—at least, as these have been extended and restricted and amended by his numerous successors: and this is a thing much to the credit of the grammar; but what bearing it has upon the language would be hard to say. If, however, we should seem to meet with a fact ignored by the grammar, or contravening its rules, we should have to look to see whether supporting facts in the language did not show its genuineness in spite of the grammar. On the other hand, there are facts in the language, especially in its latest records, which have a false show of existence, being the artificial product of the grammar's prescription or permission; and there was nothing but the healthy conservatism of the true tradition of the language to keep them from becoming vastly more numerous. And then, finally, there are the infinite number of facts which, so far as the grammar is concerned, should be or might be in the language, only that they do not happen ever to occur there; for here lies the principal discordance between the grammar and the language. The statement of the grammar that such a thing is so and so is of quite uncertain value, until tested by the facts of the language; and in this testing, it is the grammar that is on trial, that is to be condemned for artificiality or commended for faithfulness; not the language, which is quite beyond our jurisdiction. It cannot be too strongly urged that the Sanskrit, even that of the most modern authors, even that of the pandits of the present day, is the successor, by natural processes of tradition, of the older dialects; and that the grammar is a more or less successful attempt at its description, the measure of the success being left for us to determine, by comparison of the one with the other.

To maintain this is not to disparage the Hindu grammatical science; it is only to put it in its true place. The grammar remains nearly if not altogether the most admirable product of the scientific spirit in India, ranking with the best products of that spirit that the world has seen; we will scant no praise to it, if we only are not called on to bow down to it as authoritative. So we regard the Greek science of astronomy as one of the greatest and most creditable achievements of the human intellect since men first began to observe and deduce; but we do not plant ourselves upon its point of view in setting forth the movements of the heavenly bodies—though the men of the Middle Ages did so, to their advantage, and the system of epicycles maintained itself in existence, by dint of pure conservatism, long after its artificiality had been demonstrated. That the early European Sanskrit grammars assumed the basis and worked in the methods of the Hindu science was natural and praiseworthy. Bopp was the first who had knowledge and independence enough to begin effectively the work of subordinating Hindu to Western science, using the materials and deductions of the former so far as they accorded with the superior methods of the latter, and turning his attention to the records of the language itself, as fast as they became accessible to him. Since his time, there has been in some respects a retrogression rather than an advance; European scholars have seemed to take satisfaction in submitting themselves slavishly to Hindu teachers, and the grammarians' dialect has again been thrust forward into the place which the Sanskrit language ought to occupy. To refer to but a striking example or two; in Müller's grammar the native science is made the supreme rule after a fashion that is sometimes amusing in its naïveté, and the genuine and the fictitious are mingled inextricably, in his rules, his illustrations, and his paradigms, from one end of the volume to the other. And a scholar of the highest rank, long resident in India but now of Vienna, Professor Bühler, has only last year put forth a useful practical introduction to the language, with abundant exercises for writing and speaking,[8] in which the same spirit of subservience to Hindu methods is shown in an extreme degree, and both forms and material are not infrequently met with which are not Sanskrit, but belong only to the non-existent grammarians' dialect. Its standpoint is clearly characterized by its very first clause, which teaches that "Sanskrit verbs have ten tenses and modes"—that is to say, because the native grammar failed to make the distinction between tense and mode, or to group these formations together into systems, coming from a common tense-stem, Western pupils are to be taught to do the same. This seems about as much an anachronism as if the author had begun, likewise after a Hindu example, with the statement that "Sanskrit parts of speech are four: name, predicate, preposition, and particle." Further on, in the same paragraph, he allows (since the Hindus also do so) that "the first four (tenses and modes) are derived from a special present stem"; but he leaves it to be implied, both here and later, that the remaining six come directly from the root. From this we should have to infer, for example, that *dadāti* comes from a stem, but *dadātha* from the root; that we are to divide *naśya-ti* but *dā--syati*, *a-viśa-t* but *a-sic-at*, and so on; and (though this is a mere oversight) that *ayāt* contains a stem, but *adāt* a pure root. No real grammarian can talk of present stems without talking of aorist stems also; nor is the variety of the latter so much inferior to that of the former; it is only the vastly greater frequency of occurrence of present forms that makes the differences of their stems the more important ground of classification. These are but specimens of the method of the book, which, in spite of its merits, is not in its

[8] This work, somewhat recast grammatically, is about to be reproduced in English by Professor Perry, of Columbia College, New York.

present form a good one to put in the hands of beginners, because it teaches them so much that they will have to unlearn later, if they are to understand the Sanskrit language.

One more point, of minor consequence, may be noted, in which the habit of Western philology shows itself too subservient to the whims of the Sanskrit native grammarians: the order of the varieties of present stems, and the designation of the conjugation classes as founded on it. We accept the Hindu order of the cases in noun-inflection, not seeking to change it, though unfamiliar, because we see that it has a reason, and a good one; but no one has ever been ingenious enough even to conjecture a reason for the Hindu order of the classes. Chance itself, if they had been thrown together into a hat, and set down in their order as drawn out, could not more successfully have sundered what belongs together, and juxtaposed the discordant. That being the case, there is no reason for our paying any heed to the arrangement. In fact, the heed that we do pay is a perversion; the Hindus do not speak of first class, second class, etc., but call each class by the name of its leading verb, as *bhū*-verbs, *ad*-verbs, and so on; and it was a decided merit of Müller, in his grammar, to try to substitute for the mock Hindu method this true one, which does not make such a dead pull upon the mechanical memory of the learner. As a matter of course, the most defensible and acceptable method is that of calling each class by its characteristic feature—as, the reduplicating class, the *ya*-class, and so on. But one still meets, in treatises and papers on general philology, references to verbs "of the fourth class," "of the seventh class," and so on. So far as this is not mere mechanical habit, it is pedantry—as if one meant to say: "I am so familiar with the Sanskrit language and its native grammar that I can tell the order in which the bodies of similarly-conjugated roots follow one another in the *dhātupāṭhas*, though no one knows any reason for it, and the Hindu grammarians themselves lay no stress upon it." It is much to be hoped that this affectation will die out, and soon.

These and such as these are sufficient reasons why an exposition like that here given is timely and pertinent. It needs to be impressed on the minds of scholars that the study of the Sanskrit language is one thing, and the study of the Hindu science of grammar another and a very different thing; that while there has been a time when the latter was the way to the former, that time is now long past, and the relation of the two reversed; that the present task of the students of the grammar is to make their science accessible, account if possible for its anomalies, and determine how much and what can be extracted from it to fill out that knowledge of the language which we derive from the literature; and that the peculiar Hindu ways of grouping and viewing and naming facts familiar to us from the other related languages are an obstacle in the way of a real and fruitful comprehension of those facts as they show themselves in Sanskrit, and should be avoided. An interesting sentimental glamour, doubtless, is thrown over the language and its study by the retention of an odd classification and terminology; but that attraction is dearly purchased at the cost of a tittle of clearness and objective truth.

B. Book Notice of Whitney's Roots, Verb-forms and Primary Derivatives of the Sanskrit Language (1886)

Franz Kielhorn

Whitney's article naturally evoked much criticism, and most of it was well deserved. The most authoritative of his critics, Kielhorn, refers to it indirectly and rather sarcastically in a short review (in 1886) on Whitney's *Roots, Verb-forms, and Primary Derivatives of the Sanskrit Language* (which had been published in 1885 as a supplement to the *Sanskrit Grammar* and which was referred to in a footnote in Whitney's 1884 article). As is apparent from his review, Kielhorn did not count Whitney among those "who more particularly have turned their attention upon the works of the native grammarians." Kielhorn's review, which is here reproduced, appeared in the *Indian Antiquary* (15, 1886, 86–87).

Kielhorn's comparison of grammarians with potters is an implicit reference to Patañjali's *Mahābhāṣya* (ed. Kielhorn, I, 7.28–8.1): "A man who wants to use a pot goes to a potter and says 'Make a pot, I want to use it.' But a person who wants to use words does not go to a grammarian and say 'Make words, I want to use them.'" (Patañjali says this in the context of a discussion where he maintains that the grammarians' rules must account for the actual usage (*prayoga*) of the people (*loka*): quoted by Bhandarkar on page 97 of this volume). Also, elsewhere in the *Introduction* to his commentary, Patañjali produced what would be good arguments against Whitney's view that all of the uttered forms of language at least must be accessible (cf. Westergaard, quoted on page 54). In another passage quoted earlier by Bhandarkar (page 89), Patañjali discusses at length the view that there are words which are not used (*asty aprayuktaḥ*: part of a *vārttika*), ending the discussion by saying (ed. Kielhorn, I, 9.23–24): "To say that there are words which are not used without considering the enormous extent of the use of words is sheer recklessness." Patañjali was convinced that the forms of a language are infinite and cannot therefore be studied by exhaustive enumeration (as was done for the Vedic corpus in the Prātiśākhya-literature), but only with the help of a grammar consisting of rules and exceptions (the relevant passage is illustrated in Plate IV (cf. Staal 1969, 501–502).

Highly as we value the works of the native grammarians, and convinced as we are that to them is mainly due that rapid progress which the study of Sanskrit has been making during the last century, we may yet, without fear of being misunderstood, venture to say that the time has arrived when their teaching should be subjected, by a comparison with the actual usage of the language, to a thorough and searching examination. No one who has given any serious thought to the subject, would suggest that those ancient scholars of India, whose labours have been preserved by Pāṇini, Kātyāyana, and Patañjali, would willingly have misled us, or would have invented rules which they did not believe to be warranted by the language as known to them. At the same time it is possible that, in their attempt to analyse and explain the facts of the language, they may have arrived at conclusions which cannot be upheld; that their desire to generalise may have led them to lay down rules which, true in individual cases, would, if generally observed, give rise to forms or expressions that have never been in actual use; and that the commentators may have given a meaning to their dicta which was not intended by those who originated them. Moreover, it cannot be denied, that the ancient idiom of the Vedas has not received from the grammarians that careful attention and minute description which it deserves, and that their labours here at any rate must be supplemented by modern research.

But a comparison of the teachings of the grammarians with the usage of the language during its consecutive periods is likely to furnish valuable results in another direction. If it be true, that the grammarians were not like potters who fabricate their wares for those who demand them, if what they aimed at was by means of rules and exceptions to explain the existing words of the language, a careful examination and comparison of the extant literature should reveal what works must have been known to the grammarians, and assist us in fixing more accurately the place which they hold in Sanskrit literature.

It is from such considerations as these, that we welcome the appearance of the valuable work, the result of years of patient labour, by which Prof. Whitney has laid under deep obligations all who are interested in the study of Sanskrit grammar. The book is intended, to use the author's own words, especially as a Supplement to his Sanskrit grammar, giving with a fulness of detail that was not then practicable, nor admissible as part of the grammar itself, all the quotable roots of the language, with the tense and conjugation-systems made from them, and with the noun and adjective (infinitival and participial) formations that attach themselves most closely to the verb; and further, with the other derivative noun and adjective-stems usually classed as primary: since these also are needed, if one would have a comprehensive view of the value of a given root in the language. So far as the information at present available allows, everything given is dated,—whether found in the language throughout its whole history, or limited to a certain period. Veda, Brāhmaṇa, Sūtra, Upaniṣads, epic poetry, or so-called classical Sanskrit. Of the forms taught by the grammarians, which have not yet been met with in actual use, a liberal presentation is made under the different roots: such material being always distinguished from the rest by being put in square brackets. In addition, to this regular *Dhātupāṭha*, the author has given indexes of tense and conjugation-stems, from which it becomes at once apparent, whether a particular stem is found only in the earlier or only in the later language, or occurs in both; and an index of roots, arranged in reversed alphabetical order, under which we find the interesting note, that "of the more than 800 roots here recorded as making forms of conjugation, nearly 200 occur only in the earlier language, nearly 500 in both earlier and later, and less than 150 only in the later language."

For the later periods of the language Prof. Whitney has drawn his information mainly from the St. Petersburg Dictionary; but in the older language he has done much more independent work. He has, namely, himself "gone over all the texts of the earlier period accessible to him, including the as yet unpublished Kauṣītaki-Brāhmaṇa and Kāṭhaka, and the immense Jaiminīya or Talavakāra-Brāhmaṇa, which has as yet hardly been accessible to any one else; and from them he has excerpted all the noteworthy verbal forms and (less completely)the primary derivatives; thus verifying and occasionally correcting the material of the Lexicon, supplying chance omissions, and especially filling in not a few details which it had not lain in the design of that work to present in their entirety." The forms taught by the native grammarians have been given chiefly on the authority of Westergaard's *Radices*, and for this reason a few wrong forms, which had found their way into that very accurate work, have here also been repeated.

Without entering into details, for which this is not the place, we venture to maintain that Prof. Whitney's book will prove of the greatest service not only to the student of Sanskrit generally, but also to those who more particularly have turned their attention upon the works of the native grammarians. To the latter the accurate and full collections contained in the work will probably suggest additional reasons for the belief that the so-called grammarian's dialect accords in a most curious manner with the language of what Prof. Whitney calls the language of the Brāhmaṇa period.

13

Bruno Liebich (1862-1939)

Kielhorn's best pupil was Bruno Liebich, who published a series of works on the Sanskrit grammarians, ranging from Pāṇini to the non-Pāṇinian schools, in particular, the school founded by the Buddhist grammarian Candragomin (about sixth century A.D.; see pp. 21 and 106 of this volume). In his monograph *Pāṇini. Ein Beitrag zur Kenntnis der indischen Literatur und Grammatik* (1891), Liebich continued a line of research initiated by Bhandarkar (pages 91–93) and established that the stage of the language described in Pāṇini's grammar corresponds most closely to the language of two of the older Gṛhya Sūtras, i.e., *Āśvalāyana* and *Pāraskara* (see pages 91–93)434. According to Liebich, the *Aitareya-brāhmaṇa* and the *Bṛhadāraṇyakopaniṣad* are older than Pāṇini, but the *Bhagavad Gītā* is younger. One chapter of Liebich's monograph is devoted to a discussion of Whitney's views, which the author wishes to test "mit derjenigen Sorgfalt . . . welche einem Gelehrten seines Ranges gebührt" (Liebich 1891, 45). This discussion, which constitutes Chapter V of the monograph (pages 51–61) and is here reproduced, touches on a number of interesting problems, e.g., the justification for Pāṇini's classification of nominal compounds. It also points out that a grammarian, when studying his mother tongue, need not confine himself to forms encountered in texts, since he is in a position to reproduce all possible linguistic forms, whenever he needs them, "durch Reflexion"—just as a scientist may at any time obtain through experimentation what it would take him a long time to find in nature.

A. Prüfung der Argumente Prof. Whitney's (1891)

Bruno Liebich

Eine Prüfung der Gründe, welche Herrn Prof. Whitney zur Annahme eines besonderen Grammatikersanskrit geführt haben, wird uns zugleich Gelegenheit geben, unsere eigne Ansicht in einzelnen Punkten näher zu entwickeln.

Die Beweisführung Whitney's zerfällt in zwei Teile. Im ersten (Am. Journ. of Phil. V, p. 282–284) prüft er Pāṇini's Wurzelverzeichnis, unter Hinweis auf den Essay von Hjalmar Edgren: On the verbal roots of the Sanskrit language and of the Sanskrit grammarians.[1] Im zweiten (p. 284–291) behandelt er verschiedene Punkte der Formenlehre, welche aus der uns bekannten Literatur gar keine oder eine ungenügende Bestätigung erfahren.

Es war vielleicht nicht glücklich, dass Wh. grade vom Dhātupāṭha ausging. Wenn wir z. B. über einen Künstler ein Urteil gewinnen wollen, so werden wir mit einer Prüfung seiner besterhaltenen Werke beginnen, nicht mit solchen, welche vielleicht später Überarbeitungen erlitten haben. Das Śabdānuśāsana zerfällt, von diesem Gesichtspunkt aus betrachtet, in drei an Wert ungleiche Teile. Am besten erhalten und ausserdem durch das Mahābhāṣya gesichert ist der Sūtrapāṭha, der daher, wie er den Hauptteil des Werkes bildet, so auch für die Kritik der wichtigste ist. Der Gaṇa- und Dhātupāṭha bestehen aus Listen von lauter einzelnen Worten. Wie leicht in solchen Einschiebungen stattfinden konnten, liegt auf der Hand. Aber jener hat vor diesem noch voraus, dass er in der Kāśikā mit behandelt ist, und so wird sich inbezug auf ihn durch eine kritische Ausgabe derselben und mit dem Beistand, den Vardhamāna's Gaṇaratnamahodadhi gewährt, hinreichende Sicherheit schaffen lassen. Ob dies für den Dhātupāṭha je möglich sein wird, wage ich zur Zeit nicht zu entscheiden. Falls nicht neue Hülfsmittel oder neue Gesichtspunkte für die Kritik gefunden werden, so würde ich vorschlagen, bei einer neuen Ausgabe des Dhātupāṭha diejenigen Wurzeln zu notiren, welche durch den Sūtrapāṭha oder das Mahābhāṣya gesichert sind, und ausserdem bei jeder einzelnen zu vermerken, ob und in welchem Umfange sie in der Literatur nachgewiesen werden kann.

Wh. wird mir vielleicht einwenden, dass er stets von den einheimischen Grammatikern im allgemeinen rede, dass es also schliesslich gleichgültig sei, ob diese oder jene Wurzel Pāṇini selbst oder einem Späteren ihren Platz im Dhātupāṭha verdanke. Ich möchte aber grade auf den Unterschied zwischen alter und neuer Wissenschaft hinweisen, den wir ja in Indien auch auf andern Gebieten, z. B. der Astronomie treffen. Ich kämpfe hier nur für die Trias Pāṇini, Kātyāyana, Patañjali. Für die späteren Grammatiker mag alles, was Wh. tadelt, mehr oder minder zutreffend sein; für jene alten meines Erachtens nicht.

Aber der zweite Teil von Wh.'s Essay beschäftigt sich ja ausschliesslich mit Pāṇini's Sūtrapāṭha. Wenden wir uns daher jetzt zu diesem.

Den Übergang bildet der Satz: 'The principle won here is likely to prove of universal application; for we have no reason to expect to find the grammarians absolutely trustworthy in other departments of their work, when they have failed so signally in one'. Nach dem oben Gesagten ein gefährlicher Schluss, der die Befürchtung erweckt, dass Wh. an die folgenden Punkte nicht mehr mit voller Unbefangenheit herantrat.

[1] JAOS XI, 1–55.

Wh. geht nunmehr daran, 'an Beispielen den wahren Wert des einheimischen grammatischen Systems zu ermitteln' und beginnt mit der Conjugation. Sein erstes Beispiel ist das Fut. periphrast. Med.

'In der älteren Sprache', sagt er (p. 284), 'aber nicht in der ältesten (denn es fehlt im Veda), wird ein periphrastisches Futurum Activi gebildet durch Zusammensetzung eines Nomen agentis mit einem Hülfsverb, dem Präsens des Verbums *as* 'sein': so *dātā 'smi* (wörtlich *dator sum*) 'ich werde geben' etc. Es ist ganz ungewöhnlich verglichen mit dem andern Futurum, jedoch häufig genug, um zu erfordern, als ein Teil des allgemeinen sanskritischen Verbalsystems betrachtet zu werden. Zu diesem Activum geben die Grammatiker ein entsprechendes Medium, obgleich das Hülfsverbum in seinem unabhängigen Gebrauch keine mediale Flexion hat; es wird gebildet mit Endungen, die so modificirt sind, dass sie in dem gewöhnlichen Verhältnis von medialen Endungen zu activen stehen, und weiter mit Umwandlung des zur Wurzel gehörigen *s* in der 1. Sing. zu *h* — eine sehr ungewöhnliche Substitution, von welcher es, wie ich glaube, kein andres Beispiel in der Sprache giebt. Nun, welche Stütze hat dieses Medium im wirklichen Gebrauch? Nur diese: dass in den Brāhmaṇa's vier sporadische Fälle von Versuchen begegnen, durch Analogie mediale Formen für dieses Tempus zu bilden (sie sind alle aufgeführt in meiner Sanskritgrammatik, § 947; weitere Nachforschung hat keine neuen Beispiele ans Licht gebracht): zwei von ihnen sind 1. Sing., von denen eine die Form *se* für das Hülfsverbum hat, die andre *he*, wie in der Grammatik gelehrt wird; und in der ganzen späteren Literatur, der epischen und klassischen, finde ich das Vorkommen eines einzigen weiteren Falles bemerkt, *darśayitāhe* (in Naiṣ. V, 71)! Hier ist auch der klassische Dialekt der getreue Nachfolger des vorklassischen; nur im Grammatikersanskrit hat jedes Verb, das im Medium conjugirt wird, auch ein mediales periphrastisches Futurum'.

Zunächst möchte ich einen kleinen thatsächlichen Irrtum Wh.'s richtig stellen. Mit der 1. Sing., welche die Form *se* für das Hülfsverbum hat, meint er, wie aus dem bezeichneten § seiner Grammatik ersichtlich, *prayoktāse* TS. II, 6, 2, 3. Nach der einheimischen Grammatik wäre diese Form nicht 1., sondern 2. Sing., und das ist sie auch an dieser Stelle, wie der Zusammenhang ergiebt; Mādhava umschreibt sie mit *prayokṣyase*. Wir haben also in der alten Literatur nicht einen regelmässigen und einen unregelmässigen Beleg für die 1. Person, sondern je einen für die 1. und 2., beide regulär gebildet.

Mein Haupteinwand ist aber allgemeiner Natur und betrifft die meisten folgenden Punkte mit.

Wh. macht überall die stillschweigende Voraussetzung, dass den einheimischen Grammatikern für ihr Werk kein andrer Stoff zu Gebote gestanden habe als uns, oder, was auf dasselbe hinauskommt, er legt zu wenig Gewicht darauf, welche Wahrscheinlichkeit eine Form a priori habe, in der Literatur gebraucht zu werden. Das Erscheinen einer solchen ist doch nicht willkürlich, sondern richtet sich nach dem für sie vorliegenden Bedürfnis. Nun denn, das Fut. II. ist seltener als das Fut. I., da es eine beschränktere Bedeutung hat; dieses bezeichnet die Zukunft im allgemeinen, jenes nur die entferntere. Das Med. ist seltener als das Act, die 1. Person seltener als die 3. Welche Wahrscheinlichkeit haben wir also von vornherein, einer 1. Med. Fut. II. in der älteren Literatur zu begegnen?

161
Prüfung der Argumente Prof. Whitney's

Der moderne Gelehrte, der die Grammatik einer toten Sprache schreibt und ein Pāṇini, der die Gesetze des von ihm selbst gesprochenen Idioms zu ergründen sucht, arbeiten auf sehr verschiedene Weise. Jener kennt keinen Zoll breit mehr von der Sprache, als was die Gunst oder Laune des Schicksals in Denkmälern irgend welcher Art ihm aufbewahrt hat. Seine Thätigkeit, soweit sie die Gewinnung des Materials betrifft, besteht darin, die im wirklichen Gebrauch bunt durcheinander gewürfelten Formen zu sondern, zu sammeln und nach gewissen Gesichtspunkten neu zu gruppiren. Er darf streng genommen keine Form ohne Sternchen in seinen Paradigmen aufführen, die er nicht in einem Texte sicher bezeugt gefunden hat. Pāṇini kannte wahrscheinlich weniger vedische Texte als wir; ob ihm von den Upanishaden, die wir jetzt mit Bequemlichkeit excerpiren, eine einzige zugänglich war, steht dahin. Aber wie der Naturforscher durch das Experiment sich jederzeit Bildungen vor Augen stellen kann, nach denen er in der Natur lange suchen müsste, so konnte sich auch jener alle damals möglichen Sprachtypen, so oft er ihrer bedurfte, durch Reflexion herstellen und ihre Merkmale abstrahiren. Ähnliches thut noch heut jeder gelegentlich mit seiner Muttersprache.

Wenn nun Pāṇini[2] uns ausdrücklich sagt, dass die 1. Sing. in diesem Tempus und Genus die Endung *he* besass, so würde es mir danach allein schon sehr wahrscheinlich sein, dass man solche Formen vorkommenden Falls wirklich bildete, auch wenn sich in der unabhängigen Literatur kein Beleg dafür fände; denn wie in aller Welt sollte Pāṇini darauf verfallen, eine Form mit so ungewöhnlichem Lautübergang zu erfinden? Nun finden wir aber die Form thatsächlich belegt, an einer Stelle, wo sie wirklich gebraucht wird: Taitt. Ār. I, 11 lesen wir *yaṣṭāhe* 'ich werde opfern', in Gegensatz gestellt zum Präsens *yaje* und zur Vergangenheit *ayakṣi*. Ich könnte daher schliesslich die Form mit gleichem Recht für meine Ansicht in Anspruch nehmen, dass die Brāhmaṇa-Sprache und Pāṇini's Grammatik, beide unabhängig von einander entstanden, doch nur Abbilder ein und desselben Originals darstellen.

Die Form *darśayitāhe* im Naiṣadhīya ist anders zu beurteilen. Da ein Unterschied zwischen I. und II. Fut., zwischen Act. und Med. zu Harṣa's Zeit nicht mehr empfunden wurde, so verdankt sie ihre Existenz mehr dem Wunsch des Autors, seine Gelehrsamkeit zu zeigen, als einem wirklichen Bedürfnis.

Wh. geht jetzt zum Aoristsystem über und bespricht zunächst dieses im allgemeinen, alsdann speciell den Opt. Aor. oder Precativ im Med., Opt. Aor. Act., zuletzt den reduplicirten Aorist. Auf p. 286 schreibt er irrtümlich die Stellung des Precativs im System hinter den beiden Futuren und dem Conditional, vom Aorist getrennt, auf Rechnung der native grammarians; Pāṇini wenigstens und seine Schule behandeln den Precativ zusammen mit dem Potential (*liṅ*) oder vielmehr als eine Unterabteilung des letzteren (*āśīrliṅ*), also unmittelbar neben dem Aorist. Im übrigen wäre hier dasselbe zu sagen wie beim vorigen Punkte: In den Brāhmaṇa's und Sūtra's hat jedes Tempus der Vergangenheit, nicht minder der Potential und der Precativ oder Benedictiv seine bestimmte Funktion, wie diese auch von Pāṇini kurz, aber zutreffend charakterisirt wird. In den Epen ist dieses Sprachgefühl verloren gegangen, in der Kunstpoesie bei guten Schriftstellern nach der Grammatik künstlich wiederhergestellt. Wenn daher in der späteren Literatur nicht nur der Aorist, sondern alle Tempora der Vergangenheit immer

[2] VII, 4, 52.

seltener werden und die Participia auf *ta* und *tavat* an ihre Stelle treten, so hat das seinen Grund nicht in einem organisch vor sich gehenden Sprach-process, sondern einfach darin, dass diese Formen — leichter zu bilden sind. Inwieweit man dort noch von einen lebenden Sprache zu reden berechtigt ist, haben wir an dieser Stelle nicht weiter zu untersuchen.

Es folgt in Wh.'s Essay das Passivum des Aorist, Futurum I. und II., Conditional und Precativ, welches nach Angabe der Grammatiker bei gewissen Verben eine verlängerte Nebenform haben kann, z. B. *dāsyate* oder *dāyiṣyate*, *haniṣyate* oder *ghāniṣyate*. Zunächst will ich feststellen, dass von einem Missverständnis, wie Wh. gleichsam selbst entschuldigend annimmt, hier nicht die Rede sein kann. Die Bildung dieser Formen geht auf Pāṇini VI, 4, 62 zurück. Kātyāyana, der Verfasser der Kārikā's und Patañjali beschäftigen sich ausführlich mit ihr und geben eine grosse Reihe von Beispielen; kurz, diese ganze Bildung auf ein Missverständnis zurückzuführen geht nicht wohl an. Es ist aber auch gar nicht nötig. Wh. sagt: 'Was alles dieses bedeutet, ist ganz dunkel, da es keine Anwendung davon giebt, weder früh noch spät, um Licht darauf zu werfen.'[3] Aber die Seltenheit der Nebenformen würde doch nur dann seine Bedenken rechtfertigen, wenn zugleich gezeigt würde, dass im Gegensatz dazu die regulären, kürzeren Formen relativ häufig wären. Hierüber sagt Wh. nichts, auch in seiner Grammatik führt er an der betreffenden Stelle[4] keine Beispiele an, und wenn wir berücksichtigen, dass die einzige unter den oben aufgezählten Passivformen, deren Vorkommen wir a priori häufiger erwarten dürfen, die 3. Sing. Aor. für unsern Fall nicht in Betracht kommt, da sie eine Bildung für sich und gar keine Nebenform hat (*adāyi*, *aghāni*), so ist es wohl möglich, dass er überhaupt keine hat auftreiben können. Um so unbilliger aber ist es, zu verlangen, dass die besagten N e b e n f o r m e n häufiger sein sollen, und ihr Nichterscheinen den Grammatikern gewissermassen zum Vorwurf zu machen.

Nun führt Wh. selbst aus dem Jaiminīya Brāhmaṇa eine Form an, welche genau jener Regel Pāṇini's entspricht, nämlich *ākhyāyiṣyante*; 'aber diese', fügt er hinzu, 'scheint eine mit *hvayiṣyate* etc. analoge Form zu sein und beweist folglich nichts'. Ich bezweifle dass diese bequeme Art, sich unbequeme Formen vom Halse zu schaffen, allgemeinen Beifall finden wird. *hvayiṣyate* hat *hvayiṣyati* und *hvayitum* neben sich, während die entsprechenden Formen von *khyā* nie anders als *khyāsyati* und *khyātum* lauten. Wir haben daher kein Recht hier eine Analogiebildung anzunehmen. Auf solche Weise findet man die Wahrheit nicht, sondern verdeckt sie. Andre derartige Formen mögen durch die Ungeschicklichkeit der Abschreiber (vielleicht auch der Herausgeber) verwischt worden sein, da sie sich von den regulären oft nur durch das lange *ā* unterscheiden. Kurz, ich kann von diesem ganzen Passus nur den Schlusssatz unterschreiben, dass diese Formation den Anfängern im Sanskrit nicht eingeprägt zu werden brauchte.

Im folgenden Punkte (Cerebralisirung der Endungen *dhvam* und *dhve*) wird die einheimische Lehre von Wh. ungenau oder wenigstens undeutlich wiedergegeben. Die betreffenden Sūtra's von Pāṇini lauten mit Böhtlingks Übersetzung: VIII, 3, 78 *iṇaḥ ṣīdhvaṃluṅliṭāṃ dho 'ṅgāt* 'Nach einem vocalisch (jedoch nicht auf

[3] Patañjali gebraucht diese Formen mehrfach, so gleich anfangs im Mahābhāṣya (I, 11, 10) *nirghāniṣyate*.

[4] § 998. Statt *adāsi* muss es dort heissen *adiṣi*.

a) auslautenden Stamme tritt an die Stelle des *dh* in *ṣīdhvam* und in den Personalendungen des Aorists und Perfects der entsprechende cerebrale Laut'. 79 *vibhāṣeṭaḥ* 'Nach dem Augment *i* ist in diesem Falle die Substitution nicht notwendig'. Die Grammatiken von Müller und Kielhorn führen ausser den Vocalen noch *h* und die Halbvocale an, nach denen die Cerebralisirung ebenfalls stattfinden solle, und sie haben ein Recht dazu, da der Pratyāhāra *iṇ* auch diese Laute umfasst; zu Gunsten der Böhtlingk'schen Übersetzung lässt sich anführen, dass Pāṇini gewiss hauptsächlich an vocalisch auslautende Wurzeln gedacht, und dass auch die Kāśikā nur aus solchen ihre Beispiele gewählt hat. Die Formen *ajaniḍhvam* etc. sind nach diesen Regeln allerdings falsch, wenigstens nach dieser Auslegung der Regeln; sie würden richtig, sobald man, von der einheimischen Tradition abweichend, das Wort *iṇaḥ* aus 78 in der folgenden Regel n i c h t fortgelten liesse. Indessen sind dies doch nicht die einzigen hier in Betracht kommenden Bildungen, wie es nach Wh.'s Worten (it happens that all the quotable examples — are opposed to their rule) scheinen könnte; Wh. führt selbst in seiner Grammatik *astoḍhvam*, *avṛḍhvam*, *cyoḍhvam* auf, und hier erfolgt die Cerebralisirung ganz in Übereinstimmung mit der grammatischen Lehre. Es handelt sich also um einen Sprachprocess, den Pāṇini bemerkt und dessen Grenzen er festzustellen gesucht hat. Dass dieser Process wirklich vorhanden war, wird durch die in der Literatur vorkommenden Fälle genügend bezeugt. Die Grenzen richtig anzugeben, mag ihm nicht ganz gelungen sein; aber vergessen wir auch nicht, dass er sich hierbei nur nach dem Gehör richten konnte, und dass schon ein feines Ohr dazu gehört, um den Unterschied zwischen einer Endung *dhvam* mit dentalem oder cerebralem *dh* überhaupt wahrzunehmen. Wir sehen auch aus der Kāśikā, dass die Grammatiker in manchen Fällen selbst zweifelhaft waren, was das Richtige sei. Jedenfalls scheint es mir unbillig, aus einem solchen Versehen Pāṇini, dem wir grade auf dem Gebiet der Cerebralisirung eine Fülle feiner und treffender Beobachtungen verdanken, einen schweren Vorwurf zu machen.

Wie wir oben sahen, geben die Grammatiker diese Cerebralisirung auch für die Endung *dhve* des Perfectums an. Wh. findet in der Literatur dafür kein Beispiel. Er kennt zwar auch kein Gegenbeispiel, weil auch diese Form wieder ihrer Bedeutung nach so selten ist, dass man nur durch einen glücklichen Zufall hoffen darf, ihr in der Literatur überhaupt zu begegnen; aber dies hindert ihn nicht, deswegen in der stärksten Weise auf die Grammatiker loszuschlagen.[5] Warum? Weil hier für die Umwandlung des *dh* zu *ḍh* kein Grund erkennbar sei. Als ob wir in irgend einer Sprache überall die Verkettung von Ursache und Wirkung nachzuweisen vermöchten! Wenn solche Formen in der Literatur wirklich vorkämen, würde nur ein Dilettant es wagen, sie nach dem Gesetz von Ursache und Wirkung zu emendiren. Man würde sie, vorausgesetzt, dass Wh.'s Auffassung über die Ursache der Cerebralisirung im allgemeinen richtig ist, als falsche Analogiebildungen ansehen, wie wir sie überall da beobachten, wo der G r u n d eines Sprachprocesses nicht mehr deutlich empfunden wird. Wenn also dieser Fall darauf deutet, dass Pāṇini sich auch in Nebensachen davor gehütet habe, durch vorgefasste Meinungen seinen Blick trüben zu lassen, wenn ihn seine Ehrfurcht vor der 'göttlichen Sarasvatī' vor diesem schlimmsten aller Beobachtungsfehler be-

[5] Er spricht von downright unintelligent blundering, 'handgreiflichem unverständigem Gestümper.'

wahrte, so, denke ich, können wir dem gütigen Geschick dankbar sein, welches uns das Werk dieses Augenzeugen einer fernen Vergangenheit so trefflich erhalten hat.

Bis jetzt hat Wh. immer nur solche Formen zur Vergleichung herangezogen, die in der Literatur naturgemäss so selten sind, dass sie eben kaum verglichen werden können. Bei dem grossen Material, das diesem Gelehrten durch seine Sammlungen zur Verfügung steht, scheint es mir im Interesse der Sache bedauerlich, dass er nicht glücklichere Objekte ausgewählt hat, zumal er (p. 291) versichert, dass es ihm 'leicht sein würde, das Werk der Illustration viel weiter fortzusetzen'. Denn wir stehn am Ende seiner Beweisführung. Was nun noch folgt, bezieht sich nicht auf den Inhalt der Lehre Pāṇini's, sondern nur auf die Form seiner Darstellung, auf sein System.

Zunächst bemängelt Wh. Pāṇini's Einteilung der Composita. 'Nichts konnte genauer und glücklicher sein als die Unterscheidung von abhängigen, beschreibenden, besitzanzeigenden und copulativen Zusammensetzungen; nur ihre Titel — 'sein Mann' (*tatpuruṣa*), 'die Handlung stützend' (? *karmadhāraya*), 'Vielreis' (*bahuvrīhi*) und 'Paar' (*dvandva*) beziehungsweise — können kaum beanspruchen, der Beibehaltung wert zu sein. Aber es ist das Charakteristikum der Hinduwissenschaft im allgemeinen, nicht fähig zu sein innezuhalten, wenn sie genug gethan hat; und so haben uns die Grammatiker, auf demselben Einteilungsniveau mit diesen vier Hauptklassen, noch zwei andre gegeben, welche sie *dvigu* ('zweikühig') und *avyayībhāva* ('das Indeclinabelwerden') nennen; und diese haben kein Existenzrecht, sondern sind Sammlungen von Specialfällen, die zu einer der andern Klassen gehören' etc. Es ist mir nicht gelungen, festzustellen, welcher Quelle Prof. Wh. für diese Darstellung gefolgt ist. Die mir bekannten abendländischen Grammatiken führen sämtlich — nach Pāṇini's Vorbild — nicht sechs, sondern vier Hauptklassen von Zusammensetzungen auf; nämlich Tatpuruṣa, Bahuvrīhi, Dvandva, Avyayībhāva. Die Karmadhāraya sind eine Unterabteilung der Tatpuruṣa, die Dvigu nur ein specieller Fall der Karmadhāraya. Dass Pāṇini, wie jeder Systematiker, das Recht hat, Unterklassen aufzustellen und zu benennen, soweit es ihm zweckdienlich erscheint, bedarf keines Beweises. Da übrigens Wh. zu wissen wünscht, wie die Inder zu ihrer Klassifikation kamen,[6] so lasse ich ihr Einteilungsprincip folgen, welches, nebenbei bemerkt, so einfach ist, dass es Pāṇini überflüssig erschien, dasselbe im Sūtra ausdrücklich auszusprechen (cf. Kāś. zu I, 2, 57). Nur beim Bahuvrīhi findet sich ein Hinweis darauf.

Wenn man nämlich vom zweigliedrigen Compositum ausgeht, so kann man fragen, wo der Schwerpunkt (*pradhāna*) desselben ruht. Hier sind folgende Fälle möglich:

1. beide Glieder haben gleiches Gewicht (*ubhayapadārthapradhāna*);
2. der Schwerpunkt ruht auf dem ersten Teil (*pūrvapadārthapradhāna*);
3. der Schwerpunkt ruht auf dem zweiten Teil (*uttarapadārthapradhāna*);
4. der Schwerpunkt liegt ausserhalb des Compositums (*anyapadārthapradhāna*).

Alle vier Fälle kommen in der Sprache wirklich vor, ihnen entsprechen die vier Hauptklassen der indischen Grammatik, und zwar der Reihe nach die Dvandva, Avyayībhāva, Tatpuruṣa und

[6] Er gebraucht für dieselbe den nicht sehr geschmackvollen Vergleich: Tiere, Pflanzen, Mineralien und Kaktusse.

Bahuvrīhi. Was die mehrgliedrigen Composita angeht, so haben in den Dvandva auch hier, wir vorauszusehen, alle Teile gleiches Gewicht; alle übrigen lassen sich auf zweigliedrige zurückführen.

Schliesslich werden, als Repräsentanten von 'points in abundance, of major or minor consequence', die noch zu tadeln seien, von Wh. die beiden Wurzeln *grah* und *div* aufgeführt, die richtiger mit *gṛh* und *dīv* oder *dīū* hätten angesetzt werden sollen. Über diese Dinge will ich mit Wh. nicht rechten. Es ist nicht meine Absicht, das System Pāṇini's in allen Punkten verteidigen zu wollen. Ich denke mir, dass es damals, als es entstand, den Verhältnissen und Bedürfnissen am besten Rechnung getragen hat, da es alle andern aus jener Zeit stammenden verdrängte. Aber es wäre nicht gut, wenn es der heutigen Wissenschaft nicht gelingen sollte, an seine Stelle ein vollkommeneres zu setzen. Den sachlichen Inhalt seines Werkes dürfen wir, das hoffe ich gezeigt zu haben, im allgemeinen als wohlverbürgtes, zuverlässiges Material ansehen; sein System, die Art, wie er die Formen erklärt und analysirt, mögen wir beibehalten oder verwerfen, soweit wir es für gut finden.

Die grossen Verdienste des Herrn Prof. Whitney auf vielen Gebieten der indischen Philologie sind zu bekannt, als dass ich sie hier hervorzuheben brauchte; aber eben wegen der grossen Autorität, die sein Urteil dadurch besitzt, schien mir eine eingehende Widerlegung notwendig. Seine Ansicht über die indischen Grammatiker ist ihm sozusagen in Fleisch und Blut übergegangen; in seiner Sanskritgrammatik, die doch sonst vom wissenschaftlichen Standpunkt aus die erste Stelle einnimmt, kann man nicht drei Seiten weit lesen, ohne sie reflectirt zu finden; hier findet der Leser gelegentlich zu seiner Überraschung Bildungen, die Pāṇini ausdrücklich lehrt, getrost als Barbarismen bezeichnet.[7] Auch in Schriften jüngerer Sanskritisten, namentlich der amerikanischen Schule, entsinne ich mich ähnliche absprechende Urteile über die einheimische Grammatik angetroffen zu haben. Dieser Auffassung musste nachdrücklich entgegengetreten werden.

Zum Schluss giebt Prof Whitney denen, die sich mit der einheimischen Grammatik näher beschäftigt haben, einige Ratschläge, wofür ihm diese dankbar sein werden. Wenn ich mir erlauben darf, als Gegengabe gleichfalls einen Wunsch auszusprechen, so wäre es der, aus seiner Grammatik künftig alle Seitenblicke und Anspielungen auf die native grammarians zu entfernen. Er will doch in derselben nur das Sanskrit, wie es sich aus den Literaturdenkmälern abstrahiren lässt, historisch darstellen. Durch einen Verzicht auf diese höchst oberflächlichen und oft ungenauen Bemerkungen würde sein sonst so vortreffliches Werk entschieden gewinnen.

B. On Recent Studies in Hindu Grammar (1893)

William Dwight Whitney

Whitney answered promptly in an article "On Recent Studies in Hindu Grammar" of 1893, in which he discusses other works of Liebich's as well as the work of Otto Franke. It appeared in the *American Journal of Philology* (14, 1893, 171–197).

The problem of the meaning of *bhāṣā* in Pāṇini's grammar, brought up by Franke and brushed aside by Whitney, and the related problem of the meaning of *chandas* have received much attention in later studies but remain unsolved. Renou (1969, 456–457) queries still: "Is this 'spoken language' a limited and distinct dialect or did Pāṇini (outside the two zones *chandasi* and *bhāṣāyām*) hold a view on language which comprised, in an undifferentiated

[7] Cf. § 473, c und Pāṇ. V, 3, 56.

manner, the *chandas* — with the exception of archaisms — and the *bhāṣā*?" For further references see Wackernagel-Renou 1957, 88 note 317.

Nine years ago (in October, 1884) I published in this Journal a paper entitled "The study of Hindu grammar and the study of Sanskrit." It was intended to emphasize the difference between Sanskrit on the one side and Pāṇini and his successors on the other, and to point out the true place of the native grammar as an important division of Sanskrit science, requiring to be studied as such, and not as the foundation of our knowledge of the Sanskrit language. Since that time there have appeared a number of contributions to our knowledge of the Hindu grammar, from the pens of two younger scholars of decided ability, then unknown; and these contributions I propose to examine briefly, especially in order to see how they stand related to the question above set forth.

The first of them appeared in 1885, and was entitled "The case-system of the Hindu grammarians, compared with the use of the cases in the Aitareya-Brāhmaṇa"; it was a doctorate-dissertation by Bruno Liebich; the author is at present a *privat-docent* in the Breslau University. Its first part, printed in vol. X of Bezzenberger's Beiträge zur Kunde der indogermanischen Sprachen, was a digest of the system of rules laid down by Pāṇini for the use of the cases, and was very welcome, as must be every contribution to an easier understanding of the peculiarities and difficulties of the Hindu science. A few words as to the system may not be out of place here. Pāṇini does not take up the cases as forms of nouns, setting forth the various uses of each, after our manner; he adopts the vastly more difficult and dangerous method of establishing a theoretical list of modes of verb-modification by case, or of ideal case-relations (he calls them *kāraka*, 'factor' or 'adjunct'), to which he then distributes the cases. Almost as a matter of course, however, his case-relations or *kāraka* are not an independent product of his logical faculty, but simply a reflection of the case-forms; they are of the same number as the latter, and each corresponds to the general sphere of a case: they are *kartar* ('actor' = nominative), *karman* ('act' = accusative), *sampradāna* ('delivery' = dative), *karaṇa* ('instrument' = instrumental), *adhikaraṇa* ('sphere' = locative), and *apādāna* ('removal' = ablative). The genitive has no defined character, but is provided for by stating, when all the other case-uses have been rehearsed, that the remainder are those of the genitive. As for the definitions of the case-relations, it may suffice to say that the *karman* is described as belonging, first, to that which the actor in his action especially desires to obtain or attain (as in "he makes a *mat*," "he goes to the *village*"): or, second, to that which, though itself undesired or indifferent, is connected with the action in a similar manner. Anything more crude or unphilosophical than this could not well be imagined. There is not an identity between the use of a given case and the presence of its generally corresponding case-relation, because, for example, in a passive sentence, as "the mat is made by him," *mat* is still called *karman* or 'act,' though nominative, and *him* still *kartar* or 'actor,' though instrumental. Thus there is no recognition of the grammatical category of subject of a verb; and this leads, as could not be helped, to numerous obscurities and difficulties. Then, in the second part of the paper (ibid., vol. XI, 1887), the author proceeds to classify under this scheme, in all its headings and sub-headings, its general rules and its exceptions, the facts of case-use in the Aitareya-Brāhmaṇa: a careful and creditable piece of work. The results of the comparison are precisely what we should expect to find them, knowing well, as we do, the relation of the language of the Brāhmaṇas to Pāṇini's Sanskrit: there is a good degree of general agreement—as there would have been found to exist even if the Ṛg-Veda instead of a Brāhmaṇa had been compared; since changes of syntactical construction, perhaps even more than changes of form, are of slow progress in every language, leaving the main body of older usages long untouched. Alongside of this agreement are met with just the differences that could not fail to appear: constructions in the Brāhmaṇa that are unnoticed in Pāṇini, as they are wanting in classical Sanskrit; and especially a host of details in Pāṇini of which the Brāhmaṇa exhibits no examples. There is absolutely nothing to show, or even to give reason to suspect, that any special relation exists between Pāṇini and this Brāhmaṇa any more than any other of the same class of works, specimens alike of the Brāhmaṇa stage of development of ancient Indian language. The conclusion is that, whatever its defects of theory, Pāṇini's case-syntax proves to be a fairly good practical scheme; and the demonstration of the fact is to be received with thanks; it is a valuable contribution to our appreciation of the great grammarian. Whether, however, the author views it in just this light is a little questionable; for he adds as second title to his essay "a contribution to the syntax of the Sanskrit language"—which it plainly is not. Is it, forsooth, the Brāhmaṇa that he has been examining, to see whether its case-constructions are such as they ought to be? or is this part of its grammar now better understood than hitherto, or arranged in a manner which we shall be disposed to accept as preferable to, for example, Delbrück's? Nothing of all this; it is simply that Pāṇini has been tested by a bit of real language, and the test has turned out not to his disadvantage. The misapprehension that something done for Pāṇini is done for the Sanskrit language is precisely what my former paper was especially intended to discourage.

Dr. Liebich adds at the end of his own estimate of the results of his work: "I. The Aitareya-Brāhmaṇa is older than Pāṇini." This were better stated the other way: namely, that Pāṇini is later than the Brāhmaṇa; since it is really the grammarian, and not this member of the literature, that is under examination. As for the relation itself, it is not only true, but a truism; no one having any knowledge of the subject has or could have any question about it; our author's paper is not a demonstration, but merely an illustration, out of one department of grammar, of a fact already incontrovertibly established on many and sufficient grounds. The author adds as follows: "It (the Brāhmaṇa) belongs to the Vedic period, but to the close of the latter, and stands fairly near to Pāṇini (undoubtedly much nearer than to the Ṛg-Veda in the other direction)." Here again we have truths, but, since there has been no comparison made between Brāhmaṇa and Veda in the paper, they are incorrectly put forward as its "results." Further, "2. The doctrine of Pāṇini reposes upon a careful and acute observation of the actual language." Here it is a little doubtful where the stress of the assertion lies, and what counter-proposition is intended to be gainsaid. No one, certainly, would think of denying that Pāṇini observed and described with remarkable acuteness and to the best of his ability. Nor, again, I should think, that he described an actual language—"an" rather than "the," for just what language he was dealing with is one of the disputed points. The author's added remarks indicate that he thinks it a book-language; if anything in the rules is not capable of being instanced, it is, he suggests, because so much of the literature has been lost. This seems an untenable view, and has doubtless been since abandoned by him. The question will come up again further on.

Four years later (1890), in the same Journal (XVI 1–2), a kindred topic is taken up by another scholar, Dr. R. Otto Franke, now a *privat-docent* in the Berlin University. The title of his paper is "The case-system of Pāṇini compared with the use of the cases in Pāli and in the Aśoka inscriptions." He builds upon the foundation laid by Liebich, adopting the latter's scheme of Pāṇinean case-uses, and looking for correspondences to them in the dialects confessedly later than Pāṇini, as the Brāhmaṇa was confessedly earlier. Here also he finds all the agreement that could reasonably have been expected; and, as the ground has been comparatively little worked over, his work is much more truly a contribution to the syntax of the dialects of India than is that of Liebich. He brings to light one very curious thing: that for a problematic rule of Pāṇini's, declaring the future tense to be usable in describing something recently past, examples are quotable from the Pāli, though they have never been discovered in Sanskrit. But his general views as to Pāṇini and the Sanskrit seem rather strange. He calls Liebich's little work "a beginning toward the accomplishment of the very pressing task of determining by internal evidence Pāṇini's position in the literature, and so, indirectly, that of the Sanskrit"—as if nobody, before the appearance of this doctorate-dissertation, had done anything worthy of mention in that direction; or as if the position of Pāṇini's Sanskrit in the history of development of Indian language had not long been clear enough. And he points out that, in spite of the partial agreement between the case-uses in the Aitareya-Brāhmaṇa and Pāṇini's rules, we ought not to conclude that the Brāhmaṇa was the exclusive, or even the principal, foundation of the rules—as if it could ever enter into the mind of any reasonable person to draw such a conclusion. He then gives us the same warning in regard to the Pāli, which is even, if possible, more superfluous. He further admits it as possible, though on the whole less probable, that Pāṇini may have "collected the phenomena of very diverse dialects, and fused them together into an integral whole"—than which nothing could well find less to be said in its favor.

But to the question as to what the Sanskrit of Pāṇini really is the same author returns in a special paper entitled "What is Sanskrit?", dated in November, 1889 (though first published in vol. XVII, 1891, of Bezzenberger's Beiträge). Rather more than half the paper is occupied with the more specific inquiry as to what Pāṇini means by *bhāṣā*, a word that he uses only seven times, or too seldom to set forth its significance with the desirable clearness. 'Popular speech' is its natural sense; but the usages quoted from it by Pāṇini as opposed to his own approved language show that it was no Prakritic dialect (that is the chief result of the author's investigation); and it is as evidently not one of the older Vedic dialects; there seems to remain, then, only one possibility: it is essentially Sanskrit, only not what Pāṇini accepts as good Sanskrit; it includes those words and phrases which, though more or less current, he does not regard as worthy to be perpetuated.

This conclusion appears to be a reasonable and safe one.[1] The second half of the paper then deals more directly with the inquiry as to what Pāṇini's Sanskrit really is; and the author's opinion is expressed in these terms (pp. 75–76): "Pāṇini's Sanskrit is accordingly in the main *bhāṣā*. And yet, on the other hand, it is neither *bhāṣā* nor a living language." This is not particularly clear; nor is it made very much clearer by the reasonings, and the quotations of the views of others, that follow. It is to me so strange as fairly to be called unaccountable that these authors take no notice whatever of the evidence of the dramas upon the subject. In the latter we see a condition of society in which educated people talk Sanskrit, while the uneducated talk Prākrit, in dialects more or less different from one another. So far as I can perceive, there is not any reason to question that this state of things was real at the time when those dramas were produced which then set the rule for all future time. The speakers all understand one another; the difference between Sanskrit and Prākrit is not yet sufficient to prevent that; the Prākrit-speakers can even, in an emergency, put in a phrase of Sanskrit; and, on the other hand, when King Purūravas goes mad, he casts off the restraints of education, and talks in part Prākrit, like a woman. That, now, is just the present character of Sanskrit: an educated or learned dialect, kept in existence, nearly unchanged, by instruction, by learned and literary use, among languages now become so diverse from it that its knowledge is confined to a very small circle; such, too, has been its character for at least two thousand years, while the true vernaculars have been growing further and further away from it; and such must unquestionably have been its character at the outset, when their divergence, and its separate life, first began. That it was itself originally a vernacular seems to me a matter of course; nor do I see that any one has the right to say that Pāṇini's speech was not a living one, unless he then enters into a full explanation of what he means by a living language as distinguished from it. Sanskrit was the natural successor of the dialects of Veda, Brāhmaṇa, and Sūtra, and as much "living" as any of these had been, when the literary and learned class took it in hand, and, with the aid of grammatical science, fortified it against the further effect of the changes that were bringing out of it the various Prakritic dialects (taking that word in its widest sense). There is no absolute line to be drawn between living and dead languages. If the Sanskrit has never failed of being kept up by a constant tradition from teacher to pupil, though in a limited class, there is a real sense in which it has never died, but is still a living tongue. In another and equally correct sense, no language is alive that is not an out-and-out vernacular, spoken by a whole community, and having no inferior dialect below it in the same community: in this sense, to be sure, the Sanskrit of the series of grammarians of whom Pāṇini was the chief and virtually the last was not a fully living tongue; it had Prakritic dialects under it. Moreover, as soon as it took on the character of a learned dialect, it began as a matter of course to be stiffened into something a little unnatural; no dialect ever fell into the hands of grammarians without suffering from their pedantry. But I can find no reason whatever for supposing that it was not their own language, the language which they themselves

[1] It is, however, rejected by Liebich, in his Kāśikā' (p. xxv), to be described further on. Liebich suggests no substitute.

spoke and which they thought alone worthy to be spoken by others, that they set themselves to describe. Whatever Pāṇini's special original part in the work may have been, we know that he left it still abounding in errors, both of omission and of commission; the important additions and corrections of Kātyāyana and Patañjali, to say nothing of their numerous but more insignificant successors, amply prove this; and it is frankly conceded in many points by these latest students of the system, unlike the scholars of a generation or two ago. The task Pāṇini attempted was beyond the power of mortal man to accomplish, especially in the form adopted by him—which is one that no sensible man should ever have chosen, yet on account of which, it is very likely, his contemporaries and successors especially admired him, and made him their supreme authority.

Something like this, in my opinion, is what we have a right to say that we know about Pāṇini; and the investigations of Liebich and Franke, while they bring nothing to light that contradicts it, merely illustrate here and there a point in it, and do not add notably to its amount, because they ignore it all, and assume that the most fundamental facts involved have still to be established. What we really need further is added precision on a host of points as to which we have as yet only general knowledge, and particularly a comprehension of how the grammatical system, in all its details, stands related to the language of the Sanskrit classical literature, which professes to be governed by it, and yet has evidently had a traditional life of its own, simply regulated by the grammar, and has by no means been produced under the latter's dictation. To ask and answer, in all seriousness, such questions as whether a certain Brāhmaṇa, or whether the Pāli, is Pāṇini's Sanskrit, or whether that language was a living one, appears to me the wrong way to arrive at any valuable result.

In his conspectus of the views of various scholars as to the character of Sanskrit, given in the second part of his paper, Dr. Franke quotes with approval and acceptance an odd expression of opinion by Weber, made at the very outset of his career, to the effect that "the development of Sanskrit and of the Prākrit dialects out of their common source, the Indo-Aryan mother-tongue, went on with absolute contemporaneousness (*vollständig gleichzeitig*)." But I do not see why this is not an unscientific and untenable proposition. For example, *pakkhitta* and *attā* or *appā* are not contemporaneous with *prakṣipta* and *ātmā* in the historical development of language, any more than Ital. *rotto* and *rotti* with Lat. *ruptus, -um* in their various case-forms; and so *hodu* is preceded in point of time by *bhavatu*, being a later "corruption" of the latter, coming to take its place, as Fr. *était* of *stabat*, or *fûtes* of *fuistis*. And this is true of the great mass of Prākrit words, forms, and constructions; they are developed later than, and come to be substituted for, the corresponding Sanskrit words, forms, and constructions. If there were anything to be found on Indian ground that is earlier than *prakṣipta*, and from which it and *pakkhitta* should have equally descended by a parallel process, then we might have a right to speak of their contemporaneity; but that is plainly not the case; it is the Sanskrit forms themselves, and not something older and more primitive than Sanskrit, that the Prākrit words presuppose; they have passed through the stage which the Sanskrit represents. That here and there exceptions are met with, altered items for which the original is not found in Sanskrit, or is found in Vedic Sanskrit, is without any force whatever as against the great mass of material of a contrary character; such exceptions to the descent *in toto* of one dialect from another are the rule in all dialectic history, and might with equal justice be relied on to prove that Italian and French are in their development "absolutely contemporaneous" with Latin. As to the other half or side of the view already quoted, Dr. Franke adds: "That the Sanskrit had become extinct when the Prākrit dialects first began to develop themselves is false." What this means is quite unintelligible; it seems to go out of the way to deny a doctrine which no well-informed student of language could by any possibility think of maintaining, and it accordingly has no claim to be criticized, but must be simply set aside as valueless. If, for example, *ātmā* had ever become extinct, whence should *attā* or *appā* have originated? Who would say that the egg had been extinct when the chicken first began to develop itself? But, somehow or other, those whose ancestors had said *ātmā* began to say *attā* instead, the one pronunciation passing into the other, with no extinction intervening. It was, however, only a part of the community who did thus; a part, doubtless much the smaller one, continued to say *ātmā*; and the two forms went on in currency side by side, as educated and as popular speech, in the same way as in many cases elsewhere in the world; and *ātmā* was Sanskrit, and, with some help and some mishandling on the part of grammarians, has maintained itself in being to this day, in the literature which we call Sanskrit, and which, rather than the grammarians' treatment of it, is the true and proper object of the study of the Sanskrit scholar.

Next was produced by Dr. Liebich, in 1891, a valuable collection of studies entitled "Pāṇini: a contribution to the knowledge of Indian literature and grammar"; it makes a small octavo volume of 164 pages. The first study, or chapter, deals with Pāṇini's period; the author reviews briefly the opinions that have been held by different scholars respecting the matter, and, without attempting to bring any new evidence to bear upon it, comes to the moderate and sensible conclusion that only a certain degree of probability can be arrived at: "after Buddha and before Christ" represents to him the measure of this probability. The second chapter treats of the principal later grammarians who have continued and modified Pāṇini's work; in regard to the earliest and most important of them the same chronological uncertainty prevails. The third is entitled "Pāṇini and the remaining literature," and is an attempt to determine where in the succession of the ancient literature of India, from the earliest Veda down, Pāṇini comes in. It takes as starting-point the wild views of Goldstücker, with their refutation by Weber; it points out further the insufficiency of the evidences relied upon for the prevailing opinion that Yāska is earlier than Pāṇini; and it then proceeds to its principal task, of applying to the general question a new, a numerical-statistical, method of solution. The author counts off, namely, a thousand personal verb-forms occurring in succession in each of four different monuments of the literature—the Aitareya-Brāhmaṇa, the Bṛhad-Āraṇyaka, two Gṛhya-Sūtras (Āśvalāyana and Pāraskara), and the Bhagavad-Gītā; representatives respectively of the Brāhmaṇa, Upaniṣad or later Brāhmaṇa, Sūtra, and epic stages of development of Indian speech—and then applies to them the rules of the grammar, to see how many and what forms unauthorized by Pāṇini appear in the several texts. The examination is creditable to the industry and learning of its author, and its results are interesting; we can hardly go further than that and pronounce them important. For they are essentially illustrative only; they put in a numerical form peculiarities which were already familiarly known to characterize the different classes of works instanced. Not a new item, so far as I can see, is brought to light; nor is any made more certain than before. Thus, six of the seven classes of Brāhmaṇa divergencies drawn out on pages 23–4 have long been recognized as such; and how many examples of each class may chance to occur in a given amount of text is a matter of indifference. As for the seventh, represented by a single case, the lengthened final of the imperative *kṛdhī*, it is an error; such a protraction does not belong to the Brāhmaṇa language, as indeed, it has no right of occurrence anywhere except in verse; where it appears here (ii 2. 21), it is simply copied from the Ṛg-Veda verse (i 36. 14) on which the Brāhmaṇa is engaged in commenting, and of which it repeats a whole *pāda* (including *kṛdhī*) with merely the substitution of the more regular *caraṇāya* for *carathāya* in it; and the retention of the *ī* is not improbably even a misreading, such as this Brāhmaṇa has in no very small number (it may be added that the author, doubtless misled by Pāṇini, describes *kṛdhi* falsely as a present instead of an aorist imperative). And so also in each of the remaining cases. That is to say, the matter is not one to which the numerical method of investigation is well suited; this would be much better applied between, for example, different texts of the same class, as different Brāhmaṇas, to see whether it would yield any evidence as to their respective periods; and perhaps the part of the whole investigation which is of most value is the comparison which it makes possible between Aitareya-Brāhmaṇa and Bṛhad-Āraṇyaka, the latter being part of a Brāhmaṇa also, but plainly later, as was a matter of course for an Upaniṣad. Instead, again, of the Bhagavad-Gītā, which no one doubts to be a comparatively recent addition to the Mahābhārata, it were much to be wished that the author had selected something out of those parts of the epic which are most probably to be regarded as its original nucleus, in order to cast more light upon the really difficult and hitherto doubtful question how and how much the epic differs from the classical or Pāṇinean Sanskrit, and why. That Brāhmaṇa and Upaniṣad and Sūtra antedate Pāṇini we knew just as certainly before this investigation was made as we know it now; the posteriority of the Bhagavad-Gītā, again, could hardly have been questioned, however the case may stand with the earliest epic. The criteria applied to the divergences of the Gītā from grammatical strictness are of a less satisfactory and decisive character. The decided majority (21 against 16) of the irregularities concern the voice of the verb; but, though the looseness of at least the later epic in this regard is certainly excessive, it is likely that Pāṇini's rules limiting the employment of the voices are exceptionally artificial and discordant with genuine usage; our author himself so judges examples of them (e.g., p. 28) in connection with the Brāhmaṇa. As for the causative perfects with *āsa* (3 in number), Pāṇini's failure to authorize them must be either an oversight or a piece of pedantry. Any *śucas*, since this aorist occurs in Veda and Brāhmaṇa, might be deemed a sign rather of antiquity than of modern date. The harvest of results from the chapter, then, must be confessed a rather scanty one.

In the sixth and seventh chapters the author returns to the Aitareya-Brāhmaṇa and the Bṛhad-Āraṇyaka, in order to see whether any difference of period can be established among their constituent parts. Here again is, as in the particular noted above, a good and suitable application of the statistical method, and it leads to trustworthy and interesting conclusions. In the Āraṇyaka are discovered no notable indications of diversity of age; but in the Brāhmaṇa the author finds good reason to believe, as had been inferred by others before him, that the concluding chapters are more modern than the rest.

Between the parts of the volume devoted to the first and to the second examination of these two works intervene a couple of chapters, of which the former, the fourth, is headed "Pāṇini's relation to the language of India"—that is to say, the relation of Pāṇini's Sanskrit to the other dialects. The chapter is chiefly composed of a succinct statement of the views of other scholars, to which the author then appends his own view; and this is simply a summary of what he has illustrated in the preceding chapters as the relation between Pāṇini's dialect and the Brāhmaṇa and Sūtra on the one side and the epic on the other. Then (p. 50) he appends as final result a wholly new and original classification of the entire body of dialects of India. They are divided into three categories: pre-classical, classical, and post-classical. To the classical division are referred, besides "the doctrine of Pāṇini," the Brāhmaṇas and Sūtras also, which the author has himself previously recognized as pre-Pāṇinean! This leaves as pre-classical only "the saṃhitās of the four Vedas." But the third division, the post-classical, is still more wonderfully constructed: besides the "independent" epic, it contains the whole literature which we have been accustomed to know as Sanskrit, namely "Kālidāsa, etc., originated under the influence of the grammar"! What is left to constitute the classical subdivision "*b.* Doctrine of Pāṇini" is very obscure; it can be only Pāṇini's grammar itself (so that such sentences as *idamo rhil*, *gāñkuṭā-dibhyo 'ñṇinñit* are classical, as contrasted with Kālidāsa's compositions), and in addition all the works that might, could, would, or should have been written in strict accordance with it, and not merely "under its influence," if there only were any such. Now I had myself, in my former paper, laid stress on the difference between the purely hypothetical "grammarians' Sanskrit" and the Sanskrit of the literature; but I never went so far as to maintain, with Dr. Liebich, that the two even belonged to different prime divisions of the whole history of language in India (thus, II. *b.* grammarians' Sanskrit; III. *b.* Sanskrit of the literature).

Just half our author's volume (pp. 82–161) is occupied by two studies which are reckoned as Appendix I and Appendix II. The one is a digest of the teachings of the native grammar (Pāṇini, the Mahābhāṣya, and the Kāśikā) respecting the voice-inflection of the verbal roots, as active or middle or both; the other is a similar digest for the formation of feminine declension-stems from the corresponding masculines. These two appendixes constitute, in my opinion, the substantially valuable part of the volume; they exemplify what needs to be done for all the various subjects included in Pāṇini's treatise. The next step, now, should be to compare in detail the statements thus drawn out with the actual facts of the language as exhibited in the whole series of monuments of the literature, from Vedic down to classical and epic, in order to determine what is the relation between the two, and then what the former, the prescriptions of the grammar, are worth; until that is done, no contribution has yet been made to our knowledge of the language, but only to our knowledge of Pāṇini. It casts a shade of unreality over the whole subject of voice-conjugation that the voices of the thousand or twelve hundred false roots are not less carefully defined by the *dhātu-pāṭha* than those of the eight or nine hundred genuine ones.

There is left for our consideration only the fifth chapter, in which the author takes up and attempts to answer my own objections, given in my paper of nine years ago, to the confusing of the study of Pāṇini with that of Sanskrit, and the thrusting of the grammarians' dialect into the place in our attention which the real language of the recorded literature ought to occupy. I propose to examine here this reply, and see how effective it is.

Dr. Liebich's first point is, as was my own, the *dhātupāṭha*, or list of roots, which is given as part of the material of the grammar, and really even its foundation, since it is upon them that the rules of the grammar profess to go on and build up the structure of the language—and that not only grammatically but lexically, for the grammar includes the system of derivation, with definition of the modifications wrought in each root-sense and stem-sense by the added suffixes. On this point the author offers a criticism which he is obliged himself to withdraw in the next paragraph: he first accuses me of treating Pāṇini rather unfairly, since the *dhātupāṭha* was the part of his work most likely to be deformed by later corruptions; but then allows that I was perhaps (as is indeed plainly the case) criticizing the whole system of the grammarians as it lies before us, of which the list of roots objected to forms undeniably an inseparable part. Böhtlingk gives it in length and breadth in his recent second edition of Pāṇini, finding nothing else to put in its place; and it must have gone hard with him, who knows what in Sanskrit is real and what is sham better than almost any other living scholar, and who has in the Petersburg lexicons done more than any one else to make plain their distinction, to introduce into his work such a mass of worthless rubbish; I hardly comprehend how he should have prevailed on himself to do this without exercising his critical acumen upon it, and separating in some way the false from the true. Our author talks of probable interpolations, and intimates that he deems them posterior to the great trio of Pāṇini, Kātyāyana, and Patañjali, acknowledging that my criticisms may be "more or less" applicable to their successors. Well, I should think so; and more rather than less. This free and easy way of disposing of the subject is quite characteristic of the whole guild of partizans of the native grammar. It appears impossible to bring any one of them to stand up and face fairly the question of the *dhātupāṭha*. There are not far from nine hundred real authenticable roots in Sanskrit. We could believe that the uncritical interpolations of later grammarians might add to this number a dozen, or a score, or fifty, or (to take the extreme) even a hundred or two; but it is the wildest of nonsense (only strong expressions suit the case) to hold that they could swell the number to over two thousand! Such increase is thus far wholly unexplained, perhaps forever unexplainable, and certainly most unpardonable; and until it is in some way accounted for the admirers of the Hindu science of grammar ought to talk in very humble tones. If these roots are not the ones recognized by the wondrous three, when and under what circumstances and by whose influence were the additional twelve hundred foisted in, to the abandonment and loss of the old genuine list? The difficulty of explaining this seems not less great than that of supposing the whole two thousand as old as Pāṇini himself; both are hard enough; and, in either event, the taint of falsity attaches to the Hindu system as we know it and are expected to use it.

As concerns the three points of the middle periphrastic perfect, the middle precative, and the secondary passive forms, nothing that the author says tends to change at all the aspect of the case as stated by me; namely, that these are formations which, though taught by Pāṇini, are wanting in the traditional literary language—as much so as verb-forms from the thousand and more false roots; they belong to the grammarians' Sanskrit alone. Just how much or how little excuse Pāṇini may have had for setting them up, that is a different and a minor question, to be decided finally by the general result of our examination of Pāṇini's way of working, of selecting what he will adopt and what he will reject. To me they seem artificial and pedantic structures, reared on an obsolete and insufficient or misapprehended basis.

The author's well-intended correction of my estimate of *prayoktāse* in TS. ii 6. 2^3 as 1st sing. I do not find myself able to accept. The sentence is not, perhaps, absolutely clear; but the presence in it of a *te* 'for thee' is to me a tolerably certain indication that the verb is not 2d sing. ('I will employ to-morrow for thee at the sacrifice,' or 'at thy sacrifice'); no such possessive would be called for (or admissible, I think) if the person were second. And *-tāse* is obviously the true middle analogue to active *-tāsmi*, as *śāse* to *śāsmi* and the like; while *-tāhe*, as given by the grammarians, is absolutely anomalous, being unsupported, so far as I know, by a single other phonetic fact of the language. That it occurs once (but only once) in the literature, in that very late Vedic document the Taitt. Āraṇyaka, whose text is in many parts extremely faulty, is beyond question; but I would put forward the suggestion, as by no means an impossible one, that the form is corrupt, and that the 1st sing. *-tāhe* of the grammarians is founded solely on it. That the native commentary, it may be added, explains *prayoktāse* in TS. as 2d sing. is not of the smallest particle of importance; an expositor schooled in Pāṇini would of course do that, and is capable of doing it against the most incontrovertible evidence to the contrary.

Another matter which the author undertakes to defend against my objections is Pāṇini's determination of the cases where *dh* and where *ḍh* is to be used in the 2d plur. endings *dhvam* and *dhve*. He is so far successful that he is able to show the grammarians' rules to admit in part a different interpretation from that put upon them by the later Hindu authorities, and reported by the European grammars which follow these rather than the language itself. I was careful to allow for this possibility in so flagrant a case, putting in the caveat "if the Hindu grammarians are reported rightly by their European pupils (which in this instance is hard to believe)"; it now appears that a part of the reproach is capable of being shifted from the shoulders of Pāṇini to those of his later interpreters. But only a part. Pāṇini uses in the first of his two rules one of his customary algebra-like signs, *iṇ*, which is ambiguous, signifying either simply the *i*- and *u*-vowels, or these together with the *r*- and *l*-vowels, the diphthongs, the semivowels, and *h*. But such an ambiguity is itself a palpable blot upon a system that claims to be so precise, and Pāṇini's successors are little to blame, comparatively, if they have chosen the wrong meaning. Then, further, it is and must be equally a matter of uncertainty whether this same *iṇ* is or is not to be carried over by implication from the first to the second rule; and this, again, is a characteristic and a pervading difficulty, running through Pāṇini's entire work, and, as I said in my former paper, involving "a condemnation of the whole mode of presentation of the system as a failure." What are the boasted terseness and exactness of the rules really worth, when in innumerable cases you cannot tell what they mean without first knowing what they ought to mean?—that is to say, when an acquaintance with the facts of the traditional language is necessary in order to the right interpretation of the grammar's *dictum* respecting them? The present is, at the best, a case where the interpreters have been too careless of the facts and the reasons of the facts.

But, whatever improved explanation we may apply to them, there is plenty left to object to in Pāṇini's rules. The 2d pl. precative middle is plainly declared to end in *ṣīḍhvam* or in *ṣīdhvam* according to what letters precede the ṣ (which might also be s); and this is senseless. If the ending is -*ṣīḍhvam*, it is so because the form is originally -*ṣī-ṣ-dhvam*, with the special precative sibilant between mode-sign and personal ending, as in 2d and 3d sing., -*ṣī-ṣ-thās* and -*ṣi-ṣ-ta*; if it is, on the other hand, -*ṣīdhvam*, this is because, as in 1st persons and 3d plur., no such sibilant is present, and the ending is originally -*ṣī-dhvam*; and no one can speak with certainty upon the point, because, as I have pointed out, not a single example of the form has been brought to light out of the literature, earlier or later (the probabilities are altogether in favor of *ṣī-ṣ-dhvam*, and so -*ṣīḍhvam*); but it is perfectly obvious that what precedes the -*ṣī*- has nothing to do with determining the matter, any more than with determining the presence or absence of the precative sibilant in the 2d and 3d singular. It is equally plain that in the indicative of the *iṣ*-aorist we must always have *ḍhvam* (which the known texts also always give), because -*iḍhvam* necessarily results from the combination -*iṣ-dhvam*, without any reference whatever to what may precede the -*iṣ*-; and the interpreters must regulate themselves accordingly, if they wish to save Pāṇini's credit. The author thinks he catches me in an error in saying, as concerns this point, that "all the quotable examples ... are opposed to their rule," and brings up against me *astoḍhvam* etc. out of my grammar. But this only shows how carelessly or how unintelligently he has read my paper; for it is distinctly allowed there that the rule as given applies correctly to the ṣ-aorist, and there is quoted the example *aneḍhvam* (from *aneṣ-dhvam*; by the way, this example and its like seem to show that *iṇ* in the rule requires to be taken in its wider sense): one of the striking things about the matter was that a prescription suiting well the one aorist had been wantonly extended to include the other, with which it had nothing to do, its application giving in every instance a different form from the theoretically correct one found occurring in the literature.

But Pāṇini undeniably takes the perfect also into his rule, making its 2d plur. ending to be *dhve* or *ḍhve* under the same conditions as those laid down for the aorists. The impropriety of the combination and identical treatment of the two tenses is clear. The aorist has always at the end of the stem a lingual sibilant —*aneṣ*-, *apaviṣ*- — to exercise its euphonic influence upon the *dh* of the ending, while in the perfect there is none such. That is to say, none unless the endings *dhve* and *dhvam* are really by origin *sdhve* and *sdhvam*; and this is a doctrine which has found, and perhaps still possesses, some adherents. But it has no foundation whatever in the actual phenomena of Sanskrit, but solely in these blundering rules of the native grammar. Examples of the 2d plur. perfect, indeed, are of exceeding rarity; I am able at present to point to only a single one (*dadhidhve*, occurring twice in RV.) in the older language. But, if we are to recognize *sdhve* in the perfect, we plainly ought to recognize *sdhve* and *sdhvam* also in the present (indic., impv., and opt.) and imperfect; and then we should not meet with forms like *studhvam, jānīdhvam, bhavedhvam, akṛṇudhvam*, but with *stuḍhvam* and so on. It appears, then, that the only way to save Pāṇini's reputation in the matter is to strike the syllable *liṭ* (meaning 'perfect') out of his rule, as ungenuine; and I would suggest that it was perhaps intruded by the same cunning hand that thrust into the *dhātupāṭha* more than a thousand false roots without being detected or deterred; this latter trick was evidently by far the harder to execute.

But Dr. Liebich finds two other defenses to make (both on p. 58). For one thing, we are not justified in asking for a reason why *dhvam* should in certain cases be converted into *ḍhvam*. "As if," he exclaims, "we were able in any language whatever to trace everywhere the connection of cause and effect!" Begging his pardon, I assert that, on the contrary, in the combinations of stem and ending in Sanskrit euphony, we do not meet with any effect of which we may not look for a cause with good expectation of finding it. If we came anywhere upon a *ḍhvam* without a discoverable reason, we should question its correctness, and hold it probable that some one had blundered, that the text-tradition was corrupt, or the like. On the other hand, if, as is actually the case, we have no *ḍhvam* for which we cannot show a perfectly good reason (few as, unfortunately, the instances are), and no *ḍhve* at all, and can put against this only the assertion of Pāṇini and his successors and interpreters that such forms ought to occur without any reason, I submit that the sole acceptable conclusion must be that these grammarians, like grammarians everywhere else, have blundered, and need to be corrected.

Our author's remaining plea is one that, it must be confessed, gives a tinge of the comic to the whole discussion. The difference, he points out, between *dh* and *ḍh* is very slight, and it might be unfair to expect Pāṇini in every case to distinguish the one correctly from the other! That is to say, if Pāṇini prescribes a *ḍh* where there is no ground for one, it may be simply the fault of his ear, which caught the sound wrong. Now I have been accused, by the author and others, of insinuating depreciatory things about Pāṇini, but I certainly never went so far as this. If the great grammarian had too dull an ear to distinguish a lingual mute accurately from a dental (like the typical, or mythical, German, who cannot tell *t* and *d* apart), what are all his teachings worth that involve phonetic distinctions? The staff is broken over Pāṇini, and by one of his own partizans.

To conclude (after passing without notice the other points made by me; the most important was the grammarians' derivation of the reduplicated aorist from the causative stem instead of from the root directly), Dr. Liebich takes up my criticism of the Pāṇinean classification of compounds, defending and extolling this classification; and he returns to the same subject, elaborating his view still further, in the introduction to another later publication. "Two chapters of the Kāśikā."[2] According to him, the true scientific principle of arrangement of compounds, which must be regarded as underlying Pāṇini's scheme, is furnished by syntactical subordination, after the following fashion: 1. In the copulative

[2] Zwei Kapitel der Kāśikā, Breslau, 1892, 8vo, pp. xl, 80.

compounds, as *devamanuṣyās* 'gods-and-men,' neither element is subordinated to the other, but both are coördinate; 2. in the determinatives, the former element is subordinated to the latter, either as a case dependent on it or as an adjective (or its equivalent) qualifying it: examples are *housetop*, *redbird*; 3. in the possessives, both are subordinated together to a word outside the compound, which they jointly qualify in the manner of an adjective: for example, *redhead*, i.e. redheaded, or possessing a red head; then, 4. there remains only one other possibility, namely that the second element should be subordinated to the first, as in *atimātram* 'beyond measure': we might give as English parallel *aboveboard* or *overboard* (also, for the other Hindu variety, consisting of a participle governing a following noun, the English *spendthrift* or *hategood*; of this variety our author makes no account, because it is Vedic, and unnoticed by Pāṇini). If, then, we are told, the subordinated element be represented by a *minus*-sign, and the other by a *plus*, we get thus the four combinations $+ +$, $- +$, $- -$, $+ -$; and these evidently exhaust all the possibilities of the case. Now this is in the real Pāṇinean style, and proves Dr. Liebich to possess a double portion of Pāṇini's spirit, if he be not the great grammarian himself in the latter's *n*th metempsychosis. Pāṇini would have been proud to adopt it into one of his chapters, together with its algebraic notation, so akin with his own. But our author has to confess that it is not Pāṇini's own scheme; it is only brought out fully and distinctly by a much later successor. Moreover, that Pāṇini's fourth class, the so-called *avyayībhāva* compounds, is by no means limited to examples of the formula *plus-minus*, but includes a number of quite heterogeneous formations. Dr. Liebich is nevertheless confident that he recognized the unique value of the scheme, and had it plainly in mind; only he sacrificed it, "perhaps with a heavy heart" (Kāśikā, p. ix), on the altar of—brevity! This brings to our notice, and in a strikingly illustrative manner, another of Pāṇini's leading characteristics and at the same time greatest weaknesses. The prime object aimed at by him (as in no small measure in the *sūtra*-style everywhere) is brevity, brevity at the cost of every other desirable thing—of theoretic truth, of connection, and, most of all, of intelligibility. The quality may be one that recommended his work to those who had to learn it by rote (though in its degree we have the right to question even that), but it is very much the opposite of a recommendation to us, and cannot but detract very seriously from our approval and admiration. And this especially when we see how capriciously the principle is applied—how many rules are squandered on details of the most trifling consequence, far below others that are omitted; on the quotation of other grammarians (the best way to confute whom was to leave them unnoticed); on the excerption (in more than 200 rules) of scattered particulars out of the Vedic language, which are valueless because they are merely specimens, making no pretense to completeness, while the motive of their selection is in many cases beyond the reach even of conjecture—and so on. If the grammar were sharply examined with reference only to this its leading motive, it would unquestionably be found to teem with matter for unfavorable criticism.

But there is another and more fundamental difficulty lying behind Pāṇini's oversight, or possible sacrifice, in not recognizing the fourth, the *plus-minus*, class of compounds in its true character, and thus rounding out a perfect scheme of classification, namely this: there is no such class; Dr. Liebich and his authorities, the later Hindu grammarians, are deceiving themselves with a false determination and notation; the *avyayībhāva* class, however composed, is not *plus-minus*, but *minus-minus*. By this is not meant that the component parts of such compounds do not stand in a *plus-minus* relation to one another; but so also do those of the ordinary possessives stand in a *minus-plus* relation; and if the possessive is nevertheless really a *minus-minus* compound, so is, for the same reason, the *avyayībhāva*. The copulative compound, composed of two (or more) nouns or adjectives, is itself noun or adjective accordingly, and is properly reckoned as *plus-plus*; the determinative is a noun or adjective with preceding limiting word, and it also is noun or adjective accordingly, and rightly *minus-plus*. It is different with the possessive, because, though this is not less a noun with a preceding limiting word, it has passed through a transformation making of it an adjective, which is to qualify something outside: *mahābāhu* when it means 'a great arm' is determinative or *minus-plus*; but when it means 'having a great arm' it is changed to *minus-minus*. If we represent the adjectivizing influence by *a*, we shall get the equation $(minus\text{-}plus)^{a} = minus\text{-}minus$, which is good linguistic mathematics; at any rate, it is only in such a way that the possessive comes to be a *minus-minus* compound. But precisely the same is true of the *avyayībhāva*. Taking, for example, the participial compound *ābharad-vasu* 'bringing wealth,' we find it made up of a governing word and its object-noun; but it is not therefore a noun; it has been transformed to an adjective; its accus. sing. and nom. plur. are not *ābharantaṃ-vasu* and *ābharanto-vasu*, but *ābharad-vasum* and *ābharad-vasavas*; it has undergone a similar transformation to that of *mahābāhu*, and it is *minus-minus*; for its formula is again $(plus\text{-}minus)^{a} = minus\text{-}minus$. But the proper *avyayībhāva* is not an adjective, but an adverb; the phrase *ati mātrām* 'beyond measure' becomes as a compound *atimātram* 'excessively.' Here is plainly involved a similar fusion and transfer to that already described; and, if we represent the adverb-making force by *b*, the proper formula for *atimātram* is $(plus\text{-}minus)^{b} = minus\text{-}minus$. But in real truth *atimātram* is still further from being a *plus-minus* compound; for to any one who considers the class historically it must be obvious that any such adverb is simply the neuter accusative of an adjective used adverbially, as neuter accusatives, among simple words and compounds of every kind, are wont to be used. For example, the first step from *ati mātrām* is the common adjective *atimātra* 'excessive,' of which the formula is $(plus\text{-}minus)^{a}$; then from this comes by another transfer the adverb, with the formula $((plus\text{-}minus)^{a})^{b}$, or, more briefly, $(plus\text{-}minus)^{ab}$; and, as the adjective was *minus-minus*, the adverb is doubly so. Whether this double transfer be accepted or not (of course the acceptance does not imply that some of the adverbs have not been made directly, by analogy with the others of more regular development), the asserted *plus-minus* class is irretrievably lost, and with it the mathematically exhaustive and regular classification of Sanskrit compounds. It has, indeed, never been found that the facts of language could be reasoned on mathematically; and, whenever the attempt so to treat them is made, we have the right to expect to detect a misapprehension, as in the present case. We may now decline to be touched by the spectacle of Pāṇini's "heavy heart," and hold, on the contrary, that Dr. Liebich has probably done him for a second time signal injustice, in believing him capable of being deceived by an alluring though false theory. The adjective compounds with governing prior member, whether this be preposition or participle, are sub-classes, with the possessives, of the great class of secondary adjective compounds, as I have located and described them in my grammar; and the *avyayībhāvas* are no class of compounds at all, but only a group in the long list of adjective neuter accusatives used adverbially.

It may be further mentioned, as a curiously characteristic point, that our author objects (Kāśikā, p. xi, note 2) to the name "possessive" as applied by Bopp and his successors to the "much-rice" (*bahuvrīhi*) compounds, because some of them admit of being fairly rendered otherwise than by 'having' or 'possessing,' and because the Sanskrit has no verb 'have,' and therefore Pāṇini would not have cast the sense into this form. Then also, it may be inferred, we are wrong to speak of the "possessive" suffixes *in* and *vant*, and to render *balin* and *balavant* by 'having strength,' or to call *madīya* 'my' a "possessive" pronominal adjective or *tasya* 'his' a "possessive" genitive. It may be pleaded in reply that, since we name them in our own language and not in Sanskrit, we have every right to cast their real and undeniable sense into the form of nomenclature that best suits our expression: and that the Hindus themselves put the idea of possession as well as they can into the definitions of these compounds by their familiar formula *yasya . . . sa tathoktaḥ*: they say, for example, "whose arms are great" in place of our "having great arms": and it really seems to amount to the same thing.

At the close of his chapter, Dr. Liebich, conceiving himself to have broken the force of all my objections to setting Pāṇini above the Sanskrit literature, and his grammatical science above ours, regrets that I have not brought forward a happier selection of them. I, on the other hand, think myself justified in maintaining that, as they all still stand in full vigor, they are a sufficient illustration and support of my contrary estimate of the native grammar. But I am willing to add another point, which he indeed almost forces upon my attention. At the very end, namely (p. 61), he lifts up hands of horror at me (as did Speijer, in his Sanskrit Syntax, p. 189, note) for daring to stigmatize as a barbarism something which Pāṇini expressly teaches (his alarm makes him see it as double, or worse than double, and he puts it in the plural, as a thing happening "occasionally"). He ought fairly to have quoted the case, instead of merely referring to the rule about it. It is this: Pāṇini teaches that a comparative and superlative adverbial ending may be added to a personal verb: thus, *dadāti* 'he gives,' *dadātitarām* 'he gives more,' *dadātitamām* 'he gives most.' This is precisely as if one were directed to say in Greek **διδωσιτερον** (in this case, even the suffix is identical) and **διδωσιτατον**. Now I maintain, and without any fear of successful contradiction, that such formations, no matter who authorizes them, are horrible barbarisms, offenses against the proprieties of universal Indo-European speech. The total absence of anything like them, or of anything suggesting even remotely the possibility of forming them, in the pre-Pāṇinean language (one might just as successfully seek for suggestions of **διδωσιτερον** in Homer or Plato), and their rarity later (no example of *-tamām* is ever met with), among writers to whom a rule of Pāṇini is as the oracle of a god, is enough to show that they never formed any proper part of the language. Probably they were jocose or slangy modes of expression (essentially *bhāṣā*, but far below the level of decent *bhāṣā*), which some strange freak, perhaps of amusement at their oddity (and Pāṇini was entitled to some compensation for the "heavy heart" which his subserviency to brevity often cost him), led him to sanction—if indeed the rule permitting them be not another interpolation by that mischief-maker who spoiled the list of roots.

Dr. Liebich complains of the (presumably disrespectful) references to "the native grammarians" which he finds too frequent in my Sanskrit grammar, and kindly advises me to cast them all out. But this is in the highest degree unreasonable. Considering the place which those grammarians have long occupied in the study of the language, and the influence allowed them by their European successors, and that their ways of viewing and presenting things have determined in large measure the form of universal Sanskrit grammar, it is simply impossible to leave them out of account and unmentioned. I am sure I have been as respectful to them as I possibly could, and probably in the majority of cases quite successfully—at least hypothetically respectful, stating their teaching for what it may be worth, and leaving to the future the final determination of its value. It was hardly respectful for him, on his part, to pronounce (in his closing sentence) all my references to them "extremely superficial and often inaccurate," without quoting a single instance to show that they really bear that character. Perhaps, if he had done so, he would have made as signal a failure of it as he has of the attempt to refute the views and reasonings of my former paper.

An extended review of Liebich's Pāṇini, by Dr. Franke, is found in the Gött. Gelehrte Anzeigen bearing date of Dec. 1, 1891 (pp. 951–83). It is, however, less a detailed examination and criticism of the former's views than an independent discussion of some of the points involved, carried on with much learning and acuteness. Many pages are expended upon Pāṇini's classification of the compounds; and here Dr. Franke is far from supporting Liebich's answer to my criticisms; on the contrary, he takes my side, setting forth the remarkable superficialities and incongruities of Pāṇini's work in this department, especially as regards the asserted class of *avyayībhāvas*; he makes many points of detail which I have passed without notice in the above discussion of the theoretic groundwork of the classification. Though dated in the following year, Liebich's Kāśikā, and its introduction were doubtless written before the appearance of this review; he would hardly have ventured to repeat his views, or would have cast them into a very different form, if he had had before his eyes their condemnation by a fellow-partizan of Pāṇini. In other points, Franke's notice of Liebich's work is mainly laudatory. Thus, he "thoroughly approves," as "very successful" (p. 962), the latter's futile pleadings as to the ending *ḍhvam* (including, I suppose, the suggestion of Pāṇini's dullness of ear), adding, as his own contribution to the controversy, that a *ḍh* not seldom takes the place of *dh* in Prākrit, and that Prakritic changes have been known to work their way into Sanskrit. But what has that to do with Pāṇini's definite prescription of *ḍh* in certain conditions which demonstrably have nothing to do with the matter? So in Prākrit, in obedience to the same general lingualizing tendency, *n* in the majority of cases becomes *ṇ*; but that would be far from supporting a Hindu grammarian who should teach that a *r* altered the next following *n* to *ṇ* only provided it were itself preceded by the sounds included in the designation *iṇ*. As for the great question of the 1200 false roots, Dr. Franke slips smoothly over it, merely echoing the other's remark, that it was an "unfortunate proceeding" on my part to commence from that quarter my attack upon the native grammar. Unfortunate, indeed; but evidently unfortunate only for the grammar: who could help starting from that most flagrant, wanton, and inexcusable of all its many weak sides?

It is hardly worth while to say much more than has been already said with regard to Liebich's Kāśikā. It is a laborious and useful contribution to the study of Pāṇini himself and of one of the most noted comments upon his work, smoothing a little the way to their comprehension for those who shall approach it hereafter. The author's method is a narrowly restricted one; the rule in Pāṇini is given, not translated, and then follows a bald recording of the Kāśikā's exposition, with here and there brief notes added on one and another point in the latter; from any attempt at an independent explanation, and yet more from any criticism, the author carefully refrains. Thus, of the rule which introduces the whole subject, *samarthaḥ padavidhiḥ*, the Kāśikā gives two entirely discordant interpretations, illustrating, however, only the latter of them—which is a very strong indication that the commentators were themselves uncertain as to what meaning really lay hidden in its obscurity; and the translator passes the matter without a word of remark, nor does it occur to him to state whether in his opinion we ought to understand 'a word-rule is competent,' or to force into the text with extreme violence the sense 'a word in the following rules is to be taken in connection with its sense': it is only an illustration of the ordinary principle that you must first find out what a rule of Pāṇini ought to signify, and must then, at whatever cost, interpret that signification into it. And the continuation is of a piece with the beginning. No one can well avoid being moved to repugnance by the fantastic obscurity with which the subject is presented; and we know already that the underlying theory, the scheme of distinctions and of classification, is a very defective one. To claim, then, that it must be all labored through by the general body of students of Sanskrit, in order that they may duly understand the subject of Sanskrit compounds, is obviously unreasonable, not to say absurd. Pāṇini and his chief commentators must be worked over by a small class of specialists, and not simply translated—that is a mere beginning of the task—but brought into such a form as to be readily understood and assimilated by the mass of scholars. The study is excessively difficult, and on many of the points involved in it certainly seems unattainable. Dr. Liebich confesses (p. i) that he found the rendering of these two little chapters so hard that he could scarcely keep his courage up to complete the task. Speijer has been a faithful student of the native grammar; but of the discussions and criticisms of points in it on which he occasionally ventures in his Sanskrit Syntax, Böhtlingk (in a review of the work in Z.D.M.G. XLI 179 ff.) claims to refute nearly every one; and now Liebich (Kāśikā, p. iv) declares Böhtlingk, in spite of his life-long familiarity with the subject and his immense erudition, to have translated Pāṇini sometimes incorrectly. Rather discouraging that for a student who is ambitious to get his knowledge of Sanskrit directly from native sources!

I would be far from saying anything to discourage the study of Pāṇini; it is highly important and extremely interesting, and might fairly absorb much more of the labor of the present generation than has been given to it. But I would have it followed in a different spirit and for a different purpose and in a different method. It should be thoroughly dissociated from the study of Sanskrit, though never without recognition of what it may finally contribute to our knowledge of Sanskrit in addition to what we derive from the literature. As to what the literature contains, we need no help from the native grammar; it is the residue of peculiar material that we shall value, and that we should strive to separate from the mass. And the study should be made a truly progressive one, part after part of the native system being worked out to the last possible degree and the results recorded, so that each generation be not compelled to begin anew the tedious and unrewarding task.

At the beginning of the introduction to his Kāśikā, it is true, Liebich makes the claim that all Sanskrit students need to master Pāṇini, if for no other reason, because the native commentaries cannot be otherwise completely understood, it being known that they abound more or less in references to the grammar and demonstrations founded upon it. There would be more in this consideration if the grammatical discussions were not precisely the most worthless part of the comments, which can be in all cases neglected with least fear of loss. What the words mean, what allusions they contain, what is to be supplied to complete the sense, which of possible constructions is the right one—these are matters in regard to which the aid of the commentator is more or less (in proportion, namely, to the artificiality of the composition) welcome, sometimes even indispensable; but for the grammatical forms, the derivations, and everything else that Pāṇini can be quoted for, the case is different. As for Sāyaṇa and his kind, even those who make the strongest claims in his favor will hardly venture to deny that the whole grammatical part of his exposition might be expunged from his text without loss of a jot or tittle of its value.

It may be added that Dr. Franke also, in the first paragraphs of his review of Liebich briefly examined above, shows the same disposition to exaggerate and misrepresent the claims of Pāṇini to attention. He quotes once more, as Liebich had done before him, Lassen's unworthy insinuation that Bopp's growing independence of Pāṇini was owing to his ignorance of him! As if Bopp did not know Pāṇini, both at first hand and in his European representatives, sufficiently to judge with full competence what his system was worth, and how far it required to be followed! There is quite too much of Pāṇini left still in Bopp's grammar; yet to Bopp belongs the high credit of making the recorded facts of the language for the first time the basis of their orderly presentation, and of bringing the principles of European grammatical science, and those of a new and developing comparative grammar, to bear upon Sanskrit. It is owing to this that he became the real Sanskrit teacher to Europe, in a manner and degree far beyond the reach of Lassen. Dr. Franke then goes on to vindicate for Pāṇini various things to which he has not the shadow of a just title: as, 1. that not only for Sanskrit, but also for other Aryan dialects and writings, Pāṇini is of indispensable importance—which apparently means nothing more than that some of the phenomena of dialects later than Sanskrit are to be found noted in his grammar; 2. that the study of his rules has a formally educating influence—which is, I think, just the opposite of the truth, since their method is purely mechanical, sacrificing everything else to brevity, ignoring connection and proportion, lacking all recognition of the historical element, and therefore necessarily destitute of philosophy (we have seen above that too much Pāṇini has led Dr. Liebich to doubt the relation of cause and effect in Sanskrit euphony); 3. that it is

Pāṇini who has taught us to regard every word, every ending, even every letter as important—which is an accusation laid without any reason whatever against western grammatical science; and 4. that Pāṇini is going to aid literary chronology in a way that is hitherto for the most part only a matter of conjecture and of future hope—and which therefore, we may answer, it is as yet too early to say anything about; but, if there are such treasures hid in Pāṇini, why do not his partizans devote themselves to bringing them forth, instead of dwelling upon subjects which are far better understood out of the literature itself?

Just forty years ago, a German student of more than ordinary ability, in company with whom I had worked for a season under a professor of the highest eminence in Germany, took the degree of doctor of philosophy creditably with a dissertation on one of Kālidāsa's plays, and went to England for further study and for employment. He was fortified, among other things, with a letter of introduction to a Sanskrit scholar of German birth, then long resident in London. This scholar, on being consulted in regard to plans and pursuits, told him that all his hitherto acquired knowledge had no real foundation, and was essentially worthless; that, if he wished to accomplish anything, he must drop all besides and devote himself for two or three years exclusively to the study of Pāṇini; when that had been done it would be time to talk of something else. Just how much this rebuff had to do with turning my friend's attention away to other studies I do not know; but, at any rate, until his death some years after he was not heard of further in Sanskrit.

Such was, doubtless in its most intense form, the spirit of the devotees of the native Hindu grammar a generation ago. And, though it has been in some measure subdued since, it is by no means extinct, when a man of real learning and ability like Dr. Franke can still maintain (in his Casuslehre, etc., noticed above, p. 68, or p. 6 of the reprint) that our profounder knowledge of Sanskrit is to be especially proportioned to our deeper penetration into Pāṇini's teachings—against which is to be set, as antidote, the same author's exposure of Pāṇini's failure in the article of compounds. It is, of course, much to the credit of Pāṇini that he exercises such a bewildering fascination over the minds of those who involve themselves in the labyrinth of his rules—though the influence admits, I believe, of a natural explanation. I am fully persuaded that any one who should master the Hindu grammatical science without losing his head, who should become thoroughly familiar with Pāṇini and escape being Pāṇini-bitten, would be able to make exposures of the weaknesses and shortcomings and needless obscurities of the grammar on a scale hitherto unknown.

14

Otto Boehtlingk (1815–1904)

Otto Boehtlingk, the editor and translator of the *Aṣṭādhyāyī* and of Vopadeva's *Mugdhabodha*, and also the first Western linguist who applied Pāṇinian techniques in the linguistic description of another language (in his *Über die Sprache der Jakuten* of 1851), contributed to this discussion too. His article "Whitney's letzte Angriffe auf Pāṇini" deals with Pāṇini's *kāraka*-theory, the roots of the Dhātupāṭha, nominal composition, and other topics. This paper is reproduced from the *Berichte über die Verhandlungen der königlich sächsischen Gesellschaft der Wissenschaften zu Leipzig, Philologisch-Historische Classe* 45, 1893, 247–257.

The Dhātupāṭha was later the subject of special studies by Liebich (for example, Liebich 1919–1920, 1921, 1930). Nominal composition, which figures so prominently in these discussions, has of course been widely studied; for recent investigations cf. Harweg (1964), and Staal (1966a). The *kāraka* theory has only recently again received much attention (Rocher, 1964a, 1964b; Cardona; 1967; Kiparsky-Staal, 1969).

Whitney's letzte Angriffe auf Pāṇini (1893)

Otto Boehtlingk

Vor Kurzem erschien im American Journal of Philology, Vol. XIV, No. 2, S. 171–197 ein Artikel von Whitney, betitelt »On recent studies in Hindu Grammar«, der die grammatischen Schriften Bruno Liebich's und R. Otto Franke's kritisirt und bei dieser Gelegenheit auf die Schwächen von Pāṇini zu sprechen kommt. Als alter Freund und Bewunderer Pāṇini's halte ich mich für berechtigt und einigermaassen verpflichtet, zu seiner Vertheidigung die Feder zu ergreifen. Ob in diesem Versuche meine Vorliebe für Pāṇini oder Whitney's Groll auf ihn mehr zu Tage tritt, mag der geneigte Leser entscheiden.

S. 171 fg. heisst es: »Pāṇini does not take up the cases as forms of nouns, setting forth the various uses of each, after our manner; he adopts the vastly more difficult and dangerous method of establishing a theoretical list of modes of verb-modification by case, or of ideal case-relations (he calls them *kāraka*, 'factor' or 'adjunct'), to which he then distributes the cases. Almost as a matter of course, however, his case-relations or *kāraka* are not an independent product of his logical faculty, but simply a reflection of the case-forms; they are of the same number as the latter, and each corresponds to the general sphere of a case: they are *kartar* ('actor' = nominative), *karman* ('act' = accusative), *sampradāna* ('delivery' = dative), *karaṇa* ('instrument' = instrumental), *adhikaraṇa* ('sphere' = locative), and *apādāna* ('removal' = ablative). »Wenn man nicht wüsste, was *kāraka* bei P. bedeutet, würde man aus Whitney's beinahe mystischer Definition desselben sich schwerlich eine Vorstellung davon machen können. *Kāraka* ist nicht jede »case-relation«, sondern nur die Beziehung eines Nomens zu einem Verbum, und nicht jedem Casus entspricht, wie Whitney behauptet, eine ihm besonders zukommende Beziehung zu einem Verbum: der Genetiv geht hierbei leer aus, was auch Wh. nachträglich bemerkt. Auch ist Wh. im Irrthum, wenn er den *kartar* dem nominativ gleichsetzt. Das grammatische Subject kennt ja P. bekanntlich nicht, sondern nur das logische und dieses lässt er nur im Instrumental und Genetiv (subjectiven Genetiv) auftreten. Im Nominativ kann, wie auch Wh. erwähnt, sowohl der *kartar* (wenn die Personalendung diesen ausdrückt, d. i. beim Activum), als auch das *karman* (wenn das Verbum finitum dieses ausdrückt, d. i. beim Passivum) erscheinen. Mit dieser *kāraka*-Theorie, die schwierig und gefährlich genannt wird, ist Wh. nicht einverstanden. Die Schwierigkeit und Gefährlichkeit derselben hat aber den kühnen, originellen und genialen P. nicht abgeschreckt. Er hat den Versuch gemacht, und dass dieser ihm gelungen ist, werde ich in der Folge an einem Casusbegriff, am Object, klar zu machen versuchen. Dass P. auf diese Kategorien durch die Casus hingeleitet wurde, versteht sich allerdings von selbst; die Aufstellung logischer Kategorien, denen in der Sprache kein Casus entspräche, wäre ein ganz unnützes Bemühen gewesen. Es freut mich zu sehen, dass auch Delbrück, dem doch Niemand eine Voreingenommenheit für Pāṇini nachsagen oder Schärfe des Verstandes absprechen wird, in seiner so eben erschienenen Vergleichenden Syntax der indogermanischen Sprachen, Th. 1, S. 172 fgg., Pāṇini's Definitionen der Grundbegriffe der Casus seinen Lesern mitzutheilen für gut findet und ihnen seine Anerkennung nicht vorenthält. So heisst es S. 172: »An dieser Stelle glaube ich die Sache am besten zu fördern, wenn ich von den Aufstellungen der indischen Grammatik ausgehe, welche sich durch die Schärfe der Fassung vortheilhaft von demjenigen unterscheiden, was in unserer europäischen Tradition Gestalt gewonnen hat«, und S. 175: »Indem Pāṇini so den Begriff, nicht die Kasus zum Eintheilungsgrund macht, erreicht er den Zweck seiner Darstellung in höchst vollkommener Weise«.

Auf S. 172 hält Whitney ein strenges Gericht über die Definition des *karman*, des Objects. »As for the definitions of the case-relations, it may suffice to say that the *karman* is described as belonging, first, to that which the actor in his action especially desires to obtain or attain (as in 'he makes a *mat*', 'he goes to the *village*'); or, second, to that which, though itself undesired or indifferent, is connected with the action in a similar manner. Anything more crude or unphilosophical than this could not well be imagined. There is not an identity between the use of a given case and the presence of its generally corresponding case-relation, because, for example, in a passive sentence, as 'the mat is made by him', *mat* is still called *karman* or 'act', though nominative, and *him* still *kartar* or 'actor' though instrumental. Thus there is no recognition of the grammatical category of subject of a verb; and this leads, as could not be helped, to numerous obscurities and difficulties.« Ich gestehe, dass dieses ungerechte und in so schroffer Form ausgesprochene Urtheil mich geradezu verblüfft hat. Was hat nun Pāṇini in Wirklichkeit verbrochen? Er ist nicht wie unsere Grammatiker von den Casus ausgegangen, sondern von den Casusbegriffen, und hat das Object auf eine originelle und scharfsinnige Weise zu definiren versucht. Nach dieser Definition musste er in einem Satze wie *tena kaṭaḥ kriyate* den Nominativ *kaṭaḥ* Object und den Instrumental *tena* Agens benennen, und jeder Unbefangene wird zugeben müssen, dass *kaṭah* in Wirklichkeit ein logisches Object und *tena* ein logisches Subject ist. Dafür, dass das logische Object nicht in den Accusativ, und das logische Subject nicht in den Nominativ gesetzt wurde, sorgte Sūtra 2, 3, 1, und dafür, dass das logische Object im Nominativ erschien, 2, 3, 40. Zu diesem letzten Sūtra vgl. ZDMG. 41, S. 179 fg. Ich sehe also keine »numerous obscurities and difficulties«.

Nun will ich versuchen darzuthun, dass der Gedanke, vom Object und nicht vom Accusativ auszugehen, ein überaus berechtigter und geradezu nothwendiger war. In Whitney's Gr.[2] § 269 lesen wir: »The accusative is especially the case of the direct object of a transitive verb.« Dieses verstehen wir Alle, weil wir schon als Schulknaben aus einer lateinischen oder einer anderen Grammatik gelernt haben, was ein Object und was ein transitives Verbum ist. Wenn aber Pāṇini etwa gesagt hätte: *dvitīyā nediṣṭhaṃ* (oder *īpsitatamaṃ*) *karma sakarmakasya dhātor ācaṣṭe*, so würde ihn Niemand verstanden haben, da es keine Grammatik für Schulknaben gab, aus der man die Bedeutungen von *karman* und *sakarmako dhātuḥ* hätte ersehen können. Pāṇini war also genöthigt, zunächst den Grundbegriff eines zu einem Verbum in Beziehung stehenden Accusativs, das *karman*, zu definiren. Der Accusativ spielt unter den obliquen Casus die Hauptrolle; daher wurde sein Grundbegriff zuerst bestimmt. Nun mussten consequenter Weise auch die übrigen Beziehungen eines Nomens zu einem Verbum erörtert verden. Dass Pāṇini den Nominativ *prathamā* benannte, berechtigt uns wohl zu dem Schlusse, dass er auch ein Verständniss für die Wichtigkeit des grammatischen Subjects hatte. Wenn Whitney in der oben aus seiner Grammatik citirten Stelle nach »verb« noch hinzufügt: »and of any word qualifying that object, as attribute or apposition or objective predicate«, so ist dieses ein recht müssiger Zusatz, da die Congruenz eines Attributes u.s.w. auch bei anderen Accusativen und den übrigen Casus stattfindet. Solche Schwächen wird man bei Pāṇini nicht finden.

Sehr schlecht zu sprechen ist Wh. auf den Dhātupāṭha und gewiss mit einigem Recht, da hier Manches verdächtig ist. Wh. übertreibt aber die Sache ein wenig. S. 183 sagt er, dass über 2000 Wurzeln aufgezählt würden, von denen nach S. 182 800 bis 900, nach S. 183 aber »not far from nine hundred« echt seien. Die Zahl der untergeschobenen Wurzeln soll nach S. 183 zwölfhundert betragen. Nach meiner Zählung enthalten die zehn Klassen 1959 (also beinahe 2000) Wurzeln; wenn man aber die vollkommen gleichlautenden, in verschiedene Klassen und gruppen vertheilten Wurzeln einfach zählt, so erhalten wir ungefähr 1770. Von diesen wird aber noch eine bedeutende Anzahl auszuscheiden sein, da die offenbar nur orthographisch von einander abweichenden Wurzeln (wie *laḍ* und *lal*) und die nur durch Hinzufügung eines Nasals sich unterscheidenden (wie *ac* und *añc*) bei meiner Zählung als verschiedene Wurzeln figuriren. Hierzu kommt noch eine Anzahl von Denominativen (wie *kumār*), die Wh. bei seiner Zählung der echten Wurzeln wahrscheinlich ausgeschieden haben wird. Die Hunderte von verdächtigen Wurzeln werden theils Abschreiber, theils Erklärer schlechter Texte zu verantworten haben. Hat doch auch der gewissenhafte und kritische Wh. in seinem Wurzelverzeichnisse neue, höchst verdächtige Wurzel- und Verbalformen verzeichnet; vgl. ZDMG. 39, 532 fgg. Auch würde man, wenn man sich einige Mühe geben wollte, eine nicht geringe Anzahl sogenannter Wurzeln (wie z. B. *kusm*) auf ihren Ursprung zurückzuführen vermögen und ihnen vom indischen Standpunkte eine berechtigte Existenz zuschreiben müssen. An, so zu sagen, aus den Fingern gesogene Wurzeln glaube ich nicht. Wozu sollte das geschehen sein? Etwa um mit dem Reichthum der Sprache gross zu thun?

Liebich hatte die Ansicht Whitney's, dass *prayoktā́se* TS. 2, 6, 2, 3 die erste Person sei, bekämpft und darauf hingewiesen, dass die von Pāṇini gelehrte Form auf *-tā́he* im Taitt. Ār. vorkomme, was übrigens auch Wh. nicht entgangen war. Hierauf antwortet Wh. S. 184: »The author's well-intended correction of my estimate of *prayoktā́se* in TS. 2, 6, 2, 3 as 1st sing. I do not find myself able to accept. The sentence is not, perhaps, absolutely clear; but the presence in it of a *te* 'for thee' is to me a tolerably certain indication that the verb is not 2d sing. ('I will employ tomorrow for thee at the sacrifice', or 'at thy sacrifice'); no such possessive would be called for (or admissible, I think) if the person were second. And *-tāse* is obviously the true middle analogue to active-*tāsmi*, as *śā́se* to *śā́smi* and the like; while *-tāhe*, as given by the grammarians, is absolutely anomalous, being unsupported, so far as I know, by a single other phonetic fact of the language. That it occurs once (but only once) in the literature, in that very late Vedic document the Taitt. Āraṇyaka, whose text is in many parts extremely faulty, is beyond question; but I would put forward the suggestion, as by no means an impossible one, that the form is corrupt, and that the 1st sing. *-tāhe* of the grammarians is founded solely on it. That the native commentary, it may be added, explains *prayoktā́se* in TS. as 2d sing. is not of the smallest particle of importance; an expositor schooled in Pāṇini would of course do that, and is capable of doing it against the most incontrovertible evidence to the contrary.« Whitney hat hier und auch schon früher auf eine scharfsinnige und überzeugende Weise dargethan, dass *prayoktā́se* eine 1. Sg. sein könne. Aber vom sein Können bis zum Sein ist noch ein weiter Sprung. In der Stelle, welche Wh. für seine Ansicht geltend macht, könnte, wenn nicht die Grammatik dagegen Einsprache erhöbe, *prayoktā́se* eine 1. Sg. sein, braucht es aber nicht zu sein und ist es auch nicht. Dass der Commentar die Form als 2. Sg. deutet, hat auch in meinen Augen kein Gewicht, wohl aber der Umstand, dass er bei seiner Auffassung an *te*, das er durch *tvadīye* umschreibt, keinen Anstoss nimmt, da dieses nicht an das grammatische, sondern an das reale Gebiet streift. Der Opferer und der Anwender einer bestimmten Formel können, brauchen aber wohl nicht verschiedene Personen zu sein. Wenn demnach *te* fehlte, würde man nicht wissen, von wem das Opfer veranstaltet würde; mit anderen Worten: *te* ist nicht pleonastisch. Wenn aber Wh. meinen sollte, dass in einem solchen Falle nicht *te*, sondern *svasmin* stehen müsste, so hätte ich weder für noch gegen seine Behauptung etwas Entschiedendes vorzubringen. Nach meinem Gefühl sind beide Ausdrucksweisen zulässig. In Delbrück's Altindischer Syntax finde ich S. 208 Folgendes: »In P. wird, so viel ich sehe, *svā* ebenso gebraucht wie in V. Es bezieht sich natürlich in der Mehrzahl der Fälle auf dritte Personen, für eine Beziehung auf eine zweite Person habe ich (wohl zufällig) keinen Beleg notirt.« Da *prayoktáse* an und für sich nach den indischen Grammatikern und nach Wh. auch 2. Person ist, und da Wh. selbst, wie aus seinen oben angeführten Worten zu ersehen ist, nicht mit absoluter Gewissheit behauptet und behaupten kann, dass die Form in TS. die erste Person sein müsse; so ergäbe sich, wenn man seiner, ihm sehr wahrscheinlich erscheinenden Erklärung beistimmte, dass der in Frage stehende Satz sowohl »ich werde bei deinem Opfer — anwenden«, als auch »du wirst bei deinem Opfer—anwenden« bedeuten könnte. Ist dieses wohl wahrscheinlich?

Nun komme ich auf die von Pāṇini gelehrte, von Wh. aber mit aller Entschiedenheit zurückgewiesene Form *-táhe* für die 1. Person zu sprechen. Diese komme, wie er angibt, nur einmal in dem schlecht überlieferten Taitt. Ār. vor und sei falsch, und auf dieser falschen Form im Taitt. Ār. beruhe Pāṇini's *-táhe*. Damit ist implicite ausgesprochen, dass Pāṇini und auch seine Vorgänger nie in den Fall gekommen wären, in ihren täglichen Gesprächen und Disputationen mit Ihresgleichen die 1. Sg. Med. des periphrastischen Futurum anzuwenden. Credat Judaeus Apella! Hätten sie aber eine von der überlieferten verschiedene Form für die 1. Person gehabt, so würde Pāṇini, da er sie doch nicht durch einen Machtspruch aus der Welt hätte schaffen können, sie uns mitgetheilt und die im T. Ā. entdeckte neue Form als vedische erwähnt haben. Nach meinem Dafürhalten müssen wir der Form schon ihres absonderlichen, unserer Deutung sich entziehenden, aber keineswegs deshalb verdächtigen *h* wegen ein hohes Alter zuschreiben. Vielleicht, aber auch nur vielleicht, steht *he* zu *svahe* des Duals und *svahe* des Plurals in näherer Beziehung. Die 1. und 2. Person durften nicht zusammenfallen.

S. 184 fgg. erhebt Wh. eine neue Anklage gegen P. und zwar wegen des Sūtra 8, 3, 78 fg., wo von der Cerebralisirung des *dh* in den Personalendungen *dhvam* und *dhve* die Rede ist. Ich gebe gern zu, dass P. sich hier undeutlich ausdrückt, und dass für die Cerebralisirung im Perfect sich kein Grund nachweisen lässt, dass sie wissenschaftlich nicht haltbar ist. Muss aber dafür gerade P. verantwortlich gemacht werden? Ist es nicht denkbar, dass P. einen in der Sprache eingerissenen Fehler, den er nicht erkannte, wohl auch nicht so leicht wie Wh. erkennen konnte, einfach verzeichnet hätte? Es giebt doch in allen Sprachen falsche Schreibarten, die sich leicht ausmerzen liessen und doch nicht ausgemerzt werden. Schreibt doch auch Wh. *author*, obgleich er ganz gewiss weiss, dass das *h* hier keine Berechtigung hat; ob er auch *posthumous* schreibt, wage ich nicht zu behaupten, wohl aber, dass angesehene Lexicoraphen dieses thun.

Ueber alle Maassen ungehalten wird Wh. S. 192 darüber, dass P. lehrt, die adverbialen Suffixe *tarām* und *tamām* würden auch an ein Verbum finitum gefügt. »This is precisely as if one were directed to say in Greek διδωσιτερον (in this case, even the suffix is identical) and διδωσιτατον«. Ist dieses etwa ein Argument gegen P.? Ist nicht jedes Glied einer Sprachfamilie erst dadurch zu einer besonderen Sprache geworden, dass es sich selbständig und eigenthümlich veränderte und entwickelte? Wh. fährt fort: »Now I maintain, and without any fear of successful contradiction (schreckt mich nicht ab), that such formations, no matter who authorizes them, are horrible barbarisms, offenses against the proprieties of universal Indo-European speech.« Ist nicht jede Analogiebildung von Hause aus ein Barbarismus, der aber als solcher nicht empfunden wird, sonst würde er nicht Wurzel fassen können? Den Barbarismus entdecken nachträglich die Sprache kritisirende Gelehrte, die aber zum Glück bei der Bildung und Vervollkommnung einer Sprache nicht mitzusprechen haben. Kann man sich wohl ärgere Barbarismen denken als пятеро, шестеро u.s.w., wo ер als Theil des Suffixes auftritt, während es in Wirklichkeit aus dem vorangehenden четверо herübergenommen ist, wo es zum Stamme des Zahlworts gehört? An diesen Bildungen hat jedoch kein Russe bis zum heutigen Tage Anstoss genommen. Weiter heisst es bei Wh.: »The total absence of anything like them, or of anything suggesting even remotely the possibility of forming them, in the pre-Pāṇinean language (one might just as successfully seek for suggestions of διδωσιτερον in Homer or Plato), and their rarity later (no example of *-tamām* is ever met with), among writers to whom a rule of Pāṇini is as the oracle of a god, is enough to show that they never formed any proper part of the language. Probably they were jocose or slangy modes of expression (essentially *bhāṣā*, but far below the level of decent *bhāṣā*), which some strange freak, perhaps of amusement at their oddity (and Pāṇini was entitled to some compensation for the heavy »heavy heart«[1]) which his subserviency to brevity often cost him), led him to sanction—if indeed the rule permitting them be not another interpolation by that mischief-maker who spoiled the list of roots.« Ich spreche Whitney jede Berechtigung ab, sich über gut beglaubigte Erscheinungen, die er sich recht zu erklären vermag, mit solcher Geringschätzung auszusprechen und ihre Existenz sogar in Frage zu stellen, oder sie höchstens in der niedrigen Sprache gelten zu lassen. Weiss Wh. überhaupt von der Bhāṣā mehr, als er durch Pāṇini erfährt, und mit welchem Recht hat er vor dieser so wenig Achtung? Wenn sogar Schriftsteller nach Pāṇini, die doch eine von ihm gegebene Regel, wie Wh. sich ausdrückt, als das Orakel eines Gottes betrachteten, sich der in Rede stehenden Steigerung so selten bedienen, so kann daraus zunächst nur geschlossen werden, dass sich in ihren Schriften keine Gelegenheit dazu bot, nicht aber, dass dieselbe niemals »any proper part of the language« gebildet hätte. Vielleicht (aber auch nur vielleicht) waren auch P. keine Formen auf *tarām* und *tamām* in der Literatur bekannt, wird er aber nicht, wie ich schon oben bei einer anderen Gelegenheit bemerkte, in Gesprächen und Disputationen Gelegenheit gehabt haben, sich in der von Wh. gerügten Weise auszudrücken? Wohl zum grossen Entsetzen Whitney's wage ich sogar zu behaupten,

[1] Ein von Liebich gebrauchter Ausdruck.

dass die so heftig angefochtene Steigerung eines Verbi finiti gar kein arger Barbarismus ist. Die vollwichtigen, leicht anfügbaren und leicht ablösbaren Adverbialsuffixe *tarām* und *tamām* empfand der Inder beinahe als selbständige Wörter, die er an fertige Indeclinabilia anzufügen gewohnt war; vgl. *atitarā́m, abhitarā́m, jyoktamā́m, natarā́m, natamā́m, nitarā́m, pratarā́m, pratamā́m, vitarā́m, saṃtarā́m, sutarā́m, uccaistarām, uccaistamām, nīcaistarām*. Ist der Sprung von diesen Adverbien zu *pacatitarām* u.s.w. etwa gar zu kühn? Zu Gunsten meiner Ansicht kann ich auch hier den besonnenen und nie sich überhebenden Delbrück anführen; vgl. Vergleichende Syntax der indogermanischen Sprachen, Th. 1, S. 624, N. Was würde Wh. erst zu den russischen **На-те** da habt ihr! und **Ну-те** macht endlich fort! sagen? Hier ist eine Personalendung mit einer Interjection verbunden worden! Ich möchte die Bezeichnung Barbarismus auf solche Formen beschränken, die den allgemeinen Gesetzen der Grammatik widersprechen, nur in schlecht überlieferten Texten vorkommen und von keinem alten Grammatiker erwähnt werden.

S. 187–191 finden wir eine recht unerquickliche Polemik gegen Liebich's und der indischen Grammatiker Theorie der Composita, auf die ich nicht näher eingehe. Pāṇini's Dvigu und Avyayībhāva, auf die Wh. bekanntlich nicht gut zu sprechen ist, werden hier nicht wieder berührt; es sei mir aber gestattet, dieselben bei dieser Gelegenheit zur Sprache zu bringen und die Auffassung derselben bei Pāṇini und Whitney zu vergleichen. Sehen wir uns §§ 1311–1314 der Whitney'schen Gr. an, so finden wir die, zu den zwei oben genannten Compositis gehörigen Beispiele zusammengestellt und zwar in zwei Abschnitten, von denen der eine »Adjective Compounds as Nouns and as Adverbs«, der andere »Anomalous Compounds« überschrieben ist. Also auch wie bei Pāṇini von den übrigen Compositis geschieden, aber theilweise auch auf Composita ausgedehnt, die Pāṇini nicht dazu rechnet. Während bei P. der Dvigu auf das Genaueste definirt und umgrenzt wird, erblicken wir bei Wh. in § 1312 eine sehr mangelhafte Definition desselben, und doch soll es der Dvigu Pāṇini's sein. P. lehrt, dass der Dvigu ein Karmadhāraya sei und als Substantiv und Adjectiv erscheine, als Substantiv n. oder f. (*ī*) Sg. in der Bedeutung eines Collectivs, als Adjectiv nicht in der Bedeutung eines Bahuvrīhi (also *trimūrdhan* »dreiköpfig« und ähnliche Composita keine Dvigu), sondern in den verschiedensten Bedeutungen, die sonst nur durch Anfügung von taddhita's erzielt werden. Dieses ist zwar nicht wissenschaftlich ausgedrückt, besagt aber doch das, was wir wissen sollen. Hören wir nun, was Wh. in seiner Gr. vorträgt. § 1311, der beide Arten von Compositis charakterisirt, lautet: »Compound adjectives, like simple ones, are freely used substantively as abstracts and collectives, especially in the neuter, less often in the feminine; and they are also much used adverbially especially in the accusative neuter.« Ich kann mich auf kein Adjectiv besinnen, das als Neutrum zu einem Nom. abstr. geworden wäre. Die neutralen Participia auf *ta*, wie *hasitam*, werden wohl anders zu beurtheilen sein: diese stehen zu dem impersonal gebrauchten Verbum fin. in näherer Beziehung. Wenn Wh. aus substantivirten neutralen Adjectiven Collectiva entstehen lässt, so identificirt er Gattungsbegriffe mit Collectiven. Das neutrale Adjectiv kann als Substantiv, ebenso wie jedes andere Substantiv als Gattungsbegriff verwendet werden, ist aber darum kein eigentliches Collectiv. Ein grammatisches Collectiv entsteht, wenn zwei oder mehr Dinge begrifflich und sprachlich als Einheit zusammengefasst werden, und ein solches Collectiv wird im folgenden § behandelt. Dieser lautet: »The substantively used compounds having a numeral as prior member, along with, in part (was soll sich der Leser dabei denken?), the adjective compounds themselves, are treated by the Hindus as a separate class, called *dvigu*.« *triyugá*, *triyojaná*, *tridivá*, *trilokī*, *trimūlī* sollen also substantivirte Adjectiva sein! Ich möchte gern wissen, welcher Sanskritist sich mit dieser Auffassung einverstanden erklären möchte. Whitney hat den Pāṇini verbessern wollen, hat ihn aber in Wirklichkeit verballhornt. In § 1313 wird der Avyayībhāva behandelt. Auch hier ist die Zurückführung des Adverbs auf ein Adjectiv ein wenig gewagt, da ein solches bei den von P. gelehrten Avyayībhāva gar nicht nachzuweisen ist.

Whitney hat sich bei der Bewältigung des schwierigen Kapitels der Composita grosse Mühe gegeben und Manches, aber nicht Alles, richtiger untergebracht; es leidet aber seine Darstellung an unnützen Wiederholungen und an Erwähnungen und Definitionen eines Compositums an einem ganz falschen Orte. So ist in Chapter V, das von der Declination der Nomina und Adjectiva handelt, die in § 323 fg. gegebene Definition zweier Arten von adjectivischen Compositis gar nicht am Platze. Diese brauchten überhaupt nicht erwähnt zu werden, da es bei der Declination gar nicht darauf ankommt, ob ein Adjectiv einfach oder zusammengesetzt ist. In § 1294, b werden die adjectivischen Dvigu unter den Bahuvrīhi eingereiht; wozu brauchten sie noch einmal § 1312, b erwähnt zu werden? Die Collectiva hätte Wh. unter seine »Descriptive Compounds«[2] unterbringen können, Hier hätte er auch erwähnen können, was Pāṇini lehrt, aber sich nicht von selbst versteht, dass Composita wie *triyojanāni* und *trilokāḥ* nicht gestattet seien, sondern nur *triyojanam* und *trilokī*, oder nicht componirt *trīṇi yojanāni* und *trayo lokāḥ*. Das fehlerhafte *daśavarṣasahasrāṇi* trifft man bisweilen an. In § 1313, d sind *yathākārīn* und *yathācārín* an einen unrechten Ort gekommen, da sie mit *yáthākāma* und *yátkākratu* nur das mit einander gemein haben, dass sie auch mit *yáthā* beginnen.

Man kritisire Pāṇini, aber auf eine gerechte und urbane Weise. Man verliere indessen nie aus dem Auge, dass dieser geniale Mann bei der Abfassung seiner Grammatik gar kein anderes Ziel verfolgte, als seinen Standesgenossen das Verständniss der ihm bekannten Literatur zu erleichtern und sie zu lehren, wie man in gebildeter Gesellschaft zu reden (darauf hätte Wh. mehr achten sollen) und mustergültige Werke abzufassen habe. Diesen Zweck konnte er bei der in Indien herrschenden Methode des Unterrichts nicht anders erreichen, als dass er ihnen ein zum Auswendiglernen geeignetes möglichst kurzes Lehrbuch bearbeitete. Aber er hat auch mehr erreicht: ohne ihn wären unsere Grammatiker[3] und Sprachvergleicher gewiss noch nicht da angelangt, wo wir sie heut zu Tage finden. Also Ehre seinem Andenken!

[2] Der indische terminus technicus *karmadhāraya* ist, so viel ich weiss, bisher noch nicht erklärt worden. Ich vermuthe, dass das Wort »ein Object schuldend« d. i. »kein Object aufzuweisen habend« bedeutet, und dass Pāṇini damit habe sagen wollen, Composita wie *kṛtakarman*, die hier und da wohl als Karmadhāraya vorkommen, seien nach seiner Meinung nur als Bahuvrīhi zu verwenden.

[3] Hätten, um nur einen Fall zu erwähnen, unsere Grammatiker den Compositis wohl eine solche Aufmerksamkeit geschenkt, wenn ihnen nicht Pāṇini den Weg dazu geweisen hätte?

15

Georg Bühler (1837–1898)

Georg Bühler, a pupil of Benfey's, was no expert on the Sanskrit grammarians, but he contributed to many branches of Indology and, in particular, to the study of Pāli and Prākrit. He refuted Whitney with arguments of a different kind, showing that many of the roots of the *Dhātupāṭha*, though not found in extant Sanskrit literature, had to be postulated anyway in order to account for Pāli and Prākrit roots derived from them. Since many of Bühler's brilliant demonstrations would take us far beyond the scope of the present volume, only some fragments will be included here from "The Roots of the Dhātupāṭha not found in Literature," *Wiener Zeitschrift für die Kunde des Morgenlandes* (8, 1894, 17–42), also published in *Indian Antiquary* (23, 1894, 141–154 and 250–255).

The Roots of the Dhātupāṭha Not Found in Literature (1894)

Georg Bühler

In his "Review of Recent Studies in Hindu Grammar" which fills pp. 171–197 of the fourteenth volume of the *American Journal of Philology*, the continuation of an article on Hindu and European Grammar in the fifth volume of the same periodical, the late Professor Whitney reopens the discussion of a question, which used to sorely vex the soul of the Sanskritists of the last generation, but has since been dropped in Europe, because the progress of Indo-Aryan research has shewn very clearly what the solution of the problem is. Professor Whitney, engrossed with his Vedic studies, does not seem to have noticed the labours of the Prakritists. He informs us on p. 182 that there are in the Dhātupāṭha a "thousand or twelve hundred false roots," and declares that the fact of their "voices being not less carefully defined by the Dhātupāṭha than those of the eight or nine hundred genuine ones casts a shade of unreality over the whole subject of voice-conjugation." On the next page he condoles with Geheimrath von Böhtlingk, who, in his second edition of Pāṇini, has given "the whole Dhātupāṭha in length and breadth, finding nothing else to put into its place," though he ought to have known better. Next he severely blames Dr. Liebich, who "talks of probable interpolations and intimates that he deems them posterior to the great trio of Pāṇini, Kātyāyana and Patañjali, acknowledging that his (*i.e.*, Professor Whitney's) criticisms may be more or less applicable to their successors." Turning finally to the Sanskritists of the modern school in general, he throws down the gauntlet to them and winds up with the following peroration: — "This free and easy way of disposing of the subject is quite characteristic of the whole guild of partizans of native grammar. It appears impossible to bring any one of them to stand up and face fairly the question of the Dhātupāṭha. There are not far from nine hundred real and authenticable roots in Sanskrit. We could believe that the uncritical interpolations of later grammarians might add to this number a dozen, or a score, or fifty, or (to take the extreme) even a hundred or two; but it is the wildest of nonsense (only strong expressions suit the case) to hold that they could swell the number to over two thousand. Such increase is thus far wholly unexplained, perhaps for ever unexplainable, and certainly most unpardonable; and until it is in some way accounted for, the admirers of the Hindu science of grammar ought to talk in very humble tones. If these roots are not the ones recognized by the wondrous three, when and under what circumstances and by whose influence were the additional twelve hundred foisted in, to the abandonment and loss of the old genuine list? The difficulty of explaining this seems not less great than that of supposing the whole two thousand as old as Pāṇini himself; both are hard enough; and in either event the taint of falsity attaches to the Hindu system as we know it and are expected to use it."

Professor Whitney's grievances are therefore: (1) against "the guild of the admirers of Hindu grammar" that they will not—to use with Professor Whitney the language of the prize-ring—come up to the scratch and fully discuss his objections to the Dhātupāṭha, though they do answer his strictures on other and less important points: (2) against the Hindu grammarians that their Dhātupāṭha contains a very large number of verbs, which are not traceable in the accessible Sanskrit literature and which therefore must be "sham" and "false," *i.e.*, if I understand Professor Whitney rightly, inventions either of Pāṇini or of his successors.

If I venture to offer some remarks on the points, raised by the illustrious Praeceptor Columbiae, my object is to suggest a definite line of enquiry, which, I think, may lead to tangible results, valuable alike for Sanskrit and comparative philology, and to add some practical proposals. In doing so, I must premise that I do not belong to any guild of partizans of the Vyākaraṇa (if such a one exists). Eighteen years of personal intercourse with the Hindus have taught me at least something about their many excellent qualities and their weaknesses, which are all clearly discernible in their system of grammar. It shews their great acumen and their pedantry, their laboriousness and their practical sense as well as their feebleness in the struggle after an ideal, which is much too high for their strength. I am even ready to believe with the great Mīmāsṁaka Bhaṭṭa, that the Hindu grammarians occasionally resemble "horsemen who forget the existence of their steeds."[1] But, strong language on the part of a European or American authority, however great, is insufficient to persuade me that the Hindu grammarians have invented forms or roots. Such an assertion I could believe only on the evidence of stronger proof than the fact that one, or a dozen, or even a score, of scholars cannot find the forms taught. Until that has been furnished, I prefer to adhere to my own opinions, which in the main coincide with those of Professors Westergaard and Benfey. I must also express my doubts regarding the desirability of the use of strong language, in this case and in all other scientific discussions, both for personal reasons and out of regard for our special branch of learning.

Professor Whitney's first complaint seems to me well-founded. I likewise regret that the specialists in Hindu grammar and particularly the able pupils, whom Professor Kielhorn has trained, hitherto have not turned to the Dhātupāṭha, and have not availed themselves of the plentiful materials which are ready at hand in order to carry on and to supplement the work, begun in so masterly a manner by Professor Westergaard. Since the times of the great Dane the critical treatment of Pāṇini's Sūtrapāṭha has been begun, and perfectly trustworthy critical editions of the Vārttikas and of their great Commentary, as well as of the Kātantra, have been published. The Paribhāṣās, which are the key to the whole system of Hindu grammar, have been so excellently translated and so carefully illustrated by Professor Kielhorn, that even a beginner may understand their application. The Kāśikā together with its huge Vṛtti, the Padamañjarī of Haradattamiśra, Kaiyaṭa's Pradīpa, a number of Nāgojī's and Bhaṭṭojī's grammatical treatises, Bhartṛhari's Vākyapadīya, Sāyaṇa-Mādhava's Dhātuvṛtti, Śākaṭāyana's grammar and the Sārasvata have at least been printed, be it in their entirety or in part. And for those, who desire to critically examine these works, there are good old MSS. in the public libraries of India, which the liberality of the Indian Governments makes accessible to all Sanskrit students. Finally, the Grammars of Candra, Jinendra-Pūjyapāda, Buddhisāgara, Malayagiri and Hemacandra have been recovered in MSS., mostly together with their Aṅgas, as well as Jinendrabuddhi's Kāśikāvṛttinyāsapañjikā, and an apograph of Sāyaṇa's Dhātuvṛtti is lying in the library of Elphinstone

[1] *Tantravārttika*, p. 201, 11. 3–4 (Benares edition):—*sūtravārttikabhāṣyeṣu dṛśyate cāpaśabdanam / aśvārūḍhāḥ kathaṃ cāśvānvismareyuḥ sacetanāḥ/* The sermon, in which Kumārila expands this text, is highly edifying, and the best Vaiyākaraṇas living have admitted to me that the charges made there are not unfair.

College, Bombay, which has been transcribed from a MS. (at Nargunḍ), dated within a hundred years of the author's time.[2]

With these materials, which mostly were not accessible to Professor Westergaard, or only so in indifferent modern MSS., it is possible to settle the following points:—

1. Which portions of our Dhātupāṭha were certainly known to Pāṇini and the other two Munis.
2. Whether any additions have been made by the later authorities of Pāṇini's school, Vāmana, Jayāditya, Jinendrabuddhi and so forth, and what has been added by each.
3. What our Dhātupāṭha, or the list of verbs in the Dhātuvṛtti, owes to the homonymous treatises of Śarvavarman, Candragomin and the other authors of independent Śabdānuśāsanas.

Much of the work that Bühler here suggested be done for the *Dhātupāṭha* was actually done later by Liebich in various publications (e.g., 1919–1920, 1921, and 1930). A little later Bühler continues as follows:

Turning to Professor Whitney's grievance against the Hindu grammarians, his assertion that they have inserted "false," "sham," or "fictitious" forms in the list of verbs, which, as is acknowledged at all hands, has an intimate connection with their Śabdānuśāsana, is supported in his present paper by the sole argument that he cannot find the verbs, their inflexions and meanings in the literature accessible to him. In his earlier article (*Am. Journ. Phil.* Vol. V.) he refers to Professor Edgren's paper on the Verbal Roots of the Sanskrit Language (*Journ. Am. Or. Soc.* Vol. XI. p. 1–55). He greatly approves of his pupil's results and appears to wish them to be taken together with his own argument. Professor Edgren's views coincide with those of sundry authorities in comparative philology, while they disagree from those of the most competent Sanskritists of the last generation.

Briefly stated, Professor Edgren's line of argument is as follows:

1. The Dhātupāṭha contains a great many more roots that cannot be found, than such as are traceable in Sanskrit literature, and the same remark holds good with respect to the inflexions and meanings of the roots. And in spite of a "vast" progress in the exploration of Vedic and Sanskrit works, the proportion of the former had remained in 1882 virtually the same as in 1841, when Professor Westergaard expressed the conviction that every form in the Dhātupāṭha is genuine and would be found some time or other in inaccessible or unexplored works. Professor Edgren's second proposition is certainly not in accordance with the facts, as will be shewn below.

2. The roots preserved in the grammars and their Aṅgas alone, are barren and mostly have no offspring,—are not connected with derivative nouns, such as the genuine roots have produced in great numbers. Only 150 among them seem to have "a possible connection in sense with surrounding or similar nominal forms." This proposition, too, requires considerable modification.

3. Most of the roots, not found in Sanskrit literature, are *not* represented in the cognate languages. Professor Fick's *Wörterbuch* shews only 80 roots, solely known through the Dhātupāṭha, to have belonged to the common stock of the Indo-European speech, and it would seem that in some cases the evidence adduced is too

[2] See my *Rough List*, No. 120. This MS., or its original, will be used for the continuation of the edition of the *Dhātuvṛtti* in the *Benares Paṇḍit*.

weak. On the other hand, among the verified roots, 450 have representatives in Greek, or in the Iranian, the Italic, the Teutonic, the Sclavonic and the Celtic languages.

4. On a closer examination the unverified roots shew various peculiarities, which point to an artificial or fictitious origin. First, the majority of them naturally arranges itself into smaller or larger groups of forms of similar sound and identical in meaning, "the analogy of form being such as to exclude the principle of growth and decay." The first instance given is the group *kev*, *khev*, *gev*, *glev*, *pev*, *plev*, *mev*, *mlev*, *śev*, *meb*, *peb*, *mep*, *lep* with the meaning 'to honour, to serve,' and with absolutely identical inflexion. To Professor Edgren (p. 15) "it seems, as if, in coining these counterfeits, the guiding principle has been at first to model them in form and sense on some genuine radical, rightly or wrongly interpreted," and he suggests that the above group "leans on the real root *sev* as its *point d'appui*." To me it would seem that, in the case quoted, Professor Edgren has made his list unnecessarily long. *Sev* and *śev* differ only in pronunciation, and so do *pev* and *peb*, as well as *mev* and *meb*. To a Hindu the syllables *si* and *śi*, *se* and *śe* are absolutely the same thing, and our Dictionaries are full of words, which shew sometimes the one and sometimes the other. Again *ba* and *va* likewise are often exchanged. In Northern India (excepting Kaśmīr), and in the East, *va* has been lost completely and, as the inscriptions prove, since ancient times. The ten remaining forms, it would seem to me, are clearly variants of two originals, **sklev* and *plev*, and are due to the same principles of change, which are regularly operative in the Prakrits and not rarely active in Sanskrit, as well as in other Indo-European languages. The pedigree[3] stands thus:—

The form *gev* has been preserved, I think, in the noun *gevayā* 'the low ones' (Aśoka, Pillar Edict, III.), which is best explained as equivalent to *gevakāḥ* 'servitors, slaves,'[4] The same remarks apply to most of Professor Edgren's other groups, which usually consist of one or two old forms, with numerous dialectic varieties or such varieties as might be expected in the same dialect, according to the laws of Indo-Aryan phonetics. Some shew, too, an intimate con-

[3] Examples of the assumed changes are to be found in Professor E. Müller's *Simplified Pali Grammar*, and Professor Pischel's edition of Hemacandra's *Prakrit Grammar*, as well as in Sanskrit, where, e.g., the same words sometimes shew *k* and *g*, like *karta* or *garta*, *kulpha* or *gulpha*, *kirika* or *girika*, *saṃkara* or *saṃgara*, *kuha[ra]* and *guha[ra]*, *taṭāka* and *taḍāga*, *lakuṭa* and *laguṭa* and where roots are found ending in *k*, or equivalents thereof, while the corresponding ones in the cognate languages shew the media.

[4] I withdraw my former proposal to derive *gevayā* from *glep dainye*, because the Pāḷi usually preserves a *la* preceded by gutturals, and because I find in Pāḷi many cases, where *aka* is represented by *aya*.

nection with words of common occurrence in Sanskrit or in the Prakrit languages. Thus, in the second *gaṇa*, *champ gatau* is evidently the parent of the modern Gujarāti *jhāpavuṃ* and so forth, and of the Sanskrit *jhampā*, *jhampa*, *jhāmpana*. Again, in his fifth *gaṇa*, *gaj śabdārthe* bears the same relation to the common Sanskrit verb *garj* as *kaṣ* to *karṣ*, *jap* to *jalp* and so forth. And *gajati* is probably the parent of *gaja* 'elephant,' literally 'the roarer, the trumpeter.' The important fact that a very large proportion of the roots of the Dhātupāṭha is Prakritic in form, has apparently not been fully realised by Professor Edgren, though Professors Weber, Benfey and many other Sanskritists have repeatedly called attention to it, both years ago and quite lately.

The second point, which, according to Professor Edgren, makes the *introuvable* roots appear artificial, is the fact that so many of them are stated to have the same meaning. To take only the worst case, there are, according to Professor Edgren, 336 verbs, to which the explanation *gatau* is appended, and only 65 can be verified in literary works. The fact, no doubt, looks curious. But it becomes easily intelligible, if one consults the Hindu Śāstras as to the meaning of *gati* or *gamana*. The Naiyāyikas and Vaiśeṣikas say,[5] *karma pañcavidham utkṣepaṇam avakṣepaṇam ākuñcanaṃ prasāraṇaṃ gamanam*, and give us the definition of *gamanam / ukṣepaṇādicatuṣṭayabhinnatve sati karmatvavat*. They further add, *gamanaṃ bahuvidham / bhramaṇaṃ recanaṃ spandanam ūrdhvajvalanaṃ tiryaggamanam iti //* It is evident that the author, or authors, of the Dhātupāṭha hold the same opinion, and that they mean to say that the roots, marked *gatau*, denote some kind of motion. It is a matter of course that definitions like *bhāṣaṇe*, *bhāsane*, *śabdārthe* and *hiṃsāyām* are likewise intended merely as general indications of the category to which the verbs belong, not as accurate statements of their meanings.

The third point, which rouses Professor Edgren's suspicions, is that the same verbs are used according to the Dhātupāṭha *ādare/ anādare/ gatau hiṃsāyām / bhāṣaṇe bhāsane* or *vyaktāyāṃ vāci* and *avyaktāyāṃ vāci*. Nevertheless, the Sanskrit dictionaries shew that many verbs actually are used with widely divergent meanings, and he might have found without difficulty in English and in other languages a good many instances, exactly analogous to those which have appeared to him so extraordinary in Sanskrit.

The problems which the Dhātupāṭha offers, ought to be approached in a very different spirit and can be solved only by a different method. Taking as correct Professor Whitney's statement (*Am. Journ. Phil.* Vol. V. p. 5 of the reprint) that in all eleven hundred roots are awaiting verification, and likewise Professor Edgren's assertion that 150 among them are connected with nouns occurring in Sanskrit literature, and that 80 have representatives in the cognate languages, the genuineness of 870 forms has still to be proved, and the number of unverified inflexions and meanings is in all probability at least equally great.

The first question to be put is, of course, if all that can be done has been done in order to account for them, or if there are still materials unused and unexplored. The next consideration is, whether the author or authors of the Dhātupāṭha may be supposed to have drawn on other materials than those accessible in the present day and if there are circumstances which could explain the

[5] I take the following definitions from Mahāmahopādhyāya Bh. Jhalkīkar's excellent *Nyāyakoṣa* (second edition, 1893, Bo. Sansk. Ser. No. XLIX.).

apparent barrenness of so many roots as well as the absence of representatives in the cognate languages.

Professor Edgren is certainly right in maintaining that a great many Sanskrit works, and particularly the more ancient ones, have been explored lexicographically since Professor Westergaard's times. But he is as certainly in error, when he says the number of verified roots, meanings and inflexions has remained virtually the same. A comparison of the articles on roots in the *Petersburg Dictionaries* and in Professor Whitney's *Supplement* with the *Radices* proves that incontestably. Without counting those roots, which occur in Sanskrit literature, but are not found in the Dhātupāṭha, Professor Whitney has 120 verified roots, for which Professor Westergaard was only able to quote Pāṇini, the Bhaṭṭikāvya and the Nirukta, and the smaller *Petersburg Dictionary* has about a score more. Each Saṃhitā of the Vedas, the Kāṭhaka, the Maitrāyaṇīya, the Taittirīya and that of the Śaunaka Atharvavedīs has furnished its contribution. The same remark applies to the Brāhmaṇas, the Upaniṣads and the Vedāṅgas, among the Sūtras especially to the huge Kalpa of the Āpastambīyas. And it must be noted that, with the exception of the Ṛk and Atharva Saṃhitās, which have been indexed, the exploration of the printed works is not complete, and that the interpretation even of these two Saṃhitās, is not yet settled. The Ṛcas and the Mantras of the Atharvāṅgirasas are still a field *yatra yuddhaṃ kacākaci* between the strict philological school and the linguists, and will probably remain so for some time. It is not doubtful that, with an alteration of the method of interpretation, the views regarding the meanings of a certain number of roots and words, and regarding the derivation of the latter will considerably change.

After this Bühler gives some illustrations to show that there are many Sanskrit works which have been either partially explored, or not explored at all, and which can furnish facts confirming the statements of the Hindu grammarians. He then continues:

But, even after the whole existing Sanskrit literature has been fully explored, only half the task of the root-hunter has been accomplished. He has then to extend his researches to the ancient and modern Prākrits, many of which possess an extensive literature, as well as to the Mixed Language of the first centuries before and after the beginning of our era. The compositions in the oldest types of the Prākrits, which are found in Aśoka's Edicts, in the Vinayapiṭaka, the Pañca Nikāyas (e.g., in the verses of Jātakas), and other canonical Buddhist books, certainly existed in the third century B. C. This much is evident from the Maurya inscriptions on the rocks and pillars and from those on the Stūpas of Sanchi and Bharahut. Their language has preserved numerous forms older than those of the classical Sanskrit of Pāṇini, and some older than those of the Vedic dialects. Their frequent nominatives plural from masculine *a*-stems in *āse* and from neuter *a*-stems in *ā* (Professor Oldenberg's discoveries) are Vedic. The not uncommon occurrence of the subjunctive (Professor Pischel's discovery) is another remnant of the language of the Ṛṣis, and such are the imperatives like *āvajātu* (*āvrajatu*), the plural instrumentals of the *a*-stems in *ebhi* (Oldenberg), the very common first persons plural in *mase*, the infinitives in *tave*, *tāye*, *tuye*, *ase* and other forms, which may be gathered from the Pāḷi grammars, or from detached articles and notes of Professors Fausböll, Jacobi, Kern, Kuhn, Leumann, Oldenberg, Rhys Davids, Trenckner, Weber and Zachariae, as well as of Dr. Morris and M. Senart in Kuhn's

Zeitschrift, Bezzenberger's *Beiträge*, the London *Academy*, the *Journal of the Pali Text Society*, the editions of the Aśoka Inscriptions, the Mahāvastu and in other works. Among the forms, which are older even than the Vedic language, I will only mention the present participles of the Ātmanepada in *mana*, *mina*, *mīna* which the Aśoka Inscriptions offer, and which agree with the Greek, Latin and Bactrian endings, and the Aorist *addasa* 'I saw,' which goes back, not to Sanskrit *adarśam*, but to **adṛśam*, thus corresponding exactly with ἔδρακον, and which without a doubt is the older form. A careful investigation of the oldest documents reveals the existence of very many similar cases.

Now it might be expected, that such a language should have preserved verbal roots, which were dropped by the classical writers. And Professor Kern has shewn long ago in his *Bijdrage tot de Verklaring van eenige Worden in Pali-Geschriften Voorkomende*, as well as recently in his *Review of Jātakas*, Vol. V. (*Museum* of 1893, p. 100ff.) that this is the case. . . . In lately going over the Jātakas for a different purpose I have noted representatives of some more verbs, for which the explored Sanskrit literature offers no passages, and even of some which Professor Whitney in his *Supplement* expressly stigmatises as "without a doubt artificial."

The verbs which Bühler discusses and illustrates with excerpts from the *Jātakas*, but also with references to other Prakrits and to modern Indo-Aryan languages, are the following: (1) *śiṅghati* 'smell,' (2) *muṇḍati* 'crush,' (3) *śaṭati* 'pierce,' (4) *bhaṇḍate* 'deride,' (5) *kuṭati* 'curl,' (6) *amati* 'go,' (7) *irati* 'move,' (8) *kuñjati* 'whistle,' (9) *gandhayati* 'injure,' (10) *gra(n)thate* 'be hurt,' (11) *nādhati* 'fade,' (12) *maṅghate* 'start,' etc. He then continues:

The fundamental maxim, which gives their importance to these researches, is that every root or verb of the Dhātupāṭha, which has a representative in one of the Prakrits,—Pāḷi, Mahārāṣṭrī, Māgadhī, Śaurasenī, the Apabhraṃśas—, or in one of the modern Indian Vernaculars must be considered as genuine and as an integral part of the Indo-Aryan speech. Those, who consider such verbs to be "sham," "fictitious" or "artificial" have to prove their contention and to shew, that, and how, the author or authors of the Dhātupāṭha coined them. This rule, of course, holds good not only for the Indian languages, but *mutatis mutandis* for all linguistic research. If the grammatical tradition regarding the existence of a certain word is confirmed by the actualities in any dialect of a language, the presumption is that the tradition is genuine.

As I do not claim to possess prophetic gifts, I do not care to predict how many hundreds of roots will exactly be verified, when the search has been completed. But it is not doubtful that the majority of those verbs, which Prof. Whitney considers suspicious or fictitious, will turn up, and in addition a considerable number of such as have not been noted by the Hindu grammarians. On the other hand, it would be wonderful, if the whole contents of the Dhātupāṭha could ever be "belegt." For, it has been pointed out repeatedly and must be apparent to the merest *tiro* in Indian palæography that a certain proportion of the roots is the result of misreadings. This is, of course, highly probable in all cases where the Dhāṭupātha gives pairs like *yuch* and *puch* or *jhaṣ* and *ūṣ*. The characters for *jha* and *ū* are almost exactly alike in the Nāgarī alphabet of the ninth, tenth, eleventh and twelfth centuries, just as those for *ya* and *pa* in the later MSS. More important is another point, which likewise has been frequently noticed, *viz.*, the fact that only a small portion of the Vedic literature, known to Pāṇini and his predecessors, has been preserved, and that of the ancient *laukika Śāstra*, the Kāvya, Purāṇa, Itihāsa and the technical treatises only very small remnants have come down to our times. The assertion that the old literature has suffered terrible losses, is admitted by all Sanskritists. It is only a pity that their extent has not been ascertained, at least approximately, by the preparation of a list of works and authors mentioned in the Śabdānuśāsana, the Brāhmaṇas, the Upaniṣads and the Vedāṅgas. Such a list, especially if supplemented by an enumeration of the numerous references to the spoken language, which Pāṇini's Śabdānuśāsana contains, would probably bar for the future the inference that a root or form must be fictitious, because it is not found in the accessible literature. This inference is based on a *conclusio a minori ad majus*, which with a list, shewing what existed formerly and what we have now, would at once become apparent. The lost Śākhās of the Vedas and the lost works of the *laukika Śāstra* amount to hundreds. If on an average a third or a fourth of them contained each, as is perhaps not improbable according to the results of the exploration of recently recovered Saṃhitās and Sūtras, one or two of the as yet untraceable roots, that would be sufficient to account for all the lost stems.

Three other considerations, it seems to me, help to explain some of the most remarkable peculiarities, observable in the materials incorporated in the Dhātupāṭha, *viz.*, the fact that a certain proportion of the roots really is and will remain isolated, neither derivatives nor cognate forms being traceable in the Indo-Aryan or in the Indo-European languages, and the indisputable fact that many roots may readily be arranged in groups, similar in sound and identical in meaning and inflexion. Both these peculiarities, as stated above, have been used by Prof. Edgren in order to prove that the verbs, shewing them, must be fictitious. And it has been pointed out, that the number of the isolated and barren verbs is not so great as Prof. Edgren supposes, the inflected forms or representatives of a certain proportion being found in the Prakrits and in the unexplored Sanskrit literature. Nevertheless, a certain number of instances will remain, which requires accounting for. With respect to the second fact, it has been pointed out that many of the curious variants are clearly dialectic and derived from lost or preserved parent-stems in accordance with phonetic laws valid in the Prākrits and in Sanskrit.[6]

The chief considerations, which in my opinion do account for these peculiarities are (1) the great length of the period, during which the materials of the Dhātupāṭha were collected, (2) the enormous extent of the territory from which the Hindu grammarians drew their linguistic facts, and (3) the great diversity of the several sections of the Indo-Aryans inhabiting this territory.

It is admitted at all hands that Pāṇini's Śabdānuśāsana is the last link in a long chain of grammatical treatises, which were gradually enlarged and made more and more intricate, until the Hindu system of grammar became a science, which can be mastered only by a diligent study continued for years. According to the unanimous tradition of the Hindus, the Vyākaraṇa is a Vedāṅga,

[6] A perusal of Prof. Per Person's *Wurzelerweiterung und Wurzelvariation* would perhaps convince Prof. Edgren that many Indo-European roots may be arranged in *gaṇas*, similar to those in which he has arranged so many verbs of the Dhātupāṭha.

i.e., a science subservient to the study of the Veda, and it is highly probable that the older Hindu grammars exclusively or chiefly explained the Vedic forms, just like the oldest Koṣas, the Nighaṇṭus, include very little that is not derived from Vedic texts. In Pāṇini's grammar the Vedic language is of minor importance. Its chief aim is to teach the correct forms of the *laukikī bhāṣā* for the use of students of Sanskrit. The road, that leads from the Vedāṅga to the independent Śabdānuśāsana, is a long one, and has not been traversed in one or a few decades. Centuries were required in order to effect the change. For in India processes of development are particularly slow, except when extraneous impulses come into play. To the conclusion that the prehistoric period of the Vyākaraṇa was a long one, point also Pāṇini's appeals to the authority of numerous predecessors. He not only mentions ten individual earlier teachers, but also the schools of the North and the East, and his grammar shews indeed very clear traces that it has been compiled from various sources. Now, if Pāṇini's Sūtras are the final redaction of a number of older grammatical works, the same must be the case with his Dhātupāṭha. For the arrangement of all Indian Śabdānuśāsanas presupposes the existence of a Dhātupāṭha, and there is no reason to assume that the older grammars were deficient in this respect. It may be even suggested that the occasional discrepancies between the teaching of the Dhātupāṭha and rules of the Śabdānuśāsana, the existence of which has been alleged, as well as the inequality in the explanatory notes, appended to the roots, are due to an incomplete unification of the various materials which Pāṇini used. Similar instances of what looks like, or really is, carelessness in redaction[7] are not wanting in other Sūtras. In the Introduction to my Translation of Āpastamba's Dharmasūtra[8] I have pointed out that, though Āpastamba condemns in that work the raising of Kṣetraja sons and the practice of adoption, he yet describes in the Śrauta Sūtra the manner in which a "son of two fathers" shall offer the funeral cakes, and that Hiraṇyakeśin has not thought it necessary to make the language of the several parts of his Kalpa agree exactly.

But, if Pāṇini's Dhātupāṭha must be considered as a compilation from various works, dating from different centuries and composed in various parts of India, it is only to be expected that it should contain many verbs which had already in his time become obsolete and isolated, many variants or dialectic forms. This supposition becomes particularly credible, if the extent of the territory is taken into consideration, from which the ancient grammarians drew their linguistic facts. It extends from the Khyber Pass and the frontier of Sindh in the West, about 71° E. L., to beyond Patnā in the East, in 86° E. L., and from the Himālaya to the Vindhya range, where the Narmadā, the *mekhalā bhuvaḥ*, divides the Uttarāpatha from the Dakṣiṇāpatha, or roughly reckoning from the twenty-second to the thirty-first degree N. L. The Aryan population of this large tract was divided into a very great number of tribes, clans, castes and sects, as well as of schools

[7] I say advisedly 'looks like or really is carelessness,' because it is always possible that the Sūtrakāras intentionally left contradictory rules unaltered in order to indicate an option. Very clear cases of carelessness in the working up of different materials, do, however, actually occur, e.g., in the grammatical and lexicographical works of Hemacandra.

[8] *Sacred Books of the East*, Vol. II. p. xxiii p. 130, note 7.

of Vaidiks, Pandits and poets, and owed allegiance to the rulers of perhaps a dozen or more different kingdoms. In historic India tribal, sectarian, political and other divisions have always strongly influenced the development of the languages, and have caused and perpetuated dialectic differences. It seems difficult to assume that matters stood differently in prehistoric times, when there was not, as later, one single work which was generally considered as the standard authority of speech by all educated Aryans. The diversity of the words and forms in literary works and in the speech of the educated classes probably was very great and the task of the earlier grammarians, who had to make their selection from them very difficult.

This difficulty was, it might be expected, not lessened by their method of working. Even in the present day Indian Pandits rarely use any of the scientific apparatus, of which European scholars avail themselves. Indexes, dictionaries and "*Collectanea*," such as are at the service of the Europeans, are unknown to them. They chiefly trust to memory, and work in a happy-go-lucky sort of way. Even when writing commentaries, they frequently leave their quotations unverified or entrust the verification to incompetent pupils. The enormous quantity of the materials and the deficiencies in the system of working them up, explain why none of the Vedas or other old books have been excerpted completely, while the diversity of the materials and the length of the period, during which the collections were made, fully account for the occurrence of dialectic, and of isolated or obsolete, forms in the list of roots. In my opinion it is only wonderful that they are not more numerous.

I now come to the real object of my paper, the practical suggestions for the continuation of the search for roots and forms and for an organisation of this search. On the one hand it is necessary that all the unpublished Dhātupāṭhas together with their commentaries should be edited critically with good indexes and that the same should be done with the Sanskrit Koṣas, which furnish the tradition regarding the derivatives. On the other hand, all accessible Sanskrit, Pāḷi and Prakrit books and MSS., as well as the Vernacular classics ought to be read and excerpted by competent scholars, with a view to the preparation of a Dictionary of Indo-Aryan Roots. This Dictionary ought to contain, not only the roots, included in the Dhātupāṭha, together with their meanings and inflections, verified and unverified, as well with the corresponding forms of the Prakrits and Vernaculars, but also those verbs, which the grammarians have omitted, whether they are found in Vedic, Sanskrit, Prakrit or Vernacular literature or speech. If the materials are arranged methodically and intelligibly, and if a good index is added, such a book would be of very considerable use to all linguists, who study any of the Indo-European languages. And if the excerpts are made with the necessary care, a portion of them can be made useful for the Sanskrit, Pāḷi and Prakrit dictionaries of the future.

The magnitude of the undertaking would preclude the possibility of its being carried out by one or even by a small number of students. The co-operation of a great many would be required, not only of Europeans and Americans, but also of the Hindus of the modern school, who alone can furnish the materials for the very important Vernaculars. Moreover, a careful consideration of the general plan would be necessary, as well as the settlement of definite rules and instructions for the collaborators. Perhaps one of the next International Oriental Congresses will be a suitable occasion for the discussion of such a scheme, and of its details as well as of the great question of ways and means. I believe, that if the idea finds the necessary support, the appointment of a permanent international Committee will be advisable, which should supervise the preparation of the work and the indispensable preliminary labours. A small beginning has already been made with the latter by the Imperial Austrian Academy's *Series of Sources of Sanskrit Lexicography*, of which the first volume has appeared and the second, containing Hemacandra's Uṇādigaṇasūtra with the author's commentary, is ready for the press, while the third, the Maṅkhakoṣa with its commentary, has been undertaken by Prof. Zachariae. It is a matter of congratulation that the Council of the Société Asiatique has expressed its willingness to co-operate and has commissioned M. Finot to edit the Ajayakoṣa on the same principles, which Prof. Zachariae has followed in preparing the Anekārthasaṃgraha. I have hopes that the Austrian Academy will sanction the issue of some more volumes, including also some Dhātupāṭhas, *e.g.*, those belonging to Hemacandra's grammar and to the Kātantra. Prof. Lanman, the German Oriental Society, the Asiatic Society of Bengal and other corporations or individuals publishing editions of Sanskrit texts would each agree to undertake a few volumes, the necessary auxiliary editions might be prepared without too great a delay and without too heavy a strain on the resources of one single body.

At the same time it would be quite feasible to begin with the excerpts from the literary works, the results of which could be published preliminary in the *Journals* of the various Oriental Societies and in the Transactions of the Academies. The form of publication ought to be such that they could easily be used by the editor or editors of the Dictionary, and the original excerpts, done according to uniform principles, might be deposited for future reference in the libraries of the learned bodies, publishing the results. With a well considered plan, which might follow partly the lines of that, adopted for the new *Thesaurus Totius Latinitatis*, the "Dictionary of Indo-Aryan Roots" might be completed within the lifetime of those among us who at present are the *madhyamavṛddha* Sanskritists.

If the idea is ever realised and a standard book is produced, a great part of the credit will belong to Prof. Whitney. In his *Supplement*, which, in spite of my different views regarding the character of the linguistic facts handed down by the ancient Hindus and regarding various details, I value very highly and in his justly popular *Sanskrit Grammar*, the statistical method has been first applied to Sanskrit, and these two works mark a decided advance in the study of the ancient Brahmanical language.

6

The Transition

16

Bernhard Geiger (1881–1964)

The long controversies on the nature and the value of the linguistic work of the Sanskrit grammarians did not do the subject much good. Actually, Whitney's forceful opinions may have acted as a deterrent to many young Sanskritists. During a long period of transition, roughly coinciding with the first quarter of this century and marked by its paucity of contributions, only Bruno Liebich kept the torch burning by a series of discerning and valuable publications following his monograph on Pāṇini and including *Zwei Kapitel der Kāśikā: Übersetzt und mit Einleitung versehen* (1892), *Das Cāndra-vyākaraṇa* (1895), *Cāndra-vyākaraṇa: Sūtra, Uṇādi, Dhātupāṭha* (1902), *Cāndra-vṛtti: Der Original-Kommentar Candragomin's zu seinem grammatischen Sūtra* (1918), *Zur Einführung in die indische einheimische Sprachwissenschaft* I–IV (1919–1920), *Materialien zum Dhātupāṭha* (1921), *Konkordanz Pāṇini-Candra* (1928), and *Kṣīrataraṅgiṇī, Kṣīrasvāmin's Kommentar zu Pāṇini's Dhātupāṭha* (1930). Liebich did for the non-Pāṇinian school of Candragomin what had earlier been done for the Pāṇinian school. The Cāndra school, especially popular among Buddhist scholars, did not survive in India but was very influential (generally in translation) throughout the Buddhist world from Tibet to Ceylon and Java.

More directly in the Kielhorn tradition, during the period of transition, one study appeared by a pupil of Kielhorn, Bernhard Geiger. Geiger had first studied at Vienna and had written a dissertation on Arabic literature. He continued his studies in Prague, Bonn, and Göttingen, where he studied grammar with Kielhorn and Iranian with F. K. Andreas. In 1908 at the instigation of Kielhorn he published the study, reprinted here, which qualified him for an appointment at Vienna as "Privatdozent für altindische und altiranische Philologie und Altertumskunde" (Frauwallner 1961, 89–90). He also published studies on Indian music (jointly with E. Felber) and on Iranian. After the German occupation of Austria, Geiger emigrated to the United States, where he worked at the Asia Institute from 1938 to 1951, and taught at Columbia from 1951 until his retirement in 1956. He died in 1964.

The article of 1908 discusses some rules in Pāṇini's grammar as interpreted and commented upon by Patañjali in his *Mahābhāṣya* and by Kaiyaṭa in his subcommentary *Pradīpa* (of the eleventh century). In this study Geiger translates the relevant passages from the *Mahābhāṣya* and deals with, among other things, Pāṇini's concept of *asiddha*, 'regarded as not having taken effect,' which corresponds to the notion of rule ordering in contemporary linguistics.

An example of Pāṇini's technique is the following:

Rule 6.1.71 implies that the infix *t* called *tUK* (capitals stand for metalinguistic elements) is inserted after a short vowel before the suffix *ya* called *LyaP*, i.e., in the context:

short vowel __ *LyaP*. (1)

For example: *prakṛ* + *LyaP* → *prakṛtya*.

Rule 6.1.101 states that two homorganic vowels combine into one corresponding long vowel (2). For example, *daṇḍa* + *agram* → *daṇḍāgram*.

Similarly, (2) would yield: *adhi* + *i* + *LyaP* → *adhīya*. But the correct form in Sanskrit is *adhītya*. This can be obtained if (1) has also applied. But (1) is applicable only if the left context is a short vowel, and in *adhī* __ *ya* it is long. Pāṇini succeeds in deriving the correct result by postulating a metarule (6.1.86), which applies to other rules as well and which states that (2) is *asiddha* 'regarded as not having taken effect' with respect to (1). In modern linguistics this result would be obtained by ordering (1) before (2).

Another example is the following:

Rule 6.4.101 states that the imperative ending *hi* is replaced by *dhi* after the root *hu*- and after roots ending in a class of sounds denoted as *jhAL*, i.e.:

$$\text{hi} \rightarrow \text{dhi} \Big/ \begin{Bmatrix} \text{hu} \\ \text{jhAL} \end{Bmatrix} \_\_ \qquad (3)$$

(e.g., *bhind* + *hi* → *bhinddhi*).

Rule 6.4.119 states that the vowel element of the roots *dā*- and *dhā*- (together called *GHU*) and the root *as* 'be' are replaced by e before the ending *hi*, i.e.:

$$\begin{Bmatrix} \text{*GHU} \\ \text{as} \end{Bmatrix} \rightarrow \text{e} \Big/ \_\_\text{hi} \qquad (4)$$

(where *GHU denotes the vowel element of GHU; e.g., *dā* + *hi* → *dehi*).

But the imperative of *as*- is *edhi* '*be!*' Now s, but not e, is included in the class *jhAL*. Hence *edhi* cannot be derived from the underlying form *as-hi* unless (3) is declared *asiddha* with respect to (4), or (4) with respect to (3). This requirement is indeed fulfilled as a direct consequence of metarule 6.4.22.

Geiger deals with these and with similar topics in "Mahābhāṣya zu P.VI,4,22 und 132 nebst Kaiyaṭa's Kommentar: Übersetzt, erläutert und mit einem Anhang," *Sitzungsberichte der philosophisch-historischen Klasse der kaiserlichen Akademie der Wissenschaften zu Wien* (160, 1909, VIII, 1–76).

Mahābhāṣya zu P. VI, 4,22 und 132, nebst Kaiyaṭa's Kommentar (1909)

Bernhard Geiger

Vorwort

Während eines glücklichen Studienaufenthaltes in Göttingen erhielt ich bei der Lektüre des Mahābhāṣya von meinem hochverehrten Lehrer, Herrn Geheimrat Professor F. Kielhorn, die Anregung, die Abschnitte VI, 4, 22 und 132 des Mahābhāṣya zu bearbeiten. Sie empfahlen sich hiezu besonders deshalb, weil sie in sich abgeschlossen sind, die Anwendung und Bedeutung einer ganzen Reihe wichtiger grammatischer Kunstgriffe und Erklärungsmethoden kennen lehren und typische Beispiele der Vorzüge und Schwächen des Mahābhāṣya liefern. Angesichts der großen Schwierigkeiten, die das Verständnis des Mahābhāṣya bietet, schien mir eine solche Arbeit nur dann berechtigt zu sein und Nutzen zu versprechen, wenn sie imstande wäre, auch den der Methode des Mahābhāṣya Unkundigen mit ihr vertraut zu machen. Dieses Ziel schwebte mir bei der Übersetzung und den Erläuterungen vor und bestimmte mich dazu, auch den Kommentar Kaiyaṭa's vollständig zu übersetzen, trotz der Schwierigkeiten, der die Darstellung hier begegnete. Die Übersetzung des Kommentars schien mir unerläßlich zu sein, weil Kaiyaṭa's Erklärungen oft viel komplizierter und schwerer verständlich sind als das Bhāṣya selbst und die Kenntnis anderer Stellen des Mahābhāṣya und die des Paribhāṣenduśekhara voraussetzen. Leider erwies sich mein ursprünglicher Plan, den vollständigen Text von Kaiyaṭa's Kommentar beizugeben, als undurchführbar. Ich habe in den meisten Fällen nur die ersten Worte einer Anmerkung von Kaiyaṭa zitiert und hievon nur bei besonders schwierigen Stellen eine Ausnahme gemacht. Auch wichtigere Parallelstellen aus anderen Teilen des Mahbāhāṣya sowie manche schwierigere Bemerkung der Kāśikā habe ich übersetzt, den Paribhāṣenduśekhara, dessen Übersetzung von Kielhorn mir Vorbild war und für das Verständnis von Kaiyaṭa's Kommentar die größten Dienste leistete, habe ich möglichst oft herangezogen, und im Anhang gebe ich einige, wie ich glaube, notwendige Ergänzungen und Erläuterungen, die in den Anmerkungen nicht untergebracht werden konnten. Die Vārttikas Kātyāyana's habe ich zumeist unübersetzt gelassen, da Patañjali sie genau pharaphrasiert.

Für die Übersetzung des Bhāṣya habe ich Kielhorns Ausgabe [Mbh.] benützt. Kaiyaṭa's Kommentar war mir nur in der gedruckten Ausgabe Benares 1887 zugänglich, die von sinnstörenden Fehlern nicht frei ist. Den Dhātupāṭha habe ich nach der Ausgabe von Westergaard zitiert. An Abkürzungen kommen zur Verwendung:

Kāty. = Kātyāyana.
Kaiy. = Kaiyaṭa.
Pat. = Patañjali.
Kāś. = Kāśikā.
Siddh. K. = Siddhānta-Kaumudī.

Paribh. mit folgender Seitenzahl bezeichnet Nāgojībhaṭṭa's Paribhāṣenduśekhara, Text und Translation von F. Kielhorn. Bombay Sanskrit Series. Bombay 1868–74.

Paribh. Nr. = Paribhāṣā Nr. [in dem eben genannten Werke].

Ms. K. bezeichnet ein Herrn Prof. Kielhorn gehöriges Manuskript von Kaiyaṭa's Kommentar, mit dem er auf meine Bitte einige Stellen verglichen hat, an denen ich von meinem Text abweichende Lesungen vermutete.

Es empfiehlt sich, bei der Benützung dieser Arbeit überall dort, wo der Paribhāṣenduśekhara zitiert ist, auch noch Kielhorns Übersetzung dieses Werkes zu Rate zu ziehen. Die Kenntnis von

Paribh. Nr. 38 setze ich voraus. Über die in ihr enthaltenen Termini vgl. Paribh. Transl. p. 185, n. 1.

Diese Arbeit war schon abgeschlossen und ich war eben dabei, einige Verbesserungen und Bemerkungen, die Prof. Kielhorn mir wenige Tage vorher gesandt hatte, zu verwerten, als ich die erschütternde Nachricht von dem plötzlichen Tode meines lieben, unvergeßlichen Lehrers erhielt. Nun erreicht ihn mein Dank für seine so freundliche, teilnahmsvolle Förderung dieser Arbeit nicht mehr! Es war sein Wunsch, daß durch die Übersetzung und Erläuterung eines Abschnittes des Mahābhāṣya das Verständnis der indischen Grammatiker, deren größter Kenner er war und für deren Kenntnis er das meiste getan hatte, gefördert werde. Möge dies der vorliegenden Arbeit gelungen sein!

Einleitung

Obwohl Kielhorn schon im Jahre 1876 in der grundlegenden Abhandlung ‚*Kātyāyana and Patañjali*: their relation to each other, and to Pāṇini' [Bombay 1876] das wahre Verhältnis der drei großen Grammatiker endgiltig aufgezeigt hat, begegnet man noch immer einer unrichtigen Auffassung ihres gegenseitigen Verhältnisses, besonders aber einer ungerechten Beurteilung Pat.'s. So urteilt selbst Böhtlingk noch in der Einleitung [p. XVII] zu seiner Pāṇini-Übersetzung [Leipzig 1887] folgendermaßen: ‚Wenn Kāty. solche Versehen[1] [sc. Pāṇ.'s] rügt, sucht Pat. sie auf irgendeine spitzfindige Art zu bemänteln. Wer an einer solchen Kritik des großen Grammatikers Gefallen findet, möge sich in das uns jetzt in musterhafter Ausgabe vorliegende Mahābhāṣya vertiefen.' Mit dieser Behauptung bekennt sich Böhtlingk, wenigstens soweit Pat. in Betracht kommt, zu dem alten Standpunkt Webers, nach welchem Kāty. ein Gegner Pāṇ.'s und Pat. dessen Verteidiger gegen die Angriffe Kāty.'s sein soll. Es mag also nicht überflüssig sein, wenn ich an einem der hier übersetzten Abschnitte, Mbh. zu VI, 4, 22, der sich hiezu vortrefflich eignet, zeige, wie sehr die Webersche Auffassung gegen den tatsächlichen Sachverhalt verstößt. Wie verhält es sich nun in diesem Abschnitt zunächst mit der Gegnerschaft Kāty.'s gegen Pāṇ.? Die zwei ersten Vārttikas enthalten Erklärungen zweier Ausdrücke des Sūtra. Die folgenden sechs Vārtt. (3–8)

[1] Böhtlingk führt folgendes Beispiel ‚größerer Unachtsamkeit' Pāṇ.'s an: P. III, 3, 90 lehrt die Anfügung des Suffixes *naṅ* (*na*) an die Wurzel *prach*. Da dieses *na* ein *ṅit*-Suffix ist, würde sich nach VI, 1, 16 die Substitution des *Saṃprasāraṇa ṛ* für *r*, also *pṛśna*, ergeben. Kāty. bemerkt deshalb im Vārtt. 1, das Sūtra müsse durch ein Verbot des *Saṃprasāraṇa* ergänzt werden. Darauf entgegnet Pat., die Form *praśna* komme *nipātanāt* zustande, d. h. dadurch, daß Pāṇ. in III. 2, 117 das Wort *praśna* erwähnt und so ein Verbot gegen die Anwendung von VI, 1, 16 statuiert. Pat.'s Ansicht haben auch die kritische und feinfühlige Kāś. und Siddh. K. zu III, 3, 90 akzeptiert. Daß Pāṇ. sich eines so leicht auffallenden Versehens hätte schuldig machen können, halte ich für völlig ausgeschlossen. Und die Anwendung eines *nipātana* erscheint mir um nichts künstlicher als irgendeine andere Andeutung oder als so manche Paribhāṣā, deren Kenntnis und Anwendung — wie ich mit Goldstücker, *Pāṇini*, p. 114, glaube — Pāṇ. vorausgesetzt haben muß. Aber davon abgesehen, wäre der Vorwurf der Spitzfindigkeit wegen der Annahme eines *nipātana* doch auch Kāty. gegenüber gerechtfertigt, der in dem ganz analogen Falle *sarvanāman* [I, 1, 27 Vārtt. 1] und auch sonst öfters [vgl. *Ind. Ant.* vol. XVI, p. 245, n. 4] zur Rechtfertigung Pāṇ.'s ein *nipātana* annimmt.

führen Zwecke des Sūtra an, dienen also zur Verteidigung Pāṇ.'s gegen die eventuelle Behauptung, daß das Sūtra überflüssig sei. Dagegen konstatieren die Värtt. 9 (welches in 10 begründet wird), 11, 13 und 14 Ausnahmen von dem Sūtra. Värtt. 12 erklärt, daß die in 9 und 11 konstatierten Ausnahmen nicht bestehen, wenn in dem Sūtra das Wort *samānāśraya* hinzugefügt wird. Die Värtt. 15 und 16 nennen Fehler, die sich aus jeder der zwei Alternativen ‚*prāg bhāt*' (d. i. Geltung des Sūtra bis VI, 4, 129) und ‚*ā bhāt*' (= *saha tena*, d. i. Geltung bis VI, 4, 175) ergeben. Naturgemäß kann nur eines dieser zwei Värttikas gegen Pāṇ. gerichtet sein. Aus Värtt. 7 ist ersichtlich, daß Kāty. die zweite Alternative annimmt. Der größere Teil der Värttikas dieses Abschnittes dient also zu Pāṇ.'s Rechtfertigung.

Pat., der angebliche Verteidiger Pāṇ.'s, betätigt hier seine Parteinahme für Pāṇ. zunächst in der Weise, daß er die zur Rechtfertigung Pāṇ.'s bestimmten Värtt. 3–8 zum Teil auf spitzfindige Art widerlegt und hiebei einigen Regeln Gewalt antut. Er verteidigt ferner die gegen das Sūtra gerichtete Schlußbemerkung des Ślokavärttikakāra. Das Värtt. 14 — wohl das einzig berechtigte unter den kritikübenden Värttikas dieses Abschnittes — lehnt Pat. nur zur Hälfte ab, während er die zweite Hälfte akzeptiert. Andrerseits weist Pat. die Behauptung Kāty.'s [Värtt. 12] zurück, daß die in Värtt. 9 und 11 erwähnten Ausnahmen durch Hinzufügung von *samānāśraya* vermieden werden, und erklärt, daß der verlangte Zusatz schon in dem Worte *atra* des Sūtra zum Ausdruck komme. Mit demselben Argument tritt Pat. auch dem Värtt. 13 entgegen. Sub Värtt. 12 widerlegt er den im Värtt. 10 angeführten Grund *bahiraṅgalakṣaṇatvāt*. Und schließlich weist er auch die Värtt. 15 und 16 zurück. Er zeigt, daß weder die im Värtt. 15 genannten Ergänzungen durch die Annahme der Alternative ‚*prāg bhāt*' notwendig werden, noch auch die im Värtt. 16 verlangte Konstatierung von Ausnahmen durch die Wahl der Alternative *ā bhāt* (= *saha tena*).

Schon diese Inhaltsangabe lehrt, wie unzutreffend die Webersche Ansicht ist. Der eben erörterte Abschnitt bietet aber auch Gelegenheit, auf eine Eigentümlichkeit des Mahābhāṣya hinzuweisen, die bei der Beurteilung desselben nicht außer acht gelassen werden darf. Obwohl nämlich Pat. bei den Värtt. 12 bis 16 — von dem zweiten Teil des Värtt. 14 abgesehen — für Pāṇ. einzutreten scheint, fällt es doch auf, daß er hier eigentlich überhaupt nicht für Pāṇ. Partei ergreift. Denn er weist alle Värttikas, welche Zwecke des Sūtra angeben, zurück, ohne andere Zwecke namhaft zu machen. Man gewinnt infolgedessen den Eindruck, als ob Pat, das Sūtra VI, 4, 22 als gänzlich überflüssig betrachtete. In der Tat leitet er von der Widerlegung des Värtt. 8 zu den Ślokavärttikas mittels des Satzes über: *yadi tarhy ayaṃ yogo nārabhyate* (‚wenn demnach diese Regel nicht aufgestellt wird'). Und zwischen der letzten Bemerkung des Ślokavärttikakāra, die gegen die Anwendung des Sūtra gerichtet ist, und den Ausnahmen von dem Sūtra, die Kāty. aufzählt, wird die Verbindung durch den Satz hergestellt: *ārabhyamāne 'py etasmin yoge* (‚auch wenn diese Regel aufgestellt wird'). Pat. begibt sich damit plötzlich auf den Standpunkt Kāty.'s, daß das Sūtra notwendig sei, und kritisiert von diesem Standpunkt aus, ohne ihn jedoch als seinen eigenen zu bezeichnen, die folgenden Värttikas. Aus den Entgegnungen auf die Värtt. 15 und 16 ist nicht ersichtlich, welche Stellung Pat. dem Sūtra gegenüber einnimmt. Er sucht nur zu beweisen, daß die in diesen Värttikas gennanten Fehler sich aus keiner der beiden Alternativen ergeben.

Ob etwa die Annahme einer von ihnen nach Pat.'s Ansicht andere Fehler zur Folge hat, erfahren wir nicht. Und doch wäre das scheinbare Resultat der Widerlegung von Värtt. 15 und 16, d. i. der Standpunkt, daß keine der beiden Alternativen Zusätze oder Verbote notwendig mache, daß also beide korrekt sind und gleichzeitig zu Recht bestehen, widersinnig und ganz gewiß nicht der Standpunkt Pat.'s.

Pat. ist hier also ebensowenig prinzipieller, unentwegter Parteigänger Pāṇ.'s als Kāty. prinzipieller Gegner Pāṇ.'s ist. Es ist überhaupt verkehrt, zu glauben, daß Gegnerschaft oder Voreingenommenheit für Pāṇ. die Grundsätze sind, von denen Kāty. und Pat. sich leiten lassen. Kāty. macht nicht nur Zusätze und Verbesserungen; er tritt auch für Pāṇ. ein und in zahlreichen Fällen nimmt er eine gegen diesen gerichtete Behauptung durch ‚*na vā*' (‚oder auch nicht'), ‚*siddhaṃ tu*' (‚doch ist es in Ordnung') u. a. m. zurück und lehrt, auf Grund welcher Auffassung (‚*vijñānāt*'), Bedeutung (‚*vivakṣitatvāt*'), oder mit Hilfe welcher Paribhāṣā die in vorhergehenden Vārttikas genannten Schwierigkeiten vermieden werden. Viel deutlicher zeigt sich der Mangel jeglicher Voreingenommenheit bei Pat. Er macht von dem Spielraum, den das so feindurchdachte System Pāṇ.'s seiner Findigkeit noch offen läßt, den ausgiebigsten Gebrauch und erhebt bei jeder sich darbietenden Gelegenheit Zweifel und Einwendungen ‚gleichgiltig, ob es sich um eine Regel Pāṇ.'s oder eine Bemerkung Kāty.'s handelt, und ohne Rücksicht darauf, ob es eine Behauptung Kāty.'s für oder gegen Pāṇ. ist. Pat. prüft und wägt nach allen Seiten hin ab und sucht immer noch weitere Gründe, neue Auswege, andere Möglichkeiten der Erklärung ausfindig zu machen. So kommt es, daß er öfters — wie z. B. für die Form *śādhi* zu Värtt. 3 — für einen einzigen Fall gleichzeitig mehrere Möglichkeiten präsentiert. Und dies berechtigt uns zu dem Schluß, daß nicht in jeder Äußerung Pat.'s auch seine persönliche Überzeugung zum Ausdruck kommt, und daß nicht jeder Abschluß einer Diskussion auch eine prinzipielle Entscheidung bedeutet.[2] Ein typisches Beispiel möge dies veranschaulichen. Im Kapitel VI, 4, 22 [Mbh. vol. III, p. 190; s. unsere Übersetzung] behauptet der Ślokavārttikakāra, daß bei *ahāritarām* [aus *ahāri-ta* + *tarām*] die Elision der Endung *-ta* nicht als *asiddha* betrachtet zu werden brauche, damit die Elision von *tarām* verhindert werde. Es gelte nämlich aus einer früheren Regel das Wort ‚*kṅiti*' fort. Pat. verteidigt diese Ansicht. Anders verhält sich Pat. in derselben Frage im Kapitel VI,

[2] Dies ist vielfach unverkennbar und übrigens eine natürliche Folge der Methode des Mahābhāṣya, d. i. seines Diskussionsstiles. Wenn Pat. irgendeine Einwendung erhebt, so kommt darin in vielen Fällen gewiß nicht sein eigener Standpunkt zum Ausdruck, sondern eine Auffassung, die vielleicht möglich wäre, eine Meinung, die ein Teilnehmer an der fingierten Diskussion äußern könnte. Und zwar sind dies oft recht weit hergeholte Einwendungen. In manchen Fällen — wie z. B. bei *upadidīye* zu VI, 4, 22 Värtt. 14 — werden sie sofort mit einer treffenden Entgegnung abgetan. In anderen Fällen dagegen — wie bei *babhūvatuḥ* zu demselben Värtt. — sind noch weitere Erwiderungen und Verteidigungen denkbar und die Diskussion kann bei einigem guten Willen länger fortgeführt werden, bis sie schließlich in eine Sackgasse gerät. So werden scheinbare Inkonsequenzen Pat.'s leicht verständlich. In dieser Weise ist wohl auch der von Kaiy. [zu Mhb. III, 193, l. 1.] gerügte Fehler zu beurteilen, der in der Annahme einer Form *bahuśunī* (statt *bahuśvan*) besteht. In dieser Hinsicht ist die Bemerkung Kaiy.'s zu Mhb. III, 190, l. 10 beachtenswert.

4, 104 [Mbh. vol. III, p. 214]. Käty. verteidigt dort in den drei Vārttikas[3] die Regel gegen die eventuelle Behauptung, es müsse in der Regel *ta* hinzugefügt werden, damit nicht nach der Elision des *ta* auch die von *tarām* erfolge. Das erste Vārttika lehrt, daß *ta* und *tarām* nicht gleichzeitig abfallen können, weil [nach I, 1, 61] *luk* nur für ein Suffix und nicht für eine Verbindung von Suffixen eintritt. Värtt. 2 stellt fest, daß auch nachher, d. i. nach erfolgtem Abfall des *ta*, das folgende Suffix nicht abfallen könne, weil die Elision des *ta* [nach VI, 4, 22] als *asiddha* zu betrachten sei. Nach Värrt. 3 wäre auch noch ein anderer Grund möglich: das Prinzip, daß eine Handlung (Operation) bereits vollzogen sei [und nicht ein zweites Mal vollzogen werden soll]. Während Pat. das Värtt. 3 ablehnt, nimmt er mit den Worten ‚*tasmāt pūrvoktāv eva parihārau*' die zwei ersten Vārttikas ausdrücklich an, betrachtet also im Gegensatz zu der vorher erwähnten Stelle den Abfall von *ta* als *asiddha*. Aber unmittelbar nach dieser Feststellung fährt Pat. fort: ‚Oder aber [die Elision von *ta* ist nicht *asiddha*, sondern] „*kṅiti*" gilt [aus VI, 4, 98] fort'. Und er verteidigt nun diese Ansicht in derselben Weise wie Mbh. vol. III, p. 190.

Man tut aber Pat. auch unrecht, wenn man glaubt, daß seine Rolle sich in müßigen dialektischen Spielereien und spitzfindigen Haarspaltereien erschöpfe. Mag man auch bei so mancher seiner Diskussionen das Gefühl haben, daß der Scharfsinn in ihnen geradezu mißbraucht wird, so verdienen sein Scharfblick und seine Schlagfertigkeit doch an vielen anderen Stellen alle Anerkennung, seine Ansichten und Argumente den Vorzug vor denen Kāty.'s. Und zwar nicht nur dort, wo Kāty. für Pāṇ. eintritt, sondern — im Widerspruch mit Böhtlingks eingangs zitierter Behauptung — vielfach gerade in denjenigen Fällen, in welchen Kāty. Versehen Pāṇ.'s ‚rügt'. Daß der verallgemeinernde Vorwurf, Pat. bemäntele in spitzfindiger Weise die von Kāty. gerügten Versehen Pāṇ.'s, der Bedeutung Pat.'s wohl nicht gerecht wird, mögen einige Beispiele aus dem hier übersetzten Texte zeigen, die sich leicht durch solche aus beliebigen anderen Teilen des Mahābhāṣya vermehren ließen.

Was zunächst Kāty.'s und Pat.'s verschiedene Deutungen von *atra* [VI, 4, 22 Värtt. 2 und Pat. zu Värtt. 12] betrifft, so scheint zwar die Analogie von *pūrvatrāsiddham* [VIII, 2, 1] für die Auffassung Kāty.'s im Värtt. 2 zu sprechen, wonach *atra* besagt, daß eine Regel von VI, 4, 23 an ‚bis *bha*' nur ebendaselbst, d. h. nur in bezug auf eine ebendemselben Abschnitt angehörige Regel als *asiddha* zu betrachten ist. Wenn man aber erwägt, daß Pāṇ. sich sonst in *adhikāras* der größten Knappheit des Ausdruckes befleißigt, die Bestimmung der Geltungsgrenze eines *adhikāra* der Erklärung überläßt und in unserem Sūtra den Geltungsbereich schon durch den Zusatz ‚*ā bhāt*' abgrenzt, so wird man die Auffassung Pat.'s doch für möglich halten dürfen, nach welcher das Wort *atra* ausdrückt, daß eine als *asiddha* betrachtete Regel dieses Abschnittes ebendarauf beruhen muß, worauf die Anwendung der andern Regel dieses Abschnittes beruht. Dann käme der Zusatz *samānāśraya*,

[3] Diese Vārttikas, die einzigen zu VI, 4, 104, beweisen schlagend die Unrichtigkeit der Behauptung Goldstückers [*Pāṇini*, p. 120]: ‚In consequence, his [sc. Kāty.'s] remarks are attached to those Sūtras alone which are open to the censure of abstruseness or ambiguity, and the contents of which were liable to being completed or modified: he is silent on those which do not admit of criticism or rebuke.' Goldstücker meint natürlich nur die Kritik von seiten Kāty.'s.

den Kāty. verlangt, schon in *atra* zum Ausdruck. Diese Auffassung Pat. ist vielleicht nicht zwingend, aber doch annehmbar und keineswegs spitzfindig. Ihr schließen sich die Kāś. und Siddh. K. an. Dem Nachweis Pat.'s [zu Vārtt. 6], daß bei *gataḥ*, *gatavān* die Elision des Nasals [VI, 4, 37] nicht als *asiddha* betrachtet werden muß, damit die Elision des *a* [VI, 4, 48] verhindert werde, seiner Widerlegung der Vārtt. 7, 13, 16, seiner Zurückweisung des von Kāty. im Vārtt. 10 angeführten Grundes *bahiraṅgalakṣaṇatvāt* sub Vārtt. 12, sowie der Widerlegung der Vārttikas zu VI, 4, 132 wird man ohne Vorbehalt zustimmen.

Aus all dem geht hervor, daß man das Studium des Mahābhāṣya wohl nicht bloß demjenigen empfehlen darf, der an unfruchtbarer spitzfindiger Kritik Gefallen findet und damit vorlieb nimmt. Die Bedeutung des Mahābhāṣya besteht zunächst darin, daß es die Vārttikas des Kāty. in vortrefflicher Weise erläutert, vor allem aber darin, daß es das Verständnis von Pāṇ.'s Grammatik in hohem Maße fördert und einen Einblick in den wahren Sinn und Zweck einer Regel vielfach erst ermöglicht. Für ein tiefer eindringendes Verständnis des Pāṇineischen Systems ist das Studium des Mahābhāṣya zweifellos unentbehrlich. Darf ich schließlich noch einen praktischen Grund anführen, so verweise ich darauf, daß die Kāś. die zahlreichen zutreffenden Deutungen und Entscheidungen Pat.'s aufgenommen hat, und daß infolgedessen viele Stellen der Kāś. ohne Kenntnis des Mahābhāṣya schwer verständlich oder überhaupt unverständlich sind.

Der erste der hier übersetzten zwei Abschnitte des Mahābhāṣya behandelt das Sūtra VI, 4, 22. Mag nun Pat.'s Erklärung des Wortes *atra* [zu Vārtt. 12] richtig sein oder nicht, so besagt dieses Sūtra doch folgendes: Eine in dem Abschnitt VI, 4, 22 bis *bha* gelehrte, in Wirklichkeit bereits in Kraft getretene Operation ist in bezug auf eine andere Operation desselben Abschnittes, die nach der Ausführung der ersten Operation eintreten soll oder müßte, so zu betrachten, als ob sie *asiddha*, d. h. nicht in Kraft getreten wäre. Der Umstand, daß Pāṇ. in dieser Regel *asiddhavat* sagt, während es VI, 1, 86 *asiddhaḥ* und VIII, 2, 1 *asiddham* heißt, hat die Erklärer zu Erörterungen über die Bedeutung des *vat* [in *asiddhavat*] veranlaßt. Die verschiedenen Ansichten hierüber finden wir am Beginn von Kaiy.'s Kommentar zu VI, 4, 22. Es heißt dort: *Iha kvacid upamānopameyayor abhedaṃ vivakṣitvā sāmānādhikaraṇyena nirdeśaḥ kriyate: ᵓyam Brahmadatta iti. Śāstreᵓpi: ṣatvatukor asiddhaḥ; liṭ kit; goto ṇid iti ca. Tatra sāmarthyād atideśapratipattiḥ. Kvacit tu pratipattilāghavāya bhedopakrame vatinā nirdeśaḥ kriyate: Brahmadattavad ayam iti. Ihāpi: asiddhavad atrābhād iti. Anye tv āhuḥ: svāśrayam api yathā syād* [vgl. Mbh. vol. II, p. 66, l. 2] *ityevamarthaṃ vatkaraṇam; tena debhatur ity atra svāśrayaikahalmadhyagatāśrayāv ettvābhyāsalopau bhavata iti. Etad apare na mṛṣyanti. Saty asati vā vatāv atideśeṣv ātideśikāviruddhasvāśrayakāryānivṛttiḥ; siddhatvāsiddhatvayor virodhāt kathaṃ vatinā siddhatvasya prāpaṇam? kathaṃ vā siddhatvāsiddhatvayor viṣayavibhāgo labhyate? sthānivad ityādau tu vatim antareṇa saṃjñā syād iti vatkaraṇam atideśaṃ gamayat svāśrayaprāptyarthaṃ* [so Ms. K.; Text: °*artho*] *vijñāyate. Śnasor allopa iti taparakaraṇāt kvacit siddhatvaṃ śakyam anumātum; anyathā āstām, āsann ityādāv āṭoᵓsiddhatvāl lopāprasaṅgāt kiṃ taparatvena?* ,Wenn man sagen will, daß zwischen dem, womit verglichen wird, und dem Verglichenen selbst kein Unterschied besteht, so drückt man dies im Leben (*iha*) bisweilen durch die Gleichstellung aus, [indem man z. B. sagt]: ,,Dieser ist [ein zweiter] Brahmadatta." [Ebenso] auch im grammatischen

Lehrbuch [z. B. VI, 1, 86]: „In bezug auf den Eintritt von ṣ und in bezug auf das Augment *t* ist [ein *ekādeśa* als] *asiddha* [zu betrachten]"; [I, 2, 5]: „Eine Personalendung des Perfektums ist [wie] ein *kit*-Suffix [zu behandeln]"; [VII, 1, 90]: „Nach *go* ist [die Endung eines starken Kasus wie] ein *ṇit*-Suffix [zu behandeln]." In diesen Fällen erkennt man schon aus der Sachlage, daß es sich um eine Übertragung[4] [und nicht Identifizierung] handelt. Manchmal aber bedient man sich, um die Wahrnehmung [der Übertragung] zu erleichtern, der Bezeichnung durch *vat*, wenn man auf [die Betonung] des Unterschiedes abzielt, [indem man z. B. sagt]: „Dieser ist wie Brahmadatta." [So] auch hier [in VI. 4. 22]: „Bis *bha* ist [eine bereits in Kraft getretene Operation in bezug auf eine andere Operation] ebendaselbst [so zu betrachten], wie wenn sie nicht in Kraft getreten wäre." — Andere dagegen sagen: „Die Setzung von *vat* hat den Zweck, daß auch die aus ihm [d. i. dem verglichenen *siddha*] selbst sich ergebende [Operation] eintreten möge;[5] auf diese Weise erfolgen bei *debhatuḥ* [aus *dambh*] die Substitution des e und die Elision der Reduplikation, die au dem in der Mitte zwischen zwei einfachen Konsonanten stehenden [Vokal *a*] beruhen, welcher eben auf ihm [sc. dem *Siddha*-sein] selbst beruht."[6] — Dies wollen wieder andere nicht zugeben, [welche einwenden]: „Ob nun *vat* dasteht oder nicht, so wird doch bei Übertragungen [nur] diejenige aus ihm [d. i. dem Verglichenen] selbst sich ergebende Operation nicht aufgehoben, welche der übertragenen [Operation] nicht widerspricht. Wie soll man es [hingegen bei *debhatuḥ*], da doch *Siddha*-sein und *Asiddha*-sein einander ausschließen, mittels *vat* erreichen, daß [eine Operation] *siddha* sei? Oder wie soll man [wenn das aus

[4] Nämlich des für den einen Begriff Geltenden auf den andern.

[5] Hier wird der gewaltsame Versuch gemacht, dem *vat* eine ähnliche Bedeutung beizulegen, wie sie dem *vat* in *sthānivat* [I, 1, 56] eigen ist. Wenn z. B. I, 3, 28 lehrt, daß bei *han* nach der Präposition *ā* in nicht transitiver Bedeutung das *Ātmanepadam* eintritt, so gilt nach I, 1, 56 dasselbe auch für das Substitut *vadh* [II, 4, 44]. D. h. das für den *sthānin* [d. i. *han*] Geltende wird auf das Substitut übertragen; dieses hört nicht auf zu funktionieren, sondern bildet die Basis für die übertragene Operation. Man erhält also außer *āhata* auch *āvadhiṣṭa*. Das *Ātmanepadam* ist demnach nicht nur *sthānyāśrayam*, sondern auch *svāśrayam*, d. i. *ādeśāśrayam*. In unserem Falle stehen die Begriffe *asiddha* und *siddha* einander gegenüber. Das *vat* in *asiddhavat* soll auch hier angeblich ausdrücken, daß das aus *asiddha* sich Ergebende auf *siddha* übertragen werde, ohne daß dieses zu funktionieren aufhört. Hier kann natürlich nicht — wei bei *sthānivat* — eine einzige Operation in Betracht kommen, sondern außer der übertragenen, aus der Eigenschaft *asiddha* sich ergebenden Operation (*asiddhatvāśrayam*) soll auch eine andere, auf der Eigenschaft *siddha* beruhende (*svāśrayam*, d. i. *siddhatvāśrayam*) eintreten dürfen.

[6] Wenn in *da-dambh-atuḥ* nach VI, 4, 24 der Nasal elidiert worden ist, so kommt das *a* der Wurzel zwischen zwei einfache Konsonanten zu stehen und dann erfolgen gemäß VI, 4, 120 Substitution von e [für *a*] und Elision der Reduplikation. So erhält man *debhatuḥ*. Wenn jedoch — wei es VI, 4, 22 verlangt — die Elision des Nasals von *dambh* [VI, 4, 24] als *asiddha* betrachtet wird, so kann VI, 4, 120 nicht eintreten. Deshalb fordert Vārtt. 5 zu VI, 4, 120 einen Zusatz zu dieser Regel. Nach der von Kaiy. erwähnten Auffassung von *vat* dagegen kommt *debhatur* dadurch zustande, daß auch *svāśrayam*, d. i. *siddhatvāśrayaṃ kāryam* eintreten darf, d. h. die aus der in Kraft getretenen (*siddha*) Operation VI, 4, 24 sich ergebende Operation VI, 4, 120.

siddha sich Ergebende auch eintreten darf], zu einer Unterscheidung der Wirkungsbereiche des *Siddha*-seins und *Asiddha*-seins gelangen?[7] Bei *sthānivat* [I, 1, 56] dagegen wäre [das Wort *sthānī*] ohne *vat* eine Bezeichnung [des Substitutes],[8] und daraus erkennt man, daß die Setzung des *vat* die Übertragung [des für den *sthānin* Giltigen auf das Substitut] andeutet und den Zweck hat, daß [die für den *sthānin* geltende Operation] auch in bezug auf jenes [sc. das Substitut] selbst sich ergebe.[9] Daraus [jedoch], daß in [VI, 4, 111]: „*śnasor allopaḥ*" [dem *a* in *at*] ein *t* nachgesetzt ist, kann man erschließen, daß [eine Operation dieses Abschnittes trotz VI, 4, 22] bisweilen auch *siddha* sein kann. Denn welchen Zweck hätte anderenfalls das Nachfolgen des *t*, da doch bei *āstām*, *āsan* [im Augenblick der Elision des *a*] das Augment *ā* noch nicht in Kraft getreten wäre und infolgedessen die Elision [des *ā*] sich gar nicht darbieten würde?'"[10]

Hinsichtlich der Bedeutung des Wortes *asiddha* in unserem Sūtra verweist Kāty. im Vārtt. 1 auf VI, 1, 86 Vārtt. 1–5. Ich lasse hier die Übersetzung des Bhāṣya zu diesen Vārttikas folgen, da sie für das Verständnis von Kāty.'s Auffassung unseres Sūtra von Wichtigkeit sind:

P. VI, 1, 86: Ṣatva-tukor asiddhaḥ.

‚In bezug auf den Eintritt von ṣ [für s] und [die Anfügung] des

[7] D. h. wie ist es dann bei dem Gegensatz zwischen *siddhatva* und *asiddhatva* überhaupt möglich zu unterscheiden, in welchem Falle *siddhatvāśrayaṃ kāryam*, und in welchem Falle die übertragene, aus *asiddha* sich ergebende Operation eintreten soll?

[8] D. h. man würde interpretieren: unter dem *sthānin* ist der *ādeśa* gemeint. Dann entstünde aber der Fehler, daß das in I, 3, 28 gelehrte *Ātmanepadam* nur bei dem Substitut *vadh*, nicht aber bei dem *sthānin han*, eintreten würde Vgl. p. 11, Anm. 1 und Mbh. vol. I, p. 133 (Anfang).

[9] Vgl. Kāś. zu I, 1, 56: *Vatkaraṇaṃ kim? — Sthāny ādeśasya saṃjñā mā vijñāyīti svāśrayam api yathā syāt. Āṅo yamahanaḥ* [I, 3, 28]; *āhata, āvadhiṣṭety ātmanepadam ubhayatrāpi bhavati.* Hinsichtlich der Übertragung vgl. Mbh. zu I, 1, 56 Vārtt. 1: . . . *Guruvad asmin guruputre vartitavyam iti gurau yat kāryaṃ, tad guruputre 'tidiśyate. Evam ihāpi sthānikāryam ādeśe 'tisdiśyate.*

[10] Diese Bemerkung will das Zustandekommen von *debhatuḥ* erklären und bezieht sich auf das Ślokavārtt. Mhb. vol. III, p. 219: *Śnasor attve takāreṇa jñāpyate tv ettvaśāsanam.* ‚Da aber bei „*śnasor*" [VI, 4, 111] *at* vorliegt, so wird durch den Buchstaben *t* die Vorschrift angedeutet, [bei *dambh* nach VI, 4, 120 gegen VI, 4, 22] e zu substituieren.' Dazu Pat.: *Anityo 'yaṃ vidhir iti.* ‚D. h. diese Regel [VI, 4, 22] ist nicht immer giltig.' Und Kaiy. erklärt: *Śnasor attva iti | Asiddhatvasyānityatvajñāpanāya takāraḥ kṛtaḥ. Nitye tv asiddhatve āsann ityādāv āto 'siddhatvāl lopo na bhaviṣyatiti kiṃ tannivṛttyarthena takāreṇa? Tenāsiddhatvābhāvād* [Text: *tena si*°] *dambha ettvaṃ siddhyati.* ‚Das *t* [in *at*] ist gesetzt, um anzudeuten, daß das *Asiddha*-sein [einer Operation] nicht durchwegs gilt. Angenommen aber, das *Asiddha*-sein gelte durchwegs, so wird bei [der Bildung von] *āsan* usw., da ja [zur Zeit der Anwendung von VI, 4, 111] das Augment *ā* noch gar nicht vorhanden wäre [vgl. p. 24, Anm. 1], dessen Elision nicht eintreten können; wozu wäre unter diesen Umständen das *t* nötig, welches [nach I, 1, 70] ausdrücken soll, daß diese [Elision des Augmentes *ā*] unterbleiben möge? [*Āsan* usw. würden aber ohne Schwierigkeit gemäß VI, 4, 22 gebildet werden, wenn Pāṇ. in VI, 4, 111 *a-lopaḥ* statt *al-lopaḥ* gesagt hätte. Das *t* muß also noch einen anderen Zweck haben, u. zw. anzudeuten, daß VI, 4, 22 bei *debhatur* nicht gelten möge.] Auf diese Weise kommt also dadurch, daß das *Asiddha*-sein [bei VI, 4, 24] nicht stattfindet, die Substitution von e [für *a*] zustande.'

Augmentes *t* ist [ein *ekādeśa* als] *asiddha* [zu betrachten].'

Zu welchem Zweck wird dies gelehrt?

Ṣatvatukor asiddhavacanam ādeśalakṣaṇapratiṣedhārtham utsargalakṣaṇabhāvārthaṃ ca|| Värtt. 1.

Daß in bezug auf den Eintritt von *ṣ* [für *s*] und [die Anfügung] des Augmentes *t* [ein *ekādeśa*] *asiddha* sei, wird gelehrt, damit 1. die durch das Substitut bedingte [Operation] verboten werde, und 2. die durch das Ursprüngliche[11] bedingte [Operation] stattfinde. Zunächst 1., damit die durch das Substitut bedingte [Operation] verboten werde: [z. B.] *ko ᵓsiñcat, yo ᵓsiñcat.* Wenn [hier nach VI, 1, 109] die Substitution des einen Vokales [*o* für *o* + *a*] vollzogen ist, würde sich gemäß [VIII, 3, 59]: ‚Nach *iṇ*' Eintritt von *ṣ* [für *s*] ergeben. Weil [aber VI, 1, 109] als *asiddha* betrachtet wird, findet er nicht statt;[12] 2. damit die durch das Ursprüngliche bedingte [Operation] stattfinde: [z. B.] *adhītya, pretya.* Wenn [hiebei nach VI, 1, 101 und 87] die Substitution des einen Vokales [*ī*, bezw. *e*, für *i* + *i*, bezw. *a* + *i*] vollzogen ist, so würde sich das Augment *t*, [welches nach VI, 1, 71 nur] ‚an eine Kürze' [angefügt wird], nicht ergeben. Es tritt [aber] ein, weil [VI, 1, 101 und 87] als *asiddha* betrachtet werden.[13]

Ist dies der Zweck [des Wortes *asiddha*]? — Was ist denn da gegen einzuwenden?

Tatrotsargalakṣaṇāprasiddhir utsargābhāvāt|| Värtt. 2.

Dort, bei *adhītya, pretya*, kann doch die durch das Ursprüngliche bedingte Operation nicht zustande kommen. — Weshalb? — Weil das Ursprüngliche nicht mehr vorhanden ist. [In VI, 1, 71] wird gelehrt: ‚An eine Kürze [wird *t* angefügt']; aber hier [in *adhī-ya, pre-ya*] sehen wir keine Kürze mehr.

Einwurf Aber es ist doch vermöge des Wortes *asiddha* vollständig korrekt.[14]

Erwiderung Asiddhavacanāt siddham iti cen nānyasyāsiddhavacanād anyasya bhāvaḥ|| Värtt. 3.[15]

Wenn jemand sagt, es sei vermöge des Wortes *asiddha* vollständig korrekt, so trifft dies nicht zu .— Warum? — Daraus, daß

[11] *Utsarga* bezeichnet sonst eine allgemeine Regel im Gegensatz zu *apavāda*, der Spezial- oder Ausnahmsregel. [Vgl. Mbh. vol. I, p. 6 und Paribh., Transl. p. 321, n. 1]. An unserer Stelle dagegen dient *utsarga* zur Bezeichnung des *sthānin*, des ursprünglichen Elementes, das durch das Substitut aufgehoben wird. Zwischen *sthānin* und *ādeśa* besteht ja ein ähnliches Verhältnis wie zwischen *utsarga* und *apavāda*. Vgl. Kaiy. zu unserer Stelle: *Utsargaḥ sthānī sāmānyenotsṛṣṭatvāt* (‚*U.* ist der *sth.*, weil dieser als etwas Allgemeines [durch den *ādeśa*] aufgehoben wird'); Kaiy. zu VI, 4, 22 Värtt. 1: *Utsargaśabdena sāmānyaviṣayatvasādharmyāt sthāny abhidhīyate* (‚. . . weil ihm [sc. dem *sthānin*] eine generelle Funktion zukommt'); Kāś., ed. Kalkutta, p. 183: *Utsṛjyate, ādeśena bādhyata ity utsargaḥ sthānī.*

[12] Aus *kas asiñcat* wird nach VIII, 2, 66 *kar asiñcat*, nach VI, 1, 113 *ka* + *u asiñcat*, nach VI, 1, 87 *ko asiñcat*, nach VI, 1, 109 (*ekādeśa*): *ko 'siñcat.* Da diesses *o* nach VI, 1, 85 auch als Anlaut des folgenden betrachtet werden kann [*k*=*osiñcat*], müßte nun nach VIII, 3, 59 *ṣ* für *s* eintreten. Diese durch das Substitut *o* bedingte Operation wird jedoch durch VI, 1, 86 verhindert.

[13] In diesem Falle hat VI, 1, 86 nicht den Zweck, eine durch das Substitut [*ī* für *i*+*i*] bedingte Operation zu verbieten, sondern die durch den *utsarga* [*adhi*+*i*-] bedingte Operation [VI, 1, 71] zu ermöglichen.

[14] D. h.: weil das Substitut als *asiddha* bezeichnet wird, ist der *utsarga* als vorhanden zu denken.

[15] Värtt. 3–5 sind gleich I, 1, 57 Värtt. 4–6.

das eine [sc. der *ekādeśa*] als *asiddha* bezeichnet wird, folgt nicht das Vorhandensein des andern [sc. des *utsarga*]. Denn dadurch, daß das eine als *asiddha* bezeichnet wird, kommt nicht das andere wieder zum Vorschein.[16] Wenn nämlich auch der Mörder des Devadatta getötet worden ist, so kehrt doch [dadurch] Devadatta nicht in die Existenz zurück.

Tasmāt sthānivadvacanam asiddhatvaṃ ca|| Värtt. 4.

Deshalb müßte [in dem Sūtra] gesagt werden: es [sc. das Substitut] verhält sich wie der *sthānin* und es ist *asiddha*. [Und zwar] verhält es sich bei *adhītya*, *pretya* wie der *sthānin*, während es bei *ko ᵓsiñcat*, *yo ᵓsiñcat asiddha* ist.[17]

Sthānivadvacanānarthakyaṃ śāstrāsiddhatvāt|| Värtt. 5.

[Doch] ist es unnötig zu sagen ‚wie der *sthānin*'. — Warum? — Weil die Regel *asiddha* ist. Durch dieses [Wort *asiddha*] wird nicht bewirkt, daß die Operation *asiddha* ist, sondern es bewirkt, daß die Regel *asiddha* ist. Die den *ekādeśa* betreffende Regel gilt als *asiddha* in bezug auf die Regel über das Augment *t*.[18] —

Da Kāty. in dem Värtt. 1 zu VI, 4, 22 auf diese Vārttikas verweist, nimmt er offenbar auch für das Sūtra VI, 4, 22 an, daß nicht eine Operation, sondern eine Regel als *asiddha* zu betrachten sei. Denn gegen die Auffassung, daß eine Operation als *asiddha* anzusehen sei, könnte Kāty. in den Fällen *edhi*, *śādhi* [Värtt. 3], in denen das Sūtra den Zweck hat, daß die durch den *utsarga* bedingte Operation eintreten möge, geltend machen, daß nach der Ausführung der Substitution ein *utsarga* nicht mehr vorhanden ist. Demgemäß bemerkt Kaiy. zu Pat.'s Frage *asiddhavacanaṃ kimartham* am Beginn dieses Abschnittes: *Iha śāstrasya kāryārthatvāt kāryasya prādhānyād asiddhatvena bhāvyam. Tadasiddhāv api sthānino nivṛttatvāt tallakṣaṇaṃ kāryaṃ na prāpnotīty avyāptiṃ matvā praśnaḥ. Itaro vyāpakatvāc chāstrāsiddhatvaṃ pradeśāntara eva vyavasthāpitaṃ* [so Ms. K.; Text: *evaṃ sthāpitaṃ*] *manyamāna āha: asiddhava-*

[16] Kaiy.: *Kāryāsiddhatvāśrayeṇedam ucyate, ādeśena sthānino nivartitatvāt saty apy ādeśasyāsiddhatve sthāninaḥ pratyāpattyabhāvāt.* ‚Dies wird behauptet von dem Standpunkt aus, daß [die bereits vollzogene] Operation *asiddha* sei; denn da der *sthānin* durch das Substitut aufgehoben worden ist, kann der *sthānin*, auch wenn das Substitut *asiddha* ist, doch nicht wieder eintreten.'

[17] Kaiy.: *Ṣatve 'siddhatvaṃ, sthānivadbhāve tu svāśrayasyānivartanāt ṣatvaprasaṅgaḥ.* ‚In bezug auf den Eintritt von ṣ [für s] ist [der *ekādeśa*] *asiddha* [und nicht ‚wie der *sthānin*' zu behandeln]. Wenn er sich aber wie der *sthānin* verhielte, so wäre [noch immer] der Eintritt des ṣ möglich, weil das aus ihm [sc. dem *ekādeśa*] selbst sich Ergebende nicht aufgehoben wäre.' Vgl. die Erörterungen über *vat* p. 215 ff.

[18] Kaiy.: *Tataś ca pūrvaṃ tukśāstraṃ pravartate, paścād ekādeśaśāstram ity uktaṃ bhavati.* ‚Damit ist gesagt, daß zuerst die *tuk*-Regel [VI, 1, 71] eintritt und nachher die *ekādeśa*-Regel [VI, 1, 101, bezw. 87].' Diese müßte nämlich als *para*- und *nitya*-Regel gemäß Paribh. Nr. 38 früher eintreten als die *tuk*-Regel. Nach Kāty.'s Ansicht dagegen wird folgender Vorgang beobachtet: bei *adhi*+*i*+*ya* ergeben sich gleichzeitig VI, 1, 101 [*ekādeśa*] und 71 [*tuk*]; da nun in bezug auf diese Regel jene als *asiddha* [=nicht vorhanden] zu betrachten ist, tritt trotz Paribh. Nr. 38 die Regel VI, 1, 71, also die durch den *utsarga i* + *i* bedingte Operation, zuerst ein und dann erst nach 101 das Substitut *ī*. In bezug auf die Verwandlung des s in ṣ ist es natürlich gleichgiltig, ob man die Operation oder die Regel *asiddha* sein läßt. Denn hier ergibt sich VIII, 3, 59 erst nach der Ausführung von VI, 1, 109.

cana uktam iti. ‚Weil eine Regel eine Operation zum Zwecke hat, und infolgedessen die Operation die Hauptsache ist, muß [die Operation] *asiddha* sein. Weil aber, selbst wenn diese [Operation] *asiddha* ist, der *sthānin* [durch sie] aufgehoben worden ist, so ergibt sich nicht mehr eine durch diesen [*sthānin* oder *utsarga*] bedingte Operation. In der Meinung, daß aus diesem Grunde die Definition [von *asiddha*, d. i. *ādeśalakṣaṇapratiṣedhārtham utsargalakṣaṇabhāvārthaṃ ca*] zu eng sei,[19] wird die Frage [nach dem Zweck von ‚*asiddha*'] gestellt. Der andere dagegen denkt daran, daß schon an einer anderen Stelle festgestellt worden ist, die Regel [und nicht die Operation] sei *asiddha*, weil dies vollständig [d. i. für alle Teile der Definition von *asiddha*] zutrifft.' Nach Kāty.'s Auffassung würde also bei *edhi*, *śādhi* [Värtt. 3] die durch den *utsarga* bedingte Operation VI, 4, 101 früher eintreten als die sich gleichzeitig darbietenden Regeln VI, 4, 119 und 35, weil diese in bezug auf VI, 4, 101 als *asiddha* [= nicht vorhanden] zu betrachten sind. In den Fällen dagegen, in denen der Eintritt einer durch das Substitut bedingten Regel verhindert werden soll, tritt die Regel über die Substitution ein, und diese Regel wird nun in bezug auf die zu verhindernde Regel als *asiddha* betrachtet. In diesen Fällen ist also der Vorgang genau so, wie wenn die Operation selbst als *asiddha* angesehen würde. Wir werden natürlich Kāty.'s Besorgnis wegen des *utsarga* nicht teilen. Denn wenn die Substitution, d. i. die bereits vollzogene Operation, als *asiddha* betrachtet wird, ist eben trotz Kāty. der *utsarga* als noch vorhanden zu denken.

Was den Geltungsbereich unseres Sūtra betrifft, so habe ich schon oben bemerkt, daß Kāty. annimmt, es gelte einschießlich des Abschnittes über *bha* [VI, 4, 129–175], also bis VI, 4, 175. Pat. begnügt sich damit, die Vārtt. 15 und 16 zurückzuweisen und zu zeigen, daß weder aus der Annahme der Alternative ‚*prāg bhāt*' [d. i. bis VI, 4, 129], noch auch aus der Wahl der Alternative ‚*ā bhāt*' [= *saha tena*] die von Kāty. genannten Fehler sich ergeben. Eine bestimmte Antwort gibt Pat. nicht. In der Diskussion zu VI, 4, 149 Vārtt. 3 wird es als offene Frage behandelt, ob ‚*prag bhāt*' oder ‚*saha tena*' gilt. Die Kāś. zu VI, 4, 22 erklärt gleich Kāty., daß das Sūtra bis zum Schluß des Adhyāya, also bis VI, 4, 175 anzuwenden sei. Ebenso urteilt die Siddh. K. zu VI, 4, 22: *ita ūrdhvam ā pādaparisamāpter ābhīyam* ‚[eine Regel] von hier an weiter bis zum Abschluß des Pāda heißt eine bis *bha* gelehrte [Regel].' Zu dem eben besprochenen Abschnitt ist schließlich noch *Candra* V, 3, 21 [ed. Liebich, Abhandl. f. d. K. d. Morgenl. vol. 11, Nr. 4, p. 101]: ‚*Prāg yuvor avugyug asiddhaṃ samānāśraye*' zu vergleichen.

Der zweite der im folgenden übersetzten Abschnitte ist Mbh. zu VI, 4, 132. Kāty. erklärt das Wort *ūṭh* im Sūtra für überflüssig, weil Formen wie *praṣṭhauhaḥ* auch durch Substitution des gewöhnlichen Saṃprasāraṇa *u* für *v* zustande kommen. Demgegenüber erklärt Pat., *ūṭh* habe den Zweck, die Paribhāṣā ‚*asiddhaṃ bahiraṅgalakṣaṇam antaraṅgalakṣaṇe*' anzudeuten, welche verhindert, daß *praṣṭhauhaḥ* usw. auf die von Kāty. angegebene Weise gebildet werden. Diese Ansicht teilt auch die Kāśikā.

[19] *Avyāpti* bedeutet, daß ein Merkmal in einem Teile des zu Definierenden nicht vorhanden ist. Vgl. die *Dīpikā* zu *Tarkasaṃgraha* 2: *Lakṣyaikadeśāvṛttitvam avyāptiḥ, yathā goḥ kapilatvam.* In der Definition von *asiddha* trifft, wenn die Operation als *asiddha* betrachtet wird, dieses Merkmal *kāryam* (Operation) zwar für die erste Hälfte der Definition zu, nicht aber für die zweite.

Übersetzung

P. VI, 4, 22: Asiddhavad[20] atrā bhāt.

Welchen Zweck hat das Wort *asiddha*?[21]

Asiddhavacana uktam|| Värtt. 1.

[‚Es ist schon dort gesagt worden, wo von *asiddha* die Rede war'].

Was ist gesagt worden? — Dort [VI, 1, 86 Värtt. 1] ist schon gesagt worden: ‚Die Bezeichnung [des *ekādeśa*] als *asiddha* in bezug auf den Eintritt von ṣ und in bezug auf [die Anfügung] des Augmentes *t* hat den Zweck, daß die aus dem Substitut sich ergebende [Operation] verboten werde und die durch das Ursprüngliche bedingte [Operation] stattfinde.'[22] Auch hier hat das Wort *asiddha* den Zweck, daß 1. die durch das Substitut bedingte [Operation] verboten werde, und 2. die durch das Ursprüngliche bedingte [Operation] stattfinde. Zunächst 1., daß die durch das Substitut bedingte [Operation] verboten werde, [z. B. in] *āgahi*, *jahi*; *gataḥ*, *gatavān*: wenn [nach VI, 4, 37] die Elision des Nasals [von *gam*][23] und [nach VI, 4, 36] der Eintritt von *ja* [für *han*] vollzogen ist, so ergeben sich [VI, 4, 48] ‚Elision des *a*' [von *ga*- vor den *Ārdhadhātuka*-Suffixen *ta* und *tavat*][24] und [VI, 4, 105] ‚Abfall des Suffixes *hi* hinter *a*' [von *ga*- und *ja*-]. Weil [aber VI, 4, 37 und 36] als *asiddha* betrachtet werden, findet dies nicht statt. 2. Daß die durch das Ursprüngliche bedingte [Operation] stattfinde, [z. B. in] *edhi*, *śādhi*: wenn bei den Wurzeln *as* und *śās* [vor *hi* gemäß VI, 4, 119] der Eintritt von e [für das s von *as*][25] und [nach VI, 4, 35] die Einsetzung von *śā* [für *śās*] vollzogen ist, so ergibt sich nicht die [nach VI, 4, 101] durch einen Konsonanten (mit Ausnahme der Nasale und Halbvokale) bedingte Substitution von *dhi* [für *hi*]. Weil [aber VI, 4, 119 und 35] als *asiddha* betrachtet werden, tritt [das durch das Ursprüngliche, d. i. *as* und *śās*, bedingte *dhi*] ein.[26]

[20] Kaiy.'s Erörterungen über die Bedeutung von *vat* s. Einleitung, p. 215 ff.

[21] Kaiy.'s Bemerkung hiezu: *iha śāstrasya* etc. s. in der Einleitung, p. 218.

[22] Vgl. die Kāś. zu VI, 4, 22.

[23] Das Imperativsuffix *hi* ist nach III, 4, 87 nicht *pit*, also gemäß I, 2, 4 *ṅit*. — Kaiy. bemerkt zu *āgahi*, daß der Präsenscharakter *a* [*śap*: III, 1, 68] von *gam* nach II, 4, 73 abgefallen ist.

[24] Kaiy.: *Avayavalopinām ato lopo nāstīty etatparibhāṣārtham upadeśagrahaṇānuvṛttyā bhāṣyakāraḥ saṃpādayiṣyati* ‚Dies wird der Verfasser des Bhāṣya [zu Värtt. 6; p. 226] durch [die Annahme] richtigstellen, daß das Wort *upadeśa* [aus VI, 4, 37] fortgilt, um die Paribhāṣā anzudeuten: ‚Bei [Stämmen], welche [wie *gam* das *m*] einen ihrer Teile durch Elision verlieren, findet die Elision von *a* nicht statt.' Vgl. p. 227, Anm. 50.

[25] Das *a* fällt gemäß VI, 4, 111 aus, da *hi Sārvadhātuka* und *apit* [III, 4, 87], also *ṅit* [I, 2, 4] ist.

[26] Kaiy.: *Edhīti: paratvān nityatvāc ca pūrvam ettvam; śādhīty atrāpi nityatvāt pūrvaṃ śābhāvo; 'l-vidhitvāc ca dhitve nāsti sthānivadbhāvaḥ.* ‚Zuerst [d. h. vor VI, 4, 101] tritt e [VI, 4, 119] ein, weil [VI, 4, 119] eine *para*-und *nitya*-Regel ist [d. h. vor oder nach dem Eintritt von VI, 4, 101 eintreten kann; und zwar auch nach dem Eintritt des *dhi* deshalb, weil nach I, 1, 56 für das Substitut *dhi* dasselbe gilt, was für den *sthānin hi* gegolten hat]. Und auch bei *śādhi* tritt *śā* [VI, 4, 35], weil [diese Regel] *nitya* ist, zuerst ein [d, h. vor der *para*-Regel VI, 4, 101. Vgl. Paribh. Nr. 38]. Und es gilt nicht etwa hinsichtlich des Eintrittes von *dhi* [VI, 4, 101, die Regel I, 1, 56], daß [die Substitute e und *śā* sich] wie die *sthānin*'s [*as* und *śās* verhalten], da es sich [bei 101 entgegen dem Verbot in I, 1, 56] um eine Vorschrift handelt, welche auf Lauten [d. i. hier den Auslauten der *sthānins as* und *śās*] beruht.' Da also die Substitution von *dhi* nicht nach I, 1, 56 zustande

Welchen Zweck hat denn aber das Wort *atra*?[27]

Atragrahaṇaṃ viṣayārtham[28] || Värtt. 2.

[Durch *atra*] wird der Geltungsbereich zum Ausdruck gebracht. Es soll ein [in dem Abschnitt] bis *bha* gelehrte Regel hier [d. h.] in bezug auf eine ebenfalls [in dem Abschnitt] bis *bha* gelehrte Regel *asiddha* sein. [Hingegen] soll [das Sūtra] in den folgenden Fällen nicht gelten: *abhāji*, *rāgaḥ*,[29] *upavarhaṇam*.[30]

Welches sind nun aber die Zwecke dieser Regel?

Prayojanaṃ śaittvaṃ dhitve || Värtt. 3.

Der Eintritt von *śā* und von *e* ist ein Zweck hinsichtlich des Eintrittes von *dhi*, [z. B. bei] *edhi*, *śādhi*: wenn bei den Wurzeln *as* und *śās* der Eintritt von *e* [VI, 4, 119] und der von *śā* [35] vollzogen sind, so ergibt sich nicht der [nach VI, 4, 101] durch einen Konsonanten (mit Ausnahme der Nasale und Halbvokale)

kommen kann, bedürfen wir zur Bildung von *edhi* und *śādhi* der Regel VI, 4, 22.

[27] Kaiy.: *Yathāṅgasyetyādayo 'dhikārā* etc. ‚Wei sonst *adhikāras* nach Art von ‚*aṅgasya*' [VI, 4, 1] u. a. m. auch ohne die besondere Hervorhebung der [Geltungs]grenze aus ihrer Kommentierung als eine bestimmte Grenze besitzend verstanden werden, so wird auch der *adhikāra* ‚*asiddhavat*' [in unserem Sūtra als] bis *bha* [geltend] verstanden. Weil [also] dort der Ausdruck ‚*ā bhāt*' den Zweck hat, den Geltungsbereich abzugrenzen, brauchte das Wort *atra* nicht gesetzt zu werden. Dies ist der Sinn [der Frage].'

[28] Kaiy.: *viśiṣṭo yo viṣayaḥ* etc. ‚Um den [schon durch ‚*ā bhāt*'] bestimmten Geltungsbereich als charakterisiert durch [die Abhängigkeit beider Operationen von] einem gemeinsamen [Element] zu bezeichnen. Infolgedessen ist ein auf einem gemeinsamen [Element] beruhende [Operation] *asiddha*, hingegen eine nicht [auf einem gemeinsamen Element] beruhende [Operation] *siddha*: dies ist der vom Verfasser der Värttikas angenommene Zweck [des Wortes *atra*] [vgl. Värtt. 12]. Auch der Verfasser des Bhāṣya [Pat.] wird späterhin [zu Värtt. 12] eben diesen Zweck des Wortes *atra* feststellen. Jetzt dagegen nimmt er [vorläufig] an, der Ausdruck ‚*ā bhāt*' habe den Zweck, im Interesse leichterer Erkennbarkeit die Grenze des *adhikāra* anzugeben, und kommentiert [nur], durch das Wort *atra* werde ausgedrückt, daß der Bereich, in welchem [die eine Operation des Abschnittes bis *bha*] als *asiddha* zu betrachten ist, sich nur auf eine [ebenfalls in dem Abschnitt] bis *bha* [vorkommende] Regel erstrecke.' Was Kaiy. hier von Kāty. behauptet, ist unrichtig. Denn das Wort *viṣaya*, das Kāty. gebraucht, bedeutet ‚Geltungsbereich' und nichts weiter. [Vgl. III, 1, 92 Värtt. 1: *tatragrahaṇaṃ viṣayārtham*.] Und dies ist ja eben der Grund, weshalb Kāty. im Värtt. 12 den Zusatz *samānāśraya* verlangt. Vgl. p. 235, Anm. 78.

[29] In *a-bhañj-i* kann nach VI, 4, 33 der Nasal ausfallen und wir erhalten *a-bhaj-i*. Da nun *a* Pänultima (*upadhā*) des Stammes ist, tritt nach VII, 2, 116 *Vṛddhi* ein: *abhāji*. Dies wäre nicht möglich, wenn VI, 4, 33 *asiddha* wäre; denn dann wäre *a* nicht Pänultima. In bezug auf die außerhalb des Abschnittes VI, 4, 22 bis *bha* stehende Regel VII, 2, 116 ist also eine im Abschnitt bis *bha* gelehrte Regel nicht *asiddha*. — Ähnlich bei *rāgaḥ*: VI, 4, 27 und VII, 2, 116. — Kaiy.: ‚Die nach den Regeln ... [VI, 4, 33 und 27] erfolgende Elision des *n* gilt nicht als *asiddha* in bezug auf die [Substitition von] *Vṛddhi*, welche nach der Regel [VII, 2, 116]: „für *a*, welches Pänultima ist", vollzogen werden soll.'

[30] Kaiy.: *Vṛhi vṛddhāv ity asya vṛṃher acy aniṭīti nalopo guṇe siddho bhavati*. ‚Die Elision des *n* erfolgt gemäß [VI, 4, 24 Värtt. 2]: „Von der Wurzel *vṛṃh* — d. i. derjenigen, [von welcher es im Dhātup. 17, 85 heißt]: ‚*vṛhi* in der Bedeutung «stärken»' — vor einem Vokal, wenn er nicht das Augment *i* ist";

bedingte Eintritt von *dhi* [für *hi*]. Weil [aber VI, 4, 119 und 35] als *asiddha* betrachtet werden, tritt [*dhi*] ein.[31]

Einwurf Was zunächst den Eintritt von *śā* betrifft, so macht er [das Sūtra] nicht notwendig. Ich werde folgendermaßen sagen: *śā hau* [VI, 4, 35] ist gleich *śās hau*,[32] Der Laut *s* ist [nach (VIII, 2, 66 und) VIII, 3, 17] zu *y*[33] geworden. Dort [sc. bei dem Substitut *śās*] erfolgt [also] hinter dem *s* [nach VI, 4, 101] der Eintritt von *dhi*; das *s* aber wird gemäß [VIII, 2, 25]: ‚auch vor einem [mit] *dh* [anlautenden Suffix]' elidiert.[34] — Oder aber ich werde [das Sūtra ändern und] sagen: *ā hau*. Auch auf diese Weise ergibt sich für den Laut *s* [Eintritt von *dhi* nach VI, 4, 101]. Es gilt [nämlich in VI, 4, 34 und 35] ‚für die Pänultima' [aus 24] fort: wenn für die Pänultima [von *śās*] *ā* eingesetzt worden ist,[35] so erfolgt hinter dem *s* [nach VI, 4, 101] Eintritt des *dhi* und gemäß [VIII, 2, 25]: ‚auch vor einem [mit] *dh* [anlautenden Suffix]' Elision des *s*. — Oder aber ich werde sagen [das Sūtra sollte lauten]: *na hau*. Nachdem dort [in VI, 4, 35: *na hau*] der Eintritt von *i* [für das *ā* von *śās*: VI, 4, 34] verboten worden ist, erfolgt hinter dem *s* der Eintritt des *dhi* und gemäß [VIII, 2, 25]: ‚auch vor einem [mit] *dh* [anlautenden Suffix]' Elision des *s*.

Was ferner den Eintritt des *e* [in der Wurzel *as*: VI, 4, 119] betrifft, so wird man ihn als Ausnahme von der [in 111 gelehrten] Elision [des *a* von *as*] betrachten, und es ergibt sich [aus 119] nicht Elision des *s*.[36]

[diese Elision] ist *siddha* in bezug auf [die Substitution von] *Guṇa* [VII, 3, 86].' Denn sonst könnte VII, 3, 86 nicht eintreten, weil keine kurze Pänultima vorhanden wäre.

[31] So auch Kāś. zu VI, 4, 22 und Siddh. K. zu VI, 4, 119 und 35.

[32] Kaiy.: *lhetvabādhanāya śāsir* etc. ‚Der Sinn ist: hier [in VI, 4, 35] wird, um den Eintritt des [in 34 gelehrten] *i* zu beseitigen, *śās* allein als Substitut für *śās* vorgeschrieben. Da also [das Substitut] auf einen Konsonanten endigt, ist der Eintritt des *dhi* [ohne Anwendung von VI, 4, 22] vollständig korrekt.' Nach dieser Interpretation verhalten sich VI, 4, 34 und 35 folgendermaßen:
VI, 4, 34: Bei *śās* tritt unter den angegebenen Bedingungen *i* [für *ā*] ein; VI, 4, 35: vor *hi* dagegen tritt *śās* [ohne Übergang des *ā* in *i*] ein.

[33] Welches nach VIII, 3, 19 abfällt.

[34] Kaiy.: *Dhi sakāre sico* etc. ‚Es wird [hier] nicht [Ślokavārtt. zu VIII, 2, 25] angenommen, daß „bei dem *s* vor einem *dh* Elision [nur] für das *s* des Aoristes (‚*sic*') [und nicht auch für das auslautende *s* einer Wurzel] zu lehren sei". Es wird [nämlich von Pat. zu VIII, 2, 25 im Gegensatz zum Ślokavārttikakāra] ausgeführt werden, daß nur *cakādhi* [mit Elision des Wurzelauslautes *s*, und nicht *cakāddhi*] gebildet wird.'

[35] D. h. VI, 4, 34 und 35 stehen in folgendem Verhältnis:
VI, 4, 34: für [die Pänultima] von *śās* tritt *i* ein;
VI, 4, 35: vor *hi* dagegen tritt [für die Pänultima von *śās*] *ā* ein.

[36] Kaiy.: *Śnasor allopa ity asya lopasyāpavādo* etc. ‚Als Ausnahme von der in der Regel ‚*śnasor allopaḥ*' [VI, 4, 111] gelehrten Elision [des *a* von *as*] wird [in 119] Eintritt von *e* an Stelle des *a* vorgeschrieben. Weil diese Regel ‚*śnasor allopaḥ*', welche den [allgemeinen] Bereich [der Elision des *a*] ausdrücken soll, bei [119] fortgilt, so erfolgt nun durch diese [sc. 119] innerhalb des Bereiches der Elision [von *a*] Eintritt von *e* [für *a*]. Dieser Sinn ergibt sich nach seiner Behauptung.' D. h. VI, 4, 111 lehrt allgemein Ausfall des *a* von *as* vor einem *Sārvadhātuka*, welches *kit* oder *ṅit* ist; VI, 4, 119 aber lehrt die Ausnahme, daß vor dem Suffix *hi* — das ebenfalls *Sārvadhātuka* und *ṅit* ist — *a* von *as* nicht elidiert wird, sondern daß dafür *e* eintritt. VI, 4, 119 lehrt also nicht die Substitution von *e* für das *s* von *as*. Das *s* selbst fällt dann nach VIII, 2, 25 ab.

Hilopa uttve || Värtt. 4.

Die Elision von *hi* bildet eine Veranlassung [zur Anwendung von VI, 4, 22] in bezug auf den Eintritt von *u*: wenn [nämlich] bei *kuru* [nach VI, 4, 106] die Elision des [*Sārvadhātuka*] *hi* erfolgt ist, so ergibt sich nicht gemäß [VI, 4, 110]: ‚wenn auf [den Präsenscharakter] *u* ein *Sārvadhātuka* folgt' Eintritt von *u* (für das *a* von *kar-u*]. Weil [aber VI, 4, 106] als *asiddha* betrachtet wird, tritt [110] ein.[37]

Einwurf Auch dies ist keine Veranlasung. Er wird [nämlich] dort [zu VI, 4, 110 Värtt. 1, Schluß] sagen, das Wort *sārvadhātuka* [in 110] habe den Zweck, daß das *u* [für *a*] eintreten möge, auch wenn ein *Sārvadhātuka* nur eben v o r h e r d a g e w e s e n ist.[38]

Tāstilopeṇyaṇādeśā aḍāḍvidhau || Värtt. 5.

1. Die Elision [der Endung] *ta* [in der 3. sing. aor. pass.], 2. die Elision [des *a*] in der Wurzel *as*, sowie 3. die Substitution des Halbvokales für [das *i* der] Wurzel *i* (‚gehen') bieten Veranlassung [zur Anwendung von VI, 4, 22] in bezug auf die Vorschrift über die [Anfügung der] Augmente *a* und *ā*:

1. [Die Elision des *ta*, z. B.] *akāri*, *aihi*: wenn [nach VI, 4, 104] die Elision des *ta* [Substitutes für *luṅ*] vollzogen ist,[39] so ergeben sich nicht mehr die [nach VI, 4, 71 und 72 nur], vor *luṅ*' eintretenden Augmente *a* [bei *kār-i*][40] und *ā* [bei *īh-i*]. Weil [aber VI, 4, 104] als *asiddha* betrachtet wird, treten sie ein.

2. Die Elision [des *a*] in der Wurzel *as* und die Substitution des Halbvokales für [das *i* der] Wurzel *i* (‚gehen') geben Veranlassung [zur Anwendung von VI, 4, 22], bei *āsan*, *āyan*: wenn

[37] Kaiy.: *Kurv iti* etc. ‚Wenn [nach Anwendung von III, 1, 79 und III, 4, 87] *kṛ+u+hi* vorliegt, so [bieten sich gleichzeitig zwei Regeln dar: 1. VI, 4, 106: Abfall des *hi* und 2. VII, 3, 84: *Guṇa* des Wurzelvokals wegen des folgenden *Ārdhadhātuka* (III, 4, 114) *u*;] weil es später gelehrt wird [*para*] als der Abfall des *hi*, tritt zuerst *Guṇa* ein [und wir erhalten *kar+u+hi*. Nun bieten sich gleichzeitig zwei Regeln dar: 1. VI, 4, 106: Abfall des *hi* und 2. VI, 4, 110: Substitution von *u* für *a* vor einem *Sārvadhātuka*. VI, 4, 110 ist zwar *para*, doch] erfolgt noch vor dem Eintritt des *u* der Abfall des *hi*, weil dieser *nitya* ist [d. h. vor oder nach der Substitution des *u* eintreten kann]. Dann aber [sc. nach dem Abfall des *Sārvadhātuka hi*] ergibt sich der Eintritt des *u* [für *a*] nicht mehr. Doch erfolgt er dadurch, daß der Abfall des *hi* als *asiddha* betrachtet wird.' Dies ist auch die Ansicht der Siddh. K. zu VI, 4, 110.

[38] In der Diskussion zu VI, 4, 110 Värtt. 1 wird nämlich bewiesen, daß das Wort ‚*sārvadhātuke*' in dieser Regel überflüssig wäre, da aus VI, 4, 106 ‚*utaḥ*' zu ergänzen sei. Daraus schließt Pat., daß *sārvadhātuke* im Sinne von *bhūtapūrve 'pi sārvadhātuke* zu fassen sei. Man könnte nun sagen, *sārvadhātuke* sei gänzlich überflüssig, weil nach dem Abfall des *hi* die Substitution von *u* für *a* gleichwohl gemäß I, 1, 62 erfolgen könne. Dagegen wendet dort Kaiy. ein: *Atra na lumatāṅgasyeti pratyayalakṣaṇapratiṣedhād uttvaṃ na syād iti bhūtapūrvagatyā sārvadhātukagrahaṇād bhavati*. ‚Weil hier die aus dem [durch *luk* abgefallenen] Suffir [*hi*] sich ergebende [Operation VI, 4, 110] durch [die Regel I, 1, 63]: „nicht an einem Stamme [bei Ausfall des Suffixes] durch *luk*, *lup* oder *ślu* (*lumat*)" verboten wird, würde *u* [für *a*] nicht eintreten können; also tritt dieses kraft des Wortes *sārvadhātuka* ein nach dem Prinzip „wenn etwas früher dagewesen ist".' Die Kāś. zu VI, 4, 110 stimmt Pat. zu.

[39] Diese Regel tritt vor den Augmentregeln ein, ‚weil sie *nitya* ist' [Kaiy.].

[40] Der Bildungsprozeß bis zur Anwendung der Augmentregeln ist: *kṛ+cli+*(*luṅ*); nach III, 1, 66 und VII, 2,
ta
115: *kār+*(*ciṇ*)*+ta*, und nach VI, 4,
i
104: *kāri*.

in den Wurzeln *i* und *as* [die Substitution des] Halbvokales [VI, 4, 81], bezw. die Elision [des *a*: 111] vollzogen sind, so ergibt sich, da [diese Wurzeln dann] nicht mehr mit einem Vokal beginnen, nicht das Augment *ā* [VI, 4, 72]. Weil [aber VI, 4, 81 und 111] als *asiddha* betrachtet werden, tritt es ein.

Einwurf Was zunächst die Elision [des *a*] in der Wurzel *as* betrifft, so bietet sie keine Veranlassung [zur Anwendung von VI, 4, 22]. Das Vorgehen des Lehrers [Pāṇ.] läßt erkennen (*jñāpayati*), daß das Augment *ā* größere Kraft besitzt [d. h. früher eintritt] als die Elision [des *a*], da er ja in [der Regel VI, 4, 111]: ‚*śnasor allopaḥ*' [dem *a*] ein *t* nachfolgen läßt.[41]

Auch die Substitition des Halbvokales für [das *i* der] Wurzel *i* (‚gehen') gibt nicht Veranlassung [zur Anwendung von VI, 4, 22]. Hinsichtlich der Substitution des Halbvokales wird man eine Teilung der Regel [VI, 4, 82] vornehmen: [Zunächst lehrt VI, 4, 81 allgemein]: ‚Für [das *i* der] Wurzel *i* (‚gehen') tritt [vor Vokalen] der Halbvokal ein.' Hierauf [VI, 4, 82A]: ‚Für das [auslautende] *i* [des Stammes], wenn er mehr als einen Vokal enthält'; [d. h.] auch für [das auslautende] *i* [des Stammes], welcher mehr als einen Vokal enthält, tritt bei *i* (‚gehen') der Halbvokal ein. Hierauf [VI, 4, 82B]: ‚Für [ein *i*], dem nicht eine Konsonantenverbindung vorangeht, [erg. aus 81 :] tritt der Halbvokal ein', und zwar nur[42] für ein [auslautendes] *i*, wenn [der Stamm] mehr als einen Vokal [= eine Silbe] enthält.[43]

[41] D. h. Pāṇ. hätte a-*lopaḥ* sagen können. Wenn er ausdrücklich *at* setzt, so betont er [vgl. I, 1, 70], daß bei *as* das kurze *a*, nicht aber ein langes *a*, elidiert wird. Er deutet dadurch an, daß die Elision des *a* der Wurzel ausgeführt wird, nachdem das Augment *ā* eingetreteten ist. — Kaiy.: *Taparakaraṇasya prayojanam āstām, āsann ityādāv āṭi kṛte ‚vārṇād āṅgaṃ balīya' ity ekādeśaṃ bādhitvā mā bhūd ākārasya lopa iti; yadi prāg lopaḥ syāt tato 'najāditvād āṭo 'bhāvāt tallopanivṛttaye taparatvaṃ na kartavyaṃ syād ity arthaḥ*. ‚Der Sinn ist: die Nachsetzung des *t* bezweckt, baß bei [der Bildung von] *āstām, āsan* usw. **nach** erfolgtem Eintritt des Augmentes *ā* [also in *ā*+*as*+*tām* usw.] — wobei der [Eintritt des] *ekādeśā* [für *ā* + *a*: VI, 1, 90] durch [die Paribh. Nr. 55]: „Eine den Stamm betreffende [Operation, d. i. VI, 4, 111] hat größere Kraft als eine [die Verbindung von] Lauten betreffende [Operation: VI, 1, 90]" verhindert wird — **nicht das ā** [sondern das *a*] elidiert werde. Wenn dagegen vorher [d. h. vor Eintritt des Augmentes ā] die Elision [des *a* von *as*] erfolgte, dann brauchte, da [die Wurzel] nicht mehr mit einem Vokal beginnen würde, und infolgedessen das Augment *ā* garnicht eintreten könnte, nicht noch [dem *a*] ein *t* nachgesetzt zu werden, [um auszudrücken], daß nicht die Elision dieses [Augmentes *ā*] stattfinde.' *Āsan* wird also ohne Anwendung von VI, 4, 22 folgendermaßen gebildet; *as*+*an*; *ā*+*as*+*an*; *ā*+*s* +*an*=*āsan*.

[42] D. h.: während bei der ersten Teilregel [VI, 4, 82A]: ‚*er anekācaḥ*' aus 81 nich ‚*iṇaḥ*' zu ergänzen ist, gilt bei der zweiten Teilregel [VI, 4, 82B]: ‚*asaṃyogapūrvasya*' nicht mehr ‚*iṇaḥ*' aus 81, sondern nur noch ‚*er anekācaḥ*' aus 82A. fort.

[43] Die zweite Teilregel, die sich nicht mehr auf die Wurzel *i* (‚gehen') bezieht, gibt also den Sinn der ungeteilten Regel 82 wieder. Für die Bildung von *āyan* kommt die erste Teilregel [82A] in Betracht, die besagen soll, daß der Halbvokal bei der Wurzel *i* ferner eintritt, wenn der Stamm mehr als einen Vokal enthält — also schon mit dem Augment *ā* versehen ist. — Kaiy.: *Āṭam antareṇānekāj iṇ na bhavatīti pūrvam āḍ bhavatīty anumīyate; iyatur ityādau yogavibhāgam antareṇa yaṇaḥ siddhatvād āḍvidhyartham eva yogavibhāgo vijñāyate; tena nityo 'pi yaṇādeśo 'kṛta āṭi na bhavati*. ‚Ohne das Augment *ā* enthält [der Stamm

Für alle [im Vārtt. 5 genannten Fälle] aber lassen sich [Schwierigkeiten durch die Annahme] vermeiden, [aus VI, 4, 62] gelte fort ‚*upadeśe*' [d. i. ‚bei der im grammatischen System gebrauchten Grundform']. Unter dieser Voraussetzung treten die Augmente *a* und *ā* [nur] ein, solange [die Wurzeln] sich im Zustand der im grammatischen System vorliegenden Grundform befinden.[44] — Oder aber [aus VI, 4, 46] gilt fort ‚*ārdhadhātuke*, [‚vor einem *Ārdhadhātuka*'].[45] — Oder aber es handelt sich bei [der Regel VI, 4, 71]: ‚*luṅ-laṅ-lṛṅkṣv aṭ*' um eine Bezeichnungsweise, die [in *luṅ*, *laṅ*, *lṛṅ* je] zwei *l* wiedergibt;[46] [die Regel besagt demnach: die Augmente *a* und *ā* treten] bei folgendem *luṅ* usw. [ein], sofern diese [noch] mit dem Laut *l* beginnen.[47]

Einwurf Bei jeder [dieser drei Annahmen] kommen *aijyata* und *aupyata* [3. sing. impf. pass.] nicht zustande.[48]

von] *i* (‚gehen') nicht mehr als einen Vokal, also tritt [gemäß 82A] zuerst [d. i. vor der Substitution des Halbvokales] das Augment *ā* ein: so wird gefolgert. Da nun bei *iyatur* usw., [wo der Stamm ja auch mehr als einen Vokal enthält], der Halbvokal [durch die allgemeine Regel 81] ohne eine Teilung der Regel [82] zustande kommt, so ergibt sich die Auffassung, daß die Teilung der Regel einzig und allein im Interesse der Regel über das Augment *ā* [72] vorgenommen wird. Demnach findet die Substitution des Halbvokales, obwohl sie [in bezug auf 72] *nitya* ist, nicht statt, solange das Augment *ā* nicht vorgesetzt worden ist.' *Āyan* wird also gebildet: *i*+*an*; *ā*+*i*+*an*; *ā*+*y*+*an*=*āyan*. — Über *Yogavibhāga* vgl. Kielhorn, *Ind. Ant.* XVI, 247. [Cf. this volume, page 127]

44 Kaiy.: *Antaraṅgān api vidhīn bādhitvā luṅādyupadeśa evāḍāṭau bhavata ity arthaḥ*. ‚Der Sinn ist: die Augmente *a* und *ā* treten [nur] vor der im grammatischen System vorliegenden Grundform von *luṅ* usw. ein, indem sie sogar *Antaraṅga*-Regeln verdrängen.' Wenn z. B. *āsan* gebildet werden soll, so ist der *upadeśa* des *laṅ*: *as*+*laṅ*. Hier bieten sich nun, durch *laṅ* veranlaßt, gleichzeitig zwei Operationen dar: 1. die Substitution der Personalendung für *laṅ*, 2. die Vorsetzung des Augmentes. Die erste Operation ist *antaraṅga*, weil die Veranlassung zu ihrer Ausführung näher liegt [s. unten zu Mbh. III, p. 223, l. 6] als die Veranlassung zum Vollzug der zweiten Operation, die deshalb *bahiraṅga* ist. Die *Antaraṅga*-Operation sollte nun gemäß Paribh. Nr. 50 früher eintreten. Infolge der Ergänzung von ‚*upadeśe*' aber erfolgt zuerst die Vorsetzung des Augmentes; denn solange noch der *upedeśa* des *luṅ* usw. vorliegt, also die Substitution der Personalendungen für *luṅ* usw. noch nicht erfolgt ist, sollen die Augmente eintreten.

45 Kaiy.: *Ārdhadhātukagrahaṇānuvṛttisāmarthyād akṛteṣu luṅādeśeṣu lāvasthāyāṃ labdhārdhadhātukasaṃjñāyām aḍāṭau bhavata ity arthaḥ*. ‚Vermöge des Umstandes, daß das Wort ‚*ārdhadhātuka*' fortgilt, treten die Augmente *a* und *ā* ein, solange die Substitutionen für *luṅ* [usw.] noch nicht vollzogen sind, während noch der durch *la* [gekennzeichnete] Zustand [vgl. III, 4, 77] vorhanden ist, dem die technische Bezeichnung *ārdhadhātuka* eigen ist [wogegen nach III, 4, 113 die substituierten Personalendungen *sārvadhātuka* heißen].'

46 D. h. jedes *l*=*ll*.

47 Erg.: und nicht die entsprechenden Personalendungen für sie substituiert worden sind. — Dieselben drei Annahmen sowie der folgende Einwurf auch Pat. zu VI, 4, 74.

48 *Aijyata* z. B. wird [nach der Kāś. zu VI, 4, 72] gebildet: ‚Wenn *laṅ* eingetreten ist [: *yaj*+*laṅ*], so [ergeben sich] in [diesem] durch *la* gekennzeichneten Zustand [gleichzeitig 1. Substitution von *ta* für *la* und 2. Vorsetzung des Augmentes *a*; aber] vor dem Eintritt des Augmentes *a* wird die Substitution [von *ta*] für *la* vollzogen, weil sie *antaraṅga* ist [vgl. Anm. 44. — Wir erhalten *yaj* +*ta*]. Dann [bieten sich gleichzeitig 1. das Augment *a* und 2. nach III, 1, 67 das Zwischensuffix (*vikaraṇa*) *yak* dar;

Erwiderung Er [Ślokavärtt. zu VI, 4, 74] wird folgendes sagen: ‚Bei vokalisch anlautenden [Stämmen] kommt [*aijyata* usw.] mit Hilfe des Augmentes *a* [und nicht *ā*] zustande.[49]

Anunāsikalopo hilopāllopayor jabhāvaś ca || Värtt. 6.

Die Elision des Nasals gibt Veranlassung [zur Anwendung von VI, 4, 22] hinsichtlich der Elision von *hi* und *a*, sowie ferner der Eintritt von *ja* [für *han*], bei *āgahi*; *jahi*; *gataḥ*, *gatavān*: wenn [nach VI, 4, 37] die Elision des Nasals und [nach 36] der Eintritt des *ja* vollzogen sind, so ergibt sich gemäß [den Regeln] ‚Nach *a* [Elision] von *hi*' [VI, 4, 105] und ‚[auslautendes] *a* wird [vor einem *Ārdhadhātuka*] elidiert' [48], Elision [des *hi* in *āga-hi* und *ja-hi* und des *a* in *ga-taḥ* und *ga-tavān*]. Sie findet [aber] nicht statt, weil [VI, 4, 37 und 36] als *asiddha* betrachet werden.

doch] verdrängt der *vikaraṇa*, da er *nitya* ist, das Augment *a* [und wir erhalten *yaj+ya+ta*. Man könnte dagegen einwenden, daß auch die Anfügung des Augmentes *a nitya* sei, weil sie sowohl vor als auch nach dem Eintritt von *yak* erfolgen könnte; aber] das Augment *a* ist [nach Paribh. Nr. 43] *anitya*, weil sich [nach dem Eintritt von *yak*] eine andere Wortform ergeben würde. Denn nach erfolgtem [Eintritt von *yak*] hätte jenes [Augment *a*] bei dem auf das Zwischensuffix [*yak*] ausgehenden Stamm einzutreten; wenn [*yak*] hingegen nicht eingesetzt worden ist, [hätte das Augment *a*] bei der bloßen Wurzel [einzutreten]. Eine Regel ist aber *anitya*, wenn sie sich [nach dem Eintritt einer zweiten gleichzeitig sich darbietenden Regel] bei einer [hiedurch] geänderten Wortform ergäbe. — [Einwurf]: Aber gemäß [Paribh. Nr. 44]: ‚Hinter einer geänderten Wortform' wäre doch [auch die Anfügung des] *vikaraṇa* [*yak*] *anitya*, [da die Wortform, hinter welcher er eintreten würde, wenn das Augment früher eingetreten wäre, anders wäre, als vor dem Eintritt des Augmentes]? [Die Kāś. gibt keine Antwort. Man hilft sich, indem man sagt: der *vikaraṇa* ist nach Paribh. No. 46 *nitya*]. Nach erfolgtem [Eintritt des] *vikaraṇa* findet vor [dem Eintritt des] Augmentes *a* [die sich gleichzeitig darbietende Substitution des] *Saṃprasāraṇa* [i für *y* nach VI, 1, 15] statt, da diese eben *nitya* ist [und wir erhalten *ij+ya+ta*]. Da nun ein vokalisch anlautender Stamm entstanden ist, tritt nach VI, 4, 72 das Augment *ā* ein [und wir erhalten gemäß VI, 1, 90: *aijyata*].' — Diese Bildung von *aijyata* usw. wäre nach der Behauptung des Oppenenten bei keiner der drei Annahmen möglich. Vg. Kaiy.: *Triṣv api parihāreṣu* usw. ‚Bei allen drei Annahmen zur Vermeidung [von Schwierigkeiten] würden die Wurzeln *yaj* usw., da in dem durch *la* gekennzeichneten Zustand [also vor dem Eintritt des *kit*-Suffixes *yak*] *Saṃprasāraṇa* [VI, 1, 15] nicht eintritt, nicht mit Vokalen beginnen: infolgedessen könnte das Augment *ā* nicht eintreten folglich würde sich das Augment *a* ergeben.' Wir bekämen dann: *a+yaj+laṅ*; *a+yaj+ta*; *a+yaj+ya+ta* und schließlich *a+ij+ya+ta*, was jedoch nach VI, 1, 90 nicht *aijyata* ergeben kann.

[49] Kaiy.: *Āṭaś ceti yat sūtraṃ tad aṭaś ceti kriyate, acīty adhikārāc ca hali vṛddhyabhāvah. Katham āyann, āsann iti, yāvateṇastyor yaṇlopayoḥ kṛtayor vṛddhir nāsti? Antaraṅgatvād vṛddhir bhaviṣyatīty adoṣaḥ. Nānāśrayatvāc ca vārṇād āṅgaṃ balīya iti nāsti. Kṛtāyāṃ vṛddhāv āsann iti taparakaraṇād ākāralopābhāvaḥ. Iṇo 'pi vṛddher aikārasya yaṇ na bhaviṣyatīti; iṇo yaṇ er iti yogavibhāgād ikārāntasyeṇo yaṇvidhānāt tadabhāvāc cāyādeśe* [Text: *ca yādeśe* (sic!)] *kṛte āyann iti bhaviṣyati*. ‚Das Sūtra ‚*āṭaś ca*' [VI, 1, 90] wird geändert in ‚*aṭaś ca*' [d. h. auch für das Augment *a*+Vokal tritt *Vṛddhi* ein], und aus dem [hier fortgeltenden] *Adhikāra*, ‚vor einem Vokal' [VI, 1, 77] ergibt sich, daß vor einem Konsonanten *Vṛddhi* nicht eintritt. — [Einwurf]: Wie kommen aber [unter dieser Voraussetzung] *āyan*, *āsan* zustande, da sich doch bei den Wurzeln *i* und *as*, wenn [in *a+i+an* und *a+as+an*] die Substitution des Halbvokales [für *i*] und die Elision

Einwurf Was zunächst die Elision des Nasals betrifft, so gibt sie keine Veranlassung [zur Anwendung von VI, 4, 22]. Bei der Elision des *a* [VI, 4, 48] ist [nämlich] ,*upadeśe*' [aus 37] zu ergänzen.[50]

Gegeneinwurf Wenn ,*upadeśe*' zu ergänzen ist, so ergibt sich dort [III, 1, 80] nicht *dhinutaḥ*, *kṛṇutaḥ*.[51]

Erwiderung Dies bedeutet keinen Fehler. Mit dem Worte *upadeśa* wird nicht auf die ursprüngliche Form Bezug genommen, sondern auf des *Ārdhadhātuka* wird Bezug genommen. [Gemeint ist ein Stamm], welcher beim Antritt eines *Ārdhadhātuka* an die im grammatischen Lehrsystem gebrauchte Form [der Wurzel] auf *a* auslautet.[52]

[des *a* von *as*] vollzogen sind, *Vṛddhi* nicht mehr ergibt? — [Erwiderung]: Es liegt kein Fehler vor, denn [die Substitution von] *Vṛddhi* wird [noch vor diesen Operationen] eintreten, weil sie [als näherliegend: vgl. p. 225, Anm. 44] eine *Antaraṅga*-Operation ist. Und weil ferner [die beiden Operationen] auf verschiedenen [Elementen, die *Vṛddhi* auf dem Augment *a*+folgendem Vokal, der Halbvokal, bezw. die Elision, auf den Suffixen] beruhen, so gilt hier nicht [die Paribh. Nr. 55]: ,Eine den Stamm betreffende [Operation, hier: Substitution des Halbvokals, bezw. Elision des *a*] hat größere Kraft [=tritt früher ein] als eine [die Verbindung von] Lauten betreffende [Operation, hier: die Vṛddhierung].' [Vgl. dagegen Paribh. Text, p. 60, l. 9f. (Transl., p. 303): *Yat tu samānanimittikatvarūpasamānāśrayatva evaiṣeti tan na*]. ,Wenn nun *Vṛddhi* [zuerst] eingetreten ist, so findet bei *āsan* infolge der Nachsetzung des *t* [hinter dem *a* von *allopaḥ* in VI, 4, 111 nach I, 1, 70] nicht noch Elision des *ā* statt. Bei der Wurzel *i* hinwiederum wird für die *Vṛddhi ai* [aus *a*+*i*+*an*] nicht noch der Halbvokal eintreten. Da [nämlich] durch die Teilung der Regel in ,*iṇo yaṇ er*' [VI, 4, 82 A; vgl. p. 224] die Substitution des Halbvokales nur bei der Wurzel *i*, sofern sie auf *i* auslautet, vorgeschrieben wird, und weil dieses [*i* nach der Vṛddhierung in *ai*+*an*] nicht mehr vorhanden ist, wird nach vollzogener Substitution von *āy* [für *ai* gemäß VI, 1, 78] *āyan* zustande kommen.'

[50] D. h. bei einem Stamme, dessen ursprüngliche Form — d. i. die im grammatischen System gebräuchliche Form der Wurzel — auf *a* auslautet, wird dieses *a* vor einem *Ārdhadhātuka* elidiert. *Ga*- hingegen ist das Ergebnis einer an der *upadeśa*-Form *gam* vorgenommenen Operation. Hier kann also VI, 4, 48 überhaupt nicht angewendet werden. Vgl. p. 220, Anm. 24.

[51] *Dhinutaḥ* wird aus der *upadeśa*-Form *dhivi* [Dhātup. 15, 84]=*dhinv* [VII, 1, 58] gebildet, indem nach III, 1, 80 an *dhinv* das Suffix *u* angefügt und [gleichzeitig] für das auslautende *v* ein *a* substituiert wird. Wir erhalten *dhina*+*u*+*taḥ*. Das *a* wird nun wegen des folgenden *Ārdhadhātuka*-Suffixes *u* nach VI, 4, 48 elidiert, so daß sich *dhinutaḥ* ergibt. Wenn jedoch bei VI, 4, 48 *upadeśe* zu ergänzen wäre, könnte die Elision des *a* nicht erfolgen weil nicht *dhina*- *upadeśa*-Form ist, sondern *dhinv*.

[52] Eigentlich: in [dem Stadium] der *upadeśa*-Form, [wie sie] beim Antritt eines *Ārdhadhātuka* [erscheint]. — Kaiy.: *Ārdhadhātukopadeśakāle yad akārāntam aṅgaṃ, tasyārdhadhātuke parato lopa iti sūtrārthaḥ. Tatra dhinvikṛṇvyor a ceti* usw. ,. . . Weil in [der Regel III, 1, 80]: ,,Bei *dhinv* und *kṛṇv* tritt [*u* und] auch *a* [für *v*] ein'' zugleich mit dem [*Ārdhadhātuka*-]Suffix *u* [die Substitution des] *a* vorgeschrieben wird, so lauten *dhinv* und *kṛṇv* in der *upadeśa*-Form, [wie sie] beim Antritt eines *Ārdhadhātuka* [erscheint], auf *a* aus; also kommt unter jener Voraussetzung [*tatra*; d. i. gemäß der Annahme ,*ārdhadhātukopadeśe*'] die Elision des *a* [VI, 4, 48] zustande. Und weil dieser [*lopa*, welcher ein Substitut (*ādeśa*) des ursprünglichen *a* ist], durch ein folgendes [Element, sc. das *u*] bedingt ist, sich also [gemäß I, 1, 57 in bezug auf die Regel VII, 3, 86, welche den dem *sthānin* vorangehenden Laut *i* betrifft], wie der *sthānin* [sc. *a*] verhält, so erfolgt bei *dhinutaḥ* usw. nicht [die Substitution

Auch der Eintritt von *ja* [für *han*] gibt keine Veranlassung [zur Anwendung von VI, 4, 22]. Hinsichtlich der Elision von *hi* [VI, 4, 105] wird [nämlich] eine Teilung der Regel [106] vorgenommen werden. [Zunächst 105]: ,Nach einem *a* [erfolgt Elision] von *hi*.' Hierauf [106A.]: ,Auch nach *u*'; [d. h.] auch nach einem *u* findet Abfall des *hi* statt. Hierauf [106B.]: ,Wenn es ein Suffix ist'; ,wenn es ein Suffix ist', ist in beiden Fällen [sc. in 105 und 106A.] zu ergänzen.[53]

Einwurf Aber warum heißt es denn [im Värtt. 6] ,die Elision des Nasals in bezug auf die Elision von *hi* und *a*, sowie der Eintritt von *ja*', warum heißt es nicht ,die Elision des Nasals und der Eintritt von *ja* in bezug auf die Elision des *a* und *hi*?'

Erwiderung Damit nicht die [in I, 3, 10 gelehrte] Entsprechung [der in gleicher Zahl einander gegenüberstehenden Glieder des Satzes] der Zahl nach zur Anwendung komme. [Denn] die Elision des Nasals gibt Veranlassung [zur Anwendung von VI, 4, 22 auch] in bezug auf die Elision von *hi*, in: ,*Maṇḍūki tābhir āgahi*' [VS. 17, 6]; ,*rohidaśva ihāgahi*' [VS. 11, 72]; ,*marudbhir agna āgahi*' [RV. 1, 19, 1].[54]

Saṃprasāraṇam avarṇalope || Värtt. 7.

[Die Substitution von] *Saṃprasāraṇa* gibt Veranlassung [zur Anwendung von VI, 4, 22] hinsichtlich der Elision des Lautes *a*,

von] *Guṇa* [für das *i* von *dhin*-].' D. h. trotz der erfolgten Elision ist der Stamm in bezug auf VII, 3, 86 noch als auf *a* [*dhin*(*a*)+*u*+*taḥ*], also auf zwei Laute ausgehend zu denken. Das *i* ist dann nicht Pänultima, und VII, 3, 86 kann nicht angewendet werden. — Vgl. Siddh. K. zu VI, 3, 48: *Ārdhadhātukopadeśakāle yad akārāntaṃ tasyākārasya lopaḥ syād ārdhadhātuke pare*. Ebenso urteilt offenbar auch die Kāś., die zu VI, 4, 22 unter den Fällen, in denen diese Regel zur Anwendung kommt, zwar *āgahi* und *jahi*, nicht aber *gataḥ* und *gatavān* erwähnt.

[53] Kaiy.: *Samudāyāpekṣaṇāt; ,asaṃyogapūrvād' ity atra tu bhedenāpekṣaṇād ānantaryād uta saṃbadhyate, na tv ata iti* ,[*Pratyayāt* ist in beiden Fällen zu ergänzen], weil es [zum Vorhergehenden] im Verhältnis der Anreihung steht; dagegen ist hier bei ,*asaṃyogapūrvāt*', weil dessen Beziehung [zu dem Vorbergehenden] in einer Unterscheidung [d. i. Einschränkung] besteht, [nur] ,*utas*' [106A] gemeint, da [*asaṃyogapūrvāt*] unmitelbar [auf ,*utas*'] folgt, nicht aber ,*atas*' [105].' D. h. *pratyayāt* ist auch in 105 zu ergänzen, *asaṃyogapūrvāt* dagegen nur in 106A. Die Regel 105 besagt demnach: nach *a*, jedoch nur wenn es Suffix ist, erfolgt Abfall von *hi*. *Ja-hi*, bei dem dies nicht zutrifft, also nicht die Anwendung von VI, 4, 22.

[54] Wenn das Vārttika lautete,

I II 1
,*anunāsikalopa-jabhāvāv; allopa-*
2
hilopayor', so würde sich nach I, 3, 10, ebenso wie die Glieder 1 und I einander entsprechen, auch *hilopa* nur auf *jabhāva*, nicht aber auch auf *anunāsikalopa* beziehen. Doch beweist [nach Kāty.'s Ansicht] die Form *āgahi* [aus *āgam-hi*], daß *anunāsikalopa* auch in bezug auf *hilopa* als *asiddha* zu betrachten ist. — Kaiy.: *Yadyapi prayojanākhyānaparatvād* usw. ,Für diesen Satz würde zwar die Entsprechnng der Zahl nach nicht gelten, weil er [nicht ein Sūtra ist, sondern] die ausschließliche Bestimmung hat, Zwecke [eines Sūtra] anzugeben. Aber weil man auf Grund der Beobachtung, daß sonst eine Reihenfolge den Grund für ein proportionales Verhältnis [ihrer Glieder: *vyavasthā*] bildet, dasselbe auch in unserem Falle vermuten könnte, so ist, um dies gänzlich auszuschließen, [im Vārttika] diese Art des Ausdrucks gewählt worden.' — Zu *āgahi* bemerkt Kaiy.: *Atrāpi pratyayād ity asyobhayoḥ śeṣatvād dher lugabhāvaḥ sidhyati*. ,Daraus, daß ,*pratyayāt*' in beiden [Regeln: 105 und 106A.] zu ergänzen ist [vgl. oben nebst Anm. 53], ergibt sich, daß das *hi* auch hier [bie *āga-hi*] nicht abfällt.'

[z. B.] *maghonaḥ* (acc. pl.), *maghonā, maghone*. Wenn [nämlich in *magha + van + aḥ* gemäß VI, 4, 133 die Substitution des] *Saṃprasāraṇa* [*u* für *v*] vollzogen [und nach VI, 1, 108 *u* für *u + a* eingetreten] ist, so ergibt sich gemäß [der Regel VI, 4, 148]: ‚Für *i* und *a* [vor der Femininendung *ī* und vor einem *Taddhita*]' Elision [des *a* in *magha + un + aḥ* vor dem *Taddhita un* (aus *van*)].[55] Weil aber [VI, 4, 133] als *asiddha* betrachtet wird, tritt sie nicht ein.[56]

Einwurf Dies ist keine Veranlassung [zur Anwendung von VI, 4, 22]. Er wird [nämlich im Bhāṣya zu IV, 1, 7] folgendes sagen: *Maghavan* ist ein [etymologisch] nicht abgeleiteter Nominalstamm.[57]

Rebhāva āllope || Värtt. 8.

Der Eintritt von *re* [für *ire*] gibt Veranlassung [zur Anwendung von VI, 4, 22] hinsichtlich der Elision von *ā*, in: ‚*Kiṃ svid garbhaṃ prathamaṃ dadhra āpaḥ*' [vgl. RV. 10, 82, 5]. Wenn [nämlich in *da-dhā + ire* gemäß VI, 4, 76] der Eintritt von *re* [für *ire*] erfolgt ist,[58] so ergibt sich [in *da-dhā-re*] nicht gemäß [der Regel 64]: ‚*Ā* wird auch vor dem [einem *Ārdhadhātuka* vorgesetzten] Augment *i* elidiert' Elision des *ā*. Weil [aber VI, 4, 76] als *asiddha* betrachtet wird, tritt sie ein.[59]

[55] Kaiy.: *Maghona iti: magham asyāstīti cchandasīvanipau ceti vanip* ‚[*Maghavān*] bedeutet: ihm ist eine Gabe eigen [vgl. V, 2, 94]. Es est [nämlich mit dem *Taddhita*-Suffix] *van* [gebildet], nach [dem Värtt. zu V, 2, 109]: ‚Im Veda [werden] auch noch [die Suffixe] *ī* und *van* [im Sinne von *mat* (*matup*: V, 2 94) angefügt].'

[56] *Asiddhaṃ bahiraṅgam antaraṅga iti paribhāṣayā saṃprasāraṇasyāsiddhatvaṃ nāsti, — eṣā hi paribhāṣā vāha ūḍ ity atra jñāpitatvād ābhācchāstrīyā — tasyāṃ pravartamānāyām akāralopasaṃprasāraṇayor asiddhatvād antaraṅgabahiraṅgayor yugapad anupasthānān, nājānantarya iti pratiṣedhād vā.* ‚[Die Substitution des] *Saṃprasāraṇa* ist [nur gemäß VI, 4, 22 und] nicht auf Grund der Paribhāṣā [Nr. 50]: ‚‚Eine *Bahiraṅga*-Regel ist *asiddha* in bezug auf eine *Antaraṅga*-Regel'' als *asiddha* zu betrachten. Denn wenn dieses Paribhāṣā — welche nämlich eine [im Abschnitt] bis *bha* [VI, 4, 22—175] gelehrte [Regel] ist, weil sie in [der Regel VI, 4, 132]: ‚*vāha ūṭ*' [s. Pat. hiezu] angedeutet wird — zur Anwendung gelangt, so sind sowohl die Elision des *a* [d. i. die *Antaraṅga*-Operation], als auch [die Substitution des] *Saṃprasāraṇa* [d. i. die *Bahiraṅga*-Operation gemäß VI, 4, 22] als *asiddha* zu betrachten, und infolgedessen sind die *Antaraṅga*-und die *Bahiraṅga*-Operation nicht gleichzeitig zur Stelle [vgl. näheres pp. 236 ff., nebst Anm.]; oder die Paribhāṣā [Nr. 51]: ‚‚[Eine *Bahiraṅga*-Operation ist] nicht [als *bahiraṅga*, also auch nicht als *asiddha* zu betrachten, wenn die *Antaraṅga*-Operation] auf der unmittelbaren Folge eines Vokales [beruht]'' verbietet [hier die Anwendung der Paribh. Nr. 50].'

[57] *Van* ist also nicht als Suffix (*pratyaya*), und speziell *Taddhita* zu betrachten. Jene Operationen, welche sich im Falle einer etymologischen Herleitung des Wortes *maghavan* ergeben würden — hier die Elision des *a* [VI, 4, 148] — sind also unmöglich, und VI, 4, 22 hat deshalb hier keine Gelegenheit zur Anwendung. Vgl. Paribh. Nr. 22: *Uṇādayo 'vyutpannāni prātipadikāni*. — Kaiy.: *Tataś ca taddhite* usw. ‚Und deshalb tritt die vor einem *Taddhita* vorgeschriebene Elision des *a* nicht ein. Zumal da [VI, 4, 133] auch deshalb nicht [in bezug auf 148] *asiddha* sein könnte, weil [die zwei Operationen] nicht [auf einem gemeinsamen Element] beruhen [vgl. zu Värtt. 12], muß man die Alternative, daß [*maghavan*] etymologisch nicht ableitbar ist, annehmen.' — Vgl. *Uṇādisūtras* [ed. Aufrecht] I, 158.

[58] Kaiy.: *Nityatvāt*. ‚Weil [diese Operation in bezug auf VI, 4, 64] *nitya* ist [und nach Paribh. 38 zuerst eintritt].'

[59] So auch Kāś. und Siddh. K. zu VI, 4, 76

Einwurf Auch dies gibt nicht Veranlassung [zur Anwendung von VI, 4, 22]. Der Eintritt von *re* [für *ire*] ist [nämlich] vedisch. Und die Personalendungen des Perfektums[60] sind [nach III, 4, 117] im Veda auch *Sārvadhātuka*. Unter dieser Voraussetzung (*tatra*) ergibt sich aus [der Regel I, 2, 4]: ‚Ein *Sārvadhātuka*, welches nicht *pit* ist, gilt als *ṅit*-Suffix', daß [*re*] ein *ṅit*-Suffix ist, und demgemäß erfolgt die Elision des *ā* [in *da-dhā* + *re*] nach [der Regel VI, 4, 112]: ‚Für das *ā* von (*ś*)*nā* [dem Präsenscharakter der IX. Kl.] und das der reduplizierten Stämme [vor einem *Sārvadhātuka*, welches *kit* oder *ṅit* ist].[61]

Wenn demnach diese Regel [VI, 4, 22] nicht aufgestellt wird:

Zwecke des Ślokavārttikakāra[62] Ut tu kṛñaḥ katham or vinivṛttau;

‚Wie soll denn aber in *kṛ u* [für *a*] eintreten, nachdem [der Präsenscharakter] *u* verschwunden ist?'

[60] Die sonst nach III, 4, 115 *Ārdhadhātuka* sind.
[61] Kaiy.: *Sārvadhātuke śapślau dvirvacane 'ghor iti ītvaniṣedhād* [Text: itva-] *ākāralopaḥ* ‚Wenn [der Reihe nach] das *Sārvadhātuka* [*re*] eingetreten, die Abwerfung des Präsenscharakters *a* (*śap*) [III, 1, 68 wegen des *Sārvadhātuka*; II, 4, 75] und die Reduplikation [VI, 1, 10 und 8] erfolgt ist, wird das *ā* [des Stammes gemäß VI, 4, 112] elidiert, da ja durch [VI, 4, 113]: „[*ī* tritt an die Stelle von *ā* vor einem konsonantisch anlautenden *Sārvadhātuka*, jedoch] nicht bei *dā* und *dhā* (*ghu*)" der Eintritt von *ī* [für *ā*] verboten wird.'
[62] Kaiy.: ‚Nachdem die vom Verfasser der Vārttikas [Käty.] genannten Zwecke [von VI, 4, 22] widerlegt worden sind, werden die vom Ślokavārttikakāra behaupteten Zwecke vorgeführt.'
[63] In VI, 4, 110 gilt nämlich aus 106 ‚*utaḥ*' fort.
[64] Die genannten Formen werden folgendermaßen gebildet: *kṛ* + *vaḥ*; nach III, 1, 79: *kṛ* + *u* + *vaḥ*; nach VII, 3, 84, die als *para*-Regel früher als VI, 4, 108 und 109 eintritt: *kar* + *u* + *vaḥ*; nach VI, 4, 108 und 109: *kar* + $\left\{ \begin{array}{l} vaḥ \\ maḥ \end{array} \right.$ und *kar* + *yāt*. Die eben erfolgte Elision des *u* muß als *asiddha* betrachtet werden, wenn nun nach 110 *kurvaḥ* usw. zustande kommen sollen.

Kaiy.: *Ut tu kṛña iti, sārvadhātuke para iti. Atha* usw. ‚Wenn ein *Sārvadhātuka* [auf das Suffix *u*] folgt': ‚[Einwurf:] Aber warum erfolgt denn der Eintritt des *u* [für *a*] nicht [nach dem Wortlaut von VI, 4, 110], wenn nur ein *Sārvadhātuka* [ohne vorangehendes Suffix *u*] folgt? — [Erwiderung:] Dies ist nicht möglich. [Denn sonst] würde der Eintritt des *u* [für *a*] nur dort erfolgen, wo die Elision [des Suffixes] *u* vollzogen worden ist [wie in *kurvaḥ* aus *kar* + *vaḥ*], nicht aber bei *kuruta* usw., weil hier [das *u*] als Innensuffix [*kar*- und *Sārvadhātuka* trennend] dazwischentritt. Wenn man dagegen geltend machen wollte, daß ja auch bei *kurvaḥ* usw. [das Suffix *u*] noch trennend dazwischenstehe, weil [dessen Substitut *lopa*] sich [nach I, 1, 57] wie der *sthānin* [*u*] verhalte, so [antworten wir]: nein! Ein derartiges [fortdauerndes] Dazwischenstehen [eines elidierten Vokales gemäß I, 1, 57] wird [sonst nur] auf Grund eines [in einem Sūtra darauf hinweisenden] Wortes angenommen. [Nach der Interpretation „*sārvadhātuka eva parataḥ*" aber enthält VI, 4, 110 keinen Hinweis auf das Suffix *u*]. — [Einwurf:] Wenn man nun aber annimmt, [daß 110 infolge Ergänzung von „*utaḥ*" aus 106 zu interpretieren sei:] „Wenn auf [das Suffix] *u* ein *Sārvadhātuka* folgt," so wird ja doch sogar dann, wenn die Elision des [Suffixes] *u* als *nitya*-Operation [schon vor der Substitution von *Guṇa*: VII, 3, 84] vollzogen worden ist, der Eintritt des *u* [für *a*] dadurch erfolgen, daß der *lopa* für jenes [Suffix *u*] sich [nach I, 1, 57] wie der *sthānin* [*u*] verhält [also:

[Pat.] Wenn hier, bei *kurvaḥ, kurmaḥ, kuryāt*, [gemäß VI, 4, 108 und 109] die Elision des [Präsenscharakters] *u* vollzogen ist, so ergibt sich [in *kar* + *vaḥ* usw.] nicht gemäß [VI, 4, 110]: ‚Wenn auf [den Präsenscharakter] *u*[63] ein *Sārvadhātuka* folgt', der Eintritt von *u* [für das *a* von *kar-*].[64]

ṇer api ceṭi kathaṃ vinivṛttiḥ |

‚Und wie sollte denn auch *ṇi* vor *iṭ* verschwinden?'

[Pat.] Und auch hier, bei *kāriṣyate* aus *kārayati*, ergibt sich nicht [gemäß der Regel VI, 4, 51]: ‚Für [das Suffix] *ṇi* [vor einem

kṛ + *u* + *vaḥ*; VI, 4, 108: *kṛ* + *vaḥ*; VII, 3, 84: *kar* + *vaḥ* und VI, 4, 110 mit Hilfe von I, 1, 57 aus *kar* [+ *u*] + *vaḥ*: *kurvaḥ*]; geschweige denn hier, wo zuerst [nach VII, 3, 84 die Substitution von] *Guṇa* [für *ṛ*] erfolgt, weil [VII, 3, 84] *para* ist, und erst nachher [also unmittelbar vor der Anwendung von VI, 4, 110] die Elision des [Suffixes] *u* [,die nicht *nitya* ist]; und wenn dann die Vorschrift [VI, 4, 110] für [das Element *a* ausgeführt werden soll,] welches dem Vokal [d. i. dem Suffix *u*] voranging, als er noch nicht durch das Substitut [sc. *lopa*] ersetzt war [vgl. im Anhang s. *sthānivadbhāva*], so verhält sich [gemäß I, 1, 57 der *lopa* für *u*] tatsächlich wie der *sthānin* [*u*]. Hingegen soll [VI, 4, 110] nicht [auf Grund von I, 1, 62] als eine durch das [elidierte] Suffix [*u*] bedingte [Operation] eintreten; denn [diese Operation] beruht [nicht ausschließlich auf *u* als einem Suffix, sondern] auf dem Buchstaben [*u* in Verbindung mit dem folgenden *Sārvadhātuka*, also in *kurvaḥ*, aus *kar*[*u*] + *vaḥ*, auf *u-vaḥ*; vgl. im Anhang s. *pratyayalakṣaṇam*]. — [Erwiderung:] Also folgendermaßen: der Verfasser des Bhāṣya hat nicht angenommen, daß [die Elision des Suffixes *u*] sich wie der *sthānin* [*u*] verhalte, da er ein anderes Verfahren zur Vermeidung [der Schwierigkeit, u. zw. VI, 4, 22] angeben wollte. Oder aber [wir müssen, da die Anwendung von I, 1, 57 sonst berechtigt wäre, annehmen:] zuerst erfolgt die Elision des [Suffixes] *u*, weil sie *nitya* ist, und nachher [die Substitution von] *Guṇa* [für *ṛ*]. Wenn nämlich die Elision des *u* vollzogen ist, so muß gemäß [der Regel I, 1, 62], daß das durch das [elidierte] Suffix Bedingte eintritt, [die Substitution von] *Guṇa* [trotz der vollzogenen Elision des Suffixes *u*] erfolgen. Daraus ergibt sich, daß [die Substitution von] *Guṇa* nicht *nitya* ist, und zwar gemäß [der Paribh. Nr. 45:] „Eine Regel [,welche *nitya* sein sollte,] ist nicht *nitya* [tritt also nicht zuerst ein], wenn sie sich [nach dem Eintritt der zweiten sich gleichzeitig darbietenden Regel nur noch] mit Hilfe irgendeiner anderen Regel ergeben würde." [So würde sich hier *Guṇa* nach vollzogener Elision des *u* nur noch mit Hilfe von I, 1, 62 ergeben]. Dann aber [d. h. wenn also *Guṇa* erst nach der Elision eintritt] ist das *a* [in *kar-vaḥ*] ein Element, welches erst dem durch das Substitut [sc. *lopa*] ersetzten Vokal vorangeht; wenn also an einem) solchen [*a*] die Vorschrift [sc. VI, 4, 110] ausgeführt werden soll, so kann [das Substitut *lopa*] nicht [nach I, 1, 57] wie der *sthānin* [d. i. das Suffix *u*] behandelt werden. [Vgl. im Anhang s. *sthānivadbhāva*. — Demnach wird VI, 4, 22 angewendet werden, indem VI, 4, 108 und 109 als *asiddha* betrachtet werden]. — [Einwurf:] Aber es ist doch nicht moglich, daß die Elision des [Suffixes] *u asiddha* sei, da sie nicht [auf einem gemeinsamen Element] beruht; denn vor [den Buchstaben] *m* und *v* [vgl. VI, 4, 107] wird dei Elision des *u* vorgeschrieben, vor dem [auf *u*] folgenden *Sārvadhātuka* [in seiner Gänze, d. i. vor *vaḥ, maḥ*] wird der Eintritt des *u* [für *a*] vorgeschreiben? — [Erwiderung:] Dies trifft nicht zu; denn [nicht vor *m* und *v*, sondern] vor einem mit *m* oder *v* beginnenden Suffix wird die Elision des [Suffixes] *u* vorgeschreiben. Es ist also tatsächlich die Abhängigkeit [der Elision des *u*] vor einem gemeinsamen [Element] vorhanden.' [Vgl. zu Vārtt. 12.] Die Regel VI, 4, 22 wird hier also angewendet.

Ārdhadhātuka, jedoch] ohne das Augment *i*' die Elision des [Kausativ-Suffixes] *ṇi* (= *i*).[65]

Abruvatas tava yogam imaṃ syāl luk ca ciṇo nu kathaṃ na tarasya ||

,Wenn du diese Regel nicht gelten lassen willst, wie sollte da nach *ciṇ* nicht auch der Abfall von *tara* erfolgen?'

[Pat.] Und hier, bei *akāritarām*, *ahāritarām*, wie sollte da nicht [gemäß VI, 4, 104] der Abfall des auf *ciṇ* [Suffix *i* der 3. sing. aor. pass.] folgenden *tara* erfolgen?[66]

Erwiderung des Ślokavārttikakāra Caṃ bhagavān kṛtavāṃs tu tadarthaṃ tena bhaved iṭi ner vinivṛttiḥ |

,,*Ca*" [,und auch'] hat der Meister [Pāṇ.] doch nur zu dem Zwecke gesetzt, daß dadurch vor *iṭ* das Verschwinden des *ṇi* erfolge.'

[Pat.] Hier in [der Regel VI, 4, 62]: ,Vor *sya* (fut. und condit.), *sic* [*s*-aor.], *sīyuṭ* (precat.) und *tāsi* (periphr. fut.) im Impersonale und Passiv kann bei [Verbalstämmen], die in ihrer im grammatischen System vorliegenden [einfachsten] Form vokalisch auslauten, ferner bei *han*, *grah* und *dṛś* auch [so verfahren werden], als ob bei ihnen *ciṇ* [die Endung *i* der 3. sing. aor. pass.] vorläge; [dann] tritt auch noch das Augment *i* ein.' Was denn sonst noch [ca]? — U n d a u c h die Elision des [Kausativ-Suffixes] *ṇi*.[67]

Mvor api ye ca tathāpy anuvṛttau

,Sowohl ,*mvor*' wie auch ,*ye ca*' gelten noch fort.'

[Pat.] Auch hier, bei [der Bildung von] *kurvaḥ*, *kurmaḥ*, *kuryāt* [d. i. in VI, 4, 110] wird ,vor *m* und *v*' [107], sowie ,und vor *y*' [108] noch fortgelten.[68]

[65] Das Fut. pass. des Kausativums von *kṛ* ist entweder 1. gleich der *Ātmanepada*-Form *kārayiṣyate*, welche folgendermaßen gebildet wird: *kṛ* + *ṇi* + *te*; nach VII, 2, 115: *kāri* + *te*; VII, 3, 84: *kāre-te*. Dann nach III, 33, VII, 2, 70 und VIII, 3, 59: *kāre* + *i-ṣya* + *te* und schließlich nach VI, 1, 78: *kārayiṣyate*. Oder aber 2. der mit dem Kausativ-Suffix *ṇi* (*i*) gebildete Stamm *kṛ* + *ṇi*- wird so behandelt, als ob er auf *ciṇ* [d. i. das Suffix *i* der 3. sing. aor. pass.] endigte, und in diesem Falle wird an *kāri*- gemäß VI, 4, 62 im Futurum das Suffix *sya* mittels des Augmentes *i* angefügt. Wir erhalten *kāri* + *i-ṣya* + *te*. Diese Vorsetzung des Augmentes *i* muß nun als *asiddha* betrachtet werden, wenn das auslautende *i* (*ṇi*) des Stammes *kāri* gemäß VI, 4, 51 elidiert werden soll. Vgl. Mbh. vol. III, p. 206 das Ślokavārtt.: *iṭ cāsiddhas, tena me lupyate ṇir* . . . . — Kaiy.: *Prakṛtipratyayāśrayatvād* usw. ,[Die Vorsetzung des] Augmentes *i* (*iṭ*) und die Elision des *ṇi* sind von einem gemeinsamen [Element] abhängig, da sie beide auf dem ursprünglichen [d. h. nicht mit dem Augment *i* versehen] Suffix [*sya*] beruhen.' [Vgl. zu Värtt. 12].

[66] *Akāri* ist aus *akārita* entstanden, indem das auf *ciṇ* (*i*) folgende Suffix *ta* gemäß VI, 4, 104 abgefallen ist. Nach der Anfügung von *tarām* müßte derselben Regel zufolge auch das Suffix *tara* abfallen, wenn es nicht als *asiddha* betrachtet würde. Vgl. im Anhang s. *viṣayaviṣayibhāva*.

[67] Das ,*ca*' soll besagen, daß a u ß e r der Elision des *ṇi*, die aus VI, 4, 51 fortgilt, a u c h n o c h *iṭ* eintritt. Da sich also die Elision des *ṇi* schon aus VI, 4, 62 ergibt, bedarf es zu ihrem Eintritt nicht erst der Anwendung von VI, 4, 22.

[68] Danach wäre VI, 4, 110 zu interpretieren: Für *a* tritt *u* ein vor einem *Sārvadhātuka*, wenn dieses mit *m*, *v* oder *y* beginnt. Damit ist gesagt, daß diese Substitution vor den mit *m*, *v* und *y* beginnenden Endungen ohne Rücksicht auf die Elision des Suffixes *u* [vgl. Kaiy. p. 230, Anm. 64, Anfang] erfolgt. — Kaiy.: *Ata ut sārvadhātuke ity atra* usw. ,Weil in [der Regel VI, 4, 110]: ,,Für *a* tritt *u* ein, wenn ein *Sārvadhātuka* folgt" ,*mvor*' und ,*ye ca*'

ciṇluki ca kṅita eva hi luk syāt ||

,Und bei dem Abfall nach *ciṇ* soll nur der Abfall eines *kit*- oder *ṅit*-Suffixes gelten.'

[Pat.] Auch bei dem Abfall [des Suffixes] nach *ciṇ* [VI, 4, 104] gilt das vorher erwähnte Wort ,*kṅit*' fort.[69] — Wo ist es erwähnt worden? — In [der Regel VI, 4, 98]: ,[Die Paenultima] von *gam, han, jan, khan* und *ghas* wird elidiert vor einem [vokalisch anlautenden] *kit*- oder *ṅit*-Suffixe, ausgenommen vor *aṅ* [Aoristcharakter *a*].'

Einwurf Aber dieses [*kṅit* in 98] ist doch durch den Lokativ [*kṅiti*] ausgedrückt, und hier [in 104] benötigt man ein durch den Genetiv ausgedrücktes [d. i. *kṅitaḥ*].[70]

Erwiderung Dieser Ablativ *ciṇaḥ* [,nach *ciṇ*'] wird an die Stelle des Lokativs ,*kṅiti*' den Genetiv setzen,[71] indem [die Regel I, 1, 67] gilt: ,Wenn [im Lehrbuch] etwas durch den Ablativ ausgedrückt ist, so [erfolgt die Operation] an dem darauffolgenden [Element].[72] —

Selbst wenn diese Regel aufgestellt wird,[73]

Siddhaṃ vasusaṃprasāraṇam ajvidhau || Värtt. 9.

muß man [als Ausnahme] konstatieren, daß [die Substitution von] *Saṃprasāraṇa* [als] in Kraft getreten [zu betrachten ist] hinsichtlich einer Regel, welche einen Vokal betrifft. — Zu welchem Zwecke denn? — Damit bei [der Bildung der] Akkusative pluralis

fortgelten, so wird nach der vollzogenen Elision des [Suffixes] *u* der Eintritt von *u* für *a* erfolgen: dies ist der Sinn. Aber auch' — wendet Kaiy. ein — ,mit Hilfe der [ergänzten] Buchstaben *m* usw. [d. i. *v* und *y*] erfolgt bei *kurmaḥ* usw. nicht der Eintritt des *u*, weil durch sie das [Wort] *sārvadhātuka* [in 110] in einer Weise näher bestimmt wird, daß sich ein Widerspruch in der Aussage [*vākyabheda*, der Regel 110] ergibt.' D. h. durch die Ergänzung von, ,*mvor*' und ,*ye ca*' hat die Regel eine ihrem Zweck widersprechende Einschränkung erfahren; denn die Bildung von *kurutaḥ, kurvanti*, deren Endungen nicht mit *m*, *v* oder *y* beginnen, wäre nun nicht mehr möglich.

[69] Bei dieser Annahme kann nur die Endung *ta* abfallen, da sie ein *ṅit*-Suffix ist, während *tara(p)* und *tama(p)* als *pit*-Suffixe nicht abfallen.

[70] *Luk* soll ja an die Stelle des *kit*- oder *ṅit*-Suffixes treten. Dasjenige aber, an dessen Stelle ein anderes Element tritt, wird in der Grammatik nach I, 1, 49 durch den Genetiv ausgedrückt; wenn etwas hingegen im Lokativ angegeben ist, so wird nach I, 1, 66 die Operation an dem vorangehenden Element vorgenommen. Bei der Ergänzung des Lokativs *kṅiti* könnte also ein *kit*- oder *ṅit*-Suffix nicht Gegenstand der in VI, 4, 104 vorgeschriebenen Operation sein.

[71] D. h. er wird bewirken, daß der Lokativ im Sinne eines Genetivs aufzufassen ist.

[72] Vgl. die Paribh. Nr. 70: *Ubhayanirdeśe pañcamīnirdeśo balīyān* ,Wenn [in einer Regel zwei Elemente] durch beide [Kasus, das eine durch den Ablativ, das andere durch den Lokativ] ausgedrückt ist, so besitzt das durch den Ablativ ausgedrückte größere Kraft.' D. h. in einem solchen Falle gilt nicht die Regel I, 1, 66, wonach der Ablativ als Genetiv aufzufassen wäre, sondern I, 1, 67. Demnach besagt VI, 4, 104: Nach *ciṇ* tritt, wenn unmittelbar darauf ein *kit*- oder *ṅit*-Suffix folgt, für dieses Suffix *luk* ein. [Vgl. Einleit. p. 213 f.] Die Regel VI, 4, 22 wäre also auch in diesem Falle unnötig. — Im Text werden hier die Ślokavārttikas im Zusammenhang noch einmal vorgeführt.

[73] Kaiy.: *Anekaparihārāśrayeṇa* usw. ,wenn sie zu dem Zwecke angewendet wird, damit sich ein Verständnis nicht erst auf umständliche Weise dadurch ergebe, daß man mehr als eine Annahme zur Vermeidung [von Schwierigkeiten] macht.'

papuṣaḥ, tasthuṣaḥ; ninyuṣaḥ, cicyuṣaḥ; luluvuṣaḥ, pupuvuṣaḥ, wenn [nach VI, 4, 131 die Substitution des] *Saṃprasāraṇa* [*u* für das *v*] von *vas* vollzogen worden ist, gemäß [VI, 4, 64]: ‚Vor einem Vokal' [hier vor *us*] die Elision des *ā* [von *pā* und *sthā*] und die übrigen [Operationen, d. i. 82 und 77] stattfinden mögen.[74]

Aber aus welchem Grunde sollten sie denn nicht zustande kommen?

Bahiraṅgalakṣaṇatvād asiddhatvāc ca || Vārtt. 10.
[Die Substitution des] *Saṃprasāraṇa* [VI, 4. 131] ist ja doch eine *Bahiraṅga*-Regel,[75] und sie ist auch [gemäß VI, 4, 22 in bezug auf VI, 4, 64, 82 und 77] als *asiddha* zu betrachten.

Āttvaṃ yalopāllopayoḥ paśuṣo na vājān cākhāyitā cākhāyitum || Vārtt. 11.

Man muß [ferner als Ausnahme] konstatieren, daß der Eintritt von *ā* [als] *siddha* [zu betrachten] ist in bezug auf die Elision eines *y* und die eines *ā*. — Weshalb denn? — [Wegen] ‚*paśuṣo na vājān*' [RV.V, 41, 1]. Wenn [bei der Bildung von] *paśuṣaḥ* der Eintritt

[74] Der acc. pl. part. perf. act. von *pā* wird gebildet: *papā* + *vas* + *as*. Da *as* eine vokalisch anlautende Endung eines schwachen Kasus ist, ist *papāvas*- ein *bha*-Stamm, es wird also nach VI, 4, 131 *Saṃprasāraṇa* substituiert: *papā* + *uas* + *as*; daraus wird nach VI, 1, 108 und VIII, 3, 59 [wo Böhtlingk unrichtig übersetzt ‚am Anfang eines Suffixes', vgl. die Kāś.]: *papā* + *uṣ* + *as*. Die Substitution des *Saṃprasāraṇa* darf nun nicht als *asiddha* betrachtet werden, weil das *ā* nach VI, 4, 64 nur vor einem vokalisch anlautenden *Ārdhadhātuka* elidiert wird. Ähnlich verhält es sich mit den zwei anderen Gruppen von Beispielen, bei denen die Regeln 82 und 77 in Betracht kommen. — Man kann nun einwenden, daß dem *Ārdhadhātuka vas* nach VII, 2, 35 das Augment *i* vorgesetzt werden sollte. Die Ausführungen Kaiy.'s hierüber: ‚*nanu cāntaraṅgatvād iṭā bhāvyam*' usw. bis ‚*pūrvam iṇ na pravartate*' gebe ich im Anhang s. ‚*nimittāpāye naimittikasyāpy apāyaḥ*' wieder.

[75] Denn ihre Ursache liegt außerhalb der Ursache der *Antaraṅga*-Regel VI, 4, 64, wie folgende Darstellung zeigt:

papā + *vas* + *as*
papā + *us* + *as*

VI, 4, 64: Elision des *ā* bedingt durch *u*: *antaraṅga*	VI, 4, 131: *Saṃprasāraṇa u* für *v* bedingt durch *as*: *bahiraṅga*

Vgl. Paribh. Nr. 50.

[76] Kaiy. erklärt zunächst die Bildung von *paśuṣaḥ* [= *paśuṃ sanoti* ‚Vieh verschaffen']: Nach III, 2, 67 tritt an die Wurzel *san* das *kṛt*-Suffix *viṭ* (*v*) [welches nach I, 2, 46 die Wurzel zum Nominalstamm macht. Nach VI, 1, 67 verschwindet es zwar wieder, doch treten auch nachher gemäß I, 1, 62 die durch dieses Suffix bedingten Operationen ein]: *paśu-san* + (*v*) + *as*; Substitution von *ā* für *n* vor *viṭ* nach VI, 4, 41 (und von *ṣ* für *s* nach VIII, 3, 108): *paśu-ṣā* + *as*. Die Substitution von *ā* darf nun nicht als *asiddha* betrachtet werden, wenn gemäß VI, 4, 140 die Elision des *ā* erfolgen soll. — Kaiy. bemerkt ferner: *Lakṣaṇapratipadoktaparibhāṣā tv ālope nāśrīyate, avyāptiprasaṅgāt* ‚Bei der Elision des *ā* [VI, 4, 140] wird jedoch die Paribhāṣā [Nr. 105] über Ausdrücke, welche sowohl etwas erst aus einer Regel sich Ergebendes bezeichnen, als auch das durch ihren Wortlaut Gegebene, nicht angenommen. Denn sonst würde sich ergeben, daß [die Regel 140] nicht alle Fälle umfaßt [*avyāpti*, vgl. p. 219, Anm. 19].' D. h. wenn die Paribhāṣā hier gälte, würde *āt* in VI, 4, 140 nur das *ā* der auf *ā* auslautenden Wurzeln bezeichnen können, nicht aber ein sekundäres *ā*, welches nach 41 für *n* substituiert worden ist. Auf ein soches *ā* würde sich 140 dann nicht erstrecken. Aber die Bildung von *paśuṣaḥ* lehrt, daß 140 auch auf ein sekundäres *ā* angewendet wird, daß somit in diesem Falle die Paribh. 105 nicht gilt. Vgl. Paribh. Transl., p. 486, n. 2.

von *ā* [für das *n* von *san*: VI, 4, 41] als *asiddha* betrachtet wird, so ergibt sich infolgedessen nicht gemäß [der Regel 140]: ‚Für des [auslautende] *ā* einer Wurzel' die Elision des *ā*.[76]

Wenn bei [der Bildung von] *cākhāyitā*, *cākhāyitum* der Eintritt von *ā* [für *n*: VI, 4, 43] als *asiddha* betrachtet wird, so ergibt sich gemäß [der Regel 49]: ‚Für ein auf einen Konsonanten folgendes *y* [vor einem *Ārdhadhātuka*]' die Elision des *y*.[77]

Samānāśrayavacanāt siddham ‖ Värtt. 12.

‚Dadurch, daß man [in der Regel] hinzufügt „welche von dem gleichen [Elemente] abhängig ist", ist [das Sūtra hinsichtlich der erwähnten Ausnahmen] vollständig korrekt'.

[Nur eine Operation,] welche auf dem gleichen [Elemente] beruht [wie die zweite Operation], ist *asiddha*. Diese [in den Värtt. 9 und 11 genannten Regeln] aber beruhen nicht auf dem gleichen [Elemente]. Zunächst hier, in den Akkusativen pl. *papuṣaḥ*, *tasthuṣaḥ*; *ninyuṣaḥ*, *cicyuṣaḥ*; *luluvuṣaḥ*, *pupuvuṣaḥ*, beruhen die Elision des *ā* und die übrigen [Operationen] auf *-vas* [*us*], das *Saṃprasāraṇa* [dagegen] auf der Endung [*as*] des auf *-vas* ausgehenden [Stammes]. — Bei *paśuṣaḥ* [beruht] der Eintritt des *ā* [für das *n* von *san*] auf dem [Suffix] *viṭ*, die Elision des *ā* dagegen auf der Endung des auf *viṭ* ausgehenden [Stammes]. — Bei *cākhāyitā*, *cākhāyitum* [beruht] der Eintritt des *ā* auf dem [Intensivcharakter] *ya* [lies: *yaṅyāttvaṃ*], die Elision [des *y* hingegen] auf dem *Ārdhadhātuka* [*i-tṛ*] des auf *ya* ausgehenden [Stammes].

Sollte dieses [Wort *samānāśraya* in dem Sūtra] ausdrücklich hinzugefügt werden? — Durchaus nicht! — Wie soll man es aber [aus der Regel] verstehen, wenn es nicht ausdrücklich erwähnt wird? — Vermöge des Wortes *atra*.

Einwurf Aber es ist doch etwas anderes als Zweck des Wortes *atra* behauptet worden? — Was ist behauptet worden? — [VI, 4, 22 Värtt. 2:] ‚Das Wort *atra* hat den Zweck, den Geltungsbereich anzugeben.

Erwiderung Dies [sc. der Geltungsbereich] ergibt sich schon vollständig aus dem *Adhikāra* [‚*asiddhavat*'].[78]

[77] Kaiy.: *Khanater yaṅi dvirvacanāt paratvādye vibhāṣeṇyāttve dvirvacane ca tṛj irūpam* ‚Wenn an die Wurzel *khan* [nach III, 1, 22] der Intensivcharakter *ya* angefügt worden ist [: *khan-ya-*], [die Wurzel] auf die Reduplikation [VI, 1. 9] folgt usw. [d. h. nach VII, 4, 85 das Augment *nuk* (*n*) an das *a* der Reduplikationssilbe getreten ist: *caṅ-khan-ya-*], die optionelle Substitution von *ā* [für *n* zunächst an der Wurzel] und [dann] auch an der Reduplikation [VII, 4, 83] erfolgt ist [: *cā-khā-ya-*], so tritt das mit [dem Augment] *i* versehene [*Ārdhadhātuka*] *tṛc* (*tṛ*) an.' Wir erhalten [VI, 4, 48] *cākhāyitā*. Wenn aber die Substitution des *ā* als *asiddha* betrachtet würde, also noch *caṅ-khan-y-* als vorhanden zu denken wäre, müßte nach VI, 4, 49 das auf *n* folgende *y* abfallen, und wir würden fälschlich *cākhāitā* erhalten.

[78] Nach Kāty.'s Ansicht [Värtt. 2] gibt ‚*ā bhāt*' den Bereich derjenigen Regeln an, welche *asiddha* sind, und ‚*atra*' den Bereich derjenigen Regeln, in bezug auf welche jene *asiddha* sein sollen. Nach Pat. dagegen ergibt sich schon aus dem *Adhikāra* [vermittelst der Erklärung] der Abschnitt VI, 4, 22 bis *bha* als Bereich der als *asiddha* zu betrachtenden Regeln, während ‚*ā bhāt*' den Bereich der Regeln angibt, in bezug auf welche jene *asiddha* sind. ‚*Atra*' wäre also überflüssig, wenn es nicht — wie Pat. annimmt — den Zweck hätte, auszudrücken, daß beide Regeln von dem gleichen Element abhängig sein müssen. Vgl. die Kāś. zu VI, 4, 22: *Asiddhavad ity ayam adhikāro yad ita ūrdhvam anukramiṣyāma ā adhyāyaparisamāptes tad asiddhavad veditavyam*; ā bhād *iti viṣayanirdeśaḥ*: *ā bhasaṃ-*

Einwurf Hier bei *papuṣaḥ*, *cicyuṣaḥ*, *luluvuṣaḥ* wurden [Värtt. 10] zwei Gründe [dafür] namhaft gemacht [,daß die Elision des *ā* usw. nicht zustande kommen kann, nämlich]: der Umstand, daß [VI, 4, 131] eine *Bahiraṅga*-Regel und [außerdem gemäß VI, 4, 22] *asiddha* sei. [Die Annahme,] daß sie [gemäß VI, 4, 22] *asiddha* sei, mag als an jener Stelle [Värtt. 12] beantwortet gelten.[79] Auf [den Grund, daß VI, 4, 131] eine *Bahiraṅga*-Regel sei, ist aber noch nicht erwidert worden.[80]

Erwiderung[81] Dies bedeutet keinen Fehler. [Denn] eine *Bahiraṅga*- und eine *Antaraṅga*-Operation sind zwei Begriffe, die

śabdanād yad ucyate tatra kartavye [,wenn eine (zweite Operation) dort (d. h. nach einer Regel) vollzogen werden soll, welche bis zur Erwähnung von *bha* (d. i. bis VI, 4, 129 oder 175) gelehrt wird']. *Atreti samānāśrayatvapratipattyartham: tac ced atra yatra* [*bhavati* ist zu streichen!] *tad ā bhāc chāstrīyaṃ vidhīyate tadāśrayam eva bhavati, vyāśrayaṃ tu nāsiddhavad bhavatīty arthaḥ* ,. . . [Eine in dem Abschnitt bis *bha* gelehrte Operation ist *asiddha*,] wenn diese dort, wobei eine andere in dem Abschnitt bis *bha* gelehrte Operation vorgeschreiben wird, und nur eben davon abhängig ist . . .' In dem in diesem Kapitel angeführten Beispiele handelt es sich um ein gemeinsames Element, an w e l c h e m die Operation der zweiten Regel vollzogen wird; es ist zwar nicht, wie bei der ersten Operation, Ursache, aber doch ein Element, von dem die zweite Operation abhängig ist. Es kann aber auch Ursache der zweiten Operation sein, und dann haben beide Operationen die gleiche Ursache. Vgl. im Anhang s. *samānāśraya*. — Vgl. noch die Kāś. zu unserem Sūtra: *Atragrahaṇaṃ kim? Papuṣaḥ paśya* usw.

[79] Kaiy.: ,Durch die Annahme, daß es auf die Abhängigkeit von dem gleichen [Element] ankomme.

[80] Kaiy.: *Yadyapi nājānantarya ity ayam* usw. ,Obwohl hier das [in der Paribh. Nr. 51 enthaltene] Verbot zur Anwendung kommen könnte: ,,[Eine bereits ausgeführte *Bahiraṅga*-Operation ist] nicht [als *asiddha* zu betrachten, wenn die *Antaraṅga*-Operation] auf dem unmittelbaren Folgen eines Vokales [beruht;'' hier die Elision des *ā* auf dem folgenden *u* von *us*], so will dieser Zusatz [des Bhāṣyakāra] doch zu verstehen geben, daß [hier] auch die Möglichkeit der Anwendung der Paribhāṣā [Nr. 50] nicht besteht, weil [wie im folgenden gezeigt wird] eine Ursache [für ihre Anwendung] gar nicht vorhanden ist.'

[81] Das Folgende findet sich in ähnlichem Zusammenhang bei Pat. zu VIII, 3, 15 Värtt. 2.

[82] Kaiy. zu VIII, 3, 15 Värtt. 2 erklärt *pratidvandvibhāvinau: dvandvaṃ yugmam ucyate; pratikūlaṃ parasparaviruddhaṃ dvandvaṃ pratidvandvaṃ, tatra bhavataḥ.* — Zu unserer Stelle bemerkt Kaiy.: *Na hi vastvantarānapekṣaṃ antaraṅgaṃ* usw. . . . bis *padāny asminn arthe yojyante* ,Es gibt nicht irgendeine *Antaraṅga*- oder *Bahiraṅga*-Operation, die, ohne sich auf den anderen Gegenstand [d. i. auf eine zu ihr gehörige *Bahiraṅga*-, bezw. *Antaraṅga*-Operation] zu beziehen, nur für sich selbst zu Recht bestünde; denn sie liegen nur dann vor, wenn sie beide sich gleichzeitig in der Weise darbieten, daß eine von der andern abhängt, so wie bei [der Bildung von] *syona* [aus *si* + *ū* + *na* (vgl. Paribh. Transl. p. 222, n. 2) die Substitution des] Halbvokales [für *i*] und die von *Guṇa* für *i* sich gleichzeitig darbieten. Bei *papuṣaḥ* dagegen bieten sich nicht [beide Operationen] gleichzeitig dar: in dem Zeitpunkt, in welchem das *Saṃprasāraṇa* sich darbietet [d. i. so lange *-vas* noch vorliegt], besteht keine Möglichkeit für die Elision des *ā* und die übrigen [Operationen, vgl. p. 234], weil eine Ursache [für ihren Eintritt, d. i. ein Vokal] nicht vorhanden ist; und in dem Zeitpunkt, in welchem die Elision des *ā* [vor einem Vokal] sich darbietet, ist [die Substitution des] *Saṃprasāraṇa* schon ausgeführt. Und deshalb ist das *Saṃprasāraṇa* nur erst die Ursache der Elision des *ā* usw.; folglich gelangt

(einander widerstreitend) zu zweien auftreten.[82] — In welcher Weise? — Wenn eine *Antaraṅga*-Operation vorhanden ist, so ist [gleichzeitig auch] die *Bahiraṅga*-Operation da; und wenn eine *Bahiraṅga*-Operation vorhanden ist, so ist [gleichzeitig auch] die *Antaraṅga*-Operation da.[83] Hier aber [bei *papuṣaḥ* usw.] sind die *Antaraṅga*- und die *Bahiraṅga*-Operationen nicht gleichzeitig zur Stelle.[84] Wenn [nämlich] eine *Bahiraṅga*-Operation nicht in die Erscheinung getreten ist,[85] so bietet sich [auch] eine *Antaraṅga*-Operation nicht dar. Unter diesen Umständen (*tatra*) ist die [angeb-

hier die Paribhāṣā [Nr. 50] nicht zur Anwendung. Dies ist der Sinn. — [Einwurf:] Wenn es sich so verhält, so [kann man dagegen einwenden:] auch bei *pacāvedam* [aus *pacāva idam*] usw. bietet sich, so lange [die *Bahiraṅga*-Operation, d. i.] die Substitution von *Guṇa* nach *a* [für *a* + *i*: VI, 1, 87] nicht vollzogen ist, [die *Antaraṅga*-Operation, d. i.] die Substitution von *ai* gemäß ‚*ai* für e' [III, 4, 93] nicht dar; weil somit [die *Bahiraṅga*-Operation] die bedingende Ursache und [die *Antaraṅga*-Operation] das hierdurch Bedingte ist, wäre [auch hier] die Möglichkeit der Anwendung der Paribhāṣā nicht vorhanden. [In Wirklichkeit gilt sie jedoch bei *pacāvedam*. Vgl. Paribh. Transl. p. 271, n. 4.] — [Erwiderung:] Nun, dann wird [*pratidvandvibhāvinau*] folgendermaßen anders erklärt: die Paribhāṣā [Nr. 50] ‚Eine *Bahiraṅga*-Operation ist *asiddha* in bezug auf eine *Antaraṅga*-Operation' ist in [der Regel VI, 4, 132]: ‚In *vāh* tritt *ū* [als *Saṃprasāraṇa* für *v*] ein' angedeutet [vgl. Paribh. Text p. 44, l. 3 ff.; Transl. p. 235—37 samt Noten], sie ist also eine in dem Abschnitt bis *bha* gelehrte [Regel]; oder aber: obwohl [diese Paribhāṣā im Värtt. 8] zu [der Regel I, 4, 2:] ‚Bei einem Konflikt [zweier Regeln] ist die später erwähnte zu vollziehen' ergänzend hinzugefügt worden ist, so wird sie [doch auch] zu einer im Abschnitt bis *bha* gelehrten [Regel], weil [nach Paribh. Nr. 3] Termini technici und Paribhāṣās sich mit jeder Operation [bei der diese Termini vorkommen oder diese Paribhāṣās eine Rolle spielen] zu einem Satze vereinigen, somit auch die Substitution des *Saṃprasāraṇa* [VI, 4, 131] in *vas* [der Paribh. Nr. 50] eine Stätte gewährt. Wenn dann die im Abschnitt bis *bha* gelehrten Operationen, nämlich die Elision des *ā* und die übrigen, vollzogen werden sollen, so ist in bezug auf diese die [in demselben Abschnitt gelehrte] Paribhāṣā [gemäß VI, 4, 22] *asiddha*, tritt also nicht ein. Und wenn sie nicht eintritt [d. h. das *Saṃprasāraṇa* nicht als *bahiraṅga* betrachtet wird, also auch nicht *asiddha* ist], so finden [verursacht durch das *Saṃprasāraṇa*] die Elision des *ā* und die übrigen Operationen statt. Dies ist der Sinn der Auseinandersetzung [des Bhāṣya]. Die einzelnen Worte [derselben] werden in diesem Sinne [d. i. in dem der zweiten Interpretation] gebraucht.' Vgl. im Anhang s. *antaraṅga* und p. 229, Anm. 56.

[83] Kaiy. erklärt ‚*sati*' durch *buddhyāpekṣite* ‚sobald man mittels der Wahrnehmung auf sie Bezug genommen hat', d. h. sobald man sie im Bildungsprozeß der Form zum ersten Male wahrgenommen hat. Vgl. Kaiy. zu VIII, 3, 15 Värtt. 2: *saty antaraṅga iti*: *antaraṅge buddhyāpekṣite tadapekṣayā bahiraṅgaṃ bhavati, bahiraṅge cāpekṣite tadapekṣayāntaraṅgaṃ bhavaty antaraṅgavyapadeśaṃ labhata ity arthaḥ*.

[84] Nämlich im Augenblick der Anwendung des Paribhāṣā. — Kaiy. zu VIII, 3, 15 Värtt. 2 erklärt *yugapatsamavasthānam* durch: *ekasyāṃ buddhāv apekṣitaparasparam avasthānam* ‚ein Eintreten in der Weise, daß man schon bei einer einmaligen Wahrnehmung jedes auf das andere bezieht'.

[85] Nämlich deshalb, weil sie im Augenblick der Anwendung der Paribhāṣā gemäß VI, 4, 22 in bezug auf diese als *asiddha* betrachtet werden muß. Vgl. im Anhang s. *antaraṅga*.

liche] *Bahiraṅga*-Operation nichts weiter als die Ursache der [angeblichen] *Antaraṅga*-Operation.[86]

Hrasvayalopāllopāś cāyādeśe lyapi || Värtt. 13.

Man muß [als Ausnahmen] konstatieren, daß 1. die [Substitution der] Kürze, 2. die Elision des *y* und 3. die Elision des *a* hinsichtlich der Substitution von *ay* [für das Kausativ- Suffix *i*] vor [dem Suffix des Gerundiums] *lyap* (*ya*) als *siddha* zu betrachten sind, [in den Beispielen:] 1. *praśamayya gataḥ*, *pratamayya gataḥ*; 2. *prabebhidayya gataḥ*, *pracecchidayya gataḥ*; 3. *prastanayya gataḥ*, *pragadayya gataḥ*. Wenn [nämlich] 1. die [Substitution] der Kürze [für die Länge vor *ṇi*: VI, 4, 92], 2. die Elision des *y* [VI, 4, 49] und 3. die Elision des [Stammauslautes] *a* [VI, 4, 48] als *asiddha* betrachtet werden, so ergibt sich nicht gemäß [der Regel VI, 4, 56]: ‚Vor *lyap* (*ya*) nach einem auf eine Kürze folgenden [Wurzelkonsonanten]' die Substitution von *ay* [für *i*].[87]

Erwiderung Auch hier vermeidet man [Schwierigkeiten] in der Weise [,daß man erklärt]: ‚Es ist dadurch vollständig korrekt,

[86] Kaiy.: *Paribhāṣāyā asiddhatvād apravṛttāv iti bhāvaḥ* usw. ‚Damit ist gemeint: unter der Voraussetzung, daß die Paribhāṣā nicht eintritt da sie *asiddha* ist. Und zwar ist die Paribhāṣā *asiddha* [gemäß VI, 4, 22] infolge der Abhängigkeit von dem gleichen [Element], indem das *Saṃprasāraṇa* allein es ist, wovon sowohl die [Anwendung der] Paribhāṣā, als auch die Elision des *ā* und die übrigen [Operationen] abhängen.' Vgl. Paribh. Transl. p. 265, n. 2.

[87] In allen drei Fällen handelt es sich um die Bildung des kausativen Gerundiums. Und zwar werden mit Präpositionen zusammengesetzte Verba gewählt, weil nach VII, 1, 37 in der Komposition *lyap* (*ya*) für *ktvā* (*tvā*) substituiert wird.

1. Der Kausativstamm ist *praśam* + *ṇi*-, daraus nach VII, 2, 116: *pra-śām* + *i*-. Für die lange Pänultima wird nun nach VI, 4,92 die Kürze substituiert [Böhtlingk ungenau: ‚bewahrt die Kürze']: *pra-śam* + *i*-. Wenn nun [nach VII, 1, 37 statt *tvā*] das Suffix *ya* angefügt worden ist, so wird *ay* für das *i* substituiert, und wir erhalten *praśamayya*. ‚Wenn jedoch die [Substitution der] Kürze [*a*] als *asiddha* betrachtet wird, so geht dem [auslautenden Wurzelkonsonanten] *m* nicht eine Kürze voran, und infolgedessen bietet sich die Substitution von *ay* [für *i*] nicht dar' (Kaiy.). — Im Dhātup. 19, 70 erscheint *śam* unter den Wurzeln mit stummem *m* (*mitaḥ*) als ‚*mit*', sofern es nicht ‚*darśana*' bedeutet.

2. ‚Hinter dem auf das [Intensivsuffix] *yaṅ* (*ya*) ausgehenden [Stamm] von *bhid* tritt das Kausativ-Suffix *ṇic* (*i*) ein' (Kaiy.). Wir erhalten *prabebhid* + *ya* + *i*-; nach VI, 4, 48: *pra-bebhid* + *y* + *i*-; nach VI, 4, 49 [Elision des *y* vor dem *Ārdhadhātuka i*]: *pra-bebhid* + *i*-; nach VI, 4, 56: *prabebhidayya*. ‚Wenn hier die Elision des *y* als *asiddha* betrachtet wird, so folgt [in *prabebhidy* + *i*-] *ṇic* (*i*) nicht auf einen [auslautenden Wurzelkonsonanten] mit vorangehender Kürze, da ja noch das *y* dazwischen steht, und die Substitution von *ay* [für *i*] bietet sich infolgedessen nicht dar' (Kaiy.)

3. ‚Unter der Überschrift „Die auf *a* endigenden Wurzeln" wird [im Dhātup. 35, 7—8] erwähnt: „*stana* und *gada*, zur Bezeichnung himmlischer Geräusche" (Kaiy.). — Nach der Anfügung des Kausativ-Suffixes *i*, erhält man gemäß VI, 4, 48: *prastan-i*- und nach VI, 4, 56: *prastanayya*. ‚Wenn hier die Elision des *a* [VI, 4, 48] als *asiddha* betrachtet wird, ergibt sich nicht die Substitution von *ay* [für *i*: 56], da [in *prastana-i*-] ein *a* dazwischensteht [, also das *i* nicht auf einen Wurzelkonsonanten mit vorangehender Kürze folgt].'

[88] So auch die Kāś. zu VI, 4, 56.

[89] Kaiy.: *Babhūvatur iti: bhū atus vuk* usw. ‚[Zunächst] *bhū* + *atus*, [dann wird] *vuk* (*v*) [angefügt]; wenn dieses als *asiddha* betrachtet wird, bietet sich [die Substitution von] *uvaṅ* (*uv*) dar. — [E i n w u r f:] Aber [die Anfügung von] *vuk* [VI, 4, 88], die [in bezug auf einen speziellen Fall]

daß man sagt, [eine Operation sei *asiddha*,] wenn sie von dem gleichen [Element] abhängt. [Värtt. 12.] — Wieso? — Auf dem [Suffix] *ṇi* beruhen diese Regeln [VI, 4, 92; 49; 48], auf dem [Suffix] *lyap* (*ya*) hinter *ṇi* [dagegen] die Substitution von *ay*.[88]

Vugyuṭāv uvaṅyaṇoḥ || Värtt. 14.

Man muß [als Ausnahmen] konstatieren, daß die [Anfügung der] Augmente *vuk* (*v*) und *yuṭ* (*y*) hinsichtlich [der Substitution von] *uvaṅ* (*uv*) und *yaṇ* (des Halbvokales) als *siddha* zu betrachten sind. 1. *Babhūvatuḥ*, *babhūvuḥ*: wenn [hier die Anfügung von] *vuk* (*v*) [in *babhū* + *v* + *atuḥ*: VI, 4, 88] als *asiddha* betrachtet wird, so bietet sich infolgedessen [nach 77 die Substitution von] *uvaṅ* (*uv*) [für das *ū*] dar;[89] 2. *upadidīye*, *upadidīyāte*: wenn [hier die Anfügung von] *yuṭ* (*y*) [in *upadidī* + *y* + *e*: VI, 4, 63] als *asiddha* betrachtet wird, so bietet sich infolgedessen [nach 82] die Substitution des Halbvokales [*y* für *ī*] dar.[90]

vorgenommen wird, während [für diesen Spezialfall nach der allgemeinen Regel VI, 4, 77 auch die Substitution von] *uvaṅ* sich notwendigerweise [gleichzeitig]ergeben würde[*nāprāpte*], stellt doch eine Ausnahme [*apavāda*] von dieser [Substitution des *uvaṅ*] dar [und hebt diesse auf]; es gilt ja der Grundsatz [Pat. zu I, 1, 47, Värtt. 1]: ‚Wenn auch [eine allgemeine und eine Spezialregel] gleichzeitig eintreten könnten, so wird doch [jene durch diese] aufgehoben.' [Nach dem Eintritt der Spezialregel VI, 4, 88 kann also die allgemeine Regel 77, d. i. die Substitution von *uvaṅ*, nicht mehr eintreten.] — [Erwiderung:] Dies trifft [hier] nicht zu. [Denn nur] diejenige [allgemeine Regel], welche in dem Augenblick vorhanden ist, in welchem die sie verdrängende [Spezialregel] zur Anwendung gelangt, wird von der verdrängenden [Spezialregel] völlig aufgehoben und gelangt nicht mehr zur Anwendung; *uvaṅ* [nach der allgemeinen Regel] jedoch tritt nicht [gleichzeitig] in die Erscheinung, da es [gemäß VI, 4, 22] in dem Augenblick als *asiddha* [= nicht vorhanden] zu betrachten ist, in welchem *vuk* [nach der Spezialregel] eintritt, [und zwar nur deshalb eintritt,] weil es [sonst, d. i. nach dem Eintritt der allgemeinen Regel] keine Gelegenheit [zum Eintritt] hätte; [*uvaṅ*] kann also [durch die Spezialregel] nicht [ganz] verdrängt werden; und so tritt es denn, wenn [die Anfügung von] *vuk* vollzogen ist, aus dem Grunde ein, weil diese [gemäß VI, 4, 22 in bezug auf die Substitution von *uvaṅ*] als *asiddha* [= nicht in Kraft getreten] betrachtet wird.' Es werden nämlich zwei Arten von Ausnahmsregeln (*apavāda*) unterschieden: 1. Spezialregeln, die gleichzeitig mit oder nach dem Eintritt der allgemeinen Regeln zur Anwendung kommen könnten und diese gemäß der Maxime ‚*yena nāprāpte yo vidhir ārabhyate, sa tasya bādhako bhavati*' [Paribh. Text p. 65, l. 8f.; Transl. p. 321 f.] vollständig aufheben. Von solchen Spezialregeln sagt man, daß sie die allgemeinen Regeln *apavādatvāt* aufheben; 2. Spezialregeln, die nicht gleichzeitig mit oder nach dem Eintritt der allgemeinen Regeln zur Anwendung kommen könnten, und die nur deshalb, weil sie sonst überhaupt nicht Gelegenheit zur Anwendung hätten [*anavakāśatvāt*], die allgemeinen Regeln aufheben. Wenn sich nach der Ausführung einer solchen Spezialregel die allgemeine Regel noch darbietet, so gelangt sie nachher noch zur Anwendung. Vgl. Paribh. Text p. 67, l. 5: *kvacit tu sarvathānavakāśatvād eva bādhakatvam*; l. 8: *tatra bādhake pravṛtte yady utsargaprāptir bhavati tadā bhavaty eva*, und speziell Paribh. Nr. 58. Unsere Regel VI, 4, 88 ist aus den von Kaiy. genannten Gründen eine Spezialregel der zweiten Art. Nach ihrer Ausführung bietet VI, 4, 22 der allgemeinen Regel VI, 4, 77 die Möglichkeit der Anwendung. Vgl. Paribh. Transl. p. 329, n. 4.

[90] So auch Kāś. und Siddh. K. zu VI, 4, 22 und 63. Vgl. Candra V, 3, 21, wo *yuk* für unser *yuṭ* steht.

Erwiderung Was zunächst *vuk* betrifft, so ist für dieses [eine Ausnahme] nicht zu konstatieren. Ich werde [nämlich in VI, 4, 88] *vuk* überhaupt nicht erwähnen. Ich werde folgendermaßen sagen: ,,Bei *bhū* wird vor [den vokalisch anlautenden Personalendungen im] Aorist und Perfektum *ū* für die Paenultima substituiert.''[91] Hiebei wird der Eintritt von *ū* an Stelle derjenigen Paenultima erfolgen, welche vorliegt, wenn die Substitution von *uvaṅ* (*uv*) [für das *ū* von *bhū* gemäß VI, 4, 77] bereits vollzogen ist.[92]

Einwurf Aber wenn [man] auch in dieser Weise [mit VI, 4, 88 verfährt], woraus geht denn dies hervor, daß nämlich der Eintritt von *ū* für diejenige Paenultima erfolgen wird, welche vorliegt, wenn die Substitution von *uvaṅ* (*uv*) bereits vollzogen ist, daß es hingegen nicht für diejenige Paenultima eintreten möge, welche gegenwärtig vorliegt, [d. i.] für das *bh* [von *babhū-atuḥ*]?

Erwiderung Dies bedeutet keinen Fehler. [Denn] ,für *u* (*ū*)' [aus VI, 4, 83][93] gilt [hier] noch fort. Auf diese Weise wird [der Eintritt des *ū*] an Stelle des *u* [in *babhuv-atuḥ*] erfolgen.[94]

Einwurf Zugegeben, daß *babhūvatuḥ*, *babhūvuḥ* [auf diese Weise] zustande gekommen sind,[95] so kommt doch das Folgende nicht zustande, [nämlich] *babhūva*, *babhūvitha*. — Aus welchem Grunde? — Denn, wenn [in *babhū* + *itha* nach VII, 3, 84] *Guṇa* und [in *babhū* + *a* nach VII, 2, 115] *Vṛddhi* [für das *ū*] substituiert worden sind, ist der Laut *u* [für den *ū* eintreten könnte] nicht vorhanden.[96]

Erwiderung Hier bieten sich [die Substitutionen von] *Guṇa* und *Vṛddhi* gar nicht dar. — Aus welchem Grunde? — Weil [die Regel I, 1, 5:] ,Auch vor einem [Suffix] mit stummen *k* oder *ṅ*' es verbietet. — Wieso sind [*a* und *tha*] kit-[Suffixe]? — Gemäß [der Regel I, 2, 6]: ,Auch nach *indh* und *bhū*'.

Einwurf Dann weisen wir eben diese [Vorschrift], daß [bei *bhū* die Personalendungen des Perfektums als] *kit* [zu betrachten] sind, durch [die Anfügung von] *vuk* (*v*) zurück.[97]

[91] D. h. außer der Streichung von *vuk* in 88 wird auch noch eine Teilung der Regel (*yogavibhāga*) 89 vorgenommen.

[92] D. i. für die Paenultima *u* in *babhuv-atuḥ*, so daß wir *babhūvatuḥ* erhalten.

[93] *Oḥ* ist gen. sing. von *u*, welches nach I, 1, 69 zur Bezeichnung von *u* und *ū* dient.

[94] Kaiy.: *Uvarṇasyopadhāyā ūd bhavatīty evam āśrayaṇād* usw. ,Weil ja angenommen wird, für den Laut *u*, welcher Paenultima ist, trete *ū* ein; und nur wenn [die Substitution von] *uvaṅ* (*uv*) vollzogen ist, wird der Laut *u* Paenultima. — [Der Gegner aber], welcher der Ansicht ist, die Geltung [der Personalendungen des Perf. von *bhū*] als *kit* gemäß [I, 2, 6]: ,nach *indh* und *bhū*' werde [durch die Vorschrift über *vuk*] zurückgewiesen [vgl. im folgenden], sagt ,,*bhavet siddham*''.'

[95] Denn die Personalendungen des Duals und Plurals sind nicht *pit*, also nach I, 2, 5 *kit*-Suffixe, die gemäß I, 1, 5 weder *Guṇa* noch *Vṛddhi* bewirken.

[96] Hier wird die im Folgenden erwähnte Regel I, 2, 6 ignoriert, nach welcher alle Personalendungen des Perfektums von *bhū kit*-Suffixe sind, also nach I, 1, 5 *Guṇa* und *Vṛddhi* verbieten. Die Endung der 2. Sing., *thal* (*tha*), wird also, da sie nach III, 4, 82 für *sip* substituiert worden ist, als *pit* betrachtet, es tritt demnach gemäß VII, 3, 84 *Guṇa* ein. Die Endung der 3. (und 1.) Sing. ist nach III, 4, 82 *ṇal*; nach VII, 2, 115 wird also für das auslautende *ū* des Stammes *Vṛddhi* substituiert. Wenn wir so *babhav-itha* und *babhāv-a* erhalten haben, ist ein *u*, für welches *ū* eintreten könnte, nicht vorhanden.

[97] D. h. die Regel, I, 2, 6 ist überflüssig, denn die Substitutionen von *Guṇa* und *Vṛddhi* werden verhindert, wenn wir *vuk* in der unveränderten Regel VI, 4, 88 belassen. Wenn wir nämlich *vuk*

Erwiderung Aber hier [in I, 2, 6] wird doch durch [die Vorschrift], daß [die Personalendungen des Perfektums von *bhū* als] *kit* [zu betrachten] seien, [die Vorschrift über] *vuk* zurückgewiesen.[98]

Was ist nun aber hier maßgebend ?—Das Wort *vuk* ist maßgebend. Denn selbst wenn [die Personalendungen nach I, 2, 6] *kit* sind, müßten hier gleichwohl *Guṇa* und *Vṛddhi* eintreten.— Warum ? — [Denn] dies [sc. I, 1, 5] ist ein Verbot [der Substitution] von *Guṇa* und *Vṛddhi*, sofern sie [den *pratyāhāra*] *ik* betreffen. Und diese [in VII, 2, 115 gelehrte *Vṛddhi*] ist nicht eine *Vṛddhi*, welche [den *pratyāhāra*] *ik* betrifft.[99]

angefügt und *babhūvitha*, *babhūv-a* erhalten haben, sind die Regeln VII, 3, 84 und VII, 2, 115 nicht anwendbar, weil der Stamm nicht mehr vokalisch auslautet [vgl. Kāś.: *ig-*, bezw. *ajantasya*]. Und zwar erhält das Augment *vuk* den Vorzug vor den sich gleichzeitig darbietenden Substitutionen von *Guṇa* und *Vṛddhi*: *bhuvo vuko nityatvād iti nyāyāt* ,nach dem Grundsatz: weil das an *bhū* [angefügte] *vuk* (*v*) *nitya* ist' [Kaiy.]. Vgl. Mbh. zu I, 2, 6 Värtt. 1, wo erklärt wird, daß die Regel I, 2, 6 überflüssig sei, *bhuvo vuko nityatvāt: bhavater api nityo vuk; kṛte 'pi* [sc. *guṇe*] *prāpnoty akṛte 'pi*. Dazu Kaiy.: *Oḥ supīty ata or iti nānuvartata iti bhāvaḥ. Ekadeśavikṛtasyānanyatvāc ca śabdāntaraprāptyabhāvaḥ; satyām api vā śabdāntaraprāptau kṛtākṛtaprasaṅgitvād vuko nityatvam, vuki kṛte guṇasya prāptir eva nāstīti naitayos tulyabalatvam* ,Dies besagt, daß nicht aus [der Regel]: ,*oḥ supi*' [VI, 4, 83] ,*oḥ*' [,für *u*'; vgl. p. 240] fortgilt. Und da ja eine Sache, welche an einer Stelle geändert worden ist, dadurch nicht zu einer andern Sache wird, so würde sich [auch infolge der Substitution von *Guṇa*] nicht eine andere Wortform ergeben. [Wenn die Wortform mit *Guṇa* als von der ursprünglichen Wortform vershieden zu betrachten wäre, würde *vuk* nach Paribh. Nr. 44 n i c h t *nitya* sein]. Oder aber, auch wenn sich [infolge der Substitution von *Guṇa*] eine andere Wortform ergäbe, wäre *vuk* [nach Paribh. Nr. 46] auch schon deshalb *nitya*, weil es sich sowohl nach als auch vor dem Eintritt [von *Guṇa*] darbieten würde. Wenn [also] *vuk* [zuerst] eingetreten ist, ergibt sich [die Substitution von] *Guṇa* überhaupt nicht mehr. Diese beiden [Regeln VI, 4, 88 und VII, 3, 84] haben also nicht gleiche Kraft.' [Vgl. Paribn. Nr. 42.] Dasselbe gilt natürlich auch für *Vṛddhi* Vgl. Siddh. K. zu VI, 4, 88: *nityatvād vug guṇavṛddhī bādhate*.

[98] Kaiy.: *Kṅiti ceti guṇavṛddhiniṣedhād* usw. ,Weil [die Regel I, 1, 5:] ,,Auch vor einem *kit* oder *ṅit*'' *Guṇa* und *Vṛddhi* verbietet, und weil, wenn [nach VI, 4, 77] *uvaṅ* (*uv*) eingetreten ist, der Eintritt von *ū* für den Laut *u* [in VI, 4, 88 (ohne *vuk*) + 89 A] vorgeschrieben ist.' *Vuk* ist also überflüssig.

[99] Kaiy.: *Aco ñṇitīty atreka ity anupasthānād iglakṣaṇatvābhāvaḥ* ,Da in [der Regel VII, 2, 115]: ,,Für [einen Laut des *pratyāhāra*] *ac* vor [einem Suffix] mit dem *anubandha ñ* oder *ṇ*'' nicht ,,*ikaḥ*'' vorliegt, ist eine Beziehung [der dort gelehrten *Vṛddhi*] auf *ik* nicht vorhanden.' *Acaḥ* läßt vielmehr erkennen, daß für die in dieser Regel vorgeschriebene *Vṛddhi* das Verbot in I, 1, 5, welches sich nur auf *ik* bezieht, nicht gilt. Dagegen bezieht sich die *Guṇa*-Regel VII, 3, 84, welche bei *babhū-itha* in Betracht kommt, auf *ik* [vgl. die Kāś.]; das in I, 1, 5 enthaltene Verbot muß sich also tatsächlich auf VII, 3, 84 erstrecken. Deshalb ist das Wort ,*guṇa*' in dem Satze des Bhāṣya ,*syātām evātra guṇavṛddhī*' nicht am Platze. Hierüber bemerkt Kaiy.: *Guṇagrahaṇaṃ prasaṅgoccāritam; siguṇasyeglakṣaṇatvāt sidhyati hi pratiṣedhaḥ* ,Das Wort ,,*guṇa*'' ist nur wegen der Gelegenheit [d. h. nebenbei] erwähnt; denn da [die Substitution von] *Guṇa* [gemäß VII, 3, 84] vor [der Endung der 2. sing.] *si* (*sip*) [also nach, I, 1, 56 auch vor dessen Substitut *tha*] sich auf *ik* bezieht, so kommt das Verbot [von *Guṇa* durch I, 1, 5] tatsächlich zustande.' So erklärt Kaiy. zu I, 2, 6 auch die Frage des Bhāṣya nach dem Zweck dieser Regel folgendermaßen: *Vināpi sūtreṇeṣṭaṃ sidhyati saty api ceṣṭaṃ*

Erwiderung Unter diesen Umständen[100] [sage ich] folgendes: man bedarf weder des *vuk* noch auch [der Annahme], daß [die Personalendungen nach I, 2, 6] *kit* seien. *Guṇa* und *Vṛddhi* mögen hier [in *babhū-itha, babhū-a*] eintreten; für diejenige Pänultima, welche vorliegt, wenn [die Substitution von] *Guṇa* und *Vṛddhi* vollzogen, und [nach VI, 1, 78] *av* und *āv* eingesetzt sind, wird der Eintritt von *ū* erfolgen.[101] — Wieso? — In ‚*oḥ*' [VI, 4, 83] ist auch der Laut *a* (und *ā*) zum Ausdruck gebracht.[102]

Einwurf Dann bietet sich aber [VI, 4, 83] auch hier bei [der Bildung der] Akkusative pluralis *kīlālapaḥ, śubhaṃyaḥ* dar.[103]

Erwiderung Die Elision [des *ā* von -*pā* und -*yā* nach VI, 4, 140] wird in diesen Falle [die Regel VI, 4, 83] vollständig aufheben.[104]

na sidhyati, babhūvety ajlakṣaṇatvād vṛddher iglakṣaṇatvābhāvāt pratiṣedhāprasaṅgāt. Guṇamātraniṣedha eva tu babhūvitha, ahaṃ babhūveti ca ṇittvābhāvapakṣe syād iti praśnaḥ. ‚Auch ohne das Sūtra [I, 2, 6] kommt die erwartete [Form] zustande, und selbst wenn es gilt, kommt die erwartete [Form] nicht zustande; denn da bei [der Bilding von] *babhūva* [in VII, 2, 115] die Beziehung der *Vṛddhi* auf „*ac*" vorliegt, folglich eine Beziehung derselben auf „*ik*" nicht vorhanden ist, hat [das Sūtra I, 2, 6 in Verbindung mit I, 1, 5] nicht die Möglichkeit, [*Vṛddhi*] zu verbieten. Vielmehr wäre [das Sūtra] nur ein Verbot von *Guṇa* allein bei [der Bildung von] *babhūvitha* und der 1. sing. *babhūva* in dem Falle, daß [die Endung der 1. sing. *ṇal* nach VII, 1, 91] nicht *ṇit* ist [also nicht, wie die 3. sing., *Vṛddhi*, sondern nach VII, 3, 84 *Guṇa* bewirkt]. Dies ist der Sinn der Frage.'

[100] D. h. da also erwiesen ist, daß die Regel, I, 2, 6 überflüssig ist, weil zwar *babhūvitha*, nicht aber die 3. sing. *babhūva* zustande käme, wenn ihre Endungen als *kit* betrachtet würden.

[101] Der Opponent beharrt also bei der am Beginn der Diskussion gemachten Annahme eines *Yogavibhāga* mit gleichzeitiger Streichung von *vuk*.

[102] Kaiy.: *Akārokārayor ād guṇe kṛte ṅasi-ṅasoś ceti pūrvaikādeśena nirdeśāt* ‚Denn die Laute *a* und *u* [die nach I, 1, 69 zugleich ihre Längen repräsentieren] sind [in *oḥ*] in der Weise zum Ausdruck gebracht, daß, nachdem [für den Vokal *u*] hinter dem *a* [und dieses selbst] *Guṇa* [*o* allein] substituiert worden ist, gemäß [VI, 1, 110]: „Vor [der Endung] *as* des Ablativs und Genetivs singularis" das vorangehende [*o*] allein substituiert wird.' D. h. *a* + *u* + *as* nach VI, 1, 87: *o* + *aḥ*, und dies nach VI, 1, 110: *oḥ*. In Wirklichkeit ist *oḥ* natürlich gen. sing. von *u*.

[103] Kaiy.: *Oḥ supīty atrāvarṇasyāpi nirdeśād yaṇprasaṅgaḥ.* ‚Da [nach der vorausgehenden Interpretation] in [der Regel VI, 4, 83]: „Für *a* (*ā*) und für *u* (*ū*) [tritt] vor einer [vokalisch anlautenden] Kasusendung [der Halbvokal ein]" auch der Laut *ā* zum Ausdruck kommt, würde sich [die Substitution des] Halbvokales [für das *ā* von -*pā* und -*yā*] darbieten.' Dies wäre jedoch ein Nonsens.

[104] Die Regel VI. 4, 140 lehrt die Elision des auslautenden *ā* einer [durch Anfügung von *vic* (III, 2, 74; VI, 1, 67) zum Nominalstamm gewordenen] Wurzel, jedoch nur bei einem *bha*-Stamm, d. h. vor den vokalisch anlautenden Endungen der schwachen Kasus. Nach dieser Regel wird also im Acc. pl. aus *kīlāla-pā* + (*vic*) + *as*: *kīlālapaḥ*. Die Deutung von *oḥ* = *a* (*ā*) + *u* (*ū*) + *aḥ* hat aber zur Folge, daß sich gleichzeitig mit VI, 4, 140 auch VI, 4, 83 darbietet. Es fragt sich also, welche dieser Regeln zuerst eintritt. Und gelangt VI, 4, 140 zuerst zur Anwendung, so würde sich gemäß VI, 4, 22 nachher doch noch 83 darbieten. Die Antwort auf die zweite Frage ist im Bhāṣya in dem Worte *bādhaka* gegeben. Vgl. Kaiy.: *Lopo 'treti: paratvād iti bhāvaḥ. Āto dhātor iti lopasyāvakāśaḥ saṃyogapūrvākārānto dhātuḥ; akārapraśleṣasyottaratrāvakāśaḥ: babhūva, babhūvitheti. Kīlālapa ity atrobhayaprasaṅge paratvād ākāralopaḥ, vipratiṣiddhe cāsiddhatvaṃ na bhavatīti jñāpayiṣyate.* ‚Gemeint ist: weil [VI, 4, 140] eine später gelehrte [Regel] ist. Der Elision nach [140]: „Für das *ā* einer Wurzel" bietet Gelegenheit [zur

Einwurf Dann aber bietet sich [VI, 4, 83] hier dar, [nämlich bei] *kīlālapau, kīlālapāḥ* [nom. pl.][105]

Erwiderung Unter diesen Umständen [sage ich] folgendes: [Aus VI, 4, 77] gilt ,*vyor*' [d. i. ,für *u* (*ū*) und für *i* (*ī*)'][106] fort. Dadurch werden wir [in *oḥ* = *a* + *u* + *as*] den Laut *u* speziell [d. i. als allein wirksam] kennzeichnen [und VI, 4, 83 interpretieren]: ,*Oḥ*' [soweit es] ,*vyoḥ*' [ist].[107] Hier [in VI, 4, 88] gilt jetzt [nur noch] ,*oḥ*' fort, während ,*vyoḥ*' [fortzugelten] aufgehört hat.[108] —

Auch für die [Anfügung von] *yuṭ* (*y*) [in *upadidī-y-e* nach VI, 4, 63] soll nicht [eine Ausnahme] konstatiert werden. Mit Hilfe des Ausdruckes *yuṭ* wird nicht [*upadidīye*] gebildet werden. Der Aus-

Anwendung] die Wurzel [*pā*], die auf *ā* endigt, welches der erste Laut der Verbindung [*a* (*ā*) + *u* (*ū*)] ist; die Verschmelzung des Lautes *a* (*ā*) [mit *u* (*ū*) zu *o*, also *oḥ*, d. i. VI, 4, 83] hat in einem zweiten Falle Gelegenheit [zur Anwendung, nämlich bei]: *babhūva, babhūvitha*. Da sich nun bei [der Bildung von] *kīlālapaḥ* b e i d e [sc. *lopa* und *oḥ*, gleichzeitig] darbieten, tritt [nach I, 4, 2] die Elision des *ā* [VI, 4, 140 zuerst] ein, weil sie später gelehrt wird. Und daß dort, wo [zwei sonst der Bildung v e r s c h i e d e n e r Formen dienende Regeln bei der Bildung einer e i n z i g e n Form] einander im Wege stehen, [die später gelehrte, also zuerst eingetretene Regel] nicht etwa [gemäß VI, 4, 22] als *asiddha* [in bezug auf die andere] betrachtet werden darf, wird [durch die Paribh. Nr. 40] angedeutet werden.' Vgl. im Anhang s. *vipratiṣedha*.

105 Kaiy.: *Asarvanāmasthāna ity anuvartanād* usw. ,Denn da [in I, 4, 18 aus 17] ,,Nicht vor den Endungen der starken Kasus' zu ergänzen ist, also der Terminus *bha* [bei den starken Kasus *kīlālapau, kīlālapāḥ*] nicht vorliegt, bietet sich [hier] die Elision des *ā* [von *-pā*: VI, 4, 140] nicht dar.' Es würde sich also nur nach VI, 4, 83 Substitution des Halbvokales für *ā* ergeben.

106 Kaiy.: *Yad eva yvor iti prakṛtaṃ* usw. ,Was [in VI, 4, 77] als ,,*yvor*'' vorgekommen ist, dasselbe ist [hier] mit einer Umkehrung der Reihenfolge des *i* als ,,*vyor*'' bezeichnet.' *Yvor* ist gen. pl. von *i* + *u*. Die Umstellung in *vyor* hat wohl darin ihren Grund, daß das *i* bei ,*oḥ*' überhaupt nicht in Betracht kommt.

107 Wie sonst *aci* oder *anaci* u. a. m. aus früheren Regel in einschränkendem Sinne zu ergänzen sind, so soll hier ,*oḥ*' in VI, 4, 83 durch das aus 77 zu ergänzende, ,*vyoḥ*' eingeschränkt werden. *Oḥ* bedeutet ,für *a* und für *u*'; *vyor* bedeutet ,für *u* und für *i*'. ,*Or vyoḥ*' besagt also: ,für *a* und für *u*, [und zwar nur insoweit es] für *u* und *i* [geschieht].' Durch die Ergänzung von ,*vyoḥ*' wird also das in diesem nicht enthaltene *a* von ,*oḥ*' aus seiner Wirksamkeit ausgeschaltet, und solange ,*vyor*' fortgilt, bedeutet ,*oḥ*' demgemäß trotz seiner Zusammensetzung aus *a* + *u* + *as* nur ,für *u*'. Wo dagegen ,*vyor*' nicht mehr zu ergänzen ist, bedeutet ,*oḥ*' seiner Zusammensetzung gemäß ,für *a* und für *u*'. Kaiy.: *Tatrākārokārasamudāyanirdeśe 'pi* usw. ,Obwohl dort [in ,,*oḥ*''] die Verbindung der Laute *a* und *u* zum Ausdruck kommt, so tritt doch, weil [*oḥ*] durch ,,*vyor*'' näher bestimmt wird, nur für den Laut *u* der Halbvokal ein, nicht aber für *a*'. Damit ist der Einwurf betreffs *kīlālapau, kīlālapāḥ* zurückgewiesen.

108 Kaiy.: *Iheti: Bhuvo luṅliṭor ūd upadhāyā ity atra*. ,Hier, in [der Regel VI, 4, 88 (ohne *vuk*) + 89 A]: ,,Bei *bhū* tritt vor den Endungen des Aoristes und Perfektums für die Pänultima ein *ū* ein''.' Die Ausgabe von Benares 1887 hat fälschlich: *bhuvo vug luṅliṭor* usw. *Vuk* ist zu streichen, denn der Opponent hat den Standpunkt ,*nārtho vukā nāpi kittvena*' nicht verlassen. — Da ,*vyor*' bei VI, 4, 88 nicht mehr fortgilt, bedeutet das hier allein zu ergänzende ,*oḥ*' ,für *a* und für *u*', und zwar kommt für *babhūva, babhūvitha* nur das *a* in Betracht. Das Resultat dieser Diskussion ist demnach: *Vuk* wird aus VI, 4, 88 eliminiert, und diese erhält infolge eines *Yogavibhāga* und

druck *yuṭ* hat einen andern Zweck. — Welchen? — Daß zwei *y* hörbar sein mögen.[109]

Einwurf Es gibt keinen Unterschied in Bezug auf das Hören eines oder mehrerer *y* hinter einem Konsonanten.[110] —

Ist denn nun aber [eine Regel] nur vor ‚*bha*' [d. i. bis incl. VI, 4, 128] als *asiddha* zu betrachten, oder einschließlich dieses [Abschnittes mit dem Adhikāra ‚*bha*', d. i. bis VI, 4, 175]? — Woher denn aber dieser Zweifel? — Es wird dies nämlich [in VI, 4, 22] durch [die Präposition] *ā* (*āṅ*) ausgedrückt, und *āṅ* erzeugt doch einen Zweifel. So z. B. [entsteht in dem Satze]: ‚Es hat bis *Pāṭaliputra* geregnet' der Zweifel, ob [nur] vor *Pāṭaliputra* oder einschließlich desselben. Ebenso ergibt sich auch hier der Zweifel: vor ‚*bha*' oder einschließlich [der Geltung] desselben? — Und worin besteht denn da der Unterschied?

Prāg bhād iti cec śunāmaghonābhūguṇeṣūpasaṃkhyānam || Värtt. 15.

Wenn man annimmt, daß [VI, 4, 22] vor ‚*bha*' gelte, so müßte hinzugefügt werden, daß [das Sūtra] bei 1. *śunā*, 2. *maghonā* und 3. bei [der Substitution von] *Guṇa* in *bhū* [dem Substitut für *bahu*] auch noch hinzugerechnet werden möge.[111]

1. *śunaḥ* (acc. pl.), *śunā*, *śune*: wenn [in *śvan-as* nach VI, 4, 133 die Substitution des] *Saṃprasāraṇa* erfolgt ist, so bietet sich [bei *śuan-as*] ‚Elision des *a* von *an*' [VI, 4, 134] dar.[112] Wenn dagegen

der Ergänzung von ‚*oḥ*' folgende Gestalt: [*Or*] *bhuvo luṅliṭor ūd upadhāyāḥ*. *Babhūva*, *babhūvitha* werden gebildet, indem trotz I, 2, 6 *Guṇa* und *Vṛddhi* für das *ū* von *bhū* substituiert werden, und für die Pänultima *a*, bezw. *ā*, welche dann vorliegt, *ū* eintritt.

[109] Dies ist die Erwiderung auf den zweiten Teil des Värtt. 14. Der Sinn ist: wir substituieren in *upadidī-e* zunächst nach VI, 4, 82 für *ī* den Halbvokal und erhalten *upadidye*; VI, 4, 63 lehrt nur, daß hier zwei *y* hörbar sein sollen, daß also *upadidyye* gebildet werde. Da also VI, 4, 82 zuerst eintritt, bedürfen wir der Regel VI, 4, 22 auch in diesem Falle nicht.

[110] Kaiy.: *Vyañjanaparasyeti: vyañjanāt parasyeti sup supeti samāsaḥ* (‚*Vy*. ist ein Kompositum gemäß [II, 1, 4]: „Eine Kasusform mit einer Kasusform," nämlich aus *vyañjanāt parasya*'). *Śrutibhedapakṣe 'pi yaṇo maya iti dvirvacanavidhānād dhalo yamāṃ yami lopa iti pakṣe lopavidhānāt pakṣe yakāradvayaṃ bhavaty eveti nārtho yuṭeti tadvidhānasāmarthyād yaṇ na bhavati*. ‚Weil [einerseits] die Verdoppelung in [VIII, 4, 47 Värtt. 1:] „Eines Halbvokales nach einer Muta oder einem Nasal (außer *ñ*)" vorgeschrieben wird, auf der anderen Seite aber in [der Regel VIII, 4, 64]: „Nach einem Konsonanten wird ein Halbvokal oder Nasal vor einem Halbvokal oder Nasal elidiert" Elision vorgeschrieben wird, also zwei *y* tatsächlich fakultativ (*pakṣe*) eintreten, so bedarf man [hiezu] nicht noch des Augmentes *yuṭ* (*y*); also wird selbst für den Fall, daß ein Unterschied im Hören [eines oder mehrerer *y* hinter einem Konsonanten angenommen wird], nicht etwa infolge der Vorschrift dieses [*yuṭ* in VI, 4, 63] der Halbvokal [für das *ī* in *upadidī-e*] substituiert.'

[111] Denn in diesen drei Fällen handelt es sich um Regeln, die in dem Abschnitt mit dem *adhikāra* ‚*bha*' [VI, 4, 129—175] stehen.

[112] Kaiy.: *Śuna iti: śvan śas iti sthite saṃprasāraṇaṃ; vārṇād āṅgasya balīyastvāt pūrvaikādeśaṃ bādhitvāllopaḥ prāpnoti*. ‚Wenn *śvan* + *as* (acc. pl.) vorliegt, so erfolgt [die Substitution] des *Saṃprasāraṇa* [für *v*]; da nun [nach Paribh. Nr. 55] eine den Stamm betreffende [Operation: VI, 4—VII, 4 incl.] größere Kraft besitzt [also früher eintritt] als eine [die Verbindung von] Lauten betreffende, so ergibt sich [in *śuan-as*] die Elision des *a* [VI, 4, 134], mit Verdrängung der Substitution des einen vorangehenden [Lautes *u* für *u* + *a*: VI, 1, 108].' Denn VI, 4, 134 ist *āṅgam*, VI, 1, 108 aber *vārṇam*.

für diese [Substitution des *Saṃprasāraṇa* gilt], daß [eine Regel] einschließlich dieses [Abschnittes über *bha*] als *asiddha* betrachtet wird, wird dadurch, daß diese [Substitution als *asiddha* betrachtet wird, das Verbot [VI, 4, 137]: ‚Nicht aber, wenn [das *a* von *an*] auf eine Konsonantenverbindung folgt, welche auf *v* oder *m* endigt' [gegen 134] zur Geltung kommen.[113]

Erwiderung Auch wenn für diese [Substitution des *Saṃprasāraṇa*: VI, 4, 133 angenommen wird, daß nur eine Regel] vor *bha* als *asiddha* betrachtet wird [‚*Saṃprasāraṇa* also *siddha* ist], so bedeutet dies für diese [Substitution des *Saṃprasāraṇa*] keinen Fehler. — Wieso? — Es gibt hier keinen Unterschied, ob nun das Verschwinden [des *a* von *an*] durch die Elision des *a* [134] erfolgt, oder dadurch, daß [nach VI, 1, 108] der vorangehende [Vokal *u* für *u* + *a*] eintritt.

Einwurf[114] Der Unterschied besteht in folgendem: wenn das Verschwinden [des *a*] durch die Elision des *a* [VI, 4, 134] erfolgt, so würde sich [nach VI, 1, 161] notwendigerweise der durch das Verschwinden des *Udātta* bedingte Akzent [für die darauffolgende unbetonte Endung] ergeben.[115]

Erwiderung Hier bietet sich der durch das Verschwinden des *Udātta* bedingte Akzent nicht dar. — Aus welchem Grunde? — Weil [die Regel VI, 1, 182:] ‚Nicht hinter *go*, *śvan* und einem im Nominativ singularis [auf] *a* [ausgehenden Stamme]' dies verbietet.

Einwurf Dies ist nicht ein Verbot gegen den durch das Verschwinden eines *Udātta* bedingten Akzent. — Wogegen denn? — [Nur] gegen die Betonung der Endung des Instrumentals und der folgenden [Kasus, d. i. gegen VI, 1, 168].[116] Und wo es sich nun

[113] Wenn die Substitution des *Saṃprasāraṇa* als *asiddha* betrachtet wird, also noch *śvan-as* als vorhanden zu denken ist, folgt das *a* auf eine Konsonantenverbindung, welche auf *v* endigt. Die Elision nach 134 wird also durch das in 137 enthaltene Verbot verhindert.

[114] Die ‚Einwürfe' enthalten den Standpunkt desjenigen, welcher behauptet hat, daß VI, 4, 22 ausnahmsweise auch noch in den genannten drei Fällen hinzugerechnet werden müßte, wenn dieses Sūtra sonst nur vor ‚*bha*' gälte, also den Standpunkt des *Upasaṃkhyānavādin*, wie Kaiy. ihn nennt, im Gegensatz zu dem des *Pratyākhyānavādin*, des Opponenten. So bemerkt Kaiy. hier: ‚Der *Upasaṃkhyānavādin* sagt, um den Unterschied aufzuzeigen.'

[115] Kaiy.: *Anudāttanimittatvād udāttalopasya. Ekādeśe tu saty ekādeśa udāttenodātta ity ādyudāttaṃ padaṃ bhavati, śvaśabdākārasya pratyayasvareṇāntodāttatvāt.* ‚Denn die Elision des udāttierten [Vokales *a*] hat ihren Grund [vgl. ‚*yatra*' in VI, I, 161] in der unbetonten Endung. [Wir würden also aus *śuán-ā* mit falschem Akzent *śunā́* erhalten]. Wenn dagegen [in *śuán-ā* nach VI, 1, 108] die Substitution des einen [Vokales *u* für *u* + *á*] erfolgt, so ist gemäß [der Regel VIII, 2, 5]: „Ein einziger [Vokal] als Substitut [für einen unbetonten] samt einem udāttierten [Vokal] ist *udātta*" das [fertige] Wort in der ersten [Silbe] *udātta* [d. i. *śúnā* mit richtigem Akzent]; denn das *a* der Wortform *śvan* ist infolge der Betonung des Suffixes [*an*: III, 1, 3] End-*udātta*.' [Bei Böhtl. zu VIII, 2, 5 ist also das Wort ‚vorangehenden' zu streichen.]

[116] D. i. also der Kasus mit Ausnahme des Akkusativs und des Nominativs. — Kaiy.: *Upasaṃkhyānavādy āha: naiṣeti; tṛtīyādisvarasyeti: sāv ekāca iti prāptasya; tatra pratiṣiddhe 'pi tṛtīyādisvare lope saty udāttanivṛttisvaraprasaṅga iti viśeṣo 'sti, na gośvann ity asya tu niṣedhasya phalaṃ śvabhyāṃ śvabhir iti halādau vibhaktāv asti.* ‚Der *U.* sagt: „*Naiṣa*"; [dann] „[Ein Verbot] gegen die Betonung der Endungen des Instrumentals usw.": [d. i.] gegen diejenige, welche sich aus [VI, 1, 168]: „Eines im Lokativ pluralis

nicht um die Endungen des Instrumentals und der folgenden [Kasus] handelt, also bei *śunaḥ* (acc. pl.)?[117]

Erwiderung Dann [sagen wir] folgendes: wir lehren nicht, daß [VI, 4, 182] eine [bestimmte] Regel [sc. VI, 1, 168] verbiete, sondern es ist dies ein Verbot gegen die aus irgendeiner Regel sich ergebende Betonung einer Endung [überhaupt].[118]

einsilbigen [Stammes]" ergibt; obwohl unter dieser Voraussetzung (*tatra*) die Betonung der Endungen des Instrumentals usw. [durch 182] verboten wird, so liegt doch ein davon verschiedener Fall vor, wenn sich [in *śuán-ā*, *śuán-e*] nach dem Eintritt der Elision [des *á*] der durch das Verschwinden des *Udātta* bedingte Akzent [für die Endung gemäß 161] darbietet. Das Verbot „nicht nach *go*, *śvan*" [182] aber äußert seine Wirkung [nur] bei *śvábhyām*, *śvábhir* vor einer mit einem Konsonanten anlautenden Kasusendung [, vor welcher *Saṃprasāraṇa* (VI, 4, 133), also auch Elision des *á* (134) und *udāttanivṛttisvara* (VI, 1, 161) sich nicht ergeben. VI, 1, 182 erstreckt sich also nur auf Fälle, in denen der *udāttanivṛttisvara* sich nicht darbietet].'

[117] *Sa evāha: yatra tarhīti: cārthe tarhiśabdaḥ. Na kevalaṃ śunā, śune ity atra tṛtīyādisvare pratiṣiddhe 'sty udāttanivṛtti[svara]prasaṅgo, 'pi tu yatra tṛtīyādyabhāvaḥ śunaḥ paśyeti tatrāpy udāttanivṛttisvaraprasaṅga ity arthaḥ. Na hi atraitad api śakyate vaktuṃ: yena kenacid api lakṣaṇena prāptasya tṛtīyādisvarasya pratiṣedha iti.* ‚Ebenderselbe [sc. *Upasaṃkhyānav.*] sagt [ferner] „*yatra tarhi*". Das Wort *tarhi* steht im Sinne von *ca*: nicht nur bei *śunā*, *śune* bietet sich der durch das Verschwinden des *Udātta* bedingte Akzent [für die Endung] dar, selbst wenn die Betonung der Endungen des Instrumentals und der folgenden [Kasus durch VI, 1, 182] verboten wird [vgl. die vorhergehende Anm.], sondern auch dort, wo kein Instrumental oder ein folgender [Kasus] vorliegt, im acc. pl. *śunaḥ* [aus *śuán-aḥ*] bietet sich ein durch das Verschwinden des *Udātta* bedingter Akzent [für die Endung] dar. Dies ist der Sinn. Denn hier kann man nicht einmal einwenden, daß [VI, 1, 182 nicht speziell 168, sondern] diejenige Betonung der Endungen des Instrumentals usw. verbiete, die sich aus irgendeiner beliebigen Regel ergibt [also auch den nach VI, 1, 161, eintretenden *udāttanivṛttisvara*].' Nach Kaiy. wäre also der Gedankengang: VI, 1, 182 verbietet die Betonung der Endungen des Instr. usw. nur für *śvabhyām*, *śvabhir*, nicht aber für diejenigen Endungen des Instr. usw., bei denen nach 161 der *udāttanivṛttisvara* eintreten müßte [d. i. bei *śunā*, *śune*]; und (*tarhi*) dort, wo nicht ein Instr. usw. vorliegt, also beim acc. pl. *śunaḥ*, wie sollte 182 da den *udāttanivṛttisvara* verbieten? Kaiy. scheint mir aber in der Unterscheidung zwischen *śvabhyām* und *śunā* zu weit zu gehen. Ich möchte interpretieren: VI, 1, 182 verbietet nicht — wie der *Pratyākhyānav.* offenbar meint — den *udāttanivṛttisvara* bei *śvan* überhaupt, das Verbot in 182 erstreckt sich vielmehr nur auf die Endungen des Instr. und der folgenden Kasus [also auf *śunā*, *śune*, *śvabhyām* usw.]; wie sollte 182 unter diesen Umständen (*tarhi*) den *udāttanivṛttisvara* für die Endung des Akkus. pl. verbieten? Kaiy. erwähnt am Schluß dieser Diskussion des Bhāṣya, daß bisweilen [*kvacit tu pāṭhaḥ* usw.] vor ‚*yatra tarhi*' der Satz ‚*evaṃ tarhi yena kenacit prāptasya tṛtīyādisvarasya*' (‚dann [sage ich] folgendes: [182 ist ein Verbot] gegen die Betonung [der Endungen] des Instr. usw., die sich aus einer beliebigen Regel ergibt') eingeschoben erscheint. [In diesem Falle wäre Kaiy.'s Unterscheidung zwischen *śvabhyām* und *śunā* berechtigt]. Bei der uns vorliegenden Lesung aber müsse *tarhi* im Sinne von *ca* erklärt werden, weil *tarhi* sonst ein verschiedenes Subjekt zu haben pflege.

[118] Kaiy.: *Na sāv ekāca ity asyaiva* usw. ‚Dies [sc. VI, 1, 182] ist nicht nur ein Verbot gegen die Regel [168]: „Eines im Lok. plur. einsilbigen [Stammes]," sondern gegen jeden *Udātta* überhaupt, der sich für eine Endung ergibt [also auch für die des Akk. pl. *śunaḥ*]. Dies ist der Sinn. Aus dem Worte

Einwurf Wo nun aber die Betonung einer E n d u n g nicht in Betracht kommt, [wie bei] *bahuśúnī*?[119]

Erwiderung [Wie wäre es], wenn man diese [Regel VI, 1, 182] vielleicht doch als Verbot auch gegen [jedweden] durch das Verschwinden des *Udātta* bedingten Akzent betrachtete?[120]

Einwurf Solches ist nicht möglich. [Denn] es würde sich auch hier darbieten, [nämlich bei] *kumārī́*.[121]

Erwiderung Unter diesen Umständen [sagen wir] folgendes: das Vorgehen des Lehrers [d. i. Pāṇ.s] deutet an, daß sich bei *śvan* überhaupt nicht ein durch das Verschwinden des *Udātta* bedingter Akzent einstellt, da er ja [Gaṇapāṭha 81, 64] das Wort *śvan* unter *gaura* usw. anführt [und IV, 1, 41 die Bildung der Feminina dieses Wort mittels *ṅīṣ*, d. i. des betonten *ī́*, lehrt]. Er macht [also] wegen des End-*udātta* [von *śunī́*] eine besondere Anstrengung. Denn [dieser] kommt schon durch *ṅīp* (*ī*) zustande.[122]

„gegen die Betonung einer E n d u n g" [geht hervor, daß dieser [sc. der *Pratyākhyānav.*] annimmt, das Wort „*vibhakti*" gelte [in 182 aus 168 fort].'

[119] Kaiy.: ‚Hier spricht der *Upasaṃkhyānavādin* „*yatra tarhi*".' *Bahavaḥ śvāno yasyām iti* usw. ‚[*Bahuśunī*] ist ein *Bahuvrīhi* mit der Bedeutung „eine [Fahrstraße, *rathyā*; vgl. Mbh. vol. II, p. 204, l. 3 v. u.], in der sich viele Hunde befinden". Daselbst ist nach Ansicht desjenigen, welcher die Elision des *a* behauptet, [an *bahuśvan*] nach [der Regel IV, 1, 28]: „An einen auf *an* [auslautenden *Bahuvrīhi*], dessen Pänultima [*a*] elidiert wird" *ṅīp* [d. i. das unbetonte Femininsuffix *ī*, angetreten]. Weil nun nach [der Regel VI, 2, 175]: „Nach *bahu* [als erstem Glied eines *Bahuvrīhi*], wenn dadurch die Vielheit des im zweiten Gliede Ausgedrückten [bezeichnet wird], wie bei der Negation [als erstem Glied: VI, 2, 172]" [*bahuśván*] den End-*udātta* besitzt, so bietet sich [in *bahuśván-ī* infolge der Elision des *á*] der durch das Verschwinden des *Udātta* bedingte Akzent dar [und wir erhalten fälschlich *bahuśunī́*].' Da in *bahuśúnī* nach VI, 1, 68 eine Endung nicht in Betracht kommt, kann sich VI, 1, 82 auf diesen Fall nicht erstrecken, wenn es als Verbot gegen die Betonung jeder Endung von *go*, *śvan* usw. aufgefaßt wird. Der *udāttanivṛttisvara* wird also durch diese Regel nicht verhindert.

[120] Kaiy.: ‚Der *Pratyākhyānav.* sagt „*yadi punar*". Damit ist gemeint: das Wort „*vibhakti*" („Kasusendung") gilt nicht [aus VI, 1, 168 in 182] fort.' D. h. das Verbot in 182 soll sich nicht nur auf Kasusendungen, sondern auch auf jeden *udāttanivṛttisvara* bei *śvan* usw. erstrecken.

[121] D. h. wenn VI, 1, 182 den *udāttanivṛttisvara* verböte, so würde dies auch für die in der Regel erwähnten Stämme gelten, welche im Nom. sing. auf *a* ausgehen, also auch für *kumārá*, dessen Femininum nach IV, 1, 20 mittels *ṅīp* gebildet wird und nach VI, 1, 161 den *udāttanivṛttisvara* erhält: *kumārá* + *ī* = *kumārī́*. — Bei Böhtl. zu VI, 1, 182 ist das ganz unbegründete Wort ‚einsilbig' zu streichen.

[122] *Śunī́* würde auch durch Anfügung von *ṅīp* (unbetontem *ī*) zustandekommen: *śuán* + *ī* nach VI, 1, 161 = *śunī́*. Wenn Pāṇ. trotzdem die Anfügung von *ṅīṣ* (*ī́*) lehrt, so deutet er offenbar an, daß bei *śvan* niemals der *udāttanivṛttisvara* eintritt. — Kaiy.: ‚Der *Pratyākhyānavādin* sagt „*evaṃ tarhi*". Mag auch der durch das Verschwinden des *Udātta* bedingte Akzent nicht durch [die Regel VI, 1, 182]: „Nicht nach *go*, *śvan*" verboten sein, so stellt er sich doch bei *śvan* infolge eines *Jñāpaka* nicht ein. Dies ist der Sinn. So hat der Opponent (*pratyākhyānavādin*) bewiesen, daß kein Unterschied besteht [ob nun das Verschwinden des *a* von *śván* nach VI, 4, 134 oder VI, 1, 108 erfolgt].' D. h. aus der Elision des *a* nach VI, 4, 134 ergibt sich kein Fehler; das Sūtra VI, 4, 22 braucht also bei der Bildung von *śunā* usw. nicht hinzugerechnet zu werden, wenn man annimmt, daß es nur v o r ‚*bha*' gelte. *Bahuśúnī* wird mittels *ṅīp* und Elision des *á* gebildet: *bahuśuán* + *ī* [wobei man aus dem *Jñāpaka* ersieht, daß nicht nach VI, 1,

2. *Maghonaḥ* (akk. pl.), *maghonā*, *maghone*: wenn [in *maghavan-as* nach VI, 4, 133 die Substitution des] *Saṃprasāraṇa* [für *v*] vollzogen ist, so ergibt sich nach [der Regel VI, 4, 148]: ,Für *i* und für *a*' Elision [des *a* vor *-un*]. Wenn hingegen für diese [Substitution des *Saṃprasāraṇa* gilt], daß [eine Regel] einschließlich dieses [Abschnittes über ,*bha*'] als *asiddha* zu betrachten sei, so wird dadurch, daß sie als *asiddha* betrachtet wird, [VI, 4, 148] nicht eintreten.

Erwiderung Aber auch wenn für diese [Substitution des *Saṃprasāraṇa* gilt], daß [eine Regel] vor ,*bha*' als *asiddha* zu betrachten sei, bedeutet dies für diese [Substitution] keinen Fehler. — Wieso? — Er [Pat. zu IV, 1, 7] wird [nämlich] sagen: Die Wortform *maghavan* ist ein etymologisch nicht abgeleiteter Nominalstamm.[123]

3. [die Substitution von] *Guṇa* in *bhū*, [bei der Bildung von] *bhūyān*: wenn [nach VI, 4, 158] der Eintritt von *bhū* [für *bahu*] erfolgt ist, so ergibt sich [nach 146 die Substitution von] *Guṇa* für das *ū*. Wenn dagegen für diesen [Eintritt von *bhū* gilt], daß [eine Regel] einschließlich dieses [Abschnittes über ,*bha*'] als *asiddha* zu betrachten ist, wird dadurch, daß er [sc. der Eintritt von *bhū*] als *asiddha* betrachtet wird, [die Substitution von *Guṇa*] nicht erfolgen.[124]

161 Oxytonese eintritt, daß also das *u* den Ton erhält] = *bahuśúnī*. —Kaiy. bemerkt noch: *Vidyate tu viśeṣaḥ; allope* usw. ,Doch ist [in Wirklichkeit] ein Unterschied vorhanden. Wenn nämlich die Elision des *a* [VI, 4, 134] gilt, so muß [nach IV, 1, 28] *ṅīp* eintreten, weil [*bahuśván* in diesem Falle ein *Bahuvrīhi* auf *an* ist], dessen Pänultima elidiert wird: [wir erhalten also] *bahuśunī*. Wenn dagegen diese [Elision] nicht stattfindet, so wird [nach IV, 1, 12 ohne ein Femininsuffix] *bahuśvā* gebildet. [Denn] auch das für *gaura* usw. [darunter *śvan*] vorgeschriebene Suffix *ṅīṣ* [IV, 1, 41] bietet sich wegen des *Adhikāra* ,,Nicht hinter dem untergeordneten Gliede [eines Kompositums'': IV, 1, 14] nicht dar. [In dem *Bahuvrīhi bahuśvan* ist nämlich *śvan* nach I, 2, 43 *upasarjana*]. Am Schluß [unseres Kapitels] wird ja auch festgestellt werden, daß [eine Regel] einschließlich dieses [Abschnittes über *bha*] *asiddha* ist. In diesem Falle muß [weil VI, 4, 134 dann durch 137 verboten wird] eben nur *bahuśvā* gebildet werden, gleichwie *suparvā* [nach IV, 1, 12 ohne *ī*]. Dadurch aber, daß die Abfassung [dieser Diskussion] sich nur von dem einen Ziele leiten läßt, einen Unterschied hinsichtlich des Akzentes zu beseitigen, ist dies in Bhāṣya nicht richtig dargestellt worden. [D. h. es blieb unbeachtet, daß *bahuśunī* überhaupt nicht gebildet werden kann, wenn die Elision nach VI, 4, 134 nicht erfolgt.] Aber auch bei [der Regel IV, 1, 13]: ,,*Ḍāp* [das unbetonte Femininsuffix *ā*, tritt beliebig] in beiden Fällen [d. i. nach *-man* und nach einem auf *an* ausgehenden *Bahuvrīhi* ein]'' ist [von Pat. am Schluß] festgestellt worden, daß nur *bahuśvā* [und nicht *bahuśūkā*] gebildet werden darf.' — Zu der folgenden textkritischen Bemerkung Kaiy.'s vgl. p. 246, Anm. 117, Ende.

[123] Vgl. zu Värtt. 7.

[124] Kaiy.: *Nanu ca bhūbhāvasyāsiddhatvād* usw. ,Aber wenn der Eintritt des [Substitutes] *bhū* als *asiddha* betrachtet wird, so ist infolgedessen dieses [Substitut] doch [so anzusehen, als ob] noch [der *sthānin*, d. i.] das Wort *bahu* [dastünde]; es würde sich also [gemäß ,,*utsargalakṣaṇabhāvārthaṃ ca*'' (vgl. p. 217)] tatsächlich *Guṇa* [bei *bhū*] ergeben? — Dieses bedeutet keinen Fehler. Weil nämlich in bezug auf die [an *bhū*] zu vollziehende [Substitution von] *Guṇa* der Eintritt von *bhū* als *asiddha* betrachtet wird, so erfolgt der Eintritt von *bhū*, nachdem [die Substitution von] *Guṇa* schon vorher [an *bahu*] vollzogen worden ist. Und für *Guṇa* und den Eintritt von *bhū* ergibt sich nicht etwa der Fehler, daß man in einen Circulus (*cakraka*) gerät;

Erwiderung Auch wenn für diesen [Eintritt von *bhū* gilt], daß [eine Regel] vor ‚*bha*' als *asiddha* zu betrachten ist, so bedeutet dies für ihn [d. i. den Eintritt von *bhū*] keinen Fehler. — Wieso? — Wegen der Aussprache mit langem [*ū*] wird [die Substitution von *Guṇa*] nicht erfolgen.[125]

Einwurf Die Aussprache mit langem [*ū*] hat einen andern Zweck. — Welchen? — [Die Bildung von] *bhūman*.[126]

Erwiderung Dieses kommt schon infolge seiner ausdrücklichen Erwähnung[127] zustande. — Welches ist die ausdrückliche Erwähnung? — [In der Regel VI, 2, 175:] ‚*Bahor nañvad uttarapadabhūmni*.[128] —

Oder aber es gelte [die Annahme], daß [eine Regel] einschließlich dieses [Abschnittes mit dem *Adhikāra*] ‚*bha*' als *asiddha* zu betrachten sei:

Ā bhād iti ced vasusaṃprasāraṇayalopaprasthādīnāṃ pratiṣedhaḥ || Värtt. 16.

Wenn [man annimmt], daß [eine Regel] bis [einschließlich][129] zum [Abschnitt über] ‚*bha*' [als *asiddha* zu betrachten ist], so muß 1. für [die Substitution von] *Saṃprasāraṇa* in *vas*. 2. für die Elision von *y* und 3. für [die Substitution von] *pra*, *stha* usw. ein Verbot konstatiert werden:

1. [Bei der Bildung der Akkusative pl.] *papuṣaḥ*, *tasthuṣaḥ*; *ninyuṣaḥ*, *cicyuṣaḥ*; *luvuvuṣaḥ*, *pupuvuṣaḥ*:[130] nachdem [die Substitution von] *Saṃprasāraṇa* [nach VI, 4, 131] vollzogen worden ist, kommen, wenn diese als *asiddha* betrachtet wird, infolgedessen die Elision des *ā* [64] und die übrigen [Operationen, sc. 82 und 77, welche sich nur] ‚vor einem Vokal' [ergeben] nicht zustande.

Erwiderung Dies bedeutet keinen Fehler. [Im Värtt. 12] ist [nämlich] folgendes gelehrt worden: Es ist vollständig in Ordnung,

denn bei einem Circulus trifft man je nach der erwünschten [Form] eine [ihr entsprechende] bestimmte Entscheidung.' D. h. wenn die Operation a die Operation b, und diese wieder a veranlaßt, so sieht man zu, welche Form bei den Autoritäten erwünscht ist; wenn diese durch b erreicht ist, tritt a nicht wieder ein. In unserem Falle liegt ein *cakraka* nicht vor, weil der Eintritt von *bhū* nicht direkt *Guṇa* veranlaßt, sondern in bezug auf dieses *asiddha* ist, also nicht erst die ‚erwünschte Form' für das Eintritt oder Nichteintreten von *Guṇa* maßgebend ist.

[125] D. h. Pāṇini sagt ausdrücklich *bhū* mit langem *ū*, um anzudeuten, daß *Guṇa* sich nicht mehr ergibt.

[126] Kaiy.: *Bhatvābhāvād atra guṇābhāvaḥ*. ‚Weil [der Stamm vor dem Suffix *man*] nicht ein *bha*-Stamm ist, so kann hier nicht *Guṇa* eintreten.' Das lange *ū* könnte also nicht den Zweck haben, den Eintritt von *Guṇa* in *bhūman* zu verhindern. Das *ū* soll vielmehr andeuten, daß vor dem Suffix *-man* für *bahu* zwar *bhu* mit kurzem *u* substituiert wird, daß aber trotzdem *bhūman* gebildet wird.

[127] Über den Terminus *nipātana* vgl. Kielhorn, *Ind. Ant.*, vol. XVI, p. 245. [this volume, page 125]

[128] Kaiy.: *Hrasvānte 'py ādeśe kriyamāne* usw. ‚Obwohl das auf eine Kürze ausgehende Substitut [*bhu*] eingesetzt wird, so wird doch bei *bhūman* infolge der ausdrücklichen Erwähnung [dieses Wortes] die Länge eintreten. Dies ist der Sinn.'

[129] Kaiy.: *Prāg bhād ity asya pakṣasya* usw. ‚Da [*ā bhāt*] als Gegenteil der einen Alternative „*prāg bhāt*" gebraucht wird [lies: *upādīyamānatvād* statt °*mānād*], so ist [die Präposition] *ā* im Sinne des Einschlusses [*abhividhi*, vgl. II, 1, 13] zu verstehen.'

[130] Kaiy.: *Papūṣa ityādīnāṃ parihṛtānām api* usw. ‚Obwohl *papūṣaḥ* usw. [schon im Värtt. 12 als nicht in Betracht kommend] zurückgewiesen worden sind, werden sie doch wieder vorgebracht, um zu zeigen, daß der vorhin [sc. im Värtt. 9] aufgezeigte

wenn man sagt, [eine Operation sei *asiddha*,] wenn sie von dem gleichen [Element] abhängig ist. — Wieso? — Auf [dem *v* von] *vas* [beruhen] die Elision des *ā* und die übrigen [Operationen], auf der Endung des auf *vas* endigenden [Stammes die Substitution des] *Saṃprasāraṇa*.

2. Die Elision von *y* [in] *saurī balākā* [,ein mit der Sonne in gleicher Richtung (Höhe) befindlicher Kranich']: wenn dasjenige *a*, welches [nach VI, 4, 148] vor [dem *Taddhita*] *aṇ* (*a*) elidiert wird, als *asiddha* betrachtet wird, so bietet sich infolgedessen nicht nach [der Regel 149]: ,Vor *ī*' die Elision des *y* dar.[131]

Erwiderung Auch hier vermeidet man [Schwierigkeiten] in der Weise [, daß man erklärt]: Es ist dadurch vollständig korrekt, daß man sagt, [eine Operation sei *asiddha*,] wenn sie von dem gleichen [Element] abhängig ist. — Wieso? — Auf [dem *Taddhita*] *aṇ* (*a*) beruht die Elision des Lautes *a*, auf dem *ī* des auf *aṇ* (*a*) endigenden [Stammes] die Elision des *y*.[132]

Fehler sich gerade bei dieser Alternative [sc. ,,*saha tena*''] ergibt.' — Vgl. zu Värtt. 12.

[131] Kaiy.: *Sauriti : sūryeṇaikadig ity aṇ* usw. ,*Saurī*: [um auszudrücken] ,,in gleicher Richtung (Höhe) mit der Sonne befindlich'' wird [nach IV, 3, 112 an *sūrya* das *Taddhita aṇ* (*a*) gefügt [welches nach VII, 2, 117 *Vṛddhi* bewirkt]; gemäß [der Regel VI, 4, 148]: ,,Für *i* und für *a*'' erfolgt die Elision des dem *aṇ* vorangehenden *a*]; hierauf tritt [gemäß IV, 1, 15 das Femininsuffix] *ṅīp* (*ī*) ein; nun wieder gemäß [der Regel VI, 4, 148]: ,,Für *i* und für *a*'' Elision des *aṇ* (*a*) [vor *ī*]. Wenn nun hiebei beide Elisionen von *a* [d. h. nicht allein die von *aṇ* vor *ī*] als *asiddha* betrachtet werden, so ist infolgedessen das *y* nicht Pänultima [des Stammes vor *ī*, sondern drittletzter Buchstabe], und so bietet sich die Elision des *y* [149] nicht dar.— [Einwurf:] Aber auch wenn [man annimmt, daß eine Regel nur] vor ,,*bha*'' als *asiddha* zu betrachten ist, so ist, weil dann beide Elisionen [d. h. auch die des *a* vor *aṇ*] *siddha* wären, das *y* nicht Pänultima [des Stammes vor *ī*, sondern letzter Buchstabe], folglich bietet sich die Elision [des *y* (lies: *yalopa*°) hier] ebenfalls nicht dar. [Denn] auch [die Annahme, daß der für *aṇ* substituierte *lopa*] sich wie der *sthānin* [*aṇ*] verhalte [vgl. Pat. zu VI, 4, 149 Värtt. 1—2], ist [nach I, 1, 58] verboten, weil es sich um eine Vorschrift über die Elision eines *y* handelt. — [Erwiderung:] Es liegt [bei der Annahme ,,*prāg bhāt*''] kein Fehler vor, wenn man *upadhā* [in VI, 4, 149] nach der Methode ,wenn es nur vorher dagewesen ist'' auffaßt [also: ,,für *y*, wenn es auch nur vorher Pänultima gewesen ist'']. Oder auf Grund des Wortlautes [d. i. ,,für *y*, solange es Pänultima ist''] wird die [umgekehrte] Reihenfolge gewählt werden, nämlich zuerst die Elision des *y*, nachher Elision des *a* [d. i. *aṇ*], obwohl die Elision des *a* (*aṇ*) *nitya* ist [, also gemäß Paribh. Nr. 38 früher eintreten sollte]' D. h. man bildet: *sūrya* + *a*(*ṇ*) = *saury* + *a*(*ṇ*); *saury* + *a*(*ṇ*) + *ī*. Weil nach VI, 4, 149 das *y* nur elidiert wird, wenn es Pänultima eines Stammes ist, und weil es nicht mehr Pänultima wäre, wenn *a*(*ṇ*) vorher abfiele, wird zuerst *y* als Pänultima des auf *a*(*ṇ*) ausgehenden Stammes wegen des folgenden *ī* elidiert: *saur* + *a*(*ṇ*) + *ī*, und jetzt erst erfolgt die Elision des *a*(*ṇ*). So würde also nach Kaiy. derjenige, welcher ,,*prāg bhāt*'' annimmt, beweisen, daß diese Annahme keinen Fehler zur Folge hat.

[132] Dieser Auffassung stimmt auch die Kāś. zu VI, 4, 149 zu, wo es heißt: *Aṇi yo yasyeti lopas* usw. ,Diejenige Elision, welche [für das *a*] wegen des folgenden *a*(*ṇ*) gemäß [der Regel 148]: ,,Für *i* und für *a*'' erfolgt, ist nicht als *asiddha* zu betrachten, weil es nicht [von dem gleichen Element] abhängt [wei die Elision des *a*(*ṇ*)]. Dagegen wird die [Elision, welche für das *a*(*ṇ*)] wegen des folgenden *ī* eintritt, als *asiddha* betrachtet, [weil sie von demselben Element abhängt wie die Elision des *y*], und infolgedessen wird das *y* als Pänultima des auf *a*(*ṇ*) ausgehenden

3. Bei [den Substitutionen von] *pra*, *stha* usw. [in] *preyān*, *stheyān*: wenn [die Substitutionen von] *pra*, usw. [VI, 4, 157] als *asiddha* betrachtet werden, so ergibt sich nicht gemäß [der Regel 163]: ‚Ein einsilbiger [Stamm verbleibt] in seiner ursprünglichen Gestalt' das Verbleiben der ursprünglichen [d. i. unveränderten] Formen [*pra* usw.].[133]

Erwiderung Dies bedeutet keinen Fehler. Wie sich zwar dadurch, daß [die Substitutionen von] *pra*, *stha* usw. als *asiddha* betrachtet werden, das Verbleiben der ursprünglichen Formen [*pra*, *stha* usw.] nicht ergibt, ebenso wird doch auch die Elision des letzten Vokales samt dem etwa darauffolgenden Konsonanten [VI, 4, 155] nicht eintreten.[134]

P. VI, 4, 132: Vāha ūṭ.

Warum wird *ūṭ* nicht vorne angefügt? Aus [der Regel I, 1, 46, welche besagt]: ‚Vorne [wird angefügt], was ein *ṭ* zum *Anubandha* hat' ergibt sich, [daß *ūṭ*] vorne [antritt]?[135]

bha-Stammes von *sūrya* [in *saury(a)-ī*] wegen des folgenden *ī* elidiert.' Anders Siddh. K. zu VI, 4, 149: *aṅgasyopadhāyā yasya lopaḥ syāt, sa ced yaḥ sūryādyavayavaḥ*. ‚Für ein *y*, welches Pänultima eines [noch unveränderten] Stammes ist, soll [vor einem *Taddhita* oder *ī*] Elision eintreten, wenn dieses *y* einen Bestandteil von *sūrya* usw. bildet [, nicht aber für das *y* der von *sūrya* usw. abgeleiteten Stämme].' Diese Interpretation der Regel schließt sich zum Teil Pat.'s Erklärung zu VI, 4, 149 Värtt. 3 an und in der Ausdruckweise dem Kommentar Kaiy.'s zu dieser Stelle, unterscheidet sich aber von Pat.'s, bezw. Kāty.'s, Ansicht dadurch, daß dort das Wort *upadhāyāḥ* der Regel als überflüssig erklärt wird. Kaiy. erklärt dort: *Iti taddhite ca yad aṅgam anāśritarūpaviśeṣaṃ tasya yakārasya lopaḥ, sa ced yakāraḥ sūryādyavayavo bhavatīti sūtrārthaḥ*.

[133] Es müßte also nach VI, 4, 155 der letzte Vokal von *pra* usw. elidiert werden.

[134] Zum Verständnis der folgenden Ausführungen Kaiy.'s sei daran erinnert, daß nach VI, 4, 22 Värtt. 1 das Wort *asiddha* einen doppelten Zweck hat: 1. daß die durch das Substitut bedingte Operation verboten werde, 2. daß die durch das Ursprüngliche (*utsarga* = *sthānin*) bedingte Operation stattfinde. — Kaiy.: *Nanv ādeśalakṣaṇaḥ prakṛtibhāvo* usw. ‚[Einwurf:] Aber man kann doch einwenden: das durch das Substitut [*pra* usw.] bedingte Verbleiben der unveränderten Form [*pra* usw.] besteht nicht zu Recht, wenn [die Substitution] als *asiddha* betrachtet wird. Dann aber bietet sich wiederum die Elision des auslautenden Vokales samt dem etwa darauffolgenden Konsonanten [von *pra* usw.] dar, da sie sich aus dem [noch als vorhanden zu denkenden] *sthānin* [*priya* usw.] ergibt? — [Erwiderung:] Dies bedeutet keinen Fehler. [Denn] wie sollte sich Elision des auslautenden Vokales für den *sthānin* [*priya* usw.] ergeben, der gar nicht vorhanden ist, da er durch ein Substitut [*pra* usw.] aufgehoben würde, welches [noch vor der allgemeinen Regel VI, 4, 155] eingetreten ist, weil es sonst keine Gelegenheit [zum Eintreten] gehabt hätte [vgl. Paribh. Nr. 57—58]? Selbst wenn hiebei, noch bevor [die Substitute *pra* usw.] als *asiddha* betrachtet werden, die Elision des *ṭi* [von *priya* usw.] vollzogen wird, so bietet sich trotzdem nach dem Eintritt der Substitute, da diese [in bezug auf VI, 4, 155] *asiddha* sind, nicht eine durch diese [Substitute] bedingte Elision von *ṭi* dar; noch auch eine durch das Ursprüngliche [*priya* usw.] bedingte: denn bei den Ursprünglichen wäre sie schon vorher eingetreten. Und weil [infolge des *Assidha*-seins von *pra* usw.] keine Gelegenheit [für den Eintritt von *ṭilopa*] vorhanden ist, so ergibt sich für *pra* usw. auch nicht der Fehler eines Circulus (*cakraka*).' Vgl. den ähnlichen Fall p. 248, Anm. 124.

[135] Kaiy.: *Yadyapi cchvoḥ śūḍ ity atrāsya* usw. ‚Obwohl [von Pat.] bei [der Regel VI, 4, 19]: „*cchvoḥ śūḍ* [*anunāsike*

Erwiderung Durch [das Wort] ,*saṃprasāraṇam*' [VI, 4, 131] wird die Stelle des Halbvokales [*v*] in Beschlag genommen.[136]

Einwurf Wenn es sich so verhält,

Vāha ūḍvacanānarthakyaṃ saṃprasāraṇena kṛtatvāt || Värtt. 1. so ist für *vāh* das Wort *ūṭh* unnütz. — Warum? — ,Weil es durch *Saṃprasāraṇa* vollbracht wird', [d. h.] schon durch [die Substitution des] *Saṃprasāraṇa* [*u* für *v*] kommt [die zu bildende Form] zustande. — Wie kommt denn [auf diese Weise] die Form *praṣṭhauhaḥ* (acc. pl.) zustande?[137]

ca]'' dargelegt worden ist, daß dieses [*ūṭ*] mit dem Anubandha *ṭh* [und nicht *ṭ*] versehen ist, faßt er es [hier] trotzdem nach dem bloßen Gehör [als *ṭit*] und stellt demgemäß die Frage.' Vgl. die Kāś. zu VI, 4, 19: *Ūṭhaṣ ṭhitkaraṇam etyedhatyūṭhsviti viśeṣaṇārtham; vāha ūḍ ity ayam api ṭhid eva* ,Die Setzung von *ūṭh* mit dem Anubandha *ṭh* hat den Zweck, [es als das *ūṭh* der Regel VI, 1, 89] zu bezeichnen: ,,Wenn [auf *a* (*ā*) das e der Wurzeln] *i*, *edh*, oder ein *ū* (*ūṭh*) folgt, [so tritt als alleiniges Substitut *Vṛddhi* ein]''. Auch dieses [*ūṭ* der Regel] ,,*Vāha ūṭ*'' hat eben diesen Anubandha *ṭh*.' Die Bemerkung Böhtl.'s [in der ,Erklärung der gramm. Elem.' s. *ūṭh*] ,Der Ausgang ist bedeutungslos' ist demnach unrichtig.

[136] Kaiy.: *Vākyasya bhāvivarṇasya vā* usw. ,Ob nun der Terminus *Saṃprasāraṇa* als Bezeichnung des Satzes [,,*ig yaṇaḥ*'': I, 1, 45] oder des Lautes, der eintreten soll, verstanden wird [vgl. Mbh. zu I, 1, 45; *Ind. Ant.* vol. XVI, p. 244] [this volume, page 124], tritt *ūṭh* an die Stelle des Halbvokales. — Aber warum wird *ūṭh* nicht unmittelbar vor den Halbvokal gesetzt? — Weil man auch anderen Orten, an denen *Saṃprasāraṇa* erwähnt wird, annimmt, daß ,,*yaṇaḥ*'' ein Genitiv [zur Bezeichnung] der Stelle [I, 1, 49] ist, so ist auch hier nur der Genitiv, der die Stelle bezeichnet [, an der etwas eintritt], richtig angewendet. Wie es denn auch heißt: Siebzehn Substitute machen es notwendig, daß [der Genitiv zur Bezeichnung] der Stelle [an der etwas eintritt], gebraucht wird. — Die Ansetzung [von *ūṭh*] mit dem Anubandha *ṭh* aber [lies: *ṭhitkaraṇaṃ tu*] bezweckt [Substitution von] *Vṛddhi* [nach VI, 1, 89].'

[137] Die Vārttikas 2 und 3 geben an, wie die Formen *praṣṭhauhaḥ*, *viśvauhaḥ* usw. auch ohne *ūṭh* zustande kommen würden. — Kaiy.: *Praṣṭhavāh as iti sthite* usw. ,Wenn *praṣṭhavāh* [+ *ṇvi*] + *as* vorliegt, so tritt, nachdem [die Substitution von] *Saṃprasāraṇa* [*u*] für das *v* [VI, 4, 132] und die alleinige Substitution des [dem *ā*] vorangehenden [*u* gemäß VI, 1, 108] erfolgt ist, *Guṇa o* ein, welches auf dem Suffix *ṇvi* [III, 2, 64; VI, 1, 67; I, 1, 62; VII, 3, 86] beruht. Wenn sodann nach [der Regel VI, 1, 88]: ,,*Vṛddhi* [ist alleiniges Substitut], wenn [auf *a* (*ā*)] ein Diphthong folgt'' *Vṛddhi* eingesetzt worden ist, so kommt *praṣṭhauhaḥ* usw. zustande.' Man könnte nun einwenden, *ūṭh* sei unentbehrlich bei der Bildung von *śālyūhaḥ* aus *śālivāḥ* und *prauhaḥ* aus *pravāḥ*, weil sich nach der Substitution des *Saṃprasāraṇa u* für *v* und von *Guṇa śālyohaḥ* und *prohaḥ* [aus *pra* + *oh* + *aḥ* gemäß VI, 1, 94] ergeben würden. Gegen eine derartige Einwendung richten sich die folgenden Worte Kaiy.'s: *Anakārānte copapade* usw. ,Wenn ferner das Vorderglied [des Kompositums] nicht auf *a* ausgeht [*śāli-*], so erscheint im Veda nicht [wie sonst nach III, 2, 64] *ṇvi* [hinter der Wurzel *vah*]; folglich kommt auch für das Zustandekommen von *śālyūhaḥ* usw. die Vorschrift von *ūṭh* nicht in Betracht. Oder wenn man [dort *ṇvi*] anwendet, so wird doch *śālyūhaḥ* von der in der Bedeutung ,führen' auftretenden Wurzel *ūh* vor folgendem *kvip* [III, 2, 61] gebildet werden. Und auch wenn eine [auf *a* auslautende] Präposition das Vorderglied bildet [wie dies bei *pra-vāh* + *as* der Fall wäre], tritt im Veda nach *vah* nicht das Suffix *ṇvi* ein, aus dem sich [nach VII, 3, 86 *Guṇa* und dann nach VI, 1, 94 die Substitution eines einzigen Vokales] in Gestalt des [auf die Präposition] folgenden, *Vṛddhi* verdrängenden [*o*] ergeben würde, in

253 Mahābhāṣya

Guṇaḥ pratyayalakṣaṇatvāt || Värtt. 2.

Mit Hilfe der das Suffix [*ṇvi*] betreffenden Regel [VII, 3, 86] wird *Guṇa* eintreten.

Ejgrahaṇād vṛddhiḥ || Värtt. 3.

Vermöge des Wortes ‚*ej*' [‚Diphthong': VI, 1, 88] wird [sodann für *a* + *o*] *Vṛddhi* eintreten.

Erwiderung Unter diesen Umständen [sagen wir] folgendes: Wenn der Meister [Pāṇ.], obwohl [*praṣṭhauhaḥ* usw. auch ohne *ūṭh*] tatsächlich zustande kommt, *ūṭh* [als *Saṃprasāraṇa*] für [das *v* von] *vāh* lehrt, so deutet er dies speziell an, daß die folgende Paribhāṣā gilt: Eine *Bahiraṅga*-Regel ist als nicht in Kraft getreten [bezw. als nicht vorhanden] zu betrachten in bezug auf eine [zu vollziehende] *Antaraṅga*-Regel.[138] —

Welcher Zweck ist in der Andeutung dieser [Paribhāṣā] enthalten? — [Die Bildung von *pacāvedam*, *pacāmedam*: weil nämlich

welchem Falle die Vorschrift von *ūṭh* notwendig wäre [, um *Vṛddhi* zu bewirken].' Vgl. dazu Paribh. Transl. p. 235, n. 3 und p. 238 f.

[138] Kaiy.: *Saṃprasāraṇaṃ yajādipratyayanimittabhasaṃjñāśrayatvād* usw. ‚[Die Substitution des] *Saṃprasāraṇa*, die *bahiraṅga* ist ‚weil sie von dem Terminus *bha* [VI, 4, 129, also von einem vokalisch oder mit Halbvokal anlautenden Suffix] abhängt, der selbst durch die Suffixe der Wurzeln *yaj* usw. [VI, 1, 15] bedingt ist, ist als *asiddha* zu betrachten in bezug auf die zu vollziehende [Substitution von] *Guṇa*, welche *antaraṅga* ist, da sie nicht [auch vom Terminus *bha*, sondern von dem innerhalb gelegenen *ṇvi*] abhängt. *Guṇa* würde also nicht eintreten, und wenn dieses nicht vorhanden ist, würde [aus *praṣṭha* + *uh* + *aḥ*] nicht die Form [*praṣṭhauhaḥ*] zustande kommen. So deutet denn die Vorschrift von *ūṭh* die Paribhāṣā „*asiddham*" [usw.] an.' Mit *yajādipratyayanimittabhasaṃjñāśrayatvāt* meint Kaiy.: Wenn in VI, 4, 132 das *Saṃprasāraṇa* von Suffixen [u. zw. mit Vokalen oder Halbvokalen anlautenden] abhängig gemacht wird, so hat dies darin seinen Grund, daß für *yaj* usw. [darunter *vah*: Dhātup. 23, 35] in VI, 1, 15 *Saṃprasāraṇa* vor gewissen Suffixen vorgeschrieben wird. — Vgl. die graphische Darstellung Paribh. Transl. p. 236. — Kaiy. schließt mit folgender Bemerkung: *Nanu naitaj jñāpakasādhyaṃ* usw. ‚[Einwurf:] Aber zu dieser [Paribhāṣā] sollte man doch nicht erst auf Grund eines *Jñāpaka* gelangen, da sie sich schon aus dem gewöhnlichen Leben ergibt. [Vgl. Paribh. Transl., Preface, p. IV f.] Denn die Menschen beschäftigen sich [zunächst] mit dem, was ihre eigene Person betrifft [vgl. *pratyaṅgavartī loko lakṣyate*: Mbh. vol. I, p. 145, ll. 23 ff.; Paribh. Text, p. 49, ll. 10 ff.]? — [Erwiderung:] Dies trifft nicht zu. [Denn nur] dort, wo eine *Antaraṅga*- und eine *Bahiraṅga*[-Operation] sich gleichzeitig darbieten, soll die *Antaraṅga*[-Operation zuerst] eintreten, weil man die dem gewöhnlichen Leben angehörige Maxime annimmt. Hier dagegen ist die *Antaraṅga*[-Operation] durch die *Bahiraṅga*[-Operation] bedingt, die dem gewöhnlichen Leben angehörige Maxime kommt also nicht in Betracht.' D. h. wie der Mensch am Morgen der Reihe nach zuerst seine eigenen Angelegenheiten besorgt und dann die seiner Freunde usw., so geht man auch dort, wo eine *Antaraṅga*- und eine *Bahiraṅga*-Operation sich gleichzeitig darbieten, der Reihe nach vor und vollzieht zuerst die näherliegende *Antaraṅga*-Operation. In diesem Falle ist die Paribhāṣā *nyāyasiddhā*. Wo aber die *Antaraṅga*-Operation sich erst darbietet, nachdem die *Bahiraṅga*-Operation vollzogen worden ist, da ist die Paribhāṣā *jñāpakasiddhā*. Im ersten Falle bedeute *asiddham* ‚als gar nicht vorhanden zu betrachten', im zweiten Falle, ‚[obwohl schon eingetreten, doch] als nicht eingetreten zu denken'. Vgl. auch im Anhang s. *antaraṅga*. — Wir bilden also: *praṣṭha-vāh* + *aḥ*; nach VI, 4, 132 und VI, 1, 108: *praṣṭha-ūh* + *aḥ* und nach VI, 1, 89: *praṣṭhauhaḥ*.

die *Bahiraṅga*-Regel [VI, 1, 87, d. i. die Substitution von] *Guṇa* nach *a* [für dieses + *i*] als *asiddha* betrachtet wird, tritt die *Antaraṅga*-Regel [III, 4, 93, d. i.] die Substitution von *ai* [für *e*] nicht ein.[139]

Anhang

I. Antaraṅga und bahiraṅga [Zu p. 236, Anm. 82.] Kaiyaṭa trägt zwei verschiedene Deutungen des Satzes vor, daß eine *Antaraṅga*- und ein *Bahiraṅga*-Operation sich gleichzeitig darbieten müssen. Die erste Deutung gibt den Worten des Bhāṣya den Sinn: zwei Operationen sind *antaraṅga* und *bahiraṅga*, wenn ihre Vollziehung sich noch vor der Anwendung der Paribhāṣā gleichzeitig darbietet, nicht aber in dem Falle, wenn die *Antaraṅga*-Operation sich erst nach und infolge der Ausführung der *Bahiraṅga*-Operation ergibt. Wenn diese Auffassung richtig wäre, dürfte die Paribhāṣā nicht nur bei der Bildung von *pacāvedam* aus *pacāva idam* [vgl. Paribh. Transl. p. 271, n. 4], sondern auch bei der Bildung von *viśvauhaḥ* usw. [vgl. ibid. p. 236, n. 1], für welche die Paribhāṣā doch zunächst angedeutet sein soll, nicht zur Anwendung gelangen. Denn in diesen Fällen ergeben sich die *Antaraṅga*-Operationen erst nach und infolge der Ausführung der *Bahiraṅga*-Operationen. Nach der zweiten Deutung sind zwei Operationen *antaraṅga* und *bahiraṅga*, wenn im Augenblick der Anwendung der Paribhāṣā beide gleichzeitig zur Stelle sind. Dies ist nun bei *papā-us* + *as* nicht der Fall. Aus den von Kaiyaṭa genannten Gründen ist hier die Paribhāṣā nach VI, 4, 22 in bezug auf die *Bahiraṅga*-Operation als *asiddha* zu betrachten. Und in dem Augenblick, in welchem die Paribhāṣā angewendet würde, wäre die *Bahiraṅga*-Operation [d. i. die Substitution des *Saṃprasāraṇa*] als *asiddha* zu betrachten, und infolgedessen würde sich auch ihr Korrelat, die *Antaraṅga*-Operation, nicht darbieten. Daß die zweite Interpretation auch der Ansicht Patañjalis entspricht, geht aus dem Bhāṣya zu VIII, 3, 15 Värtt. 2 hervor, wo ein ähnlicher Fall erörtert wird. Dort behauptet Patañjali von einer *Antaraṅga*-Operation [VIII, 3, 15] und einer *Bahiraṅga*-Operation [VII, 2, 117], daß sie sich nicht gleichzeitig darbieten, und nennt als Grund: *asiddhatvāt*. Nach Kaiyaṭas Erklärung bedeutet dies: weil die *Antaraṅga*-Regel VIII, 3, 15 gemäß VIII, 2, 1 als *asiddha* zu betrachten ist in bezug auf die in VI, 4, 132 angedeutete Paribhāṣā; weil also die *Antaraṅga*-Regel nicht vorhanden ist, so ist auch VII, 2, 117 nicht eine zu ihr in Beziehung stehende *Bahiraṅga*-Regel; die *Bahiraṅga-Paribhāṣā* gelangt also nicht zur Anwendung, und infolgedessen ergibt sich VII, 2, 117. — Auch die Kāś. zu VI, 4, 22 akzeptiert die zweite Deutung und bemerkt: *Eṣā hi paribhāṣā ā bhāc chāstrīyā; tasyāṃ pravartamānāyāṃ vasusaṃprasāraṇādīnam ā bhāc chāstrīyāṇām evāsiddhatvād antaraṅgabahiraṅgayor yugapatsamupasthānaṃ nāstīti paribhāṣā na pravartate.* — ‚*Yugapatsamupasthānam*' bedeutet also nicht, daß beide Operationen sich vor der Anwendung der Paribhāṣā noch unausgeführt darbieten müssen, wie bei *syona*. Die *Bahiraṅga*-Operation darf vielmehr bereits vollzogen sein, wie bei *pacāvedam*. Dies stellt Nāgojībhaṭṭa, Paribh. Text, p. 43, l. 15 ausdrücklich fest in dem Satze: *Antaraṅge kartavye jātaṃ tatkālaprāptikaṃ ca bahiraṅgam asiddham ity arthaḥ*. ‚In bezug auf eine zu vollziehende *Antaraṅga*-Operation ist eine *Bahiraṅga*-Operation,

[139] In *pacāvedam* gilt nämlich der *ekādeśa* *e* [für *a* + *i*] nach VI, 1, 85 auch als Auslaut des Vorangehenden. — Vgl. Paribh. Transl. p. 271, n. 4.

sowohl wenn sie bereits zustande gekommen ist, als auch wenn sie sich gleichzeitig mit jener darbietet, als *asiddha* zu betrachten.'

II. Nimittāpāye naimittikasyāpy apāyaḥ [Zu p. 234, Anm. 74.] Kaiy.: *Papuṣa iti: nanu cāntaraṅgatvād iṭā bhāvyam* usw.:[140] Aber [vor *vas*] müßte doch [nach VII, 2, 35 und Paribh. Nr. 50] das Augment *i* (*iṭ*) eintreten, da es *antaraṅga* ist [, das *Saṃprasāraṇa* für *v* in *vas* aber *bahiraṅga*]? Und das *iṭ* verschwindet auch dann nicht mehr, wenn [seine Ursache, daß *v* von *vas* verschwunden ist, d. i. die Substitution des] *Saṃprasāraṇa* [für *v*] vollzogen worden ist. Denn der Verfasser des Bhāṣya [Pat.] hat die Paribhāṣā [Nr. 56] nicht angenommen [, welche lehrt]: ,Wenn [beim Eintritt einer *Bahiraṅga*-Regel] die Ursache [einer *Antaraṅga*-Operation] verschwindet, so verschwindet auch das durch jene Ursache Bewirkte'.[141] Und ebenso ist auch [im Bhāṣya] zur [Regel VI, 3, 138]: ,Vor *ac* (*cu*) [wird der Endvokal des Vordergliedes verlängert]' gelehrt worden: ,Hier stellen andere [Lehrer] ein Verbot gegen [den Eintritt des] *pratyaṅga* [d. i. der *Antaraṅga*-Regel VI, 1, 77] vor *ac* (*cu*) auf; dies müßte doch auch hier [d. i. in der Regel selbst, irgendwie] bewerkstelligt werden [,wenn VI, 3, 138 überhaupt eintreten soll].' Dies ist deshalb gesagt worden, weil die Substitution des Halbvokales [für das *i* in *prati-ac* + *as* nach VI, 1, 77] usw. [d. i. die Substitution von *ā* für *a* + *a* in *pra-ac* + *as* nach VI, 1, 101, welche Regeln *antaraṅga* sind,] nicht aufgehoben werden, auch wenn [ihre Ursache, d. i.] das *a* [von *ac* infolge des Eintrittes der *Bahiraṅga*-Regel VI, 4, 138] verschwunden ist.[142] — Und ebenso ist auch [im *Bhāṣya* zum Vārtt. 2] bei [der Regel VI, 4, 19]: ,Für *cch* [= *t* + *ch*] und *v* [wird auch vor einem Nasal *ś*, bezw. *ū* substituiert]' bemerkt worden: ,Hier muß notwendigerweise eine besondere Bemühung gemacht werden, damit nicht [in *praśna* aus *prach* + *na* nach VI, 1, 73] das Augment *t* (*tuk*) vorhanden sei; denn [die Anfügung von *tuk*: VI, 1, 73] bietet sich

[140] Den korrekten Text findet man Paribh. Transl. p. 313, n. 1.

[141] Vgl. Paribh. Text p. 65, l. 3: *Kiṃ caiṣā bhāṣye na dṛśyate. Tad uktam asiddhavatsūtre* [VI, 4, 22] *Kaiyaṭena: nimittāpāye naimittikasyāpy apāya iti paribhāṣāyā bhāṣyakṛtānāśrayaṇād iti.* — Durch *nimittāpāye* usw. gibt Kaiy. die Paribh. Nr. 56 wieder, welche lautet: *Akṛtavyūhāḥ Pāṇinīyāḥ* ,die Anhänger des Pāṇini stellen keine besonderen Erwägungen [über das Eintreten einer Regel] an [d. h. kümmern sich nicht um ihr Eintreten, wenn eine Ursache derselben verschwindet].' Nach Paribh. Text p. 61, l. 9 ff. ist der Sinn dieser Paribhāṣā, daß eine *Antaraṅga*-Operation überhaupt nicht stattfindet, wenn nachher, infolge des Eintretens der *Bahiraṅga*-Regel, die Ursache der *Antaraṅga*-Operation verschwände. Nach Kaiy.'s Auffassung [*nimittāpāye* usw.] dagegen besagt die Paribhāṣā, daß das bereits eingetretene Resultat einer *Antaraṅga*-Operation wieder verschwindet, wenn seine Ursache verschwindet. Weil aber diese Paribhāṣā — so folgert Kaiy. — weder von Pat. erwähnt, noch auch in den folgenden Beispielen [*ac* und *tuk*] angewendet wird, kommt sie auch in unserem Falle, d. i. für *iṭ*, nicht in Betracht. ,*Iṭ* müßte also als *antaraṅga* eintreten, und durch dieses [nicht aber durch das *u* in *papā* + *i-us* + *as*] würde dann [nach VI, 4, 64] die Elision des *ā* bewirkt werden. Unter diesen Umständen wäre jene [Bemerkung Pat.'s ,*saṃprasāraṇe kṛte*' zu VI, 4, 22 Vārtt. 9] ganz ungereimt.' [Paribh. Text p. 64, l. 9 f.] Wenn aber *iṭ* einträte, würden wir *papyuṣaḥ* erhalten.

[142] D. h. weil die Paribh. Nr. 56 nicht anerkannt wird. Anstatt von dieser Gebrauch zu machen, antwortet Pat., Pāṇini habe in VI, 3, 138 durch die Vorschrift der Länge für den dem *ac* vorangehenden Vokal angedeutet, daß

deshalb [zuerst, d. i. vor VI, 4, 19] dar, weil sie *antaraṅga* ist.[143] Auch dies ist auf Grund der Ansicht behauptet worden, daß das [als *antaraṅga*] bereits eingetretene *t* (*tuk*) nicht verschwindet, auch wenn [dessen Ursache *ch* verschwunden, d. h. gemäß der *Bahiraṅga*-Regel VI, 4, 19] *ś* [für *ch*] substituiert worden ist.[144]

Erwiderung Unter diesen Umständen[145] [sagen wir] folgendes: wenn man, indem man das fertige Wort[146] [*papuṣaḥ*] vor Augen hält, die Auflösung [desselben in seine Bestandteile] vornimmt und die einzelnen Teile [nebeneinander] hinstellt, so liegt nicht eine *Antaraṅga*- und eine *Bahiraṅga*[-Regel] vor. Wenn nämlich [die Teile] *papā* + *vas* + *as* dastehen, so tritt [zunächst] das *Saṃprasāraṇa* [für *v* von *vas*] ein, indem dieses, weil es *nitya* ist,[147] das *iṭ* verdrängt. Und da es sich [, wenn nachher gemäß VII, 2, 35 *iṭ* eintreten soll] um eine auf einen Laut [d. i. *v* des *sthānin vas* beruhende] Regel handeln würde, gilt nicht [die Regel I, 1, 56], daß [das Substitut *u*] sich wie der *sthānin* [*v*(*as*)] verhält, und infolgedessen bietet sich [die Anfügung von] *iṭ* nicht dar. — Oder aber[148] [die Substitution des] *Saṃprasāraṇa* [VI, 4, 131] und dasjenige, was darauf beruht [d. i. die Elision des *ā*] besitzt als [*Pratipadavidhi*] größere Kraft [als VII, 2, 35] und in diesem Bereich [sc. einer *Pratipada*-Regel] tritt *iṭ* nicht früher ein.[149]

die *Antaraṅga*-Regel VI, 1, 77 [Substitution des Halbvokales für diesen Vokal] nicht eintritt. Vgl. Paribh. Text p. 64, l. 10 ff. und Transl. pp. 317 f. und 318, n. 1.

[143] Die besondere ‚Bemühung' besteht darin, daß Pāṇ. in VI, 4, 19 die Substitution von *ś* für *cch*, und nicht für *ch*, lehrt. Vgl. Paribh. Transl. p. 306, n. 1.

[144] D. h. Pat. hat dies behauptet, weil er die Paribhāṣā nicht annimmt. Denn wenn er sie angenommen hätte, würde *t*(*uk*) überhaupt nicht eintreten, oder es würde [nach Kaiy.'s Deutung der Paribh.] das schon eingetretene *t*(*uk*) wieder verschwinden. Dann aber hätte die Bemerkung Pat.'s keinen Sinn, daß [durch die Schreibung *cchvoḥ* statt *chvoḥ*] eine besondere Bemühung gemacht werden müsse, damit man nicht *pratśna* statt *praśna* erhalte. Vgl. Paribh. Text p. 64, l. 12 und Transl. p. 306, n. 1; p. 318 f. und 318, n. 2.

[145] D. h. da die Paribh. 56 nicht gilt und infolgedessen *iṭ* eintreten müßte.

[146] *Nityaḥ śabdaḥ* ‚das [beim Sprechen für einen Begriff einzusetzende] fertige Worte', im Gegensatz zu *kāryaḥ śabdaḥ*, ‚dem [mit Hilfe grammatischer Regeln erst] zu bildenden Wort', Vgl. Mbh. vol. I, p. 3, l. 18; p. 6, l. 12 und p. 7 (unten) f.

[147] Denn das *Saṃprasāraṇa* kann sowohl vor als auch nach der Anfügung von *iṭ* eintreten; *iṭ* dagegen ist *anitya*, weil es gemäß ‚*valādeḥ*' in VII, 2, 35 nur v o r der Substitution des *Saṃprasāraṇa* angefügt werden kann.

[148] Auch hier zerlegt man zunächst das fertige Wort in die Bestandteile *papā* + *vas* + *as*, aus denen es hervorgegangen ist.

[149] Daß hier *pratipadavidhānāt* oder *pratipadavidhitvāt* zu ergänzen ist, ergibt sich aus Kaiy. zu IV, 1, 82 [vgl. Paribh. Transl. p. 311, n. 2]: . . . *Tatra saṃprasāraṇaṃ balīyaḥ pratipadavidhānād iti tatra kṛte valāditvābhāvād iṇ nāstīti siddhaṃ papuṣa iti.* ‚Im diesem Falle besitzt [die Substitution des] *Saṃprasāraṇa* größere Kraft, weil sie für den Ausdruck [*vas:* VI, 4, 131] in seiner durch den Wortlaut gegebenen Bedeutung vorgeschrieben wird. Wenn demnach [das *Saṃprasāraṇa*] substituiert worden ist, so tritt *iṭ* nicht mehr ein, weil [das *Ārdhadhātuka*] nunmehr nicht mit [einem Laut des *pratyāhāra*] „*val*" [hier *v*] beginnt. So kommt denn *papuṣaḥ* tatsächlich zustande.' Vgl. zu dem analogen Beispiel *seduṣaḥ* Paribh. Text p. 63, l. 10 ff.: . . . *pratipadavidhitvāt pūrvaṃ saṃprasāraṇe valāditvābhāvād iṭaḥ prāptir eva neti* . . . Dazu Transl. p. 313 f. — In VI, 4, 131 erscheint ‚*vas*' in eben dieser, durch den Wortlaut gegebenen Gestalt, ist also *pratipadoktam*, während es sich bei der Anwendung von VII, 2, 35 aus dem Terminus

III. Pratyayalakṣaṇam [Zu p. 230, Anm. 84] Zu Kaiy.'s Bemerkung ‚*Pratyayalakṣaṇaṃ tu varṇāśrayatvān mā bhūt*' vgl. Mbh. vol. I, p. 161, l. 12: *Atha dvitīyaṃ pratyayagrahaṇaṃ kim artham? Pratyayalakṣaṇaṃ yathā syād, varṇalakṣaṇaṃ mā bhūd iti.* ‚Aber welchen Zweck hat denn [in I, 1, 62] das zweite Wort *pratyaya*? — Daß [nur] die aus dem Suffix selbst [in seiner Eigenschaft als Suffix] sich ergebende [Operation] eintreten möge, [hingegen] soll nicht [eine Operation] stattfinden, die sich aus [ihm als] einen [bloßen] Buchstaben [und Bestandteil des folgenden] ergibt.' Dazu Kaiy.: *Pratyayalope tallakṣaṇam ity ucyamāne pratyayasya yatra kārye nimittabhāvaḥ pratyayarūpāśrayeṇa varṇarūpatāśrayeṇa vā tat sarvaṃ syāt sarvanāmno vastumātraparāmarśitvāt. Pratyayagrahaṇe tu sati pratyayanimittam eva kāryaṃ pratyayalope bhavati, na varṇarūpatānimittam. Raikulam iti: avayavadvāreṇātra pratyayasyāpy ādeśaṃ prati nimittatvam asty eva, pratyayāśrayas tv āyādeśo na bhavatīti na pravartate.* ‚Wenn [in der Regel] gelehrt würde: Nach der Elision eines Suffixes [tritt gleichwohl] das durch dieses (*tad*) Bedingte [ein]', so würde überall dort, wo ein Suffix bei einer Operation eine Ursache bildet, jede derartige [Operation] stattfinden, ob sie nun auf [jenem in seiner Eigenschaft] als Suffix beruht, oder ob sie auf ihm nur zum Teil und] insofern beruht, als es in Form eines Lautes [und Bestandteiles der Gesamtursache] erscheint; denn das Pronomen [*tad*] vergegenwärtigt ausschließlich den Gegenstand [d. i. *pratyaya* im allgemeinen, ohne eine einschränkende Bestimmung]. Wenn dagegen das Wort *pratyaya* vorhanden ist, so [besagt dies, daß] nur eine durch das Suffix [selbst] bedingte Operation nach der Elision des Suffixes eintritt, nicht aber [eine Operation], die [nur] insofern [durch das Suffix bedingt ist], als es in Gestalt eines Lautes erscheint. *Raikulam* [aus *rāyaḥ kulam*]: [Wenn in *rāyaḥ kulam* nach II, 4, 71 das Kasussuffix *as* abgefallen ist, sollte in *rai-kulam* gemäß I, 1, 62 die durch das abgefallene Suffix bedingte Operation VI, 1, 78, d. i. die Substitution von *āy* für *ai* eintreten]. Das Suffix [*as*] ist zwar tatsächlich mittels eines Teiles [d. i. des Vokales *a*] Ursache für die Substitution [von *āy* für *ai*], doch beruht die Substitution von *āy* nicht auf dem Suffix [selbst] und tritt deshalb nicht ein.' Vgl. Paribh. Nr. 21.

IV. Vipratiṣedha [Zu p. 242, Anm. 104.] Die Definition von *vipratiṣedha* ist in dem Värtt. 1 zu I, 4, 2 enthalten, welches Pat. folgendermaßen wiedergibt: *Dvau prasaṅgau yadānyārthau bhavata ekasmiṃś ca yugapat prāpnutaḥ sa vipratiṣedhaḥ.* ‚Wenn zwei [Regeln] sich [sonst] zur [Bildung] verschiedener [Formen] darbieten und bei [der Bildung] einer einzigen [Form] sich gleichzeitig ergeben, so ist dies ein *vipratiṣedha*.' In einem solchen Verhältnis stehen, wie Kay. zeigt, die Regeln VI, 4, 140 und 83, die verschiedenen Zwecken dienen und sich bei der Bildung von *kīlālapaḥ* gleichzeitig darbieten. Nach

‚*val*', also erst aus einer Regel, ergibt. Die Substitution des *Samprasāraṇa* [VI, 4, 131] ist also eine *pratipadavidhi*. Und da sich ein *pratipadoktam* früher darbietet [‚*śīghropasthitikatvāt*'], der abgeleitete Ausdruck aber später [‚*vilambopasthitikaḥ*': vgl. Paribh. Text. p. 104, l. 11 f.], so tritt naturgemäß auch eine *pratipadavidhi* früher ein. Dies drückt Kaiy. zu VII, 2, 98 dadurch aus, daß er für das Wort *apavāda* der Paribh. Nr. 38 *pratipadavidhi* einsetzt: *Paranityāntaraṅgapratipadavidhayo virodhisaṃnipāte teṣāṃ mithaḥprasaṅge parabalīyastvam.* D. h. je zwei dieser Arten von Regeln stehen einander im Wege, wenn sie zusammentreffen. Wenn sie sich gleichzeitig darbieten, besitzt jene Art größere Kraft, welche [in obiger Aufzählung] später genannt ist. Vgl. Paribh. Transl. p. 314, n. 2.

I, 4, 2 tritt also die *para*-Regel VI, 4, 140 zuerst ein. Indem nun die Paribh. Nr. 40: ,*Sakṛdgatau vipratiṣedhe yad bādhitaṃ tad bādhitam eva*' bestimmt, daß bei einem *vipratiṣedha* die durch die *para*-Regel aufgehobene *pūrva*-Regel als vollständig aufgehoben zu betrachten ist und nicht mehr angewendet werden kann, deutet sie gleichzeitig an, daß die *pūrva*-Regel — hier VI, 4, 83 — auch dann nicht noch eintritt, wenn in bezug auf sie die *para*-Regel nach VI, 4, 22 als *asiddha* betrachtet werden müßte. Im Bhāṣya weist Pat. durch das Wort *bādhaka* auf die Paribhāṣā [,. . . *tad bādhitam eva*'] hin. Mit dem Wort *jñāpayiṣyate* aber nimmt Kaiy. nicht auf ein in einer Regel Pāṇ.s enthaltenes *Jñāpaka* bezug. Denn auch Pat. meint zu I, 4, 2 Värtt. 7 nicht Pāṇini, sondern einen andern *ācārya*, wenn er bemerkt: *Paṭhiṣyati hy ācāryaḥ: sakṛd gatau vipratiṣedhe yad bādhitaṃ tad bādhitam eveti*. [Vgl. Kielhorn, *Kātyāyana and Patañjali* p. 24f.] Diese Paribhāṣā, welche Paribh. Transl. p. 189ff. erschöpfend erklärt ist, erwähnt Pat. zu VI, 3, 42; 139; VI, 4, 62; VII, 1, 26; 54.

V. Viṣayaviṣayibhāva [Zu p. 232, Anm. 66.] Pat. zu VI, 4, 104: ,In [der Regel über] den Abfall [des Suffixes] hinter *ciṇ* müßte das Wort *ta* gesetzt werden. — Zu welchem Zwecke? — Damit [der Abfall] nicht auch hier, in *akāritarām*, *ahāritarām* erfolge.

Ciṇo luki tagrahaṇānarthakyaṃ saṃghātasyāpratyayatvāt || Värtt. 1.

In [der Regel über] den Abfall des [Suffixes] hinter *ciṇ* ist das Wort *ta* unnötig. — Weshalb? — ,*Saṃghātasyāpratyayatvāt*': [d. h.] warum erfolgt nicht der Abfall eines Komplexes [von Suffixen, d. i. -*ta* + *tara* + *ām*]? Weil [dies] nicht ,ein Suffix' ist. Es wird ja [I, 1, 61] gelehrt: ,[Das Verschwinden] eines Suffixes heißt *luk*, *ślu* oder *lup*', und ein Komplex [von Suffixen] ist nicht ,ein Suffix'.

Einwurf Wenn dem so ist, so bietet sich doch, nachdem die Elision des [ersten Suffixes] *ta* vollzogen ist, die das folgenden [Suffixes *tara*] dar?

ErwiderungTalopasya cāsiddhatvāt || Värtt. 2.

Die Elision des *ta* wird als *asiddha* betrachtet, und weil sie *asiddha* ist, wird [auch die des folgenden Suffixes *tara*] nicht erfolgen.

Hiezu bemerkt Kaiy.: *Tagrahaṇam iti: idam asminn asiddham iti bhedanibandhanatvād viṣayaviṣayibhāvasya ciṇo lug ity asya lakṣaṇasya bhedābhāvād akāritarām ity atra lopasyāsiddhatvābhāvāt tarapo 'pi luk prāpnoti; evaṃ sati pratyayatrayātmakasya samudāyasya lukprasaṅgaḥ. Itaras tu yugapat pratyayatrayasya lukprasaṅgo 'nenokta iti matvāha ciṇo lukīti . . . Pratilakṣyaṃ lakṣaṇabhedād asti viṣayaviṣayibhāvaḥ*. ,Weil ein Objekt [einer Operation in einer und derselben Regel] selbst auch ein Objekt [in bezug auf welches es *asiddha* ist] nur unter der Bedingung hat, daß die Teilung vorgenommen wird ,,[und] dieses gilt als *asiddha* in bezug auf jenes'', und weil eine [derartige] Teilung der Regel ,*ciṇo luk*' nicht vorhanden ist, so ergibt sich bei *akāritarām*, dadurch daß die Elision [des *ta*] nicht *asiddha* [in bezug auf den Abfall von *tara*] ist, auch der Abfall [des Suffixes] *tara*. [*Ta* wäre nämlich sonst *viṣaya* der ersten Operation (*luk*) und gleichzeitig, als *asiddha*, *viṣayin* in bezug auf den Abfall von *tara*]. Unter diesen Umständen würde sich der Abfall des aus drei Suffixen bestehenden Komplexes [*ta* + *tara* + *ām*] darbieten. — Der Opponent aber glaubt, jener habe behauptet, daß der Abfall der drei Suffixe sich gleichzeitig darbiete, und sagt deshalb [im Värtt. 2] ,*ciṇo luki*' [u.s.w.] . . .; [zu Värtt. 2:] Man muß dagegen [d. i. gegenüber der Behauptung, daß *ta* in der Regel notwendig sei] darauf hinweisen, daß infolge [der tatsächlichen Annahme jener] Teilung dieser Regel das Objekt [*ta*] tatsächlich [innerhalb dieser Regel] selbst ein Objekt [d. i. den Abfall von *tara*] hat [, in bezug auf welchen sein eigener Abfall als *asiddha* betrachtet wird].' Noch deutlicher setzt dies Pat. zu I, 1, 57 Vārtt. 6 auseinander. Dort wird nämlich zunächst behauptet, daß zur Erklärung von *vāyvoḥ* usw. wegen der Regel VI, 1, 66 die Regel VI, 1, 77 interpretiert werden müsse: Für *i, u, ṛ, ḷ* und ihre Längen werden vor einem Vokal die entsprechenden Halbvokale substituiert, [und diese Regel ist als *asiddha* zu betrachten, wenn sich die Elision der Halbvokale (*y* oder *v*) darbietet]. Dagegen wird eingewendet, daß nur eine Regel in bezug auf eine andere Regel *asiddha* sein könne (*anyad anyasmin*), während hier die Regel VI, 1, 77 in bezug auf sich selbst *asiddha* wäre. Darauf wird erwidert: *Tad eva cāpi tasminn asiddhaṃ bhavati. Vakṣyati hy ācāryaḥ: ciṇo luki tagrahaṇānarthakyaṃ saṃghātasyāpratyayatvāt talopasya cāsiddhatvād iti. Ciṇo luk ciṇo luky evāsiddho bhavati.* ‚Es ist doch auch eine bestimmte [Regel] in bezug auf sie selbst [ohne daß dies in der Regel ausdrücklich gesagt wird] *asiddha*. Denn der Lehrer [Kāty.] wird [VI, 4, 104 Vārtt. 1] sagen ‚*Ciṇo luki*' usw. [d. h.]: Der Abfall [des Suffixes] nach *ciṇ* ist in bezug auf den Abfall [eines anderen Suffixes] nach *ciṇ asiddha*. Kaiy. zu I, 1, 57 nennt die wörtliche Auffassung der Regel ‚*sakṛtpāṭha*' [‚einmalige Lesung'. *Viṣayabhedāt tu bhedāśrayaṇād asiddhatvam āśrīyate.* ‚Infolge der Teilung des Objektes [der Regel in ein Objekt und Subjekt] aber gelangt man auf Grund der Annahme der Teilung dazu, daß [das Objekt] *asiddha* ist.' Vgl. Kāś. zu VI, 4, 104: *Akāritarām, āhāritamām ity atra talopasyāsiddhatvāt taraptamapor na lug bhavati, ciṇo lug ity etadviṣayabhedād bhidyate.*

VI. Samānāśraya [Zu p. 231, Anm. 64 (Schluß).]

1. *samānāśraya:*

$$kur\ [+\ u] + \begin{cases} va\,ḥ \\ ma\,ḥ \end{cases}$$
(a)

2. *vyāśraya:*

$$kur\ [+\ u] + \begin{cases} va\,ḥ \\ ma\,ḥ \end{cases}$$
(a)

1. Die Elision des *u* [VI, 4, 108 und 109] beruht auf dem [ganzen] mit *v*, bezw. *m*, anlautenden *Sārvadhātuka*-Suffix *vaḥ*, bezw. *maḥ*. Auf dem gleichen Element beruht die zweite Operation [VI, 4, 110]. Die Elision des *u* ist demnach *samānāśraya*.

2. Nach dieser Auffassung beruht die Elision des *u* nicht auf dem ganzen Suffix *vaḥ*, bezw. *maḥ*, sondern nur auf ihren Anfangsbuchstaben *v*, bezw. *m*, welche bei der zweiten Operation [VI, 4, 110] nicht in Betracht kommen; denn diese beruht auf dem ganzen Suffix *vaḥ*, bezw. *maḥ*. Die Elision des *u* ist in diesem Falle *vyāśraya*, also nicht *asiddha*.

VII. Sthānivadbhāva [Zu p. 231, Anm. 64 (Mitte und gegen Schluß).]

Zu den Bemerkungen Kaiy.'s: ‚*Tataś cānādiṣṭād acaḥ pūrvasya...*' und nachher: ‚*tataś cādiṣṭād acaḥ pūrvo 'kāra iti tadvidhau nāsti sthānivadbhāvaḥ*' vgl. Pat. zu I, 1, 57 Vārtt. 1: *Yo 'nādiṣṭād acaḥ pūrvas tasya vidhiṃ prati sthānivadbhāva ādiṣṭāc caiṣo 'caḥ pūrvaḥ.* ‚In bezug auf die Operation an einem [Element], welches dem Vokal vorangeht, solange er noch nicht durch das Substitut ersetzt ist, verhält sich [das Substitut] wie der ursprüngliche [Vokal]; dieses aber geht [erst] dem durch das Substitut ersetzten Vokal voran.'

7 The Modern Period

Plate V

A page from a manuscript in the India Office, London, of Patañjali's *Mahābhāṣya* with Kaiyaṭa's subcommentary *Bhāṣyapradīpa*, reproduced by courtesy of the Secretary of State for Foreign and Commonwealth Affairs. This manuscript was written in A.D. 1787–1788 (see No. 4981, Catalogue Keith 1935). It is MS. B of Kielhorn's edition.

The four lines in the middle of the page constitute the following passage from the beginning of the Introduction of the *Mahābhāṣya*: **śabdaḥ yenoccāritena sāsnālāṃgūlakakudakhuraviṣāṇināṃ saṃpratyayo bhavati sa śabdaḥ athavā pratītapadārthako loke dhvaniḥ śabda ity ucyate tadyathā śabdaṃ kuru mā śabdaṃ kārṣīḥ śabdakāryayaṃ māṇavaka iti dhvaniṃ kurvann evam ucyate tasmāt dhvaniḥ śabdaḥ kāni punar asya śabdānuśāsanasya prayojanāni . rakṣohāgamalaghvasaṃdehāḥ prayojanaṃ rakṣārthaṃ vedānām adhyeyaṃ vyākaraṇaṃ lopāgamavarṇavikārajño hi samyag vedān paripālayiṣyatīti ūhaḥ** "(What then is) the word 'cow'? That by means of which, when uttered, there arises the notion of creatures with dewlap, tail, hump, hooves, and horns. Or else the sound, which in everyday life conveys a particular meaning, is called a word. One refers to sounds when saying "produce a word," "do not produce a word," "the boy produces words." Therefore a word is sound. Now what are the fruits of this teaching of words? Preservation, modification, tradition, abbreviation, and removal of doubt constitute its fruit. We should study grammar for the preservation of the Vedas. For he who knows the linguistic zero, the verbal augment, and the ways in which sound is modified will be in a position to properly protect the Vedas. Modification (. . .)."

The beginning of this passage with its inquiry into *śabda* has given rise to a great many interpretations and controversies (see, for example, Brough's interpretation, page 405.

The five lines at the top of the page continuing with the five lines at the bottom constitute Kaiyaṭa's subcommentary on this passage of the *Mahābhāṣya*.

नित्यतरमाह येनोच्चारितेनेति वैयाकरणा वर्णव्यतिरिक्तस्य पदस्य वाक्यस्य च वाचकत्वमिच्छन्ति वर्णानां प्रत्येकं वाचकत्वे द्वितीयादिवर्णोच्चारणा नर्थक्यप्रसंगात् आनर्थक्ये तु प्रत्येकमुत्पत्तिपक्षे यौगपद्येनोत्पत्त्यभावाद् अभिव्यक्तिपक्षे तु क्रमेणैवाभिव्यक्तत्वात् समुदायाभावादेकस्मृत्युपारूढा

च नां वाचकत्वे सरो रस इत्यादावर्थप्रतिपत्त्यविशेषप्रसंगात्तद्व्यतिरिक्तः स्फोटो नादाभिव्यंग्यो वाचको विस्तरेण वाक्यपदीये व्यवस्थापितः उच्चारितेनेत्य प्रकाशितेनेत्यर्थः अथवेति अन्यत्र ध्वनिस्फोटयोरभेदस्य व्यवस्थापितत्वादिहाभेदेनापि व्यवहारे न दोषः द्रव्यादेर्पि न शब्दः शब्दवाच्यत्वात् तात्प र्येण ध्वनिं कुर्वन्निति विधिनिषेधयोः प्रवृत्तिविषयत्वात्कथमस्य क्रियाभिः संबन्ध उच्यते शब्दं कुर्वन्नपि शब्दं कुर्विति उच्यते विरामार्थं ... कामोतान्निह

शब्दः येनोच्चारितेन सास्नालाङ्गूलककुदखुरविषाणिनां संप्रत्ययो भवति स शब्दः अथवा प्रतीतपदार्थको लोके ध्वनिः शब्द इत्युच्यते तद्यथा शब्दं कुरु मा शब्दं कार्षीः शब्दकार्ययं माणवक इति ध्वनिं कुर्वन्नेवमुच्यते तस्मात् ध्वनिः शब्दः कानि पुनरस्य शब्दानुशासनस्य प्रयोजनानि रक्षोहागमलघ्वसंदेहाः प्रयोजनं रक्षार्थं वेदानामध्येयं व्याकरणं लोपागमवर्णविकारज्ञो हि सम्यग्वेदान्परिपालयिष्यतीति कहः ७

त्वये नयानभिमतशब्दश्रवणोद्विजितेनोच्यते मा शब्दं कार्षीरिति कानि पुनरिति किं संध्योपासनादिवत् व्याकरणाध्ययनं नित्यं कर्म अथ काम्यमिति प्रश्नः पारं पर्येण पुरुषार्थसाधनतामस्याह रक्षेति लोके लोपाद्यदृष्टं वेदे दृष्ट्वा अस्पष्टं वैयाकरणाः वैयाकरणास्तु नः प्रमतिं वेदार्थे बोध्यमस्यति तत्र लोपागमयोरुदाहरणं देवा अदुह्र इति दुहेर्लङि झस्यादादेशे कृते लोपस्त आत्मनेपदेष्विति तलोपः बहुलं छन्दसीति रुट् सति रूपमितत् वर्णविकारो यथा उद्ग्राभं च निग्राभं चेति हृग्रहोर्भश्छन्दसि हस्येति वक्तव्यमिति हस्य भकारः उदियर्ति इत्यत्र उद्ग्राभमित्याभौ च छन्दसि इति उद्गि पूर्वाङ्क्तेः स्रुगुद्यमननिपातनयोरिति वचनात् घञ् कहः ७

17

Leonard Bloomfield (1887–1949)

Under the heading "The Modern Period," a final selection of papers will now be presented which together illustrate a remarkable diversity of approaches. The "modern period" includes roughly the years 1925–1960. At the beginning of this period there are two publications which can hardly be regarded as very important contributions themselves, but which contrast in significant and instructive ways when considered together.

Leonard Bloomfield (1887–1949), the well-known linguist who is generally regarded as the founder of American structural linguistics, was the nephew of the Sanskritist, Maurice Bloomfield. Leonard studied Indo-European and especially Germanic at Harvard, Wisconsin, Leipzig, and Göttingen. He studied Sanskrit with Herman Oldenberg (mainly in Indo-European perspective) and Karl Brugmann. That Leonard Bloomfield held the Sanskrit grammarians in high regard is clear from many passages in his works. In *Language* (1933), for example, he called Pāṇini's grammar "one of the greatest monuments of human intelligence" and substantiated this as follows: "It describes, with the minutest detail, every inflection, derivation, and composition, and every syntactic usage of its author's speech. No other language, to this day, has been so perfectly described" (page 11). In *Linguistic Aspects of Science* (1939), he characterized the contribution of the Sanskrit grammarians to linguistics in the following sentences: "Around the beginning of the nineteenth century the Sanskrit grammar of the ancient Hindus became known to European scholars. Hindu grammar described the Sanskrit language completely and in scientific terms, without prepossessions or philosophical intrusions. It was from this model that Western scholars learned, in the course of a few decades, to describe a language in terms of its own structure" (page 2). It is interesting to note that Bloomfield was attracted to the Indian grammarians in the first place because of their alleged positivism. Moreover, the *Linguistic Aspects of Science*, from which these lines are quoted, forms part of the *International Encyclopedia of Unified Science*, the neopositivist series which derived great inspiration from the Vienna Circle, and in which such scholars as Rudolf Carnap played an important part. In turn, construing praise by Bloomfield as an indisputable symptom of taxonomic leanings, later linguists have erroneously regarded Pāṇini as the embodiment of the taxonomic approach (e.g., Lees 1963², xix).

Bloomfield made a more technical contribution to the study of Pāṇini's grammar in a paper published in 1927, when he was Professor of German and Linguistics at Ohio State University. The discussion mainly deals with an apparently "unwonted repetition" in the *sūtra* and in the accompanying *gaṇa* list. Bloomfield's "whimsical humor" (Bernard Bloch in Sebeok 1966, II, 517) is apparent in a excursus on undergarments. What is generally striking in this paper is his purely technical and atheoretical approach. What is perhaps more specifically characteristic of Bloomfield is his empiricism, which becomes apparent at the end of section IV of the paper. There Bloomfield assumes, "as would any modern linguist," that it is only natural that Pāṇini "did not concern himself with such far-fetched theoretical possibilities as someone's taking it into his head to say *śvaliḍ ḍhaukate*" (the expression means 'to come near licking like a dog'). But the Sanskrit grammarians were always looking out for possible examples (*udāharaṇa*) and counterexamples (*pratyudāharaṇa*), for precisely such cases.

Unlike Pāṇini, Bloomfield does not seem to have thought of these predictive implications of the notion of grammatical rule.

Bloomfield's paper "On some rules of Pāṇini" was published in the *Journal of the American Oriental Society* (47, 1927, 61–70).

On Some Rules of Pāṇini (1927)

Leonard Bloomfield

I

In the first chapter of the first book of his Grammar, Pāṇini sets up the term pronoun (*sarvanāman*) as a designation of certain words. He does this so that in other passages he may, without repeating the list of these words, describe their inflectional and other peculiarities (*e. g.*, dative singular masculine and neuter, pronominal *sarvasmai*, as opposed to nominal *pade*, *devāya*, 7, 1, 14). These passages are of course listed in the Indices of Boehtlingk's second edition (Leipzig, 1887)[1].

The rules defining the term pronoun read as follows (1, 1):

27. *sarvādīni sarvanāmāni*,	27. *sarva* etc. are pronouns,
28. *vibhāṣā diksamāse bahuvrīhau*,	28. option in direction-compound exocentric,
29. *na bahuvrīhau*,	29. not in exocentric,
30. *tṛtīyāsamāse*,	30. instrumental-compound,
31. *dvaṃdve ca*,	31. and copulative,
32. *vibhāṣā jasi*,	32. option before nom. pl. *-as*,
33. *prathamacaramatayālpārdhakatipayanemāś ca*,	33. and *prathama*, *carama*, *-taya*, *alpa*, *ardha*, *katipaya*, *nema*.
34. *pūrvaparāvaradakṣiṇottarāparādharāṇi vyavasthāyām asaṃjñāyām*,	34. *pūrva*, *para*, *avara*, *dakṣiṇa*, *uttara*, *apara*, *adhara* in spatial relation not name,
35. *svam ajñātidhanākhyāyām*,	35. *sva* not in kinsman or property appellative,
36. *antaraṁ bahiryogopasaṁvyānayoḥ*.	36. *antara* in conjunction with outside and undergarment.

The list (*gaṇa*) Sarva Etc. that goes with Rule 27 reads with Boehtlingk's numbering, as follows:

1. *sarva*; 2. *viśva*; 3. *ubha*; 4. *ubhaya*.
5. *ḍ-atara*; 6. *ḍ-atama*; 7. *itara*; 8. *anya*; 9. *anyatara*.
10. *tvá*; 11. *tva*; 12. *nema*; 13. *sama*; 14. *sima*; 15. *pūrva-parā-'vara-dakṣiṇo-'ttarā-'parā-'dharāṇi vyavasthāyām asaṁjñāyām*; 16. *svam ajñātidhanākhyāyām*; 17. *antaraṁ bahiryogopasaṁvyānayoḥ*.
18. *tyad*; 19. *tad*; 20. *yad*; 21. *etad*; 22. *adas*; 23. *idam*; 24. *eka*.
25. *dvi*; 26. *yuṣmad*; 27. *asmad*; 28. *bhavat-u*; 29. *kim*.

Bhaṭṭojidīkṣita, *Siddhāntakaumudī* (ed. Vasu, Allahabad, n. d.) places 7 after 9, 22 after 23, and reads *tvat* for 10. This last variant is mentioned by Jayāditya, *Kāśikā* (my copy is a reprint of the Benares 1876–8 edition), which otherwise agrees with Boehtlingk's reading.

The traditional interpretation of these rules, as given, e.g., in the two books just named, and, except for one detail, accepted by Boehtlingk, is as follows:

(*a*) Whatever word is designated as a pronoun will nevertheless not be a pronoun (*i.e.*, lack pronominal characteristics) in an exocentric compound, in an instrumental determinative compound, and in a copulative compound; except that it may (optionally) have pronominal characteristics in an exocentric compound of points of the compass (*e. g. northeast*) and in the nominative plural masculine (in the other genders the nominal and pronominal inflections here coincide) of a copulative compound.

[1] Apart from Pāṇini himself and his commentators, my obligation is to Boehtlingk's indices and to the writings of B. Liebich: Pāṇini (Leipzig, 1891); *Zwei Kapitel der Kāśikā* (Breslau, 1892); *Candra Vṛtti* (AKM 14, Leipzig, 1918); *Zur Einführung in die indische Sprachwissenschaft*. I-IV (Heidelberg *SB*, 1919 ff.).

(*b*) Designated as pronouns are the words in the List *Sarva* Etc.; numbers 15, 16, 17 with the limitations there stated. To this constituency is to be *added* the fact that the first six words in Rule 33 (which are not otherwise treated as pronouns) optionally have pronoun character in the nominative plural masculine, e. g. *prathame* beside *prathamāḥ*. And from this constituency is to be *subtracted* the fact that (12) *nema* and the words under 15, 16, 17 (in the senses there stated; in other senses they are not pronouns) optionally lack pronoun character in the nominative plural masculine, e. g. *nemāḥ* beside *neme*, *pūrvāḥ* beside *pūrve*.

In the case of (17) *antara* the restriction means that this word is a pronoun when it is a synonym of *outside* and in the sense of *undergarment*.

II

What first strikes one in this passage is the repetitious and clumsy treatment of the words in 15, 16, 17 of the List. They are there cited not in stem form, but as inflected neuters, and restrictions of meaning are added, contrary to the usual form of the Lists. The option for nom. pl. masc. is stated by repeating in Rules 34, 35, 36 not only the entire section of the List, but also the restrictions of meaning,—in contrast with Pāṇini's usual elegant brevity. No wonder that Kātyāyana's one comment on Rule 34 is, "And needlessness of repetitive citation in the Text of Rules of *avara* etc., owing to reading in the Text of Lists." (I cite from S. D. Kudāla's edition of Patañjali's *Mahābhāṣya*, vol. 1, Nirnaya Sagar Press, Bombay 1917, which contains also Kaiyaṭa's *Pradīpa*, Nāgeśa's *Uddyota*, and selections from a *Chāyā*, commentary).

Patañjali tries to discover what Pāṇini meant to indicate by this unwonted repetition. Did he mean to set up the restrictions under which these words have pronoun character? No, for that has been attained by the List. Did he mean to show that these words are not to be included when he tells us (5, 3, 2) that (25) *dvi* etc. are in certain cases excepted from pronominal treatment? (We interrupt to ask why anyone could be tempted to include 15, 16, 17 in a statement about "25 and the following"; of this more, immediately). No, says Patañjali, for Pāṇini permits himself exceptions in matters of sequence. Pāṇini's real intent, he concludes, was to show us, by a repetition which otherwise would be purposeless, that the words in 15, 16, 17 and Rules 34, 35, 36 belong with Rules 32 and 33, *i. e.*, have option of nominal form in the nom. pl. masc.,—*e. g.*, *pūrvāḥ* beside *pūrve*.

The second of the suppositions which Patañjali rejects would be intelligibile only if in the List 15, 16, 17 came after (25) *dvi*, etc. Only if that were the order could anyone suppose, even for a moment, that they were included in the "*dvi* etc." of Rule 5, 3, 2, and only then could one suppose, be it mistakenly, that Pāṇini's repetition was meant to indicate that the words in 15, 16, 17 constitute a special group and are not to be involved when an exception is stated for (25) *dvi* etc. And, indeed, Kaiyaṭa tells us that by some scholars (13) *tyad* and the following (including therefore (25) *dvi* and its successors) are read before (15) *pūrva* and the following. This shows us that since Patañjali's time the order of the List has been changed.

Patañjali's reason for rejecting this second possible motive is of interest. The reason is that when Pāṇini at 5, 3, 2 makes a statement about "*dvi* etc." this need not include the subsequent *pūrva* and its followers, for Pāṇini permits himself exceptions in matters of sequence. The Master, says Patañjali, has given us a formal indication of this by making an obvious and otherwise inexplicable exception to the sequence announced in 8, 2, 1. This rule says that from there to the end of the Grammar each rule is to be taken as uneffected with regard to preceding rules. Yet, at 8, 3, 13 he gives a rule which can apply only if the subsequent rule 8, 4, 41 be taken as already effected, and apply within just limits only if 8, 4, 53 be taken as already effected. He points out that Kātyāyana recognizes this in his comment on 8, 3, 13.

The motive which Patañjali finally attributes to Pāṇini seems inadequate. If Pāṇini meant to tell us that the words in 15, 16, 17 allowed of nominal nom. pl. masc., he could have added the word "*pūrva*-etc." to Rule 33. He would not even have had to specify the extent of "*pūrva*-etc.", since these words stood at the end of the List. Kātyāyana seems to have the better of the argument: his objection is valid.

It is noteworthy that Kātyāyana cites our words not as "*pūrva* etc.", but as "*avara* etc." Kaiyaṭa says that he (or rather, Patañjali in paraphrasing him) does this *prakārārtham* "for the sake of the special meaning" (*i. e.*, to symbolize that Rules 34, 35, 36 are *avara* "posterior" to the reading of the same words in the List, which is *pūrva* "preceding"). Nāgeśa, however, says that in reality Kātyāyana says "*avara* etc." because *avara* ought properly to precede, since its syllables are short (Kātyāyana on Pāṇini 2, 2, 34) and because it begins in a vowel and ends in short *a* (Pāṇini 2, 2, 23: the edition reads *ajādyantatvāt*, for *ajādyadantatvāt*).

Patañjali touches upon the peculiar form of Kātyāyana's citation. He opens his discussion of Kātyāyana's critique by asking: How do we know that the Text of Lists comes first and that therefore the reading of 34 in the Text of Rules is a repetition? By the symbolism that in the former we have "*pūrva* etc.", that is, "preceding etc." and in the latter "*avara* etc.", that is, "following etc."? No, for in the latter, too, we have "*pūrva* etc." Yet it is true that the Lists come first, the Rules second. The Master indicates this to us by his later reference (7, 1, 16) to "the nine beginning with *pūrva*."—That is, the fact that Pāṇini says "nine" decides for Patañjali that the List is meant, since only there does *pūrva* head a group of nine words, and since the mention of "nine" could have no other motive than to refer us explicitly to the List: what with the final position of *pūrva* etc. in the List, the word "nine" would otherwise be superfluous. The fact that Pāṇini's reference is to the List and not to the Rules apparently decides for Patañjali that the List is to be read first.

This shows that Patañjali, at any rate, read *pūrva* and not *avara* as the first word in Rule 34. We shall find reason to believe that this was Pāṇini's own reading. Accordingly, Kātyāyana's "*avara* etc." remains unintelligible except as a laconic indication of a flaw, namely that Pāṇini's wording disagrees with the rules of order in copulative compounds (as above cited from Nāgeśa). From Pāṇini's general practice it appears that he did not begin his rule with *avara* (or with one of the other words with initial vowel) because to do so would have added a syllable (though not a mora) to the length of his rule; he arranges his words so as to merge or elide as many vowels as possible. Beyond this, I cannot account for the order in which Pāṇini cites these stems.

III

Beside the repetition, the strange form of numbers 15, 16, 17 in the List, their historic change of place, and the later reference with "nine," our rules contain several peculiarities which the commentators do not mention. Why does Rule 33 cite its words in the masculine, when the normal form of citation is neuter (Rules 34, 35, 36)? Why does the word *ca* "and" stand in Rule 33? The commentators ignore these points, probably because their discussion of Pāṇinean methods had worked out the principles that the gender in which Pāṇini cites words is not necessarily significant, and that the placing of *ca* "and" does not necessarily indicate the end of an enumeration. At least, these decisions are given by Nāgojī (Nāgeśa) in his *Paribhāṣenduśekhara*, Numbers 73 and 78 (Kielhorn's translation, Bombay Sanskrit Series, No. 2, 1868–74).

Finally,—a point which lay outside the view of the ancients,—in the light of historical linguistics the doctrine of the rules as they are traditionally interpreted is most surprising. In the first six words of Rule 33 we see the lapse, widespread in Indo-European languages, of nominal words into pronominal inflection, especially in the nom. pl. masc. In Latin and Greek this has, of course, involved all the *o*-stems (and gone on even to the *ā*-feminines); in Germanic it has involved the whole strong adjective declension. The pronominal form of the nom. pl. masc. is favored also in the copulative compounds, Rule 32. But in the case of *nema* in Rule 33 and of the words in Rules 34, 35, 36 we are taught the opposite: *nema* has pronominal forms throughout, but in the nom. pl. masc. may have nominal form, *nemāḥ* beside *neme*; and the other words have pronominal forms throughout (except for an option in the ablative and locative singular, masculine and neuter, 7, 1, 16), but in the nom. pl. masc. also nominal form, e. *g.*, *pūrvāḥ* beside *pūrve*.

IV

Pāṇini and Kātyāyana recorded the facts of a standard colloquial language spoken by them as their mother-tongue and as the medium of everyday life; if, like ours, it was archaic in comparison with the normal dialects of the time, it was, like ours, native to many speakers, who with a little training were able to decide what could and what could not be spoken. The later grammarians, including, I venture to say, Patañjali, were in no position to criticize the facts thus given by their predecessors; for them Sanskrit was a second language, spoken to be sure, but preserved and by them acquired through a literary tradition, much as was classical Latin for a learned Italian of, say, the fifth century A.D. They could judge only of the form of Pāṇini's presentation. What is more, the text of Pāṇini was canonical. If Patañjali found a repetition in our passage, it was his task to divine what the Master could have meant by this unusual proceeding. If he found a discrepancy in the order of the rules in the Eighth Book, he could at best take it as an intentional and formal indication on the part of the Master, to the effect that exceptions of order occur in the Text. He could not like Boehtlingk, see in the order of 8, 3, 13 and 8, 4, 41 one of the slips inevitable in a human construction of such size and complexity. He could not, as would any modern linguist, conclude from the order of 8, 3, 13 and 8, 4, 53 that Pāṇini did not concern himself with such far-fetched theoretical possibilities as someone's taking it into his head to say *śvaliḍ ḍhaukate*. For later students, Pāṇini, Kātyāyana, and Patañjali were the Three Seers, and especially the ultimate interpretation of Patañjali was canonically binding. If Nāgojī found a single passage where, under Patañjali's interpretation, the gender in which a word is cited is indifferently chosen, or a single passage where, under Patañjali's interpretation, the word "and" has no particular bearing, then he was obliged to conclude that Pāṇini could not have intended these features to be generally significant.

V

Probably the peculiarities of our passage are to be explained as follows.

The citation of the words in Rule 33 is in masculine form because it is only the masculine nominative plural that is involved in the rule. This helps to set off these words from the following, and incidentally saves a short vowel.

The word *ca* "and" in Rule 33 has the same value as in Rule 31 and in many other passages of the *Grammar*: it is used in the last of a series of (two or more) rules that are additively coordinated. This habit, taken from ordinary speech, serves in the Grammar to show where such an enumerative series ends. Thus, in Rule 31 "and in a copulative," the word "and" shows that "in a copulative" is the last of the three places where *sarva* etc. are not pronouns. Technically, we may phrase this by saying that the word "and" shows the continued validity (*anuvṛtti*) up to this point, and the cessation of validity (*nivṛtti*) at this point of the word *na* "not" in Rule 29. Similarly in Rule 33: the word "and" concludes the series of rules (two in number) which tell where option in the nom. pl. masc. is given. In technical language: the word "and" in Rule 33 marks the continued validity in this rule of the words "option before nom.-pl. *-as*" of Rule 32 and the cessation of this validity at the end of Rule 33. This indication is reinforced by quoting the words in masculine form. Thus the subsequent rules, 34, 35, 36, have nothing to do with option in the nom. pl.

The words in these subsequent rules were not intended by Pāṇini to stand in the List. These three rules simply state that these words, with these restrictions of sense, are pronouns. These words are treated in the Text and not in the List because they require restriction: they are pronouns only in the meanings here given. After Pāṇini's time and before Kātyāyana's, some tinkerer added them bodily, without reducing them to stem form, and with the statements of restriction, to the end of the List *Sarva* Etc. There Kātyāyana and Patañjali, and, according to Kaiyaṭa, some later students found them. This corruption of the List involved not only the repetition which Kātyātyana criticized and Patañjali tried to explain, but also another discrepancy: Rule 5, 3, 2 excludes "*dvi* etc." from a characteristic of pronouns which almost any page of Sanskrit shows to hold good for *pūrva* and its group (adverbial forms like *pūrvatra*). Patañjali explains this, as we have seen, as an exception to order. A later arranger of the List solved this difficulty by moving these final numbers of the List back to a place before 18 *tyad*; here they no longer interfered with "*dvi* etc." of Rule 5, 3, 2 or with rules about "*tyad* etc."

Pāṇini's reference at 7, 1, 16 to "the nine beginning with *pūrva*" would have lacked the mention of "nine" and would have read simply "*pūrva* etc.", had he intended these words to stand, as

Patañjali found them, at the end of the List *Sarva* Etc. We have seen how Patañjali tries to explain the mention of the number "nine." In reality, 7, 1, 16 refers to Pāṇini's Text at 1, 1, 34, 35, 36, and the number "nine" is necessary to secure inclusion of all the words. This reference shows, incidentally, that for Pāṇini *pūrva*, and not *avara*, actually stood first in Rule 34.

The word *nema* in Rule 33 repeats number 12 of the List. The traditional interpretation, then, has it that the first six words in Rule 33, not being in the List, are normally nouns, but are in the nom. pl. masc. capable of pronominal inflection; but that *nema*, being in the List, is normally a pronoun, but is in the nom. pl. masc. capable of nominal inflection. Not to repeat the other arguments, one may surmise that if Pāṇini had meant this, he would have put *nema* into a separate rule. Probably *nema* did not stand in Pāṇini's List; he treated it in Rule 33 on a par with the six other words there cited: in Pāṇini's language *nema* had nominal character except for the option of a pronominally formed nom. pl. masc. In Sanskrit literature the word *nema* is little used, certainly not enough to carry on a (literary) tradition of its Pāṇinean inflection. Later grammarians were dependent for information on this point upon their interpretation of Pāṇini's statements and upon whatever examples they could find in old books. Probably some scholar who knew pronominal forms of the word in Vedic texts (perhaps *nemasmin* RV 10, 48, 10) inserted it in the List.

Boehtlingk in his edition of Pāṇini and more fully in the Petersburg Dictionary, *s. v. antara*, suggests the correct interpretation of *bahiryoga-* in Rule 36: "in conjunction with 'outside'" means "in contrast with 'outside.'" The word *yoga* is used in the same way at 4, 1, 48; everywhere else in Pāṇini it means "in (actual) context with" so that the only possible alternative meaning of *bahiryoga-* would be "in connection with the word *bahiḥ*, 'outside.'" There is no parallel for Kaiyaṭa's interpretation, "as a synonym of 'outside.'" which was taken over by Bhaṭṭojī and Jayāditya. This faulty interpretation does not go back to Kātyāyana and Patañjali. The former says: "The mention of 'undergarment' is purposeless, because this effect is attained by *bahiryoga*.—No, for, rather, it has the purpose of applying to a pair of petticoats and the like." Patañjali expands these remarks, rejecting the latter. The Chāyā points out that this discussion was necessitated by the absence of the word *ākhyā* "appellative" in the rule, which otherwise could have been interpreted like Rule 35, giving "in an appellative for *undergarment*." Now, Kātyāyana's second sentence is obscure, and Patañjali's interpretation of it seems far-fetched,[2] but so much is clear, that these scholars did not know *antara* in a sense of "outer," but interpreted *bahiryoga* as "inner."

[2] Kātyāyana's remarks may perhaps be interpreted thus: In his and Pāṇini's speech one could say "an inner" for "an undergarment." K. questions whether this need be specially stated, since this usage would seem to be included under the definition "in contrast with outside" (Vārtika 1), but decides that, after all, it needs to be stated, since "an inner" refers to either of two petticoats or the like, worn one over the other, while "in contrast with outside" might be taken as appropriate only to the inside one (Vārtika 2).

This, however, is not Patañjali's interpretation. He paraphrases the two Vārtika's and explains and refutes the second by saying: Where this is not known: which is the inside one (*antarīyam*) and which the outside one (*uttarīyam*), here, too, that person who has first made examination, for him it is decided: this is the inner and

VI

In our view, then, the List *Sarva* Etc. should be read without (12) *nema*, (15) *pūrva* etc., (16) *sva*, (17) *antara*; and the Rules would be interpreted thus:

(a) As interpreted by the ancients.

(b) Designated as pronouns are the words in the List. Also the words *pūrva, para, avara, dakṣiṇa, uttara, apara, adhara* in the sense of a spatial or temporal relation when not specialized appellatives; the word *sva* when not an appellative for "kinsman" or "property"; the word *antara* when meaning "inner" or "undergarment." (Later, at 7, 1, 16, we learn that these nine words have optionally nominal inflection in certain forms; the nom. pl. masc., however, in the pronominal senses, is always *pūrve*, etc., never *pūrvāḥ*). The words *prathama, carama, -taya* (*i. e.*, words formed with this suffix), *alpa, ardha, katipaya, nema* optionally have the pronominal form in the nom. pl. masc., but otherwise have only nominal forms.

this the outer. (Kaiyaṭa's gloss: In the case of a pair of petticoats of equal size and not donned, it is not known whether a given one is the outer or inner.—"Here too"; as soon as the identity of the undergarment is determined by forethought, then, too, it is a case of "conjunction with outside"). Thus it appears that Patañjali's interpretation of Kātyāyana's second Vārtika is: An undergarment is still an undergarment even when not recognized as belonging inside. His refutation is that, as soon as one recognizes it as an undergarment, one also recognizes that it belongs inside. He has underestimated Kātyāyana's point, probably because the expression "an inner" for an undergarment was unfamiliar to him.

A different interpretation is quoted by Kaiyaṭa: But others say: The word "and so forth" is included in the Vārtika 2: this means that in the case of a set of three or four petticoats, since the third and fourth are not in "conjunction with outside," the word "undergarment" deserves separate mention.

18

Barend Faddegon (1874–1955)

Barend Faddegon, Professor of Sanskrit at the University of Amsterdam, was the author of a few papers in linguistics and of numerous studies in the field of Sanskrit (mainly concerning Indian philosophy, the *Sāmaveda*, and Pāṇini). Though hardly known as a linguist, he had sound judgment in linguistic matters. Faddegon was original both as a scholar and as a man and wrote in a very personal style. The more temperate of his contemporaries reacted to his publications with mixed feelings. Perhaps Renou's judgment on Faddegon's *Studies on Pāṇini's Grammar* (1936) may be taken as representative and just: "ouvrage un peu fantasque, mais séduisant" (1940, 10, note 1). Earlier Renou had commented on Faddegon's *Studies* in the following terms: "il a du goût pour les formules algébriques et verse lui-même aisément dans ces enchaînements par association qu'il a relevés chez l'auteur qu'il décrit" (*Orientalistische Literaturzeitung* 40, no. 5, 1937, 319).

A good specimen of Faddegon's style and outlook is the motto of his *Studies on Pāṇini's Grammar*:

> Goldstücker has admirably attacked Böhtlingk, but for Böhtlingk we forget Goldstücker;
> and Whitney had admirably attacked Pāṇini, but for Pāṇini we forget Whitney.
> I adore Böhtlingk because he reveals to us the spirit of Pāṇini,
> I adore Pāṇini because he reveals to us the spirit of India,
> I adore India because it reveals to us the Spirit, the Spirit.

A more specific and very insightful comment on Pāṇini's syntactic-semantic theory of *kāraka* is also characteristic:

> Evidently Pāṇini tries in this analysis to separate the ideational aspect from the linguistic expression, an attempt which the Occidental linguists of the latter half of the nineteenth century have condemned, misled as they were by the hope of being able to understand language through the exclusive study of its phonal and morphological aspect, i.e. its articulative utterance and the association-system underlying declension and conjugation, as if the application and imitation of physics and a mechanistic psychology were the last word of moral science. And so besides the injustice done to a pioneer of grammar who lived about twenty-five centuries ago by associating with him supposed results of modern grammar, it is even questionable whether Pāṇini has not something still to say to us [from page 18 of the same book].

Faddegon had one outstanding pupil in the field of Pāṇinian studies: Herman Eldert Buiskool (1884–1963), at first a schoolteacher and later a civil servant who was mostly engaged in committee work relating to the frequent proposals for spelling reform in Dutch. Buiskool wrote one book, his dissertation for Faddegon, entitled *Pūrvatrāsiddham. Analytisch onderzoek aangaande het systeem der Tripādī van Pāṇini's Aṣṭādhyāyī* (1934), republished in 1939 as *The Tripādī, being an English Recast of Pūrvatrāsiddham (An Analytical-Synthetical Inquiry into the System of the Last Three Chapters of Pāṇini's Aṣṭādhyāyī)*. In this work Buiskool gave a penetrating analysis of some of the fundamental techniques of Pāṇini's grammar, largely relating to the relative strength of rules and to the concept of *asiddhatva* (see page 207).

Probably the earliest of Faddegon's contributions to the study of the Sanskrit grammarians was a paper read at the First International Congress of Linguists on April 13, 1928: "The Mnemotechnics of Pāṇini's Grammar I: The Śiva-Sūtra," *Acta Orientalia* 7, 1929, 48–65. It is a remarkable, although perhaps unintentional, indication of each author's evaluation of the Sanskrit grammarians, that the Sanskritist Faddegon's paper was read at a linguistic congress, whereas the linguist Bloomfield's paper was published in an orientalist journal.

There are inaccuracies in this paper. For example, it is argued in §13 that *v* may be dispensed with, but that this is not so follows from a rule mentioned earlier: Without *v* it is impossible to state 8.3.7, which amounts to

n → ṃ⁀śAR/ _______ # chAV⁀aM.

Hence we have *bhavāṃś cinoti*, *bhavāṃs tarati*, but *bhavān karoti*.

The *Śivasūtra* has been the subject of a number of studies by modern authors. Apart from Sköld (1926), mentioned by Faddegon, there are studies by Breloer (1929), K. C. Chatterji (1934a), Thieme (1935a: beginning of Chapter 4), C. K. Raja (1957), Staal (1962a), Misra (1966, section 2.1), Cardona (1969; cf. Staal 1970b). Sköld had defended the view that the *Śivasūtra* was not the work of Pāṇini, but it has become increasingly clear that this list of sounds is very closely interrelated with many of Pāṇini's grammatical rules. The traditional view that the *Śivasūtra* was revealed to Pāṇini by Śiva is related to some of the legends connected with Patañjali (see this volume page 3).

The Mnemotechnics of Pāṇini's Grammar I: The Śiva-Sūtra (1929)

Barend Faddegon

The subject I have chosen for my paper does not seem to possess any actuality.[1] Even Prof. Liebich, who has given so much time to the interpretation of Pāṇini, acknowledges the study of this grammar to be exclusively the work of the specialist.[2] It is many years ago since the study of Pāṇini was used in Europe as a grammatical guide for Sanskrit. At the present time one need only understand the technical expressions borrowed from Pāṇini by the commentators of Indian literature; Pāṇini's grammar itself has lost its general interest.

And yet Böhtlingk praised Pāṇini as a genius and his grammar as a masterpiece, thus claiming for it a lasting value. But before giving up the modest attitude of Liebich, we must consider whether Böhtlingk is right, for in his laudation he is more assertative than argumentative. To prove this I shall now read out to you a quotation from Böhtlingk's preface bearing on this matter.

"The order of the sūtras may here and there seem strange to us, but it is planned and carried out in a consistent and admirable manner. A perfect conciseness and complete avoidance of all repetitions has been the aim of the author and without any doubt he has attained this. The more thoroughly one studies Pāṇini's grammar, the more one is struck by the acuteness and the successful mastery of the vast matter, shown in it. It is in its kind a masterpiece of the first rank. The more recent grammars in which the unchangeable order of Pāṇini's sūtras has been tampered with in order to string together everything bearing on the same matter, cannot be understood without the aid of extensive commentaries, which of necessity continually refer to passages either long past by or not yet arrived at; indeed these grammars must be considered as failures."

So runs the quotation from Böhtlingk. The reader, however, who reads Pāṇini for the first time, will be painfully struck by the fact that the text of the first chapters totally contradicts the assertion of Böhtlingk. Numerous references to later passages are also needed here and are indeed given by Böhtlingk himself in his translation. And even these references are not sufficient in number. Already at the second chapter of the first book the reader is overwhelmed by its grammatical intricacies; and when he has finished the eight books, he only possesses a chaotic impression of details. The help afforded by Böhtlingk is insufficient in order to determine the merits of Pāṇini exactly; we want more insight into the total plan, the execution of details, and the idea underlying the pregnant form of expression.

Here I shall restrict myself to the last-mentioned point, Pāṇini's mnemotechnical system, and again specially to the mnemotechnics of the introductory Śiva-Sūtra.

By the Śiva-Sūtra is understood a collection of 14 formulae of phonetical contents, which precedes the eight books, the Aṣṭādhyāyī. Each formula, also called a sūtra, contains a group of speech-sounds, to which sūtra is added at the end a mute letter, a so-called *anubandha*, which possesses a mnemotechnic function.

With reference to this Śiva-Sūtra[3] I have two propositions which I wish to defend:

Proposition I. The Śiva-Sūtra has a double purport. The chief

[1] See Supplement § 16.

[2] Cf. B. Liebich, *Zwei Kapitel der Kāśikā*, Breslau 1892, p. I sq.

[3] In order to simplify my argumentation I purposely treat the author of the Śiva-Sūtra and the author (or more correctly the authors) of the Aṣṭādhyāyī as one and the same person. Cf. Supplement § 2.

purport is a phonetical classification. The sūtra presupposes the traditional alphabet and together with this alphabet affords the means for a concise phonetical terminology. In this respect the Śiva-Sūtra deserves praise.

Proposition II. The subordinate purport of the Śiva-Sūtra is to afford the means of formulating concisely euphonic and morphological rules. Although on the whole very interesting and ingenuous, this grammatical use of the Śiva-Sūtra in many cases degenerates into subtlety.

In order to prove my first proposition I have put together three tables: table A, containing the Śiva-Sūtra; table B, showing the phonetical basis of this sūtra; and table C which explains the phonetical basis of the traditional alphabet.[4]

Alphabet and Śiva-Sūtra complement each other. For we see that Pāṇini forms from both his *pratyāhāras*, i.e. technical denotations of phonetical classes. He uses *ku* for denoting the group of the five velars *k*, *kh*, *g*, *gh*, *ṅ* as found in the alphabet; similarly *cu*, *ṭu*, *tu*, *pu* respectively for the four other groups. From the Śiva-Sūtra Pāṇini forms several *pratyāhāras* all according to the same method; for denoting a group he takes the first consonant of this group and then adds to it the mute letter, the *anubandha* which closes the group; for instance the *pratyāhāra ak* denotes *a*, *i*, *u*, *ṛ*, *ḷ*, the five original monophthongs of Sanskrit; the *pratyāhāra ec* denotes e, *o*, *ai*, *au* of which the two first were originally diphthongs and the two last are still diphthongs; in the same way (see sūtra 5 and 6) the *pratyāhāra yaṇ* is a denotation for the semivowels as defined by the Hindus, i.e. our semivowels and liquids.

An additional rule bearing on the indication of the quantity of vowels may be omitted here (see Supplement § 6).

The alphabet which Pāṇini used as complement to the Śiva-Sūtra was not his own invention. If it had been so, this fact would have been carried down to us by tradition. But, since we are neither sure that Pāṇini was the author of the sūtra, in this way we cannot settle their chronological order. However, when we compare the alphabet with the sūtra, we see that the former is the older of the two and that the latter is derived from it. In the case of the contact-consonants, namely, the alphabet shows a more logical order than the sūtra, while at the same time we can prove that the illogical order of the sūtra is due to the desire of obtaining *pratyāhāras* which may be useful for the formulation of the phonetical and morphological rules. Thus the alphabet enunciates the contact-consonants in regular order from the velar series up to the labial series; on the other hand the Śiva-Sūtra places for instance the *jh* and *bh* before the *gh*, and the *ph* before the *ch*.

Putting aside this irregularity of order[5] I shall show with a few examples the phonetical importance of the Śiva-Sūtra. For this purport I have composed the table B. This table differs from table A, i.e. the sūtra itself, in so far as all the mute letters of minor importance are left out. The partial sūtras 1 and 2 are arranged in one line, which contains the sounds of the *pratyāhāra ak*; the sūtras 3 and 4 are combined into *ec* with omission of the *anubandha ṅ*; the *h* of sūtra 5 is put apart; the rest of sūtra 5 is put together with sūtra 6 as *yaṇ*; sūtra 7 remains the same, as *ñam*; sūtra 8 and 9 are conjoined as *jhaṣ*; sūtra 10 remains the same as *jaś*; sūtra 11 requires a special hypothesis, namely, that in the first mental plan-

[4] See Supplement § 1.

[5] See below the discussion on P. 7, 3, 101–102, and Supplement § 5.

ning of the sūtra the *anubandha v* followed *th* and not *t*; as a result of this surmise the five first consonants of sūtra 11 form the *pratyāhāra khav* and its three remaining consonants together with sūtra 12 the *pratyāhāra cay*; finally the sūtras 13 and 14 remain the same.

The proof for the hypothesis concerning the original place of the *anubandha v* is given in the Supplement § 12 and 13; for the present I want to draw the following conclusions from table B.

1st conclusion. In the alphabet voiced and voiceless speech-sounds alternate without order; but the author of the sūtra, by reversing the order of the consonants and by placing the *h* twice (once in sūtra 5 and again in sūtra 14), enables us to denote all the voiced speech-sounds by the *pratyāhāra aś*, and all the voiceless speech-sounds by the *pratyāhāra khar*, whilst at the same time we can combine the four continuants into the one *pratyāhāra śal*.

2nd conclusion. In the new arrangement, as met with in the sūtra, the nasals can be combined with the semivowels into the *pratyāhāra yam*, which is an advantage when considering the great acoustic affinity between semivowels and nasals.

3rd conclusion. Table B shows a remarkable regularity in the choice of the *anubandhas* as technical consonants. The stops *k* and *c* are used for the two divisions of the vocalic sounds; the nasals *ṇ* and *m* for the acoustically connected semivowels and nasals; the continuants *ṣ* and *ś* for the two divisions of the voiced stops; the semivowels *v* and *y* for the two divisions of the voiceless stops; the liquids *r* and *l* for the two classes of the continuants.

4th and final conclusion. The Śiva-Sūtra is an old and meritorious classification of the speech-sounds as met with in Sanskrit.

With this last conclusion the proof for the first proposition is completed. I shall now repeat my second proposition:

The Śiva-Sūtra affords in its subordinate purport the means for formulating very concisely euphonic and morphological rules. Although this grammatical use of the sūtra is on the whole ingenious and interesting, in many cases it degenerates into subtlety and artificiality.

The *merits* of the Śiva-Sūtra in its grammatical aspect are very evident. For instance, the *pratyāhāra eṅ* in the third partial sūtra and the *pratyāhāra aic* in the fourth sūtra enable the author to formulate concisely the rules for the *guṇa* and *vṛddhi* of *ĭ* and *ŭ*. Similarly the *pratyāhāra yaṇ*, contained in the 5th and 6th sūtra, and the *pratyāhāra ik*, contained in the 2nd and 3rd sūtra, by their correspondence in order facilitate the formulation of the rules bearing on the changes of semivowels into their correspondent vowels and vice versa. Many other similar examples in the entire sūtra prove its grammatical usefulness.

The *weak side* of the sūtra, its subtlety, requires a fuller explanation. As an example I have chosen the *pratyāhāra yañ*, contained in the sūtra 5 up to 8. This *pratyāhāra* is only once made use of, namely in P. 7, 3, 101–102, which runs as follows: *ato dīrgho yañi* and *supi ca*. It would take up too much time to explain in full the algebraic expression of these sūtras; in ordinary language they express the rule that a long *ā* is substituted for the short *ă* of the thematic conjugation and the thematic declension in those cases where the personal ending or the case-ending begins with one of the consonants contained in the *pratyāhāra yañ*. When in order to apply this rule we compare all the beginnings of the personal endings and case endings with the consonants of the *pratyāhāra yañ*, then we find that these two series have only four consonants in common, namely, *m*, *v*, *y* and *bh*. Thus when we follow the general rules of these sūtras 101 and 102 and at the same time apply the exceptions to those rules, as given by the sūtra 103 and following, we arrive at the fact that the Sanskrit language possesses such forms as *pacāmi*, *pacāvaḥ*, *pacāmaḥ*; *vṛkṣāya* and *vṛkṣābhyām*.

Evidently, Pāṇini was obliged here to change in the Śiva-Sūtra the alphabetical order of the contact-consonants and to insert the *anubandha ñ* after the 8th sūtra; for, if he had used the *pratyāhāra yaṣ*, then he had to formulate a separate exception for the second person plural of the *ātmanepada*, such as *pacadhve* and *apacadhvam*.

The method of formulating the rules too broadly and then leaving it to the reader to find out from the context the proper limitations to these rules has, no doubt, always roused enthusiastic admiration among Hindu grammarians; on the contrary the modern European, who does not cultivate oral memorizing to such an extent as the Hindu does, and even when memorizing does not appreciate the saving of a syllable, will consider the process artificial and misleading.

And now I have proved my two propositions, the first one maintaining that the Śiva-Sūtra as a phonetical classification deserves the highest praise, and the second that the Sūtra in grammatical respects, although often ingenious, shows a tendency towards artificiality.

Liebich considers Pāṇini's grammar a work of interest only for the specialist; this modest attitude, we may already conclude, is too modest. For, although Pāṇini is no longer used for grammatical instruction, he still claims the attention of every linguist who feels interested in the history of his own study; and, in doing so, at the same time he rewards the reader with a sudden insight into two typical features of the Hindu mind, its acute originality and its queer subtlety.

Böhtlingk has on his own authority praised Pāṇini's grammar, in its composition, as a masterpiece of its kind. Whether he is right or wrong in his judgment, cannot be decided by a mere discussion on the Śiva-Sūtra. Still I am inclined to think that a more complete analysis of only this introductory sūtra might show that even in the subtlety of Pāṇini there lies genius.

Supplement to Chapter I

§1. Tables showing the phonetical basis of the Śiva-Sūtra and the traditional alphabet.

A. The Śiva-Sūtra.

Speech-sounds		Anu-bandhas	Speech-sounds		Anu-bandhas
1	*a i u*	*ṇ*	9	*gh ḍh dh*	*ṣ*
2	*ṛ ḷ*	*k*	10	*j b g ḍ d*	*ś*
3	*e o*	*ṅ*	11	*kh ph ch ṭh th*	
4	*ai au*	*c*		*c ṭ t*	*v*
5	*h y v r*	*ṭ*	12	*k p*	*y*
6	*l*	*ṇ*	13	*ś ṣ s*	*r*
7	*ñ m ṅ ṇ n*	*m*	14	*h*	*l*
8	*jh bh*	*ñ*			

B. The Phonetical Basis of the Śiva-Sūtra.

Character of sound	Ś.-S.	Place of articulation: glottal	pharyngal	palatal	labio-velar: lab.	vel.	labial (2)	palatal (2)	mūrdhanya	dental	Anubandhas
I vowels	1–2		*a*	*i*	*u*				*ṛ*	*ḷ*	*k*
	3–4			*e*	*o*						
				ai	*au*						*c*
	5	*h*									
III semivowels	5–6			*y*	*v*				*r*	*l*	*ṇ*
II nasals	7			*ñ*	*m*	*ṅ*			*ṇ*	*n*	*m*
II voiced stops	8–9			*jh*	*bh*	*gh*			*ḍh*	*dh*	*ṣ*
	10			*j*	*b*	*g*			*ḍ*	*d*	*ś*
II voiceless stops	11					*kh*	*ph*	*ch*	*ṭh*	*th*	[*v!*]
	11							*c*	*ṭ*	*t*	
	12					*k*	*p*				*y*
IV continuants	13							*ś*	*ṣ*	*s*	*r*
	14	*h*									*l*

C. The Phonetical Basis of the Traditional Alphabet.

Character of sound	Place of articulation: glottal	pharyngal	velar	palatal	labio-velar	mūrdhanya	dental	labial
I vowels		*a ā*		*i ī*	*u ū*	*ṛ ṝ*	*ḷ ḹ*	
				e ai	*o au*			
II stops			*k kh g*	*c ch j*		*ṭ ṭh ḍ*	*t th d*	*p ph b*
			gh ṅ	*jh ñ*		*ḍh ṇ*	*dh n*	*bh m*
III semivowels				*y*		*r*	*l*	*v*
IV continuants	*h*			*ś*		*ṣ*	*s*	

§2. The authorship of the Śiva-Sūtra.

Pāṇini begins the first sūtra of his grammar with the word *vṛddhi* as a kind of precative formula or *maṅgala* and the last sūtra of his work "*a a*" is a clear reference to this first sūtra. For in free paraphrase this sūtra means "in the beginning of my work I made the fictitious supposition that *a* and *ā* are homogeneous sounds and thus I called *ā* the *vṛddhi* of the *a*, but now I take back this supposition and give to the *a* its real phonetical value."

This beginning and this end stamp the eight books as a complete composition, from which the Śiva-Sūtra is exempted. Should Pāṇini have intended to claim it as its own, he would have inserted it in his work.

The name Śiva-Sūtra, i.e. Sūtra taught by the god Śiva, moreover shows that Indian tradition does not ascribe these introductory formulae to Pāṇini himself. This legendary name, which is of more recent origin than the names *akṣara-sūtra* or *pratyāhāra-sūtra* (according to Böhtlingk, edition, p. 1), is also interesting, because it reminds us of the narrative which proclaims Śiva to be Pāṇini's teacher in grammar (Böhtlingk, edition, Einleitung, p. VIII and Kathāsaritsāgara, 4, 20 sqq.).

Most likely the Śiva-Sūtra is of earlier date than the Aṣṭādhyāyī. However, from this conclusion we must draw another conclusion, namely, that Pāṇini must have borrowed many of his grammatical rules from his immediate predecessors, for the Śiva-Sūtra is closely interwoven with the grammar and many of its *anubandhas* are inserted for the purport of facilitating the formulation of grammatical rules.

When I mention Pāṇini in my article, I really mean the grammarians to whom we are indebted for Śiva-Sūtra and Aṣṭādhyāyī.

For the prehistory of Pāṇini's grammar cf. B. Liebich, *Zur Einführung in die indische einheimische Sprachwissenschaft*, II, Sitzungsber. d. Heidelberger Akad. d. Wissensch., phil.-hist. Kl., 1919, 15. Abh., especially p. 43–45, and Th. Goldstücker, *Pāṇini*, London 1866, p. 181. Further see below §16.

§3. The order of the contact-consonants in the Śiva-Sūtra.

When we compare the useful alphabetical arrangement of the contact-consonants in their rows and columns with the Śiva-Sūtra, then we notice that the columns of the alphabet in reverse order (nasals, voiced aspirates, &c.) become the rows of the sūtra.

§4. The phonetical principles of alphabet and Śiva-Sūtra.

A glance at the tables of §1 shows

that each of the four phonetical classes of the alphabet moves forward from the pharynx to the lips, the only exception to this being the *u*-group;

that the Śiva-Sūtra follows two systems of arrangement, the order palatal, labial, velar, &c. for the voiced consonants, and the order velar, labial, palatal, &c. for the voiceless stops.

§5. The reason for the irregularity of order in the Śiva-Sūtra.

The author of the *Śiva-Sūtra* has here and there deviated from the logical order of the alphabet in order to arrive at a mnemotechnical system.

Thus *e-o*, *ai-au*, *y-v* are grouped into pairs like *i-u* in order to facilitate the rules for *guṇa*, *vṛddhi* and *saṃprasāraṇa*.

ñ and *m* are placed in front of the nasals to obtain the *pratyāhāra ṅam*, the three nasals which at the end of a word are doubled according to the same rule.

For the place of *jh* and *bh* see §9; for *kh*, *ph*, *k* and *p* §11.

§6. The indication of the vowel-quantity.

At, *it*, *ut*, *ṛt*, *ḷt* indicate the short monophthongs, *āt*, &c. the long monophthongs. *A* represents both *a* and *ā*, and according to the commentators likewise the nasalized *a* and *ā*, and the *ā* lengthened by *pluta*. The same rule holds good for the other monophthongs.

§7. The insertion of the anubandhas of subordinate importance.

The principal *anubandhas* afford the means for a phonetical classification; the *anubandhas* of subordinate importance have only a grammatical significance, see §§8–11.

§8. The anubandha *ṇ* at the end of the first sūtra.

We may distinguish the *anubandhas* *ṇ* at the end of the first and sixth *sūtra* as $ṇ_1$ and $ṇ_2$; and accordingly the *pratyāhāra aṇ* as $aṇ_1$ and $aṇ_2$.

The *pratyāhāra aṇ*$_1$ is used in

P. 6, 3, 111 : *a, i, u* are lengthened through the loss of a following *ḍh* or *repha* (*punārakta*, &c.);

P. 7, 4, 13 sq. : *ā, ī, ū* are shortened before the *taddhita*-suffix *ka* (*jñakā, kumārikā*, &c.);

P. 1, 1, 51 : a *sūtra* bearing on the alternations *ṛ̆̄* : *ăr*, *ṛ̆̄* : *ĭr*, *ṛ̆̄* : *ŭr*;

P. 8, 4, 57: a rule for the nasalization of final monophthongs.

§ 9. The anubandha *ṅ*.

Cf. § 5 on the group *e-o*.

§ 10. The anubandha *ṭ*.

This *anubandha* is only used in the *pratyāhāra aṭ*, which contains the vowels, the *h* and the semivowels with the exception of *l*. See:

P. 8, 3, 3 and 9: a Vedic *sandhi*-rule;

P. 8, 4, 2: a rule for the transition of *n* into *ṇ*; here the reader is obliged by the context to eliminate the *repha*. This artifice of formulating a rule too broadly and leaving the reader to find the restrictions himself in the context, may be termed "implied restriction." It is a device, used by Pāṇini with virtuosity and care, and which leads to conciseness and avoids ambiguity;

P. 8, 4, 63: a facultative *sandhi*-rule for *ś*, followed by vowel, *y, v* or *r*; *ś* + *h*, of course, does not occur.

§ 11. The anubandha *ñ*.

The *anubandha ñ* is only met with in the *pratyāhāra yañ*, P. 7, 3, 101–102. The first of these two *sūtras* is interesting as implying two "implied restrictions." On the one hand the *pratyāhāra yañ* is limited to *y, v, m, bh*; and on the other hand the technical term *sārvadhātuke* (taken from 7, 3, 95) is restricted in meaning by its context.

In the sūtra *ato dīrgho yañi* [i.e. *sārvadhātuke*] the genitive means "is substituted for," the *t* of *at* indicates the short *a* as such; the locative means "when follows." The translation accordingly runs: the [correspondent] long vowel, [namely *ā*] must be substituted for *ă* before a *sārvadhātuka*-suffix beginning with *y, v, m* and *bh*.

Now there are three classes of *sārvadhātuka*-suffixes: 1. the suffixes of the present tense (*a* accented and unaccented, *nu, nā*, &c., with the exception of *u*); 2. the personal endings with the exception of those of the perfect; 3. a small class of suffixes which form nouns from the stem of tenses, e.g. the participle-suffixes *-āna* and *-ant*; the Vedic infinitive-suffix *-adhyai*; all the suffixes of this third class begin with a vowel.[6]

Of these three classes of *sārvadhātuka*-suffixes the third is excluded because of its beginning with a vowel; the first is excluded, because the rule applies only to such suffixes which follow an *a*, namely the *a* of the present system. Thus the term *sārvadhātuka* is limited by the context to the meaning of personal ending.

Note. In *abhavam* and *bhavanti* the last *a* is short, because Pāṇini analyses here *abhav-am* and *bhav-anti*; according to 6, 1, 97 the *a* of the stem is elided before the *a* of the ending.

§ 12. The anubandha *v*, its original place and the advantages of its removal.

As the Śiva-Sūtra is in principle a phonetical classification, one would expect to find the *anubandha v* after *th*. What has been the reason for placing it after *t*? In other words, what advantage

[6] See Böhtlingk's edition of Pāṇini, p. 183* s. v. *śit* 2.

has there been in removing it, and are there no disadvantages connected with doing this?

In searching for an answer to these questions, we notice that the strange position of *v* and the irregular order of the voiceless contact-consonants are due to the same cause, the wish of Pāṇini to form the *pratyāhāra chav*, which includes the two series *ch*, *ṭh*, *th*, and *c*, *ṭ*, *t*. A peculiarity which strikes us in these two series is their parallelism to the series *ś*, *ṣ*, *s*. And further we notice that the *pratyāhāra chav* is only once met with, P. 8, 3, 7, *naś chavy apraśān*, i.e. (*padasya*)[1] *no* (*ru*)[2] *chavy* (*ampare*)[3], *apraśān*.

padasya[1] = *padasyānte*, P. 8, 1, 16; *ru*[2] = the indication of an (unoriginal) final *r* or one of its substitutes such as *visarga*, *s*, &c., P. 8, 3, 1; *ampare*[3], P. 8, 3, 6. The entire sūtra is closely connected with 8, 3, 2 and 4.

Translation: *ru* (i.e. *s* before *t*, *th*, *ṣ* before *ṭ*, *ṭh*, *ś* before *c*, *ch*, see 8, 2, 66; 8, 3, 15 and 34; 8, 4, 40 sq.) is substituted for *n* at the end of a word, when the next word begins with one of the consonants of the *pratyāhāra chav* followed by one of the speech-sounds of the *pratyāhāra am*. At the same time the preceding vowel is nasalized or is followed by an additional *anusvāra*. The rule does not apply to the word *praśān*.

For instance in *bhavān* + *chādayati*, the *ā* of *bhavān* becomes either *āṃ* or *ām̐*, and the *n* is changed into *ś*.

Note I. The technical substitutions of Pāṇini's are evidently no "laws of sound change" in our sense of the word.

Note II. The rule affords again an example of "implied restriction." For *am* in *ampara* contains as a *pratyāhāra* the vowels, the *h*, the semivowels and nasals. But practically speaking[7] the voiceless contact-consonants are only followed by vowels and semi-vowels, the only exception to this being *tman*. On the other hand, if we examine the consonants not included by *am* and which form the *pratyāhāra jhal*, then we see that there is only one case in which a *chav*-consonant is followed by a *jhal*-consonant, namely the word *tsarati*. Thus the rule given by the addition *ampare* amounts to this, that in *bhavān tsarati* the *ā* and *n* remain unchanged. For the rest, since *ampare* is only a supplement taken from the precedent sūtra, we are not quite sure whether Pāṇini himself intended to state this exception.

§13. No disadvantages connected with the removal of *v*.

No difficulties arise from the removal of *v*. For instance, if we want to express that under certain circumstances an aspirate loses its aspiration, we simply say that *jhaṣ* becomes *jaś* and *khav* (or even *khay*) becomes *cay*; for in the latter case the *cav*- (or *cay*-) consonants are eliminated from the *khav*- (or *khay*-) group by "implied restriction." See P. 8, 4, 53 sqq. and 8, 2, 39 for the form in which this principle is applied.

§14. The ingenious pregnancy in Pāṇini's use of the Śiva-Sūtra. First example.

The imperative 2nd pers. sing. of the verbs *lih* and *dviṣ* is *līḍhi* and *dviḍḍhi*. How can we construct these forms with the aid of Pāṇini's grammar?

Note. A modern linguist would explain these forms with the aid of "phonetical laws" and psychical "associative influences,"[8]

[7] For the following see the dictionaries.

[8] See the excursus.

but from Pāṇini we only expect grammatical description in pseudo-mathematical form.

**lih-dhi* > **liḍh-dhi*; P. 8, 2, 31 : *h* > *ḍh*, if *h* is *saṃyogādi*, i.e. the first component of a consonant-group (8, 2, 29), whilst the suffix begins with a *jhal*-consonant (any consonant with the exception of nasal or semivowel), 8, 2, 26;

**liḍh-dhi* > *liḍh-ḍhi*; P. 8, 4, 41 : mūrdhanyizing[9] owing to assimilation;

**liḍh-ḍhi* > *līḍhi*; P. 8, 3, 13: *ḍh* dropped before *ḍh*; 6, 3, 111: *i* > *ī* through the loss of a following *ḍh*.

On the other hand:

**dviṣ-dhi* > **dviḍ-dhi*; P. 8, 4, 53: *jhal*-consonant changed into the nearest related *jaś*-consonant before *jhaś*-consonant;

dviḍ-dhi > *dviḍḍhi*; P. 8, 4, 41 : mūrdhanyizing through assimilation.

(The *ḍ* is preserved before *ḍh*; cf. P. 8, 3, 13.)

§ 15. Second example of pregnancy in Pāṇini's use of the Śiva-Sūtra.

How to build up with the aid of Pāṇini's grammar the flexion of the stem and root *lih*; especially of *-liṭ*, nom. sing.; *-liṭsu*, loc. pl.; *aleṭ*, 2nd pers. sing. imperf.; *lekṣi*, 2nd pers. sing. present.

The nominative *-liṭ* and the 2nd person *aleṭ* follow the same explanation. We start from the theoretical forms **lih-s* and **aleh-s*

**lih-s* > **lih*, and **aleh-s* > **aleh*; P. 6, 1, 68: the flexional *s* is dropped after a consonant;

**lih* > **liḍh*, and **aleh* > **aleḍh*; P. 8, 2, 31 : *h* > *ḍh* "*ante*" = at the end of a word;[10] (8, 2, 32-35 state special rules which do not apply to our case);

**liḍh* > *liḍ*, and **aleḍh* > *aleḍ*; P. 8, 2, 39: *jhalāṃ jaśo 'nte*, a *jhal*-consonant becomes the nearest related *jaś*-consonant at the end of a word;[10]

liḍ remains *liḍ* or > *liṭ*, and *aleḍ* remains *aleḍ* or > *aleṭ*; P. 8, 4, 56: free choice between *jaś*-consonant (a voiced non-aspirate) and *car*-consonant (*car* really means both voiceless non-aspirate and voiceless continuant, but here only voiceless non-aspirate owing to "implied restriction").

We now turn to the construction of the verbal form *lekṣi* and start for that purport from the theoretical form **leh-si*.

**leh-si* > **leḍh-si*; P. 8, 2, 31 : *h* > *ḍh* (cf. *saṃyogādi* 8, 2, 29 and *jhali* 26);

**leḍh-si* > *lekṣi*; P. 8, 2, 41 : *ḍh* > *k* before *s*, and P. 8, 3, 57 and 59: *s* > *ṣ* after *k*.

The construction of the form *liṭsu* is more difficult. One would expect **likṣu* according to the same argumentation as given for the verbal form *lekṣi*. Here the rule of sūtra 8, 2, 41 is annulled by other rules and principles.

P. 1, 4, 14: *sup-tiṅ-antaṃ padam*, a *pada* is that which ends in a declinational or conjugational ending; 17: *sv-ādiṣv asarvanāmasthāne*, the term *pada* is also applied to the nominal stem when it precedes a flexional ending provided no "ending of a strong case" follows; 18: *yaci bham*, the term *bha* is applied to the nominal stem

[9] I leave the term *mūrdhanya* untranslated, although Prof. Lanman has suggested the very near translation "domal" for it; "concave-linguals" would be the best phonetical term; and the conversion of dental into concave-lingual might be called concavation.

[10] A fuller explanation of these sūtras is given below.

before a suffix which begins with *y* or *ac* (= a vowel). The last two of these three sūtras must be explained in agreement with the general principle laid down in P. 1, 4, 1 for the chapters 1, 4 sqq. According to this principle sūtra 18 contains a restriction to sūtra 17. Consequently the sūtras 1, 4, 14; 17 and 18 give an exhaustive classification for the nominal stem-forms into α strong forms or stem-forms before *sarvanāmasthāna* (1, 1, 42-43), β *pada* or weak forms the ending of which begins with *bh* or *s*, and γ "*bha*" or weak forms the ending of which begins with a vowel or *ya* (this last condition refers to the rules for derivation).

The fact that the same term *pada* is applied to a "complete word," i.e. a word with a flexional ending, as well as to the weak nominal stem before a consonantal ending means in Pāṇini's pregnant language that the *pada*-stem follows the same euphonic rules as the "complete word" in the phonetical coherence of the sentence.

Now P. 8, 1, 16 runs *padasya*, which means that up to 8, 3, 54 we must supplement the expression *padasya* to all the sūtras which by their context demand this.

Consequently P. 8, 2, 31 *ho ḍhaḥ* (... *ante ca*) and 8, 2, 39 *jhalāṃ jaśo 'nte* must be understood as *padasyānte*, which expression includes the end of a nominal stem before a consonantal ending: **lih-su* > **liḍh-su* > **liḍsu* > *liṭsu* (cp. P. 8, 4, 55 and 42).

Note. Since Pāṇini does not mention the stem *dviṣ* explicitly, one might think that he has overlooked the declension of the stem *dviṣ*, in which case I have beaten Pāṇini in subtlety. But considering the great care which he has bestowed on the description of the consonantal declension, this is not likely.

§16. The publication on Pāṇini by Hannes Sköld.

When preparing my paper for the Congress of Linguists I had forgotten that Sköld had already published his penetrating studies on Pāṇini (*Papers on Pāṇini and Indian grammar in general*, Lund 1926). In the chapter Facts and conjectures about the Śiva-Sūtras Sköld has treated the same matter as myself, but according to a different method and with a different aim.

Excursus

The forms *dviḍḍhi* and *līḍhi*.

A strictly phonetical development of the imperatives of *dviṣ* and *lih* would have made them similar. For modern comparative linguistics teach us the following series:

IE. **dvis-dhi* → **dvizdhi* → **dviẓdhi* → **dviẓḍhi* → Skr. **dvīḍhi*.

IE. ***liĝh-dhi* → **liĝdhi* → **liždhi* → **liẓḍhi* → Skr. *līḍhi*.

In the transition *ždh* → *ẓḍh* (the 3rd transition of the 2nd series), or in general in the transition from the combination palatal continuant + dental contact-consonant into the combination mūrdhanya continuant + mūrdhanya contact-consonant we have to do with a reciprocal assimilation. In the palatal continuant the tongue is only raised in the middle whilst the point is lowered towards the back of the bottom teeth; in the mūrdhanya continuant both the middle and the point of the tongue are raised whilst the surface between is concave. Under the influence of the following dental stop the palatal continuant is changed into the mūrdhanya continuant, and owing to this mūrdhanya continuant the dental itself is changed into a mūrdhanya stop.

Note. Both the palatal continuant and the mūrdhanya continuant occur in the individual pronunciation of English *sh*. Other examples of the same assimilation: IE. *oḱtou > *ośto- > Skr. aṣṭa-; IE. *viḱto- > Skr. viṣṭa-; IE. *uĝdhi (imperative of √ weḱ) > *uždhi > *uẓḍhi (> Skr. uḍḍhi).

The ẓ originated from ž before dh was transferred by "phonetical analogy" to forms in which ž was followed by bh; thus *ližbhis > *liẓbhis.

A second normal sound change converted z before the voiced stops g, bh, j into d (whilst dj > jj), and ẓ before the voiced stop bh into ḍ; thus *dviẓbhis > dviḍbhis and *liẓbhis > liḍbhis. Dialectically ẓ was converted into ḍ also before the homorganic ḍh; thus *dviẓḍhi > dviḍḍhi, *uẓḍhi > uḍḍhi (cf. J. Wackernagel, *Altindische Grammatik* I, Göttingen 1896, p. 251, § 271).

By a third normal and general sound change z was dropped before d and dh, and ẓ before ḍ and ḍh with simultaneous lengthening of the precedent vowel; thus *liẓḍhi > līḍhi.

To summarize, līḍhi is the regular phonetical form of the universal language, and dviḍḍhi and uḍḍhi are preserved formations of an old dialect (other explanations are given by Wackernagel, I, p. 175 sq., § 149 c and p. 177, § 150 in fine).

19

Kshitish Chandra Chatterji (1896–1961)

A prominent feature of the work of the modern period is the large number of contributions made by Indian scholars. This is only natural; an Indian Sanskritist is in a much better position to study the Indian grammatical tradition than is a Western scholar. The reason that this feature is nevertheless inadequately represented in this volume is that most Indian contributions have been of a rather technical nature. On the one hand, Indian papers often deal with the interpretation of specific rules and are thus beyond the more general scope adopted here. On the other hand, they often presuppose such a high degree of fluency in Sanskrit that they could not be incorporated here without being largely rewritten.

Among early monographs written by Indian scholars, special mention may be made of I. S. Pawate's *The Structure of the Aṣṭādhyāyī* (1935?), a rare work in which the author argues that many rules of Pāṇini's grammar are not by Pāṇini. This line of research was developed much later by Robert Birwé, especially in *Studien zu Adhyāya III der Aṣṭādhyāyī Pāṇinis* (1966).

Kshitish Chandra Chatterji (1896–1961), who studied in Calcutta and taught comparative philology and Sanskrit at Calcutta University for thirty-five years, wrote several papers on the Indian grammarians as well as a monograph, *Technical Terms and Technique of Sanskrit Grammar* (1948), and a lively annotated translation into English of the *Paspaśā* or "Introduction" to Patañjali's *Mahābhāṣya* (second edition 1957). These works are full of valuable information and relate interesting and often amusing traditions among the grammarians. The article reproduced here deals with various criticisms directed at the Sanskrit grammarians by scholars of other schools, in particular the ritualist philosophers of the *Mīmāṃsā* (who themselves had contributed in a very original way to the study of Sanskrit syntax and semantics; see Edgerton 1928, 1929; Staal 1962b). These criticisms had never been the subject of a separate study, though they were not unknown (for example, Kumārila's *sūtravārttikabhāṣyeṣu dṛśyate cāpaśabdanam* 'ungrammatical expressions occur in the rules, the *vārttikās* and the commentary' was quoted by Bühler, see this volume, p. 195, note 1).

Chatterji quotes from several *Mīmāṃsā* sources: the *Mīmāṃsā Sūtra* attributed to Jaimini (abbreviated J.S.), of uncertain date; Śabara's commentary on this *sūtra*, probably written in the fifth century A.D.; Kumārila's *Tantravārttika* (T.V.), of the eighth century; and Pārthasārathi Miśra's *Śāstradīpikā*, of the fourteenth century. He also quotes a logical work, the *Nyāyamañjarī* (N.M.), probably written in the tenth century. The controversies among the grammarians and the logicians have only recently begun to be studied (see Matilal 1966, 1968).

Chatterji quotes rather extensively from his sources and provides free translations, which for that reason are not placed within quotes. In fact, his article consists very largely of such free translations and summaries of the texts. I have omitted most texts quoted in the footnotes, retaining the references, but I have added a number of translations, always in square brackets. "The Critics of Sanskrit Grammar" is reproduced from the *Journal of the Department of Letters, University of Calcutta* 24, 1934, 3.1–21.

The beginning of this article refers to Patañjali's discussion on *śiṣṭa*, where this circularity is also mentioned (see above page 100). The references to incorrect words also echo Patañjali (see above page 97). The final mention of the fact that there are always people who are cleverer than others is a well-known theme in philosophical texts (for example in Śaṅkara, and Bhartṛhari).

The Critics of Sanskrit Grammar (1934)

Kshitish Chandra Chatterji

Pārthasārathi Miśra in his Śāstradīpikā sums up the charges against grammar in the following Kārikā:
nirmūlatvād vigītatvān naiṣphalyād vedabādhanāt/
pūrvaparavirodhāc ca nāsya prāmāṇyasambhavaḥ//

No authority can possibly attach to grammar, for it has nothing authoritative as its basis, because its adherents themselves differ widely in their opinions and cast aspersions on each other, because it serves no useful purpose, because its teachings are in conflict with the Vedas and lastly because it is self-contradictory.

1. Now as regards the first point. We derive all our knowledge of grammar from the writings of the three sages Pāṇini, Kātyāyana and Patañjali whence grammar is described as *trimuni-vyākaraṇam* ['the grammar of the three sages']. But Pāṇini and others are human beings and as such cannot be regarded as free from the four defects — *bhrama* (mistake), *pramāda* (carelessness), *vipralipsā* (desire to deceive) and *karaṇāpāṭava* (defect of the senses). Thus grammar being a product of the human brain must, in order that its authority may be established, be shown to be based on the Vedas, which it is not possible to do. No doubt we find mention of many technicalities of grammar, of *śabda* ['correct expression'] and *apaśabda* ['incorrect expression'] in the Vedas themselves. We find, for instance, such texts as *tasmād brāhmaṇena na mlecchitavai* ['therefore brahmans should not speak barbarously'], *mleccho ha vā eṣa yad apaśabda* ['a barbarism, i.e., an incorrect expression'], *ekaḥ śabdaḥ samyak prayuktaḥ svarge loke kāmadhug bhavati* ['a single expression well pronounced fulfills one's wishes in heaven'], *āhitāgnir apaśabdaṃ prayujya prāyaścittīyāṃ sārasvatīm iṣṭiṃ nirvapet* ['when the Āhitāgni priest uses an incorrect expression he should, for expiation, perform an oblation to Sarasvatī'] *tasmād vyākṛtā vāg udyate* ['therefore speech is manifest'], etc. But these texts refer to the Prātiśākhyas which deal exclusively with Vedic words and accents and have nothing to do with grammar in the sense in which we are considering it here.

Should you say that the science of grammar like the science of medicine is based on the usage of the Śiṣṭas or experts, we must ask you to define clearly what you mean by Śiṣṭa. Do you mean by Śiṣṭa those who use correct words like *go*, etc., or those who use corrupt words like *gāvī*, etc., or those who use both? In the first case the vicious circle is inevitable, for grammar is based on the usage of the Śiṣṭas and Śiṣṭas are those who are versed in grammar. In the second case, it has to be admitted that coachmen and others who use such corrupt words as *gāvī*, etc., are Śiṣṭa and that grammar based on the usage of these coachmen[1] who habitually use corrupt words lays down rules for the formation of correct words —a statement which is self-contradictory.[2] In the third case it is difficult to conceive what useful purpose would be served by grammar which prescribes a heterogeneous mass of correct and corrupt words.

[1] By the same brilliant process of reasoning a philosopher arrived at the following conclusion as to the origin of language: "The first men as yet speechless came together in order to invent speech, and to discuss the most appropriate names that should be given to the perceptions of the senses and the abstractions of the mind."

[2] In the Mahābhāṣya, however, we find the tables turned on the grammarian who discovered an *apaśabda* in the language of his charioteer (ed. Kielhorn, Vol. II, p. 557).

Śiṣṭas such as the authors of the Kalpa-sūtras, Smṛti-texts, Mīmāṃsā and Gṛhya-sūtras have been found to use any number of "incorrect" words. The nom. neut. sing. of *itara* ['other'] is not *itaram* but *itarat* — a form found in such sentences as *samānam itarac chyenena* ['the other similar to a falcon'], yet Maśaka in various places uses such incorrect expressions as *samānam itaraṃ jyotiṣṭomena* ['the other similar to the *jyotiṣṭoma* sacrifice'] and the author (of the Chāndogya-sūtras) himself has said: *samānam itaraṃ gavaikāhikena* ['the other similar to the Gavaika descending node']. According to Pāṇini's rule *svaritañitaḥ kartrabhiprāye kriyāphale* (1.3.72) a root with an indicatory svarita vowel or a root with an indicatory *ñ* takes the Ātmanepada when the benefit of the action accrues to the agent, yet in the text *bahiṣpavamānaiḥ sadasi stuvīran* ['they chant with *Bahiṣpavamāna* praises in the sacrificial hut'] where the nom. to *stuvīran* is three priests and where, consequently, the benefit of the action does not accrue to the agent (the merit arising from the performance of the sacrifice going to the *yajamāna* ['patron of the sacrifice'] and thus where we should expect Parasmaipada as in the sentence *yajanti yājakāḥ* ['the priests sacrifice'] Ātmanepada has been used regardless of grammar. Similarly in the sūtra *pratyasitvā prāyaścittaṃ na juhuyaḥ* ['having sat down in the opposite direction they should not perform the expiation ceremony'] Āśvalāyana has not used *lyap* ['the suffix *-ya*'] in *pratyasitvā* though it is a compound in direct violation of Pāṇini's rule: *samāse 'nañpūrve ktvo lyap* (VII.1.37). In *ājyenākṣiṇo ājya* ['having anointed the eyes with clarified butter'] on the other hand, *lyap* has been used in *ājya* even though it is not a compound. Similarly in his work on Śikṣā, Nārada writes[3] *pratyuṣe brahma cintayet* ['at dawn (*pratyuṣasi*) he should meditate on *brahman*'] where the expression *pratyuṣe* is on a par with words like *gāvī*, etc. Similarly in the line *jñātāraḥ santi mety uktvā* ['having said: they are my witnesses'] (VIII. 56) where we should expect *jñatāraḥ santi ma ity uktvā* Manu has joined *me ity uktvā* into Sandhi regardless of the doctrines of grammar. Similarly in the Mīmāṃsā-sūtra *gavyasya ca tadādiṣu* ['and in cases like that of *gavya*'] (I.1.18) the word *gavya* which can be correctly used only in the sense of *gor vikāraḥ* ['modification of cow'] or *gor avayavaḥ* ['part of cow'] has been used in quite a different sense, *viz.*, *gavām ayana* ['going of cows']. Similarly in the sūtra *dyāvos tatheti cet* ['and if you say it is similar of the two heavens'] (J.S., IX. 3. 18) instead of saying *dyāvāpṛthivyoḥ* ['of heaven and earth'], *dyāvoḥ* has been used against all canons of grammar. Similarly, the author of the Gṛhya-sūtras has made use of the expression *mūrdhany abhijighrāṇam* ['smelling at another's forehead' (as a token of affection)] where he should have said *mūrdhani abhighrāṇam*, the substitute *jighra* (for *ghrā*) being out of place, for Pāṇini in his rule *pāghrādhmā* ... (VII.3.78) distinctly lays down that *jighra* is to be substituted for *ghrā* only before *sārvadhātuka* affixes and *lyuṭ* ['the suffix *-ana*'], as every schoolboy knows, is an *ārdhadhātuka* affix. Even in the Nirukta which is the complement of grammar there are many uses which do not conform to the rules of grammar, such as *brāhmaṇo bruvaṇāt* (Brāhmaṇa is so called because he speaks). While stating the derivative meaning of the word Brāhmaṇa as applied to the frogs in the stanza *saṃvatsaraṃ śaśayānāḥ* ['after lying low for a year ...'], Yāska with a view to show that

[3] In the printed text the reading is *uṣasi brahma cintayet* (II.8.1).

this particular application of the word Brāhmaṇa is due to their habit of speaking, uses the word *bravaṇa* instead of substituting *vac* for *brū* according to Pāṇini's rule *bruvo vaciḥ* (II.4.53) and saying *vacana*. (In the printed texts of the Nirukta, however, we find *brāhmaṇā vratacariṇo'bruvāṇāḥ*.)

There is no end of incorrect words in *itihāsas* and *purāṇas*. We also find words like *ubhābhyam* ['by, for, from both' (for, *ubhābhyām*)], etc., used by the author of works like the Hastiśikṣā.

Vālmīki, for example, uses such an expression as *tad anantaraṃ tubhyaṃ ca rāghavasya ca* ['immediately after that for you and of Rāghava'] and Dvaipāyana such a sentence as *janme janme yad abhyastam* ['what is accumulated in birth in birth'].[4] In sentences like *yugapad ubhābhyāṃ dantābhyāṃ yaḥ prahāraḥ sa ubhābhyaḥ* ['striking with both tusks at the same time is with both (plural)'], etc., words have been used by Pālakāpya, Rājaputra and others regardless of grammar.[5]

Nor can Grammar be held authoritative because it is generally recognised as a *vedāṅga* [auxiliary science to the Veda] for, according to us, it is not *śikṣā* [phonetics], *kalpa* [ritual], etc., that constitute the six Vedāṅgas but the group of six, *viz*., *śruti* [verbal authority], *liṅga* [evidence], etc. Or if this does not satisfy you, if you insist on the generally accepted enumeration of the six Vedāṅgas in which grammar is included, even then we have no objection, but grammar must be held to mean not grammar in general but the grammatical speculations scattered in Vedic literature or the Prātiśākhyas. The text *tasmād brāhmaṇena niṣkāraṇaṃ ṣaḍaṅgo vedo'dhyeyo jñeyaś ca* ['therefore the Veda and its six auxiliaries must be disinterestedly studied and known by a brahman'] may refer to either of these two.

Thus we find the science of grammar is not based on solid granite but on heaps of sand.

2. Now we come to the next point.[6] It is well-known that Sanskrit grammar is based on the sūtras of Pāṇini, the vārttikas[7] of Kātyāyana which explain, criticise and supplement the rules of Pāṇini, and the Bhāṣya of Patañjali which explains the rules of Pāṇini and Kātyāyana and often severely criticises the latter. Of these three Patañjali is regarded as more authoritative than the two other sages, as he, coming much later than they, had an opportunity of observing a much greater number of actual forms.[8] Kaiyaṭa says (on II. 4. 26) *munidvayāc ca bhāṣyakāraḥ pramāṇataram adhikalakṣyadarśitvāt* ['the author of the commentary (i.e. Patañjali) has greater authority than the other two sages because he has observed more linguistic usage']. . . .

Now these three sages often differ from one another. Kātyāyana is openly hostile to Pāṇini. He subjects the rules of Pāṇini to a rigorous test, finds many of them wanting, rejects some of them and suggests supplementary rules to remedy the defects of others. His rules often end with *iti vācyam* or *iti vaktavyam* ['thus it should be said'] meaning that Pāṇini ought to have said this but has not said.

[4] N.M., p. 414.

[5] T.V., p. 259.

[6] For the sake of convenience, the second and fifth points have been taken up together.

[7] *uktānuktaduruktārthavyaktikāri tu vārttikam* ['the vārtikkas explain the meaning of what is said, not said or imperfectly said' (in a *sūtra*)]

[8] Haradatta's Padamañjarī, Benares ed., p. 7.

The Bhāṣyakāra professes the highest regard for Pāṇini, thinks his rules perfection itself, says at the beginning of his treatise: *pramāṇabhūta ācāryo darbhapavitrapāṇiḥ śucāv avakāśe prāṅmukha upaviśya mahatā yatnena sūtraṃ praṇayati sma tatrāśakyaṃ varṇenāpy anarthakena bhavituṃ kiṃ punar iyatā sūtreṇa* ['the competent teacher, having sat down facing East with purifying *darbha* grass in his hand in a pure place, composed the rules with great care — hence it is impossible that a single sound should be without meaning, much less an entire rule'] (ed. Kielhorn, Vol. I, p. 39) and further on (under Pāṇini, VI. 1, 77) —

nitye yaḥ śākalabhāk samāse tad artham etad bhagavāṃś cakāra sāmarthyayogān na hi kiñcid asmin paśyāmi śāstre yad anarthakaṃ syāt

['If the compound is obligatory according to the followers of Śākalya, the preceptor has fixed the appropriate meaning by way of the meaning of the context, for I don't see anything in this treatise which is without meaning']. Yet he takes all sorts of liberties with the rules of Pāṇini, sometimes rejects them wholesale (as the seven rules in the *apādāna* section), sometimes goes out of his way to change them (as in *upasargād anotpara*, VIII, 4, 28, which he changes to *upasargād bahulam*), splits up single rules of Pāṇini into two — one part prescriptive and the other merely illustrative (as in the case of *samānasya cchandasy amūrdhaprabhṛtyudarkeṣu* VI. 3. 84, etc.), sometimes charges Pāṇini with carelessness as when he speaks of the repetition of *tad* in *tad adhīte tad veda* (IV. 2. 59) as *pramādakṛtam ācāryasya* ['a mistake has been made by the preceptor'] and so on, and turns and twists the rules of Pāṇini in all conceivable ways. Sometimes he raises objections which he cannot solve; like the Frankenstein monster they prove too strong for him. Let us take some more concrete examples.

It has been pointed out that in the very first rule of Pāṇini the canons of both grammar and rhetoric have been violated. The rule is *vṛddhir ād aic* meaning *ā*, *ai* and *au* are to be known as *vṛddhi* vowels. Now it is a commonplace of grammar and rhetoric that of the subject and the predicate, since the subject is more or less known to us and the predicate supplies some new information about the subject, it is the subject that is to be placed first, for we always find it easy to pass from the known to the unknown. The violation of this rule constitutes the defect known as *vidheyāvimarśa*.[9] In the rule *vṛddhir ād aic* the predicate *vṛddhi* ought to have been placed after *ād aic*, just as Pāṇini himself says *ad eṅ guṇaḥ*. Patañjali points out the defect and apologises for Pāṇini — *idam ekam ācāryasya maṅgalārthaṃ mṛṣyatām māṅgalika ācāryo mahataḥ śāstraughasya maṅgalārthaṃ vṛddhiśabdam āditaḥ prayuṅkte / maṅgalādīni hi śāstrani prathante vīrapuruṣakāṇi bhavanty āyuṣmat puruṣakāṇi ca, adhyetāraś ca vṛddhiyuktā yathā syuḥ* ['let the preceptor be forgiven for this once on account of auspiciousness. The preceptor, intent on auspiciousness, uses the word *vṛddhi* at the beginning of his great compilation of science for the sake of auspiciousness. For only such works as have auspiciousness at the beginning thrive well and make mankind strong, long-lived, and prosperous'] (ed. Kielhorn, Vol. I, p. 40).

This apology is lame and completely breaks down in the case of the rule *apṛkta ekālpratyayaḥ* (I.2.41) where commentators are

[9] The commentator of the Vyaktiviveka (Trivandrum ed., pp. 15–16) tries to show that there are indications in the writings of Pāṇini, Kātyāyana and Patañjali about many of the rhetorical defects.

forced to admit, the inversion of the order of the subject and predicate merely serves to show that the grammarians do not recognise the defect known as *vidheyāvimarśa*.

The non-mutation of the final palatal into the corresponding guttural is the other defect in this rule. This also Patañjali explains away with the help of a rule applicable only to the Vedas for according to him *chandovat sūtrāṇi bhavanti* ['sūtras are like the Veda'] (ed. Kielhorn, Vol. I, p. 37, 1.4).

Frequently we find sharp differences of opinion among the grammarians themselves on many points.[10] The word *pāṭita* for instance is to be derived with the suffix *ita* according to Pāṇini and *ta* according to Patañjali. From the sūtra *yat tad etebhyaḥ parimāṇe vatup* (V.2.39) it appears that in *tāvān* the affix is *vatup*, but from the vārttika *ḍāvatāv arthavaiśeṣyāt* the suffix appears to be *ḍāvatu*.[11] According to Pāṇini the compound of *nañ* with a substantive is optional, whereas according to Kātyāyana it is obligatory.[12]

Further, according to Patañjali those words are to be regarded as correct the precise meanings of which may be easily ascertained from the practice of experts and which have been in use in these particular senses from time immemorial. And what do we find in Pāṇini?[13] From the beginning to the end his work abounds with words and expressions like *ṭi*, *ghu*, *bha*, etc., which were never in use before his time and which must consequently be regarded as 'apaśabdas.' A strange sight this—the work of an exponent of correct words bristling with incorrect words!

What is stranger still is that Pāṇini himself has violated his own rules at almost every step. Take for instance such a simple rule as *janikartuḥ prakṛtiḥ* (I.4.30). In this rule the word *janikartuḥ* may well be regarded as an instance of the maximum of error in the minimum of space. According to the dictum *ikstipau dhātunirdeśe* (III.3. 198.2) *ik* has been tagged on to *jan* to indicate that the writer is speaking of the root *jan*. The sūtra does not certainly prescribe ablative ending for the producer of the root. The word *jani* has here evidently been used in the sense of "the act of being born" a meaning which it can never have according to the rules of grammar. Further the rule *tṛjakābhyāṃ kartari* (II.2.15) forbids the compounding of an objective genitive with a word ending in the agent suffix *tṛc* or *aka*.[14] Pāṇini has gone out of his way to compound *jani* with *kartuḥ* and thereby violated one of his own rules. He has violated another rule of his, *viz*., *gamahanajanakhanaghasāṃ lopaḥ kṅity anaṅi* (VI.4.98) by not dropping the vowel of the root *jan* and changing *n* into *ñ*.

Then again Pāṇini uses the expression *saṃjñāpramāṇatvāt* (I.2.35) where the *samāsa* in *saṃjñāpramāṇatva* is absolutely indefensible for he himself has forbidden such compounds in his rule *pūraṇaguṇa* ... (II.2.11). In this instance his noble example has been followed even by his commentator and critic Kātyāyana who constantly uses such expressions as *dambherhalgrahaṇasya jātivācakatvāt siddham* (I.2.10.1), *ānyabhāvyaṃ tu kālaśabdavyavāyāt* (I. 1.2.11), etc.

Then again he frames the rules *lakṣaṇahetvoḥ kriyāyāḥ* (III.2.126) and *samudrābhrād ghaḥ* (IV.4.118) in direct violation of

[10] Tantravārttika, Ānandāśrama ed., p. 246

[11] Śabdakaustubha, p. 6.

[12] Śabara on J. S., X. 8. 4.

[13] Sāyaṇa on Taittirīya Saṃhitā, I.1.1.

[14] Another provision of this rule had been violated in *tatprayojako hetuś ca* — Pāṇini, I.4.55.

his own teaching *alpāctaram* (II.2.3), *i.e.*, in a Dvandva compound, a word with a smaller number of vowels is to precede.

Then again he has his rules *samāṃ samāṃ vijāyate* (V.2.12) and *bandhuni bahuvrīhau* (VI.1.14) in direct violation of all known canons of number and gender, for *bandhu* substantive is never neuter and *samā* is always plural. In the rule *grīvābhyo'ṇ* (IV.3.57) it is difficult to understand why he uses the plural number.

Many of his rules are ambiguous — and ambiguity is the one fault a sūtra should not labour under. In the case of his use of the pratyāhāras *aṇ* and *iṇ* we do not know whether he intends the first or the second *ṇ*.

The writings of Kātyāyana are also full of such ungrammatical words as śāsvata, etc.

And Patañjali does not lag behind his two masters in his use of incorrect words and expressions. In *aviravikanyāyena* ['the saying about *avi* and *avika*' — both *avi* and *avika* mean 'goat,' but an expression meaning 'goat's flesh' can be derived from the latter only (i.e., *āvikam*)] grammar requires that the first component of the compound should drop its *vibhakti* ['ending,' i.e., resulting in *avyavikanyāyena*]. In *anyathā kṛtvā coditam anyathā kṛtvā parihāraḥ* ['having done it one way, an injunction, having done it another way an exclusion'] the rule *anyathaivaṃkathamitthaṃsu siddhāprayogaś cet* (III.4.27) requires the addition of *ṇamul* ['the suffix *-am*', i.e., *anyathākāraṃ kṛtvā . . .*]. Then again such expressions as *śivabhāgavata*, *śakyañ cānena śvamāṃsādibhir api kṣut pratihantum* ['it is possible with this with dog-flesh etc. even to trample strike'], etc., clearly violate the fundamental rules of grammar. *Śabdānāṃ śabdapārāyaṇam* ['going over the grammatical expression of the grammatical expressions'] is manifestly tautologous.[15]

Let us now examine in some detail the first few lines of the great commentary of this highest authority on grammar. He begins his book with the sentence *atha śabdānuśāsanam* ['now (begins) the investigation into grammatical expressions']. Critics have taken exception to the compound *śabdānuśāsanam* on the ground that a compound with the objective genitive in such cases is barred by the rule *karmaṇi ca* (II.2.14). He then asks *keṣām śabdānām* ['whose grammatical expressions']? This *śabdānām* cannot refer to the word *śabda* in the compound *śabdānuśāsanam* for the simple reason that it is a subordinate member of a compound.[16] Then again Patañjali's division of words into two classes 'laukika' and 'vaidika' is not correct as most of the words and forms current in the language are common to both Vedic and classical Sanskrit, the only distinction between them consisting in the abandonment by the latter of many superfluous Vedic expressions. Further instead of adducing *gauḥ* ['cow'], *aśvaḥ* ['horse'], *puruṣaḥ* ['man'], *hastī* ['elephant'], etc., as instances of *laukika* words, he should have mentioned some words or grammatical forms which are peculiar to classical Sanskrit and which have been described by ancient grammarians as occurring in the bhāṣā only. As instances of Vedic words Patañjali mentions *śan no devīr abhiṣṭaye* ['peace be the goddess to us, to our aid' (beginning of the Atharvaveda)], etc.— words which are also of frequent occurrence in classical Sanskrit whereas he should have mentioned *gṛbhṇāmi* ['I grasp'], *dattvāya* ['having given'], etc., which are purely Vedic. It cannot be urged,

15 T.V., p. 260 See also N.M., p. 143, 11. 18 ff.

16 T.V., p. 261.

in his defence, that these are sentences, not words, and as such differ in their very nature from classical Sanskrit where the order of words is free, whereas the order of words is fixed and immutable in the Vedas, for, the order of words in popular speech also is fixed in many cases as *indrāgni* ['Indra and Agni'], *pitāputrau* ['father and son'], etc., and secondly grammar lays down rules for words only and has nothing to do with sentences. Then again strictly speaking it is *gāvī*, *goṇī*, etc., that are *laukika śabda*'s and not *go* and it is these words that ought to be explained in grammar, for can you point out a single person who even though versed in the Vedas, even though conversant with the text 'one should use correct words only,' even though devoted to the practice of virtuous conduct, even though of refined intellect, even though averse to the practices prohibited in the Śāstras, even though a Brāhmaṇa learned in the Vedas, uses correct words only?[17] And their examples have been followed by later writers on grammar. Bhaṭṭi wrote an epic poem to illustrate the rules of grammar and the very first word that he composed is grammatically indefensible. In the line *abhūn nṛpo vibudhasakhaḥ parantapaḥ* ['there was a king, a friend of the gods, a destroyer of his enemies'], *abhūt* should have been *babhūva* for the king lived long long ago and was beyond the range of vision of the poet (*rajñaś cirātītatvat, kaveḥ parokṣatvāc ca*). At the beginning of his *Pradīpa* on the *Mahābhāṣya*, Kaiyaṭa writes *bhāṣyābdhiḥ kv atigambhīraḥ* ['the ocean of the commentary is exceedingly deep'] where the epithet *atigambhīraḥ* vitiates the compound *bhāṣyābdhiḥ* for according to the rule *upamitaṃ vyāghrādibhiḥ sāmānyāprayoge* (II.1.56) an object of comparison is compounded with words like *vyāghra*, etc., provided the common quality is not stated in words. Kārttikeya Siddhānta begins his commentary[18] on the Mugdhabodha thus:—

yady aham śrīkārttikeyo mandabuddhis tathāpi ca
pūrvakovidapanthānam avalambyācikīrṣiṣam
dhīrā vaḥ prāñjalir yāce varam ekam padāntataḥ
yadarthaṃ yasya sañcintya tasya kāryā pariṣkriyā

['Now I, Śrī Kārttikeya, slow-witted as I am, wished to follow the path of earlier scholars, I beg you with folded hands, o wise ones, to grant me finally one wish, that the task which I carefully considered for its own sake may be fully accomplished'].

Here *pūrvakovidapanthānam* ought to be °*patham*, for *pathin* at the end of a compound is changed into *patha*, and *vaḥ* in the third line ought to be *yuṣmān* for these enclitics cannot be used at the beginning of a sentence nor immediately after a vocative which begins the sentence. Similarly Bhaṭṭojī while explaining the rule *halo'nantarāḥ saṃyogaḥ* (I.1.7) writes *ajbhir avyavahitāḥ* ['adjoining (to) *aj*', i.e., adjoining vowels]. Here *ajbhiḥ* is a grammatical blunder, it should have been *agbhiḥ*. No doubt *ga* might lead to confusion with the instrumental plural of *ak*. Bhaṭṭojī should therefore have written *svaraiḥ* ['(to) vowels']. As Nāgeśa says: *atra kutvaṃ nyāyam / ata eva hayavasūtre 'aco'kṣu' iti bhāṣyaprayoge kutvaṃ dṛśyate / svarair avyavahitā iti tūcitā vṛttiḥ*. The same remark applies to *ac-sandhi* and *anusvārasyāpy ac-tvāt*.

As a matter of fact some curse seems to be connected with the study of grammar. Just as in our Catuṣpāthīs when students are lectured on the *śuddhitattva* (which prescribes the period of mourning in the case of death of one's kin) some bereavement to

[17] N.M., p. 406.

[18] MS. in the collection of the Asiatic Society of Bengal.

either teacher or pupil is inevitable, just as when lessons are given on the *vyadhikaraṇa* ['difference of locus'] section of Nyāya dealing with *abhāva* ['negation'], some calamity is sure to befall the scholars or their teacher; similarly lessons on grammar are sure to impair the mental efficiency of the teacher and the taught. It has been said:

vṛttiḥ sūtraṃ tilā māṣāḥ kapatrī kodravodanaḥ
ajaḍāya pradātavyaṃ jaḍīkaraṇam uttamam

['glosses, rules, sesame seeds, beans, an evil bird, . . . (?) when this is to be imparted it causes utter stupidity even to a clever person'].

3. As for the utility of the science of Grammar.

Grammar serves no useful purpose for the very simple reason that Pāṇini who may be regarded as the father of this science has not stated any.

In the case of Mīmāṃsā and allied sciences the authors themselves have stated in no ambiguous terms the utility of the study of these particular sciences. It cannot be said that the purpose of the study of grammar is too well-known to be stated, for how can it be well-known when we with all our efforts cannot discover it and when no two men agree on what it is.[19] Of the four ends of human existence—virtue, wealth, love and salvation—not one can be said to be promoted by the study of grammar. Religious merit accrues from the performance of sacrifices, making of gifts, speaking the truth, offering oblations to the fire and so on and we learn about these not from grammar but from Vedic injunctions, from the Smṛtis of Manu, Yājñavalkya and others, from the practice of the pious and from the epics and Purāṇas. It is well-known that economics and politics teach one of the best means of acquiring wealth and not grammar, for we find scholars well-versed in grammar suffering the pangs of poverty throughout their lives. Success in love may be secured by a study of Vātsyāyana's Kāmaśāstra. It is absurd to suppose that a repetition of *tiḍḍhāṇañ*, etc., and a knowledge of the distinction between dental 'n' and cerebral '*ṇ*' will raise a man's worth in the eyes of his beloved. And lastly self-knowledge has been held to be the means of attaining salvation and not grammatical rules. As Śaṅkarācārya says *prāpte sānnihite'tra maraṇe na hi rakṣati ḍukṛñ karaṇe*. When death which is always near us comes, grammatical aphorisms like *ḍukṛñ karaṇe* cannot save us.[20]

Kātyāyana after racking his brains to find out the purposes served by grammar mentions the following:— (*i*) the preservation of the Vedas, (*ii*) *ūha*, (*iii*) *āgama*, (*iv*) simplicity and (*v*) absence of doubt.

i. The preservation of the Vedas. It is not knowledge of grammar but connexion with the preceptor that helps in the preservation of the Vedas. The preceptor gives lessons on the Vedas and as soon as the pupil while repeating the lessons makes the slightest deviation in pronunciation or accentuation, his fellow pupils at once come down upon him and by rebukes, ridicule and repeated instructions make him properly recite the Vedas.[21]

ii. Ūha. In the books dealing with sacrifices all the sacrifices are not treated in detail; one sacrifice of each class is dealt with in detail (this is known as *prakṛti*) and only the variations in the case of the others of that type are mentioned. These are known as *vikṛti*'s. In certain cases, in the *vikṛtiyāga*'s the *vibhakti* ['ending'],

[19] T.V., p. 256. N. M., p. 411.
[20] N.M., p. 411.
[21] T.V., p. 262.

etc. have to be changed. Kātyāyana and Patañjali are of the opinion that one cannot make the necessary changes in the case of the *vikṛti* sacrifices unless he is conversant with grammar. This also is not true. Ūhas may relate to *mantras*, *sāmans* and *saṃskāra* (different modes of purification). Grammar cannot possibly have anything to do with the last variety, and as for the first two, the practice of the *yājñika*'s or those versed in sacrificial lore will be enough to instruct us in the changes to be introduced. So grammar is superfluous.

iii. Vedic Texts. There is the Vedic text *brāhmaṇena niṣkāraṇo dharmaḥ ṣaḍaṅgo vedo'dhyeyo jñeyaś ca* which means a Brāhmaṇa should study *dharma*, *i.e.*, the Veda with the six *aṅgas* or subsidiary studies and understand them and of the six *aṅgas* grammar is the most important.

We have already dealt with the text and shown how *ṣaḍaṅga* here means the group of six—*śruti*, *liṅga*, etc., and how even supposing it to refer to *śikṣā* ['phonetics'], etc., *vyākaraṇa* as included in the group of six refers either to the grammatical speculations in Vedic literature or to the Prātiśākhyas.

It may be pointed out in this connection that it is absurd to say that the text *brāhmaṇena*, etc., shows one of the purposes of the study of the Vedas. It would be more correct to say the text tells of the reason why we should study the Vedas.

iv. Simplicity. It is absurd to speak of grammar as the simplest means of acquiring a knowledge of words when it is common experience that even after years of patient labour one fails to master the science. One feels inclined to suspect that what the Vārttikakāra meant was *gaurava* ['heaviness'] or cumbrous means and has euphemistically used the word *lāghava* ['simplicity'] (by what is known as *viparītalakṣaṇā* ['metaphorical usage of opposites']).[22]

v. Removal of doubts. It has been said that when a doubt arises as to the meaning of certain words and expressions, a knowledge of grammar helps us to take into account the accents, etc., and to determine the correct meaning. This is hardly correct, for it is well-known the various doubts that every sentence gives rise to are dispelled not by grammar but by Mīmāṃsā.[23] Grammar deals with words only, whereas Mīmāṃsā deals with words as well as sentences. When we come across the Vedic text *aktāḥ śarkarā upadadhāti*, *i.e.*, anointed pebbles are to be placed and are in doubt whether the pebbles are to be anointed with ghee or oil, it is Mīmāṃsā that comes to our help and tells us that the subsequent mention of ghee in the *arthavāda* makes it quite clear that in the present case it is ghee that has to be used as the ointment and not oil. And what do the grammarians themselves do when they are in doubt as to the precise meaning of an expression in their precious rules? Do they not rely on the authoritative explanations on the point? What harm is there, therefore, in relying on traditional explanations for determining the meaning of such compounds as *sthūlapṛṣatī* ['coarsely spotted (cow)'; when accentuated differently, 'coarse, spotted cow'], etc.? Where then does grammar come in?

Thus to say that *rakṣā* ['preservation'], etc., are the purposes served by a study of grammar is an insult to the intelligence. We may summarily dismiss the further reasons adduced in support of the study of grammar, for since these principal purposes have

[22] N.M., p. 412. Tantravārttika, pp. 265–66. VI. 1–2.

[23] N.M., p. 412.

failed to establish the utility of grammatical studies, it would be like leaning on a broken reed to expect anything from the subsidiary reasons.[24]

It has been said by Bhartṛhari that the true nature of sounds (words) can only be learnt with the aid of grammar (*tattvāvabodhaḥ śabdānāṃ nāsti vyākaraṇāṭṭate*). This is entirely wrong. What he ought to have said is *tattvāvabodhaḥ śabdānāṃ nāsti śrotrendriyāṭṭate* ['the true nature of words can only be learnt with the aid of the sense of hearing']—(T.V., p. 260).

5. Lastly the rules of grammar are, in many cases, in conflict with the Vedas. To explain the formation of the word *kāleya* [name of a chant in the Sāmaveda] Pāṇini has laid down the rule *kaler ḍhak* (IV.2.8) which means that the affix *ḍhak* is to be added to the word *kali* in the sense of *dṛṣṭaṃ sāma* ['intuited chant']. Similarly *vāmadevya* is formed according to the next rule *vāmadevāḍ ḍyaḍḍyau ca* (IV.2.9), in the sense *vāmadevena dṛṣṭaṃ sāma* ['chant intuited by Vāmadeva']. In the Vedas, however, we find *yad akālayat tat kāleyasya kāleyatvam* ['that which drives forward is the essence of *kāleya*'] from which it is clear that *kāleya* is not derived from the base *kali* but from the causal verb *kāli*. Similarly we find *āpo ṛtviyam ārchaṃs tāsāṃ vāyuḥ pṛṣṭe vyavartata / tato vāmaṃ vasu samabhavat / tan mitrāvaruṇāv apaśyatām tāv abrūtāṃ vāmaṃ vā idaṃ devebhyo'jani tasmād vāmadevyam* ['the waters came in proper time and the wind set on their back. Then Vasu joined the lovely one (*vāma*). Mitra and Varuṇa saw him and they said, verily, this Vāma is born from the gods. Hence (the name) *vāmadevya*'].

Thus we see that the waters in their monthly courses had connection with the air and gave birth to treasure which accrued to the gods. Hence the name *vāmadevya* (*vide Mayūkhamālikā* on Śāstradīpikā, I.3.9). Similarly for the etymology of the word *yūpa*. In the *Uṇādisūtra*'s the word *yūpa* is derived from the root *yu* with the suffix *-p* (*kuyubhyāñ ca* III.27). In the Vedas however it is derived from the root *yup—yad ayopayat tad yūpānāṃ yūpatvam* ['what conceals that is the essence of *yūpa*'s']. And so on.

Now since in all cases of conflict between a *śruti* ['revelation'] and a *smṛti* ['tradition'] it is the *smṛti* that must go to the wall, we must reject grammar. Thus it has been said[25]—Only those who are possessed by the devil, or afraid of the royal rod or cursed by their parents need take pains in the study of grammar.

The Nyāyamañjarī concludes the Mīmāṃsaka's diatribe on grammar with the following words:—

sarvathā durvyavasthitaṃ śabdānuśāsanam / yaś ca vyākhyātṝṇām uktānuktaduruktanirīkṣaṇaprayatno yaś ca vācakamātrāvarṇādhikyamiṣapuraḥ saralakṣaṇaparicodanaprakāro yac cedaṃ vyākhyātṛvacanam 'iha na bhavaty anabhidhānāt' iti, yac ca vyāptisiddhau saralam upāyam apaśyatām ākṛtigaṇavarṇanaṃ yac ca pade pade bahulavacanaṃ tat sutarām apariśuddhim anuśāsanasya darśayatīti / anye tu śobheti cīrṇam iti na yāti pratibhettum iti mātur anuharatīti phalinabarhiṇau dhāsīti kāndiśīka iti bhrājiṣṇur iti gaṇeya iti vareṇḍa iti lakṣyasaṃgrahabahiṣkṛtasmṛtisandehaviparyayapratipādakatvalakṣaṇaskhalitaṃ viplataṃ pāṇinitantraṃ manyamānās tatra mahāntam ākṣepamatāniṣuḥ sa tu sthūlodaraprāya itīha granthagauravabhayān na likhyate / nanu yadi lakṣaṇasya praṇetā pāṇinir na samyag darśayaty atra vivaraṇakārāś ca nātinipuṇaṭṭaśaḥ, kāmam anyaḥ sūcīkṛtabuddhir bhaviṣyati vṛttikārāś ca prauḍhataraṭṭaṣṭayo bhaviṣyanti tebhyaḥ śabdalakṣaṇam aviplutam avabhotsyāmaha iti /

[24] N.M., p. 412.

[25] N.M., p. 418.

naitad asti, teṣām apy abhiyuktatarāḥ kecit prekṣanta eva doṣaṃ teṣām apare teṣām apy apare / tad evam anavasthāprasaṅgān nāsti nirmalam anuśāsanam iti kleśāyaiva vyākaraṇādhyayanamahāvrata-grahaṇam / tathā ca bṛhaspatiḥ — pratipadam aśakyatvāl lakṣaṇasyāpy avyavasthānāt tatrāpi skhalitadarśanād anavasthaprasaṅgāc ca maraṇānto vyādhir vyākaraṇam iti //

The science of grammar is not final by any means. The fact that commentators try to find out what has been said, what has been omitted and what has been wrongly asserted, the fact that faults are found with the rules under the pretext that a word contains more mātrās or more letters than are absolutely necessary, the words of the commentator 'the particular thing prescribed does not take place here because such a word is not in use,' the mention of *ākṛtigaṇa*'s (*i.e.*, lists which are not exhaustive but which have to be supplemented from usage) as no easy way is found for including all words, the use of the word *bahulam* ['variously'] at every step—all this shows clearly and distinctly the utter inadequacy of the science of grammar.

Others have found fault with the science of Pāṇini thinking it to be worthless as it labours under the defects of ambiguity and falsity inasmuch as it does not include within its scope such expressions as *śobhā* ['splendid'], *cīrṇam* ['conduct'], *na yāti pratibhettum*, *mātur anuhārati* ['he resembles his mother'], *phalinabarhiṇau dhāsi*, *kāndiśīka* ['running away'], *bhrājiṣṇu* ['shining'], *gaṇeya* ['calculable'], *vareṇḍa*, etc. That is patent on the surface and so is not discussed here for fear of increasing the bulk of the volume.

Well should you say, 'If Pāṇini, the composer of the rules does not expound properly and if the commentators are also far from being very clear-sighted in these matters, it must be admitted that there will be others whose intellect is as clear as the needle, and the writers of the vṛttis will also be men of clearer insight, from them we shall learn the rules for the formation of words correctly;' that is not possible. People more learned than they find fault with what they say, and these in their turn are subjected to criticism by people more learned and they by others. So since there is thus no finality there can be no instruction of words free from defects and consequently the taking of the great vow of the study of grammar merely brings on distress. As Bṛhaspati says: As it is not possible to lay down rules for every word, as the rules again are not perfect, and as even in them slips and errors are found and consequently there is no finality in the science, grammar is a fatal disease, which baffles the skill of the physician at every step, the symptoms of which again are not permanent, and in the diagnosis of which the physician is apt to make mistakes.

20

Paul Thieme (born 1905)

Paul Thieme, who studied at Göttingen with the German Sanskritist E. Sieg, considers himself connected through *upadeśaparamparā* (uninterrupted tradition of teaching) with Kielhorn (Thieme 1957b, 47). Thieme spent the years from 1933 to 1935 in India, where he studied grammar and was taught in particular by Paṇḍit Kamalākānta Miśra, who was then at Deraganj near Allahabad. Thieme taught Sanskrit at Göttingen, Breslau, Halle, Frankfurt, and Yale (from 1954); at present he is back in Tübingen.

In 1935 he published *Pāṇini and the Veda: Studies in the Early History of Linguistic Science in India*, a rare book printed and published by the Globe Press at Allahabad. With this publication Thieme joined the ranks of the great Pāṇiniya scholars of the past; he also re-embodied the forcefulness and argumentativeness of his predecessors. In his later work, he continued to concentrate on the two areas mentioned in the title of his book, the Sanskrit grammarians and the Veda.

In the same year that *Pāṇini and the Veda* was published in India, there appeared a long study in the *Nachrichten von der Gesellschaft der Wissenschaften zu Göttingen, Philologisch-historische Klasse* (Neue Folge, Bd. 1, Nr. 5, 1935, 171–216), entitled "Bhāṣya zu vārttika 5 zu Pāṇini 1.1.9 und seine einheimische Erklärer. Ein Beitrag zur Geschichte und Würdigung der indischen grammatischen Scholastik." This study, included in this volume, shows how a grammatical discussion on the homorganic status of *ṛ* and *ḷ* was developed by the commentators through the centuries.

The primary issues are whether the rule which is under discussion is adequate to cover the relevant facts of the language and whether it is required, or whether other rules which have already been adopted suffice to account for these facts. Mere descriptive adequacy is not considered enough; the results have to be obtained in the correct manner. Thieme notes how the grammarians' technical use of certain terms captures this difference (*prāpnoti* 'obtains (but) incorrectly,' *sidhyati* 'obtains correctly'). The discussion is carried out in two rounds and made explicit in Thieme's translations. In the first round it takes place between an opponens, a defensor and the *ācārya* who "settles the doubt"; in the second, between the *ācārya* and the *ekadeśin*, who voices new criticisms but who is only partly familiar with the facts. The examples and counter-examples are on a par with such forms as *śvaliḍ ḍhaukate* 'to come near licking like a dog,' to which Bloomfield had taken such exception (see page 270). Thieme notes that even a pandit "wallowing in Sanskrit" would rarely have occasion to say *hotṛkāraḥ* 'the vowel *ḷ* of the Hotṛ priest' or *upalkārīyati* 'he wants in addition an *ḷ*.' But he rightly enlarges upon the relevance of the discussion for grammatical theory.

The discussion starts with Patañjali's *Mahābhāṣya* and culminates in Nāgojībhaṭṭa's *Uddyota* and *Laghuśabdenduśekhara* (LŚŚ), works which constitute the foundation of the so-called new school of grammar in the eighteenth century. Thieme translates the relevant passages of the difficult LŚŚ in full. The intervening stages, representing the old school, are the *Kāśikā* (seventh century), which Thieme describes as a practical but not always consistent manual; Kaiyaṭa's *Pradīpa* (not earlier than the eleventh century), "pedantically meticulous"; Haradatta's *Padamañjarī* and Bhaṭṭojīdīkṣita's *Śabdakaustubha* (seventeenth century), the latter full of artificial anxieties; and Bhaṭṭojidīkṣita's *Siddhāntakaumudī* with its "subtle ingenuity."

A. Bhāṣya zu vārttika 5 zu Pāṇini 1. 1. 9 und seine einheimischen Erklärer (1935)

Paul Thieme

Nachdem Kātyāyana Pāṇini's Definition: *tulyāsyaprayatnaṃ savarṇam* (1. 1. 9) so geändert, beziehungsweise interpretiert hat, daß sich der Sinn ergibt: „Was die gleiche Artikulationsstelle[1]) und die gleiche Artikulationsweise im Munde[2]) wie etwas anderes hat, heißt mit Beziehung auf dieses 'gleichlautig'", fügt er ein Postulat hinzu:
ṛkāraḷkārayoḥ savarṇavidhiḥ (värtt. 5 zu Pāṇ. 1. 1. 9)[3]).

An dieses värtt. schließt Patañjali eine Erörterung, die ich nebst ihren Reflexen in der einheimischen Literatur erläutern möchte, da sie ein typisches Beispiel der Darstellungs- und Argumentationsmethode der indischen Grammatiker liefert, als wie gering immer sich ihr sachliches Interesse herausstellen mag. Sie zerfällt in drei Teile:

I. Paraphrase (*vākyādhyāhāra*) des värtt. und Beispiel (*udāharaṇa*).

II. Diskussion, ob für das värtt. eine 'notwendigmachende Veranlassung' (*prayojana*) besteht.

Die Teilnehmer an der Diskussion nenne ich in der folgenden Übersetzung 'Defensor [des värtt.]' und 'Opponens [des värtt.]', den Verkünder der [Zweifel-]Beschwichtigung (*samādhāna*), 'Ācārya'. Der Ācārya gibt mit dem *samādhāna* eine vollständigere Erklärung des värtt., als sie in I angedeutet ist.

III. Diskussion, ob sich bei der Annahme des *samādhāna*, d. h. des konsequent interpretierten värtt., Fehler (*doṣa*) ergeben.

Ich nenne den Verteidiger des *samādhāna* 'Ācārya', seinen Opponenten, 'Ekadeśin'. Dem Ekadeśin ist nur ein Teil der Wahrheit bekannt, und er befürchtet deshalb, daß Fehler resultieren, wenn man das värtt. anwendet. Er wird schließlich mit einer richtigen Antwort widerlegt, die er selbst auf eine Frage des Ācārya erteilt[4].

[1] Die Artikulationsstellen sind: Hals (*kaṇṭha*), Schlund (*tālu*), Kopf[mitte] (*mūrdhan*), Zähne (*danta*) usw.

[2] Die Artikulationsweisen im Munde: verschlossen (*spṛṣṭa*), halbverschlossen (*īṣatspṛṣṭa*), offen (*vivṛta*), bedeckt (*saṃvṛta*) usw. Die Verschlußlaute sind '*spṛṣṭa*', die Halbvokale '*īṣatspṛṣṭa*', die einfachen Vokale '*vivṛta*', kurzes a '*saṃvṛta*' usw. Vgl. Pat. zu värtt. 3 zu 1. 1. 10 und zu värtt. 10 zu ŚS. 3, 4.

Von diesen 'Artikulationsweisen im Munde' sind zu unterscheiden die außerhalb des Mundes gelegenen, wie Tonhaftig- und Tonlosigkeit, Aspiriert- und Unaspiriertheit usw. Vgl. Pat. zu värtt. 2 zu 1. 1. 9.

[3] „[(Wenn die in den vorhergehenden värtt. geforderte Formulierung von Pāṇ. 1. 1. 9 angenommen wird, dann) muß ausdrücklich gelehrt werden, daß] für 'gleichlautige' Laute gültige Regeln [auch] für *ṛ* und *ḷ* [gültig sind]".

Zur Ausdrucksweise vgl. z. B. värtt. 2 zu ŚS. 3, 4: *plutyādiṣv ajvidhiḥ* „[(Wenn die in värtt. 1 geforderte Hinzufügung von *t* getätigt wird) dann muß ausdrücklich gelehrt werden, daß] für '*ac*' gültige Regeln [auch] für 'plutierte' [Diphthonge] [gültig sind]". — värtt. 13 zu ŚS. 3, 4 *tulyarūpe saṃyoge dvivyañjanavidhiḥ* „[(Wenn Teile eines Lautes durch Nennung des ganzen Lautes nicht mitgenannt werden) dann muß ausdrücklich gelehrt werden, daß] für zwei aufeinanderfolgende Konsonanten gültige Regeln [auch] für eine gleichgestaltige Konsonantengruppe (z. B. *tt*, *kk*) [gültig sind]".

[4] Die Abtrennung von Rede und Gegenrede ergibt sich unzweideutig aus dem Text und ist von der einheimischen Tradition bereits richtig durchgeführt. Daß meine Benennung der Teilnehmer willkürlich ist, habe ich schon angedeutet: Sie dient lediglich praktischen Zwecken.

Übersetzung des Bhāṣya zu vārtt. 5 zu 1. 1. 9.

I. (Paraphrase und Beispiel) ,,Der Name 'gleichlautig' muß für *ṛ* und *ḷ* [ausdrücklich][5] gelehrt werden.
hotṛ + ḷkārah > hotṝkāraḥ.''

II. (Erste Diskussion) Opponens: ,,Was ist die notwendigmachende Veranlassung [für diese spezielle Angabe]''?

Defensor: ,,[Dies muß gelehrt werden,] damit Substitution des langen Vokals [in *hotṝkāraḥ* aus *hotṛ + ḷkāraḥ*] nach *akaḥ savarṇe dīrghaḥ* (Pāṇ. 6. 1. 101)[6] statthabe''. (Erstes Argument.)

Opponens: ,,Dies (i. e. die Substitution des langen Vokals in *hotṝkāraḥ* aus *hotṛ + ḷkāraḥ*) [bildet] nicht eine notwendigmachende Veranlassung. [Denn Kātyāyana (selbst)] wird lehren: '*savarṇadīrghatve ṛti *ṛ*[7] *vāvacanam, ḷti *ḷ*[7] *vāvacanam*[8] (vārtt. 1 und 2 zu 6. 1. 101)''[9]. (Erstes Argument.)

[5] Kaiyaṭa: *ṛkāraḷkārayor iti sthānabhedān na prāpnotīty ārambhaḥ* ,,Dies vārtt. muß speziell unternommen werden, da [für *ṛ* und *ḷ* der Name 'gleichlautig'] sich nicht ergeben würde, insofern sie verschiedene Artikulationsstellen haben''.

ṛ und *ḷ* haben die gleiche Artikulationsweise im Munde: *vivṛta*.

Die Artikulationsstellen jedoch sind beziehentlich 'Kopf[mitte]' (*mūrdhan*) und 'Zähne'.

[6] ,,Nach einem *ak* (*a, i, u, ṛ, ḷ* nebst ihren Längen) vor einem gleichlautigen Laut wird der lange Vokal allein für den vorhergehenden und den folgenden Laut substituiert''.

[7] Ich gebe die hier zitierten Laute durch **ṛ* und **ḷ* wieder, da sie weder mit gewöhnlichem kurzen, noch mit gewöhnlichem langen *ṛ* und *ḷ* identisch sind, wie sich aus der Diskussion des Bhāṣya selbst und auch aus der Behandlung der einheimischen Tradition deutlich ergeben wird.

Trapp, Die ersten fünf Āhnikas des Mahābhāṣyam ins Deutsche übersetzt und erklärt (Leipzig 1933) S. 264 (nebst Anm. 180, 181) hat das nicht bemerkt und folglich die ganze Diskussion nebst Kaiyaṭa mißverstanden. Auch hat er übersehen, daß Kielhorn in den zitierten vārtt. nicht die gewöhnlichen Zeichen für *ṝ* und *ḹ*, sondern eigens geschaffene *akṣara* verwendet.

[8] ,,Zu Pāṇ. 6. 1. 101 muß gelehrt werden, daß vor kurzen *ṛ* entweder **ṛ*, und vor kurzem *ḷ* entweder **ḷ* substituiert wird [oder der 'lange' Vokal]''.

[9] Da *ḷ* niemals ans Ende eines Wortes oder Namens zu stehen kommt, muß sich das zweite vārtt. auf einen Fall wie *hotṛ + ḷkāraḥ* beziehen. Es lehrt demnach die Formen *hot*ḷkāraḥ* und *hotṝkāraḥ* für *hotṛ + ḷkāraḥ* und wir brauchen nicht vārtt. 5 zu 1. 1. 9 um *hotṝkāraḥ* nach 6. 1. 101 zu bilden, wie Defensor (1. Arg.) behauptet hat.

Kaiy.: . . . *tatra ḷvāvacanam ity atra dīrgha ity anuvartate. tatra ḷti *ḷśabde vikalpite 'prāpta eva pakṣe dīrgho bhaviṣyati* ,,In dieser [Hinzufügung Kāty.'s zu 6. 1. 101] gilt in dem Satz 'es muß gelehrt werden, daß entweder **ḷ* substituiert wird' fort: 'der lange Vokal' (aus 6. 1. 101 *akaḥ savarṇe dīrghaḥ*) [sodaß zu ergänzen ist: 'oder der lange Vokal']. Indem also vor kurzem *ḷ* [die Substitution von] **ḷ* als Alternative gegeben ist, wird der 'lange' Vokal beliebig substituiert, obgleich er sich [ohne dies] nicht ergeben würde''.

Zur Entscheidung der Frage, welcher 'lange' Vokal substituiert wird, haben wir uns an Pāṇ. 1. 1. 50 *sthāne 'ntaratamaḥ* ,,im Falle einer Substitution tritt der nächstbenachbarte Laut an Stelle [des Originals]'' zu halten. 'Nächstbenachbart' dem Original *ṛ + ḷ* (in *hotṛ + ḷkāraḥ*) würde entweder ein langes *ṝ* oder ein langes *ḹ* sein. Der letztere Laut fehlt der Sprache. Es kann also nur *ṝ* substituiert werden.

Kaiy.: *sa ca bhavann ḷvarṇasya dīrghābhāvād ṛvarṇasyāntaratamyād dīrgha ṝkāro bhaviṣyati* ,,Wenn nun der 'lange' Vokal substituiert wird, so wird, da ein zu *ḷ* gehöriger 'langer'

Defensor: „[Gut. Du magst recht haben. Die Substitution des 'langen' Vokals (ṝ) in *hotṛ* + *ḷkāraḥ* > *hotṝkāraḥ* ergibt sich aus dem vārtt. zu 6. 1. 101. Sie kann also nicht die notwendig machende Veranlassung für unser vārtt. sein. Aber es ergibt sich eine andere notwendig machende Veranlassung:] Daß diese [alternativische Substitution des 'langen' Vokals (ṝ) und des **ḷ* vor *ḷ*, die durch das vārtt. zu 6. 1. 101 erreicht ist] vor (nach unserm vārtt.) 'gleichlautigem' Laut (i. e. vor *ḷ* nach *ṛ*) statthabe, nicht aber in den folgenden Fällen: *dadhy ḷkāraḥ*, *madhv ḷkāraḥ* (aus *dadhi* + *ḷkāraḥ*, *madhu* + *ḷkāraḥ*, wo *ḷ* dem vorausgehenden Laut unter keinen Umständen 'gleichlautig' ist)[10]. (Zweites Argument.)

Opponens: „Was [Kāty. als] '*savarṇadīrghatve ṛti*' [gelehrt hat], das werde ich als '*ṛtaḥ*' („nach kurzem *ṛ*") lehren[11] (i. e.: ich werde vārtt. 1 zu 6. 1. 101 formulieren: *ṛta *ṛvāvacanam*). Und dann [werde ich lehren] *ḷti* (**ḷvāvacanam*). 'Auch vor *ḷ* wird entweder **ḷ* substituiert [oder der lange Vokal]'. (Das gilt jedoch) nur [unter der Voraussetzung] '*ṛtaḥ*' (nach *ṛ*)[12]". (Zweites Argument.)

Defensor: „Diese [alternativische Substitution des 'langen' Vokals und des **ṛ* bezw. **ḷ* vor *ṛ* und *ḷ*, die in den vārtt. zu 6. 1. 101 gelehrt wird] muß nicht [ausdrücklich] gelehrt werden [wenn

Vokal nicht vorhanden, das 'lange' *ṝ* substituiert werden, da es dem *ṛ* [in *hotṛ* + *ḷkāraḥ*] nächstbenachbart [unter den 'langen' Vokalen] ist".

[10] Kaiy.: . . . *yady avidhāya savarṇasaṃjñāṃ tad ucyate 'gmātrasya ḷti tatkāryaṃ syāt: dadhy ḷkāra iti. tasmād vidheyā savarṇasaṃjñā* „Wenn dieses [vārtt. zu 6. 1. 101] gelehrt wird, ohne daß man den Namen 'gleichlautig' [für *ṛ* und *ḷ*] gelehrt hat, dann würde die durch dieses vārtt. veranlaßte Operation schlechtweg für '*ak*' vor kurzem *ḷ* gelten, z. B. [für *i* + *ḷ* in] *dadhy ḷkāraḥ* etc. Deshalb muß der Name 'gleichlautig' [für *ṛ* und *ḷ*] gelehrt werden".

Trapp meint, der Defensor wolle einem andern Zweck des vārtt. zu 6. 1. 101 angeben. Abgesehen davon, daß die Diskussion sich darum dreht, einen Zweck (eine 'notwendigmachende Veranlassung') für vārtt. 5 zu 1. 1. 9, und nicht für irgend ein anderes vārtt., zu finden, vermag man nicht einzusehen, wie die Veranlassung für das vārtt. zu 6. 1. 101 sein könnte, die von ihm gelehrte Operation auf bestimmte Fälle einzuschränken, ohne daß diese Einschränkung in der Formulierung enthalten wäre.

[11] Nicht 'werde ich *beifügen*' (Trapp), und nicht *ṛtaḥ* gen.: 'für *ṛ*' (Trapp), sondern abl.: 'nach *ṛ*'. Vgl. Śabdakaustubha zu Pāṇ. 1. 1. 9 . . . *ṛty ity apanīya ṛta iti pañcamyantapāṭhenaiva sarvasāmañjasyam* „Alles ist schon in Ordnung, wenn man '*ṛti*' [aus dem vārtt.] entfernt und den Ablativ '*ṛtaḥ*' einsetzt ('liest')".

[12] Kaiy. kommentiert die Form, in der der Opponens die vārtt. zu 6. 1. 101 *akaḥ savarṇe dīrghaḥ* lehrt.

1. *ṛta *ṛvāvacanam* „es muß gelehrt werden, daß nach *ṛ* entweder **ṛ* substituiert wird (oder der 'lange' Vokal)".

Kaiy.: *ṛkārasya ṛkāra eva savarṇa ity ṛty eva bhaviṣyati* „[Die Substitution] wird statthaben nur vor *ṛ* (obgleich das nicht ausdrücklich gelehrt wird), da eben nur *ṛ* einem *ṛ* 'gleichlautig' ist" (i. e. er läßt '*savarṇe*' aus dem sūtra fortgelten).

2. *ḷti *ḷvāvacanam* „es muß gelehrt werden, daß vor *ḷ* entweder **ḷ* substituiert wird (oder der 'lange' Vokal)" „nur nach *ṛ* ('*ṛtaḥ*' gilt fort aus dem ersten vārtt.)".

Kaiy.: *idaṃ cāsavarṇārtham. tena ḷti rūpadvayaṃ siddham* „Und dies [vārtt.] wird für ungleichlautige Laute [gelehrt]" (i. e. er läßt *savarṇe* nicht mehr fortgelten). „Folglich sind die zwei Formen vor *ḷ* (nach *ṛ*) korrekt".

. . . *ṛkāre . . . hotṝkāraḥ, hot*ṛkāra iti rūpadvayam. ḷkāre . . . hotṝkāraḥ, hot*ḷkāra iti rūpadvayam* „Vor *ṛ* (i. e. in *hotṛ* + *ṛkāraḥ*) ergeben sich zwei Formen: *hotṝkāraḥ* und *hot*ṛkāraḥ*, und vor *ḷ* (i.e. in *hotṛ* + *ḷkāraḥ*) ergeben sich zwei Formen: *hotṝkāraḥ* und *hot*ḷkāraḥ*".

unser värtt. gelehrt wird, da die betreffenden Operationen sich in diesem Falle von selbst ergeben][13]. (Drittes Argument).

Opponens: ,, Diese [alternativische Substitution des langen Vokals (*ṝ*) und des **ṛ* und **ḷ*] muß unter allen Umständen (i. e. ob man värtt. 5 zu 1. 1. 9 ablehnt, wie der Opponens, oder annimmt, wie der Defensor) gelehrt werden. [Die Ansicht, daß wir bei Annahme von värtt. 5 zu 1. 1. 9 die värtt. zu 6. 1. 101 streichen können, ist unrichtig.]

,, [Nach 6. 1. 101 wird der 'nächstbenachbarte' 'lange' Vokal substituiert. Nun] wird gelehrt, daß ein '*ac*' genannter Laut je nachdem er die Länge von *u*, *ū* oder *ū*3 hat, 'kurz', 'lang' oder 'plutiert' heißt (1. 2. 27). Und weder **ṛ* noch **ḷ* heißt '*ac*'[14] [kann demnach auch nicht 'lang' heißen, und folglich nicht nach 6. 1. 101 substituiert werden, obgleich es dem Original 'nächstbenachbart' ist]''. (Drittes Argument.)

Defensor: ,,Ich werde [ausdrücklich] lehren,[15] daß **ṛ* und **ḷ* '*ac*' heißen[16]. [Dann kann ich ihre Substitution nach 6. 1. 101 auch ohne värtt. 1, 2 erreichen.]

,, Und zwar muß das unter allen Umständen (*i. e.* ob man die zwei värtt. zu 6. 1. 101 ablehnt, wie der Defensor, oder annimmt, wie der Opponens) gelehrt werden. [Die Ansicht, daß wir **ṛ* und **ḷ* nicht '*ac*' zu nennen brauchen, wenn wir die värtt. zu 6. 1. 101 lehren, ist unrichtig.] [Es muß gelehrt werden,] damit die Substitution des plutierten Vokals statt hat. (Z. B.:) *hotṛ* + *ṛkārah* > *hot*ṛkārah*, (nach Pāṇ. 8. 2. 86 wird gebildet:) '*hotṛ3kāra!*'; *hotṛ* + *ḷkārah* > *hot*ḷkārah*, (nach Pān. 8. 2. 86 wird gebildet:) '*hotl3kāra!*'[17]''. (Viertes Argument.)

[13] Trapp mißversteht den Defensor wiederum. Er meint, es handle sich darum, die vom Opponenten vorgeschlagene Änderung des värtt. zu 6. 1. 101 zurückzuweisen, wobei dann das folgende Argument völlig seinen Sinn verliert. Die Frage ist vielmehr, die Formen *ṝ*, **ṛ*, **ḷ* für *ṛ* + *ṛ* und *ṛ* + *ḷ* mit Hilfe des värtt. 5 zu 1. 1. 9 auch ohne värtt. 1, 2 zu 6. 1. 101 zu erhalten.

Kaiy.: *dvāv apy etau dīrghau *ṛ *ḷ iti. tatra ṛkāre kadācid ṛ iti dīrghaḥ kadācid *ṛ iti. ḷkāre 'pi ṝ *ḷ ity etau bhaviṣyataḥ satyāṃ savarṇasaṃjñāyām iti bhāvaḥ* ,,Die Meinung ist: Diese [in värtt. 1, 2 zu 6. 1. 101 genannten Laute] **ṛ* und **ḷ* sind alle beide 'lang'. Insofern sich das so verhält (*tatra*), wird vor *ṛ* manchmal der 'lange' Vokal *ṝ* und manchmal [der 'lange' Vokal] **ṛ* (als 'nächstbenachbarter' 'langer' Vokal nach 6. 1. 101) substituiert. Und auch vor *ḷ* werden *ṝ* und **ḷ* (nach 6. 1. 101) substituiert, unter Voraussetzung, daß der Name 'gleichlautig' [für *ṛ* und *ḷ*] statt hat (und somit 6. 1. 101 auf *ṛ* + *ḷ* Anwendung finden kann)''.

[14] '*ac*' heißt ein Laut entweder, wenn er in ŚS. 1–4 aufgeführt ist, oder, wenn er einem der dort aufgeführten Laute 'gleichlautig' ist (nach 1. 1. 69).

Es ist demnach klar, daß die Laute, von denen hier die Rede ist, weder mit gewöhnlichem *ṛ* und *ḷ*, die ŚS. 2 tatsächlich aufgeführt sind, identisch, noch ihnen 'gleichlautig' sein können. Das heißt, sie haben entweder andere Artikulationsstellen, oder eine andere 'Artikulationsweise im Munde.' Die Entscheidung dieser Frage behalte ich für später vor, wie auch die Behandlung der Bemerkungen Kaiy.'s die Trapp (Anm. 185 zu S. 265) grausam entstellt hat.

[15] Nicht 'ich behaupte' (Trapp).

[16] Kaiy.: *saty actve dīrghasaṃjñanayor bhaviṣyati* ,,Wenn die beiden [Laute *ṛ und *ḷ] '*ac*' heißen, dann wird der Name 'lang' für sie statt haben.''

[17] Da nach Pāṇ. 1. 2. 27 ebenfalls nur ein '*ac*' den Namen 'plutiert' empfängt, ist die Substitution von überlangem **ṛ* und **ḷ* nach 8. 2. 86 nur unter der Voraussetzung möglich, daß diese überlangen Laute '*ac*' heißen.

Kaiy.: *tvayāpi *ṛvāvacanam *ḷvāvacanam iti bruvatā 'ctvam anayor vaktavyam. anyathā vidhānamātram*

(Hiermit ist die Diskussion abgeschlossen.)

Der Opponens will värtt. 5 zu 1. 1. 9 ablehnen, aber die zwei värtt. zu 6. 1. 101 beibehalten.[18]

Der Defensor will värtt. 5 zu 1. 1. 9 biebehalten, aber die zwei värtt. zu 6. 1. 101 ablehnen.

Beide, Defensor und Opponens, sind gezwungen ausdrücklich zu lehren, daß *ṛ und *ḷ '*ac*' heißen.

Ihre Vorschläge scheinen sich ungefähr die Wage zu halten[19], da värtt. 5 zu 1. 1. 9 (21½ Moren) und die värtt. zu 6. 1. 101 (24 Moren) beinahe gleich 'schwer' (*guru*) sind.)

[Zweifelsfrage (*ākṣepa*):]

,,Was aber ist unter diesen Alternativen (*atra*) besser''?

[Zweifel-Beschwichtigung (*samādhāna*):]

Ācārya: ,,Est ist besser, lediglich den Namen gleichartig [für *ṛ* und *ḷ*] zu lehren [als lediglich die värtt. zu 6. 1. 101].

,,Denn dann ist nicht nur die Substitution des langen Vokals[20] [*ṝ* und *ḹ für *ṛ* + *ḷ*] schon (ohne weiteres värtt.) in korrekter Weise erreicht (nach 6. 1. 101)[21].

,,sondern es wird (dann) außerdem durch Nennung von *ṛ* [in der Grammatik] Nennung von *ḷ* impliziert[22] (nach Pān. 1. 1. 69).

,,[Zum Beispiel:] Nach *ṛty akaḥ* (Pān. 6. 1. 128)[23] [erhält man] *khaṭva ṛśyaḥ* (für *khaṭvā* + *ṛśyaḥ*), *māla ṛśyaḥ* (für *mālā* + *ṛśyaḥ*). [Bei Annahme des värtt. 5 zu 1. 1. 9] ergibt sich auch das folgende in korrekter Weise: *khaṭva ḷkāraḥ*, *māla ḷkāraḥ*.

anayoḥ syāt nāckāryaṃ plutaḥ. sati tv actve tābhyāṃ trimātrayor api sāvarṇyād grahaṇe sati plutasaṃjñā bhaviṣyatīti plutasiddhiḥ ,,Auch du, der du die värtt. zu 6. 1. 101 lehrst, mußt lehren daß *ṛ und *ḷ '*ac*' heißen. Wenn das nicht geschähe, dann würde für sie lediglich statt haben, was gelehrt ist (daß sie nämlich fakultativ für *ṛ* + *ṛ* und *ṛ* + *ḷ* substituiert werden), aber nicht die für ein '*ac*' gültige Operation, nämlich [die Substitution] des 'plutierten' Vokals. Wenn sie jedoch '*ac*' heißen, dann werden sie auch die dreimorigen Laute (*ṛ3 und *ḷ3) einbegreifen, da sie 'gleichlautig' sind (nach 1. 1. 69). [Diese werden also ebenfalls '*ac*' heißen und] folglich wird der Name 'plutiert' [für sie] statt haben, und da der Name 'plutiert' statt hat, ergibt sich in korrekter Weise die Substitution des 'plutierten' Vokals (nach 8. 2. 86)''.

[18] In der Fassung: *ṛta *ṛvāvacanam, ḷti *ḷvāvacanam*. Gegen die Änderung des Wortlauts ist nichts einzuwenden, da sie die Zahl der Moren nicht vermehrt.

[19] Kaiy.: *ekaikasmin saṃhitāyām . . . rūpadvayaṃ sādhyam. taccobhayathā sidhyati . . . iti sāmyam ubhayoḥ pakṣayoḥ* ,,Vor *ṛ* sowohl als vor *ḷ* müssen zwei (Substitutions)formen erreicht werden, wenn Sandhi statt hat. Und diese ergeben sich korrekt auf beiderlei Weise. Deshalb sind die beiden Alternativen im Gleichgewicht''.

[20] Nāg.: *īṣatspṛṣṭavivṛtarūpo dīrgho varṇa ity arthaḥ*. ,,Der Sinn ist: 'Substitution des langen Vokals in der Form '*īṣatspṛṣṭa*' (*ḹ) und '*vivṛta*' (*ṝ)''. Über die Ausdrücke *īṣatspṛṣṭa* und *vivṛta* s. u.

[21] Beachte, daß der Ācārya mit dem Ausdruck *dīrghatvaṃ caiva hi siddhaṃ bhavati* die Behauptung des Defensors (1. Arg.) *akaḥ savarṇe dīrgha iti dīrghatvaṃ yathā syāt*, die bereits im 'Beispiel' (I) angedeutet war, aufnimmt, jedoch in einem weiteren Sinne, indem nunmehr nicht nur *hotṝkāraḥ* (für *hotṛ* + *ḷkāraḥ*) sondern auch *hot*ḹkāraḥ* (für *hotṛ* + *ḷkāraḥ*) 'notwendigmachende Veranlassung' ist.

[22] Hierdurch ergibt sich eine weitere Serie von Veranlassungen, wodurch erst die Schale wirklich zu Gunsten des Defensors sinkt.

[23] ,,Vor kurzem *ṛ* nach einem '*ak*' wird ein einzelner Laut nicht substituiert, aber der 'kurze' Vokal [für etwaiges 'langes' '*ak*'], nach der Lehre des Śākalya''.

„Nach *vā supy Āpiśaleḥ* (Pāṇ. 6. 1. 92)[24] [erhält man] *uparkārīyati* und *upārkārīyati* (für *upa* + *ṛkārīyati*). [Bei Annahme des värtt. 5 zu 1. 1. 9] ergibt sich auch das folgende in korrekter Weise: *upalkārīyati* und *upālkāriyati* (für *upa* + *ḷkārīyati*)".

III. (Zweite Diskussion) Ekadeśin: „Wenn denn durch Nennung von *ṛ* Nennung von *ḷ* impliziert ist (und wir also überall, wo Pāṇ. '*ṛ*' nennt, zu ergänzen haben 'und *ḷ*'), ergibt sich nach *ur aṇ raparaḥ* (Pāṇ. 1. 1. 51)[25] [fälschlich][26], daß auch ein für *ḷ* [substituiertes *a*, *i*, *u*] von *r* gefolgt ist." (Erste Befürchtung.)

Ācārya: „Ich werde [ausdrücklich][27] lehren, daß ein für *ḷ* [substituiertes *a*, *i*, *u*] von *l* gefolgt ist.

„Und zwar muß das unter allen Umständen (i. e. ob das värtt. 5 zu 1. 1. 9 besteht oder nicht) gelehrt werden. [Die Befürchtung, daß die Annahme des värtt. ein falsches Resultat verschulde, ist nichtig.] Wenn *ṛ* und *ḷ* nicht 'gleichlautig' heißen, wird [meine Regel] dazu dienen eine positive Vorschrift aufzustellen[28] (in diesem Falle würde ein Substitut für *ḷ* eben zunächst nur *a*, *i* oder *u* lauten, und es müßte gelehrt werden, daß ein *l* zu folgen hat: *al*, *il*, *ul*), und wenn sie 'gleichlautig' heißen, wird ebendieselbe [Regel] dazu dienen, *r* zu verhindern[29] [in diesem Falle würde ein Substitut für *ḷ* zunächst *ar*, *ir*, *ur* lauten, und es müßte gelehrt werden, daß es nicht so, sondern *al*, *il*, *ul* zu lauten hat)".

Ekadeśin: „[Gut. Da der Ācārya ausdrücklich lehren wird, daß *a*, *i*, *u* als Substitute für *ḷ* von *l* gefolgt werden, ergibt sich bei Annahme unseres värtt. nicht fälschlich nach 1. 1. 51, daß sie von *r* gefolgt sind. Und da der Ācārya gezeigt hat, daß er es, auch wenn unser värtt. nicht gilt, lehren muß, kann ich auch nicht einwenden, daß värtt. 5 zu 1. 1. 9 eine 'Erschwerung' des Wortlauts der grammatischen Regeln bedingt.] Zur folgenden Regel denn: *raṣābhyāṃ no ṇah samānapade* (Pāṇ. 8. 4. 1)[30] ist Nennung von *ṛ* gefordert[31] (värtt. 1 zu 8. 4. 1 *raṣābhyāṃ ṇatva ṛkāragrahaṇam*[32]), um [Substitution von *ṇ* für *n* in] *mātṝṇām*, *pitṝṇām* zu erreichen. Diese [Substitution] ergibt sich (bei Annahme unseres värtt., auf Grund dessen durch Nennung von *ṛ* auch *ḷ* impliziert ist) [fälschlich] auch

[24] „Nach einem Präverb vor einer mit kurzem *ṛ* anlautenden denominativen Verbform wird entweder *vṛddhi* oder *guṇa* allein substituiert, nach der Lehre des Āpiśali".

[25] „Wenn *a*, *i* oder *u* für *ṛ* substituiert werden, sind sie [je] von *r* gefolgt".

[26] *prāpnoti* 'erbigt sich fälschlich' ist im Bhāṣya und der grammatischen Literatur stets das Gegenteil von *sidhyati* 'ergibt sich in korrekter Weise'.

na prāpnoti 'ergibt sich fälschlich nicht', *na sidhyati* 'ergibt sich nicht in korrekter Weise'.

[27] Zu Kaiy.'s Deutung von *vakṣyāmi* s. u.

[28] '*vidhyartham*'. Unrichtig Trapp: 'Zur Regelung der Vorschrift'.

[29] i. e. eine spezielle Ausnahme (*apavāda*) zu einer generellen Vorschrift (*utsarga*) aufzustellen.

Ein '*vidhi*' lehrt eine Operation, die sich fälschlich nicht ergibt; in Sanskrit mag man '*vidhi*' erklären mit '*aprāptavidhānam*'.

Ein '*apavāda*' verhindert eine Operation, die sich fälschlich ergibt; in Sanskrit mag man '*apavāda*' erklären mit '*prāptabādhanam*'.

[30] „Nach *r* und *ṣ* wird für *n*, wenn es sich im gleichen Wort befindet, *ṇ* substituiert" [ob es nun unmittelbar folgt, oder durch einen Vokal, Halbvokal. Guttural, Labial usw. getrennt ist: 8. 4. 2].

[31] '*coditam*' meint stets 'in einem värtt. gefordert'.

[32] „In Pāṇ. 8. 4. 1 muß *ṛ* [ausdrücklich] genannt werden."

im folgenden Fall: '*kḷpyamānaṃ*[33] *paśya*''. (Zweite Befürchtung.)

Ācārya: ,,Nun denn, auch wenn *ṛ* und *ḷ* nicht 'gleichlautig' heißen, warum hat [die Substitution von *ṇ* für *n*] nicht statt im folgenden Fall: *prakḷpyamānam*[34] *paśya*''?

Ekadeśin: ,,Ich werde [ausdrücklich] lehren: 'Wenn [*n* von *r* oder *ṣ*] durch einen Palatal, einen Lingual, einen Dental, ein *l*, ein *śar* (i. e. ein *ś*, ein *ṣ* oder ein *s*) getrennt ist, [wird] *ṇ* nicht [substituiert] (i. e. ich werde Kāty.'s vārtt. 1 zu 8. 4. 2 annehmen, dessen Notwendigkeit trotz vārtt. 2 zu 8. 4. 2 durch vārtt. 3 zu 8. 4. 2 etabliert ist.)

,,Ein anderer sagt: ,,Ich werde [ausdrücklich] lehren:

'[*ṇ* wird] nicht [für *n* substituiert,] wenn es [von *r* oder *ṣ*] durch die drei mittleren Gruppen (Palatale, Linguale, Dentale) oder durch *l*, *ś*, *s* getrennt ist'[35]. (Halbvers).

,,Und außerdem [werde ich lehren] (*ca*!), daß durch Nennung von Lauten Teile von Lauten [ebenfalls] gennant werden[36]. (Ich werde die von Kāty. zu ŚS. 3, 4 behandelte Frage, ob diese Paribhāṣā anzunehmen ist (vārtt. 6–10) oder nicht (vārtt. 11–13), im erstern Sinne entscheiden.)

,,[Dann kann ich erklären:] das *l*, das in *ḷ* (phonetisch = *ələ*) enthalten ist, wird den Grund dafür abgeben, daß [in *prakḷpyamānam*] das Verbot gilt [daß bei Trennung durch *l* nicht *ṇ* für *n* substituiert wird]''.

Ācārya: ,,Wenn das so ist[37] [daß nämlich daß in *ḷ* enthaltene *l* die Substitution von *ṇ* verhindert], dann ist die [im vārtt. 1 zu 8. 4. 1 geforderte] Nennung von *ṛ* in 8. 4. 1 zwecklos. [Da du sagst:] 'Außerdem [werde ich lehren], daß durch Nennung von Lauten Teile von Lauten [ebenfalls] genannt werden', wird das *r*, das in *ṛ* (phonetisch = *ərə*) enthalten ist, den Grund dafür abgeben, daß [in *mātṝṇām* etc.] *ṇ* [für *n*] substituiert wird] [nach der Regel 8. 4. 1,

[33] In diesem Fall ist *n* nur durch einen Labial, Halbvokal und einen weiteren Labial von *ḷ* getrennt. 8. 4. 1 in der von Kāty. geforderten Form würde demnach nach 8. 4. 2. statthaben müssen.

[34] Kaiy.: *prakḷpyamānam iti kṛtyaca iti ṇatvaprasaṅgaḥ* ,,In '*prakḷpyamānam*' ergibt sich eine zu weite Anwendung der Substitution von *ṇ* nach Pāṇ. 8. 4. 29.''

Pāṇ. 8. 4. 29 *kṛty acaḥ* 'Für ein *n* in einem *kṛt*-Suffix, welches auf einen Vokal folgt (in diesem Fall für das *n* von *-māna-*) wird *ṇ* substituiert nach einem *r* [nicht nur wenn es sich im gleichen Wort befindet, sondern auch] nach einem Präverb [mit *r*] (in diesem Falle *pra*)''.

[35] Kaiy.: *pūrvasmād ayaṃ viśeṣaḥ: pūrvatra śarantarbhūto 'pi ṣakāraḥ sākṣāṇṇatvanimittatvād vyavadhāyakatvena nāśrīyate. iha tu tasyānupādānam eva* ,,Der Unterschied [dieser zweiten Formulierung] zur ersten ist der folgende: In der ersten Formulierung wird *ṣ* nicht als eine Trennung konstituierend aufgefaßt, obgleich es in dem Ausdruck *śar* enthalten ist, da es [auf Grund von Pāṇ. 8. 4. 1] direkte Ursache der Substitution von *ṇ* ist. In der zweiten Formulierung ist es gar nicht erst erwähnt.''

In andern Worten: Zwischen den zwei Formulierungen besteht kein sachlicher Unterschied.

[36] Zur näheren Erläuterung s. u.

[37] Es steht nicht fest, ob die angeführte Paribhāṣā wirklich gültig ist. Zu 8. 4. 1 werden deshalb zwei weitere Möglichkeiten erwähnt, mit deren Hilfe vārtt. 1 zu 8. 4. 1 abgelehnt werden kann (vgl. Pat. III p. 452 Z. 15 ff. und Z. 19 f.).

Patañjali nimmt übrigens auch Kāty.'s Vorschlag, Pāṇ. 8. 4. 2 negativ zu formulieren (vārtt. 1 u. 8. 4. 2), nicht an, wie der 'Ekadeśin'. Auch das macht keinen Unterschied, da er durch Interpretationsmanöver dasselbe erreicht, was Kāty. und der 'Ekadeśin'durch Änderung erreichten.

daß nach *r* ein *ṇ* für *n* substituiert wird]. (Da du also värtt. 1 zu 8. 4. 1 nicht zu lehren brauchst, kannst du dein Argument nicht aufrecht erhalten, daß sich bei Annahme von värtt. 5 zu 1. 1. 9 etwas Falsches aus värtt. 1 zu 8. 4. 1 ergibt)".

Aus den übersetzten Diskussionen haben wir gelernt, daß bei Annahme des värtt. 5 zu 1. 1. 9 *ṛkāraḷkārayoḥ savarṇavidhiḥ*, 'erwünschtes (*hotṛ* + *ḷkāraḥ* > *hotṝkāraḥ*, *hot*ḷkāraḥ*; *mālā* + *ḷkāraḥ* > *māla ḷkāraḥ* (neben *mālalkāraḥ*); *upa* + *ḷkārīyati* > *upalkārīyati*, *upālkārīyati*) sich in korrekter Weise ergibt' ('*iṣṭasiddhiḥ*'), und Befürchtungen, bei seiner Annahme ergäben sich Fehler ('*doṣaprāptiḥ*'), nichtig sind.

Vom praktischen Standpunkt aus gesehen ist das 'erwünschte' Resultat gewiß völlig belanglos. Auch ein im Sanskrit schwelgender Paṇḍit hat wohl selten Gelegenheit z. B. von dem 'vokalischen *ḷ* des Hauptpriesters' zu sprechen oder 'sich außerdem ein *ḷ* zu wünschen', und sicherlich wird er nicht das Bedürfnis empfinden, für solche Ausdrücke gleich zwei, alternativ korrekte, Formen von der Grammatik geliefert zu bekommen.

Um so interessanter ist die Erörterung selbst. Sie zeigt die ganze Kunst patanjaleischer Darstellung. In abstraktester Form werden die Gesichtspunkte für und wider gegeneinander ausgespielt, werden uns die verschiedenen Überlegungen in ihren R e s u l t a t e n vorgeführt. Die Ausdrucksweise ist knapp genug, Mißverständnisse des Interpreten entschuldbar zu machen, und doch wieder so genau, daß die falsche Auffassung eines Arguments sich unweigerlich beim nächsten verrät und rächt. Uns lädt sie schließlich noch deshalb zu näherer Betrachtung ein, weil die sprachlichen Tatsachen, um die es sich handelt, leicht zu überblicken sind, und wir uns gänzlich auf die logischen Schwierigkeiten konzentrieren können, die uns auf einer kurzen Wanderung durch die panineische Literatur begleiten werden.

Zunächst haben wir uns klar zu machen, welcher Art die Laute sind, die nach värtt. 1, 2 zu 6. 1. 101 für *ṛ* + *ṛ* und *ṛ* + *ḷ* substituiert werden. Ich habe sie durchgängig mit **ṛ* und **ḷ* umschrieben; in den Ausgaben des Bhāṣya und der Kommentare finden wir sie teils durch spezielle *akṣara* bezeichnet, teils durch gewöhnliches langes *ṝ* und *ḹ*, und, am öftesten, durch gewöhnliches kurzes *ṛ* und *ḷ*, die nur gelegentlich durch diakritische Zeichen markiert sind. Wir werden sehen, daß jedenfalls die Autoren der Prakriyā- und der Siddhāntakaumudī sicherlich selbst kurzes *ṛ* und *ḷ* verwendeten, als sie ihre Werke fixierten.

Was Kātyāyana, der Autor der värtt., sich vorgestellt hat, mag vorsichtigerweise dahingestellt bleiben. Seine Ausdrucksweise ist zu kurz und nicht eindeutig genug, um sichere Schlüsse zuzulassen.

Patañjali's Erörterungen (oben unter II) dagegen zeigen deutlich, wie er die beiden Laute auffaßte, obgleich er es nicht a u s d r ü c k l i c h feststellt. Der 'Defensor' und der 'Opponens' sind sich nämlich darüber einig,

1. daß die beiden Laute nicht '*ac*' heißen, wenn sie nicht ausdrücklich durch Hinzufügung einer Angabe so gennant werden. (Opp. 3 und Def. 4.)

Sie sind also weder in den ŚS. aufgeführt, noch den dort aufgeführten Lauten *ṛ* und *ḷ* 'gleichlautig' (ob. S. 301 Anm. 2).

2. daß sie nur deshalb nicht 'lang' heißen, weil sie nicht '*ac*' heißen. (Opp. 3 und Def. 4.)

Sie sind also nicht 'kurz', sondern 'zweimorig' und heißen 'lang', sobald ihnen der Name '*ac*' zugeteilt wird.

3. daß sie — neben *ṝ* — nach 6. 1. 101 substituiert werden können, sobald sie den Namen 'lang' erhalten, vorausgesetzt, daß värtt. 5 zu 1. 1. 9 gelehrt wird. (Def. 3 und Opp. 4.)

**ṛ* gilt also für ebenso 'nächstbenachbart' zu *ṛ* + *ṛ* wie *ṝ*, und **ḷ* gilt für ebenso 'nächstbenachbart' zu *ṛ* + *ḷ* wie *ṝ*.

Wenn nun **ṛ* einem *ṛ* nicht 'gleichlautig' ist, und gleichzeitig einem *ṛ* + *ṛ* für ebenso 'nächstbenachbart' gilt wie *ṝ*, kann es sich von *ṛ* nur durch die 'Artikulationsweise im Munde' unterscheiden, nicht aber durch die 'Artikulationsstelle'. Im letzteren Fall könnte es nämlich einem *ṛ* + *ṛ* nicht für ebenso 'nächstbenachbart' gelten wie *ṝ*, auf Grund der Paribhāṣā '*yatrānekavidham āntaryaṃ tatra sthānata āntaryaṃ balīyaḥ*'[38].

Ähnliches gilt für **ḷ*: Es kann sich von *ḷ* nur durch die 'Artikulationsweise im Munde' unterscheiden, da es sonst einem *ṛ* + *ḷ* nicht für ebenso 'nächstbenachbart' gelten könnte wie *ṝ*.

Die 'Artikulationsweise im Munde' von *ṛ* und *ḷ* ist 'offen' (*vivṛta*), wie die aller einfachen Vokale außer *a*. Diejenige von **ṛ* und **ḷ* muß, wie wir gesehen haben, verschieden sein. Das nächstliegende ist, sie als 'halbverschlossen' (*īṣatspṛṣṭa*) zu betrachten, wie die Halbvokale (*y*, *v*, *r*, *l*), und anzunehmen, daß Pat. sich etwa das folgende gedacht hat:

In *ṛ* and *ḷ* ist ein halbvokalischer[39] und ein vokalischer Bestandteil[40] hörbar. Wenn nun einmoriges *ṛ* oder *ḷ* gelängt wird, so mag man entweder durch Längung des vokalischon Bestandteils eine 'offene' (*vivṛta*) Länge erhalten (*ṝ*), die im Fall des *ḷ* in der Sprache nicht existiert, oder durch Längung des halbvokalischen Bestandteils eine 'halbverschlossene' (*īṣatspṛṣṭa*) Länge: **ṛ* bzw. **ḷ*.

Diese so gebildeten Laute entsprechen den oben genannten Erfordernissen.

1. Als 'halbverschlossen' sind sie 'offenem' *ṛ* und *ḷ* nach 1. 1. 9 nicht 'gleichlautig';

2. als zweimorig erhalten sie nach 1, 2. 27 den Namen 'lang', sobald sie '*ac*' genannt werden;

3. als von gleicher Artikulationsstelle wie *ṛ* bzw. *ḷ* sind sie ebenso 'nächstbenachbart' zu *ṛ* + *ṛ* bzw. *ṛ* + *ḷ* wie *ṝ*:

1. *ṛ* + *ṛ*, *ṝ*, **ṛ* sind zweimorig und lingual,
2. *ṛ* + *ḷ* ist zweimorig und halb lingual, halb dental,
**ṝ* ist zweimorig und lingual,
**ḷ* ist zweimorig und dental.

Die einheimischen Erklärer

Bevor wir uns dazu wenden, einen kurzen Blick auf die Reflexe der behandelten Bhāṣyastelle in einigen Hauptwerken der panineischen Literatur zu werfen, möchte ich mich über zwei prinzipielle Punkte aussprechen, die im einzelnen an der zur Erörterung stehenden Diskussion zu demonstrieren die eigentliche Absicht dieses Aufsatzes ist. Es handelt sich dabei um nichts Neues, aber um etwas das, wie mich bedünkt, in der Praxis oft vergessen oder vernachlässigt wird, und das auch schon deshalb von Wichtigkeit ist, weil

[38] Vgl. Paribhāṣenduśekhara 13.

[39] Bezeichnet als '*repha*' und '*la*', siehe oben S. 305.

[40] Genannt '*bhakti*', z. B. Pat. zu värtt. 2 zu 8. 4. 1 (III 452 Z. 9).

es an eine Frage rührt, die uns in ähnlicher Weise bei der Erklärung jedes alten indischen Textes entgegentritt: die Frage einer kritischen und gerechten Würdigung der einheimischen 'Tradition.'

Erstlich: Was wir die grammatische 'Tradition' nennen, ist offenbar nicht eine Tradition in dem Sinne, daß in ihr einfach alte, auf Patañjali selbst zurückgehende Erklärungen zugänglich werden, die durch *śiṣyaparaṃparā* sich mündlich fortgeerbt hätten. Eine strikte 'Tradition' besitzen wir in der Überlieferung des Vedatexts seit der Zeit der Redaktoren: Man kann Lieder und sogar Bücher auswendig lernen, und der heilige Text konnte sich völlig unversehrt erhalten ohne andere Hilfe als den mündlichen Unterricht und die übliche chorusmäßige Rezitation, die als korrigierender Faktor nicht unterschätzt werden darf. Gedanken und Inhalte jedoch kann man nicht mechanisch überliefern, wie die traurige Verfassung der einheimischen Vedainterpretation zeigt[41].

'Traditionell' in der einheimischen Grammatiker-Literatur ist lediglich die Methode: Das überaus ernste Bemühen, die Lehren des grammatischen Dreigestirns in der richtigen Weise zu interpretieren, das heißt, durch Anwendung der im Mahābhāṣya selbst entwickelten Prinzipien die korrekten Sprachformen durch korrekt formulierte Regeln zu erhalten. Die außerordentlichen Erfolge der einheimischen Auslegung sind zu danken einmal dem Scharfsinn und der Intelligenz der 'Paṇḍits', zum andern der Bescheidenheit und Geduld, mit der man innerhalb dieser hochentwickelten Gelehrtenkaste sich um eine wirklich gründliche Kenntnis der klassischen Texte vor allem andern bemüht. Unsere 'kritisch-historische' Erklärungsweise verfügt über reichere Fragestellung und vielfältigere Arbeitshypothesen, es pflegt ihr jedoch, von glänzenden Ausnahmen abgesehen, die solide Grundlage zu fehlen, die dem Paṇḍit selbstverständliche Voraussetzung ist, und die leider auch ein Kursus bei einem modernen Śāstrī uns nicht verschaffen kann.

Zweitens: Einem grammatischen Kommentator kommt es meistens nicht auf die einfache Erklärung des Wortsinns an. Er hat seine eigenen Lehrmeinungen, die er entweder denen seiner Vorgänger gegenüberstellt, oder ihnen unterschiebt. Die kritisch-apologetischen Bemühungen Kātyāyana's und Patañjali's finden ihre Fortsetzung in folgenden Jahrhunderten. Kātyāyana's ständige Fragen, ob eine bestimmte Formulierung einer Lehrmeinung unkorrekt, ungenügend oder überflüssig sei, sind nicht verstummt bis auf den heutigen Tag. Er eröffnet den Reigen der nachpanineischen 'Aufsteller gültiger Lehrmeinungen' (*siddhāntasthāpakāḥ*), als dessen wichtigstes und praktisch letztes Glied wir Nāgojībhaṭṭa betrachten dürfen, der heutzutage als der Begründer der 'neuen Schule' (*navyāh*) im Gegensatz zur älteren (*prācīnāḥ*: Kaiyaṭa und Bhaṭṭoji Dīkṣita) gilt.

Die neue Schule nun unterscheidet sich von der älteren in einem wesentlichen Punkt: in der Stellung zu Patañjali. Auch die Vertreter der älteren Schule glauben an seine Autorität. Sie handhaben jedoch seine Methode verhältnismäßig unabhängig, indem sie versuchen, durch Einführung neuer — sozusagen nur im

[41] Daß der durchschnittliche Ṛgvedin, der den gesamten Text in makelloser Reinheit zu rezitieren versteht, nicht im Stande ist, über ein Lied etwas zu sagen, das nicht in der Anukramaṇī steht, kann ich aus persönlicher Erfahrung bezeugen. Man kann von ihm nicht einmal erwarten, daß er mit Sāyaṇa vertraut ist, oder daß er sich in Sanskrit auszudrücken versteht.

Geist patanjaleischer — Kunstgriffe, das Lehrgebäude Pāṇini's auf eigene Faust zu erweitern und veränderten Umständen anzupassen. Nāgojībhaṭṭa geht von der Voraussetzung aus, daß alles zur 'Interpretation' Pāṇini's Notwendige im Bhāṣya vorgebracht ist, daß wir also keine Autorität besitzen, neue Gesichtspunkte einzuführen, oder Sprachformen zu rechtfertigen, die im Bhāṣya nicht erwähnt oder gebraucht sind. Es kommt infolgedessen nur darauf an, die Lehrmeinungen Patañjali's zu erfassen und herauszuarbeiten. Auf diese Aufgabe konzentriert er denn seine ganze Aufmerksamkeit und seinen ganzen Scharfsinn. Es gelingt ihm in der Tat, nicht nur die gesamte Bhāṣya-Interpretation, die bis dahin von Kaiyaṭa beherrscht war, von Grund auf zu reformieren, sondern auch das Lehrgebäude der 'Pāṇinīyāḥ' von zahlreichen 'Ausklügeleien' (*phakkikā*) und manch einer 'gequälten Interpretation' (*kliṣṭaṃ vyākhyānam*) panineischer Regeln zu säubern. In seinen, in der üblichen Weise als Kommentare oder Subkommentare eingekleideten Darstellungen pflegt er nach Auseinandersetzung der Ansicht Kaiyaṭa's oder Bhaṭṭoji Dīkṣita's seine eigene, fast stets schlagend originelle und richtige Auffassung mit der bescheidenen Wendung einzuleiten: *pare tu* ... 'Andere jedoch [sagen]', die von seinen Erklärern treffend paraphrasiert wird: *bhāṣyatattvavidas tu* ... 'Diejenigen jedoch, die die wahre Meinung des Bhāṣya kennen...'

1. Die Kāśikā[42] (Erste Hälfte des 7. Jahrhunderts n. Chr.)
Kāṣ. zu Pāṇ. 1. 1. 9 ... *ṛkāraḷkārayoḥ savarṇasaṃjñā vaktavyā. hotṛ + ḷkāraḥ, hotṝkāraḥ. Ubhayor ṛvarṇasya ca ḷvarṇasya cāntaratamaḥ savarṇo dīrgho nāstīty ṝkāra*[43] *eva dīrgho bhavati.*

Der erste Satz ist identisch mit Patañjali's 'Paraphrase' (I). Da die Kāśikā '*hot*ḷkāraḥ*' hier nicht erwähnt, dürfen wir schließen, daß des Defensors Lehrmeinung (Arg. 3) nicht angenommen ist, das heißt, daß der Verfasser es nicht für richtig hält, diese Form bereits aus värrt. 5 zu 1. 1. 9 abzuleiten und folglich die värrt. zu 6. 1. 101 zu streichen.

Andrerseits befindet er sich im Widerspruch mit dem Opponenten, mit dem er nur darin übereinstimmt, daß die värtt. zu 6. 1. 101 gelehrt werden müssen. Denn der Opponens erhält auch die Form '*hotṝkārah*' aus eben diesen värtt. und lehnt värtt. 5 zu 1. 1. 9 ab (Arg. 1 und 2).

Die Kāśikā fährt fort: „Da für beide, nämlich das *ṛ* und das *ḷ* [in *hotṛ + ḷkārah*] ein 'nächstbenachbarter' 'gleichlautiger' 'langer' [Vokal] nicht vorhanden ist [da ein langes *ḷ* der Sprache fehlt], wird lediglich *ṝ* als 'langer' [Vokal] (nach 6. 1. 101 *akaḥ savarṇe dīrghaḥ*) substituiert". Diese Erklärung der Substitution von *ṝ* in *hotṛ + ḷkāraḥ* > *hotṝkāraḥ* ist im Bhāṣya als offenbar selbstverständlich nicht gegeben. Kaiy. formuliert ähnlich[44]; wir werden sehen, daß man später noch genauer ist.

Kāś. zu Pāṇ. 6. 1. 101 lehrt, wie erwartet, die beiden värtt. und erhält durch sie: *hot*ṛkāraḥ* neben *hotṝkāraḥ* für *hotṛ + ṛkāraḥ* und *hot*ḷkāraḥ* neben *hotṝkāraḥ* für *hotṛ + ḷkāraḥ*.

Dann fährt sie fort: *ṛkāraḷkārayoḥ savarṇavidhir ukto; dīrgha-*

[42] Zitiert nach der Ausgabe von Paṇḍit Bāla Śāstrī, Benares[2] 1898. — Sie ist leider, wie auch die Ausgaben der folgenden von mir zitierten Werke, durchaus nicht frei von Druckfehlern, in denen sich in einer für uns recht lästigen Weise des Paṇḍits souveräne Verachtung des geschriebenen Wortes ausdrückt.

[43] Ausgabe: *ṛkāra*.

[44] S. oben S. 300 Anm. 9.

pakṣe tu samudāyāntaratamasya ḷvarṇasya dīrghasyābhāvād ṝkāra eva kriyate.

,,Es ist gelehrt worden (zu 1. 1. 9), daß ṛ und ḷ 'gleichlautig' heißen. (Daraus ergibt sich, daß *ṛti* und *ḷti* in den värtt. richtig paraphrasiert werden als 'vor einem gleichlautigen ṛ' und 'vor einem gleichlautigen ḷ': Def. Arg. 2.) Senn die Substitution des 'langen' (Vokals) gewählt wird, dann wird lediglich ṝ getätigt, da ein der Summe (ṛ + ḷ) [ebenfalls] nächstbenachbartes 'langes' ḷ nicht vorhanden ist''.

Aus der Ausdrucksweise geht unzweideutig hervor, daß *ṛ und *ḷ nicht für 'lang' gelten. Damit ist jedoch nichts über ihre tatsächliche Dauer ausgesagt. Es bedeutet lediglich, daß der Vorschlag des Def. (Arg. 4), für sie den Namen '*ac*' zu lehren, abgelehnt ist, und zwar offenbar deshalb, weil die Substitution des 'plutierten' Vokals in dem gewiß absurden Satz: 'He, du ḷ des Hauptpriesters', ein verzichtbares Resultat erscheint. Wenn man aber das 4. Argument des Def. nicht annimmt, dann muß man dem Opp. folgen, welcher behauptet, daß die zwei värtt. zu 6. 1. 101 unter allen Umständen zu lehren sind, ob man nun värtt. 5 zu 1. 1. 9 annimmt oder nicht (Arg. 3).

Die Kāśikā stimmt also den Argumenten 2 des Defensors und 3 des Opponenten zu, während sie die Argumente 3 und 4 des Defensors ablehnt, und demnach auch den Siddhānta des Ācārya. Die Begründung können wir ihren knappen Sätzen nicht unmittelbar entnehmen, es ist jedoch offensichtlich, daß praktische Rücksichten der Deutlichkeit und Einfachheit für eine Lösung verantwortlich zu machen sind, die in keiner Weise Patañjali's wirkliche Ansicht wiederspiegelt.

2. Kaiyaṭa[45] (frühstens 11. Jahrhundert n. Ch.) Wir haben Grund anzunehmen, daß in Kaiyaṭa's 'Bhāṣyapradīpa' nicht viel originelle Arbeit steckt. Der Autor selbst versichert, daß er 'traditionsgemäß' erklären will und gibt Bhartṛhari als seine Quelle an[46]. Seine Knappheit und Übersichtlichkeit, und wahrscheinlich auch seine kluge Beschränkung auf einfache und naheliegende Interpretationen haben dem Pradīpa jedoch den Vorrang vor anderen Bhāṣyakommentaren erobert. Auch wir tun gut, Kaiyaṭa als erste Hilfe zum Verständnis vorzugsweise zu behandeln.

Er gibt uns freilich nicht eine einfache Erklärung des Wortsinns, er paraphrasiert nur gelegentlich. Das Bhāṣya ist ja in leichtem Sanskrit abgefaßt, und es kommt verhältnismäßig selten vor, daß wir Wendungen oder Ausdrücke nicht verstehen. Eine einfache Übersetzung der Worte bereitet kaum eine Schwierigkeit. Diese beginnt erst später: Nachdem wir den Wortsinn (*artha*) verstanden haben, müssen wir uns die Meinung (*bhāva*) klar machen, die Motivierungen der Argumente und Behauptungen, die im Bhāṣya kurz und nackt hingesetzt sind. Bei diesem Versuch, das Skelett des Textes mit Leben zu erfüllen, hilft uns Kaiyaṭa mit seinen Deutungen.

Ich habe bereits in den Fußnoten zu meiner Übersetzung alle die Bemerkungen Kaiyaṭa's aufgeführt, die ich für richtig halte, und auch meine eigenen Hinzufügungen durchweg auf ihn gegründet. Der Beweis der Richtigkeit wird durch die Tatsache

[45] Zitiert nach der Ausgabe von Paṇḍit Śivadatta D. Kuddāla: Patañjali's Vyākaraṇa Mahābhāṣya with Kaiyaṭa's Pradīpa, Bombay 1917.

[46] Einleitung Vers 5 und 7. — Zum Verhältnis Kaiyaṭa's und Bhartṛhari's vgl. Kielhorn, Mahābhāṣya II² Preface S. 19, Anm. 1.

geliefert, daß nur unter der Voraussetzung dieser Motivierungen das Bhāṣya einen konsistenten Sinn hat: Nur wenn *ṛ* und *ḷ* verschiedene Artikulationsstellen haben, braucht das värtt. 5 zu 1.1.9 gelehrt zu werden; nur wenn aus 6. 1. 101 der Ausdruck *dīrghaḥ* in den värtt. fortgilt, und nur wenn *ṝ* allein der 'lange' 'nächstbenachbarte' Vokal zu *ṛ* + *ḷ* ist, hat das Argument 1 des Opponens, nur wenn sich ohne värtt. 5 zu 1. 1. 9 als Substitut für *dadhi* + *ḷkāraḥ* etwas Falsches nach värtt. 2 zu 6. 1. 101 ergibt, hat das Argument 2 des Defensors einen Sinn usw.

Aber auch Kaiyaṭa hat nicht darauf verzichtet, Deutungen in seinen Kommentar aufzunehmen, die wir teils ablehnen, teils als nicht notwendigerweise richtig dahingestellt bleiben lassen müssen

1. Der Ācārya (1. Antwort) sagt, daß er ausdrücklich lehren will, daß ein *a*, *i* oder *u* als Substitut für *ḷ* von *l* gefolgt ist. Wir erhalten z. B. für *upa* + *ḷkārīyati* zunächst: *up* + *guṇa* + *kārīyati* (Pāṇ. 6. 1. 92); *guṇa* meint *a*, *e* oder *o* (Pāṇ. 1. 1. 2); als zu wählender Vokal ergibt sich *a* als dem *a* + *ḷ* 'nächstbenachbart' (Pāṇ. 1. 1. 50): *up* + *a* + *kārīyati*; und schließlich soll resultieren: *upalkārīyati*.

Patañjali löst jedoch das Versprechen des Ācārya nicht ein, wie er auch nicht den Namen '*ac*' für **ṛ* und **ḷ* tatsächlich lehrt. Sein Bhāṣya hat eben nur die Aufgabe zu diskutieren, was im Text der Grammatik hinzugefügt oder geändert werden sollte und was nicht: die resultierenden Lehrsätze sind nicht formuliert. Es bleibt Spätern überlassen, die Folgerungen zu ziehen. Bezüglich **ṛ* und **ḷ* einigt man sich denn, wie wir noch sehen werden, sie in den ŚS. aufzuführen, als das kürzeste und beste Mittel zu erreichen, daß sie *ac* heißen.

Bezüglich der Substitute für *ḷ* hilft man sich seit der Kāśikā in der folgenden Weise: Man faßt das *a* in ŚS. 6 (*laṇ*) als nasaliert, d. h. nach 1. 3. 2. als *anubandha*, auf[47] und läßt in der Regel Pāṇ. 1. 1. 51 *ur aṇ raparaḥ* das *ra* mit diesem *anubandha* gebildet sein, sodaß es also die in ŚS. 5 und 6 genannten Laute *r* und *l* einbegreift. Dem betreffenden Substitut wird dann nach 1. 1. 50 beziehentlich *r* oder *l* folgen, je nachdem es für *ṛ* oder *ḷ* steht. Anstatt also 'ausdrücklich zu lehren', interpretiert man mit einem Kunstgriff.

Kaiyaṭa projiziert nun diese künstliche 'Interpretation' ins Bhāṣya. Er erklärt den Ausdruck des Ācārya (1. Antwort) *vakṣyāmi* 'ich werde [ausdrücklich] lehren' mit *vyākhyāsyāmīty arthaḥ* „Der Sinn ist: Ich werde interpretieren", und fährt fort: *rapara ity atra ra iti laṇ iti sakārākāreṇa pratyāhāra āśrīyate. tatrāntaratamyād ṛkārasyāṇ raparaḥ, ḷkārasya laparaḥ* „In dem Ausdruck *raparaḥ* (in Pāṇ. 1. 1. 51) wird '*ra*' [nicht als der Name des Konsonanten *r*, sondern] als ein Sammelausdruck (*pratyāhāra*) aufgefaßt, (der nach 1. 1. 71 gebildet ist) mit dem ebenfalls (als *anubandha*) wirkenden *a* in ŚS. 6 (*laṇ*). Bei dieser Auffassung wird (nach Pāṇ. 1. 1. 51) für *ṛ* ein von *r* gefolgtes, für *ḷ* ein von *l* gefolgtes *a*, *i* oder *u* substituiert." Aber er gerät in die Brüche: bei dieser Interpretation von *vakṣyāmi* wird der folgende Satz des Ācārya logisch unkorrekt: *asatyām savarṇasaṃjñāyāṃ vidhyartham ... bhaviṣyati*, denn die Interpretation von *ra* in 1. 1. 51 als *r* und *l* hilft uns nichts, wenn *ṛ* und *ḷ* nicht 'gleichlautig' heißen, da dann in dem *uḥ* in 1. 1. 51 nur *ṛ* und nicht auch *ḷ* genannt ist. Kaiyaṭa ist also gezwungen gegen das Bhāṣya, das dasselbe (*tad eva*) Mittel für beide Fälle — ob nun värtt. 5 zu 1. 1. 9 aufrecht steht oder nicht — anwenden will, zu behaupten:

[47] Das ist möglich, insofern die Nasalierung eines Vokals in der Aṣṭādhyāyī niemals schriftlich bezeichnet, sondern aus der Interpretation zu folgern ist: *pratijñānunāsikyāḥ Pāṇinīyāḥ*.

asatyāṃ savarṇasaṃjñāyām ur aṇ rapara ity atra ḷkāragrahaṇaṃ kartavyaṃ bhavati ,,Wenn [für _ṛ_ und _ḷ_] der Name 'gleichlautig' nicht [gelehrt] ist, dann muß in Pāṇ. 1. 1. 51 der Ausdruck _ḷ_ hinzugefügt werden[48]''.

2. Die vom Ācārya zitierte Regel 6. 1. 128[49] wird nicht nur so interpretiert, daß man nach ihr beliebig _māla ṛśyaḥ_ etc. statt _mālarśyaḥ_ (nach 6. 1. 87) für _mālā + ṛśyah_, sondern auch so, daß man _hotṛṛśyaḥ_ statt _hotṝśyaḥ_ (und _hot*ṛśyaḥ_) (nach 6. 1. 101) erhält (vgl. värtt. 1 und Bhāṣya zu 6. 1. 128). Wenn nun _hotṛṛkāraḥ_ nach 6. 1. 128 korrekt ist, dann, muß auch _hotṛḷkāraḥ_ korrekt sein: Sofern _ḷ_ und _ṛ_ 'gleichlautig' heißen, nach 6. 1. 128; im andern Fall mag man Pāṇ. 6. 1. 127 in Ansprach nehmen. Kaiyaṭa zu Opponens 2 operiert demnach mit je drei Sandhiformen: _hotṛṛkāraḥ_, _hotṝkāraḥ_, _hot*ṛkāraḥ_ und _hotṛḷkāraḥ_, _hotṝkāraḥ_, _hot*ḷkāraḥ_, und je einer Außersandhiform: _hotṛ ṛkāraḥ_ und _hotṛ ḷkāraḥ_.[50] Nāgojībhaṭṭa gelingt es im Uddyota zu zeigen, daß Kaiyaṭa diesem komplizierten Spiel nicht ganz gewachsen ist und sich in seinen selbstgeschaffenen Schwierigkeiten verfängt (unten S. 320 f.).

Die Kernfrage der ersten Diskussion (II) bildet, wie wir sahen, die Auffassung der Laute _*ṛ_ und _*ḷ_. Kaiyaṭa bemerkt richtig, daß das dritte Argument des Defensors nur einen Sinn hat unter der Voraussetzung, daß er beide Laute für 'lang' und somit ihre Substitution nach 6. 1. 101 für gegeben hält. Der Opponens bekämpft diese Ansicht mit dem Hinweis, daß beide Laute nicht '_ac_' heißen, was wiederum nur einen Sinn hat unter der Voraussetzung, daß sie weder mit gewöhnlichem _ṛ_ und _ḷ_ identisch, noch ihnen 'gleichlautig' sind (o. S. 301 Anm. 2). Deshalb sagt Kaiyaṭa zu Opp. 3: _anye tv īṣatspṛṣṭakaraṇatvād anayor ṛkāraḷkārayośca vivṛtatvāt tābhyām tayor agrahaṇād anactvam āhuḥ_ ,,Andere jedoch [deren Ansicht ich teile] sagen, daß jene beiden (i.e. _*ṛ_ und _*ḷ_) nicht '_ac_' heißen, weil sie von [den in ŚS. 2 als '_ac_' aufgeführten] _ṛ_ und _ḷ_ nicht (nach 1. 1. 69) einbegriffen werden, da ihre Artikulation 'halbverschlossen' ist, _ṛ_ und _ḷ_ jedoch 'offen' sind.''[51]

Wie wir uns weiter bei Ablehnung der värtt. zu 6. 1. 101 und bei Annahme von värtt. 5 zu 1. 1. 9 die Substitution von _ṛ_, bzw. _*ṛ_ und _*ḷ_, nach 6. 1. 101 vorzustellen haben, erörtert er später (zum '_ākṣepa_') in folgender Weise: _dvayor ṛkārayo rephadvayayuktatvād vivṛtatvāc ca kadācid rephadvayayukta *ṛ_[52] _bhavati kadācid vivṛta ṝkāraḥ_[53] _ḷkāre 'pi kadācid ṛkārāntaratama ṝkāraḥ kadācid ḷkārāntaratama *ḷkāraḥ_.[54] ,,Da die zwei _ṛ_-Vokale [in _hotṛ + ṛkāraḥ_] zwei konsonantische _r_ enthalten, und da sie [zu gleicher Zeit] ,offen' sind, wird manchmal das zwei konsonantische _r_ enthaltende _*ṛ_ [als 'nächstbenachbarter' 'langer' Vokal], und manchmal 'offenes' _ṝ_ [als 'nächstbenachbarter' 'langer' Vokal] (nach 6. 1. 101) substituiert. Und auch wenn _ḷ_ folgt [in _hotṛ + ḷkāraḥ_], wird manchmal das dem _ṛ_ [von _hotṛ_] 'nächstbenachbarte' _ṝ_, manchmal

[48] Die korrekte Interpretation der Bhāṣyastelle erst bei Nāgojībhaṭṭa, siehe unten S. 320.

[49] Oben S. 303.

[50] Die Tendenz, mit fakultativer Regeln möglischst viele Sandhiformen zu gewinnen, wächst seit Patañjali. Den Rekord hält wohl Bhaṭṭoji Dīkṣita, der sich in der Siddhāntakaumudī zu 8. 3. 34 gleich 108 verschiedene Aussprachemöglichkeiten für das Wort _saṃskartā_ ausrechnet!

[51] Trapp übersetzt (Anm. 185): 'weil ṛ und ḷ zugleich leicht berührt und offen gesprochen werden und wegen dieser beiden sich widersprechenden Eigenschaften nicht als Vokale erfaßt werden können'. (sic!)

[52] Ausgabe: _ṛ_.

[53] Ausgabe: _ṛkāraḥ_.

[54] Ausgabe: _ḷkāraḥ_.

das dem ḷ [von ḷkaraḥ] 'nächstbenachbarte' *ḷ [als 'langer' Vokal] (nach 6. 1. 101) [substituiert]."

Kaiyaṭa gibt also dieselbe Deutung, zu der wir oben[55] unsere Zuflucht nahmen: Nur wenn ṝ als 'offen,' *ṛ und *ḷ jedoch als 'halbverschlossen' gilt, hat die Argumentation des Bhāṣya einen Sinn. Kaiy. ist nur etwas genauer in der Bestimmung der Laute *ṛ und *ḷ, als wir es zu sein wagten: Wir begnügten uns mit der Annahme, die Längung von ṛ und ḷ zu *ṛ und *ḷ sei erreicht durch Längung des in ṛ und ḷ enthaltenen konsonantischen Bestandteils. Kaiyaṭa rechnet aus: In ṛ ist ein konsonantisches r = ½ Mora, und in ḷ ein konsonantisches l = ½ Mora enthalten. Da ein 'kurzer' Vokal (nach 1. 2. 27) eine Mora beträgt, bleibt je ½ Mora für den vokalischen Bestandteil. In *ṛ und *ḷ dagegen sind, nach seiner Meinung, bezeihentlich zwei konsonatische r = 1 Mora, und zwei konsonantische l = 1 Mora enthalten, sodaß eine Mora für den vokalischen Bestandteil bleibt.

Wenn sich demnach Kaiy.'s Erklärung im wesentlichen mit der unsern deckt, so fragt sich, ob er oder seine Quelle sie auf demselben Wege erreicht, das heißt, ob er sie ebenfalls durch Interpretation erschlossen hat, oder ob sie sich auf mündliche Tradition gründet, in dem Sinne, daß die Aussprache, die Patañjali selbst für *ṛ und *ḷ im Unterricht verwendete, durch *śiṣyaparaṃparā* noch bekannt gewesen wäre. Auch abgesehen davon, daß es sich offensichtlich mehr um eine theoretische als um eine praktische Eigentümlichkeit handelt, können wir unumwunden die erste Alternative bejahen.

Kaiyaṭa kennt nämlich auch eine andere Ansicht. Ihre Vertreter erklären, daß *ṛ und *ḷ deshalb nicht '*ac*' heißen, weil sie zwei und eine halbe Mora betragen.[56] Sie haben also die Auffassung von *ṛ und *ḷ als 'halbverschlossen' entweder nicht gekannt oder nicht geteilt: *ardhatṛtīyamātratvād iti kecid āhuḥ* „Manche sagen [daß *ṛ und *ḷ nicht '*ac*' heißen], weil sie [je] 2½ Moren betragen". Nach Pāṇ. 1. 2. 27 hat nun ein '*ac*' entweder ein (*u*), oder zwei (*ū*), oder drei (*ū*3) Moren.

Die zitierten Gelehrten müssen also die Längen des ṛ etwa in der folgenden Weise analysiert haben:

ṛ + ṛ (= 1½ə + ½ r + 1½ ə + ½ r) = ṝ(3ə + 1 r) = 2 Moren
ṛ + ṛ (= 2ə + ½ r + 2ə + ½ r) = *ṛ(4ə + 1r) = 2½ Moren.

Kaiy. zeigt nun, daß diese Deutung des Satzes: *na ca ṛkāra ḷkāro vāj asti*, falsch ist, da sie sich späterhin in der Interpretation nicht bewährt. Er sagt nichts über eine tatsächliche, feststehende Aussprache, der sie zuwiderliefe:

saty actve dīrghasaṃjñānayor bhaviṣyati. yeṣāṃ tu matam ardhatṛtīyamātrāv etāv iti teṣāṃ mate saty apy actve dvimātratvābhāvād etayor dīrghasaṃjñā na prāpnoti. tasmād dvimātrāv etāv abhyupagantavyau „[Er (i.e. der Defensor) sagt: 'Ich werde lehren, daß *ṛ und *ḷ '*ac*' heißen', indem er voraussetzt:] Wenn *ṛ und *ḷ '*ac*' heißen, dann werden sie den Namen 'lang' (nach 1. 2. 27) empfan-

[55] S. 307.

[56] Nach Trapp (Anm. 185) werden gewöhnliches ṛ und ḷ von einigen Grammatikern als 'zweieinhalbzeitig' angesehen! — In derselben Anmerkung bemerkt er, daß eine Vorschrift, die nur von einigen Grammatikern vertreten wird, immer wahlfrei sei. Wir werden sehen, daß die Ansicht, *ṛ und *ḷ seien zweieinahlbzeitig, von Kaiy. unzweideutig abgelehnt wird. Es handelt sich eben gar nicht um eine 'Vorschrift', sondern um eine 'Ansicht'. Falsche Ansichten jedoch werden auch in Indien bekämpft und abgewiesen: sie gelten nicht als fakultativ ebenfalls richtig.

gen [und demnach nach 6. 1. 101 substituiert werden]. — Diejenigen jedoch, die da annehmen, daß *ṛ und *ḷ je zwei und eine halbe Mora enthalten, müssen annehmen, daß, auch wenn *ṛ und *ḷ '*ac*' heißen, der Name 'lang' sich für sie nicht ergibt, da sie nicht zwei Moren [sondern zwei und eine halbe] enthalten (und demnach 1. 2. 27 nicht Anwendung finden kann). Deshalb müssen *ṛ und *ḷ als zweimorig angesehen werden."

Wie ich an diesem Beispiel vor allem zeigen wollte, ist also Kaiyaṭa's 'Lampe' zur Aufhellung der Meinung des Bhāṣya auch für uns von unschätzbarem Wert. Nicht jedoch, weil seine Deutungen auf alte Tradition zurückgehen, sondern vielmehr, weil sie auf wohlerwogenen Gründen der Interpretation beruhen, deren Gewicht wir nachzuprüfen durchaus imstande sind, wenn wir in der Grammatik und im Bhāṣya selbst genügend Bescheid wissen. Wir dürfen natürlich seine Deutungen verwerfen, wie zum Beispiel seine Erläuterung zu *vakṣyāmi* (oben S. 311), falls wir nämlich nachweisen können, daß sie keine Wurzel im Bhāṣya haben. Wir dürfen uns jedoch nicht übermütig über sie hinwegsetzen, oder gar unterlassen, sie überhaupt erst zu verstehen. Sonst laufen wir Gefahr, aufs neue mißzudeuten, was indische Gelehrte bereits vor Jahrhunderten richtig herausgefunden haben, und Übersetzungen zu liefern, deren wir uns vor dem durchschnittlichsten Vyākaraṇa-Śāstrī zu schämen hätten.

3. Haradatta's Padamañjarī[57] (später als Kaiyaṭa) und Bhaṭṭoji Dīkṣita's Śabdakaustubha[58] (17. Jahrhundert) In der Padamañjarī zu Kāś. zu Pāṇ. 1. 1. 9 (p. 55 ff.) am Ende (p. 58 f.) gibt Haradatta zunächst eine Erklärung des Siddhānta der Kāśikā. Er ist dabei, wie es übrigens schon Jinendrabuddhi war, genauer in der Motivierung der Substitution des langen ṝ, als Kaiyaṭa und die Kāśikā: „Der Sinn des Satzes der Kāśikā '*ubhayoḥ*' usw. ist: Da für beide (*ṛ* + *ḷ*) [zusammen] ein 'nächstbenachbarter' 'langer' Vokal nicht existiert,[59] und da auch für *ḷ* ein 'nächstbenachbarter' 'langer' Vokal nicht existiert, wird für beide lediglich *ṝ* (nach 6. 1. 101) substituiert".

Dann geht er dazu über, eine Paraphrase des Bhāṣya zu vārtt. 5 zu geben. Den Wert solcher Paraphrasen in der Padamañjarī hat schon Kielhorn betont.[60] Sie ergänzen Kaiyaṭa in vorzüglicher Weise. Während Kaiy. in seinem Kommentar gewissermaßen nur Antworten auf unausgesprochene Fragen gibt, die man zum Text des Bhāṣya stellen kann, gibt Haradatta eine zusammenhängende, knappe aber übersichtliche Darstellung der Diskussionen. Er benutzt Kaiyaṭa, mit dem er teilweise wörtlich übereinstimmt, sucht ihn jedoch in logischer Schärfe zu übertreffen.

So fügt er zu Kaiy.'s Deutung, daß *ṛ und *ḷ 'halbverschlossene' 'zweimorige' Laute seien, welche zwei konsonantische *r* bezw. *l* enthalten, eine noch genauere Angabe über ihre tatsächliche Konstitution hinzu: *madhye dvau rephau* (bezw.: *lakārau*), *tayor ekā mātrā. abhito 'jbhakter aparā* „In der Mitte von *ṛ (bezw. *ḷ) befinden sich zwei konsonantische *r* (bezw. *l*), welche eine Mora

[57] Zitiert nach der Ausgabe von Bhāradvāja Damodara Śāstrī (Reprint from Pandit), Benares 1898.

[58] Zitiert nach der Ausgabe von Rāma Kṛṣṇa Śāstrī, Benares 1898.

[59] Vgl. vārtt. 18 zu 1. 1. 50 und Bhāṣya: *ubhayor yo 'ntaratamas tena bhavitavyam.*

[60] Mahābhāṣya II² p. 11 f. — Trapp hat zu seinem Schaden auf diese Hilfe gänzlich verzichtet.

ausmachen ($\frac{1}{2}$ Mora + $\frac{1}{2}$ Mora = 1 Mora). Die vokalische Partikel auf beiden Seiten [des *rr* bezw. *ll*] macht eine Mora aus."[61] Wir können also umschreiben: **ṛ* = *ərrə*, **ḷ* = *əllə*.

Wie Kaiyaṭa das Argument 1 des Opponens versteht, wird nach dessen Ansicht '*dīrghaḥ*' aus 6. 1. 101 in värtt. 2 zu 6. 1. 101 fortgelten, und deshalb beliebig auch der 'lange' Laut *ṝ* in *hotṛ* + *ḷkāraḥ* substituiert. Haradatta macht sich Sorge, wieso sich das notwendigerweise ergibt, und beschwichtigt sie mit der Annahme, daß in *ḷti *ḷvāvacanam* der Ausdruck '*vā*' im Sinne der Hinzufügung[62] stehe, d. h. 'und' bedeute.[63]

Rühmt sich Haradatta im Eingang seines Kommentars 'von dem Mangobaum[64] der Grammatik die Blütendolde der (richtigen) Worte gepflückt zu haben' (V. 4), so hat Bhaṭṭoji Dīkṣita im Śabdakaustubha vor 'das Kaustubhajuwel des (richtigen) Wortes aus dem Ozean des von der Schlange[65] verkündeten Bhāṣya herauszuholen [wie die Götter den Kaustubha aus dem gequirlten Ozean]' (V. 3). Zuvor erweist er seine Ehrerbietung dem grammatischen Dreigestirn: Pāṇini, Kātyāyana und Patañjali, und den Auf- oder Feststellern der gültigen Lehrmeinungen (*siddhāntasthāpakāḥ*) Bhartṛhari usw. (V. 2).[66] Den Sinn, den man nur mühevoll und durch Bewältigung vieler Werke erhalten kann, sollen sich die 'Guten' restlos und ohne Mühe aus seinem Buch aneignen (V. 4).

Der Dīkṣita hat also nicht die Absicht, die Interpretation eines alten Werkes zu erleichtern, sondern vielmehr die, es zu ersetzen, und zwar durch Darstellung und Untersuchung der Lehrmeinungen nicht nur des ursprünglichen Verfassers, sondern auch anderer, folgender '*siddhāntasthāpakāḥ*.' Der 'Sinn,' den man sich aneignen soll, ist nicht einfach das Verständnis des Bhāṣya sondern der endgültige Sinn aller bisher geleisteten grammatischen Arbeit: Die Bildung der korrekten Wortformen auf Grund korrekt formulierter Regeln. Der bekannte auf Haradatta's Werk gemünzte Nyāya[67] gilt auch für den Śabdakaustubha.

Die Erklärung des värtt. 5 zu 1. 1. 9 im Śabdakaustubha (S. 151 ff.) ist also zu verstehen als eine Widergabe nicht nur der Erörterung Patañjali's, sondern auch der Feststellungen Kaiyaṭa's und Haradatta's, mit denen sie oft wörtlich übereinstimmt, und die

[61] Daß man auch diese Ansicht im Bhāṣya begründen kann, zeigt Nāgojībhaṭṭa, siehe unten.

[62] Auf Grund von Nirukta 1. 4 *veti vicāraṇārthe ... athāpi samuccayārthe bhavati*, ist eine entsprechende Angabe in die Kośa aufgenommen.

[63] *tatra ḷti *ḷvāvacanam ity atra vāśabdo dīrghasya samuccayārthas. tenāprāpta eva dīrgho bhaviṣyati* „In diesen värtt. steht nun das Wort '*vā*' in värtt. 2 um die Hinzufügung von '*dīrghaḥ*' zu erreichen. Deshalb wird der 'lange' Vokal (*ṝ*) [für *ṛ* + *ḷ*] substituiert werden, obgleich er sich [fälschlich] nicht (nach 6. 1. 101) ergibt (insofern *ṛ* und *ḷ* nach meiner Meinung nicht 'gleichlautig' heißen)".

Die Ausgabe liest statt *ḷti *ḷvāvacanam* : *ṛti *ṛvāvacanam*, was nicht richtig sein kann, da der 'lange' Vokal (*ṝ*) sich als Substitut für *ṛ* + *ṛ* korrekt nach 6. 1. 101 ergibt, ob man nun *ṛ* und *ḷ* als 'gleichlautig' betrachtet oder nicht.

[64] *sahakārapādapāt*: Der Sahakāra ist eine besonders süß duftende Abart des gewöhnlichen Āmra.

[65] Patañjali wird gern als Schlange (*sarpa, phaṇin, nāga, śeṣa*) vorgestellt.

[66] Vgl. die ähnliche Gegenüberstellung von *munitraya* und *vaiyākaraṇasiddhānta* im Einleitungsvers der Siddhāntakaumudī.

[67] Siehe G. A. Jacob, Laukikanyāyāñjali III² (Bombay 1911), S. 7: *Anadhīte Mahābhāṣye vyarthā syāt Padamañjarī, adhīte 'pi Mahābhāṣye vyarthā sā Padamañjarī*.

sie völlig ausbeutet, jedoch ihrerseits in Genauigkeit und logischer Schärfe übertrifft.

Kaiyaṭa's Bemerkung zu Opp. 2, daß nach dessen Ansicht im värtt. 1 zu 6. 1. 101 *'savarṇe'* aus 6. 1. 101 fortgelte, während värtt. 2 *'asavarṇārtham'* gegeben sei (o. S. 301 Anm. 12), wird mit einem negativen Beleg (*pratyudāharaṇa*) gerechtfertigt: *dhātṛ* + *aṃśaḥ* ergibt nur *dhātraṃśaḥ* nach 6. 1. 77.

Seit Def. 3 wird gefordert (außer von der Kāśikā, s. o. S. 310), daß für **ṛ* und **ḷ* der Name *'ac'* gelehrt werden muß, damit sie (nach 1. 2. 27) 'lang' heißen können, und damit Substitution des plutierten Vokals (nach 8. 2. 86) für sie statthabe, insofern der Name 'plutiert' (nach 1. 2. 27) nur einem *'ac'* gegeben werden darf (Kaiy., Haradatta). Dīkṣita präzisiert: insofern ein 'plutierter' Vokal nach 1. 2. 28 (*acaś ca*) nur für ein *'ac'* substituiert werden kann. *tadvidhāne hy acaś ceti paribhāṣayā aca ity upatiṣthati* „Denn wenn Substitution des plutierten Vokals gelehrt wird, so tritt auf Grund der Interpretationsregel 1. 2. 28 'für ein ac' hinzu[68] (sodaß wir also 8. 2. 86 zu interpretieren haben: „Für ein *ac*, welches 'lang' usw. ist ... wird der 'plutierte' Vokal substituiert").

Wir erreichen jedoch nicht die Substitution des r i c h t i g e n 'plutierten' Vokals. Wenn nämlich lediglich gelehrt wird, daß **ṛ* und **ḷ* *'ac'* heißen, so ist damit nicht gesagt, daß sie auch *'aṇ'* sind. Dann können sie aber überlanges **ṛ3* und **ḷ3* nicht (nach 1. 1. 69) einbegreifen, diese heißen also nicht (nach 1. 2. 27) 'plutiert.' Folglich wird man fälschlich als 'nächstbenachbarten' 'plutierten' Vokal *ṝ3* substituieren: *ata eva acsaṃjñāmātreṇāpi na nistaraḥ* „Deshalb ist die Schwierigkeit auch nicht damit beseitigt, daß man für **ṛ* und **ḷ* lediglich den Namen *'ac'* lehrt." Sie müssen vielmehr in den Śivasūtra unter den *'ac'* a u f g e f ü h r t werden (*varṇasamāmnāye tau paṭhanīyau*); dann erst gelten sie auch als *'aṇ'* und begreifen (nach 1. 1. 69) auch die überlangen Vokale **ṛ3* und **ḷ3* ein, die dann als 'nächstbenachbarte' 'plutierte' Vokale richtig nach 8. 2. 86 substituiert werden.

4. Die Siddhāntakaumudī[69] In der äußeren Anlage seiner Werke zeigt der Dīkṣita wenig Erfindungsgabe: Der Śabdakaustubha ist im Grunde nichts als ein 'Haradatta redivivus.' Und auch die Siddhāntakaumudī ist nach einem bekannten Muster gearbeitet, sie folgt in Plan und Darstellung engstens der Prakriyākaumudī[70] Rāmacandra's (15. Jahrh.).

Wie Rāmacandra lehrt Bhaṭṭoji Dīkṣita alle drei värtt. (värtt. 5 zu 1. 1. 9 und värtt. 1, 2 zu 6. 1. 101) in der Siddh. Kaum., setzt also die im Śabdakaustubha festgestellte Lehrmeinung, die die theoretisch beste Möglichkeit darstellt, nicht in die Praxis um. Sonst müßte er **ṛ* und **ḷ* in den ŚS. lehren und die beiden värtt. zu 6. 1. 101 streichen.

Värtt. 5 zu 1. 1. 9 erscheint (Siddh. Kaum. p. 8) in der Formulierung: *ṛḷvarṇayor mithaḥ sāvarṇyaṃ vācyam.* die der Prakr. Kaum. (p. 26) entlehnt ist.

Zu diesem Wortlaut—*'vācyam'* ist nicht mitzurechnen—, ist zunächst zu bemerken, daß *mithaḥ* 'gegenseitig' hinzugefügt ist.

[68] Auf Grund der Paribhāṣā: *kāryakālaṃ saṃjñāparibhāṣam* (Paribh. Induś. 3).

[69] Zitiert nach der Ausgabe von Paṇḍit Śivadatta Śāstrī, Bombay 1926.

[70] Ed. K. P. Trivedi, Bombay 1925. — Ich schulde es dem gelehrten und sorgfältigen Herausgeber zu betonen, daß diese Ausgabe in dem oben (S. 309 Anm. 42) geäußerten Urteil nicht inbegriffen ist. Sie wird allen wissenschaftlichen Ansprüchen gerecht.

Kaiy.'s, im Śabdakaust. gebilligte, Ansicht[71], daß *mithaḥ* sich aus der Interpretation ergebe, ist also nicht angenommen. Die Hinzufügung schafft natürlich unmittelbarere Klarheit. Da sie jedoch das värtt. 'schwerer' macht, ist in anderer Beziehung abgekürzt worden. Statt *savarṇavidhiḥ* (8½ Moren) heißt es: *sāvarṇyam* (7 Moren), und statt *ṛkāraḷkārayoḥ*:*ṛḷvarṇayoḥ*, wobei durch Auslassung des ersten *-kāra* 4 Moren, und durch Ersetzung von *kārayoḥ* durch *varṇayoḥ* eine halbe Mora, gespart sind.

In der Prauḍhamanoramā[72], die er selbst eine '*vyākhyā*' der Siddh. Kaum. nennt (Einleitungsvers), die jedoch in Wahrheit lediglich eine Rechtfertigung der Formulierungen und Lehrmeinungen der Kaumudī ist[73], erklärt Bhaṭṭoji (p. 15), wie das Kompositum *ṛḷvarṇayoḥ* aufzulösen ist. Nämlich entweder als Genetiv eines Kompositums: 'die beiden Laute *ṛ* ('*ā*' = Nom. von *ṛ-*) und *ḷ* ('*ā*' = Nom. von *ḷ-*)', oder als Kompositum des Genetivs: 'des *ṛ* ('*uḥ*') und des *ḷ* ('*ul*'), der beiden Laute'. Hiermit vermeidet er den Vorwurf, daß das Kompositum gegen Pāṇ. 2. 2. 11 verstoße.

Die värtt. zu 6. 1. 101 *ṛti *ṛvāvacam, ḷti *ḷvāvacanam* erscheinen in der Prakr. Kaum. (p. 67f.) als *ṛti savarṇe ṛ vā, ḷti ḷ vā*[74], und in der Siddh. Kaum. (p. 27) als *ṛti savarṇe ṛ vā, ḷti savarṇe ḷ vā*[74].

Die Formulierung des Dīkṣita ist 'schwerer', hat jedoch den Vorteil, seine Lehrmeinung klar erkennen zu lassen: Er nimmt das Arg. 2 des Def. an, daß die värtt. nur unter der Voraussetzung, daß *ṛ* und *ḷ* 'gleichlautig' heißen, einen korrekten Sinn haben, aber auch das Arg. 3 des Opponens, daß die värtt. gelehrt werden müssen, da **ṛ* und **ḷ* nicht '*ac*' sind. Die Wiederholung von *savarṇe* im zweiten värtt. macht es ganz deutlich, daß er *dīrghaḥ* n i c h t fortgelten läßt.

Dem Einwand, daß für **ṛ* und **ḷ* der Name '*ac*' gelehrt werden muß, oder, wie er selbst im Śabdakaust. sagt, daß **ṛ* und **ḷ* in den ŚS aufgeführt werden müssen, um die Substitution des plutierten Vokals (nach 8. 2. 86) zu erreichen, mag er mit der Antwort begegnet haben, daß der plutierte Vokal nur in Vokativen, und auch hier in nicht-letzter Silbe nur fakultativ, substituiert wird, nie-

[71] Kaiy. zu Pat. *ṛkāraḷkārayoḥ savarṇasaṃjñā vidheyā: atra cānayor eva śrutatvān mithaḥ savarṇasaṃjñā vijñāyate, na tv etayor anyena saheti bodhyam* ,,Da in diesem värtt. eben nur *ṛ* und *ḷ* gehört werden, wird erkannt, daß der Name 'gleichlautig' gegenseitig gilt; nicht jedoch hat man zu verstehen: [der Name 'gleichlautig'] für diese zwei und einen andern [Laut].''

[72] Zitiert nach der Ausgabe von Paṇḍit Rāma Śāstrī Mānavallī, Benares 1885.

[73] Wie übrigens im Titel auch angedeutet: *Prauḍhamanoramā* = 'Die üppige Geliebte' und = '[Der Kommentar (*vyākhyā*)] der das Denkorgan (*manaḥ*) der Fortgeschrittenen (*prauḍha*) beschwichtigt (*ramā*)'.

Belvalkar vermutet (Systems of Sanskrit Grammar p. 47), daß der Kommentar 'Prauḍhamanoramā' genannt sei, um ihn von der 'Bālamanoramā' zu unterscheiden, die er eine verkürzte Fassung (agridgement) der Prauḍham. nennt, und zweifelnd ('perhaps') demselben Autor zuschreibt (vgl. Generalindex unter Bālamanoramā). Das mag jedoch auf sich beruhen bleiben, da der Autor der Bālam. sich selbst Vāsudeva nennt, von Bhaṭṭoji als einer von ihm verschiedenen Persönlichkeit spricht (vgl. Bālam. ed. Trichinopoly 1910 p. 2: *tac ca Prauḍhamanoramāyāṃ svayam eva mūlakṛtā prapañcitam eva*), und schließlich sogar Nāgojībhaṭṭa zitiert (z. B. p. 13: *śāstrāsiddhatvakāryāsiddhatvayoḥ phalabhedas tu Śabdenduśekhare vyaktaḥ*, vgl. LŚŚ. p. 40 f.), noch auch die Bālamanoramā ein 'abridgment' der Prauḍhamanoramā genannt werden darf.

[74] Ich verzichte absichtlich auf diakritische Zeichen!

mand jedoch praktische Gelegenheit hat, z. B. den Vokal '*ḷ*' anzureden oder anzurufen.

Ich kann nicht sagen, ob Bhaṭṭoji diesen eigentlich recht vernünftigen Einwand[75] irgendwo ausdrücklich vorgebracht hat. Daß er bestand, ergibt sich aus Nāg.'s Bemerkung zu värtt. 5 zu 1. 1. 9 (Bhāṣya I): *ḷkāraśabdo devatāvācīty eke.* „Einige [sagen], das Wort '*ḷkāra*' bezeichne eine Gottheit". Das kann nur als eine Antwort auf einen derartigen Einwand verstanden werden.

Da der Dīkṣita *ṛ und *ḷ nicht '*ac*' nennt, kann er sie auch nicht 'lang' heißen. So sagt er: „Zu beiden värtt. muß [ausdrücklich] gelehrt werden, daß es sich [bei diesen Lauten] um je eine Lautdoppelheit handelt, die zwei Moren beträgt (aber nicht 'lang' heißt, da die Lautdoppelheit nicht den Namen '*ac*' trägt). Die erste Lautdoppelheit (**ṛ*) hat zwei konsonantische *r* in der Mitte. Diese machen eine Mora aus. Auf jeder Seite [dieses *rr*] ist eine Vokalpartikel. Diese macht eine weitere Mora aus (ə + *rr* + ə). Die zweite Lautdoppelheit (**ḷ*) hat zwei konsonantische *l* in der Mitte. Alles weitere wie im ersten Fall."

Der aufmerksame Leser wird noch eine weitere Konsequenz beobachten. Da der Dīkṣita **ṛ* und **ḷ* nicht als '*ac*' ansieht, läßt er keinen Sandhi eintreten und sagt: *savarṇe ṛ, savarṇe ḷ*. Gewiß, auch Kātyāyana sagt *ṛti *ṛ . . ., ḷti *ḷ. . .* Dies kann man jedoch, auch wenn *ṛ* und *ḷ* '*ac*' heißen, nämlich mit 6. 1. 127, rechtfertigen.

Schließlich braucht Bhaṭṭoji nicht anzugeben, daß **ṛ* und **ḷ* 'halbverschlossen' sind. Diese Angabe ist ja nur notwendig, wenn man zeigen will, daß sie zwar gewönlichem *ṛ* und *ḷ* nicht 'gleichlautig', jedoch ihnen 'nächstbenachbarte' 'lange' Laute sind.

Die Prauḍhamanoramā verteidigt die Beschreibung von **ṛ* und **ḷ* als 'zweimorige Lautdoppelheiten': *yat tu prācā vyākhyātaṃ dīrghe prāpte hrasva ṛkāra ḷkāraś ca vidhīyata iti tad Bhāṣya-Kaiyaṭādivirodhād upekṣyam.* „Was jedoch der 'Frühere' erklärt hat: '[In den värtt. *ṛti . . . ṛ vā* etc.] wird der 'kurze' *ṛ*- und *ḷ*-Vokal gelehrt in einem Fall, wo ein 'langer' Vokal sich ergeben würde', das ist nicht zu beachten, da es im Widerspruch zum Bhāṣya und zu Kaiyaṭa usw. steht."

Der 'Frühere', der so fälschlich **ṛ* und **ḷ* als 'kurze' Laute auffaßt und — offenbar vom Schriftbild verführt — sie mit gewöhnlichem *ṛ* und *ḷ* identifiziert, ist Viṭṭhala, der Kommentator der Prakriyākaumudī (siehe Prakr. Kaum. p. 67). Er steht mit seinem Irrtum allein in der gesamten panineischen Literatur, die zwar überwiegend **ṛ* und **ḷ* in der Schrift mit *ṛ* und *ḷ* wiedergibt, sich jedoch über die besondere Natur dieser Laute mindestens seit Patañjali völlig einig ist.

5. Nāgojībhaṭṭa (18. Jahrhundert) Seinen Ruhm als Grammatiker verdankt Nāgojībhaṭṭa vor allem drei Werken: dem Uddyota[76], einem Kommentar zum Pradīpa und zum Mahābhāṣya, dem Laghuśabdenduśekhara[77] einem Kommentar zur Siddhāntakaumudī und dem Paribhāṣenduśekhara[78], einer Monographie über die grammatischen Interpretationsregeln, die von Pāṇini nicht ausdrücklich gelehrt sind. Dies letztere Werk ist durch

[75] Den wir ja auch für die Kāśikā voraussetzten, oben S. 310.

[76] Zitiert nach der ausgabe von P. Śivadatta D. Kuddāla (Mahābhāṣya, Bombay 1917).

[77] Zitiert nach der Ausgabe von Narahari Śāstrī Pendse, Benares 1927 ff. (Abgekürzt = LŚŚ.)

[78] Ed. Kielhorn, Bombay 1868. (Abgekürzt: PŚ.)

Kielhorn's meisterhafte Übersetzung[79] und Erklärung allgemein zugänglich, und deshalb hervorragend geeignet als Einführung in die Grammatik, wie sie in Indien betrieben wird, zu dienen.

Der Ehrenplatz, den Nāgojībhaṭṭa als der Begründer der 'neuen' Schule der indischen Grammatik hält, seine fast autoritative Geltung bei den modernen Grammatikern[80], kommt ihm mit Recht zu. Er beherrscht das Bhāṣya unendlich viel besser, als irgend jemand vor ihm, und überragt seine Vorgänger gleicherweise in Gründlichkeit, Scharfsinn und Originalität. Kaiyaṭa sagt von sich, daß er den Ozean des Bhāṣya langsam ausschreitend gleich einem Lahmen auf der von Bhartṛhari gezimmerten Brücke überquert habe (Einleitung V. 7), womit er nicht nur seine Sorgfalt in der Auswahl der richtigen Interpretation charakterisiert, sondern auch die Vorsicht, mit der er fast gänzlich an der Erklärung der einzelnen Stelle klebt, mit der er darauf verzichtet, eigene neue Interpretationen zu versuchen. Wir haben an einem kleinen Beispiel gesehen, daß Haradatta und Bhaṭṭoji Dīkṣita wesentlich auf ihm beruhen, daß auch sie keine entscheidenden Neuerungen einführen: Sie verschärfen, verfeinern, treiben auf die Spitze — gelehrte aber inspirationslose Grübler. Ganz anders verhält es

[79] Paribhāṣenduśekhara, Part II: Translation and Notes, Bombay 1873 ff.

[80] Natürlich versucht man auch, über ihn hinauszukommen und seine Gedanken fortzuentwickeln. Die Freude am 'Zerbrechen' (*khaṇḍana*) früherer Lehrmeinungen — ein Kunst, die Nāg. erfolgreichst in seiner Kaiyaṭa-Kritik entwickelt — und am Beseitigen von Unstimmigkeiten durch interpretatorische Spitzfindigkeiten (*phakkikā*) ist, namentlich in Benares, auch heute noch lebendig. Wer sich von der modernsten Richtung einen Begriff machen will, mag sich in die Vijayā vertiefen, den beliebtesten Kommentar zum PŚ.

Ich gebe je ein Beispiel für ein 'Zerbrechen' und einen Interpretationskunstgriff. — a) Einige Grammatiker meinen, der Grundsatz, daß ein Augment (*āgama*) ein Teil des Elementes wird, zu dem es hinzugefügt wird, und deshalb bei Nennung des augmentlosen Elements auch das Element mit Augment genannt ist (Paribh. 11), komme nicht in Anwendung, wenn es sich um ein Augment zu einem Laut handelt. Nāg. zu Paribh. 11 verwirft diese Ansicht, da sie drei Bhāṣyastellen widerspreche (vgl. Translation p. 57 ff.), und begnügt sich lediglich mit der Feststellung, daß Paribh. 11 keine allgemeine Gültigkeit hat. Die Vijayā sucht nun zu zeigen, daß die von Nāg. angezogenen Bhāṣyastellen anders zu interpretieren seien, und jene Ansicht doch zu Recht bestehe.

b) Die Bemerkung Nāg.'s zu Paribh. 6: *ḍādiviṣaye tu sarvādeśatvaṃ vinānubandhatvasyaivābhāvenānupūrvyāt siddham* „Insoweit *ḍā* usw. in Frage kommen, ergibt sich aus der Reihenfolge [der grammatischen Operationen] (daß sie für das ganze Original und nicht für seinen letzten Laut substitutiert werden), insofern der Name '*anubandha*' überhaupt nicht vorhanden ist, solange *ḍā* usw. nicht für das Ganze substitutiert sind", steht im Widerspruch zu seiner eigenen Ansicht (vgl. Translation p. 34 Anm. 1 Abs. 2), die im LŚŚ (zu Pāṇ. 7.1.17, p. 281) und bei Kielhorn l. c. auseinandergesetzt ist. Man interpretiert den zitierten Satz deshalb, indem man *vinā* statt mit *sarvādeśatvam* mit *abhāvena* konstruiert, in der folgenden künstlichen Weise: „Auch ohne das Nichtvorhandensein des Namens '*anubandha*' (i. e. auch wenn *ḍ* in *ḍā* usw. schon von vornherein '*anubandha*' heißen, wie es nach LŚŚ in der Ordnung ist) ergibt sich korrekt, daß *ḍā* usw. für das Ganze substituiert werden auf Grund der Aufeinanderfolge (von *ḍā* und *ā*, die in *ḍā* verborgen ist, und dem Suffix den Charakter eines aus mehreren Lauten bestehenden Substituts: *ā* + *ā* gibt)".

sich mit Nāgojībhaṭṭa. Er hat den Unterschied selbst gefühlt und in seiner bescheidenen Weise zum Ausdruck gebracht: Dem Versprechen Kaiyaṭa's, das Bhāṣya 'traditionsgemäß' (*yathāgamam*) erklären zu wollen (Einleitung V. 5), stellt er sein eigenes Prinzip im Uddyota gegenüber (Einleitung V. 4):

... *Bhāṣya-Pradīpavyākhyānaṃ kurve 'ham tu yathāmati.*

„Ich jedoch interpretiere das Bhāṣya und den Pradīpa (nicht traditionsgemäß, sondern) wie ich es für richtig halte".

Er braucht keine Brücken und Krücken. Wie ein großer Virtuose handhabt er mit scheinbarer Leichtigkeit und mit absoluter Sicherheit Patañjali's schwieriges Werk, spielt er mit den im Bhāṣya vorgebrachten Gesichtspunkten, Möglichkeiten und Lehrmeinungen — ein kongenialer Denker, der sich niemandem beugt als dem 'Herrn der Schlangen' (LŚŚ. V. 3: *natvā Phaṇīśam* ...), das heißt dem Gott Śiva, dem Offenbarer der Grammatik, und dem Patañjali[81].

Siegreich behauptet denn Nāg. das Feld gegen Kaiy. auch bei der Erklärung unserer Bhāṣyastelle im Uddyota. Es muß fallen zunächst Kaiy.'s Deutung des *vakṣyāmi* des Ācārya (oben S. 311): *vacanasya kvāpy adarśanād āha vyākhyāsyāmīti. anye tu laṇsūtrasthākārasyānunāsikatve 'ato lrāntasya' ity atra bhagavān Pāṇinir lakāraṃ noccārayet pratyāhāreṇaiva nirvāhāt. tasmād apūrvaṃ vacanaṃ kāryam ity eva Bhāṣyāśaya ucita ity āhuḥ* „Kaiy. sagt: '[Der Sinn von '*vakṣyāmi*' ist:] Ich werde interpretieren', da sich der Lehrsatz (daß ein *aṇ* als Substitut für *ḷ* von *l* gefolgt ist) nirgends [tatsächlich ausgesprochen] findet. Andere jedoch [deren Meinung ich teile] sagen: Wenn das in ŚS. 6 (*laṇ*) stehende *a* nasaliert wäre [und demnach (nach 1. 3. 2) den Namen *it* empfangen würde], dann würde der Erhabene Pāṇini in der Regel '*ato lrāntasya*' (7. 2. 2) kein *l* aussprechen, da er [in diesem Fall] lediglich durch einen (nach 1. 1. 71 gebildeten) *pratyāhāra* ('*rā*') [in welchem sowohl *r* als *l* enthalten wären] seine Absicht erreichen könnte. Deshalb ist allein als Ansicht des Bhāṣya angemessen, daß ein neuer Lehrsatz aufgestellt werden muß[82].

Unrichtig sind auch einige der Bemerkungen Kaiy.'s zu Opp. 2 (oben S. 311f.), wo es heißt: *asaṃhitāyām ṛkāre hotṛ ṛkāra iti rūpam* ... *ḷkāre 'saṃhitāyāṃ hotṛ ḷkāra iti* „Wenn nicht engster Zusammenschluß (vgl. Pāṇ. 1. 4. 109) vorliegt, so ergibt sich, falls *ṛ* folgt, die Form *hotṛ ṛkāraḥ*, falls *ḷ* folgt, *hotṛ ḷkāraḥ* (insofern die auf Pāṇ. 6. 1. 72 folgenden Regeln nur unter der Voraussetzung '*saṃhitāyām*' gültig sind)". Nāg. bemerkt, daß in einem Kompositum stets 'engster Zusammenschluß' [der Glieder] statt haben muß (*samāse saṃhitā nityā*), und daß eine solche Form (wie *hotṛ* + *ḷkāraḥ*) außer in einem Kompositum nicht vorkommt (*asamāse tv īdṛśaṃ rūpaṃ durlabham*). Das im Bhāṣya stehende *hotṛ ḷkāraḥ* (p. 62 Z. 28, 63 Z. 7) ist [nicht eine in der Sprache verwendete Form[83], sondern] das

[81] Zu Patañjali als Schlange vgl. oben S. 315 Anm. 65. — Kontrastiere die Anrufung des grammatischen Dreigestirns und der *siddhāntasthāpakāḥ* bei Bhaṭṭoji Dīkṣita oben S. 315.

[82] Ausführlicher LŚŚ. (p. 9 ff.) zu Siddh. Kaum. zu den ŚS. (*laṇsūtre 'kāraśca* „auch das *a* in ŚS. 6 heißt '*it*'"). Hier heißt es am Ende der von *pare tu* ... *ity āhuḥ* eingeklammerten Erörterung: „Deshalb (i. e. aus den hier dargelegten Gründen) ist die Annahme, das *a* in ŚS. 6 sei nasaliert, ohne Autorität. In der Regel *ur aṇ raparaḥ* (1. 1. 51) muß *l* [ausdrücklich] genannt werden, wie auch die 'Gleichlautigkeit' von *ṛ* und *ḷ* [ausdrücklich gelehrt werden muß]".

[83] Vgl. Nāg. zu Pāṇ. 6. 1. 72 in LŚŚ (p. 185): „Und zwar ist '*saṃhitā*' die Aussprache mit einer natürlichen Trennung [der Worte] durch die Zeit

Aussprechen des Zustandes, in welchem die Substitution des langen Vokals zu erfolgen hat (*bhāṣye tu hotṛ ḷkāra iti dīrghapravṛttiyogyadaśoccāraṇam*). Das heißt, es handelt sich hier um eine grammatische Abstraktion. Ich habe diese Tatsache in meiner Übersetzung angedeutet, indem ich in diesen Fällen *hotṛ* + *ḷkāraḥ* etc. umschrieben habe.

Wichtiger ist das Folgende: Kaiy. meint, daß bei Annahme der von Opp. 2 vorgetragenen Ansicht sich nicht nur *hot***ḷkāraḥ*, sondern auch beliebig *hotṛḷkāraḥ* als Sandhiform für *hotṛ* + *ḷkāraḥ* korrekt ergäbe: *Śākale hotṛḷkāraḥ* "Wenn man der Ansicht des Śākalya (Pāṇ. 6. 1. 127f.) folgt, ergibt sich *hotṛḷkāraḥ*". Hierzu Nāg.: *evaṃ Śākale hotṛḷkāra ity api cintyam, savarṇatvavidhāyakavacanābhāve etadvicārasattvena tatra ṛty aka ity asyāprāpteḥ. iko 'savarṇa ity api na samāsa iti niṣiddham. nityagrahaṇaṃ tu tatra bhāṣye pratyākhyātam ity āhuḥ* „Man sagt [mit Fug], daß ebenso auch Kaiy.'s [Satz] '*Śākale hotṛḷkāraḥ*' bedenklich sei, da Pāṇ. 6. 1. 128 ([*Śākalyasya*] *ṛty akaḥ*) sich hier nicht ergibt, insofern der Lehrsatz, der den Namen 'gleichlautig' [für *ṛ* und *ḷ*] lehren wird, [noch] nicht existiert, insofern seine Existenz erst noch überlegt wird. (Wir können also *ṛti* in 6. 1. 128 noch nicht als 'vor *ṛ* und *ḷ* interpretieren.) [Auch kann man nicht sagen, daß die Sandhiform *hotṛḷkāraḥ* sich bei Ablehnung von värtt. 5 zu 1. 1. 9 aus Pāṇ. 6. 1. 127 (*iko 'savarṇe Śākalyasya hrasvaśca*) ergäbe. Denn] auch das Eintreten von 6. 1. 127 ist durch [die zusätzliche Bemerkung] 'nicht in einem Kompositum' verboten. [Man könnte freilich sagen, daß värtt. 1 zu 6. 1. 127, welches diese zusätzliche Bemerkung lehrt, nur von 'ewigen[84] Komposita spricht]. Der Ausdruck 'ewig' [des värtt.] ist jedoch im Bhāṣya zu 6. 1. 127 zurückgewiesen."

Die Sandhiform *hotṛḷkāraḥ*—wohl zu unterscheiden von der grammatischen Abstraktion *hotṛ* + *ḷkāraḥ*—ergibt sich folglich erst bei Annahme des värtt. 5 zu 1. 1. 9 durch den Ācārya nach 6. 1. 128. Nāg. sagt deshalb zum '*samādhāna*': *khaṭva ḷkāra iti hotṛḷkāra ity asyopalakṣaṇam* '[Durch Nennung des Falles] *khaṭva ḷkāraḥ* ist [der Fall] *hotṛḷkāraḥ* elliptisch (ebenfalls) genannt[85]".

einer halben Mora. Diese Regel (Pāṇ. 6. 1. 72 *saṃhitāyām* 'in engstem Zusammenschluß') dient zur Verhinderung der in diesem Kapitel gelehrten Operationen im Falle man [mit einer Trennung der Worte] durch die Zeit einer weiteren halben Mora ausspricht. Die alten [Erklärer] sagen jedoch, daß bei einer Trennung vin über einer halben Mora weder Korrektheit (der gesprochenen) noch Verständnis (der gehorten Worte) [von Pāṇ.] angenommen werde. Für diese hat denn Pāṇ. 6. 1. 72 kein (spezielles) Anwendungsgebiet. (Wenn man nämlich Worte im Gebrauch stets im engsten Zusammenschluß aufeinanderfolgen lassen müßte, wie etwa die Glieder eines Kompositums oder Stamm und Suffix, müßte die Regel so interpretiert werden, daß sie in der ganzen Grammatik gültig ist.) Dies ist der Sinn (der Feststellung Bhaṭṭoji's '*iti adhikṛtya*' 'nachdem 6. 1. 72 als Kapitelüberschrift gegeben worden ist')".

[84] i. e. durch Anfügung eines *taddhita* unauflöslich gewordenen.

[85] Wenn wir der Ausgabe der Padamañjarī trauen dürften, würden wir annehmen müssen, daß diese Interpretation auf Haradatta zurückgeht. Hier lesen wir nämlich (S. 59): *idam api siddhaṃ bhavati 'ṛty akaḥ' khaṭva ḷkāraḥ mātṛ ḷkāraḥ* "[Wenn värtt. 5 2u 1. 1. 9 gelehrt wird] ergibt sich auch das folgende korrekt nach 6. 1. 128: *khaṭva ḷkāraḥ*, *mātṛḷkāraḥ*." Leider verdankt das Beispiel *mātṛḷkāraḥ* sein Dasein ganz offenbar lediglich einer Liederlichkeit des Herausgebers, und steht für das dem Bhāṣya entnommene *māla ḷkāraḥ*. Man beachte die Ähnlichkeit der *akṣara* für *tṛ* und *la*!

Nāg. bleibt jedoch nicht bei der Kritik Kaiy.'s stehen. Seine treffende Bemerkung zum Ausdruck '*dīrghatvam*' im '*samādhāna*' habe ich mir (oben S. 303 Anm. 20, 21) angeeignet, da sie erst die wirkliche Pointe herausbringt. Anderes ist weniger naheliegend, und hat für uns den Wert einer Kritik des Bhāṣya, das doch nicht alle Seiten des komplizierten Problems in Betracht gezogen hat. Nāg. hat freilich ein Mittel zur Hand, diese Unterlassungssünden zu rechtfertigen, ein Mittel, das natürlich in strikter Weise 'patanjaleisch' ist.

Zu Opp. 2 heißt es im Uddyota: *tena ḷtīti. siddhānte 'pi vyavasthitavibhāṣayānabhidhānena vā hotṛ + ḷkāre pūrvavārttikaṃ gamḷ + ḷkāre cottaravārttikaṃ na pravartate. evam kṝ iti dīrghasya ṛkāre pare pūrvasya tasyaiva ḷkāra uttarasya cāpravṛttis tata eva iti bhāvaḥ* ,,Kaiy. sagt: '[Wenn man värtt. 5 zu 1. 1. 9 streicht und die värtt. zu 6. 1. 101 in der Form lehrt, die Opp. 2 vorschlägt] dann [ergibt sich richtig] vor *ḷ* usw.' [Er schweigt über die Frage, ob sich dasselbe ergibt, wenn man Kāty. folgt.] Die (diesem Schweigen) [zu Grunde liegende] Meinung[86] ist:

,,Auch wenn man die värtt. zu 6. 1. 101 in der Form, in der sie von Kāty. gegeben sind, und außerdem värtt. 5 zu 1. 1. 9 lehrt ('*siddhānte 'pi*') (und folglich värtt. 1 zu 6. 1. 101 *ṛti *ṝvā . . .* interpretieren muß 'vor 'gleichlautigem' kurzen *ṛ* oder *ḷ* wird beliebig **ṝ* substituiert', und weiter annehmen muß, daß beide värtt. auch dann gelten, wenn *ḷ* oder *ṝ* vorausgehen, da *ṛ* und *ḷ* ja auch diesen 'gleichlautig' sind), hat das erste värtt. (zu 6. 1. 101) nicht statt in *hotṛ + ḷkāraḥ*, und das zweite värtt. nicht in *gamḷ + ḷkāraḥ* ('der *ḷ*-Vokal der Wurzel *gamḷ*'), da es sich (in värtt. 1 und 2 zu 6. 1. 101) um eine *vyavasthitavibhāṣā* handelt, oder aber weil die Meinung nicht ausgedrückt ist. So hat, aus eben demselben Grunde, das erste värtt. nicht statt, wenn der lange Vokal der Wurzel *kṝ* von *ṛ* gefolgt ist, noch das zweite värtt., wenn derselbe Vokal von *ḷ* gefolgt ist.''

Daß also für *ṛ + ḷ* und *ṝ + ṛ* nicht **ṝ*, und für *ḷ + ḷ* und *ṝ + ḷ* nicht **ḹ* substituiert wird — Möglichkeiten, die das Bhāṣya völlig außer Acht gelassen hat — erreicht Nāg. zunächst durch die Annahme einer '*vyavasthitavibhāṣā*'. Wenn eine *vibhāṣā* '*vyavasthitā*' ist, hat die durch diese *vibhāṣā* als beliebig statthabend gelehrte Operation in gewissen Fällen nicht, oder aber in gewissen Fällen alleinig statt.[87] Inwieweit der Geltungsbereich solcher *vibhāṣā* beschränkt ist, hat man aus der Richtigkeit der sich ergebenden Formen festzustellen (*lakṣyānusārād vyavasthā bodhyā*, PŚ. p. 101). In unserm Falle hätte man also festzustellen, daß die in värtt. 1, 2 zu 6. 1. 101 als beliebig statthabend gelehrte Substitution von **ṝ* und **ḹ* in den genannten Fällen nicht statthat, da das Resultat **ṝ* für *ṛ + ḷ* usw. und **ḹ* für *ḷ + ḷ* usw. falsch wäre.

Nāg. hat jedoch selbst im LŚŚ. (zu Pāṇ. 6. 1. 123, p. 151) nach Aufzählung der Fälle, in denen das Bhāṣya eine *vyavasthitavibhāṣā*

[86] Nāg. ist ein ritterlicher Gegner. Solange Kaiy. sich nicht durch eine unzweideutige Äußerung bloßgestellt hat, nimmt Nāg. an, daß er etwas Richtiges meint. In dieser Hinsicht ist er typisch 'scholastisch'. Er unterscheidet sich von andern wesentlich nur dadurch, daß er niemals dem Wortsinn Gewalt antut.

[87] Vgl. PŚ., Paribh. 99 und Translation p. 471 ff. — Z. B.: nach Pāṇ. 8. 2. 56 dürfen wir bilden *trāṇa* benen *trāta*, in '*devatrātaḥ*' hat jedoch die als beliebig gelehrte Operation nicht statt. Nach 6. 1. 123 dürfen wir bilden *gavāgram* neben *go'gram* und *goagram* (6. 1. 122) usw., in *gavākṣam* hat jedoch die als beliebig gelehrte Operation alleinig statt.

annimmt, festgestellt, daß wir keine Autorität haben, mit diesem Interpretationsmittel auf eigene Faust zu operieren[88].

Deshalb versucht er eine andere Interpretation und sagt: *anabhidhānena vā* „oder aber [und das ist die richtige Auffassung] weil [der Sinn] nicht ausgedrückt ist". Den Schlüssel zum Verständnis dieser Worte bietet uns der PŚ. Zu Paribh. 13 heißt es dort (p. 13 Z. 13): *sthānyarthābhidhānasamarthasyaivādeśateti siddhāntāt* . . . „nach dem Prinzip, daß nur dasjenige ein Substitut werden kann, was fähig ist, den Sinn des Originals auszudrücken . . .". Die an sich grammatisch korrekten Formen *hot**ḷ*kāraḥ* usw. werden demnach nicht für *hotṛ* + *ṛkāraḥ* usw. substituiert, da sie nur fähig sind, den Sinn von *hotṛ* + *ḷkāraḥ* usw. auszudrücken.

Es handelt sich hier nicht um eine grammatische Interpretationsmaxime, sondern um einen sprachphilosophischen Grundsatz, der natürlich seine Wurzel ebenfalls im Bhāṣya hat. Wenn Nāg. meint, daß ein Substitut fähig sein muß, den Sinn des Originals auszudrücken, spricht er nicht von einzelnen Lauten, die nach der Ausdrucksweise der Grammatik für einzelne Laute substituiert werden. Denn nicht einzelne Laute, sondern nur Lautgruppen haben einen Sinn (vgl. z. B. Pat. zu värtt. 15 zu ŚS. 5, bes. p. 32 Z. 7 ff.). Er faßt also *hot**ḷ*kāraḥ* als Substitut für *hotṛ* + *ḷkāraḥ* auf, und nicht **ḷ* als Substitut für *ṛ* + *ḷ*. Daß dies der sprachphilosophisch richtige Standpunkt ist, geht z. B. aus dem Bhāṣya zu värtt. 5 zu 1. 1. 20 (p. 75 Z. 10 ff.) hervor, wo sich der berühmte Vers findet:

sarve sarvapadādeśā Dākṣīputrasya Pāṇineḥ
ekadeśavikāre hi nityatvaṃ nopapadyate.

„Alle [Substitute] des Sohns der Dākṣī, Pāṇini, sind Substitute für g a n z e Worte. Denn wenn nur ein T e i l [eines Wortes] geändert wird, stimmt die [Annahme der] Ewigkeit [des Wortes] nicht".

Ausführlicher und vielseitiger als im Uddyota sind die Lehrmeinungen, die man aus unserer Bhāṣya-Diskussion abstrahieren kann, im LŚŚ. untersucht und dargestellt. Da es sich um vielleicht besonders schwierige Stellen handelt, gebe ich eine vollständige Übersetzung.

1. LŚŚ. (p. 45) zu Siddh. Kaum. (p. 8): *ṛḷvarṇayor mithaḥ sāvarṇyaṃ vācyam.*

„[Das Kompositum] '*ṛḷvarṇayoḥ*' ist zu zerlegen: '*ṛ* und der *ḷ*-Laut[89]. Unterbleiben der Substitution [in *ṛḷ*-] ist korrekt nach Pāṇ. 6. 1. 128[90].

[88] „. . . Und man darf nicht sagen, daß Pāṇ. 6. 1. 124 (*indre ca* „*vor Indra* wird immer *ava* für das *o* von *go* substituiert") zwecklos sei, insofern die ständige Substitution von *ava* vor *Indra* sich durch [Annahme einer] *vyavasthitavibhāṣā* korrekt (nach 6. 1. 123) ergebe (wie die ständige Substitution von *ava* in *gavākṣa*, s. oben Anm. 1). [Und zwar deshalb nicht] da diese Regel (6. 1. 124) gegeben ist um anzudeuten, daß für [die Annahme] von] *vyavasthitavibhāṣās*, die im Bhāṣya (zu 7. 4. 41 usw.) nicht ausdrücklich gelehrt sind, keine Autorität besteht".

[89] Richtet sich gegen die Ansicht der Prauḍhamanoramā (ob. S. 317).

[90] Identisch mit Prauḍhamanoramā *ad l. c.* und Uddyota zu *ṛkāraḷkārayoḥ* (Bhāṣya I), an welch letzterer Stelle auch eine andere Ansicht erwähnt ist: *vārttike 'py evam eva pāṭha iti prāmāṇikāḥ* „Diejenigen, für die [der tatsächliche Gebrauch in einem Lehrsatz] Autorität ist, sagen: '[Pat. sagt *ṛkāraḷkārayoḥ*] da es ebenso im värtt. steht'". Das wird wohl deshalb zugefügt, weil es wunderlich erscheint, daß Pat. diesen Sandhi nicht von vornherein als '*prayojana*' vorgebracht hat, und ihn auch später nicht

„Allein um dieses vārtt. willen wird *ḷ* in den ŚS. namentlich aufgeführt [nämlich in ŚS. 2: *ṛ ḷk*] (nicht aber um der Substitution des 'plutierten' Vokals in *kḷ3ptaśikha*! (nach 8. 2. 86) willen, wie im Bhāṣya zu ŚS. 2 behauptet wird[91]. Gilt nämlich dieses vārtt., würde *ḷ* auch dann '*ac*' heißen, wenn es in den ŚS. nicht aufgeführt wäre, indem es als 'gleichlautig' nach 1. 1. 69 in der Nennung von *ṛ* einbegriffen wäre. Es würde demnach auch dreimoriges *ḷ3* nach 1. 2. 27 'plutiert' heißen und für das '*ac*' *ḷ* nach 1. 2. 28 substituiert werden können). [Denn] wenn *ḷ* in der ŚS. nicht namentlich aufgeführt wäre, könnte dieses vārtt. [durch welches dann der Grund, den Pat. für die Aufführung von *ḷ* angibt, hinfällig wird] überhaupt nicht gelehrt werden, da man befürchten müßte, daß *ḷ* nicht existiert.

„(Nun könnte man einwenden, daß diese Auffassung gegen Pat. gehe, da ja dieses '*prayojana*' für die Aufführung von *ḷ* im Bhāṣya zu ŚS. 2 nicht berücksichtigt ist. Das ist jedoch nicht der Fall.) [Daß sich dies so verhält] das ist am Ende des Bhāṣya zu ŚS. 3 auch angedeutet (wenn auch nicht ausdrücklich ausgesprochen). (Und zwar in der folgenden Weise:)

„Nachdem man die Befürchtung vorgebracht hat, daß sich (wenn man das Prinzip ablehnt, daß durch Nennung von Lauten Teile von Lauten ebenfalls genannt werden) eine durch das Vorhandensein zweier Konsonanten bedingte Operation[92] fälschlich

erwähnt. Wie wir sahen, ist er ja nach Nāg.'s Ansicht im *samādhāna* elliptisch genannt (oben S. 321).

[91] Im Bhāṣya zu ŚS. 2 wird untersucht, warum *ḷ* in den ŚS. namentlich aufgeführt wird. Ich gebe eine kurze Paraphrase:

ḷ kommt nur in Ableitungen von der Wurzel *kṛp* wirklich vor, z. B. in *kḷpti-*; *kḷpta-*. Das *ḷ* dieser Formen ist nun nach 8. 2. 18 für *ṛ* substituiert, ist also wie alle nach 8. 2. 1 gelehrten Substitutionen in Rücksicht auf eine vorhergehende Regel als nicht vorhanden zu betrachten. Alle vorhergehenden Operationen werden folglich an dem *ṛ* von √*kṛp* getätigt, für welches dann (nach 8. 2. 18) der jeweils 'nächstbenachbarte' *ḷ*-Laut eintritt. In 8. 2. 86 dagegen ist das Substitut *ḷ* bereits vorhanden, da 8. 2. 18 vorhergeht, und es ist deshalb notwendig, auch *ḷ* '*ac*' zu nennen.

Kāty. erklärt aus diesem Grunde im vārtt. 1 zu ŚS. 2, daß *ḷ* aufgeführt sei, um die Substitution des plutierten Vokals zu erreichen. Er entrkäftet das in vārtt. 4 mit dem in Paribh. 37 formulierten Prinzip, daß etwas, das eine Änderung in Bezug auf einen seiner Teile erfahren hat — in diesem Fall ist *ərə* (*ṛ*) zu *ələ* (*ḷ*) geworden — nicht als etwas Anderes betrachtet wird, als was es vorher war. Insofern *ḷ* in *kḷpta-* demnach immer noch als *ṛ* betrachtet wird, heißt es '*ac*'.

Pat. lehnt es jedoch ab, die Substitution des plutierten Vokals in *kḷ3ptaśikha*! auf diese Wiese zu erklären, da wir so zwar erreichen würden, daß *ḷ* '*ac*' heißt, andrerseits aber das für *ṛ* gegebene Verbot der Substitution des plutierten Vokals (8. 2. 86 . . . *anṛto* . . .) auch für *ḷ* gelten müßte. *ḷ* ist also nach seiner Meinung in den ŚS. notwendig.

Kāty. will freilich die genannte Schwierigkeit durch Änderung der Formulierung von 8. 2. 86 beseitigen (vārtt. 5 zu ŚS 2.) Pat. bemerkt dazu: Die Aufführung des *ḷ*-Lautes in ŚS. 2, die den Zweck hat die Substitution des plutierten Vokals (nach 8. 2. 86) möglich zu machen, ist von Kāty. unter Änderung einer Regel (nämlich 8. 2. 86) zurückgewiesen worden. Das ist, als ob man eine *laṭvā*(?) von einem hohen Bambusstamm herunterholt (i. e. eine unverhältnismäßige Anstrengung).

Die übrigen Gründe, die Kāty. im vārtt. 1 für die Notwendigkeit, *ḷ* in den ŚS. aufzuführen, angibt, sind in den vārtt. 2 und 3 nebst Bhāṣya widerlegt.

[92] Wie die in 8. 2. 86 gelehrte Substitution des plutierten Vokals, die für einen 'positionslangen' Vokal statt-

nicht ergäbe in *saẙyantāḥ* usw. (i.e. *saẙvatsaraḥ, yal̊lokam*)[93] (sodaß man also nicht *saȝẙyantaḥ!* usw. bilden könnte),

,,da (zwar *kk* in *kukkutaḥ!* nicht '*hal*' heißt, sondern '*saṃyoga*', insofern das in den ŚS. genannte *k* nicht das 'gleichlautige' *kk'* mitnennt, da *k* nicht '*aṇ*' heißt, *ẙy* usw. jedoch den Namen '*hal*' erhalten müßten, da)

,,durch Pāṇ. 1. 1. 69 (*aṇ udit savarṇasya cāpratyayaḥ*) bei Nennung von *y* usw. (i. e. *v, l*) [die im *hal* von Pāṇ. 1. 1. 7 *halo 'nantarāḥ saṃyogaḥ* genannt sind] auch das Doppel-*y* usw. (i. e. *ẙy, v̊v, l̊l*), das eine ganze Mora beträgt, mitgenannt ist[94],

,,insofern Pāṇ. 1. 1. 69 sich auch auf die Konstituenten eines *pratyāhāra* (in diesem Fall '*hal*' in 1. 1. 7) erstreckt[95] [soweit sie '*aṇ*' heißen, in diesem Fall also *y, v, l*],

,,wird dort nämlich gesagt:

,,Da ein eine [ganze] Mora betragender Konsonant nicht gelehrt ist, und da etwas, das nicht gelehrt ist, nicht existiert, und da etwas, das nicht existiert, nicht erhalten werden kann, ist Doppel-*y* usw. wenn 1. 1. 69 statthat, nicht mitgenannt[96] (kann also auch in dem *hal* von Pāṇ. 1. 1. 7 nicht mitgenannt sein, und ist deshalb als 'Doppelkonsonanz' zu erkennen).

,,Auch [kann man] nicht [gegen dieses vārtt. einwenden], daß sich die Substitution des 'plutierten' Vokals (nach 8. 2. 86) in *kl̥ȝptaśikha!* fälschlich nicht ergebe, da [wenn *r̥* und *l̥* gleichlautig heißen] das Verbot 'nicht für ein kurzes *r̥*' (8. 2. 86) [auch für *l̥*] gelten müsse[97]. Denn es ist kein Fehler, wenn man vermutet, daß *r̥* und *l̥* sich m a n c h m a l gegenseitig nicht erfassen (obgleich sie 'gleichlautig' heißen), da sie verursachen, daß [die Wurzeln mit

haben darf. 'Positionslang' (*guru*) ist ein Vokal vor einer 'Konsonantenverbindung' (*saṃyoga*). Den Namen '*saṃyoga*' erhalten nach 1. 1. 7 aufeinanderfolgende '*hal*' genannte Laute.

[93] Aus sam + yantā usw. nach 8. 4. 58.

[94] Pat. zu vārtt. 13 zu ŚS. 3 (p. 26 Z. 24 ff.): *iha tu kathaṃ 'saẙyantā, saẙvatsa raḥ, yal̊lokam, tal̊lokam' iti yatraitad asty aṇ savarṇān gr̥hṇātīti.*

Uddyota: *yatraitad astīti Bhāṣye. halo 'nantarā ity atra yakārādibhir asya grahaṇe haldvayābhāva iti bhāvaḥ.* ,,Im Bhāṣya (i. e. n i c h t im Pradīpa) [heißt es]: *yatraitad asti* usw. Die zugrundeliegende Meinung ist: Da in Pāṇ. 1. 1. 7 auch *ẙy* usw. durch *y* usw. genannt sind, [in *ẙy* usw.] nicht zwei [sondern nur e i n '*hal*'] vorhanden''.

[95] Bezüglich der in Pāṇ. 1. 1. 10 (*nājjhalau* ,,ein '*ac*' und ein '*hal*' sind nicht gleichlautig'') genannten *pratyāhāra* hat zwar 1. 1. 69 nicht statt, da erst nachdem die Definition der 'Gleichlautigkeit' vollständig gegeben ist, der Ausdruck *savarṇasya* in 1. 1. 69 verstanden werden kann. An andern Stellen der Grammatik, wo ein *pratyāhāra* genannt wird, hat jedoch 1. 1. 69 statt, und nennen die in den *pratyāhāra* enthaltenen Laute auch ihre 'gleichlautigen' Partner, z. B. das in *akaḥ* 6. 1. 101 enthaltene *i* auch langes *ī* Vgl. Bhāṣya zu vārtt. 4 zu 1. 1. 10 (p. 64 Z. 11–18).

[96] Bhāṣya (zu vārtt. 13 zu ŚS. 3 (p. 26 Z. 26 f.) *anupadiṣṭaṃ sat kathaṃ śakyaṃ vijñātum asac ca kathaṃ śakyaṃ pratipattum* ,,Wie kann etwas, das nicht gelehrt ('gezeigt') worden ist, als existierend erkannt werden? Und wie kann etwas, das nicht existiert, erhalten werden''?

Uddyota: *anena l̥kārāpāṭhe tasyāsattvaśaṅkayā tayoḥ sāvarṇyavidhir apy aśakya iti sūcitam* ,,Hierdurch ist angedeutet, daß, wenn *l̥* [in den ŚS.] nicht aufgeführt wäre, auch der Lehrsatz, daß [*r̥* und *l̥*] 'gleichlautig' heißen, nicht gelehrt werden könnte, da man zu befürchten hatte, daß *l̥* nicht existiert''.

[97] Derselbe Einwand wird im Bhāṣya gegen die Anschauung erhoben, daß *l̥* in den ŚS. nicht gelehrt zu werden braucht, insofern es als von *r̥* nicht verschieden aufgefaßt werden kann. (Siehe oben S. 324 Anm. 91).

symbolischem *ṛ* und *ḷ*] verschiedene *anubandha* haben''[98].

2. LŚŚ. (p. 148) zu Siddh. Kaum. (S. 27): (1) *ṛti savarṇe ṛ vā: hotṛkāraḥ, hotṝkāraḥ. ḷti savarṇe ḷ vā: hotḷkāraḥ, pakṣe ṝkāraḥ sāvarṇyāt: hotṝkāraḥ.*

ṛti ṛvā, ḷti ḷvety ubhayatrāpi vidheyaṃ varṇadvayaṃ (2) *dvimātram. ādyasya madhye* (3) *dvau rephau, tayor ekā mātrā.* (4) *abhito 'jbhakter aparā. dvitīyasya tu madhye* (5) *dvau lakārau. śeṣaṃ prāgvat* . ...

(1) ,,[Bhaṭṭ. sagt:] 'vor einem gleichlautigen *ṛ*', da er will, daß das im Sūtra (6. 1. 101 *akaḥ savarṇe dīrghaḥ*) stehende Wort 'gleichlautig' fortgilt. Er erreicht damit, daß die värtt. in Fällen wie *dadhy ṛkāraḥ* (für *dadhi* + *ṛkāraḥ*) usw. nicht statthaben[99].

Die auf Grund dieser värtt. (als Substitute) herzustellenden Laute heißen '*ac*', da sie [in den ŚS.] unmittelbar nach *a i uṇ* (ŚS. 1) aufgeführt werden (müssen)[100]. Daraus ergibt sich, daß für sie der

[98] Kaiy. sagt (zum Schluß des Bhāṣya zu värtt. 5 zu 1. 1. 9): *ṛditāṃ ḷditāṃ ca bhedenānubandhanireśād bhedena copādānād anubandhakāryeṣu paraspara-grahaṇābhāvād vyatikarābhāvaḥ.* ,,Die Wurzeln mit dem *anubandha ṛ* und die Wurzeln mit dem *anubandha ḷ* werden nicht gegenseitig durcheinandergebracht, weil, da die *anubandha* [*ṛ* und *ḷ*] als verschieden [im Dhātupāṭha] aufgeführt sind und als verschieden [in der Grammatik] zitiert werden, *ṛ* und *ḷ* sich gegenseitig nicht erfassen, sofern von *anubandha* bedingte Operationen in Betracht kommen''.

Hiegegen hat schon Dīkṣita im Śabdakaustubha (zu ŚS, 2, p. 51) eingewendet, daß wir daraus, daß die Verschiedenheit der *anubandha ṛ* und *ḷ* einen Sinn haben muß, zwar schließen dürfen, daß ein für eine Wurzel mit dem *anubandha ḷ* gelehrte Operation nicht auch für eine Wurzel mit dem *anubandha ṛ* gilt. Nachdem wir dies geschlossen haben, hat jedoch die Verschiedenheit einen Sinn, und wir dürfen nicht noch weiter schließen, daß auch eine für eine Wurzel mit dem *anubandha ṛ* gelehrte Operation nicht für eine Wurzel mit dem *anubandha ḷ* gilt. Deshalb — und wegen der Form *kḷ3ptaśikha*! — nimmt er an, daß die Aufführung von *ḷ* in den ŚS. den Zweck hat, anzuzeigen, daß die 'Gleichlautigkeit' von *ṛ* und *ḷ* nicht allgemein gültig ist (l. c. ... *ṛkāraḷkārayoḥ sāvarṇyasyānityatāṃ jñāpayituṃ kartavya eva ḷkāropadeśaḥ*).

Nāg. hat oben eine andere 'Veranlassung' für die Aufführung von *ḷ* gegeben, die er mit dem Bhāṣya begründen zu können glaubt. Auch scheut er sich spezielle Vermutungen als berechtigt anzuerkennen, die nicht im Bhāṣya ausdrücklich geäußert sind. Er entnimmt als der Tatsache, daß *ṛ* und *ḷ* verschiedene *anubandha* sind, die allgemeine Vermutung, daß sie sich manchmal nicht erfassen. Nach der Erklärung eines Kommentators (LŚŚ p. 45 Anm.) beruht seine Ansicht auf dem logischen Prinzip: *asati bādhake pramāṇānāṃ sāmānye pakṣapātaḥ* ,,Wenn nicht eine spezielle Einschränkung vorhanden ist, haben 'Erkenntnismittel' ['Schlußfolgerung' (*anumāna*) usw.] eine Tendez zum Allgemeinen''. — In diesem Fall handelt es sich um ein '*kalpana*' (Vermutung), eine Abart des *anumāna*. Wie man z. B. aus dem Vorhandensein von Rauch auf Feuer im allgemeinen, nicht aber auf ein bestimmtes — großes oder kleines — Feuer schließen kann, ist auch in diesem Fall nur eine allgemeine Vermutung möglich.

[99] Vgl. oben S. 301 (Def. Arg. 2).

[100] Das ist zwar in der Siddh. Kaum. nicht geschehen, im Śabdakaust. wird jedoch Aufführung unter den '*ac*' verlangt (siehe oben S. 316). Nāg. definiert die Stelle, an der **ṛ* und **ḷ* zu denken sind. — Man erinnere sich, daß nach värtt. 6 ff. nebst Bhāṣya zu ŚS. 5 auch die 'unangeschirrt ziehenden' Laute (*visarjanīya, jihvāmūlīya, upadhmānīya, anusvāra* usw.) in den ŚS. aufzuführen sind, was ebenfalls niemals in die Praxis umgesetzt wird. Im Uddyota bemerkt Nāg. zu Kaiy. zu Def. 4: ,,[Kaiy. sagt]: 'Wenn **ṛ* und **ḷ* '*ac*' heißen'. Die zugrunde liegende Meinung ist: 'da sie unter

plutierte Vokal korrekt substituiert wird[101], und daß sie (wenn sie für ṛ + ṛ bezw. ṛ + ḷ substituiert werden) nicht von r gefolgt sind (was nach 1. 1. 51 der Fall sein müßte, wenn man sie vor dem ersten *anubhandha* der ŚS. (*ṇ*) lehren würde).

(2) ,,[Bhaṭṭ. sagt: 'in beiden Fällen ist ein] zweimoriger [Doppellaut herzustellen]'.

,,Eben weil sich das so verhält, sind diese zwei värtt. im Bhāṣya zu Pāṇ. 1. 1. 9 zurückgewiesen, indem man sich darauf stützt, daß sich das erwünschte Resultat, welches darin besteht, daß [die Substitution von *ṛ bezw. *ḷ für ṛ + ṛ bezw. ṛ + ḷ] beliebig statt hat, sich [auch ohne diese värtt.] allein durch 6. 1. 101 korrekt ergibt,

,,insofern sich [als 'nächstbenachbarte' 'lange' Substitutionsvokale] korrekt ergeben

,,A. für die zwei ṛ (in *hotṛ* + *ṛkāraḥ*)

1. zuweilen der zwei konsonantische *r* in sich tragende Laut (*ṛ), insofern er 'nächstbenachbart' ist auf Grund der Eigenschaft[102] welche darin besteht, daß er (wie das Original) zwei konsonantische *r* enthält
[ṛ (ərə) + ṛ (ərə) benachbart zu *ṛ (ərrə)],

2. zuweilen der 'offene' Laut (ṝ), insofern er nächstbenachbart ist auf Grund dessen (i.e. der Eigenschaft), daß er (wie das Original) offen ist
[ṛ (ərə) + ṛ (ərə) benachbart zu ṝ (əərəə)];

,,B. wenn ḷ folgt (in *hotṛ* + *ḷkāraḥ*)

1. zuweilen der zwei konsonantische *l* enthaltende Laut (*ḷ), insofern er 'nächstbenachbart' ist auf Grund dessen (i. e. der Eigenschaft), daß er (wie das Original) ein konsonantisches *l* enthält
[ṛ (ərə) + ḷ (ələ) benachbart zu *ḷ (əllə)],

2. zuweilen der offene Laut ṝ, insofern [er 'nächstbenachbart' ist, insofern] er [dem Original] ähnlich[103] ist auf Grund dessen (i. e. der Eigenschaft), daß er offen ist, und insofern er [dem Original]

den '*ayogavāha*' (*visarjanīya* usw.) aufzuführen sind'.'' Das heißt: da sie als aufgeführt zu d e n k e n sind.

[101] Vgl. Śabdakaust., oben S. 316.

[102] Nachbarschaft kann beruhen auf Artikulationsstelle (*sthāna*), Sinn (*artha*), Eigenschaft (*guṇa*) und Zeitdauer (*pramāṇa*). Vgl. PŚ. zu Paribh. 13. — Eine Eigenschaft ist auch die 'Artikulationsweise'. — Nāg. zählt im folgenden nicht alle 'nächste Nachbarschaft' begründenden Faktoren auf, sondern nur diejenigen, die uns veranlassen unterschiedliche und doch gleichwertige 'nächste Nachbarschaft' anzunehmen. ṝ und *ṛ sind dem Original gleich nächst benachbart, soweit Artikulationsstelle und Zeitdauer in Betracht kommen, die in beiden Fällen die gleichen sind. Außerdem haben sie je eine Eigenschaft, die dem andern fehlt. Von diesen Eigenschaften ist die Rede.

[103] 'Nahe benachbart' und 'ähnlich' sind synonym. Vgl. z. B. die Gleichung *antaratamaḥ* = *sadṛśatamaḥ*, Siddh. Kaum. zu 1. 1. 50 (p. 13). Da *āntaryam* als Abstraktum zu *antaratamaḥ* 'nächst benachbart' vergeben ist, verwendet Nāg. *sāmyam* 'Ähnlichkeit' als Abstraktum zu *antaraḥ* 'nahe benachbart'.

Während *ḷ schon insofern es *l* enthält, 'nachstbenachbart' zu ṛ + ḷ ist, da es keinen andern 'langen' *l*-haltigen Laut gibt, ist ṝ insofern es *r* enthält nur 'nahe benachbart' zu ṛ und ḷ, da es diese Eigenschaft mit *ṛ teilt. Daß es 'nächstbenachbart' ist und deshalb mit Ausschluß von *ṛ substituiert wird, verdankt es der weiteren, unterscheidenden Eigenschaft, daß es 'offen' ist.

Man vergleiche das Schulbeispiel für 'nächste Nachbarschaft' auf Grund einer Eigenschaft: *vāg gharih* nach 8. 4. 62 für *vāg* + *hariḥ*. Hier ist das dem *g* 'gleichlautige' *gh* substituiert, insofern es als 'tönend' und 'aspiriert' dem *h* 'nächstbenachbart' ist, während das dem *g* ebenfalls 'gleichlautige' *kh* nicht substituiert wird,

ähnlich ist auf Grund dessen (i. e. der Eigenschaft), daß er ein konsonantiches *r* enthält
[*ṛ* (ərə) + *ḷ* (ələ) benachbart zu *ṝ* (əərəə)].

(3) „[Bhaṭṭ. sagt: 'In der Mitte des ersteren Lautes (*ṛ) befinden sich] zwei konsonantische *r*. [Diese machen eine Mora aus]'.

„Die Autorität auch für diese Angabe ist die nämliche Bhāṣyastelle. Denn nur wenn *ṛ z w e i konsonantische *r* enthält, ergibt sich in korrekter Weise die Einschränkung[104], daß dieser Laut (*ṛ) substituiert wird, wenn das Original zwei *r* enthält (*ṛ* + *ṛ*), der andere Laut (*ḷ), wenn das Original ein *l* enthält (*ṛ* + *ḷ*).

(4) „[Bhaṭṭ. sagt:] 'Um herum [befindet sich je eine Vokalpartikel usw.]'. Es ist zu ergänzen 'die zwei konsonantischen *r*-Laute'. Und zwar steht dieser [aus dem vorhergehenden zu ergänzende Ausdruck] im Akkusativ, da er mit dem Wort 'um herum' konstruiert ist.

„Die [der Angabe, daß sich in *ṛ eine Vokalpartikel (ə̄) auf jeder Seite der zwei konsonantischen *r*-Laute [*rr*] befindet, zu Grunde liegende] Meinung ist:

„Da, insofern eine Vokalpartikel von je einer halben Mora (ə̄) auf jeder Seite (des konsonantischen Bestandteils) in den in ŚS. 2 gelehrten Lauten [*ṛ* und *ḷ*] angenommen wird, es billig ist, daß es sich ebenso verhält[105] [soweit *ṛ in Frage kommt].

„[Daß sich eine Vokalpartikel auf beiden Seiten des konsonantischen Bestandteils von gewöhnlichem *ṛ* und *ḷ* befindet, i. e. 1) daß *ṛ* und *ḷ* nicht mit einem *r* bezw. *l* b e g i n n e n, sondern mit einem ə, und 2) daß *ṛ* und *ḷ* nicht mit einem *r* bezw. *l* s c h l i e ß e n, sondern ebenfalls mit ə, wird angenommen aus folgenden Gründen:]

1. „Bei Erörterung der Alternative, daß durch Nennung eines Lautes ein [diesem Laut identischer] Teil eines [andern] Lautes [mit] genannt ist ist[106], welche Alternative auf jeden Fall anzunehmen ist, damit z. B. die Substitution von *ṇ* in einer Form wie *mātṝṇām* sich korrekt (nach 8. 4. 1) ergibt (insofern dann '*r*' in 8. 4. 1 auch den dem *r* identischen Teil des *ṛ* (ərə) und *ṝ* (əərəə) mitnennt, und wir somit zu interpretieren haben '*n* nach *r*, mag dieses *r* nun allein stehen oder in *ṛ* bezw. *ṝ* enthalten sein'),

„wird im Bhāṣya zu ŚS. 3 zwar

„[erstlich] die Befürchtung ausgesprochen, daß

„in [einer Form wie] *pralūya* [Hinzufügung von] *tuk* (nach Pāṇ. 6. 1. 71) [sich ergeben würde] (insofern nach dem genannten Prinzip auch der zweite Teil des *ū* (= *u* + *u*) in dem Ausdruck 'kurzer Vokal' einbegriffen wäre)[107],

„in [einer Form wie] *khaṭvābhiḥ* [Substitution von] *ais* [für

insofern es als lediglich 'aspiriert' dem *h* nur ähnlich ('nahe benachbart') ist. Siehe LŚŚ. zu 1. 1. 50 (p. 84): „Warum ist [in 1. 1. 50] das Superlativsuffix (*antara-tamaḥ*) verwendet? Damit in *vāg gharih* usw. nicht das dem vorhergehenden Laute 'gleichlautige' *kh* (nach. 8. 4. 62) substituiert wird, welches getätigt werden würde, da es [dem Original] ähnlich ist auf Grund dessen, daß es aspiriert ist."

[104] '*vyavasthā*': *viśiṣṭe viṣaye 'vasthā* 'Statthaben in speziellen Fällen', 'Beschränktsein'. 'Beschränkung' im transitiven Sinn ist '*niyamaḥ*'.

[105] Während für irgend eine andere Annahme keine 'billige' Begründung gegeben werden könnte.

[106] värtt. 6 zu ŚS. 3 *varṇaikadeśā varṇagrahaṇena cet* . . . „Wenn durch Nennung von Lauten Teile von Lauten [ebenfalls genannt werden] . . .". Das heißt, z. B. durch Nennung von konsonantischem *r* auch der in *ṛ* (ərə) steckende konsonantische Teil, durch Nennung von *a* auch die Teile des langen *ā* = *a* + *a*.

[107] Pat. zu värtt. 7 (p. 24 Z. 6 f.): . . . *ālūya, pralūya. hrasvasya piti kṛti tug bhavatīti tuk prāpnoti.*

bhis] (nach Pāṇ. 7. 1. 9) [sich ergeben würde] (insofern nach dem genannten Prinzip auch der zweite Teil des *ā* (= *a* + *a*) in dem Ausdruck 'kurzes *a*' einbegriffen wäre)[108], und

,,in [einer Fügung wie] *vācā tarati* [Eintritt] des durch [das Vorhandensein von] zwei '*ac*' genannten Lauten bedingten [Suffixes *ṭhan*] (nach Pāṇ. 4. 4. 7) [sich ergeben würde] (insofern nach dem genannten Prinzip auch die beiden Teile des *ā* (= *a* + *a*) in dem Ausdruck '*ac*' einbegriffen wären, und somit *vāc*- zwei '*ac*' enthielte)[109],

,,und [zweitens] eine Beschwichtigung gegeben,

,,welche darin besteht, daß [man annimmt, daß] die Vermutung notwendig gemacht ist, daß [obgleich der genannte Grundsatz besteht] eine grammatische Operation, die bedingt ist durch einen Teilen [eines andern] Lautes ähnlichen, selbständigen Laut, nicht statt hat, wenn diese Teile des [andern] Lautes nicht als abgetrennt wahrgenommen werden[110]),

,,da es einen Sinn haben muß, daß *tuk* ausdrücklich als [in gewissen Fällen] nach einem langen Laut (6. 1. 75) [anzufügend] gelehrt ist[111],

[108] Pat. zu värtt. 8 (p. 24 Z. 11 f.): *khaṭvābhiḥ, mālābhiḥ. ato bhisa ais* (7. 1. 9) *ity aisbhāvaḥ prāpnoti.*

[109] Pat. zu värtt. 8 (p. 24 Z. 26 f.): *ekavarṇavac ca dīrgho bhavatīti vaktavyam. kiṃ prayojanam? vācā taratīti dvyajlakṣaṇaṣ ṭhan mā bhūd iti.*

[110] Pat. zu värtt. 9 (p. 25 Z. 4): *nāvyapavṛktasyāvayavasyāvayavāśrayo vidhir bhavati.* Z. B. wird *u* in *ū* nicht als von dem ersten Bestandteil des *ū* getrennt wahrgenommen, es wird nur abstrahiert; *r* in *ṛ* (ərə) dagegen wird als von dem vokalischen Bestandteil getrennt wahrgenommen, man hört in *ṛ* tatsächlich zwei verschiedene Laute. Soweit *u* in *ū* in Frage kommt, gilt also eine durch einen 'kurzen' Vokal bedingte Regel nicht, während für den konsonantischen Bestandteil des *ṛ* eine durch *r* bedingte Regel Anwendung findet.

Dieser Grundsatz ist im Bhāṣya durch einen Beleg (*dṛṣṭānta*) aus dem täglichen Leben gerechtfertigt, ist also '*lokanyāyasiddha*' (vgl. zu diesem Terminus Kielhorn, PŚ. Translation p. IX f.). Da es jedoch möglich und erlaubt ist — wenn auch nicht notwendig — auch für einen solchen Grundsatz ein '*jñāpaka*' zu finden, bemerkt bereits Kaiy., daß die verschiedenen *jñāpaka*, die von Patañjali zu värtt. 7 und 8 in einem speziellen Sinn genommen werden (siehe im folgenden!). den allgemeinen Satz vermuten lassen, der im värtt. 9 durch einen *lokanyāya* begründet ist, und stellt Nāg. an unserer Stelle das Prinzip als '*jñāpakasiddha*' dar.

[111] Pat. zu värtt. 7 (p. 24 Z. 7 ff.): ,,Das von Pāṇini eingeschlagene Verfahren macht die Vermutung notwendig (*jñāpayati*), daß (obgleich das in värtt. 6 formulierte Prinzip gilt) eine durch einen 'kurzen' Vokal bedingte Regel nicht statt hat, wenn ein 'langer' Vokal vorliegt, insofern er [ausdrücklich] (in 6. 1. 75) verordnet, [daß das Augment] *tuk* vor *ch* nach einem 'langen' Vokal [angefügt wird] (wofür keine notwendig machende 'Veranlassung' bestünde, wenn dies sowieso nach 6. 1. 73 geschähe. Die Regel 6. 1. 75 würde also ohne das erschlossene Prinzip sinnlos sein, und erhält einen Sinn, wenn es gilt.)

(Opponens:) ,,Das ist nicht 'etwas, das eine Vermutung notwendig macht' ('*jñāpaka*', Trapp: 'beweiskräftig'! — Kielhorn Paribh. Ś. Translation p. V: ,,*Jñāpaka* . . . is applicable to any term employed by Pāṇini, or to any rule given by him, or in short to any proceeding of his, which would be meaningless or superfluous (*vyartha*), or for which it would be absolutely impossible to assign a reason, if a particular Paribhāṣā did not exist, but which appears necessary and serves a purpose (i. e. is *charitārtha*), as soon as and only when that Paribhāṣā has been adopted, and which on that account indicates the existence of that Paribhāṣā etc.''). Denn diese Regel hat eine andere

„da es einen Sinn haben muß, daß [an das in 7. 1. 9 genannte *a*] ein *t* angefügt ist[112], und

„da es einen Sinn haben muß, daß das in 4. 4. 7 stehende (Wort) '*nau-*' ausdrücklich genannt ist[113];

„jedoch wird

„weder die Befürchtung ausgesprochen, daß

„z. B. in *prātar ṛtam* sich [nach] Pāṇ. 8. 3. 14 (Schwund des *r* vor *r*) [ergeben müßte] (insofern nach dem genannten Prinzip der konsonantische Bestandteil des *ṛ* durch den Ausdruck 'vor *r*' mitgenannt wäre), und

„z. B. in *tad ḷkārah* sich [nach] Pāṇ. 8. 4. 60 [*l* für den Dental (*d*)] [ergeben müßte] (insofern nach dem genannten Prinzip der konsonantische Bestandteil des *ḷ* durch den Ausdruck 'vor *l*' mitgenannt wäre),

„noch auch eine Beschwichtigung (solcher Befürchtung) gegeben[114].

(Hieraus geht denn klärlich hervor, daß der konsonantische Bestandteil des *ṛ* und *ḷ* sich nicht am Anfang dieser Laute befindet, somit *r* in *prātar ṛtam* überhaupt nicht vor *r*, sondern vor einen Vokal (ə), und *d* in *tad ḷkāraḥ* überhaupt nicht vor *l*, sondern vor einen Vokal (ə) zu stehen kommt.)

2. „Andrerseits heißt es im Bhāṣya zu ŚS. 5[115]: 'die (Laut) partikel, welche auf *r* (in *ṝ*) folgt'.

'notwendig machende Veranlassung'.

„Was ist diese Veranlassung?

(Opponens:) „[Die Veranlassung ist, daß Pāṇini im Sinn hat:) 'Ich werde in 6. 1. 76 lehren, daß [nach einem 'langen' Vokal an Ende eines Wortes Antritt von *tuk*] beliebig ist. (6. 1. 75 muß demnach gelehrt werden, um 6. 1. 76 möglich zu machen.)

„[Wenn sich das so verhält,] dann [macht das von Pāṇ. eingeschlagene Verfahren die Vermutung des obigen Prinzips notwendig] insofern er zwei Regeln lehrt (wo eine einzige genügen würde). Denn wenn das Prinzip nicht bestände (*itarathā*), würde er nur (in einer einzigen Regel) formulieren *dīrghāt padāntād vā* [statt: *dīrghāt. padāntād vā*]". (Daß es schwerer ist, zwei Regeln statt einer zu lehren geht aus Paribh. 121 hervor, wenn auch das hier aufgestellte Prinzip als zu weitgehend abzulehnen ist.)

112 Pat. zu värtt. 7 (p. 24 Z. 12): *taparakaraṇasāmarthyān na bhaviṣyati* „Da es einen Sinn haben muß, daß [an *a* in *ato bhisa ais* (7. 1. 9)] ein *t* angefügt ist, wird [Substitution von *ais* für *bhis* in *khaṭvābhiḥ*] nicht statthaben. (Wenn nämlich der Ausdruck 'nach *at*' ('kurzem' *a*) auch den zweiten Teil des *ā* bezeichnen sollte, würde es genügen, einfach zu sagen 'nach *a*'".

113 Pat. zu värtt. 8 (p. 25 Z. 1 f.): . . . *naugrahaṇaṃ jñāpakaṃ dīrghād dvyajlakṣaṇo vidhir na bhavatīti* „Die Nennungen von *nau-* (in 4. 4. 7) ist ein *jñāpaka*, daß eine Operation die durch [das Vorhandensein von] zwei '*ac*' bedingt ist, nicht nach einem 'langen' Vokal statt hat [obgleich es bei Annahme des genannten Grundsatzes als zwei '*ac*' enthaltend gelten muß]. (Wenn nämlich solche Operation statt hätte, würde die spezielle Nennung von *nau-* in 4. 4. 7 sinnlos sein.)"

114 Man könnte sagen, daß die Fälle '*pralūya*' usw. die Fälle '*prātar ṛtam*' usw. elliptisch mitbezeichnen. Dagegen spricht die sorgfältige Behandlung, die Pat. jeder einzelnen der aufgeführten Befürchtungen zu teil werden läßt, und — entscheidend — die Tatsache, daß die für *pralūya* vorgebrachte Beschwichtigung für angebliches *prātar* + *rətan* nicht in Frage käme. Es hätte eine andere Beschwichtigung vorgebracht werden müssen, die uns auch darüber aufklärt, warum in *mātṝṇām* usw. der in värtt. 6 gelehrte Grundszta gilt, in *prātar ṛtam* (angeblich = *pratar* + *rətam*) aber nicht.

115 Dies ist ein merkwürdiger Irrtum: der angeführte Satz findet sich im Bhāṣya zu ŚS. 3 (p. 26 Z. 4 f.). — Vgl.

(Hieraus geht klärlich hervor, daß der konsonantische Bestandteil der in ŚS. 2 gelehrten Laute sich auch nicht am Ende dieser Laute befindet.)

(5) „[Bhaṭṭ sagt: 'In der Mitte des zweiten Lautes (*ḷ)] sind zwei konsonantische *l*'.

„Die [zu Grunde liegende] Meinung ist: da *ḷ ein Genosse des erstgenannten Lautes (*ṛ) ist, welcher zwei Konsonanten enthält[116] (insofern *ṛ und *ḷ in värtt. 1, 2 zu 6. 1. 101 in gleichem Atem gelehrt werden).

„Wenn[117] dieses (värtt. 1, 2 zu 6. 1. 101) gelehrt wird (*atra*), so ist die Substitution des ersten Lautes (*ṛ) korrekt nur dann, wenn es sich um ein Einzelsubstitut handelt, dessen Original zwei kurze *ṛ* sind (*ṛ* + *ṛ*); und die des zweiten Lautes (*ḷ) nur dann, wenn es sich um ein Einzelsubstitut handelt, dessen Original ein kurzes *ṛ* und ein *ḷ* ist[118].

„Eben weil sich das so verhält (ist durch '*ṛti*' im ersten värtt. nicht auch *ḷ* genannt, und durch '*ḷti*' im zweiten värtt. nicht auch *ṛ*[119], und) wird, wenn *ḷ* folgt nicht *ṛ, und wenn *ṛ* folgt, nicht *ḷ substituiert.

„Eben weil sich das so verhält, ist im ersten värtt. ausdrücklich gelehrt vor 'kurzem' *ṛ*, und hat der Ausdruck 'vor kurzem *ḷ*' im zweiten värtt. einen Sinn.

„Und [eben weil es sich so verhält] ist es logisch einwandfrei, wenn im Bhāṣya zu 1. 1. 9 gesagt wird: 'Für '*ṛti*' werde ich '*ṛtaḥ*' lehren', und: 'indem man sich auf diese värtt. stützt braucht man nicht zu lehren, daß *ṛ* und *ḷ* 'gleichlautig' heißen [um *hotṝkāraḥ* für *hotṛ* + *ḷkāraḥ* zu erhalten][120].

„Jene beiden Laute (*ṛ und *ḷ) sind 'halbverschlossen' [zu nennen], da wir keine Autorität dafür besitzen, die (gegenüber *ṛ* = *ərə* und *ḷ* = *ələ*] hinzugetretene Artikulationsweise, welche die eines konsonantischen *r* ist [*ṛ = *ərrə*, *ḷ = *əllə*], zu ignorieren. Wenn sie nämlich 'offen' wären, dann würden auch sie [wie *ṝ*] durch offenes *ṛ* und *ḷ* mitgenannt, und bereits das värtt. [zu 6. 1. 101] würde sinnlos sein[121], insofern [das Resultat] sich bereits aus 6. 1. 101 korrekt ergeben würde".

auch Bhāṣya zu 8. 4. 1 värtt. 2 (p. 452 Z. 9).

[116] Im PŚ. zu Paribh. 103 zeigt Nāg., daß wir aus dem Bhāṣya zu 2. 3. 8 lernen, daß nur ähnliche Dinge als Genossen behandelt werden (p. 103 Z. 8 f.: *tena* [*karmapravacanīyayukte dvitīyā* (2. 3. 8) *iti sūtre bhāṣyena*] *hi sadṛśānām eva prayoge sahāyabhāvo bodhitaḥ*).

[117] Nachdem Nāg. die Bemerkungen Bhaṭṭ.'s erläutert hat, geht er dazu über, zwei Feststellungen zu treffen, die sich nicht bei Bhaṭṭ. finden.

[118] Warum sich das so verhält, ist im Uddyota erörtert (siebe oben S. 322).

[119] Daß wir zu solcher Annahme berechtigt sind, hat Nāg. zu värtt. 5 zu 1. 1. 9 (siehe oben S. 326) erörtert.

[120] Während alle die in den mit 'eben weil sich das so verhält' (*ata eva*) eingeleiteten Sätze die Richtigkeit der Behauptung voll bestätigen, die sich demnach im Einklang mit dem Bhāṣya befindet, kann man nicht sagen, daß die Formulierung Kāty.'s oder auch die des Opponens ein '*jñāpaka*' enthält, das uns ein Prinzip vermuten läßt. Alles angeführte autorisiert uns jedoch, die Substitutionen nur in den von Pat. genannten Fällen für richtig zu halten. Danach haben wir dann die Interpretation einzurichten.

[121] Wenn Kāty. das värtt. lehrt, sind *ṛ und *ḷ noch nicht '*ac*' genannt. Erst nachdem das geschehen ist, kann man es zurückweisen. Es ist jedoch nicht von Anfang an sinnlos. Wenn *ṛ und *ḷ 'offen' wären, würde es überhaupt nicht vorgeschlagen worden sein.

Es ist ein langer und ein dorniger Weg, der vom '*Phaṇīśa*' zum '*Nāgeśa*' führt, und es ist nicht zu verwundern, daß er oft gescheut, und immer wieder der Versuch unternommen wird, das Bhāṣya ohne die Hilfe gründlich verstandener Kommentare zu meistern. Ich habe hier dartun wollen, daß es nicht nur notwendig ist, die Werke jener 'Späteren' zu lesen: wir müssen auch ihren individuellen Charakter verstehen, ihre verschiedenartigen Betrachtungsweisen werten und in Rechnung stellen. Es besteht ein gewaltiger Unterschied zwischen der kurzen, aufs Praktische gerichteten und nicht immer konsistenten Kāśikā und der messerscharf formulierten, spitzfindigen und geschlossenen Siddhāntakaumudī; zwischen Kaiy.'s pedantisch-genauem Pradīpa, in dem die Schwierigkeiten des Bhāṣyatexts mit nüchternem Bemühen angegriffen werden, und dem Uddyota, der sie meisterhaft beherrscht; zwischen dem Śabdakaustubha mit seinen grüblerischen Überlegungen und selbsterfundenen *phakkikās*, und dem Śabdenduśekhara mit seiner originellen und sicheren Virtuosität, seinen strikten Prinzipien.

Sind auch die Glieder der Kette, die Bhartṛhari und Nāgojībhaṭṭa verbindet, von unterschiedlichem direkten Wert für die Interpretation des Bhāṣya, so können wir doch kaum eines vernachlässigen, wollen wir nicht das Verständnis des nächsten in Frage stellen. Und wenn auch Nāg. nicht wirklich das letzte Wort haben soll, und für unseren Geschmack immer noch zu viele Annahmen macht, so scheint es mir doch außer Frage, daß der Weg ins Bhāṣya über das gründliche Kennenlernen dieses genialen Scholastikers führt. Es hat seine tiefere Bedeutung, daß Kielhorn den Paribhāṣenduśekhara übersetzte und erläuterte, bevor er an die Herausgabe des Bhāṣya ging.

Als ein Ausdruck der brahmanischen Civilisation, jener Lebenseinrichtung, die Indiens hervorstechendste Eigenart bildet, hat 'die Weisheit des Paṇḍits', der diese Seiten gewidmet waren, schließlich noch ein höheres Interesse, als die einer schätzenswerten Hilfe, die sie uns bei unsern philologischen Bemühungen sein kann. Sie zeigt uns harte Züge: wir finden in ihr all den Stolz, all die Unnahbarkeit des Brahmanen, der fern von der Masse eifersüchtig seinen alleinigen Besitz, seinen einzigen Schatz hütet, die Wissenschaft, welche s e i n e n Schutz gesucht hat, und die den Uneingeweihten sich nicht ergeben mag. Wir finden in ihr aber auch die fromme Bescheidenheit des 'Zweigeborenen', dessen höchstes Glück es ist, die heiligen Schriften seiner Vorväter zu studieren und sich möglichst Wort für Wort anzueignen, der die Siege und Niederlagen weltlicher Reiche auf indischem Boden vergessen, aber die Sprache der Urzeit seines Volkes bewahrt hat bis auf den heutigen Tag.

B. On the Identity of the Vārttikakāra (1937–1938)

Paul Thieme

In *Pāṇini and the Veda*, Thieme had dealt, among other things, with the conceptual and historical relationships between Pāṇini's grammar and the Prātiśākhya literature, the treatises attached to each of the schools or branches (*śākhā*) of the Veda. Among these, the *Vājasaneyi Prātiśākhya*, which belongs to the White Yajurveda, is attributed to a certain Kātyāyana. This raises the problem of the relationship between this Kātyāyana and the Kātyāyana who was the author of the *vārttikas* on Pāṇini's *sūtras*. Though Goldstücker had defended the identity of the two Kātyāyana's, this view had been generally rejected by Western scholars. Thieme returned to it, and brilliantly defended it in "On the Identity of the Vārtti-

kakāra," here reproduced from *Indian Culture* 4, 1937–1938, 189–209. The demonstration culminates in the analysis by Kātyāyana, the *vārttikakāra*, of the description of the pronunciation of the *Subrahmaṇyā*,* a Vedic chant which plays an important role in the Vedic ritual. Here Kātyāyana, the *vārttikakāra*, shows himself to be not only a linguist conversant with the technicalities and theoretical issues raised by Pāṇini's rules, but equally at home in the technicalities of the more practical realm of the Vedapāṭhaka, the priest who recites the Veda at the sacrifice.

In my little book 'Pāṇini and the Veda' I have raised afresh, amongst other points, the question of the relative age of Pāṇini's work and the so-called Vājasaneyi Prātiśākhya (properly to be styled: Kātyāyanīya Prātiśākhyasūtra). Following others I thought a comparison of such rules of the two Sūtras as agree in their purport, but show a somewhat different wording, to be especially helpful towards a final settlement of this old problem. I arrived at the conclusion that the rules of the Prātiśākhya, though often lacking in that utmost brevity observable in the Aṣṭādhyāyī, at several instances appear to reveal a deliberate endeavour to improve on formulations of Pāṇini's. Particularly convincing in this respect seemed to me the difference of Pāṇini 1. 1. 9 *tulyāsyaprayatnaṃ savarṇam* and V. Pr. 1. 43 *samānasthānakaraṇāsyaprayatnaḥ savarṇaḥ*, since this latter definition adds to the former an essential element (*sthānakaraṇa*), which also the Vārttikakāra proposes to supply when expressing in vārtt. 2 on Pāṇini 1. 1. 9 the desire to replace Pāṇini's rule by the more accurate one: *āsye tulyadeśaprayatnaṃ savarṇam*, his expression *deśa* comprising the terms *sthāna* and *karaṇa*[1].

Yet my arguments have not been able to carry conviction. Even in face of an instance as the one given just now, Prof. Keith still maintains that 'it is easy to explain his (Pāṇini's) deviations from the V. Pr. by the desire to condense the matter of the latter.' [2] Now I am ready to admit for argument's sake that, as matters stand, the decision of the dilemma essentially rests on the appreciation of certain general considerations and, in the end, must be of subjective nature.[3] Prof. Keith holds Pāṇini 1. 1. 9 to be a condensation of V. Pr. 1. 43; I hold V. Pr. 43 to be an improvement on Pāṇini, but though having the weighty support of the Vārttikakāra,

* [The translation of the *Subrahmaṇyā* runs as follows: "Subrahmaṇyom! Subrahmaṇyom! Subrahmaṇyom! O Indra, come! O possessor of bay horses, come! O ram of Medhātithi, o wife of Vṛṣaṇaśva! O cow impregnator! O lover of Ahalyā! O Brahman of the Kauśika family! O usurper of the name of Gautma! Today (respectively: tomorrow, in two days, in three days) come to the Soma pressing, O generous one! Gods, Brahmans, come, come, come!" The inserted piece (*asau yajate* . . .) means: "N. sacrifices, the son of N. sacrifices, the grandson of N. sacrifices, the descendant of N. sacrifices, the father of N. sacrifices, the grandfather of N. sacrifices, the greatgrandfather of N. sacrifices, the father, the grandfather, the greatgrandfather of those that will be born sacrifices." Specimens of the *Subrahmaṇyā* as they are still chanted can be heard on an LP record album *The Four Vedas* (Asch Mankind Series, New York 1969).]

[1] *o.c.*, p. 92f.

[2] *Indian Culture*, Vol. II, p. 741.

[3] Thus O. Strauss, Deutsche Literaturzeitung 1936, p. 880, who is inclined however to accept my view as the more probable one.

I can see no short way to convince my opponent that my appreciation of the facts is correct. For the briefer wording *is* Pāṇini's, and for somebody who takes brevity of expression to be probably a sign of young age, this may be a sufficient argument.

I

If, then, the correctness of my contention be still open to doubt, this much my lengthy discussions must have shown, that it is at least possible to accept Pāṇini's priority, and to consider it on par with the contrary assumption. This being, at least for argument's sake, admitted, we are faced with the further question, whether the author of the Vārttika and the author of the V. Pr., who is referred to by his commentator Uvaṭa as '*Kātyāyanācārya*,' may not be identical, after all. For it is hard to agree with Prof. Keith's view that the identity of a name like Kātyāyana creates 'no probability at all' with reference to the identity of the authors.[4] The probability created may be a faint one, it may even be altogether, deceptive, but anyone thinking the V. Pr. to be later than Pāṇini, must feel a keen suspicion, which he wants to be either removed or confirmed by good reasons. Prof. Keith is persuaded that the Vārttika and the V. Pr. are by quite different hands: 'It seems to have been forgotten by Dr. Thieme that Weber [note: Ind. Stud., V, 103ff.; XIII, 444; Keith, TS., I, p. CLXXI] long ago adduced points in which the two works differed in terminology, and that unless and until the facts in question are explained away, they form a very powerful argument against the identity of the two authors.'[5]

When Albrecht Weber wrote the 5th volume of the 'Indische Studien'[6] he was not yet in possession of either a manuscript or an edition of the Mahābhāṣya. Whatever he knew of the work of the Vārttikakāra was culled from the old Calcutta edition of Pāṇini, where a number of 'vārttikas' are quoted, and from Goldstücker's 'Pāṇini'. He wrote the 13th volume[7] after just having gone through the whole Bhāṣya for the first time, and many are the misunderstandings that occurred to him in the difficult, really temerous, task of mastering the great and intricate work in one sitting. As a matter of fact, he added here nothing new to what he said in the 5th volume with respect to our problem: which merely proves that arguments do not lie on the surface. It must be remembered that all notions about the Vārttikakāra had to be of the haziest description until Kielhorn, after having shown a way to distinguish the part of the Bhāṣya belonging to Patañjali from that belonging to Kātyāyana,[8] presented our science with his monumental edition.[9] Weber's arguments—like those of Goldstücker—are nevertheless still of interest. But this interest is almost altogether a historical one. There is something truly pathetical about the passion with which these great pioneers tried to wring evidence from witnesses they could not really understand half; there is something truly admirable in the acumen by which now Goldstücker and then Weber somehow managed to find a way-mark in the all-overspreading darkness.

Prof. Keith has summed up those points of Weber that in his

[4] Keith, *l.c.*, p. 742.
[5] *l.c.*
[6] Berlin, 1862.
[7] Berlin, 1873.
[8] Kātyāyana and Patañjali, Bombay 1876.
[9] BSS. 1880–1885.

opinion still hold good in his Translation of the TS., I p. CLXXI, to which he refers me. They run as follows:

'1. The term *jit* occurs in both [the Vārttika and the V. Pr.] with a different sense; 2. the terms used in the Prātiśākhya (*sim, mud, dhi, bhāvin*) are not found in the Vārttikas; 3. the Vārttika (on II. 4. 54) makes *khyā* have the original form of *kśā*; the Prātiśākhya (IV. 164) repudiates this view; 4. the Prātiśākhya (IV. 120) provides for the regular change of a mute before a nasal into a nasal; the Vārttika (on VIII. 4. 45) leaves it optional except in the Bhāṣā before a nasal affix.'

It is not difficult to show that Weber's points even in this sifted form do not at all deserve the value Prof. Keith attaches to them.

Let us start with points 3 and 4.

For point 3 Prof. Keith relies on Weber, Ind. Stud. V, p. 119, who quotes *asiddhe śasya yavacanaṃ vibhāṣā* as the *first* värtt. on Pāṇini 2. 4. 54. But from Kielhorn's edition it becomes clear that this is only the third vārtt. while the first runs thus: *cakṣiṅaḥ kśāñkhyāñau*, which means: '[If a suffix called *ārdhadhātuka* follows,] both *kśāñ* or *khyāñ* are substituted for *cakṣiṅ* [not only *khyāñ* as Pāṇini teaches].' The following vārtt.s say that instead of *kśāñ* and *khyāñ*, there might also be taught one single substitute starting with *kh* and *ś* (i.e. *khśāñ*), from which are to be derived the forms with *khyā* and *kṣā-* by means of an optional rule to be inserted in Pāṇini somewhere after 8. 2. 1. Further vārttikas discuss the benefit that might be derived from our doing so.

V. Pr. 4. 164 *khyāteḥ khayau kaśau*[10]*G ārgyaḥ sakhyokhyamukhyavarjam.* 'Gārgya changes the *kh* and *y* of root *khyā* to *k* and *ś* respectively—except in *sakhya, ukhya, mukhya.*' This cannot be said, as Prof. Keith appears to believe, to repudiate the view that *khyā* is derived from *kśā*; it is, on the contrary, in perfect agreement with the first vārtt. on 2. 4. 54, which recognizes *khyā* and *kśā* side by side, while Pāṇini knows only *khyā*.

Point 4. Having as its chief and immediate object to give rules for the conversion of the VS. Padapāṭha into the Saṃhitāpāṭha, the V. Pr. naturally has to teach only such *sandhi* phenomena as are observable in the latter.[11] Hence it says in 4. 120 [*sparśo' pañcamaḥ* 4. 117] *pañcame pañcamam* 'a mute is changed into a nasal if a nasal follows', having explicitly stated before that this rule does not apply inside a word (4. 116 *nāntaḥpade svarapañcamāntaḥsthāsu*).

Having as its object to define the *sandhi* phenomena of a spoken language and several Saṃhitās, the Aṣṭādhyāyī naturally has to teach optional validity of its rules rather often[12]. So in 8. 4. 45. It is clearly in no way surprising that Kātyāyana, even if he be the author of the V. Pr., does not take exception to it. The fact of this rule being strictly observed in his own Saṃhitā could give him no reason to forbid its optional validity in other Saṃhitās or in the Bhāṣā. And when adding to Pāṇini 8. 4. 45 that it is always

[10] Thus correctly Weber's ms. A.

[11] *cf.* AV. Pr. 1, 2 *evam iheti ca vibhāṣāprāptaṃ sāmānye* with the commentator's exposition as given by Whitney.

[12] *cf.* Patañjali I, p. 400 l. 9ff. *avaśyaṃ khalv asmābhir idaṃ vaktavyaṃ 'bahulam, anyatarasyām, ubhayathā, vā, ekeṣām' iti. sarvavedapāriṣadaṃ hīdaṃ śāstram. tatra naikaḥ panthāḥ śakya āsthātum.* 'We can indeed not -avoid teaching [with general expressions like:] 'often', 'on one alternative', 'both ways', 'optionally', 'according to the teaching of some'. For this Śāstra [of Pāṇini] is a grammar of the *whole* Veda. This being so, he cannot take one way only [and imply that other usages are incorrect].'

applied in the Bhāṣā if the consonant is followed by a suffix (*yaro 'nunāsike pratyaye bhāṣāyāṃ nityavacanam*), he distinctly suggests that it is not always applied in a Saṃhitā (*cf. e.g. vāgmin*): if he had failed to add *bhāṣāyām* to his own teaching, then and only then we should have a right to speak of a contradiction, *viz.* to V. Pr. 4. 116.

Now we may turn to point 2. The expression *sim* (= Pāṇini's *āk*), *mud* (= Pāṇini's *śar*), *dhi* (= half vowels and nasals), *jit* (= Pāṇini's *khar*) and *bhāvin* (= all vowels except *a*, *ā*) are all used in the V. Pr., that is true enough. But they all are explicitly defined. Who would have been able to understand them otherwise? When commenting on the Aṣṭādhyāyi, Kātyāyana could not but prefer the short expressions formed by Pāṇini's rules. When writing the V. Pr., he could not employ Pāṇini's *pratyāhāras* without having given also the Śiva Sūtras and some further rules teaching how to put them to their proper use. The rules which serve this purpose in Pāṇini (1. 3. 3, 1. 1. 71, 1. 3. 9) are at the same time useful also in other respects (for the formation of *sup*, *tiṅ*, *etc.*): in the V. Pr. they would have been given just for the sake of a few sound-*pratyāhāras*.

Occasionally there occur in the Vārttika expressions like *svara* (instead of *ac*), *vyañjana* (instead of *hal*), *sandhyakṣara* (instead of *ec*), *sparśa*, *prathama*, *dvitīya*, *tṛtīya*, *caturtha*, *jihvāmūlīya*, and *upadhmānīya*, all of which can be found also in the V. Pr. Such terms, of course, were common property, they were understood by everybody. The Vārttikakāra occasionally even employs *samānākṣara* (*ec*), when the V. Pr. says *sim*, *aghoṣa* (*khay*), when the V. Pr. says *jit*.[13]

As the compiler of the V. Pr., Kātyāyana did not want, I assume, to presuppose acquaintance with the Aṣṭādhyāyi in those Veda students likely to study his book. Most probably they knew as little of it as modern Vedapāṭhakas would. As the commentator of the Aṣṭādhyāyī, Kātyāyana did not want, I assume, to presuppose acquaintance with his little treatise on the V.S. in his readers. Why should he have meant the Vārttika only for Vājasaneyins? I cannot see any inherent impossibility in such assumptions.

The only really decisive argument against the identity of the two Kātyāyanas in Weber's opinion is of course the fact that *jit* has a different sense in a vārttika (vārtt. 7 on 1. 1. 68) and in the V. Pr. (here = Pāṇini's *khar*), though Pāṇini does not employ the term *jit* himself. Prof. Keith also accords this point precedence before the others.

Now it is somewhat misleading to say that *jit* is a term with the Vārttikakāra. This would suggest that he uses it the way he uses *ḍu* (vol. I p. 304 = Pāṇini's *ṣaṣ*) or *taṇ* (vol. I p. 488, vol. II pp. 99 and 221 = *saṃjñāchandasī*)[14], which two terms he nowhere explains and may have taken from some other source.[15] In reality the case of *jit* in vārtt. 7 on 1. 1. 68 is of a different character.

In his Vārttika on Pāṇini 1. 1. 68, Kātyāyana discourses on the difficulty that a word given by Pāṇini in his rules sometimes denotes only words for the representatives of the different kinds of the conception named by the word, as for example *vṛkṣa* in 2. 4. 12, where we have to understand that the rule is to be applied only to the different names of the trees like *plakṣa*, *nyagrodha etc.*,

[13] All the above quoted terms from the Vārttika have been collected by Kielhorn, *Ind. Ant.*, XVI, p. 106.
[14] Kielhorn, *l.c.*
[15] Do they not resemble curiously the *sim*, *mud*, *dhi*, *jit* of the V. Pr. with their apparent arbitrariness.

but not to the word *vṛkṣa* itself; sometimes its synonyms, like *sva* in 3. 4. 40, where we have to understand the word *sva* or any other word for 'property'; sometimes its synonyms only, like *rājan* in 2. 4. 23, where we have to understand any word for 'king' but the word *rājan* itself; and sometimes words for the representatives of the different kinds of the conception named and the word given itself, like *matsya* in 4. 4. 35, where we have to understand the different names of fish and the word *matsya* itself. To remove this difficulty, he proposes to teach the following rules in addition to Pāṇini 1. 1. 68: (1) A word to which an *s* is attached as *anubandha* belongs to the first class (vārtt. 5); (2) a word to which a *p* is attached, to the second (vārtt. 6); (3) a word to which a *j* is attached, to the third (vārtt. 7); (4) a word to which a *jh* is attached, to the last (vārtt. 8). Consequently we must add an *s* to *vṛkṣa* in 2. 4. 12; a *p* to *sva* in 3. 4. 40; a *j* to *rājan* in 2. 4. 23; and a *jh* to *matsya* in 4. 4. 35.

The terms *sit, pit, jit, jhit* are, then, not terms Kātyāyana takes so to speak from his own private vocabulary, but terms he *would* use if Pāṇini had taught the rules proposed. I cannot see, why Kātyāyana in considering this possibility of an addition to Pāṇini's grammar should feel bound to choose another sound but *j* for his third rule, just because he has employed *jit* in the V. Pr. in a different sense. I should find it much more astonishing that he does not mind proposing as *anubandha p*, though Pāṇini has already employed *p* as *anubandha* for a different purpose.

But quite apart from all this, I do think arguments like Weber's 'decisive *jit*' are all but worthless. Even if Kātyāyana were not consistent, we should be quite wrong to press the point. Does not Pāṇini himself use homonymous terms over and over again? What valid inference could be drawn from *jit* being used in the Vārttika in the sense of 'having *j* as *anubandha*', and in the V. Pr. in the sense of 'surd mutes and sibilants' when Pāṇini in his work uses *aṇ* as a *pratyāhāra* for *a, i, u, and* as a term for a *kṛt* (3. 2. 1 *etc.*) and a *taddhita* (4. 1. 83 *etc.*); or *āp* as a term for the feminine endings in *ā* (4. 1. 1. *etc.*), *and* as a *pratyāhāra* for all case terminations from the *ā* of the instrumental singular up to the *sup* of the locative plural (7. 2. 112); or *ak* as a *pratyāhāra* for *a, i, u, ṛ, ḷ, and* in the sense of 'having no *k*' (6. 1. 132 *etc.*), *etc. etc.*: examples lie on the way of anybody who is ready to take the trouble to look.

I cannot regret having 'forgotten' Weber's points as referred to by Prof. Keith. The instances supposed to show that the author of the V. Pr. and the Vārttika 'in several important respects completely differ in opinion on phonetic points'[16] were taken from misinterpreted passages. The deviation in the terminology recognizable as far as *sim, mud, dhi, jit* are concerned throws no light. Nobody can deny an author the right to express himself the way he chooses and thinks appropriate to the particular occasion. If I should see anything significant in terminological usages, it would be the circumstance that the Vārttikakāra does use Prātiśākhya terms occasionally: *svara* 'vowel', *vyañjana* 'consonant', *sandhyakṣara* 'diphthong', *sparśa* 'mutes and nasals', *prathama* 'surdmute', *dvitīya* 'surd aspirate mute', *tṛtīya* 'sounding mute', *caturtha* 'sounding aspirate mute,' *jihvāmulīya*, and *upadhmānīya*;[17] that

[16] Keith, TS., I, p. CLXXI.
[17] To these above mentioned terms I only want to add one more: *vikāra* in vārtt. 16 on Pāṇini 1. 1. 66, 67 stands for the Pāṇinean term *ādeśa* (1. 1. 48, 56, 8. 3. 59), as *vikāra* in V. Pr. 1. 1. 33, *etc.*

beside *at*, *et*, *ot*, *etc*. he also has the Prātiśākhya way: *akāra*, *ekāra*, *okāra etc*., and that the V. Pr. sporadically employs Pāṇinean terms like *tiṅ* 1. 27; *luk* 3. 12; *lup* 1. 114; *et*, *ot* 1. 114; 4. 58. Is it not so that at least this last point has to be 'explained away' by rather far-fetched assumptions if we are to believe the V. Pr. to be older than Pāṇini?

II dvirbaddhaṃ subaddhaṃ bhavati (Patañjali III, p. 119, 1.l 21)

But I shall not rely on terminological usages. Again I am ready to admit for argument's sake that they cannot prove either theory. They just open out the possibility of that identity I suspect. To get a solid philological base from which we may approach the hard task of proving it conclusively, we have to confront single rules of Pāṇini and the V. Pr. Since my former endeavours have proved unconvincing, I shall again take a number of rules and ask again and again the decisive questions: Is it likely that Pāṇini has condensed the formulation of the V. Pr., or is it likely that the V. Pr. has wanted to improve on Pāṇini? And: Is it possible to recognize any connection between the deviations of the V. Pr. and vārttikas of Kātyāyana's? I need not apologize for the following discussions in part being rather intricate. He who wants to understand old Indian grammarians, must follow them into their subtleties, and he who wants to settle their relative age with better arguments than were at the command of Weber and Goldstücker, must understand them.

1. Pāṇini says in 1. 1. 66, 67 *tasminn iti nirdiṣṭe pūrvasya, tasmād ity uttarasya* 'when something is given in the locative case, the rule applies to what is preceding it; when in the ablative case, to what is following it.' Hence we have to understand when we read for example the loc. *aci* in 6. 1. 77, that this rule applies to what is preceding *ac*; when the abl. *dvyantarupasargebhyaḥ* in 6. 3. 97, that this rule is preceding *ac*; when the abl. *dvyantarupasargebhyaḥ* in 6. 3. 97, that this rule applies to what is following *dvi*, or *antar*, or a preposition.

The V. Pr says in 1. 134, 135 *tasminn iti nirdiṣṭe purvasya, tasmād ity uttarasyādeḥ*, which is longer by the word *ādeḥ*. But should we apply here the theory of condensation, we would be badly advised. For Pāṇini, in order to complete his second rule, has to teach besides in 1. 1. 54 *ādeḥ parasya* 'when [a substitute is taught to step] in the place of something that is following [something given in the ablative case], [the substitute steps] in the place of its first sound.' Only now we can construct correctly Pāṇini 6. 3. 97 *dvyantarupasargebhyo 'pa īt* 'long *ī* is substituted for the *first* sound of *ap* that is following *dvi*, or *antar*, or a preposition.' The V. Pr. need not give this rule.

One might ask, why it stopped at changing the second rule. Why did it not say correspondingly in 1. 134: *pūrvāntasya*, especially as it does not teach a rule like Pāṇini 1. 1. 52 *alo 'ntyasya* 'when [a substitute is taught to step in the place of something; it steps] in the place of the last sound'? An answer to this question I should not be able to give, if I had not the first vārttika on Pāṇini 1. 1. 66, 67: *nirdiṣṭagrahaṇam ānantaryārtham*, which means that the expression *nirdiṣṭe* in 1. 1. 66 can have only the purpose of making it clear that a rule containing a locative applies only to that which is preceding *immediately* the word put in the locative, that is the last sound. Else Pāṇini could have simply said '*tasminn iti pūrvasya.*'

Yet this may not be obvious enough.

Looking ahead, we find a rule that complements V. Pr. 1. 134, 135. In V. Pr. 1. 145 we read: *purvottarayor uttarasya* 'when [a rule would apply simultaneously] to what is preceding and to what is following, it [has to be understood to refer only] to what is following.'[18] This rule has, strange to say, no application in the Prātiśākhya. Nor does Pāṇini give it. Did he omit it as useless? This can hardly be. For in the Aṣṭādhyāyī there are sundry rules containing both a locative and an ablative case. Hence Kātyāyana formulates the vārtt. 3 on 1. 1. 66, 67: *ubhayor nirdeśe vipratiṣedhāt pañcamīnirdeśaḥ* 'when both (a locative and an ablative case) are given, the giving of the ablative [will be the stronger one according to Pāṇini 1. 4. 2 *vipratiṣedhe paraṃ kāryam*], since there is a conflict.' Those on the lookout for contradictions between the Vārttika and the V. Pr. might, however, point out that this vārtt. just shows that Pāṇini need not have taught a special rule like V. Pr. 1. 145, since the dilemma can be solved already by 1. 4. 2. Further they might point out that the V. Pr. in 1. 159 teaches a rule of identical purport with Pāṇini 1. 4. 2[19], hence the man who wrote the vārttika could not have thought 1. 145 necessary in the V. Pr. either. I must however disappoint them: Kātyāyana rejects in vārtt. 13 his first view that in a dilemma the giving of the ablative must be stronger according to Pāṇini 1. 4. 2, by showing that technically there would be no 'conflict'[20], and gives as his final view (*siddhānta*) in vārtt. 17 that both the operations, the one concerning what is preceding and the one concerning what is following, would have to apply if Pāṇini 1. 1. 66, 67 is left as it stands—even if one should have recourse to some special assumption. I need not enter into the technical details of this assumption, which anyhow would not be applicable in the V. Pr. What I wanted to draw attention to, is the fact that there exists a connection between V. Pr. 1. 145 and vārtt. 3ff. on Pāṇini 1. 1. 66, 67. They are children of the same thought.

2. Pāṇini says in 1. 1. 11 *īdūded dvivacanaṃ pragṛhyam* 'an *ī* or *ū*, or *e* expressing duality is called *pragṛhya.*'

The V. Pr. says in 1. 92, 93 *pragṛhyam, ekārekārokārā dvivacanāntāḥ.*

Again, at a first look, the theory of condensation appears to work. There are however other points worth consideration.

I need not be long on the V. Pr. saying *ekāra etc.* instead of *e etc.* Also the AV Pr., which is later than Pāṇini even in Prof. Keith's opinion,[21] uses the former expressions, quite apart from the fact that the Vārttikakāra himself does not avoid them.

On the assumption that Pāṇini reformulated V. Pr. 1. 92, 93, we should have to account for Pāṇini not leaving the order of the vowels as it was given in the V. Pr. by saying *edīdūd* ... We could easily do so by suggesting that he preferred to follow the order of the alphabet.

On the assumption that the V. Pr. modelled its rules on

[18] Of identical construction is V. Pr. 1. 144 *saṃnikṛṣṭaviprakṛṣṭayoḥ saṃnikṛṣṭasy* and e.g. Pātañjali I, p. 71, 1. 16 *lakṣaṇapratipadoktayoḥ pratipadoktasyaiva.*

[19] See below.

[20] As defined in vārtt. 1, 2 on 1. 4. 2.

[21] *Indian Culture*, Vol. II, p. 741.

Pāṇini, we should have to account for its changing the natural order as reflected in a supposable *īkārokāraikārāḥ*. We could easily do so by pointing out that there exist dual forms in e (type: *māle*, *pacete*) as well as *ai* (type: *pacāvahai*). A formulation *īkārokārai-kārāḥ* would leave it doubtful, whether the former or the latter type was meant.

Is Pāṇini's *dvivacanam* a condensation of *dvivacanāntam*?

Pāṇini's rule may be translated as above. In this case *īdūdet* is the subject of the proposition, *dvivacanam*, the attribute of the subject. This seems obvious, but creates a difficulty: the rule does not apply to the ending e of a form like *pacete*, since here we have not an e expressing duality, but an *ete*. Neither has Pāṇini called *ete* '*pragṛhya*', nor has he stated that an e that happens to stand in the end of an element expressing duality, is also called 'pragṛhya'. This is formulated by the first vārtt. on Pāṇini 1. 1. 11: *īdādayo dvivacanaṃ pragṛhyā iti ced antyasya vidhih* 'if [Pāṇini means to say that] *ī etc*.., when expressing duality, are called '*pragṛhya*', a special rule must be given for [an e] that forms the end [of an element expressing duality].'

Pāṇini's rule may also be constructed by taking *dvivacanam* as subject, and *īdūdet* as its attribute. If we do so, *īdūdet* can, according to Pāṇini 1. 1. 72, be understood to denote something ending in *ī*, *ū*, e. This possibility is considered in vārtt. 2 and accepted as unobjectionable in vārtt. 3.

A third possibility is to understand 'word' as subject, and both *īdūdet* and *dvivacanam* as its attribute. Now we can translate according to Pāṇini 1. 1. 72: 'a word that ends in *ī*, *ū*, e and in an element expressing duality.' This possibility is considered in vārtt. 4 and accepted as unobjectionable in vārtt. 5.

Now everybody will agree that Pāṇini must have meant what I have translated first. For both alternative constructions create a serious difficulty with respect to the next rule (1. 1. 12 *adaso māt*), where only *īdūdet* can be the subject, and is taken as such by the Pāṇinīyas, who yet, following Patañjali's *siddhānta* (I. p. 68, l. 6f.), make *dvivacanam* the subject in 1. 1. 11. It is obvious that Kātyāyana's vārttikas 2 ff. are nothing but scholastic devices in defence of Pāṇini's wording.

On the assumption that Pāṇini condensed the *dvivacanāntam* of the V. Pr. into *dvivacanam*, we have to believe that he did not notice that he was putting the worse for the better.

This is the more unlikely as the V. Pr. wording removes with one stroke all difficulty. It may be noted that it is the only formulation that cannot be projected by any interpretative device into Pāṇini's rule. For *dvivacanāntāḥ* 'as endings of [a word] expressing duality' is a *tatpuruṣa*, and for Pāṇini 1. 1. 11 can be got from Pāṇini 1. 1. 72 only the *bahuvrīhi*: *dvivacanānta* 'whose end is [something] expressing duality'.

3. Pāṇini says in 6. 1. 158 *anudāttaṃ padam ekavarjam*. This admits of two interpretations. Either: 'a word has no *udātta* but one' (so Patañjali III, p. 98, l. 25 f.). Or: 'a word is *anudātta* except for one [vowel].'

It is only this latter interpretation that Kātyāyana considers in the Vārttika.

He is not satisfied with the rule. When forming a word like *āmalakīja*, we ought to make its first vowel *udātta* according to 6. 2. 82, and the last but one vowel of the element preceding *ja* according to 6. 2. 83 also. It is desirable that only the latter rule applies: *āmalákījaḥ*. In order to obtain this result, it would be necessary to recognize a 'conflict' between 6. 2. 82 and 6. 2. 83, which would allow us to apply Pāṇini 1. 4. 2. *vipratiṣedhe paraṃ kāryam.* Yet according to the definition of 'conflict' (*vipratiṣedha*) as given by Kātyāyana in vārtt. 1 and 2 on Pāṇini 1. 4. 2, there is no 'conflict' between 6. 2. 82 and 83, since it is quite possible for both rules to apply simultaneously—the one concerning the first and the other the third vowel, and the *eka* in 6. 1. 158 being understandable only in the sense of 'the one [for which an *udātta* (or primary *svarita*) is explicitly taught]'. This[22] is expressed by the first vārtt.: *anudātte vipratiṣedhānupapattir ekasmin yugapatsaṃbhavāt* 'if [we define with Pāṇini a word to be] *anudātta*, we do not obtain a 'conflict' [in cases where several *udāttas* are taught], since [several *udāttas*] might be substituted at the same time'.

The second vārtt. proposes to remove the difficulty by changing Pāṇini's definition: *siddhaṃ tv ekānanudāttatvāt* 'but it is alright if we teach [instead of *anudāttaṃ padam ekavarjam*]: *ekānanudāttaṃ padam* ('a word has only one vowel that is not *anudātta*').' Now there *is* a 'conflict' between 6. 2. 82 and 83 (and between similar rules), for now they cannot apply simultaneously, since from 6. 2. 82 we have to learn that the first vowel *alone* is *udātta*, and also from 6. 2. 83 that the last but one before *ja alone* is *udātta*.

Kātyāyana is careful not to propose *ekodāttaṃ padam*, for this would neglect the cases where a primary *svarita* is taught (6. 1. 185, *etc.*).

The reflection of Pāṇini 6. 1. 158 is found in V. Pr. 2. 1 *svaritavarjam ekodāttaṃ padam.* The decision whether this has been condensed by Pāṇini, or whether it is meant as an improvement on Pāṇini might have been doubtful if we had not the Vārttika. Having the Vārttika we cannot but recognize that V. Pr. 2. 1 wants to avoid what could be objected to Pāṇini. Its formulation equals the one proposed by the Vārttikakāra, only that in the Vārttika there has been found out a more concise form of a truly cunning simplicity. We may compare the three definitions in the following way:

Pāṇini 6. 1. 158 *anudāttaṃ padam ekavarjam*: concise, but objectionable (from Kātyāyana's point of view).

V. Pr. 2. 1. *svaritavarjam ekodāttaṃ padam*: not concise, but unobjectionable.

Vārttikakāra *ekānanudāttaṃ padam*: both concise and unobjectionable.

Here I may be forgiven if I quote what I wrote in my 'Pāṇini,' p. 93, after discussing Pāṇini 1. 1. 9 with vārtt. 1 and 2, and V. Pr. 1. 43:

'Pāṇini 1. 1. 9: *tulyāsyaprayatnaṃ savarṇam*: concise, but not precise.

V. Pr. 1. 43: *samānasthānakaraṇāsyaprayatnaḥ savarṇaḥ*: not concise but precise.

Vārttikāra: *āsye tulyadeśaprayatnaṃ savarṇam*: both concise and precise.'

4. A vocative is not accented except in the beginning of a sentence or of a line of a verse.

This is expressed by Pāṇini thus: 8. 1. 16 *padasya* 17 *padāt* 18 *anudāttaṃ sarvam apādādau* 19 *āmantritasya ca.*

By the V. Pr., thus: 2. 2. *anudāttam* 17 *padapūrvam āmantritam anānārthe 'pādādau.*

[22] I hope to have fathomed Kātyāyana's meaning correctly. His objection is, no doubt, very subtle, and Patañjali has easy play in showing that it may be dropped (III, p. 98, l. 20 ff.).

There are the following differences: (*a*) The V. Pr. has left out a word corresponding to *padasya*; (*b*) *āmantrita* is put in the genitive case by Pāṇini, in the nominative in the V. Pr.; (*c*) the V. Pr. has *padapūrvam* instead of *padāt*; (*d*) it has left out the expression *sarvam*; (e) it has added *anānārthe*.

a. It is not quite correct to say that the V. Pr. has left out a word corresponding to *padasya*. For a corresponding word *is* taught, only it need not be repeated. It is valid from 2. 1 *svaritavarjam ekodāttaṃ padam*, which equals Pāṇini 6. 1. 158 *anudāttaṃ padam ekavarjam*.

Here lies no argument. We could say, of course, that the V. Pr. has deliberately tried to arrange matters so as to be enabled to save one '*padam*'. But it could well be maintained that Pāṇini, for reasons of his own, has deliberately chosen a different disposition of the accenting rules; and that in any case he could not imitate the procedure of the V. Pr. since he wanted to put *pada* the first time in the nominative case and the second time in the genitive.

b. We have, then, in reality two nominatives in the V. Pr. and two genitives in the Aṣṭādhyāyī. This difference of construction cannot prove much. It is well known that when Pāṇini says: 'for *x* (gen.) [is substituted] *y* (nom.)', the V. Pr. say: *x* (nom.) [is changed] to *y* (acc.).' We are quite used to that.

It must, however, be pointed out that the Vārttikakāra is at pains of setting right the significance of the genitive *padasya*. If it is understood as 'in place of a *pada*' (according to Pāṇini 1. 1. 49), we have to construct the rule 8. 2. 4 *udāttasvaritayor yaṇaḥ svarito 'nudāttasya* thus: 'a *svarita* vowel is substituted for the last sound (according to 1. 1. 52) of a word that ends in an *anudātta* vowel (according to 1. 1. 72) that is following a *yaṇ* which has been substituted for an *udātta* or *svarita* vowel (according to 6. 1. 77).' This means that we can obtain the correct accent of forms like *kumāryàu* and *kiśoryàu*, but not of forms like *kumāryòḥ* and *kiśoryòḥ* (*cf*. värtt. 4 on 8. 1. 16, 17 with Patañjali). Consequently, *padasya* must be taken as an attributive genitive (vārtt. 5) and added as such throughout the chapter. *Padasya . . . sarvam* in 8. 1. 18 hereby receives the meaning: 'the whole of a *pada*', *padasya. . . anudāttasya* in 8. 2. 4: 'in the place of an *anudātta* vowel of a *pada*' etc.

It must be admitted, of course, that there lies no obvious argument here either.

c. The V. Pr. has *padapūrvam* instead of *padāt*. This is, no doubt, due to its having taught in 1. 135 that if something is given in the ablative case, the rule applies to the first [sound] of what is following. It is for the same reason that the V. Pr. says, for example, in 6. 11 *ākhyātapūrvam*, when Pāṇini could have used the ablative (*cf*. *atiṅaḥ* in 8. 1. 28). Pāṇini is free to use the ablative because he has employed the word *sarvam* in 8. 1. 18.

d. By leaving out *sarvam* the V. Pr. becomes, then, really more cumbrous.[23] As if foreseeing this objection against the formulation

[23] It should be noted, however, that it may use the ablative whenever a misunderstanding cannot arise. In V. Pr. 2. 17 and 6. 11 one might understand that only such vocatives and verb forms are meant as start with an *udātta* vowel before the rule is taught, type: *ágne*, *ápacat*. In 2. 9. *yáthā gr̥bhobhuvo' gnibhyaḥ*, for example, the ablative is unobjectionable, since the rule could not possibly be concerned with the first sound of *yáthā*.—Somewhat different is the case of the ablative in 4. 134 *udāttāc cānudāttaṁ svaritam*, since *udātta* means here a syllable 'containing an *udātta* vowel', and *svarita* a syllable 'containing a *svarita* vowel' according to V. Pr. 4. 1.

of the V. Pr. Kātyāyana tries to prove in the Vārttika that Pāṇini need not have employed the word *sarvam* in 8. 1. 18: *sarvavacanam anāder anudāttārtham iti cel luṭi pratiṣedhāt siddham* 'if [one should maintain that] 'the word *sarvam* has been employed [in 8. 1. 18] for the purpose [of obtaining substitution] of an *anudātta* vowel that is not the first [of what is following, in spite of 1. 1. 54]', [the answer would be that the substitution of an *anudātta* for such vowel] is already in order because of the prohibition [given in 8. 1. 29] with respect to a periphrastic future [which prohibition would be without any purpose if an *anudātta* had to be substituted only for the first vowel according to 8. 1. 29, since the first vowel in a periphrastic future is necessarily always *anudātta*]'. Against this one might object that Pāṇini 1. 1. 54, according to Kātyāyana's own words (vārtt. 1 on 1. 1. 54), is a special exception (*apavāda*) to the general injunction (*utsarga*) pronounced in 1. 1. 52: *alo 'ntyasya* 'a substitute steps in the place of the last sound', and if Pāṇini by his prohibition in 8. 1. 29 had indicated that in this chapter he did not want 1. 1. 54 to apply, he might yet have meant 1. 1. 52 to apply, and that consequently the word *sarvam* in 8. 1. 18 *is* necessary to remove this wrong impression. This objection is voiced in vārtt. 2 on 8. 1. 18 *alo 'ntyavidhiprasaṅgas tu* '[if *sarvam* were not employed in 8. 1. 18] there yet would wrongly apply Pāṇini 1. 1. 52.' Now Kātyāyana sets out to show in vārtt. 3 and 4 that Pāṇini has given an indication that 1. 1. 52 should not apply either in this chapter. For if it applied, he need not have taught the rule 8. 1. 51, since the last vowel of an ordinary future form is always *anudātta* (vārtt. 3), nor need he have employed the expression *anta* in 8. 2. 7, but could simply have said *nalopaḥ prātipadikasya* (instead of *prātipa-dikāntasya*), since it would anyway be clear from 1. 1. 52 that *lopa* could be substituted only for the end of a *prātipadika* (vārtt. 4 on 8. 1. 18 and vārtt. 6 on 8. 1. 16, 17). In fact it may be suspected that vārtt. 6 on 8. 1. 16, 17 has only been given as an alternative solution, beside the one mentioned in vārtt. 5 (above *b*), of the difficulty pointed out in vārtt. 4, because Kātyāyana could not take *padasya* as an attributive genitive in 8. 1. 18 if he cancelled the expression *sarvam*.[24]

But we need not insist on the latter point. We only ask: Why ever does the Vārttikakāra try so hard to prove that *sarvam* in Pāṇini 8. 1. 18 is superfluous? Can it be anything else but the special reason suggested above?

Even this point may not be obvious enough. Let us, then, turn to the last.

e. Vārtt. 5 on Pāṇini 8. 1. 18: *samānavākye nighātayuṣmadasma-dādeśāḥ* (= vārtt. 11 on Pāṇini 2. 1. 1) says that the loss of accent (according to 8. 1. 18, 19 *etc.*) and the substitution of *vām* and *nau* etc. (according to 8. 1. 20ff) ought to have been taught [not only for the case of a vocative and the respective forms of *yuṣmad* and *asmad* following a word, but also for the case of their standing] in the same sentence [as the word they follow].

130, 131 *savritavānt svaritaḥ; udātta-vān udāttaḥ*.—On the other hand, in order to prevent the ablative in Pāṇini 8. 4. 66 (and in other cases) from causing a wrong application, Kātyāyana has to give the rule of interpretation: *halsvaraprāptau vyañjanam avidyamānavat* (vārtt. 2 on 6. 1. 223), which again is not quite sufficient in Patañjali's opinion (III, p. 119, l. 21ff.). Without defect is T. Pr. 14. 29 *udāttāt paro 'nudāttaḥ svaritam*, 30 *vyañjanāntarhito'pi*.

[24] Patañjali explains vārtt. 6 in a different way, without accounting for Kātyāyana's *vā*.

Now we have an obvious argument. It suffers no doubt that the *one* additional expression in V. Pr. 1. 17: *anānārthe* and this vārttika are children of the same thought, though the formulation of the vārttika: *samānavākhye* seems by far happier. But then, Kātyāyana, in order to make it clear had to give a definition of the concept *vākya* in värtt. 9 and 10 on Pāṇini 2. 1. 1: *ākhyātaṃ sāvyaya-kārakaviśeṣaṇaṃ vākyam*; *ekatiṅ*. That the V. Pr.'s *anānārthe* may be taken strictly in the sense of 'in one sentence', appears from Mī. S. 2. 1. 46 *arthaikatvād ekaṃ vākyam* . . .

5. The Vārttikakāra is not satisfied with Pāṇini 1. 2. 39 [*ekaśruti* 33] *svaritāt saṃhitāyām anudāttānām*. If we take the plural *anudā-ttānām* at its face value 'for several *anudātta* vowels', the rule applies only when more than two *anudātta* vowels follow a *svarita* (vārtt. 1 on 1. 2. 39); if we take it to mean 'for *anudātta* vowels' = 'for any *anudātta* vowel', we can apply it only to the next that follows the *svarita*, since the plural would be void of any special force (vārtt. 2). A solution of the dilemma is given in vārtt. 3: *anekam apīti tu vacanāt siddham* "it is in order if we teach: 'also several *anudāttas*'."

Everybody will admit the difficulty of construing this additional *anekam api* in Pāṇini's rule. In reality we could only say either: *svaritāt saṃhitāyām anudāttanām anekānām api*, or: . . . *anudātta-syānekasyāpi*.

V. Pr. 4. 138 reflects Pāṇini 1. 2. 39 thus: *svaritāt param anudā-ttam udāttamayam*. Here Kātyāyana's addition would fit perfectly Rather, it does! For 4. 139 actually runs: *anekam api*.

Only very powerful arguments indeed could make me believe that this is a coincidence created by chance.[25]

The other differences between Pāṇini's wording and that of the V. Pr. (*saṃhitāyām: param, ekaśruti: udāttamayam*) yield no obvious arguments.

6. Pāṇini says in 1. 4. 2: *vipratiṣedhe paraṃ kāryam* 'when there is a conflict [between two rules], the one that comes later must be applied.'

The V. Pr. in 1. 159: *vipratiṣedha uttaram balavad alope*.

There are three deviations: (*a*) Instead of *kāryam*, the V. Pr. reads *balavat;* (*b*) the V. Pr. has added the expression *alope;* (*c*) Pāṇini says *param*, the V. Pr. *uttaram*.

a. It is certainly not obvious whether *kāryam* or *balavat* should be preferable.

But it is interesting, though it proves nothing by itself, that when referring to what is expressed in Pāṇini 1. 4. 2 by *kāryam*, the Vārttikakāra does not use this word, but *balīyas* 'stronger': vārtt. 9 on 7. 1. 1: *vipratiṣedhāt tu ṭāpo balīyastvam*, and on 1. 4. 2 itself tells us that Pāṇini has given his rule because whenever there arises a conflict of two rules, neither would apply since both would have the same *strength*: vārtt. 5 on 1. 4. 2: *apratipattir vobhayos tulyabalatvāt*. In vārtt. 8 on 1. 4. 2 he adds that Pāṇini ought to have taught beside *param* 'the one that comes later', also *antaraṅgam* 'the one the cause of which presents itself first.' He refers to this addition in vārtt. 9 on 6. 1. 108 by the expression *antaraṅgabalīya-stva*. Even when he does not employ the expression *balīyas* itself, his construction shows that in his mind he had a formulation not like: *vipratiṣedhe paraṃ kāryam, antaraṅgaṃ ca*, but like: *vipra-*

[25] Also the fact of V. Pr. 4. 138 being taught *after* 4. 134 (corresponding to Pāṇini 8. 4. 66) is in accordance with the remarks of the Vārttikakāra on 1. 2. 32.

tiṣedhe paraṃ balīyaḥ, antaraṅgaṃ ca. Thus in vārtt. 9 ff. on 1. 4. 2 we have a number of constructions of the type *svaro lopāt* (vārtt. 18): '[a rule on] accent [is stronger] than [a rule on *lopa*]', and throughout the Vārttika, whenever Kātyāyana feels called upon to state that an *x* is effected (according to 1. 4. 2) and not a *y*, because there is a 'conflict' between the two, he always says: '*x* (nom.) [is stronger] than *y* [abl.] since there is conflict [between the two and *x* is the one that comes later]' (*cf.* vārtt. 1 on 1. 2. 5; vārtt. 4 on 2. 1. 69; vārtt. 1 on 6. 2. 121, *etc.*).

b. The addition of *alope* in V. Pr. 1. 159 is instructive.

It certainly cannot be accounted for by the argument that the more archaic author has not yet found out means of arranging his rules in such a way as to make our rule universally valid. On the contrary, the V. Pr. avoids a fault of Pāṇini's. The Vārttikakāra not only has to add *antaraṅgaṃ ca* (vārtt. 8) to the latter's rule (with many applications set forth in vārtt. 10 ff. on 1. 4. 2), but also to teach in vārtt. 25 that *luk* is stronger than *lopa*, substitution of *yaṇ* etc., and, on a number of occasions, to name cases where the rule has to be inverted: vārtt. 4 on 3. 4. 77; vārtt. 1 on 5. 1. 2; vārtt. 9 and 10 on 6. 1. 12; vārtt. 1 on 6. 4. 48; vārtt. 10 and 11 on 7. 1. 96. It is well known that Patañjali evades the embarrassment created by Pāṇini's rule and procedure contradicting each other so frequently, by taking *para* in the sense of *iṣṭa* 'desirable' and understanding Pāṇini 1. 4. 2 to mean: 'if there is a conflict of two operations the one that is desirable must be applied' (I, p. 306, l. 9 f. and often).

c. If Pāṇini says *param* and the V. Pr. *uttaram*, the theory of condensation would of course maintain that Pāṇini has deliberately chosen the shorter word *param* for the longer word of his predecessor. But I would be at a loss to explain why Pāṇini left unchanged *uttarasya* of V. Pr. 1. 135 in 1. 1. 67, where *parasya* would have been the more fitting as *parasya* is employed just a few rules before (in 1. 1. 54) synonymously.

Nor can I easily account for the V. Pr. having replaced *param* by *uttaram*, for it also uses *para* (*e.g.* in 3. 3) synonymously with *uttara*.

Both authors, this is the only possible inference, did not mind whether they said *para* or *uttara*—notwithstanding the latter being the longer expression.

It is necessary to emphasize this point. It appears as if scholars, when talking of the 'brevity' of grammatical rules, do not always take an altogether correct view of the character of this brevity. I think, because there is always in their mind that last Paribhāṣā of Nāgojībhaṭṭa's collection: 'Grammarians rejoice over the saving of [even] the length of half a short vowel as over the birth of a son.' Enjoying the sublime irony of this witticism, which seems to voice what we feel when faced with Pāṇinean rules like *iko yaṇ aci* (6. 1. 77) or *a a* (8. 4. 68), we are apt to forget that, like any witticism, it ought to be taken with a pinch of salt.

It would be wrong, of course, to rely only on the comparative recency of our maxim. For it can be shown that already Patañjali held somewhat similar views. So, when he maintains that Pāṇini having produced his work with great care—holding a bushel of *darbha* grass in his hand, sitting on clean ground, his face to the east—, it would be impossible that even one sound be without purpose (I, p. 39 l. 10 ff.); or when he calculates that the expression *yvoḥ* has the length of 3½ short vowels, while the synonymous expression *iṇaḥ* would count only 3, and asserts that Pāṇini must have had a special reason to choose the former lengthier one, instead of the latter (I, p. 35 l. 12 ff.).

On the other hand, however, Nāgojībhaṭṭa is, no doubt, right when remarking that 'the question raised [in the Bhāṣya] is generally only, whether in a rule which is made up of several words a word can be saved, but not whether a *mātrā* (or half a *mātrā*) can be economized.'[26]

It is not difficult, in point of fact, to recognize that Pāṇini, though striving after brevity with great eagerness, often does not mind employing long words when he easily could have avoided them. He is ingenious in finding out ways of being brief, but he is not pedantic about it.

Be this however as it may. Essential for us now is the question, whether the Vārttikakāra can be supposed to share the view of 'brevity' implied in our Paribhāṣā. The answer can only be a decided 'No'. Whenever the Vārttikakāra is about to shorten some rule of Pāṇini's, he proposes to cancel a whole expression that appears superfluous. Never does he want to replace some word by a shorter synonym. He is a logician of no small acumen, and sometimes his pruning-knife appears to cut rather too sharp. But he raises no point that would be, materially or logically, altogether irrelevant. Looking at things in a natural way, it does seem irrelevant whether one should say *e.g. parasya* or *uttarasya* in 1. 1. 67. He who thinks that to Kātyāyana it was not, must prove it. It is simply wrong to ascribe to him a view for which we only have later authorities, and which, even with them, is only occasionally and for distinct purposes brought to bear upon the interpretation of Pāṇini. If Kātyāyana really thought *parasya* preferable to the *uttarasya* of Pāṇini 1. 1. 67, why did he not say so in his Vārttika?

These specimens may suffice. They are not meant to exhaust the arguments, and on request I could easily increase them. They were meant as a series of experiments executed to test several theoretical possibilities. For only such possibility can be accepted as likely as holds good if applied to single facts.

Several tests led, as might have been foreseen, to ambiguous results. We cannot decide, for example, whether the expression *param* in Pāṇini 1. 4. 2 is meant as an improvement on *uttaram* in V. Pr. 1. 159, or *vice versa* (6 *c*).

We did not detect a single point, where Pāṇini would have been shorter and better at the same time.

A few tests favoured the theory of V. Pr. being younger: *dvivacanāntam* in V. Pr. 1. 93[27] is better than *dvivacanam* in Pāṇini 1. 1. 11 (2); the addition *alope* in V. Pr. 1. 159 is better than Pāṇini's silence about the exceptions to his rule 1. 4. 2 (6 *b*).

The majority of facts, however, only revealed their significance after the deviations of the V. Pr. from Pāṇini had been looked at in the light of vārttikas. It was only a vārttika that made plausible the additional rule V. Pr. 1. 145 (1); the formulation of V. Pr. 2. 1 (3); the expression *anānārthe* in V. Pr. 1. 17 (4 e).

On the other hand, only the formulation of V. Pr. 4. 138, 139 made understandable the wording of vārtt. 3 on Pāṇini 1. 2. 39 (5).

Leaving aside all other points and questions, we have to admit that the Vārttikakāra must have well known the rules of the V. Pr., and that he must have thought them to compare favourably with

[26] *cf.* Kielhorn's edition of the Paribhāṣenduśekhara, p. 115, l. 12 ff.; Translation, p. 526.

[27] *cf.* also AV. Pr. 1. 75, 76 [*īkārokārau* 74] *dvivacanāntau, ekāraś ca.*

Pāṇini's. So much so that he puts himself out to prove that Pāṇini 6. 1. 158 contains an objectionable definition (3), which is by no means obvious; that the expression *sarvam* in Pāṇini 8. 1. 18 is superfluous (4 *d*), which nobody will admit easily.

Pondering over all this I cannot help feeling that all those who think identity of such a name as Kātyāyana to create any, however slight, probability at all, will be forcibly inclined to believe that the V. Pr. and the Vārttika are by the same hand. Those who do not—well, they may assume that the Vārttikakāra's father, or grandfather, or great-grandfather, or cousin, or uncle, or any other male relation of his in the ascending line, has composed the V. Pr., and that Kātyāyana has devoted careful study to it. All this is, as yet, by no means ruled out.

But, I think, everybody will have to admit: (1) that the Vārttikakāra knew the V. Pr. well; (2) that the probability of the V. Pr. being younger than Pāṇini is stronger than the contrary, if detailed comparisons can yield any result at all.

III te khalv api vidhayaḥ suparigṛhītā bhavanti yeṣu lakṣaṇaṃ prapañcaś ca (Patañjali I, p. 400, l. 8)

I know that I have been unfair in taking Prof. Keith by his word and pretending to believe that it is Weber's arguments that prevent him from accepting the identity of Kātyāyana, the author of the V. Pr., and Kātyāyana, the Vārttikakāra. As a matter of fact, he cannot lay much store by them, since that he did not think it worthwhile to examine them with the help of Kielhorn's Mahābhāṣya text—neither in 1914, nor in 1936. He will hardly feel sorry now they are shown to be of no value; he will be convinced that there are other, better arguments available to close the breach. I am even afraid lest he should heed all the interpretative details I have given here above, as little as those I gave before. He may still think that I am trying to prove what cannot be, and that my diving into technical subtleties only tends to obscure a clear issue. What is it that makes Prof. Keith accept any argument put forward in favour of the priority of the V. Pr., bad as it may be, and that makes him take easy any argument to the contrary? It can be nothing else but the general impression he has derived from the study of Pāṇini's work, the Vārttika, and the V. Pr.

As to the first, Prof. Keith's impression can only be that, may Pāṇini be a genius or a more or less skilful compilator, the Aṣṭādhyāyī evinces a very considerable degree of knowledge and acumen, of insight into the structure of the language it describes, of technical routine in arranging and representing facts—in brief, that it testifies to a high stage reached by the science of grammar in his time.

As to the V. Pr., his impression must be that it reveals in part an endeavour to define certain grammatical facts by general rules, similar to those given in Pāṇini's grammar; and in part a deplorable incapacity of grasping the significance of others, which seem very simple. To give only two examples: In 6. 1 the V. Pr. teaches that a verbform is *anudātta* if it follows another word belonging to the same sentence; in 2. 14 it teaches that *śrutam* is *anudātta* when preceded by *iha*, aiming at V. S. 7. 9 *máméd ihá śrutaṁ hávam*, where *śrutam* must be a verbform. In 4. 164 the V. Pr. teaches that Gārgya changes the *kh* and *y* of root *khyā* to *k* and *ś* respectively; in the same rule it puts down the absurd addition: 'except in *sakhya, ukhya, mukhya*.'

Led by this impression, which, no doubt, will be shared by many, he thinks it quite unlikely that the V. Pr. should be younger than Pāṇini. The facts seem to allow of one interpretation only. The science of grammar as represented in the V. Pr., is on its march towards the perfection attained at the time of Pāṇini. The V. Pr. is Pāṇini's precursor, as the dawn is the precursor of the day.

As to the Vārttikakāra, Prof. Keith's impression must be that its author being later than Pāṇini, it must be more perfect than the Aṣṭādhyāyī. Hence it is impossible to ascribe it to the same author as the V. Pr.

These impressions appear very plausible, and the conclusions formed on them seem to simply compel acceptance. When in some places Pāṇini's formulation obviously is less happy than the one of the V. Pr., it becomes very easy to account for it by such assumptions as: Pāṇini has borrowed unintelligently, or: in Pāṇini's grammar the consideration of brevity is allowed to override even intelligibility and logical correctness.

It is difficult, if not impossible, to prove such like assumptions to be wrong in every single case.

Yet I think we can look at things in a somewhat different way. Let us try to see, whether it leads us to absurd consequences.

If I should state the general impressions I have derived from the study of Pāṇini and the V. Pr. in a few short sentences, I should say:

Admirable as Pāṇini's work is as a whole, I cannot deny that he has overdone his ingenuity and partly fallen sacrifice to it. He is so brief as to be often obscure and not seldom even illogical: he is so subtle as to be ambiguous, and not seldom even incomprehensible. In order to understand rules of his that are not exceptionally simple, it is necessary first to know what they are supposed to teach: to-day, when his language does not any longer live, but has to be learned in school, a scholar who wants to freely handle and master his injunctions, must possess a stupendous memory and a tremendous amount of learning in the vast literature discussing the implicit suggestions, silent assumptions and principles underlying his formulations or supposed to underlie them.

There is hardly anything admirable in the V. Pr. But I cannot but acknowledge that if it is not quite free, it is yet more free than Pāṇini, of the defects of indistinctness, ambiguity, and obscurity. It may contain some hard passages, but nowhere is it necessary to make its author implicitly suggest, or silently assume, anything, or establish by some artificial device any principle that would adjust his formulation. In order to apply its teaching it is necessary to know the Padapāṭha of the V.S., to have a certain idea of the meanings of the words occurring therein, and to observe carefully what the author says.

Pāṇini addresses subtle intellects, scholars with scientific rather than practical interests; the V. Pr., just any ordinary Vājasaneyin.

Led by these impressions, I think it quite natural to assume that the V. Pr. is written by someone who knew Pāṇini, but did not want to follow too closely his risky ways of teaching. Doubly so, if I bear in mind that as far as the Bhāṣā is concerned an incorrect form, even when used at a public occasion, is no serious matter, while even *one* incorrect sound uttered in the recitation of a vedic verse, is bound to bring down bad misfortune. Is not Pāṇini himself inclined to be careful when referring to vedic forms (e.g. in 3.1.123; 3.1.42; 7.1.43)?

I can find no difficulty in accounting for the deviations of the V. Pr. from Pāṇini. They all may be based on reasonable motives, as I have taken some trouble to show. There remain the cases where the V. Pr. appears to contradict itself, where it appears to follow two distinctly different methods, of which the one looks archaic (V. Pr. 2. 14; 4. 164 second half), the other modern (V. Pr. 6. 1; 4. 164 first half). The most natural course to explain contradictions of this kind in a work, is to trace them to the individuality of its author. Consequently I should say:

There are two souls living in the breast of Kātyāyana, the author of the V. Pr. The one aspires high: it strives to vie with Pāṇini in the abstract sphere of scientific thinking and logical acumen. It makes him give the *definition (lakṣaṇa)* 6. 1 *anudāttam ākhyātam āmantritavat* 'a verb is unaccented after the way of the vocative'; and 4. 164 *khyāteḥ khayau kaśau* . . . . The other one is bound down by the practical necessities of life: it keeps in the low region where the Vedapāṭhaka breathes, who knows the text of his Saṃhitā and nothing else, who does not care about the sense of what he recites, relying on a dogma expressed by Mī. S. 1. 2. 39 (*mantrānarthakyam*) or by Kautsa as quoted in Nir. 1. 15 (. . . *anarthakā hi mantrāḥ*). It is this soul that makes him give an *amplification (prapañca)* to his definition 6. 1 in the seemingly superfluous rule 2. 14; that makes him add to his definition 4. 164 the absurd exception *sakhyokhyamukhyavarjam*, which guards against any wrong application of his teaching on the part of the unintelligent.

If I were asked to give my general impression of the Vārttikakāra in one short sentence, I should say:

These two souls live also in Kātyāyana, the Vārttikakāra.

This wants some proof. I will give it in detail, for it forms my strongest argument. Without it, I should probably have left matters as they stand, considering Prof. Keith's view as possible, though not likely.

Throughout his work the Vārttikakāra does not deem it necessary to add a wealth of vedic details to Pāṇini's rules. He is satisfied, for example, with adding to Pāṇini 6. 1. 94 in vārtt. 6 the general remark: *emanādiṣu cchandasi*, which sums up V. Pr. 4. 53 *sumudrasyemaṁs, tvemaṁs, tvodmann iti ca;* or with adding to Pāṇini 2. 1. 2 in vārtt. 6: *param api cchandasi*, which reflects the circumstantial rules V. Pr. 2. 18 and 19. Occasionally he explicitly states that it is impossible so to complement by one short rule an injunction given by Pāṇini as to make it comprise the vedic detail: vārtt. 1–4 on 6. 1. 7.[28] In vārtt. 1 on 1. 1.6 he wants to cancel the expressions *dīdhī* and *vevī* because these roots occur only in the Veda, and because for the Veda [no general rules can be given but only] rules that describe afterwards what has been observed to occur (*dṛṣṭānuvidhitvāc ca cchandasi*) . . . .[29] For a student of the Aṣṭādhyāyī it is sufficient to know that such and such phenomena do occur in the Veda, he need not trouble about their exact where and when. The attempt to reformulate Pāṇini's vedic rules with a view of making them a safe guide for Vedapāṭhakas of any description, would indeed be utterly impossible.

It is different when Pāṇini expounds on some vedic detail that is easy of verification, because it only can occur in one special context.

[28] Quoted by Wackernagel, Altindische Grammatik, I, p. LXV n. 1.

[29] Compare e.g. Patañjali on vārtt. 1 on 6. 4. 141 (III, p. 225, l. 3), quoted by Wackernagel o.c., p. LXV n. 5.

With such a detail are concerned Pāṇini's rules on the accent of the Subrahmaṇyā formula, 1. 2. 37, 38.

The Subrahmaṇyā runs thus:

subrahmaṇyo3m—subrahmaṇyo3m—subrahmaṇyo3m indrāgaccha hariva āgaccha medātither meṣa vṛṣaṇaśvasya mene—gaur āvaskandinn ahalyāyai jāra—kauśika brāhmaṇa gautama bruvāṇa—ityahe (*i.e.*: *adya*, *śvaḥ*, *dvyahe*, or *tryahe*) *sutyām āgaccha maghavan devā brahmāṇa āgacchatāgacchatāgacchata.*[30]

During the Agniṣṭoma, on the day preceding the pressing of the Soma, there is on a certain occasion (Lāṭy. Ś. 1. 3. 18; Drāhy. Ś. 1. 3. 18; Āp. Ś. 11. 20. 3; Mān. Ś. 2. 2. 5. 9; Kāty. Ś. 8. 9. 12) inserted in the Subrahmaṇyā, before the sentence *śvaḥ sutyām āgaccha*. . . (Lāṭy. Ś. 1. 3. 20; Drāhy. Ś. 1. 3. 22), the following piece:

asau (*i.e.* the Yajamāna 'N. N.') *yajate—amuṣya* (*i.e.* 'N.N.'s') *putro yajate—amuṣya pautro yajate—amuṣya naptā yajate—amuṣya pitā yajate—(amuṣyāḥ pitā yajate—) amuṣya pitāmaho yajate—(amuṣyāh o o—) amuṣya prapitāmaho yajate—(amuṣyāḥ o o—) janiṣyamāṇānāṃ pitā pitāmahaḥ prapitāmaho yajate.*[31]

Pāṇini's rules run thus:

1. 2. 37 [*ekaśruti dūrāt saṃbuddhau* (1. 2. 33)] *na subrahmaṇyāyāṃ svaritasya tūdāttaḥ* 38 *devabrahmaṇor anudāttaḥ* '[Everything is] of equal pitch when it is a case of calling from afar, [but] not in the Subrahmaṇyā formula. Here, however, an *udātta* vowel is substituted for a *svarita*; an *anudātta* is substituted for a *svarita* in the words *deva* and *brahman*'.

They are supposed to teach the following accentuation:

subrahmaṇyóm índrā́gáccha, háríva ā́gáccha, médā́tither meṣa, vṛ́ṣáṇaśvasya mene, gaúr ā́vaskandinn, áhályāyai jāra, kaúśíka brāhmaṇa, gaútáma bruvāṇa, śváḥ (*dvyahé* etc.) *sutyā́m ā́gáccha maghavan dévā bráhmāṇa ā́gácchata.*

The Vārttikakāra has two possibilities of viewing and examining these rules. This reveals what I have called his two souls.

His *first* possibility is to examine the logical indemnity of Pāṇini's teaching itself. He indulges in it in his Vārttika on Pāṇini 1. 2. 32. He says:

'Pāṇini 1. 2. 32–40 ought to be taught after Pāṇini 8. 4. 66 in order to make apply correctly Pāṇini 1. 2. 39' (vārtt. 1). This means: The substitution according to 8. 4. 66 of a (dependent) *svarita* for an *anudātta* that follows an *udātta*, has to be considered as not having taken effect in any preceding rule according to 8. 2. 1. Hence Pāṇini 1. 2. 39 would apply only to such *anudātta* vowels as follow an (independent) *svarita* that has been substituted according to a rule like 6. 1. 185.

[30] ŚB. 1. 1. 10, 11 omits *āgacchatāgacchatāgacchata*.—ŚB. 3. 3. 4. 7ff. quotes *subrahmaṇyo3m* only twice; omits *āgaccha maghavan*; quotes *āgacchata* only once.—TĀ. 1. 12. 3ff. gives the text only till *bruvāṇa*.—Lāṭy. Ś. 1. 3. 1ff. has *etāvadahe* instead of *ityahe* (1. 3. 1); leaves optional the sentence *devā brahmāṇa āgacchatāgacchatāgacchata* (1. 3. 3); leaves it optional to say *āgaccha maghavan* (1. 3. 5), or simply *āgaccha* (1. 3. 4), or to leave out both words.—I have marked by hyphens the places where one must insert a pause (according to Lāṭy. Ś. 1. 3. 6, 7). Drāhy. Ś. 1. 3. 2ff. substantially agrees.—See also Caland-Henry, L'Agniṣṭoma, p. 65.

[31] A more elaborate form is given by Caland-Henry, *o.c.*, p. 119. I have tried to keep closely to the wording suggested by Lāṭy. Ś. 1. 3. 18-20; Drāhy. Ś. 1. 3. 18-20. The hyphens are inserted according to Lāṭy. Ś. 1. 3. 9; Drāhy. Ś. 1. 3. 9. The other śrautasūtras (quoted above) allow no inference as to the exact wording.

'And also for the sake of the second part of Pāṇini 1. 2. 37 (*svaritasya tūdāttaḥ*)' (vārtt. 2). This means: The substitution of an *udātta* for a *svarita* in the Subrahmaṇyā would apply again only to an independent *svarita*. Consequently we should get only *subrahmaṇyóm* instead of *subrahmaṇyòm* (with *svarita* according to 6. 1. 185), but not *ágáccha etc.* for *ágàccha etc.* (with *svarita* according to 8. 4. 66).

'And also in order to prevent substitution of a *svarita* (according to 8. 4. 66) for [the *anudātta*] following the *udātta* that is substituted for a *svarita* (according to 1. 2. 37)' (vārtt. 3). This means: If 8. 4. 66 follows 1. 2. 37, it has to apply after 1. 2. 37 again. We should consequently get first *ágáccha* for *ágàccha*, and afterwards *ágácchà* for *ágáccha*.

'And also for the sake of Pāṇini 1. 2. 40' (vārtt. 4). This means: Also this rule would apply only to such *anudātta* vowels as precede an *udātta* or a *svarita* that is taught in rule standing before Pāṇini 8. 2. 1.

All these objections are perfectly correct. Pāṇini has not followed his own plan with all desirable care. The V. Pr. is in this respect blameless: the rules corresponding to Pāṇini 1. 2. 39 (V. Pr. 4. 138) and 1. 2. 40 (V. Pr. 4. 135) follow the rule corresponding to Pāṇini 8. 4. 66 (V. Pr. 4. 134).

But Kātyāyana knows how to free Pāṇini of the net he has thrown over him. In his last vārttika on 1. 2. 32 he gives as his final view this:

'The fact of Pāṇini teaching the substitution of an *anudātta* [for a *svarita*] in the words *deva* and *brahman* (*dévāḥ* for *déváḥ*, *bráhmāṇaḥ* for *bráhmáṇaḥ*) gives an indication that Pāṇini 8. 4. 66 has [to be considered to have] taken effect [as far as Pāṇini 1. 2. 32–40 is concerned, in spite of Pāṇini 8. 2. 1].' This means: Since Pāṇini 1. 2. 38 would be perfectly void of sense and purpose if it did not concern the secondary *svarita*, and if Pāṇini 8. 4. 66 would apply afterwards again, we are entitled to infer that this paragraph (1. 2. 32–40) is *meant* to follow 8. 4. 66.

As often, Kātyāyana's subtlety has been a match for Pāṇini's. He has scrutinized his great predecessor's formulation, pointed out a logical flaw, and hit on a striking solution for the difficulties resulting: the rules in question are put in the wrong place. Then he has topped it all by finding out that Pāṇini himself has given an indication that he wanted us to interpret him as if he had proceeded correctly. Taken all in all, a neat specimen of scholastic acumen!

His *second* possibility is to examine the practical usefulness of Pāṇini's rules from the point of view of a priest who has to recite the subrahmaṇyā. He might say, firstly, that it is not clear whether *dūrāt saṃbuddhau* is still valid from 1. 2. 33, and, secondly, that it is not clear which accentuation is really the correct one. Having formulated a negative rule by just forbidding to recite with equal pitch, Pāṇini has, strictly speaking, left open manifold possibilities. Theoretically, an accentuation like *indrá āgáccha* would answer his definition also. Kātyāyana must have thought likewise. In his Vārttika on 1. 2. 37 he actually rewrites the whole rule. He puts a *prapañca* in the place of Pāṇini's *lakṣaṇa*. It runs thus:

subrahmaṇyāyām okāra udāttaḥ (vārtt. 1) *ākāra ākhyāte, parādiś ca* (vārtt. 2) *vākyādau ca dve dve* (vārtt. 3) *maghavanvarjam* (vārtt. 4) *sutyāparāṇām antaḥ* (vārtt. 5) *asāv ity antaḥ* (vārtt. 6) *amuṣyety antaḥ* (vārtt. 7) *syāntasyopottamam ca* (vārtt. 8) *vā nāmadheyasya*.

'[Pāṇini ought to have said thus:] In the Subrahmaṇyā the vowel *o* is *udātta* (1); the vowel *ā* when followed by a verbform [is *udātta*]; also the first of the following [syllables] (2); also the two first [syllables] in the beginning of each sentence [are *udātta*] (3); except [those of the word] *maghavan* (4); the end [of the words] followed by *sutyā* [is *udātta*] (5); the end of [the word designated by] 'N.N.' [is *udātta*] (6); the end of [the word designated by] 'N.N.'s' [is *udātta*] (7); [the end] and the last but one [syllable] of [a word] ending in *sya* [is *udātta*] (8); [the last but one syllable] of a name [is *udātta*] or [not] (9).'

The last 4 rules must be concerned with the piece inserted on the last day before the pressing: it is open to doubt, whether Pāṇini wanted to include it in his rule.

Let us try, then, to apply Kātyāyana's teaching to the whole!

Vārtt. 1: The vowel *o* is actually always *udātta* in the Subrahmaṇyā. Not only in *subrahmaṇyó3m*, which is given as example by Patañjali, but also in the inserted piece: *putró* [*yajate*], *pautró* [*yajate*], *pitāmahó* [*yajate*], *prapitāmahó* [*yajate*].

Vārtt. 2a: The vowel *ā* is always *udātta* when followed by a verbform. Not only in *ā́gaccha*, which is given as example by Patañjali, but also in the inserted piece: *naptā́* [*yajate*], *pitā́* [*yajate*], and in the end: *ā́gacchata*.

Vārtt. 2b: The first of the following syllables is also *udātta*, says Kātyāyana. Obviously we have to accent not only *ā́gáccha*, which is given by Patañjali, but also: *naptā́ yájate pitā́ yájate*. We even must go a step further, and construe *parādiś ca* not only with *ākāra*, but also with *okāra* (as may be indicated by the *ca*). For if we accent *naptā́ yájate*, it is only logical that we accent likewise: *putró yájate*, *pautró yájate*, *pitāmahó yájate*, *prapitāmahó yájate*.

Vārtt. 3: The two first syllables of each sentence are *udātta*. This provides us with the accentuation: *índrā́gáccha*, *hárīva* [*ā́gáccha*], *médā́tither meṣa*, *vŕ̥ṣáṇaśvasya mene*, *gaúr ā́vaskandin*, *áhályāyai jāra*, *kaúśika brāhmaṇa*, *gaútáma bruvāṇa*.

All the following vārttikas are special exceptions (*apavāda*) to this last general statement (*utsarga*), for they teach only the accent of words that happen to stand in the beginning of sentences of the Subrahmaṇyā.

Vārtt. 4: *maghavan*, which of course in reality belongs to the sentence *ityahé sutyā́m ā́gáccha*, and not to *dévā bráhmāṇa ā́gácchata*, is unaccented.

Vārtt. 5: *adyá*, *dvyahé*, *tryahé*, which do start a sentence, are accented on their last syllable only.

Vārtt. 6: The end of the word designated by 'N.N.' (*asau*) is *udātta*. For simplicity's sake, let 'N.N.' be called by a name used by Patañjali in his examples: *gārgyá*, *dā́kṣi*, or *devadattá*.

First of all, the rule informs us that in sentences like *gārgyo yajate*, *dākṣir yajate*, *devadatto yajate*, vārtt. 3 is superseded. For *gārgyó yájate*, *devadattó yájate* we do not want any further ruling: their accents result already from vārtt. 1 and 2. Nor is it possible to say that vārtt. 6 would supersede them. For neither is it an *apavāda* with respect to vārtt. 1 and 2, since it applies also in cases that do not fall under the jurisdiction of these rules, nor can it be stronger by virtue of its being taught later, since there is no 'conflict'[32].

dākṣir yajate is different. The name has normally an *udātta* in the *first* syllable. We get, however, by vārtt. 6 only *dākṣír yajate*. And while everywhere else the syllable following an *udātta* becomes *udātta* itself before an *anudātta*, we seem to have a single

[32] See above.

udātta here. I think it is obvious that Kātyāyana has given his last vārttika for an instance like this. As translated above,[33] it gives us permission to accent the last but one syllable of a name. Who wants to use the name *dākṣi* can consequently say: *dā́kṣír yajate*, getting the first *udātta* from vārtt. 9 and the second from vārtt. 6. Now everything is in order.

Vārtt. 7: The end of a word designated by 'N.N.'s' (*amuṣya*) is *udātta*. We learn from this, again first of all, that in sentences like: *gārgyasya putro yajate, devadattasya putro yajate*, vārtt. 3 is superseded. Secondly, that *dākṣeḥ*, which may have an *udātta* in the first syllable according to vārtt. 9, is also accented on the last: *dā́kṣéḥ putró yájate*.

Vārtt. 8: The end and the last but one syllable of a word ending in *sya* is *udātta*: *gārgyásyá putró yájate, devadattásyá putró yájate*.

Vārtt. 9: See on vārtt. 6 and 7.

The accents of the inserted piece are, then, according to Kātyāyana:

gārgyó (devadattó) yájate (dā́kṣír yájate); gārgyásyá (devadattásyá, dā́kṣéḥ) putró yájate; naptā́ yájate; pitā́ yájate; pitāmahó yájate; prapitāmahó yájate.[34]

It thus becomes obvious that the lengthy vārttikas do not add or change anything with respect to the content of Pāṇini's rule: In the Subrahmaṇyā a *svarita* is replaced by the *udātta*. The one point on which the Vārttikakāra differs is the accent of *dévāḥ* and *bráhmāṇaḥ*. According to Pāṇini 1. 2. 38 the *svarita* in these words is replaced by the *anudātta*. According to Kātyāyana vārtt. 1 on 1. 2. 38 this is only the opinion of some authorities. Consequently he wants himself to accent: *dévā́ḥ, bráhmā́ṇaḥ*, which restores complete analogy of accent throughout the Subrahmaṇyā.

For our particular investigation, however, it is not essential what Kātyāyana is teaching, but *how* he is teaching it. We may even leave the question open whether he actually is quite distinct and unambiguous. We saw that without some interpretative efforts,

[33] Patañjali understands vārtt. 9 in a different way. He believes it to teach optional correctness of *devadattasyá pitā́ yájate* beside *devadattásyá pitā́ yájate*, which is evidently wrong.

[34] It would apparently be wrong to apply Kātyāyana's teaching to the last sentence, which would have to be accented thus: *jánı́ṣyamāṇānāṃ pitā́ pitāmahā́ḥ prapitāmahó yájate*. It is possible that Kātyāyana did not know the use of it, seeing the many variations in the Subrahmaṇyā as pointed out in Lāṭy. Ś. (above p. 350 n. 30). Nor does he appear to have considered the cases *amuṣyāḥ pitā yajate etc.*

Drāhy. Ś. 1. 3. 23ff. also teaches the accentuation of the inserted piece. It differs from Kātyāyana in considering also the accent of feminine genitives and of the last sentence. It does, moreover, not provide for any name that is not *antodātta*. It runs thus:

1. 3. 23 *arthanirvacanam uccāntam* 'what expresses [only] the sense [of the nominal stem] (*i.e.* a nominative) has a high-pitched (*i.e. udātta*) end' (the name, *putráḥ, putrā́ḥ, naptā́, pitā́, pitāmaháḥ, prapitāmaháḥ*).

1. 3. 24 *vaibhakte ca syādau vaibhaktaś caiva* 'what is preceding a *sya* etc. (*i.e. yāḥ*) that belongs to a case termination, and [the vowel] belonging to the case termination [is high-pitched] also' (*-ásyá, -ā́yā́ḥ pitā́ etc.*).

1. 3. 25 *uccāc ca nīce nīcam* 'a low-pitched (*i.e. anudātta*) syllable that is following a high-pitched and preceding a low-pitched syllable (*i.e.* a *svarita*) [is high-pitched] also' (. . . *pitā́ pítāmaháḥ prápitāmahó* . . .).

1. 3. 26 *janiṣyamāṇānām iti madhye dve* 'the two [syllables] in the middle of '*janiṣyamāṇānām* [are high-pitched]' (*janiṣyámā́ṇānām*).

1. 3. 27 *yajeś cādiḥ* 'the beginning of root *yaj* [is high-pitched] also' (*putró yájate, pitā́ yájate etc.*).

his last vārttika is misunderstandable, and that if I am right, Patañjali *did* misunderstand it. Moreover, Patañjali hardly realized the full bearing of the first vārttikas, as interpreted above. For us is only essential Kātyāyana's unmistakable intention of being distinct, and his obvious impression that Pāṇini was not distinct enough.

Let us admit that theoretically Pāṇini's formulation is ambiguous. We have to acknowledge, at the same time, that it reveals insight into the linguistic phenomenon as such. It clearly grasps the essential feature of the accenting particularity of the Subrahmaṇyā. In this respect it is unsurpassable.

Let us admit that theoretically Kātyāyana's formulation is clearer. We have to acknowledge, at the same time, that it is much more circumlocutory, and that it does not reveal any insight into the linguistic phenomenon. It is superficial and mechanical to the last degree, though in its own way ingenious enough.

Is it not the author of the Prātiśākhya who spoke to us in these Vārttikas?

Let us, to facilitate our argument, apply one last test.

Let us suppose the Vārttika and Bhāṣya on Pāṇini 1. 2. 37 had been lost, and by some lucky chance there had been found, in our days, some palmleaf containing only Kātyāyana's 9 rules without Patañjali. What would philologists do with it?

Some would say: 'These rules must be pre-Pāṇinean, for the expressions *okāra, ākāra, ākhyāta* have been replaced by Pāṇini by the shorter ones: *ot, āt, tiṅ.*' I am afraid Prof. Keith would be amongst them. For in his opinion 'everything points to the condensation of the Aṣṭādhyāyī as the carrying to perfection of an endeavour to attain brevity for its own sake [note: *e.g. ku* for *kavarga*].'[35] And if he finds it 'quite impossible to believe that V. Pr. 1. 55 *amātraḥ svaro hrasvaḥ* [*etc.*] is an attempt to improve on Pāṇini [1. 2. 27 *ūkālo 'jjhrasvadīrghaplutaḥ*]',[36] he cannot believe that our rules are an attempt to improve on Pāṇini 1. 2. 37 either. Not only is Pāṇini's rule about five times shorter, to us it appears also to contain the clearer formulation. And how much more clever is its point of view! Prof. Keith thinks Pāṇini 1. 2. 27 'absurd', yet he maintains it to be a 'refinement', though a 'not very happy' one. Pāṇini 1. 2. 37 is not absurd at all. It just looks a very happy refinement of our rules.

Most scholars should say: 'These rules must be taken from some of the Prātiśākhyas, in which terms like *okāra, ākāra, ākhyāta* are in permanent use—be they young (as the AV. Pr.) or old (as the V. Pr.). If so, they must belong to either a Sāmaveda Prātiśākhya, since the priest reciting the Subrahmaṇyā is a Sāmavedin, or a Prātiśākhya to the White Yajurveda, since according to the Vājasaneyins it is the Adhvaryu himself who recites the Subrahmaṇyā.'[37] Upon this they would find that the V. Pr. not only indeed uses the terms quoted above, but also that it is well acquainted with expressions of the type '*maghavanvarjam*' (*cf. e.g.* V. Pr. 1. 87; 1. 131 *sāmajapanyūṅkhavarjam:* Pāṇini 1. 2. 34. . . . .*ajapanyūṅkhasāmasu;* V. Pr. 2. 1; 4. 21; 4. 164). Further they would ask themselves, which word is referred to by the neuters *dve dve* (vārtt. 3) and *upottamam* (vārtt. 8), and they could not but recognize that it must be *akṣara* n. They would now remember that V. Pr. 1. 99 says: *svaro 'kṣaram* 'a vowel is called *akṣara* [together with the

[35] *Indian Culture*, Vol. II, p. 745.
[36] *l.c.*, p. 746.
[37] Caland-Henry, *o.c.*, p. 64, No. 49 n. 2.

preceding consonants]', and uses *akṣara* in this sense in 4. 129, and makes us supply *akṣaram* to *svaritam* in 4. 132, 134 *etc. etc.*

Now as regards 'doctrine, which is the sole criterion available',[38] they would certainly be struck by the fact that the beginning of our rules does not seem to presuppose acquaintance with the most simple grammatical facts and categories. But soon they would come across the terms *ākhyāta* and *vākya*, which betray quite a decent standard of grammatical knowledge. After just having forgiven the author his unintelligent first rules, they would hit on the fourth, which shows that either the author or those for whom he wrote were not able to discern that *maghavan* belongs to the sentence: *ityahé sutyā́m ā́gáccha maghavan*, though its accent forbids to construe it with the following: *dévā́ bráhmā́ṇa ā́gácchata*. Again they would remember that the V. Pr., too, though presupposing acquaintance with the concept *ākhyāta* (finite verb) in 6.1, does not expect in 2. 14 its students to realize that *śrutam* in V.S. 7. 9 *is* an *ākhyāta;* that the V. Pr., though presupposing acquaintance with the concept *āmantrita* (vocative) and *ṣaṣṭhī* (genitive) in 2. 17, 18, does not expect in 2. 19 its students to realize that *apā́m nápāt* in V.S. 8. 24 is not a vocative, but a nominative; that the V. Pr., though presupposing acquaintance with the grammatical abstraction *khyāti* (root *khyā*) in 4. 164, does not expect in the same rule its students to realize that the *khy* of *sakhya*, *ukhya*, *mukhya* has to do nothing whatsoever with the *khy* of root *khyā*.

Those would not be the worst of our hypothetical scholars, who try to find a place in Sanskrit literature for our hypothetical palmleaf, that would insist on the circumstance that just this contradictory side by side of a respectable standard of knowledge and mechanical, insipid pedantry, which we find in our rules, gives its individual character to the V. Pr.; and that the two fighting tendencies of stating each single case by itself and of giving general, comprehensive directions eventually spoil each other's game as well in our rules as in the V. Pr.

Sceptics might rely on the Subrahmaṇyā not occurring in the V.S. But theirs would be a weak argument: the author of the V. Pr. could well have taken special interest in it, since it is recited by the Vājasaneyin Adhvaryu. They might point out, further, that once we allow the author to take his point of view as he chooses, these rules are quite a *chef-d'œuvre* in their skilful arrangement and artful disposition, which makes use of the really surprising accident that all the vowels *o*, and all the vowels *ā* before a form of a verb, are *udātta* in the Subrahmaṇyā. In this respect hardly one piece of the V. Pr. can compare with them. Yet these sceptics certainly would have a hard stand.

If, however, anyone should suggest that our rules are really taken from the Vārttika—he might refer to the expressions *okāra*, *ākāra*, *vākya* and the type *maghavanvarjam* being not foreign to its style—, he would be answered by the same argument, on which Prof. Keith declines[39] to believe in the identity of the Vārttikakāra and the author of the V. Pr.: 'The plain fact is that the Vārttikakāra is far advanced in grammatical knowledge beyond the author of these rules.'

Fortunately we have not to deal with an anonymous palmleaf. Fortunately we are not placed in the awkward position of having to prove that our 9 rules were written by the Vārttikakāra. Fortunately by indulging in his Vedapāṭhaka inclinations, Kātyāyana

[38] Keith, *l.c.*, p. 746.

[39] *l.c.*, p. 742.

himself has led *ad absurdum* all the arguments by which Prof. Keith still wants to settle the relative chronology of the Prātiśākhyas. Kātyāyana's rules show distinctly that in chronological questions we can rely neither on the brevity of technical terms, nor on the brevity of expression in general, nor on the more or less 'advanced' doctrine.

They show more. They show that the suspicion of Kātyāyana, the Vārttikakāra, and Kātyāyana, the author of the V. Pr., being identical was not vain. It is not only easy to assume that the scholar who penned the Vārttika on Pāṇini 1. 2. 37 is responsible also for the V. Pr., it is almost unavoidable when it is considered that the Vārttika shares, in its expressions as well as in its method of representing linguistic facts, marked peculiarities with the V. Pr. I defy scholars to find out a similarly close relationship between any two other grammatical works of Indian antiquity.

The proof that the Kātyānācārya, who wrote the V. Pr., is not the Vārttikakāra now lies with the sceptics. With Weber's arguments they cannot defend their case. They have to explain away the relationship of the terminology of the Vārttika and the V. Pr., which was unknown to Weber, and the surprising coincidences of a number of deviations of the V. Pr. from Pāṇini with objections raised by Kātyāyana against the very points of Pāṇini's grammar that are removed by these deviations, coincidences, which are far more numerous and characteristic than those pointed out by Goldstücker. They have to explain how, if their idea of the development of linguistic studies and teaching technique in India is right, Kātyāyana could ever have written the Vārttika on Pāṇini 1. 2. 37. Will they not rather admit that their simple and seemingly easy assumptions (a lucid work: early, obscure: young; diffuse: early, brief: young, *etc.*), have not taken in account the complicated nature of historical development, which seldom, if ever, follows a straight line? Is it not obvious that they have neglected to consider that books are not written by schools, but by single men, by individuals, who naturally had their own taste, their own inclinations and preferences, and little cared when adopting new styles, new methods, and new points of view, whether to later centuries their procedure meant progress or not? Unfortunately, in Indian literature it is but seldom possible to recognize the author behind his work. In the case of Kātyāyana, I think, we can do so; but as soon as we catch a glimpse of his personality, his writings cease to be measurable by the simple standards generally accepted, and thus prove them to be arbitrary and utterly unreliable.

21

Pierre Boudon

We have seen that the first information available in Europe on the Sanskrit grammarians was due to the French Jesuit Jean François Pons (see pages 30–32). Pons' Sanskrit grammar, available in manuscript, enabled A. L. de Chézy to occupy the first chair for Sanskrit at the Collège de France in 1814. But despite the excellent traditions of Sanskrit studies which developed in Paris during the nineteenth century, there were hardly any French scholars who contributed directly to the study of the Indian grammarians.

Of course, the Sanskrit grammarians were studied for the historical data they provide. The well-known French Sanskritist and Indologist Sylvain Lévi (1863–1935; cf. Renou 1936) for example in a brief communication of 1891, ingeniously demonstrated that Kātyāyana must have been a contemporary of one of the few kings (e.g., Piyadasi) who were referred to in inscriptions with the honorific title *devānāṃpriya* 'dear to the gods.' What is remarkable about this compound is that its first member retains the Genitive ending. According to Pāṇini 3.6.21, it must therefore have a pejorative meaning. Kātyāyana, however, allows for an honorific use by listing *devānāṃpriya* among the exceptions to Pāṇini's rule. Since Patañjali again reverts to Pāṇini's view and accepts only pejorative meanings for compounds of this kind, and since later usage continues to confirm these meanings only, Kātyāyana must have been a contemporary of those few kings which were honored with the title *devānāṃpriya*. This fixes his date around the middle of the third century B.C.

In another note (Lévi 1906–1908), Sylvain Lévi analyzed Pāṇini's treatment of preverbs in 1.4.80–82, together with Kātyāyana's *vārttikās* (but omitting Patañjali's comments, "qui supposent une extrême familiarité avec les détails du système de Pāṇini," page 277). He concluded that Pāṇini treated a stage of the language intermediate between Vedic and "le terrain encore anonyme du sanscrit qui naît" (page 279).

Sylvain Lévi also directed the excellent dissertation of a visiting Indian scholar, Vasudeva Gopala Paranjpe, *Le Vârtika de Kâtyâyana. Une étude du style, du vocabulaire et des postulats philosophiques* (1922). But it was his best pupil and eventual successor, Louis Renou (see pages 432–525), who restored the balance almost singlehandedly and placed French Indology in the forefront of Indian grammatical studies.

At the time Renou was beginning to contribute to the study of the grammarians, another French Sanskritist, Pierre Boudon, worked in the same field. Boudon contributed only one publication: the following article, entitled "Une Application du raisonnement par l'absurde dans l'interprétation de Pāṇini (les *jñāpakasiddhaparibhāṣā*)", which appeared in the *Journal asiatique* (230, 1938, 65–121). Like Buiskool's book, Boudon's article was based in the first place on Kielhorn's edition of the *Paribhāṣenduśekhara*, the one publication that still provides the best introduction to the study of the later grammarians. Boudon's article deals with metarules (*paribhāṣā*), some of them artificial, and also with problems connected with the relative strength of rules. The application of Pāṇini's rules sometimes gives rise to contradictions. These are interpreted as apparent contradictions which in fact serve a purpose; they are devices indicating (*jñāpaka*) that a *paribhāṣā* is needed. Such a *paribhāṣā*, which is inferred from a *jñāpaka*, is called a *jñāpakasiddhaparibhāṣā*.

Une Application du raisonnement par l'absurde dans l'interprétation de Pāṇini (les jñāpakasiddhaparibhāṣā) (1938)

Pierre Boudon

I "ardhamātrālāghavena putrotsavaṃ manyante vaiyākaraṇāḥ"

C'est un postulat admis par les commentateurs grammaticaux sanscrits que Pāṇini n'a jamais employé une demi-mātrā qu'elle ne fût indispensable. Or on rencontre de loin en loin dans l'*Aṣṭādhyāyī* une lettre, un mot, parfois tout un sūtra, ou encore un procédé de composition, qui à première vue sont inutiles ou inexplicables.

Ce qui fait croire à l'inutilité de ces éléments, dans la règle où ils se trouvent, c'est le plus souvent l'existence d'une autre règle (ou d'une maxime) qui semble exprimer la même idée. Ailleurs telle énonciation paraît superflue en ce que l'objet qu'elle vise aurait pu, semble-t-il, être atteint sans elle, vu l'apparence d'une double possibilité d'interpréter ou d'appliquer une règle (ou une série de règles), l'une avec, l'autre sans cette énonciation.

Les commentateurs de Pāṇini—en premier lieu Patañjali—qui ne pouvaient admettre une dérogation à leur postulat, se sont efforcés de donner un sens à ces énigmes : ils ont, selon le cas, soit nié la valabilité universelle de la règle ou maxime apparemment concurrente, soit rejeté l'une de deux possibilités d'interprétation, pour ne laisser subsister que celle qui comporte l'utilisation de l'élément autrement superflu.

Et la maxime ou interprétation gênante est réfutée par l'absurde : sa fausseté (au moins partielle) résulte de ce qu'elle aboutirait à une conséquence inadmissible, la présence d'un mot ou procédé inexplicable dans les sūtras de Pāṇini. Le mot ou procédé ainsi sauvegardé devient le signe révélateur d'une maxime d'interprétation, d'une *paribhāṣā*.

Une maxime tout à fait générale (paribh. 5[1] : *ekāntā anubandhāḥ*) enseigne que les anubandha[2] font partie de ce à quoi ils sont attachés. Si cette maxime était toujours vraie, le mot *śit* de 1, 1, 55 : "*anekāl śit sarvasya*"[3] serait inutile. Car un substitut multilittère

[1] La numérotation suivie est celle du recueil de Nāgojībhaṭṭa, *Paribhāṣenduśekhara* (Ed. Kielhorn, Bombay, 1868; —Part II. Translation and notes, Bombay, 1874). Cet ouvrage étant fréquemment cité dans ce qui suit, les abréviations PŚ. et Kielh. renvoient, la première au texte sanscrit, la seconde à la traduction, que j'ai généralement suivie pour la partie technique des sections I et II de ce travail.

[2] Les anubandha sont des lettres supplémentaires que Pāṇini attache aux suffixes, substituts, augments, racines, pour en marquer les différentes propriétés quant à l'accentuation, modification du thème, etc. Ainsi les désinences e, *as*, *as*, *i* des datif, ablatif, génitif et locatif singulier, figurent dans Pāṇini sous les formes techniques *ṅe*, *ṅasi*, *ṅas*, *ṅi* avec l'anubandha commun *ṅ*, dont le rôle est de rappeler conventionnellement les caractéristiques communes à ces quatre désinences et définies par les règles 1, 4, 6, 7, 3, 111, etc. (L'anubandha *i* de *ṅasi* distingue la désinence de l'ablatif de celle du génitif).—"*Anubandha*" a pour synonyme dans Pāṇini le mot "*it*", lequel est toujours employé comme second terme du bahuvrīhi désignant le mot qui a pour anubandha la lettre constituant le premier terme du composé. Les quatre désinences ci-dessus sont des "*ṅit*", i.e. des éléments qui ont pour *it* (pour anubandha) la lettre *ṅ*. Le mot "*ṅit*" sert par suite de désignation collective dans les règles relatives à ces désinences.

[3] 1. 1. 55: "Un substitut multilittère (*anekāl*) er un substitut *śit* prennent la place de tout (l'original)". — Ce sont là deux exceptions à la règle générale de substitution "*alo 'ntyasya*" (1, 1, 52), qui enseigne qu'un substitut prend la place de la dernière des lettres de l'original.

(sous sa forme technique) pourrait ne consister qu'en un substitut réel d'une seule lettre accompagné de son anubandha, et la catégorie des *śit* rentrerait dans celle des *anekāl*. Mais si le mot *śit* était inutile, Pāṇini aurait violé son principe d'économie; ceci étant une absurdité, il faut conclure que la paribhāṣā 5 est fausse, au moins en ce qui concerne la règle 1, 1, 55.

Telle est la réfutation par l'absurde et sa conclusion limitée, á partir de laquelle,—par une deuxième démarche qui se présente sous les dehors d'une induction, mais qui n'est peut-être qu'une citation—est invoquée une maxime nouvelle destinée è corriger la première. C'est la paribhāṣā 6: "*nānubandhakṛtam anekāltvam*", "La multilittérité n'est pas créée par les anubandha".

Le mot *śit*, de superflu qu'il apparaissait d'abord, prend maintenant sa valeur et même une double valeur, puisqu'en même temps qu'il indique la paribhāṣā 6, il apparaît indispensable aussitôt qu'on admet celle-ci. De *vyartha* ce mot devient *caritārtha*[4]. Il est dit le *jñāpaka* i. e. l'indice de la paribhāṣā[5].

La jñāpakasiddhaparibhāṣā, avec le raisonnement qui prétend l'établir, est introduite dans le Bhāṣya, soit dans le sūtra même qui contient le jñāpaka, à propos d'une critique faite au texte du sūtra, texte que la paribhāṣā vient justifier, soit, plus souvent, ailleurs, en réponse à diverses objections.

C'est ainsi que dans le Bhāṣya, 1, 3, 9, est soulevée la question: les anubandha font-ils partie de ce à quoi ils sont attachés? L'un des interlocuteurs répond qu'ils en font partie. Sur quoi un autre fait observer qu'il en résulte trois difficultés . . . l'une relative au sarvādeśasūtra (1. 1, 55). Avec cette thèse en effet tous les substituts seraient *anekāl*; par suite le substitut *aut* (= *au*) prescrit par 7, 1, 84[6], par exemple, serait par 1, 1, 55 substitué à la totalité du thème *div*, alors qu'il doit être substitué, par 1, 1, 52, à la finale seulement. L'objection est en fin de discussion écartée par Patañjali au moyen de la paribhāṣā 6 appuyée sur son jñāpaka: "*yad apy uktaṃ sarvādeśa iti tatrāpy ācāryapravṛttir jñāpayati nānubandhakṛtam anekāltvaṃ bhavatīti yad ayaṃ śit sarvasyety āha*". "En ce qui concerne l'objection introduite par le mot *sarvādeśe*, à cela aussi (il y a réponse car) il est une procédure de Pāṇini qui nous

[4] Ces deux conditions sont nécessaires — au moins selon Nāgoj. — pour qu'il y ait véritable jñāpaka. Car il n'admet pas qu'une paribhāṣā puisse être indiquée d'une manière conventionnelle par un mot ou procédé qui, la maxime adoptée, ne serait pas caritārtha. (Voir PŚ. réfutation des jñāp. de 93, 119, justification du jñāp. de 28). — D'autre part, si le mot ou procédé a une raison d'être dans l'hypothèse de l'inexistence de la paribhāṣā, il n'est pas valable non plus comme jñāpaka. (Voir réfutation des jñāp. de 52 [premier jñāp. allégué], 90, 120, justification des jñāp. de 17, 28, 53, 55).

[5] Le raisonnement qui procède du jñāpaka trouve son illustration la plus intéressante dans l'établissement des jñāpakasiddhaparibhāṣā, qui ont en général pour but de défendre, en l'interprétant, le texte des sūtra. Mais ce mode d'argumentation revient sans cesse dans le dialogue du Bhāṣya, où il est également employé, pour étayer la critique des sūtra, soit, le plus souvent à tort, par l'interlocuteur qui n'est que partiellement informé (ekadeśin), soit, valablement, par celui qui, sachant à fond la doctrine (siddhāntin), exprime la pensée de Patañjali. De ces jñāpaka de sūtra on trouvera deux exemples ci-après, pages 382–385 et 386–388.

[6] 7, 1, 84: *diva aut* (*sau*) "*au* est substitué à (la finale de thème) *div* devant *su* (= s, désinence du nominatif singulier)": *dyauḥ*.

suggère cette maxime: "La multilittérité n'est pas créée par les anubandha", à savoir le fait qu'il a dit *śit sarvasya*".

Cette formule, à peu près invariable, dont Patañjali se sert pour introduire une jñāpakasiddhaparibhāṣā, présuppose le rejet de la thèse contradictoire par une réduction à l'impossible qui, pour n'être pas toujours exprimée[7], n'en est pas moins l'opération capitale de l'argumentation qui prétend fonder la paribhāṣā.

Autre exemple. La paribhāṣā 30 *vyapadeśivad ekasmin*[8] enseigne: "Une opération subie par un mot complexe à raison d'une désignation spéciale (par exemple du type *tadādi* ou *tadanta*) qui définit cette complexité, est subie de même par le mot simple correspondant". Ainsi la règle 4, 1, 95, *ata iñ* "(dans le sens de descendant), le suffixe *iñ* vient après un thème *a*", (c'est-à-dire, par 1, 1, 72[9], *adanta*) s'applique non seulement dans le cas *Dakṣa* +

[7] Deux fois (pour ne parler que des jñāpaka de paribhāṣā), on rencontre la majeure du syllogisme conditionnel explicitement formulée:

Bh., 1, 1, 1 (paribh. 109 — jñāp.: *udāttaḥ* de 7, 1, 75): "*yadi bhedakā guṇāḥ syur udāttam evoccārayet*". "Si leurs qualités suffisaient à différencier les lettres, Pāṇini aurait (simplement) prononcé *udātta* (le substitut *anaṅ*, sans lui assigner cette qualité par le mot "*udāttaḥ*")".

Bh. 7, 2, 98 (paribh. 52 — jñāp. : anuvṛtti ex (7, 2, 91 per) 7, 2, 95, 96 in 7, 2, 98 de "*maparyantasya*" : *yady atrānya ekavacanādeśāḥ syur maparyantānuvṛttir anarthikā syāt*". — Il s'agit des composés du type *tvatputraḥ* ou *tvaddhitam* de:

yuṣmad + *ṅas* + *putraḥ* > *yuṣmad* + *putraḥ* (2, 4, 71) > *tvatputraḥ* (7, 2, 98); *yuṣmad* + *ṅe* + *hitam* > *yuṣmad* + *hitam* . . . > *tvaddhitam* . . .

L'élision par *luk* (2, 4, 71) de la désinence du génitif (*ṅas*) ou du datif (*ṅe*) est effectuée en premier lieu. Après quoi, par 7, 2, 98, *tva* est substitué à la partie du pronom qui a pour limite inclusive *ma* (*maparyanta*), c'est-à-dire à *yuṣma*. La validité, littéralement le passage par roulement (*anuvṛttir*) de "*maparyantasya*" dans 7,2, 98 est indispensable, pour empêcher que *tva*, substitut multilittère (*anekāl*), ne soit substitué, en vertu de 1, 1, 55, à la totalité du pronom *yuṣmad*, — Le raisonnement de Patañjali nous dit à quelle condition (inadmissible) la validité de "*maparyanta*" serait inutile.

"[Si l'antaraṅgaparibhāṣā s'appliquait ici, 7, 2, 95 (96), antaraṅga, l'emportant sur 2, 4, 71, bahiraṅga, et par suite] S'IL POUVAIT Y AVOIR D'AUTRES SUBSTITUTS DU SINGULIER [— à savoir *tubhya*, *mahya* de 7, 2, 95 (*tava*, *mama* de 7, 2, 96) — que les substituts *tva*, *ma* de 7, 2, 98 (d'où conflict), ces derniers l'emporteraient en qualité d'apavāda, et en vertu de la maxime que les substituts d'un apavāda correspondent au même original que les substituts d'un utsarga], L'ANUVṚTTI DE "MAPARYANTASYA" SERAIT INUTILE". — L'anuvṛtti de *mapary*° ne peut qu'être indispensable. Il s'ensuit que les substituts *tva*, *ma* de 7, 2, 98 sont les seuls possibles, et ce parce que, dans le conflit 2, 4, 71 — 7, 2, 95 (96), c'est la règle 2, 4, 71 qui s'applique en premier lieu, élidant par *luk* les désinences du génitif et du datif et supprimant du même coup la possibilité des substituts prescrits par 7, 2, 95 (96) au devant de ces désinences. Par là se trouve établie la paribhāṣā 52 "*antaraṅgān api vidhīn bahiraṅgo lug bādhate*". "Une règle de *luk* bahiraṅga l'emporte même sur des règles antaraṅga". — La paribhāṣā 52 est une restriction à l'antaraṅgaparibhāṣā (paribh. 50) expliquée ci-après pages 362–366 les notions d'apavāda et d'utsarga sont définies ci-après p. 375, n. 67.

[8] Littéralement : "comme le désigné, (ainsi) dans le cas du simple".

[9] 1, 1, 72 : "*yena vidhis tadantasya*", littéralement : "à l'occasion de quoi il y a règle, (règle vaut) pour ce qui a pour fin cela", c'est-à-dire "Une opération grammaticale prescrite pour tel élément (lettre, suffixe etc.) s'applique à ce qui finit par cet élément".

iñ = *Dākṣi*, mais aussi dans le cas *A* (*Viṣṇu*) + *iñ* = *I* (un descendant de *A*), bien que le thème *A*, étant fait d'une seule lettre ne soit pas capable par lui-même de recevoir la désignation "*adanta*".

Si cette paribhāṣā était universellement valable, la séparation des deux règles 5, 2, 86 "*pūrvād iniḥ*"[10] et 87 "*sapūrvāc ca*"[11] n'aurait aucun sens. Car une règle applicable à ce qui finit par *pūrva* (ici 5, 2, 87, où, *sapūrvapūrva* = *pūrvānta*) serait aussi applicable au simple *pūrva*, et il aurait suffi de dire "*pūrvāt sapūrvād iniḥ*". La séparation des deux règles ne peut qu'être indispensable. C'est donc que *pūrva* n'est pas traité comme *pūrvānta*. Cette constatation suggère une maxime nouvelle, qui limite la précédente : "*vyapadeśivadbhāvo 'prātipadikena*", "Le traitement vyapadeśivad (i. e. la paribh. 30) ne s'applique pas à un thème nominal". Ceci est la paribhāṣā 32[12].

Les deux paribhāṣā 6 et 32 ont un caractère limitatif et n'existent qu'en fonction d'autres maximes. C'est là le caractère du plus grand nombre des paribhāṣā qui reposent sur un jñāpaka. Il y a conflit entre l'utilité d'un mot ou procédé de Pāṇini et la valeur, au moins universelle, d'une maxime (paribhāṣā des recueils ou paribhāṣāsūtra) ; ce conflit se résout par une maxime nouvelle qui corrige la première, formulée en termes trop absolus.

Les autres jñāpakasiddhaparibhāṣā sont des maximes indépendantes, mais on peut faire ici une nouvelle distinction.

Certaines de ces maximes (9, 87, 88, 89, 50 [cas 1]) peuvent se ramener au type restrictif en ce qu'elles constituent des dérogations à ce qu'on serait tenté de prendre pour des vérités premières grammaticales. Par exemple, on croirait que l'énonciation d'un

[10] 5, 2, 86 : le suffixe *ini* (= *in*) vient après le mot *pūrva*" (dans le sens de *anena kṛtam*, c'est-à-dire en vue de désigner la personne qui est la première à accomplir une action quelconque). Example: *pūrvaṃ gatam* (*bhuktam*, *pītam*, etc.) *anena* = *pūrvī*.

[11] 5, 2, 87 : "(le suffixe *ini*) vient aussi après (le mot *pūrva*) précédé d'un autre mot" (dans le même sens). Exemple : *kṛtapūrvī* (*kaṭam*).

[12] La paribhāṣā 32 apparaît dans la discussion du vārt. 15 "*tasya ca*" à 1. 1, 72, vārt. nécessaire pour expliquer le dérivé *rauṇa*, de *roṇī* + *aṇ* (4, 2, 78), à la formation duquel s'oppose précisément la paribhāṣā 32. Celle-ci a sa raison d'être dans les énonciations *sūtrānta* (4, 2, 60), *daśānta* (5, 2, 45), où l'emploi de "*anta*" indispensable, vu le vārt. 3 à 1, 1, 72 "*samāsapratyayavidhau pratiṣedhaḥ*" (qui enseigne que dans les règles de composés et de suffixes un prātipadika ne désigne que lui-même et non ce qui finit par ce prātipadika), ne peut pas indiquer qu'il y a dérogation à la paribhāṣā 30, ni par dispenser de la paribhāṣā 32. La discussion se termine ainsi : "*ācāryapravṛttir jñāpayati vyapadeśivadbhāvo 'prātipadikeneti yad ayaṃ pūrvād iniḥ sapūrvāc cety āha. — naitad asti jñāpakaṃ/ asti hy anyad etasya vacane prayojanam. — kim — sapūrvāt pūrvād iniṃ vakṣyāmīti — yat tarhi yogavibhāgaṃ karoti./ itarathā hi pūrvāt sapūrvād inir ity eva brūyāt.*" "Il est un procédé de Pāṇini qui indique : "Le traitement vyapadeśivad ne s'applique pas à un prātipadika", à savoir le fait qu'il a dit "*pūrvād iniḥ*" (quand d'autre part il disait) "*sapūrvāc ca*" [celui qui parle comprend : "après un mot (quelconque) précédé d'un autre mot"]. — Cela n'indique rien, car il y a un motif autre à cette énonciation. — Lequel ? — (Le motif est que Pāṇini a ceci en tête :) C'est après le *sapūrva* "*pūrva*" (i. e. c'est lorsque le mot à élément antécédent est *pūrva*), que je veux prescrire le suffixe *ini*. ("*pūrva*" de 5, 2, 86 est donc destiné à passer dans le sūtra suivant; n'étant pas vyartha, ce mot ne peut pas être jñāpaka). — Alors c'est la séparation des deux règles (qui est le jñāpaka), car autrement (i.e. si la paribh. n'existait pas), Pāṇini dirait (en une seule règle) "*purvāt sapūrvād iniḥ*".

suffixe individuel ne dénote que ce suffixe : la paribhāṣā 87 enseigne que le suffixe *aṇ*, lorsqu'énoncé au locatif il est la cause d'une opération grammaticale, dénote aussi le *ṇa tācchīlika*[13].

Les autres paribhāṣā du même type autonome (79, 80, 81, 82, 86, 90, 50 [cas 2]) n'ont pas à proprement parler un caractère restrictif, mais déterminent le choix dans un cas douteux. La racine *pā*, dans Pāṇini, dénote-t-elle *pāti* ou *pibati* ? Selon la paribhāṣā 90, elle ne peut dénoter que *pibati*[14].

Dans l'une comme dans l'autre de ces deux catégories de maximes indépendantes, il s'agit de deux possibilités *a priori* d'interprétation ou application des règles (ou suites de règles). Dans l'une tel élément est indispensable, dans l'autre il serait superflu ; une réduction à l'impossible rejette celle des deux hypothèses qui ne tient pas compte de ce qui se trouve devenir ainsi le jñāpaka de l'autre hypothèse.

L'antaraṅgaparibhāṣā (paribh. 50), à deux aspects et deux jñāpaka correspondants, offre un exemple de chacune de ces deux dernières variétés de paribhāṣā. Elle enseigne que la succession naturelle des règles n'est pas toujours possible (cas 1) et permet de choisir entre deux opérations qui se présentent simultanément (cas 2). Un premier jñāpaka est le mot *ūṭh* de 6, 4, 132[15]. *Ūṭh* (= *ū*) est un saṃprasāraṇa spécial qui a pour but la formation d'un accusatif pluriel comme *viśvauhaḥ*. Or il semble qu'on pourrait y arriver aussi bien par le saṃprasāraṇa ordinaire, comme le montre la comparaison que voici :

viśva + vāh + ṇvi + śas	*viśva + vāh + ṇvi + śas*
viśva + uāh + O + aḥ 6, 4, 132 "*vāhaḥ*"	*viśva + ūāh + O + aḥ* 6, 4, 132 "*vahā ūṭh*"
viśva u h O aḥ 6, 1, 1, 108 [17]	*viśva ū ḥ O aḥ* 6, 1, 108
viśva o h O aḥ 7, 3, 86[16]	*viśv au h aḥ* 6, 1, 89[19]
viśv au h O aḥ 6, 1, 88[18]	

13 87 : "*tācchīlike ṇe 'ṇkṛtāni bhavanti*" "(Les opérations) déterminées par le suffixe *aṇ* ont lieu aussi devant le *ṇa tācchīlika*" (*ṇa* de 4, 4, 62).

14 90 : "*lugvikaraṇālugvikaraṇayor alugvikaraṇasya*" "De deux (possibilités d'interprétation:) racine à vikaraṇa *luk* (= racine de la 2° classe), racine à vikaraṇa autre que *luk*, (c'est la seconde qui prévaut et une règle ne vaut que) pour la racine à vikaraṇa autre que *luk*".

15 6, 4, 132 : *vāha ūṭh* (*saṃprasāraṇam — bhasya*) "*ū* est le saṃprasāraṇa de la demi-voyelle de *vāh*, lorsque *vāh* est un thème *bha* (i. e. devant suffixe commençant par *y* ou une voyelle. Pāṇ., 1, 4, 18).

16 7, 3, 86 : *pugantalaghūpadhasya ca* (*iko —aṅgasya—guṇaḥ—sārvadhātukārdhadhātukayoḥ*). Traduction ordinaire : "guṇa devant sārva- et ārdhadhātuka (Pāṇ., 3, 4, 113 et 114) de l'*ik* (*i, u, ṛ, ḷ*) d'une base (aṅga) qui a l'augment *puk* (= *p*) comme finale ou une brève comme pénultième". — Mais la règle ainsi comprise s'appliquerait indûment à *bhinatti*, *chinatti*, etc. Par suite, Patañj. interprète "*pugantalaghūpadhasya*" comme le génitif d'un samāhāradvandva de *puganta* (tatpuruṣa) + *laghūpadhā* (karmadhāraya), génitif d'un substantif en apposition à *iko* au lieu de génitif d'un adjectif qui qualifierait *aṅgasya*. D'où, la traduction : "guṇa devant sārva- et ārdhadhātuka de l'*ik* d'un aṅga, quand cet *ik* est soit un *puganta*, soit une *laghūpadhā*". — Sur *puganta* étiqueté "tatpuruṣa" voir Nāgoj., *Uddyota*, ad 1, 1, 3, vārt. 6.

17 6, 1, 108 : *saṃprasāraṇāc ca* (*ekaḥ pūrvaparayoḥ — pūrvaḥ*) "Après la voyelle d'un saṃprasāraṇa (et devant voyelle de la racine), la précédente, i. e. la voyelle du saṃprasāraṇa est le simple substitut de la précédente et de la suivante". Cela veut dire : Le saṃprasāraṇa, i. e. la transformation en voyelle de la demi-voyelle qui précède la voyelle *a*, s'accompagne de la disparition de cet *a* de la racine.

363 Raisonnement par l'absurde dans Pāṇini

Étant donné que le suffixe *ṇvi*[20] (3, 2, 64) n'est ajouté à la racine *vah* que si celle-ci est en composition avec un premier terme terminé par *a*, il n'y aurait jamais d'autre substitution à opérer, après saṃprasāraṇa et guṇa, que celle de *au* pour *a* + *o*, et cette substitution serait réalisée par 6, 1, 88, sans le secours d'un second procédé de formation. L'avantage de celui-ci, c'est qu'il permet d'arriver à *viśvauhaḥ* sans passer par le guṇa de 7, 3, 86.

Il semblerait naturel qu'une succession de règles applicables à un thème dût s'effectuer sans obstacle dans l'ordre des transformations du thème, chaque état intermédiaire tombant automatiquement sous la règle nouvelle dont il réaliserait les conditions. Si ce principe s'appliquait ici, i. e. si le guṇa de 7, 3, 86 était possible après le saṃprasāraṇa de 6. 4, 132 (lue "*vāhaḥ*"), le mot *ūṭh* serait inutile. Ceci ne pouvant être, on conclut qu'est seul praticable le procédé qui part d'une règle "*vāha ūṭh*". Pourquoi l'opération de 7, 3, 86 n'est-elle pas réalisable après celle de 6, 4, 132, condition nécessaire et suffisante de la première[21] ? Explication : le saṃprasāraṇa, bien qu'effectué, est considéré par convention comme irréel (asiddha) au moment où il s'agit d'opérer la substitution du guṇa. Et ce qui détermine l'*asiddhatvam* de 6. 4, 132 en face de 7, 3, 86 est révélé par l'examen des conditions des deux règles dans leur application au cas

viśva + *vah* + *ṇvi* + *as*
u h
o h
7, 3, 86 Antar°
6, 4, 132 "vāhaḥ" Bahir°

7, 3, 86 dépend du suffixe *ṇvi* dont l'effet subsiste en vertu de 1, 1, 62 même après substitution du lopa. 6, 4, 132 dépend du suffixe *as*, au moins médiatement, puisque c'est l'initiale vocalique de ce suffixe qui fait que *vah* est un thème *bha*.[22] Les deux causes sont

[18] 6, 1, 88 : *vṛddhir eci* (*āt — ekaḥ pūrvaparayoḥ*) "Après *a* (finale du mot précédent) et devant diphtongue (initiale du mot suivant), la vṛddhi est le simple substitut de la précédente et de la suivante".

[19] 6, 1, 89 : *etyedhatyūṭhsu* (*āt — vṛddhir — ekaḥ — pūrvaparayoḥ*) "Après *a* (finale du mot précédent) et devant e de *eti* ou *edhati* ou devant *ūṭh* (= *ū* de 6, 4, 132), la vṛddhi est le simple substitut des deux: précédente et suivante".

[20] *ṇvi* (= *v*) est un suffixe pour lequel la règle 6, 1, 67 prescrit la substitution d'un lopa (ce que je représente par un zéro), i. e. un suffixe qui n'apparaît pas dans la réalité. En vertu de 1, 2, 45, aucune racine ne peut être thème nominal, à moins (cf. 1, 2, 46) qu'un suffixe primaire n'y soit ajouté : d'où nécessité de suffixes imaginaires pour opérer, sans aucun changement réel, le passage dhātu > prātipadika. Bien que le *v* qui constitue le suffixe lui-même disparaisse complètement par 6, 1, 67, l'effet du suffixe n'en subsisterait pas moins en vertu de 1, 1, 62 : le guṇa de l'*ik* pénultième prescrit par 7, 3, 86 aurait lieu, n'était la paribhāṣā 50, comme si le *v* de l'ārdhadhātuka *ṇvi* était réellement présent.

[21] Le saṃprasāraṇa et la substitution 6, 1, 108, qui en est inséparable, peuvent être considérés comme une seule opération. Cf. texte de la paribhāṣā 119, où 6, 1, 108 est désignée simplement par sa relation avec le saṃprasāraṇa : "*saṃprasāraṇaṃ tadāśrayaṃ ca kāryam* . . . ", "Le sampr. et l'opération qui en dépend . . . ".

[22] Il faut donc admettre ici avec Nāg., sur l'autorité de Patañj., qui fait du mot *ūṭh* le jñāpaka de l'antaraṅgaparibhāṣā (voir note 24), la possibilité de la causation médiate (*paramparayā nimittatvam*). — Cf. (*Kielh.*, p. 232–233) le

l'une par rapport à l'autre intérieure et extérieure. 7, 3, 86, dont la cause est intérieure, est dite *antaraṅga* ; 6, 4, 132, *bahiraṅga*.[23] D'où la maxime : "Un bahiraṅga déjà effectué est considéré comme irréel lorsqu'un antaraṅga doit être effectué."[24] C'est le premier aspect de l'antaraṅgaparibhāṣā, caractérisé par l'antériorité du bahiraṅga. Cet aspect comporte deux possibilités : 1° A exige l'application préalable de B. L'effet de celui-ci étant asiddha, c'est-à-dire virtuellement suspendu, A est inapplicable ; 2° L'effet de B constitue un obstacle pour A ; B devenant asiddha, A devient applicable.[25] — C'est la première de ces possibilités qu'illustre la formation de *viśvauhaḥ*. Ainsi s'explique la nécessité dans 6, 4, 132 du mot *ūṭh*, qui permet la vṛddhi de 6, 1, 89, celle de 6, 1, 88 étant impossible, à cause de l'inapplicable guṇa intermédiaire de 7, 3, 86.

cas *vṛtrahan* + *kvip* + *bhyām*, où cette possibilité, faute de la même autorité, n'est pas admise : l'élision de l'*n* final d'un *pada* (8, 2, 7) n'est pas considérée comme bahiraṅga, bien qu'elle soit causée médiatement par le suffixe *bhyām*, lequel est cause que *vṛtrahan* est un *pada* (voir Pāṇ., I, 4, 14).

[23] PŚ., p. 41, 1. 12 : "*atrāṅgaśabdena śabdarūpaṃ nimittam eva gṛhyate śabdaśāstre tasya pradhānatvāt*". — Cf. Kielh, p. 223 : "The word aṅga in this (Paribhāṣā) denotes only a formal cause (such as a letter or a combination of letters), because in a work which teaches the formation of words main importance attaches to the wordform."

[24] L'antaraṅgaparibhāṣā est introduite par Patañj. dans le commentaire de 6, 4, 132 en réponse à trois vārt. qui déclarent le mot *ūṭh* inutile, vu que son objet pouvait être réalisé par l'application successive de 7, 3, 86 et 6, 1, 88. La réplique est donnée dans cette fin de dialogue : "*evaṃ tarhi siddhe sati yad vāha ūṭhaṃ śāsti taj jñāpayaty ācāryo bhavaty eṣā paribhāṣāsiddhaṃ bahiraṅgalakṣaṇam antaraṅgalakṣaṇa iti. — Kim etasya jñāpane prayojanam — pacāvedaṃ pacāmedam/ asiddhatvād bahiraṅgalakṣaṇasyād guṇasyāntaraṅgalakṣaṇam aitvaṃ na bhavatīti*", "Eh bien (puisque l'objet du mot *ūṭh* serait réalisé ainsi) le fait que Pāṇini prescrit *ūṭh* (comme saṃprasāraṇa spécial) du thème *vāh* indique l'existence de la maxime "*asiddham* . . . ." — Quel est le cas (par exemple) qui peut motiver cette indication ? — *pacāvedam* (de *pacāva* + *idam*), *pacāmedam* (*pacāma* + *idam*) : étant donné l'irréalité (conventionnelle) du bahiraṅga i. e. de la substitution de guṇa prescrite après *a* (6, 1, 87), l'antaraṅga, i. e. la substitution de *ai* (3, 4, 93) n'a pas lieu." — Par 3, 4, 93, *ai* est substitué à e faisant partie des suffixes de la première personne à l'impératif. La diphtongue e qui résulte du sandhi *a* + *i*, équivalant en vertu de 6, 1, 85 à la première des deux voyelles, c'est-à-dire à l'*a* final de *pacāva*, *pacāma*, appartient à l'impératif et de ce fait tomberait sous 3, 4, 93. Par l'antaraṅgaparibhāṣā cette diphtongue devient asiddha, et par suite 3, 4, 93 inapplicable.

[25] De cette seconde variété d'application du cas 1, on peut citer, à défaut d'exemple réel que je n'ai pas rencontré, une illustration théorique : la formation de *adhītya* de *adh* + *i* + *ktvā* > *adhi* + *i* + *tvā* > *adhī* + *tvā* (2, 2, 28 et 6, 1, 101) > *adhī* + *ya* (7, 1, 37) > *adhītya* (6, 1, 71). Cette dernière opération, insertion de l'augment *tuk* (= *t*) prescrite après voyelle brève, ne devrait pas avoir lieu dans le cas *adhī* + *ya*. Un moyen de résoudre la difficulté serait de faire appel à la paribhāṣā 50, à laquelle ressortit le conflit des règles 6, 1, 101 et 6, 1, 71 dans le cas

adhi + *i* + *t* + *ya*
B — A
6, 1, 101 — 6, 1, 71

6, 1, 101, qui est B parce qu'elle porte sur deux mots (v. infra, p. 366, n. 30) étant considérée comme irréelle, le composé *adhī* serait censé revenir à l'état *adhī* + *i* et l'addition du *tuk* serait normale. — En fait Pāṇini a fait appel à une autre solution : la mention du mot *tuk* dans 6, 1, 86 "*ṣatva-tukor*

La paribhāṣā 50 a un second aspect, suggéré par un jñāpaka particulier, le monosyllabe *āṅ* de 6, 1, 95, mot indispensable pour arriver à une forme comme *khaṭvoḍhā*. Or il semble tout d'abord que Pāṇini aurait pu faire l'économie de ce monosyllabe, vu les deux possibilités théoriques que voici :

khaṭvā + *ā* + *ūḍhā*	*khaṭvā* + *ā* + *ūḍhā*
khaṭv *ā* + *ūḍhā* 6, 1, 101[26]	*khaṭvā* + *o* *ḍhā* 6, 1, 87
khaṭv *o* *ḍhā* 6, 1, 87[27]	*khaṭv* *o* *ḍhā* 6, 1, 95[28]

Il s'agit ici de deux opérations (6, 1, 101 et 6, 1, 87) qui se présentent simultanément. Par laquelle commencer ? Si l'ordre 6, 1, 101 — 6, 1, 87, était permis, le second procédé, c'est-à-dire le mot *āṅ* de 6, 1, 95 serait superflu. Le premier procédé est donc illicite. Et l'explication est celle-ci : en face de 6, 1, 87, 6, 1, 101 est asiddha, mais dans un sens différent. Dans le cas 1, l'une des règles (B) était déjà effectuée quand se présentait l'autre. La suspension artificielle de B faisait que A pouvait ou non s'appliquer, selon que l'effet de B constituait pour A un obstacle ou une condition préalable. Ici les deux règles se présentent ensemble ; aucune des deux n'exige l'application ou la suspension de l'autre. Le caractère asiddha du bahiraṅga consiste à céder le pas à l'antaraṅga, qui est effectué d'abord.

La raison de l'*asiddhatvam* est donnée par l'examen des conditions respectives des deux règles dans leur application au cas

khaṭvā + *ā* + *ūḍhā*
B A
6,1,101 6,1,87

6. 1. 87 est antaraṅga parce que ses causes (*ā* + *ū*) se présentent d'elles-mêmes en premier lieu ; 6, 1 ; 101, bahiraṅga, parce que se causes (*khaṭvā* + *ā-ūḍhā*) se présentent en second lieu (voir Kielh., p. 243, n. 2). L'exemple *khaṭvoḍhā* illustre une nouvelle maxime : "Un bahiraṅga qui est applicable en même temps qu'un antaraṅga est asiddha en face de celui-ci". C'est l'aspect 2 de la paribhāṣā 50 : A est effectué en premier lieu ; après quoi, si les causes de B subsistent, B est effectué, sinon non.

asiddhaḥ (ekādeśaḥ)", "Un ekādeśa (i. e. un substitut à forme simple d'un original constitué de deux éléments, cf. 6, 1, 84) est asiddha quand il s'agit de substituer *ṣ* ou d'ajouter le *tuk*". Par là, dit Nāg. (PŚ., p. 53, 1. 4) le mot *tuk* de 6, 1, 86 indique l'inconstance de l'antaraṅgaparibhāṣā. — Si, dans le cas *adhītya*, l'antaraṅgapar ne s'applique pas pour la seule raison qu'elle est anitya, elle peut s'appliquer ailleurs dans un cas analogue ; autrement dit cette possibilité où A devient applicable du fait de la suspension de B, rentre dans le mécanisme de la paribhāṣā.

[26] 6, 1, 101 : *akaḥ savarṇe dīrghaḥ (ekaḥ pūrvaparayoḥ)* "Après une *ak* (*a, i. u, ṛ, ḷ*) et devant homophone, la longue est le substitut des deux : précédente et suivante".

[27] 6, 1, 87 : *ād guṇaḥ (ekaḥ pūrvaparayoḥ)* "Après *a* (finale du mot précédent et devant voyelle autre que *a*, initiale du mot suivant), le guṇa est le substitut de la précédente et de la suivante".

[28] 6, 1, 95 : *om-āṅoś ca (āt — pararūpam — ekaḥ pūrvaparayoḥ)* "Après *a* et devant *om* et *āṅ* (i. e. la diphtongue qui résulte du sandhi : préfixe *ā* + voyelle initiale d'une forme verbale), le simple substitut des précédente et suivante est constitué par la suivante"

L'antaraṅga 6, 1, 87 effectué, on a *khaṭvā* + *oḍhā*. Ceci, par 6, 1, 88, donnerait* *khaṭvauḍhā*, d'où nécessité de la mention spéciale "*āṅ*" dans 6, 1, 95, qui prévoit le substitut à forme de la lettre suivante (pararūpam) pour les cas du type *khaṭvā* + *oḍhā*. Le monosyllable *āṅ* est ainsi le jñāpaka de la paribhāṣā 50, cas 2. Les deux aspects de cette paribhāṣā ont été réunis sous une seule formule: "*asiddhaṃ bahiraṅgam antaraṅge.*[29]"

II L'Argumentation Basée sur le Jñāpaka et sa Valeur Logique

La réduction à l'absurde n'est pas autre chose qu'un syllogisme conditionnel du type tollendo-tollens: la destruction du conséquent dans la mineure entraîne comme conclusion la destruction de l'antécédent. Ce raisonnement pour être rigoureux suppose une condition essentielle: il faut que la mineure qui énonce le postulat préalable, pivot du raisonnement, soit vraie.

Que vaut ce postulat selon lequel il n'y a pas de mot vyartha dans l'*Aṣṭādhyāyī*? "Vyartha," entendu au sens strict qui l'oppose à caritārtha, qualifie une énonciation ou un procédé de Pāṇini, qui en l'absence de telle paribhāṣā, ne serait pas indispensable, ou

[29] La paraphrase de Nāgoj. (PŚ., p. 43, l. 15) distingue nettement les deux cas : "*antaraṅge kartavye jātaṃ tatkālaprāptikaṃ ca bahiraṅgam asiddham ity arthaḥ*". Chaque cas comportant deux possibilités d'application, on a les quatre schèmes suivants:
cas 1 : B, non A
B, A
cas 2 : A, B
A, non B

Le cas 2 de la paribhāṣā 50 est suggéré clairement, mais sans indication de jñāpaka, dans le Bhāṣya 6, 1, 108, à propos de la formation *adya* + *ā* + *ūḍhā* : "*Kim punar ihāntaraṅgaṃ kiṃ bahiraṅgaṃ yāvatā dve pade āśritya savarṇadīrghatvam api bhavaty ādguṇo 'pi. — Dhātūpasargayor yat kāryaṃ tad antaraṅgam — kuta etat — pūrva upasargasya hi dhātunā yogo bhavati nādyaśabdena — kim arthaṃ tarhy adyaśabdaḥ prayujyate — athādyaśadb asyāpi tu samudāyena yogo bhavati*". — "Mais quel est donc ici l'antaraṅga, quel, le bahiraṅga, puisque, l'une et l'autre portant sur deux mots (et donc étant théoriquement B[30] l'une et l'autre), et la substitution de longue homophone s'applique, et la substitution de guṇa prescrite après *a*? — L'opération qui porte sur la racine et son préfixe, celle-là est l'antaraṅga. — Comment cela? — L'opération première en effet c'est l'union du préfixe avec la racine, non avec le mot *adya*. — Dans quel but alors le mot *adya* est-il employé? — Du mot *adya* à son tour il y a union avec l'aggrégat (*oḍhā*)."

[30] Bien qu'il ne soit pas explicitement enseigné par Patañjali que ce qui est *padadvayāśraya* est bahiraṅga (cf. Kielh., p. 269, n. 3), cela ressort de passages comme celui qui précède. C'est en tout cas admis par Kaiyaṭa dans son commentaire à 7, 2, 98, à propos du composé *gomatpriyaḥ* de *gomat* + *su* + *priya* : "*gomatpriya iti atrāntaraṅgā ekapadāśrayatvāt sulopādayaḥ syuḥ padadvayāśrayatvād bahiraṅgo lug iti gomānpriya iti syāt...*", "(Si l'antaraṅgaparibhāṣā s'appliquait) ici, auraient lieu le lopa du suffixe *su* (6, 1, 88) et autres opérations qui sont antaraṅga parce qu'elles dépendent d'un seul mot, le *luk* (du même suffixe par 2, 4, 71) étant bahiraṅga parce qu'il dépend de deux mots [au moins indirectement, vu que 2, 4, 71 prescrit le *luk* du suffixe casuel d'un mot qui devient prātipadika, c'est-à-dire qui entre en composition], et on obtiendrait **gomānpriyaḥ*". — Si le suffixe disparaissait par lopa, toutes les opérations liées au suffixe (7, 1, 70, etc,) auraient lieu, en vertu de 1, 1, 62, même après disparition du suffixe. Mais la paribhāṣā 52 enseigne qu'une règle de *luk* l'emporte même sur un antaraṅga. Du fait de sa disparition par *luk*, l'effet du suffixe disparaît avec ui (1, 1, 63).

serait inexplicable, quand à sa valeur grammaticale. Et de fait (sinon en théorie) "vyartha" n'équivaut pas toujours à "inutile absolument" : on peut citer, d'après le témoignage indirect, sinon explicite, de Patañjali ou de Nāgoj, eux-mêmes trois exemples de mots grammaticalement vyartha à la fois et de par ailleurs utiles.

C'est d'abord le prétendu jñāpaka de la paribhāṣā 56 "*akṛta-vyūhāḥ Pāṇinīyāḥ*,"[31] le mot "*samarthānām*" de la règle 4, 1, 82 "*samarthānāṃ prathamād vā*," dont la traduction ordinaire est celle-ci : "(Les suffixes prescrits par les règles qui suivent s'ajoutent) après le premier des mots en construction (d'une locution de l'un des types 4, 1, 92, 4, 2, 1, etc., la locution n'étant pas exclue par le dérivé, vu que le suffixe n'est prescrit que) facultativement." Le sūtra ainsi compris est un adhikāra (règle gouvernante) dont l'influence s'étend jusqu'à la fin de 5, 2, i.e. sur toutes les règles des suffixes taddhita. Mais il ne gouverne celles-ci que par l'intermédiaire d'un certain nombre d'adhikāra subordonnés, dont chacun indique le sens d'une série de suffixes. Ainsi 4, 1, 92 "*tasyāpatyam*" gouverne les règles des suffixes patronymiques (4, 1, 83 et suiv.). Les "mots en construction" de l'adhikāra général sont les énonciations — *tasyāpatyam* (4, 1, 92), *tena raktaṃ rāgāt* (4, 2, 1), *tatra bhāvaḥ* (4, 3, 53), etc. — des adhikāra inférieurs. En conséquence, chaque règle de suffixe taddhita doit être interprétée à travers les deux adhikhāra superposés. Ainsi 4, 1, 95 "*ata iñ*" signifie : "Le taddhita *iñ* s'ajoute facultativement après un thème finissant par *a*, quand ce thème correspond au premier des mots en construction d'une expression du sens de "*tasyāpatyam*." De *sūtthita*, par exemple, on forme, au sens de "*sūtthitasyāpatyam*," un dérivé *sūtthita* + *iñ* = *sautthitiḥ*.

Mais c'est un autre sens que Patañjali attribue à l'adjectif *samartha*. Il désignerait selon lui les mots "capables d'exprimer un sens," c'est-à-dire les mots sous leur forme définitive, tels qu'ils sont après sandhi de leurs parties constituantes.[32] Ainsi *sūtthita* et *vīkṣamāṇa* sont dits *samartha* par opposition á *su-utthita* et *vi-īkṣamāṇa*, formes *asamartha*. L'adhikāra 4, 1, 82 signifierait donc que le taddhita *iñ*, par exemple, doit s'ajouter à *sūtthita* et non à *su-utthita*. C'est sur cette interprétation de *samartha* comme synonyme de *kṛtasandhi* que repose le jñāpaka "*samarthānām*."

A supposer en effet que pour arriver à *sautthitiḥ* on parte d'un asamartha *su-utthita*, auquel cas deux opérations, 6, 1, 101[33]

[31] "Les Pāṇinéens ne soutiennent pas (la thèse : persistance de l'effet d'une règle quand les causes de celle-ci ont disparu)".

[32] Bhāṣya, 4, 1, 82 : . . . *kiṃ punaḥ samartham — arthābhidāne yat samartham — kiṃ punas tat — kṛtavarṇānupūrvikaṃ padam* . . . Kaiyaṭa explique: *kṛtavarṇānupūrvikam iti/tasyaiva loke 'rthapratipādanāya prayogāt samarthatvam iti bhāvaḥ*. ". . . parce qu'on n'emploie dans le langage ordinaire en vue d'exprimer un sens que le mot de cette espèce (le mot qui est *kṛtavarṇa*), ce mot a qualité de *samartha*." — *kṛtavarṇa* = *kṛtasandhi*, voir Nāgoj. PŚ., p. 64, l. 2. — Il faut supposer, si l'on veut que *samarthānām* se rapporte à *prathamād*, que la seconde acception n'est pas exclusive mais ne fait que se superposer à la première : "Les taddhita s'ajoutent après le premier des mots en construction d'une expression analytique . . .étant entendu d'autre part qu'il ne peut s'agir que de mots "capables de sens" i. e. de mots à forme définitive.

[33] 6, 1, 101 : *akaḥ savarṇe dīrghaḥ* V. *supra*, p. 365, n. 26.

antaraṅga et 7, 2, 117[34] bahiraṅga, sont simultanément applicables,[35] la règle 6, 1, 101 est, en vertu de la paribhāṣā 50 (cas 2), effectuée en premier lieu et le taddhita *iñ* ne peut que s'ajouter à *sūtthita*. Autrement dit, si l'antaraṅgaparibhāṣā s'applique, *samarthānām* est superflu. On devrait conclure que la paribhāṣā ne s'applique pas. C'est ce que font certains grammairiens. Constatant en outre que le conflit des deux règles en question a ceci de particulier que les causes de l'antaraṅga 6, 1, 101 (à savoir *u* + *u*) disparaîtraient par l'application de bahiraṅga, si celui-ci s'appliquait en premier lieu, ces grammairiens ont voulu faire du mot *samarthānām* le jñāpaka d'une paribhāṣā (56) qui prétend qu' "un antaraṅga voit son effet disparaître (ou n'a pas lieu), dans le cas où ses causes disparaissent ultérieurement (ou même par la simple considération qu'elles disparaîtraient) par l'application du bahiraṅga."[36] Mais paribhāṣā et jñāpaka sont rejetés par Nāgoj., qui déclare que l'antaraṅgaparibhāṣā s'applique réellement dans la formation de *sautthitiḥ*, et s'exprime ainsi sur le mot *samarthānām*: "Bien qu'il ne soit que la répétition de ce que nous savions déjà par l'antaraṅgaparibhāṣā, ce mot nous met en garde contre l'erreur qui consisterait à croire qu'il en est pour tous les taddhita comme pour *na*, qui dans *viṣuṇa*, etc., est ajouté à une forme (*viṣu* + *ak*) où n'a pas été fait le sandhi."[37] Par là Nāgoj. reconnaît 1° que *samarthānām* est vyartha du point de vue strictement grammatical, puisqu'il

[34] 7, 2, 117 : *taddhiteṣv acāmādeḥ* (*ñṇiti* — *vṛddhih*) "La vṛddhi est substituée à la première voyelle du thème devant taddhita *ñit* ou *ṇit*".

[35] Il y a conflit exactement entre 6, 1, 101, d'une part et, d'autre part, 4, 1, 95 immédiatement suivie de 7, 2, 117. (Cf. paribh. 50 où de même l'opération B était en réalité double : 6, 4, 132 + 6, 1, 108.) Commence-t-on par 6, 1, 101, *iñ* s'ajoute à *sūtthita*, d'où *sautthitiḥ;* si l'on commençait par le suffixe, celui-ci s'ajouterait à *suutthita*, d'où **sāvutthitiḥ*.

[36] Telle est la double portée que donnent à la paribh. 56 ses partisans. Voir PŚ., p. 61, l. 10 "*bahiraṅgenāntaraṅgasya nimittavināśe paścāt saṃbhāvite 'ntaraṅgaṃ na*" et p. 62, l. 8 "*etatpravṛttau ca nimittavināśasaṃbhāvanāpi nimittam*".

[37] PŚ., p 64, l. 1.6 et suiv: "*samarthānām iti sūtrasthasamarthagrahaṇaṃ tu viṣuṇa ity ādāv akṛtasandheḥ pratyayadarśanena sarvatra tathābhramavāraṇāya nyāyasiddhārthānuvādaiva*", (Sur *viṣuṇa*, voir vārt. 2 à 5, 2, 100.)

Selon Kaiyaṭa, *samarthānām* est destiné à empêcher la vṛddhi qui s'appliquerait en vertu de la paribh. 55, d'après laquelle une règle de l'aṅgādhikāra (ici, 7, 2, 117) est plus forte qu'une règle de sandhi (ici 6, 1, 101). Ainsi si la Paribh. 55 s'applique, *samarthānām* empêche la vṛddhi. Si la paribh. 55, par inconstance, ne s'applique pas, c'est la paribh. 50 qui s'applique normalement, et le mot *samarthānām* a même objet que la paribhāṣā. Dans un cas comme dans l'autre ce mot n'est pas jñāpaka de 56. Cf. Kielh., p. 316, n. 1.

La paribh. 56 est mentionnée dans Kaiyaṭa mais non dans Patañjali. Kaiy. (6. 4, 22) signale même qu'elle n'est pas admise par Patañjali. Certains invoquent la paribh. 56 pour expliquer la forme *papuṣaḥ* d'où l'augment *iṭ* (préfixé au suff. *vas* par 7, 2, 35, antaraṅga) disparaîtrait lorsque sa cause, l'initiale *v* du suff. *vas*, a disparu par le saṃprasāraṇa de 6, 4, 131, bahiraṅga. Kaiy. répond ainsi : "*papuṣa iti/nanu cāntaraṅgatvād iṭā bhāvyam. /na ca saṃprasāraṇe kṛte 'pīṭo nivṛttir nimittāpāye naimittikasyāpy apāya ity asyāḥ paribhāṣāyā bhāṣyakāreṇānāśrayaṇāt . . .*" "L'augment *iṭ* n'est-il pas possible en qualité d'antaraṇga? Et il n'est pas vrai que même après le saṃprasāraṇa (opération B qui détruit ici la cause de A, l'effet de A, i.e.) l'augment *iṭ* disparaisse, car la maxime "à disparition de la cause, disparition de l'effet" n'est pas admise par l'auteur du Bhāṣya . . ."

est une répétition (anuvāda); 2° que cette répétition a néanmoins une utilité.

Tel est encore le cas du soi-disant jñāpaka de la paribhāṣā 93[10], le mot *sthāne* de 7, 3, 46,[38] exprimé après *ātah*, alors qu'il est sous-entendu, conformément à 1, 1, 49,[39] après *ataḥ*. *ataḥ* désigne l'objet de la règle : *a* original du substitut prescrit; *ātaḥ* désigne ce qui qualifie l'objet de la règle : *ā* original de l'ex-substitut *ă* devenu original du substitut prescrit. L'emploi par Pāṇini du mot *sthāne* après *ātaḥ* indiquerait, au dire de certains, que *sthāne*, c'est-à-dire le paribhāṣāsūtra 1, 1. 49, ne pouvait pas être suppléé ici, et par suite qu'une paribhāṣā se sous-entend avec ce qui est enseigné dans une règle, non avec ce qui ne fait que donner un renseignement touchant l'objet de la règle.[40] La paribhāṣā est rejetée par Nāgoj., qui déclare que 1, 1, 49 ne signifiant pas que *sthāne* doive être suppléé avec tous les génitifs, la mention expresse de *sthāne* dans une règle n'indique rien.[41] Si le mot est exprimé ici, c'est seulement dans un but de clarté : "*tatra sthānegrahaṇaṃ tu spaṣṭārtham eva*" (PŚ., p. 97, l. 2).

Un troisième exemple est le mot *ubhayeṣām* de 6, 1, 17.[42] Ce mot aurait pu être omis, car il désigne deux catégories de verbes énoncées dans 6, 1, 15 et 16, dont la validité dans 6, 1, 17 allait de soi. Le mot étant vyartha, on a voulu en faire le jñāpaka d'une paribh. (119), selon laquelle "le saṃprasāraṇa et l'opération qui en dépend (= 6, 1, 108) ont plus de force que les opérations concurrentes,"[43] paribhāṣā qui expliquerait la formation du parfait des deux groupes de verbes en question. Lorsqu'en effet a été opéré le redoublement de *vyadh* par exemple, deux règles sont applicables à l'état *vya* + *vyadh* + *a* : 6, 1, 17 (saṃprasāraṇa) et 7, 4, 60 (halādiśeṣaḥ), qui enseigne que des consonnes de la redoublée seule la première est retenue. En vertu de 1, 4, 2, 7, 4, 60 devrait s'appliquer d'abord puisque postérieure (para), et le *y* de la syllabe redoublée étant ainsi élidé, le saṃprasāraṇa serait alors substitué au *v* de la même syllabe, ce qui donnerait* *uvyādha*. C'est le contraire qui a lieu et cela s'expliquerait par la paribhāṣā 119. Mais le mot *ubhayeṣām* est un jñāpaka sans valeur car il ne devient pas caritārtha après adoption de la paribhāṣā. Celle-ci est rejetée par Nāgoj., qui déclare, d'après le Bhāṣya, que le mot

[38] 1, 1, 49 : *ṣaṣṭhī sthāneyogā* "La sixième (vibhakti, i. e. le génitif), implique (en grammaire) la relation dénotée par le mot "*sthāne*", "à la place de".

[39] 7, 3, 46 : *udīcām ātaḥ sthāne yakapūrvāyāḥ* (*ata id — na*) "*i* n'est pas substitué à la place de *a* qui est substitué (par 7, 4, 13) à la place d'un *ā* (du féminin) précédé de *y* ou *k*. (Interdiction conforme à la doctrine) des Septentrionaux (et par suite facultative"). Exemple : *kṣatriyakā* ou *kṣatriyikā*. 7, 3, 46 est une exception à 7, 3, 44, d'après laquelle *i* est le substitut de *a* qui précède le *k* appartenant à un suffixe, quand suit la terminaison féminine *ā*, excepté à la fin d'un bahuvrīhi. Exemple : *kāraka* + *ā* = *kārikā*.

[40] Paribh. 93[10] : *vidhau paribhāṣopatiṣṭhate nānuvāde*.

[41] Si 1, 1, 49 n'enseigne pas que *sthāne* doive être sous-entendu avec tous les génitifs, *sthāne* peut ne pas être sous-entendu (peut être exprimé) sans que 1, 1, 49 cesse de s'appliquer. La mention expresse de *sthāne* après *ātaḥ* ne peut donc pas signifier la non-application de 1, 1, 49, ni par suite indiquer la paribh. 93[10].

[42] 6, 1, 17 : *liṭy abhyāsasyobhayeṣām saṃprasāraṇam*) "sampras. de la syllabe du redoublement des deux (groupes de verbes : *vacyādi* (6, 1, 15) et *grahādi* (6, 1, 16)), quand les suff. de *liṭ* suivent" (i. e. au parfait).

[43] Paribh. 119 : *saṃprasāraṇaṃ tadāśrayaṃ ca kāryaṃ balavat*.

ubhayeṣām a le même objet qu'aurait la paribhāṣā, vu qu'il a le sens de *eva* et indique que des deux règles applicables au redoublement des verbes en question, seul le saṃprasāraṇa doit avoir lieu.[44]

A ces mots auxquels est assignée par Patañjali ou Nāgoj. une valeur conventionnelle,[45] on peut ajouter une autre catégorie, certainement aussi fort restreinte, de mots techniquement vyartha ceux que Pāṇini peut avoir employés dans une intention pédagogique. Si cette intention coïncidait en général avec la recherche de la concision, elle pouvait exiger de temps en temps qu'il y fût fait dérogation. Ainsi peut-on essayer de justifier deux ou trois éléments dont à cause de leur inutilité proprement grammaticale on a voulu faire des jñāpaka.

Soit la paribhāṣā 84 "*samāsāntavidhir anityaḥ*."[46] Elle aurait pour jñāpaka la présence de mot *rājan* dans le gaṇa *aṃśvādi*, qui intervient dans 6, 2, 193 : "*prater aṃśvādayaḥ tatpuruṣe* (*antodāttāḥ*) " Dans un tatpuruṣa dont le premier terme est *prati*, les mots *aṃśu*, etc. ont l'aigu sur la finale." Or le mot *rājan*, quand il figure à la fin d'un tatpuruṣa, prend le suffixe *ṭac* par 5, 4, 91,[47] et ce suffixe étant *cit*, un mot comme *pratirāja* est déjà antodātta par 6, 1, 163.[48] On raisonne donc comme suit : si la règle 5, 4, 91 était d'une application constante, il n'y aurait pas d'autre composé *pratirāja* que celui qui est formé au moyen du *ṭac*, et la mention de *rājan* dans les *aṃśvādi* serait superflue. Il s'ensuit que la règle du *ṭac* est anitya, comme le sont, dit la maxime ainsi suggérée, toutes les règles des suffixes samāsānta (de 5, 4, 68 à la fin du pāda).

Il est bien vrai que l'objet direct (prescription de l'aigu sur finale) de la mention du mot *rājan* dans le gaṇa *aṃśvādi* était obtenu sans cela. Mais ce rappel est-il inutile ? Il est probable que Pāṇini (si Pāṇini est l'auteur des gaṇa)[49] a inséré à dessein le mot *rājan*, de manière à faire un gaṇa complet de tous les mots accentués sur la finale dans les mêmes conditions (i.e. dans un tatpuruṣa à premier terme "*prati*"), y compris un mot qui, portant dans son suffixe samāsānta l'indice de cette accentuation, aurait pu à la rigueur être omis. Si l'on admet cette explication, le mot *rājan*

[44] Cf. Bhāṣya, 6, 1, 17 : . . . *idaṃ tarhy ubhayeṣāṃ grahaṇasya prayojanam / ubhayeṣām abhyāsasya saṃprasāraṇam eva yathā syād yad anyat prāpnoti tan mā bhūd iti. — kiṃ cānyat prāpnoti — halādiśeṣaḥ — . . .*

[45] Il y a lieu de signaler aussi les quelques éléments rejetés par Patañjali, ainsi que ceux qui, bien que réellement vyartha, ne sont pas discutés dans le Bhāṣya, et au sujet desquels Nāgoj. (PŚ., p. 94, l. 10 et suiv.) s'exprime ainsi : "*bhāṣyācāritaprayojanānāṃ sautrākṣarāṇāṃ pārāyaṇādāv adṛṣṭamātrārthakatvakalpanāyā evaucityāt*". — Nāgoj. vient de dire que les paribh. 93[1–5] sont à rejeter parce qu'elles ne figurent pas dans le Bhāṣya et que nous ne sommes pas autorisés à considérer comme correcte une maxime, même établie par un jñāpaka, si elle n'est pas donnée dans le Bhāṣya. Il ajout : "et parce que la seule manière convenable (d'expliquer) certaines lettres employées dans les sūtra et dont le motif n'a pas été discuté dans le Bhāṣya, c'est de supposer qu'elles ont simplement pour but de procurer à celui qui les étudie des mérites religieux".

[46] " Une règle de suffixe samāsānta (= suff. que prend un mot en fin de composé) est inconstante."

[47] 5, 4, 91 : *rāja-ahas-sakhibhyaṣ ṭac* (*tatpuruṣasya*) " Le suffixe *ṭac* s'ajoute aux thèmes *rājan, ahas, sakhi* en fin de composé, quand le composé est un tatpuruṣa".

[48] 6, 1, 163 : *citaḥ* (*antodāttaḥ*) " Les (mots terminés par un suffixe) *cit* sont accentués sur la finale".

[49] Sur ce point, voir Goldstücker, *Pāṇini*, p. 131, n. 154. [see this volume 264].

du gaṇa *aṃśvādi* ne peut pas suggérer la paribhāṣā 84, qui se révèle d'ailleurs comme une fausse paribhāṣā.

Patañjali, qui termine le commentaire du sūtra 6, 2, 197 par la formule "*vibhāṣā samāsānto bhavati*," où, l'on peut voir une première forme de la paribhāṣā "*samāsāntavidhir anityaḥ*," ne parle pas du prétendu jñāpaka *rājan*, mais constate que Pāṇini a employé le composé *pāddanmūrdhasu* sans suffixe samāsānta. La règle 6, 2, 197 "*dvitribhyāṃ pāddanmūrdhasu bahuvrīhau (antodāttaḥ)*" enseigne qu'après *dvi* et *tri* les mots *pād*, *dat* et *mūrdhan* ont l'aigu sur la finale dans un bahuvrīhi. Deux vārttika observent que si Pāṇini a voulu désigner le thème *mūrdha*, il faut ajouter *mūrdhan*; s'il a voulu dire *mūrdhan*, il faut ajouter *mūrdha*, puisque l'aigu se rencontre également sur la finale de *trimūrdhā* et sur celle de *trimūrdhaḥ*. D'accord avec un troisième vārt. Patañjali déclare[50] que l'énonciation au moyen du thème *mūrdhan* suffit à englober les deux cas, car l'accent prescrit par 6, 2, 197 pour la finale d'une forme *trimūrdhā* se retrouve, en vertu de 6, 1, 161,[51] après addition au thème *mūrdhan* du samāsānta *ṣa* (5, 4, 115),[52] sur la finale de *trimūrdhaḥ*. Suit une discussion sur le conflit des règles 6, 2, 197 et 5, 4, 115. Accentue-t-on la finale du thème avant d'ajouter le samāsānta, ou ajoute-t-on d'abord le samāsānta, qui se trouve ainsi recevoir l'accent? Les deux règles étant *nitya*,[53] 6, 2, 197 l'emporte *paratvāt* (Pāṇ. 1, 4, 2), et l'on a la succession: 6, 2, 197 (accent sur la finale de *mūrdhan*), 5, 4, 115 (samāsānta), 6, 4, 144 (élision du *ṭi*, i.e. de la partie *an* de *mūrdhan*), 6, 1, 161 (accent sur le samāsānta). La conclusion est donnée de la façon suivante:[54]

"Mais convient-il de discuter cela? [la question de savoir si 6, 2, 197 doit être effectuée avant ou après le samāsānta, car même après addition du samāsānta, le second terme du composé n'en est pas moins *mūrdhan*. Or, 6, 2, 197 concerne le second terme, non le composé.] N'est-il pas vrai que Pāṇini a employé de façon non équivoque le thème à finale *n* puisqu'il a dit °*mūrdhasu*? S'il avait employé le thème à finale *a*, il aurait dit °*mūrdheṣu*.

— C'est le suffixe samāsānta qu'a pour objet (en définitive) cette discussion; car (en agissant) ainsi (qu'il le fait, c'est-à-dire en disant °*mūrdhasu*), Pāṇini nous indique que le samāsānta est facultatif."

Patañjali parle-t-il du seul samāsānta *ṣa*, ou du samāsānta en général? Il est probable qu'il s'est servi à dessein d'une formule générale qui justifiait les dérogations déjà courantes de son temps aux règles des samāsānta, tel le féminin *supathī*, formé sans le *kap*

[50] Ce qui suit n'est pas la traduction littérale, mais seulement un abrégé du Bhāṣya.

[51] 6, 1, 161 : *anudāttasya ca yatrodāttalopaḥ (udāttaḥ)* "Reçoit aussi l'udātta une voyelle non accentuée qui détermine l'élision de la voyelle accentuée précédente".

[52] 5, 4, 115 : *dvitribhyāṃ ṣa mūrdhnaḥ (bahuvrīhau)* "Le suffixe *ṣa* (= *a*) vient, dans un bahuvrīhi, après le thème *mūrdhan* venant après un premier terme *dvi* ou *tri*".

[53] Il s'agit de la notion technique de *nitya*, définie par la paribh. 42 : *kṛtākṛtaprasaṅgi nityaṃ tadviparītam anityam* "Une règle qui s'appliquerait aussi bien avant (après) qu'elle s'applique après (avant) l'effectuation d'une règle concurrente est nitya; daus le cas contraire, anitya". Cf. Kielh., p. 209, n. 1.

[54] *Yuktaṃ punar idaṃ vicārayitum / nanv anenāsaṃdigdhena nakārāntagrahaṇena bhavitavyaṃ yāvatā mūrdhasv ity ucyate yady akārāntagrahaṇaṃ syān mūrdheṣv iti brūyāt — saiṣā samāsāntārthā vicāraṇā / evaṃ tarhi jñāpayaty ācāryo vibhāṣā samāsānto bhavatīti.*

de 5, 4, 152, et qu'on rencontre Bhāṣ., 7, 1, 17 (*supathī nagarī*). Quoi qu'il en soit, le composé en °*mūrdhasu* employé par Pāṇini n'implique rigoureusement que la non-application du samāsānta *ṣa*. Quant à la présence de *rājan* dans le gaṇa *aṃśvādi*, elle n'a pour Patañjali aucune valeur d'indice puisqu'il ne la mentionne pas ; ce n'est probablement qu'un pseudo-jñāpaka inventé par ceux qui dans la suite ont donné sa forme définitive à la fausse paribhāṣā.[55]

Un autre souci qu'a pu avoir Pāṇini dans la rédaction de ses sūtra, c'est celui de simplifier l'explication des formes rares ou difficiles. Si dans son système l'économie des règles a plus d'importance que l'économie des mots (voir paribh. 121 : "*padagauravād yogavibhāgo garīyān*"), il a dû juger, du point de vue du lecteur, comme également entachée de *gaurava* la procédure qui obligerait à recourir à deux règles pour expliquer une forme, alors qu'une seule moyennant une légère addition suffirait. De cette manière peut-on essayer d'expliquer les deux prétendus jñāpaka de la paribh. 92.

L'énonciation *jā*, au moyen de la longue, dans 7, 3, 79,[56] permet d'expliquer les formes *jānāti*, *jāyate*, etc., par cette seule règle ; avec l'énonciation *jă*, ces formes exigeaient l'application successive de 7, 3, 79 et 7, 3, 101.[57] — De même, grâce au monosyllabe *āt*, la règle 6, 4, 160 "*jyād ād īyasaḥ*"[58] suffit pratiquement (la fusion des deux homophones allant de soi) à rendre compte de *jyāyān*, qui ne s'expliquerait autrement que par l'application de 6, 4, 160 (lue "*jyād īyasaḥ*" avec anuvṛtti de "*lopaḥ*" ex 6, 4, 158) et de 7, 4, 25[59] (allongement de *a* de *jya*).[60]

[55] L'inauthenticité de la paribh. 84, déjà signalée par Goldstücker (*Pāṇini*, p. 113, n. 131), se trouve confirmée par l'examen des justifications auxquelles la fait servir l'auteur de la *Durghaṭavṛtti*, livre de casuistique grammaticale, où elle n'est pas invoquée moins de sept fois. Voir *Durghaṭavṛtti of Śaraṇadeva, edited with notes by T. Gaṇapati Śāstrī*, Trivandrum, 1909 :

2, 2, 30 : *apetamaithilīm*, solécisme contre 2, 2, 30 (*upasarjanaṃ pūrvam*), si tatpuruṣa selon 2, 1, 38, est interprété comme un bahuvrīhi qui n'a pas pris le suff. *kap* (5, 4, 153).

4, 1, 44 : *ananyagurvyās* ex *ananyagurvī* (*ṅīṣ* licite par 4, 1, 44) est interprété comme un bahuvrīhi sans le *kap*.

5, 4, 78 : *brahmavarcasaḥ*, ablatif au lieu de °*varcasāt*, forme normale avec le samāsānta *ac* de 5, 4, 78. L'explication par l'inconstance est ici d'autant plus inadmissible qu'il s'agit d'une règle faite expressément pour le mot *varcas*.

5, 4, 92 : *āgāmivartamānāhar* est interprété comme un viśeṣaṇasamāsa sans le *ṭac* de 5, 4, 92.

5, 4, 132 : *dhṛtadhanuṣam* est interprété comme un bahuvrīhi sans le suffixe *anaṅ* de 5, 4, 132.

5, 4, 153 : *varatanu*, et

7, 3, 108 : *sutanu*, solécismes contre 7, 3, 108 si thèmes en *u*, deviennent réguliers par 7, 3, 107, parce qu'interprétés comme des vocatifs de bahuvrīhi terminés par des thèmes *nadī* (voir 1, 4, 3) qui n'ont pas pris le suffixe *kap* (5, 4, 153).

[56] 7, 3, 79: *jñājanor jā* (*śiti*) "*jā* est substitué à *jñā* et *jan* devant un suffixe *śit*".

[57] 7, 3, 101 : *ato dīrgho yañi* (*sārvadhātuke*) "*ā* est substitué à *a* devant un sārvadhātuka commençant par une lettre du pratyāhāra *yañ* (= demi-voyelles + nasales + *jh* et *bh*).

[58] 6, 4, 160 : *jyād ād īyasaḥ* "après *jya*, *ā* est substitué à (la première lettre de) *īyas*". Cf. 1, 1, 54

[59] 7, 4, 25 : *akṛtsārvadhātukayor dīrghaḥ* (*yi kṅiti*) "Une longue est substituée à la voyelle finale du thème devant suffixe commençant par *y*, qui est *kit* ou *ṅit*, mais non devant un *kṛt* ou un sārvadhātuka".

[60] Une forme un peu compliquée est le plus souvent le résultat de plusieurs règles, celles-ci étant des règles d'une certaine généralité. Mais il convient

Ce sont là explications aussi satisfaisantes que celles qui font du monosyllabe *āt* et de l'énonciation *jā* les jñāpaka d'une paribhāṣā "*aṅgavṛtte punarvṛttāv avidhiḥ*," selon laquelle de deux règles successives de l'aṅgādhikāra[61] qui portent sur le même mot seule la première peut avoir lieu. Patañjali (Bhāṣ., 7, 1, 30) qui formule cette paribhāṣā avec l'addition du mot "*niṣṭhitasya*," indique par là qu'elle ne rend compte que des formes qui sont correctement établies sans l'intervention d'une seconde règle de l'aṅgādhikāra,[62] celles où l'on constate l'application de deux règles successives s'expliquant par l'inconstance de la paribhāṣā : ainsi "*dvayoḥ*" obtenu par 7, 2, 102 et 7, 3, 104 et deux fois employé dans les sūtra (1, 2, 59 et 5, 3, 92), ce qui semble bien indiquer que la paribhāṣā 92 était inconnue de Pāṇini.[63]

Il n'y a qu'un petit nombre de cas où il soit possible de donner d'un mot d'apparence inutile une explication extra-grammaticale. C'est dire que les quelques mots réellement superflus, du point de vue technique de la grammaire, qu'on peut rencontrer dans Pāṇini ne peuvent pas infirmer pratiquement le postulat de l'économie pāṇinéenne, et le raisonnement qui repose sur ce postulat

de considérer à part le cas des formes rares ou d'exception : si Pāṇini était amené à faire une règle en vue du seul comparatif *jyāyān*, ou en vue des temps *śit* des deux racines *jñā* et *jan*, il devait être tenté de la faire unique, d'y inclure, si possible, tout ce qui concernait la formation de ce comparatif ou de ces temps exceptionnels.

[61] L'adhikāra "*aṅgasya*" (6, 4, 1) gouverne le quatrième pāda du livre 6 et les quatre pāda du livre 7.

[62] En fait le Bhāṣya ne cite que deux cas où la paribhāṣā 92 pourrait s'appliquer (et dans aucun des deux elle n'est indispensable); elle expliquerait :

1° La non-application de 7, 3, 86 après 7, 3, 78 dans *pibati*, ce qui rendrait inutile le vart. 1 "*pibater guṇapratiṣedhaḥ*" à 7, 3, 78. (Bhāṣ., 6, 4, 160 et 7, 3,79). Lorsque de *pā* + *śap* + *tip* on a obtenu, par 7, 3, 78, *pib* + *a* + *ti*, le guṇa devrait être substitué à la pénultième *i* en vertu de 7, 3, 86; celle-ci étant une seconde règle de l'aṅgādhikāra, on peut dire qu'elle est exclue par la paribh. 92. — Mais une autre explication est possible : le substitut prescrit par 7, 3, 78 est *piba* (au lieu de *pib*), auquel cas 7, 3, 86 est inapplicable et la paribh. 92 inutile.

2° La non-application de 7, 3, 103 après 7, 2, 90 dans la formation de *yuṣmabhyam* (Bhāṣ., 7, 1, 30). Cette forme peut être ainsi obtenue : *yuṣmad* + *bhyas* > *yuṣmad* + *bhyam* (7, 3, 30 lue "*bhyaso bhyam*") > *yuṣma* + *bhyam* (7, 2, 90). Ici par 7, 3, 103, e devrait être substitué à l'*a* de *yuṣma* devant *bhyam*. 7, 3, 103 étant une seconde règle de l'aṅgādhikāra, on peut recourir à l'explication de la paribh. 92. — Autre explication : 7, 1, 30 est lue "*bhyaso 'bhyam*". La forme en question est alors ainsi obtenue : *yuṣmad* + *bhyas* > *yuṣmad* + *abhyam* (7, 1, 30) > *yuṣma* + *abhyam* (7, 2, 90) > *yuṣmabhyam* (6, 1, 97), et la paribh. 92 est inutile.

[63] D'après certains (*ke cit*), dit Nāgoj., il n'y aucune forme en vue de laquelle cette paribhāṣā soit indispensable (. . . *anayā paribhāṣayā na kiṃcil lakṣyaṃ sādhyate*) et les assertions contenues dans le Bhāṣ. 6, 4, 160, 7, 3, 79 et 7, 1, 30 doivent être considérées comme paroles de celui qui n'est que partiellement instruit de la doctrine (*ekadeśyuktir*). — Kielh., p. 440, n. 1, signale : d'après Pāyaguṇḍa, "*ke cit*" indique que Nāgoj. n'approuve pas cette thèse; d'après d'autres, "*ke cit*" signifierait "*bhāṣyatattvavidaḥ*". D'où le point d'interrogation dont Kielh. fait suivre le mot "rejected" dans sa liste des jñāpakasiddhaparibhāṣā (préface, p. ix). — "*ke cit*" ne peut pas désigner Nāgoj., vu que l'opinion de celui-ci est toujours introduite par "*pare tu*". Néanmoins, comme Nāgoj. expose la thèse du rejet sans la faire suivre de réfutation on peut supposer qu'il la considère comme vraisemblable.

est généralement valable. Mais ce raisonnement ne permet qu'une conclusion limitée. De la maxime générale invoquée, la constatation faite dans la règle du jñāpaka ne constitue qu'un cas particulier. Comment s'opère le passage du cas particulier à la maxime ? Y a-t-il induction ? Et d'abord que vaudrait cette induction ? Parce que le thème "*pūrva*" de 5, 2, 86 ne dénote pas *pūrvānta* (*supra*, p. 361), s'ensuit-il que tout thème nominal échappe à la maxime "*vyapadeśivad ekasmin*" ?

L'induction n'est possible, disent les logiciens, que s'il y a énumération suffisante de données singulières, l'induction à partir d'un cas unique n'étant valable que si l'attribut du jugement singulier est essentiel au sujet. Or dans les propositions de la grammaire il n'y a pas d'attribut essentiel, ni par suite d'induction valable à partir d'un cas singulier.[64] La maxime 32, si elle n'avait pas d'autre fondement que son jñāpaka n'aurait qu'une valeur de probabilité : on soupçonnerait qu'il en est pour tous les thèmes nominaux comme pour le thème "*pūrva*," faute de voir pourquoi Pāṇini aurait agi de telle manière dans tel cas et non ailleurs.

La valeur de probabilité des maximes à formule universelle ne serait encore acceptable comme telle qu'à condition de s'appuyer strictement sur la constatation première. Condition en fait réalisée le plus souvent. C'est la compréhension de la règle du jñāpaka qui détermine celle de la paribhāṣā. Par exemple, le mot *kārma*, dérivé de *karman* par le suffixe *ṇa tācchīlika* (4, 4, 62) est traité par Pāṇini dans 6, 4, 172 comme un dérivé par *aṇ* ; maxime correspondante (paribh. 87) : les opérations déterminées par le suffixe *aṇ* le sont aussi par le *ṇa tācchīlika*.[65]

Mais il est des paribhāṣā qui n'auraient même pas valeur de vraisemblance ; ce sont celles dont la formule ne procède pas exactement des indications du jñāpaka, soit qu'elle les dépasse (paribh. 66), soit qu'elle reste en deçà (paribh. 106).

La paribhāṣā 66 a pour jñāpaka le mot "*akitaḥ*" de 7, 4, 83 "*dīrgho 'kitaḥ*" : "Une longue est substituée à (la voyelle finale du) redoublement à l'intensif moyen et actif (littéralement : devant *yaṅ* [= *ya*, suffixe de l'intensif] et devant *luk* de *yaṅ*), quand ce redoublement ne prend pas d'augment *kit*." "*Akitaḥ*" a pour but

[64] Je mets à part un cas comme celui de la paribh. 27, qui énonce un principe allant de soi : *saṃjñāvidhau pratyayagrahaṇe tadantagrahaṇaṃ nāsti*" "Dans une règle de définition, la mention d'un suffixe n'équivaut pas (contrairement à 1, 1, 72) à la mention de ce qui finit par ce suffixe". Un suffixe pour être défini comme tel, doit nécessairement être distingué de ce qui finit par le suffixe. Dans ce cas l'esprit passe sans hésiter, et même sans faire d'induction, de la constatation singulière faite dans la règle-jñāpaka (1, 4, 14 : *suptiṅantaṃ padam*) à la maxime générale.

[65] 87 : *tācchīlike ṇe 'ṇkṛtāni bhavanti*. Cette paribhāṣā a pour jñāpaka le mot *kārma* de 6, 4, 172 "*kārmas tācchīlye*" "(Existe le mot) *kārma* dans le cas d'habitude caractéristique" (c'est-à-dire pour désigner celui qui a l'action [*karman*] pour habitude, un homme d'action).

6, 4, 144 enseigne : "d'un thème bha (v. Pāṇ. 1, 4, 18) le *ṭi* (partie commençant avec la dernière voyelle) est élidé devant taddhita". — 6, 4, 167 enseigne : "d'un thème finissant par *an*, la syllabe *an* demeure inchangée devant le suffixe *aṇ*". — Pāṇini, par la règle 6, 4, 172, veut fixer la forme *kārma* (de *karman* + *ṇa tācchīlika*) ; or l'élision du *ṭi* de *karman* serait régulière par 6, 4, 144. Si 6, 4, 172 a un sens, autrement dit si le dérivé *kārma* mérite une mention spéciale, c'est qu'il est comme irrégulier par rapport à 6, 4, 167 : par conséquent les opérations déterminées par le suffixe *aṇ* le sont aussi par le *ṇa tācchīlika*.

de séparer du domaine de 7, 4, 83[66] le domaine des règles 7, 4, 84, 85, etc., qui enseignent l'addition d'augments à anubandha *k* (*nik*, *nuk*, etc.) au redoublement de l'intensif de certains groupes de verbes, toutes règles qui seraient des apavāda,[67] par rapport à un utsarga 7, 4, 83 formulé "*dīrghaḥ*." Soit 7, 4, 85,[68] qui prescrit l'augment *nuk* (= *n*) après l'*a* bref d'un redoublement à l'intensif moyen et actif, quand la racine finit en nasale. Si, dans la formation de l'intensif de *yam*, par exemple, la prédominance du supposé apavāda (qui serait ici un anavakāśa) s'exerçait normalement, c'est-à-dire si 7, 4, 85 s'appliquait d'abord, la forme *yaṃyamyate* une fois pourvue du *nuk* n'aurait plus un redoublement en voyelle finale et ne courrait aucun risque de tomber sous l'utsarga "*dīrghaḥ*." Autrement dit, "*akitaḥ*" serait superflu. — Conclusion inadmissible. Ce qui oblige à constater que dans le cas des deux règles 7, 4, 83 (lue "*dīrghaḥ*") et 7, 4, 85, qui ont trait l'une et l'autre au redoublement intensif, la prédominance normale eût été renversée : l'utsarga aurait précédé (et par là rendu impossible) l'apavāda. D'où, nécessité dans 7, 4, 83 de "*akitaḥ*" pour empêcher cela.[69]

[66] 7, 4, 83 : *dīrgho 'kitaḥ* (*abhyāsasya — yaṅlukoḥ* [= *yaṅi yaṅluki ca*]).

[67] Un apavāda ou règle particulière (par opposition à utsarga, règle générale) est défini par la maxime "*yena nāprāpte yo vidhir ārabhyate sa tasya bādhako bhavati*". "Alors qu'une règle (générale) s'appliquerait nécessairement (à un mot), une règle (particulière) faite (en vue du même mot) exclut la règle (générale)". Il y a deux variétés d'apavāda :

1° L'anavakāśa (cf. paribh. 58), règle particulière "dépourvue d'occasion" d'application, et donc de raison d'être, à moins qu'elle ne soit appliquée de préférence à la règle générale. L'exclusivisme d'un anavakāśa a son principe dans le conflit avec l'utsarga (PŚ., p. 55, l. 1 : *virodhe bādhakatvam*); par suite une telle règle n'est exclusive qu'autant qu'elle doit s'appliquer elle-même : l'utsarga s'applique ensuite s'il est encore applicable;

2° L'apavāda au sens strict (cf. paribh. 57), règle particulière qui serait applicable même après la règle générale (les deux étant donc sāvakāśa). Elle exclut l'utsarga absolument (PŚ., p. 55, l. 2 : *vināpi virodhaṃ saty api saṃbhave bādhakatvam*).

Si le mot *apavāda* peut désigner l'une ou l'autre des deux variétés de règles particulières, il va de soi que l'instrumental *apavādatvena* (ou l'ablatif *apavādatvāt*) ne désigne que l'apavāda au sens strict, en s'opposant à *anavakāśatvena* (°*tvāt*). Cf. Kielh., p. 329, n. 4.

[68] 7, 4, 85 : *nug ato 'nunāsikāntasya* (*abhyāsasya — yaṅlukoḥ* [= *yaṅi yaṅluki ca*]).

[69] Nāgoj. (PŚ. p. 73–74) explique ainsi le jñāpaka : "*dīrgho 'kitaḥ* (7, 4, 83) *ity akidgrahaṇam asyā jñāpakam* / *anyathā yaṃyamyata ity atra nuki kṛte 'najantatvād dīrghāprāptau tadvaiyarthyaṃ spaṣṭam eva*" "L'emploi du mot "*akitaḥ*" de la règle "*dīrgho 'kitaḥ*" est le jñāpaka de cette paribhāṣā. Autrement (i. e. si la paribhāṣā n'existait pas), une fois, dans *yaṃyamyate* par exemple, le *nuk* ajouté (à la syllable du redoublement, cette syllable) ne se terminerait plus en voyelle; étant donné par suite l'inapplicabilité de la longue. "*akitaḥ*" serait manifestement superflu". (La réduction à l'absurde qui dans Patañjali aboutit à la paribhāṣā se transforme naturellement en une preuve par l'absurde de la paribhāṣā dans le PŚ., recueil de monographies sur les maximes supposées connues.) — Kielh., dans sa paraphrase de Nāg. (p. 349, n. 2), commet une erreur en disant que "*akitaḥ*" a pour but d'empêcher que 7, 4, 83 ne soit appliquée après 7, 4, 85. Kielh. suppose donc qu'en vertu de la paribh. 66, l'utsarga "*dīrghaḥ*" deviendrait applicable après l'apavāda. Or cela est inadmissible. Si 7, 4, 85 a pour effet de créer une situation (redoublée terminée en consonne et non plus en voyelle) qui rend 7, 4, 83 inapplicable, ce n'est pas une pari-

Une généralisation naturelle à partir de cette constatation aurait consisté à dire : "Quand il s'agit de modification du redoublement intensif, un apavāda n'exclut pas un utsarga." Or. la paribhāṣā 66 est ainsi conçue : "*abhyāsavikāreṣu bādhyabādhakabhāvo nāsti*," "Quand il s'agit de modification du redoublement les règles ne s'excluent pas l'une l'autre," tous les genres de conflit étant supprimés. Cette formule, si elle était donnée comme le résultat d'une induction ne se justifierait pas, car elle dépasse en compréhension la constatation du jñāpaka.

Il y a d'autre part des paribhāṣā dont la portée n'est pas universelle mais limitée à quelques cas. Telle la paribhāṣā 106, qui a pour jñāpaka l'anubandha *p* de *daip*.[70] Étant donné que, par 6, 1, 45,[71] *ā* est substitué à la diphtongue finale des racines du Dhātupāṭha, et qu'en vertu de la paribhāṣā 7,[72] l'anubandha *p* n'empêche pas *daip* d'être considérée comme racine en *ai*, l'anubandha commun ne peut avoir pour but que d'inclure les deux racines *dāp* et *daip* dans une énonciation commune, celle de l'exception *adāp* de la règle 1, 1, 20 "*dādhā ghv adāp*".[73] Mais cette explication se heurte à la paribhāṣā 105 "*lakṣaṇapratipadoktayoḥ pratipadoktasyaiva grahaṇam*" "Lorsqu'une énonciation pourrait dénoter à la fois quelque chose d'original et quelque chose résultant d'une règle grammaticale, elle ne dénote que ce qui est original."[74] Si cette maxime était universellement valable, l'énonciation *dā* (de *dādhā*) ne pourrait pas dénoter la racine *daip*, qui n'est qu'une

bhāṣā qui peut faire que 7, 4, 83 devienne applicable après 7, 4, 85. Et "*akitaḥ*" ne peut pas être destiné à empêcher ce qui est impossible. — En réalité le cas *yaṃyamyate* se présente de la façon que voici. Normalement, i. e. en l'absence de la paribh. 66, 7, 4, 85 exclurait 7, 4, 83 ("*dīrghaḥ*") *anavakāśatvāt*. En vertu de la paribh. 66, la préséance seriat renversée : c'est 7, 4, 83 qui, s'appliquant d'abord, rendrait 7, 4, 85 impossible. Le rôle de "*akitāḥ*" consiste, en séparant le domaine des deux règles, à supprimer le conflit (et la solution qu'en donne la paribh. 66); il n'y a plus ni apavāda ni utsarga et le redoublement de *yam* ne relève que de la règle d'augment 7, 4, 85. — A noter que dans les quatre exemples donnés dans le Bhāṣya 7, 4, 82, l'effet de la paribh. 66 consiste dans le renversement de la prédominance:

Normalement:

ḍoḍhaukyate : 7, 4, 83 para
exclurait 7, 4, 59
acīkarat : 7, 4, 94 para
exclurait 7, 4, 79–93
mīmāṃsate : 3, 1, 6 antaraṅga
exclurait 7, 4, 79
ajīgaṇat : 7, 4, 97 anavakāśa
exclurait 7, 4, 60

En vertu de 66, on a :

1°	2°
7, 4, 59	7, 4, 82
7, 4, 79–93	7, 4, 94
7, 4, 79	3, 1, 6
7, 4, 60	7, 4, 97

[70] Le jñāpaka, même quand il est cité, comme ici, indépendamment de tout sūtra, n'en est pas moins lié à un sūtra. Le jñāp. de 106, c'est en réalité l'anubandha *p* de la racine *daip*, en tant que celle-ci intervient dans 1, 1, 20.

[71] 6, 1, 45 : *ād eca upadeśe 'śiti* (*dhātoḥ*) "*ā* est substitué à la finale d'une racine qui dans l'enseignement (de Pāṇini, i. e. dans le Dhātupāṭha) finit en diphtongue (*ec*), sauf quand suit un suffixe *śit*". Exemple de *glai*, on a *glātā*, *glātum*, mais *glai* + *śap* + *tip* = *glāyati*.

[72] 7 : *nānubandhakṛtam anejantatvam*, littéralement : "la non-terminaison en diphtongue (*ec*) n'est pas créée par les anubandha".

[73] "Les différentes racines *dā* et *dhā* s'appelent "*ghu*", excepté les racines *dā* pourvues de l'anubandha *p*"

[74] Ce n'est là qu'une des deux significations que comporte cette paribhāṣā. Cf. Kielh., p. 486.

racine *dā* dérivée (par application de 6, 1, 45), et la racine *daip* s'exclurait d'elle-même. Inutile dès lors de l'inclure dans *adāp*, d'où inutilité de l'anubandha *p*. Force est de conclure que la paribhāṣā 105 ne s'applique pas ici : "*dā*" peut dénoter les racines dérivées (*do, deṅ*) aussi bien que les racines originales (*dāṇ, dudāñ*).

Si à partir de cette constatation il s'agissait de faire une induction analogique, on établirait qu'il en est de même pour toutes les racines capables de dénoter, à côté de la forme originale, une forme dérivée par application de 6, 1, 45, c'est-à-dire pour toutes les racines en *ā*. Au lieu de cela, la paribhāṣā invoquée (106 : *gāmādāgrahaṇeṣv aviśeṣaḥ*) n'accorde ce privilège qu'à trois racines. Induction qui serait absolument arbitraire ; ce n'est qu'*a posteriori*, après avoir lu tout Pāṇini, qu'on pourrait déterminer le domaine de cette paribhāṣā.[75]

Enfin il est une maxime qui dans Patañjali n'existe qu'à l'état de constatation singulière. C'est la paribhāṣā 91 "*prakṛtigrahaṇe ṇyadhikasyāpi grahaṇam*,"[76] qui a pour jñāpaka le mot *acaṅi* de 7, 3, 56 "*her acaṅi (ku-has-abhyāsāt)*." Ce sūtra nous dit qu' "Une gutturale est substituée à la lettre *h* de *hi* (*hinoti*) après un redoublement, mais non au *caṅ* (aoriste redoublé du causatif)." Or le sūtra 3, 1, 32 "*sanādyantā dhātavaḥ*" enseigne que le thème du désidératif et tous autres thèmes dérivés sont des "racines" et, en cette qualité, indépendants de la racine primitive et exclus par la simple énonciation de celle-ci. Si ce paribhāṣāsūtra s'appliquait à 7, 3, 56, le *caṅ*, forme à redoublement fait sur le thème du causatif, s'exclurait de lui-même, et le mot *acaṅi* serait superflu. Il s'ensuit que le paribhāṣāsūtra ne s'applique pas. C'est à cette constatation que se borne Patañjali, à la fin de la discussion sur le sūtra 7, 3, 56 et ses deux vārttika, dont le Bhāṣya ne fait que reprendre la conclusion[77] :

"Quand Pāṇini dit "*acaṅi*", qu'est-ce qu'il a en vue? (Il pense à des expressions comme) "*prājīhayad dūtam*".

[75] La paribh. 106 est énoncée dans le Bhāṣya 1, 1, 20, sans indication de jñāpaka, à la fin de la discussion sur l'interprétation de "*dādhā*". — L'école de Bhāradvāja enseigne que la définition des "*ghu*" doit comporter le mot "*prakṛti*" : l'appellation "*ghu*" doit s'appliquer aux énonciations *dā* et *dhā*, en tant qu'elles sont des thèmes "originales" (*prakṛti* s'oppose ici à *anukaraṇa*, "imitatif", i.e. énonciation purement matérielle). Cela 1° à cause des suffixes *śit*, qui ne permettent pas la transformation diphtongue > *ā* de 6, 1, 45, ce qui n'empêche pas les racines en diphtongue qui se trouvent au devant d'un *śit* de se comporter en racines *ghu* (ainsi concernant 8, 4, 17); et 2° à cause des racines *vikṛta*, i. e. transformées par 6, 1, 45, qui dans l'application de 8, 4, 17 se comportent également en racines *ghu*. L'interprétation de *dādhā* à l'aide de la notion de *prakṛti* explique dans ce second cas la dérogation à la paribh. 105.

Cette thèse est réfutée par Patañjali de la façon suivante. Inutile de faire intervenir le mot *prakṛti* dans 1, 1, 20. En ce qui concerne les suffixes *śit*, cette intervention est indispensable, il est vrai, dans 8, 4, 17, en vue de la racine *mā*, qui doit être lue "*prakṛtimā*", mais "*prakṛti*" doit être en même temps rapporté au mot "*ghu*" qui précède (ce qui dispense d'employer "*prakṛti*" dans 1, 1, 20). — En ce qui concerne les *vikṛta*, la dérogation à la paribh. 105 trouve sa justification dans la paribh. 106, qui corrige 105 : ". . . *vikṛtārthena cāpi nārthaḥ/ doṣa evaitasyāḥ paribhāṣāyā lakṣaṇapratipadoktayoḥ pratipadoktasyaiveti gāmādāgrahaneṣv aviśeṣa iti*".

[76] "Une racine employée (en grammaire) dénote non seulement la racine simple, mais aussi tout ce qui résulte de l'addition à cette racine du suffixe *ṇi* (suffixe du causatif)".

[77] Bh., 7, 3, 56 : "*acaṅīti kim artham — prājīhayad dūtam/* Vārt. I. *heś caṅi pratiṣedhānarthakyam aṅgānyatvāt.*

Vārt. I. L'interdiction de la racine *hi* au *caṅ* est superflue, vu qu'(au *caṅ*) il s'agit d'une base différente.

"L'interdiction de la racine *hi* au *caṅ* (dit Kātyāyana) est superflue.

Pourquoi?

Parce qu'(au *caṅ*) il s'agit d'une base différente. La base (sur laquelle est formé le *caṅ*) est terminée par *ṇi*; elle est différente (de la racine primitive).

Après qu'un lopa a été substitué (par 6, 4, 51) au suffixe *ṇi*, ce n'est pas une base différente.

En vertu de la règle (ici 1, 1, 59) qui veut qu'un substitut se comporte comme l'original, (le lopa étant considéré comme équivalent au suffixe *ṇi*) il s'agit d'une base différente."

Vārt. II. Ou plutôt (l'interdiction au *caṅ*) est un jñāpaka, qui a pour but de nous faire connaître que la gutturalisation du causatif a lieu ailleurs (qu'au *caṅ*).

"Alors en agissant ainsi, Pāṇini nous indique que (dans le domaine) du causatif, ailleurs (qu'au *caṅ*), la gutturalisation a lieu.

Quel est l'objet pratique de cette indication?

C'est que dans *prajighāyayiṣati* la gutturalisation se trouve correctement établie."

Ainsi donc l'exception à 3, 1, 32, indiquée par le jñāpaka, ne vaut, selon Kātyāyana et Patañjali, que pour la racine *hi* et seulement en tant qu'elle tombe sous la règle 7, 3, 56.[78] Et la paribhāṣā 91, sous la forme qu'elle a dans le PŚ., n'est qu'une généralisation arbitraire dont la fausseté est confirmée par la formule sous laquelle se présente le vārt. 2 à 8, 4, 34 : ce vārt. enseigne qu'aux racines énumérées dans la règle il y a lieu de faire l'addition des mêmes racines "*ṇyantānām*", ce qui n'aurait aucun sens si la racine simple dénotait aussi le causatif[79].

Bh. : *heś caṅi pratiṣedho 'narthakaḥ — kiṃ karaṇam — aṅgānyatvāt / ṇyantam etat / aṅgam anyad bhavati — lope kṛte nāṅgānyatvam — sthānivadbhāvād aṅgānyatvam.*

Vārt. II. *jñāpakaṃ tu anyatra ṇyadhikasya kutvavijñānārtham.*

Bh. : *evaṃ tarhi jñāpayaty ācāryo 'nyatra ṇyadhikasya kutvaṃ bhavatīti. — kim etasya jñāpane prayojanam — prajighāyayiṣatīty atra kutvaṃ siddhaṃ bhavati.*"

Le *caṅ* de *hi* est ainsi obtenu :

hi + *ṇic* +
cli + *luṅ* > *a* + *hāy* + *i* + *caṅ* + *t*
(6, 4, 71, 3, 1, 48, 7, 2, 116)
a + *hāy* + *O* + *a* + *t*
(6, 4, 51)
a + *hay* + *O* + *a* + *t*
(7, 4, 1)
a ja + *hay* + *O* + *a* + *t*
(6, 1, 11, 1, 1, 59)
a ji + *hay* + *O* + *a* + *t*
(7, 4, 93, 7, 4, 79)
a jī hay a t
(7, 4, 94).

Le suffixe du causatif élidé par 6, 4, 51 est, en vertu de 1, 1, 59, considéré comme présent en vue du redoublement prescrit par 6, 1, 11. Ce redoublement est donc fait sur le thème du causatif.

[78] D'après Nāg., la paribhāṣā 91 a pour domaine les règles qui enseignent la substitution d'une gutturale, c'est-à-dire le groupe 7, 3, 54–59 (PŚ., p. 92, l. 15 : *iyaṃ ca kutvaviṣayaiva*). Mais le vārt. de Kātyāyana et la phrase de Patañjali ne peuvent se rapporter, du fait du mot "*anyatra*", qu'à une règle du domaine de laquelle le *caṅ* est exclu, c'est-à-dire à 7, 3, 56; ce qui laisserait supposer que les formes à gutturalisation qui, se justifiant par la paribhāṣā 91, sont obtenues par d'autres règles que 7, 3, 56 (par exemple le *caṅ* de *han*, *ajīghanat*, obtenu par 7, 3, 55) n'étaient pas en usage aux temps de Kātyāyana et Patañjali.

[79] Nāg., qui cite d'ordinaire tous les textes propres à confirmer ou infirmer une paribhāṣā, ne mentionne pas

Intéressante est la comparaison des trois dernières paribhāṣā et des trois jñāpaka correspondants. Ceux-ci (*akitaḥ* de 7, 4, 83, — l'anubandha *p* de *daip*, c'est-à-dire en réalité le mot *adaip* inclus dans *adāp* de 1, 1, 20, — *acaṅi* de 7, 3, 56) ont même caractère : il s'agit de trois *nañsamāsa* dont l'emploi par Pāṇini indique que tel mot (ou telle opération, cas de *akitaḥ*) n'est pas exclusif de tel autre comme on l'attendrait normalement. Les trois jñāpaka ont aussi même valeur. Or du premier Patañjali passe à une maxime générale, et qui dépasse même, en compréhension, la constatation du jñāpaka, du deuxième, à une maxime applicable à trois racines, et du troisième, à une proposition qui ne vaut que pour la règle du jñāpaka. Il est manifeste que dans chacun des cas la portée de la maxime était connue par Patañjali indépendamment du jñāpaka. Et de fait les paribhāṣā, quand le texte ne varietur n'en était pas connu par la tradition (cas des paribhāṣā authentiques), ont été établies a posteriori, d'après le plus ou moins grand nombre de faits qu'elles devaient servir à expliquer. C'est ce que semble bien indiquer le principe de Pāyaguṇḍa "*yāvatā vinānupapattis tāvato jñāpyatvam*" "Autant est suggéré par un jñāpaka qu'il est nécessaire pour éviter une incorrection". Cela revient à dire que le jñāpaka n'a aucune valeur d'inférence générale. Il indique selon le cas une maxime universelle ou particulière; il peut même, si besoin est, comporter une double conclusion. (Voir Kielh., p. 37, n. 2 et p. 172, deux exemples de jñāpaka à double fin).

De l'examen des exemples qui précèdent il résulte que le raisonnement basé sur le jñāpaka, alors même qu'il aboutit à la constatation rigoureuse d'un fait particulier, ne permet pas d'aller au delà. Il ne pourrait légitimement fonder ni les paribhāṣā à portée limitée (83, 106, etc.), ni les paribhāṣā à formule générale, qui ne seraient alors que des généralisations de vraisemblance. Si les jñāpaka sont impuissants à faire connaître les maximes d'interprétation, il convient d'admettre que Patañjali et autres commentateurs ou tenaient ces maximes d'une tradition sûre, ou bien les ont inventées de leur propre chef. Tel est en effet le principe de la distinction entre paribhāṣā authentiques, remontant à Pāṇini, (et même probablement, comme on essaiera de le démontrer, antérieures à Pāṇini) et paribhāṣā inauthentiques, inventées après Pāṇini.

III Paribhāṣāsūtra et Paribhāṣā Authentiques non Formulées par Pāṇini. L'Antériorité de Celles-ci prouvée par l'Impuissance du Jñāpaka à les Inférer

Pourquoi Pāṇini a-t-il formulé certaines paribhāṣā et non les autres, bien qu'il y en ait parmi celles-ci qui ne soient pas moins importantes que les paribhāṣāsūtra.

Une première réponse est donnée par la paribhāṣā 116 : "*jñāpakasiddhaṃ na sarvatra*" "Ce qui est fondé sur un jñāpaka ou un nyāya [selon Nāg. le mot jñāpaka a ici ce double sens] n'est pas d'une application constante." Ce que Nāgoj. commente ainsi : "La

celui-là. Le vārt. 2 à 8, 4, 34 est signalé dans la *Durghaṭavṛtti* (1, 2, 2), à propos de la forme *udvejita*, où l'on constate le guṇa malgré la règle 1, 2, 2 "*vija iṭ* (*ṅit*)", qui enseigne qu'après la racine *vij* un suffixe précédé de l'augment *iṭ* est *ṅit* et par suite (en vertu de 1, 1, 5) exclut guṇa et vṛddhi. L'auteur justifie "*udvejita*" en disant qu'il s'agit d'une forme du causatif. Réfutant ensuite l'objection qu'en vertu de la paribhāṣā 91 l'énonciation de la racine *vij* inclurait aussi le causatif, l'auteur cite le vārt. qui détruit la paribhāṣā.

mention par Pāṇini de certaines maximes, alors même qu'elles étaient établies par un jñāpaka ou un nyāya, a pour but de faire connaître que les autres sont anitya.[80]" L'explication de la paribhāṣā 116 n'aurait en soi rien d'inadmissible. Mais elle suppose qu'il y a deux catégories absolument distinctes de maximes, avec coexistence des caractères constant et formulé dans l'une, inconstant et non formulé dans l'autre. Or l'une des plus importantes paribhāṣā de Pāṇini, le vāsarūpasūtra (3, 1, 94)[81], est considéré par Pāṇini lui-même comme anitya. C'est sur cette constatation que Nāgoj fonde la paribhāṣā 68, dépourvue de jñāpaka direct[82]. Il y a là une objection sérieuse contre l'explication de la paribhāṣā 116. D'autre part cette explication présuppose que toutes les maximes

[80] PŚ., p. 110, l. 9 : *nyāyajñāpakasiddhānām api keṣāṃcit kathanam anyeṣām anityatvabodhanāya ity arthaḥ.*

Cf. Kielh., p. 509 : "When some (rules such as 1, 1, 56) have been actually given (by Pāṇini) although they are established by jñāpakas and nyāyas they must be understood (to have been given by him) for the purpose of informing us that other rules (which are similarly established but have not been actually given by him) are not universally valid."

Le paribhāṣāsūtra 1, 1, 56 : "*sthānivad ādeśo 'nalvidhau*" ,si Pāṇini ne l'avait pas formulé, pouvait être restitué comme suit : La partie positive "*sthānivad ādeśaḥ*" ("un substitut se comporte comme l'original") est établie par une maxime de sens commun (nyāya) : Celui qui prend la place d'un autre en prend aussi les attributs (*tatsthānāpanne taddharmalabhaḥ*). Quant à la restriction "*analvidhau*" elle serait suggérée par un jñāpaka, le mot "*lyap*" de 2, 4, 36 "*ado jagdhir lyap ti kiti* (*ārdhadhātuke*)", "*jagdh* est substitut de *ad* devant *lyap* et devant un ārdhadhātuka qui commence par *t* (voir paribhāṣā 33) et a *k* pour anubandha" (exemple *ktvā*). *Lyap* (+ *ya*) est substitut de *ktvā* (= *tvā*) quand le verbe est pourvu d'un préverbe sauf *a* (7, 1, 37). Si *lyap* se comportait toujours comme *ktvā*, il eût été superflu, dans 2, 4, 36, de l'énoncer à part. Cette énonciation ne peut qu'être indispensable : *lyap* ne se comporterait donc pas comme *ktvā* concernant l'opération de 2, 4, 36, qui a lieu devant suffixe COMMENÇANT PAR T. D'où la restriction "*analvidhau*", "... sauf quand l'opération dépend des lettres (de l'original)".

[81] 3, 1, 94 : *vāsarūpo 'striyām* (*dhātoḥ*) "Après une racine (i. e. quand il s'agit d'un suffixe *kṛt*), un (suffixe prescrit par un apavāda) non uniforme (avec un suffixe prescrit par un utsarga) n'est que facultativement exclusif, sauf s'il s'agit du féminin." — Exemple : 3, 1, 133 (utsarga) prescrit *ṇvul* (= *aka*) et *tṛc* (= *tṛ*) après toutes les racines; 3, 1, 135 (apavāda) prescrit *ka* (= *a*) après racines à pénultième *ik*, etc. — Le suffixe *ka*, vu qu'il est *asarūpa*, n'exclut pas les suffixes *ṇvul* et *tṛc* : on a *vikṣeptṛ* et *vikṣepaka* à côté de *vikṣepa*

[82] PŚ., paribhāṣā 68 (*ktalyuṭṭumunkhalartheṣu vāsarūpavidhir nāsti*) — *idaṃ ca vāsarūpavidher anityatvāt siddham / tadanityatve jñāpakaṃ cārhe kṛtyatṛcaś ca* (3, 3, 169) *iti / tatra hi cakārasamuccitaliṅā kṛtyatṛcor bādhā mā bhūd iti kṛtyatṛjgrahaṇaṃ kriyate ...*

"Cela (paribhāṣā 68) est établi par l'inconstance du vāsarūpavidhi. Et ce qui indique l'inconstance de celui-ci, c'est la règle 3, 3, 169 "*arhe kṛtyatṛcaś ca* (*liṅ*)", où la mention des suffixes *kṛtya* et *tṛc* empêche qu'ils ne soient exclus par le suffixe *liṅ*, coordonné (ex 3, 3, 168) par le mot *ca*." — Si le vāsarūpavidhi s'appliquait ici, i. e. si *liṅ*, suffixe d'apavāda, n'excluait que facultativement les suffixes d'utsarga *kṛtya* (3, 1, 95) et *tṛc* (3, 1, 133), il serait superflu de mentionner ceux-ci dans 3, 3, 169.

[83] Goldstücker, *Pāṇini : his place in Sanskrit Literature*. London, Berlin, 1861, p. 107–118.

[84] Goldstücker (p. 110) signale pour le réfuter un autre argument qu'à son avis on pourrait être tenté d'invoquer en faveur de la postériorité des paribhāṣā par rapport à Pāṇ. Mais cet argument, tiré de la définition par Vaidyanātha

— formulées et non formulées — ont pour inventeur Pāṇini, thèse qui sera réfutée dans ce qui suit.

Une autre explication est celle de Goldstücker[83]. Si les recueils de Nāgoj. et autres, dit-il en substance, pouvaient être considérés comme un tout indivisible, les "vieux grammairiens" que Nāgoj., dans l'introduction du PŚ., cite comme son autorité ne pourraient pas avoir précédé Pāṇini, puisqu'il y a une paribhāṣā qui contient le mot "pāṇinīyāḥ". Mais ces recueils, pour diverses raisons, n'étant pas originaux, on ne peut juger de l'âge des maximes que par leur contenu (p. 110–113)[84]. Cette constatation faite, Goldstücker argumente comme suit (p. 113–115). Des deux hypothèses, antériorité, postériorité des paribhāṣā par rapport à Pāṇini, la première est la plus probable, vu l'indispensabilité du grand nombre de ces maximes pour une correcte application des sūtra. Néanmoins l'hypothèse de la postériorité des paribhāṣā ne serait pas impossible si Pāṇini n'en avait formulé aucune. Or il en a formulé un certain nombre. L'omission des autres n'est donc pas affaire de principe: l'explication n'est donnée que par l'hypothèse selon laquelle les paribhāṣā omises sont celles qui existaient déjà[85].

des mots *jñāpaka* et *nyāya*, ne serait possible que si cette définition pouvait être étendue aux paribhāṣā elles-mêmes, ainsi que le fait Goldstücker. Vaidyanātha, commentant les mots "*jñāpakanyāyasiddhāni*" employés par Nāgoj. dans l'introduction du PŚ, s'exprime ainsi : "*tatraitacchāstrīyaliṅgaṃ jñāpakam / etacchāstralokatantrāntaraprasiddhayuktir nyāyaḥ*". Goldstücker (p. 108) explique : "The paribhāṣās . . . have been defined by Vaidyanātha . . . as "axioms (the existence and authority of) which are established by certain sūtras of Pāṇini, and axioms (the existence and authority of) which are established by the method that governs other works, but is applicable to Pāṇini also . . . In other words, these paribhāṣās are, according to the grammarians quoted, special axioms referring to Pāṇini exclusively, and general axioms which avail for his grammar as well as for other works. The "certain" sūtras of Pāṇini which indicate that such Paribhāṣās are in existence and are required for a proper application of the rules, are called jñāpaka and the method of other authors which indicates that those paribhāṣās are applied as well to them as to Pāṇini, bear the name of Nyāya." (Cf. p. 118, où G. réfute la définition de Vaidyan. et la remplace par une autre). Sans entrer dans l'examen de la traduction même de G., je note seulement que ce que vise Vaidyan. dans sa double définition, ce n'est pas la paribhāṣā, mais le procédé qui la fonde. Ce qu'a certainement vu G., qui applique néanmoins à la paribhāṣā elle-même ce qui est dit du procédé. Or la distinction est ici d'importance, du moins en ce qui concerne la première partie de la définition. Si les jñāpakasiddhaparibhāṣā pouvaient être qualifiées d'"exclusivement pāṇinéennes" (telle est l'interprétation — contestable — qu'en définitive donne G. du mot "*etacchāstrīya*"), cela signifierait qu'elles on été inventées par Pāṇini et donc formulées après lui, conclusion qui pourrait ensuite être appliquée avec quelque vraisemblance à la totalité des paribhāṣā [ce n'est qu'ainsi que j'arrive à comprendre la portée de l'argument en question]. Mais les jñāpaka peuvent être dits "exclusivement pāṇinéens", que les paribhāṣā authentiques aient été formulées avant ou après Pāṇini, puisque dans les deux cas Pāṇini les a appliquées, les jñāpaka étant les traces d'application. La définition de Vaidyan., qui (dans sa première partie) concerne les seuls jñāpaka, ne peut donc, même entendue à la façon de G., fournir aucun argument touchant l'âge des paribhāṣā.

85 Il y a lieu de distinguer soigneusement la question de l'authenticité des paribhāṣā, et celle de la prémière formulation des paribhāṣā authentiques. On constate dès l'abord qu'il y a des paribhāṣā qui n'ont pu qu'être connues de Pāṇini (par exemple

Selon Goldstücker, en effet, Pāṇini ne serait pas l'inventeur de tout le système grammatical qui nous est parvenu sous son nom. Il aurait repris l'œuvre et les procédés de ses devanciers, se contentant d'y faire additions et perfectionnements. En ce qui concerne les paribhāṣā, il n'aurait formulé que celles qui étaient indispensables pour l'interprétation de son seul ouvrage, omettant celles qui existaient dans la tradition grammaticale et pouvaient servir à l'interprétation des œuvres de ses prédécesseurs aussi bien que de la sienne propre.

Goldstücker trouve une confirmation de son hypothèse dans le sens qu'a constamment le mot *jñāpaka* dans les vieux commentateurs et notamment dans Patañjali. Ce mot désigne un sūtra qui se réfère à un autre sūtra (sūtra ordinaire ou paribhāṣāsūtra), celui-ci toujours antérieur. La même relation, conclut Goldstücker, doit exister entre jñāpaka et paribhāṣā non formulées : celles-ci ont dû exister avant ceux-là, si l'on veut que Patañjali soit d'accord avec lui-même dans la définition du mot *jñāpaka*.

Sur l'autorité de cette définition, qu'il croit trouver dans la formule *yogāpekṣaṃ jñāpakam* qui clôt le commentaire de Patañjali sur le vārt. 10 à 1, 1, 23[86], Goldstücker déclare : qu'un jñāpaka concerne l'application d'une règle ; et par suite ne peut pas précéder mais doit suivre la règle qu'il indique.

Qu'un jñāpaka concerne toujours, directement ou indirectement, selon une distinction qui sera faite dans la suite, l'application d'une règle, c'est certain, mais tel n'est pas le sens de l'expression invoquée par Goldstücker, dont la méprise se double d'une fausse distinction entre le sūtra 5, 1, 23 d'une part et les sūtra 5, 2, 51, 52, (53)[87], d'autre part. Selon Goldstücker ces derniers seulement seraient jñāpaka de 1, 1, 23, parce que seuls ils concerneraient l'application de cette règle. Or le sūtra 5, 1, 23, considéré dans sa relation avec 1, 1, 23 ne diffère en rien de l'un quelconque des trois autres ; qu'il suffise de comparer

paribhāṣā 6), et d'autres qui lui sont non moins certainement étrangères (par exemple paribhāṣā 84). Dresser la liste exacte des deux catégories supposerait résolu le problème de l'authenticité, lequel ne peut être étudié que dans le cadre de chaque paribhāṣā. Tout à fait indépendante est la question de la formulation, qui n'a de sens qu'en ce qui concerne les paribhāṣā authentiques (les fausses paribhāṣā ne pouvant qu'être entièrement — fond et forme — postérieures à Pāṇini). Le problème est celui-ci : les paribhāṣā authentiques ont-elles été formulées avant ou après Pāṇini ? Dans la première hypothèse, Pāṇini les a connues par une tradition ou des ouvrages grammaticaux antérieurs où elles étaient déjà formulées. Dans la seconde, Pāṇini, inventeur des paribhāṣā, les aurait appliquées pour la première fois ; elles auraient été extraites de son livre au moyen des jñāpaka et formulées après lui, soit par Patañjali, soit par d'autres (par exemple les "vieux grammairiens" de Nāg.) chez qui Patañjali les aurait trouvées.

[86] 1, 1, 23 ; *bahu-gaṇa-vatu-ḍati saṃkhyā* "Les mots *bahu*, *gaṇa*, les mots en *vatup* (c. *tāvat*), les mots en *ḍati* (*kati*, etc). sont des *saṃkhyā* (+ des numéraux)".

[87] En réalité G. n'oppose 5, 1, 23 qu'à 5, 2, 51 et 52, parce que le manuscrit de Kaiyaṭa qu'il cite ne mentionne que ces deux sūtra. Mais 5, 2, 53 ne peut pas être séparé des deux autres ; les trois sūtra ont exactement même caractère quant à la relation avec 1, 1, 23 :

5, 2, 51 : *ṣaṭ-kati-katipaya-caturāṃ thuk* (*ḍaṭ* > *ḍaṭi parataḥ*).
52 : *bahu-pūga-gaṇa-saṅghasya tithuk* (*ḍaṭ* > *ḍaṭi parataḥ*.)
53 : *vator ithuk* (*ḍaṭ* > *ḍaṭi parataḥ*).

5, 1, 23: *vator iḍ vā* (ex 22: *kan* > *kanaḥ*)[88]
et 5, 2, 53: *vator ithuk* (ex 48: *ḍaṭ* > *ḍaṭi parataḥ*)[89]

Dans les deux sūtra le collectif *vatup* est traité conformément à la dénomination de *saṃkhyā* qu'il a reçue par 1, 1, 23, les augments prescrits étant là applicable à un suffixe (*kan*) ici déterminé par un suffixe (*ḍaṭ*), qui l'un et l'autre n'appartiennent qu'aux *saṃkhyā*. Si Pāṇini, dans la définition 1, 1, 23, avait omis le mot *vatup*, le lecteur était à même de le suppléer en s'appuyant à son gré sur 5, 1, 23, ou 5, 2, 53, car l'un et l'autre sūtra seraient également inexplicables si les mots en *vatup* n'étaient pas des *saṃkhyā*. Les deux sūtra ont donc en droit même valeur de jñāpaka. Et l'équivalence est la même entre 5, 1, 23 et 5, 2, 51 ou 52.

En pratique il existe une différence entre 5, 1, 23 et le groupe 5, 2, 51–53. Ceux-ci s'opposent à celui-là, non comme des jñāpaka à un non-jñāpaka (ainsi que le croit Goldstücker) mais comme des jñāpaka particuliers et rigoureux à un jñāpaka à inférence générale et indéterminée. C'est, dans l'esprit de Patañjali, un jñāpaka conventionnel, relatif à l'usage verbal concernant la notion de nombre, c'est-à-dire destiné à justifier toutes les expressions où un mot, même étranger à la catégorie des numéraux ordinaires, est traité comme un numéral. Tel est le sens de l'expression *yogāpekṣaṃ jñāpakam*, qui clôt la discussion sur le vārt. 10 (*bahvādīnām agrahaṇaṃ jñāpakāt siddham*) entre maître et élève, l'un A(dversaire), l'autre D(éfenseur du sūtra, ou tout au moins faisant des objections à la suppression du sūtra):

A. „L'emploi des mots *bahu*, etc, pouvait être évité (i.e. le sūtra 1. 1. 23 peut être supprimé).[90]

D. Par quel moyen alors dans les règles d'opération (*pradeśa*)[91] applicables aux *saṃkhyā*, y aura-t-il une correcte interprétation du mot *saṃkhyā*?

A. Cette interprétation est assurée par un jñāpaka.

D. Quel jñāpaka?

[88] 5, 1, 23 : "*iṭ* est facultivement l'augment du suffixe *kan* venant après un numéral qui finit en *vat*." Exemple *tāvatkaḥ* ou *tāvatikaḥ*.

[89] 5, 2, 53 : "*ithuk* est l'augment d'un thème finissant en *vat*, quand suit *ḍaṭ*" (suffixe des ordinaux, voir 5, 2, 48). Exemple *yavatāṃ pūraṇaḥ* = *yāvatithaḥ* — *iṭ* se place au devant de *kan; ithuk* après le mot en *vatup*. Cf. 1, 1, 46: *ādyantau ṭakitau*. — *kanaḥ* (5, 1, 23) et *vator* (5, 2, 53) sont des génitifs, — *vator* de 5, 1, 23 est un ablatif au sens de 1, 1, 67.

[90] A. *bahvādīnāṃ grahaṇaṃ śakyam akartum.*

D. *kenedānīṃ saṃkhyāpradeśeṣu saṃkhyāsaṃpratyayo bhaviṣyati.*

A. *jñāpakāt siddham etat.*

D. *jñāpakaṃ kim.*

A. *yad ayaṃ vator iḍ veti saṃkhyāyā vihitasya kano vatvantād iṭaṃ śāsti.*

D. *vator eva taj jñāpakaṃ syāt.*

D. *nety āha / yogāpekṣaṃ jñāpakaṃ.*

[91] *pradeśa* désigne la règle d'opération par opposition soit à la règle de définition, soit à la règle (ou maxime) d'interprétation, qui intervient comme subordonnée dans la première. Ce sens apparaît nettement dans le passage du PŚ consacré aux paribh. 3 et 4 (yathoddeśa° et kāryakālapakṣa), où le mot *pradeśa* revient plusieurs fois, toujours opposé à saṃjñā ou à paribhāṣā. Cf. notamment PŚ., p. 3, l. 7 : *saṃjñāśāstrasya tu kāryakālapakṣe na pṛthagvākyārthabodhaḥ kiṃ tu pradeśavākyārthena sahaiva*, "Une règle de définition, au kāryakālapakṣa, n'a pas de sens considérée isolément, mais seulement en union avec le sens exprimé par la règle d'operation (où elle intervient)", et l. 10 ". . . *kāryajñānaṃ ca pradeśadeśa eva* . .", "la connaissance d'une opération (grammaticale) n'a lieu qu'à l'endroit du *pradeśa*".

A. Le fait que Pāṇini par la règle *vator iḍ vā* (5. 1. 23) enseigne qu'après un mot finissant en *vatup*, *iṭ* est l'augment du suffixe *kan* prescrit (par 5, 1, 22) après une *saṃkhyā*.

D. Ce jñāpaka ne vaudrait que pour les *vatup*.

A. Non, un jñāpaka vaut pour l'usage,[92],,

Cette dernière réplique est commentée par Kaiyaṭa de la façon suivante: "Parce que ce jñāpaka (5, 1, 23) sert á la réfutation de cette règle, qu'on ne comprenne pas pour cela qu'il existe en vue de cette (seule) règle. Au contraire (le sens est:) il concerne les usages (verbaux, dans le domaine de la catégorie nombre), d'où son nom "relatif à l'usage". (En ce qui concerne les mots définis par la règle 1, 1, 23) le fait que Pāṇini, par les règles 5, 2, 52, 53, 51, prescrit (tel ou tel) augment, "quand *ḍaṭ* suit", indique qu'il y a opération de *saṃkhyā*"[93].

Cette dernière phrase n'oppose donc pas les trois sūtra 5, 2, 51–53 au sūtra 5, 1, 23 comme des jñāpaka à un non-jñāpaka. La méprise de G. est d'autant plus surprenante que la phrase de Kaiy., telle qu'il la cite, ne mentionne comme jñāpaka de 1, 1, 23 que les deux règles 5, 2, 52 et 51. Texte point inadmissible et qui supposerait ceci: c'est parce qu'il considère 5, 1, 23 comme jñāpaka particulier des *saṃkhyā* en *vatup* que Kaiy. se dispense de faire appel à 5, 2, 53. Autrement dit, 5, 1, 23, indépendamment de son rôle de jñāpaka général, aurait la même valeur précise relativement aux *vatup* que 5, 2, 52, 51 relativement à *bahu-gaṇa* et les mots en *ḍati*. Et dans ce cas raison de plus de ne pas l'opposer à celles-ci comme un non-jñāpaka à des jñāpaka. — Cette variante sur la citation des jñāpaka par Kaiy. est d'importance minime. L'intérêt est dans le mot *yogāpekṣam*. Qu'il n'y ait pour Kaiy. qu'une façon de le comprendre, c'est ce que confirme Nāgoj.

Nāgoj., en désaccord avec Patañj., n'admet pas le rejet du sūtra 1, 1, 23, parce que, même en conversant la FORMULE du sūtra, c'est-à-dire même si n'existe pas, comme donnée à inférer, la DONNÉE formulée par le sūtra, les règles 5, 2, 51–53 ne sont pas vyartha, mais indispensables pour indiquer la possibilité du suffixe *ḍaṭ* après *pūga*, etc., et par suite ne peuvent pas être jñāpaka de 1, 1, 23[94]. Ayant ainsi donné son opinion personnelle sur le Bhāṣya, Nāg. passe à l'interprétation de Kaiy.: "D'après certains, dit-il[95], le sūtra *vator iḍ vā* indique (et justifie) le caractère *saṃkhyā* des autres opérations, même caractérisées (en elles-mêmes) par l'absence de cause consistant en dénombrement, dont on constate dans les formes usuelles qu'elles ont eu lieu comme si déterminées par la qualité de *saṃkhyā*. Par là est établi le caractère *saṃkhyā* des opérations subies par *adhika*, etc[96]. Voilà pourquoi Patañjali dit *yogā-*

[92] Goldstücker fond les répliques 4, 5, 6 en une seule. La phrase *yad ayam* . . ., qui affirme la valeur de jñāpaka de 5, 1, 23, devient dans sa traduction interrogative et se trouve ainsi niée par la réplique finale.

[93] Kaiy. : *yogāpekṣam iti / asya yogasya pratyākhyānād etadyogāpekṣam iti na boddhavyam / kiṃ tu yogān apekṣata iti yogāpekṣam / yad ayaṃ bahupūgagaṇa-saṅghasya tithuk* (5, 2, 52) *vator ithuk* (53) *ṣaṭkati* (51) *iti ḍaṭi parata āgamaṃ śāsti taj jñāpayati bhavati saṃkhyākāryam iti.*

[94] Nāg. : *yad ayam iti . . . pūgādibhyo ḍaḍarthaṃ bahugaṇeti sūtre kṛte 'py jñāpakāvaśyakatvam iti bhāvaḥ.*

[95] Nāg : *ke cit tu vator iḍ vety anena saṃkhyānakaraṇatvābhāvavatām apy anyeṣāṃ prayogeṣu dṛśyamānasaṃkhyākāryāṇāṃ saṃkhyakāryaṃ jñāpyate / tenādhikādīnām api siddhaṃ tad āha yogāpekṣam iti prayogāpekṣam ity arthaḥ / etena pūgādibhyaḥ śasādiprasaṅgo 'pi vārita ity āhuḥ.*

[96] Bien qu'aucune règle ni jñāpaka de Pāṇini ne permette d'attribuer au mot *adhika* la qualité de *saṃkhyā*, un com-

385
Raisonnement par l'absurde dans Pāṇini

pekṣam; "relatif à l'usage" (*prayogāpekṣam*), voilà ce qu'il veut dire. Grâce à cette interprétation se trouve écartée du même coup (*api*) l'application indue des suffixes *śas*, etc. après *pūga*, etc. Ainsi disent (Kaiy. et autres, commentant la pensée de Patañjali)".

Nāgoj. approuve-t-il tacitement l'interprétation selon Kaiy. du jñāpaka 5, 1, 23 et de son qualificatif *yogāpekṣam*? La considère-t-il comme suspecte comme le laisserait croire la formule "*ke cit tu*"? Une traduction plus simple de *yogāpekṣaṃ jñāpakam*, qui vient en réponse à l'objection "Ce jñāpaka ne vaudrait que pour les *vatup*", serait "Non, il vaut pour (toute) la règle". Mais c'est là pour Kaiy. un contresens contre lequel il met en garde avec une insistance qui mérite d'être prise en considération. D'autre part cette traduction ne résout aucune des difficultés que pose le sūtra 1, 1, 23; elle en crée de nouvelles. De quel droit un jñāpaka qui n'implique la qualité de *saṃkhyā* que pour les *vatup*, vaudrait-il pour les autres mots de 1, 1, 23. Si son inférence peut être arbitrairement étendue à trois mots qui sont hors de son domaine, mieux vaut alors l'appliquer partout ou il est utile de le faire, c'est-à-dire à tous les mots que l'usage traite comme des *saṃkhyā*. C'est cette solution qu'a probablement choisie Patañjali.

Le sūtra 1, 1, 23 soulevait en effet deux difficultés, l'une antérieure au rejet du sūtra—et l'une des causes du rejet— : c'est que ce sūtra est incomplet, vu qu'il omet *adhika* et autres mots qui ne diffèrent en rien quant à l'application des *saṃkhyāpradeśa* des quatre mots qu'il mentionne. Comme pour ceux-ci la qualité de *saṃkhyā* est impliquée par des jñāpaka, Patañj., à la suite de Kātyāyana, avait deux raisons de condamner le sūtra. Mais le rejet de 1, 1, 23 par les règles 5, 2, 51–53 soulevait une deuxième difficulté: il fallait empêcher que l'inférence des trois jñāpakasūtra ne s'etendît, comme le voudrait la logique, à tous les mots qu'ils contiennent. Autrement *pūga*, *saṅgha*, *katipaya* subiraient inévitablement, tout comme *bahu* et *gaṇa*, etc., les opérations déterminées par la qualité de *saṃkhyā*, par exemple l'adjonction des suffixes *śas* (5, 4, 43), *dhā* (5, 4, 20), *kṛtvasuc* (5, 4, 17), etc. Or il se trouve qu'il y a deux règles, à même valeur de jñāpaka, qui impliquent l'une et l'autre la qualité de *saṃkhyā* pour les mots en *vatup*: 5, 1, 23, et 5, 2, 53. Une seule suffisant à cet office, Patañjali fait jouer à l'autre le rôle de jñāpaka conventionnel qui lui permet d'échapper aux difficultés susdites. Du moment en effet que Patañjali attribue à 5, 1, 23 une capacité d'inférence indéterminée, signifiant qu'il y a opération de *saṃkhyā* pour tous les mots qui, différents des numéraux ordinaires, sont traités par l'usage à l'égal de ceux-ci, sont exclus du même coup tous les mots exclus de ce traitement par l'usage. Ainsi s'explique que les jñāpaka particuliers 5, 2, 51 et 52 impliquent la qualité de *saṃkhyā* sans restriction pour les mots *bahu*, *gaṇa*, *kati*, tout en n'impliquant que la possibilité de prendre le suffixe *ḍaṭ* pour les mots *pūga*, *saṅgha*, *katipaya*.

En résumé, le sūtra 1, 1, 23 serait tacitement rejeté au moyen des trois jñāpaka 5, 2, 51–53; mais Patañjali se contenterait pratiquement de faire appel au jñāpaka conventionnel 5, 1, 23, qui englobe les trois autres et en même temps supplée à ce qu'ils ont d'insuffisant. Parce que Patañjali devait être tenté de recourir à cette convention, il est probable que Kaiy. interprète exactement

posé comme *adhikaṣāṣṭika* n'en est pas moins conforme aux règles 2, 1, 51 et 7, 1, 15, qui concernent l'une et l'autre les composés dont le premier terme est une *saṃkhyā* (cf. vārt. 9 à 1, 1, 23). — Même cas pour *adhyardha* et *ardha* par rapport aux règles 2, 1, 51 et 5, 1, 22 (Cf. vārt. 5 et 7 à 1, 1, 23).

la pensée de Patañjali. — La formule *yogāpekṣaṃ jñāpakam*, au moins selon Kaiyaṭa (or c'est à travers Kaiy. que Goldstücker prétend comprendre Patañjali), ne signifie donc pas qu'un jñāpaka concerne l'application d'une règle, mais bien qu'un jñāpaka concerne "les usages". Cette façon de comprendre l'interprétation de Kaiyaṭa est encore confirmée par le mot *prayoga*, par lequel Nāgoj.—traduisant la pensée de Kaiyaṭa[97] — glose *yoga*, car *prayoga*, qui s'oppose à *śāstra* comme la pratique à la théorie, ne peut désigner ici que l'usage verbal qui tend à échapper aux règles, et ne s'y ramène qu'au moyen d'artifices comme celui qu'on vient de voir[98].

Une règle-jñāpaka, ajoute Goldstücker, ne peut pas précéder mais doit suivre la règle qu'elle indique. Qu'en fait il en soit ainsi, cela résulte de l'arrangement des sūtras de Pāṇini. Mais on ne peut pas dire qu'il doit en être ainsi. Dans un ordre des sūtra qui serait différent, le jñāpaka pourrait précéder sans cesser d'être jñāpaka. En ce qui concerne en particulier les jñāpita qui sont des saṃjñā- ou des paribhāṣāsūtra, la position antécédente ne se conçoit inévitable (et encore du seul point de vue de Pāṇini, extérieur ici à la notion de jñāpaka) que par rapport aux jñāpaka que l'on peut appeler directs, ceux que constitue un cas d'application du saṃjñā- ou du paribhāṣāsūtra. Il en va tout autrement pour les jñāpaka à inférence indirecte, tel celui qui est cité par Goldstücker p. 117 n. 136 et qu'on rencontre dans le commentaire du vārt. 1 à la règle 1, 1, 3 *iko guṇavṛddhī*.

Ce vārt. (*iggrahaṇam ātsandhyakṣaravyañjananivṛttyartham*) enseigne que 1, 1, 3 a une triple valeur négative: il exclut de la substitution de guṇa et vṛddhi la lettre *ā*, les diphtongues et les consonnes. Sous son troisième aspect, 1, 1, 3 signifie donc "*na vyañjanasya guṇo bhavati*".—Mais, dit le contradicteur[99], cette vérité n'a pas besoin d'être formulée; elle est impliquée par un jñāpaka: la caractérisation par l'anubandha *ḍ* (*ḍitkaraṇam*) du suffixe *ḍa* prescrit par 3, 2, 97[100] après la racine *jan* composée avec un mot représentant un locatif. Le *ḍ* signifiant l'élision du *ṭi* (partie du thème qui commence avec la dernière voyelle, cf. 1, 1, 64), on a par

[97] G. (p. 116, n. 134) cite la glose *yogāpekṣam iti prayogāpekṣam iti arthaḥ* comme si c'était l'opinion personnelle de Nāgoj. En réalité, cette glose, étant comprise entre les mots *ke cit* . . . *āhuḥ*, est censée celle de Kaiy. dont Nāg., dans tout ce passage, ne fait qu'interpréter l'interprétation.

[98] Il faut reconnaître que l'interprétation de Kaiy. peut soulever des objections, l'une constituée par l'emploi de *yoga* (au moins au pluriel : cf. Kaiy.: *yogān apekṣate* et Nāg. : *prayogeṣu*) au sens de *prayoga*. — Qu'on préfère l'interprétation de Kaiy. ou l'interprétation plus facile (trop facile) selon laquelle "ce jñāp. concerne toute la règle", une chose est certaine, c'est que la traduction de Goldstücker est inadmissible. D'ailleurs "application de règle" est une expression complexe, dont l'équivalent sanscrit ne peut être qu'un composé. Ce composé existe. C'est *śāstrapravṛttiḥ* (v. Mahābhāṣyam, Introd., comm. du vārt. 15), ailleurs *lakṣaṇapravṛttiḥ* (texte de la par. 111 : *parjanyaval lakṣaṇapravṛttiḥ*) ou encore *sūtrapravṛttiḥ* (PŚ., p. 3, l. 12), composé à premier terme variable selon le mot choisi pour signifier "règle", mais dont le second terme est *pravṛtti* pour signifier "application".

[99] Bhāṣya *ad* 1, 1, 3, vārt. 1 : . . . *vyañjananivṛttyarthenāpi nārthaḥ / ācāryapravṛttir jñāpayati na vyañjanasya guṇo bhavatīti yad ayaṃ janer ḍaṃ śāsti — kathaṃ kṛtvā jñāpakam — ḍitkaraṇa etat prayojanaṃ ḍitīti ṭilopo yathā syāt / yadi vyañjanasya guṇaḥ syād ḍitkaraṇam anarthakaṃ syāt.*

[100] 3, 2, 97 *saptamyāṃ janer ḍaḥ*. "Le suffixe *ḍa* vient après la racine *jan*, au sens d'un locatif" (i. e. quand la racine *jan* est composée avec un mot représentant un locatif).

387 Raisonnement par l'absurde dans Pāṇini

exemple au sens de "*upasare jātaḥ*", *upasara* + *jan* + *ḍa* = *upasarajaḥ*. Or si le guṇa prescrit devant sārva- et ārdhadhātuka pouvait être substitut d'une consonne, cette "ḍitisation" du *ḍa* serait superflue, car après substitution du guṇa, les trois voyelles, celle de la racine, celle du guṇa, celle du suffixe, se ramèneraient par 6, 1, 97 à la dernière d'entre elles, d'où la même forme *upasarajaḥ*.

Mais comme le *ḍ* du suffixe *ḍa* de 3, 2, 97 ne peut qu'être indispensable, ce suffixe *ḍit* doit représenter l'unique procédé de formation praticable. Conclusion : le guṇa d'une consonne est illicite. — Ce jñāpaka est discuté et finalement rejeté dans le dialogue que voici[101] :

"Cette prescription du suffixe *ḍa* après *jan* — que vous invoquez — n'indique rien (*jñāpakaṃ na*). C'est seulement si (l'objet de la règle 3, 2, 97, i.e. la formation de *upasaraja*, etc.) pouvait être obtenu par application d'un principe "guṇa est substitut de consonne" que la règle établie par Pāṇini aurait valeur de jñāpaka. Or (les formes en question) ne peuvent pas être obtenues par le guṇa (de la finale) de *jan*. D'où peut-on savoir en effet que le guṇa prescrit est *a* et non pas plutôt *e* ou *o*[102]?

— En vertu de l'affinité (prosodique), une consonne, valant une demi-mātrā, ne peut pas avoir d'autre substitut que la lettre *a*, d'une mātrā.

— Même ainsi, c'est la voyelle nasalisée qui se substitue (ce qui est incorrect).

— Par sa fusion avec la voyelle suivante la nasalisée reviendra à l'état pur.

[101] "*yad apy ucyate janer ḍavacanaṃ jñāpakaṃ na vyañjanasya guṇo bhavatīti siddhe vidhir ārabhyamāno jñāpakārtho bhavati na ca janer guṇena sidhyati / kuto hy etajjaner guṇa ucyamāno 'kāro bhavati na punar ekāro vā syād okāro veti.*
— āntaryato 'rdhamātrikasya vyañjanasya mātriko 'kāro bhaviṣyati.
— evam apy anunāsikaḥ prāpnoti.
— pararūpena śuddho bhaviṣyati.
— evaṃ tarhi gamer apy ayaṃ ḍo vaktavyaḥ / gamer ca guṇa ucyamāna āntaryata okāraḥ prāpnoti / tasmād iggrahaṇaṃ kartavyam//

[102] Celui qui faisait appel au jñāpaka supposait deux possibilités d'arriver à *upasaraja*, etc. La prescription par Pāṇini de l'une (3, 2, 97) impliquait l'exclusion de l'autre (guṇa de la consonne par une règle 7, 3, 84 conçue sans le mot "*ikaḥ*"). Réponse : c'est seulement si le guṇa de la finale de *jan* représentait bien une première possibilité que la règle 3, 2, 97, à moins d'être vyartha, impliquerait que le guṇa de la consonne est illicite. Mais en fait le guṇa ne permet pas d'obtenir *upasaraja*. En d'autres termes, 3, 2, 97 serait indispensable même si d'une manière générale le guṇa de la consonne était licite. Elle ne peut donc pas être jñāpaka de la proposition contraire : "*na vyañjanasya guṇo bhavati*".

Je traduis d'après l'édition Kielhorn. Le texte de l'édition Śivadatta D. Kudāla (Bombay, 1917) est le suivant "*yad apy ucyate — janer ḍavacanam? — na vyañjanasya guṇo bhavatīti//siddhe . . .*" L'éditeur qui considère les mots "*janer ḍavacanam*" comme une interpolation, pense avec la *Chāyā* que Patañjali reprend simplement la donnée 3 du vārt. : "*na vyañjanasya guṇo bhavati*". Il est plus probable que c'est le jñāpaka qui est d'abord rappelé et nié avant d'être réfuté en forme. On peut ainsi conserver les deux mots suspects en coupant "*yad apy ucyate janer ḍavacanaṃ na*", le fragment "*vyañjanasya guṇo bhavati*" se construisant alors avec *siddhe*. Mais de quelque façon qu'on ponctue, il n'y a qu'une interprétation possible de *siddhe*, qui a pour sujet, comme *sidhyate* de la ligne suivante, ce qui est l'objet de la règle 3, 2, 97, c'est-à-dire la formation de *upasaraja*, etc. — Cf. Bhāṣya, 7, 2, 102, jñāp. discuté après la troisième kārikā et où le mot *siddhe* a même valeur.

— (S'il en est) ainsi (pour les dérivés de *jan*, i.e. si l'on peut arriver à *upasaraja*, etc., par le guṇa de la consonne, il reste) alors (une autre objection: rappelez-vous que) le même suffixe *ḍa* doit être prescrit (par 3, 2, 101) après la racine *gam*. Or si l'on applique ici le procédé du guṇa, c'est la lettre *o* qui, en vertu de l'affinité (selon l'organe de prononciation) se substitute indûment à la consonne. (La *ḍit*isation du *ḍa*, lequel est valide de 3, 2, 97 dans 3, 2, 101, est donc l'unique possibilité de former les dérivés de *gam* et ne peut pas avoir la valeur de jñāpaka que vous lui attribuez). Voilà pourquoi le mot *ik* (en ce qui concerne le sens 3 que lui donne le vārt.) devait être employé dans 1, 1, 3".

Ainsi la "*ḍit*isation" par Pāṇini du suffixe *ḍa* n'est pas jñāpaka de 1, 1, 3 (3°), car si même *ḍa* peut être regardé comme inutile en ce qui concerne les dérivés de *jan*, il est destiné à passer de 3, 2, 97 dans 3, 2, 101, où il représente l'unique possibilité de former certains dérivés de la racine *gam*. Parce qu'il aurait une raison d'être même en l'absence de la vérité enseignée par 1, 1, 3 (3°), il n'est pas jñāpaka de cette vérité, qui par suite devait être formulée par Pāṇini[103]. C'est là un exemple de ces pseudo-jñāpaka qu'invoque si souvent l'un des interlocuteurs à l'appui d'une objection contre un sūtra ou un vārt. et qui sont finalement rejetés par Patañjali.

[103] La règle 3, 2, 101 "*anyeṣv api dṛśyate*" (traduction ordinaire : "(Le suffixe *ḍa*) se rencontre (après la racine *jan*) même quand elle est en composition avec d'autres (mots que ceux qui sont énumérés dans les précédents sūtra)" est comprise par Patañjali de la façon suivante : "(Le suffixe *ḍa*) se rencontre aussi dans le cas d'autres (racines que *jan*)", l'une de ces racines étant *gam*.-Trapp (*Die ersten fünf Āhnikas des Mahābhāṣyam ins Deutsche übersetzt u erklärt*, Leipzig, 1933, p. 215, n. 76), croyant que Patañjali fait allusion à la règle 3, 2, 48, qui prescrit le suffixe *ḍa* après la racine *gam* précédée de différents mots (par exemple *sarva*, d'où *sarvagaḥ*), explique ainsi l'objection de la dernière réplique : "Es müsste also für das *m*, *o* eintreten und das stumme *ḍ* wäre zwecklos." — C'est exactement le contraire que serait la conclusion de Patañjali (même s'il s'agissait de 3, 2, 48) : c'est parce que le guṇa, en tant que représenté ici par *o*, ne permettrait pas d'arriver à *sarvaga* et autres formes semblables, que l'anubandha *ḍ* de *ḍa* serait déclaré indispensable (comme il l'est en fait) en tant qu'unique moyen de formation. Ce n'est pas l'inutilité du *ḍ* — ce qui en ferait un jñāpaka —, mais au contaire son indispensabilité — ce que l'empêche d'être un jñāpaka —, que Patañj. a besoin de démontrer. Car Patañj. défend ici la formulation du sūtra 1, 1, 3 (aspect 3) et la formulation du sūtra n'est défendable qu'autant que la chose formulée n'est pas suggérée par un jñāpaka.

Mais ce n'est pas du *ḍa* de 3, 2, 48 qu'il s'agit. L'anubandha *ḍ* de ce *ḍa* a beau être indispensable, Patañj. n'en serait pas plus avancé, si le *ḍ* du *ḍa* de 3, 2, 97 était reconnu inutile. C'est l'indispensabilité de celui-ci qui est mise en cause par le contradicteur et qu'il s'agit de démontrer. Or Patañj. vient de faire une concession : il a implicitement reconnu que, le guṇa de la consonne permettant d'obtenir *upasaraja*, etc., la *ḍit*isation du *ḍa* de 3, 2, 97 pouvait être considérée comme INUTILE EN CE QUI CONCERNE LES DÉRIVÉS DE *JAN*. Il s'agit néanmoins de lui trouver une raison d'être pour l'empêcher d'être un jñāpaka. Le suffixe *ḍa* est valide dans les règles suivantes jusqu'à 3, 2, 101 inclusivement. Si dans toutes ces règles il s'agit de la racine *jan* et par suite d'une dérivation uniforme, l'inutilité du caractère *ḍit* du suffixe se trouve reconnue une fois pour toutes. Si au contraire, "*anyeṣu*" de 3, 2, 101 signifiant "dans le cas d'autres racines" (il n'importe en rien que ce soit ou non l'intention de Pāṇini; il ne s'agit ici que de l'intention de Patañj.), la racine *gam* est

389 Raisonnement par l'absurde dans Pāṇini

C'est en même temps un exemple de jñāpaka indirect. Le raisonnement part d'une hypothèse affirmative ("si le guṇa de la consonne était licite") que le jñāpaka exclut parce qu'il en représente l'équivalent pratique; d'où, conclusion négative. Par suite 3, 2, 97 (pour celui qui invoque le jñāpaka) est en relation avec le principe contenu dans 1, 1, 3, non comme illustration directe, vu qu'en soi elle n'a rien à voir avec l'application des substituts guṇa et vṛddhi, mais simplement parce qu'elle exclut le principe contraire[104].—Inverse est le mouvement dans le cas des sūtra 5, 2, 51–53, jñāpaka directs de 1, 1, 23: on part d'une hypothèse négative ("si *bahu*, etc., n'étaient pas des *saṃkhyā*"), contredite par les jñāpakasūtra, qui sont des cas d'application de la définition des *saṃkhyā*; d'où, conclusion affirmative.

Or si dans ce dernier cas les jñāpaka ne peuvent que suivre le jñāpitasūtra, le fait (dans 5, 2, 51–53) de traiter comme numéraux d'autre mots que les numéraux ordinaires exigeant de la part de Pāṇini (pour qui 5, 2, 51–53 n'avaient pas valeur de jñāpaka) un avertissement préalable à ses lecteurs, à savoir la définition 1, 1, 23, il n'en est pas de même pour un jñāpaka indirect comme celui de 3, 2, 97. Celui-ci pourrait, sans inconvénient pour lui-même, précéder le prétendu jñāpitasūtra, vu qu'il en est indépendaut. Il vient après parce qu'en vue d'un certain arrangement des sūtra qui présentait des avantages didactiques Pāṇini a placé dans le premier pāda le plus grand nombre de ses saṃjñā- et paribhāṣāsūtra. Qu'au lieu de faire ainsi il les eût distribués par petits groupes selon les adhyāya où, ils devaient intervenir: le sūtra "*iko guṇavṛddhī*" (1, 1, 3) pourrait être numéroté 7, 1, 3: le *ḍ* du suffixe situé dans 3, 2, 97 (pour celui qui l'invoque) n'en en serait pas moins le jñāpaka.

susceptible de prendre le *ḍa*, on est en présence d'un cas différent: le guṇa de la consonne étant inapte à former de *gam* les dérivés voulus, le caractère *ḍit* du suffixe est ici indispensable. Mais *ḍa* n'est valide dans 3, 2, 101 que parce qu'il est énoncé dans 3, 2, 97. Ainsi le *ḍ* du *ḍa* de 3, 2, 97 aurait une raison d'être même en l'absence de la proposition "*na vyañjanasya guṇo bhavati*." Il ne peut pas être le jñāpaka de cette proposition, qui par suite devait — sous les espèces du mot *ik* — être formulée par Pāṇini. Telle est la seule manière, d'ailleurs conforme aux commentaires de Kaiy. et Nāg., de comprendre la réfutation par Patañj. de ce pseudo-jñāpaka. — A noter que l'interprétation qu'admet ici Patañj. de "*anyeṣu*" n'a pas été inventée pour la circonstance; elle est conforme au commentaire qui est fait en son lieu du sūtra 3, 2, 101: "*anyebhyo' pi dṛśyata iti vaktavyam / ihāpi yathā syāt / akhā utkhā parikhā*." La Kāśikā est encore plus catégorique: "*apiśabdaḥ sarvopadhivyabhi cārārthaḥ . . .*" "Le mot *api* signifie que (la prescription du suffixe *ḍa*) est indépendante de toute condition". Formule reprise par Nāg. qui, plus logiquement, attribue cette valeur au mot *dṛśyate* ". . . *anyeṣv api dṛśyata iti sūtre dṛśigrahaṇasya sarvopadhi-vyabhicārārthatvena* . . ." L'interprétation de "*anyeṣu*" comme impliquant (entre autres choses) "*anyebhyas*" "après d'autres racines," semble donc appartenir à la tradition des commentateurs.

[104] Les jñāpaka appelés ici indirects le sont en ce sens seulement que la conclusion, étant négative, ne peut pas être prouvée par une trace positive d'application du principe nié, mais seulement par la non-application du principe contraire. Ce que Kielh. en parlant des jñāpaka de paribhāṣā appelle jñāpaka indirects (3, 3, 169, jñāp. de 68 (v. *supra*, p. 380, n. 82); *atiṅ* de 2, 2. 19, jñāp. de 75) ce sont des jñāpaka qui ne permettent d'arriver à la paribhāṣā que par l'intermédiaire d'une première inférence dont la paribhāṣā est une conséquence.

Il y a des jñāpaka qui pourraient être situés après la règle qu'ils impliquent (ou sont censés impliquer). Et même dans le cas des jñāpaka qu'on a appelés directs, parce qu'ils consistent en une trace positive d'intervention d'une autre règle, l'ordre suivi par Pāṇini ne correspond pas à une nécessité absolue. On ne voit donc pas comment la position relative dans la grammaire de Pāṇini du jñāpita- et du jñāpakasūtra pourrait impliquer une relation parallèle entre la paribhāṣā et son jñāpaka. Au lieu de se placer sur le plan des données écrites, peut-être convient-il de se mettre dans l'esprit de celui qui, dans le dialogue de Patañjali, fait appel au jñāpaka. (Il n'est ici question que des jñāpaka qui se rélèrent à un sūtra). Cet interlocuteur (cas général) a commencé par nier la raison d'être d'un sūtra (ou d'une partie de sūtra); il en suppose l'inexistence. "Telle règle (ou partie de règle), dit-il, aurait pu être omise: tel mot (ou procédé) d'une autre règle en implique l'objet". La véritable relation qui existe entre le jñāpaka comme tel et le sūtra ou élément censé inexistant et par là même jñāpya, c'est la relation logique du connu à l'inconnu. La relation de fait notée par Goldstücker est quelque chose d'accidentel qui ne peut rien prouver touchant la relation jñāpaka-paribhāṣā. Que les paribhāṣā aient précédé Pāṇini, c'est-à-dire leurs jñāpaka, ou qu'inventées par Pāṇini et formulées après lui, elles aient suivi leurs jñāpaka, l'ordre: règle impliquée, règle indicatrice, peut se concevoir tel qu'on le constate dans Pāṇini. L'hypothèse de l'antériorité des paribhāṣā par rapport à Pāṇini, fondée par Goldstücker sur la nécessité d'expliquer leur absence de l'*Aṣṭādhyāyī* et sur le fait général que Pāṇini n'est pas l'inventeur de tout son système grammatical, n'est donc pas confirmée par la constatation que, dans le corps des sūtras, le jñāpita précède le jñāpaka. Par contre elle trouve une confirmation dans la conclusion de l'analyse du procédé d'argumentation qui a pour point de départ le jñāpaka: les jñāpaka étant inaptes à faire connaître exactement les paribhāṣā, il serait invraisemblable que Pāṇini, s'il en était l'inventeur, les eût omises systématiquement pour laisser à la sagacité de ses commentateurs le soin de les extraire de son texte, puisque c'est chose impossible; si les paribhāṣā ont été omises, c'est parce qu'elles étaient déjà connues[105]. Ainsi peut se défendre la thèse de Goldstücker même privée de son principal argument.

La discussion de la formule "*yogāpekṣaṃ jñāpakam*" a donné l'occasion de voir des jñāpaka (ceux de 5, 2, 51–53) dont l'inférence était rigoureuse. Il ne peut en être autrement lorsque le jñāpitasūtra est une définition (cas de 1, 1, 23), et que chacun des mots définis a son jñāpaka. Comme il ne s'agit de tirer de celui-ci qu'une constatation singulière, l'applicabilité à tel mot de telle désignation, il ne saurait être question d'induction et le *prasaṅgānumāna* (réduction à l'absurde) suffit à donner la conclusion voulue. D'autre part on a vu que les paribhāṣā ne peuvent pas, en tant que formules générales, être fondées sur les jñāpaka. Faut-il en conclure que le mot *jñāpaka* aurait deux valeurs différentes selon le cas, ou qu'il aurait dans les deux cas (incorrectement dans le second cas) la même valeur précise de *hetu* ou *sādhana*? Ni l'une ni l'autre de ces deux suppositions n'est admissible.

[105] Cette conclusion ne vaut rigoureusement que pour les jñāpakasiddhaparibhāṣā (les plus importantes et les plus nombreuses). Mais on peut, comme le fait Goldstücker de sa propre conclusion, l'étendre sans trop de risque à l'ensemble des paribhāṣā.

En réalite les mots *jñāpaka* et *jñāpayati* ne se rapportent pas étroitement à l'opération d'inférence. Il est probable que Patañjali a employé à dessein un mot d'ample acception pour désigner une opération qui, comportant toujours à sa base une inférence (celle du *prasaṅgānumāna*), tantôt n'était pas autre chose (cas de certains jñāpitasūtra, par exemple, 1. 1, 23), tantôt était plus qu'une inférence (inférence singulière + rappel de la maxime : cas notamment des paribhāṣā)[106]. En ce qui concerne ce dernier cas, ce n'est qu'au moyen de la figure pars pro toto que l'argumentation de Patañjali a pu être traitée d'*anumāna* et la paribhāṣā d'*anumānikī*, mots qu'on rencontre dans Nāgoj[107]. Cette évolution qui tendait à faire du mot *jñāpaka* le synonyme exact de *hetu* était favorisée par le fait qu'on avait dû attribuer au jñāpaka une capacité d'inférence totale pour justifier les fausses paribhāṣā : ainsi la paribhāṣā 91 qui, n'existant dans Patañjali qu'a l'état de constatation singulière, est indûment passée dans la suite au rang de formule générale. L'emploi par Nāgoj, des mots *anumāna*, *anumānikī*, pas plus que l'emploi des mots *jñāpaka*, *jñāpayati* par Patañjali, ne prouve rien touchant l'origine des paribhāṣā authentiques. Il reste établi qu'elles ne peuvent pas être inférées par leurs jñāpaka. Car ces jñāpaka ne sont en réalité que des indices rappelant les maximes sous-jacentes, que Pāṇini avait suivies, mais que Patañjali et autres connaissaient par la tradition grammaticale avant même d'en retrouver la trace dans les sūtra. Ceci ne vaut naturellement que pour les paribhāṣā authentiques, celles qu'a connues Pāṇini. En ce qui concerne les fausses paribhāṣā, le jñāpaka n'est que le prétexte qui leur a donné naissance, prétexte constitué par un fait mal interprété, à partir duquel on établissait une maxime d'une extension suffisante pour recouvrir tous les cas de la même espèce qui ne s'accordaient pas autrement avec Pāṇini. C'est de même que de nos jours les juristes sont obligés d'"interpréter" les codes pour les adapter à des situations que le législateur n'avait pas prévues. Tout comme les institutions et les mœurs les langues évoluent ; des formes nouvelles s'imposent qui ne tiennent pas compte des grammairiens. Mais il était admis que les sūtra du ṛṣi Pāṇini détenaient la clef du langage. Il suffisait de savoir les interpréter. L'aide des maximes traditionnelles ne le permettait pas toujours : de là les fausses paribhāṣā.

[106] Kielh. (préf. p. v, n. 3) remarquant que Patañjali considère exceptionnellement comme jñāpaka un mot ou procédé que la paribhāṣā correspondante ne rend pas caritārtha (par exemple l'emploi de l'anubandha *ṇ* dans deux Śivasūtra, jñāp. de I, le mot *apratyayaḥ* de 1, 1, 69, jñāp. de 19 observe que dans ce cas le mot *jñāpayati* est employé par Patañjali dans un sens moins limité. Il est probable que *jñāpayati* est toujours employé dans le même sens et que ce n'est jamais un sens limité. Il semble que ce soit Nāgoj. qui ait cherché à systématiser la notion de jñāpaka. Dans son commentaire de la paribhāṣā I, par exemple, il a soin d'employer le mot *bodhyate* (non *jñāpyate*), parce que cette paribhāṣā ne possède pas un jñāpaka selon l'idée rigoureuse qu'il s'en est faite (cf. Kielh., p. 2, n. 3). — On a vu d'autre part qu'il n'admet pas que les règles 5, 2, 51-53 soient jñāpaka de 1, 1, 23, parce que, étant indispensables comme jñāp. de l'adjonction du suffixe *ḍaṭ* après *pūga*, etc., elles ne seraient pas vyartha même en l'absence de l'inférence que leur attribue Patañjali.

[107] Notamment PŚ., paribh. 50 (p. 45, 1. 2: *kiṃ ca pūrvatrety asya pratyakṣatvena tenānumānikyā asyā bādha evocitaḥ*), où Nāg. oppose la paribhāṣā, qui repose sur une inférence (*anumānikī*) et le sūtra 8, 2, 1, objet de perception, celui-ci par suite l'emportant sur celle-là (cf. PŚ., p. 45, 1. 9 et suiv.).

22

K. A. Subramania Iyer (born 1896)

A unique place in the grammatical tradition is occupied by the grammatical philosopher Bhartṛhari. His commentary on Patañjali's *Mahābhāṣya* and his *Vākyapadīya* were already known to I-Tsing (pages 15–16), but his work is only now beginning to receive due attention again. The reason is two-fold. On the one hand, only one incomplete manuscript of the commentary on the *Mahābhāṣya* is known; it is now preserved in Berlin. Kielhorn published a few fragments of this manuscript, and also established that Bhartṛhari "had access to a very extensive commentational literature, superseded by his own work as his own writings have in turn been superseded by those of later authors" (Preface to the second volume of the first *Mahābhāṣya* edition: Kielhorn 1880–1885; this Preface has unfortunately been omitted from the third revised edition of 1965). The first volume of an edition of the Berlin manuscript has only recently been published for the first time (Swaminathan 1965). Bhartṛhari's *Vākyapadīya*, on the other hand, was not only badly edited and published in parts; it remained largely unintelligible. This was partly due to the fact that this text, unlike most other grammatical works, disappeared from the traditional curriculum at an early date and had rarely been studied.

The foremost authority on the *Vākyapadīya* is K. A. Subramania Iyer (born in Kerala in 1896), who studied in Paris with Sylvain Lévi and Foucher, and in London with Barnett, Rhys Davids, and de la Vallée Poussin (a refugee in London during the First World War). Subramania Iyer, who for many years has been Professor of Sanskrit at Lucknow University, has occupied many distinguished positions in the Indian academic world. He has edited parts of the text of the *Vākyapadīya* (Kāṇḍa I, Poona 1966; Kāṇḍa III, Part 1, Poona 1963), translated the first chapter (Poona 1965) and published a monograph on Bhartṛhari (Poona 1969). Earlier, when working with the published texts then available to him, containing "many passages where the text was very doubtful and did not make much sense" (1963, vii), he published some articles on the *Vākyapadīya*, namely, "The Conception of Guṇa among the Vaiyyākaraṇas," *New Indian Antiquary* (5, 1942, 121–130; dealing with the philosophical notion of *guṇa* 'quality' as refined by the grammarians, not with the linguistic notion of *guṇa* as introduced in Pāṇini 1.1.2); and "The Point of View of the Vaiyākaraṇas," *Journal of Oriental Research* (18, 1948, 84–96, Madras University). The latter is reproduced here with the omission of almost all of the textual material quoted in the footnotes and with the addition of some translations within square brackets.

"After failing for many years to attract the attention due to such an important work, the *Vākyapadīya* is now at last coming into its own" (Gray 1968, 70); see, apart from Subramania Iyer's works and Brough (1951b; see pages 401–423 of this volume), Ruegg (1959), Sastri (1959), Bhattacharya (1962), Pandeya (1963), Kunjunni Raja (1963), Biardeau (1964a and 1964b), Joshi (1967), and Aklujkar (1969). For reviews of Pandeya and Kunjunni Raja see Staal (1966b). For a general survey of the Sanskrit philosophy of language, see Staal (1969).

The Point of View of the Vaiyākaraṇas* (1948)

K. A. Subramania Iyer

To explain the forms of a language is the main purpose of the science of grammar. For this, it is necessary to isolate and analyse the notions which are expressed by the forms of that language. As these notions are, to a great extent, the products of the social factors which govern that language, they may or may not be the same as those of other languages. Grammar is not the only discipline which is concerned with notions. Logic and philosophy are equally concerned with them. Hence the influence of logic and philosophy on grammar in the West until the 19th century when the method of observation of facts, already in operation in the physical sciences, was extended to linguistic phenomena. In India, as elsewhere, logic and philosophy share with grammar a partly common vocabulary. Countless are the passages in Sanskrit grammatical literature where the concepts of this or that system of philosophy are brought in for explaining the facts of the Sanskrit language. And yet our grammarians knew that the point of view of grammar was quite distinct from that of the systems of philosophy.

This distinction is pointed out by Helārāja on many occasions in his commentary on the Vākyapadīya. But, before we present his views on the subject, it is necessary to study the few passages in the Mahābhāṣya on which the views of Helārāja are based. Vyākaraṇa is a Vedāṅga, but it is not attached to any particular Veda. It is common to all of them. Patañjali makes this point clear in connection with the use of the word *bahulam* ['variously'] in P. II. 1.57 and P. VI. 3.14. Though the word *bahulam* found in the sūtras is traditionally interpreted in four ways[1] so as to include all the facts and details which can come under the sūtras in question, Pāṇini actually mentions some of these details in the subsequent sūtras. In addition to the word *bahulam* he sometimes uses other words like *vā*, *ubhayathā*, *anyatarasyām*, *aikaṣām*. Patañjali explains the diversity of usage by saying that the science of Vyākaraṇa is common to all the Vedas and this diversity of usage is necessary to cover all the facts found in the various branches of the Vedas.[2] All that we have to note here is that, according to Patañjali, the science of grammar is not attached to any particular Veda or to any branch of it, but is common to all. It is *sarvavedapāriṣada*. We will see, in a little while, what form this idea assumes in the later grammatical literature.

Another statement of Patañjali which throws light on the grammarian's point of view is found in the Bhāṣya on vt. 13, of the Paspaśāhnika. To the objection that if the knowledge of the correct word leads to spiritual merit, a knowledge of corrupt forms, inevitable in a close study of grammar, must necessarily lead to demerit, Patañjali answers:—*śabdapramāṇakā vayam / yac chabda āha tad asmākam pramāṇam / śabdaś ca śabdajñāne dharmam āha nāpaśabdajñāne'dharmam/*[3] ['We go by the authority of *śabda*. What *śabda* says is our authority. And *śabda* says that merit accrues from the knowledge of correct expressions, not that demerit accrues from the knowledge of incorrect expressions'].

Here Patañjali means the Vedas by the word *śabda* and refers to the well known *śruti*: *ekaḥ śabdaḥ samyag jñātaḥ śāstrānvitaḥ suprayuktaḥ svarge loke kāmadhug bhavati/*[4] [one word properly

* Paper read in the Classical Sanskrit Section of the 15th All-India Oriental Conference, Bombay.

[1] Nyāsa on Pāṇini III.3.1.

[2] M. Bhāṣya on II. 1.58 (57).

[3] M. Bhā. on Vt 13, Paspaśāhnika.

[4] M. Bhā. on P. VI. 1.84.

known and well pronounced in accordance with the theory will grant wishes in heaven'].

The śruti speaks only of merit resulting from a knowledge of the correct words, and not of demerit due to a knowledge of incorrect ones. But in another similar context containing the same words, śabda does not mean the Vedas. It means merely the word in general. The point is raised whether in the sentence *ayam daṇḍo harānena* ['this (is a) stick, take with it'], the daṇḍa is the agent (*kartā*) of the action of 'being', the meaning of the word *asti* which is understood here, or the instrument of the action of taking (*hara*). Against the view that it is the former, the objection is raised that it is, after all, with the daṇḍa that the action of taking is done and that, therefore, it should be considered to be the instrument of that action rather than as the agent of an action which is not mentioned in the sentence. To this objection the answer is given that, for grammarians, it is the word which is pramāṇa, authority. Whatever the word presents, they accept.[5] In the sentence in question, the words as they stand, present the daṇḍa as the agent of the action of "being", which, though not mentioned, is understood here, as in all other cases where no other action is openly expressed. Thus the daṇḍa is, at first, the agent of the action of 'being' and then only does it become the instrument of the action of taking. This is at least the case if we go by what the words present, apart from what the reality may be.

Thus we see two ideas in Patañjali: (1) that Vyākaraṇa is not confined to any particular Veda: (2) that the grammarians go by what the words present rather than by how things really are. By śabda, Patañjali means sometimes the Vedas and sometimes the word in general.

These two ideas are made use of frequently by Helārāja while explaining Bhartṛhari's Vākyapadīya and we need not doubt that they were quite familiar to Bhartṛhari himself. But both these ideas have undergone modifications:—

The idea that the science of grammar is common to all the Vedas is changed into the idea that it is common to all the systems of philosophy. It is found that Bhartṛhari in his Vākyapadīya often expounds a grammatical doctrine, not only from his own point of view, but also from the point of view of some system of philosophy or other. Often an idea belonging to some system of philosophy is made use of to explain and justify a particular idea of grammar. The question arises: Why should he do it? Why did he not content himself with explaining it as an Advaitin which he was? Helārāja justifies this by saying that Vyākaraṇa as a śāstra belongs to all the disciplines. If linguistic facts can be explained from as many points of view as possible, so much the better for the science of grammar. This does not preclude a particular author from having a preference for his own point of view. Bhartṛhari, for instance, has a preference for the Advaitic point of view, and he has tried to explain most of the facts and notions of grammar from that point of view.[6] But his work is remarkable for the bringing in of other points of view on

[5] *śabdapramāṇaka vayam / yac chabda āha tad asmākam pramāṇam / śabdaś ceha sattām āha – ayaṃ daṇḍa / astīti gamyate / sa daṇḍaḥ kartā bhūtvānyena śabdenābhisaṃbadhyamānaḥ karaṇaṃ saṃpadyate* ['we go by the authority of the word. What the word says is our authority. And the word says here that something is — this (is a) stick; "is" is implied. That stick which is agent, when combined with another word, becomes instrument']. M.Bhā. on P. II, 1.1.

[6] Helārāja on Vāk III. Jā. verse 35.

many occasions. A few examples will make this point clear:—

It is the view of the Vaiyākaraṇas that, when words are used, three things are understood by us:—(1) the form of the word, consisting of an entity over and above the sequence of sounds heard; (2) the meaning; (3) the intention of the speaker.[7] Of these, the first one is closest to the word. It is understood by the hearer in any case, even if he does not understand the second and the third. Between this and the second meaning the relation is *vācyavācakabhāva*. The first is *vācaka* ['expressing'] and the second is *vācya* ['expressed']. This is usually understood as referring to the objects of the world. Between the first and the third, the intention of the speaker, the relation is said to be *kāryakāraṇabhāva* ['relation between cause and effect']. It is the intention of the speaker which calls up particular words for use. They are, therefore, looked upon as the effects of that intention.[8] The question now arises: Why should Bhartṛhari speak about *kāryakāraṇabhāva* at all, considering that grammar, as a science, is chiefly concerned with the other relation namely, *vācyavācakabhāva*, between the word and the meaning? The answer given is that Vyākaraṇa as a discipline is common to all the systems of philosophy. Its notions and explanations must be such that they can be acceptable to the followers of all the systems of philosophy.[9] Some hold that the word does not point to any external object, but only refers to the intention of the speaker. It is in order to respect their views (*tanmatopaskārārtham*) that Bhartṛhari speaks about *kāryakāraṇabhāva*. If meaning is nothing more than the intention of the speaker, the relation between the word and the meaning is naturally *kāryakāraṇabhāva*, because it is the intention of the speaker which calls up this word or that in speech.[10]

Another doctrine which is expounded in the Vākyapadīya is *sattādvaita*, the view that all words, nay, even parts of a word like roots and suffixes, ultimately have *sattā* or "Being" as their meaning. This 'Being' is the Supreme Universal which is found in all the objects of the world and which binds them all together in one reality. The distinctive features of each object are comparatively unreal. In this view, even negative entities are credited with a kind of 'Being'.[11] This 'Being' is essentially identical with Brahman. It is clear that Bhartṛhari here speaks as an Advaitin. But he further points out that the Sāṅkhya Philosophy is also in keeping with the doctrine of *sattādvaita*. According to this system, the first evolute from Prakṛti is Mahat or Buddhitattva, as it is called. It is to be regarded as "the most universal stage which comprehends within it all the buddhis of individuals and potentially all the matter of which the gross world is formed. Looked at from this point of view, it has the widest and the most universal existence, comprising all creation and is thus called 'mahat', (the great one)".[12] All the other evolutes proceed from this principle and are absorbed into it at the time of dissolution. This great principle is essentially 'Being' and all the evolutes proceeding from it share this 'Being'. Thus the Sāṅkhya system also, Helārāja points out, favours the doctrine of *sattādvaita*.[13]

Side by side with the view that the science of grammar is *sarvapārṣada* and, therefore, brings in notions and ideas current in

[7] Helārāja on Vāk. III. Saṃ. verse 1.
[8] Helārāja on Vāk. III. Saṃ. verse 1.
[9] Helārāja on Vāk. III. Saṃ. verse 1.
[10] Helārāja on Vāk. III. Saṃ. verse 1.
[11] Helārāja on Vāk. III. Jā. verse 34.
[12] Das Gupta. A History of Indian Philosophy, Vol. I, p. 249.
[13] Helā. on Vāk. III. Jā. verse 34.

other śāstras to explain grammatical notions, there is the other view that grammar is not bound to accept an idea simply because it is current in some other discipline or in the world. Whether such an idea should be made use of by Vyākaraṇa is a matter of convenience only. It was utilised if it was convenient to do so. Otherwise it was not. Thus the Vaiśeṣika conception of Guṇa[14] has been utilised by Vyākaraṇa in explaining some forms:— The word *guṇavacana* occurring in P. IV. 1.44; V. 1. 124; in a vār. on V. 2, 94. and in VIII. 1.12. refers to this Vaiśeṣika conception.[15] But this conception is not enough to explain all the forms which occur in the Sanskrit language. Another conception of it is mentioned here and there in the Bhāṣya and it is explained in the guṇasamuddeśa of the 3rd kāṇḍa of the Vākyapadīya. It is a conception peculiar to Vyākaraṇa and it is derived from the forms of the Sanskrit language, and it is meant to explain them.[16] Similarly, the popular conception of 'liṅga': *stanakeśavatī strī syāl lomaśaḥ puruṣaḥ smṛtaḥ / ubhayor antaraṃ yac ca tadabhāve napuṃsakam //*[17] ['women possess (long) hair and breasts, men are known for hairiness, / what is different from both and does not have these (qualities) is neuter'] is found inadequate to explain all the diversity of forms relating to liṅga found in the Sanskrit language. Patañjali therefore rejects it and says: *tasmān na vaiyākaraṇaiḥ śakyaṃ laukikam liṅgam asthātum / avaśyaṃ ca kaścit svakṛtānta āstheyaḥ //*[18] ['therefore the ordinary concept of *liṅga* cannot be used by grammarians; and some self-made notion has to be set up'] that Vaiyākaraṇas must evolve their own conception of 'liṇga' and proceeds to do so. This idea that Vaiyākaraṇas have a right to evolve their own notions is expressed by later writers also. P. I. 2.58 teaches the use of the plural number after a word which primarily expresses *jāti* ['genus; class']. But for this sūtra, only the singular number could be used, because *jāti* is one and so it would be normal to use the singular number. Now one can say, *brāhmaṇaḥ pūjyaḥ* ['a brahman should be honored'] or *brāhmaṇāḥ pūjyāḥ* ['brahmans should be honored'] in the same sense. To this somebody objects that it is wrong to say that 'jāti' is one. Jāti has no number at all. It is the dravya or 'vyakti' in which the jāti resides which has number.[19] This is answered by saying that in these matters grammarians do not accept the views of other śāstras. They evolve their own notions.[20] To them jāti is one because the word presents it as such, and it is, therefore, natural to use the singular number after a word expressive of it.

This reference in the Bhāṣya and in the later literature to *svakṛtānta* ['self-made (notion)'], the particular doctrine of the Vaiyākaraṇas suggests that they have their own point of view from which their doctrines and notions are derived. What this point of view is has been indicated by Patañjali in that passage where he says:— *śabdapramāṇakā vayam / yac chabda āha tad asmākaṃ pramāṇam /* ['we go by the authority of the word. What the word says is our authority']. The idea contained in this passage has been utilised by Helārāja very frequently in his commentary on the Vākyapadīyam. For the grammarian, 'artha' does not mean the external reality but whatever the word brings to the mind.

[14] Kaṇāda-Vaiśeṣika-Sūtra I. 1.16.
[15] Kaṇāda-Vaiśeṣika-Sūtra I. 1.16.
[16] *See* the author's paper on "The Conception of Guṇa among the Vaiyākaraṇas" (N. I. A., Vol. V., No. 6, Sept. 1942).
[17] M. Bhā. on P. IV. 1.3.
[18] M. Bhā. on P. IV. 1.3.
[19] Helārāja on Vāk. III. Jā. verse 52.
[20] Helārāja on Vāk. III. Jā. verse 52.

Artha does not mean vastvartha but śabdārtha, not reality, but the meanings of words. Individual words bring something to the mind and the sentence as a whole also brings something to the mind. Both these things are included in the expression 'śabdārtha'. Grammar studies both these things in order to evolve notions which will explain the forms of the language. Grammar is satisfied if these notions conform to what we understand from words, no matter whether they conform to reality or not. Grammar does not look at reality directly in the face. As Helārāja puts it:

śabdapramāṇakānāṃ hi śabda eva hi yathārtham abhidhatte tathaiva tasyābhidhānam upapannam / na tu vastumukhaprokṣatayā / [21] ['for to those whose authority is the word, the word designates what it corresponds to, and its designation is accordingly appropriate; but it is not for looking reality directly in the face'].

Not to look at reality directly in the face is as good as not philosophising and Helārāja sometimes makes it quite clear that the grammarian is really not concerned with philosophy proper. Thus while explaining the different conceptions of Time mentioned by Bhartṛhari in the Kālasamuddeśa such as that it is an entity which exists apart from the mind or that it is a mere construction of the human mind, Helārāja says that Bhartṛhari is not really concerned with what time is philosophically, but that he is anxious to examine and analyse that something which is responsible for our putting the Sanskrit verb in different tenses as in *abhūt* ['was'], *asti* ['is'] and *bhaviṣyati* ['will be']. That something may not be able to stand close philosophical scrutiny, but if it serves the purpose of explaining the different tenses, one would have to accept it.[22] Similarly in the kriyāsamuddeśa, the question is: What is action? The answer given by Bhartṛhari on the basis of the Bhāṣya passages is that it is a process, something having parts arranged in a temporal sequence. It is not directly perceptible, but it is to be inferred. Each moment or part may be looked upon as action, in which case, it will also be inferrible only and not directly perceptible. These parts may be further subdivided and the smaller parts will also be actions. There will come a time when the part cannot be further sub-divided. It cannot then be called action at all. Such an atomic point may be directly perceptible but that will not make actions so because such a point cannot be called action at all. Only that can be called action which has parts arranged in a temporal sequence. After having clearly explained all this, Helārāja adds that for grammarians the real question is not whether an action has actually parts or not, but whether the verb presents it as such. The answer is that verbs do present action, however momentary, in nature, as something having parts which cannot co-exist, but are arranged in a temporal sequence. And Vaiyākaraṇas go by what the words present to us.[23]

It is pointed out that a notion arrived at by the Vaiyākaraṇas from their own point of view, may sometimes agree with popular ideas rather than with those accepted by some system of philosophy. Vaiśeṣikas think of the whole, the avayavī, as existing in the parts, the avayavas. That is an idea to which they have come by a logical analysis of reality. They also specify the particular relation by which the whole exists in the parts. It is samavāya, inherence. The popular conception, however, is that the horn of a cow exists in the cow and not vice versa. The part exists in the whole. Helā-

[21] Helārāja on Vāk. III. Saṃ. verse 66.
[22] Helārāja on Vāk. III. Kā. 58.
[23] Helārāja on Vāk. III. Kri. 10.

rāja points out that the language follows the popular conception in this matter. In the expression *gavi śṛṅgam* ['the horn is in the cow'] the locative suffix is affixed to the word *go* ['cow'] which denotes the whole of which *śṛṅga* is a part. If one followed the Vaiśeṣikas in this matter, one would have to say *śṛṅge gauḥ* ['the cow is in the horn'] and *śākhāyāṃ vṛkṣaḥ* ['the tree is in the branch'].[24]

It is mainly this point of view which the Vaiyākaraṇas adopt in defining the various grammatical categories such as the different kārakas, gender, number, person, aspect (*upagraha*) etc. dealt with in the 3rd kāṇḍa of the Vākyapadīya. This naturally results in certain distinctive notions. It will not be out of place here to draw the attention of the reader to a few of these distinctive notions.

Regarding the meaning of individual words, there are two views current among grammarians, associated with the names of two ancient grammarians mentioned in the Vārttikas of Kātyāyana, namely, Vājapyāyana and Vyāḍi. One view is that all words, nay, even parts of words, denote primarily the Universal and only secondarily the Particular. If we apply the same word, say, 'cow' or 'tree' to a large number of objects it is because we see some common characteristic in all of them. This common characteristic is the universal or 'jāti' as it is called. The word 'aśva' ['horse'], therefore, primarily denotes 'aśvatva' ['horseness'], the word 'go' ['cow'] denotes gotva ['cowness'] and so on. If this is true, then the word 'jāti' must also denote a universal present as a common characteristic in all the universals. But such a view goes against the Vaiśeṣika view that there cannot be a universal in a universal. They argue that to accept a universal in a universal. would lead to anavasthā or 'regressus ad infinitum'. Where would one stop in the process of postulating universals? Why not postulate a third universal in the second one and so on? The best thing would be to stop at the very first universal and not go any further. But the grammarian replies that this kind of reasoning might be all right from the Vaiśesika point of view, but not for himself. He has his own point of view. His chief concern is to find out the nature of meanings conveyed by words. What he finds is that in all universals as conveyed by words, there is a common characteristic which can be looked upon as another universal. The existence of the first universal was postulated just because a common characteristic was experienced in the individuals or particulars, followed by the use of the same name to all the individuals. A similar common characteristic is experienced in all the universals as conveyed by words and that justifies the use of the word 'jāti' for all of them. Where there is identity of cognition and of name, a universal has to be postulated and in the universals as presented by words there are both. And for grammarians, it is what words convey which matters.[25]

If we go by what words present, there can be not only a universal in a universal but many other things which are ordinarily looked upon as guṇa ['quality'] or kriyā ['activity'] may turn out to be universals. If a guṇa is presented by words as something which persists as a common feature in many things, it becomes a universal for the grammarians.[26] That is probably the reason why Pāṇini has applied the word sāmānya to the meaning expressed by the word 'śyāma' "dark" in the compound 'śastrī-

[24] Helārāja on Vāk. III. Jā. 11.

[25] Helārāja on Vāk. III. Jā. 11.

śyāma' "dark like a knife" formed according to the sūtra *upamānāni sāmānyavacanaiḥ*.[27] Samānya is another name for 'jāti'. In the compound śastrīśyāmā the word śyāma expresses a guṇa and, as it expresses a common feature between a śastrī and whatever is compared to it, the grammarians look upon it as jāti.

Similarly, action can be presented as jāti by words. We use the expression 'pacati', 'he cooks', in a variety of circumstances. The person who cooks, the thing cooked, the fuel and the utensils used for cooking, may all be different and yet the notion of cooking and the expression 'pacati' persist. This also shows that the word presents action as 'jāti'.[28]

Even though philosophers like Vaiśeṣikas make a distinction between jāti, guṇa, kriyā, and dravya, the grammarians believe that it is all a question of how words present them and the words can present the first three also as dravya ['substance']. They have their own definition of dravya. Anything which is presented by words as something to be characterised, distinguished from other things (*bhedya*) is a dravya. Whatever can be referred to by the demonstrative pronouns *idam* "this" and *tad* "that" is a dravya: *vastūpalakṣaṇaṃ yatra sarvanāma prayujyate / dravyam ity ucyate so'rtho bhedyatvena vivakṣitaḥ //* Vāk. III. Dra. verse 3. "where a pronoun is used to refer to a thing it refers to a substance and its meaning is expressed by differentiation (from other things)". If words present 'jāti' as something to be differentiated, as a viśeṣya, then it becomes a dravya: *sarvanāmapratyavamarśayogyatvam*, the fitness to be referred to by a pronoun as 'this' is the characteristic of a dravya. This view is traced by Helārāja to so ancient a writer as Yāska, whose statement: *ada iti yat pratīyate tad dravyam* "what is inferred from 'that' is a substance" is quoted by him.[29] The expression is significant because it makes the whole thing dependent upon the 'vivakṣā' of the speaker. It makes it quite clear that what is defined in the verse quoted above is not the artha called dravya, but the meaning of the word 'dravya' or rather the nature of the thing presented by the word 'dravya'.[30] Anything can be presented by words as something to be differentiated. For instance, movement or action is so presented in "sukhaṃ sthīyate" ['it is pleasant to stand'] where the action of standing is presented as a thing and it is determined or modified by the word 'sukham'. The meaning of the verb "sthīyate" is, therefore, dravya. In the sentence, "śuklataram rūpam" ['the color is whiter'] a quality is so presented. Here 'rūpa', though a quality, is presented by words as a thing to be qualified or determined by white. It is, therefore, a dravya. The action in 'sthīyate' can be referred to by the pronoun "kim", another indication that it is a dravya. It is easy to see that this conception of dravya is very different from the Vaiśeṣika conception of it.

The essence, then, of the Vaiyākaraṇa point of view is that it does not look at reality in the face directly, but only at reality as presented by words. But while they knew this distinctiveness of their point of view, their literature is full of passages which make one wonder whether they did not often forget this and indulge in a direct analysis of reality. Whether they are discussing the nature of 'jāti' or 'guṇa' or 'kriyā', their language often makes one think that they are discussing, not reality as presented by words,

[26] *Ibid.*
Vāk. III. Kri. 20.
[27] P. II. 1 55.
[28] Helārāja on Vāk. III. Jā. verse 11.
[29] Helārāja on Vāk. III. Dra. verse 3.
[30] Helārāja on Vāk. III. Dra. verse 3.

but reality itself. It is true that a writer like Helārāja frequently reminds himself and his readers that, for grammarians, artha is 'śabdārtha' and not 'vastvartha'. But this frequent reminder to himself is perhaps the best proof that it is not easy to discuss the nature of śabdārtha, without unconsciously straying into a consideration of the nature of 'vastvartha'. Perhaps the fact that the word 'artha' in Sanskrit can and does mean both 'vastvartha' and 'śabdārtha' also made it difficult to separate the two. Some of the problems discussed in Vaiyākaraṇa literature and the answers given also show that the grammarians did not always succeed in keeping the two kinds of 'artha' absolutely distinct. One set of such questions which they have discussed relates to action. What is action? Is it perceptible or can it only be inferred? Is there such a thing as action apart from that which is active? And they are answered as follows. Action is something which has parts arranged in a temporal sequence. It cannot be directly seen but has to be inferred. It is quite distinct from 'dravya'. These questions are more appropriate to philosophy than to grammar. The same thing can be said of the grammarians' treatment of gender. In languages like English, we have two words, sex and gender, to denote the distinction found in the objects of the world and that found in words respectively. In Sanskrit, 'liṅga' has to denote both, and this fact may have ultimately led to the grammarians coming to the conclusion that what is called 'liṅga' is a property of things and not of words. And they have invoked the Sāṅkhya philosophy in determining this property of things. The idea that it is a property of words was also known to them. They discuss it only to reject it.

Thus Vyākaraṇa oscillates between philosophy and linguistics, while it is conscious all the time that its proper sphere is something distinct from that of philosophy.

23

John Brough (born 1917)

During the century and a half after Colebrooke, the Sanskrit grammarians were studied in England by continentals (Kielhorn and Goldstücker; cf. Bhandarkar, this volume, page 82). In such a handbook as *The Sanskrit Language* (1955) by T. Burrow, the Boden Professor of Sanskrit at Oxford, Pāṇini is referred to only in passing. This situation began to change when John Brough (born 1917), who had studied at Edinburgh and Cambridge and who became Professor of Sanskrit, first at London and now at Cambridge, directed attention to the Sanskrit grammarians. Brough published three articles within the span of three years, in which he made some use of contemporary linguistics as it was then being developed by his colleague at London, J. R. Firth. Brough writes about the problems discussed by Indian grammarians: "it is to a large extent the rediscovery of these problems by modern linguistics during the last twenty or thirty years which renders possible a better understanding of the Indian theories."

Brough's articles deal mainly with Patañjali and Bhartṛhari. During the same period another English scholar, W. S. Allen, directed attention to the Prātiśākhya and Śikṣā literature, which resulted in *Phonetics in Ancient India* (1953). This work was in fact preceded by S. Varma's *Critical Studies in the Phonetic Observations of Indian Grammarians* (1929).

Brough dealt with the stories and legends connected with the origin and development of the Indian grammarians (such as were related by Tāranātha, see pages 25–26) in a different context. In his *Selections from Classical Sanskrit Literature* (1951) he published and translated a relatively little-known section of the *Haracaritacintāmaṇi* (of the twelfth century) dealing with the origin of grammar (pages 2–21). This episode, entertaining and eminently readable as it is, is beyond the scope of this volume.

In "Audumbarāyaṇa's Theory of Language," *Bulletin of the School of Oriental and African Studies* (14, 1952, 73–77) Brough dealt with Bhartṛhari's thesis that language consists of sentences, while words are merely artificial abstractions. He made it seem probable that this thesis was already held by Audumbarāyaṇa, an ancient authority referred to in the *Nirukta*.

In "Theories of General Linguistics in the Sanskrit Grammarians," *Transactions of the Philological Society* (1951, 27–46), which is reproduced here, Brough discusses the notion of *sphoṭa*, the distinction between use and mention (or antonymy) and other fundamental semantic concepts. For a recent study on *sphoṭa*, together with the text and translation of a seventeenth-century text on semantics, see Joshi (1967).

The passage dealing with the definition of *śabda* occurs on Plate V. Brough's emendation *apratītapadārthaka* is not supported by the recently published text of Bhartṛhari's *Mahābhāṣyaṭīkā* (Swaminathan 1965, 5).

A. Theories of General Linguistics in the Sanskrit Grammarians (1951)

John Brough

It is well known that the discovery of Sanskrit by the West at the end of the 18th century provided the operative stimulus for the development of the comparative study of the Indo-European languages. It has also been recognized that the Pāṇinean analysis of Sanskrit into a system of roots, stems, and suffixes pointed the way to the method which has prevailed in Indo-European studies to the present day. It is true that roots and suffixes were not entirely new concepts to Europe, but it remains doubtful whether the method would have been applied with such thoroughness if it had not been for Pāṇini's example. It is customary to add at this point the deprecatory remark that Pāṇini was, of course, aided in his analysis by the extraordinary clarity of structure of the Sanskrit language; but we are apt to overlook the possibility that this structure might not have seemed so clear and obvious to us if Pāṇini had not analysed it for us.

But while we in the West have acknowledged a debt to Pāṇini in the matter of formal analysis, we have paid less attention to the theories of general linguistics and linguistic philosophy to which the Indians devoted much thought.[1] I wish in this paper to discuss a few of the most important aspects of the Indian theory, not merely as a matter of antiquarian curiosity, but because in their extraordinary linguistic and philosophic acumen these ancient authors are still, I believe, worthy of our respect.[2] As Bhartṛhari himself puts it, the Goddess of Learning does not smile on those who neglect the ancients.[3]

As has been said from time to time,[4] linguistics is faced at the outset with the difficulty that in making statements about language, language is apparently turned back on itself. At first sight the situation is similar to the old philosophical problem of how consciousness can be conscious of itself. The difficulty here, however, is not, I believe, a fundamental philosophical one. It is merely that the habits of everyday language make it troublesome to state the matter in a clear manner. At the same time, everyday language has already provided us with the method of dealing with linguistic facts, by permitting words not only to be used but also to be quoted. The point is so obvious and familiar that it is difficult to realize its cardinal importance, and even to be aware of it in ordinary grammatical discourse. The discussion of this topic in

[1] It is clear from scattered references that many of these problems were discussed as early as Yāska and Pāṇini; and the *Saṃgraha* of Vyāḍi, known only from quotations, and Patañjali's *Mahābhāṣya* both dealt incidentally with such topics. The earliest extant work specifically devoted to the philosophy of grammar is the Vākyapadīya (VP) of Bhartṛhari (*c.* 7th century A.D.). Later writers elaborated Bhartṛhari's exposition, but while continuing the tradition of "the Grammarians" as a definite school of thought opposed to the standard philosophical schools, added little of first-rate significance.

[2] I do not, of course, wish to exaggerate in this matter. The majority of the problems discussed by the Indians are in fact familiar in modern linguistics and logic (though still perhaps insufficiently appreciated by many professional teachers of languages); and it is to a large extent the rediscovery of these problems by modern linguistics during the past twenty or thirty years which renders possible a better understanding of the Indian theories. In this connection I am particularly grateful to my colleague Professor J. R. Firth, with whom I have had numerous informal discussions on these topics.

[3] VP ii.493, anupāsita-vṛddhānāṃ vidyā nātiprasīdati.

[4] For example, J. R. Firth, *TPS.*, 1948, p. 128.

Sanskrit centres round Pāṇini's statement[5] *svaṃ rūpaṃ śabda-syāśabdasaṃjnā*, "A word (in a grammatical rule) which is not a technical term denotes its own form." The immediately obvious interpretation is, of course, that a statement about a particular word is not to be taken as applying also to its synonyms. Thus, Renou explains it,[6] "(... il s'agit) du mot en tant que forme propre, (non en tant que porteur d'un sens, autrement dit: qu'il n'englobe pas les mots de mêmes sens que lui)." This follows closely Kātyāyana's preliminary statement (*vārttika* 1): *śabdenārthagater, arthasyāsaṃbhavāt, tadvācinaḥ saṃjñāpratiṣedhārthaṃ svaṃrūpagrahaṇam.* "Since by the word is understood the thing-meant,[7] and since the thing-meant is impossible (in this context), the expression 'its own form' is to prevent the word being taken as a name denoting any word which expresses the same thing-meant." As Patañjali says, with a touch of humour, when we say "Fetch the cow", or "Eat the curds", it is a thing which is fetched, and a thing which is eaten; but when we say "*Agni* (fire) has the suffix-*eya*",[8] we clearly cannot add the suffix to the embers.[9] But since the use of the word *agni* in the sūtra brings to mind the fire, the inference might then be that "words meaning *fire*" are intended. This, however, seems to be merely a prima facie view (*pūrvapakṣa*), since Kātyāyana continues in *vārttika* 2: *na vā, śabdapūrvako hy arthe saṃpratyayas, tasmād arthanivṛttiḥ.* "Alternatively, this is not the real intention of the sūtra, for the understanding of the thing-meant is preceded by the word; hence, in the grammatical context, the thing-meant is ruled out of court." The question of synonyms therefore does not arise, since when the word *agni* is used in the grammatical statement the *signatum* is not the fire, but is (apparently) the same as the *signans*. The difference in logical status is obvious if we compare "A sheep is grazing in the field", with "'Sheep'[10] has an anomalous plural". The *svaṃ rūpam* reference (in the logician's terminology, the autonymous use of a word) is conventionally marked in our writing by quotation-marks. As Bhartṛhari puts it, "Just as a technical term like *vṛddhi*, while linked to its own form, is also attached to what is named by it, viz. the speech-entities symbolized by *ādaic* (i.e. *ā*, *ai*, *au*), so likewise this word *agni* (in the sūtra), while linked to the word *agni* (in everyday use, i.e. the meaning 'fire'), is also attached to the sound *agni*, which (in this context) has the word *agni* as the thing-expressed. The word which is uttered (in ordinary usage) is certainly not the one which partakes of the operation (of adding the suffix). But in conveying this other sense, its power (to

[5] i.1.68.

[6] *La Grammaire de Pāṇini* (Paris, 1948), p. 13.

[7] The Sanskrit *artha* is as many-sided as the English "meaning", and "thing-meant" is a convenient device to indicate what I understand to be the sense of the Sanskrit here. The term was first introduced, I believe, by Sir Alan H. Gardiner (*Theory of Speech and Language*, p. 29). Its use here, however, does not imply an acceptance of Gardiner's consequent application of the term "meaning".

[8] Pāṇini, iv.2.33, *agner ḍhak.*

[9] śabdenoccāritenārtho gamyate: gām ānaya dadhy aśānety artha ānīyate 'rthaś ca bhujyate. *arthasyāsambhavāt*: iha vyākaraṇe 'rthe kāryasyāsambhavah. agner ḍhag iti na śakyate 'ṅgārebhyaḥ paro ḍhakkartum (Kielhorn, vol. i, pp. 175–6).

[10] Note that English does not permit the autonym to take an article.

convey the normal sense) is not impeded."[11] This is important, since otherwise grammatical discussion would be futile. Although *agni* and '*agni*' symbolize in different ways, they are indissolubly connected, '*agni*' being the name (*saṃjñā*) while *agni* is the thing-named (*saṃjñin*). Both the name and the thing-named, it seems, must be understood as members of classes.[12] Otherwise extraordinary complications of thought arise. Bhartṛhari notes two such possible interpretations: "Some consider that the sūtra 'A word denotes its own form' means that the particular (which appears when the grammarian utters the rule *agner ḍhak*) is the name, and that it is the class attached to the particular which (is the thing-named and which) undergoes the grammatical operations. Others hold that it is the particular as the thing-named which is the purport of the sūtra (and that it is the class which is the name; the grammatical operations being thus attached to the particular, since) in any given instance there appears only a particular whose understanding is brought about by the class."[13]

It is, of course, easier to be clear in such discussions where the grammar of one language is described in another language. Thus, a translation into English of a Sanskrit passage on Sanskrit grammar shows at once which words are autonymous, since these, of course, remain in Sanskrit. This is also obvious in the case of a two-language dictionary: the heading-words, in the first language, are clearly autonymous (*svaṃ rūpam*), while the defining words in the second language express their own meanings. The distinction, though not so immediately apparent, is, of course, equally present in a one-language dictionary, and in logical and mathematical definitions, as well as in everyday usage ("What does '*x*' mean?"; "What did you say?"—"I said '*x*'").[14] The importance of this for logic is very considerable.[15] It is fundamental in the discussion of the possibility of stating the syntax of a logical language in that language itself, and is important for the theory of a hierarchy of languages.[16] But these matters must be reserved for a later discussion.

[11] VP i.59–61:—
vṛddhyādayo yathā śabdāḥ
svarūpopanibandhanāḥ
ādaic-pratyāyitaiḥ śabdaiḥ
saṃbandhaṃ yānti saṃjñibhiḥ,
agni-śabdas tathaivāyam
agni-śabdanibandhanaḥ
agni-śrutyaiti saṃbandham
agni-śābdābhidheyayā.
yo ya uccāryate śabdo
niyataṃ na sa kāryabhāk,
anya-pratyāyane śaktir
na tasya pratibadhyate.

[12] This is not stated directly, but seems plausible from the relation of normal words with things, VP i.15, *yathārtha-jātayāḥ sarvāḥ śabdākṛti-nibandhanāḥ*, "Just as all thing-classes depend upon word-classes . . ."; VP iii.1.6, *svā jātiḥ prathamaṃ śabdaiḥ sarvair evābhidhīyate, tato 'rthajāti-rūpeṣu tadadhyāropakalpanā*, "All words first of all express their own class, thereafter they are fictionally superimposed on the forms of classes of things."

[13] VP i.68, 69:—
svaṃ rūpam iti kaiścit tu
vyaktiḥ saṃjñopadiśyate,
vyaktau kāryāṇi saṃsṛṣṭā
jātis tu pratipadyate.
saṃjñinīṃ vyaktiṃ icchanti
sūtragrāhyām athāpare,
jātipratyāyitā vyaktiḥ
pradeśeṣūpatiṣṭhate.

[14] Cf. *MBh.* i. p. 176, yo 'pi hy asāv āhūyate nāmnā, nāma yadānena nopalabdhaṃ bhavati tadā pṛcchati, kiṃ bhavān āheti. VP i.57, ato 'nirjñāta-rūpatvāt kim āhety abhidhīyate.

[15] See for example Carnap, *The Logical Syntax of Language*, p. 156.

[16] Bertrand Russell, *An Inquiry into Meaning and Truth*, p. 62. Some at least of the paradoxes, however, which are used as arguments for the hierarchy, appear to be capable of a different solution.

What then can be said of the nature of these words which as linguists we quote and discuss? The definition given at the beginning of the *Mahābhāṣya* is well known: "What then is this word (*śabda*) 'cow'? . . . It is that by means of which, when uttered, there arises an understanding of creatures with dewlap, tail, hump, hooves, and horns."[17] In this definition, however, the word "uttered" (*uccārita*) must mean something more than the mere production of sounds, since Patañjali proceeds to contrast it with a commonsense view held by non-linguists, namely that the word consists of the actual sounds of the instance. The commentators therefore are doubtless right in understanding the sense to be that the word is the symbol which, when brought to light (*abhivyakta*) by the pronunciation of the sounds, brings about the understanding of the meaning. The naïve view, that the word is the sound, is usually read as follows: *atha vā pratītapadārthako*[18] *loke dhvaniḥ śabda ity ucyate, tadyathā, śabdaṃ kuru, mā śabdaṃ kārṣīḥ, śabdakāry ayaṃ māṇavaka iti dhvaniṃ kurvann evam ucyate*. This is perhaps possible if we take the author to mean that the popular view looks on the sound itself as the direct conveyor of the meaning. But *pratītapadārthaka* merely repeats the sense of *saṃpratyaya* in the first definition, and it seems to me that the intended contrast is better brought out if we understand it as *apratītapadārthaka*. The sense would thus be, "Alternatively, in everyday life the actual *sound*, which does not itself convey the meaning, is called *śabda*, e.g. 'Make a noise', 'Don't make a noise', 'This boy is noisy'—so it is said when one makes (linguistic?) sounds."

The tradition of the commentators interprets the first definition here as concerning the *sphoṭa*, a term which is normally opposed to the speech-sound, *dhvani* or *nāda*. This, however, can be accepted only with the reservation that the *sphoṭa* for Patañjali was a rather different conception from that found in the later grammarians, however pardonable the commentators' assumption may be that the fully-fledged theory is already present in the Mahābhāṣya. This term *sphoṭa*, which is of prime importance for Indian linguistic theory, has unfortunately been subjected by modern writers to a great deal of unnecessary mystification. Thus, for example, Keith[19] describes the *sphoṭa* as "a mysterious entity, a sort of hypostatization of sound, of which action sounds are manifestations". Similarly, S. K. De[20] writes, "Some philosophers propounded and the grammarians took it for granted that a word has intrinsically a word-prototype corresponding to it. The *sphoṭa* is not exactly this word-prototype, but it may be explained as the sound of a word as a whole, and as conveying a meaning apart from its component letters (*varṇas*). The *sphoṭa* does not contain exactly the sounds of the word in the order peculiar to the letters, but the sounds or something corresponding to them are blended indistinguishably into a uniform whole. When a word is pronounced its individual sounds become reflected in some degree in the order of the *sphoṭa* in which the particular sounds are comprised; and as the last sound dies away, the *sphoṭa*, in which the idea corresponding to all these sounds is comprised, becomes manifest and raises to our consciousness the idea thus associated. The sounds

[17] MBh. i. p. 1. atha gaur ity atra kaḥ śabdaḥ? . . . yenoccāritena sāsnālāṅgūla-kakuda-khura-viṣāṇināṃ saṃpratyayo bhavati sa śabdaḥ.

[18] Kielhorn, in his edition, adds a punctuation mark after this word, but this has no authority from the commentators.

[19] A. Berriedale Keith, *A History of Sanskrit Literature*, p. 387.

[20] *Studies in the History of Sanskrit Poetics*, vol. ii, p. 180.

of a word as a whole, therefore, and apart from those of the constituent letters, reveal the *sphoṭa*."

It is not surprising that Professor De goes on to describe this as a "somewhat mystical conception"; but with all respect, I feel that this statement hardly does justice to the grammarians' theory; and, indeed, it is hardly to be wondered at if the western reader, in the face of numerous comparable accounts, should come to the conclusion that the *sphoṭa*-theory represents a departure from lucidity which, coming as it does from men whose professional task was the clear presentation of linguistic facts, is quite inexplicable.

First, it must be made clear that the *sphoṭa* is not a "hypostatization of sound". Its fundamental attachment is to the other side of the linguistic situation, namely, the meaning. In its non-technical sense *sphoṭa* means simply "a bursting, a splitting open", and it is normally defined in its linguistic sense as "that from which the meaning bursts forth, i.e. shines forth, in other words the word-as-expressing-a-meaning (vācaka)".[21] The *sphoṭa* then is simply the linguistic sign in its aspect of meaning-bearer (*Bedeutungsträger*). The suggestion of the commentators that Patañjali's first definition of *śabda* refers to the *sphoṭa* is therefore true to the extent that it is the meaning-bearer which is in question. But the essential nature of the meaning-bearer was not seen by Patañjali in the same light as it was by later thinkers.[22] This is clear from his discussion of Pāṇini i.1.70 (*taparas tatkālasya*), where he explicitly distinguishes speech-sound (*dhvani*) and *sphoṭa*. The Pāṇinean system uses the convention that a statement about a short vowel applies also to the corresponding long vowel (and where necessary the prolated, *pluta*). Where, however, it is necessary to restrict a statement to the one length, a *t* is added. Thus, *a* = *a* and *ā*; *at* = *a* only. The sūtra, however, states that the *t* restricts the vowel to the same time-length; and Kātyāyana (*vārttika* 4) raises the possible objection that if a rule containing this *t* is uttered in the rapid style of diction (*druta*) it will be necessary to add that the medium (*madhyama*) and slow (*vilambita*) styles are also included, since they differ in time-length. This he answers in *vārttika* 5, by stating that the vowels themselves are fixed (*avasthitā varṇāḥ*) and that the styles of diction (*vṛtti*) depend upon the speech-habits of the speaker. Patañjali's discussion of this is interesting[23]:—

vaktā kaścid āśv abhidhāyī bhavati, āśu varṇān abhidhatte, kaścic cireṇa kaścic ciratareṇa, tadyathā: tam evādhvānaṃ kaścid āśu gacchati kaścic cireṇa gacchati kaścic ciratareṇa gacchati. rathika āśu gacchaty āśvikaś cireṇa padātiś ciratareṇa.—viṣama upanyāsaḥ. adhikaraṇam at rādhvā vrajati-kriyāyāḥ. tatrāyuktaṃ

[21] Koṇḍabhaṭṭa, *Vaiyākaraṇa-bhūṣaṇa* (Bombay, 1915), p. 236; Nāgeśabhaṭṭa, *Sphoṭavāda* (Adyar Library, 1946), p. 5: *sphuṭati prakāśate 'rtho 'smād iti sphoṭo vācaka iti yāvat.* Mādhava, *Sarvadarśanasaṃgraha* (ed. Abhyankar, p. 300), gives the double explanation that the *sphoṭa* is revealed by the letters, and itself reveals the meaning: *sphuṭyate vyajyate varṇair iti sphoṭo varṇābhivyaṅgyaḥ, sphuṭati sphuṭībhavaty asmād artha iti sphoṭo 'rthapratyāyakaḥ.*

[22] There is no evidence to show that Pāṇini knew the term *sphoṭa* or any meaning-theory comparable to the later discussions. The term itself occurs first in the Mahābhāṣya. Nāgeśa, it is true (*Sphoṭavāda*, p. 102), ascribed the doctrine to Sphoṭāyana, who is quoted by Pāṇini (vi. 1.123) on a point of morphology. But this is rather like ascribing a theory of roots to Racine.

[23] Kielhorn's edition, i. p. 181.

yad adhikaraṇasya vṛddhiḥ rāsau syātām.—evaṃ tarhi, sphoṭaḥ śabdo, dhvaniḥ śabdaguṇaḥ. katham?

bheryāghātavat.[24]

tadyathā bheryāghātaḥ. bherīm āhatya kaścid viṃśati padāni gacchati kaścit triṃśat kaścic catvāriṃśat. sphoṭaś ca tāvān eva bhavati, dhvanikṛtā vṛddhiḥ.

"One speaker is rapid in his utterance, pronounces the sounds rapidly, another is slow, and a third still slower. Similarly, one man travels the same road rapidly, a second slowly, a third still more slowly. Thus, a charioteer goes rapidly, a horseman slowly, and a pedestrian still more slowly. (The pupil objects:) 'The analogy is inexact. In this case the road forms the (unchanging) substratum of the action of going. But in the other case this is not applicable, since the length and shortness belong to the substratum itself.' (The teacher answers:) It is the same in the other case also, the *sphoṭa* (the unchanging substratum) is the word, the sound is merely an attribute of the word. How? Like a drum-beat. When a drum is struck, one drum-beat may travel twenty feet, another thirty, another forty. But the *sphoṭa* is of precisely such and such a size, the increase in length is caused by the sound."[25]

From this context it is clear that the word as the *sphoṭa*, in Patañjali's view, consists of a fixed pattern of letters, with long and short vowels; and this is confirmed by his statement that "the *sphoṭa* is of precisely such and such a size". In the more developed theory of Bhartṛhari, such an attribution of size to the *sphoṭa* would be unthinkable. I trust that this explanation does not attribute too much significance to *tāvān eva*. Puṇyarāja, it is true, in commenting on *Vākyapadīya* i.49, uses the expression *tāvān eva sphoṭo vicitrāṃ vṛttim anuvidhatte*; but I suspect that this is a direct reminiscence of the *Mahābhāṣya* passage, and that it is strictly incompatible with the later theory. The principal argument for my interpretation, however, is that Patañjali's problem here is the distinction between vowel-length as ordinarily understood in linguistic analysis, and absolute vowel-length of instances such as might be measured instrumentally. This in the later theory is the distinction between the *prākṛta-dhvani* and the *vaikṛta-dhvani*; while the *sphoṭa* in *Bhartṛhari's* sense is really irrelevant to the problem. It would thus seem that Patañjali's *sphoṭa* (except in so far as it is for him the meaning-bearer) is really comparable to Bhartṛhari's *prākṛta-dhvani*. The commentators, being acquainted with the later theory, naturally point out that the speed of utterance belongs to the *vaikṛta-dhvani*, but fail to observe that the contrast of the latter with Bhartṛhari's *sphoṭa* does not answer Patañjali's problem.

For Patañjali, then, it would seem that a word as a *sphoṭa* is fundamentally a structure consisting of a series of consonants and long or short vowels, in other words a structure which can be analysed as a succession of phonematic units. In the same way it is possible for him to talk of the *sphoṭa* of a single letter (*varṇa*). Thus, in discussing Pāṇini's statement *kṛpo ro laḥ*[26] ("in the root *kṛp-*, *r* is replaced by *l*", hence for **karpta* we have *kalptā*, etc.), he points

[24] This should be printed as a *vārttika*.

[25] The analogy here is clearly suggested by the literal meaning of *sphoṭa*, so that in the case of the drum it might be taken as the "burst" of sound. But whether or not this is the starting-point of the doctrine, the later discussions, as already noted, are more concerned with the "burst" of meaning occasioned by the linguistic sign.

[26] viii.2.18; MBh. vol. i, pp. 25–6.

out that strictly this does not make allowance for such forms as *kḷpta* < **kṛpta*, since only the consonant *r* is mentioned in the rule, and not the vowel *ṛ*. He ingeniously suggests that the sūtra may be analysed as *kṛpa* (for *kṛpe*?) *uḥ raḥ laḥ*, where *uḥ* and *r-aḥ* are respectively the genitives of *ṛ* and *r*, while *la-ḥ* is the nominative of *l*. This, however, is not completely satisfactory, as *ḷ* still does not appear. The final solution is: *athavobhayataḥ sphoṭamātraṃ nirdiśyate: raśruter laśrutir bhavatīti*, "alternatively, in both cases (*r* and *l*) it is only the *sphoṭa* which is taught in the sūtra, i.e. 'an[27] *r*-sound is replaced by an *l*-sound'." This can be approximately rendered in modern terminology, "In both cases the phoneme is meant, i.e. 'an allophone of the *r*-phoneme is replaced by an allophone of the *l*-phoneme'." It is of interest to observe that Patañjali realized that for the phonology of Sanskrit it is convenient to regard *r* and *ṛ* as belonging to the same phoneme.

Bhartṛhari, like Patañjali, starts from the observation that the word can be considered under two aspects, as sound, or as meaning-bearer (VP i.44):—

dvāv upādānaśabdeṣu śabdau śabdavido viduḥ
eko nimittaṃ śabdānām aparo 'rthe prayujyate.

"In meaningful language, linguists recognize two (entities which can be called) words: one is the underlying cause of words, the other is attached to the meaning." Here the "underlying cause of words" is clearly to be interpreted as the abstract sound-pattern which underlies instances of the utterance of the word, while the other which this utterance reveals is the *sphoṭa*, which in turn gives rise to the meaning. Thus, for Bhartṛhari, the sound (*dhvani*) is something more than the instance, and the *sphoṭa*, so far from being a time-series pattern is, in fact, repeatedly stated to have neither time nor parts. The time-order of the *dhvani* is merely a means (upāya) for revealing the timeless and indivisible *sphoṭa* (VP i.48):—

nādasya kramajātatvān na pūrvo na paraś[28] ca saḥ
akramaḥ kramarūpeṇa bhedavān iva gṛhyate.

"The fact that the sound is produced serially is no argument for considering the *sphoṭa* to be (capable of the predicates) 'before' or 'after': having no order itself, it is only apparently perceived under the disguise of order and as possessing parts."

This concept of the *sphoṭa* appears to have arisen under the influence of arguments in the philosophical schools. The Nyāya philosophers, for example, held that the meaning of a word was presented to the mind by the last sound, aided by the memory-impression of the preceding sounds. This, however, is linguistically unsatisfactory. Even granting the hypothesis that the data are received as a series of atomic perceptions, it is necessary to postulate in addition that we remember not only the impressions, but also their order; and even then all that would be present to the mind is a collection of sounds in a given order, and not a meaning-bearing

[27] V. Trapp, *Die ersten fünf Āhnikas des Mahābhāṣyam* (Leipzig, 1933), p. 89, seems to me to obscure the matter by importing the definite article: "An Stelle *der* Gehörsempfindung 'r' tritt *die* Gehörsempfindung 'l'".

[28] So both India Office MSS.; Benares edition, *nāparaś*; Puṇyarāja, *pūrvatraparatva-*; cf. MBh. i. p. 355, *pūrvaparayoḥ*, Laghumañjūṣā, p. 162, *ayaṃ pūrvo 'yaṃ para iti*. On the other hand, *paurvāparya* is the regular form; and cf. also (dependent on this) *pūrvāparābhāvāt*, MBh. i, 356, vārttika. There is probably a reference here to Pāṇini i. I. 66–7, *tasminn iti nirdiṣṭe pūrvasya*; *tasmād ity uttarasya*.

word. The sounds by themselves have clearly no capacity to attach themselves directly to a meaning, otherwise the collection of the first three sounds of the word *manage* would present to the mind the word *man*; and this, in fact, does not happen. To deal with the situation adequately, it is necessary to postulate a meaning-bearer which is not identical with the collection of sounds, but is related to this collection in such a way as to be capable of being revealed by it. In other words, for linguistic purposes the word must be considered as a meaning-bearing unit, a single symbol whose parts are not relevant to it *qua* symbol, just as the fact that the written symbol *y* contains a part similar in shape to *v* is strictly irrelevant to its symbolic employment. Thus the *sphoṭa* is simply the word considered as a single meaningful symbol. In this conception of the *sphoṭa*, it seems to me that there is nothing "mysterious": it is merely an abstraction to assist us in the handling of our linguistic material. In fact, most linguistic discussions implicitly assume such a *sphoṭa*, if only as a point of reference. The fact that the *sphoṭa* itself cannot be pronounced is a characteristic shared with the phoneme and any other linguistic abstraction. And the fact that the Indians themselves appear to have given "ontological status" to this abstraction, and to have considered it as a sort of quasi-Kantian "Wort-an-sich", does not detract from the linguistic appropriateness of their observations.

This *sphoṭa*, the word located in the mind (*śabdo buddhisthaḥ*, VP i.46) is revealed by the sounds produced in a fixed sequence (VP i.85, 86):—

nādair āhitabījāyām antyena dhvaninā saha
āvṛtti[29]-paripākāyāṃ buddhau śabdo 'vadhāryate.
asataś cāntarāle yāñ chabdān astīti manyate
pratipattur aśaktiḥ sā grahaṇopāya eva saḥ.

"With the last sound, the word is grasped in the mind (of the hearer) where the seed has been sown by the sounds, and which has been brought to ripeness by the telling over in order (*āvṛtti*) of the sounds. And as for the non-existent words which the hearer considers to be present in the interval (before the utterance is completed)[30]—this is merely the incapacity of the hearer: it is simply a means to the comprehension (of the word actually being uttered)."

The false attribution of time to the *sphoṭa* may arise in two ways: either we may measure the actual time of an instance, or we may construct an abstract phonological time-pattern (VP i.75–8):—

sphoṭasyābhinnakālasya dhvanikālānupātinaḥ
grahaṇopādhibhedena vṛttibhedaṃ pracakṣate.
svabhāvabhedān nityatve hrasva-dīrgha-plutādiṣu
prākṛtasya dhvaneḥ kālaḥ śabdasyety upacaryate.
varṇasya grahaṇe hetuḥ prākṛto dhvanir iṣyate
vṛttibhede nimittatvaṃ vaikṛtaḥ pratipadyate.
śabdasyordhvam abhivyakter vṛttibhede tu vaikṛtāḥ
dhvanayaḥ samupohante sphoṭātmā tair na bhidyate.

"According to the differences in the specific cause of its comprehension (in individual instances), men attribute differences in speed of utterance (vṛtti) to the *sphoṭa* which is not divided in time, and merely reflects the time of the sound. Similarly, in the case of the short, long, and prolated vowels—since, on the view that these are permanent, they are intrinsically distinct—it is the time-pattern

[29] Benares edition and India Office MSS., *āvṛtta-*.

[30] In examples such as *man*: *manage*.

of the primary sound which is metaphorically attributed to the word (the *sphoṭa*) itself. The 'primary sound' (*prākṛta-dhvani*) is defined as the cause of the perception of the letters (phonemes), the 'secondary sound' (*vaikṛta-dhvani*, literally 'modified') is the causal factor underlying differences of diction. But it is only after the word has been revealed that the secondary sounds are presented to the mind as differences of diction; hence (*a fortiori*) the essential nature of the *sphoṭa* is not disrupted by these." This last observation is most important. I may, for example, hear two utterances identical in absolute length, but it is only after I have understood the words themselves that I can interpret one as *śita* and the other as *śīta*. The same consideration can, of course, also be applied to other linguistic happenings. In my own speech, for example, I normally distinguish in pronunciation the three words *poor*, *pore*, and *paw*. Many speakers of Southern English, however, pronounce all three (in certain contexts) as **phɔ:**. But it is only when I have understood which word is intended that I can start to consider the nature and extent of the *vaikṛta-dhvani* modifications which such a speaker has imposed on the pattern of my own pronunciation, which by an understandable prejudice I consider to be identical with the *prākṛta-dhvani*.

Bhartṛhari's analysis therefore envisages three aspects of the language situation: (1) the integral linguistic symbol, the *sphoṭa*, which we may for convenience distinguish typographically as *AGNI*. This, of course, is not the "pronunciation" of the *sphoṭa*, since it cannot be pronounced, but is merely the name of it, just as we say, for example, "the *t*-phoneme." (2) The *prākṛta-dhvani*, *agni*, the phonological structure, the sound-pattern of the norm; or, from another point of view, the name of the class of which the various instances are members. (3) The *vaikṛta-dhvani*, **agni**, the individual instance, noted in purely phonetic terms. This, of course, we do not normally perceive in language-communication, since we receive it as a series of sense-data which the brain is conditioned to elaborate and interpret as a finished *Gestalt*. Accordingly, in a given instance it is apparently the *prākṛta-dhvani* which is presented to the consciousness of the hearer. Even so, it is not felt by the hearer as something separate from the *sphoṭa*: and normally, in everyday conversation, all that we are immediately conscious of is the meaning (VP i.82):—

sphoṭarūpāvibhāgena dhvaner grahaṇam iṣyate
kaiścid dhvanir asaṃvedyaḥ svatantro 'nyaiḥ prakāśakaḥ.

"Some consider that the perception of the *dhvani* is indissolubly linked with (the perception of) the form of the *sphoṭa*; others hold that the *dhvani* itself is not perceived (as such) [i.e. we are not normally aware of the phonemes when we hear a word]; and others consider the *dhvani* to be an independent manifesting agent" [as is clearly seen in the speech of a parrot or a gramophone record]. The three views are, of course, not mutually exclusive, and in differing circumstances one or other will commend itself.

It will thus be seen that the *sphoṭa*-doctrine, so far from being something "mysterious", is in fact of central importance for the theory of language-symbolism. The fact that it has been so generally neglected by western Sanskritists appears to be due for the most part to two reasons. The first is the unfortunate mistranslation of *śabda* as "sound". Thus, Cowell[31] translates Mādhava's statement *varṇātirikto varṇābhivyaṅgyo 'rthapratyāyako nityaḥ śabdaḥ sphoṭa*

[31] *Sarva-darśana-saṃgraha*, translated E. B. Cowell and A. E. Gough, p. 211.

iti tadvido vadanti, as "And . . . (say the wise in these matters) . . . this *sphoṭa* is an eternal sound, distinct from the letters and revealed by them, which causes the cognition of the meaning". This is hardly an incentive to further investigation. A retranslation, however, removes the objection: "The abiding word which is the conveyor of the meaning . . . is called the *sphoṭa* by the grammarians." The second reason for neglect has been the fact that on the basis of the *sphoṭa*-theory there was erected a metaphysical superstructure, in which the transcendental Word was seen as the first-principle of the universe, in a manner somewhat analogous to the *λόγος* doctrine of St. John's gospel. It has therefore been assumed that the theory was in all respects mystical, and that the translation of *sphoṭa* as "transcendental word"[32] was entirely adequate in all circumstances. Hence, it has been overlooked that the doctrine is in the first place founded upon observation and interpretation of the actual speech situation. In fact, when an opponent questions the existence of the *sphoṭa*, the grammarian replies, not that it requires a mystical insight to perceive it, but that its justification is direct perception of the facts.[33] Similarly, Nāgeśa-bhaṭṭa says[34]. *idam ekaṃ padam ekaṃ vākyam iti pratyayaḥ sphoṭasattve tadekatve ca pramāṇam*, "The justification for the existence of the *sphoṭa* and for its unity is the realization 'This is *one* word, *one* sentence'."

The later development of the theory details eight classified varieties of *sphoṭa*[35]:—

1. varṇa-sphoṭa
2. pada-sphoṭa
3. vākya-sphoṭa
4. akhaṇḍa-pada-sphoṭa
5. akhaṇḍa-vākya-sphoṭa

} (vyakti-sphoṭas)

6. varṇa-jāti-sphoṭa
7. pada-jāti-sphoṭa
8. vākya-jāti-sphoṭa

Here also the fundamental argument is meaningfulness (*vācakatvam*). Thus, the letter-*sphoṭa* (1) is justified on the grounds that a meaning is understood, for example, from suffixes such as *-ḥ*, *-ti*, in *rāmaḥ*, *pacati*. Similarly the alternations in *kar-*, *kār-*, *kur-*, *cakar-*, are clearly functional.[36] On the other hand, the impossibility of

[32] E.g. O. Strauss, *Altindische Spekulationen über die Sprache und ihre Probleme*, ZDMG, N.F. 6, 1927, pp. 99–151. B. Liebich, *Über den Sphoṭa*, ZDMG, N.F. 2, 1923, pp. 208–219, contributes nothing to the understanding of this question. A. Foucher, *Le Compendium des Topiques — Tarkasaṃgraha — d'Annambhaṭṭa* (Paris, 1949), Introd., p. xix, describes the *sphoṭa* as "La mystérieuse et fulgurante relation qui éclate entre le son et le sens, entre le mot et l'idée". The *sphoṭa*, however, is not a relation, but the word itself.

[33] *Sarvadarśanasaṃgraha* (ed. Abhyankar), p. 299, pratyakṣam evātra pramāṇaṃ, gaur ity ekaṃ padaṃ iti nānāvarṇātiriktaikapadāvagateḥ sarvajanīnatvāt.

[34] *Mahābhāṣya-pradīpoddyota* (Bibl. Ind.), vol. i, p. 11.

[35] See, for example, Nāgeśa-bhaṭṭa, *Sphoṭavāda* (Adyar Library, 1946); Bhaṭṭoji-dīkṣita, *Śabda-kaustubha* (Chowkhamba Skt. Ser., Benares, 1933), pp. 7 ff.

[36] The discussion of the question as to whether or not the individual letters in a word have meaning is not far removed from modern discussions on the phoneme. Thus, it may be said that letters are meaningful on the grounds that meaning can be understood from roots, suffixes, and particles which consist of a single letter; and also since the substitution of a different letter can produce a different word, while the non-perception of a single letter may make it

discriminating exactly how much of the word conveys the thing-meant, and how much the case-relationship (e.g. in *rāmāya, rāmeṇa, haraye, harau, harīn*), makes it necessary to postulate a word-*sphoṭa* (2). Similarly, sandhi-forms such as *dadhīdam*, "this is curds," point to the desirability of a sentence-*sphoṭa* (3). But inasmuch as the word is still thought of as consisting of stem and suffix, and the sentence as consisting of words, these *sphoṭas* (2 and 3) do not satisfy the linguist's requirements. As Bhartṛhari had already shown, in language as we find it in the world as an object of study, there are no letters in the word, and no words in the sentence.[37] The analysis into letters and the distribution of meanings between stem and suffix, or between the words in the sentence—these proceedings, as Nāgeśa says, are the occupation of grammarians.[38] In actual usage, the word conveys its sense as a unit, and hence the undivided-word-*sphoṭa* (4) takes the place of (2). Even this is not completely satisfactory, since isolated words (*padas*) do not occur as meaningful utterances in ordinary language (apparent exceptions being one-word sentences). Therefore the grammarian admits the reality only of the undivided-sentence-*sphoṭa* (5). The preceding *sphoṭas* are merely fictional (*kālpanika*) constructs of the grammarian.

Here there arises a philosophical controversy as to whether the *sphoṭa* is a particular (*vyakti*) or a universal (*jāti*). To meet the needs of those who believe in the latter, the class-*sphoṭas* (6, 7, and 8) are provided. V. Krishnamacharya[39] states that the ancients held the *jāti-sphoṭa* view, the moderns (i.e. Nāgeśa and his contemporaries) the *vyakti-sphoṭa*. The ascription of the *jāti-sphoṭa* view to Bhartṛhari is supported by Bhaṭṭoji-dīkṣita,[40] who quotes in this connection some stanzas from VP. iii. 1.33:—

saṃbandhibhedāt sattaiva bhidyamānā gavādiṣu
jātir ity ucyate tasyāṃ sarve śabdā vyavasthitāḥ.

"Being divided into cows and so forth through distinctions of those things in which the relationship subsists, it is Existence which is called *the* Class (*par excellence*); and in this class all words have their being." This, however, is no argument for holding that Bhartṛhari accepted the *jāti-sphoṭa* theory, and still less is the other passage quoted by Bhaṭṭojī (VP i.94):—

anekavyaktyabhivyaṅgyā jātiḥ sphoṭa iti smṛtā
kaiścid vyaktaya evāsyā dhvanitvena prakalpitāḥ.

In this stanza, Bhaṭṭoji presumably took the first line as a complete statement; but the interpretation of Nāgeśa-bhaṭṭa,[41]

impossible to understand the meaning. But from another point of view the letters are meaningless in themselves, since the hearer does not perceive a meaning from each letter separately. (MBh. I. 220. arthavanto varṇā dhātu-prātipadika-pratyaya-nipātānām eka-varṇānām arthadarśanād varṇavyatyaye cārthāntaragamanād varṇānupalabdhau cānarthagateḥ; anarthakās tu prativarṇam arthānupalabdheḥ.) In similar fashion some modern writers have considered their phonemes to be the smallest significant segments of a word, their "significance" lying in their differentiation-value.

[37] VP i. 73:—
pade na varṇā vidyante
varṇeṣv avayavā na ca
vākyāt padānām atyantaṃ
praviveko na kaścana.

[38] Nāgeśa, *Laghumañjūṣā*, p. 5, *tat tad arthavibhāgaṃ śāstramātraviṣayam.*

[39] Introd. to his edition of Nāgeśa's *Sphoṭavāda*, p. 24.

[40] *Śabda-kaustubha*, p. 9.

[41] *Sphoṭavāda*, p. 99.

which takes the first phrase down to *kaiścit*, seems preferable[42]: "Some consider that the *sphoṭa* is the class revealed by the various individual instances, and they consider that the members of this class are the *dhvanis*." Thus, on this view, as Nāgeśa explains,[43] there appears in the particular only the sounds and nothing more. The distinction between the two views, therefore, is not quite what it would appear at first sight. Both sides, in fact, accepted the concept of the class, but while the *jāti*-school considered the *sphoṭa* to be merely a class whose members were not themselves *sphoṭas*, the other school maintained that the *sphoṭa* was in fact present in the particular. That Bhartṛhari held the latter views is further supported by the fact that in his discussion of the definition of a sentence he appears to give preference to the view that the sentence is *eko 'navayavaḥ śabdaḥ*, "a single integral language-symbol," i.e. a *vyakti-sphoṭa*, rather than a *jātiḥ saṃghātavartinī* "a class residing in a collocation (of words)".

Thus the class-*sphoṭa* theory is closely similar to a modern view put forward by Kaplan and Copilowish,[44] who define a sign (including a linguistic sign) as "a class of sign-vehicles all having one and same law of interpretation". Merely as terminology, this is extraordinarily awkward—Russell, for example, stumbles over this awkwardness and talks of the loudness of a "sign", forgetting for the moment that a "class of sign-vehicles" cannot have loudness. But the authors themselves have not taken their definition seriously, for they discuss the conditions under which a sentential sign may be true. Clearly a class cannot be true or false. Thus they have propounded a jāti-*sphoṭa* theory, but implicitly assume in their discussion a vyakti-*sphoṭa* view. It would seem, in fact, that the jāti-*sphoṭa* view is philosophically unworkable.

In Bhartṛhari's view, then, the primary linguistic fact is the undivided sentence-*sphoṭa*. Just as a bare root has no meaning in the world,[45] so also the meanings of individual words are merely hints or stepping stones to the meaning of the sentence. This is a plain linguistic fact, which has none the less been clear to very few philosophers, either in India or elsewhere; and though familiar enough in modern linguistics, is still constantly overlooked in many discussions on meaning. Until it is thoroughly understood, no real progress can be made in the central linguistic problem of semantics. Bhartṛhari's discussions of these questions is full of valuable observation, and it is hoped to offer an account of these on a later occasion. The present paper is intended merely as an introduction to some of the aspects of the Indian theory which are still of vital importance to us to-day.

In this very difficult field I can hardly hope to have rendered the subtle arguments in so brief a compass in an entirely satisfactory manner. To quote yet again from Bhartṛhari (i.34):—
yatnenānumito 'py arthaḥ kuśalair anumātṛbhiḥ
abhiyuktatarair anyair anyathaivopapādyate.
"When clever logicians have with great pains deduced a result to their own satisfaction, then others still more able come along, and

[42] This is also in accordance with Puṇyarāja's commentary on Bhartṛhari, which introduces the stanza as *matāntaram āha*.

[43] *ibid.*, tadvyañjakavyaktayaś ca dhvanaya eva, na tadatiriktā iti.

[44] *Mind*, Oct. 1939; discussed by Russell, *Inquiry into Meaning and Truth*, p. 184.

[45] VP ii. 212, dhātvādīnāṃ viśuddhānāṃ laukiko 'rtho na vidyate.

reach a totally different conclusion." If nothing else, I trust that this preliminary presentation will offer an incentive to those more able to prosecute this study further.

Brough reverted to Indian semantics in the following article, "Some Indian Theories of Meaning," *Transactions of the Philological Society* (1953, 161–176). This paper paved the way for later work by K. Kunjunni Raja, for example, *Indian Theories of Meaning* (1963).

B. Some Indian Theories of Meaning (1953)

John Brough

In a paper to the Society in 1951,[1] I gave some account of ancient Indian theories on the relationship between sounds and meaningful words which is summed up in the doctrine of *sphoṭa*. The present paper is intended to supplement that discussion and to indicate those aspects of Indian theory on the more general topics of meaning which I feel preserve the greatest interest for modern linguistic theory.

One of the earliest pieces of practical linguistics of which we have any record is the composition of the *pada* text of the Ṛgveda. This is an analysis of the *saṃhitā*, or connected text as uttered in recitation, into its constituent words in the form in which they would appear in isolation. This involved the resolution of the rather complicated junction-features which the connected Sanskrit sentence exhibits, and in many places the *pada* text did in fact amount to an interpretation at a time when the connected text was beginning to suffer from obscurity. Alongside this analysis of words from the sentence there was developed the study of the meanings of the words thus derived, and the results of this etymological study is summed up for us in the *Nirukta* of Yāska. It is clear that just as phonetics arose in India chiefly as a means to preserve the mode of utterance of the Vedic hymns, so the study of words and of the meanings of words was undertaken in the first place primarily to meet the needs of Vedic ritual and the text material required by it. It was thus on a basis of words and of word-meanings that the study of Vedic exegesis took shape in what was later known as the Mīmāṃsā school of philosophy. And, indeed, throughout the development of Indian linguistic thought, the relationship between word and sentence, between the word-meaning and the sentence-meaning, remains a central problem. The Mīmāṃsā school developed elaborate canons of interpretation, and this organized body of linguistic doctrine later played an important part in the discussions of lawyers when interpreting legal injunctions, and on the other hand did much to stimulate the development of logic. In passing, one might note that the Mīmāṃsā preoccupation with the injunctions of Vedic texts with regard to religious duties was not without its effect on logical theory. The typical sentence with which they are concerned is in the imperative mood, and although later Indian logic deals largely in indicative sentences, the linguistic thought of philosophers in India was not so strictly confined to indicative propositions as that of logicians in the west. This influence can be traced in the terms *vidhi* and *pratiṣedha*, originally meaning injunction and prohibition, but in later texts occasionally used also to apply simply to positive and negative statements.

I do not propose here to give a detailed account of all the types

[1] Theories of General Linguistics in the Sanskrit Grammarians, *TPS* 1951, pp. 27–46. [This volume, pages 402–414]

of definitions of a sentence which occur in Indian writings; but mention should be made of the main types. As early as the *Kātyāyana-śrauta-sūtra* the Mīmāṃsā type of definition appears, in a purely ritual manual. A sentence, it is said, is that which is *nirākāṅkṣam*[2]: that is to say, something which has no requirement or expectation of words outside itself to complete its meaning. It is, of course, realized that the expectancy which holds between words in the sentence is a grammatical one, since, for example, a sentence containing a pronoun requires the evidence of a neighbouring sentence to identify the pronoun. Accordingly a commentator on this passage interprets the rule which follows, *mithaḥ saṃbaddham* "it is mutually linked (with other sentences)" to mean that it may be necessary to complete the meaning of the sentence by understanding words from preceding sentences. The fact that the requirement of *ākāṅkṣā* is a grammatical one was not always fully understood and we find even Bhartṛhari criticizing the Mīmāṃsā definition on the grounds that its *ākāṅkṣā* would imply that a passage of several grammatical "sentences" would have to be considered as one sentence.[3] Later the normal statement of the conditions for a sentence is that it must be a collection of words possessing *ākāṅkṣā*, *yogyatā* and *āsatti*. In effect, however, it is only the first which is of real linguistic importance. It is the desire or requirement of an individual word or words in the sentence for others to complete the meaning, the factor which distinguishes a sentence from a string of words "cow horse man elephant". The second factor, *yogyatā*, really involves a judgment on the truth or falsity of a statement, or the sense or nonsense of a sentence. The example quoted most frequently as a breach of this condition is "He wets it with fire". Into this category also fall such logical puzzles as "the round square". The third condition, *āsatti* or *saṃnidhi*, is that the words should be contiguous in time. It is said that words uttered with the interval of a day intervening between each word cannot produce a sentence. This again is not a linguistic condition. It is of course only to be expected that the early stages of linguistic theory in India, as elsewhere, should show a certain *naïveté* and it is not surprising to find generally current in Indian philosophy, outside the writings of the professional grammarians, the idea that an individual word possesses an individual word-meaning or, in the case of nouns, that the word is the name of a thing. This view is fossilized in the regular philosophic term for thing or object, namely *padārtha*, literally "meaning of a word, that which a word means".

The two main schools of the later Mīmāṃsā were sharply opposed in their theories of the sentence. The Bhāṭṭa school on the whole seems to preserve the more primitive attitude. According to them words have in themselves meanings, and as the words are uttered in a sentence, each word performs its task of expressing its meaning, and the sentence is the summation of these meanings. The Prābhākara school, on the other hand, held the more sophisticated theory that the individual words did not express any meaning until they were united together into a sentence. This was upheld by an appeal to the method whereby a child learns its own mother tongue. They pointed out that it was by hearing sentences "fetch the cow", "fetch the horse", and so forth, that the child came

[2] KŚS i. 3. 2 teṣāṃ (*sc.* mantrāṇāṃ) vākyaṃ nirākāṅkṣam.
[3] VP ii. 3 ff. The grammatical sentence is here identified on the basis of the Vārttika definition, *eka-tiṅ* "possessing one finite verb".

gradually to understand that the animal which he saw on each several occasion was, in fact, either a cow or a horse and that the action performed by his elders was the act of fetching. These two views were named respectively *abhihitānvaya-vāda* and *anvitābhidhāna-vāda*, terms which are troublesome to translate by concise English expressions. Roughly speaking, the first is the theory that the sentence is "a series of expressed word-meanings", and the second is that the sentence is "the expressed meaning of a series (of words)".

At the beginning of the second book of the *Vākyapadīya*, Bhartṛhari gives a list of definitions and quasi-definitions of a sentence. Five of these are grouped by the commentator under the traditional Mīmāṃsā designations. Thus the view that the sentence is a unified collection (*saṃghāta*) and the view that it is an ordered series (*krama*) are aspects of the *abhihitānvaya-vāda*; while the other three belong to the *anvitābhidhāna-vāda*. These are, that the sentence is defined by a verbal expression (*ākhyāta-śabda*) or by the first word (*padam ādyam*) or by all the words taken separately with the feature of mutual requirement or expectancy superadded (*pṛthak sarvapadaṃ sākāṅkṣam*). All these views, of course, imply the feature of expectancy, and the first and second are to be explained with reference to this feature, since the verb or the first word is only what it is in view of its ties with the other words in its own sentence. All these theories are adversely criticized by Bhartṛhari and they need not be considered in detail here. They are none the less of some interest as evidence of very vigorous argument and debate on linguistic topics in ancient India.

All these earlier discussions on the nature of the sentence accept without question the fact that there are such things as words (*pada*), and that it is possible to attribute to these words something which can be called their meaning (*artha*). The most developed theory, namely that of the *anvitābhidhānavāda*, did to some extent foreshadow the later development in the grammatical schools, since it denied the words conveyed a meaning except in the context of a sentence. Like the other views, however, this theory continued to regard the words as real and actual constituents of language. They were the units which in fact operated in linguistic communication, and since they were actually present, it merely remained for the grammarian to detect their presence by means of a grammatical analysis. The statement of procedure is quite in accordance with many modern statements. Thus a root or suffix is analysed out on the basis of a paradigm, and complete words were recognized on the basis of substitution in sentences. It remained for the professional grammarians, of whom Bhartṛhari is the leading ancient spokesman, to draw attention to the fact that although this process of analysis could give some account of language from the formal aspect, and though it possessed a distinct value for teaching and for the explanation of texts, it was entirely inadequate as a basis for a theory of language-meaning. To Bhartṛhari and his school words were, in fact, artificial constructions of the grammarian, and looked on from the point of view of language functioning in the world, they were unreal (*asatya*).

This extraordinary relegation of words to the realm of fictions is not at all easy to grasp at first sight, and I hope I may be pardoned if I dwell at some length on this topic, since it seems to me of considerable importance for fundamental linguistic theory, and hence also for philosophy, in so far as the latter may be a "critique of language".

It is, of course, a commonplace in modern linguistics that the sentence is the primary datum. But such a statement may imply no more than an attitude comparable with the *anvitābhidhāna-vāda*. I suspect that it is the latter type of view which is often implicit in statements described as "analysis at the word level".[4] It demands something of an effort for the beginner brought up on an alphabetic system of writing to appreciate fully that a word is not a succession of letters or phonemes or segments which are then rammed together—"realized" has been a popular term in this connection. But on the contrary the word is what it is, and any account in terms of syllables, letters, phonemes, segments, prosodies, is merely an analysis, an attempt at *description* which may be more or less adequate. A similar effort, though perhaps a still more difficult one, is required to grasp the significance of Bhartṛhari's theory of the unreal nature of words. It is important to realize that this theory is not derived from *a priori* speculation, but is the result of a careful examination of what happens when we speak or listen in ordinary conversation. We do not in fact express ourselves or understand what is spoken in a series of meaning-units. After a sentence has been understood we may look back at it, analyse it into words, and maintain that we discern words in it. But if we do so during the course of the utterance itself, we are apt to lose the meaning of the sentence. The situation is perhaps analogous to the experience which some of us had at the recent International Congress of Linguists (London, 1952) when Professor Delattre played to us records of series of synthetic vowels, each vowel being made up of two musical formants. According to the method of focusing the attention, one could hear the record either as a series of vowels or as two converging musical scales, but not as both simultaneously. The essence of the matter lies in discriminating clearly between language in operation, and language-material considered and described by a grammarian. Bhartṛhari's view is simply that words and "word-meanings" belong to the latter sphere. They constitute an apparatus (not necessarily adequate) for the description of language events, but (roughly speaking) do not themselves "exist" in the events described.

This theory of the non-reality of words not unnaturally met with strong opposition from other Indian philosophers, and Bhartṛhari provides us with a number of the arguments which they brought against it. Typical of these is the argument from our experience of sentences which contain an unknown word. If for example a townsman, who has not previously heard of the bird in question, hears the sentence, "Fetch a cuckoo from the woods," he instinctively assumes that he has not understood the sentence because he does not know the word "cuckoo"; and as the objector points out, he does know the words "Fetch . . . from the woods". On Bhartṛhari's view, however, a better description of the situation

[4] Such an analysis may be justified where the forms of words are the chief concern; but considerable contortions and an embarrassing set of fictions (e.g., the "central core of meaning" of a word) seem to be needed if we attempt to construct a descriptive statement of meaning on the basis of a word analysis. Such a wholesale rejection of word-meanings from scientific discussion does not of course mean the advocacy of the abolition of lexicography, but rather the recognition of the essentially practical and pragmatic nature of lexicographical statements of meaning.

would be that he cannot understand the word—that is, he cannot attribute a word-meaning to it—because he has not understood the sentence. This is, at first sight, perverse and paradoxical, but if patiently considered it will be seen to have much in its favour. It follows as a corollary that the piece "Fetch . . . from the woods" is not the same as similar phrases which occur in other sentences, for example, "Fetch a tree from the woods"; and this situation Bhartṛhari unreservedly accepts.[5] It is of course clear that any meaning which we attribute to the fragment "Fetch . . . from the woods" is different in the two cases, since for example the method of transport will be different. At the most, therefore, we can say that the apparently identical fragments in the two sentences are similar but not the same.

On this view, the distinction between "formulae" and "free expressions" is not so clear-cut as Jespersen would have us believe.[6] Of the former category, he says, "One may indeed analyse such a formula and show that it consists of several words, but it is felt and handled as a unit, which may often mean something quite different from the meaning of the component words taken separately." But this holds also for free expressions, and as Jespersen himself realizes elsewhere,[7] the "meaning of the component words taken separately" is something which cannot be determined apart from a context; and once this is granted, the distinction between the two categories amounts to little more than this: that a word-meaning analysis is more congenial to a grammarian in the one case than in the other. The apparently objective criterion upon which Jespersen relies to diagnose a free expression, namely, substitution in sentential functions, is as we have seen explicitly rejected by Bhartṛhari as being in fact illusory.

The occurrence of homophones in a language has always provided grammarians with an interesting problem, and almost all writers on the theory of grammar have discussed the factors which enable a language to tolerate such homophones without giving rise to ambiguities. Bhartṛhari gives a list of such factors, of which the most important are *vākya*, sentence-context, and *prakaraṇa*, situational context. As a typical modern statement of the same matter I might quote Sir Alan Gardiner: "The *polysémie* of words . . . does not matter in the least, because the hearer always has the situation to guide him in choosing that type of meaning which is appropriate to the context."[8] This statement conveys the position roughly; but it seems unlikely that the hearer actually chooses

[5] The objection is raised in VP ii. 74, and answered in ii. 94. The naïve person (*mūḍha*) thinks that he perceives the same meaning in the parallel portions of the two sentences (*vanāt* pika *ānīyatām; vanād* vṛkṣa *ānīyatām*); but this, as the commentator remarks, is a misconception due to the serial nature (*krama-vaśāt*) of the linguistic sentence-symbol. [Thus for Bhartṛhari the naïve view is completely analogous to the suggestion that in *y* and *v* —due to the linear nature of our writing—there is a common part. Cf. also VP ii. 416 : just as the letters in a word are in themselves meaningless, so also are the words (*pada*) in a sentence.] Thus the substitution of the word *pika* for *vṛkṣa* produces an entirely different sentence; and if there is doubt as to the meaning of one word, then the whole sentence is not understood (*pikādiyogāt sakalam evātyantavilakṣaṇam; ekapadārthasaṃdehe sakalam evājñātaṃ vākyam ity ucyate*).

[6] O. Jespersen, *The Philosophy of Grammar*, p. 18 f.

[7] Op. cit., p. 66.

[8] TPS 1951, p. 60.

between the various meanings or types of meaning of the *word*—he certainly does not do so consciously in his native language; and it might be better to say that the hearer does in fact understand the sentence, and that this understanding, if afterwards utilized by the lexicographer (who also must "understand" the sentence), will enable the latter to state that, in such-and-such a situation, in such-and-such a verbal context, etc., the given word can be extracted analytically, and such-and-such a "word-meaning" attributed to it, this word-meaning being different from other meanings of the same "word" in different contexts and different situations. Further, it is necessary to recognize that when we talk of "the word *x* with meaning *A*", "the word *x* with meaning *B*", the identification of the two *x*'s as "one word" is a mere practical convenience for lexicography and exegesis, something which belongs not to the material but to one method of describing the material, and that this method is not necessarily the best approach to a satisfactory description of language in operation.

We are apt to say from time to time, when struggling with a difficult passage in a foreign text, that we know all the words, but that the meaning of the sentence escapes us. This however is a delusion. In such circumstances we are presumably attributing to one or more of the words a "meaning" which has not been extracted from this particular context, and the obvious comment is that we do *not* know all the words, since our knowledge does not include the manner of their occurrence in the context in question. In practice, of course, a more general, if vaguer, aura of meaning extracted from *similar* contexts frequently gives us a sufficient clue; but this leads us in the first place to an understanding of the meaning of the sentence as a whole, and only afterwards, by an analysis of this understanding, to the attribution of meanings to the individual words.

These considerations are of the first importance for those of us who are concerned with ancient texts and hypothetical forms in Indo-European or other conjectural languages. The pursuit of the meanings of words in ancient texts is a highly skilled art, and the best work which has been done in this field has substantially added to our understanding of texts. But it is an art which requires a delicate tread. When we inquire into the meaning of a word in an ancient language we are really juggling with possible translations of sentences in which the word occurs, until we finally succeed in finding a mode of translation in which a single word or phrase of the English appears to correspond more or less to the ancient word in question. We then say that this English word or phrase is a meaning of the ancient word. Here we at least have in the texts sentences which by one means or another we understand after a fashion; and historical and comparative studies frequently enable us to glean from texts in related languages useful hints towards this understanding—though it is important to remember that these methods can at best protect us, as a near-scientific control, against specific errors, but can never prove a positive case. When we come to the prehistory of words, however, we have no sentences at all. The only conclusion that we can reach is that it is therefore impossible to talk of the meanings of, for example, Indo-European roots, except in a very different sense of the term "meaning". Indeed the vagueness of the meanings attributed to Indo-European roots by writers on this subject is an indication of the vagueness of what is meant by meaning in this context.

Having characterized the sentence as "a single undivided utterance" which conveys a single undivided meaning, Bhartṛhari proceeds to indicate what he understands to be the nature of this sentence-meaning. One cannot claim that what he says is a definition, and indeed the theory itself really implies that definition as ordinarily understood is an impossibility. The important point is that the sentence-meaning is grasped as a unity. The situation is compared to our apprehension of a picture. This we perceive as in some sense a unity, and although we can analyse the field of vision, and say that this part of the picture is blue, this part white, and so forth, none the less, we are normally aware of the integrated whole. If on this analogy we proceed to explain the sentence on the basis of an analysis into words, we are in fact merely giving a commentary on it in what are ultimately other words, not words of the sentence itself. The idea here is closely similar to that expressed by Wittgenstein when he maintains that a proposition can only *show* what it has in common with the fact, and that this cannot be *said* in language, since any attempt to do so can only produce other propositions sharing the same logical form.[9] In the end the utmost that can be said of the meaning of a sentence according to Bhartṛhari is that it is grasped by an instantaneous flash of insight (*pratibhā*).[10] The same word is used in later times with reference to the insight of a great poet, and in such contexts may be reasonably translated as poetic genius. We are all, in fact, in a greater or lesser degree poets in our composition of sentences and in our understanding of the utterances of our fellows. And when we have understood a sentence, we cannot explain to another the nature of this understanding.[11] Although it is an acquired faculty, understanding a language is in its operation very similar to the instinctive behaviour of animals.[12]

It is unnecessary to labour the point that the meaning of a sentence is not necessarily grasped from a knowledge of the dictionary meaning of the words. A few examples, however, may be given of the way in which sentences frequently produce an "implied" sense over and above what appears to be the literal sense. As Bhartṛhari's commentator points out, when a mother says, "The tiger eats little boys who cry," she does not in fact literally mean that there will follow an actual eating by a tiger. Rather she

[9] *Tractatus*, 4.12–4.1212.

[10] VP ii. 119, 145.

[11] VP ii. 146: *idaṃ tad iti sānyeṣam anākhyeyā kathaṃcana : pratyātmavṛttisiddhā sā kartrāpi na nirūpyate:* "This (*pratibhā*) cannot in any way be explained to others in terms such as 'It is this'; its existence is ratified only in the individual's experience of it, and the experiencer himself cannot describe it."

[12] Bhartṛhari points the analogy in a pair of verses (VP ii. 151, 152):—

svaravṛttiṃ vikurute
madhau puṃskokilasya kaḥ :
jantvādayaḥ kulāyādi-
karaṇe kena śikṣitāḥ.
āhāraprītyabhidveṣa-
plavanādikriyāsu kaḥ
jātyanvayaprasiddhāsu
prayoktā mṛgapakṣiṇām.

"Who alters the note of the cuckoo in spring? Who teaches the spider to weave its web? Who impels the birds and beasts in their eating and mating, in their enmities, or in their flight, and in all the other actions determined by heredity?" The commentator on the latter verse in fact uses the term *pratibhā*, where we should say "animal instinct" (*pratiprāṇyāhārādikriyā niyatānādipratibhāvaśāt*, "The actions of animals, eating, etc., differing from one animal to another, are determined by a beginningless *pratibhā*," i.e., a *pratibhā* which is not learnt).

means what is meant by the sentence, "Don't cry."[13] Similarly, if a traveller says to his companion, "We must go, look at the sun," the meaning conveyed is not simply that of looking at the sun, but rather that the companion should realize how late in the day it is.[14] Again, in response to the command, "See that the crows do not steal the butter," not even a child is so literal-minded as to interpret it to mean that he can allow the dogs to steal the butter.[15] Examples of this sort are a direct invitation to formulate a theory on the hypothesis that a sentence can be said to have a literal meaning. This is something which in our normal linguistic discussions we are very apt to take as axiomatic; but it will be apparent after what has been said that from Bhartṛhari's point of view it is more of the nature of a postulate which we ourselves lay down as the condition for constructing specific systematic statements, as a practical convenience in handling the material. For Bhartṛhari himself, the examples quoted above were probably simply further indications of the unsatisfactory nature of a theory depending upon word-meanings. But the commentator does in fact interpret them on the basis of metaphorical transfer of meanings (*lakṣaṇā*). This was the standard interpretation in later grammatical writings, and we find for example the explanation that "crows" in the sentence quoted stands metaphorically for "crows and other animals which might steal the butter."[16]

The theory of literal and metaphorical meaning was further extended in the 9th century by Ānandavardhana in the *Dhvanyāloka*. This is primarily a treatise on poetics; but as the basis of his aesthetic theory, the author carries out an elaborate analysis of poetic meaning. He had inherited from earlier theorists the distinction between primary and transferred or metaphorical senses of words (*abhidhā* and *lakṣaṇā*), and in addition to these he postulated a third potency of language which he called the capacity to imply or reveal a meaning other than the literal meaning (*vyañjanā*). The central term of the theory, namely *dhvani*, which has frequently been translated as suggestion, is said by Ānanda himself to be directly taken from the grammarians, though the relationship between his use of it and the use in grammar has perhaps been insufficiently clarified by modern writers. In brief, just as the sound of utterances (*dhvani* in the grammarians' sense) reveals the word (*sphoṭa*), so a poem is said to be *dhvani* when it reveals a meaning over and above the literal meaning and when the revealed or implied meaning has at the same time aesthetic value. In this theory we thus leave the more abstruse levels of philosophic linguistics, and come to more practical affairs, namely, the description and classification of meaning types as they occur in literature. Ānanda's work in fact seeks to unite the two traditions of the grammarians on the one hand and the formal rhetoricians on the other.

Ānanda's basic postulate is that utterances possess a literal meaning, and can also convey a further meaning. The scheme of classification which he adopts is fairly detailed and I can give only the outlines of it here. The main subdivision is into two types, first, the type where the literal sense is not intended (*avivakṣita-*

[13] Commentary to VP ii. 322: *yathā rudantaṃ vyāghro bhakṣayatīti bālasyocyate, na tatra vyāghrabhakṣaṇaṃ vastusthityā saṃbhavi, kevalaṃ mā kadācit tvaṃ rodīr iti rodananiṣedha eva tasya kriyate . . .*

[14] VP ii. 312.

[15] VP ii. 314: *kākebhyo rakṣyatāṃ sarpir iti bālo 'pi coditaḥ: upaghātapare vākye na śvādibhyo na rakṣati.*

[16] So far example Nāgeśa Bhaṭṭa, *Laghumañjūṣā*, p. 123 (*kākādi*).

vācya); and second, the type where the literal sense is in fact intended, but subserves the implied sense (*vivakṣitānyapara-vācya*). The first of these is again subdivided into two: the type where the literal sense is completely set aside (*atyantatiraskṛta-vācya*), and the type where the literal meaning is shifted (*arthāntarasaṃkramita-vācya*). The first of these embraces what we should normally call metaphor; but it is, so to speak, motivated metaphor, where the metaphorically used words are employed with the definite intention of conveying their associations, or producing a striking effect. The second sub-variety is an interesting one, and covers cases where a word is used in an enhanced or diminished sense. Edgerton[17] compares this with the "emphasis" of the classical western rhetoricians, quoting Quintilian's definition; though in fact the point of view here is somewhat different. Typical examples are, "Only when favoured by the rays of the sun are lotuses *lotuses*"; "Let men continue to give the moon as a simile for her face; none the less, in the final analysis, the poor moon is the *moon*."[18]

Of much greater interest is the second main subdivision, where the literal sense is intended. The chief type here is that where poetic emotion or mood (*rasa*) is conveyed. It is of great interest to see the term *artha* "meaning," enlarged to include all that is conveyed by a poem. In accordance with the grammarians' views on the unity of the sentence-meaning, the *dhvani*-theory to a large extent operates in terms of larger unities and not individual words. At the same time it is possible from another point of view to indicate that the operative factor in producing the overtones of the implied meaning may on occasion be a single word or phrase. Thus in one example an old hunter says to a tradesman who is seeking merchandise, "How can you expect us to have elephants tusks or tiger skins, so long as my daughter-in-law wanders about the house with dishevelled hair?" Here, says Ānanda, the *dhvani* arises not from the sentence as a whole, but from the phrase "dishevelled hair," since this indicates to the hearer that the hunter's son, who ought to be out hunting, is in fact spending his time in dalliance with his newly wedded wife.[19] Similarly, when in a drama the king Udayana is told that the queen has perished in a fire, he calls to mind in his anguish her beauty: "*Those* eyes of hers glancing wildly round in terror . . ." Here the word "those" heightens the emotion conveyed by the stanza and underlines for the sensitive audience the poignancy of the king's memories of very different circumstances.[20] But though it is reasonable for analysis to take account of features of this sort, Ānanda fully realizes that in other cases we must take the whole stanza,

[17] F. Edgerton, "Indirect Suggestion in Poetry: A Hindu Theory of Literary Aesthetics," *Proc. American Philosophical Society*, lxxvi, 1936, p. 700. Edgerton seems to imply that the whole of the *avivakṣita-vācya* category could be compared with *emphasis*, though in fact only the *arthāntarasaṃkramita* type is really analogous to the first of Quintilian's two varieties of *emphasis* (*Institutio*, viii, 3, 83 ff.).

[18] To bring out the idea, we can offer paraphrases such as "i.e., lotuses in the fullest sense of the word; lotuses with all the qualities of beauty which make them worth calling lotuses"; and in the second example, "i.e., *only* the moon and nothing else."

[19] *Dhvanyāloka*, iii. I, *vṛtti*.

[20] Ibid. iii. 4.

or even the whole poem, as instrumental in conveying the poetic meaning.[21]

The extant Sanskrit writings on linguistic theory and on rhetoric form a very extensive literature, and the foregoing account is necessarily a mere outline sketch of some of the most interesting aspects of the Indian theories. One important point which I should like to stress is the realization of the Sanskrit rhetoricians of the need for an explicitly formulated theory of language-meaning as a basis for a theory of poetics. Most philosophic discussions of meaning confine themselves to a relatively small portion of language behaviour, namely, statements which describe or report a state of affairs—the propositions of the natural sciences, or, more generally, such statements as are traditionally handled by logic. This part of language possesses enormous importance and prestige, and is also the least difficult to deal with in a more or less clear fashion. But its treatment frequently suffers from a forgetfulness of the fact that propositions (or the formulae of symbolic logic) are none the less language; and I would suggest that a wider linguistic understanding is most desirable, both for philosophy and for poetic theory. Of colloquial language, Wittgenstein remarks[22] that it is "a part of the human organism and not less complicated than it. The silent adjustments to understand colloquial language are enormously complicated." This is sufficient to dismiss the subject from the consideration of logic, and it is of course quite reasonable that the logician should limit his field in this way. The linguist however must include within his survey all types of language behaviour, from logic to literature. Wittgenstein's implication clearly is that logic can construct a logical language which can be understood without these "silent adjustments"; and it has frequently been claimed in modern times that the aim of logic should be the construction of syntactical rules which will prevent nonsense. I trust that the present paper will show that the former hope is certainly a vain illusion, and that the latter is probably so. Logic, mathematics, linguistics, science in general, all convey their messages in language, and this language, however technical, *cannot be understood* save in a manner which is fundamentally similar to the understanding of everyday language. As the ancient Indian might say, the utterances of the costermonger, the language of the great poet, and the formulae of the atomic physicist are all in some sense manifestations of the same divine Vāk.

[21] See the discussion in the early part of book iii (summed up in iii. 2), where the types of *dhvani* are classified as arising from individual sounds (*varṇa*), words (or parts of words, suffixes), sentences, "stylistic structure" (*saṃghāṭanā*, i.e. the style measured by the incidence of compound words), or the whole poem or epic.

[22] *Tractatus*, 4.002.

24

Yutaka Ojihara (born 1923)

Buddhism was officially introduced in Japan in the sixth century. Buddhist scholarship developed in its wake, and Sanskrit studies began to flourish within the larger framework of research on Indian Buddhism. While much information on India used to reach Japan through Chinese intermediaries, the eighteenth century brought a revival that broke away from this dependence. Though the Japanese interest has largely remained confined to Buddhist studies (just as the Indian interest itself remains largely confined to Brahmanical studies), Sanskrit scholarship has rapidly increased in depth and width ever since this time. Among non-Buddhist topics treated by Japanese Sanskritists, the Hindu philosophical systems rank first; these had in fact influenced Buddhist philosophy in India, and some had even become part of the Buddhist canon in China (for a general evaluation of Sanskrit and Indological studies in Japan, see Renou 1956a).

The leading contemporary Japanese expert on the Sanskrit grammarians is Yutaka Ojihara (born 1923), who studied in Philadelphia and Paris (with Louis Renou), and at the Bhandarkar Institute in Poona. He now teaches at Kyoto University. Ojihara has contributed a series of very careful specialized articles (including several translations) to Japanese journals, some of them written in Japanese, others in French. Among the latter are the "Causeries Vyākaraṇiques," I–IV, in different issues of the *Journal of Indian and Buddhist Studies* during the period from 1958 to 1967. Together with Louis Renou, Ojihara published two volumes of a translation of the first *pāda* of the *Kāśikā*; the third volume is by Ojihara alone.

The fourth of the "Causeries Vyākaraṇiques," "*Jāti* 'genus' et deux définitions pré-patañjaliennes," is reproduced here. It deals with a problem which led the grammarians to invoke two different notions of *jāti* 'genus, generic term.' In Sanskrit a *bahuvrīhi* compound may be formed to express "he whose wife (*bhāryā*) is a young girl (*kumārī*)" (in analyzed form: *kumārī bhāryā yasya*). Since the description itself refers to a man, the compound stem cannot have a feminine ending (as in *kumārī-bhāryā*) but must be provided with a masculine ending. The "masculinization" may be confined to the end of the compound (as in *kumārī-bhārya*), but it may also affect the ending of its first member (as in *kumāra-bhārya*). The two definitions of *jāti* are invoked to account for such alternatives.

Ojihara's study is reprinted, with the author's corrections, from the *Journal of Indian and Buddhist Studies* (16, 1967, 459–451 [Japanese reverse pagination]).

Jāti 'genus' et deux definitions pré-patañjaliennes (1967)

Yutaka Ojihara

Le mot *jāti* figure vingt trois fois au total dans la Grammaire de Pāṇini, et cela, à une seule exception près, manifestement au sens de "genre" ou "espèce."[1] Cet ètat de choses donnera en lui-même à présumer que les *śiṣṭa* "hommes de culture" de l'époque de Pāṇini étaient déjà familiers avec des éléments de logique plus ou moins élaborée. Quant au rôle capital que joue chez Patañjali le même mot dans ladite valeur, il ne serait guère opportun de le décrire ici dans tous ses détails. Bornons-nous à noter que, en posant la fameuse quadripartition des mots, Patañjali reconnaissait en *jāti* "genus" la première des quatre "causes de production (des mots)" '(*śabda*) *pravṛttinimitta*' bien que ce dernier terme tel quel soit d'origine post-patañjalienne.[2]

Ce n'est évidemment point à l'auteur de ces lignes, dont le souci habituel se concentre sur l'aspect "opératoire" de la Grammaire, qu'incombe la tâche d'exposer comment la notion de *jāti* "genus" allait revêtir une importance croissante, ceci sur le plan décidément philosophique, chez les théoriciens ultérieurs représentant diverses branches ou tendances de l'érudition indienne. Il sera, par contre, assurément de notre devoir de rappeler expressément que le plus ancien essai connu de définir le terme en question remonte à une époque pré-patañjalienne, étant attesté sous la forme de deux *kārikā* citées au début du Bh. ad 4. 1. 63.[3] Nous marquerons désormais par [A] et [B] respectivement, soit les deux *kārikā* elles-mêmes, soit les définitions qu'elles donnent du terme *jāti* tel qu'il est énoncé (JĀTEḤ à l'Ablatif) dans le sū. 4. 1. 63.[4] Voici maintenant le texte de la portion intéressée du Mahābhāṣya (éd. Kielhorn, II, 225, 13-21):—

JĀTER ity ucyate, kā jātir nāma / apara āha /

[A] '*ākṛtigrahaṇā jātir*
liṅgānāṃ ca na sarvabhāk /
sakṛdākhyātanirgrāhyā
gotraṃ ca caraṇaiḥ saha //'

[B] '*prādurbhāvavināśābhyāṃ*
sattvasya yugapad guṇaiḥ /
asarvaliṅgāṃ bahvarthāṃ
tāṃ jātiṃ kavayo viduḥ //'
gotraṃ ca caraṇāni ca //

kaḥ punar etayor jātilakṣaṇayor viśeṣaḥ/ yathā pūrvaṃ jātilakṣaṇam* (A). *tathā* kumārībhārya *iti bhavitavyam/ yathôttaraṃ* (B). *tathā* kumārabhārya *iti bhavitavyam //

[1] Cf. O. Böhtlingk, *Pāṇini's Grammatik* (Leipzig, 1887²), p. 232*, s. u. *jāti* La seule exception est JĀTYANTĀT dans le sū. 5. 4. 9: il s'agit ici du mot *jāti*- pris en tant que pure forme.

[2] Bh. ad praty.-sū. 2 vt. 1 (éd. Kielhorn, I, 19, 20 sq.): *catuṣṭayī śabdānāṃ pravṛttiḥ. jātiśabdā guṇaśabdāḥ kriyāśabdā yadṛcchāśabdāś caturthāḥ.*

[3] Le fait n'a que peu retenu, semble-t-il, l'attention des spécialistes modernes de la philosophie indienne du langage (d'autant moins peut-être que Bhartṛhari, pas davantage que Helarāja, ne reprend ces *kārikā* dans son "*jātisamuddeśa*", ainsi que s'intitule le chapitre initial du 3e *kāṇḍa*, "*pada-k*°" ou "*prakīrṇaka-k*°", du Vākyapadīya). Parmi les plus récents ouvrages, on ne trouve aucune référence à ces *kārikā* chez MM. D. Seyfort Ruegg, B. Bhattacharya, R. C. Pandeya et Kunjunni Raja; une référence chez Mlle M. Biardeau, v. ci-dessous n. 5; une référence chez M. H. Scharfe, v. ibid.

[4] Sū. 4. 1. 63: JĀTER ASTRĪVIṢAYĀD AYOPADHĀT // (ATAH 4) (PRĀTIPADIKĀT 1) (STRIYĀM 3) (ṄĪṢ 40).— La mention médiane du sū. soulève un problème extrêmement compliqué: cf. notre *Sur l'énoncé pāṇinéen ASTRĪVIṢAYA* (4. 1. 63) : *deux interprétations et leur rapport avec le Gaṇapāṭha* (*Adyar Library Bulletin, vols.* 31–32=V. *Raghavan Felicitation Volume*, p. 125 sqq.)

Nous estimons aussi de notre devoir de présenter ici un nouvel essai de traduction des *kārikā*, d'autant plus que les traducteurs qui nous ont précédé ne semblent pas en avoir saisi la portée implicite compte tenu de l'observation terminale de Patañjali,[5] où, doivent entrer en jeu des considérations bel et bien "opératoires."

Définition (A)[6]: "Est une *jāti*: (1°) ce dont la compréhension surgit en fonction d'une forme corporelle (déterminée)[7]; (2°) ce qui (a) n'est pas susceptible de (valoir à travers) la totalité des (trois) genres (grammaticaux)[8] et qui, (b) une fois (qu'on l'a) signalé nommément (, à titre d'instruction, par référence à, un individu donné), (nous) est (désormais) reconnaissable (sur d'autres

[5] Il n'existe à notre connaissance que deux essais de traduction savante des *kārikā*:

1° L. Renou, *Terminologie grammaticale du sanskrit* (Paris, 1942), p. 148: [A] "ce qui se laisse percevoir par sa forme (*ākṛti*; ou comprendre comme forme N.), ce qui ne participe pas à tous les genres (= n'est pas un adjectif), se laisse sitôt énoncé reconnaître (en d'autres individus Pr.), et (désigne en particulier) la famille (*gotra*) ainsi que les sectes (*caraṇa*)" . . . [B] "ce qui fait apparaître et disparaître l'objet, est en connexion avec les qualités en même temps (qu'avec l'objet), ne comporte pas tous les genres, a des sens multiples (atteignant tous individus Pr.)".

2° M. Biardeau, *Théorie de la connaissance et philosophie de la parole dans le brahmanisme classique* (Paris, La Haye, 1964), p. 48: [A] "La *jāti*, c'est ce que fait appréhender l'*ākṛti*, et elle ne participe pas de tous les genres (grammaticaux). Reconnue après avoir été éconcée une seule fois, elle est aussi le *gotra* et les différentes écoles védiques". . . . [B] "Du fait que chaque être individuel apparaît et disparaît en même temps que ses qualités, les poètes savent que la *jāti* comporte une multiplicité d'objets".

H. Scharfe, *Die Logik im Mahābhāṣya* (Berlin, 1961), p. 141 se contente de reproduire la traduction Renou—'wegen ihrer [=zwei Zitatverse] Schwierigkeit', dit-il.

[6] La *kārikā* [A] se retrouve citée et commentée non seulement, comme il va de soi, dans les deux sous-comm(entaires) du Mahābhāṣya, à savoir Pr(adīpa) de Kaiyaṭa et Ud(dyota) de Nāgeśa, mais dans plusieurs autres ouvrages: ainsi, pour ne nommer que ceux que nous avons consultés, la Kāśikā sous 4. 1. 63 et le N(yāsa) ad loc.; la S(iddhānta) K(aumudī) 518 avec ses sous-comm., notamment le Laghuś(abdenduśekhara) de Nāgeśa et la B(āla)M(anoramā); le Śabdakalpadruma (s.u. *jāti*) contenant une très utile citation de Durgādāsa, grammairien du début 17e s. (citation puisée de toute évidence à sa "*Subodhā*", comm. sur le Mugdhabodha de Vopadeva: cf. Aufrecht, *Cat. Cat.*, I, p. 256); le Nyāyakośa (s.u., la *kārikā* n'étant d'ailleurs expliquée qu'en partie). Ces textes, toutefois, ne laissent sentir la divergence des opinions que sur le deux points signalés ci-dessous nn. 9 et 10, si bien que, dans les notes qui suivent, nous n'indiquons en principe que celle d'entre les gloses indigènes qui constitue la source la plus directe du passage concerné de notre article.

[7] '*ākṛtigrahaṇā*' = *avayavasaṃniveśaviśeṣavyaṅgyā* (Pr.) A côté d'*avayavasaṃniveśa*, le mot *saṃsthāna* est employé non moins souvent pour gloser '*ākṛti*'.

Il semble que, en ce qui concerne un animal, seul passe pour un *avayava* ce qui fait partie de son ossature: les deux cornes sont censées être des *avayava* d'une vache, ayant donc rapport à l'*ākṛti* de cette dernière, alors que nos cheveux sont considérés comme choses extérieures n'affectant point notre *ākṛti* (cf. ci-dessous nn. 17 et 22). Ainsi donc, nous rendons '*ākṛti*' délibérément par "forme corporelle".

Les auteurs ultérieurs citent surtout souvent ce premier quart de la *kārikā* [A], en le rapprochant non sans raison du Nyāya Sūtra 2. 2. 67: '*ākṛtir jātiliṅgākhyā*'.

[8] '*liṅgānāṃ na sarvabhāk*' = (scil. *yā*) *sarvāṇi liṅgāni na bhajate* (N.).

individus)[9]; ou encore, (3°) une appellation patronymique conjointement à (chacune des appellations des) diverses écoles de science sacrée,[10]

Définition (B)[11]: (1°) "Ce qui (a) (, bien qu'étant d'existence pérenne, se manifeste et se cache) à mesure que naît et périt une substance (donnée, tout en s'unissant à cette dernière) en même temps que diverses qualités (s'y unissent comme on le sait),[12] qui (b) n'assume pas tous les (trois) genres (grammaticaux), et qui (c) vise à plusieurs (individus de manière à en être concomitant),[13] c'est là ce que les sages comprennent sous le nom de *jāti*" — (2°) (il faut comprendre,) en outre, une appellation patronymique, et (chacune des appellations des) diverses écoles de science sacrée.

La définition [A] est tripartite:[14] la clause [1°] détermine la notion de *jāti* proprement dite de telle façon que, pour peu qu'il satisfasse la présente condition, un mot donné s'intitulera un "nom générique" (*jātiśabda*) sans qu'il y ait plus à considérer s'il satisfera ou non les conditions ultérieures (notamment [2°a]); la clause [2°] a pour effet de réhabiliter au rang de *jāti*, ceci sous la double condition [a + b], les mots qui ont été éliminés par [1°][15]; la clause [3°] réhabilite encore, à titre d'ailleurs nettement accessoire, certains d'entre les mots qui ont été éliminés à deux

[9] '*sakṛdākhyātanirgrāhyā*' = *ekasyāṃ vyaktau kathanād vyaktyantare kathanaṃ vinâpi sugrahā* (SK.).

D'après Durgādāsa (cf. ci-dessus n. 6), ainsi que le N. du moins en puissance, la présente teneur se rattache aussi à la clause [1°], d'une manière d'ailleurs toute différente de celle dont elle fait partie de la clause [2°]. Śabdakalpadruma (s.u. *jāti*): . . . *ajñātahaṃsasya haṃsaṃ dṛṣṭavato 'pi tasya saṃsthānena haṃsatvaṃ vyañjituṃ na śakyate, iti haṃsasyâpi jātitvaṃ nâyātam iti pūrvalakṣaṇasya doṣaḥ. evam . . . iti dvitīyalakṣaṇasya doṣaḥ. iti doṣadvayam apākartuṃ dvayor lakṣaṇayor viśeṣaṇam āha* sakṛd. . .*iti*. . .*tena, īdṛśo haṃsa ity upadeśe haṃsaṃ dṛṣṭavatas tasya saṃsthānena haṃsatvaṃ vyañjituṃ śakyata evêti pūrvalakṣaṇasya na doṣaḥ*.

[10] '*gotraṃ caraṇaiḥ saha*' = *apatyapratyayāntaḥ śākhādhyetṛvācī ca śabdaḥ* (SK.). Pour ce que la glose *adhyetṛ* implique au sujet de '*caraṇa*', cf. ci-dessous n. 26. Le terme '*gotra*' est à prendre ici dans sa valeur "courante", signifiant donc '*apatya(mātra)*'. Le seul dissident, à ce dernier propos, est Nāgeśa dans son Laghuś., qui veut même ici la valeur "technique" du terme. Pour l'opposition *laukikagotra/pāribhāṣikagotra*, cf. notre *Kāśikā-Vṛtti (adhyāya I, pāda 1) traduite et commentée*, 3e partie (Paris, 1967), p. 108, n. 13.

[11] A part Pr. et Ud., le Laghuś. est le seul à commenter la *kārikā* [B] parmi les oeuvres nommées ci-dessus n. 6.

[12] '*prādurbhāvavināśābhyāṃ sattvasya*' = *sattvasya* [=] *dravyasya prādurbhāvavināśābhyāṃ yāvirbhāvatirobhāvau prāpnoti. yâvaddravyabhāvinîty arthaḥ* (Pr.). āvirbhāvêtyādi. *nityatvād utpattivināśāsaṃbhavād evam uktam* (Ud.).

'*yugapad guṇaiḥ*' = *guṇair yugapad* (scil. *yā*) *dravyeṇa saṃbadhyate. yathā nirguṇasya dravyasyôpalambho na bhavati, evaṃ jātirahitasya* (scil. *dravyasya*) *apîty arthaḥ* (Pr.).

L'essence de la clause réside dans la première moitié de la teneur, par contraste avec la moitié restante qui ne constitue qu'une constatation explicative. Ud.: *guṇair iti. idam atra lakṣaṇe svarūpakathanam eva.*

[13] '*bahvarthām*' = *sarvavyaktivyāpinīm . . . arthaśabdo 'tra viṣayavācī* (Pr.) viṣayavācîti . . . *jātyāśrayatvād vyaktīnāṃ viṣayatvoktiḥ* (Ud.).

[14] BM.: . . . *iti cet, na* [!] . . . *bhāṣyoktatrividhajāter vivakṣitatvād — ity abhipretya bhāṣyoktatraividhyaṃ prapañcayati* — ākṛtigrahaṇā jātir *iti, prathamêti śeṣaḥ* . . .

[15] Pr.: *aprāptaprāpaṇārthaṃ cêdaṃ vacanam.* Ud.: *pūrveṇa* (scil. *vacanena*) *yatrâprāptaṃ jātitvaṃ, tadartham idam* (scil. *vacanam*) *ity arthaḥ*.

reprises par [1°] et par [2°]. La définition [B] est bipartite si l'on y intègre la clause complémentaire [2°], due peut-être à Patañjali lui-même (et de fait identique à [A 3°]) : la clause [1°], propre à la *kārikā* et remarquable par son étendue, vise à unifier deux clauses distinctes dans l'autre définition, à savoir [A 1°] et [A 2°], en sorte qu'un mot donné passera pour être un "nom générique" s'il satifait à la fois la triple condition [a + b + c], dont le terme essentiel, malgré sa teneur trop elliptique pour ne pas être obscure, est évidemment [a], surtout sa première moitié[16] (tandis que, en substance, [b] ne diffère pas de [A 2° a], ni [c] de [A 2° b]). Illustrons maintenant comment fonctionnent l'une et l'autre définition.

Définition (A):

[1°] légitime comme "nom générique" *go* "vache", étant donné une "forme corporelle" spécifique (caractérisée par deux cornes, etc.)[17]; *taṭa* "rivage" pour la même raison, ceci sans tenir compte de [2° a], càd., que le mot vaille ou non à travers les trois genres grammaticaux (cf. ci-dessous [B 1°][18]).

[2°] légitime comme "nom générique" *brāhmaṇa* "brâhmane', mot qui, bien qu'éliminé par [1°] (la "forme corporelle" dont il s'agit n'étant pas autre chose que celle d'un être humain quelconque),[19] satisfait [a] par l'absence de genre nt.,[20] ainsi que [b] du fait que l'état de brâhmane, signalé sur un individu donné, ne manquera jamais de s'appliquer, sinon à ses enfants (qui peuvent être d'une caste mixte), du moins, à ses parents, grands-parents, etc.[21]

Un nom de qualité ou adjectif (*guṇaśabda*), ainsi *muṇḍa* "chauve," est éliminé, non seulement par [1°] (la "forme corporelle" de ce dont il est question n'étant pas changée par l'absence ou la pousse des cheveux),[22] mais aussi par [2°] — ceci à défaut de satisfaire [a].[23] Ce n'est donc pas un "nom générique."

Un nom propre (*saṃjñāśabda*), ainsi *Devadatta*, est éliminé, non seulement par [1°] (pour la même raison que celle notée ci-dessus pour *brāhmaṇa*), mais aussi par [2°] — ceci à défaut de satisfaire [b].[24] Ce n'est donc pas un "nom générique," sauf là où s'applique [3°].

[3°] légitime comme "nom générique" *Aupagava*, nom patronymique d'*Upagu*, tiré avec le suffixe [aṇ] *-a-* selon 4. 1. 83 et 92[25]; *Kaṭha*, nom d'un des *caraṇa yajurvedin*.[26]

16 Cf. ci-dessus n. 12, in fine.
17 N.: *gotvâdayo hi viṣāṇâdimatsaṃsthānavyaṅgyatvād ākṛtigrahaṇāḥ.*
18 BM.: *jalasamīpapradeśa ākṛtiviśiṣṭas taṭaḥ, atas taṭatvam ākṛtivyaṅgyatvāj jātiḥ.*
19 N.: *etena lakṣaṇena brāhmaṇatvâdayo jātiviśeṣā na saṃgṛhītāḥ. na hi te saṃsthānavyaṅgyāḥ. . . yādṛśam hi saṃsthānaṃ brāhmaṇasya, kṣatriyâdeḥ saṃsthānam api tādṛśam eva. . .*
20 Ceci conformément à Amara 3. 5. 37: '*strīpuṃsayor . . . dvicatuḥṣaṭpadoragāḥ*'.
21 BM.: *brāhmaṇatvaṃ tu putrapautrâdau yady api na sugamam — brāhmaṇāt kṣatriyâyām utpannasya brāhmaṇatvâbhāvāt* (scil. *kiṃ tu mūrdhâvasiktatvāt*)—, *tathâpi pitrâdau sugamam eva.*
22 BM.: *muṇḍatvaṃ nāma viluptasarvakeśatvam. tat tu nâkṛtivyaṅgyam, keśadaśāyām api tadākṛteḥ sattvāt.*
23 BM.: *sarvaliṅgatvāt*. Le mot, en effet, est attesté assez souvent au nt., comme dans *śiro muṇḍam*.
24 Ud.: *na devadattatvaṃ kvacit piṇḍântare pratīyate. yady api piṇḍântarasya devadatta iti saṃjñā, tathâpi vācakasādṛśyam eva, na tv arthasādṛśyaṃ tatra pratīyate.*

Définition [B]:

[1°] légitime d'un seul coup *go* et *brāhmaṇa* chacun comme "nom générique," [a] étant évidemment satisfait de part et d'autre, aussi bien que [b] (= [A 2°a], v. ci-dessus); le genre nt. fait défaut également à *go*) et [c] (= [A 2°b], v. ci-dessus); de même, *taṭa* malgré le triple genre assigné au mot (depuis Amara 1. 9. 7) — ceci du fait ou bien que la condition [b] n'est que de nature approximative (*prāyika*), ou bien que ledit triple genre (notamment, la reconnaissance de *taṭa-* nt.) n'est dû, qu'à une erreur chez des lexicographes.[27]

Les noms propres sont définitivement éliminés par [1°], à défaut de satisfaire [c] (= [A 2°b], v. ci-dessus) — exception faite d'ailleurs de ceux d'entre eux qui font l'objet de [2°] (= [A 3°], v. ci-dessus); les adjectifs le sont également, ceci à défaut de satisfaire [b] (=[A 2°a], v. ci-dessus).

Tout cela veut-il dire que l'une et l'autre définition mènent partout à un même résultat? La réponse doit être négative, puisque Patañjali nous y contraint par sa remarque terminale (d'ailleurs fort énigmatique). Considérons le cas mis en cause, celui du mot *kumāra* "jeune homme," à la lumière des deux définitions:

Voici un "nom générique" suivant la définition [A], le mot s'accommodant avec la clause capitale [1°] du fait que la jeunesse est bel et bien dotée d'une "forme corporelle" spécifique, caractérisée par la finesse dans l'ensemble des membres.[28]

A en juger par la définition [B], ce n'est pas là un "nom générique" — ceci à défaut de satisfaire [1°a], en ce sens que la jeunesse n'est pas du tout de nature à se manifester aussi longtemps que dure telle ou telle "substance" ('*sattva*' = *dravya*[29]).

Voilà donc au moins un cas de divergence entre les deux définitions de *jāti*, et cette divergence n'ira pas sans se répercuter, le cas échéant, sur le plan "opératoire":

Au mot *kumāra-*, conçu comme "nom générique" suivant la

[25] Le mot est éliminé par [2°], ceci non pas en raison de [b], qu'il pourra satisfaire d'une façon analogue à celle notée plus haut pour *brāhmaṇa*, mais du moins en raison de [a]: un mot patronymique s'emploie bel et bien même au nt., ainsi *aupagavaṃ kulam*. Cf. Amara 3. 5. 45 sq.: '*aṇādyantās . . . triṣu*'.

[26] A en juger par certaines observations indigènes, il n'est plus question ici, semble-t-il, de discuter comment le mot sera éliminé tant par [1°] que par [2°]. Le mot en cause n'est, strictement parlant, pas la même chose que le nom du Sage *Kaṭha* mais, il en est un dérivé lointain, réalisé en passant par 4. 3. (104 et) 107 ainsi que 4. 2. (59 et) 64, le sens littéral étant donc "celui qui récite le texte promulgué par (le Sage) *Kaṭha*" (Laghuś.); se rapportant ainsi à l'action de réciter sur le plan de sa "cause de production", le mot est par définition un *kriyāśabda* et non un *jātiśabda* (N. = Durgādāsa), et ce n'est que grâce à la mention '*caraṇaiḥ saha*' dans la présente définition de *jāti*, que lui sera transférée la qualité de "mot générique" (Laghuś.).—N.: *caraṇaśabdas tv adhyayanakriyāsaṃbandhena pravṛttatvāt kriyāśabda eva [na tu] jātiśabda ity atas tadarthasya jātitvapratipādanāya* caraṇaih sahêty *uktam*. Ajouter les éléments mis entre crochets au texte, éd. Chakravarti, I, 862, 16.

[27] Laghuś.: *liṅgānāṃ ca na sarvabhāk* [A 2°a] *iti . . .tac ca prāyikam iti kecit. . . .taṭaṃ triṣu* [Amara 1. 9. 7] *ityādi kośakṛtāṃ pramādaḥ, ity anye.*

[28] Pr.: *kaumāram. . .ākṛtigrahaṇatvāj jātir. . .* Ud.: ākṛtigrahaṇatvād *iti. bālyagatasūkṣmâvayavasaṃniveśasya sarvatraîkajātīyatvād iti bhāvaḥ.*

[29] Pr.: *uttare tu lakṣaṇe kaumāraṃ jātir na bhavati, ayāvaddravyabhāvitvāt.*

définition [A], s'appliquera comme de juste le suffixe fém. [ṅīṣ] -ī- selon le sū. 4. 1. 63 (en raison de l'énoncé JĀTEḤ), d'où le dérivé fém. *kumārī-* "jeune fille" (en liaison avec 6, 4. 148): spécifions cette dernière forme comme *kumārī*-[A].

A la même base, estimée toutefois non "générique" suivant la définition [B], le suffixe fém. applicable ne sera plus le suffixe [ṅīṣ] 4. 1. 63 (à défaut de satisfaire JĀTEḤ), mais le [ṅīp] -ī- que le sū. 4. 1. 20 enseigne pour une base notant le "premier âge" (VAYASI PRATHAME), d'où, *kumārī-* au fém. (comme précédemment): mettons ici *kumārī*-[B].

Aucune différence,[30] protestera-t-on sans doute. Mais qu'on garde présent à l'esprit ce fait d'importance capitale, à savoir que *kumārī*-[A] est un "nom générique" tandis que *kumārī*-[B] ne l'est point.

Or, lorsqu'il s'agira de former selon 2.2.24 un composé *bahuvrīhi* correspondant à l'expression analytique '*kumārī bhāryā yasya*' "celui qui a pour épouse une jeune fille (avant la puberté)," il y aura certes lieu d'étudier comment la forme provisoire *kumārī-bhāryā-* va être affectée par la "masculinisation" (*puṃvadbhāva*) dont traite la section 6. 3. 34-42. Le mot fém. *kumārī-*, étant ici apposé à l'autre fém. *bhāryā*-qui suit, fera-t-il bien l'objet du sū. 6. 3. 34 enjoignant la "masculinisation" précisément pour un tel élément?[31] Mais attention! — cette "masculinisation" sera prohibée à son tour par le sū 6. 3. 41, quand le mot fém. en question est un "nom générique.[32] C'est dire que tout dépend maintenant de la nature du fém. *kumārī-*:

S'agit-il ici de *kumārī*-[A], "nom générique"? Alors, c'est la règle négative 6. 3. 41 qui doit entrer ici en vigueur de manière à entraver la "masculinisation" selon 6. 3. 34: *kumāri-bhāryā-* passe à *kumārī-bhārya-* par application du sū. 1. 2. 48 tout seul.

S'agit-il de *kumārī*-[B], qui n'est pas un "nom générique"? La "masculinisation" selon 6. 3. 34 doit alors y prendre effet, sans que la prohibition posée par 6. 3. 41 intervienne en aucune manière: *kumārī-bhāryā-* passe à *kumāra-bhāryā-* d'abord, puis à *kumāra-bhārya-* selon 1. 2. 48.

Nous voici parvenu, espérons-nous, à éclaircir toute la section intéressée du 4. 1. 63 Bh. Il ne restera qu'à savoir, à titre d'épilogue, si Patañjali portait ou non sa préférence tacite à l'une ou à l'autre de ces deux définitions de *jāti*.

Rappelons, tout d'abord, que ce qui a été observé ci-dessus concernant le mot *kumāra-* (fém. *kumārī-*) vaut aussi bien pour le mot *yuvan-* "jeune" (fém. *yuvati-*, selon 4. 1. 77 en liaison avec 1. 4. 17 et 8. 2. 7), dans la mesure où il est dit d'un être humain.[33]

Or, Patañjali lui-même cite, dans son Bh. ad 4. 1. 1 vt. 19 (éd. Kielhorn, II, 195, 7), la forme *yuvatitarā-* ou la base présuffixale

[30] Ceci même au point de vue accentuel: *kumārī́*-[A], le ton suffixal -ī́- dû à 3. 1. 3 étant seul maintenu selon 6. 1. 158 (et vt. 9 ad loc.); *kumārī́*-[B] = *kumār°'*,-ī-[*kumārá-ī-*, le [ṅīp] -ī- étant atone selon 3. 1. 4, tandis que l'uṇādi-sū. 418 (numérotation d'après SK.) fait valoir l'oxyton *kumārá-* en tant que nom d'agent dérivé de *kam-* "briller" (!).

[31] Sū. 6. 3. 34: STRIYĀḤPUṂVAD. . . SAMĀNĀDHIKARAṆE STRIYĀM . . . // (UTTARAPADE 1.).

[32] Sū. 6. 3. 41: JĀTEŚ CA// (STRIYĀḤ PUṂVAD 34) (NA 37).

[33] Noter toutefois que ces deux mots ne sont pas tout à fait synonymes, *yuvan* appartenant à un stade de maturité plus avancée que *kumāra*: '*mṛdusaṃsthānavyaṅgyā kumāratva-jātiḥ, kaṭhinasaṃsthānavyaṅgyā yuvatvajātiḥ*', ainsi qu'il est dit dans un sous-comm. du Laghuś.

yuvati- se trouve maintenue à l'abri de la "masculinisation" selon 6. 3. 35[34] — ceci, force nous est de l'entendre, par l'application à *yuvati-* de la règle prohibitive 6. 3. 41 portant sur un "nom générique" fém.: autrement dit, la définition [A] de *jāti* est sous-jacente au présent emploi patañjalien. S'il en est ainsi, va-t-on conclure avec Kaiyaṭa que Patañjali était partisan implicite de la définition [A]?[35]

Non, déclare Nāgeśa: qu'on n'ignore pas un autre emploi patañjalien, qui va précisément à l'encontre d'une telle conclusion: à savoir la forme *yuvajāni-* qui figure dans le Bh. ad 1. 1. 57 (éd. Kielhorn, I, 142, 11 sq.) en tant que composé *bahuvrīhi* représentant '*yuvatir jāyā yasya*,[36] et qui doit présupposer la définition [B] de *jāti*, puisque la "masculinisation" 6. 3. 34 s'est bel et bien effectuée sur le membre antérieur *yuvati-*, au mépris total de la prohibition 6. 3. 41 portant sur un "nom générique" fém. La conclusion de Nāgeśa est que, étant donné ces deux témoignages contradictoires émanant d'un même maître Patañjali, les deux définitions de *jāti*, [A] et [B], sont à estimer égales en autorité.[37] *

[34] Sū. 6. 3. 35: TASILĀDIṢV Ā KṚTVA=SUCAḤ// (STRIYĀḤ PUṂVAD . . . 34). Le suffixe comparatif *-tara-*, [tarap] 5. 3. 57, est enjoint certes dans les limites inclusives 5, 3, 7 (enseignant [tasil] *-tas*) — 5. 4. 17 (einseignant [kṛtvasuc] *-kṛtvas*).

[35] Pr.: *pūrvoktam eva lakṣaṇaṃ bhāṣyakārasyâbhimatam. . .tathā ca* yuvatitarā *iti* ṄYĀP *sūtra udāharaṇaṃ dadau*, TASILÀDIṢU *iti prāptasya puṃvadbhāvasya* JĀTEŚ CA *iti niṣedhāt.*

[36] Le passage de °*jāyā* -à °*jāni-* s'explique par 5. 4. 134 et 6. 1. 66.

[37] Ud.: *vastutas tu lakṣaṇadvayapraṇetṛkarṣidvayaprāmāṇyāj jātikāryasya yuvaśabdādau vikalpaḥ. ata eva* yuvajāniḥ (*ity atra puṃvattvam*, Laghuś.), yuvatitarā (*ity atra tadabhāvaś ca*, ibid.) *ityādau dvividham apy anuṣṭhānaṃ bhagavataḥ.*

* Nos plus vifs remerciements sont dus à M. Jacques May pour avoir donné tous ses soins à mettre au point la présente rédaction française.

25

Louis Renou (1896–1966)

This selection of readings is completed with some specimens of the work of Louis Renou (1896–1966), the late Professor of Sanskrit at the Sorbonne, who was not only the greatest Western Sanskritist of the last decades (and "the most complete Sanskritist," as V. Raghavan aptly called him: 1956, 20) but also the leading expert on the Sanskrit grammarians. Renou, who had studied with Sylvain Lévi, contributed to all branches of Sanskrit and Indology (see Filliozat 1967a and 1967b for an evaluation of his work and for a bibliography). In the field of *vyākaraṇa* he published and translated a very technical text of the twelfth century, Śaraṇadeva's *Durghaṭavṛtti* (in two volumes, each in three fascicles, 1940–1956). He published a dictionary in two parts, one dealing with *vyākaraṇa* and the other with the Vedic linguistic treatises: *Terminologie grammaticale du sanskrit* (1942; 1957[2] cf. Thieme 1958). This finally fulfilled Schlegel's wish (see page 57), though it was in fact preceded by Hamilton's booklet of 1814 (see page 54). He brought out a new translation of Pāṇini (1948–1954; re-edited together with the text of the *sūtras*: 1961; cf. Thieme 1956), largely based upon the interpretations of the *Kāśikā* and of Puruṣottamadeva's *Bhāṣāvṛtti* (twelfth century). He translated, together with Ojihara, the beginning of the *Kāśikā*.

Apart from these major publications, Renou published numerous important monographs, smaller studies, and articles. Basic information and references are contained in three contributions which provide together the best introduction presently available to the study of the Sanskrit grammarians: (1) the Introduction to the *Durghaṭavṛtti* (1940); (2) Section VII of the "Introduction générale," an annotated re-edition in French of the *Einleitung* of Wackernagel's *Altindische Grammatik* (1957); and (3) the article "Pāṇini" in *Current Trends in Linguistics*, volume 5 (1969). Renou also completed two series of studies: *Études pāṇinéennes* (five articles in the *Journal asiatique* in 1953 and 1956) and *Études védiques et pāṇinéennes* (16 volumes, 1955–1967).

It is clear from this incomplete sketch that it is difficult to make a representative selection from Renou's work on the Indian grammarians. Four articles will be republished here. Renou devoted a number of studies to the place which the *vyākaraṇa* occupies in the whole of Sanskrit technical and scholarly literature. Since few have been as qualified as Renou to cover authoritatively so wide an area, and since this volume has so far concentrated mainly on the Sanskrit grammarians themselves without effectively showing what an important role they played in Indian culture and civilization, three of these not primarily historical but conceptual and comparative studies, are included. They relate to ritual studies, philosophy, and poetics, respectively. The fourth article deals directly with Pāṇini's treatment of a grammatical topic.

In all his work Renou made use of numerous abbreviations. Those with which only Sanskritists may be expected to be familiar are in the list of abbreviations on pages xxii–xxv.

The first and longest of Renou's comparative studies on grammar is devoted to the ritual. We have seen on page 90 that Patañjali compared grammatical rules for forms that are not in use with the rules framed by the ritualists for the performance of sacrificial rites that are in fact never performed. Indeed, the existence of the Sanskrit grammatical tradition would be wholly unintelligible without the equally unparalleled background of the Vedic ritual. In the following study, Renou relates the analysis of grammar to the practice of Veda recitation; shows how the concept of *sūtra* 'rule' is used in ritual and grammatical texts and how the concept of *paribhāṣā* 'metarule' arose; studies the use of a number of technical expressions in ritual and grammatical *sūtras*; and finds parallels in the ritual literature for many of the basic concepts and terms of grammar.

Renou's article bristles with names and references to this ritual literature, which is vast and complex. A brief sketch of the structure of this collection of texts may therefore be in order. The four Vedas themselves—Ṛgveda (RV), Yajurveda (YV), Sāmaveda (SV), Atharvaveda (AV)—are subdivided into various schools or recensions, many of which have developed around a corpus of four collections of texts: the *saṃhitā* (S) consisting mainly of hymns and ritual formulas (*mantras*); the *brāhmaṇa* (B) consisting mainly of prose interpretations of the *saṃhitā*, often from a ritualistic perspective; the *āraṇyaka* (Ā), appendixes to the former; and the *upaniṣads* (U), further appendixes tending toward more general speculation. Each of the schools possesses technical texts in *sūtra* form which describe the ritual in precise detail. The most fundamental among these are the *śrautasūtras* (ŚS), dealing with public ceremonies. Next come the *gṛhyasūtras* (GS), dealing with domestic ritual. Next come a variety of texts, for example, the *dharmasūtras* (DS), relating to religious law, or the *prātiśākhyas* (Pr), dealing with recitation, pronunciation, and phonetics of the particular Vedic school to which they belong. The following table provides a simplified outline of the main names.

Many of the *sūtra* texts belong to the period 500–200 B.C. (cf. Liebich's conclusions with regard to *Pāraskara-* and *Āśvalāyanagṛhyasūtra*, page 158). Ritualism developed later into a full-fledged system of philosophy, the *Mīmāṃsā* (see page 286).

Renou reverted several times to the topics treated in the following study, last perhaps in "Sur le genre du *sūtra* dans la littérature sanskrite," *Journal asiatique* (251, 1963, 165–216). The article reproduced here is "Les Connexions entre le rituel et la grammaire en sanskrit," *Journal asiatique* (233, 1941–1942, 105–165).

Table 1. The Four Vedas and Their Subdivisions.

Veda	Saṃhitā	Brāhmaṇa	Āraṇyaka	Upaniṣad	Śrautasūtra	Gṛhyasūtra	Prātiśākhya
Ṛgveda	Ṛk	Aitareya	Aitareya	Aitareya	Āśvalāyana	Aśvalāyana	Ṛk
		Kauṣītaki	Kauṣītaki	Kauṣītaki	Śāṅkhāyana	Śāṅkhāyana	
Yajurveda	Taittirīya	Taittirīya	Taittirīya	Taittirīya	Baudhāyana	Baudhāyana	Taittirīya
(black)					Bhāradvāja	Bhāradvāja	
					Āpastamba	Āpastamba	
					Hiraṇyakeśin	Hiraṇyakeśin	
	Kāṭhaka-	Kaṭha	Kaṭha	Kaṭha	Kāṭhaka	Kāṭhaka	
	Maitrāyaṇi			Maitri	Mānava	Mānava	
(white)	Vājasaneyi	Śatapatha	Śatapatha	Bṛhadāraṇyaka	Kātyāyana	Pāraskara	Vājasaneyi
Sāmaveda	Kauthuma-	Pañcaviṃśa		Chāndogya	Lāṭyāyana	Gobhila	Ṛktantra
	Rāṇāyanīya	Ṣaḍviṃśa			Drāhyāyana	Drāhyāyana	Puṣpasūtra
	Jaiminīya	Jaiminīya		Kena	Jaiminīya	Jaiminīya	Pañcavidha
Atharvaveda	Atharva	Gopatha		Muṇḍaka, etc.	Vaitāna	Kauśika	Atharva

A. Les Connexions entre le rituel et la grammaire en sanskrit (1941-1942)

Louis Renou

Si la datation de la grammaire de Pāṇini[1] demeure aujourd'hui encore incertaine, malgré les efforts qui ont été faits depuis longtemps pour la fixer,[2] en revanche la situation de ce texte relativement à la littérature indienne en général ne laisse guère de place au doute. On a eu depuis longtemps le sentiment,[3] et plus précisément depuis les travaux de Liebich,[4] que la description pāṇinéenne s'applique à un état de langue qui, en littérature, est représenté au plus près par les traités du rituel domestique. On peut dire: du rituel en général, si l'on élimine dans les Sūtra du culte solennel les archaïsmes nombreux, provenant des *mantra* qu'ils recèlent, dans les *dharmasūtra* les vulgarismes ou dialectismes qui ont porté à croire que certains de ces traités échappaient à la norme des grammairiens.[5] Comme enfin la littérature des Brāhmaṇa n'est pas au fond sur un autre plan que celle des Sūtra rituels et qu'on a renoncé à instituer une période des Sūtra indépendante de la période des Brāhmaṇa, on peut mettre en fait que les sources littéraires de Pāṇini sont la prose védique dans sa totalité.[6]

Sans doute on rencontre de temps en temps l'affirmation que Pāṇini décrirait une *bhāṣā*, une "langue parlée" distincte de la langue religieuse. Mais en réalité les règles de sa grammaire qu'il donne pour applicables à la *bhāṣā* sont de nombre et d'importance minimes; on n'a jamais su linguistiquement en tirer aucune donnée précise. A l'exception des quelque 250 sūtra à validité védique, qui sont signalés par la mention *chandasi* ou un terme analogue, l'ensemble de la description englobe indistinctement la langue

[1] Abréviations : les abréviations usuelles des textes sanskrits, et notamment P. Pāṇini, M. Mahābhāṣya, RV. Ṛgveda, AV. Atharvaveda, Br. Brāhmaṇa (AB. Aitareya Br., ŚB. Śatapatha Br., etc.), ŚS. Śrautasūtra (KŚS. Kātyāyana ŚS. etc.), Pr. Prātiśākhya (RPr. Rk Pr., APr. Atharva Pr. etc.), Mī. Mīmāṃsā(sūtra), Ve. Vedānta(sūtra).

[2] C'est plutôt par l'effet d'une conviction subjective que par suite de preuves directes qu'on maintient P. au IVe s. avant l'ère, date où avaient conduit à le situer les premières recherches, fondées sur des indices incertains. Voir sur ce problème la bibliographie chez Winternitz Ind. Litt. III p. 383 Keith Skt Liter. p. 425, auxquels ajouter plus récemment Pathak Ann. Bhand. XI p. 59 Sköld Papers on P. p. 24 Man. Ghosh P.-Śikṣā p. LII C. V. Vaidya Skt Liter. 3 p. 146.

[3] Bradke ZDMG. XXXVI p. 470 Kielhorn IA. XV p. 87 Bhandarkar JBoRAS. XVI (1885) p. 20 Wackernagel Ai. Gr. I p. XXXIII; les réserves de Delbrück Ai. Synt. p. VII Franke BB. XVI p. 74 demeurent théoriques.

[4] Dans son Pāṇini (1891) notamment, où, se fondant sur les formes verbales attestées, il établit que la description de P. repose sur un état très voisin de, sinon identique à, celui des *gṛhyasūtra* et que AB. et BĀU. en particulier sont antérieurs à P. Dans un article des BB. XI p. 308 il précise que toutes les règles casuelles de P. concordent avec l'usage de l'AB.: résultats qui ont été à leur tour étendus par Wecker (BB. XXX p. 91) aux Upaniṣad anciennes, en sorte qu'on admet couramment depuis lors que BĀU. ChU. au moins sont prépāṇinéennes, et probablement l'ensemble des Up. dites "anciennes".

[5] Sans qu'il faille nécessairement en tirer les conclusions chronologiques que Bühler Sacred Books of the Āryas I. p. XLVI ZDMG. XL p. 705 croyait pouvoir formuler. Aussi bien avant qu'après P., tout un côté de la littérature sanskrite demeure hors de l'influence des règles des grammairiens.

[6] Les essais qu'on a faits pour délimiter les textes connus de P. aboutissent à des conclusions analogues : cf. depuis Weber Ind. Stud. I p. 141 et Goldstücker Pāṇ. p. 129 jusqu'à R. Mookerji IA. LII p. 21 et surtout Thieme Pāṇ. and the Veda, passim.

religieuse et la langue profane ou *bhāṣā*. Bien loin que la *bhāṣā* s'oppose à la langue religieuse, elle en est si proche qu'une même description, sauf dans des cas exceptionnels, suffit à rendre compte des deux domaines : autrement dit l'Aṣṭādhyāyī se situe en un point de l'évolution indienne où la langue profane commençait à peine à manifester son autonomie en regard des disciplines du culte, de l'exégèse et de l'école brâhmaniques.

Les monographies qui ont été consacrées à étudier tel ou tel trait de langue mènent presque invariablement à souligner les accointances de l'Aṣṭādhyāyī avec les faits de la prose védique pris dans leur ensemble, expurgés de leurs résidus archaïques.[7]

Il est vrai que la plupart des traits de langue anciens que nous trouvons chez Pāṇini sont attestés à nouveau dans la littérature classique, à quelque moment de son développement : mais c'est que cette littérature s'est emplie peu à peu, par purisme ou par pédantisme, de formes qui ont été calquées sur les enseignements grammaticaux. La manière même dont Pāṇini les présente, en jonction avec les faits du domaine védique, par exemple la "tmèse" du préverbe et du verbe (BSL. XXXIV p. 96), laisse déceler qu'il les puise dans une tradition toute voisine de l'état ancien, à "la frontière entre le domaine suranné du *chandas* et le terrain encore anonyme du sanscrit qui naît" (S. Lévi MSL. XIV p. 279).

Quelques-uns de ces traits, d'ailleurs, n'ont pas survécu à la prose védique ; leur présence chez Pāṇini prend dès lors une portée chronologique éminente : tel est le cas pour les dérivés en *-uka-* (avec construction accusative), qui sont limités aux Brāhmaṇa ; pour l'emploi du génitif partitif, qui n'a guère débordé la tradition védique ; de façon moins stricte, pour la valeur "hors la vue" (*paro'kṣe*) du parfait, la valeur "d'aujourd'hui" (*adyatane*) de l'aoriste, ainsi que pour nombre de prescriptions particulières visant l'emploi de la voix moyenne.

Inversement les sūtra ignorent les faits de langue que nous voyons attestés à partir de l'épopée : ainsi il limite la formation des noms-racines en °*han-* aux trois termes *brahmahan-*, *bhrūṇahan-*, *vṛtrahan-*, ce qui reflète exactement, *mantra* mis à part (cf. le *bahulam* III 2 88), l'usage védique.[8] Il ne mentionne que l'auxiliaire *kṛ-* dans la formation du parfait périphrastique : c'est aussi le seul qu'utilise normalement la prose ancienne.[9] Il ignore en fonction de prohibitif l'impératif avec *mā*, et à plus forte raison le futur : le second emploi est inconnu aux textes védiques, le premier n'y figure que très accidentellement. De même il ne donne pas la construction accusative pour le verbal en *-tavant-*, laquelle est postvédique ; il ne parle pas (sauf dans un cas d'espèce) de l'utilisation

[7] Voir, pour le subjonctif ou l'infinitif, nos Monogr. sktes I p. 43 ou II p. 57. Dans quelques cas, il est vrai, la description de P. ne coïncide pas entièrement avec ce que les textes nous livrent, ainsi quant à l'absolutif en *-am* dit *ṇamul* (cf. MSL. XXIII p. 373) ou quant à l'adverbe en *-tarām* (IHQ. XIV p. 132) : mais le principe de la formation est tout de même ancien, l'image qui en résulte est archaïsante et au total des cas de ce genre ont nettement moins d'importance que les faits inverses de concordance.

[8] Quelques formes nouvelles, visiblement empruntées à la langue familière, apparaissent ChU. VII 15 2 sq. ; par ailleurs on ne trouve guère qu'une formation instantanée, *matsyahan-* ŚB., ou analogique de formes mantriques, *yajñahan-*.

[9] L'auxiliaire *as-* apparaît de façon très isolée dans des textes récents ŚŚS. GB. et portion finale de AB. ; *bhū-* est plus récent encore. On sait que Patañjali a réintroduit artificiellement la mention de *āsa* et de *babhūva* dans la teneur des sūtra.

comme prédicat du participe en *-vas-*, qui a disparu après les *mantra* pour ne reparaître qu'avec l'épopée; il n'autorise pas les formes du type *dantena, pādena* qui supplantent en skt classique les formes radicales *datā, padā*, et qu'enseigneront les grammairiens à partir de Candra; il ne mentionne pas l'usage, si habituel à partir de l'épopée, du génitif en fonction du datif d'attribution.[10] Il est vrai qu'en revanche quelques faits propres à la prose ancienne sont ignorés de Pāṇini, ainsi l'optatif en *-ayīta* des Brāhmaṇa tardifs et des Kalpasūtra. Mais il est à présumer qu'il s'agit là d'un état de choses que Pāṇini entendait ne pas sanctionner. On n'en saurait dire autant des faits précédemment cités.

Il y aurait lieu d'examiner l'ensemble des mots donnés en exemple chez Pāṇini ou qui dérivent expressément d'une règle[11] : on verrait qu'une portion notable d'entre eux se retrouve dans les textes védiques ou appartient à la zone védique de la phraséologie.[12]

On a fait valoir que plusieurs prescriptions de Pāṇini se rapportent à un usage parlé (Wackernagel Ai. Gr. I p. XLIII): combien plus visent des aspects religieux. Le nom de *patnī* IV I 33 est défini par la participation de l'épouse au sacrifice, *yajñasaṃyoge* : définition qui surprend Patañjali et l'amène à expliquer une expression comme *vṛṣalasya patnī* "épouse d'un hors-caste" par : femme "assimilée à une *patnī*"; les grammairiens ultérieurs, ainsi Candra II 3 30 ou Hemac. II 4 51 trouvent plus simple d'adopter une définition profane. Les allusions aux faits rituels sont nombreuses dans l'Aṣṭādhyāyī : on en trouve à propos du terme *saṃstāva-* III 3 31 (et cf. *prastāra-* 32), des dérivés en *-ya-* bâtis sur un nom de *yajus* IV 4 125, en *-ika-* sur un nom de sacrifice V 1 95, en *-īya-* sur un nom d'officiant 135 (et cf. le suffixe *-tva-* 136), à propos des *dvandva* désignant des écoles ou des rites II 4 3 sq. Le phénomène de la *pluti*, qui n'est pour ainsi dire pas attesté hors de la langue sacrée (Wackernagel op. c. p. 298), résulte de l'observation des récitations liturgiques, de même que l'ensemble si minutieusement ordonné des règles sur l'accentuation, que les grammairiens postérieurs,

[10] Usage que Candra notera de manière adventice. Les exemples à date ancienne sont très rares, ainsi ChU. I 11 3 : cf. Oertel SBBayer. 1937 8 p. 132 KZ. LXIII p. 206.

Le mot *bhaviṣṇu-* n'est donné par P. que comme védique : il ignore l'emploi qu'en fait l'épopée; au reste, dans l'ensemble de la formation en *-iṣṇu-*, l'adhésion à la prose ancienne est sensible.

Les adjectifs en *-ima-*, ceux en *-trima-* mis à part, datent de l'épopée et comme il est naturel ne sont enseignés que chez Patañjali; de même les adjectifs du type *sudarśana-, duryodhana-*; de même l'emploi de *paraspara-*, le type *ātmanātṛtīya-*, la construction avec l'accusatif des prépositions *ṛte* et *vinā*. Tout le traitement des prépositions chez. P. est archaïque; cf. aussi le fait que les dérivés en *-as-* sont transférés massivement dans les *uṇādi* au lieu d'être traités avec les autres suffixes primaires dans le *sūtrapāṭha*.

[11] Cette recherche n'a guère été reprise depuis que Schroeder ZDMG. XXXIII p. 194 XLIX p. 161 a signalé les termes émanant de MS. et de KS.; cf. aussi quelques indications de Bradke ibid. XXXVI p. 470 pour les textes Mānava, de Thieme Pāṇ. and the Veda passim pour les *mantra* en général.

[12] Bornons nous à signaler les noms en *-āyya-*, à élément *-āy-* radical, que P. cite III 1 127 sqq. : la plupart sont des termes rituels : *sāṃnāyyaparicāyya-kuṇḍapāyya- dhāyyā- upacāyya-* (sur ce dernier, v. Schroeder l. c. p. 163 et HirŚS. XXV 4 47). Kātyāyana ad P. I 1 6 signale comme superflue la mention des racines *dīdhī- vevī-*, parce qu'elles sont limitées au Veda.

dans la mesure où ils en tiennent compte, rangeront parmi les faits védiques[13]; de même encore l'extension donnée à la théorie du *gotra*, les prescriptions relatives aux astérismes, etc.

Lorsque Wackernagel op. c. p. LXIV n. conteste que la grammaire soit sortie de l'étude du Veda, la remarque est juste dans la mesure où il appert que Pāṇini vise à une description systématique qui dépasse les cadres de l'exégèse et les besoins d'un *śrotriya*; mais on ne saurait douter que sa grammaire ne plonge dans un milieu où les préoccupations religieuses étaient au premier plan et dont elle a conservé l'empreinte là même où elle s'en est émancipée. Et d'abord dans l'enseignement de la phonétique: la théorie de la gémination dans les sūtra se fonde visiblement sur le *varṇakrama* (le terme lui-même de *krama* "marche pas à pas" est l'un des modes de récitation du Veda) tel qu'il est exposé dans les Prātiśākhya. Peu importe que ces textes soient antérieurs ou, comme l'affirmait récemment M. Thieme avec des raisons très valables, postérieurs à Pāṇini (le peu qu'ils apportent de terminologie grammaticale proprement dite a toutes les apparences d'être emprunté aux grammairiens). Il existait un courant puissant d'études sur la phonétique appliquée au Veda, et la grammaire "générale", le *sāmānya* que vise APr. I 2, en a subi l'effet: comment expliquer autrement la théorie du *pragṛhya* chez Pāṇini, dans laquelle plusieurs règles n'ont de valeur que pour le *padapāṭha*,[14] et dont le nom même et son analyse par *pra-grah-* rappellent nécessairement la technique du *padapāṭha*[15]?

[13] L'un de ces sūtra accentuels est commun à P. et au KŚS I 8 19 (cf. aussi VPr. I 130 sq.), comme l'a reconnu Weber ISt. X p. 423 qui conclut à une source commune aux trois textes. Il s'agit de la description de la monotonie (*ekaśruti*) et, sauf peut-être la première mention (*dūrāt saṃbuddhau*), tout ce qu'en dit P. n'a d'application que dans la liturgie, comme le précisera Kātyāyana ad P.1 2 37 (v. le détail chez Thieme Ind. Cu. IV p. 205 [this volume, pages 351–356]). En l'empruntant comme il est probable à P., le KŚS. a restitué au rituel un bien qui lui est propre. *L'aikaśrutya* est défini ĀśvŚS. I 2 9 "rapprochement maximum (*paraḥ saṃnikarṣaḥ*) des tons *udātta*, *anudātta*, *svarita*" : cette définition singulière s'inspire peut-être de celle de P. I 4 109 sur la *saṃhitā*.

[14] C'est ce qui demeure de plus certain après la polémique qui a opposé Bat. Ghosh IHQ. X p. 665 Ind. Cu. IV p. 387 NIA. II p. 59 (qui voyait dans P. I 1 16 un emprunt direct à RPr.) à Thieme IHQ. XIII p. 329 Ind. Cu. V p. 363 Chaṭṭopādhyāya IHQ. XIII p. 343 Keith Ind. Cu. II p. 742 Chaturvedi NIA. I p. 451.

[15] Ces dérivés en °*graha* (*pragṛhya* se dit *pragraha* dans TPr. et HirŚS. XXI 2 33) sont d'ailleurs propres aux Pr. où ils désignent des faits du *pada*-ou du *krama-pāṭha* : *avagraha*, que P. emploie incidemment, avec la même nuance que VPr., pour désigner le phonème après lequel intervient une "séparation" dans un mot complexe du *padapāṭha* (cf. *avagrah-* "tenir séparé" PB. VI 7 22 et l'emploi plus technique de l'expression *padāvagrāham* AB. ŚŚS. "en séparant les mots" au cours d'une récitation); *vigraha* "état disjoint" d'un mot, i. e. son emploi simple, hors de la composition : terme que la grammaire reprend au sens de "résolution, analyse" d'un composé; *parigraha* "entourage" de *iti* par un mot répété, terme emprunté au rituel qui désigne par là l'encerclement de la *vedi* au moyen de tracés concentriques; *upagraha* "annexion" d'un -e en finale LŚS, VII 8 11 DŚS. II 2 4 Puṣpasū. p. 518, ou d'un *visarga* SaṃhUB. p. 17 : terme propre aux "anciens maîtres" d'après la Kāś. ad P. VI 2 134 comme désignation du génitif, ou d'après Helār. ad Vākyapad. III 12 1 comme nom de la "voix", de la diathèse verbale. Il y a encore *udgrāha*, nom d'un *saṃdhi* chez RPr., et *nigraha*, nom d'un *doṣa* dans le même texte.

Ce n'est pas un hasard si le mot *saṃhitā* qui désigne la "diction continue" chez Pāṇini désigne aussi un mode de récitation du Veda: survivance manifeste en grammaire d'un vaste emploi élaboré dans les cercles de phonéticiens du Veda, et qui a sa résonance mystique particulière dans les Āraṇyaka (AĀ. III 1 5 ŚĀ. VII 2 sqq. et cf. aussi TĀ. VII 3 1, où l'enseignement de la *saṃhitā* est qualifié d'*upaniṣad* "doctrine secrète").[16] Le mot *anārṣa* chez Pāṇini "propre (au texte, i. e. au *padapāṭha*) n'émanant pas d'un *ṛṣi*" appartient aux mêmes milieux, et il faut observer que la plupart des mentions de docteurs cités dans les sūtra de Pāṇini sont faites à propos de données de phonétique: ç'a été là visiblement le point de départ de l'enquête grammaticale.

La structure de l'Aṣṭādhyāyī est la même que celle des textes rituels: c'est la composition en *sūtra* ou "aphorismes" comme on traduit conventionnellement[17]: phrases en prose dominées par le souci de la concision, qui lui-même résulte d'exigences mnémoniques. A vrai dire ce nom de sūtra couvre des textes de type assez divers: par exemple dans la tradition du rituel le Vādhūlasūtra ou le Baudhāyana ne sont que des Brāhmaṇa affublés du nom de sūtra; inversement le Sāmavidhānabrāhmaṇa et les Brāhmaṇa mineurs du Sāmaveda laissent transparaître la composition en sūtra. Ce mode de rédaction a dû se constituer à une époque précise; il répond à la pensée de verser en manuels la masse des enseignements, oraux condensés dans les écoles védiques; ce qui ne veut pas dire qu'on n'ait pas de tout temps, et quelquefois par simple pastiche, continué à compiler des sūtra: ainsi les tardifs sūtra du Sāṃkhya faits à l'imitation des textes des autres *darśana*, ou bien les sūtra des grammairiens hétérodoxes, depuis le Kātantra jusqu'au Saupadma, faits à l'imitation de Pāṇini, ou encore les sūtra de Ruyyaka traitant de la rhétorique,[18] les Śilpasūtra de Nārada,

[16] Il est probable aussi que le terme tout voisin de *saṃdhi*, évité dans P. et, relativement encore, dans M., et que le Pradīpa ad Śivasū. 3–4 déclare emprunté aux "anciens maîtres", remonte aussi à l'enseignement védique où nous le voyons, à travers les Pr., avec des inflexions beaucoup plus riches que dans les textes grammaticaux. Comme *saṃhitā*, *saṃdhi* comporte dans les Āraṇyaka un jeu mi-grammatical, mi-mystique édifié sur la notion de "jonction", AĀ. III 1 2, 2 2.

[17] Le terme sort apparemment de la technique du tisserand, comme *tantra* qui désigne les actes auxiliaires du processus rituel, qui se retrouvent toujours les mêmes d'un rite à l'autre et constituent la "trame" du sacrifice (le terme apparaît aussi en grammaire à partir de M. avec une légère translation de sens: "valeur normative" d'une désinence, etc., dans un énoncé; et cf. *svatantra* P. dit de l'agent, "qui a sa propre trame", donc autonome); cf. aussi les multiples métaphores de la langue védique fondées sur la racine *tan-* associée à *yajña- adhvara- dhī-* etc. (et, absolument, ŚB. XIII 2 5 2) et sur lesquelles repose l'emploi généralisé de cette racine dans le Kāvya. Même acception rituelle pour *tantu* ŚB. XI 5 5 13. — Une définition tardive du sūtra est celle du Madhvabhāṣya (éd. C. Palle p. 10) "ce qui a aussi peu de mots que possible, ne prête pas à amphibologie, contient l'essence, est universel [*viśvatomukha*: ou "multiface", comme propose Ghate Vedānta p. 5], n'a pas de (mots superflus comme sont les) *stobha*, est au-dessus de toute critique". [Depuis Vāyup. LIX 142].

[18] Mais les autres rhétoriciens rédigent sous forme de "versets" ou *kārikā*; il n'y a pas lieu de présumer que ces *kārikā* remontent à des sūtra perdus, même pour ceux, tels Vāmana ou Mammaṭa, dont les manuscrits ou les commentaires donnent souvent l'œuvre comme étant faite de sūtra.

les Bhaktisūtra et les Śaivasūtra qui traduisent les spéculations des religions sectaires.[19]

Les sūtra de haute époque sont, outre ceux de Pāṇini (auxquels on peut joindre les Phiṭsūtra qui les suivent de très près par le style et par la terminologie), les Prātiśākhya et leurs annexes (Upalekha, Bhāṣika, Upanidāna, etc.) et plusieurs Anukramaṇī, celles de Kātyāyana notamment. Les sūtra de Piṅgala sont de type plus archaïsant qu'archaïque. Dans le rituel l'apogée du genre est marquée par le *śrautasūtra*, relativement tardif, de Kātyāyana, mais tous les traités du culte solennel ou privé, textes *śrauta*, *gṛhya*, *dharma*, *śulba* (etc.) y participent, bien qu'avec de notables différences de forme. Aux dharmasūtra on peut rattacher les aphorismes d'*arthaśāstra* attribués à Bṛhaspati.

Le style nominal, représenté de façon rigoureuse par les sūtra grammaticaux[20] et que reprendront les sūtra philosophiques,[21] cède la place, dans le rituel, à un style verbal caractérisé par l'indicatif descriptif, l'optatif prescriptif, l'absolutif d'enchaînement temporel : cet état de choses décèle l'influence védique, marque une période que n'a pas encore atteinte la prévalence de l'expression abstraite. L'ablatif de cause dans les noms abstraits, dont les origines en sanskrit ne semblent pas remonter au-delà des Upaniṣad

En revanche, les *naṭasūtra* mentionnés par P. (à côté des *bhikṣusūtra*, ceux-ci d'interprétation incertaine) semblent, concuremment à d'autres indices, autoriser à poser un Nāṭyaśāstra primitif de forme sūtra, cf. De Skt Poetics I p. 27. On l'a revendiqué aussi pour le Kāmaśāstra et l'Arthaśāstra: nos textes de Vātsyāyana et de Kauṭilya présentent en effet des traces de réfection, et les anciens sūtra percent çà et là sous le revêtement de *bhāṣya*. De même, dans les parties introductoires du Nirukta, le style sūtra est encore reconnaissable sous la prose continue. Le procédé consistant à noyer des sūtra ou des *vārttika* dans un *bhāṣya* a été fréquent dans la littérature technique, depuis le Mahābhāṣya jusqu'à certains commentaires du Nyāya par ex. Une autre forme de dégradation des sūtra est la mise en *śloka*: ainsi dans le Ṛkprātiśākhya, où il est assez aisé de déceler les sūtra primitifs, conformes à ceux de tous les autres Pr.

Dans les textes rituels aussi le sūtra et le *bhāṣya* alternent; plusieurs *śrautasūtra* sont écrits, en totalité ou en partie, dans une prose de type *brāhmaṇa*. Mais comme ce sont les textes les plus anciens de la série, il est difficile de croire que le style sūtra y a été aboli au profit du style *brāhmaṇa*. Peut-être y aurait-il profit à rechercher dans un *śrautasūtra* comme celui de Baudhāyana s'il y a effectivement des traces de forme sūtra: Hillebrandt GGA. 1903 p. 949 l'affirme et a même relevé des éléments de *vārttika* (il cite Bau. II 15), qui montreraient que la dialectique des grammairiens et des logiciens a existé aussi, du moins à titre fragmentaire, dans la littérature rituelle.

[19] Pāṇini n'emploie comme forme personnelle du verbe que *dṛśyate* (en regard de *darśanāt* préféré par les sūtra rituels ou philosophiques, qui font grand usage du terme et avec des implications plus ou moins chargées de sens); toutefois il utilise volontiers le verbe personnel pour définir des valeurs de suffixes, *tad gacchati*, *tad adhīte*, *tad veda*, *tad arhati*, etc.

[20] Cf. encore les tardifs Āyurvedasūtra. Il existe des Śaktisūtra, ainsi que des sūtra tantriques, ceux-ci en consciente imitation du *kalpa* védique, à savoir les Pārānanda, Agastya, Bhārgava. Jusque la Bhaktamāla du vieux hindī qui s'inspire du style sūtra (Grierson JRAS. 1909 p. 608).

[21] Il n'y a pas un seul verbe expressif, par exemple, dans les Yogasūtra. Les deux Mīmāṃsā, et surtout la seconde, ont d'assez nombreuses formes verbales, mais de valeur faible, comme *darśayati bravīti pratiṣedhati upapadyate śāsti smaryate*.

(Oldenberg Ai. Prosa p. 29 n. 1 et Br. Texte p. 229 note comme exceptionnel l'emploi d'*avināśitvāt* BĀU. IV 3 23 sqq.), fait défaut dans les sūtra grammaticaux, lesquels, fidèles apparemment aux exigences premières du genre, décrivent et ne justifient pas[22]. Il est connu des Prātiśākhya, mais d'un usage très limité[23]. Dans le rituel l'ablatif de cause est usité, mais de façon inégale: on le trouve surtout dans les portions de *paribhāṣā;* à tout prendre il est plus fréquent dans le *dharma* que dans le *śrauta*, où toutefois Kātyāyana, Hiraṇyakeśin et Āpastamba notamment (sur ce dernier, v. Garbe éd. III p. xv) le présentent de manière assez suivie. Il est probable que son développement a une valeur chronologique. L'opposition si tranchée qui se marque à cet égard entre les sūtra de la grammaire ou de la phonétique et ceux du rituel ou de la philosophie répond à celle qui, dans la grammaire même, sépare les sūtra des *vārttika*. Les sūtra rituels et surtout les sūtra philosophiques combinent avec l'ancien schéma du sūtra descriptif le schéma nouveau du sūtra dialectique et interprétatoire, dont le modèle parfait est fourni par le grammairien Kātyāyana.

Une des exigences du style sūtra est la formulation des *paribhāṣā* ou règles générales d'interprétation: c'est l'une des six sortes de sūtra reconnues pareillement par la grammaire et par la Mīmāṃsā. On sait que Pāṇini a disséminé dans l'Aṣṭādhyāyī, et surtout dans le premier *pāda*, des sūtra qui constituent des axiomes à valeur générale, "illuminant comme une lampe la grammaire entière" (Pradīpa ad M. I 1 49 vt. 4) et que la tradition appelle des *paribhāṣāsūtra*. L'un des plus notables est *vipratiṣedhe paraṃ kāryam* I 4 2 "lorsqu'il y a prohibition mutuelle (entre deux règles simultanément applicables, la règle) à effectuer est celle qui est ultérieure".[24] Les philosophes du rituel ont emprunté cette *paribhāṣā*; les Mī. XII 4 37 donnent la formule *vipratiṣedhe*

[22] La formule est de Thieme ZII. VIII p. 24. Ce principe suffit à nous permettre de juger comme interpolés les sū. I 2 53 à 57 de P. (sur lesquels v. en dernier lieu Faddegon Stud. on P. p. 57) qui, outre les ablatifs de cause, contiennent un emploi moderne du mot *pramāṇa* au sens de "norme" (P. n'a que le sens de "mesure", de même RPr. "mesure" d'un mètre); le sens de "norme", rare encore dans M., apparaît dans un passage de PGS. I 8 13 (qui se réfère à la *śruti*) et dans LŚS.-DŚS. ainsi que dans une kār. Kauś. CXLI 24. Ils contiennent aussi un emploi moderne de l'optatif *syāt*, qu'on retrouve dans la Mīmāṃsā et déjà dans le rituel, notamment dans KŚS. I 2 17, 6 18 IX 9 19 et plus spécialement dans *syād vā* I 5 3, 8 14 VIII 2 19 etc.

[23] On l'a au début de VPr. (ainsi que l'optatif *syāt*), portion peut-être surajoutée au texte primitif; ainsi que VPr. V 43 sq. APr. IV 6 RPr. X 19 et notamment XI 66 sq. où figure une discussion implicite entre un *pūrvapakṣin* et un *siddhāntin* à la manière des *vārttika*. La phraséologie par *na* + ablatif figure VPr. I 3 comme KŚS. I 4 18, 5 8 et sera reprise abondamment par les sūtra philosophiques, qui font usage aussi de l'idiome *iti cen na*, emprunté aux *vārttika* grammaticaux (l'emploi de *ced* dans P. et dans les Pr. est tout différent). Sauf erreur, on n'a dans aucun texte en sūtra l'instrumental servant à justifier la cause fournie à l'ablatif, instrumental dont useront tous les *bhāṣya* tardifs.

[24] Le terme *vipratiṣedha* apparaît aussi dans le rituel en concurrence avec *virodha* (qui le glose chez M.) et, isolément, avec *vibādhamāna* ĀpŚS. XXI 1 20 (qui montre un cas, rare à date ancienne, de la racine *bādh-* dite de règles qui s'entravent: emploi de M. et des grammairiens en général, repris aussi Mī. III 3 8), et de là dans les sū. philosophiques: toutefois, dans les NySū. le mot a le sens de contre-objection V 1 41 sq. ou même d'un

param, infléchie d'ailleurs vers une valeur différente "lorsqu'il y a prohibition mutuelle (entre ce qui est en vue du rite et ce qui est en vue de l'homme), c'est l'autre (i.e. ce qui est en vue du rite) qui est à effectuer".[25] Mais les sūtra philosophiques connaissent aussi la prévalence de l'ultériorité en un sens voisin de celui où l'entendent les grammairiens. Elle est constante au fond de la notion d'*uttara-mīmāṃsā* appliquée au Vedānta en tant que spéculation postérieure et supérieure à la fois à la Mīmāṃsā première; elle est latente dans nombre d'argumentations de Śaṅkara. Un des Mī. sū., à savoir VI 5 54, en fait état lorsqu'il enseigne *paurvāparye pūrvadaurbalyaṃ prakṛtivat* "lorsqu'il y a connexion entre élément antérieur et élément ultérieur, l'antérieur est le plus faible, comme dans l'archétype"; l'archétype en effet, bien que prescrit antérieurement aux ectypes, est plus faible que ceux-ci, doit autrement dit céder le pas à toute règle particulière: ici encore il s'agit de l'application d'un principe grammatical bien connu, aux termes duquel la règle générale (*utsarga, nyāya, sāmānya*) cède le pas à la règle particulière (*apavāda, viśeṣa*), cf. la paribh. 57 et le sū. I 2 101 du Sarasvatīkaṇṭhābhar. *utsargāpavādayor apavādo vidhir balavān*.[26]

Pāṇini, on le sait, n'a pas formulé toutes les *paribhāṣā* auxquelles son œuvre pouvait donner cours: certaines, qui étaient nécessairement présentes à son esprit, ont été laissées de côté, soit parce qu'évidentes, soit parce qu'existant dans des recueils séparés. En fait nous avons des recueils de *paribhāṣā*, mais de date généralement tardive et qui englobent avec ces authentiques axiomes des maximes nouvelles qui sont de simples généralisations, d'autres qui sont déduites d'une règle de grammaire en vue d'obtenir certains résultats pratiques. Le problème se pose, qu'on ne peut aborder ici,[27] de savoir lesquelles de ces *paribhāṣā* sont d'origine pāṇinéenne ou pré-pāṇinéenne.

Rappelons seulement que les *paribhāṣā* grammaticales sont plus rigoureuses que celles des techniques voisines: elles désignent des règles dont l'existence est requise par un indice révélateur (*jñāpaka*) puisé dans la substance même d'un sūtra; elles supposent un raisonnement d'inférence, fondé sur le postulat implicite du caractère nécessaire de toute teneur pāṇinéenne.

Hors de la grammaire, les *paribhāṣā* se présentent dans des conditions diverses. Dans les Prātiśākhya elles sont assez rares et mal circonscrites; leur place, leur manque partiel de nécessité, d'autres indices encore, invitent à les considérer comme de simples emprunts aux écoles de grammairiens. Dans l'APr. nous n'en trouvons qu'une, à savoir *āntaryeṇa vṛttiḥ* I 95 "le traitement (des phonèmes) a lieu d'après l'affinité": cet axiome joue le même

simple *pratiṣedha* II 1 14. A *arthavipratiṣedha* et *śabda(para)*° de M. répondent les mêmes expressions dans Mī. I 2 36 III 3 36 V 1 26; cf. aussi *rūpa*° HirŚS. I 1 16 *dharma*° VŚS. I 1 1 70 Mī. III 3 40 *kalpa*° ŚŚS. XIII 14 5.

[25] L'argument du *parārthatva* se retrouve ailleurs, avec des nuances diverses: Mī. I 1 18 il sert à justifier la théorie de la pérennité des mots. Dans le rituel même on le trouve appliqué aussi à un cas de conflit entre deux possibilités contradictoires: (*pāṭhakramārthakramayor*) *virodhe 'rthas tatparatvāt* KŚS. I 5 5 "lorsqu'il y a conflit entre l'ordre de la teneur et l'ordre du sens, le sens l'emporte parce que la teneur dépend du sens"; de même I 4 16 *arthadravyavirodhe 'rthasāmānyaṃ tatparatvāt*.

[26] Inversement il y a *paradaurbalya* Mī. III 3 14 dans une séquence de facteurs, qui rappelle celle de la paribh. grammaticale 38.

[27] Cf. en dernier lieu Boudon J. as. 1938 1 p. 101. [this volume, pages 379–391].

role que *vikārī yathāsannam* VPr. I 142 (et cf. aussi *yathāntaram* RPr. I 56) et repose comme ce dernier sur P. I 1 50 *sthāne 'ntaratamaḥ*. Dans le TPr. les sū. I 50 *padagrahaṇeṣu padaṃ gamyeta* et 51 *api vikṛtam* rappellent respectivement le pbh. sū. P. I 1 68 et la pbh. 37 *ekadeśavikṛtam ananyavat*.[28]

Le Ṛktantra et le Sāmatantra n'ont pas de *paribhāṣā*. Le RPr. compte une maxime généralisante, à savoir *nyāyair miśrān apavādān pratīyāt* I 53 (Müller 54), qui est toute proche des paribh. grammaticales 62 et 63 : l'emploi du mot *apavāda* "exception, règle particulière-entravante" (qu'on retrouve plusieurs fois en ce sens RPr. et APr. dans la recension de Vishva Bandhu Śâstrî) sent son origine grammaticale.[29] Une autre maxime *sarvaśāstrārthaṃ pratikaṇṭham uktam* I 54 donne le même enseignement que la paribh. 110; la formule *padavac ca padyān* I 61 (Müller 62) vulgarise P. I 1 62, enfin *padaṃ padāntādivad ekavarṇam* II 6 (Müller 110) rappelle *ādyantavad ekasmin* de P. I 1 21 (et cf. VPr. I 152 *sa evādir antaś ca*).[30]

Dans les textes rituels, les *paribhāṣā* forment des séries plus ou moins compactes de sūtra situées généralement en tête de la portion *śrauta*; elles sont d'autant plus complètes, semble-t-il que le texte est plus récent. Dans Āpastamba et Baudhāyana elles se groupent dans une section finale. Les *gṛhyasūtra*, qui ne font que prolonger les *śrauta* en guise d'annexe, n'avaient pas besoin de *paribhāṣā* spéciales, et de fait n'en possèdent pas; toutefois quelques maximes de caractère secondaire marquent le début de plusieurs textes, Āpastamba, Gobhila, Khādira, ainsi que Kauśika qui n'a pas de *śrauta* derrière lui; dans Hiraṇyakeśin les *paribhāṣā* sont dispersées au hasard des cas particuliers auxquelles elles s'appliquent, conformément à l'axiome grammatical (pbh. 3) *kāryakālaṃ*

[28] Seul le sū. I 25 avec son annexe 26 n'a pas de correspondant en grammaire: *āsannaṃ saṃdehe*. Le sū. I 23 (avec 24) est plutôt un *saṃjñāsūtra*, définissant la valeur du nominatif dans un énoncé. La pbh. grammaticale *yanthāntaram* est reprise dans un texte de *kalpa*: Kauś. VIII 10.

[29] De même *nyāya*, qui a aussi chez les grammairiens tardifs le sens de "règle générale" opposé à *apavāda*; Nāg. ad M. III 4 67 vt. 7/8 Pradīpa ad M. II 3 1 vt. 1 (imprimé: *nyāyya*). Le terme plus usuel est *utsarga*. Le sens d'*utsarga* est proprement "ce dont l'application est sujette à être levée (par une règle particulière, par l'*apavāda*)", valeur qui est sensible aux commentateurs (cf. Prad. VI 1 86 vt. 1 et la pbh. citée M. I p. 463 2) et qui explique aussi l'acception d'"élément original" (donc sujet à être levé par le substitut) que revêt quelquefois le terme. Tout ceci dérive du sens de "levée, suspension" connu par le rituel (v. les ex. chez BR.), d'où "renonciation" Mī. IV 1 3, "remplacement" d'une idée fausse par une idée vraie Śaṅk ad. VeSū. III 3 9. Le sens de "règle générale" n'a guère débordé les commentaires grammaticaux; cf. cependant Śabarasv. III 7 41.

[30] Le VPr. est assez riche en *paribhāṣā*, par quoi ce texte souligne son adhésion plus marquée aux traditions grammaticales. Certaines de ces maximes sont empruntées littéralement à P.: à savoir celles sur la valeur des cas, sur le locatif I 134 = P. I 1 66, sur l'ablatif 135 = P. I 1 67, sur le génitif 136 = P. I 1 49, à quoi VPr. ajoute l'accusatif 133 et l'instrumental 139. D'autres ont trait à la manière de citer les phonèmes I 36 sq. (cf. aussi TPr. I 19 sqq.), au sens de *iti* ibid. (TPr. I 16 sq.), à la manière de désigner un *varga* 64, à la valeur englobante d'une voyelle brève 63 (RPr. I 55). La pbh. *vipratiṣedha uttaraṃ balavad alope* I 159 suit de très près P. I 4 2; *pūrvottarayor uttarasya* 145 est analogue à M. I 1 66 vt. 3. Enfin *saṃkhyātānām anudeśo yathāsaṃkhyam* 143, presque identique à P. I 3 10, se retrouve quant au fond dans la pbh. rituelle *bahuṣu bahūnām anudeśa ānantaryayogaḥ* ĀśvŚS. II 1 6.

saṃjñāparibhāṣam "*saṃjñā* et *paribhāṣā* (entrent en fonction non au moment où elles sont enseignées, mais) au moment où les opérations (qu'elles concernent sont prescrites)". Le ŚāṅkhGS. présente V 10 3 une *paribhāṣā* noyée dans la description.[31]

Il est probable que plusieurs de ces maximes ont précédé le texte où elles figurent: on les retrouve sous des formes similaires dans la plupart des écoles. La *paribhāṣā* enseignant qu'on reconnaît l'endroit où prend fin un *mantra* par le commencement du *mantra* suivant, *parādinā pūrvāntaḥ* KŚS. I 3 9, se laisse attester sous un aspect moins concis dans *uttarādiḥ pūrvāntalakṣaṇam* LŚS. I 1 3 DŚS. I 1 3, *uttarasyādinā pūrvasyāntaṃ vidyāt* HirŚS. I 1 30, *u° pūrvasyāvasānam* BhārŚS. I 2 1, *u° p° vidyāt* ĀpŚS. XXIV 2 4, *ādinottarasya pūrvasyāntaṃ vidyāt* MānŚS. I 1 1 5. Ces expressions rappellent curieusement les termes *parādi*, *pūrvānta* qui dans le Mahābhāṣya définissent la place des "accréments" entre le thème et le suffixe. Mais le schéma dominant est celui qui met en relief une prévalence entre deux notions contradictoires (cf. déjà ci-dessus p. 441), soit le type *dravyasaṃskāravirodhe dravyaṃ balīyaḥ*/ *arthadravyavirodhe 'rtho balīyān* ĀpŚS. XXIV 3 47 sq., *mantracodanayor mantrabalam* KŚS. I 5 7, *vipratiṣedha ṛtur nakṣatraṃ ca balīyaḥ* HirŚS. III 2 30; analogue III 8 28 et toute la série débutant avec le sū. 32, dans laquelle en particulier la juxtaposition *aṅgāt pradhānam* fait réplique exacte à ce que serait un **upasarjanāt pradhānam* en grammaire. Ce schéma de prévalence est réalisé aussi dans la Mīmāṃsā: *vipratiṣiddhadharmāṇāṃ samavāye bhūyasāṃ syāt sadharmatvam* XII 2 22, *aṅgaguṇavirodhe* 25. Il est très fréquent dans les paribh. grammaticales. C'est ainsi que la maxime *prasaṅgād apavādo balīyan* ĀśvŚS. I 1 22 "la règle particulière (ou: exception) prévaut sur la règle qui devait se présenter" (i. e. sur la règle générale, *sāmānyavidheḥ* Nār.) reparaît dans la grammaire et indirectement dans les Mī. Sū., v. ci-dessus p. 442. De même la paribh. *śrutir balīyasy ānumānikād ācārāt* HirŚS. XXVI 1 127 "un enseignement exprès prévaut sur un traitement résultant d'une inférence" (analogue *vipratiṣedhe śrutilakṣaṇaṃ balīyaḥ* XXVI 8 9), coïncide avec la paribh. pāṇinéenne n° 104 *śrutānumitayoḥ śrutasaṃbandho balavān*, qui elle-même retentit dans l'opposition *śruti* / *liṅga* Mī. III 3 14.

Ces règles générales que nous venons de citer pour la Mīmāṃsā ne constituent cependant à aucun égard un corpus de *paribhāṣā* analogue à celui de la grammaire ou du rituel. Les sūtra philosophiques sont de deux types, ou bien explicites (Nyāya, Vaiśeṣika, Yoga), et ils n'ont que faire des implications que les *paribhāṣā* ont pour rôle de développer; ou bien elliptiques (les deux Mīmāṃsā) et apparemment dédaigneux de faciliter au lecteur l'intelligence du texte. La concision dans les deux Mīmāṃsā, qui conduit à supprimer des éléments essentiels et amoindrit en fait l'intelligibilité (Deussen Syst. d. V. p. 29 Ghate Vedānta p. 5 Thibaut Ved. Sū. transl. I p. XIV) est aux antipodes de la concision pāṇinéenne, où tout ce qui importe est formulé.

[31] Par contre, ce qu'on appelle le *paribhāṣāsū.* de Bau(GS.) n'est qu'un fragment de *brāhmaṇa* superposé à un complément au GS., Caland Über d. Sū. d. Bau. p. 30. Sont aussi de simples maximes introductoires les sū. initiaux de plusieurs textes de *dharma*, Baudh., Vās., etc. Hors de là on trouve encore des *paribhāṣā* dans l'introduction à la Sarvānukramaṇī, dans SVB. I 5 2 dans les *śulbasūtra* (Thibaut On the Śu. p. 6), dans le début de Piṅg. Chandaḥsū., dans la seconde strophe de l'Āryabhaṭīya (trad. Clark p. X), chez Amara et d'autres lexicographes, dans les Pāranandasūtra du tantrisme, chez Candra Liebich Konkordanz p. 49, chez Kaumāra Lüders SBB. 1930 p. 526.

La composition en sūtra, sous sa forme la plus stricte, entraîne l'omission des mots qui se laissent déduire tacitement du sūtra antérieur et valent ainsi dans le sūtra suivant par l'effet de ce qu'on appelle *anuvṛtti* ou "récurrence".[32] Les commentateurs du rituel font état quelquefois de l'*anuvṛtti*, par emprunt évident aux choses de la grammaire (ainsi ad KŚS. I 6 16, 8 8 et 46 VII 1 33, 2 1, ad HirŚS. XXIV 8 37): mais il est clair qu'elle est loin de s'appliquer dans le rituel avec la rigueur que lui donnent les grammairiens, où les gloses en arrivent à justifier, abusivement d'ailleurs, toute répétition de mots. Ici au contraire la répétition[33] n'est nullement évitée et n'est jamais justifiée. Les *adhikāra* ou "rubriques gouvernantes" de la grammaire, avec leur validité soigneusement mesurée, n'ont qu'un assez faible écho dans le rituel, où la notion plus banale de "chapitre", "tête de chapitre"[34] l'a emporté sur celle de rubrique à portée précise, se confondant en fait avec une *anuvṛtti* de longue durée. Dans la langue rituelle, *adhikāra* est normalement la "qualification" à effectuer un rite, le "droit", dit le Mī. Nyāyaprak. 225 (et cf. Śaṅk. ad VeSū. I 3 25), à jouir du fruit qu'on attend de l'acte rituel. Mais c'est là un aspect de l'emploi plus général de "concernement" qui rend compte aussi du sens grammatical. Il est dit ainsi d'un certain puisage, qui n'est qu'une modification du puisage du *dadhi*, qu'il n'"est pas concerné" ou "commandé" par les ordonnances valant pour le *soma*, *anadhikṛtaḥ somadharmair dadhigrahavikāratvāt* ĀpŚS. XII 7 15 (analogue ŚŚS. XVI 20 3 DŚS. XII 2 12).[35]

Tous les commentaires de sūtra raffinent sur la valeur des particules, *ca vā tu api eva hi atha*: ils cherchent à introduire par le biais de ces mots certaines indications sémantiques qu'a manqué à exprimer la composition lacunaire du sūtra. Le cas le plus remarquable est celui de la particule *vā*, à laquelle les sūtra grammaticaux confèrent constamment le sens de "à titre facultatif", qui repose en somme sur l'omission d'une des deux parties de l'alter-

[32] Le terme est du M. et ne paraît pas avoir franchi la zone des commentaires grammaticaux; cf. toutefois Śaṅkara ad VeSū. I 1 24. Mais le verbe *anuvṛt-* figure dans le rituel avec un sens très voisin, ainsi ĀśvŚS. V 3 11 au causatif: "faire valoir à nouveau" dans une prière une divinité déjà invoquée.

[33] *Punargrahaṇa* KŚS. I 4 6 sq., *punaḥprayoga* ĀpŚS. IX 1 7, *anuvāda* KŚS. IV 3 18, *abhyāsa* passim: mêmes termes que chez les grammairiens. Les Mī. sū. ont aussi *abhyāsa* passim, *anuvāda* II 4 25 III 4 12 (qui est comme en grammaire une "remarque complémentaire" sans valeur prescriptive, un "résumé" d'une chose déjà dite); en outre, *dvirukta* III 6 2 *punarukta* II 4 8 *punarvacana* II 4 15.

La *nivṛtti* "cessation" d'*anuvṛtti* apparaît ĀpŚS. XXIV 1 41 dans un sens presque identique à celui que donneront à ce mot les grammairiens.

[34] Marquée par l'expression *atha . . . vakṣyāmaḥ*, que nous retrouvons dans les textes de philosophie. Le terme du rituel est *prakaraṇa* ("contexte" en grammaire et dans la Mī.: *ekavākyatām āpanno vākyasamūhaḥ* définit le Jaim. Nyāyamālāvistara en termes nettement grammaticaux), celui de la philosophie *adhikaraṇa* (en grammaire: "référence, plan"). Mais *adhikāra* est connu de TPr. XXII 6 (VPr. IV 177 incertain) — APr. I 1 utilise le terme *prātijñā* — et de quelques commentateurs du rituel, ainsi Nār. ad ĀśvŚS. II 3 24 III 1 1 VIII 7 17 Dhanv. ad DŚS. XIII 1 1; le sens de "sujet" d'un passage persiste dans les VeSū. II 3 12, 21 III 3 3 et Śaṅkara I 1 19.

[35] Emploi analogue dans la Mī.: ainsi III 8 31 où le terme se dit de détails de l'archétype qui n'ont pas "place" dans l'ectype, ou 22 de directives "concernant" une autre personne, ou encore III 3 1 de mots "qui visent" une espèce; analogue III 2 20, 7 35 VI 1 4 VII 1 13.

native. Avec cet emploi caractéristique coïncide un changement dans la fonction du mot: *vā* cessant d'être enclitique peut figurer à l'initiale du sūtra.[36] Cette acception se retrouve dans les Pr., quoique sensiblement moins développée: on relève un exemple dans APr. (IV 27), un dans VPr. (I 132), plusieurs dans les Phiṭsū. et dans le RPr., et dans ces deux textes, aussi, comme chez Pāṇini, à l'initiale du sūtra ou du *pāda*, à savoir Phiṭsū. I 12 et 16 RPr. VI 9 et 26. Le même emploi a été noté il y a longtemps (dans le BR.) pour le KŚS. où il est assez fréquent, et où il apparaît également l'initiale, ce que Böhtlingk omet de dire, soit I 1 13 XII 1 26 XXII 3 5 XXIV 7 8. Il ne semble pas qu'aucun autre traité de *kalpa* l'atteste. C'est un cas remarquable de convergence entre un texte rituel et les écoles de grammairiens.[37]

La particle *ca* a pour effet d'attirer dans l'énoncé où elle figure un élément de l'énoncé qui précède: c'est *l'anukarṣaṇa* de Kātyāyana et de Patañjali (le Tribhāṣyaratna se sert du terme *anvākarṣaṇa*), l'*anvādeśa* de TPr. XXII 5. Les commentaires rituels en font état, eux aussi, d'ordinaire par l'expression *ākarṣaṇa* ou par la simple mention *caśabdāt*.[38] L'emploi le plus notable est l'*anuktasamuccayārthatva*, c'est-à-dire *ca* = "etc.": il y a là comme on sait une valeur dont les grammairiens postérieurs à Patañjali ont fait grand usage (Kielhorn IA. XVI p. 251 [this volume, p. 133]) et qui leur a permis d'enrichir à peu de frais l'enseignement des sūtra. La question s'est posée il y a longtemps si ce sens vaut également pour les sūtra rituels et philosophiques, où les commentaires le donnent quelquefois (Vās. XI 2 Vaiśes. I 1 6 NySū. V 2 1 d'après les Navya, etc.).[39] Il faut reconnaître qu'aujourd'hui où la littérature rituelle est mieux connue, nulle part l'interprétation d'un *ca* par "etc." ne paraît s'imposer. Le rituel et la philosophie ne sont

[36] P. fait usage aussi des mots *anyatarasyām* et *vibhāṣā* (ce dernier, substantif figé), qui ne semblent guère avoir dépassé la grammaire: cependant *vibhāṣā* est attesté isolément dans Puṣpasū. VI 241 APr. I 2, et VPr. V 15 a *anyatarataḥ*. Les commentateurs de sūtra ainsi que les sūtra philosophiques (parfois déjà ceux du rituel, v. BR. et cf. encore DŚS. VIII 3 29, 4 1) ont souvent *vikalpa* (*vikalpena*, *vikalpate*) que les grammairiens utilisent aussi, mais qui est encore rare dans M. On trouve aussi, à basse époque, *pakṣe* (*pakṣeṇa*), éventuellement *dvaidha*. ĀpŚS. XIII 1 15 emploie *kṛtākṛta*, glose *vaikalpika*.

Les termes inverses *nityam* et *sarvatra* "de façon nécessaire" sont en usage dans le rituel comme en grammaire.

[37] Par ailleurs les commentaires donnent à *vā* le sens de *avadhāraṇe* (BR. s. v. *vā* n° 4), *pakṣavyāvṛttau* ou *pūrvapakṣanirāsārthe*, *vikalpe*. Yājñik. ad. KŚS. II 1 17 III 3 25 VIII 5 25, Nār. ad ĀśvŚS. I 12 5 connaissent le sens de *vyavasthitavikalpa* comme les grammairiens depuis Candra (Kielhorn IA. XVI p. 251 [this volume, p. 132]). Il y a aussi un *vā cārthe* Nār. ad ĀśvŚS. I 1 25 Śrībhāṣya II 2 38 III 3 54 *samuccayārthaḥ* Ślokavā., codanāsū. 109. *Api vā* et *na vā*, propres aux vārtt. grammaticaux, figurent dans les textes rituels ainsi que dans la Mī. (Paranjpe p. 58).

[38] *Ca* est aussi *samuccayārthe* "visant à englober" (le terme grammatical de *samuccaya* se trouve aussi dans le rituel, v. BR.); accessoirement *vārthe* Yājñ. ad KŚS. I 1 10, *avadhāraṇārthe* I 3 29, *tvarthe* HirŚS. IX 7 9 Śrībhāṣya II 1 2, *ivārthe* HirŚS. I 1 14 *vikalpārthe* II 3 4 etc.

[39] Cf. à ce sujet la vieille controverse entre Bühler WZKM. I p. 13 affirmant l'authenticité de cette acception, et Knauer Fest. Böhtlingk p. 62 Böhtlingk ZDMG. XXXIX p. 484 XL p. 145 (ad Bühler XXXIX p. 706) XLI p. 516 Sächs. Ber. 1895 p. 152, qui ne voient là qu'une habile invention des commentateurs; cf. encore Franke Genuslehren p. 49 ZDMG. XLVIII p. 84 Aufrecht LII p. 273.

pas comme la grammaire des domaines où la pression de la réalité et l'évolution de la langue tendent constamment à faire éclater les anciens cadres.[40]

Maintenant le vocabulaire : et d'abord les termes qui, sans être des noms techniques de grammaire, se rencontrent à la fois chez les grammairiens et chez les ritualistes. Ainsi *vidhi* "règle prescriptive". Le mot en grammaire s'oppose à *pratiṣedha* "règle prohibitive" en tant qu'il souligne le caractère positif de la prescription ; il s'oppose à *niyama* "règle qui restreint (une autre règle antérieure)" en tant qu'il comporte un enseignement nouveau : *apūrvo vidhiḥ* M. I. p. 312 16. Ces oppositions se retrouvent dans le rituel, tel que l'élabore du moins la Mīmāṃsā : le seul trait qu'elle ajoute est que dans le *vidhi* le verbe est à l'optatif ou à l'impératif — et ce fait concorde avec Pāṇini chez qui l'emploi fondamental de ces deux modes se note par le mot *vidhi*. Quant au reste, le *vidhi* de la Mīmāṃsā est *apūrva* comme celui des grammairiens (est *apūrva* aussi la *prakṛti* KŚS. IV 3 21), cf. *vidhir vā syād apūrvatvāt* Mī I 2 19, mais *l'apūrva* est érigé en un principe d'effet surnaturel de l'acte rituel (cf. le terme voisin *adṛṣṭa*). Ceci est de la spéculation : à l'origine *apūrva* glose en quelque sorte le terme *codanā* "injonction" (cf. Śabarasv. ad II 1 5), qui lui-même est un équivalent de *vidhi*[41] et que les grammairiens emploient sous la forme *codita, codyate* avec le sens de "requérir au moyen d'un *vārttika*". D'autre part l'opposition *vidhi/ pratiṣedha* est présente aussi bien dans le rituel (où *pratiṣedha* s'applique naturellement aussi à l'interdiction d'une chose concrète, d'un mets, etc.) qu'en philosophie (cf. l'index du Mī. Nyāyaprak. ou l'Arthasaṃgraha p. VII ; "objection" NySū.).[42]

[40] Mêmes conclusions au sujet de *iti*, pour lequel les commentaires connaissent aussi le sens de "etc.": mêmes références, et en outre Keith JRAS. 1910 p. 1317 Gaastra JŚS. p. XXVII. Le commentaire de HirŚS. III 1 11, l'Upaskāra ad VaiśSū. X 1 4 connaissent un *iti prakāre* conforme aux grammairiens ; *iti hetau* ad HirŚS. XXVII 3 57. L'emploi de *iti* pour noter la fin d'une section est propre à date ancienne au traité de Piṅgala et au VPr. (Weber ISt. IV p. 92) ; on le note dans les VaiśSū. en fin des sections II VI et X, ainsi qu'à la fin des YoSū. L'expression *itikaraṇa* de M. et des Prātiśākhya (R., V., Upalekha) se retrouve aussi ŚŚS. I 2 25.

Yājñik. ad KŚS. I 7 8, 8 46 recourt à l'artifice de l'*avibhaktiko nirdeśaḥ* des grammairiens (Kielhorn IA. XVI p. 249). L'emploi prégnant des cas qu'enseignent pour les sūtra grammairiens et phonéticiens n'avait guère l'occasion de s'appliquer dans le rituel : cependant un génitif *sthāne* est reconnu par ex. par Agnisv. ad LŚS. VII 10 4. Un emploi remarquable chez. P. est relui de *ā* et de *prāk* référant à un sūtra ultérieur : on les retrouve dans le rituel, appliqués à la fois à un rite ultérieur et au passage textuel qui le décrit : ainsi pour *ā* ĀpŚS. VIII 14 20 KŚS. II 22 XII 4 1, pour *prāk* ĀpŚS. X 21 5 XIX 1 18.

Le *bahulam* de P. n'a pas dépassé le domaine voisin des Pr. : APr. (dans les deux versions) VPr. Nir. avec un très petit nombre d'attestations.

[41] *Codanā* est attesté déjà dans le rituel (*codana* KŚS.) et glosé en général par *vidhi*. Le *codanāśabda* KŚS. I 10 1 est l'impératif des *praiṣa*. Le terme est défini *kriyāyāḥ pravartakaṃ vacanam* Śabarasv. I 1 2, c'est-à-dire *śruti*. *Vidhi* désigne aussi un texte de *brāhmaṇa* (Mī. I2 53 II 1 30), alors que dans PGS., à côté de *vidheya* = *mantra* et de *tarka* = *brāhmaṇa*, il semble se référer au *kalpa*.

[42] Le mot *niṣedha* n'apparaît pas en grammaire avant Kaiyaṭa et Puruṣotama (on le trouve aussi dans quelques Śikṣā), bien que la forme verbale *niṣidh-* soit védique et que *niṣedha* même s'applique à des *sāman* dans les écoles du SV. Il est fort rare dans les sūtra philosophiques : un seul ex. NySū. et cf. *niṣiddha* VaisSū. V 2 23.

Quant à *niyama*, le mot est aussi du rituel : comme en grammaire, *niyamaśabda* KŚS. I 4 8 désigne la particule *eva*, et *vākyaniyama* Mī. I 2 32 vise la "fixation (de l'ordre des mots) dans une phrase (de *mantra*)"; la définition du Mīm. Nyāya-Prak. *pakṣe 'prāptasya yo vidhiḥ* 243 "prescription (non de ce qui n'était absolument pas acquis auparavant, comme dans le cas du *vidhi* proprement dit, mais) de ce qui n'était optionnellement pas acquis" est conforme à l'esprit des grammairiens. *Aniyama* (VeSū. II 3 37, 51 et déjà KŚS. I 3 6 ainsi qu'*aniyata*) équivaut à "arbitraire" comme *yāthākāmī* ĀpŚS. III 15 3 DŚS. II 2 20 (et v. BR.; °*kāmya* ŚŚS.) : le Mahābhāṣya use du terme voisin *kāmacāra* qui dérive de ŚB.[43]

Le rituel ne fait pas grand usage au sens de "règle" des termes *yoga*, *lakṣaṇa*, *śāstra* qui de façon variable ont accédé à cette acception chez les commentateurs grammaticaux. Cependant on a pour *yoga* (d'ordinaire "connexion," comme d'ailleurs chez P. même) KŚS. I 2 16 (mais : *saṃbandha* Yājñik. ad loc.), pour *śāstra* Mī. I 3 24; *lakṣaṇa* ("règle" M. et RPr. XIII 31 : 739), qui garde son sens propre de "caractéristique" et que le Ślokavā. II 9 glose par *nimitta/pramāṇa*, a été supplanté par *liṅga*.

On sait le rôle essentiel que jouent les notions d'*antaraṅga/bahiraṅga* dans l'argumentation des grammairiens à partir de M. Ces termes n'apparaissent guère hors de la grammaire qu'en un passage des YoSū. (cf. aussi Vācaspatim. ad YoSū. II 45 Sāṃkhya-prav. III 35 IV 8 VI 15) : cette coïncidence est même l'un des arguments sur lesquels on s'est appuyé pour tenter d'établir l'identité des deux Patañjali (Liebich SBHei. 1919 4 p. 7, 1921 7 p. 57). Mais la valeur de ces termes est sensiblement différente dans les YoSū. de ce qu'elle est en grammaire, à savoir "moyens internes (immédiats)" et "externes (indirects)" pour atteindre au *yoga*.[44]

Des termes importants du raisonnement grammatical se fondent sur les dérivés de la racine *diś-* : *nirdeśa* est l'"énoncé" M. (cf. déjà *nirdiṣṭa* P.), c'est-à-dire l'énoncé par excellence, les sūtra en tant que principe d'autorité. Dans le rituel et la philosophie rituelle, l'"énoncé" est naturellement le texte de la *śruti*, extérieur aux sūtra et qui les commande. De cette translation résulte qu'a disparu dans le rituel tout le côté étonnamment formaliste de la grammaire, l'autorité attachée à la lettre même de l'enseignement, et les vastes conséquences qu'en tirent les écoles grammaticales. Le rituel, qui situe au delà et hors des sūtra le principe d'autorité, n'a pas connu dans sa forme et dans sa teneur l'extrême exigence et les multiples implications qui ont été le fait de la doctrine grammaticale.[45]

[43] *Niyama* "règle" en général, NySū. III 2 11; "règle de composition, *nibandhana*" Mī. I 3 12.

Vyavasthā note de part et d'autre soit une fixation qui est à instaurer séparément pour tel et tel cas d'espèce KŚS. I 3 4 Mī. II 4 26, soit une restriction, équivalent passif de *niyama*.

[44] *Sākṣātsvarūpopakārakatvāt/pāraṃparyeṇopakārakatvāt* Maṇiprabhā ad loc. : d'autres commentaires mettent en évidence le caractère de nécessité de l'*antaraṅga*.

[45] *Nirdeśa* est usité aussi de manière plus lâche, en un sens voisin de *vyapadeśa* (un autre dérivé de *diś-* commun à la grammaire et au rituel) "désignation, énonciation", ainsi VeSū. II 3 36, 1 22 Mī. II 4 26; "assignation" d'une oblation à la divinité Mī. IV 1 29 etc.

D'autres noms de l'"énoncé" ou "teneur" communs à tous les sūtra sont *vacana* et *grahaṇa*. Le premier sens de *grahaṇa* a dû être la valeur concrète de "fait du puiser, de saisir pour l'oblation une part du liquide", attestée à partir de ŚB.; de

Le mot *uddeśa*, que les NySū. opposent à *nirdeśa* comme "donnée générale" à "donnée particulière", a pour contrepartie en grammaire, soit *upadeśa* (même sens, kār. chez M. IV 1 73; ou "explication directe" par opposition à *uddeśa* "explication par description" M. I 3 2 init.), soit *anudeśa*: l'*uddeśa* est alors un élément de teneur qui "désigne par avance" un élément ultérieur corrélatif appelé *anudeśa*.[46] *Upadeśa* est d'ordinaire "enseignement": toutefois le sens propre de "référence" est conservé P. I 4 70 (= *parārthaḥ prayogaḥ* Kāś.) et repris NySū. II 1 65, 2 39 etc.; le Nir. I 1 III 21 entend par ce terme le pronom soit déictique, soit anaphorique;[47] enfin le mot est rangé VaiśSū. IX 2 4 parmi les synonymes de *hetu* "cause". *Ādeśa* est également, au point de départ, "indication, prescription" (Nār. ad ĀśvŚS. II 1 8 glose par *vidhi*), notamment dans la formule rituelle *anādeśe* ŚB. ŚS. passim "lorsqu'il n'y a pas d'indication (contraire)"; le même sens a pénétré dans plusieurs Prātiśākhya (et dans des textes annexes de même époque). Mais d'une part le terme tend à fonctionner en corrélation avec *anvādeśa* pour désigner "une première affectation", *prathamādeśa*, ainsi Nir. IV 25 où il sert pour les faits d'anaphore pronominale, et ĀśvŚS. III 4 10 (cité dans la n. précéd.) où il vise l'emploi d'un *mantra* dans l'archétype. D'autre part *ādeśa* dans la langue des grammairiens a revêtu dès l'origine le sens de "substitut". On voit bien comment cette acception s'est établie: le substitut est la chose effectivement "énoncée" en regard du primitif qui s'efface devant lui: M. I 1 56 après vārtt. 11 le définit pertinemment *yo 'bhūtvā bhavati* "ce qui est maintenant, n'ayant pas été auparavant".[48]

Le terme inverse est *sthānin* "élément primitif", proprement "ce qui (était) à telle place" (et n'y est plus), sens que confirme l'autre valeur du mot, également pāṇinéenne, "élément sous-entendu", opp. à *prayujyamāna* "élément effectivement employé". Le rituel ne connaît le terme qu'au sens de "qui est à sa place" (ĀśvŚS. III 13 19 dit d'une *devatā* et glosé *kasmiṁś cit karmaṇi yaṣṭavyā*; ĀpŚS. XXI 1 18 dit d'une donnée qui "a sa place" dans tel rite).

là "fait de saisir, de noter, notation, mention": *aliṅgagrahaṇe* KŚS. XV 2 13 "quand il n'y a mention d'aucun signe particulier", *mantravidhiś cādigrahaṇena* LŚS I 1 2 "un *mantra* noté par le début est prescrit (comme valant) dans sa totalité"; le terme est glosé *pramāṇa* ad HirŚS. III 1 2.

[46] Même sens d'*anudeśa* VPr. I 143, qui concerne plus précisément l'anaphore pronominale II 7. La valeur propre "indication" est conservée KŚS. XVIII 6 15. *Uddeśa* "description" Nir. I 15 (= *upadeśa* Skand.); "explication" XII 40 (= *pratijñā* Skand.); "tradition" ŚŚS. I 1 11.

[47] Glosé *uccāraṇa, abhivyakti* Skand. Ailleurs le Nir. se sert au même sens d'*anvādeśa*, qui est aussi un terme de P., qui dans TPr. I 58 traduit de manière plus générale une "référence à un élément antérieur" et qui dans le rituel, ainsi ĀśvŚS. III 4 10, concerne l'emploi dans l'ectype d'un *mantra* appartenant en propre à l'archétype, c'est-à-dire relevant de l'*ādeśa*. Il y a ici comme ailleurs correspondance exacte entre les termes de la grammaire et ceux du rituel, si éloignées les unes des autres que soient les notions qu'ils circonscrivent. *Upadeśa* syn. de *vidhi* Ślokavā., autp. sū. 11.

[48] Hors de la grammaire ce sens de "substitut" n'est passé que dans les tardifs Pr. de l'AV. ainsi que dans le Pratijñ. 22 et la YājñavŚikṣā 152. Il y est fait allusion NySū. II 2 39. Les Mī. I 1 16 emploient *varṇāntara* et l'on a plus souvent, dans le rituel et dans la philosophie, *pratinidhi*, qui chez P. signifie "réplique, contre-partie"; cf. aussi *upaliṅgin* Nir. X 17.

Enfin *atideśa*, règle de grammaire comportant un transfert d'application, figure avec une valeur analogue ĀśvŚS. IX 1 2 sq. (et cf. *atidiś-* ŚB. ŚS. cités chez BR.); le mot est repris VeSū. III 3 46 (mais simplement "référence à" NySū. V 1 6). C'est dans les Mī. Sū. qu'il atteint toute son ampleur : il désigne les règles qui, formulées pour l'archétype, sont transférées à l'ectype sans avoir à être à nouveau énoncées à l'occasion de chaque cas particulier.

Un autre terme d'origine grammaticale, qui a pris une grande importance dans la Mīmāṃsā, est celui de *śeṣa*. En grammaire il caractérise certaines formations comme le *bahuvrīhi* selon P. II 2 23, le génitif selon II 3 50, un groupe de *taddhita* selon IV 2 92 en tant qu'elles valent pour les cas "restants", dans les emplois qui "restent" à couvrir, n'ayant pas été prévus par les sūtra antérieurs. Une valeur analogue se retrouve dans le rituel, ainsi VŚS. I 4 1 10 (rare) et dans les Mī. II 1 33 III 7 19. Mais en général, dans ce dernier texte, *śeṣa* désigne un élément auxiliaire du rite, ce qui n'entre pas dans le schéma du *pradhāna*; c'est un autre nom de l'*aṅga*, et qui s'est donné un corrélatif dans *śeṣin* = *pradhāna* Mī. Nyāyaprak. 105; il est défini par la notion de *parārthatva* Mī. III 1 2 "(ce qui existe) en vue d'une autre chose". A vrai dire les ritualistes hésitent sur l'amplitude exacte du terme et Śabarasv. ad III 1 1 évoque les deux interprétations de "auxiliaire" et de "cas restants", qui audit passage se trouvent coïncider. Le Vedānta à son tour oriente l'antithèse *śeṣa*/*śeṣin* vers des valeurs spéculatives.[49]

Reste le vocabulaire proprement grammatical. Ici le travail de Liebich nous précède. Dans un mémoire paru en 1919 dans les Sitz. Ber. de l'Académie de Heidelberg sous le titre Historische Einführung und Dhātupāṭha, le regretté savant a signalé de remarquables concordances entre les termes techniques de la grammaire et ceux des textes religieux. Mais son étude était nécessairement incomplète puisque d'une part elle se fondait presque exclusivement sur la théorie du verbe, que d'autre part elle ne faisait guère intervenir le rituel et son prolongement mīmāṃsiste. Les faits replacés dans un plus vaste ensemble confirment les résultats auxquels Liebich était arrivé.

L'unité auquel le grammairien a affaire est le mot. Le terme *śabda* qui signifie "mot" dans la langue courante n'est pas véritablement un terme grammatical. C'est, dit M. I p. 18 19, "un point dans l'espace comportant perception auditive, susceptible d'être saisi par l'entendement, éclairé par l'emploi". Mais ceci est une définition élaborée; le sens premier est "son" : l'oreille est le lieu des *śabda* ŚB. XIV 5 4 11 (BĀU. II 4 11), 6 2 6 (III 2 6) : c'est la base des phonèmes TPr. XXII 1 (où le Tribhāṣy. glose *dhvani*) et, joint aux phonèmes, c'est la base du langage XXIII 3 : il est produit par l'air avec mélange (*saṃkara*) [d'autres éléments] VPr. I 6. Mais bien qu'en védique (où le terme apparaît depuis la VS.) *śabda*

[49] Cf. sur l'emploi en Mī. Strauss SBB. 1931 p. 265.
Les formes si usuelles *prāpta* et *siddha*, qui scandent l'argumentation dans M. (d'une part "ce qui est acquis" à titre provisoire ou de manière inadéquate, d'autre part "ce qui est acquis" à titre définitif), et que reprendront les *bhāṣya* ultérieurs de toute espèce, n'ont pas laissé grande trace dans le rituel (*prāpti* KŚS. cité BR.; *siddha* dans la formule de Mān. Āp. Bhār. passim *siddham iṣṭiḥ saṃtiṣṭhate* "l'*iṣṭi* menée à terme d'après (le paradigme déjà acquis"), ni dans les sūtra philosophiques (*prāpta* Mī. III 6 3 *aprāpta* I 2 9 *asiddha* VaiśSū. II 2 29; *vikāraprāpta* NySū. II 2 45).

Sur *utsarga* et *apavāda*, v. ci-dessus p. 442.

désigne aussi un simple bruit,[50] il s'identifie de bonne heure à la parole, *yaḥ kaś ca śabdo vāg eva sā* ŚB. XIV 4 3 10 (BĀU. I 5 3) "tout ce qui est son est parole". Chez les grammairiens et les phonéticiens, *śabda* est un élément, mais non pas nécessairement un mot: un suffixe, une désinence (VPr. III 17), une syllabe (Bhār Śikṣā 26, 30, etc.), un phonème (P. IV 3 64 VIII 3 86); en tant que mot, il s'applique à toutes les formes (désinentielles et même dérivées) d'un thème donné.[51] C'est *śabda*, non *pada*, qui figure dans les spéculations relatives à la pérennité des mots (*śabdanityatva*, M. passim, Mī. I 1 5 VaiśSū. II 2 32); le *śabdārtha* "sens des mots (en tant que groupes phoniques)" se distingue du *padārtha* "sens du mot" opposé au *vākyārtha* "sens de la phrase". *Śabda* apparaît dans plusieurs passages du rituel où il est question de substituer tel "mot" à tel autre dans un *mantra* ou un *vidhi*: il s'agit du mot en tant que forme énoncée, non en tant qu'unité grammaticale: l'expression *śabdavikāra* ŚŚS. VI 1 3 définit ainsi l'*ūha*, la formule *śabde 'vipratipattiḥ* KŚS. I 4 9 signifie qu'en tel cas "il n'y a pas lieu de modifier un mot" du *mantra* pour l'adapter à un acte nouveau.[52]

Le terme grammatical est *pada*, qui désigne une forme achevée en regard de *prakṛti* ou *aṅga* (v. ci-après) "base", une forme *une* en regard de *vākya* "ensemble constituant un énoncé complet, phrase".[53] C'est ce qui se termine par une désinence, enseigne P. I 4 14 — définition que reprendront les NySū. II 2 56

[50] Encore "son" dans *śabdakarman* P., et aussi Nir. IX 12. AĀ. III 2 5 joue avec le double sens de "son" du luth et "son articulé" émis par le corps humain.

[51] Du moins dans le RPr. IV 23 : 242. Plus fréquemment en ce sens on a *pravāda*, en plusieurs passages de RPr., de l'Upalekha et dans TPr. XIII 9 où le Tribhāṣy. glose "énoncé (valable non seulement pour la forme telle qu'elle est posée, mais pour toute forme qui s'en distingue par) une différence de genre et de désinence, par (adjonction d'un membre de) composé ou d'un suffixe secondaire". Le sens de *pravāda* dans le rituel est "mention" faite dans un mantra ĀpŚS. XVIII 22 10 XIX 18 4 MŚS. V 1 4 14 HirŚS. II 7 68 (où le comm. glose *pada*). Ce sens est à l'origine de l'emploi des Pr. Le Nir. donne au mot la nuance d'"expression" (et pratiquement "désignation qualificative, épithète" II 13). On a *śabda* au sens de "thème nominal" RPr. IV 52 : 271 Uvaṭa; "terme technique" de la grammaire TPr. XXII 3, glosé *śāstra* Tribhāṣy.

[52] De même dans les sūtra philosophiques où le terme, demeuré en grande partie voisin de *dhvani*, s'oppose à *artha* "sens"; "témoignage oral", c'est-à-dire *śruti*, NySū. II 2 2.

[53] Le sens précis de "phrase", i. e. "verbe avec adverbes, déterminants casuels et leurs appartenances", éventuellement "verbe (seul)" M. II 1 1 vt. 9 sq. n'est réalisé que par la grammaire, où d'ailleurs la valeur prédominante demeure celle d'"expression analytique" (à peu près ce que RPr. appelle *vigraha*), opposée à *vṛtti* "expression synthétique". Mais les Mī. Sū. n'infléchissent en somme qu'assez légèrement le terme lorsqu'ils emploient *vākyabheda* "dissociation d'une phrase en deux" (expression fréquente des comm. grammaticaux) I 2 25 II 1 47 III 1 19, 21 par opposition à *ekavākya(tā)* III 1 20, 4 9 (et même VeSū. III 4 24), *vākyārtha* I 2 40, *vākyasamāpti* II 1 48, *guṇavākya* "phrase secondaire, subordonnée" II 3 2, (*vākyānvaya* "connexion de phrases" VeSū. I 4 19) et surtout *vākyaśeṣa* I 2 22, 29, 3 13, 4 24 (VeSū. I 4 12) qui désigne un "complément à un *vidhi*", formant avec ce *vidhi* une seule unité de sens et d'emploi rituel, et qui repose sur la doctrine grammaticale de l'"ellipse" que rend le même terme dans Nir. XII 22 par ex. (= P. *vākyādhyāhāra*) : ainsi les sūtra du rituel sont dits, par contraste avec le *vidhi* (= Brāhmaṇa), *avākyaśeṣa*, en ce sens que leur teneur ne comporte

sous la forme *te vibhaktyantāḥ padam*; ou, dit plus précisément Kāt. I 1 20, l'ensemble de la base et du suffixe accompagnant la perception d'un sens. L'intervention du "sens" dans la définition remonte à VPr. III 1, qui traduit *pada* par *artha* "(ce qui comporte un) sens", tout en maintenant l'autre définition, purement phonétique, *akṣarasamudāya* "agrégat de syllabes" VIII 50 (et: *akṣaraṃ vā* "ou bien encore syllabe unique" ou, comme dira Śabarasv. I 1 5 p. 48 *akṣarāṇy eva padam*).[54]

D'où dérive cet emploi ? L'étymologie indienne par *padyate* = *gamyate* (*'rtho 'nena*), que donne par exemple Uvaṭa ad VPr. III 1 et qu'illustre AA. II 2 2, ne mène évidemment à rien. Il faut situer le terme dans les conditions védiques de son emploi. Le sens de "mot" est relativement tardif. Il est vrai que Geldner, dans son souci de moderniser le Veda, a soutenu que l'acception était déjà

aucun élément (prescriptif) à suppléer. La formule *saṃdigdheṣu vākyaśeṣāt* Mī. I 4 29 est une véritable *paribhāṣā* "dans les cas douteux, (on décide) sur la base du complément d'énoncé".

Autres ex. de *vākya* Mī. II 2 23, 26, 3 7, 4 17 III 3 14 VaiśSū. VI 1 1 NySū. II 1 59. La définition *saṃhatyārtham abhidadhāti padāni* Śabarasv. III 3 14 est empruntée à la grammaire, et l'explication du *vākya* comme *arthaikatvād ekaṃ vākyaṃ sākāṅkṣaṃ ced vibhāge syāt* Mī. II 1 46 "la phrase est une unité en raison de l'unicité d'objet, si, lorsqu'on l'analyse, (les parties) requièrent (chacune un supplément)". Le *vākya* est l'un des six *pramāṇa* de l'interprétation verbale Mī. III 3 14. Le terme n'est pas ancien dans l'usage : rare encore chex P., il ne figure, outre Nir., que dans des textes védiques tardifs comme Bṛhaddev., APr. (recension Vishva Bandhu), Bhāṣikasū., Sarvānukram. Pour le rituel, BR. ne cite aucun exemple : cependant le *vākyabheda* est mentionné KŚS. XXVI 2 13, qui en un autre passage note que l'énoncé des *yajus* forme une "phrase" lorsqu'une fois dit, il ne requiert aucun mot de plus (*vākyaṃ nirākāṅkṣam* I 3 2 : aspect complémentaire de Mī. II 1 46 précité). On a *vākyaśeṣa* HirŚS. XXV 3 12, °*samāpti* XXVI 4 4. Mais simplement "énoncé" de *mantra* ĀpŚS. VIII 13 7 XXIV 3 51. A partir des DhSū., le sens classique de "paroles, ordre verbal, etc." est acquis.

[54] Plus précisément encore, *pada* chez P. vise le traitement de fin de mot; le terme corrélatif est alors *bha*, terme fictif, peut-être abrégé de *bhakta* "faisant partie de", qui désigne le traitement interne. Dans l'usage que font les grammairiens du terme *pada*, la notion de finale est prépondérante (cf. *padya* APr. au sens de *padāntya* "relatif à la fin de mot"). Le membre de composé est senti comme un mot parce que sa finale est traitée comme fin de mot, d'où les expressions *pūrva*= et *uttara-pada*, que connaissent aussi les Pr. (RPr. forme même le dérivé *pūrvapadya* "relatif au membre antérieur") et, partiellement, Nir.; la tentative d'exprimer le membre par *parvan* "articulation" APr. (notamment dans *jaratparvan*) VPr. Nir. (*eka*= et *aneka-parvan*) dans la langue plus imagée de ces textes, n'a pas eu de succès.

D'autres composés, purement grammaticaux, sont *ātmane*= et '*parasmaipada* "mot pour soi" (moyen) et "mot pour autrui" (actif), d'où *pada* "voix" dans *padavyavasthā*, remplaçant le terme désuet *upagraha*. Des formes analogues — mais qui d'après Prad. ad M. VI 3 8 vt. 1 appartiennent à la langue non technique — sont *ātmane*= et *parasmaibhāṣa* que M. cite à titre d'exemples et qu'emploie APr. dans la recension Vishva Bandhu; cf. aussi *adhyātmam* "par référence à soi", i. e. "à la voix moyenne" Rktan. 196. *Prātipadika* "thème nominal", proprement "ce qui est (pareil à soi-même) en chaque mot" est repris APr. ainsi que GB. I 24 et 26. *Pañcapadī* "les cinq formes (fortes du nom fléchi)" APr. repose sur l'emploi précité de *pada*/ *bha*. *Upapada* "mot annexe" ou "adjoint", repris VPr., figure en un passage au moins du rituel, HirŚS. XXV 4. 2.

établie dans le RV. I 72 6, à la faveur d'un double sens (cf. la note ad loc.; dans le Glossar il ajoute à ce passage RV. VII 87 4 AV. X 8 6). C'est fort peu probable: il n'y a pas lieu de dissocier ces quelques phrases des nombreux passages où le terme désigne en contexte plus ou moins mystique le "séjour" de la divinité (Bergaigne Rel. Véd. II p. 76 et cf. ci-après). Le sens de "mot" est probablement connu d'un Br. tardif, KB. XXVI 5, où *pada* se juxtapose à *ṛc, ardharca, pāda, varṇa*. Cette énumération a subi une réfection: la forme ancienne en est préservée ŚB. X 2 6 13 où le terme *pāda* fait défaut et où *akṣara* figure au lieu de *varṇa*: il n'est nullement certain, par suite, que *pada* y signifie autre chose que "vers". Dans le même Br. XI 5 6 19 il est recommandé, si on ne peut lire un texte entier, de lire au moins *ekaṃ devapadam*, c'est-à-dire sans doute moins "un mot divin" qu'un "passage de texte sacré" (*devatāvācy ekaṃ vaidikapadam* Sāy.). Enfin les insertions liturgiques sont qualifiées PB. XII 13 22 d'*ekapada* et *tryakṣara*: ici encore le sens de "mot" donné par BR. ("one-footed" Caland) est improbable.

D'après Liebich un emploi intermédiaire a acheminé *pada* "séjour" à *pada* "mot": celui de "quart de strophe", soit "vers" au sens restreint du terme, "pied" selon la conception indienne. Le vers est le "pied" ou le "pas" de Sarasvatī comme telle région du ciel ou de la terre est le "pas" d'Agni et de Soma. En cet emploi, *pada* a été progressivement remplacé par son doublet *pāda* qui, signifiant "pied" au propre, repose sur la comparaison de la strophe typique à quatre vers avec l'animal quadrupède (la vache), par l'entremise de "quartier, quart".[55]

Au contraire, dans *pada*, l'acception "quart de strophe" est ancienne: on la trouve déjà dans l'hymne à énigmes I 164 du RV., appliquée au "pied" du mètre *jagat(ī)*, au v. 23; dans le même hymne, au v. 45, il est dit que le langage consiste en quatre *pada* ou "quartiers", dont l'un est le langage des hommes: cette valeur archaïque est méconnue par M. qui dans la Paspaśā entend par ces quatre *pada* les quatre parties classiques du discours (nom, verbe, préverbe, particule). AV. IX 10 19 il est question du *pada* de la strophe ("step", traduit encore Whitney); d'autres mentions sont à relever dans VS. ainsi que dans plusieurs Br. et Sūtra, mais l'emploi est dans l'ensemble en disparition devant *pāda*. C'est certainement par archaïsme que la Bṛhaddev. le donne, ainsi que le Nirukta où l'expression *padapūraṇa* I 4 sqq. et 9, qui répond au *pādapūraṇa* de P., s'oppose à *vākyapūraṇa*.[56]

En fait, *pada* comme *pāda* sont les formes thématiques tirées du nom racine *pad/ pād* qui dès l'origine de la tradition désignait des "quarts de strophes" lorsqu'il figurait au dernier membre de composés numériques: ainsi *aṣṭāpadī* épithète de *vāc* RV. VIII 76 12, *dvipad* et *catuṣpad* épithètes de *vāka* RV. I 164 24 (et dans le même hymne, v. 41 *ekapadī, dvi°* etc.); par extension *apad* ŚB. XIV

[55] *Pāda* au sens de "quart de strophe, vers" n'apparaît pas avant KB. précité, où *pada* et *pāda* sont en contiguité, et AB. IV 4. Ce sens est courant dans les Pr. et P. en porte la trace dans l'expression *pādapūraṇa* qu'il a en commun (quoique avec une valeur grammaticalement un peu différente) avec VPr. RPr. (et cf. Bṛhaddev. II 90). Figurément *pāda* = *mūla* AśvŚS. I 1 17.

[56] En outre, en fin de composés désignant une structure strophique, *ekapadā, dvi°, tri°* et dans *padapaṅkti*, nom d'un mètre, RPr. VS. ŚŚS., qui est à analyser en *pañcapada paṅktiḥ* RPr. ŚB. Le dérivé *padya* signifie "qui consiste en *pada* = vers" KB. ou "envisagé du point de vue des *pada*" RPr. PB.

8 15 10 = BĀU. V 14 7 (à côté d'*ekapadī*, etc.) et *padanuṣaṅga* ŚB. VIII 6 2 3 "appendice d'un vers".

Le contact évident entre *pad* et *pada* (doublé par *pāda*) n'exclut pas que le sens de "mot" ait pu se constituer directement sur *pada* "séjour" du Veda. La notion de "séjour" dans les *mantra* confine souvent à celle d'une désignation, d'un nom, le nom (*nāman*) inversement est un autre aspect du "séjour" ou plutôt nom et séjour superposés caractérisent la personnalité divine (Geldner ZDMG. LXXI p. 317): les expressions *padaṃ goḥ, padaṃ veḥ, druhas padam*, etc. sont des périphrases qui circonscrivent le "nom" même de la vache, de l'oiseau, du dol; au v. VII 87 4 les *triḥ sapta nāma* "les trois fois sept noms" de la vache sont étroitement reliés aux *padasya guhyā*, aux "arcanes du séjour", comme *mahat padam* AV. X 8 6 "le grand séjour" glose en quelque sorte *jaran nāma* "le nom antique" ("substance antique" Henry) qui précède. D'autre part, dans les *mantra* ṛgvédiques, *pada* et *akṣara* sont plusieurs fois rapprochés (III 31 6, 55 1 X 13 3): ce rapprochement est significatif, à un stade de la langue où ces deux termes s'acheminent vers des notations linguistiques en partant l'un et l'autre de valeurs abstraites, "séjours" et "élément impérissable".

Le mot *dhātu* "racine verbale"[57] est une création de la grammaire; les deux APr., RPr., et VPr., ainsi que le Rktantra et le Nirukta emploient incidemment le mot, mais il est visible que c'est là un simple rappel de la théorie grammaticale. *Dhātu* paraît d'abord n'avoir aucun tenant dans la littérature védique. Les plus anciens emplois du mot sont des composés numériques tels que *tridhātu* (et *triviṣṭidhātu*), *saptadhātu* (et aussi, sans doute par analogie, *sudhātu*) qui ne sont autres que des adjectifs ou des adverbes de répartition "triple(ment), septuple(ment), multiple(ment)". La valeur répartitive n'est pas moins nette dans le dérivé adverbial *dhātuśas* du ŚB. Kāṇva (Caland I p. 54) et de BauŚS. XX 11. La situation est donc analogue à celle de *pada* (*pāda*) qui au sens de "vers" apparaît postérieurement aux composés numériques *ekapadā*, etc.; on retrouvera des faits parallèles à propos de *guṇa*.

Sans doute il existe un *dhātu* sous la forme simple RV. V 44 3, exemple unique pour ce texte (et douteux d'ailleurs, cf. Oldenberg Noten ad loc.); il ne nous semble pas exclu que la phrase *sac ca dhātu ca* ne contienne la tmèse d'un ancien **saddhātu* équivalent de *sudhātu*. En tout cas les autres emplois du mot en simple qu'on trouve dans le rituel sont clairement déduits de l'emploi compositionnel: les expressions *tridhātu, pañcadhātu* ĀpŚS. II 9 2 (analogue I 4 10 VŚS. I 2 1 21 sq. HirŚS. I 8 4 sq.) sont reprises par la formule distributive *dhātau dhātau* (4) qui en dérive, et sur laquelle les commentateurs n'ont aucune explication plausible à fournir. La phrase de ChU. VI 5 1–3 *tredhā vidhīyate/ tasya yaḥ sthaviṣṭho dhātuḥ* ". . . se répartit en trois: la portion la plus grossière . . ." souligne que le mot relève de la catégorie distributive sous sa forme la plus abstraite: *dhātu* est pour ainsi dire la nominalisation d'un adverbe en *-dhā*; de même *tridhātu* JUB. IV 23 6 rappelle *caturdhā* qui précède et entraîne à son tour un pluriel *dhātavaḥ* au sens de "parts".[58] Il ne faut donc voir dans le terme grammatical de *dhātu* autre chose

[57] Pratiquement aussi "verbe", notamment dans le Nir. Ce sens est à la base des termes grammaticaux *ārdhadhātuka* et *sārvadhātuka* "qui appartient à la forme verbale (réduite de) moitié" ou "entière".

[58] Même valeur dans *prathamaṃ dhātum ādadhāti* KŚS. XVI 3 27; le comm. interprète par *mṛtprakṣepa*. Même origine numérique dans *ayujo dhātūn kurvan* Kauś. II 22 *ayugdhātūni yūnāni* KŚS. I 3 14.

que "part", "élément d'un tout sécable". Comme dans le cas de *pada*, un emploi d'origine abstraite, associé à des représentations numériques. L'acception de "racine" dans GB. I 1 26 sq., passage connu de mystique du langage, dérive naturellement de la grammaire.

Le terme *guṇa* désigne, comme on sait, un aspect *a*(*r*) *e o* du vocalisme, substitué dans des cas déterminés aux formes de base *ṛ i u*, qui ne portent pas de nom spécial, et qui sont susceptibles aussi de se "renforcer" en *ā*(*r*) *ai au*, sous le nom de *vṛddhi*.[59] Ce sens, qui est propre aux grammairiens, et qui de là a passé furtivement dans RPr. XI 10: 622 et dans Nir. X 17, s'explique par une spécialisation en partant de "caractéristique secondaire", valeur bien connue du terme, qui a diversement évolué et que présentent aussi les textes grammaticaux. Dans l'acte rituel on distingue l'élément fondamental ou *pradhāna*, l'élément secondaire ou *guṇa*.[60] La notion de *guṇa* s'applique à des choses très diverses, depuis un processus rituel "auxiliaire" jusqu'à un simple qualificatif: ainsi il est dit KŚS. VI 7 23 qu'en guise de *sviṣṭakṛt* pourvu de qualificatif on aura en telle circonstance un *sviṣṭakṛt* sans qualificatif, *saguṇasthāne 'guṇaḥ*. Le terme s'oppose aussi à *dravya* "substance sacrificielle" (gâteau, etc., comm. ad KŚS. I 5 13) et il est défini (comm., passim) *upakāraka* ou *sādhanabhūta*; il précise le terme *vikṛta* ĀpŚS. XXI 24 1 ou *vikāra* XIV 1 1. Le nombre est un *guṇa* KŚS. XXII 8 14. Ces nuances de "qualifiant" (Yājñik. ad KŚS. I 4 17 glose *guṇa* par *kṛṣṇatvādi* "fait d'être noir et autres qualités"), cette opposition avec *dravya* se retrouvent en grammaire où *guṇa* tend à désigner l'adjectif, *dravya* le substantif; l'expression *guṇavacana* figure dans les deux domaines. La "qualité" est conçue de part et d'autre comme un attribut "secondaire", "auxiliaire" à partir de la substance. Les mêmes caractères s'appliquent au mot *guṇa* dans les Mī. Sū. qui confrontent eux aussi le terme avec *dravya*, ainsi II 1 8 où il est défini *yair dravyaṃ cikīrṣyate*; avec *pradhāna* II 1 6; avec *mukhya* III 3 9. En outre, parallèlement aux *paribhāṣā* grammaticales, il désigne l'emploi secondaire, figuré d'un mot I 2 47 (cf.

[59] Le mot *vṛddhi* s'explique de lui-même. Outre sa valeur littérale il a peut-être une nuance auspicieuse que met en évidence l'emploi du terme au début de l'Aṣṭādhyāyī et aux fins d'*adhyāya* dans VPr. Hors des grammairiens, on le trouve dans VPr. V 29 et (*vṛddha*) APr. IV 55 Puṣp. III 1; *vṛddha* au sens de *pluta* Rktantra 44 et 68 SaṃhUB. p. 29 LŚS. VII 8 5 Pañcavidh. I 40. *Vṛddhi* opposé à *nirhrāsa* HirŚS. XXV 1 10, à *hrāsa* avec le sens d'"allongement" (de voyelle) NySū. II 2 55. Augmentation du volume sonore d'un mot prononcé par plusieurs personnes à la fois Mī. I 1 11 et 17.

Saṃprasāraṇa, qui désigne soit une voyelle issue de semi-voyelle, soit le processus de vocalisation, est l'"extension" : c'est le sens du groupe *saṃprasṛ-* en védique, et notamment dans l'emploi plus technique de l'Anupadasū. (cité BR. s. v.). Autre explication Edgerton JAOS. LXI p. 222.

[60] Un autre nom du *guṇa* est *aṅga*, qui s'oppose aussi à *pradhāna* et désigne les portions du rite, comme les *prayāja* et les *anuyāja*, qui se répètent sans changement d'un sacrifice à l'autre et constituent le *tantra*. C'est sans doute cet aspect d'"invariant" qui a déterminé l'emploi du terme en grammaire pour désigner chez P. la portion du mot "après laquelle un suffixe est prescrit, en présence dudit suffixe", soit la "base" nominale ou verbale.

Śabarasv. *yat saṃbandhini stotavye saṃbandhyantaraṃ stūyate* I 2 10); analogue VeSū. I 1 6 II 3 3, 4 2 NySū. IV 1 56.[61]

On sait d'autre part que dans la philosophie Sāṃkhya (Yoga) le mot *guṇa* note l'un des trois "aspects" ou "états" de la *prakṛti*. Bien que l'usage associe parfois cette notion avec la valeur commune du mot comme "qualité" (cf. Woods Yogasū. p. 148 n.), il semble qu'il faille partir d'une donnée plus abstraite, de caractère numérique et répartitif, comme celle qu'on a posée à la base de *dhātu* et de *pada*. En effet dans les textes védiques les expressions *dviguṇa, triguṇa* se présentent fréquemment au sens de "double, triple" (*triguṇa* ĀpŚS. VII 1 1 2 équivaut à *trivṛt* du passage parallèle ŚB. III 7 1 20). A côté figure quelquefois *guṇa* à l'état simple, au sens de "fil, élément d'un cordage tressé", en sorte qu'une expression comme *triguṇa* aurait pour sens original "(corde) à trois fils". Il y a toute apparence cependant pour que ce mot *guṇa* soit déduit du composé multiplicatif, comme l'a pensé par exemple Oltramare Théos. brahm. p. 239 n. 2: le mot a très peu de vitalité, il figure toujours à côté du composé, ainsi *uttaram uttaraṃ guṇam uttamaṃ karoti* BhāŚS. VII 9 3 avoisine *dviguṇa, triguṇa* 8 19 et 9 2. Même dans TS. VII 2 4 2 où *guṇa* apparaît seul, la formule *guṇe guṇam* donne l'impression de résoudre un ancien multiplicatif *dviguṇa* ou un itératif *guṇaṃ-guṇam*. Bref le terme en cet emploi concret n'a pas plus d'authenticité que n'a *dhātu* dans *tridhātu*, que n'aurait *vṛt* ou *varttu* dans *trivṛt* et *trivarttu*.

Reste le passage — également numérique — AV. X 8 43 où l'on a voulu voir une allusion anticipée aux trois *guṇa* du Sāṃkhya (*guṇa* pré-sāṃkhya, dit Senart J. as. 1915 2 p. 158); il est parlé là du *puṇḍarīka*, figurant sans doute le corps humain, avec ses neuf portes (*navadvāram*), fermé par (les) trois *guṇa* (*tribhir guṇebhir āvṛtam*). Le vers est à entendre en liaison avec un autre passage (X 2 29) où il est question de la citadelle (du *brahman*) fermée par l'*amṛta* et, un peu plus loin (32), du réceptacle (*kośa*) à trois rais, à trois étais. Rien de tout celane rappelle les *guṇa* de la philosophie classique: nous sommes en pleine fantasmagorie numérique de type essentiellement védique, et l'expression *tribhir guṇebhiḥ* ne fait que résoudre un plus ancien *triguṇam* "triplement".

Le terme *pradhāna*, qui est antérieur à Pāṇini (selon qui I 2 56 la notion de *pradhāna* est *aśiṣya*, n'a pas à être enseignée), désigne en grammaire, par opposition à *upasarjana*[62] la relation "principale" en regard de la relation "subordonnée"; dans un composé en particulier, le "déterminé" en regard du "déterminant", *puruṣa-* en regard de *rājan-* dans *rājapuruṣa-* (ou de *rājñaḥ* dans

[61] En tant que caractéristique secondaire, *guṇa* désigne l'accent NySū. II a 55, la propriété d'un phonème (sonorité, aperture, etc.) RPr. XIII 21 : 7 29, (le lieu et le mode articulatoires, etc.) Uvaṭa ad RPr. XIII 19 : 727, (l'état de *saṃdhi* et de *pada*) APr. I 1. Dans un passage du Nir. I 12 et 14 II 1 il est question des mots dans lesquels "la formation et l'accent se signalent par un *guṇa* propre à la base (dont ils sont issus)", c'est-à-dire par une modification radicale (la variante de *guṇa* auxdits passages est significativement *vikāra*); Strauss ZDMG. VI (1927) p. 115 rend "par une propriété qui réfère au verbe de base".

[62] Qui semble être resté à peu près confiné dans les disciplines grammaticales. Le mot désigne le "versement" de l'oblation KŚS. XII 5 9 et cf. l'expression *upasarjanī* (*āpaḥ*), l'eau qu'on a versée sur la farine, l'eau de pétrin. Il est notable cependant qu'Ānart. ad ŚŚS. I 17 5 connaisse le terme comme synonyme d'*upasarga* et de *guṇa* : on le retrouvera dans les comm. de la Mī., ainsi que dans l'Āpadevī.

l'expression analytique *rājñaḥ puruṣaḥ*). Dans le Nirukta et la Bṛhaddev., le terme caractérise une strophe en tant qu'elle s'adresse à la divinité à titre "primaire", c'est-à-dire de manière "directe": c'est un équivalent de *pratyakṣa* (Nir. VII 1 sqq.) et le terme opposé est ici *nipāta* ou *naighaṇṭuka* (aussi *paro'kṣa*). Dans le rituel, d'où l'emploi semble émaner, le mot désigne par opposition à *aṅga* (v. ci-dessus p. 450) les portions essentielles du rite, celles qui lui donnent son individualité et qui varient de sacrifice en sacrifice: sorte de "pré-établi" rituel (telle est la valeur étymologique)[63].

Prakṛti signifie "base": le mot est glosé *mūla*, *yoni* (le comm. de HirŚS. XXV 1 10 le donne pour un équivalent de *nimitta* ou de *kāraṇa*) et désigne les rites qui une fois décrits ne seront plus répétés quand on traitera d'autres cérémonies. C'est par rapport à la *prakṛti* qu'est instruite la *vikṛti* ou "variété", l' "ectype" si l'on préfère par rapport à l' "arché-type". Le Mī. Nyāyaprak. 107 sq. définit *prakṛti* "(forme rituelle) d'où la *vikṛti* tire ses éléments auxiliaires (*aṅga*)" et aussi "acte dans lequel les *aṅga* ne sont pas atteints par une injonction de transfert", autrement dit, dans lequel ils sont directement prescrits. La même valeur de "base" existe chez les grammairiens et les phonéticiens: donc "radical" opposé à *pratyaya*, ou bien "état primitif, originel" du mot, opposé à son "état modifié" que note le terme *vikṛti* et plus souvent *vikāra* (le *vikāra* est signalé dans la teneur des sūtra par une désinence d'accusatif, enseignent VPr. I 133 TPr. I 28). C'est sur la base d'une disquisition grammaticale que les Mī. I 1 10 emploient *prakṛti* au sens de "forme originelle" = *sthānin*, et *vikṛti* de "forme substituée" = *ādeśa*. L'instrumental adverbial *prakṛtyā* est fréquent aussi bien en grammaire qu'en rituel (et cf. Mī. III 3 34, 6 2), avec le sens de "dans l'état primitif", pratiquement "sans modification": le sens premier est nécessairement "conformément à l'archétype": l'usage du terme en grammaire se décèle donc comme un emprunt à la langue rituelle.[64]

On a vu que *pratyaya* est le terme opposé à *prakṛti*. Le sens de "suffixe" s'est instauré en grammaire de manière stable et constante,[65] mais hors là il n'apparaît que dans des commentaires tardifs ou bien dans un passage de GB. (I 24, 26) dont les attaches avec la grammaire sont évidentes. Dans le Nirukta I 15 il est dit qu'on ne peut sans le secours de l'analyse étymologique reconnaître le sens (*arthapratyaya*) d'une strophe védique; *pratyayārthe* RPr.

[63] Dans les NySū. IV 1 56 *pradhāna* désigne par opposition à *guṇa* le sens "propre" du mot, qui en grammaire est noté plus souvent par *mukhya*. La terminologie du Sāṃkhya, dont nous avons vu ci-dessus l'application peu correcte qu'elle fait du mot *guṇa* à la désignation de substances (alors que partout ailleurs *guṇa* et *dravya* s'opposent rigoureusement), utilise le terme *pradhāna*, de manière peu adéquate, comme un équivalent de *prakṛti* "matière (originelle)".

[64] *Vikaraṇa* désigne aussi à l'origine une "modification" : on retrouve ce sens, appliqué à un phonème, dans une citation faite chez Uvaṭa ad VPr. III 135; appliqué au sens d'un mot, dans Nir. I 3; appliqué à l'accentuation du verbe, dans Bhāṣikasū. II 1. Dans la grammaire proprement dite, à partir de M., le mot se spécialise pour désigner les affixes du présent et de l'aoriste, proprement les "modificateurs".

[65] Il apparaît aussi, par emprunt à la grammaire, dans l'APr. (les deux recensions) et peut-être dans VPr. V 13 (*vibhaktipratyaye*); dans TPr. V 7 en tout cas l'acception serait plus large qu'en grammaire puisque le mot englobe l'augment verbal. "Suffixes" se dit *antakaraṇa* ou *nāmakaraṇa* dans le Nir., aussi *ibid.*, *upabandha*, qui dans le rituel signifie "connexion"; peut-être *aṅga* Ṛktantra 127.

VI 34: 410 semble signifier "quant à la fonction". Dans les Sūtra rituels où le terme apparaît quelquefois, une acception non technique, "fait ou moyen de reconnaître, de réaliser (une notion)" est généralement décelable: ainsi dans *lokapratyayāt* (et *pratyayāt* seul XXII 3 44) "du fait que (la chose) est reconnue dans l'usage profane" KŚS. XIII 1 9; *āmnāyapratyaya* "ce qui a la tradition pour (domaine) reconnu" Kauś. I 2; "signe distinctif" BDhS. I 20 12. Les commentaires glosent le plus souvent par *pratīyate*, c'est-à-dire *jñāyate*; celui de ŚŚS. XII 13 6 glose par *prati* "concernant", ce qui fournirait pour *pratyaya* un point de départ abstrait qui irait de pair avec celui de plusieurs autres termes grammaticaux. De même le comm. de BŚS. XXIV 1 : 185 1 et 12 glose *pramāṇa* "critère".[66]

Est-ce de là que peut sortir l'acception de "suffixe"? Sans doute les grammairiens exposent (M. III 1 1 vt. 3) que le suffixe est *pradhāna*, l'élément essentiel dans le mot, parce qu'il n'a pas fait l'objet d'un "enseignement antérieur", et le Mī. Nyāyaprak., développant cette idée, dit que la racine ou le thème est subordonné au *pratyaya*. Plus généralement *pratyaya* est glosé dans la grammaire "ce qui est enseigné, ce qu'on a fait comprendre, fait se réaliser" (*pratyāyyamāna*), ainsi M. et Prad. I 1 69 init.: "on appelle *pratyaya*, dit le Prad. ad III 1 1, ce dont le sens est réalisé par le radical". Mais tout ceci semble avoir été construit sur la valeur non technique du terme, celle dont le rituel a conservé la trace et que reprendront les Mīmāṃsistes (Śabarasv. I 1 5 p. 44 *pratyāyakaḥ śabdaḥ* "le mot est ce qui fait comprendre, ce qui communique (un sens)"; dans le même contexte, *pratyaya* équivaut à "signification"). Il semble que, pour rendre compte de l'acception de "suffixe", il faille plutôt partir du sens de "qui s'agrège à, qui suit", sens qui est attesté pour le groupe verbal *prati-i-* dans le RV., et duquel serait sorti à son tour le sens d'"atteindre, de réaliser". Or ce sens de "qui suit" est précisément attesté dans plusieurs Prātiśākhya (largement dans RPr., ainsi que VPr. et Puṣpasū.) où le locatif *pratyaye* équivaut à *pare* "quand (tel mot ou tel élément d'un autre mot) suit". Il existe dans les mêmes textes un emploi parallèle pour un autre dérivé de la racine *i-*, à savoir *udaya*, et cet emploi est même accidentellement passé chez Pāṇini. Dans l'usage qu'elle fait du mot *pratyaya*, la littérature des Prātiśākhya nous paraît donc plus archaïque que Pāṇini, chez qui cependant le *sū*. III 1 2 *paraś ca* marque à la fois que la dissociation *pratyaya* / *para* était effectuée, et que persistait le souvenir d'une identité.

L'origine est plus apparente dans *vibhakti* "désinence", dont Liebich a reconnu exactement l'emploi premier. Hors de la grammaire le mot est attesté au sens de "désinence" dans les deux recensions d'APr., dans VPr., Rktan., Nir., Bṛhadd. (et plus tard NySū. II 2 38 et 56 Mī. I 3 29); on retrouve aussi le sens grammatical dans GB. I 24 et 26 sq. et dans NidSū. III 9 IV 13. *Vibhakti* est connu dans toute la prose védique, soit au sens général de "distribution" ("répartition" du gâteau entre Agni et Viṣṇu AB. I 1 6, "division" de la victime animale VII 1 6, "distinction" entre les trois pressurages VI 5 3; analogues TS. TB.); soit par spécialisation sémantique, pour désigner les modifications, la "fragmentation" que subit un mot tel qu'*agni-* dans divers *mantra* où il figure, identiques par ailleurs, au cours des récitations de *yājyā*. C'est à la fois la division casuelle d'un nom et la discrimination qui grâce à cette division s'opère entre les *mantra* qui portent ces diverses formes. On dira

[66] Autres exemples du rituel : KŚS. XXII 3 46 XXV 1 3 BŚS. XXII 2 : 118 10 XXIII 12 : 169 7 LŚS. X 4 4 BDhS. I 11 24 Pitṛme. Caland p. 40 8.

donc "prononcer une *vibhakti*" (*vibhaktim uktvā*) ĀpŚS. V 28 8 TS. I 5 2 3, "faire une *vibhakti*" TS. ibid. ou encore "placer (*dadhāti*) des *vibhakti*" BŚS. III 2 : 70 4, 3 : 70 17, c'est-à-dire réciter les *mantra* en *agne*, *agnim* etc. Telle *iṣṭakā* est appelée *vibhakti* BŚS. (passim) du fait qu'elle s'accompagne d'un *mantra* à modifications (*vibhaktimantra*). Qu'en cet emploi le mot ne fasse que spécialiser le sens de "variété" ou "variation", on le voit par PB. qui signale une *vibhakti* du ton dans un *sāman* X 9 1, une *vibhakti* dans la modulation de la finale 10 1, dans l'*iḍā* 11 1, et qui donne parallèlement une *vibhakti* du nom d'Agni 7 1 et 5 ou d'Indra 8 1. Ibid. IV 8 7 le dixième jour du rite, qui reprend des motifs antérieurs, est dit "consister en *stoma*, en mètres, en *vibhakti* déjà utilisés" (*āptastoma*, *āptacchandas*, *āptavibhaktika*) : il s'agit moins des désinences que des formes en lesquelles un nom se divise : mais il n'est pas douteux que la valeur grammaticale du terme ne soit en quelque manière devancée dans cette affectation rituelle.[67]

Un autre terme où l'influence religieuse est sensible est *upasarga* "préverbe", terme connu de la grammaire ainsi que des Prātiśākhya et du Nirukta. On le trouve aussi GB. I 24 et 27 et dans la section des GS. relative au nom à donner à l'enfant (Āp. XV 9 Hir. II 4 10 Bau. II 1 27). Le sens propre est "chose versée en sus, accessoire" (cf. ci-dessus *upasarjana*) : cette valeur est directement conservée dans le rituel, où une divinité est *upasṛṣṭa* ŚŚS. I 17 5 lorsqu'elle est *saguṇa* (vṛ.), c'est-à-dire accompagnée d'épithètes, par exemple Agni dans *agniṃ tapasvantam* ; on reconnaît ici déjà un domaine touché par la grammaire. Analogue ŚŚS. XVIII 1 12 ĀśvŚS. VI 3 15 où *upasṛjet* est glosé *miśrayet*. *Upasargin* LŚS. IV 8 21 désigne un jour qu'on "ajoute" aux trente jours du mois. D'autre part, dans la liturgie, *upasarga* signifie "interpolation" : PB. XII 13 22 vise l'insertion de groupes "unipèdes" et trisyllabiques comme *pra vaha*, *mitro ṇa* (dans SV. I 302–304). Chez les Aitareyin (AB. IV 4 1) ce sont les *śakvarī* qui servent d'*upasarga*, c'est-à-dire des portions de strophes *mahānāmnī*.[68]

C'est aussi vers le sens de "mention incidente" qu'est orienté à l'origine le mot *nipāta*, qui dans la tradition grammaticale désigne les particules, ainsi appelées d'après Nir. I 4 en ce qu'elles "tombent" en des sens divers, ou plutôt en ce qu'elles "tombent" au cours d'une phrase comme des éléments tout faits, sans processus formatif. Le sens de "particule" est attesté dans plusieurs Pr. ainsi que dans GB. I 24 et 26. Mais la valeur plus ancienne d'"incidence" est à la base des expressions *pūrvanipāta* chez P., *paranipāta* chez M. ainsi que de la racine *nipat-*, du dérivé *nipātana*.[69] D'autre part

[67] Autres références TS. I 1 5 6, 5 2 2 V 7 1 1 KS. VIII 5 IX I XXII 8 MS. I 6 4, 7 3 TB. I 1 5 6, 8 5, 3 1 1 et 6 TĀ. I 9 5 JB. III 330 KB. I 4 ŚB. II 2 3 26 ĀpŚS. V 28 6 et 9, 29 5 MŚS. I 6 5 10 V 1 2 6 ĀśvŚS. I 3 6, 6 3 II 8 5 LŚS. IV 5 11 8 BŚS. X 23 sq. ; en outre M. dans la Paspaśā, not. p. 3 10. Mais *vaibhakta* DŚS. I 3 24 se dit d'une finale comme *-sya* "appartenant à la désinence" du génitif sing. Le Bhāṣya ad NySū. II 2 38 entend *vibhakti* = *vibhāga* "distinction".

[68] Cf. encore NidSū. II 12 (cité Caland ad PB. p. 306). Un vers de neuf syllabes est *upasṛṣṭa* KB. XVII 1 ; analogue ŚĀ. II 1.

[69] Qui désigne en grammaire une forme que l'auteur d'un sū. ou d'un vārtt. a "laissé tomber" toute faite dans la teneur, et qui par suite revêt d'après les *paribhāṣā* une autorité particulière. Le terme n'apparaît qu'une fois dans la littérature technique non proprement grammaticale, à savoir RPr. XII 26 : 708 où il sert de glose étymologisante à *nipāta*. *Nipātana* au sens pāṇinéen se dit *pratikaṇṭha* dans ce texte.

le Nir. (et à sa suite la Bṛhadd.) désigne par *nipāta* la "mention incidente" d'une divinité dans un hymne, par opposition à *pradhāna*. Enfin ĀśvŚS. VI 14 14 note par *nipātita* des expressions comme *meda uddhṛtaṃ pārśvataḥ śroṇitaḥ* qui sont "tombées" au milieu d'un *mantra*.[70]

Les phonèmes n'ont en principe pas de nom, sauf les phonèmes accessoires (les *ayogavāha* des phonéticiens) qui, étant de prononciation malaisée à l'état isolé, avaient besoin d'une désignation particulière. Seul le phonème *r* comporte un nom spécial, parce que dans le traitement phonétique il posait certains problèmes (du point de vue notamment du *padapāṭha*) dans ses relations avec le *visarga* et avec la sifflante. Le terme de *repha* est connu de M. et glosé *ra* + *ipha*; l'analyse rappelle celle de TPr. I 19 et de HVPr. I 39 en *r* + *epha*, et suppose que les liens rattachment le mot à la racine *riph-* se sont relâchés: en effet, dans les Prātiśākhya, le verbal *riphita* (quelquefois aussi *rephin*) désigne le *visarga* du *saṃhitāpāṭha* "changé en *r*, rhotacisé". Cet emploi remonte aux ŚS. où figure *riphita* ŚŚS. I 2 9 sq. (*viriphita* AB. V 4 3 au sens probable de "démuni de *-r-*"), *riphyate* ĀśvŚS. I 5 10, ainsi que *repha* ŚŚS. l. c. ĀśvSS. I 2 18 HirŚS. XXI 2 34 SaṃhUB. p. 17 *rephin* ĀśvŚS. I 5 11 sq. Le Vaidikābharaṇa ad TPr. I 19 connaît pour *riphyate* le sens de "être déchiré", dit d'une étoffe, ce qui confirme l'origine onomatopéique du terme ("gratter" ĀpŚS. XII 22 7? Cf. Caland ad loc.).

La désignation du phonème a lieu par le mot *kāra* attaché à *a*, *i*, *u*, *ka*, *ta*, etc.: cet emploi, enseigné M. III 3 108 vt. 3 (où *kāra* est senti comme suffixe), remonte à TPr. I 16 VPr. I 37, mais il n'est pas connu de Pāṇini qui, par souci de brièveté, pose le phonème à l'état nu, ainsi *uḥ* "après un *-ṛ-*" etc. L'emploi de *kāra* après un nom de phonème apparaît dans les Brāhmaṇa de la seconde période AB. (V 32 2) KB. (XI 5 XIV 3) JB. (n° 182) et se poursuit dans les Sūtra rituels, les Āraṇyaka, les Upaniṣad et d'autres textes. Il sort de la notation des interjections rituelles *hiṅkāra*, *oṃkāra*, *svāhākāra*, *vaṣaṭkāra*, *svadhākāra*, etc. qui sont attestées dès le YV. et l'AV. et demeurent fréquentes dans toute la littérature védique; les formes verbales correspondantes *svāhākṛ-* et *hiṅkṛ-* sont même connues depuis le RV., qui désigne ou figure le nom de l'"éclair" par une forme *haskāra*, soit peut-être "ce qui fait (ou: fait faire) *has!*": on aurait là une première ébauche de la catégorie en *kāra*. Le même mot *kāra* a servi à étayer des particules, *cakāra*, *evakāra*, éventuellement même une forme verbale *ayāṭkāra*, ŚB. I 7 3 12. Nous n'avons en somme, dans le type *akāra*, *kakāra*, qu'une spécialisation incidente.

Le nom véritable du phonème est *varṇa*. Pāṇini l'emploie fort peu, à l'encontre des Prātiśākhya où il abonde. Il est bien établi dans la prose religieuse à partir d'AB.-KB., dans plusieurs sūtra de type *śrauta* et dans les Āraṇyaka. Bien qu'à l'état simple il désigne

[70] Un terme grammatical de contenu analogue à *upasarga*, mais plus compréhensif, est celui de *gati*: on entend par *gati* tous les éléments, par ex. les formes en *-ī* ou un adverbe comme *sat*, qui fournissent avec le verbe *kṛ-* un groupe composé. Il n'est guère douteux qu'il ne s'agisse du mot banal *gati* "moyen d'accès, voie" (cf. la glose *gamyate* Padamañj. I 4 60 "ce par quoi sens est obtenu" et cf. *pratyaya*), encore qu'en tant que nom grammatical il soit du masculin, anomalie notée Padamañj. VI 2 49. C'est par emprunt évident à la grammaire que l'APr. édité par Vishva Bandhu Śāstri I 1 11 emploie le terme. En phonétique, sāmavédique, *gati* est l'étirement d'une syllabe de *stobha* par addition de *i*, *u* Puṣpasū. p. 520 Rktantra (Van der Hoogt Vedic Chant p. 20).

le plus souvent les phonèmes en général (et aussi dans des composés comme *sarvavarṇa* TPr., *varṇasāmāmnāya* Nir.), il ne figure guère, après un nom particulier de phonème, que pour des voyelles brèves : constatation que confirme l'enseignement de TPr. I 20 aux termes duquel *varṇa* désigne les trois premières voyelles. De fait, P. et M. n'ont que les formes *avarṇa*, *ivarṇa*, *uvarṇa* (aussi *ṛvarṇa*) ; de même les Pr. ; de même encore le Kātantra (Burnell Aindra School p. 112 Goldstücker Pāṇ. p. 37) ; il faut descendre à basse époque pour rencontrer des composés comme *kavarṇa*, *ṣavarṇa*. Partout la voyelle brève devant *varṇa* implique la longue correspondante, autrement dit *avarṇa* = *akāra* + *ākāra* (+ *ā3kāra*). Cette limitation semble bien indiquer que le sens au départ n'était autre que "coloration".[71]

Un nom analogue, d'origine manifestement religieuse et plus encore mystique, est le nom de la "syllabe", *akṣara*.[72] La valeur étymologique du terme est pleinement ressentie par les textes : *na kṣarati* "ce qui ne s'écoule pas" est attesté Nir. XIII 12 Vaidikābhar. ad TPr. I 2 M. (*kārikā* citée n. précéd.), ainsi que dans plusieurs ouvrages rituels. Le RV. ici encore prélude à ce rapprochement verbal lorsqu'il juxtapose *kṣaraty akṣaram* dans l'hymne ésotérique I 164 42.[73]

Le sens de "syllabe" est fixé depuis l'AV. et le YV. ; le mot est affecté surtout aux choses de la métrique ; on sait le rôle considérable que jouent les mètres et les noms des mètres dans la spéculation religieuse, et que les mètres se fondent sur un décompte rigoureusement syllabique. C'est dans ce domaine, comme on l'a rappelé, que s'est constituée sans doute la notion du "mot". Dans le RV. l'emploi d'*akṣara* fait difficulté. Il n'est guère douteux qu'au premier plan le mot ne désigne en tant qu'"impérissable" la parole sacrée. Mais la question est de savoir si cette affectation mystique présuppose ou non une valeur grammaticale. Bergaigne le croyait (Études sur le lexique du RV. s. v.) ; Oldenberg aussi inclinait à l'admettre (ZDMG. LXIII p. 293), tout en pensant que le sens de "syllabe" était visé de manière assez indirecte pour laisser place à d'autres connotations ; Neisser (Wörterb. s. v.) se suffit avec "parole du sacrifice", à côté de quoi il maintient à la suite d'Oldenberg, pour le fém. *akṣarā*, le sens de "vache". Geldner

[71] Cf. *rakta* "coloré", *raṅga* "coloration", pour désigner dans plusieurs Pr. et Śikṣā les phonèmes nasaux et spécialement les voyelles nasalisées.
[72] Le terme est parfois employé au sens de "phonème" : d'après une *kārikā* chez M. I p. 36 10 *akṣara* est le nom du "phonème" dans un sūtra antérieur, sūtra que Kaiyaṭa cite sous la forme *varṇā akṣarāṇi*. Il désigne aussi la voyelle, en tant qu'élément essentiel et support de la syllabe (la consonne est *svarāṅga* TPr. XXI 1). Cette double coïncidence s'exprime dans les définitions de l'*akṣara* des Pr. : "voyelle avec consonne ou anusvāra, ou bien voyelle seule" RPr. XVIII 32 : 1033 (analogue VPr. I 99 sqq.) et simplement "voyelle" APr. I 93 Rktan. 46 ; d'autre part "conglomérat de phonèmes ou phonème unique" VPr. VIII 48 sq. Les composés *samānākṣara* "voyelle pure" proprement "de type égal" (terme des anciens maîtres d'après le Pradīpa et attesté de fait dans les Pr.), *saṃdhyakṣara* "diphtongue" M. (Prad., même remarque ; proprement "phonème de jonction") Pr., ainsi que ŚŚS. I 2 4 (qui oppose de terme à *prakṛtyākṣara* "phonème originel") ĀśvŚS. I 5 9 MŚS. V 1 1 11 GB. I 27, gardent la trace de cette valeur. Pour "diphtongue", RPr. a aussi de façon imagée *dviyoni*.
[73] Śaṅk. ad VeSū. I 3 10 reprend la formule *na kṣarati* ; il y ajoute *aśnute* qui émane aussi de M. I p. 36 9. On trouve encore *na kṣīyate* Nir. et M. I. c., JUB. I 43 11.

Glossar propose "parole éternelle" et aussi "élément primitif de la strophe" (au fém. "discours"), mais dans sa traduction il rend par "syllabe" I 164 39 et 41. Il nous semble que le sens de "syllabe" n'est pas encore formé, qu'on s'y achemine en partant de "(base) impérissable (du discours)" et par association avec *pad* "pied" qui, comme on l'a vu, se dirige en même temps vers "ligne métrique". Les deux termes sont voisins en plusieurs passages: il est dit III 31 6 que Saramā, la femme "aux beaux pieds" (lisez en même temps: "aux beaux vers"), "a dirigé les *akṣara*" i. e. les paroles: ce doit faire allusion, comme le pense Geldner, à la joûte oratoire entre Saramā et les Paṇi; il est dit ailleurs (I 164 41) que la bufflesse (symbolisant apparemment la parole comme tonnerre) a mugi, devenant *ekapadī dvipadī*, c'est-à-dire se fragmentant en les multiples versets de la poésie sacrée, devenant enfin *sahasrākṣarā* dans l'espace suprême. Pareillement "la parole faite de mille (éléments)" VII 15 9 se dirige vers Agni pour l'hommage. Le terme voisin est même *pada* III 55 1 lorsqu'il s'agit de rappeler qu'au temps où apparurent les premières aurores "le grand *akṣara* s'est propagé au séjour de la vache", *mahad vi jajñe akṣaram pade goḥ*, ce qui, transcrit en moderne, donnerait "la grande syllabe est née dans le domaine de la parole". Bien loin de présupposer un *akṣara* "syllabe", ces passages mettent en évidence un emploi cosmogonique qui, favorisé par la jonction avec *pad(a)* et la technique métrique, s'engagera dans la désignation de la "syllabe".

Toute cette imprégnation mystique a survécu, s'est développée dans les Upaniṣad et les Āraṇyaka, où il s'est établi une sorte d'équivalence entre *akṣara* et *brahman*; on sait qu'à l'origine le mot même de *brahman* servait à noter la "parole sacrée". Les deux termes ont achevé leur jonction, cf. BĀU. III 8 8 sqq. ChU. I 1 5 et 9. L'expression *jīvākṣara* AĀ. II 3 8 équivaut à *jīvātman*. Cf. aussi VeSū. I 3 10.

Sur les noms de groupes de phonèmes; il y a peu à dire: *vyañjana* "consonne", qui n'est usité en grammaire qu'à partir de M., mais que connaissent les phonéticiens (et qui figure comme terme grammatical dans plusieurs ouvrages rituels ŚŚS. I 1 19, 2 12 XIII 1 8 ĀśvŚS. I 5 9 LŚS. VI 10 16 HirŚS. XXI 2 34), signifie en propre "chose qui suggère, signe visible".[74] C'est le sens qui est à la base de RV. *vyañjana* "ornement, parure" (à coté d'*abhyañjana*), et plus directement d'ĀśvŚS. VIII 12 13 "expression qui suggère" (*sūcaka śabda* vṛ.) ou Nir. VII 13, dit de l'épithète en tant qu'elle "suggère" un nom personnel (ainsi Vṛtrahan comme *vyañjana* d'Indra). Par ailleurs, le terme désigne en védique les "signes caractéristiques" de la femme (seins, etc.) ou de l'homme ĀpŚS. VIII 6 1 BhāŚS. VIII 6 5, les "marques de puberté" ĀpDhS. II 26 12 HirŚS. XXVII 5 207, les symptômes de maladie HirŚS. XXVII 3 36, les condiments ĀpŚS. VIII 4 11, les règles (cf. *lakṣaṇa*) X 15 13; ŚĀ. superpose dans le même emploi la valeur de "consonne" à celle d'"indices corporels". La parole, dit AĀ. II 3 6, "se manifeste par les occlusives et les spirantes" *sparśoṣmabhir vyajyamānā* (*vāk*): c'est tout le contenu de *vyañjana* qu'implique cette formule.[75]

[74] Non pas "ce qui est manifesté par la voyelle adjacente" Tribhāṣy. ad TPr. XXI 1 Vaidikābhar. ad I 6, ni même "ce qui manifeste" (le sens) Uvaṭa ad RPr. I 5, mais "signe" permettant de caractériser un mot dont la "tonalité" est fournie par la voyelle (*svara* "voyelle" et "ton").

[75] Un autre dérivé de la même racine est *vyakti* qui a abouti à "genre" chez P.; c'est d'après la Kāś. I 2 51 une expression des anciens maîtres pour *liṅga*. Le mot est rare chez les gram-i-mairiens et l'emploi connu de "man

Les voyelles sont dites *svara* "son, résonance", mot qui a abouti parallèlement à "ton", ton musical, ou ton accentuel. Pāṇini n'emploie pas *svara* au sens de "voyelle", vu qu'il utilise un *pratyāhāra*, mais ce sens est connu de plusieurs ŚS. ainsi que du SaṃhUB. Un passage mystique d'AĀ. III 2 5, repris ŚĀ. VIII 8 sq., montre un usage ambivalent du terme: les *svara* sont comparés aux "tons" du luth divin, dont les *sparśa* ("occlusives", proprement "contact") seraient les touches. SaṃhUB. p. 23 enseigne que les consonnes sont traversées (*vyāpta*) par le *svara*.[76]

Le "composé" se dit *samāsa*, terme passé à plusieurs Pr. (APr. dans les deux recensions, VPr., RPr., Nir.). Le sens propre est "combinaison", et l'on peut discerner à travers le RPr. (ainsi X 16: 605) un emploi un peu plus large du mot englobant toutes les formes divisibles par *avagraha*, c'est-à-dire ce qu'ailleurs les Pr. appellent *iṅgya* "amovible". Dans le rituel le sens est "unification de deux choses" (*ekīkaraṇa* glose ad HirŚS. XXV 1 26 sq.), ainsi

festation individuelle, individu" opposé à *jāti* est assez tardif. Plusieurs Śikṣā emploient *vyakti* au sens d'"hiatus".

Liṅga est aussi un nom du "signe" devenu nom du "genre" (grammatical), ce dernier sens ayant passé dans la recension nouvelle d'APr., dans VPr. IV 170, Bṛhadd. GB. I 24. On est parti de *puṃliṅga* et *strīliṅga* Kauś. LX 15 PitṛmeSū. p. 29 6, 45 2, "signe distinctif" da masculin, du féminin. Le *liṅga* est dans toute la littérature rituelle (ainsi que dans Nir. Bṛhadd. Sarvānukram.) la "caractéristique" d'un mantra, le Stichwort consistant d'ordinaire en la divinité qui est désignée, mais qui éventuellement peut consister aussi en le "genre" de la personne à laquelle le *mantra* s'adresse: ainsi au passage cité de Kauś. le *yajus* adressé à l'homme (au donateur) est dit *puṃliṅga*, celui adressé à la femme (l'épouse) est *strīliṅga*. Ce sens est repris et développé diversement dans les sūtra philosophiques, notamment dans Mī. III 3 3, 3 33 et 42, 4 31 VIII 1 27 X 5 5; le Mī. Nyāyaprak. 90 le définit par *sāmarthya*. De même *vacana* "(ce) qui exprime" (cf. *guṇavacana*, etc.) en est venu à signifier "nombre (grammatical)" (également d'après Kāś. I 2 51 un nom des anciens maîtres) parce que le mot était associé à *eka*, *dvi* et *bahu*.

Les noms des genres sont fondés sur la répartition des être animés en "mâles" et "femelles"; le neutre *napuṃsaka* (AĀ. emploie *astrīpumān* II 3 8) est ce qui n'est "ni mâle[, ni femelle]". Les tentatives par *vṛṣan*/*yoṣā* AB. ŚB., qui amorçaient des nuances grammaticales, n'ont pas abouti. Le ŚB. X 5 1 2 parle des briques de l'autel qui portent des noms masculins, féminins ou neutres comme les membres de l'homme, et il ajoute (3) qu'on dit *iṣṭakā* ("brique"), non *iṣṭakaḥ* ou *iṣṭakam*, car (les briques) sont appelées d'après la forme de langage (*vāc*) et tout ici-bas est *vāc*, qu'il soit féminin (femelle), masculin (mâle) ou neutre (ni l'un ni l'autre). Ce passage montre clairement la coïncidence du genre naturel et du genre grammatical; il indique le point où commence une notion de grammaire, se dégageant avec peine d'une notion de la langue courante. Cf. sur ce problème Oertel SBBay. 1943 n° 7.

[76] Diverses triades de phonèmes s'instaurent dans des contextes analogues: aux passages cités d'AĀ. ŚĀ. (et aussi ChU. II 22 3), le groupe *svara*/ *sparśa*/ *ūṣman*. Ailleurs (AĀ. II 2 4) les *ūṣman* ou "spirantes" sont opposés aux *vyañjana* (peut-être compris en un sens restrient : occlusives sourdes) et aux *ghoṣa* "phonèmes sonores" comme le souffle (*prāṇa*) est opposé au corps et à l'âme. L'*ūṣman* est identifié ou *prāṇa* aussi AĀ. III 2 1. Ceci confirme la valeur première du mot "souffle (chaud), vapeur". *Prāṇa* même a failli atteindre une valeur grammaticale RPr. Introd. 4 (et cf. AĀ. III 2 6 ŚĀ. VIII 11) où il est dit que le phonème -ṣ- (une spirante!) s'appelle *prāṇa*, comme -ṇ- s'appelle *bala* (selon ChU. II 22 5 ce sont les voyelles qui sont à prononcer avec "force").

AB. I 1 14 où il est dit que les saisons sont cinq par *samāsa* de l'hiver et de la saison froide, ou bien LŚS. X 12 14 qu'il y a *samāsa* (du rôle de l'*adhvaryu*, dans la description ultérieure) avec (ce qui a été dit précédemment) du *hotṛ*. Une nuance voisine est "résumé": ainsi KB.IV 5 enseignant que tel sacrifice est le *samāsa* de tel autre, d'où l'adverbe *samāsena* "sommairement". Noter que la définition du composé comme "unification" se retrouve en grammaire: *samāsasyaikārthatva* M. I 2 42 vt. 1. *Samāsa* au sens de *samudāya* NySū. II 2 38 d'après le Bhāṣya.

Les noms des composés sont tantôt des exemples de la formation, *tatpuruṣa*, *bahuvrīhi*, *dvigu*,[77] tantôt des formes qui suggèrent ce dont il s'agit, ainsi *avyayībhāva* ou *karmadhāraya*.[78] *Dvandva* signifie "paire, couple": du *dvandva* "couple" naît le *mithuna* "accouplement" AB. III 50 4 et passim. Il s'agit dans le rituel d'objet associés par paire, mais non nécessairement composés TS. I 6 9 4 ŚB. I 1 1 22 V 3 3 14; les huit *dvandva* alludés Nir. VII 4 IX 35 sont les n° 29 à 36 de Nigh. V 3 et comprennent des formes comme *ārtnī* ou *devī joṣṭrī*. Noter qu'en passant en grammaire le mot est devenu masculin (masculin aussi au sens rituel NidSū. VII 7), d'après les autres noms de composés, sauf dans VPr. II 48, 55 V 28 qui conserve le genre neutre.

Les cas grammaticaux ne portent pas de désignations spéciales: ils sont notés par des indices numériques, *prathamā*, etc.[79] Ce mode de désignation doit provenir du rituel où une foule de notions (jours, rites, modes musicaux, etc.) étaient évoquées par des ordinaux. En revanche les fonctions que notent les cas dans leur relation avec le procès verbal, les *kāraka* (proprement "ce qui fait s'effectuer l'action verbale"), portent des noms d'aspect fortement individualisé, parmi lesquels prédomine un groupe de dérivés de la racine *kṛ-*[80]: *karman*, *karaṇa*, *kartṛ*, *adhikaraṇa*. *Karman* "action (en tant qu'objet direct, objet du verbe transitif)" appartient aux milieux rituels où le mot, depuis le RV., désignait l'acte par excellence, c'est-à-dire le rite. De même *kartṛ* qui dans les deux do-

[77] Même type de désignation dans *nadī*, nom des thèmes en *-ī-* (*-ū-*) P., dans *śraddhā* Kāt. II 1 10, *agni* II 1 8. Cf. ci-après *kṛt* et *kṛtya*.

[78] Nom obscur : il s'agit d'un composé formé de l'apposition de deux noms, donc peut-être "(fait de deux noms) qui portent l'acte (le procès verbal)" [de manière égale], qui sont en *sāmānyādhikaraṇya*.

[79] Cf. aussi *pañcamī* "impératif" Kāt. III 1 18 et 26 Hem. III 3 8, *saptamī* "optatif" Kāt. III 1 20 et 25 Hem. III 3 7.

[80] Cette racine, que est aussi à la base de *kāraka*, fournit chez P. les noms du suffixe primaire (*kṛt*) et du verbal d'obligation (*kṛtya*), lesquels sont d'ailleurs aussi des exemples de la formation. En outre chez M. *kārita* "causatif" (nom des anciens maîtres d'après le Dhātuprad. X 170 et attesté en effet Nir. I 13 et APr. IV 91); *carkarīta* "intensif" (actif) M. ainsi que Nir. II 28 VI 22, également un nom des anciens maîtres d'après le Dhātuprad. II 71; *cekrīyita* "intensif" (moyen) Kāt. III 2 14 et 43, 3 7 : ce nom est pareillement donné comme des anciens maîtres Prad. IV 1 78, mais le Nir. l. c. qui désigne le verbe *coṣkūyate* comme un *carkarīta* montre ainsi que *cekrīyita* a dû être fabriqué secondairement. Le même texte VI 1 a aussi *cikīrṣita* "désidératif". Les formes *kurvant kṛta kariṣyant* de l'AB. IV 31 3, 29 3 V 1 3 n'ont pas été retenues par l'usage comme désignations temporelles : les formes en *bhū-* et *vṛt* l'ont emporté.

Un mot tel que *taddhita* "suffixe secondaire" ne constitue pas un exemple de la formation, mais donne l'une des valeurs qui selon V 1 5 commandent l'emploi d'un tel suffixe. Cf. aussi P. *tadrāja*, APr. IV 29 *tanmānin*. Nir. VI 28 *tatprepsu* (APr. IV 29 *prepsu*).

maines est l'"agent". *Karaṇa*, d'après l'usage général en védique, devait être un équivalent plus banal de *karman*: "acte" dans les *mantra*, "fait d'exécuter" dans la prose: l'emploi en grammaire au sens de "(notion d') instrument" provient du fait que de nombreux noms à suffixe *-ana-* comportaient une valeur instrumentale. *Adhikaraṇa* est plus difficile: en grammaire c'est la notion locative, la "location", mais le sens propre, révélé par l'expression *samānādhikaraṇa*, est "référence, plan". C'est en gros la valeur dans les textes religieux: dans TĀ. VII 3 1 *adhikaraṇa* définit la série de "références" qu'impliquent les termes *adhilokam, adhijyotiṣam*, etc.: c'est en somme la nominalisation du préverbe *adhi* "en ce qui concerne".[81]

Apādāna "notion d'ablatif, ablation" fait contre-partie à *saṃpradāna* "notion dative, dation", comme *apādātṛ* à *pradātṛ* TB. I 7 3 1. *Saṃpradāna* est la "tradition", mais l'attache du mot au verbe *saṃprayam-* "donner" est sensible, ainsi ŚĀ. IV 15.

Hetu "cause" est aussi un *kāraka*: c'est l'incitation à agir transcrite grammaticalement par le causatif. Le terme est rare en védique, bien que le livre X du RV. présente déjà l'expression prépositionnelle banale *hetoḥ* génitif "à cause de". Il est probable que Pāṇini sent la forme comme un nom d'agent, "celui qui incite".

Niṣṭhā qui désigne le verbal en *-ta-* est un terme de la langue religieuse, au sens d'achèvement: il se dit HirŚS. XXVII 3 58 = ĀpDhS. II 15 24 d'une cérémonie qui marque la "limite" (à partir de laquelle commence la capacité à suivre le *dharma*), c'est-à-dire qui constitue un "achèvement"; de même HirŚS. XXVII 6 24 — ĀpDhS. II 29 11 "complément", dit des connaissances propres aux femmes et aux *śūdra*, qui ne sont qu'un complément à celles des hommes. C'est aussi "achèvement" qui convient ChU. VII 20 1, où le mot est rattaché à la racine verbale *niḥ-sthā-*.[82]

Avasāna "pause" est proprement le "dételage", le relais et le relâche. La pause est marquée, on le sait, par la relaxation des effets du *saṃdhi*. Wackernagel Ai. Gr. I p. 301 estime avec raison qu'on est parti de la notion de *pāda* et qu'*avasāna* désignait d'abord la fin du *pāda* (et dans le *padapāṭha* la fin du mot, puisque tout mot dans cette récitation est suivi d'une pause). C'est cette affectation ancienne qu'il faut voir sans doute dans le dérivé *avasānya* VS. XVI 33, épithète de Rudra en tant qu'"ayant rapport avec le *pāda*": le terme contigu est *ślokya* "ayant rapport avec la strophe".

Lopa "perte", amuissement d'un phonème (cf. aussi la racine verbale *lup-*, attestée notamment dans les Pr., reprise par M. et surtout par le Kāt. etc.; le verbal *lupta*, les termes *lup luk ślu lumant* forgés par P.) est attesté plus largement dans le rituel pour désigner quelque élément du rite, tel jour sacrificiel, etc., qu'on omet, mais souvent aussi déjà tel mot, tel groupe de mots, telle syllabe qu'on "saute" dans une récitation.[83] La valeur ancienne

[81] Mais = *sthāna* DŚS. 1 4 2 BŚS. XXIV 12 : 196 8; = *sādhanadravya* BŚS. XXIV 2 : 186 2 (cf. chez P. où *adhikaraṇa* est glosé par *dravya* Kāś. passim et M. II 1 1 vt. 21); "fonction" ŚŚS. I 1 8 BhāŚS. V 14 13 VIII 6 17; "section" d'ouvrage dans les sū. philosophiques.

[82] Glosé *guruśuśrūṣādi* Śaṅk., d'où "attention on a tutor" Müller; "Hervorwachsen" Deussen (qui propose aussi : "Wurzelung"), d'où "growing forth" Hume; "pratique parfaite" Senart. Mieux "Abschluss" Böhtlingk.

[83] TS. III 2 9 5 KB. XXVI 4 ĀpŚS. I 10 21 II 19 3 VIII 8 5 XXIV 4 14 (opposé à *vivṛddhi*) BhāŚS. I 10 15 DŚS. XV 3 15 HirŚS. VIII 8 26 KŚS. IV 3 22 ŚŚS. III 19 2 LŚS. III 7 7 VI 1 14. Avec une valeur plus grammaticale ŚŚS. I 2 10 XIII 1 8 XIV 40 18 ĀśvŚS. I 5 12 VŚS. I 1 1 67 DŚS. IV 3 20 XV 4 7 LŚS. I 3 21 II 5 22 III

est "rompre": elle figure sous la forme du causatif *ropayati*, *rūrupat* en des passages de TS. TB. (cités chez BR.) où il est mis en garde contre telle pratique qui aurait pour effet de "rompre" une partie du sacrifice: Sāy. glose *mohayati*, *bhrāntiṃ janayati*, mais l'idée est celle d'une continuité rompue, et par suite d'une déperdition.

Pluti (*pluta*) désigne chez les grammairiens et surtout chez les phonéticiens la prolongation de la durée d'une voyelle jusqu'à trois mores. Le terme figure avec cette valeur dans plusieurs textes rituels, qui connaissent même les formes causatives *plāvana* MŚS. V 1 1 11 ĀpDhS. I 5 17 *plāvayati* MŚS. l. c. HirŚS. XXI 2 34 ŚŚS. I 2 1 ĀśvŚS. I 5 7 dont la grammaire n'use pas. Le sens originel est "flotter, nager", d'où "se mouvoir" (à la façon de quelque chose qui flotte ou nage): le ŚB. XI 5 5 13 parle des jus de soma qui "coulent" entrelacés à des jus de soma, *somāḥ somair vyatiṣaktāḥ plavante*, des atomes lumineux qui "nagent" (dans l'air) IX 4 1 8, de l'homme qui "se meut" avec ses membres, restant immobile avec (le gros de) son corps XII 2 4 8, etc. Il semble qu'il y ait là un emploi imagé, lequel permet d'induire que le mot est passé des Prātiśākhya à la grammaire et non l'inverse.[84]

Cette série de concordances entre les habitudes linguistiques du rituel et de la théorie grammaticale atteste qu'on a affaire à des disciplines issues des mêmes milieux, répondant à des besoins complémentaires. L'une et l'autre ont pour norme la pratique des *śiṣṭa*, des spécialistes (GobhGS. III 3 29, 5 38 d'une part, M. VI 3 109 de l'autre). En présence de tel mot particulier, il n'est pas aisé de reconnaître s'il sort des cercles de grammairiens ou des cercles de ritualistes: l'absence de toute chronologie textuelle, le parallélisme général des techniques dans l'Inde ancienne, rendent cette recherche aléatoire. Dans beaucoup de cas cependant il est visible que le point de départ est dans les textes religieux, la valeur grammaticale apparaissant comme une spécialisation à l'intérieur d'une acception rituelle mieux articulée. La masse, l'importance de la littérature religieuse, l'indéniable priorité des *mantra* et des

4 17 VI 10 14 sq. VII 11 6 KŚS. XIX 7 6 SaṃhUB. p. 16 sq. NidSū. II 10. La racine *cyu-* au même sens GB. I 26 n'a rien donné. Les NySū. II 2 55 emploient *upamarda* (*ekarūpanivṛtti*).

[84] *Nam-* (*saṃnam-*) se dit dans le rituel d'un *mantra* qu'on "incline", c'est-à-dire qu'on modifie pour l'adapter à un besoin nouveau : c'est une désignation imagée de l'*ūha*. L'emploi (relevable ĀpŚS. XIV 1 9 XIX 26 6 XXIV 3 25 HirŚS. IX 2 4 XX 4 9 Kauś. LX 20 LXIII 12 ĀśvGS. III 8 7) a peut-être incité les phonéticiens à utiliser la forme *nam-* (*nati nāmin vināma*) pour désigner l'"inclinaison" d'une dentale en cérébrale.

Le terme technique *pratyāhāra* a son domaine préparé par l'usage que fait le rituel du groupe verbal *pratyāhṛ-* : ainsi selon DŚS. XV 4 7, dans le mantra *ā vājaṃ vājino agman*, le préverbe *ā* tombe et l'on ramène à sa place (*pratyāhṛtya*) la forme *agman*, de manière à obtenir un nouveau mantra *agman vājaṃ vājinaḥ*.

L'*abhinidhāna*, défini par RPr. VI 17 : 393 comme la ségrégation et le voilage de consonne devant consonne, c'est-à-dire une articulation incomplète de la première consonne par opposition à *saṃyoga* qui désigne la "jonction" normale (cf. RPr. VI 24 : 400), est dans le rituel "le fait de déposer à côté ou dessus" (donc, contact sans jonction) KŚS. V 1 31 XXV 3 13 et cf. *abhinidhā-* ŚB. *Abhinihita* est le nom d'un *saṃdhi* où l'*a-* initial s'est "rapproché" de *-e -o* final (pour être absorbé par ceux-ci): "mis en contact" ŚB. I 3 4 12.

formes liturgiques qu'ils présupposent, invitent à voir de ce côté l'origine.

Hors même des correspondances de vocabulaire, cette littérature révèle par ses préoccupations générales comment des notions de grammaire ont pu sortir peu à peu de valeurs religieuses. Dès un hymne du Ṛgveda, l'hymne à la Parole (*vāc*) X 71, nous voyons la parole magnifiée comme art de l'expression : cet hymne qui fait prévoir pour ainsi dire le développement de la grammaire est en même temps le plus vieux texte de la poétique indienne. L'origine du langage est reportée aux temps primitifs où sous l'égide de Bṛhaspati "le maître de la parole sacrée", il fut "imparti des noms aux choses", et qu'ainsi "se révéla avec amour ce qu'il y avait en elles de meilleur, de pur, et qui demeurait caché". Ainsi que les Brāhmaṇa le réaffirmeront souvent, le langage est conçu comme la partie extériorisée, explicite (*nirukta*) de l'ensemble mystérieux (*paro'kṣa*) des choses informulables (*anirukta*). Les vieux Sages ont imposé la parole à la pensée "comme on clarifie les grains par le crible" : ce qui est évoqué ici, c'est donc la constitution d'une langue raffinée, d'un "sanskrit" grâce auquel "la beauté s'imprima sur la parole". Cette langue raffinée est au service du rite : ce n'est pas un hasard si le terme *saṃskṛta* et la série qui s'y apparente désignent les préparations rituelles, les actes matériels (*adhiśrayaṇa*, *paryagnikaraṇa*, *pātrapratapana*, etc.) qui ornent et ajustent un rite, et aussi les cérémonies de consécration ou "sacrements" qui marquent les étapes de la vie d'un *ārya*. Mais cette parole, poursuit l'hymne X 71, n'est pas donnée à tous : les uns ne la voient pas ni ne l'ententent : ils cheminent dans l'"illusion" (*māyā*) et leur langage est "sans fleur et sans fruit" ; ils ne connaissent pas le chemin de l'acte, entendez : du rite. D'autres au contraire la réalisent : à eux la parole "a ouvert son corps comme à son mari une femme aux riches atours".

Le problème de la répartition de la parole a maintes fois occupé les Brāhmaṇa. La plus ancienne mention s'en trouve dans l'hymne à énigmes I 164 du RV. ; au v. 45 il est dit que le discours "mesure quatre parties", dont "trois sont tenues secrètes, on ne les met point en branle" ; seule est connue la quatrième : c'est le langage des hommes. Il ne faut pas voir ici, naturellement, d'allusion aux quatre parties du discours, comme croit ou feint de croire la Paspaśā (p. 3 l. 26) — encore que précisément cette distribution quadripartite a dû être présente à l'esprit de Yāska et des auteurs des Prātiśākhya quand ils ont réparti les mots en noms et verbes, particules et préverbes. Il ne faut pas davantage en croire le ŚB. IV 1 3 16, selon qui les quartiers cachés sont le langage des bêtes, quadrupèdes, oiseaux, animalcules. Il s'agit bien plutôt, pensons nous avec Geldner (RV. ad loc.) et Strauss (ZDMG. VI 1927 p. 102), de la partie transcendante du langage, ce qu'à date ultérieure on dénommera le *brahman*, dont il est dit, comme de la *vāc*, que l'homme n'est en état d'en reconnaître qu'une minime partie.

Car toute la spéculation sur le *brahman* se fonde en dernière analyse sur une différenciation linguistique où le *brahman* "parole sacrée, mot magique" englobe à la fois le mot matériel (ce qu'on appelle significativement *śabdabrahman*, et dont l'*ātman* est une manifestation) et le mot transcendant, le *parabrahman*. C'est cette distinction qui dans les cercles de philosophes du langage fournira la base de l'opposition *dhvani* : *sphoṭa*. Du point de vue védique, le nom (*nāman*) est l'essence des choses, et le "mot" (*pada*) est le lieu conçu comme une entité. La réalité est la parole divine exprimée. *Manas* et *vāc* forment une unité ŚB. I 4 4 15. La pensée (*mati*), c'est la parole, car c'est par la parole que pense tout être ici-bas VIII 1 2 7. C'est le plus puissant des souffles KS. XIX 10. Lorsqu'on respire, ce n'est pas par la respiration, c'est par la parole qu'on dit : j'ai respiré KB. II 7. Le Soi tout entier entre dans la parole et est fait de parole, ibid. D'autre part, la parole joue un rôle primordial dans la création : elle est créatrice, elle est le démiurge. La création est l'œuvre de la parole, c'est par la parole que tout a été fait ici-bas ŚB. VIII 1 2 9. Les trois mots sacrés *bhūḥ bhuvaḥ svaḥ* deviennent les trois mondes XI 1 6 3. On pourrait multiplier ces citations, dont on trouvera d'autres spécimens encore chez Deussen Gesch. Philos. I 1 p. 205 Hopkins Connecticut Acad. XV p. 26 S. Lévi Doctrine du sacrif. p. 22 Oldenberg Weltanschauung p. 78 Scharbau Idee der Schöpfung p. 123.

Il n'est pas surprenant si dans ces conditions la grammaire et les théories grammaticales ont joui dans la pensée indienne d'un prestige unique. La grammaire est considérée comme un membre du Veda, un Vedāṅga,[85] voire le plus important et le premier : *pradhānaṃ ṣaṭsv aṅgeṣu vyākaraṇam* M. I p. 1 19, *prathamaṃ chandasām aṅgam* Vākyapad. I 11 ; ce dernier texte ajoute que la grammaire est "la science suprême, filtre-purifiant de toutes les sciences" (*pavitraṃ sarvavidyānām adhividyam*), "la voie royale exempte de détours" (*ajihmā rājapaddhatiḥ*). Le Sarvadarśanasaṃgraha, qui mettra le Pāṇinimata sur le plan d'un *darśana*, dit à la fin de la section afférente que la grammaire "vise à réaliser l'objet suprême de l'homme" (*paramapuruṣārthasādhanatayā*). Elle est le Veda des Veda, ChU. VII 1 2 et 4, 2 1.

Lorsque la Paspaśā (p. 1 14) veut définir les buts fondamentaux de la grammaire, elle ne trouve à faire valoir que des notions d'ordre religieux : la *rakṣā* ou préservation du texte sacré, l'*ūha* ou modification apportée à un *mantra* pour qu'il s'adapte à un besoin nouveau, l'*āgama* ou tradition. D'ailleurs tout ce qui dans la Paspaśā est dit de la grammaire se réfère en fait au Veda. Lorsqu'au värtt. 5 il est enseigné que le domaine d'application des mots est constitué par les quatre Veda, ceci est à entendre au sens littéral. L'adjonction même que Patañjali propose à ce sujet souligne la prééminence des choses védiques : car les domaines annexes qu'il mentionne, la *vākovākya*, l'*itihāsa*, le *purāṇa*, le *vaidyaka* sont certainement des aspects particuliers de la littérature sacrée.[86] Ceci montre que, même à l'époque de Patañjali, après le grand effort vers la constitution d'une *bhāṣā* que trahit son œuvre, la grammaire était encore définie par rapport aux besoins de l'exégèse, comme une sorte d'*ancilla theologiae*, appelée d'ailleurs à jouer aussi le rôle d'une maîtresse.

La pensée indienne a pour substructure des raisonnements d'ordre grammatical. La Mīmāṃsā, en tant que prolongement et pour ainsi dire jurisprudence du rituel, implique une masse de données philologiques qui remontent en fin de compte à la gram-

[85] En fait l'Aṣṭādhyāyī, qui est largement sécularisée, est probablement le reflet d'un traité antérieur, plus proche du *chandas*. Les noms des *pūrvācārya* cités chez Pāṇini sont pour la plupart des noms de phonéticiens du Veda, connus par les Pr., et en même temps de ritualistes.

[86] *Vākovākya*, qui pourrait faire doute, désigne d'après Kaiyaṭa les énigmes rituelles.

maire[87]: d'abord par ses discussions sur la pérennité du mot (et le caractère périssable des phonèmes),[88] sur la relation entre le mot et le sens et le problème du *saṃbandha* ou "connexion" (Strauss SBB. 1932 p. 486), sur le prototype éternel du mot ou *sphoṭa*,[89] lesquelles coïncident avec celles du Mahābhāṣya (p. 483) et représentent le fonds le plus ancien de la Mīmāṃsā (p. 470). Ensuite par toute son organisation interne, par le lien qu'elle établit entre l'injonction védique ou *vidhi* et son aspect linguistique, à savoir l'optatif ou *liṅ*, par le rôle qu'elle attribue à la force de réalisation incluse dans la forme verbale de l'injonction, la *bhāvanā*, contrepartie du *kārakatva* et de la *śakti* des écoles grammaticales (v. là-dessus Edgerton Language IV p. 174). Il y a là une véritable scolastique grammaticale sous-jacente à l'herméneutique ritualiste.

Le Vedānta semble à première vue bien éloigné de ces problèmes. Mais il suffit de lire attentivement Śaṅkara ou Rāmānuja pour constater que leur pensée est constamment étayée et nourrie de raisonnements grammaticaux. Rappelons la théorie du *śeṣa*, élevé à la hauteur d'un principe éthique (et élaboré d'ailleurs sur une armature de Mīmāṃsā), la notion de *bheda* "différenciation", de *vyāpti* "extension (d'un phonème, d'une fonction, transitivation)"; la notion de *guṇa* "attribut" ou "qualification" commande le problème du *brahman*. Le postulat du primat de l'ultériorité émane des *paribhāṣā* grammaticales. Le principe du *sāmānyādhikaraṇya* ou "communauté de référence (de deux noms par rapport à l'action verbale)" (symbolisée en grammaire par le *karmadhāraya*) est à la base du monisme, où l'axiome *tat tvam asi* se résout en une relation de sujet à prédicat. Toute glose indienne, dans son détail, dans son cheminement littéral, est pétrie de grammaire, mais c'est aussi la grammaire qui relie et domine quelques-unes des démarches les plus hautes de la pensée indienne.

[87] Dans sa discussion sur la question si le mot désigne l'espèce ou l'individu, M. I 2 64 vt. 35–59 (traduit Strauss ZDMG. LXXXI p. 137) est un avant-coureur de la Mī. depuis Jaimini, Upavarṣa et Śabarasvāmin, du Nyāya depuis Gotama et Vātsyāyana (Strauss l. c. 151). De même il y a des contacts étroits entre tel passage de M. sur le genre grammatical et le genre naturel (M. IV 1 3, traduit Strauss Festg. Garbe p. 84) et l'argumentation des logiciens. Sur les analogies entre M. et les Yogasū., v. en particulier l'Introd. de Woods p. 15.

[88] Ce problème crucial est abordé Mī. I 1 6–23 et repris dans les NySū. et les VaiśSū., cf. notamment Abegg Festschr. Wackernagel p. 255. Le point de départ en réside dans une réflexion toute primitive sur la nature et la fonction du Veda, dont on retrouverait sans peine la trace jusque dans les Hymnes. En tout cas la discrimination entre le mot *kārya* "opératoire" et *śāśvatika* "éternel" est déjà formulée RPr. XIII 14 : 722. C'est à une date bien postérieure que se sont élevés chez les Mīmāṃsistes des critiques de la grammaire, sentant en celle-ci une adversaire de la révélation (quelques textes réunis ici Ksh. Ch. Chatterjee J. Dep. Letters XXIV [this volume, pages 287–297]). — Noter que les NySū. II 2 55 usent d'une terminologie grammaticale, mais non pāṇinéenne: *guṇa* au sens d'"accent", *upamarda*, *hrāsa*, *vṛddhi* au sens d'"allongement", *leśa*, *śleṣa*.

[89] Littérature : Abegg Fest. Windisch p. 188 Liebich ZDMG. LXXVII p. 212 Strauss p. 131 Jacobi LVI p. 399 Chakravarti Ling. Specul. p. 42, 127 et passim Philos. Skt Gr. p. 84 Varma Critical Studies p. 172 Dasgupta Study of Pat. (Appendice 1). [See this volume, pages 405–414]. La doctrine, à laquelle sauf le Yoga aucune école philosophique n'a vraiment adhéré, émane des grammairiens; la discussion la plus attentive sur ce sujet est celle de Kumārila, dans le chapitre du *sphoṭavāda* du Ślokavārttika.

B. Grammaire et Védānta (1957)

Louis Renou

The second comparative study presented here is "Grammaire et Védānta," *Journal asiatique* (245, 1957, 121–133). Renou takes one of the most well-known philosophical texts in Sanskrit (part of which he translated in *Śaṅkara: Prolégomenes au Védānta*, 1951) and studies concepts and patterns of reasoning that may be traced back to the grammarians. Śaṅkara's commentary on the *Brahmasūtra* or *Vedāntasūtra* was probably written in the eighth century A.D.

Prenant pour exemple le commentaire de Ś[aṅkara] sur les [Brahma]sū[tra] — par commodité, nous ajouterons aux références par adhyāya, pāda et sū. les pages de la traduction Thibaut —, essayons de voir l'usage que fait Ś. de notions ou de formes de raisonnement émanant ou susceptibles d'émaner des écoles grammaticales.

À vrai dire, les citations expresses de textes grammaticaux sont en nombre très réduit : l'index de Thibaut(-Winternitz) n'en livre que trois : a) P[āṇini] I. 4,30 sur l'Abl. de cause matérielle (*prakṛti*), appuyant la thèse que le *b*[*rahman*] est bien la cause matérielle du monde (I. 4,23 p. 285). b) P. VI. 4,158 sur le sens du mot *bhūman* ("fait d'être beaucoup"), mot que le sū. lui-même (et en tout cas Ś. ad loc.) I. 3,8 p. 162 interprète comme un des noms du *b*. (le terme vient de ChU. VII. 23 et 24). c) Ad I. 4,11 p. 260 enfin, l'expression *pañcajanāḥ* de la BĀU. (impliquée dans le sū. suivant n° 12) est interprétée à l'aide de P. II. 1, 50, aux termes duquel de pareils composés ayant un nom de nombre au membre antérieur sont des *saṃjñā* : *pañcajanāḥ*, en l'occurrence, désignera une classe d'êtres et nommément, en vertu du sū. 12, "le souffle et autres (essences) analogues".

Beaucoup plus souvent, les règles pāṇinéennes demeurent à l'état latent, comme il est d'ailleurs naturel, dans la trame du commentaire. D'ordinaire, dans la portion initiale du développement consacré à tel ou tel sū., celle qui contient la paraphrase. Comme dans les cas précédents, l'allusion aide à élucider quelque forme, quelque emploi embarrassant du sū. ou, plus souvent encore, de l'Up. visée par ce sū.[1]

C'est l'emploi des cas (à quoi se réfère déjà I. 4,23 précité) qui donne lieu au plus grand nombre de remarques. Au cours des efforts faits par Ś. pour réduire à l'unité les propositions upaniṣadiques et étendre les identifications avec le *b*.,[2] il s'agissait en effet

[1] Mentionnons pour mémoire les allusions à des données qui sont moins de grammaire que de "philosophie grammaticale", encore que Patañjali y ait touché le premier. Ainsi sur le *sphoṭa* I. 3,28 p. 204 considéré comme le mot (perçu globalement, par opposition aux phonèmes successifs qui le composent), *tasmāt sphoṭa eva śabdaḥ* p. 206. Ou bien sur le *dhvani*, ibid. p. 208, considéré comme la "tonalité", d'où dépendent les distinctions d'*udātta*, *anudātta* et autres, *tannibandhanāś codāttādayo viśeṣāḥ*. Ibid. enfin, dans ce même riche contexte de réflexions paralinguistiques (p. 202), il est dit que la connexion des mots est avec l'espèce ou le genre, non avec l'individu, *ākṛtibhiś ca śabdānāṃ saṃbandho na vyaktibhiḥ* : thème bien connu de discussion, depuis Patañjali.

[2] Ici joue à l'occasion le concept du *paryāya*, de la synonymie. Ainsi I. 1,22 p. 83, après qu'il a eu montré qu'*ākāśa* signifiait *b*., Ś. ajoute que les synonymes d'*ā*° signifient également *b*. En revanche, les "symboles" (*pratīka*) tels que le "nom" ne sont pas aptes à exprimer le *b*. IV. 1,4 p. 341 ; la coordination grammaticale (*sāmānyādhikaraṇya*) qui lie éventuellement ces symboles au mot "*b*." n'est pas

de montrer que tel cas grammatical équivaut à tel autre, ou du moins n'entrave pas l'assimilation. Ainsi le Loc. de séjour (*ādhāra*, mot qui chez P. I. 4,45 glose *adhikaraṇa*) "dans le ciel" équivaut à l'Abl. de limite (*maryādā*)[3] "au-dessus du ciel" I. 1,27 p. 96. De même le Loc. et l'Instr. III. 2,7 p. 142: dans "il s'unit avec l'Être", un Loc. ("dans l'Être") est entendu, en raison de passages complémentaires où figure effectivement "dans l'Être": ainsi dit-on dans l'usage profane "il va vers la mer par le Gange" ou "dans le Gange", indifféremment.

Mais, au moins au titre de *pūrvapakṣa*, une différence entre Nom. et Loc. est admise I. 2,5 p. 112. Il ne fallait pas que le *kārakatva* grammatical fût un obstacle dirimant aux équivalences notionnelles.

Ailleurs (II. 3,10 p. 21), Ś. a jugé utile de préciser la valeur de l'Abl. afin d'expliquer le texte "de l'air naquit le feu" *vāyor agniḥ* de la TU., texte qui semble en contradiction avec d'autres affirmant que le feu naquit du *b.*, *tejaso brahmajatve*. La difficulté est résolue en invoquant la différence entre origine immédiate et origine ultime.

D'autres passages montrent la nécessité de respecter la distinction casuelle: dans *pituḥ pitā* ou *prāṇasya prāṇaḥ*, Gén. et Nom. ont chacun leur rôle I. 1,23 p. 87 Ailleurs (III. 2,22 p. 169), Ś. note que le *b.*, dans tel passage de la BĀU. (II. 3,1), n'est mentionné qu'au Gén., en sorte qu'il n'est pas dominant, mais figure seulement en tant que déterminé par ses propres formes, *brahma tu rūpaviśeṣaṇatvena ṣaṣṭyā nirdiṣṭam . . . na svapradhānatvena*.[4] Enfin (IV. 2,12 p. 373), le *pūrvapakṣin* discute sur l'équivalence entre Gén. et Abl. dans *na tasya/na tasmāt prāṇā utkrāmanti* BĀU. IV. 4,5: le Gén., qui exprime la relation, la connexion en général,[5] est ici "déterminé dans le sens d'une relation spécifique par l'Abl.", *pañcamyā saṃbandhaviśeṣe vyavasthāpyate*.

Hormis ces faits d'emploi casuel, qui prolongent et justifient la nette séparation qu'opérait P. entre catégorie casuelle et emploi des cas, seuls sont à relever des traits dispersés. Le *pūrvapakṣin* I. 1,13 p. 66 discute sur le sens de *-maya-* dans *ānandamaya* TU.: est-ce un *vikāraśabda*,[6] est-ce un élément notant "abondance" (*prācurya*)[7] ? Après une longue disquisition, Ś. se décide à conserver le sens usuel "fait de félicité" (sū. 19).

Le même sū (I. 1,19) fournit la matière de quelques autres allusions de grammaire: Ś. p. 76 autorise qu'un mot masculin — en l'occurrence, un pronom — se réfère au mot *b.*, lequel est neutre: ainsi seront acquis pour le Vedānta une série de passages décrivant un être qui en apparence est hétérogène au *b.* Le même contexte

une identification, pas plus que la coordination théoriquement exprimable dans la phrase *gaur aśvaḥ* "le bœuf (est) un cheval" n'aboutit à identifier réellement le bœuf au cheval.

[3] L'Abl. est noté par *avadhi* "limite" dans la Kāś. I. 4,24 et le mot *maryādā* lui-même figure P. I. 4,89.

[4] Le Nom. exprime le *svātantrya* ou "autonomie", comme chez les grammairiens, I. 1,5 p. 49–50, ainsi dans "(le soleil) brûle, donne la lumière".

[5] *Saṃbandhasāmānyaviṣayā hi ṣaṣṭhī.* Cf. encore I. 1,2 p. 16. Le terme *saṃbandha* figure dans la Kāś. II. 3,50. — Noter la distinction que fait Ś. entre Gén. du *karman* et Gén. du *śeṣa* pour expliquer le composé *brahmajijñāsā* I. 1,1 p. 12 : le *karman*, "désir de connaître le *b.*" s'accorde mieux à l'Écriture que le *śeṣa* "désir de connaître lié au *b.*".

[6] Mot employé par la Kāś. IV. 3,143 et qui d'ailleurs reprend une teneur de P. lui-même IV. 3,134.

[7] Mot reprenant le *prācuryeṇa prastutam* de Kāś. V. 4,21.

cite les noms techn. *prātipadika* p. 74, *anukarṣaṇa* p. 73 (*ananukṛṣya* "sans qu'il y ait lieu d'attirer [dans un texte un élément emprunté à un texte antérieur]"), *adhikāra* p. 72, qui, au sens de "influence gouvernante (d'un mot mis en tête d'un développement)", reflète l'emploi grammatical du terme.[8]

Ailleurs: *upapada* I. 1,7 p. 57 au sens de "mot servant d'attribut ou de détermination accessoire". *Sarvanāman* "pronom" I. 1,24 p. 93. *Bahuvrīhi* I. 1,2 p. 16 (avec l'épithète *tadguṇasaṃvijñāna*, cf. Terminol. s. u. *guṇa*°). *Karmadhāraya* I. 3,15 p. 180, passage où Ś. propose d'expliquer *brahmaloka* par "le monde (qui est) *b.*", afin d'éviter l'attribution au *b.* d'une notion concrète distinctive. L'explication du désidératif *pipatiṣati* "elle va tomber" (dit de la berge du fleuve) I. 1,5 p. 52 sert à montrer comment les Sāṃkhya s'entendent à poser que le *pradhāna*, entité notoirement dénuée d'intelligence, est la cause du monde; l'exemple est connu en grammaire, Kāś. III. 1,7.

Le recours à l'étymologie, malgré les facilités qu'il donnerait à l'argumentation, est évité. Un exemple est le mot *setu* "pont" MuU. II. 2,5: Ś. enseigne que ce terme n'implique pas nécessairement l'idée d'une "autre rive", idée qui aurait pour conséquence fâcheuse que le séjour du ciel et de la terre serait distinct du *b.*: conformément à l'étymologie par *si-* "lier", l'idée est celle de "tenir ensemble", "soutenir" I. 3,1 p. 156.[9]

Les cas qui précèdent sont des emprunts à la Grammaire, valables pour des besoins limités, pour alimenter des gloses particulières. Tout autres et plus intéressants sont les cas qui suivent, où un raisonnement de type grammatical entre en jeu. Ici se pose une question de principe. Ces mêmes procédés se retrouvent dans les commentaires sur la Mīmāṃsā, parfois aussi dans ceux sur le Nyāya. On ne peut strictement démontrer qu'ils aient pris naissance chez les grammairiens, sauf là où le contenu est nettement grammatical. Nous savons que Ś. était nourri de Mīmāṃsā, nous constatons que des tranches entières de son argumentation en dérivent. Là même où l'on pense atteindre un élément grammatical, c'est à travers la Mīmāṃsā qu'il a pu parvenir à Ś. À vrai dire, il existait un mode de raisonnement élémentaire, dont la plus

[8] Ailleurs, *adhikāra* est simplement "subject-matter", sens attesté dans les sū. mêmes II. 3,12 et 21 III. 3,3, et qui avoisine celui de *prakaraṇa*, plus fréquent. — Le mot *anuvṛtti* figure notamment I. 1,24 p. 91 ; 3,40 p. 232. — Notons en passant qu'il y'n a pas de glose "grammaticale" sur des particules telles que *ca* ou *vā* (*vā* III. 1,7 sert à écarter une objection, comme plus souvent *tu*); des gloses sans portée grammaticale affectent *atha* (au début de l'œuvre), *iti* (passim), *eva* (passim), *tathā* II. 4,1.

[9] Des paribhāṣā grammaticales sont mises en jeu III. 1,25 p. 131 *utsargāpavādayoś ca vyavasthitaviṣayatvam* "la règle générale et l'exception ont des domaines délimités", axiome d'ailleurs en contexte mīmāṃsiste (Garge Citations in Śabara-bhāṣya p. 264) : "ne fais pas violence à la créature" et "qu'il offre un animal à tel dieu" ont des sphères d'application distinctes. Ou bien I. 1,4 p. 39 où Ś. traite des deux types de négation; *prasajya* et *paryudāsa*, également dans le cadre mīmāṃsiste, Garge p. 265 et note de Thibaut ad loc. D'origine non moins grammaticale est un axiome tel que *itaretaraviśeṣaṇaviśeṣyabhāva* IV. 3,1 p. 383; 2 p. 385 "relation réciproque entre attribut et terme pourvu d'un attribut"; passim aussi *dharmadharminor abhedaḥ*, cf. Terminol s. u. *dharma*. La notion d'*abheda* "non-différence" a un substrat grammatical patent.

ancienne expression se trouve dans le Mahābhāṣya,[10] mode qui comportait l'usage d'un certain nombre de paribhāṣā ou clefs interprétatoires; beaucoup de ces paribhāṣā sont passées à haute époque dans le Mahābhāṣya lui-même. Les autres systèmes n'en offrent pas l'équivalent, et elles ont fait loi, mutatis mutandis, dans le domaine philosophique, tout au moins dans l'une et l'autre Mīmāṃsā qui, plus qu'aucun autre système, exigeaient un code de conventions.

L'argument préliminaire, chez Ś., se fonde volontiers sur le sens établi (*prasiddha*), sur l'usage (*prayoga*) attesté (*darśana*), tout comme les grammairiens font état de l'usage (*loka*), de l'aptitude à exprimer (*abhidhāna*). Ce "sens établi" fournit des valeurs directes, immédiatement sensibles. Il repose en principe sur la convention ou *rūḍhi* I. 3,40 p. 232. Entre deux valeurs établies, il advient que l'une "monte (plus) vite à la conscience" *śīghraṃ buddhim ārohati* I. 1,22 p. 82. C'est l'emploi profane ou usuel du mot. La méthode védântique, sur le plan de la sémasiologie, consiste pour une bonne part à écarter ce sens naturel, à retrouver une valeur indirecte, à outrepasser en somme l'usage: ainsi le mot *anna* signifiera, non "nourriture", mais "terre" (dans ChU. VI. 2, 4) II. 3,12 p. 23. On reconnaît ce forçage linguistique si commun à la scolastique indienne depuis le Nirukta: l'exégèse du Ṛgveda en a fourni le prétexte et en a accrédité l'habitude. Mais, ici comme ailleurs, le recours à la grammaire forme le propre du pūrvapakṣa; le Vedāntin accompli le transcende: c'est ce que font, plus ou moins ouvertement, toutes les disciplines classiques de l'Inde.

D'autres considérations priment en effet l'usage ou l'apparence. Ainsi le *prakaraṇa* ou "contexte". Toutefois il y a un risque à abandonner le sens direct au profit du contexte I. 3,8 p. 166 *tatra prakaraṇānurodhena śrutiḥ parityaktā syāt*: on contrevient au principe bien connu de la Mīmāṃsā (Garge op. c. p. 276), alludé par Ś. lui-même III. 3,49 p. 262, aux termes de quoi la valeur directe (*śruti*) a plus de force que le signe-caractéristique (*liṅga*), le *liṅga* plus que la connexion syntactique (*vākya*), le *vākya* enfin plus que le *prakaraṇa*. On reconnaît là cette scrutation sur la "force" de tel type de règles par rapport à tel autre, domaine essentiel de la théorie des paribhāṣā.

[10] Qu'on pense à la séquence à peu près obligatoire : paraphrase littérale, exposé du problème en litige (*saṃśaya*), thèse antérieure, thèse définitive (faisant suite à des objections partielles, des répliques, des aperçus ne comportant qu'une part de vérité Thieme GN. 1935 [this Volume page 299]). Cette séquence se retrouve dans toute la scolastique indienne; mais nulle part, sauf peut-être chez Śabarasvāmin, elle n'est si voisine du modèle patañjalien que chez Ś., en dépit des siècles qui séparent ces deux maîtres. L'entrée en matière si commune chez Ś., telle que I. 1,22 p. 81 "une question se pose : le mot Ether (ChU. I. 9,1) désigne-t-il le *b.* suprême ou bien l'éther-élément? — Pourquoi cette question? — Parce que l'un et l'autre sont attestés" *kim ākāśaśabdena paraṃ brahmābhidhīyata uta bhūtākāśam iti/ kutaḥ saṃśayaḥ/ ubhayatra prayogadarśanāt* rappelle tant d'attaques toutes semblables chez Patañjali. L'emploi de *prāpta* pour désigner un résultat apparemment, provisoirement, acquis, en fait annulable par un raissonement ultérieur, est aussi fréquent chez Ś. qu'en Grammaire. Cf. encore l'usage du terme *prayojana* I. 1,4 p. 38 "motivation" (non "final end" Thibaut) et une formule familière comme *kiṃ tava tena syāt* (ibid.) *kiṃ kṛtaṃ syāt* (passim).

La "valeur directe" comporte elle-même des aménagements; on peut faire appel d'une interprétation moins informée à une autre mieux informée, ainsi IV. 2, 1 p. 364 où le pūrvapakṣin tient que c'est la parole même qui se résorbe dans la pensée (au moment de la mort), cette explication seule faisant justice au "sens direct"; mais le siddhāntin comprend "la fonction de la parole se résorbe . . .": fonction et chose affectée de fonction sont comprises comme non-distinctes, *vṛttivṛttimator abhedopacārāt*. En réalité, Ś. use, suivant les convenances, de l'un ou l'autre de ces procédés. Il fait état, très souvent, du *prakaraṇa*, malgré la faiblesse relative de cet argument. Ainsi, dans un passage (I. 1, 24 p. 90) où il entend montrer que la lumière (*jyotiṣ*, ChU. III. 13, 7) est bien le *b*. Les "signes caractéristiques" sont également invoqués, ainsi dans le développement I. 1, 23 p. 85 où Ś. aboutit à l'équation *prāṇa* = *b*. Si le personnage sis dans le disque solaire est le *b*. même (I. 1, 11 p. 63), c'est en raison du *liṅga*, à savoir, "le fait de n'être associé à aucun mal".[11]

La "connexion syntactique" joue un rôle éminent (Garge op. c. p. 262). Si le mot "lumière" (au passage déjà cité, p. 93) signifie *b*., c'est que la phrase où il figure est liée à la précédente par le pronom *yad*, qui forme un *sāmarthya*, une "communauté sémantique". Ce qui compte est moins la force d'une donnée initiale I. 4, 19 p. 274 que la valeur du développement entier, ibid. p. 275, ou bien la pluralité des connexions I. 1, 29 p. 99, où le terme *saṃbandhabhūman* figure déjà dans le sū. Ainsi en Grammaire, où l'*adhikāra* initial est souvent perdu de vue à mesure qu'on avance dans le chapitre qu'il commande. C'est la connexion de tel élément avec tel autre qui peut rendre un texte intelligible I. 1,26 p. 96. Le *vākya* peut provoquer un transfert en propulsant un mot hors de son domaine naturel I. 1, 24 p. 93 (contexte déjà cité), *svaviṣayāc chakyā pracyāvayitum*. Le mot *atideśa* "transfert" joue un rôle éminent en Mīmāṃsā (Garge p. 280) comme en Grammaire. On le trouve encore I. 1, 20 p. 78 et 79, où il est dit que le *puruṣa* sis dans le disque solaire a des caractères qui se laissent transférer au *puruṣa* sis dans l'œil (passage déjà cité).[12]

Toute interprétation qui préserve l'unité d'une phrase vaut mieux que celle qui entraîne une scission: principe connu des grammairiens (Terminol. s. u. *ekavākya*), chez qui une paribhāṣā invite à ne déduire de la "scission de règle" (*yogavibhāga*) que les résultats "souhaitables". Mais d'après la Mīmāṃsā (Garge p. 256), le *vākyabheda* a une signification un peu différente: l'axiome entre en vigueur là où une même proposition semble contenir deux injonctions distinctes. C'est le risque que commande d'éviter Ś. I. 2, 2 p. 108; 3, 14 p. 177; III. 3, 58 p. 279 (cf. aussi I. 1, 31 p. 103) et qui lui permet de réfuter un pūrvapakṣa. En ce dernier passage (III. 3, 58), l'argumentation consistant à unir plusieurs données en un même ensemble syntactique est rejetée en posant que les phrases successives ne possèdent aucun indice qui marquerait l'"appétence" (*ākāṅkṣā*) de l'une d'elles vers un élément complétif: chacune d'elles se suffit à elle-même, preuve qu'on a bien

[11] La notion de *liṅga* émane du Rituel plutôt que de la Grammaire, JA, 1941-1942, p. 153 [this Volume page 463]. En Grammaire, l'emploi à peu près corrélatif est celui de *lakṣaṇa*.

[12] Une conséquence de la connexion non-observée est l'erreur consistant à abandonner un sujet en cours pour en attaquer un nouveau I. 1, 15 p. 68; 24 p. 90 et passim. *prakṛtahānāprakṛtaprakriye*.

affaire à une "phrase": la notion d'*ākāṅkṣā* est connue aussi en Grammaire.

La "connexion" est plus que la simple proximité, qui en Grammaire peut servir de base à une interprétation, tout en passant pour moins "forte" que le *sāmarthya* (Terminol. s. u. *pratyāsatti*). Ś. use çà et là de l'argument de proximité; il distingue une proximité moins grande et une plus grande (*saṃnihitatara*) I. 1, 19 p. 75. Mais il enseigne I. 1, 23 p. 86 que la proximité ne prévaut pas contre la force d'une "proposition complémentaire" (*vākyaśeṣa*), en vertu de quoi, par exemple, *prāṇa* sera identifiable à *b*. Cette notion du *vākyaśeṣa* repose, du point de vue grammatical, sur l'ellipse, cf. le Mahābhāṣya, Terminol. s. u., comme l'indique clairement l'expression *iti vākyaśeṣaḥ* I. 1, 2 p. 16. C'est un aspect particulier de la connexion. A côté des "propositions absolues" (dont certaines sont dites "décisives", *nirṇayavākya* I. 1, 2 p. 19), il y a les *vākyaśeṣa*: le mot figure dans les sū. mêmes, I. 4, 12, ainsi que dans les MīSū. C'est souvent le *vākyaśeṣa* qui donne la clef d'un Texte, ainsi la signification du composé (déjà cité) *pañcajanāḥ* I. 4,12 p. 260 est précisée par le *v*° "ceux qui connaissent le souffle du souffle", d'où suit que *pañcajana* (sur le plan védântique) égale *prāṇa*. La complémentarité résulte d'un même emploi rituel et d'une unité sémantique, cf. le passage mīmāṃsiste I. 1, 4 p. 23. La *śruti* ou valeur directe l'emporte, comme de juste, sur la proximité III. 3, 55 p. 273, laquelle est faible par nature III. 3, 25 p. 224, passage également d'inspiration mīmāṃsiste.

Ainsi l'emploi simultané de la Grammaire et de la Mīmāṃsā, ou si l'on préfère de la Mīmāṃsā à substructure grammaticale, permettra de saisir des gradations, partant des préférences, des applications privilégiées pour telle proposition qu'on cherche à distinguer par rapport à telles autres.

Un autre artifice, plus productif encore, est la différence qui s'opère entre valeur primaire (*mukhya*) et valeur secondaire (*gauṇa*). Il s'agit là d'une des tendances fondamentales, la plus importante même sans doute, de toute la sémantique indienne, de toutes les théories fondées de près ou de loin sur la sémantique, à commencer par l'Alaṃkāraśāstra.[13] L'origine s'en trouve clairement du côté des écoles grammaticales. Une paribhāṣā conservée chez Patañjali pose que "si un mot a une valeur secondaire en même temps qu'une valeur primaire, l'opération le concernant se réfère à sa valeur primaire (seule)". Ceci rappelle d'un peu loin l'axiome précité de la Mīmāṃsā, aux termes duquel la *śruti* ou "valeur directe" prévaut sur toute autre interprétation.

Chez Ś. aussi le sens primaire est préférable au sens impliqué I. 1, 22 p. 82; 26 p. 96;[14] IV. 2, 1 p. 364 (passage déjà cité). La distinction entre sens "dérivé" et sens primaire ne s'avère que là où existe une différence de fait entre les choses énoncées I. 1, 4 p. 42 *prasiddhavastubhedasya gauṇatvamukhyatvaprasiddheḥ*. Il est vain de poser avec les Sāṃkhya un sens figuratif au mot "il considéra"

[13] Le sens "secondaire" n'entrave pas le principe, connu aussi des grammairiens, de l'*ekārthatva* du vocabulaire (racines verbales exceptées) : principe rappelé par Ś. I. 1, 7 p. 56; 22 p. 82. Les grammairiens ont le juste sentiment que les acceptions secondaires d'un mot, si aberrantes soient-elles, ne contredisent pas son unité sémantique essentielle.

[14] Il s'agit ici de la connotation du mot *b*. dans ChU III. 12, 7 : "sens primaire" veut dire que le mot *b*. ne signifie "rien d'autre que *b*.". C'est autour et par rapport au mot *b*. que s'agite tout l'effort sémasiologique du Vedānta śaṅkarien.

de l'Up. pour justifier que le sujet de ce verbe soit le neutre *sat* "l'Être" I. 1, 6 p. 53.[15]

Ce qui paraît devoir désigner des essences extérieures au *b.*, par exemples les vocables "rive", "mesure", "connexion", "séparation" III. 2, 31 p. 175 — et qui les désigne selon le pūrvapakṣin — n'est en réalité que métaphore; c'est ainsi que le *b.* est appelé "rive" parce qu'il ressemble à une rive d'une certaine manière.

Soit le Texte relatif à l'éther II. 3, 1 p. 3 et suiv., lequel est tantôt donné comme sans origine, tantôt comme né du Soi. Comment expliquer cette contradiction? A-t-on le droit d'unir syntactiquement les deux propositions? On se ralliera plutôt à la position d'un "sens secondaire": le Texte admettant une certaine origine de l'éther (sū. 3 p. 5) à un sens secondaire, autrement dit figuratif. Tel mot — ainsi *saṃbhūtaḥ* (sū. 5 p. 7) — peut être primaire dans telles conditions, secondaire dans telles autres. Le mot *b.* lui-même est pris secondairement quand il se réfère à la nourriture, primairement quand il vise la félicité (ceci dit à propos de TU. III. 2-6, ibid.). L'équivalence, au même passage, "*tapas* = *b.*" est figurée, c'est une *bhakti* ou "participation" assimilatrice. Les mots "naissance" et "mort", lorsqu'ils s'appliquent au Soi, sont *bhākta* ou purement métaphoriques, d'après le sū. même II. 3, 16 p. 28: leur emploi primaire entacherait la permanence du Soi.

Faut-il reconnaître le sens figuré dans le cas de choses pour lesquelles les mots (védiques) sont notre seul instrument de connaissance (*pramāṇa*)? Ce point de vue est rejeté par Ś. I. 1, 7 p. 56, qui y voit le risque d'un "manque de confiance" généralisé, *sarvatrānāśvāsaprasaṅgāt*; il consent que certains mots aient l'une ou l'autre valeur suivant les circonstances.[16] Il discute encore III. 1, 10 p. 120 sur le sens direct du mot *caraṇa* "conduite" et le sens connotatif "résidu des œuvres": ici les t. techn. employés sont *śrauta* d'une part, *lākṣaṇika* de l'autre, qui font penser aux paribhāṣā grammaticales bien connues opérant avec *śruta/lākṣaṇika* ou *śruta/anumita* (Terminol. s. uu.).

Un autre aspect de la valeur "secondaire" est celui qu'on observe III. 3, 42 p. 255: on évoque là ce principe mīmāṃsiste qu'un *arthavāda* ou "proposition énonçant un état de fait" ne forme qu'une matière secondaire, alors que les portions concernant le résultat ou "fruit" d'un acte enjoint forment une "matière principale" et du point de vue linguistique sont à entendre au sens direct, littéral, *tathā hi guṇavāda āpadyeta phalopadeśe tu mukhyavādopapattiḥ*.

Parfois le sens secondaire est à préférer. On enseigne IV. 4, 4 p. 408 que l'âme délivrée est indivise avec le Soi suprême: là où un Texte énonce une séparation, c'est la non-séparation qu'on

[15] Audit sū. est attesté le mot *gauṇa*, que Ś. glose par *aupacārika* "résultant d'une approximation (métaphorique)".

[16] Toutefois il ne faudrait pas prendre un seul et même mot, tantôt au sens primaire avec tel attribut, tantôt au sens secondaire avec tel autre, en un seul et même développement; il en résulterait un "manque d'uniformité", vice qu'il faut à tout prix éviter II. 4, 3 p. 77, *na hy ekasmin prakaraṇa ekasmiṃś ca vākya ekaḥ śabdaḥ sakṛd uccarito bahubhiḥ saṃbadhyamānaḥ kvacid mukhyaḥ* kvacid *gauṇa ity adhyavasātuṃ śakyam/ vairūpyaprasaṅgāt.*

Le sens secondaire est admis à titre optionnel (*vā* du sū.) III. 1, 7 p. 110 : il s'agit du mot *anna* dans "les Vaiśya sont l'*anna* des rois" *viśo 'nnaṃ rājñām*, et analogues. Aussi III. 2, 4 p. 4 à propos de l'individu qui, en dormant, "crée des chariots, etc." selon BĀU. III. 3, 9 et 10.

admettra, sur la base du "sens secondaire", *bhedanirdeśas tv abhede 'py upacaryate.*

L'objet propre du Védānta, tel que l'entend Ś., est de ramener à l'unité les Textes et les notions inscrites, Thibaut p. LXVI. De manière analogue, l'objet de la Smṛti savante est de résorber les conflits virtuels entre les sources écrites ou ceux entre droit et coutume. Celui des commentaires pāṇinéens est de concilier l'usage avec les règles, quand ce n'est pas de permettre l'application non contrariée de deux règles afférentes à une même opération.

On ne peut accepter l'idée d'un conflit, même entre les mantra et les brāhmaṇa I. 1, 15 p. 68, *mantrabrāhmaṇayoś caikārthatvaṃ yuktam/avirodhāt*: pas davantage entre les diverses Écritures.[17] De là l'emploi du *vākyaśeṣa* (ci-dessus décrit) et du "sens secondaire", qui évoque de loin l'*antaraṅgatva* et le *bahiraṅgatva* des raisonnements grammaticaux. Un axiome banal est la "conformité de vues des textes révélés" *śrutisāmānya* I. 1, 21 p. 81.

Toutefois, il faut distinguer. De même que certaines règles de grammaire sont de simples développements (*prapañca*) d'une règle antérieure, que d'autres sont des définitions, d'autres enfin des rappels d'une chose établie (*anuvāda*),[18] non pas des injonctions proprement dites, de même il y a dans la Mīmāṃsā des *arthavāda* (Ś. y fait allusion I. 1, 4 p. 23 et cf. III. 3, 42 cité ci-dessus), lesquels n'ont d'autorité que par l'effet de leur enchaînement à tel ou tel *vidhi*.

De même aussi que dans les sū. grammaticaux le répétition d'un mot, d'une règle donnée à une règle prochainement consécutive, serait une faute si elle n'avait quelque motivation (*prayojana*) particulière, de même en Śruti la répétition de deux Textes indique qu'il faut les séparer l'un de l'autre, sinon la validité de l'un des deux serait compromise III. 3, 35 p. 242. Pareillement, rappelle encore Ś., la répétition dans la Mīmāṃsā montre que deux actes rituels sont distincts. La reprise du mot *b.* I. 2, 15 p. 127, a une incidence sur la valeur du mot prédicat, en l'occurrence *ka* et *kha*: le prédicat serait conçu comme une simple qualité et ne pourrait servir de support à une méditation. La répétition oriente la sémantique: le mot "félicité" étant repris dans TU. au sens de "*b.*", il s'ensuit que le "Soi fait-de-félicité" n'est autre que le *b.* I. 1, 12 p. 65. Chez Ś., comme chez les grammairiens, l'attitude initiale, vis-à-vis des teneurs répétées, est celle d'un "doute" qui se déclanche, d'un problème qui se pose.

[17] Le conflit est admis, du moins à titre préliminaire, I. 4, 14 p. 263 et 265, pour un domaine n'intéressant pas la doctrine, celui des choses créées. La *śrutivipratipatti* de III. 2, 31 p. 175 demeure au niveau des apparences. — Noter que certains mantra et brāhmaṇa, au début des Up., n'appartiennent pas à la *brahmavidyā*, bien qu'elles en avoisinent l'enseignement, III. 3, 25 p. 223 : ceci exprime un fait dont nous avons aujourd'hui le sentiment, à savoir que le début des Up. plonge encore dans la substance des Brāhmaṇa et n'échappe que progressivement à cette gangue.

[18] Le terme figure chez Ś. I. 1, 4 p. 27; 3, 42 p. 234 ("Qui est le Soi?" Réponse "Celui qui est dans le cœur" : s'agit-il là d'un *anuvāda* sur la nature du Soi migrant, déjà connue par d'autres sources; ou bien le passage vise-t-il à établir la nature dudit Soi? Argumentation qui fait penser à l'*aprāpta* = et à la *prāpta-vibhāṣā* des écoles grammaticales) II. 3, 47 (les Textes visent à enseigner la non-différence; sur la différence, il n'y a que des *anuvāda*, comme on en a sur les choses naturellement établies, *svabhāvaprāpta*).

Nous venons de mentionner l'expression "pour servir de support à la méditation": Ś. en effet fait intervenir la "méditation" pour rendre compte de certains attributs qu'au premier examen la Śruti confère au *b.*: ces fantômes ont été évoqués simplement, nous dit-on, "pour servir à la méditation", *upāsanārtham*: ainsi I. 1, 24 p. 91 à propos des pseudo-localisations du *b.* En Grammaire, les mentions de lieux (*udīcām*, etc.), les noms de maîtres figurent *pūjārtham* "honoris causa": elles sont dénuées de valeur injonctive par elles-mêmes. Il ne serait pas excessif de montrer que les artifices de la *māyā* ou "altérité (phénoménale)" I. 1, 20 p. 80, de la *līlā* ou "jeu (phénoménal)" II. 1, 33 (sū.!), du *nāmarūpa* ou "nom-et-forme" II. 2, 2 p. 369, considérés comme autant d'obstacles à l'identification fondamentale, reposent lointainement sur des postulats grammaticaux: la distinction entre la forme opérationnelle (*kārya*) et la forme réalisée (*siddha*), ou encore cette "non-réalisation" technique que résume en des perspectives illimitées le célèbre *pūrvatrāsiddham* de Pāṇini. Toutes les démarches de Ś. postulent la recherche d'un état second permettant d'annuler la multiplicité que fournit l'état élémentaire. C'est aussi, en un sens, l'effort de la Grammaire.

C. Grammaire et Poétique en sanskrit (1961)

Louis Renou

The third comparative study is "Grammaire et poétique en sanskrit," *Études védiques et pāṇinéennes* (8, 1961, 105–131). Here Renou takes a basic treatise on poetics, the *Kāvyaprakāśa*, and studies some of the relationships between poetics and syntax. The *Kāvyaprakāśa* was written by a Kashmir brahman, Mammaṭa, who lived in the eleventh century A.D. Renou deals with discussions on the grammaticality of poetic forms; poetic analysis of long nominal compounds; expressions for poetic comparison or analogy; ellipsis; cases where a member of a compound is syntactically related to words outside the compound; and other topics.

§1. Prenant pour base le Kāvyaprakāśa (KP.),[1] notre objet limité est de rechercher ce que la Poétique ajoute à notre connaissance de la grammaire, telle qu'elle résulte de P(āṇini) et de son école.

[1] Texte cité d'après l'éd. du Bhandarkar Oriental Research Institute (1950); par *sū(tra)*'s et, éventuellement, par pages. Le découpage des *kār(ikā)* en *sū.*'s, ajoutons-le, n'a pas de justification interne (cf. en dernier Sivaprasad Bhattacharyya, éd. du KP. 1, p. LXIV), pas en tout cas celle que peut posséder le Rk-Prātiś. — l'autre texte où cette double division est attestée —, à savoir de nous rappeler qu'un sectionnement ancien en *sū.*'s a été refondu en forme de *kār.*'s. La seule raison d'être des pseudo-*sū.* du KP. est qu'ils coïncident avec des développements distinctifs de la *v(ṛtti)*; c'est la *v.* qui, par sa disposition même, commande cette fragmentation en *sū.*'s ou qui, à l'inverse, amène à grouper deux ou plus de deux *kār.* en une seule masse, laquelle est paradoxalement considérée aussi comme un *sū.* — Sur les relations de la *kār.* et du *sū.*, cf. la définition de Bharata 6.11 (éd. p. 264 du vol. I[2] et cf. K. M. Varma Seven Words in Bharata p. 69). — Le KP. occupe une position centrale en Poétique, centrale en ce sens qu'il condense et repense tous les problèmes précédemment abordés; mais ce n'est pas un texte "de base", car le destin de l'Alaṃkāraśāstra a voulu qu'il n'existât point, au départ de cette tradition, un corpus de *sū.*'s comme il y en avait à l'orée de la plupart des disciplines érudites ou spéculatives.

Il convient de distinguer ici deux points. On trouve des allusions dispersées — plus nombreuses dans certains chapitres, ainsi dans celui des Défauts, VII — à des faits de morphologie, avec renvoi explicite ou implicite, à P.,[2] allusions qui servent à appuyer quelque interprétation, à illustrer quelque trait du sémantisme "poétique". On trouve ensuite des faits de langue donnés indépendamment du *vyākaraṇa*, pour en développer les enseignements ou même en déborder le cadre. C'est ce qu'on pourrait appeler les faits "linguistiques", par contraste avec l'autre série, qui rassemble les faits "grammaticaux". Ce second aspect doit évidemment nous retenir davantage, étant plus intéressant et plus novateur. Encore faut-il noter tout de suite qu'il n'est pas toujours aisé de voir le moment exact où la Poétique se dissocie de la Grammaire.

Nous laisserons de côté, comme de peu d'importance, les apports de phonétique,[3] qui se résument en de menues disquisitions sur des cas de *sandhi* et d'*asandhi*, en des appréciations sur le caractère expressif de certaines consonnes. On peut omettre aussi les axiomes touchant la nécessité des études grammaticales pour l'apprentissage de la matière poétique: axiomes qui font défaut, au surplus, dans le KP., traité strictement préoccupé de technique et qui limite au minimum les exordes qui s'étalaient dans la littérature antérieure.[4]

[2] Ni dans le KP., ni dans les autres Traités que nous avons pu parcourir, il ne semble surgir d'enseignement remontant à une source autre que P. et son école (Mahābhāṣya, accessoirement Kāśikā-v.). Isolé et sans portée est le fait que le Sāh. Darp. 10.19 (*v*). signale que chez les Kalāpa on désigne par *yinn-āyi-ṇam* ce que P. rendait par *kyac-kyaṅ-ṇamul*.

[3] Sur l'accent (védique) et les très rares allusions qui y sont faites en Poétique, cf. Ruyyaka cité H. Jacobi ZDMG. 62, p. 420 note, P. V. Kane History of Sanskrit Poetics[2] p. 70 (cas de *indraśatru*, qui d'ailleurs est allégué en Poétique, non en partant du Veda, mais à travers Patañjali).

[4] Ainsi d'après Bhām. 1.9 la Grammaire vient en tête des savoirs requis pour le poète : *śabda* la désigne, juxtaposé à *abhidhāna* et *artha* (ou *abhidhānārtha*?), qui vise l'étymologie (et éventuellement la sémantique). Vām. 1.3,4 parle aussi de *śabda*(*smṛti*), suivi d'*abhidhāna*(*kośa*). Naturellement le *kāvya* lui-même est défini le plus souvent par la combinaison de *śabda* et d'*artha*, mais où il s'agit de "forme" et de "sens", non pas de "morphologie" et de "sémantique" Chez Bharata (chap. 6, début), il y a une utilisation imprévue du mot *nirukta*, au sens probable de "définition reposant sur une analyse grammaticale" (cf. Varma, op. cit., p. 69 qui a étudié en détail cette notion), dans les préliminaires à la théorie du *rasa :* il s'agit d'un souvenir du "*nirukta*" védique, mais détourné de son sens ancien. Il y a en outre (éd., chap. 14 = trad. Man. Ghosh chap. 15) une brève description des principes de la Grammaire, comme préliminaire aux règles de prosodie. Déjà donc chez Bharata comme dans la Poétique proprement dite, la Grammaire est traitée en simple "servante", en dépit des éloges dont çà et là elle fait l'objet : sur ces éloges ou l'affirmation de la nécessité de l'étude grammaticale, v. des références chez Kane op. cit., p. 374 ou S. K. De Sanskrit Poetics 1, p. 10. Le texte le plus explicite sans doute, avec insertion d'un passage entier emprunté à la Paspaśā, est la Kāvyamīmāṃsā. D'autre part, on semble éprouver une certaine antinomie entre Poétique et Grammaire, depuis l'instant où se développe la théorie du *dhvani* (cf. S. K. De 2, p. 162) : car, si la Grammaire se fonde sur les valeurs expresses du langage, le *dhvani* s'évertue à dégager les valeurs latentes.

Une indication plus précise est celle que donne le chap. grammatical de Bhām. 6.29, à savoir qu'on peut

§2. A l'inverse de certains Traités plus anciens — il s'agit, en fait, des œuvres de Bhām[aha] et de Vām[ana] —, qui groupent des faits de langue, grammaire aussi bien que lexique, dans un chapitre terminal, le KP. ne comporte aucun développement linguistique autonome. Les citations de P. manquent à l'intérieur des *kār(ikā)*, vouées à la formulation la plus abstraite, la plus elliptique; elles sont rares dans la *v(ṛtti)*. D'autant plus utile demeure-t-il de relever l'emploi que fait ce texte de valeurs linguistiques.

Mais voyons d'abord en quoi consistent ces chapitres terminaux de Bhām. et de Vām.? Ils ont peu à voir avec la poétique proprement dite, si ce n'est par cet attribut général qu'on y pourvoit le poète de conseils pratiques concernant des emplois à préférer, d'autres à éviter. A part quelques généralités, on n'y trouve en effet qu'une suite de cas concrets, suite succincte chez Bhām., beaucoup plus ample chez Vām. Ces cas sont allégués dans l'ordre même où ils devraient figurer s'ils étaient traités dans l'Aṣṭādhyāyī,[5] ce qui confirme bien l'origine exacte de cet enseignement. Ceci dit, Bhām. et Vām. sont assez différents l'un de l'autre, malgré quelques concordances de détail. Bhām, a souci de marquer que la formation dont il traite est non seulement acceptable, mais recommandable; il reste, à cet égard, voisin de la Poétique dans son ensemble, laquelle se fonde sur le choix. Ainsi pose-t-il que les suffixes "*yuc*", "*kurac*", "*varac*", "*iṣṇuc*" sont "singulièrement" (*viśeṣeṇa*) utilisables en poésie (48). Ou bien, désireux de préciser une option pāṇinéenne, il enseigne qu'on doit préférer *mārjanti* à *mṛjanti* (31). Il admet l'emploi du participe parfait dans la *bhāṣā* (42), alors que les Grammairiens laissent souvent la ques-

recourir à l'*upasaṃkhyāna* et à l'*iṣṭi*, qui sont des "additifs" quasi normaux faits à P. dans le Bhāṣya, mais qu'il faut éviter d'user du *yogavibhāga* ou "scission de règle", cet artifice qui, bien qu'étant connu parfois du Bhāṣya lui-même, se développe surtout chez les commentateurs postérieurs et tend à l'abus; une *paribhāṣā* (n° 114) cherche à en limiter les effets, *yogavibhāgād iṣṭasiddhiḥ* "d'une (nouvelle règle obtenue par) scission (en deux) d'une règle (ancienne, on ne peut tirer que) les résultats (qui apparaissent) souhaitables (pour tel cas d'espèce)" (la *paribhāṣā* n'est pas reprise, à l'inverse de tant d'autres, dans les *sū.* du Traité grammatical de Bhoja. Bhām. fait aussi allusion au Nyāsa, ci-dessous § 8. Des détails aussi précis font défaut chez Vām. — Il n'est que naturel que des allusions de grammaire dans une strophe poétique soient considérées comme un défaut, ainsi KP. *sū.* 81, p. 413, à moins, ajoute l'auteur, que la strophe incriminée ne soit mise dans la bouche d'un grammairien. Quant aux aoristes de la str. citée p. 414, ils sont à la fois rudes phoniquement (*kaṣṭa*) et insolites, comme peuvent l'être en français certains imparfaits du subjonctif.

[5] Ceci a été déjà relevé pour Vām. par Cappeller Stilregeln p. ix (dont nous suivons ici la numérotation des *sū.*), mais c'est également vrai de Bhām. Il s'agit donc d'une "*durghaṭavṛtti*" à l'état embryonnaire; les données de Bhām. et de Vām. offrent du reste plus d'un point de contact avec le texte de Śaraṇadeva; nous en signalerons plusieurs. Mais le grammairien va plus loin que ses devanciers dans l'effort de "conciliation". Ad P. 3.2,162, il cite un enseignement de Vām. (40) concernant la nuance du dérivé en *-ura-*: en fait, Vām. s'était borné à instaurer sous forme d'une *iṣṭi* une indication déjà donnée dans la Kāśikā, indication qui n'avait pas laissé de provoquer quelque remous parmi les commentateurs, cf. nos Études de gr. skte 1, p. 122. Ainsi la grammaire de Bhoja (1.4,233) pose d'emblée la valeur réfléchie (*karmakartari*), mais ajoute que, selon certains, la valuer active (-transitive) est seule correcte.

tion controversée.[6] Il arrive aussi qu'il restreigne, sur la foi de l'usage poétique, un emploi qui chez P. se tenait dans un cadre trop large : importante est son observation (40) touchant les formations "*kvip*", qu'il souhaite voir se limiter à l'Instr. sing. et au Loc. pl. Il circonscrit aussi (39) le droit qu'on a théoriquement de tirer des formes nouvelles en partant d'un *gaṇa* pāṇinéen.[7] Il pose enfin (32) qu'on ne peut, d'une règle générale comme P. 1.2,64 (sur les *ekaśeṣa*), déduire qu'un nombre déterminé de formes, celles à savoir qui expriment la relation définie par P. 67, comme *varuṇau, indrau, bhavau, śarvau, mṛḍau* : il s'agit donc d'endiguer un usage qui risquait de dépasser les bornes permises.[8] Jamais Bhām. n'écarte de front un enseignement de l'école pāṇinéenne ; ses rares énoncés négatifs sont conformes à des *pratiṣedhasūtra* de P., ainsi ceux qui visent le *ṣaṣṭhītatpuruṣa* d'un nom en *-tṛ-*(36) ou en *-aka-*.[9] Les deux *kār.* ultimes sont orientées un peu différemment, attirant notre attention sur une formation verbale assez rare, au sujet de quoi l'étudiant pourrait trébucher, l'aspect en *-at-* du participe des présents redoublés, et la 3e pers. plur. corrélative en *-ati*, ou bien encore le *-i-* de liaison du type *roditi, svapiti*.

§3. Chez Vām., la théorie grammaticale a plus clairement l'allure d'une *śabdaśuddhi* ou d'un *sauśabdya*, une "purification des formes du langage", comme les données qu'égrènent tout au long des *sū.* pāṇinéens les commentateurs tardifs — ainsi la Bhāṣāvṛtti, et déjà, timidement, la Candravṛtti et la Kāśikā —, et qui se déploient à plein dans la Durghaṭavṛtti. On trouve d'abord chez Vām. des formations que l'auteur tient pour incorrectes, ainsi *avaihi* 71, *apāṅganetrā* 72, *śliṣṭapriya* 73 (cité aussi Durgh. ad 6.3,34, qui justifie la forme), *nidrādruk* 88, *niṣpanda* 89, *aṅgulisaṅga* 90 ; à propos de *śārvara* 52, Vām. n'a pas fait l'effort qu'on pouvait attendre pour justifier la dérivation, effort auquel se livre sans peine Durgh. ad P. 4.3,11. Ces mots et plusieurs autres sont-ils considérés par Vām. comme absolument incorrects, ou seulement comme sujets à caution ? On peut se le demander, voyant les vocables fort divers dont l'auteur se sert pour stigmatiser ces emplois, tantôt *anveṣya, cintya, durlabha*, tantôt *avadya*, ou encore *a(niṣedhya)* ou simplement (88) *na*.[10]

Dans la majorité des cas, les formes, vicieuses selon l'explication grammaticale obvie, peuvent cependant se concilier avec la Grammaire au prix d'une explication moins apparente. Ainsi en va-t-il de *sudatī* 69 : ou bien l'on donnera une valuer cumulative au *CA* de P. 5,4,145 (ce que fait déjà la Kāś., reprise par la Bhāṣāv.), ou

[6] Les cas de *mṛjanti*/ *mārjanti* résulte en partie de P. (7.2,114), en partie (et surtout) d'une *iṣṭi* dans Bhāṣya 1.1,5 (trad. Ojihara-Renou p. 28). — Quant au participe parfait, question fort embarrassée, cf. nos Études de gr. skte 1, p. 99 et 133 et, en dernier lieu, notre article sous presse du JAs. 1961 sur la Théorie des temps d'après les grammairiens sanskrits [see pages 500–525 of this volume].

[7] Sur l'*ākṛtigaṇatva* de P. et les problèmes que pose la présence des *gaṇa*, cf. l'introduction à l'éd. critique du Gaṇapāṭha, ouvrage (sous presse) de R. Birwé.

[8] Cf. Durgh. ad P. 67 et le long *bhāṣya* ad P. 64, notamment autour du *vt.* 46 (*liṅga-vacanasiddhiḥ*).

[9] Cf. ci-dessous § 8. Ibid., également, la question, un peu obscure, de l'*avyayībhāva*.

[10] Plusieurs de ces mots sont repris Durgh., passim. Le *NA* pāṇinéen ne signifie jamais qu'une forme (en usage) est à éviter, mais seulement que là où les règle(s) positive(s) précédemment énoncée(s) cesse(nt) de valoir dans les cas d'espèce qui sont énoncés ensuite.

bien l'on considérera *sudatī* comme un "nom" (*saṃjñā*) et l'on recourra à P. 5.4,143 (passage où justement la Bhāṣāv. cite le mot en exemple); la Durgh. ad 5.4,141 connaît encore un autre biais. Vām. 45 fait appel aussi au *CA*, comme il se retranche ailleurs (79) derrière le *BAHULAM*, comme il fait état du *nipātana* 43 (pour *śobhā*, mot étudié aussi Durgh. ad 3.3,102) et 85 (pour *virama*).[11] La technique des *gaṇa* illustratifs (*ākṛtigaṇa*) permet de "justifier" plusieurs formes embarrassantes, ainsi sous 14, 16, 18, 33, 75. Il advient qu'on ait à utiliser une analyse (autre que celle normalement attendue) 37, 38, 84, une étymologie distincte 76, 77, 78 (ainsi dans *prapīya*, qui viendrait, non de la racine *pā-*, mais de la racine *pī*), un découpage du mot incriminé (ainsi 82, où le futur *vetsyasi* est expliqué par *vetsy asi*). Certaines formes relèvent d'une interprétation par l'analogie (c'est là une tentative plutôt rare d'explication de type scientifique): ainsi l'Instr. *mukhena* dans *mukhena trilocanaḥ* 26 est donné comme une extension licite de P. 2.3,20, *akṣṇā kāṇaḥ*; *āha* en fonction de prétérit (46) résulte de l'analogie des autres formes verbales en *-a*, toutefois Vām. ajoute aussitôt que les bons écrivains usent de *āha* au sens de présent. Enfin il y a des explications qui, sans faire état d'une règle de grammaire spéciale, prennent prétexte d'une valeur "générique" (*sarvatra*), ce qui permet à la forme litigieuse d'échapper à l'application d'un *sū.* grammatical: ainsi pour *dṛḍhabhakti* 73 bis (manque Cappeller) ou *śakya* 25 (avec appui d'une citation tirée du Mahābhāṣya.[12]

Plus intéressants, de notre point de vue, sont les cas où une forme est déclarée correcte, malgré la Grammaire, sur la foi de l'usage qui l'accrédite. Cette pression de l'usage vivant a été une tendance naturelle, que le temps n'a pu que renforcer: de fait, il est peu d'auteurs de *kāvya* qui, à tel ou tel moment, n'outrepassent les limites de la stricte adhésion à P. Ainsi Vām. 83 admet *kāmayāna* au lieu de *kāmayamāna*, pourvu, ajoute-t-il curieusement, qu'un pareil emploi repose sur une tradition, autrement dit, ne fasse pas novation.[13] De même pour *śāsvata* 53 (cf. Durgh. ad 4.3,23); *te* et *me* au sens de *tvayā* et *mayā* 11. Mais ces cas sont peu fréquents. Vām. est dominé par le souci de "concilier", plus encore, par celui de maintenir la pureté du langage en attirant l'attention sur les barbarismes, *apabhraṃśo rakṣyaḥ* 23. Il se tient ainsi à mi-chemin entre les tendances quelque peu mécanistes des grammairiens et le comportement qualitatif des poéticiens. L'option qu'il donne entre *sāmagrya* et *sāmagrī* (58) ne fait que codifier un enseignement de *vyākaraṇa*.[14] Quelques notations de caractère plus global ont lieu au *sū.* 62, où Vām. marque que le suffixe *-tara-* sert aussi pour des valeurs non strictement "comparatives"; ou bien, dans l'*adhyāya* 1 (du 5e *adhikaraṇa*), quand il expose le sens de la double négation (9) ou l'emploi du duel (17, avec recours à l'autorité, non de P., mais de la Mīmāṃsā). Ce sont là les rares

[11] Sur *virama*, cf. un cas analogue cité dans Bhāṣāv. ad P. 7.3,34 et dans Durgh. ibid., p. 109 (*udyama, uparama*).

[12] Sur *dṛḍhabhakti*, cf. Durgh. ad P. 6.3,34; sur *śakya* suivi d'un infinitif, v. nos Monogr. sktes 2, p. 48, touchant la doctrine des grammairiens.

[13] *Anādiś ced*. Il est donc probable que l'auteur a eu en vue, non le cas spécial de *kāmayāna* (mot épique), mais le groupe des formations similaires. La *v.* s'appuie sur une (pseudo-) *paribhāṣā*, n° 93/2, dont on a fait grand abus par ailleurs.

[14] Cf. les références chez Debrunner Suffixe p. 397 bas.

données qui ne reposent pas sur l'exercice d'un artifice technique.[15]

§4. Dans le KP. comme dans la majorité des Traités de poétique, les composés nominaux sont de beaucoup la catégorie grammaticale la plus souvent alléguée.[16] Non pas que ces textes aient du neuf à nous apprendre sur la structure interne du composé; ce n'est pas leur rôle. Mais justement, par contraste avec la Grammaire qui ne met en œuvre que des formations élémentaires, des cellules bimembres,[17] la Poétique, elle, traite des composés longs, ou plutôt elle en confirme l'existence, l'importance stylistique, elle en mesure la densité.

Considérant les Qualités en tant qu'elles se réfèrent au mot (*śabdaguṇa*) — car, remarque-t-on au *sū*. 95, les Qualités résident en fait dans les sentiments et ne sont présentes que secondairement dans les mots —, le KP. (*sū* 98) enseigne qu'elles ont pour facteur "suggérant" (*vyañjaka*), soit les phonèmes, soit le composé nominal, soit enfin l'arrangement (*racanā*: entendez, une sorte d'harmonie pouvant résulter de l'arrangement des mots dans la phrase).[18] Or, il est aisé de voir que le composé nominal est un indice plus important que les phonèmes ou même que l'arrangement; en fait, si l'on prend l'ensemble des Traités, on s'aperçoit qu'il est présent dans toutes les définitions, alors que les autres signes n'y figurent que temporairement.

Des trois Qualités que distingue le KP., le *mādhurya* ou "suavité", typique du "sentiment" Érotique et plus encore, nous dit-on, du Pathétique, du Frustratif (à l'intérieur de l'Érotique), du Quiescent, comporte soit absence totale de composés (*avṛtti*),[19] soit du moins présence de composés de dimension moyenne (*madhyavṛtti*), *sū*. 99: ceci va de pair avec la présence de phonèmes doux, l'absence de phonèmes rudes, l'allure "coulante" de la diction.

[15] Nous relèverons quelques autres faits empruntés à ces mêmes sections de grammaire (§ 8).

[16] Cf., outre les §§ 4 à 8, l'emploi des composés dans l'*upamā* §§ 9 et 10 dans la théorie des Défauts § 12. Bharata (15.34 et 35 trad. Man. Ghosh = 14.34 de l'éd.) croit devoir définir le composé (*luptavibhaktir nāmnām ekārthaṃ saṃharat samāso'pi*) au terme de sa brève exposition de grammaire (ci-dessus p. 106 n. 2). C'était pour lui une manière de conclusion.

[17] Le principe dans l'Aṣṭādhyāyī (cf. BSL. 52, p. 103 et n. 1) est de laisser la formation libre, tout au moins pour le *bahuvrīhi* et le *dvandva* (à l'exception du *dvandva* singulier, qui est réglementé); bien que limité en apparence, le *tatpuruṣa* est aussi, en fait, largement ouvert, cf. notamment P. 2.1,57 2.2,6 et 8, comme le montrent, par preuve inverse, les interdictions énoncées sous P. 2.2, 10 à 17. Enfin *SAHA SUPĀ* 2.1,4 pouvait frayer la voie à diverses facilités. Les composés plurimembres ne sont signalés que rarement par les cc., ainsi quelques *dvandva* donnés en contre-exemples ad P. 2.4,6; cf. aussi (pour les *dvandva*) Bh. ad 2.2,34 *vtt*. 1–3 et 6; pour les *bahuvrīhi*, Bh. ad 2.2,24 *vt*. 1, spéculant sur la teneur quelque peu équivoque *ANEKAM* de P. (ad loc.). Le type *śākapārthiva* 2.1,69 *vt*. 8 atteste indirectement la présence de trimembres (*uttarapadalopin*).

[18] Disposition ternaire qu'on retrouve ailleurs §§ 9 et 11.

[19] *Vṛtti* au sens de "composé" est un emploi qu'on trouve çà et là en Grammaire, ainsi Bh. 2.1,1 init. ou Kāś. 2.1,34 et 40: c'est un aspect particulier du mot au sens de "expression synthétique", englobant donc la dérivation nominale, d'où la formule *samāsataddhitānāṃ vṛttiḥ* Bh. ad 2.1,18 *vt*. 2.

La Qualité de "force" ou d'"ampleur puissante" (*ojas*, glosé *prauḍhi*)[20] exige, à l'inverse, des composés longs (*vṛttidairghya*), indice que corrobore l'emploi de certaines consonnes ou combinaisons consonantiques, *sū.* 100; on ajoute parfois aussi: la construction tendue ou heurtée. La troisième Qualité, le *prasāda* ou "limpidité", *sū.* 101, ne possède pas de critères formels, ou du moins pas de critères positifs: à nous de les déduire par comparaison avec les deux autres Qualités. Le *prasāda* est utilisé pour exprimer tous les *rasa* (à l'inverse de l'*ojas* qui exprime l'Héroïque, plus encore le Répugnant, plus enfin le Furieux) et convient à toutes les dictions.

§5. Cette théorie a une assez longue histoire. Les trois Qualités du KP. se sont substituées (comme le note expressément la *v.*) aux dix catégories de Vām., catégories qui étaient démunies de signes linguistiques directs. Mais ces signes surgissent ailleurs, de temps à autre: ainsi déjà chez Bharata (16.100 = trad. Man. Ghosh 17.99) la Qualité dite *samatā* "égalité" comporte des traits négatifs: pas trop de mots "broyés" (ou: pas de mots "broyés" à l'extrême), pas d'expressions redondantes ou difficiles à comprendre, *nāticūrṇapadair yuktā, na ca vyarthābhidhāyibhiḥ/durbodhanaiś ca . . .*, ce qui semble signifier: pas trop de mots non composés (qui laissent une impression hachée au discours)[21]: l'absence d'excès, l'unité à l'intérieur de la stance est recommandée, unité que viole un contre-exemple cité Vām. 3.1,12, où nous voyons un premier hémistiche fait de mots simples, le second ayant un composé très long.

Toutefois la situation du composé nominal n'apparaît de plein fouet qu'à propos de la description de l'*ojas*. Dès Bhar. 16.105 (= trad. 17.102), on enseigne que l'*ojas* abonde en mots composés, *samāsavadbhir bahubhiḥ . . . padair yutam* (les épithètes qui suivent, *vicitraiḥ, sānurāgaiḥ, udāraiḥ*, n'ont pas d'incidence directe sur le langage). Daṇḍin 1.80 définissait l'*ojas* par le mot "*samāsabhūyastva*, dominance (en nombre) des composés".[22] Vām. 3.2,2 reconnaissait pour l'une des manifestations de l'*ojas* — envisagé comme Qualité de sens — le *samāsa*,[23] c'est-à-dire, non pas directement, comme son nom l'indique, un type mixte prose/vers ou une prose versifiée, est ici (1.10) caractérisé par des composés point trop difficiles (*utkaṭa*). Remontant jusqu'à Bharata (éd. 14.38 = trad. Man. Ghosh 15.35), nous voyons que *cūrṇa, cūrṇapada*, est simplement contrasté à *nibaddha* (*bandha*): la question des composés demeure non explicitée.

[20] Sur *ojas* et les implications du mot en Poétique, v., outre les Manuels d'ensemble, la monographie de J. Gonda Ancient-Indian *ojas*, notamment p. 37.

[21] Le mot *cūrṇa* sert de t. techn. pour désigner un certain type de composition en prose (Vām. 1.3,24) comportant des composés "point trop longs" (ainsi que des mots empreints de "douceur"), par contraste avec le type dit *utkalikā(prāya)* 25. D'après l'Agni Pur. 1.13, le *cūrṇaka* (caractérisé selon 1.9 par le petit nombre de composés; composé se disant *vigraha*, mot qui en Grammaire désigne plutôt l'analyse des membres du c°) domine le genre littéraire appelé *ākhyāyikā*, cf. ci-dessous § 6 fin., alors que l'*utkalikā* (1.9) a des composés longs. Le *vṛttagandhi*, qui chez d'autres théoriciens est simple-

[22] L'expression est reprise, par ex., dans SKĀbh. 1.71, le *mādhurya* étant ici signalé par l'existence de mots séparés 1.68, la *suśabdatā* reposant sur la "clarté des *sup* et des *tiṅ*" 1.72: c'est l'équivalent du *prasāda* qu'on a ailleurs. Dans Sāh. Darp. n° 608 sqq., le *mādhurya* a peu ou point de composés, l'*ojas* en a beaucoup; rien n'est dit sur le *prasāda*.

[23] Ce *samāsa* de Vām. est alludé KP. *sū.* 96 (*v.*).

tement le "composé" au sens grammatical, mais la faculté de resserrer en un mot (ce qu'on pourrait aussi dire en plusieurs): c'est le *saṃkṣepa* de Bhoja, le *śleṣa* de Bharata. Il y a là un essai, normal chez Vām., pour dépasser le niveau linguistique, tout en s'appliquant à le transcrire autrement. Le Sār. K. Ābhar. 1.36, définissant l'antonyme de l'*ojas*, parle d'une structure brisée (*khaṇḍayan rītim*) et ajoute "*asamasta*, absence de composés". Quant au rôle majeur de l'*ojas* dans la littérature, il suffit d'évoquer ce que dit Daṇḍin, loc. cit.: l'*ojas* est l'âme de la prose; même en poésie, les auteurs (autres que les Méridionaux) y trouvent leur unique recours, *etad (ojas) gadyasya jīvitam/padye 'py adākṣi-ṇātyānām idam ekaṃ parāyaṇam.*[24]

§6. Une autre classification où interviennent les composés nominaux est celle des Styles ou *rīti* (parfois *mārga* ou "chemin"). Ils y sont même la marque fondamentale, tout autant que dans les Qualités; au surplus, il y a un lien étroit entre Qualités et Styles, comme on le constate du premier abord. Ces styles à dénominations régionales (ou censément telles, comme les noms des prâkrits) nous sont décrits, non dans le KP., mais dans les traités antérieurs, dès Daṇḍin 1.42, qui note que les dix Qualités — au nombre desquelles figure l'*ojas* — sont l'âme du *vaidarbha mārga*, l'inverse de ces Qualités étant le propre du *gauḍa vartman.*[25] C'est après Daṇḍin que se fait l'association entre *ojas* et Gauḍa's (ou *gauḍīyā rīti*): cette *gauḍīyā rīti* selon Vām. 1.2,12 a les Qualités d'*ojas* (et de *dīpti* ou "éclat"), d'où l'on peut inférer la présence de composés longs. A cette *rīti* s'oppose la *vaidarbhī* (Vām. 19) qui, du moins sous sa forme "pure", est exempte de composés; enfin la *pāñcālī* (ibid. 13) qui, ayant les Qualités de suavité et de tendresse (*saukumārya*), doit (est-on amené à penser) se comporter, quant aux composés nominaux, comme la Qualité *mādhurya*. La *vaidarbhī* répond donc à la Qualité *prasāda*, malgré un certain décalage.

Dans les textes ultérieurs, les caractères formels se précisent et durcissent. Ils sont très explicites dans le Sār. K. Ābhar. 2.28 sqq. qui définit la *vaidarbhī* comme dénuée de composés, la *pāñcālī* comme ayant des composés de cinq ou six membres, la *gauḍīyā* comme faite de mots composés "très vigoureux", *samastātyudbha-ṭapada*; les trois autres "styles" sont l'*āvantikā*, qui a des composés de deux à trois membres, la *lāṭīyā*, qui mélange les mots composés aux mots simples, enfin la *māgadhī*, avec son "style brisé", *khaṇḍarīti*. Analogue dans le Śṛṅg. Prak. 3 p. 212 sqq.[26]: *gauḍīyā*, composés très longs, *pāñcālī*, composés point trop longs, *vaidarbhī*, pas de composés, *lāṭīyā*, peu de composés. Dans le Sāh. Darp. n° 625 sqq., la *vaidarbhī*, peu ou pas de composés, *gauḍīyā*, beaucoup de composés, *pāñcālī*, des formations de cinq ou six membres, *lāṭī*, intermédiaire entre *vaidarbhī* et *pāñcālī*. De même dans l'Agni Pur. 4.9. Daṇḍin qui, nous l'avons rappelé, ignore ces subdivisions, admet pourtant (1.46) que les Gauḍa préfèrent ce qui n'est pas "trop conventionnel, *nātirūḍham*", ce qui revient à

[24] Il s'agit des Orientaux (cf. 1.83), ce qui rejoint la répartition entre Gauḍa's et Vaidarbha's; les Vaidarbha sont assimilables aux Méridionaux d'après 1.60.

[25] Daṇḍin admet qu'il y ait plusieurs *mārga*, mais n'en décrit que deux, *vaidarbha* et *gauḍa*. Il signale le premier (1.44) comme étant fait de *bandhagaurava* "compactness of (syllabic) binding" Belvalkar, ce qui ne s'accorde guère aux caractéristiques qui seront instruites plus tard.

[26] Cf. V. Raghavan, Analyse du Śṛṅg. Prak., p. 200, qui cite encore d'autres textes.

dire qu'ils s'intéressent aux formations analysables : l'exemple cité à l'appui atteste en effet un composé long, comportant une "analyse" morphologique et sémantique relativement complexe.[27]

§7. Ici intervient dans KP., *sū*. 102, un élément nouveau de quelque intérêt, qui n'appartient pas aux Traités surtout descriptifs des époques antérieures, mais puise dans le Dhvanyāloka. Les caractères servant à définir les Qualités sont modifiables selon le sujet parlant (*vaktṛ*), la chose dont on parle (*vācya*), le genre littéraire (*prabandha*) : ainsi l'*ojas*—et partant, le composé lourd—est admissible quand parle Bhīma(sena), personnage incarnant le *rasa* Furieux, même si le contenu de la strophe ou le genre dont elle relève ne s'accordent pas à l'*ojas*. De même a-t-on l'*ojas* là où le sujet traité le commande (en l'occurrence, la décapitation du démon Kumbhakarṇa), bien que le sujet parlant soit un simple héraut (*vaitālika*) et le genre un *nāṭaka*, type peu propice aux longs composés.[28]

En effet, le genre littéraire affecte l'aspect du langage, en ce sens, dit la *v*., que dans les œuvres dramatiques les composés lourds sont à éviter même s'il s'agit de rendre le *rasa* Furieux : fait, ajoute-t-on, qui n'est cité qu'à titre d'exemple.[29]

Le Dhvanyāloka formule à ce point une remarque assez pénétrante (3.5) : on distingue d'abord la structure de phrase, *saṃghaṭanā*, selon qu'elle est dénuée de composés, ou "parée" de composés moyens, ou enfin pourvue de composés longs : nous voyons ici la morphologie poussée au premier plan, sans mixture d'autres facteurs, stylistiques non plus que phonétiques. Un peu après (3.6) est notée la diversité du langage en fonction du *rasa* : c'est à nouveau la question des composés qui la signale, composés longs dans l'Érotique, mots simples dans le Furieux (et autres *rasa*), même s'il est admis qu'en principe l'*ojas* convienne au Furieux, la suavité ou la placidité à l'Érotique ou à certains dérivés de l'Érotique. Cette constatation contradictoire amène aussitôt une question : étant acquis (par d'autres Traités) que l'*ojas* est caractérisé par les composés longs, comment une structure sans composés sera-t-elle apte à rendre la "force" ? La *dīpti* qui se manifeste à l'occasion du *rasa* Furieux n'est autre que la force ou *ojas* : y a-t-il donc une "force" qui peut se manifester sans composés ?

[27] Selon la KāvMī (trad. fr. p. 49), la *gauḍī* est riche en composés, la *pāñcālī* pauvre, la *vaidarbhī* en est démunie. Le même ouvrage, p. 101 et suiv., développe une indication du Viṣṇudharmott. 3.4, suivant laquelle les diverses catégories d'êtres surnaturels ont chacune leur langage ; là encore, les composés (du moins dans KāvMī., non dans Viṣṇudharmott.) sont signalés au nombre des caractéristiques éminentes, aussi bien de la langue des dieux que de celles des Vidyādhara, des Gandharva, des Yoginī, enfin des Nāga, sans qu'il y ait d'ailleurs (et pour cause !) des variations très marquées de l'une à l'autre. — Ce texte précieux montre bien comment le problème des composés est au centre nerveux de la théorie "ancienne" de l'Alaṃkāra, au carrefour de la description des *guṇa*, des *rīti*, des *rasa*, et même des *vṛtti*, qui sont associées aux *rīti* dans le chap. 3 de la KāvMī.

[28] Ceci est résumé dans Hem. *sū*. 103 : la structure se conforme parfois au sujet traité sans égard pour la personne qui parle ni le genre littéraire, parfois en revanche elle est adaptée au genre en négligeant sujet parlant et sujet traité, *kva cid vaktṛprabandhānapekṣayā vācyaucityād eva . . . kva cid vaktṛvācyānapekṣāḥ prabandhocitā eva*.

[29] Sur un plan plus général, il y a la différence entre poésie et prose (différence effleurée Daṇḍin 1.80 déjà cité) et celle entre les divers types de prose, ci-dessus p. 484 n. 21.

Là-dessus cette remarque: la structure linguistique et les caractères à exprimer sont deux choses distinctes. Il arrive qu'une structure à composés longs entrave la perception d'un *rasa*; s'il s'agit de rendre la tristesse ou la souffrance d'amour, on aurait tort de préférer les composés longs, les moyens y sont bons. Les composés longs peuvent n'être pas hors de propos pour dépeindre un caractère noble-et-fier, *dhīroddhata*, entendez: même dans le contexte de l'Érotique où on ne les attend guère.[30] Ce qui importe, c'est la qualité de "limpidité" ou "placidité": s'il n'y a pas "placidité", une structure même exempte de composés sera inapte à évoquer la tristesse où la souffrance d'amour; s'il y a cette qualité, des composés moyens n'y feront pas obstacle. Tel est le sens vers lequel le poète doit porter son effort.

Quant aux genres littéraires étudiés en fonction du *rasa*, le Dhvany. note que même dans l'*ākhyāyikā* (où l'on s'attend à des composés longs),[31] ces composés sont à éviter s'il s'agit d'un *rasa* ne les comportant pas: le *rasa* prévaut sur le "genre". Dans les drames, on s'abstiendra de composés en tout cas: ici le "genre" l'emporte. Mais c'est pour rendre le Furieux ou l'Héroïque qu'il convient surtout d'en tenir compte: ainsi, il ne saurait y avoir uniquement des mots simples dans l'*ākhyāyikā*, ou des composés trop longs dans le drame, quelles que soient par ailleurs les règles présidant à ces deux *rasa*.

Tel est l'enseignement, rudimentaire par certains côtés, mais insistant et tout de même fondamental par d'autres, que livrent les théoriciens. La question du composé nominal, bien que présentée de manière moins pressante, est abordée de nouveau à propos de la Comparaison (§§ 9 et 10), elle revient dans le chapitre sur les Défauts (§ 12). Mais reprenons d'abord les quelques données résultant des chapitres grammaticaux de Bhām. et de Vām., chapitres dont nous avons déjà brièvement parlé.[32]

§8. Ces données n'intéressent certes pas l'essence même de la poétique; mais elles sont utiles du point de vue linguistique. Il est clair que Bhām. et surtout Vām. s'appliquent à limiter l'usage de certains composés dont la Grammaire à leurs yeux tient l'éventail trop ouvert. D'abord chez Bhām.: limitation des *avyayībhāva* quant à la forme casuelle (c'est un raffinement, d'ailleurs assez obscur, apporté par Bhām. 6.34 à P. 2.4, 83 et 84, raffinement s'appuyant sans doute sur le *BAHULAM* du grammairien). Limitation du *gaṇa tiṣṭhadgu* Bhām. 35, cf. P. 2.1, 17, règle au sujet de laquelle le *vt.*

[30] KP. *sū.* 81, p. 431 donne le cas d'un composé long qu'on n'attend pas dans une ambiance d'Érotique. Sous-entendre: il est tout de même acceptable, servant à intensifier le déplaisir ressenti par l'amant qui souffre.

[31] Autre avis sur l'*ākhyāyikā* dans l'Agni cité p. 112 n. 1. Sur ce terme techn., v. en dernier S.K. De Problems of Skt. Poetics p. 65 qui rappelle (p. 74) que ce genre littéraire est en prose de type *cūrṇa*. Pourtant le modèle convenu de l'*ākhyāyikā* n'est-il pas le Harṣacarita (cf. KP., fin du chap. VIII), qui consiste presque tout entier en composés immenses? Hem. loc. cit.: dans l'*ākhyāyikā*, même pour l'Érotique, il ne doit pas y avoir trop de mots "suaves"; dans la *kathā*, même pour le Furieux, il n'y a pas à user d'un style "sauvage"; dans le drame, même pour le Furieux, il n'y a pas de composés longs.

[32] Répartition des composés selon les mètres, cf. Suvṛttatilaka 2.17 (on note l'absence de composés en *vaṃśastha*); 23 (c° en premier hémistiche, en *mālinī*); 27 (pas de c° en *pṛthvī*); 37 (c° au second hémistiche, en *śārdūla*°); tout cela paraît bien arbitraire, comme les particularités euphoniques adjointes, et la mention inattendue du participe présent (11).

1 donnait déjà la spécification d'emploi "*kālaviśeṣe*", celle même qu'exploite ensuite Bhām. Interdiction (Bhām. 36) du *ṣaṣṭhītatpuruṣa* pour un nom en *-tṛ-*, interdiction conforme à P. 2.2,15, mais avec cette précision notable que, aux dires du poéticien, les personnes "cultivées" et l'auteur du Nyāsa admettraient un tel composé: de fait, le Nyāsa instaure (ad P. 2.2,16) un "*kva cid*", succédant à l'artifice du *jñāpana*, et cite en exemple la forme *bhayaśokahartṛ* (variante: °*hantṛ*), qui ressemble fort à l'exemple *vṛtrahantṛ* que donnera Bhām. dans des conditions similaires, pour le rejeter il est vrai, alors que le Nyāsa le déclarait acceptable.[33]

La description chez Vām. est plus articulée. La remarque la plus instructive concerne la distinction entre *bahuvrīhi* et *tatpuruṣa*, distinction sur laquelle la Grammaire était muette, si ce ne'st l'enseignement indirect qu'on pouvait tirer du fait que le champ des *samāsānta* y était ouvert de manière quasi illimitée pour les *bahuvrīhi* (*ŚEṢĀT* P. 5.4,154), alors qu'il était maintenu dans des bornes assez serrées pour les *tatpuruṣa*. Il est donc significatif que Vām., dès le début de son exposé (5.1,7 et 8), déconseille l'emploi des *karmadhāraya* susceptibles d'être pris pour des *bahuvrīhi* (et l'inverse): *vīrapuruṣa* ne saurait signifier "qui a de valeureux serviteurs" (il y faut *vīrapuruṣaka*); cf. aussi la discussion sur *caturasraśobhin* 5.2,59 et la *v.* afférente.

Quant à l'ordre des membres, la tendance chez Vām. est, comme nous l'avons vu, à concilier: on attend **adharabimba* "lèvre (semblable au) *bimba*" par P. 2.1,56, mais *bimbādhara*, qui est l'expression usuelle (Vām. 5.2,16), s'explique par référence au *g. śākapārthiva*, ce refuge trop commun pour maintes difficultés, à l'intérieur même de la tradition vyākaraṇique. Au *sū.* 23, Vām. se résigne à admettre certains manquements à la séquence normale des éléments du *dvandva*, manquements qui sont d'ailleurs couverts d'avance par le trouble même que jette dans la théorie lapidaire de P. 2.2,34 la multiplicité des *vtt.* subrogés audit *sū.* Seul *kharoṣṭrau* (Vām. 28, au lieu de *uṣṭrakharau*) est censuré comme intolérable.

Plusieurs types de mots ne peuvent entrer en composition, ainsi le type *madhupipāsu* (14) ne ressortit à aucune catégorie reconnue, mais peut s'expliquer par P. 2.1,24 *vt.*1 (*gaṇa gami-gāmi*). *Dhānyaṣaṣṭha* (19) a l'air incorrect à cause de P. 2.2,10, comme aussi *pattrapītiman* et analogues (2) à cause de P. 11: Vām. maintient la seconde prohibition, lève la première. Pour *arihan* (et analogues, 37) *brahmavid* (et analogues, 38), qui pareillement contreviennent, quoique de façon diverse, à P. 3.2,87, le premier groupe est taxé d'incorrect, le second peut être réaménagé si l'on appelle au secours P. 2.2,8 + 3.2,76.

Un composé d'apparence malaisé à expliquer, tel que *āmūlalola* (18) pourra s'intégrer dans un *gaṇa*: en l'occurrence, sous la rubrique commode des *mayūravyaṃsakādi*. En revanche, on ne sait trop sur quelle base Vām. 21 interdit les *bahuvrīhi* dont les membres sont en relation discordante entre eux (les *vyadhikaraṇa bahu*°), interdiction qui n'est levée que pour les seuls °*janman* et analogues: le *vt.* 10 ad P. 2.2,24 paraît bien rejeter de tels *bahuvrīhi* d'une manière générale, mais le rejet est ensuite jugé superflu (*vt.*18), du fait que l'usage d'ores et déjà ignore de telles formations (*anabhidhānāt*). On voit que Vām. a estimé utile de prohiber ce qui,

[33] Ceci montre que le Nyāsa juge des faits en grammairien, incorporant à la rigueur des formes de type épique et purāṇique; plus puriste, Bhām. se tient aux normes du *kāvya*, qui exclut soigneusement ces mêmes formes.

au niveau de langue du Bhāṣya, passait encore pour insolite.[34]

§9. Revenant aux enseignements de poétique proprement dite, on observera qu'un groupe massif de traits linguistiques est mentionné à propos de la Figure qui vient généralement en tête de l'exposé sur les Alaṃkāra, à savoir l'*upamā* ou Comparaison.[35] Alors que les autres Figures, qui toutes ont un lien de dépendance implicite par rapport à l'*upamā*, sont décrites sans qu'interviennent des critères morphologiques, l'*upamā* au contraire est mise d'emblée en connexion avec la structure grammaticale. Ainsi le KP., *sū*. 127, enseigne que, sous sa forme "pleine" (*pūrṇā*), l'*upamā* se présente, soit en phrase (analytique), soit en composé nominal, soit dans un dérivé (secondaire). On retrouve ici le classement ternaire qui prévaut en Poétique, alors qu'il est absent en Grammaire. On retrouve aussi le composé parmi les facteurs ou indices de l'*upamā*.

La Comparaison de phrase (*vākyagā*) est celle qui est introduite par les particules *iva*, *yathā*, *vā* et analogues.[36] La Comparaison par dérivé (*taddhitagā*) s'exprime au moyen du suffixe adverbial -*vat*. Ces deux premiers types *d'upamā* sont tantôt direct ou perceptible (*śrautī*), tantôt indirect ou reposant-sur-le-sens (*ārthī*). Subdivision d'apparence purement "poétique", voire philosophique, mais qui ne laisse pas, au moins quant à -*vat*, d'utiliser une donnée pāṇinéenne. En effet, P. 5.1,116 avait posé le suffixe -*vat* au sens du Locatif (*mathurāvat* "comme à Mathurā") : ou du Génitif (*devadattavat* "comme [celui] de Devadatta") : -*vat*, observent les poéticiens, équivaut ici à *iva* et déclanche comme *iva* une Comparaison directe : le pouvoir-inhérent (*sāmarthya*) à cet élément engendre l'idée d'une relation, par le seul fait qu'on le "perçoit" dans la phrase, tout comme les désinences du Génitif engendrent l'idée d'une connexion ou *saṃbandha*, de par

[34] D'autres cas sont mentionnés, touchant l'expression du féminin au membre antérieur (73), touchant aussi le *samāsānta* (60 déjà cité, 66 et suiv.), la forme du membre ultérieur (84), la phonétique jonctionnelle (90–92), le genre dans un *dvandva* (27), enfin la relation du pronom avec un membre subordonné de composé (5.1,11), question qu'on peut retenir de préférence aux autres, ne serait-ce que parce qu'elle n'est pas traitée (et ne pouvait guère l'être) en grammaire (description des faits chez Wackernagel 2.1, p. 32).

[35] L'*upamā* pleine consiste en quatre éléments; l'*upamāna* ou objet auquel on compare qqch., ainsi le visage, l'*upameya* ou sujet de la comparaison, ainsi la lune, le terme "commun" (tertium), appelé *sāmānya*, *sādhāraṇa* ou *dharma*, enfin la particule comparative (*upamāpratipādaka* ou °*dyotaka*, *upamā* tout bref, *vādi*). Il est notable que P. mentionne plusieurs fois des faits de langue à portée comparative, ainsi quand il dit que la particule *cid* (en védique) est *upamārthe* 8.2,101 ; de façon plus importante, quand il enseigne que les *upamāna* se composent avec le tertium (appelé *sāmānyavacana*); au *sū*. suivant figure le mot *upamita* = *upameya*. Cf. encore 2.2,24 *vt*. 12 cité plus loin.

[36] Sur *vā* comparatif, cf. Böhtlingk-Roth n° 3: emploi des lexiques, de l'Épopée, du *kāvya*, peut-être par influence du *vă* moyen indien (et, éventuellement, ṛgvédique?) = *iva*, références Debrunner Ai. Gr. 1², p. 27 bas. — Quant à *iva* "pour ainsi dire", il est distingué de *iva* "comme" KP. p. 784: le premier a sa place dans la Figure appelée *utprekṣā*, qui comporte une "vision" directe, alors que *iva* "comme", ou *yathā*, même sens, suggère un tertium qui serait inapproprié dans l'*utprekṣā*.

leur seule présence.[37] Au contraire, la Comparaison indirecte est celle qui s'exprime, soit par le mot *tulya* ou un mot analogue, soit par un autre emploi du suffixe *-vat*, celui que décrit P. 5.1,115. D'abord le cas de *tulya*: ici la propriété engendrée par ce mot n'est pas directement "perçue", elle est indirectement sensible, à travers l'idée de similitude. Une telle *upamā* affecte trois variétés, "le visage (de telle personne) est pareil à (la lune)", où la similitude est par rapport à l'objet comparé; "ce (lotus, là-bas) est pareil à (ce visage, ici)", où elle a lieu par rapport à la chose à quoi l'on compare; "ce (visage) et ce (lotus) sont pareils", où l'une et l'autre relations se présentent à la fois. Quant au cas du suffixe *-vat*, exemple *brāhmaṇavat* "(il se conduit) comme un brâhmane", la propriété commune ou tertium comparationis est une action verbale, la similitude est le propre de l'action (sous-entendue), d'où l'on "infère" la similitude des personnes agissantes.[38]

Le troisième et dernier type de Comparaison est celui qui se fonde sur un composé nominal (*samāsagā*). On s'attendrait ici à rencontrer la vaste catégorie des *tatpuruṣa* porteurs d'une valeur comparative (P. 2.1,55 déjà cité), mais c'est là une division de l'*upamā* "elliptique", puisque le signe extérieur de la comparaison y fait défaut. La Comparaison "pleine" est concernée, sous la forme directe, par l'emploi de *tulya* et termes analogues, placés au second membre du composé[39]; sous la forme directe, les poéticiens font état, d'une manière qui peut légitimement surprendre, d'un type d'expression où la particule *iva* forme composé avec le nom qui la précède. Cet enseignement remonte, lui aussi, à la Grammaire, P. 2.1,4 *vt.* 2: le composé ainsi formé révèle sa singularité par la manière même dont il est défini: on nous dit en effet que la désinence du membre antérieur y est maintenue, et que l'accent reste celui du nom isolé.[40]

[37] Au lieu de *sāmarthya*, Jagannatha (d'après J°, by V. A. Ramaswami Sastri, p. 166) parle d'une *lakṣaṇā*: mais en ce cas, la distinction entre *upamā* expresse et *upamā* implicite risque de perdre sa raison d'être.

[38] Le mot décisif est *kriyā* "action (verbale)", qui figure déjà dans le Bhāṣya ad loc. — Sāh. Darp. 10.15-16, n° 649–650 suit de prés KP. et explique ainsi la différence entre *śrautī* et *ārthī* (*upamā*): les mots *tulya* et analogues sont "épuisés" (*viśrāmyanti*) après avoir servi de qualifiants à l'*upamāna*, ils sont ainsi incapables de rendre une notion supplémentaire, c'est-à-dire la similitude entre deux objets ayant une propriété commune.

[39] Voire, d'un composé nécessaire (*nitya*), c'est-à-dire non résoluble, précise KP. (repris Hem. *sū.* 114), alors que le *vt.* 2.1,4, n° 2 ne disait rien de pareil. Y aurait-il là une doctrine non pāṇinéenne? C'est peu probable, vu que les textes de poétique obéissent en général au système de P.

[40] Le Bh. ad P. 2.2,18 in fin., qui englobe peut-être un *vt.*, ne fait que reprendre 2.1,4 *vt.* 2. Les commentaires de KP. ad loc., p. 557 se réfèrent en outre à P. 2.4,71. — Il s'agit apparemment d'une survivance védique: tous les *padapāṭha* (cf. Whitney ad Ath. Prāt. 1.82) combinent *iva* avec le mot qui précède, *udadheḥ-iva* remplace ainsi *udadher iva* (qui devrait être découpé *udadheḥ/iva*); cf. aussi Weber ISt. 13, p. 5 sqq. De là l'habitude de considérer *iva*, tantôt comme mot indépendant tantôt comme membre ultérieur. Noter aussi que la présence de *iva* affectait la finale des *pragṛhya* RkPrāt. 2.55. Tout ceci reflète une situation d'enclise archaïque, mais pourquoi maintenue pour le seul *iva*? — En Poétique, il semble qu'on ait arbitrairement *iva* compositionnel et *iva* autonome, celui-ci plutôt quand le lien avec le nom est plus lâche, celui-là quand *iva* interrompt par exemple une séquence au cas oblique formée d'une épithète, de *iva*, du substantif afférent.

§10. A côté de la Comparaison pleine, la Comparaison "elliptique".[41] Les sous-groupes sont à peu près les mêmes. Du point de vue grammatical, qui seul ici nous requiert, nous avons à citer l'ellipse du tertium comparationis: processus qui entraîne une *upamā* indirecte, soit avec composition nominale (ex. *amṛtopamā* "semblable à l'ambroisie"), soit avec dérivation secondaire (ex. *viṣakalpa* "analogue à du poison"). L'ellipse du terme auquel on compare l'objet donne lieu, comme il est naturel, à un composé: c'est la catégorie normale. Plus instructive (encore qu'étroitement fondée sur le *vyākaraṇa*, comme toute cette doctrine de l'*upamā*) est l'ellipse de la particule comparative, laquelle aboutit à l'emploi de plusieurs formations verbales relativement singulières (fort connues d'ailleurs dans le *kāvya*): le dénominatif en "*kyac*",[42] dans lequel le thème de base a valeur d'objet-transitif, ex. *sutīyati* "il traite (quelqu'un) comme son fils", ceci suivant P. 3.1,10 qui pose dans son *sū.* le terme *UPAMĀNĀT*; dans lequel aussi le thème de base a valeur de Locatif (*ādhāra* = *adhikaraṇa* du *vt.* 1 ad P., même sū.), *antaḥpurīyati* "il se meut comme dans le gynécée". Le dénominatif en "*kyaṅ*", suivant P. 3.1,11, ex. *nārīyate* "il agit comme une femme" (P. reconduit ici, au témoignage des commentaires, le mot *UPAMĀNĀT*).[43] L'absolutif en *-am*, appelé "*ṇamul*", où le thème de base est soit un objet-transitif (P. 3.4,25 et 29), type *gharmāṃśudarśam* "comme on voit le soleil", soit un sujet de phrase, *pārthasaṃcāram* "comme Arjuna se meut" (P. 3.4,43); l'emploi "comparatif" est assuré par la mention *UPAMĀNE* chez P. 45. Enfin le composé nominal, ex. *kāminīgaṇḍapāṇḍu* "pâle comme la joue de l'amante".[44]

Suivent des cas où l'on reconnaît une double ellipse, ellipse du tertium et ellipse de la particule comparative: c'est la formation dite en "*kvip*", ex. *vidhavati* (sur *vidhu* "lune"), "il se comporte comme la lune": formation qui repose, sinon expressément sur P., du moins sur un élargissement de P. 3.1,11 dû au Bhāṣya, lequel mentionne l'éventualité d'un dénominatif sans affixe après une racine quelconque et cite *aśvati*, *gardabhati*, où la nuance comparative ("il se comporte comme un cheval, comme un âne")

[41] La notion d'ellipse en Poétique est fuyante et multiforme, comme d'ailleurs, bien qu'avec des aspects très différents, en Grammaire. Cf. Vām. 5.1,14 qui fait dépendre l'ellipse de l'usage. On a vu § 12 des cas de pronom ellipsé. Parmi les Défauts de phrase, il en est un qui réside en l'absence de certains mots attendus (*nyūnapada*), cf. la strophe citée KP. *sū.* 75, p. 339, Regnaud p. 163, où manquent *asmābhiḥ* et *ittham*. Mais rien de tout cela ne ressemble à la théorie du *lopa* qui domine plus d'un développement en Grammaire.

[42] Sāh. Darp. 10.19 = n° 653, éd. Kane[5], p. 96, conteste que "*kyac*" soit un cas d'ellipse de la particule. Il y voit une ellipse du *dharma*, car les affixes verbaux, dit-il, expriment d'eux-mêmes la ressemblance: allusion implicite à la Grammaire! — Hem. *sū.* 115 et autres, suivent KP.

[43] Le cas de "*kyac*" et de "*kyaṅ*" est cité pour la première fois par Udbhaṭa 1.36.

[44] Sāh. Darp. loc. cit. cite encore l'*upamā* reposant sur le suffixe *-in-*, autrement dit la *ṇinigatā* (*upamā*), qui s'appuie sur P. 3.2,79; c'est un cas d'ellipse de la particule, comme celui de la *kangatā* (*upamā*), qui remonte à P. 5.3,98. Dans la *chagatā* (*upamā*), qui reflète le cas traité par P. 5.3,106, suffixe *-īya-*, il y aurait ellipse de l'*upamāna*. Ce dernier procédé est traité tout au long dans Kuval. 1.7 qui allègue l'exemple bien connu en Grammaire, *kākatālīya* "comme (les choses se passent pour) la corneille et le fruit du palmier".

résulte du *sū.* même.[45] En second lieu, dans des conditions analogues, apparaît à nouveau le procédé compositionnel, ainsi *rāja-kuñjara* "un roi semblable à un éléphant", qui correspond à la formation *puruṣavyāghra* bien connue en grammaire, P. 2.1,56, qui fait état, sinon d'une ellipse double, du moins de l'ellipse (*APRA-YOGE*) du tertium.

Cette même ellipse du tertium, combinée à celle de l'objet auquel on compare, aboutit à un procédé nécessairement compositionnel, ex. *kusumasadṛśa* "semblable à la fleur". L'ellipse de la particule et de l'objet comparé donne un cas d'affixe "*kyac*", ex. *sahasrāyudhīyati* "il se comporte comme Sahasrāyudha".[46]

Enfin les théoriciens les plus avancés croient discerner—c'est le cas extrême, et d'authenticité bien contestable, il faut l'avouer—une ellipse des trois éléments cités. Ceci donne un composé tel que *mṛganayanā* "(une fille) aux yeux de gazelle", composé que KP. (*v.*) explique en fonction de P. 2.2,24 vt.12: à cet endroit de la Grammaire il est fait état d'un *bahuvrīhi* avec chute du membre ultérieur, le membre antérieur consistant en un "*upamāna*", *saptamyupamānapūrvapadasya bahuvrīhir uttarapadalopaś ca*, ex. *uṣṭramukha* = *uṣṭramukham iva mukham* "dont la figure est comme la figure du chameau". En l'occurrence, *mṛganayanā* reposerait sur une proposition telle que "*mṛganayane iva cañcale nayane yasyāḥ*".[47]

On voit que, sans comporter d'innovations, la théorie de la Comparaison en tant que Figure de style, telle que la définit Mammaṭa, prend fond sur des catégories grammaticales, sur des *sūtra* ou des *vtt.* de l'école pāṇinéenne; c'est une mise en système des données éparses dans le *vyākaraṇa*. Les Traités postérieurs admettent tous, plus ou moins, cette classification complexe et les critères linguistiques qu'elle entraîne. Quelques auteurs cependant protestent: la Citramīmāṃsā (p. 27) fait valoir qu'un tel classement, reposant sur des principes grammaticaux, n'a pas sa place (*na vyutpādyatām arhati*) dans un Traité de poétique; elle ajoute que, au surplus, des divisions de ce genre ne sont pas valables. Cette contestation isolée pourrait trouver argument sur les Traités antérieurs à KP., qui pour la plupart ignorent les indices de langue: c'est le cas au moins de Daṇḍin, de Bhām., de Vām. Daṇḍin, nous l'avons vu, ne connaît qu'une énumération de caractère lexical, qui par son ampleur présente un assez vif intérêt, mais qui n'est accompagnée d'aucune doctrine morphologique. Udbhaṭa se borne à distinguer (1. 32 sqq.) l'*upamā* pleine et l'*upamā* elliptique, avec double ou triple ellipse, vingt et une variétés en tout, mais sans entrer dans le détail.[48] Rudraṭa va un peu plus loin (8.4) en

[45] D'après Sāh. Darp. 10.10 = n°. 655, la différence entre "*kvip*" et "*kyaṅ*" est que "*kyaṅ*" laisse une trace dans le verbe (à savoir, un affixe explicite), "*kvip*" non.

[46] Sāh. Darp. n° 658 voit là une ellipse de l'*upameya*. On peut se demander quelle est la différence entre *sahas-rāyudhīy-* et *nārīy-* (précité): c'est que, dans le premier de ces dénominatifs, l'*upameya* n'est pas le sujet de la phrase (*saḥ* . . .), mais l'objet implicite (*ātmānam*), dans le second (qui lui est identique de notre point de vue), il n'y a d'autre ellipse que celle de la particule (remplacée par "*kyaṅ*"), Kane trad. p. 102.

[47] Cf. Hem. *sū.* 115, Jagann. op. cit., p. 164, Sāh. Darp. 10.22. Kane op. cit., p. 104 rappelle que certains auteurs, justement inquiets de cette analyse, rejettent la *trilopopamā*. Cf. aussi S.V. Dixit éd. (1959) de KP., p. 214.

[48] Vingt-quatre variétés dans SKĀbh., vingt-sept Sāh. Darp., trente-deux Kuval.

distinguant d'abord entre *samāsa* et *pratyaya*, comparaison compositionnelle et comparaison dérivative, puis en sériant trois types de la première, selon que l'*upamāna* est composé avec le tertium (17) ou avec l'*upameya* (21), ou enfin l'*upameya* avec le tertium (19). Plus explicite est l'Agni Pur. qui (8.5 et 6) distingue deux *upamā*, celle à composé, celle hors de la composition; il ajoute (7 et 8) que la première est de trois espèces suivant que l'élément mis en composition est l'*upamādyotaka* (c'est-à-dire la particule), l'*upameya*, ou les deux à la fois. C'est le KP. qui, sur le plan grammatical, développe en somme les virtualités de ce qui figurait à l'état de germe dans la littérature antérieure.[49]

§11. Autre chapitre où apparaissent des traits de langue: celui de la "suggestion" considérée comme facteur poétique dominant. C'est l'objet du chapitre IV du KP.; il n'y a rien de correspondant au chapitre V, d'ailleurs écourté, qui traite de la forme poétique où la suggestion n'est qu'un élément secondaire. Rien non plus au chap. VI, qui concerne la forme inférieure, celle où la capacité suggestive fait défaut.

Après avoir décrit le *rasa* et ses environnements, Mammaṭa pose qu'il est susceptible d'être "suggéré" (*dyotyate, vyajyate*) au moyen de trois indices formels: au moyen de certaines portions de mot—c'est-à-dire, pratiquement, soit du thème, soit plus souvent du suffixe (ou désinence)—, au moyen de l'arrangement (*racanā*), enfin au moyen des phonèmes, *sū*. 61. On reconnaît la disposition ternaire, comme ci-dessus § 4 et dans des conditions similaires. La question de l'arrangement et des phonèmes sera traitée par KP. à propos des Figures, soit au chap. VIII; elle ne porte qu'incidemment sur des points de grammaire.

Au contraire, la question des "portions de mot" (*padaikadeśa*) intéresse des faits morphologiques et lexicologiques combinés. Parmi eux, il en est qui ne nous concernent pas directement ici, ainsi lorsqu'on enseigne que *jayati* "il l'emporte" (p. 169) suggère le *rasa* Érotique, ce que n'eût pas obtenu le terme plus simple, apparemment plus banal, *śobhate* "il est beau"; on nous affirme p. 170 que *pada* "pas" suggère l'anxiété amoureuse mieux que n'eût fait *dvāra* "porte". Mais c'est à peine si l'on peut parler de qualification lexicale; c'est en vérité le contexte, l'ambiance de la strophe tout entière, qui amène à préférer tel mot à tel autre, sans que le vocable sélectionné ait plus de vertu intrinsèque que le terme évincé.

Cette remarque s'applique pareillement aux cas où la morphologie est en jeu. Telle désinence, dans une str. donnée, passe pour être mieux apte qu'une autre à suggérer quelque *rasa* (le *rasa* Érotique, comme dans tous les exemples des théoriciens, a un rôle indûment privilégié); entendez par là la désinence, en tant

[49] Les critères de langue font défaut en effet dans les plus anciens Traités, ceux de Daṇḍin, de Bhām., d'Udbhaṭa; aussi chez Ruyyaka, qui est singulièrement sommaire touchant l'*upamā*. Bhām. 2.31 se bornait à citer le cas de *yathā* et *iva*, puis le *kriyāsāmya* (donc, = P. 5.1,115) avec *-vat* (2.33); *-vat* est mentionné sommairement par Daṇḍin 2.57 et Udbh. 1.37 (en valeur de *karman*), 38 (en valeur de Gén. et de Loc.). Rien chez Vām. Mais Daṇḍin expose une remarquable liste de substantifs, d'adjectifs, de verbes, entraînant une valeur "comparative", 2.57–65: cela, certes, se limite au lexique, sans entrer dans la doctrine grammaticale, mais c'est la matière première du *kāvya*, et, sous l'angle de la documentation, c'est plus proche de notre conception moderne de la stylistique que les analyses périmées de la Poétique sanskrite ultérieure.

qu'elle exprime soit une relation casuelle ou temporelle, soit une personne, soit un nombre; il s'agit donc du contexte, non de l'aspect morphologique. On enseigne ainsi que le présent *kirati* (p. 171, Regnaud p. 87) note un acte en train de se réaliser (*sādhyamāna*; cf. *pravṛttasyāvirāme* dans la définition du présent chez P. 3.2, 123 *vt.*1), que le nom verbal *atīta* note un acte accompli (*siddha*: cf. les caractères bien connus de la *niṣṭhā* P. 1.1,26), si bien que le suffixe *-ta-* "suggère" le caractère révolu de l'acte désigné par le verbe; "or, ces deux actes sont dans un rapport logique de cause et d'effet qui se trouve interverti grammaticalement, puisqu'en vertu des suffixes en question, l'effet aurait précédé la cause. Mais cette erreur apparente a pour résultat de suggérer la rapidité avec laquelle les blessures de l'Amour sont suivies de leurs conséquences, et par cela même de faire naître le *rasa* érotique" (Regnaud loc. cit.). De même (p. 173), dans *likhann āste bhūmim* "il se tient grattant la terre", le participe joint à *āste* (là où l'on attend, paraît-il, **likhaty āsitaḥ*) suggère un acte qui se poursuit jusqu'à apaisement de l'esprit (*prasāda*): ceci, joint à l'Accus. *bhūmim* (là où l'on attend paraît-il, le Loc. *bhūmau*), suggère que l'acte de "gratter" a lieu sans intention particulière (*na hi buddhipūrvakam*).[50] Cette indication sur le participe de continuité descriptive, en locution periphrastique, n'est pas sans valeur du point de vue linguistique; non plus celle du Locatif envisagé comme cas "intentionnel", ce qui évoque sans doute la *nimittasaptamī* souvent mentionnée dans les commentaires grammaticaux. Mais, dans la strophe citée, de tels phénomènes émanent d'une interprétation psychologique a posteriori, bien plutôt que des formes grammaticales, qui n'ont aucun contenu expressif par elles-mêmes.

Les autres traits allégués sont de caractère plus élémentaire encore: si l'Instr. *divasena* "suggère" l'idée que le fruit souhaité est atteint (p. 179) "au terme de la journée" (et non "au cours de la journée"), il y a bien là le rappel implicite de l'*APAVARGE* de P. 2.3,6, expression que justement la Kāśikā glosait par *phalaprāpti* (comme fait KP. ici même): mais l'emploi serait à peine digne d'être relevé si l'entourage de la strophe ne donnait quelque impulsion à dégager cette nuance. De même p. 180 (Regnaud p. 91), où le KP. note que le suffixe *-ka-* dans *aṅgaka* "membre" suggère l'idée de compassion, conformément à P. 5.3,76.[51] Rarement la doctrine puise chez Patañjali: pourtant p. 178 sur l'ordre des membres dans le *dvandva*, commandé par le *prādhānya* ou "primauté" relative des éléments en présence: enseignement qui émane de P. 2.2,34 *vt.* 4.

Des données de ce genre n'ajoutent pratiquement rien à notre connaissance de la grammaire, ni même n'expliquent l'affectation stylistique dont telle ou telle formation peut bénéficier dans le

[50] Regnaud dit très bien: "*tracer le sol*, sens exprimé par une construction qui ne permet pas d'admettre l'ellipse d'un régime direct destiné à désigner ce qu'on s'applique à y tracer, indique un acte machinal résultant du trouble éprouvé par la personne qui l'accomplit; au lieu que *tracer sur le sol* supposerait l'ellipse d'un régime direct à l'accusatif, exprimant ce qu'on y tracerait (des caractères, etc.), et impliquant par là un acte accompli avec réflexion".

[51] Importance relative des nuances d'affectivité chez P., telles que *ākrośe*, *lipsāyām*, *āśiṣi*, *praśaṃsāyām*, non seulement dans la théorie des modes du verbe (où cet apport affectif est pour ainsi la base de la description), mais ailleurs. La Poétique n'a pas manqué de faire son profit de telle de ces notations, ainsi naturellement celle concernant le "*manye*" (= *manyase*) *prahāse* de P. 1 4,106.

kāvya.[52] Retenons toutefois comme de quelque valeur — parce que la chose est inattestée dans la littérature grammaticale — la remarque touchant l'emploi de *ca* réitéré : emploi défini comme un état d'équilibre (*tulyayogitā*) entre deux actions simultanées, dont en réalité la première est la cause et la seconde est l'effet : "*et* ton esprit s'est tourné vers la fierté *et* nos ennemis ont été détruits", c'est-à-dire "ton âme a montré de la fierté et cela a suffi pour que nos ennemis fussent détruits" (KP. p. 181, Regnaud p. 92) ; comme dit Regnaud, "de cette suggestion résulte la promptitude avec laquelle le roi a anéanti ses adversaires ; et par là apparaît un sentiment (*bhāva*) en rapport avec le *rasa* héroïque". Le cas est déjà signalé dans le Dhvany. loc. cit. Il rentre, de notre point de vue, dans les voies et moyens de l'expressivité linguistique.[53]

Le caractère "suggestif" est attribué, entre autres, au suffixe d'abstrait *-iman-*, avec l'exemple *taruṇiman* "jeunesse" (Regnaud p. 93). P. 5.1,122 fait dépendre d'un *gaṇa* l'apparition du suffixe d'abstrait *-iman-*, autrement dit il s'agissait d'une formation relativement rare, surtout si on la compare aux autres dérivés abstraits tels que ceux en *-tva-* et *-tā-*, voire en *-yă-*. Mais ceci n'aurait pas suffi à nous permettre de penser que *-iman-* comportait une nuance qualitative, si nous n'avions le témoignage corroborant de Bhām. 6.54, qui recommande en poésie l'usage de ce suffixe, alors que Vām. 5.2,56 écarte certains emplois, peut-être simplement parce qu'on en abusait. Le fait que le suffixe *-iman-* (en tant que suffixe secondaire) ait été rattaché à la série des noms en -(*ī*)yas- et *-iṣṭha-* et à certains dénominatifs en *-ayati* a contribué à accentuer le caractère concret de cette petite catégorie, qui à l'origine était à peine distincte de la classe des noms en *-man-* et dépourvue de valeur affective ; *-īyas-* lui aussi est déclaré particulièrement souhaitable en poésie, Bhām. loc. cit.

§12. Le chapitre des Défauts (chap. VII) est riche en notations grammaticales, souvent plus novatrices, en tout cas moins déconcertantes, que celles que nous venons d'examiner. Ici d'abord on retrouve la question des composés, qui forme vraiment l'épine dorsale de la théorie grammaticale en Poétique. Il est vrai que KP. est plus libéral en détails que les autres textes.

Certains des défauts portant sur un mot ne se rencontrent qu'en composition nominale, *samāsagatam eva* KP., *sū.* 72 p. 266 et 284. Observation qui, de notre sentiment, est sans portée appréciable, car il est clair que les défauts sont les mêmes, qu'il s'agisse d'un mot simple ou d'un composé (le composé, sur le plan sémantique, est un mot comme les autres), ainsi le défaut appelé *kliṣṭa* "(expression) difficile ou obscure". Tout ce qu'on peut dire est qu'un terme mis en composé rend d'emblée l'expression plus difficile, moins tolérable parfois l'ambiguïté : d'où cette catégorie spéciale.

Mais il y a un défaut au moins qui est spécifique à la composition nominale, c'est l'*avimṛṣṭavidheyāṃśa*, p. 266 et 285 : tel élément

[52] Il n'y a guère à tirer non plus des remarques de l'Aucityavic. 20 sqq. concernant la "propriété" ou "convenance" (*aucitya*) de divers cas, genres, nombres, celle des adjectifs, préverbes, particules, temps verbaux. On est là dans un domaine trop fluent.

[53] Sur l'emploi de *ca* réitéré, cf. J. Gonda Vâk 5, p. 37 et notamment p. 41.

de phrase qui devrait figurer comme prédicat (*vidheya*)[54] demeure à l'état non-autonome ou subordonné (*guṇībhūta*), c'est-à-dire sous la forme d'un membre de composé. Ainsi *mithyāmahiman* "faux prestige" (cité aussi Regnaud p. 146), là où le mouvement de la phrase exigeait *mithyā mahimā* "mon prestige (s'avéra) inane"; *dvitīyamaurvī* "deuxième corde d'arc" (aussi Regnaud, ibid.), expression qui passe inaperçue, alors qu'il fallait dire *dvitīyāṃ maurvīm* "(sa ceinture était comme) une corde d'arc (qui eût été paradoxalement) la deuxième (portée par Amour, lequel n'en a qu'une d'ordinaire)"; *alakṣyajanmatā*, où eût convenu *alakṣitā janiḥ* "sa naissance est inconnue"; *amuktā* "non délaissée" (Regnaud, ibid.), quand on attendait *na muktā* "elle n'a pas été délaissée".[55] Il s'agit bien là d'un fait de style, mais à fondement linguistique: la tendance "resserrante" de la strophe, l'abus du composé nominal, le mouvement inéluctable qui conduit l'expression en *kāvya* à revêtir l'allure d'un *sūtra* versifié, tout cela aboutit à masquer le prédicat (comme est masqué ou même ellipsé, bien souvent, le sujet même de la phrase); il important au théoricien d'attirer l'attention là-dessus, même si les exemples allégués sont inégalement propres à assurer la démonstration.

§13. Le même défaut apparaît un peu plus loin (*sū*. 74 p. 306) à l'occasion, non plus du composé, mais de la phrase. Il s'agit ici encore d'un prédicat qui n'est pas mis en évidence, mais est laissé dans la pénombre, voire, complètement omis. Les exemples cités, qui sont relativement nombreux — il est visible que Mammaṭa a entendu donner quelque ampleur à une thèse qui n'avait été formulée avant lui ni en Poétique ni en Grammaire —, concernent la phrase corrélative, cette structure majeure de la phrase sanskrite. Le KP. considère comme un défaut l'absence de pronom corrélatif

[54] *Vidheya* en ce sens n'appartient pas à la Grammaire (dans le Bhāṣya, le mot ne signifie rien de plus que "ce qui fait l'objet d'une règle, ce qui est à instruire sous forme de *vidhi*"). En Poétique, le terme s'oppose à *anuvādya* (non attesté en Grammaire), "ce qui exprime une référence à quelque chose qui a été antérieurement émis". Le contraste *vidhi/ anuvāda* se trouve dans les Nyāyasūtra 2.1,62, mais il appert que cet emploi d'*anuvād(y)a* relève de la Mīmāṃsā, cf. Mī. Kośa, s.u.; *anuvādya*, glosé *uddeśya*, *prāptenāvagata*, équivaut sur le plan grammatical à "sujet (de la phrase, en tant que désignant qqch. de connu)", d'où *vidheya* "prédicat (en tant que la chose à faire connaître)". Le Tantravārtt. (cité dans le c. moderne de KP., p. 285) parle des phrases corrélatives, où l'*anūdyatā* (= *anuvādyatā*) caractérise la proposition en *yad*, comme se situant en protase et désignant la chose "acquise", par rapport à la *vidheyatā*, qui caractérise la proposition en *tad*, placée en apodose et désignant la chose "à réaliser", *yacchabdayogaḥ prāthamyaṃ siddhatvaṃ cāpy anūdyatā/ tacchabdayoga auttaryaṃ sādhyatvaṃ ca vidheyatā.*

[55] Sāh. Darp. n°. 574 reprend ces exemples et souligne le cas de *amuktā/ na muktā*, qui illustre la fameuse théorie sur les deux espèces de négation, le *prasajya* = et le *paryudāsa-pratiṣedha*. — Un peu plus loin (p. 304), KP. cite l'exemple (aussi repris Sāh. Darp.) *svargagrāmaṭikāviluṇṭhanavṛthocchūnaiḥ kim ebhir bhujaiḥ* "à quoi bon mes bras qui se sont en vain gonflés des dépouilles du hameau céleste!" (on attendait: c'est en vain que . . .). — Le rapport entre *vidheya* et *anuvādya* est également en jeu dans la str. *nyakkāraḥ* KP. *sū*. 74, p. 304 (repris Sāh. Darp.), mais il s'agit ici d'un "ordre troublé" (le *vyākīrṇa* de SKĀbh. 1.23): on attend *ayam eva nyakkāraḥ*, avec l'*anuvādya* (*ayam*) avant le *vidheya* (*nyak*°). Ceci concerne d'ailleurs le style bien plutôt que la syntaxe, comme le Défaut similaire appelé *saṃkīrṇa* KP. *sū*. 75, p. 362.

dans la séquence attendue *yaḥ . . ./saḥ . . .*: il dit que le pronom *asau* (qu'on a dans un élément strophique *tanoti yo 'sau subhage tavāgataḥ*) ne saurait remplacer *saḥ*, qu'il faudrait donc *yaḥ . . ./ sa āgataḥ*, cf. Regnaud p. 148. Car *asau*, est-il précisé, sert simplement à désigner un objet en tant que la chose à laquelle on se réfère (*anuvādyamātra*), il n'a pas, dirions-nous, force corrélative.[56]

Si la structure fondamentale *yaḥ . . ./ saḥ . . .* requiert la stricte corrélation, la structure inverse (moins bien accréditée ou, du moins plus faible en tant que système corrélatif) n'exige pas aussi fermement le démonstratif: on peut dire *sādhu kṛtam . . . yad . . .* "c'est une chose bien faite, (à savoir) que . . .", au lieu de *tat sādhu kṛtam . . . yad . . .* (Regnaud p. 150). Pourquoi? C'est que le relatif a pouvoir-inhérent (*sāmarthya*) (d'assurer à lui seul la valeur corrélative). On constate en effet aisément que *ya* postérieur est plus fort que *ya* antérieur, en ce qu'il entraîne souvent avec lui une valeur complétive, loin de couvrir à titre purement formel, comme *ya* antérieur, un simple "adjectif syntaxique" (suivant l'expression de M. Benveniste).

Cette notion de pouvoir-inhérent est, il est vrai, dangereuse à manier; c'est une de ces abstractions que poéticiens et grammairiens aiment évoquer. Mammaṭa observe qu'en vertu du *sāmarthya* il arrive que *ya* ou *ta* puissent manquer; on cite un exemple où l'un et l'autre pronoms font défaut, *utpatsyate/ 'sti mama ko 'pi samānadharmā* = *ya utpatsyate/ taṃ praty asti . . .* (Regnaud, ibid.). On rentre ici dans une autre abstraction commode, celle de l'ellipse.

Une double objection se présente quant à la nécessité de la rigoureuse liaison *yaḥ . . ./ saḥ . . .*: (a) ne peut-on supposer que (dans la phrase déjà citée) *asau* joue le rôle de *saḥ*, de même qu'on trouve ailleurs *yaḥ . . ./ asya . . .*, là où l'on comptait sur *yaḥ . . ./ tasya . . .*? Réponse: non, car alors, dans un cas tel que *yo 'sau . . . saḥ . . .*, le pronom *saḥ* serait superflu, ce qui n'est nullement avéré; ensuite, si *asau* était corrélatif, il viendrait en tête de la seconde proposition; donc *yo 'sau* agit comme *sa yaḥ*, pour indiquer la personne en tant qu' "inconnue". On notera incidemment que l'ordre des mots, pourtant si arbitraire dans le *kāvya*, est une exigence de la Poétique: sans doute y a-t-il là le souvenir d'un état de langue plus rigoureux, tel celui de la prose védique, où peu de liberté était laissé aux auteurs de changer la place d'un mot.

(b) si l'on escompte une corrélation stricte, comment se fait-il qu'on ait telle strophe où *tad* (seul) répond à *yad-yad*? Réponse: *tad* renvoie à une entité unique, qui équivaut justement à cette unicité qu'exprime (d'autre manière) le complexe *yad-yad*.[57] Ces indications ont leur prix, même si on les applique (comme ç'a été sûrement l'intention de Mammaṭa) à la structure un peu relâchée qui est celle du sanskrit classique, fût-ce même à l'intérieur du *kāvya*.

§14. Dans ce même cadre, la question de la phrase relative revient au *sū.* 75 p. 347, afin d'illustrer le Défaut appelé *abhavanmatayoga* = *abhavanniṣṭasaṃbandha* (Regnaud p. 169): la relation

[56] A ce propos, KP. énumère judicieusement les nuances du *tad* non corrélatif: désigner l'objet dont traite le contexte, *prakṛta*; l'objet connu, *prasiddha*; l'objet dont le sujet parlant a l'expérience personnelle, *anubhūta*.

[57] De même un peu plus loin (p. 349) *yad. . ./ tadānīm*, au lieu de *yadānīm . . ./ t°* ou de *yad . . ./tad*. Pour éviter cette rupture d'uniformité, Mammaṭa préfère corriger *yad* en *ced*. L'exemple *yad-yad/tad* est repris Sāh. Darp., n° 574.

qu'on souhaite (entre relative et principale) n'a pas lieu. Dans l'exemple cité, il s'agit de démons (*kṣapācāriṇām*) par la puissance desquels (*yeṣām*) . . . (et) par qui (*yaiḥ*) . . ., enfin dont (*yeṣām*) . . .: l'antécédent est au Génitif, ce qui, selon Mammaṭa, ne s'accorde pas avec l'Instr. *yaiḥ*, commandé par la syntaxe de l'apodose. Il n'y a rien là que de régulier à notre sens; tout au plus estimera-t-on que cette mixture de pronoms relatifs entraîne de prime abord quelque obscurité. Toutefois le KP. n'hésite pas à taxer de défectueux le rapport *kṣapācāriṇām*/ *yaiḥ*, ce qui, si l'on généralisait la remarque, conduirait à rejeter nombre de structures présentant une disparité analogue, ne gardant comme correctes que celles où, par une sorte d'attraction (ici mal concevable), l'antécédent a été apparié au cas grammatical du relatif. Chose curieuse, l'objection faite à cette phrase prend appui, non sur un grammairien (la Grammaire, on le sait, se soucie fort peu des structures), mais sur Jaimini: la Mīmāṃsā, tout bien considéré, n'est-elle pas la vraie "syntaxe" du sanskrit, une *vākyamīmāṃsā* ou disquisition sur les propositions, tout comme la grammaire est une *padamīmāṃsā*, une disquisition sur les mots.[58]

De fait, Jaimini 3.1,22 donne l'axiome *guṇānāṃ ca parārthatvād asaṃbandhaḥ samatvāt syāt* "il ne peut y avoir de relation (entre des rites secondaires), étant donné que (lesdits rites) servent à quelque chose d'autre (= n'ont pas leur fin en eux-mêmes) et qu'ils sont égaux (entre eux à cet égard par rapport à l'acte primaire)". Transposé en langage grammatical, ceci signifie: quand il y a plusieurs subordonnants (*yac-chabdanirdeśya*), ils servent à quelque chose d'autre et ne sauraient être en corrélation mutuelle. Conclusion pratique, et d'ailleurs irréalisable: à côté de *yeṣām* . . . *kṣapācāriṇām*, il faudrait un *yaiḥ* . . . *kṣapācāribhiḥ* (d'autant plus que *yaiḥ* est en corrélation avec *taiḥ* au 4ᵉ *pāda*).

Un autre exemple, assez différent, du même Défaut est encore donné p. 350 (Regnaud p. 170): la strophe citée commence par "écoute (le récit de) tout ce qui (*yad-yad*) a été (atteint, obtenu ou conquis, *samāsāditam*) par telle et telle (chose respective, *tena-tena*): ainsi les flèches (Nomin.) (furent obtenues) à l'aide de l'arc (Instr.), par les flèches (fut conquise) la tête de l'ennemi, etc.". La phrase paraît irréprochable. Mammaṭa trouve à y redire et pose une alternative: ou bien les mots "flèches, arc, tête, etc." sont les régimes de "écoute" et doivent être pareillement à l'Accus.; ou bien l'on admet que "écoute" n'a pas de mot particulier pour régime, mais seulement le sens-global ou sens-de-la-phrase, *vākyārtha*, et alors on attend une proposition autonome commençant avec "les flèches" et la mise au Nomin. de tous ces mots. Double solution qui nous paraît spécieuse, sinon absurde, mais qui recèle tout de même un germe de réalité. Le poéticien préconise la correction de *yena yena* . . . *yad yad* en *kena kena* . . . *kiṃ kim*.[59] Du moins, voit-on par des détails de ce genre, par

[58] Cf. nos Études 6, p. 66. Les *paribhāṣā* mīmāṃsistes ont affaire au *vākya* (lequel fait partie, soit dit en passant, des six critères ou *pramāṇa*). Elles ont aussi une incidence grammaticale, cf. JAs. 1941–42, p. 121. [this volume, page 442]—Sur l'influence de la Mīmāṃsā sur la Poétique, Kane, op. cit., p. 375.

[59] "Flèches", etc. ne saurait ni être apposé à *ya*, ni être inclus dans le sens du relatif (KP.). — Exemple accessoire concernant la rupture d'uniformité dans le pronom: *tadvisṛṣṭa* est à corriger en *anena vi*°, la référence étant à Śiva, qui vient d'être nommé: ceci confirme que *tad* est senti comme pronom de référence lointaine ou même abstraite.

l'excès même du purisme syntaxique, l'intérêt que prennent certains théoriciens à la théorie de la phrase, théorie dont l'absence, constitue une grave lacune, la seule grave peut-être, dans l'enseignement des grammairiens.[60]

Ainsi, sans aborder de front les problèmes de langue, la Poétique sanskrite ouvre tout de même quelques perspectives nouvelles, du moins chez ses représentants les plus pénétrants, Ānandavardhana et surtout Mammaṭa.

On peut observer encore ceci : là où la Grammaire prescrit ou interdit — ne connaissant en guise d'"options" (*vikalpa*) que des faits de pure indifférence linguistique (par ex. il est indifférent qu'on forme *śiśvāya* ou *śuśāva*, selon P. 6.1,30) —, la Poétique, intervenant qualitativement, indique certains choix, certaines préférences, notamment dans le domaine de la Dérivation nominale, qui de tous les compartiments du *vyākaraṇa*, a toujours été le plus évoluant, le plus mobile. Elle connaît des nuances expressives, éventuellement affectives, même s'il lui advient trop fréquemment d'attacher la vertu de "suggestion" à tel ou tel élément grammatical qui, pris en soi, est parfaitement inerte.

En dépit du caractère de bonne heure stéréotypé qu'ont revêtu les enseignements de poétique, on y découvre encore la recherche d'une certaine hiérarchie dans les valeurs du langage, recherche qui demeure très éloignée des préoccupations de la grammaire traditionnelle.

[60] Les Défauts portant sur un mot isolé ne nous concernent pas ici, étant affaire de lexique, sauf le n° 2 (*sū.* 73, p. 268) dénommé *cyutasaṃskṛti*, glosé *vyākaraṇalakṣaṇahīna*, "échappant aux règles de grammaire", qui répond au *śabdacyuta* de Bhar. trad. Man. Ghosh 17.94, au *śabdahīna* de SKĀbh. 1.111 dont on nous dit qu'il peut se muer en Qualité s'il s'agit d'une imitation, *anukaraṇa*, c'est-à-dire si l'on veut imiter le parler défectueux d'un homme sans culture: tel pourrait être le cas, souvent cité, de la phrase *paśyaiṣa ca gav iti* KP. *sū.* 80, p. 412 (l'exemple *gav iti* est d'origine grammaticale, il est signalé Kāś. ad 1.1,16, justement comme cas d'"imitation", cf. la trad. Ojihara-Renou p. 63; sur le principe de l'*anukaraṇa* en Grammaire, v. quelques références dans Terminol. s.u. et Durgh. Introd., p. 134). Ainsi *anunāthate* contrevient à P. 1.3,21 *vt.*7, vu que la str. où cette forme figure n'implique pas de nuance précative (*āśiṣi*); moins pusillanime, Durgh. ad P. 1.3,21 parvient à justifier la forme; cf. de même *ājaghne* Sāh. Darp. 7.4 SKĀbh. 1.20 Durgh. ad P. 1.3,28. — Il semble qu'en Poétique l'incorrection grammaticale, le solécisme, n'appartienne jamais qu'au mot, non à la phrase, car on nous dit (KP. p. 296) que le Défaut de phrase répondant à la *cyutasaṃskṛti* n'existe pas: ceci montre bien que la pureté grammaticale était affaire de mot, non de phrase. — Tel Défaut concernant une "portion de mot" (cf. ci-dessus § 11) effleure un problème grammatical, ainsi le n° 3 (*nirarthaka*) *sū.* 74, p. 321; pourquoi le plur. *dṛśām* "des yeux", s'agissant d'une seule femme? Ou encore le moyen *kurute*, là où manque toute nuance rétroflexe? A propos de *dṛśām*, la *v.* note assez finement que le pluriel est injustifiable, car dans une notion unitaire il n'est admissible que s'il y a diversité de fonctions (*vyāpāra*), or ce n'est pas le cas quand il s'agit des "yeux". Inversement un singulier "générique" est plausible Vām. 5.1,17 (avec recours de la *v.* à la notion de "genre" d'après la Mīmāṃsā).

D. La Théorie des temps du verbe d'après les grammairiens sanskrits (1960)

Louis Renou

The last article is Renou's "La Théorie des temps du verbe d'après les grammairiens sanskrits," *Journal asiatique* (248, 1960, 305–337). The related treatment of verbal moods is the subject of a more recent monograph by Rocher (1968a). Many of the rules discussed here occur on Plate III.

§1. Rien[1] n'est plus simple, en apparence au moins plus élémentaire, que la façon dont Pāṇini décrit les valeurs temporelles dans le verbe. En fait, une lecture plus attentive, un recours aux commentaires, aux grammairiens non-pāṇinéens, permettent de constater que, sur beaucoup de points, l'enseignement était précis et souvent même pénétrant.

L'indice qui désigne les formations temporelles — ou, plus exactement, les désinences afférentes — est un indice à *L* initial.[2] Les signes conventionnels *Ṅ* et *Ṭ* marquent respectivement les temps secondaires — imparfait *LAṄ*, aoriste *LUṄ*, conditionnel *LṚṄ*[3] — et les temps primaires (ou mieux: non-secondaires) — présent *LAṬ*, parfait *LIṬ*,[4] futur périphrastique *LUṬ*, enfin futur (simple) *LṚṬ*. A cette série s'ajoutent les indices modaux: c'est l'optatif (avec l'indice des temps secondaires) *LIṄ*,[5] puis le subjonctif

[1] Abréviations: Bh. = Mahābhāṣya; BM. = Bālamanoramā; C(V). = Candra(vṛtti); H. = Hemacandra (avec la Bṛhadvṛtti); J. = Jainendra (avec la Mahāvṛtti); K. = Kāśikāvṛtti; Kai. = Kaiyaṭa; Kt. = Kātantra (avec le c. de Durgasiṃha); N. = Nyāsa; Ng. = Nāgeśa; P. = Pāṇini; SK. = Siddhāntakaumudī; ŚK. = Śabdakaustubha; SKĀ. = Sarasvatīkaṇṭhābharaṇa; sū. = sūtra's; vt(t). = vārttika('s). — Nos investigations dans la littérature grammaticale ne sont pas complètes; il est peu probable que des faits importants se laissent déceler chez les post-Pāṇinéens; nous n'avons rien trouvé de remarquable chez Śākaṭāyana, ni dans la Bhāṣāvṛtti ou la Prakriyākaumudī. Vopadeva a ceci de curieux qu'il supprime les règles élémentaires, ne gardant que quelques curiosités; de même le Sārasvata, qui se limite à *lunīhi lunīhi* (= P. 3.4,2), *yajati sma* (= 3.2,123), *supto 'haṃ vilalāpa* (= 3.2,115 vt.), *yāvat karoti* (= 3.3,4), *smarasi* (avec *yad*, = 3.2,113). Il n'entrait ni dans nos vues ni dans nos moyens de faire intervenir les philosophes de la grammaire; la Śabdaśaktiprakāśikā a tout un prakaraṇa sur les valeurs "*la*" du verbe qui transcende pour ainsi dire les données grammaticales tout en conservant les articulations de P. Au contraire, dans le Vākyapadīya (3me Livre, *kālasamuddeśa*), on a une exposition abstraite sur le temps grammatical, où les faits de langue sont à peine dégagés de la spéculation.

[2] Emanant de *kāla* "temps," comme l'a noté Ksh. Ch. Chatterji Techn. Terms 1 p. 9. Le *kālaviśeṣa* ou "spécification du temps" est l'une des deux raisons d'être du "*la*(*kāra*)," l'autre étant l'*arthaviśeṣa* ou spécification du sens K. ad 3.4,77. — Les autres indices en *L* sont étrangers à la théorie temps.

[3] Ce sont les trois temps à augment (*bhūtakaraṇavatī*) que Kt. 3.1,14 appelle *rūḍha* "transmis par la tradition," pensant aux noms qui les désignent dans cette Grammaire.

[4] Le parfait n'est pas, à proprement parler, un temps primaire, mais il se comporte comme tel, tant pour les formes que pour l'emploi (cf. Brugmann 2². 3 p. 769), et tout d'abord en ce qu'il est démuni d'augment; ni pour le véd. ni pour le "class.", P. ne reconnaît un plus-que-parfait, cf. le silence à ce sujet de Thieme Plusquamperfektum.

[5] Le soi-disant précatif n'est qu'une variante de l'optatif, du point de vue sémantique aussi bien que formel; P. le caractérise par *LIṄ ĀŚIṢI* 3.4,116, d'où la dénomination *āśīrliṅ* des Pāṇinéens, *āśiṣ* seul des non-Pāṇinéens.

LEṬ, enfin l'impératif *LOṬ*[6] (ces deux-ci, avec l'indice primaire).[7]

Un tel ensemble traduit d'abord cette vérité que, dans l'organisation du verbe sanskrit, il n'existe pas de catégorie modale qui serait distincte par nature d'une catégorie temporelle, comme le Veda avait tenté d'en constituer une[8]; dans la prose védique de type "récent" (celle même que vise P.),[9] aussi bien qu'en sanskrit ultérieur, l'expression verbale dans la phrase subordonnée, c'est-à-dire dans le domaine par excellence du mode, se répartit entre l'optatif, le futur (théoriquement aussi, le conditionnel) et le présent.

§2. La théorie des temps chez Pāṇini s'insère à l'intérieur de l'exposé sur la dérivation nominale (primaire).[10] La chose se comprend de soi si l'on considère que les désinences verbales, de même que les suffixes primaires, s'attachent à la racine (ou au thème verbal, *DHĀTOḤ*). Le parallélisme entre l'une et l'autre formations se marque déjà dans la terminologie: désinences et suffixes s'appellent *pratyaya* "ce qui s'attache, ce qui s'affixe à qqch."[11] L'expression *KARTARI* vise, dans le nom, la fonction "agentis" et, dans le verbe, la voix active (c'est-a-dire, non-passive): de fait, les noms d'agent sont glosés uniformément par le verbe actif, *karotīti kṛt* "qui fait", *pacatīti pacaḥ* "qui cuit." L'expression *KARMAṆI* désigne, dans le nom, l'Accus. et, dans le verbe ou le nom verbal, la voix passive: le passif ne repose-t-il pas sur le transfert (au Nomin.) d'un objet direct qui, dans la phrase normale, c'est-à-dire à la voix active, s'inscrivait à l'Accus.? Enfin le terme *BHĀVE* concerne les dérivés nominaux "actionis" et, dans le verbe, il s'applique à la catégorie de l'impersonnel.[12]

[6] L'impératif, lui aussi, et une formation primaire, en dépit de désinences spéciales (la finale -*u* répondant à l'-*i* des temps primaires). Quand au subionctif, qui est mixte, les formes en sont claires là surtout où les désinences primaires les caractérisent. — P. use, à l'occasion, d'indices diminués, *LṚ* qui englobe *LṚṄ* et *LṚṬ*; *LI* qui associe au parfait (*LIṬ*) les morphèmes d'aoriste désignés génériquement par *CLI*.

[7] Il est notable que P. n'ait pas senti le besoin de poser la catégorie de l'indicatif (dont les critères modaux sont purement négatifs); s'il l'avait fait, il l'aurait définie sans doute un peu comme, dans le nom, il définit le Nomin. 2.3,46 (cf. Thieme JAOS. 76 p. 4), ce que C. 2.1,93 résume par *arthamātre* "ce qui note le sens et rien d'autre".

[8] Avec un subjonctif bien défini, un optatif et un "injonctif", ce dernier, il est vrai mixte entre le temps et le mode.

[9] Celle des Br. expurgée de ses archaïsmes, des Sūtra, des Up. en prose.

[10] Chez les non-Pāṇinéens, elle se dégage parfois du chapitre de dérivation, ainsi Vop. a un "*kti-pādaḥ*" (chap. 25) qui traite des valeurs personnelles, abstraction faite des suffixes.

[11] Autre interprétation du mot chez les Gramm., v. Termin. s.u. *pratyaya* et JAs. 1941–42 p. 144 [see pages 457–458 of this volume]. *Prakṛti* est également commun à la morphologie nominale et verbale, ibid.

[12] Ainsi *padyate 'neneti pādaḥ* "le pied est ce avec quoi on marche" CV. 1.3,7 = P. 3.3,18. Ceci ne veut pas dire qu'au sentiment des Gramm. les "actionis" reposent nécessairement sur un impersonnel; P. 19 les connaît aussi notant un régime verbal quelconque (autre que le régime d'agent, càd. le Nomin.), avec cette restriction importante que le domaine dudit sū.19 est celui d'une *saṃjñā*, n. propre ou n. techn. — Au début de 3.1,67, le Bh. est amené à distinguer le *bhāva* noté par un verbe et le *bhāva* noté par un suffixe : le premier indiquant temps, personne et voix, étant lié à un agent, assimilable à un acte (*kriyāvat*), le second étant dénué de ces spécifications et assimilable à un objet concret (*dravyavat*).

A quel endroit du troisième Livre (lequel traite de la dérivation primaire) commence l'exposé sur les valeurs temporelles? A l'occasion des suffixes valables au sens du "passé" (*BHŪTE* P., *atīte* Kt. et ailleurs), l'expression *bhūte* étant à compléter en *dhātvarthe bhūte* K. ad 3.2,84 "quand le sens de la racine est celui du passé". Cette précision, comme la plupart de celles qu'apporte K., remonte au Bh.: Patañjali proposait d'abord de sous-entendre *kāle* "quand le temps est celui du passé", mais son interlocuteur observe qu'il n'y a point de rubrique gouvernante (*adhikāra*) sur le temps chez Pāṇini.[13] Il propose alors de sous-entendre *dhātau*, mais l'objection est qu'une "racine verbale" est un mot et qu'un mot ne saurait être présent, passé ni futur. Il propose enfin *dhātvarthe* "sens de la racine," autrement dit *kriyāyām* "quand l'action (verbale) est passée," et cette façon de formuler est à l'abri de toute objection.[14]

De telles indications locatives, en Grammaire, ne servent pas nécessairement à définir un emploi "sémantique". Une spécification comme *KARTARI* ou *BHĀVE* (nous l'avons rappelé) indique une catégorie très générale ("quand il s'agit de . . ."). Les mentions *BHŪTE* ou *BHAVṢIYATI* marquent la nuance (éventuellement) passée ou future propre à tel ou tel dérivé nominal, quels que soient les caractères qui, par ailleurs, distinguent telle formation de telle autre. On voit l'importance de ces critères temporels à propos des suffixes *auṇādika* que P. évoque au début du troisième pāda: ces suffixes sont valables, nous dit-il, *BAHULAM* "diversement," notion qui peut s'entendre, évidemment, sur plus d'un plan, mais que le grammairien a sûrement entendue aussi sous l'angle temporel, puisqu'il pose au sū. 2 *BHŪTE 'PI DṚŚYANTE* "on les rencontre également au sens du passé", et au sū. 3 *BHAVIṢYATI* "au sens du futur." Le Bh. n'enseigne rien à ce sujet dans son commentaire sur le sū.l, mais K. glose *vartamāne 'rthe* "au sens du présent", ce qui est sans portée pratique, mais a l'avantage d'être logique avec le système.[15]

[13] Cf. encore ci-dessus § 10. — P. évitait ces *adhikāra* qui ne sont pas strictement grammaticaux, ce qui n'empêchera pas, plus tard, Kt. 3.1,10 de formuler un "*kāle*" qui se justifie, ajoute le c., quand il y a doute si le qualifiant appartient au verbe ou à l'objet (*dravya*); le temps, qui est *un* par nature, se divise, lorsqu'il réside dans un objet ayant forme matérielle, en présent, passé, futur, du fait de l'action (qui est elle-même présente, passée, future).

[14] Une autre remarque dans Bh. ad vt.4 conduirait à supprimer *BHŪTE*, sous prétexte que les suffixes désignent le passé par nature. La réponse est qu'on a besoin que le sens passé soit spécifié dans certains cas d'espèce, ainsi dans *kumāraghātin* et *śīrṣa*° (3.2,86 et cf. 51), *ākhuhan* (76 et 87), *sutvan* (103 et 132), *suṣupvas* (172 et 107), *anehas* (3.3,1 et cf. 3.1,133), enfin dans véd. *agnim ā dadhānasya* (3.2,106 et 129).

[15] Toute une tranche de la Dérivation primaire est ainsi subordonnée aux valeurs temporelles: *BHŪTE* vaut de 3.2,84 à 122 inclus (mais la K. ne l'allègue expressément que pour 85–87, 102, 104, 105, 110–122; cf. en outre 3.3,2 et 140, 141); *VARTAMĀNE* vaut de 3.2,123 à 188 inclus (cf. K. 3.3,131), mais K. ne reconduit le terme que sous 123; *BHAVIṢYATI* vaut de 3.3,3 à 15 inclus (et en outre 136–139), mais n'est cité par K. que pour 3–13 et 15; *triṣu kāleṣu* K. ad 3.3, 16 (et 3.4,6) et suiv.; enfin *BAHULAM* (3.3,1) implique en partie au moins une valeur temporelle, tout comme l'indice de "transfert" *-VAT* (3.3,131 132 135). — Pratiquement, on le voit, la validité est restreinte; elle le serait davantage si l'on ôtait des listes les sū. relatifs aux formes personnelles du verbe. Si bien qu'on a moins lieu de s'étonner de l'importance allouée par

Or, il y avait une série de formations nominales qui, au moins pour l'expression du prétérit, traçaient une ligne de force temporelle: ce sont les absolutifs en *-tvā*, les noms verbaux en *-ta-* et *-tavant-*, les participes parfaits (le participe aoriste est obsolet et, d'ailleurs, n'avait jamais eu nettement le sens d'un passé). C'est là précisément que P. accroche la théorie du verbe personnel.

§3. La transition est marquée par le participe parfait (3.2,106), le sū. "védique" 105 — qui anticipe sur le sū. "commun" 115 — servant pour ainsi dire de prélude. Ce participe, tant au moyen (106) qu'à l'actif (107), est envisagé, non en tant que paradigme, mais bien plutôt comme substitut (optionnel) du parfait personnel, *agniṃ cikyānaḥ* "*il a* empilé (les briques de l'autel du) Feu". Limitée au Veda,[16] cette disposition est ensuite (108) étendue à la bhāṣā, où toutefois on nous apprend qu'elle se limite à trois verbes, *sad-*, *vas-*, *śru-*.[17] Enfin le sū. 109 installe à titre de formes

les Gramm. à l'expression du temps dans les suffixes primaires (d'ailleurs la règle *DHĀTUSAṂBANDHE* ci-dessous note 20 vient encore en limiter les effets). Elle s'explique par l'extension même de la phrase nominale, qui transfère aux dérivés primaires tout le poids de l'expression temporelle : tout dérivé primaire ("agentis") est plus ou moins, en sanskrit, un *participe*.

[16] La mise en exergue d'un enseignement védique n'est nullement sans parallèles. Elle se justifie ici parce qu'il a été question du participe au 104 et que le cas du participe revient dans 106 et 107 (qui commandent à leur tour 108 et 109): or 106 et 107 dépendent de 105.

[17] Ainsi, au 124, le participe présent est substitut du *LAṬ*. Les exx. cités pour 106–108 sont bien des exx. où le participe joue le rôle de prédicat (non pas 109, bien que K. donne pour contre-exemple à *anāśvān* par ex.: *nāśīt / nāśnāt / nāśa* "il ne mangeait ou ne mangea point"). Pourtant le sū. 124 justement nous laisse dans le doute : si l'Accus. *pacamānam* est traité en substitut du *LAṬ*, s'il est précisé que le Nomin. *pacan* ne peut être employé qu'au sens de *pacati* (il faut dire *devadattaḥ pacati*, non d° *pacan* [mais K. ad 3.3,14 autorise au participe futur *kariṣyan devadattaḥ*]; l'interdiction est d'ailleurs ensuite atténuée déjà dans Bh. in fin., que reprend K.), on en déduira analogiquement que le *jakṣivān* de K. 107 signifiera "ayant mangé" tout autant que "j'ai (ou : il a) mangé". Le sū. 109, sous l'apparence de poursuivre le même théorie, vise surtout à instruire des formations "irrégulières".

Les non-Pāṇinéens, qui conservent 108 en ignorant 105–107, considèrent par la force des choses que ledit sū. concerne, non le participe, mais le parfait: ainsi C. 1.2,73 pose qu'avec *śru-sad-vas-* le parfait s'emploie au sens d'un prétérit indifférencié (englobant donc le *pārokṣya* BM., ce qui résulte de Bh. 108 in fin.), concurremment à l'aoriste et au parfait, tout comme P. 105 enseignait le sens du prétérit indifférencié pour le *LIṬ* védique. Il est vrai que C. 74 connaît aussi un participe parfait substitut optionnel du parfait personnel, c'est-à-dire qu'il admet la validité non védique de P. 107, possibilité qu'évoque encore la Bhāṣāv. J. 2.2,88 atteste que "selon certains" *-vas-* et *-āna-* sont usités après toutes racines aux lieu et place du parfait personnel. H. 5.2,1 est celui qui transcrit avec le plus de détail cette situation assez trouble : il pose d'abord le parfait en valeur se prétérit pur avec *śru- sad- vas-*, concurremment aux temps requis par d'autres règles, mais il ajoute que certains réclament *-vas-* seul valable, non le parfait personnel; que d'autres admettent aussi l'imparfait (comme forme indifférenciée?). Ensuite (2), que *-vas-* et *-āna-* valent seulement dans le domaine du parfait personnel, *-vas-* au sens "agentis", *-āna-*, en outre, en emploi passif et impersonnel; les exx. son tirés de verbes divers. H. ajoute encore que *-āna-* manque parfois, que "selon certains" *-vas-* lui-même n'est valable qu'après *śru- sad- vas-* (*-āna-* étant

toutes-faites (*nipātana*) trois participes parfaits, soit qu'il les entende aussi comme substituts optionnels de l'indicatif (ce qu'indiquent les exemples, ainsi *upasedivān kautsaḥ pāṇinim* "Kautsa a été l'élève de P."), soit (ce qui devait être la véritable intention de P.) qu'il attire, l'attention sur certaines anomalies morphologiques. Tout cela ne laisse pas de créer une situation un peu trouble, que les commentateurs exploiteront en des directions diverses.

§4. C'est à cet instant que Pāṇini introduit le verbe personnel. D'abord le *LUṄ* (110), c'est-à-dire l'aoriste considéré comme notant un passé pur (ou mieux: indifférencié). Sitôt après, le *LAṄ* ou imparfait (111), un peu plus loin le *LIṬ* ou parfait (115), qui expriment des aspects spécialisés du prétérit; dans l'intervalle et après, sont indiqués quelques autres procédés pour rendre le prétérit sans sortir du verbe personnel.[18]

Suit la théorie du présent ou *LAṬ* (123), à quoi s'annexent aussitôt les substituts du présent personnel, c'est-à-dire les participes (jusqu'à 133); on peut, lato sensu, y rattacher les suffixes décrits ensuite, tels que *-tṛ-* (134 et suiv.), dont les fonctions sont, en grande partie, celles d'un duratif, donc, indirectement au moins, d'un "présent". D'autres suffixes viennent après, qui sont sans support temporel, mais ont en commun avec la série précédente d'appartenir à la classe des "agentis". Le troisième pāda fait alors retour aux valeurs temporelles, et plus particulièrement à l'expression du futur: celle-ci concerne, outre certaines formes du verbe personnel, des dérivés nominaux en *-tu-* (infinitifs), en *-aka-* (10) et quelques autres. Le futur proprement dit n'est allégué qu'au sū. 13 (et encore, de manière indirecte, cf. § 14 ci-dessous), c'est-à-dire après qu'auront été décrites d'autres expressions personnelles ayant valeur ou faisant fonction de futur (4-9). Suit presque immédiatement (15) le futur périphrastique: formation d'origine nominale, qui donc nous achemine assez naturellement à l'exposé de nouveaux dérivés primaires, qui sont, cette fois-ci, des "actionis." Le retour à la théorie des temps du verbe se produira plus loin (131): il s'agit ici, derechef, du futur personnel, mais orienté vers des nuances modales: précisé en effet par le conditionnel (139-141) — qui est morphologiquement un temps, syntaxiquement un mode —, combiné avec l'optatif, lequel apparaît d'abord timidement aux sū. 134, puis 143, plus fermement à partir de 147, encore que ses caractères fondamentaux ne soient formulés qu'au sū. 161. Les six aspects de l'optatif sont ensuite transférés à l'impératif (162), qui en possède trois

tout à fait rejeté); selon d'autres, on aurait *-vas-* partout, mais non *-āna-*. Les poètes, dit SK. 3095, usent "diversement" — c'est-à-dire librement — de *-vas-* (et de *-āna-*?), exx. *tasthivāṃsam, adhijagmuṣaḥ* (donc: hors de la fonction de prédicat). BM., rappelant que d'après Bh. *-vas-* est védique (comme *-āna-*), admet implicitement l'usage de *-vas-* dans la langue non védique. Il ressort de tout cela que les Gramm. ultérieurs ont exploité P. 3.2, 106 sqq. pour ébaucher un emploi général du participe parfait, perdant de vue le rôle de prédicat. Cf. encore nos Etudes de gr. skte (à propos de CV.) 1 p. 98.

[18] P. part de la fonction, non de la catégorie; de là s'explique d'ailleurs qu'il juxtapose les dérivés nominaux à nuance (accessoirement) temporelle et les formations de participe ou de verbe personnel. Ainsi, dans le nom, part-il des *kāraka* ou modalités de recton casuelle (liée au verbe), pour aboutir aux désinences (*vibhakti*) aptes à exprimer ces modalités.

autres à titre singulier (163). Le pāda s'achève par l'exposé du précatif et du dé-précatif (autrement dit, du prohibitif).

§5. Là se termine la description des formes personnelles: elle comporte, on le voit, un passage nuancé des valeurs temporelles aux valeurs modales. Cette manière de présenter les faits répond, en somme, à ce que les textes littéraires ont à nous apprendre sur la déperdition du mode après l'époque des mantra védiques (l'impératif étant à part, en tant qu'il est par nature impropre à la subordination): disparition rapide du subjonctif (et de pseudo-injonctif à nuance modale), restriction de l'optatif aux emplois d'éventuel ou de prescriptif — donc, à des emplois très faiblement modaux — si bien que l'indicatif, sous ses divers aspects, deviendra le mode par excellence, entraînant dans son sillage des résidus d'optatif.

Seul déborde sur le pāda 4 de l'Aṣṭādhyāyī un fait de langue curieux (à peine attesté d'ailleurs en littérature), à savoir la répétition (*āmreḍita*) d'un impératif, type *lunīhi lunīhīty evāyaṃ lunāti* "il coupe de façon répétée," "il coupe et recoupe".[19] Enfin les sū. 6 à 8 n'intéressent que le domaine védique: 6 constatant l'indifférence au temps des trois prétérits personnels; 7 et 8 décrivant l'emploi du subjonctif; autrement dit, la notion de mode l'emporterait en expressivité, dans le Veda, sur celle de temps, ce qui ne laisse pas d'être exact. La théorie pāṇinéenne est ainsi encadrée par les faits védiques, le sū. terminal 3.4,6 ne faisant que reprendre, sous une autre perspective, le sū. 3.2,105 par lequel cette description avait commencé.[20]

[19] Il fallait bien inscrire l'enseignement 2–5 à cette place insolite de la Grammaire, puisqu'il est censé dépendre du *DHĀTUSAṂBANDHE* 1. — L'indicatif (présent) est intéressé à ce même emploi (selon 3 et 5.), à titre facultatif, puisqu'on peut dire *chando 'dhīṣva* (etc.) ou *chando 'dhīte* (etc.). . . *ity evāyam adhīte* "il étudie continûment la métrique" (littéralement: comme qq'un dont on dirait "il étudie, il étudie. . . "). Mais c'est certainement l'impératif qui est typique (cf. JAs. 1959 p. 70 pour les quelques références littéraires connues), l'indicatif n'est qu'un subrogat. Les formules en *lunīhi-lunīhi* s'apparentent aux composés tels que *jahistamba* (Wack. 2.1 p. 315), *ehi-yavam* (p. 328) et surtout *utpacanipacā* (ibid.).

[20] La question se pose donc de la compatibilité mutuelle de ces deux règles encadrantes. K. est formelle: 3.2,105 vaut pour un passé non spécifié (*aviśeṣeṇa*); 3.4,6 vaut dans le cadre du *DHĀTUSAṂBANDHE* 1, c'est-à -dire là où sens du verbe est conditionné par sa "relation avec un verbe" voisin, *padāntarasaṃbandhe*, dit CV. 1.3,128 un peu différemment. L'adduction de ce *DHĀTU*° pour le sū. 6 paraît hautement artificielle (et d'ailleurs les exx. de K. ne comportent que des verbes isolés, comme *adyā mamāra* "il est mort aujourd'hui", exception à 3.2,115); elle se comprend bien, en revanche, dans le cas cité par Bh. (1 ad vt. 2), *agniṣṭomayājy asya putro janitā* "celui qui célébrera un Agniṣṭoma aura un fils", où °*yājin*, qui devrait signifier "ayant célébré" (3.2,85), reçoit une acception temporelle conforme à celle, du verbe voisin (*janitā*): cas intéressant — s'il est linguistiquement authentique — d'une concordance de temps, sur un plan non morphologique, mais syntaxique. Bh. ajoute que c'est le qualifiant (en l'occurrence, le dérivé primaire) qui, du fait de son caractère secondaire, se plie au temps du qualifié ou verbe personnel; ce n'est pas l'inverse (raisonnement repris N., SK. 2824 et ailleurs); BM. évoque le primat de l'acte. Toutefois H. 5.4,41 cite une phrase (du Śiśupāla) où l'on voit un futur (*yaiḥ plāvayiṣyanti*) s'adapter au prétérit qui suit (*sa dadarśa*) au point de perdre le sens futur (ex. attesté aussi SKĀ. 2.4,224). Le Bh. étend cette sorte d'"attraction" temporelle aux

§6. L'énoncé des valeurs fondamentales requiert chez P. un minimum de mots: l'aoriste s'emploie [*BHŪTE*] 3.2,110, l'imparfait [*BHŪTE*] *ANADYATANE* 111, le parfait [*BHŪTĀNADYATANE*] *PARO'KSE* 115, le présent *VARTAMĀNE* 123, le futur simple [*BHAVIṢYATI*] 3.3,13, l'autre futur [*BHAVIṢYATI*] *ANADYATANE* 15; enfin le conditionnel est décrit par un "actionis" *KRIYĀTI PATTAU* 139, avec reprise de [*BHAVIṢYATI*] ou (140) *BHŪTE*. Avec ce laconisme contraste l'ampleur relative donnée aux nuances modales, y compris à celles du subjonctif (bien que le subjonctif soit védique et, partant, sujet à une formulation abrégeante). Certes, la concision est l'un des traits majeurs de l'Aṣṭādhyāyī. Elle a l'avantage, en l'occurrence, de souligner le côté rudimentaire des emplois temporels en sanskrit commun, dans cette langue mal définie qui englobe d'un seul mouvement l'état védique (archaïsmes exclus) et l'état "classique."[21] Mais, si l'on fait entrer en jeu des faits, des opinions, des tendances que révèle la littérature grammaticale post-pāṇinéenne, on s'aperçoit que la théorie des temps était relativement étoffée et qu'elle a conservé plus d'un trait intéressant.

§7. L'aoriste est considéré comme temps du passé (sans plus), par opposition à l'imparfait et au parfait: cela, parce que ces deux derniers comportent des spécifications qui manquent à l'aoriste, non parce que l'aoriste pāṇinéen indiquerait le "procès pur et

dérivés secondaires, considérant que *gomān*, mis à côté de *āsīt*, pourra signifier "il était possesseur d'une vache", donc "il possédait. . .", alors que, pris en soi, le suffixe *-mant-* désigne le temps présent, *TAD ASYĀSTY ASMIN* 5.2,94. Il y a là, bien entendu, de notre point de vue un raisonnement spécieux. D'ailleurs le vt. 2 précise lui-même que le changement de temps ne porte pas sur le suffixe en tant que tel, mais affecte le dérivé en tant que mot complémentaire (*upapada*) du verbe; autrement dit, c'est la phrase seule qui reçoit la notation temporelle. La remarque est assez fine. Bh. analyse en conséquence l'ex. précité (en *agniṣṭomayājin*) "quelqu'un, ayant célébré l'A°, . . .qqch. se passera en lui. . . en qui?. . . en celui qui aura un fils. . . quand? . . . quand il y aura une célébration d'A° faite par lui".

[21] Nous avons vu que l'intrusion du Veda, dans la théorie des temps, se bornait à deux passages, fidèles l'un et l'autre au principe du *BAHULAM* qui domine toute la description védique : (a) selon 3.2,105 (sū. non commenté Bh.), le parfait véd. s'emploie au sens du prétérit (pur), ce qui, d'une part, élargit l'usage du sanskrit commun (115), d'autre part fait opposition, par avance, à 3.4,6 (ci-après); les exx. choisis, *aham... dadarśa*, *aham. . .ā tatāna* (K., mais empruntés à Bh. 106–107), sont en effet conçus en fonction de 115. Cette manière d'énoncer les faits peut sembler sommaire; mais il faut avouer que, compte tenu des intentions de P. en matière de védisme, elle reflète bien l'impression globale que laissent les mantra;
(b) selon 3.4,6, ce sont les trois formations personnelles du prétérit qui sont utilisées "pour tous les temps" (K.; sū. non commenté Bh.). Extension un peu surprenante, dont K. a voulu peut-être limiter les conséquences en ajoutant *dhātusaṃbandhe*. Mais cette adjonction est ici inopérante (cidessus n. 20). Tout aussi bien les exx. retenus sont ceux où n'existe aucune "relation" extérieure, ce sont *akarat akaram* en fonction de présent (ou d'imparfait?); *avṛṇīta*, d'aoriste; *mamāra*, de présent (mais aussi bien, d'aoriste), les temps normaux étant valides optionnellement (K.). On retiendra ce témoignage sur l'arbitraire temporel prévalant dans la langue des mantra et des yajus. Reste à concilier 3.2,105 et 3.4,6 pour ce qui est du parfait : ce sont deux perspectives légèrement différentes d'une même réalité.

simple", au sens où Meillet Introd.[7] p. 250, définissait l'aoriste indo-européen. En réalité, bien que l'aoriste soit affecté au prétérit en général, les Grammairiens ont été amenés, pour en délimiter le domaine par rapport aux autres formations du passé, à lui allouer le passé "récent", voire le passé "d'aujourd'hui": de là, le nom d'*adyatanī* (*vibhaktiḥ*) "formation-désinentielle relative au (passé) d'aujourd'hui" que donnent à l'aoriste Kt. et d'autres grammairiens. Au sū. 110, Bh. se demande si l'aoriste, du fait même qu'il est instruit sans spécifications, ne forme pas une exception-entravante (*apavāda*) à l'emploi de l'imparfait; autrement dit, si, dans *apāma payaḥ* "nous avons bu du lait", l'imparfait attendu par 111 (car il s'agit d'un fait d'hier, comme on peut le supposer) ne sera pas nécessairement évincé par l'aoriste selon 110; mais il ajoute qu'il ne s'agit pas là d'une "entrave", disons plus clairement, d'une opposition d'où résulterait un choix nécessaire: si l'on emploie l'aoriste *apāma*, c'est qu'on n'a pas *voulu* rendre un passé antérieur à aujourd'hui, qu'on a choisi de rendre un passé indifférencié.[22] C'est reconnaître l'importance de la *vivakṣā*, de l'"intention", dans le domaine des fonctions grammaticales: on n'est jamais tenu d'employer une forme "spécifiée". C'est reconnaître aussi (de notre point de vue) que l'aoriste, tout en s'adaptant particulièrement à noter l'aujourd'hui, demeure une forme générale, propre à noter tout événement dont l'emplacement temporel n'est pas précisé. — Dira-t-on, ajoute encore Bh., qu'en disant "nous avons bu du lait", on sait très bien à quel jour cet événement s'est situé (seul le futur, si l'on admet cette objection, aurait le droit d'être "général")? La difficulté se résout par la *vivakṣā*: tout dépend si l'on *veut* employer une forme générale

[22] Le principe de la *vivakṣā* (Termin. s.u., Introd. à Durgh. p. 131), relativement évité dans Bh., se développera chez les Gramm. ultérieurs, tant il offre de commodités, au moins pour les faits d'emploi et de syntaxe. A propos de la théorie des temps, cf. surtout CV. 1.2,81; 3,3 Kt. 3.1,16 H. 5.2,5 et ailleurs; H. va jusqu'à introduire la *vivakṣā* dans le sū. même, en spécifiant qu'on a l'aoriste là où il n'y a pas intention de différencier. A suivre CV., on conclurait que des tranches entières de la théorie s'expliquent — ce qui veut dire, dans la vraie pensée de C., s'éludent — en faisant appel à la *vivakṣā*. Le principe se fonde évidemment sur le *VĀ* pāṇinéen, dont l'extension n'est nulle part aussi sensible que dans le chapitre des valeurs temporelles, mais quel énoncé de grammaire résisterait s'il fallait en soumettre l'application à la "volonté" que peut avoir le sujet d'employer telle forme plutôt que telle autre? — Un autre procédé, non incompatible avec le précédent, est de considérer que la position morphologique précède la constitution de la phrase, c'est-à-dire a lieu sans tenir compte de la phrase; il y a là un paralogisme, qui permettra à K. 3.3,131 de dire que *śvaḥ kariṣyati* "il fera demain" est correct, *kariṣyati* se situant sur le plan formel, l'addition de *śvas* sur le plan du sens-de-la-phrase : c'est le conflit entre le *pada*- et le *vākya-saṃskāra* (Termin. s.uu.). A ce passage, K. raisonne ainsi: celui qui estime que, dans la forme *gacchāmi* (employable selon ledit sū. au sens de "j'irai dans un avenir proche"), c'est purement et simplement le sens du présent qu'on a, et que la notion d'un autre temps résulte de la phrase; — or, au moment où l'on forme un mot, on ne met pas en exercice le temps connu par la phrase; — (nous répondrons que) ce n'est pas à un interprète tel que celui-là, au courant du sens de la phrase, qu'est destiné le problème ici entrepris (mais à un étudiant ordinaire, auquel on a donc à faire savoir que *gacchāmi* signifie bien "j'irai"). Le présent sū., précise N., est fait pour les *mandabuddhi*, les gens à l'esprit lent.

pour noter un fait particulier, ou si l'on préfère recourir à une forme spécialisée, telle l'imparfait.

§8. La discussion qui s'engage autour de la racine *vas-* "passer la nuit" (110 vt. 3) éclaire bien le sens qu'il faut donner au [*BHŪTE*] du sū. Le vt. en question ajoute à la théorie de l'aoriste le cas de la racine *vas-* sous deux conditions: (a) si l'on a à dire "j'ai passé la nuit (dernière à tel endroit)", donc [*kva bhavān uṣitaḥ?*] *aham amutrāvātsam*, la nuit étant arrivée à son terme; ou encore (b) "j'ai passé la nuit (sans dormir)". Le premier de ces deux emplois constitue une exception à l'imparfait: on attend en effet l'imparfait pour noter un procès qui n'appartient plus à l'aujourd'hui[23]; si l'on a ici l'aoriste, c'est bien parce que l'aoriste concerne un prétérit qui est d'aujourd'hui même ou qui confine à l'aujourd'hui.[24] On rejoint alors une valeur linguistique connue: l'aoriste de constatation, dont l'usage privilégié a lieu au cours du dialogue, quand les personnages, bien entendu, parlent d'événements qui leur sont survenus à eux-mêmes ou dont ils ont été les témoins.

Dans le second exemple (b), s'il y a "veille continue" (vt.4, *jāgaraṇasaṃtatau*), le sujet qui dit "j'ai passé la nuit (à tel endroit, sans dormir)"[25] croit avoir affaire à aujourd'hui et emploie l'aoriste. C'est donc bien par leur opposition réciproque que les Grammairiens définissent imparfait et aoriste.[26]

§9. Dès lors, contrairement aux apparences, c'est l'imparfait qui est la forme non-*marquée*, n'étant ni actuel (comme l'est l'aoriste), ni hors la vue (comme nous verrons qu'est le parfait). Ceci répond assez fidèlement aux tendances littéraires, où nous voyons que l'imparfait ne peut guère se définir sinon négativement, soit par rapport à l'aoriste, soit par rapport au parfait.

Il est un cas toutefois oû l'imparfait, d'après les Grammairiens (111 vt. 2), empiète sur le territoire du parfait: il désigne en effet un événement du passé hors la vue, à condition qu'il s'agisse d'un fait notoire[27] et qui (par sa date: *aruṇad yavanaḥ sāketam* "les Grecs assiégèrent Sāketa")[28] pouvait être perçu du sujet parlant: on souligne ainsi, par anticipation, que le parfait sera approprié

[23] L'aujourd'hui, disent les cc. depuis K., va du lever normal au coucher normal, en incluant la demi-nuit de part et d'autre, ainsi H. 5.2,7; lever normal signifie quatrième veille Kai. — *rātriviśeṣe* K. est une mauvaise leçon, bien que connue de N. (rien dans la Padamañj.).

[24] Pour désigner un acte englobant hier et aujourd'hui (ou laissant le choix entre ces deux temps,) l'aoriste prévaut sur l'imparfait, *adya hyo 'bhukṣmahi* "nous avons mangé aujourd'hui (et) hier" (peu importe si Bh. III vt.1 tire cette disposition d'un artifice technique, à savoir du mot *ANADYATANE* compris comme composé possessif). De même, le futur non spécifié prévaut sur le futur périphr. quand il y a mixture entre l'aujourd'hui et le demain. La forme la plus générale l'emporte.

[25] S'il a dormi, fût-ce un instant, il est tenu d'user de l'imparfait (Bh.).

[26] C'est bien par rapport à l'aoriste que l'imparfait, appelé temps du non-aujourd'hui chez les Pāṇinéens, est dénommé *hyastanī* "temps de l'hier" chez Kt. et H.; c'est aussi parce que les exx. grammaticaux serrent au plus près les confins de la temporalité.

[27] P. *LOKAVIJÑĀTE*, H. 5.2,8 *khyāte*.

[28] CV. rajeunit l'exemple (que K. maintient par tradition tel qu'il l'a trouvé dans Bh. : souci d'autonomie, du moins en matière d'exemple, chez les Gramm. hétérodoxes) en *ajayaj japto* (lire : *gupto?*) *hūṇān*, cf. Liebich éd. Kṣīratar. p. 266 (JAs. 1932, 1, p. 152); H. loc. cit. *aruṇat siddharājo 'vantīn*. — Il demeure au moins ceci dans l'usage littéraire que l'imparfait fonctionne comme une sorte de doublure (plus rare) du parfait, tout en débordant largement sur l'*aparo'kṣa*.

aux faits lointains, on marque aussi que l'acte noté par l'imparfait n'est pas un acte indifférent; dans le choix, apparemment libre, voire arbitraire, que font les auteurs, en littérature, entre les diverses expressions du passé, l'imparfait convient aux événements de caractère "notoire", ceux auquels le sujet porte, a priori, quelque intérêt. Les contre-exemples précisent ce point: "le soleil s'est levé", *udagād ādityaḥ* (aoriste: fait d'expérience); "Devadatta a fait une natte", *cakāra kaṭaṃ devadattaḥ* (parfait: fait hors la vue, mais nullement notoire); "Vāsudeva a tué Kaṃsa *jaghāna kaṃsaṃ kila vāsudevaḥ* (parfait "mythologique": fait hors la vue, notoire, mais éloigné dans le temps; *kila* souligne la nuance "dit-on communément").[29]

Pāṇini traite à cet endroit (112-114) d'un procédé occasionnel pour rendre le sens du passé au moyen du futur grammatical; si cet enseignement succède à celui de l'imparfait, c'est qu'il concerne également le passé du non-aujourd'hui, et qu'au surplus il comporte l'imparfait à titre de variante, soit nécessaire (113), soit optionnelle (114). C'est le futur qu'on trouve dans une phrase du type *abhijānāsi devadatta kaśmīreṣu vatsyāmaḥ* "te souviens-tu (que) nous résidions (en ce temps-là) au Kaśmīr?". Peu importe en ce moment l'origine de cette phraséologie singulière, qui en littérature est quasiment inattestée: s'agit-il d'un futur au sens d'un éventuel du passé? Ou d'un tour direct (à quoi fait penser l'ellipse de *yad*) "te souviens-tu (de ce que nous disions alors, à savoir:) nous allons résider au K.?". En tout cas, la présence de *yad* suffit à rétablir la norme, c'est-à-dire l'imparfait (. . . *yat kaśmīreṣv avasāma*), tout comme elle rétablit l'optatif (forme attendue en contexte modal) dans 3.3,147-151 155 168.[30]

§10. Climax des emplois temporels, le parfait pāṇinéen est le temps du passé "hors la vue". Bh. se demande si c'est le "temps" qui est hors la vue, mais *kāle* n'étant pas rubrique-gouvernante (ci-dessus § 2), mieux vaut suppléer le *DHĀTOḤ* de 3.1,91 et entendre que c'est la "racine" donc le "verbe" qui est hors la vue. Objection: "racine" n'est qu'un mot, comment un mot serait-il sous la vue ou hors la vue? — *DHĀTOḤ* signifie: le sens noté par la

[29] Kt. 3.1,16 introduit ici la *vivakṣā*: l'imparfait est valable si l'on n'entend pas traiter l'événement comme étant hors la vue, tout en maintenant l'idée d'un temps historique. N. et ŚK. précisent qu'un contemporain de Kṛṣṇa pouvait seul dire à l'imparfait "il a tué Kaṃsa".

[30] Mais Sār. 2.34,5 cite *smarasi yad upakariṣyati* au sens de *upakuruthāḥ* [sic]. Avec ou sans *yad*, le futur (114) reprend ses droits (concurremment à l'imparfait) quand le verbe affecté requiert lui-même un autre verbe à sa suite (*SĀKĀṄKṢE*; Vop. 25.30 libelle tout autrement, *anekasmārye*); autrement dit (K.) s'il n'est qu'un signe (*lakṣaṇa*) annonçant une chose signifiée (*lakṣya*), notée par un verbe ultérieur (lequel sera donc éventuellement entraîné au futur). L'ex. de ŚK. est plus pertinent que celui de Bh. ou de K.: "te souviens-tu que nous résidions à Prayāga [simple "signe" de ce qu'on a à dire ensuite], que nous faisions l'ablution du mois de Māgha [chose réellement signifiée, chose qui *seule* devrait déclencher le souvenir]?" *abhijānāsi devadatta prayāge vatsyāmaḥ (/avasāma), tatra māghaṃ snāsyāmaḥ (/asnāma)*. En fait, précise Bh., la notion de "chose requise" vaut des deux côtés: le second verbe requiert le premier, comme le premier requiert le second. La position d'*ĀKĀṄKṢĀ* est rare chez P.; on la retrouve à propos d'une phrase (ou d'un verbe) complémentaire (par la présence duquel ou de laquelle la règle a son plein effet) 3.4,23 8.1,35; 2,96 et 104. — Sur les attestations littéraires (rarissimes) du futur de "souvenir", v. ma Gramm. scte p. 462 JAs. 1959 p. 73.

racine.... Quel est ce sens ? — C'est l' "action" (*kriyā*) : c'est donc l'action qui sera hors de vue. — Ne risque-t-on pas alors d'avoir le parfait dans "il a cuit (un mets) hier" (où l'on attend l'imparfait selon 111, *hyo 'pacat*), car il s'agit là d'une action non point vue, mais inférée, qu'on ne peut montrer à l'instar d'un objet mis en boule[31] ? Bh. adopte la thèse finale selon laquelle ce qui est hors la vue, ce n'est pas l'action elle-même, mais les instruments (*sādhana*) permettant de l'effectuer[32] ; un *sādhana*, en tant que totalité des "qualités", mais distinct d'elles, peut être atteint par voie d'inférence ; il est capable d'exprimer un état sous la vue ou hors la vue.

Suit une discussion sur la question de savoir si *PARO'KṢE* "hors la vue" vise qqch. qui a eu lieu il y a cent ou mille ans, qqch. qui est séparé (du sujet parlant) par un mur ou une natte, enfin (retour au *paro'kṣa* temporel, entendu sous forme atténuée) qqch. qui a eu lieu il y a deux ou trois jours (seulement). Bh., comme si souvent, ne décide pas : ce qui importe, conclut Kai., est qu'il s'agisse d'un acte du passé non-d'aujourd'hui, réalisé par des instruments sis hors de la portée des sens.[33]

§11. Corollaire empirique : la première personne se trouve exclue, sauf, ajoute Bh., au cas où le sujet parle de quelque événement qui lui est arrivé pendant qu'il dormait ou quand il était en état d'ébriété : *supto 'haṃ* (ou : *matto 'haṃ*) *kila vilalāpa* "il paraît que j'ai parlé, étant endormi ou ivre". Il se peut d'ailleurs que, même éveillé (et non ivre), on ne perçoive pas le temps : ainsi le grammairien Śākaṭāyana, assis sur le chemin, ne vit pas la caravane passer [distraction des grammairiens !]. Les objets des sens sont intrumentaux pour la perception quand ils sont attelés par la conscience ; s'il n'y a pas conscience, il y a un état de fait "hors la vue".

Autre cas, plus inattendu, où le parfait est licite, bien qu'a la première personne (vt.1) : le cas d'une dénégation absolue (*atyantāpahnava*), exemple "il n'est pas vrai que je sois allé au Kaliṅga" *no* (. . .) *kaliṅgāñ jagāma* (entendez : je n'ai pu commettre le crime qu'on m'impute au K°, n'ayant jamais mis les pieds en ce pays).[34]

[31] *piṇḍībhūta* : même "mise en boule" on ne peut voir cette action car, étant donné le caractère instantané de ses éléments constitutifs, il n'y a pas là de "mise en boule" (véritable) (Ng.).

[32] Kai. glose "les éléments pourvus d'un pouvoir expressif", mais Bh. *guṇasamudāya* ensemble des qualités. C'est le *sādhana*, ajoute K., qui cause le fait que les gens croient en le caractère sous-la-vue (*pratyakṣa*) d'une action, alors que, prise en soi, toute action est *paro'kṣa*. De même H. 5.2, 12 : toute idée verbale est *paro'kṣa*, les *sādhana* seuls sont susceptibles d'être sous-la-vue. Analogue J 2.2,95. Une autre objection est donnée Bh. : quel temps employer lorsqu'on a vu sur le chemin l'eau de riz (ayant servi à la cuisson)? On ne sait d'abord, précise Kai., si ce riz a été cuit ou offert-en-sacrifice ou battu, mais après on réalise qu'il s'agissait d'une cuisson et l'on dit "il a cuit (du riz)". Les instruments de l'action étant demeurés hors la vue du sujet, on devra dire *papāca*; de même encore, si sont hors la vue les particularités nées de l'action, tels les grondements et sifflements (du chaudron). — En dernier sur le parfait dans les textes littéraires (kāvya), JAs. 1959 p. 70.

[33] Ces derniers mots sont complétés par Kai.

[34] Précision fournie par H. 5.2,11 (c.); il s'agit du meurtre d'un brâhmane (acte explicable au pays Kaliṅga); une dénégation partielle comme "je n'ai pas tué. . ." auriat entraîné l'imparfait. — Noter que dans l'ātmastuti Ṛgv. 10.48 (–49), la première personne du parfait est à peu près exclue, mais on la trouve dans les emplois dénégatifs *ná párā jigye*, *na. . . áva tasthe* "il n'est pas vrai que j'aie. . ." : cas d'*atyantāpahnava*. Cf. Valeur du parfait p. 83 85 87.

C'est la négation d'un fait situé sous la vue (*pratyakṣa*), comme dit Kt. 3.1,16.

Il n'existe guère de catégorie fermée, du moins dans le domaine de la fonction. On ne peut donc s'étonner si Pāṇini ouvre la voie à l'expression du hors la vue par l'imparfait, non seulement dans le cas dont nous avons traité § 9, mais encore au sū. 116, où il autorise l'imparfait, concurremment au parfait, lorsqu'il y a pour terme "adjacent" (*upapada*) la particule *ha* ou *śaśvat*, ex. *iti ha cakāra* (ou : *iti hākarot*), *śaśvac cakāra* (ou : *śaśvad akarot*) "il a fait (ainsi dans un passé du non-aujourd'hui, sis hors la vue)".[35] La même disposition s'étend ensuite (117) à la phrase interrogative, en tant qu'elle se réfère à un passé proche[36] (encore que situé hors la vue) : on peut donc dire *iyāja* (ou : *ayajad*) *devadattaḥ* "Devadatta a-t-il sacrifié (à date récente) ?" (les conditions étant les mêmes que pour le sū. 116). Nous en conclurons que le parfait était mieux adapté à exprimer un temps lointain, mais que, en phrase interrogative (ce qui revient à dire : en discours direct), l'usage était indécis.[37] Nous voyons bien, dans la linguistique contemporaine, l'intérêt qu'il y a à distinguer, quant à l'expression temporelle, entre la narration (ou la description) et le discours.[38]

§12. Fidèle au principe de partir des fonctions, Pāṇini poursuit la notation du prétérit en traitant de l'indicatif présent avec *sma*. Cet emploi concorde avec celui du parfait (118),[39] ou bien traduit un *aparokṣatva* (*APARO'KṢE* 119), autrement dit coïncide avec l'imparfait. Double validité qui reflète assez bien l'usage classique, où nous voyons le présent avec *sma* doubler le prétérit de narration, sans comporter de référence à l'actuel ou de participation au discours.[40]

Mais le présent (sans *sma*) figure lui-même pour noter un passé non spécifié (c'est-à-dire un passé de type aoristique), lorsqu'il

[35] Il s'agit du *śáśvat* des Br., signifiant "peut-être" ou "certes", non du *śáśvat* des mantra "toujours" (que connaît seul Amara); cf. Minard Trois énigmes 1 § 589*b* sur cette évolution de sens inattendue, à quoi l'on peut comparer *dvitā* passant de "de deux manières" à "assurément", ou fr. *toujours* au sens de "encore" ou "du moins". H. 13 enseigne l'imparfait seul (avec *ha* et *śaśvat*) dans le domaine répondant à P. 112.

[36] Passé proche (*alpakāle 'pi* Sār. 2.34,3) signifie : moins de cinq ans (N., se référant aux Naiyāyika); *yugāntar* H. 13.

[37] H. 14 met au crédit de la *vivakṣā* (ci-dessus n. 22) l'usage de formes variées en une même phrase, comme *anvanaiṣīt / nyakṣipat / proce*, pour un passé hors la vue. Ceci se rencontre en effet abondamment en littérature, surtout peut-être dans le kāvya jaina (que H. a en vue); le même auteur cite encore *abhaiṣīt / ayuyutsayat / yuyutsayāṃcakre*. ŚK. ad 115 rappelle que les poètes peuvent user de l'aoriste si, même dans le domaine du *LIṬ*, ils entendent n'exprimer qu'une tranche de passé indifférenciée. Durgh. cite ici un aoriste en valeur de parfait.

[38] Nous avons noté à propos du kāvya l'intérêt qu'offre la distinction entre narration (impersonnelle) et discours, JAs. 1959 p. 2 et *passim*. Cf. pour le français même (dans la répartition des temps du passé), l'exposé magistral de Benveniste BSL. 54 (1959) p. 74.

[39] Kai. justifie la reconduction de *PARO'KṢE* dans 118 : si elle n'avait pas lieu, *ANADYATANE* (qui lui est associé) cesserait de valoir; d'autre part, il fallait une règle indépendante *APARO'KṢE CA* 119 afin de révéler la validité de l'*anadyatana*. — Noter que *sma* sert aussi à entraver l'optatif attendu, au profit de l'impératif, selon 3.3,165–166.

[40] Sur le présent avec *sma*, en dernier JAs. 1959 p. 71 ; mentionné Gaṇaratnam. p. 15.

s'agit de répondre, soit avec *nanu* "certes" (120: *akārṣīḥ kaṭaṃ devadatta/nanu karomi bhoḥ* "as-tu fait la natte? Oui, je l'ai faite"), soit avec *na* seul "non" ou *nu* seul "certes" (121)[41] (*na karomi bhoḥ* ou *ahaṃ nu karomi*, concurremment à *nākārṣam, ahaṃ nv akārṣaṃ* "non, je ne l'ai pas faite", "oui, je l'ai faite"), à une interrogation qui a été posée à l'aoriste. C'est là un nouveau témoignage (cf. § 11) du souci que prend P. à relever les emplois propres au discours, un témoignage aussi de la tendance qu'ont certaines particules à modifier la forme du verbe qu'elles accompagnent: c'est ce qui se produisait tout à l'heure avec *sma*. On notera ici que les particules plus neutres (*na* ou *nu*) admettent l'option, la plus appuyée (*nanu*) commande un choix strict.

C'est enfin le présent (122) qui rend le sens du passé non-d'aujourd'hui (donc, en filiation directe avec le sū. 119) lorsque la particule adjacente est *purā*,[42] ex. *vasantīha purā chātrāḥ* "les écoliers résidaient ici (antérieurement à aujourd hui)". La restriction par rapport à 118 est que, si la phrase comporte à la fois *sma* et *purā*, 118 s'applique par préférence à 122; que, d'autre part, l'aoriste est admis à titre optionnel dans le champ du sū. 122 (*avātsuḥ*...).[43]

[41] Il s'agit du *nú* Böhtl.-Roth sous 1) g), issu du *nú* ou *nū́* des mantra; c'est le *nu prativacane* de Gaṇaratnam. p. 8–9. — H. 17 et 18 connaît *nanu kurvantam, nu k°, na k°* à côté de *nanu karomi, nu k°, na k°* (par application de P. 3.2,124); emploi fictif. J. 2.2,100 considère ces deux sū. comme inutiles, l'emploi du présent s'expliquant par le (désir de noter) le non-achèvement.

[42] Emploi connu de Gaṇaratnam. p. 16. — H. 5.3,7: si l'on a à la fois *purā* (ou: *yāvat*) et *śvaḥ*, on a le présent. En fait, cet auteur (5.2,15) semble d'abord ignorer le présent, instaurant avec *purā* (et *tadā*! Cf. "*purādau*" dans la teneur de sū.) les temps du passé; toutefois le présent cumule avec ces temps selon 16, le présent vaut seul avec *sma purā* comme avec *ha sma, ha śaśvat, ha sma purā* (ce dernier conglomérat étant attesté dans la prose véd., cf. un ex. de la Taitt. Saṃh. cité dans Bh. 122, où figure *ha sma purā́ śáśvat* avec verbe au présent). Enfin on peut se poser la question de savoir si ces temps passés "de remplacement" sont identiques aux temps de base, ainsi H. 15 rappelle que certains auteurs rejettent l'aoriste avec *purā* si le sens est celui d'un passé hors la vue. Ces temps valent chacun en son domaine propre, enseigne K., qui admet l'imparfait, que CV. 1.2,81 donne aussi, mais simplement en fonction de la vivakṣā. Bh. ne cite d'exemples (pour le prétérit) qu'avec l'aoriste.

[43] Dans la prose véd., *purā́* s'utilise en effet avec le présent pour noter des événements typiques du passé (mais engageant l'actuel) selon Delbrück Ai. Syntax p. 278 Idg. Syntax 2. p. 266. Plus fréquent est *sma purā́* (ou plus exactement *ha sma purā́*) qui, avec un présent, note un passé indifférencié (Ai. Syntax p. 502 Idg. Syntax *loc. cit.*; ci-dessus, n. 42). Comme on l'a montré depuis longtemps, l'habitude d'avoir un présent avec *sma* au sens du passé découle de l'emploi plus ancien avec *sma purā́*.

On peut se demander si la reconduction d'*ANADYATANE* 122 — qui n'est acquise que par l'artifice du Saut de Grenouille — est vraisemblable, car elle aboutit à créer un aoriste du non-aujourd'hui, càd. opposé aux valeurs habituelles de l'aoriste. En outre, les exx. de *sma purā* donnés par K. 118 sont mal venus; on attendrait des exx. avec *sma* seul, comme en ont CV., Bhāṣāv., SK. et autres. Toutes ces dispositions reflètent les éléments de discussion de Bh. 118 vt. 1, qui proposait d'abord d'entendre le présent avec *sma purā* au sens d'un passé pur (non au sens d'un passé d'aujourd'hui), vt. qui sera rejeté ensuite (vt. 2), la reconduction étant déclarée valide aussi bien avec *purā* qu'avec *sma*.

Pareil flottement doit correspondre à un certain usage : la langue hésitait, en présence de *purā*, entre deux tendances : maintenir le temps requis par le contexte, ou imiter l'emploi avec *sma*, c'est-à-dire généraliser le présent, considérant que la particule suffit à évoquer la nuance temporelle exacte.

§13. C'est alors seulement (123) qu'est introduite la théorie du présent (indicatif) ès-qualités : l'acte qu'il note se place "en ce moment même" (*saṃprati* Kt. 3.1, 11 ; *sati* "dans l'étant" H. 5.2, 19), d'où l'appellation *vartamānā* donnée au temps présent (Kt.), ou encore *bhavantī* (qui est un nom des anciens Maîtres, d'après Kai.).

Deux propositions additionnelles dans Bh. :

a. L'indicatif présent note également un acte qui, ayant été entrepris (dans le passé), n'a pas cessé encore (au moment où l'on parle), *ihādhīmahe* "nous sommes en train d'étudier" : c'est, dit Śk., la valeur "suggérée" (*dyotya*) du présent. Bh. observe que cette addition est inutile, car cet acte inachevé au moment où l'on parle n'est autre qu'un acte "présent". D'ailleurs la cessation a lieu de toutes manières, car lorsqu'on dit "Devadatta est en train de manger", il advient nécessairement qu'il rie ou cause ou boive en mangeant.[44] On peut donc gloser *VARTAMĀNE* par "entrepris et non encore achevé" (comme fait K. d'emblée), sans avoir à postuler aucune valeur additionnelle ;

b. L'indicatif présent sert à noter aussi un acte permanent, ainsi "les montagnes se tiennent (immobiles)" *tiṣṭhanti parvatāḥ*, proposition qui ne comporte aucun fractionnement temporel (et suppose donc un additif au moins mental à l'énoncé de P.). Réponse : on peut concevoir des fractionnements temporels dans cette locution, ainsi "les montagnes se tiendront, se sont tenues".—Mais est-ce en usage ?—Ce n'est pas affaire d'usage. Sur terre, les actions des rois passés, futurs et présents sont le lieu (*adhikaraṇa*) où se situe "se tenir" ; on dit "les montagnes se tiennent" quand ont lieu les actions des rois de maintenant ; ". . . se tiendront" quand auront lieu les actions des rois à venir, etc.—Cette discussion aboutit, si nous comprenons bien, à dégager l'idée d'un temps relatif, idée très souhaitable en matière syntaxique et à quoi P. lui-même avait songé en posant son *DHĀTUSAṂBANDHE* (ci-dessous, n. 21). Quant à la situation du présent grammatical, elle se trouve élargie par l'admission d'un temps "général", admission d'autant

[44] Dans "nous sommes en train d'étudier," le fait d'étudier n'est pas interrompu par l'acte (éventuel) de manger, ou plutôt ce dernier est traité comme partie intégrante de l'étude (Kai.). K. résume grossièrement ce développement en glosant *VARTAMĀNE* par *ārabdho 'parisamāptaś ca*, ce qui semble exclure toute autre nuance de présent. Plus précis est SK. 2151 (c.) qui tient compte du présent "permanent." H. 19 considère à part le cas d'une phrase négative, *jīvaṃ na mārayati* "(on) ne fait pas périr un être vivant," où c'est l'ordre formulé négativement (le *niyama*) qui est "en cours et non achevé." Mais, dans "les montagnes se tiennent (debout)" (b), H. ne voit qu'une application du mêmes présent de la chose "en cours" ; si l'on dit *tasthuḥ, sthāsyanti* en cette formule, c'est qu' "on se réfère aux actions qui ont pris place ou prendront place en présence des montagnes." Déjà CV. 1.2,82, citant *tiṣṭhanti girayaḥ*, s'appuyait sur le présent "en cours" ; de là vient, sans doute, le silence de K. Selon J. 2.2,101 le temps présent est celui qui va depuis le commencement (d'un acte) jusqu'à sa non-cessation, c'est un temps intermédiaire, *tanmadhyaṃ kālam*.

plus utile que ni l'"actuel" de P., ni le "non-achevé" de Bh. n'y préparaient.

Mais Bh. soulève une objection contre la notion même de "présent": on ne saurait dire valablement "les fleuves coulent vers la mer", *syandante saritaḥ sāgarāya*, car l'actuel—non plus que le passé ou l'avenir—ne comporte pas de mouvement. Autrement dit, ajoute Kai., l'instant seul est perçu, en l'occurrence l'instant actuel, qui ne saurait recouvrir l'acte de "se mouvoir". Réponse de Bh.: cet acte a lieu en vue d'un certain but, qui est la cause même de l'effectuation de l'acte; c'est en considérant un tel but qu'on pourra employer l'expression "il marche".[45]

§14. Reste à voir l'expression grammaticale du fait à venir. Elle est dévolue par privilège au temps grammatical appelé *bhaviṣyantī* (nom des anciens Maîtres selon Kai.) chez les non-Pāṇinéens, mais simplement *LṚṬ*, comme nous avons vu, chez P. La valeur en est décrite au début du troisième *pāda*, c'est-à-dire à propos des suffixes (primaires) désignant une chose à venir (3). Mais P., selon un procédé qui lui est assez familier, traite d'abord du présent employé au sens du futur (4).[46] De même, en effet, que certaines particules inclinent l'indicatif présent — formation éminemment instable — vers le sens du prétérit, quelques autres, nommément *yāvat* et *purā*,[47] l'orientent à noter une chose à venir, ainsi *yāvad*

[45] Kai.: si l'on considère l'enchaînement des actes consistant en le cumel des instants (notion d'instantanéité, de provenance sans doute bouddhique). — ŚK. utilise l'exemple *pacati* "il cuit": la racine *pac-* vise un faisceau d'actes, commençant avec l'idée de "mettre au feu" et circonscrits par le but unique qu'on veut atteindre. BM. note que la notion de présent ne fait que qualifier le sens du verbe, non pas l'agent ou autres instruments qui, eux, peuvent appartenir au passé. ŚK. se demande aussi — dans l'hypothèse où le présent consiste en un acte "en cours" — pourquoi on dit "l'*ātman* est, était, sera"? Réponse: dans cette essence unique qu'est l'*ātman*, une différenciation se manifeste, qui dépend des conditions particulières et repose sur telle ou telle activité.

Bh. voit encore une autre manière d'échapper à l'objection précédente: il existe certes un présent, mais on ne le perçoit pas plus qu'on ne perçoit la marche du soleil; aussi peu qu'on voit se modifier chacune des fibres de lotus en train de brûler en masse, aussi mal voit-on se modifier l'entrée-en-acte en appréhendant un à un les instants dans l'afflux des *kāraka* ou éléments qui participent à l'achèvement d'une action verbale. Seuls les Tribhāva (Kai.: Yogin's pour qui existe une réalisation dans les trois temps) perçoivent une telle modification. — Kai. précise encore: de l'idée verbale ayant forme d'acte, idée comportant plusieurs instants, on infère qu'il existe une valeur de présent, parce que ces instants ne se manifestent pas tous ensemble. Et Ng.: en saisissant chaque instant, on est hors d'état de percevoir l'entrée en-acte qui se modifie par la différenciation des instants. Mais, si ténu que soit chaque instant, leur total n'est-il pas perceptible aux sens? Réponse: l'acte est accessible aux sens, soit comme partie, soit comme totalité; en l'occurrence, le temps présent s'accrédite si l'on impute dans l'idée verbale une totalité, l'acte en question comportant une pluralité d'instants perceptibles par inférence. — Durgh. 115 connaît un présent d'"imputation-secondaire," qui, en fait, est fonction d'un verbe voisin.

[46] Éventuellement, du futur périphr. (vt.).

[47] Ces mots *yāvat* et *purā* posent un petit problème, que les commentaires grammaticaux n'aident guère à résoudre. Il s'agit de particules, précise P. (*NIPĀTA*), donc probablement de *purā* au sens de "avant peu," *yāvat* au sens de "cependant" (ou simplement, l'un et l'autre au sens de "assurément"). Les attestations litté-

bhuṅkte ou *purā bhuṅkte* au sens de *bhokṣyate* "il mangera". Même orientation, mais optionelle seulement,[48] après les adverbes interrogatifs *kadā* et *karhi* (5), après le pronom *ka* et ses appartenances (*KIṂVṚTTE*, 6), ex. *kadā bhuṅkte* ou *kadā bhokṣyate* "quand mangera-t-il?". C'est l'exact pendant du temps présent employé au sens du passé (§ 12); c'est aussi une évidence nouvelle du rôle atténuateur des particules, permettant l'usage du temps le moins marqué, alors même qu'existe une nuance désidérative implicite (*LIPSĀYĀM* 6, ex. *kataro bhikṣāṃ dadāti* "lequel de vous deux donnera l'aumône?", aumône que le sujet interrogeant "a désir d'obtenir"). La participation effective est évoquée encore au sū. 7, lequel admet (hors de la phrase interrogative) l'emploi du temps présent pour noter un fait á venir qu'on inscrit comme actuel afin d'encourager (*protsāhayati* K.) celui dont on décrit l'acte ("celui qui donnera la nourriture, il ira au ciel", *yo 'annaṃ dadāti sa svargaṃ gacchati*, *LIPSYAMĀNASIDDHAU*, quand on réussit à atteindre ce justement qu'on désire atteindre).[49] L'un et l'autre verbes sont mis au présent (à titre, il est vrai, optionnel), tout comme, dans l'Atharvaveda magique, nous voyons l'aoriste employé pour noter des événements à venir dont la réalisation est censée d'ores et déjà acquise.

§15. Ainsi accède-t-on aux valeurs modales du présent grammatical quand il s'agit de noter un fait à venir: elles sont posées concurremment au futur grammatical. En premier lieu (8), on a affaire à une action (à venir) qui est le signe (*LAKṢAṆE*)[50] d'une

raires sont rares (JAs. 1959 p. 79 sur *purā*). BM. renvoie à Amara où *yāvat* a plusieurs sens; de même Gaṇaratn. p. 11. Pour SK. 2783, qui sans doute a vu juste, ces particules suggèrent la certitude (*niścaya*). Mais CV. 1.3,3 (et d'autres) voi(en)t dans ce *purā* la conjonction "avant que..." (celle de P. 8.1,42) et de fait N. ad 8.1,42 évoque 3.3,4: ex. *purā vidyotate vidyut* "avant qu'il ne fasse un éclair," conjonction bien connue (Böhtl.-Roth I) c)) avec présent au sens futur. En ce cas, *yāvat* pourrait être aussi la conjonction subordonnante qu'enseigne P. 8.1,36 "jusqu'à ce que..." (mais CV. ad. loc.: *yāvad bhuṅkte tato vrajati* "il mange d'abord, puis s'en va"); Sār 2.34,4 *purā karoti* et *yāvat k°* = *kariṣyati*. Il faut se tenir au *NIPĀTA* de P.

[48] Ceci dépend de la *vivakṣā* (ci-dessus, n. 22) N., principe que CV. 1.3,3 étend à tout un groupe de règles relatives au futur. — C'est en prenant ce sū. pour exemple que Kt. 3.1,17 énonce *prayogataḥ* dans le sū. même: le c. constate que si, au lieu de dire *yāvad bhuṅkte*, on voulait employer le futur, il suffirait de ne pas poser *yāvat*. C'est reconnaître la sollicitation qu'exercent les particules. Plus généralement, c'est "l'usage" qui doit enseigner la spécification du temps; mais on aboutit alors à une notion qui, en Grammaire, est tout aussi destructive de règles que peut l'être celle de *vivakṣā* ou de *saṃskāra* (n.22).

[49] Traduit selon la lettre, mais K. distingue l'homme [le donateur] qui réussira à gagner (le ciel) et l'homme [le donataire] qui souhaite obtenir (la nourriture). SK. 2786 développe K.: le sujet parlant encourage le donateur en exprimant l'espoir que, à partir du riz — objet désiré — le succès écherra au donateur, sous la forme du *svarga*. Noter que rien n'indique dans le sū. même la présence d'une phrase incluant une proposition relative.

[50] Nous avons déjà rencontré le "signe" à propos d'actions corrélatives (ci-dessus, n. 30). *Lakṣaṇa* chez P. désigne un signe matériel, servant à reconnaître qqch., indice (ainsi 2.3,21) ou but (ainsi 2.1,14) ou, plus abstraitement, cause (1.1,62; 2,65). Le terme sert indirectement à décrire le Loc. absolu (2.3,37, "ce par l'être de quoi il y a signe d'un [autre] être"). Mais il a aussi une acception purement lexicale = "au sens de," ainsi 3.4,16.

autre action (connectée), notée par un impératif, ex. "si le maître vient, apprends la métrique" *upādhyāyaś ced āgacchati, atha tvaṃ chando 'dhīṣva*; autrement dit. la venue du maître est le "signe" (*nimitta* N., *hetu* H. 5.3,11) de l'exhortation à apprendre (*adhyayane praiṣata* N.). Nous constatons là la tendance des phrases hypothétiques à renoncer à l'expression précise que conseille leur intention propre, cela parce que la conjonction (*ced*) dispense en quelque sorte de noter le mode attendu (les autres types d'hypothétiques seront abordées plus loin, § 22). On remarquera que rien dans l'énoncé de P. n'imposait de croire que le sū. se limitait à ce type de phrases : c'est la glose des commentaires qui nous l'apprend.

Le sū. 9 est une variante mineure de 8, instituant qu'il y a choix libre entre présent et optatif pour noter un acte situé dans un avenir relativement proche,[51] ainsi *upādhyāyaś ced āgacchet* (ou : *āgacchati*, aussi d'ailleurs *āgamiṣyati* ou *āgantā*), *atha tvaṃ chando 'dhīṣva* "si le maître vient à arriver (dans un certain délai)...". Ici apparaît pour la première fois l'optatif, dont la description ne sera reprise que vers la fin du pāda en cours, d'abord dans des emplois "concurrents", ensuite seulement dans des emplois autonomes. Le sū. 9 correspond à ce qu'on a dit ci-dessus (§ 12), touchant le présent à valeur de prétérit proche.

Jusqu'ici donc nous avons des valeurs "à venir" notées par des temps autres que le futur grammatical. Ce dernier ne sera instruit qu'au sū. 13 : encore l'enseignement s'y combine-t-il avec celui d'une expression "intentionnelle". En effet, poursuivant la description entamée aux sū. 10-12, P. se préoccupe d'abord de montrer que le futur est parallèle à l'infinitif ou au datif final des noms d'action, ex. *naṭaṃ drakṣyāmīti vrajati* "il va voir la comédie", littéralement "il va (donnant pour motif à sa marche cet élément de discours :) j'ai l'intention de voir...".[52] Mais, au cours de la même règle, P. introduit le temps futur "pur et simple" (*śuddhe* K.) avec cette formulation soustractive à quoi il incline, *ŚEṢE CA*,[53] c'est-à-dire "les désinences du futur sont valables aussi, pour noter un fait à venir, dans les cas restants", soit "dans les cas non couverts par le *KRIYĀYĀṂ KRIYĀRTHĀYĀM* 10". Les exemples des com-

[51] *muhūrtād ūrdhvakālīne* BM. : il s'agit, sans doute, d'un délai supérieur de peu à un *muhūrta*.

[52] Autrement dit, "*iti*" n'est pas éprouvé par les Gramm. comme nous l'éprouverions, c'est-à-dire interrompant le sentiment d'une subordination; *drakṣyāmīti* est pour eux un équivalent pur et simple de *draṣṭum*. Ex. analogue K. 3.3,156, l'exemple normal (K. 14) étant *arjayiṣyamāṇo vasati* "il habite (là) dans l'intention d'acquérir (des biens)". On aurait tort, en effet, dans bien des cas, de voir dans *iti* autre chose qu'un outil grammatical, avec lequel le discours direct est pur formalisme.

[53] *ŚEṢE* se dit presque toujours des emplois "restants", ceux qui n'ont pas été couverts par la description antérieure: ainsi, la voix active 1.3,78, le *bahuvrīhi* 2.2,23, le Génitif 2.3,50, les suffixes *ārdhadhātuka* 3.4,114, etc.: ceci épargne une définition, qui risquerait d'être longue. Une acception différente du mot ne se présente qu'une fois, 7.4,60 "(qui subsiste) seul". Il n'empêche que la formulation de P. est un peu cryptique; SK. 2193 cherche à la clarifier en posant *asatyāṃ satyāṃ ca* (*kriyāyāṃ kriyārthāyām*) "qu'il y ait ou non action faite en vue d'une (autre) action"; mais un état pédagogiquement satisfaisant n'est atteint que chez un grammairien tel que H. qui énonce par un sū. distinctif *bhaviṣyantī* 5.3,4. L'avantage du libellé pāṇinéen est, comme nous le disions, d'impliquer ce qu'on pourrait appeler une vision historique des faits. — J. 2.3, donne deux sū. distincts, *lṛṭ* (11), puis *śeṣe* (12).

mentaires confirment bien qu'il s'agit du futur en son emploi le plus ordinaire, *kariṣyati* "il fera" (sans spécification de délai ni d'intention). Le Bh. s'interroge sur l'interprétation de ce *ŚEṢE* (*CA*): le vt. 1 propose d'y voir une allusion au sū. 10 (Kai.: le sū. 10 cessant de valoir dans 13): s'il n'y avait pas *ŚEṢE*, ajoute le vt. 2, le futur serait entravé par l'application de 3.1,94 (plus précisément, par l'infinitif BM.). Le point de vue décisif est le suivant: la portion *LṚṬ* du sū. veut dire que le futur vaut dans le champ de 10; la portion *ŚEṢE* — dont on pourrait aussi bien faire un sū. distinct — que le futur est valable "ailleurs" (*CA* étant superflu). Laissons de côté cette technique et retenons seulement que Pāṇini fait sortir en somme le temps futur de l'emploi "intentionnel", ce qui concorde avec les conditions historiques: le futur normal du sanskrit commun n'est qu'un futur "des cas restants", une sorte de privation du caractère intentionnel.

§16. Sitôt après est posé le futur périphrastique (15), défini comme un futur du non-aujourd'hui, *ANADYATANE*: c'est la réplique exacte de l'imparfait (§ 10). Et de même que l'imparfait trouvait son terrain privilégié dans l'événement "d'hier", ce futur a le sien dans l'événement "de demain" (*śvaḥ kartā* "il fera demain"), d'où son nom de *śvastanī* "le temps de demain", nom que connaissent déjà les vtt.[54]

A ce propos s'engagent deux vārttika destinés à élargir l'emploi du futur périphrastique:

a. Ce futur remplace le futur simple quand il s'agit d'une action causant un chagrin (*paridevane*): "quand donc marchera cette (femme malade), qui pose ainsi les pieds?" *iyaṃ nu kadā gantā yaivaṃ pādau nidadhāti*. On redoute une attente vaine; l'expressivité du contexte, la nuance implicite de "chagrin", permettent d'employer un temps qui n'eût convenu normalement que si l'acte s'inscrivait dans un avenir spécifié par des mots tels que "demain" ou "après-demain"[55];

b. L'autre vt. n'est qu'une interprétation différente (et contournée) de l'exemple précédent: du fait même du temps qui passe, l'idée surgit d'une comparaison, "elle est pareille à quelqu'un qui marche", d'où "elle ne marchera pas (vraiment)" *ganteveyaṃ gantā, neyaṃ gamiṣyati*. Sous la pression de l'usage, ajoute Kai., le futur périphrastique s'accrédite ainsi dans une valeur secondaire (soumise à la présence virtuelle d'une particule comparative).[56]

[54] Développant Bh., Ng. note que, selon certains, il est incorrect d'avoir le futur (simple) au sens du non-aujourd'hui, ceci n'étant valable qu'au participe (pourquoi ce privilège du participe? est-ce simplement parce qu'il n'y a pas de participe répondant au futur périphr.? Le décalage entre indicatif et participe est, en tout cas, un détail à retenir). Ex.: *śvo 'gnīn ādhāsyamānena* "par lui devant placer les feux demain". Bh., qui cite cet ex., obtient ce résultat en scindant le sū. 15 en *ANADYATANE* (a) et *LUṬ* (b): peu importe.

[55] N. montre qu'on est bien dans le champ d'action de la *śvastanī*, mais SKĀ. 2.4,13 dit *adyatanārtha ārambhaḥ*. L'emploi de *gantā* est indépendant du sens de la phrase, poursuit N., rappelant que la cause-efficiente dans la formation d'un mot est son sens propre, non le sens de la phrase où il est appelé à figurer (cf. n. 22 ci-dessus). Pour Ng. aussi, on est dans le domaine du non-aujourd'hui.

[56] Il n'y a point de comparaison possible avec un verbe personnel, dit Bh. — De ce vt. on peut retenir qu'il a été senti un lien entre "comme" et la négation: ceci rappelle l'emploi ṛgvéd. bien connu de *ná* particule tantôt négative, tantôt comparante; avec raison, sans doute, Vendryès BSL. 46, 1950 p. 10, enseignait l'identité foncière des deux emplois.

§17. Un dernier faisceau (le plus massif) de règles temporelles est celui qui commence au sū. (3.3,)131 : concernant essentiellement le futur, il s'agrège sans peine au groupe antérieur.[57]

Toutefois, le sū. initial (131) aborde, de façon plus large, la question du passé proche et de l'avenir proche, notions qui comportent à titre optionnel l'emploi du présent grammatical. C'est la tendance bien connue du présent à empiéter sur les zones limitrophes, sur le passé proche par continuation ou reconduction (*ayam āgacchāmi* "je viens d'arriver"), sur le futur proche par anticipation (*eṣa gacchāmi* "je vais (y) aller"). Pāṇini dit, non pas "(l'affixe en vigueur est optionnellement) le présent", mais "...est traité comme un présent".[58] Cette manière de s'exprimer sert, d'après Bh., à empêcher que les affixes ici prescrits ne s'attachent qu'à la racine pure et simple (il faut qu'ils puissent s'attacher aussi à un thème verbal); mais la motivation réelle du *-VAT* est de permettre d'intégrer dans la règle les substituts du présent, tels que le participe. C'est ce que K. résume en disant que *-VAT* marque la similitude absolue[59] : quelle que soit la qualification avec laquelle les affixes ont été prescrits en valeur de présent (entre 3.2,123 et 3.3,1), c'est-à-dire quelle que soit la base, quel le membre de composé accolé, quelles les conditions d'emploi — ce sont ces affixes mêmes et non d'autres qui sont ici valables. Il est permis de penser que les grammairiens avaient surtout en vue le *LAṬ* 123, même si quelques exemples supplémentaires sont donnés avec le participe (présent : *āgacchantam eva māṃ viddhi* "sache que je viens d'arriver") ou avec un dérivé primaire comme *alaṃkariṣṇu* "qui a récemment orné; qui va bientôt orner".[60]

§18. A partir du sū. 132, le futur grammatical est en jeu (Bh.), d'abord avec la nuance semi-modale d'"espoir" (*ĀŚAṂSĀYĀM*); le verbe notant l'acte espéré figure soit, comme il est normal, au futur (*upādhyāyaś ced āgamiṣyati/ ete vyākaraṇam adhyeṣyāmahe* "si le maître venait (dans un avenir espéré), nous apprendrions la grammaire" (cf. le contre-exemple *āgamiṣyati* K.); soit, par une sorte de subrogation, au présent ou à l'aoriste; le vt. 1 exclut nommément l'imparfait et le parfait, parce que l'énoncé en *-VAT* implique qu'on a affaire à un temps "général", non à un temps parti-

[57] La transition est l'exposé sur le suffixe *KHAL* (et ses dépendances) 126-130, suffixe qui est proche du verbe, en ce sens que, par ex., *īṣatkaro bhavatā* confine à (*īṣat*) *kriyate* ou *kariṣyate bhavatā*. Dans CV. 1.3,106, *khal* joint à *yuc*, est englobé sans discontinuité dans la description du futur: c'est pousser à l'extrême la disposition de P.

[58] On a donc affaire à l'un de ces sū. d'extension ou, pour mieux dire, de transfert (*atideśa*, Termin. s.u.), dont l'interprétation est souvent d'autant plus malaisée à retrouver que les cc. la chargent d'enseignements latents.

[59] Donnée reprise SKĀ. 2.4,187 H. 5.4,1 Prakr. Kaum. 3.2,131 SK. 2789, etc. — Noter, est-ce un hasard?, que les ex. sont empruntés au discours, non à la constatation impersonnelle.

[60] N. discute une fois de plus sur l'opposition qui peut se produire entre *pada*° et *vākya-saṃskāra* (ci-dessus, n. 22): il faut appliquer le temps requis par la phrase au moment même où l'on forme le mot, sinon l'on obtiendrait le groupement fautif *śvaḥ kariṣyati* au lieu de *śvaḥ kartā* (groupement que semble admettre pourtant K. elle-même, citée n. 22, et plus tard H.). — CV. 1.3,106 explique que ce qui est proche du présent n'est autre qu'un présent, car les fruits de l'acte y sont reconduits; le futur de même, parce qu'on met en œuvre (au moment où l'on parle) les moyens propres à atteindre ces fruits. Incidence grammaticale de la doctrine philosophique du *karman*!

cularisé.[61] Nous sommes donc en plein flottement temporel, ce qui n'a rien d'étonnant puisque ces phrases à nuance d' "espoir" sont, si l'on en juge par les exemples des commentaires, des hypothétiques, correspondant à celles des sū. 8 et 9 déjà vus.[62] On notera, une fois de plus, le soin que prend P. à éviter de donner directement la structure de la phrase hypothétique; en matière de syntaxe, ce qui lui importe est la nuance psychologique appelant telle ou telle structure.

Le sū. 133 est une annexe au précédent: le voisinage de l'adverbe *kṣipram* (ou d'un mot analogue) entraîne le retour exclusif du futur, autrement dit du temps normal.[63] Pareillement (134), l'optatif est seul possible si la nuance d' "espoir" est inscrite dans la phrase même par un mot précis (les commentaires citent les formes verbales *āśaṃse*, *avakalpaye*, *kāmaye*, non suivies de *yad*). De notre point de vue, c'est 132 qui est une exception à 133–134, du point de vue des grammairiens 133–134 sont des exceptions à 132.

Le vt. 2 (poursuivi par 3) connaît un emploi du temps "achevé" pour noter un acte qu'on admet par avance comme réalisé[64]; au lieu de dire "s'il pleut, le riz sera abondant" *devaś ced vṛṣṭaḥ saṃpatsyante śālayaḥ*, on dira ainsi "...est abondant" *saṃpannāḥ*. Le riz étant encore en épillet, on s'attend bel et bien qu'il soit battu (Bh. ad vt. 4). Là-dessus, Bh. (vt. 5) développe la thèse suivant laquelle toutes les désinences valent au sens du présent quand il s'agit d'un verbe d'existence: le sujet parlant sait à quoi s'en tenir

[61] Id SK. 2790; la Bhāṣāv. ajoute le futur périphr. et l'optatif et cite un ex. littéraire plutôt hardi, *mām upāyaṃsta* "(j'espère qu'elle) m'épousera". H. 5.4,2 donne: aoriste, verbal en *-ta-*, présent, les deux futurs.

[62] Quel sens donner à *ĀŚAṂSĀ* "espoir", par rapport à *SAṂBHĀVANA* (154) "supposition", se demande le vt. 3? Le vt. 4 établit qu'*āśaṃsā* fait partie intégrante de *saṃ*°, le premier terme étant susceptible ou non de réalisation, le second étant seulement réalisable (si tel est bien le sens de [*an*]*abhinīta*, mot que Kai. rend par "capable (ou incapable) d'être atteint par l'appropriation des causes"); l'*āśaṃsā* est *pradhāritā* "réifiée par la pensée qui se dit: puisse cela m'arriver!", le *saṃ*° est *apradhārita* (si telle est bien la leçon) = "indéterminé par nature". — Notable est l'emploi possible du verbal en *-ta-* comme substitut du futur, soit, dans le cadre syntaxique cité, *āgataḥ* et *adhītavantaḥ*. K.: cet emploi (comme, déjà, celui de l'aoriste) montre que, dans le domaine de la subordination, les formes verbales sont régies par l'intention générale de la phrase et perdent pour ainsi dire leur valeur propre: ainsi l'imparfait fr., au sens futur, en proposition hypothétique.

[63] H. 5.4,3 connaît le présent, l'aoriste, les deux futurs; il imagine un conflit avec P. 15 (coexistence de *śvaḥ* et *śīghram*), d'où résulte la prévalence du futur simple. Le vt. 1 note, quant à lui, le conflit éventuel entre 133 et 134: 134 l'emporte en vertu du principe "ce qui est énoncé après l'emporte (sur ce qui est énoncé avant)", l'une des *paribhāṣā* fondamentales de la Grammaire. Pour K. l'énoncé *LṚṬ* vise à indiquer que le futur simple couvre aussi le domaine du futur périphr.: tel est le risque qu'entraînent les enseignements implicites, d'abolir par endroits les règles les mieux établies.

[64] SKĀ. met même cette disposition en sū. (2.4,191): pour un acte non réalisé, on emploie les mêmes affixes que pour un acte réalisé, quand il y a *saṃbhāvanā* (glosé *śaktiśraddhāna* "croyance en une possibilité de réalisation"), avec l'ex. (que donne aussi H. 5.4,4) "s'il faisait effort en temps utile, le succès se produirait", *samaye cet prayatno 'bhūt, udabhūvan vibhūtayaḥ*.

quand il a vu une fois un puits; même s'il n'observe pas de dénivellation, il n'en réalise pas moins en pensée l'existence permanente de ce puits et il dit "*il y a* (ici) un puits".[65] — En fait, toute désinence est employée avec le temps qui convient, pourvu qu'elle ne soit pas enseignée à titre optionnel ou que l'usage inverse ne soit pas acquis (par une autre règle): personne ne dira "il fut un puits" *kūpo 'bhūt*, quand il faudrait dire "il y a un puits" *kūpo 'sti*.[66] L'activité des sens donne simplement un contact, c'est la conscience qui décide. Quelqu'un voulant aller à Pāṭaliputra dit "sur le chemin menant à P° il y aura un puits" *yo 'yam adhvā gantavya ā pāṭaliputrād etasmin kūpo bhaviṣyati* (futur simple); quand il aura marché et envisagera un temps (précis) du non-aujourd'hui, il dira "il y aura là un puits (demain)" *bhavitā* (futur périphr.); quand il aura atteint l'endroit, "il y a un puits" *asti* (présent); le point une fois dépassé, "il y avait un puits" *abhūt* (aoriste); la nuit une fois écoulée, "il y avait là un puits" *āsīt* (imparfait); la chose oubliée, "il y eut là un puits" *babhūva* (parfait). Les désinences sont ce qu'est l'activité des sens; c'est l'activité de la conscience qui décide qu'on a affaire à un présent.

§19. Une règle d'apparence déconcertante est 135, enseignant aoriste et futur (simple) aux lieu et place de l'imparfait et du futur périphr. quand il y a à rendre un procès continu (*KRIYĀPRABANDHA*) ou une proximité (dans le temps, *SĀMĪPYA*). Exemples: *a*) "il a donné (ou: donnera) de la nourriture sa vie durant" *yāvajjīvam annam adāt* (*dāsyati*; K. précise la nuance en ajoutant *bhṛśam*); *b*) *yeyaṃ paurṇamāsy atikrāntā* (ou: *yeyam āmāvāsyāgāminī*), *etasyām upādhyāyo 'gnīn ādhita* (ou: *ādhāsyate*) "lors de la pleine lune précédente (ou: de la nouvelle lune prochaine), le maître a disposé (ou: disposera) les feux". C'est donc une entorse faite à l'expression normale du non-aujourd'hui. Le *SĀMĪPYA* a cet intérêt pour nous de dégager un aoriste de constatation — c'est un peu ce que nous attendions, mais en vain, en lisant 3.2,111 sans le secours des commentaires.[67] D'autre part, le *PRABANDHA* étend heureusement le

[65] Ceci repris (en forme de sū.!) SKĀ. 192, d'où suit qu'on dira indifféremment *mārge kūpo 'bhūt, āsīt, babhūva*, etc.; de même H. 5.2,19 toutes désinences sont valables avec les verbes d'existence. C'est se limiter à la position première de Bh., sans tenir compte du siddhānta.

[66] Cf. Bh. ad 1.4,80 vt. 4 "nul ne dit *pacati pra*, quand il faudrait dire *pra pacati*", d'où suit que la Grammaire n'est pas faite pour interdire ce qui par nature est étranger à l'usage, *prayuktānām eva lakṣaṇenānvākhyānāt* "car seules les choses en usage sont à expliquer par voie de règle" Kai. ad 1.1,24 fin. Sage précepte, que les commentateurs ne semblent pas avoir toujours fidèlement suivi!

[67] Il est vrai qu'un aoriste de continuité semble contradictoire avec l'idée que nous nous faisons de ce temps: il faut y voir un aspect de l'aoriste notant un passé fait d'instants répétés, allant jusqu'à l'actuel. — La règle, une fois de plus, est soumise à la *vivakṣā* CV. 1.3,106. Quant aux deux négations qu'elle contient (*NA* et *AN*°), Bh. observe que l'enseignement inverse se trouve par là même impliqué, à savoir que, en cas de futur ou de passé d'aujourd'hui, on devra employer les temps prescrits; ainsi, il n'est pas à redouter qu'on ait le *LṚṬ* dans le domaine du *LUṄ*, le *LUṄ* dans celui du *LṚṬ*. N. dit: si P. avait dit que, dans les circonstances énoncées, le traitement serait conforme à celui d'un passé ou d'un futur d'aujourd'hui, le présent sū. serait prescriptif et il y aurait confusion des temps; mais, en fait, le sū. est prohibitif simplement: il prohibe les temps du non-aujourd'hui et eux seuls; ce point acquis, les temps normaux valent chacun en son domaine. Selon certains, dit encore H. 5.4,5, ce sū.

domaine du futur simple, dont nous savons assez par l'usage littéraire qu'il est parfaitement compatible avec une datation rapprochée ou avec l'idée d'une continuité.

Le sū. suivant (136) donne un autre cas où le futur (simple) remplace le futur périphr. attendu par 15 : c'est, à savoir, si'l y a mention d'une limite en deçà de laquelle se situe l'acte, ex. "nous mangerons deux fois du riz en deçà de Kauśāmbī sur la route menant à Pāṭaliputra" *yo 'yam adhvā gantavya ā pāṭaliputrāt tasya yad avaraṃ kauśāmbyās tatra dvir odanaṃ bhokṣyāmahe* (et non : *bhoktāsmahe*). Cet empiètement peut surprendre : il s'explique justement parce que la précision temporelle est suffisamment marquée dans la phrase. Au sū. 136 s'annexe naturellement 137, qui contredit l'enseignement précédent quand la limite est de caractère temporel (non plus spatial) *yo 'yaṃ saṃvatsara āgāmī tatra yad avaram āgrahāyaṇyās tatra yuktā adhyeṣyāmahe* "nous étudierons ensemble dans l'année qui vient (jusqu'à la période qui est) en deçà de l'Āgrahāyaṇī". 138 laisse le choix entre l'un et l'autre futurs quand ladite limite (de temps) est celle au-delà de laquelle l'action se situe (*tasya yat param āgra°*). Le vt. 1 ad 136 précise que ledit sū. (évidemment aussi 137 et 138) ne comporte pas la validité récurrente de *KRIYĀ°* 135.

§20. Intervient à ce point le conditionnel (139). Le conditionnel est traité comme un temps du futur et appelé à cet endroit de la Grammaire par l'allusion aux phrases hypothétiques que contiennent les sū. 132 à 134. Il se définit par le fait que le sujet passe outre à l'action (*KRIYĀTIPATTAU*)[68] : c'est là une manière indirecte, plus appropriée peut-être à rendre l'intention psychologique, de noter ce que nous désignons par "irréel". Le Bh. propose d'énoncer "outrepassement (non de l'acte, mais) des instruments de l'acte", puis il rejette cette modification, car tout outrepassement des moyens propres à réaliser un acte contient nécessairement l'outrepassement de l'acte lui-même. On notera, une fois de plus, que Pāṇini ne définit pas en termes grammaticaux la phrase irréelle ; il renvoie seulement par avance (*LIṄNIMITTE*) à la mention *HETUHETUMATOḤ* 156, laquelle ne définit pas davantage une structure, mais invite à reconnaître l'existence d'une relation de cause à effet. A nous d'insérer cette mention dans un cadre syntaxique ; comme dit K., l'outrepassement se laisse comprendre par la phrase (non par les termes mêmes d'un sū.).[69] Dans l'exemple "s'il appelait (à l'aide) Kamalaka, son chariot ne se renverserait pas" *yadi kamalakam āhvāsyan na śakaṭaṃ paryābhaviṣyat*, l'appel fait à K° (ou plutôt : l'appel que le sujet outrepasse l'occasion de faire à K°) est la cause (*hetu*), le non-renversement du chariot est l'effet (*hetumant*). Le

interdit le parfait et autres temps, même s'ils sont prescrits par une autre règle, en tant qu'indiquant spécialement le non-aujourd'hui.

[68] Glosé *anabhinirvṛtti* K. ; H. 5.4,9 du fait de l'autorité que revêtent les notions de cause et d'effet, le sujet parlant, ayant compris qu'il doit se produire une non-réalisation de l'acte, dit "s'il appelait . . .". — Noter que le conditionnel chez. P. est défini au moyen d'un nom d'action, alors que les autres valeurs temporelles sont définies par des participes ou des noms verbaux ; c'est bien ce qui montre l'attache du conditionnel aux modes, car les modes eux aussi sont définis par des noms d'action indiquant des catégories psychologiques.

[69] Toutefois, K. dit *ity evamādikam*, ce qui peut viser 157 ; pour 140, elle allègue à la suite du vt. 1 l'optatif 152 "et suivant(s)". — Durgh. 139 met l'emploi de *syāt* au compte de la *vivakṣā* (ci-dessus, n. 22).

sujet, dit N. (précisant K.), ayant vu par des appels antérieurs répétés faits à K° que le char ne se renversait pas, ayant reconnu qu'un appel futur à K° serait également la cause du non-renversement (ayant donc vu là, comme dit K., un rapport entre signe et chose signifiée), comprend par quelque évidence extérieure (comme le fait que K° va dans un autre pays, etc.) qu'il y a "outrepassement" de l'appel, et prononce la phrase en question; K. considère que si le cocher s'abstient ainsi d'appeler, c'est "par suite de quelque défectuosité mentale" (*vaiguṇya*).

Le sū. 140[70] transporte au passé le cadre précédemment acquis, donc "s'il avait appelé K°, le chariot ne se fût pas renversé". Ceci n'est pas une modification accessoire du sū. 139, c'est bien plutôt la reconnaissance du caractère éminent du conditionnel: on sait assez, par l'usage littéraire, que ce mode est pratiquement réservé à l'expression d'un irréel du passé.

Ainsi défini, le conditionnel (selon 140) est censé valoir, entre 143 et 152, en concurrence aux temps directement enseignés auxdits sū., c'est-à-dire surtout à l'optatif, parfois au présent et au futur: il suffit, pour qu'apparaisse le conditionnel, que l'acte soit conçu comme "outre-passé". Ceci élargirait singulièrement la zone de cette formation, la ferait déborder hors du cadre des phrases hypothétiques. De fait, le conditionnel dans la prose védique n'est pas limité à de telles phrases, il dépend moins d'une structure que d'une notion à rendre.[71] Les commentateurs sont donc justifiés à enseigner le conditionnel entre 143 et 152; tout ce qu'on peut dire, ici comme ailleurs, est que ces emplois obtenus par le jeu de la "concurrence" ont moins de poids que les enseignements sortant directement d'un sū.; ils sont sujets à quelque automatisme.[72] Mais le principe en est difficilement contestable.

§21. Le sū. 142, faisant retour au temps présent (*LAṬ*), instruit ce temps lorsque la phrase comporte une idée de "blâme" (*GARHĀYĀM*), l'exemple de base étant "se peut-il que vous fassiez faire un sacrifice par un *śūdra* (acte éminemment blâmable)?" *api* (ou: *jātu*) *tatrabhavān vṛṣalaṃ yājayati* / *garhāmahe*. A vrai dire, ce sū. n'est valable que si l'on rejette l'hypothèse que le sū. *VARTAMĀNE LAṬ* s'appliquerait déjà à noter le présent comme temps indifférencié. Les particules *api* et *jātu* interviennent ici (selon le processus déjà observé) pour autoriser par leur seule présence une forme du verbe moins marquée qu'elle l'eût été en leur absence.[73]

[70] 140 succède à 139 uniquement parce que 139 est en dépendance des sū. antérieurs, mais P. n'a pu manquer de réaliser que le conditionnel du passé est incomparablement plus important que celui du futur.

[71] Il manque une étude sur le conditionnel, mais les indications de Delbrück Ai. Syntax p. 365 pour la prose védique (ce mode manque presque totalement dans les mantra) montrent la souplesse de la formation au stade ancien; plus tard (Speyer, etc.) vient une sorte de normalisation, coïncidant avec une raréfaction.

[72] En fait, 146 est exclu, ainsi que 151 (K.); cf. CV. 1.3,108 à 116 (*bhūte liṅviṣaye*). Le conditionnel futur est donné comme nécessaire (*nitya*) pour 143–145, 147–150, 152; le conditionnel passé comme optionnel (*vā*) pour 144, 145, 147–150 (mais comme nécessaire pour 152); cf. Prakr. Kaum. 3.2,143 *lṛḍ bhaviṣyati nityam, bhūte vā*. Voici quelques exx. dans K., empruntés au type *vṛṣalaṃ yājayati* (§ 21): *ko nāma vṛṣalo yaṃ tatrabhavān ayājayiṣyat* 144, *nāvakalpayāmi tatrabhavān nāma vṛṣalam ayājayiṣyat* 145 (plus loin K. renonce aux exx. de conditionnel).

[73] Bh. ad vt. 1 note que le sū. était inutile, car il s'agit là d'une action non achevée, où le présent est valable par définition. Dira-t-on que ce sū. sert à empêcher les substituts du présent (participe, etc.) d'y valoir? Non, vu

143 et 144 sont des corollaires à 142: il y a concurrence entre présent et optatif si la phrase comporte l'interrogatif *katham* "comment se peut-il que . . . ?"; concurrence entre optatif et futur s'il y a le pronom *ka* ou ses dérivés (*KIṂVṚTTE*). Les mots interrogatifs sont moins sélectifs que les particules, ces dernières imposant un temps précis, ceux-là permettant un choix (cf. déjà une répartition analogue aux sū. 5 et 6, ci-dessus § 14).[74]

Suivent (145) deux nuances accompagnant l'emploi optionnel de l'optatif et du futur: c'est, à savoir, si le sujet considère l'acte, soit comme impossible (ou du moins, invraisemblable, sur le plan moral), soit comme intolerable: les exemples montrent qu'on est toujours en face d'une variante à 142, "je ne crois pas possible ou tolérable que vous fassiez faire un sacrifice..." *nāvakalpayāmi* (ou: *na marṣayāmi*) *tatrabhavān nāma vṛṣalaṃ yājayet* (ou: *yājayiṣyati*): le mot *ANAVAKḶPTI* est rendu par *aśraddhā* C. 1.3,111, plus expressif que *asaṃbhāvanā* K. et correspondant, d'ailleurs, au *na śraddadhe* de l'exemple afférent; de même *krodha* C. est plus précis que l'*akṣamā* K. glosant P. *AMARṢA*. La présence d'un mot adjacent tel que *kiṃkila* ou d'un verbe d'existence (à valeur atténuée, *vidyate nāma* "se peut-il que... ?") suffit selon 146 à écarter l'optatif: on en conclura que, dans tout ce développement, l'optatif était bien le mode normal, dont le futur est un substitut conditionné par le contexte.[75]

La portion qui suit concerne l'optatif seul et ne nous intéresse pas ici.[76] Le futur reparaît au sū. 151, comme substitut de l'optatif (selon 150), là où l'idée prévalente est celle d'une chose "étonnante" (*CITRĪKARAṆE*), mais sans qu'il y ait de mot adjacent (à savoir, sans la conjonction *yac ca* ou *yatra* prévue pour 150, à quoi s'ajoute encore *yadi*),[77] donc en subordonnée implicite (comme le sont d'ailleurs les phrases citées sous 145 et. 146), ex. "il serait surprenant qu'un sourd apprît la grammaire", *āścaryam / badhiro nāma vyākaraṇam adhyeṣyate*.

Le sū. 155 introduit un futur optionnel quand l'idée est celle d'une chose qu'on "suppose" (*SAṂBHĀVANA*), mais en fait, d'après les exemples cités, d'une chose qu'on présume devoir se produire et même sur laquelle on compte,[78] ainsi après *saṃbhāvayāmi*, *ava-*

que ces substituts sont souhaitables, ainsi *api māṃ yājayantaṃ paśya* "me vois-tu en train de faire faire un sacrifice . . .?".

[74] H. 13 (= P. 143) donne ici "tous les temps", ainsi *kathaṃ bhakṣayet bhakṣayati ababhakṣat abhakṣayat bhakṣayāṃcakāra bhakṣayitā bhakṣayiṣyati abhakṣayiṣyat*. Au contraire, le sū. suivant (H. 14) entrave toutes désinences, il ne reste que *brūyāt vakṣyati avakṣyat*. De même 145 (H. 15). — Gaṇaratn. p. 12.

[75] *kiṃkila* Gaṇaratn. p. 11–12. — Il y a cette restriction que les exx. sous 145 comportent, non seulement l'idée d'une chose non possible ou non tolérable, mais les formules expresses *nāvakalpayāmi* et analogues (tout comme 155 et cf. ci-dessus. §18) "je ne crois pas, je ne supporte pas que", sans l'intervention de la conjonction *yad*; qu'ensuite, d'après 147, la particule *jātu* suivie de *yad* maintient l'optatif (le vt. 1 adjoint à *yad yadā* et *yadi*). On remarquera l'importance de la subordination, implicite dans tous ces schémas (depuis 145); c'est là surtout où apparaît le libre choix des formes temporelles.

[76] 147 entrave le futur (H. 17).

[77] Mais *AYADAU* est inutile selon le vt. 1, car avec *yadi* il n'existe pas de nuance d'étonnement, mais simplement de supposition. — 151 vaut *sarveṣu kāleṣu* d'après SKĀ. 2.4,208, mais entrave tous autres temps d'après H. 20. — *yac ca* cité Gaṇaratn. p. 10.

[78] "Croyance en la capacité ou possibilité (d'agir), faculté de discriminer une convenance dans les actes (à faire)" K.

kalpayāmi, śraddadhe (...*bhuñjīta bhavān / bhokṣyate bhavān* "je présume qu'il mangera" : toujours avec subordination implicite) : si la conjonction *yad* intervient, on retombe sur le tour normal, c'est-à-dire l'optatif.[79]

§22. Déjà traitée indirectement sous 132–134 (ci-dessus, § 18), 139–140 (§ 20), la phrase hypothétique est abordée de front au sū. 156; la protase est appelée *HETU* "cause", l'apodose *HETUMANT* "effet",[80] termes qui font bien sentir le lien étroit entre les deux parties du diptyque, mais n'accusent pas *a priori* l'aspect syntaxique. L'optatif y este le mode habituel, mais, s'agissant d'un fait à venir — car ce sū. continue à être sous la récurrence de *BHAVIṢYATI* comme tous les sū. environnants — le temps futur peut être employé.[81] Les exemples allégués montrent bien qu'il s'agit d'un "potentiel" corrélatif à l'irréel de 139, "s'il fait appel à Kamalaka, son chariot ne se renversera pas" *yadi kamalakam āhvayen na śakaṭaṃ paryābhavet* (ou : *āhvāsyati... paryābhaviṣyati*) : la théorie du futur s'achève sur cet encadrement de formules parallèles, qui donne à la description son style propre.

Cette théorie est relativement longue, comparée à celle du prétérit ou du présent. On notera toutefois que le futur n'est enseigné, le plus souvent, qu'à titre optionnel : concurremment au présent 5-8, au présent et à l'optatif 9, de nouveau au présent 131–132, au futur périphr. 138, au présent et à l'optatif 143, enfin à l'optatif seul 144–145, 155–156, sans compter quelques cas conditionnés. Ainsi le futur pāṇinéen est essentiellement un temps facultatif, enclin à empiéter sur le mode ou à se laisser empiéter par lui.[82] C'est bien l'impression que nous en donnent aussi les textes classiques.

Cette fin du troisième pāda marque aussi le terme de la théorie d'ensemble des valeurs temporelles. Demeure seul un emploi secondaire, un peu à part, emploi qu'incitait à placer ici la mention du précatif (173 et 174) : c'est la question du prohibitif. Elle occupe deux sū. fort brefs, 175 et 176 : on y apprend le choix que laisse la Grammaire entre l'aoriste (inaugmenté, 6.4,74) avec *mā* et l'imparfait (id.) avec *mā sma*, ce dernier doublé par l'aoriste (donc, *mā kārṣīt/mā sma karot* ou *kārṣīt* "qu'il ne fasse pas !") : la forme verbale la moins expressive choisit la double particule. Il est difficile

[79] Il y a présent implicite dans le domaine de 153, le mot adjacent étant *kac cid*. Futur implicite dans le domaine de 154, le mot adjacent étant *alam* : ici encore, la particule entraîne avec elle une forme verbale moins marquée.

[80] *phala* C. 1.3,120 SKĀ. 2.4,213 et ailleurs; *hetumant* Sāṃkhyakār. 10 "ayant une cause".

[81] Les autres temps sont exclus K., mais SKĀ. *loc. cit.*, donne *yāyāt yāsyati yāti ayāsīt*, avec les correspondants dans l'apodose. D'après CV., repris K., la règle ne s'applique pas à un emploi tel que *varṣatīti dhāvati* "étant donné qu'il pleut, il court", où il ne s'agit pas du futur et où, note CV., *iti* entrave l'optatif. N. pose la *vivakṣā* (ci-dessus, n. 22), qui fait préférer le présent; enfin, SKĀ. dit que le *hetu* et le *phala* sont suggérés par *iti*, si bien que le présent suffit. C'est un cas tout analogue à celui de *drakṣyāmīti*, ci-dessus, § 15.

[82] Si le futur tend au mode (Delbrück Ai. Syntax p. 289 Idg. Syntax 2 p. 243 Brugmann 2².3 p. 784), peut-être parce qu'il est l'indicativisation d'une ancienne forme modale, il arrive que l'optatif tende au présent : ainsi *icchet* donné comme équivalent d'*icchati* 160 : c'est dans ce cas très limité que les Gramm. ont aperçu la vaste équivalence entre optatif et indicatif, équivalence qui d'ailleurs est surtout sensible après l'époque védique. Un autre cas également très spécial atteste une concurrence entre impératif et indicatif (ci-dessus, n. 19).

de mesurer à quel degré les textes confirment cette répartition; de toutes manières, et dès l'origine, l'aoriste est fortement prédominant.[83]

§23. Un regard, même rapide, sur tout cet enseignement, porte à croire que Pāṇini a noté exactement, bien que, en partie, de manière rudimentaire, les valeurs temporelles du verbe; que, à côté de règles très compréhensives, il a pris soin de relever des détails fort menus, souvent insaisissables pour nous (peut-être simplement parce qu'ils appartiennent à un usage oral ou familier dont nous n'avons plus de témoignage). Cette disparité dans la présentation des faits se retrouve, du reste, dans d'autres portions de la Grammaire. Mais l'école pāṇinéenne, prise dans son ensemble, fortifiée çà et là par les faits nouveaux qu'enregistrent les non-Pāṇinéens (notamment Hemacandra, le plus novateur de tous, du moins dans le domaine qui nous a retenu ici), rétablit un certain équilibre. C'est ainsi que Patañjali a conservé de précieuses données, avec un arrière-plan philosophique, sur la signification du "présent"; il nous a permis de voir plus distinctement quelles étaient, selon Pāṇini même, les délimitations entre les temps du passé. Il demeure, certes, une disproportion entre le futur et les autres formations personnelles, mais il faut voir que le futur est en partie un substitut de mode et que, au surplus, la plupart de ses emplois sont donnés à titre de "concurrence". Peut-être les commentateurs ont-ils poussé jusqu'à l'arbitraire une tendance qui n'était pas à ce degré déductible des sūtra; ils ont cherché, là comme ailleurs, à égaliser et balancer les enseignements, à multiplier les indices de reconduction. Il est vrai que, dans le chapitre de la syntaxe verbale, ils avaient des excuses: rien n'est plus flou, surtout postérieurement à l'époque védique, que l'usage des formes verbales dans la littérature; il faudra toute la rigueur, l'ascèse grammaticale du kāvya, pour y mettre quelque ordre.

Parmi les observations à retenir, notons le rôle modificateur (atténuateur) attribué à certaines particules. Le parti pris de mettre en avant la fonction et non la catégorie, a été salutaire pour l'unité de l'exposé et pour sa fermeté. Il a permis de dégager plusieurs notations psychologiques, qui ont été des facteurs de syntaxe. Il y a donc chez les grammairiens un ensemble de faits dont l'interprétation n'est pas toujours facile, mais qui enrichit notre connaissance de la langue, qui rend justice aussi à cet instinct d'harmonie interne qu'on dirait avoir présidé à sa structuration.

[83] K. cite comme incorrect — donc, bien établi dans l'usage — l'emploi de *mā bhavatu, mā bhaviṣyati*. Les Gramm. soucieux de conciliation le justifient en posant une particule *mā* distincte du *MĀṄ* de P.; cet artifice est repris, entre autres, par Kt. 3.1,22 SK. 2219 H. 5.4,39 Durgh. (ad 175). BM. ajoute que, dans *māstu, astu* est lui-même une particule à apparence (*pratirūpaka*) de forme verbale. Vop. 25.27 met sur le même plan *mā viraṃsīt*/ *mā viramatu*/ *mā viraṃsyati*. Kt. admet aussi "selon certains" l'interversion *sma karon mā*. — Sur l'usage véd., v. BSL. 43, 1946 p. 46, n. 2 JAs. 1959 p. 74; plus anciennement, Delbrück Ai. Syntax p. 358, 361, 501.

Bibliography

Aklujkar, Ashok (1969). "Two Textual Studies of Bhartṛhari," *Journal of the American Oriental Society* 89, 547–563.

Allen, W. S. (1953). *Phonetics in Ancient India*. London.

Aufrecht, Th. (ed.) (1859). *Ujjvaladatta's Commentary on the Uṇādi-Sūtras*. Bonn.

Ballantyne, J. R., and the pandits of the Benares College (eds.) (1856). *The Mahábháshya with Its Commentary, the Bháshya-pradípa and the Commentary Thereon, the Bháshya-pradípodyota*, vol. I. Mirzapore.

Beal, Samuel (trans.) (1885). *Si-yu-ki. Buddhist Records of the Western World*, by Hsüan Tsang, vol. 1, Boston. See pp. 6–7.

_____ (1911). *The Life of Hiuen-Tsiang*, by Hwui Li, London. See pp. 7–10.

Belvalkar, S. K. (1915). *An Account of the Different Existing Systems of Sanskrit Grammar*. Poona.

Benfey, Theodor (1874). *Einleitung in die Grammatik der vedischen Sprache*. Göttingen.

Bhandarkar, R. G. (1864, 1877). "Review of Goldstücker's *Pāṇini, His Place in Sanskrit Literature*," *Indian Antiquary* 6, 108–113. See pp. 72–78.

_____ (1872). "On the Date of Patañjali and the King in whose Reign He Lived," Native Opinion, 1864, and *Indian Antiquary* 1, 299–302. See pp. 78–81.

_____ (1873a). "Note on the Above" [See Weber 1873c], *Indian Antiquary* 2, 59–61. See p. 84.

_____ (1873b). "Reply to Professor Weber" [Weber 1873c], *Indian Antiquary* 2, 238–240. See pp. 84–85.

_____ (1876). "Ācārya, the friend of the student, and the relations between the three Ācāryas," *Indian Antiquary* 5, 345–350. See pp. 86–87.

_____ (1883–1885a). "The Date of Patañjali. A Reply to Professor Peterson," *Journal of the Bombay Branch of the Royal Asiatic Society* 16, 199–222.

_____ (1883–1885b). "Development of Language and of Sanskrit," *Journal of the Bombay Branch of the Royal Asiatic Society* 16, 245–274. See pp. 87–93.

_____ (1883–1885c). "Note" [on Peterson 1883–1885], *Journal of the Bombay Branch of the Royal Asiatic Society* 16, 343–345.

_____ (1883–1885d). "Relations between Sanskrit, Pāli, the Prākṛits and the Modern Vernaculars," *Journal of the Bombay Branch of the Royal Asiatic Society* 16, 314–342. See pp. 94–101.

_____ (1889). "My Visit to the Vienna Oriental Congress," *Journal of the Bombay Branch of the Royal Asiatic Society* 17, 72–95. Also in Ṇ. B. Utgikar, ed., *Collected Works of Sir R. G. Bhandarkar* 1933, vol. 1, 332–360, Poona. See pp. 81–83.

Bhattacharya, B. (1962). *A Study in Language and Meaning: A Critical Examination of Some Aspects of Indian Semantics*. Calcutta.

Biardeau, M. (1964a). *Théorie de la connaissance et philosophie de la parole dans le brahmanisme classique*. Paris/La Haye.

——— (1964b). *Bhartṛhari Vākyapadīya Brahmakāṇḍa avec la vṛtti de Harivṛṣabha*. Paris.

al-Bīrūnī. See Sachau (1887) and (1910).

Birwé, Robert (1966). *Studien zu Adhyāya III der Aṣṭādhyāyī Pāṇinis*. Wiesbaden.

Bloch, Bernard (1949). "Leonard Bloomfield," *Language* 25, 87–98. Reprinted in Sebeok 1966, II, 508–518.

Bloomfield, Leonard (1927). "On Some Rules of Pāṇini," *Journal of the American Oriental Society* 47, 61–70. See pp. 266–272.

——— (1933). *Language*. New York.

——— (1939). "Linguistic Aspects of Science," *International Encyclopedia of Unified Science* (Otto Neurath, ed.) 1, no. 4, Chicago.

Boehtlingk, Otto (ed.) (1844). *Die Uṇādi-affixe*. St. Petersburg.

——— (ed.) (1847). *Vopadeva's Mugdhabodha*. St. Petersburg.

——— (1851). *Über die Sprache der Jakuten*. St. Petersburg.

——— (1876a). "Kâtjâjana oder Patańgali im Mahâbhâshja," *Zeitschrift der deutschen morgenländischen Gesellschaft* 29, 183–190.

——— (1876b). "Das Verhalten der drei kanonischen Grammatiker in Indien zu den im Wurzelverzeichniss mit ṣ und ṇ anlautenden Wurzeln," *Zeitschrift der deutschen morgenländischen Gesellschaft* 29, 483–490.

——— (ed., trans.) (1887). *Pāṇini's Grammatik*. Leipzig (the edition of the text first appeared in 1839; reprint Hildesheim 1964).

——— (1893). "Whitney's letzte Angriffe auf Pāṇini," *Berichte über die Verhandlungen der königlich sächsischen Gesellschaft der Wissenschaften zu Leipzig, Philologisch-Historische Classe* 45, 247–257. See pp. 186–192.

——— **and Rudolf Roth** (1855–1875). *Sanskritwörterbuch*, vols. 1–7. St. Petersburg.

Bopp, Franz (1816). *Über das Konjugationssystem der Sanskritsprache*. Frankfurt am Main.

——— (1827). *Ausführliches Lehrgebäude der Sanskrita-Sprache*. Berlin.

——— (1867³). *Glossarium comparativum linguae sanscritae in quo omnes sanscritae radices et vocabula usitatissima explicantur et cum vocabulis graecis, latinis, germanicis, lituanicis, slavicis, celticis comparantur*. Berlin.

Boudon, Pierre (1938). "Une Application du raisonnement par l'absurde dans l'interpretation de Pāṇini (les *jñāpakasiddhaparibhāṣā*)," *Journal asiatique* 230, 65–121. See pp. 358–391.

Breloer, B. (1929). "Studie zu Pāṇini," *Zeitschrift für Indologie und Iranistik* 7, 114–135.

Brough, John (1951a). *Selections from Classical Sanskrit Literature*. London.

——— (1951b). "Theories of General Linguistics in the Sanskrit Grammairians," *Transactions of the Philological Society* 27–46. See pp. 402–414.

______ (1952). "Audumbarāyaṇa's Theory of Language," *Bulletin of the School of Oriental and African Studies* 14, 73–77.

______ (1953). "Some Indian Theories of Meaning," *Transactions of the Philological Society* 161–176. See pp. 414–423.

Bühler, Georg (1894). "The Roots of the Dhātupāṭha Not Found in Literature," *Wiener Zeitschrift für die Kunde des Morgenlandes* 8,17-42. Also in *Indian Antiquary* 23, 141–154, 250–255. See pp. 194–204.

Buiskool, Herman E. (1934). *Pūrvatrāsiddham: Analytisch onderzoek aangaande het systeem der Tripādī van Pāṇini's Aṣṭādhyāyī*. Amsterdam.

______ (1939). *The Tripādī, being an English recast of Pūrvatrāsiddham (An analytical-synthetical inquiry into the system of the last three chapters of Pāṇini's Aṣṭādhyāyī*). Leiden.

Burnell, A. C. (1875). *Essay on the Aindra School of Sanskrit Grammarians*. Mangalore.

Burrow, T. (1955). *The Sanskrit Language*. London.

Cannon, Garland H. (1958). "Sir William Jones' Persian Linguistics," *Journal of the American Oriental Society* 78, 262–273. Reprinted in Sebeok 1966, I, 36–57.

Cardona, George (1967). "Pāṇini's Syntactic Theories," *Journal of the Oriental Institute (Baroda)* 16, 201–215.

______ (1969). "Studies in Indian Grammarians I: The Method of Description Reflected in the Śivasūtras," *Transactions of the American Philosophical Society* 59, part 1, 3–48.

Carey, W. (1806). *A Grammar of the Sungskrit Language/ . . . /to Which are Added Examples for the Exercise of the Student and a Complete List of the Dhatoos, or Roots*. Serampore.

Chatterji, K. C. (1934a). "The Śiva Sūtras." *Journal of the Department of Letters, University of Calcutta* 24 (2), 1–10.

______ (1934b). "The Critics of Sanskrit Grammar," *Journal of the Department of Letters, University of Calcutta* 24 (3), 1–21. See pp. 287–297.

______ (1948). *Technical Terms and Technique of Sanskrit Grammar*. Calcutta.

______ (ed. and trans., 1957²). *Patañjali's Mahābhāṣya: Paspaśāhnika*. Calcutta.

Chatterji, S. K. (1951). "Al-Bīrūnī and Sanskrit," *Al-Bīrūnī Commemoration Volume, A.H. 362–A.H. 1362*, Calcutta, 83–100.

Chomsky, Noam (1964). *Current Issues in Linguistic Theory*. The Hague.

______ (1966). *Cartesian Linguistics*. New York/London.

Colebrooke, H. T. (1803). "On the Sanskrit and Prácrit Languages," *Asiatic Researches* 7, 199–231. See pp. 33–45.

______ (1805). *A Grammar of the Sanscrit Language*, vol. 1. Calcutta.

______ (1823). "Essay on the Philosophy of the Hindus," *Transactions of the Royal Asiatic Society* 1: 19–43, 92–118, 439–466, 549–579; 2: 1–39.

Dasgupta, Surendranath (1922). *A History of Indian Philosophy*, vol. I. Cambridge.

Delbrück, Berthold (1904–1905). "Otto Böhtlingk," *Indogermanische Forschungen* 17, 131–136. Reprinted in Sebeok 1966, I, 261–268.

Dove, Alfred (1881). "Humboldt," *Allgemeine deutsche Biographie* 13, 338–358. Reprinted in Sebeok 1966, I, 71–101.

Edgerton, F. (1928). "Some Linguistic Notes on the Mīmāṅsā System," *Language* 4, 171–177.

——— (1929). *The Mīmāṅsā-Nyāya-Prakāśa or Āpadevī*. New Haven and London.

Eggeling, Julius (1887). *Catalogue of the Sanskrit Manuscripts in the Library of the India Office*, vol. I, part I, Vedic Literature. London.

Eliade, Mircea (1954). *Le Yoga, Immortalité et liberté*. Paris.

Emeneau, M. (1955). "India and Linguistics," *Journal of the American Oriental Society* 75, 145–153.

Faddegon, Barend (1929). "The Mnemotechnics of Pāṇini's Grammar I: The Śiva-Sūtra," *Acta Orientalia* 7, 48–65. See pp. 275–285.

——— (1936). *Studies on Pāṇini's Grammar*. Amsterdam.

Fa Tsang. See van Gulik (1956).

Filliozat, J. (1937). "Une grammaire sanscrite du XVIIIe siècle et les débuts de l'indianisme en France," *Journal Asiatique* 229, 275–284.

——— (1967a). "Louis Renou et son œuvre scientifique," *Journal Asiatique* 255, 1–11.

——— (1967b). "Bibliographie des travaux de Louis Renou," *Journal Asiatique* 255, 13–30.

Foster, Henry P. (1810). *An essay on the principles of Sanskrit Grammar*, Part 1. Calcutta.

Frauwallner, Erich (1959). "Dignāga, sein Werk und seine Entwicklung," *Wiener Zeitschrift für die Kunde Süd- und Ostasiens und Archiv für indische Philosophie* 3, 83–164.

——— (1960). "Sprachtheorie und Philosophie im Mahābhāṣyam des Patañjali," *Wiener Zeitschrift für die Kunde Süd- und Ostasiens und Archiv für indische Philosophie* 4, 92–118.

——— (1961). "Geschichte und Aufgaben der Wiener Indologie," *Anzeiger der österreichischen Akademie der Wissenschaften, Philosophisch-historische Klasse* 98, 77–95.

Geiger, Bernhard (1909). "Mahābhāṣya zu P. VI, 4, 22 und 132 nebst Kaiyaṭa's Kommentar: übersetzt, erläutert und mit einem Anhang," *Sitzungsberichte der philosophisch-historischen Klasse der kaiserlichen Akademie der Wissenschaften zu Wien* 160, VIII: 1–76. See pp. 209–259.

Goldstücker, Theodor (1861). *Pāṇini: His Place in Sanskrit Literature*. London. Reprinted Varanasi 1965, Osnabrück 1966.

——— (1874a). *Patañjali's Mahābhāṣya, a MS dated Saṃvat 1751, as reproduced by photo-lithography*. London.

——— (1874b). *Patañjali's Mahābhāṣya with Kaiyyaṭa's Bhāṣyapradīpa, an undated MS, as reproduced by photo-lithography*. London.

Gopinatha Rao, T. A. (1916). *Elements of Hindu Iconography*, vol. II. Madras.

Gray, J. E. B. (1959). "An Analysis of Nambudiri Ṛgvedic Recitation and the Nature of the Vedic Accent," *Bulletin of the School of Oriental and African Studies* 22, 499–530.

______ (1968). Reviews of Biardeau 1964a and 1964b, and of Subramania Iyer 1965, *Foundations of Language* 4, 70–77.

van Gulik, R. H. (1956). *Siddham. An Essay on the History of Sanskrit Studies in China and Japan*. Nagpur. See pp. 18–19.

Hamilton, Alexander (1814). *Terms of Sanskrit Grammar*. London.

Harle, J. C. (1963). *Temple Gateways in South India*. Oxford.

Harweg, R. (1964). *Kompositum und Katalysationstext vornehmlich im späten Sanskrit*. The Hague.

Hsüan Tsang. see Julien (1857–1858), and Beal (1885).

Humboldt, Wilhelm von (1832). *Über die Kawi-Sprache auf der Insel Java*. Berlin.

______ (1836). *Über die Verschiedenheit des menschlichen Sprachbaues und ihren Einfluss auf die geistige Entwickelung des Menschengeschlechts*. Berlin. See pp. 60–64.

Hwui Li. See Beal (1911), Julien (1853), and Li (1959).

Ingalls, Daniel H. H. (1960). "On the study of the past," *Journal of the American Oriental Society* 80, 191–197.

I Tsing. See Takakusu.

Jones, William (1807). "A Dissertation on the Orthography of Asiatick Words in Roman Letters," *The Works of Sir William Jones*, vol. III, London, 253–318.

Joshi, S. D. (ed. and trans.) (1967). *The Sphoṭanirṇaya of Kauṇḍa Bhaṭṭa*. Poona.

______ (1968). *Patañjali's Vyākaraṇa—Mahābhāṣya: Samarthāhnika (P.2.1.1). Edited with Translation and Explanatary Notes. Poona.*

______**, P. Kiparsky and J. F. Staal** (in preparation). *The Sanskrit Grammarians*.

Jouveau-Dubreuil, G. (1937). *Iconography of Southern India*. Paris.

Julien, Stanislas (1853). *Historie de la vie de Hiouen-Thsang et de ses voyages dans l'Inde par Höei-li et Yen-thsong*. Paris.

______ (1857–1858). *Mémoires sur les contrées occidentales, traduits du sanscrit en chinois, en l'an 648, par Hiouen-Thsang, et du chinois en français par M. Stanislas Julien*, vols. I–II. Paris.

Keith, Arthur Berriedale (1935). *Catalogue of the Sanskrit and Prakrit Manuscripts in the Library of the India Office*, vol. II, part I. London.

Kielhorn, F. (ed. and trans.) (1866). *Śāntanava's Phiṭsūtra. Mit verschiedenen indischen Commentatoren, Einleitung, Übersetzung und Anmerkungen*. Leipzig.

______ (ed. and trans.) (1868–1874). *Paribhāṣenduśekhara of Nāgojībhaṭṭa*, vols. 1–4. Trans. and re-edited 1960, Poona.

——— (1876a). *Kātyāyana and Patañjali: Their Relation to Each Other and to Pāṇini.* Bombay. Reprinted Varanasi 1963, Osnabrück 1965.

——— (1876b). "On the *Mahābhāṣya*," *Indian Antiquary* 5, 241–251.

——— (ed.) (1880–1885). *The Vyākaraṇa-Mahābhāṣya of Patañjali*, vols. 1–3. Bombay. Second edition 1892–1909, third revised edition 1962 (vol. 1), 1965 (vol. 2). Poona.

——— (1883). "On the grammarian Bhartṛhari," *Indian Antiquary* 12, 226–227.

——— (1885). "Der Grammatiker Pāṇini," *Nachrichten von der Königlichen Gesellschaft der Wissenschaften und der Georg-Augusts-Universität zu Göttingen* 5, 185–190. See pp. 103–105.

——— (1886a). Book Notice of Whitney's *Roots, Verb-forms and Primary Derivatives of the Sanskrit Language, Indian Antiquary* 15, 86–87. See pp. 155–157.

——— (1886b). "Indragomin and other Grammarians," *Indian Antiquary* 15, 181–183.

——— (1886c). "The *Cāndra-Vyākaraṇa* and the *Kāśikā-Vṛtti*," *Indian Antiquary* 15, 183–185.

——— (1886d). "*Ācāryadeśīya*" or Notes on the *Mahābhāṣya* 1, *Indian Antiquary* 15, 80–81.

——— (1886e). "Gōṇikāputra and Gōnardīya" or Notes on the *Mahābhāṣya* 2, *Indian Antiquary* 15, 81–84.

——— (1886f). "On Some Doubtful *Vārttikas*" or Notes on the *Mahābhāṣya* 3, *Indian Antiquary* 15, 203–211.

——— (1886g). "Some Suggestions Regarding the Verses (*Kārikās*) in the *Mahābhāṣya*" or Notes on the *Mahābhāṣya* 4, *Indian Antiquary* 15, 228–233.

——— (1887a). "The Authorities on Grammar Quoted in the *Mahābhāṣya*" or Notes on the *Mahābhāṣya* 5, *Indian Antiquary* 16, 101–106. See pp. 106–114.

——— (1887b). "The Text of Pāṇini's Sūtras as Given in the *Kāśika-Vṛtti*, Compared with the Text Known to Kātyāyana and Patañjali" or Notes on the *Mahābhāṣya* 6, *Indian Antiquary* 16, 178–184. See pp. 115–123.

——— (1887c). "Some Devices of Indian Grammarians" or Notes on the *Mahābhāṣya* 7, *Indian Antiquary* 16, 244–252. See pp. 123–134.

Kiparsky, Paul (1970). "From paleogrammarians to neogrammarians," *Essays in the History of Linguistics* (Dell Hymes, ed.). Bloomington.

———**, and J. F. Staal** (1969). "Syntactic and Semantic Relations in Pāṇini," *Foundations of Language* 5, 83–117.

Krishna Sastri, H. (1916). *South-Indian Images of Gods and Goddesses.* Madras.

Kulke, H. (1969). *Cidambaramahātmya. Eine Untersuchung der religionsgeschichtlichen und historischen Hintergründe für die Entstehung der Tradition einer südindischen Tempelstadt.* Wiesbaden.

Kunjunni Raja, K. (1963). *Indian Theories of Meaning*. Madras.

Lanman, Charles Rockwell (1897). "Memorial Address," *The Whitney Memorial Meeting: A Report*, 7–27. Reprinted in Sebeok 1966, I. 426–439.

Lassen, Christian (1830). "Über Herrn Professor Bopps grammatisches System der Sanskrit Sprache," *Indische Bibliothek* 3.1.1–113.

Lees, Robert (1963²). *The Grammar of English Nominalizations*. The Hague.

Leitzmann, Albert (ed.) (1908). *Briefwechsel zwischen Wilhelm vom Humboldt und August Wilhelm Schlegel*. Halle a.S.

Lévi, S. (1891). "Notes de chronologie indienne, Devānāṃpriya Aśoka et Kātyāyana," *Journal Asiatique* 181, 549–553.

______ (1906–1908). "Des préverbes chez Pāṇini," *Mémoires de la Societé Linguistique de Paris* 14, 276–279.

Liebich, Bruno (1891). *Pāṇini. Ein Beitrag zur Kenntnis der indischen Literatur und Grammatik*. Leipzig. See pp. 159–165.

______ (1892). *Zwei Kapitel der Kāçikā: Übersetzt und mit Einleitung versehen*. Breslau.

______ (1895). *Das Cāndra-vyākaraṇa*. Göttingen.

______ (1902). *Cāndra-vyākaraṇa. Sūtra, Uṇādi, Dhātupāṭha*. Leipzig.

______ (1918). *Candra-Vṛtti, der Original-Kommentar Candragomin's zu seinem grammatischen Sūtra*. Leipzig.

______ (1919–1920). *Zur Einführung in die indische einheimische Sprachwissenschaft*, vols. I–IV. Heidelberg.

______ (1921). *Materialien zum Dhātupāṭha*. Heidelberg.

______ (1928). *Konkordanz Panini-Candra*. Breslau.

______ (1930). *Kṣīrataraṅgiṇī, Kṣīrasvāmin's Kommentar zu Pāṇini's Dhātupāṭha*. Breslau.

Li Yung-hsi (trans.) (1959). *The Life of Hsuan-Tsang*, by Hui-Li. Peking.

Lohmann, J. (1960). "Über den paradigmatischen Charakter der griechischen Kultur," *Die Gegenwart der Griechen im neueren Denken. Festschrift H.-G. Gadamer*, 171–187. Tübingen.

Master, Alfred (1956). "Jones and Pāṇini," *Journal of the American Oriental Society* 76, 186–187.

Matilal, B. K. (1966). "Indian Theorists on the Nature of the Sentence (*vākya*)," *Foundations of Language* 2, 377–393.

______ (1968). *The Navya-nyāya Doctrine of Negation. The Semantics and Ontology of Negative Statements in Navya-nyāya Philosophy*. Cambridge, Mass.

McCawley, James D. (1967). "The phonological theory behind Whitney's *Sanskrit Grammar*," *Language and Areas. Studies presented to George V. Bobrinskoy* 77–85. Chicago.

Misra, V. N. (1966). *The Descriptive Technique of Pāṇini*. The Hague-Paris.

Mukherjee, S. N. (1968). *Sir William Jones: A Study in Eighteenth-Century British Attitudes to India*. Cambridge.

Müller, F. Max (1866, 1870²). *A Sanskrit Grammar for Beginners.* London. See pp. 138–139.

——— (1869). *Rig-veda-prātiśākhya, das älteste Lehrbuch der vedischen Phonetik.* Leipzig.

——— (1883). *India, What can it teach us?* London.

Ojihara, Yutaka (1958, 1960). "Sū. 1.1.62 vis-à-vis de sū. 1.1.56," or Causerie Vyākaraṇique I (unfinished), *Journal of Indian and Buddhist Studies* 6, 305–302; 8, 370–369.

——— (1959, 1963). "Antériorité du Gaṇapāṭha par rapport au Sūtrapāṭha" or Causerie Vyākaraṇique II, *Journal of Indian and Buddhist Studies* 7, 797–785; 11, 852–846.

——— (1961, 1962). "Incohérence interne chez la Kāśikā" or Causerie Vyākaraṇique III (unfinished), *Journal of Indian and Buddhist Studies* 9, 753–749; 10, 776–766.

——— (1967a). "*Jāti* 'genus' et deux définitions pré-patañjaliennes" or Causerie Vyākaraṇique IV, *Journal of Indian and Buddhist Studies* 16, 459–461. See pp. 425–431.

——— (trans.) (1967b). *La Kāśikā-Vṛtti* (Adhyāya I, Pāda 1), vol. 3. Paris.

———**, and Louis Renou** (trans.) (1960–1962). *La Kāśikā-Vṛtti* (Adhyāya I, Pāda 1), vols. 1–2. Paris.

Pandeya, R. C. (1963). *The Problem of Meaning in Indian Philosophy.* Delhi-Varanasi-Patna.

Paranjpe, V. G. (1922). *Le Vārtika de Kātyāyana. Une étude du style, du vocabulaire et des postulats philosophiques.* Paris.

Pawate, I. S. (1935?). *The Structure of the Aṣṭādhyāyī.* Hubli.

Peterson, P. (1883–1885). "Note on the Date of Patañjali," *Journal of the Bombay Branch of the Royal Asiatic Society* 16, 181–189.

Pillay, K. K. (1953). *The Śucīndram Temple.* Madras.

Pischel, R. (1885). "Der Dichter Pāṇini," *Zeitschrift der deutschen morgenländischen Gesellschaft* 39, 95–98.

Pons, J. F. (1743). in *Lettres édifiantes et curieuses, écrites des Missions Étrangères, par quelque Missionaires de la Compagnie de JESUS,* XXVI Recueil, 222–227. Paris. See pp. 30–32.

Pott, August Friedrich (1833–1836). *Etymologische Forschungen auf dem Gebiete der indo-germanischen Sprachen,* vols. 1–2. Lemgo.

Raghavan, V. (1956). *Sanskrit and Allied Indological Studies in Europe.* Madras.

Raja, C. K. (1957). "The Śiva Sūtras of Pāṇini," *Annals of Oriental Research,* Centenary number, Sanskrit section, 65–81.

Rājarāmaśāstri and Bālaśastri (eds.) (1871). *Patañjali's Mahābhāṣya with Kaiyyaṭa's Bhāṣyapradīpa.* Benares.

Regnier, Adolphe (ed.) (1856–1858). "Études sur la Grammaire védique. Prâtisâkhya du Rig-Véda," *Journal Asiatique* ser. 5: 7, 163–239, 344–407, 445–474; 8, 255–315; 482–526; 9, 210–247; 10, 57–111, 374–450, 461–474; 11, 289–379; 12, 137–220, 329–394, 535–593.

Renou, Louis (1931). *Bibliographie Védique*. Paris.

______ (1936). "Sylvain Lévi et son oeuvre scientifique," *Journal asiatique* 228, 1–59.

______ (1937). "Review of Faddegon's Studies on Pāṇini's Grammar," *Orientalistische Literaturzeitung* 40, no. 5, 318–319.

______ (ed. and trans.) (1940–1956). *La Durghaṭavṛtti de Śaraṇadeva; Traité grammatical en sanskrit du XIIe siècle*, Introduction; I, 1–3; II, 1–3. Paris.

______ (1941–1942). "Les Connexions entre le rituel et la grammaire en sanskrit," *Journal asiatique* 233, 105–165. See pp. 434–469.

______ (1942, 1957²). *Terminologie grammaticale du sanskrit*. Paris.

______ (trans.) (1948–1954). *Aṣṭādhyāyī of* Pāṇini, vols. I–III. Paris. Re-edited with text of *sūtras*, 1961.

______ (trans.) (1951). *Śaṅkara: Prolégomènes au Védānta*. Paris.

______ (1953a). "Les Transitions dans la grammaire de Pāṇini" (Études Pāṇinéennes I), *Journal asiatique* 241, 417–427.

______ (1953b). "Le Véda chez Patañjali" (Études Pāṇinéennes II), *Journal asiatique* 241, 427–464.

______(1955–1967). *Études védiques et pāṇinéennes*, vols. 1–16. Paris.

______(1956a). "L'indianisme au Japon," *Kratylos* 1, 99–103.

______(1956b). "Les uṇādisūtra" (Études Pāṇinéennes III), *Journal asiatique* 244, 155–165.

______(1956c). "Amarasiṃha et Pāṇini" (Études Pāṇinéennes IV), *Journal asiatique* 244, 369–377.

______(1956d). "Le Véda chez les grammairiens non-pāṇinéens" (Études Pāṇinéennes V), *Journal asiatique* 244, 377–389.

______(1957). "Grammaire et Védānta," *Journal asiatique* 245, 121–133. See pp. 470–478.

______(1957). See Wackernagel, J., and L. Renou.

______ (1960). "La Théorie des temps du verbe d'après les grammairiens sanskrits," *Journal asiatique* 248, 305–337. See pp. 500–525.

______(1960–1962). See Ojihara, Yutaka, and Louis Renou.

______(1961). "Grammaire et Poétique en sanskrit." *Études védiques et pāṇinéennes* 8, 105–131. See pp. 478–499.

______(1963). "Sur le genre du *sūtra* dans la littérature sanskrite," *Journal asiatique* 251, 165–216.

______(1969). "Pāṇini," *Current Trends in Linguistics* 5, 481–498.

Rocher, Rosane (1964a). "'Agent' et 'Objet' chez Pāṇini," *Journal of the American Oriental Society* 84, 44–45.

______(1964b). "The Technical Term 'hetu' in Pāṇini's Aṣṭādhyāyī," *Vishveshvaranand Indological Journal* 2, 31–40.

______ (1967). Review of Birwé 1966, *Journal of the American Oriental Society* 87, 582–588.

______(1968a). *La Théorie des voix du verbe dans l'école pāṇinéenne (le 14e āhnika)*. Bruxelles.

______(1968b). *Alexander Hamilton (1762–1824). A Chapter in the Early History of Sanskrit Philology.* New Haven, Conn.

______(1970). "New Data for the Biography of the Orientalist Alexander Hamilton," *Journal of the American Oriental Society* 90, 426–448.

Roth, Rudolph (ed.) (1852). *Jāska's Nirukta, sammt den Nighaṇṭavas.* Göttingen.

Ruegg, D. S. (1959). *Contributions à l'histoire de la philosophie linguistique indienne.* Paris.

Sachau, Edward C. (ed.) (1887). *Al-Bīrūnī's India. An Account of the Religion, Philosophy, Literature, Chronology, Astronomy, Customs, Laws and Astrology of India.* London. Reprinted Leipzig 1925.

______(trans.) (1910). *Alberuni's India, An Account of the Religion, Philosophy, Literature, Geography, Chronology, Astronomy, Customs, Laws and Astrology of India,* vols. I–II. London. See pp. 20–22.

Sastri, G. N. (1959). *The Philosophy of Word and Meaning: Some Indian Approaches with Special Reference to the Philosophy of Bhartṛhari.* Calcutta.

Schiefner, Anton (trans.) (1869). *Tāranātha's Geschichte des Buddhismus in Indien.* St. Petersburg. See pp. 23–26.

Schlegel, August Wilhelm von (1820). "Ueber den gegenwärtigen Zustand der Indischen Philologie," *Indische Bibliothek* 1, 1–49. See pp. 51–52.

______(1832). *Réflexions sur l'étude des langues asiatiques.* Bonn-Paris. See pp. 54–57.

Schlegel, Friedrich von (1808). *Über die Sprache und Weisheit der Inder.* Heidelberg.

Schwab, Raymond (1950). *La Renaissance Orientale.* Paris.

Sebeok, Thomas A. (ed.) (1966). *Portraits of Linguists. A Biographical Source Book for the History of Western Linguistics,* 1746–1963, vols 1–2. Bloomington-London.

Seymour, Thomas Day (1894). "William Dwight Whitney," *American Journal of Philology* 15, 271–298. Reprinted in Sebeok 1966, I, 399–426.

Sköld, H. (1926). *Papers on Pāṇini and Indian Grammar in General.* Lund.

Somasundaram, J. M. (1955). *The University's Environs.* Annamalainagar.

Staal, J. F. (1962a). "A Method of Linguistic Description: the Order of Consonants According to Pāṇini," *Language* 38, 1–10.

______(1962b). "Negation and the Law of Contradiction in Indian Thought," *Bulletin of the School of Oriental and African Studies* 25, 52–71.

______(1965a). "Context-sensitive Rules in Pāṇini," *Foundations of Language* 1, 63–72.

______(1965b). "Euclid and Pāṇini," *Philosophy East and West* 15, 99–116.

______(1966a). "Room at the Top in Sanskrit: Ancient and Modern Descriptions of Nominal Composition," *Indo-Iranian Journal* 9, 165–198.

______(1966b). "Indian Semantics, I," *Journal of the American Oriental Society* 86, 304–311.

______(1967). *Word Order in Sanskrit and Universal Grammar*. Dordrecht.

______(1969). "Sanskrit Philosophy of Language," *Current Trends in Linguistics* 5, 499–531.

______(1970a). "Origin and Development of Linguistics in India," *Essays in the History of Linguistics* (Dell Hymes, ed.). Bloomington.

______(1970b). "Review of Cardona (1969)," *Language* 46, 502–507.

Subramania Iyer, K. A. (1942). "The Conception of Guṇa among the Vaiyyākaraṇas," *New Indian Antiquary* 5, 121–130.

______(1948). "The Point of View of the Vaiyākaraṇas," *Journal of Oriental Research* 18, 84–96. See pp. 393–400.

______(ed.) (1963). *Bhartṛhari's Vākyapadīya*, Kāṇḍa III, Part 1. Poona.

______(trans.) (1965). *The Vākyapadīya of Bhartṛhari with the Vṛtti*, Chapter I. Poona.

______(ed.) (1966). *Bhartṛhari's Vākyapadīya*, Kāṇḍa I. Poona.

______ (1969). *Bhartṛhari. A Study of the Vākyapadīya in the Light of the Ancient Commentaries*. Poona.

Swaminathan, V. (ed.) (1965). *Bhartṛhari's Mahābhāṣyaṭīkā*, vol. I. Varanasi.

Takakusu, J. (transl.) (1896). *A Record of the Buddhist Religion as Practised in India and the Malay Archipelago*, by I-Tsing. Oxford.

Tāranātha. See Schiefner.

Thieme, P. (1935a). *Pāṇini and the Veda: Studies in the Early History of Linguistic Science in India*. Allahabad.

______(1935b). "Bhāṣya zu vārttika 5 zu Pāṇini 1.1.9 und seine einheimischen Erklärer. Ein Beitrag zur Geschichte und Würdigung der indischen grammatischen Scholastik," *Nachrichten von der Gesellschaft der Wissenschaften zu Göttingen, Philologisch-historische Klasse Neue Folge*, 1, 5, 171–216. See pp. 299–332.

______(1937–1938). "On the Identity of the Vārttikakāra," *Indian Culture* 4, 189–209. See pp. 333–356.

______ (1956). "Pāṇini and the Pāṇinīyas", *Journal of the American Oriental Society* 76. 1–23.

______(1957a). "Pāṇini and the Pronunciation of Sanskrit," *Studies Presented to Joshua Whatmough on his Sixtieth Birthday* (Ernst Pulgram, ed.), 263–270. 's-Gravenhage.

______(1957b). "The Interpretation of the Learned," *Felicitation Volume presented to Professor Sripad Krishna Belvalkar* (A. S. Altekar, ed.). 47–62. Banaras.

______(1958). Review of Renou 1957², *Göttingische Gelehrte Anzeigen* 212, 19–49.

Varma, S. (1929). *Critical Studies in the Phonetic Observations of Indian Grammarians*. London. Second ed. 1961. Delhi.

Vasu, S. C. (ed. and trans.) (1891). The *Ashṭādhyāyī of Pāṇini*. Allahabad. Reprinted 1962, Delhi-Varanasi-Patna.

Verburg, P. A. (1950). "The Background to the Linguistic Conceptions of Franz Bopp," *Lingua* 2, 438–468. Reprinted in Sebeok 1966, I, 221–250.

Wackernagel, J. (1908). "Franz Kielhorn (†19 März 1908)," *Nachrichten der K. Gesellschaft der Wissenschaften zu Göttingen, Geschaftliche Mitteilungen* 1, 1–22.

——— **and L. Renou** (1957). *Altindische Grammatik: Introduction générale*, 34–42, 112–125. Göttingen.

Waley, Arthur (1952). *The Real Tripitaka and other pieces*. London.

Weber, Albrecht (1858). "Das Vâjasaneyi-Prâtiçâkhyam," *Indische Studien, Beiträge für die Kunde des indischen Alterthums* 4, 65–171, 177–331.

———(1862). "Zur Frage über das Zeitalter Pāṇini's," *Indische Studien, Beiträge für die Kunde des indischen Alterthums* 5, 1–176.

———(1873a). "Das Mahābhāshya des Patañjali," *Indische Studien, Beiträge für die Kunde des indischen Alterthums* 13, 293–496.

———(1873b). "Remarks on Parts X and XI," [including on Bhandarkar 1872], *Indian Antiquary* 2, 57–59.

———(1873c). Professor Weber on Patañjali, &c [reply to Bhandarkar 1873a], *Indian Antiquary* 2, 206–210.

———(1877). To the Editor of the Indian Antiquary [reply to Kielhorn 1876b], *Indian Antiquary* 6, 301–307.

Westergaard, Niels (1841). *Radices linguae sanscritae*. Copenhagen.

Whitney, William D. (ed., trans.) (1862). *The Atharvaveda Prātiśākhya or Śaunakīyā Caturādhyāyikā*. New Haven, Conn. (reprinted 1962, Varanasi).

———(ed., trans.) (1871). "The Tâittirîya-Prâtiçakhya with Its Commentary, the Tribhâshyaratna," *Journal of the American Oriental Society* 9, 1–469.

———(1874). *Oriental and Linguistic Studies*. New York.

———(1879, 1889²). *Sanskrit Grammar*. Leipzig.

———(1884). "The Study of Hindu Grammar and the Study of Sanskrit," *American Journal of Philology* 5, 279–297. See pp. 142–154.

———(1893). "On Recent Studies in Hindu Grammar," *American Journal of Philology* 14, 171–197. See pp. 165–184.

Wilson, H. H. (1819, 1832²). *Dictionary in Sanskrit and English*. Calcutta.

Windisch, Ernst (1917–1920). *Geschichte der Sanskrit-Philologie und indischen Altertumskunde*, vols. I–II. Strassburg.

———(1921). "Philologie und Altertumskunde in Indien," or Geschichte der Sanskrit-Philologie und indischen Altertumskunde III, *Abhandlungen für die Kunde des Morgenlandes* XV: 3, 1–38.

Woods, J. H. (1914, 1927²). *The Yoga-system of Patañjali*. Cambridge, Massachusetts.

Index of Names

Index of Sanskrit Terms

Sanskrit alphabet:
a, ā, i, ī, u, ū, ṛ, ṝ, ḷ, ẹ, o, ai, au, k, kh, g, gh, ṅ, c, ch, j, jh, ñ, ṭ, ṭh, ḍ, ḍh, ṇ, t, th, d, dh, n, p, ph, b, bh, m, y, r, l, v, ś, ṣ, s, h

Index of Sūtras

6.1.90, 133, 224, 226